D1518409

ENCYCLOPEDIA OF
FREE BLACKS
AND
PEOPLE OF COLOR
IN THE AMERICAS

VOLUME II

ENCYCLOPEDIA OF
FREE BLACKS
AND
PEOPLE OF COLOR
IN THE AMERICAS

VOLUME II

Editor:
STEWART R. KING

Associate Editor:
BEVERLY C. TOMEK

Facts On File
An Infobase Learning Company

Encyclopedia of Free Blacks and People of Color in the Americas

Facts On File, Inc.
An imprint of Infobase Learning
132 West 31st Street
New York NY 10001

Library of Congress Cataloging-in-Publication Data
Encyclopedia of free Blacks and people of color in the Americas / edited by Stewart R. King.
    v. cm.
  Includes bibliographical references and index.
  Contents: v. 1. Entries A-J— v. 2. Entries K-Z.
  ISBN 978-0-8160-7212-5 (acid-free paper) 1. Free blacks—America—History—Encyclopedias. 2. Free African Americans—History—Encyclopedias. 3. Blacks—America—History—Encyclopedias. 4. America—Race relations—Encyclopedias. I. King, Stewart R., 1960-
  E29.N3E53 2011(2012)   305.896'07303—dc23
              2011017152

Facts On File books are available at special discounts when purchased in bulk quantities for businesses, associations, institutions, or sales promotions. Please call our Special Sales Department in New York at (212) 967-8800 or (800) 322-8755.

You can find Facts On File on the World Wide Web at http://www.infobaselearning.com

Text design by Annie O'Donnell
Composition by Publication Services
Cover printed by Yurchak Printing, Landisville, Pa.
Book printed and bound by Yurchak Printing, Landisville, Pa.
Date printed: December 2011

Printed in the United States of America

10 9 8 7 6 5 4 3 2 1

This book is printed on acid-free paper.

Contents

Entries K–Z

KANSAS

Like other states of the western portion of the Midwest, the territory that would become Kansas saw relatively few free black settlers before the AMERICAN CIVIL WAR (1861–65). Although the question of whether slavery would be allowed in Kansas provoked much political conflict and actual bloodshed in the decade before the Civil War, the number of blacks, whether free or enslaved, who resided in the territory was minimal.

Free black settlers and traders probably traversed the Kansas Territory in the late 18th and early 19th centuries, but few of them settled permanently in the region. The first well-documented case was Ann Davis Shattio, born in Illinois in 1817. Davis Shattio was the wife of Clemet Shattio (or Claymore Chattilon), a settler of French descent, born in St. Louis. Davis Shattio, although free-born, had been kidnapped and sold into slavery in MISSOURI, and although the circumstances of her rescue and marriage to Shattio are unclear, the couple are known to have married and settled by 1852 in the Topeka region, where they remained until the 1880s.

Kansas-Nebraska Act of 1854 posed the question of whether to allow slavery in the Kansas Territory. Sponsored by the Illinois senator Stephen A. Douglas, the act divided the Nebraska Territory into two territories, NEBRASKA in the North and Kansas in the South. The bill also voided the Missouri Compromise of 1820, which had prohibited slavery in the former Louisiana Territory north of 36°30', the southern border of Missouri. Thus, slavery in Kansas and Nebraska, both north of 36°30', was no longer off-limits. On the basis of the concept of popular sovereignty, or the people's will, residents of Kansas and Nebraska would choose whether to allow or prohibit slavery. The Kansas-Nebraska Act, however, failed to define just who constituted "the people." The question drew competing pro- and antislavery forces into Kansas in the mid-1850s to try to sway the state either toward or away from allowing slavery. The bloody conflict that ensued became known as "Bleeding Kansas."

In 1855, pro-slavery forces sacked the town of Lawrence, and in retaliation, the radical abolitionist John Brown and his sons murdered five pro-slavery settlers. As the conflict continued between 1855 and 1861, the pro-slavery and antislavery forces battled one another, not just over the future of slavery in the state, but also over land claims in the territory.

In 1858, a pro-slavery state constitution known as the Lecompton Constitution was proposed at the same time an antislavery territorial legislature was elected. The legislature called for a popular vote on the Lecompton Constitution, which decisively defeated the proposed pro-slavery constitution. Calling the results of the popular vote fraudulent, President JAMES BUCHANAN's administration tried to force the Lecompton Constitution through Congress, effectively making Kansas a slave state. The Lecompton Constitution and the seeming repudiation of popular sovereignty were condemned by Senator Douglas, a position that further drove a wedge between Northern and Southern Democrats on the eve of the Civil War.

For all of the conflict over slavery, the number of black residents in the territory remained relatively small. In 1860, just one year before official Kansas statehood, the federal census recorded only 625 free black residents in the Kansas Territory and two slaves, of a total population of more than 100,000. Most of the free black residents lived in the towns of Leavenworth, Atchison, and Quindaro.

During the American Civil War, which began in 1861, fugitive slaves entered the state, many of whom enlisted in Kansas military units. Recruitment for black units began in Kansas as early as 1861, far in advance of the federal government's call for black soldiers. The 1st Kansas Colored Volunteer Infantry was officially mustered into federal service in January 1863—the same month President ABRAHAM LINCOLN issued the EMANCIPATION PROCLAMATION—followed by the 2nd Kansas Colored Volunteers in June. Although not all black soldiers who served in Kansas regiments formally resided in the state or returned after the war, the war drew significant numbers of black settlers to the state.

With the official abolition of slavery in 1865 and the removal of restrictions on black mobility outside the

AFRICAN-AMERICAN POPULATION OF KANSAS, 1860–1900

Year	Slaves	Free People of Color	Free People of Color as a Percentage of Total Population	Total Population
1860	2	625	0.6%	107,206
1870		17,108	4.7%	364,399
1880		43,107	4.3%	996,096
1890		49,710	3.5%	1,427,096
1900		52,003	3.5%	1,470,495

South, the post–Civil War black migration to Kansas was also significant, and there were several all-black communities in the state. In 1877, the first exclusively black settlement was established at Nicodemus, in Graham County in the northwestern portion of the state. The 1880s census counted more than 300 residents in the town. By 1890, the community had grown to nearly 500. The town of Nicodemus still exists as a living community, as well as a National Historic Site.

In the late 1870s, dissatisfied with post-Reconstruction social and economic conditions, more black settlers from the South began a brief but significant migration to Kansas known as the EXODUSTER MOVEMENT. The largest migration of blacks in the United States before the Great Migration of the early 20th century, the Exoduster Migration took thousands of Southern black migrants, many of them former slaves, into the prairie. Between 1879 and 1880, an estimated 20,000 Exoduster migrants swelled the existing black population. Originally promoted by railroad and land speculators, the movement took on a millenarian character as destitute Southern blacks began to see Kansas as the new Promised Land for former slaves.

The addition of the Exoduster migrants was only part of the much larger growth in the black population of the state. By the time of the Exoduster migration, the black population of Kansas was already undergoing exponential growth. From just 627 black residents in 1860, the black population grew to 17,108 by 1870, and to 43,107 by 1880.

By the final decade of the 19th century, white hostility to the increasing numbers of black settlers in Kansas increased the incidence of racial violence. In 1889, a black accused of murder was lynched in Topeka, and across the state, white opinions hardened against the black population. As in many areas across the nation, by the turn of the 20th century, black Kansans had experienced discrimination and segregation in most aspects of public life. This marked a major change in Kansas, as the state had generally been more tolerant of its black population than others in the Midwest.

Janet Maclellan

FURTHER READING

Athearn, Robert G. *In Search of Canaan: Black Migration to Kansas, 1879–80.* Lawrence: Regents Press of Kansas, 1978.

Chu, Daniel. *Going Home to Nicodemus: The Story of an African American Frontier Town and the Pioneers Who Settled It.* Morristown, N.J.: J. Messner, 1994.

Cox, Thomas C. *Blacks in Topeka, Kansas, 1865–1915.* Baton Rouge: Louisiana State University Press, 1982.

Painter, Nell Irvin. *Exodusters: Black Migration to Kansas after Reconstruction.* New York: Alfred A. Knopf, 1977.

KENTUCKY

Kentucky is a state of the United States. It is located on the southern bank of the Ohio River west of the Appalachian Mountains. The eastern third of the state is mountainous; the north-central and western sections are a fertile river valley, suitable for the production of plantation crops such as cotton and tobacco. The central portion of the state, the Bluegrass district, is fertile and produces horses as well as being suitable for tobacco cultivation. The indigenous inhabitants of Kentucky were agriculturalists who were organized into several tribal confederations when American settlers began to enter the territory across the mountains from VIRGINIA AND WEST VIRGINIA in the 1760s, after the British victory in the SEVEN YEARS' WAR. A pair of treaties with the local Indians in 1768 and 1775 permitted settlement to proceed relatively peacefully, and a reasonably dense population of whites, with some slaves and free blacks, had grown by the outbreak of the WAR OF AMERICAN INDEPENDENCE, 1775–83. The Shawnee Indian nation, located to the north of the Ohio River in modern OHIO and INDIANA, opposed American settlement in the area and joined with the British in the War of American Independence. American victories along the Ohio ensured the survival of the Kentucky settlements. The far western portion of the state, along the Mississippi River, was only opened for settlement after 1818, after General ANDREW JACKSON's defeat of large Indian nations to the south. At first, Kentucky was administered as a part of the state of

Virginia, but the Kentucky settlers were unhappy with rule from Richmond and explored a number of possibilities, including separate independence and Spanish colonial rule. Finally, in 1792, Kentucky was admitted to the United States as the 15th state.

The Antebellum Period

As in many frontier areas, the situation of blacks in Kentucky in the early days of settlement was much less harsh than that found in more settled eastern areas. Some settlers took slaves with them—for example, the prominent settler Daniel Boone (1734–1820) took in three—but there was little possibility for plantation agriculture since communication with the East was so difficult. Slaves lived and worked alongside poor white farmworkers, and some found opportunities to gain their freedom by saving money and ransoming themselves or by simply running away across the open frontier. The census only counted 114 free blacks in the state in 1790, while by 1800, 741 were enumerated. This is no doubt an understatement of their total numbers, both because some people of mixed race were not counted as black and because RUNAWAY SLAVES and people LIVING "AS FREE" would avoid the census taker. The following table traces the development of the black population in Kentucky through the 19th century, as reported by the national census bureau.

In 1803, the U.S. government took an important step that changed the lives of Kentucky people of color when it purchased the LOUISIANA territory from France. In the succeeding decades, the introduction of steamship transportation also greatly improved Kentucky's trade. Up to that point, Kentucky farmers had tenuous con-

nections to the global marketplace through the port of NEW ORLEANS, LOUISIANA, administered until 1802 by SPAIN. Spanish authorities would occasionally prohibit American merchants from transiting their territory, and navigation on the Ohio and Mississippi was difficult. With the opening of the Mississippi route to trade, Kentucky became an important part of the plantation complex. As the plantation sector became more important to the state's economy, more and more slaves were imported, and in a process familiar throughout the plantation Americas, the situation of free blacks worsened.

The state government passed a number of laws restricting the free black population. In 1807, a law prohibited the immigration of free blacks from other states, however, this law was widely ignored and was in fact reenacted in the 1850s. Free blacks were required to register annually with local officials according to an 1832 law; for this registration they were required to pay a substantial sum, which apparently varied by county and over time but could amount to several dollars in a period when an adult male worker's daily pay might be no more than 10 cents. Free blacks were, at various times, prohibited from owning firearms, selling alcohol, meeting with slaves in large numbers (an attempt to hinder the growth of black churches), and violating other rules that did not apply to whites. Free blacks could testify in court against a white person except in capital cases, but nonetheless, their access to the courts to defend what rights they did have was severely limited by long-held customs—white juries discounted their evidence, and fear of reprisals frequently made them unwilling to use the courts. They were denied the vote and could not serve in

AFRICAN-AMERICAN POPULATION OF KENTUCKY, 1790–1900

Year	Slaves	Free People of Color	Free People of Color as a Percentage of Total Population	Total Population
1790	12,430	114	0.2%	73,677
1800	40,343	741	0.3%	220,995
1810	80,561	1,713	0.4%	406,511
1820	117,302	2,939	0.5%	564,317
1830	165,213	4,917	0.7%	687,917
1840	128,258	7,317	0.9%	779,828
1850	210,981	10,011	1.0%	982,405
1860	225,483	10,684	0.9%	1,155,681
1870		222,210	16.8%	1,321,011
1880		271,451	16.5%	1,648,690
1890		268,071	14.4%	1,858,635
1900		284,706	13.3%	2,147,174

the MILITIA or hold most other public jobs. Oppression increased in Kentucky, as throughout the South, after the DENMARK VESEY plot in SOUTH CAROLINA in 1822 and Nat Turner's revolt in neighboring Virginia in 1831, as free blacks were suspected of conspiring with slaves to overthrow slavery.

Despite these legal handicaps, free blacks in Kentucky established a range of cultural institutions that cemented their community and prepared them to provide leadership to all of Kentucky's blacks after the abolition of slavery. Starting in 1812 in Lexington, black churches soon appeared in most of the larger towns of the state. There were nine in Louisville by 1860. These churches also offered education to black students, an important function in a state that offered little formal opportunity for education even to whites. Free blacks also formed secular fraternal organizations, including the United Brothers of Friendship, founded in Louisville in the 1860s, which became one of the largest black fraternal organizations by 1900.

The population of free blacks grew to almost 11,000 by 1860, or about 5 percent of the black population of the state. By this time, most of these people lived in the cities and towns. There were sharp restrictions on landowning, and an outright ban on free blacks' owning or managing slaves other than their own relatives (whom they were presumably seeking to liberate) passed in 1850. These laws meant that blacks had difficulty sharing directly in the state's agricultural wealth. Instead, some worked as ARTISANS or small businesspeople, while the majority were laborers or servants. Many worked in commerce, as boatmen, steamship crewmen, stevedores, carters, warehousemen, and the like. One special condition in Kentucky that contributed to the growth of the free colored population was the widespread practice of slave hiring. This was common throughout the slave societies of the Americas, but conditions in Kentucky made the practice even more common than in neighboring states. Farms were generally small. Tobacco cultivation, in particular, has a highly variable labor demand, with many workers needed at harvest and planting and smaller workforces required at other times. The great economic diversity of the state, without one large crop and with many population centers, meant that labor demands fluctuated very significantly. Therefore, to achieve flexibility in their workforce, masters commonly rented slaves to each other or permitted slaves to seek employment on their own account, often in return for a regular payment to the master. This meant that slaves had greater mobility and access to capital. Moreover, the fluctuating labor demand provided niches for free colored workers. At the same time, the fact that free blacks were working alongside slaves, doing the same tasks and sometimes being paid the same wages, blurred the distinction between free and enslaved and lowered the social status of free blacks. Another condition common to all the states of the Upper South was that their black populations were growing faster than the demand for their labor. As a result, many enslaved blacks were "sold down the river" to the Lower South, where the rapidly expanding COTTON CULTIVATION sector demanded as many laborers as it could get. Free people of color were somewhat immune, but REENSLAVEMENT was always a threat.

A prominent black Kentuckian during this period was James C. Cunningham (1787–1877). Cunningham had been born free in Bermuda and had immigrated to the United States as a young man. He studied violin in PHILADELPHIA, PENNSYLVANIA, and moved to Louisville in the 1810s. He became quite popular as a musician, forming the city's most famous cotillion orchestra and training both black and white students. By 1870, he had a personal estate valued at above $4,000, a significant sum for the era, making him one of the wealthiest blacks in the state. His daughter, Mary Cunningham Smith, sued the streetcar company over segregation in public transportation and won a landmark ruling in state courts in 1872. Another prominent free black at this time was London Ferrill (1789–1854), pastor of the First Baptist Church for Colored Persons in Lexington. He gained his freedom as a young man in Virginia, joined the Baptist Church, and became a preacher. He established his church in Lexington in 1822 and is said to have baptized 5,000 persons of all races during his career—a number that is significantly greater than the entire free black population of the state at that time and reflects, at the same time, frontier-sized storytelling and the impact he had on religious practices of blacks and whites alike (see also BAPTISTS AND PIETISTS). Pastor Ferrill's role as a community leader reflects the importance of the black church as a community institution providing a variety of services. Ferrill's church fed poor people, both blacks and whites; provided education to blacks; helped people keep their farms during an agricultural depression; and quietly helped slaves who wished to gain their freedom move to free territory.

The Civil War and Reconstruction
The AMERICAN CIVIL WAR had a profound and ambiguous impact on Kentucky's free blacks. Kentucky did not vote to join the Confederate States of America in 1861. The eastern counties, in particular, and the large towns where the free black population was concentrated were very strong for the Union, and the western counties where the plantations were centered had less voting strength than their populations would have indicated since a slave under the U.S. Constitution was only counted as 60 percent of a free person for representation purposes. The state government tried to remain neutral,

hoping that the storm would pass quickly and leave all as it had been before. This was not to be. In September 1861, first Confederate and then Union forces invaded the state. By this time, Unionist majorities controlled the state government, and tens of thousands of white Kentuckians had enrolled in the U.S. Army. U.S. forces rapidly consolidated their control of most of the state, although there were several Confederate attacks in the area in 1862 and 1863.

The pro-Union position of Kentuckians did not signal a change of heart on the subject of slavery or equal rights for free blacks, however. Kentucky continued vigorously to enforce the FUGITIVE SLAVE ACT OF 1850; however, Southern masters loyal to the Confederacy could not reclaim their slaves, and Union army camps generally protected RUNAWAY SLAVES from Kentucky law enforcement officials. Slaves continued to be an important part of Kentucky's labor force during the war years. The discriminatory laws against free people of color continued in force. Kentucky at first refused to accept black enlistments in the armed forces, so in 1863, at least 4,000 black Kentuckians crossed the border to Ohio, ILLINOIS, or Union-controlled Memphis, TENNESSEE, to enlist in the newly forming black regiments. Including these men, more than 28,000 black Kentuckians enrolled in the U.S. Army, making them the largest single state contingent of black troops during the Civil War. President ABRAHAM LINCOLN approached the Kentucky state government, and other border state governments, several times during the war, hoping for voluntary acceptance of the idea that slavery was dying, but unlike their fellow border states of MISSOURI, MARYLAND, and West Virginia, the Kentucky legislature rejected any form of even compensation or gradual abolition on several occasions. Slavery ultimately ended in Kentucky with ratification of the Thirteenth Amendment to the U.S. Constitution in December 1865, and thus it was the last place in the United States to have slavery. Kentucky did not formally ratify the Thirteenth Amendment until 1976.

The antiblack tendencies of Kentucky white elites were not restrained in the immediate postwar era by a Reconstruction government, as was the case in the states that had joined the Confederacy. Federal laws, such as the Civil Rights Act of 1866, constrained Kentucky to some extent, and the courts offered blacks some protection during the era of RECONSTRUCTION IN THE UNITED STATES, as in the antisegregation lawsuit brought by Mary Cunningham Smith in 1870. However, the Kentucky government remained determined to keep blacks in "their place" through laws, where that was possible, and, if not, through informal constraints, including police brutality and toleration of mob violence. There were more than 200 lynchings of blacks in Kentucky between the Civil War

and the 1940s, almost none of them investigated as crimes by state officials.

Kentucky blacks did not submit tamely, using the courts and appeals to public opinion to fight segregation during the Jim Crow era. Leaders in this struggle were often former free people of color, including Henry Adams (1802–72), leader of the Fifth Street Baptist Church in Louisville, who organized the Convention of Kentucky Baptists in 1865 (see also NEGRO CONVENTION MOVEMENT IN THE UNITED STATES). In addition, as did Pastor Adams, blacks worked to build up the segregated institutions that were given them. The Kentucky legislature grudgingly established a public school system for blacks in 1874. Black schools were chronically underfunded, despite contributions from the FREEDMEN'S BUREAU in the immediate postwar period and philanthropic Northerners in later years. A black normal school, Ely Normal in Louisville, trained teachers for the black schools. Black teachers and principals were important community leaders. The black churches maintained their role in sponsoring education, with one of the most important black high schools in the state, Central High in Louisville, sponsored by the AFRICAN METHODIST EPISCOPAL CHURCH. The national leader Bishop DANIEL A. PAYNE spoke at the inauguration of the school. The ROMAN CATHOLIC CHURCH was establishing a separate school system for its followers at this time and saw an opening for service and evangelization in the education of black students of all religions. The Sisters of Loretto, a Catholic order of teaching nuns, formed in Kentucky in 1812 with the mission of educating the poor, created schools for black students in Lexington and Louisville, and also enrolled black women in its ranks. The Kentucky legislature tried to enact a law in 1870 forbidding private and parochial schools to educate black children, but the law was not applied to the Catholic school system because of political repercussions were feared and because it was thought to represent an unconstitutional interference in the work of a religious group. Many of these educators were also prewar free people of color. Among these was Jordan C. Jackson, a Louisville undertaker, who had started a free colored benevolent society (which offered burial insurance) in 1843 and who was the chairman of the board of Berea Literary Institute, an integrated high school, from 1879 to 1894.

Stewart R. King

FURTHER READING

Bogert, Pen. "Mary Victoria Cunningham Smith: A Woman of Courage." Kentucky Center for African-American Heritage. Available online. URL: http://www.kcaah.org/site/essay/c/maryvictoriacunningham.htm. Accessed December 28, 2010.

Lucas, Marion B. *A History of Blacks in Kentucky: From Slavery to Segregation, 1760–1891*. Frankfort: Kentucky Historical Society, 2003.

"Notable Kentucky African Americans Database." University of Kentucky Library. Available online. URL: http://www. uky.edu/Libraries/NKAA/index.php. Accessed December 28, 2010.

KINGSLEY, ANNA (ANTA MAJIGEEN NJAAY)
(ca. 1793–1870) *Senegalese planter, resident in the United States and Haiti*

Anna Kingsley, a black freedwoman born in Senegal, was a successful planter in FLORIDA and Hispaniola in the 19th century.

Anna Kingsley was born Anta Majigeen Njaay about 1793 in a Wolof state of present-day Senegal (maybe Jolof or Kajoor), where her family was probably socially prominent. Captured and transported to Havana, CUBA, in 1806, she was purchased by Zephaniah Kingsley, a planter and captain of English Quaker origins. Zephaniah married her in Havana and anglicized her name to Anna Magigine Jai Kingsley.

Zephaniah took Anna back to his Laurel Grove plantation along the St. Johns River near Jacksonville, Florida, which was then Spanish territory. Laurel Grove was a large plantation of about 100 slaves and specialized in Sea Island COTTON CULTIVATION. Anna bore three mixed-race children, George, Martha, and Mary (Zephaniah also had common-law unions with other slaves), and served as de facto manager of the plantation since her husband was often overseas. Zephaniah emancipated his wife on March 4, 1811, after which she moved with her children and a dozen slaves to a nearby plantation in Mandarin that she owned in her name.

The 1812 Patriot Rebellion, during which U.S. sympathizers challenged Spanish control of Florida, was keenly felt around Jacksonville. Patriots took over Laurel Grove and forced Zephaniah to embrace their cause; the plantation was then ravaged in a retaliatory raid by Seminole Indians allied with SPAIN. Mandarin was also attacked, forcing Anna to burn her plantation and flee with her children and slaves.

In March 1814, the Kingsleys established themselves on a new plantation on St. George Island (the buildings are well preserved and can still be visited today). Anna spent more than 20 years there as a matriarch and businesswoman; a second son, John, was born there in 1824. The U.S. takeover of Florida after the 1819 Adams-Onís Treaty, however, threatened her prominent status. New laws were introduced to make MANUMISSION more costly, ban interracial sex and marriages, and prevent mixed-race offspring from inheriting (the laws were not retroactive, but they affected John and generally reflected racial views more stringent than those prevalent under Spanish rule).

Zephaniah, a slave owner but also a supporter of humane treatment of slaves and free-colored rights, opposed these new laws, then arranged to purchase land in Mayorasgo de Koka near Puerto Plata in Hispaniola. The area, now part of the DOMINICAN REPUBLIC, was then under the rule of the black Republic of Haiti, whose president, Jean-Pierre Boyer, encouraged free-colored immigration from the United States. Anna and her two sons moved to Haiti in 1837, along with 60 slaves, who were emancipated in exchange for long-term labor contracts.

Political turmoil in Puerto Plata, the death of Zephaniah in 1842, and ensuing lawsuits to secure his inheritance convinced Anna to moved back to the Jacksonville area in 1847. John remained in Puerto Plata to manage the estates; her other son, George, died in a shipwreck. Anna, who again moved to Point St. Isabel in 1860, presided over an extensive mixed-race kinship network and various plantations. After the AMERICAN CIVIL WAR began, Anna to moved to New York City. Back in Florida, she died in July 1870.

Philippe R. Girard

FURTHER READING
May, Philip S. "Zephaniah Kingsley, Nonconformist." *Florida Historical Society* 23 (January 1945): 145–159.
Schafer, Daniel L. *Anna Kingsley.* 1994. Reprint, Saint Augustine, Fla.: Saint Augustine Historical Society, 1997.
Stowell, Daniel, ed. *Balancing Evils Judiciously: The Proslavery Writings of Zephaniah Kingsley.* Gainesville: University Press of Florida, 2000.

KU KLUX KLAN
The Ku Klux Klan, also referred to simply as the "KKK," was formed in Giles County, Pulaski, TENNESSEE, shortly after the AMERICAN CIVIL WAR. KKK tradition held that the organization was founded by six Confederate veterans who met on December 24, 1865, but the exact date is still not clearly defined—not even by the original founders of the Klan. By 1866, however, it became known as a terrorist group that led the fight to oppress—often violently—and restrict the rights of newly emancipated African Americans. In this capacity it attracted a number of defenders of the pre-emancipation Southern social order, most notably the Confederate general Nathan Bedford Forrest, who was known for leading his troops in the mass murder of black Union soldiers who had been captured at Fort Pillow (April 12, 1864).

Briefly calling themselves "The Circle," the six founding members of the Klan were James Crowe, Richard Reed, Calvin Jones, John Lester, Frank McCord, and John Kennedy. However, perhaps to add a sense of originality

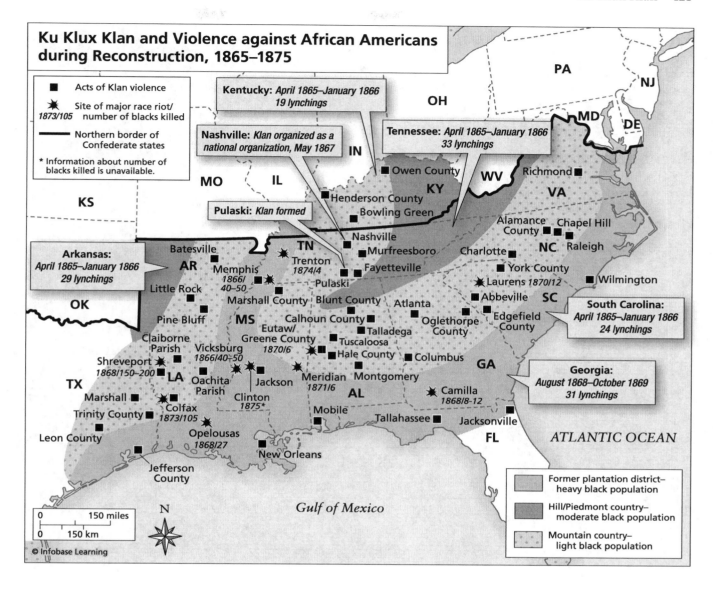

Ku Klux Klan and Violence against African Americans during Reconstruction, 1865–1875

■ Acts of Klan violence

✶ Site of major race riot/
1873/105   number of blacks killed

— Northern border of Confederate states

* Information about number of blacks killed is unavailable.

Kentucky: *April 1865–January 1866 19 lynchings*

Nashville: *Klan organized as a national organization, May 1867*

Tennessee: *April 1865–January 1866 33 lynchings*

Pulaski: *Klan formed*

Arkansas: *April 1865–January 1866 29 lynchings*

South Carolina: *April 1865–January 1866 24 lynchings*

Georgia: *August 1868–October 1869 31 lynchings*

Former plantation district–heavy black population

Hill/Piedmont country–moderate black population

Mountain country–light black population

Gulf of Mexico

ATLANTIC OCEAN

© Infobase Learning

and uniqueness to the name, they quickly decided to change the name to the Greek word for circle, *kuklos*. After further modifications to this name, *Kuklux* was agreed upon, and the word *Klan,* based on the Scots-Irish descent of the members, was added. The group members dressed in sheets, mimicking the appearance of ghosts as they rode out into the night. They also adopted occult symbols that had no meaning—at least to them—and made themselves look taller and more ominous simply by wearing longer articles of clothing.

As the Klan spread throughout all of the Southern states and grew to include a wide range of white society, from common folk to local officials such as sheriffs, judges, and mayors, the organization developed a formal structure. Six formal offices were created, including the "Grand Cyclops," or president; the "Grand Magi," or vice president; and the "Grand Turk." Also included

in this hierarchy were the two "Night Hawks" and the "Lictor," who enforced order in the Klan meetings. As the Klan expanded, auxiliaries known as dens began to form. In April 1867, a new "Prescript" of rules for the Klan established a military hierarchy with "Provinces," "Dominions," and "Realms." The overall leader in charge of the "Invisible Empire" was deemed the "Grand Wizard."

Many of the Klan's rules were left purposely vague to allow for a broad interpretation depending on the given situation. Passwords were used, but with no standard set of passwords, variations frequently occurred from den to den. Furthermore, ideas and concepts from other secretive organizations were borrowed or stolen by the KKK—the 19th century in America was a time when secret societies, most of which had more peaceful and positive goals, were common. To increase public awareness of the

A gang of Southern whites assaults a black woman in 1867 during the struggle over Reconstruction in the United States. The men are not wearing Ku Klux Klan regalia, so it is unclear whether they are members of a formal Klan cell, but there were many informal or local groups who also carried out terrorist attacks on blacks as part of the white resistance to Reconstruction. *(North Wind Picture Archives via Associated Press)*

KKK and to invite publicity, the Klansmen often held parades and had their first public announcement of their meeting on March 29, 1867.

By 1868, the Klan became known as a vigilante organization and launched a reign of terror upon the newly free blacks. Their main targets were generally black politicians and political social leaders, but they spared few members of the black community. They terrorized the newly freed in a systematic effort to prevent them from voting or fighting for their rights to fair treatment as laborers. Thousands of Southern African Americans were beaten, whipped, and murdered for a number of "offenses" that generally amounted to challenging the social order that strove to

keep them in conditions that mirrored slavery. The murders were very brutal and committed either publicly or in the presence of family members. Black intellectuals and teachers often found themselves targeted, as did black landowners and those who sought any degree of education or independence. Black schools and churches were often burned down. Since these social institutions in black communities were often led by prewar free people of color, they were more likely to be targets of KKK terrorism.

The white public throughout the South had no interest in punishing the Klansmen, so squelching their activities was rather difficult, even though some state governments tried. Republicans in Tennessee and ARKANSAS organized police forces to deal with the Klan, and the Texas governor, Edmund Davis, went a step further by creating a police force that was 40 percent black and managed to arrest more than 6,000 Klansmen. Blacks and whites also united in the Carolinas to fight the Klan.

Even so, local resistance was seldom sufficient. Often, jurors were members of the KKK, so if a fellow Klansman happened to be put on trial, a conviction rarely resulted. Also, many businesses are said to have caught "Ku-Klux Fever," finding clever ways of using the three Ks in advertising in order to increase their revenue.

However, the U.S. government did make efforts to end Klan violence since the group's activity directly violated the Fifteenth Amendment to the Constitution (which granted black male suffrage) by intimidating voters. In 1870 and 1871, the federal government enacted four Ku Klux Klan acts, also called the Force Acts, to put an end to the KKK. These laws were enforced with considerable severity by federal troops, present in the South as part of the military occupation force that was a part of the congressionally led program of radical Reconstruction in the United States. Trials took place before military tribunals, not civilian courts, and convictions were easier to obtain. Hundreds of Klan members were convicted, and many were sentenced to harsh fines or imprisonment. As a result, Klan activity generally ended by 1872, and the founders formally disbanded the group that year. It remained dormant until a "Second Ku Klux Klan" emerged in 1915, directed this time more at immigrants than blacks.

Other terrorist groups with similar agendas played an important role in the overthrow of Republican governments in the South, once the threat of federal military intervention was removed with the negotiated outcome of the election of 1876. Federal troops withdrew, and the progress that blacks had achieved in the South was rapidly reversed. Terrorism played a role in this process, but the secretive sort of assassination and sabotage that the Klan had used was no longer necessary once white elites had regained control of local and state government. Law enforcement and public opinion, coupled with semiofficial lynchings of blacks who got "above themselves" or committed offenses against prevailing racial standards, were sufficient to protect white supremacy in the South until the 1960s.

Tim Stringer

FURTHER READING
Budiansky, Stephen. *The Bloody Shirt: Terror after Appomattox.* New York: Viking, 2008.

MacLean, Nancy. *Behind the Mask of Chivalry: The Making of the Second Ku Klux Klan.* New York: Oxford University Press, 1994.

PBS. "The Rise and Fall of Jim Crow: The Ku Klux Klan (1866)." Available online. URL: http://www.pbs.org/wnet/jimcrow/stories_events_kkk.html. Accessed December 28, 2010.

Wade, Wyn Craig. *The Fiery Cross: The Ku-Klux Klan in America.* New York: Oxford University Press, 1987.

Williams, Lou Falkner. *The Great South Carolina Ku Klux Klan Trials, 1871–1872.* Athens: University of Georgia Press, 1996.

Wilson, Charles Reagan. *Baptized in Blood: The Religion of the Lost Cause, 1865–1920.* Athens: University of Georgia Press, 1980.

LA ESCALERA PLOT

In 1843, a series of slave revolts broke out in the Spanish colony of CUBA. The presumed conspiracy behind the revolts became known as La Escalera Plot and led to a period of brutal government repression of slaves and free people of color. Uprisings in March and November were located on plantations in the rich western SUGAR CULTIVATION region of Matanzas, and revolts in May took place in Santiago de Cuba, in the East. The rebels destroyed several plantations and killed and wounded numerous white planters and their families. To end the November insurgency, Captain General Leopoldo O'Donnell sent regular military troops to the countryside, where they captured and hanged dozens of slaves. Suspicious of these increasingly organized uprisings, Cuban officials connected the rebellions to a conspiratorial plot among slaves, free people of color, and British abolitionists designed to overthrow slavery and Spanish colonial rule. Historians have debated whether or not a conspiracy actually existed, with some suggesting that the government fabricated the plan, and others asserting that slaves and free people of color had already established a precedent for allied revolt. These debates aside, historical witnesses and contemporary scholars agree that the ensuing violence produced the most notorious repression in Cuban history.

In January 1844, authorities implemented an intense investigation to uncover the details of the suspected conspiracy. During this yearlong period of repression, officials arrested more than 4,000 people, mainly slaves and free people of color, and some foreign whites. Suspicious of those connected to past uprisings and the abolitionist movement, authorities accused David Turnbull, the former British consul in Havana, and Domingo del Monte and José de la Luz y Caballero, two of Cuba's important intellectuals, of being key organizers of the conspiracy and enemies of Spain. They avoided arrest, but others did not. Despite protests by diplomatic representatives, Cuban police imprisoned French planters, British merchants, and American skilled workers. However, the Military Commission ultimately acquitted most whites who had been formally charged.

Slaves and free people of color bore the brunt of the repression. Military officials traveled throughout the countryside harassing the African-descended population, extorting confessions from them, and seizing their furniture, livestock, and other property. To extract information, administrators tortured suspects by tying them to a ladder, *la escalera*, and whipping them until they confessed or died. Andrés Dodge, a free MULATTO and a prominent Havana dentist, withstood suffering on the ladder three times before officials executed him for refusing to confess. After beating the free black Pedro Núñez, authorities suspended him from a house ceiling. Given its level of violence, some observers equated the repression of La Escalera to the Spanish Inquisition. Torture on the ladder became the primary image of colonial efforts to suppress resistance and gave rise to the events' name, the La Escalera Plot.

The government set up a Military Commission to try to sentence accused conspirators and accomplices. At least 78 people were executed by firing squad, including the poet Plácido (GABRIEL DE LA CONCEPCIÓN VALDÉS); the suspected ringleader, the dentist Andrés Dodge; the tailor Francisco Uribe; and numerous other influential free people of color. Juan Francisco Manzano, author of Cuba's only slave narrative, published in the 19th century, spent several months in jail during the repression. In order to remove rebellious influences from Cuba, the Military Commission banished more than 400 free people of color from the island, including the popular orchestra leader and militia officer Claudio Brindis de Salas. Harsh conditions forced hundreds more into exile in MEXICO, the United States, and other locales in the Caribbean. To curtail suspicious activities, authorities placed slaves and free people of color under constant surveillance and restricted their employment opportunities and social gatherings. Particular constraints were placed on skilled workers of color. For instance, authorities barred María del Pilar Podeva, Plácido's mother-in-law, from working as a midwife, and the medical establishment petitioned to prevent free people of color from practicing dentistry. By the end of the sentencing in January 1845, more than

1,200 people had been subjected to execution, imprisonment in Cuba and overseas, or hard labor for their connection to the conspiracy.

News of the violent repression received international attention. Accounts by U.S. consulate officers, Spanish onlookers, and British travelers described horrific scenes of the torture and destruction but also rationalized the Cuban administrator's actions as the only way to restore order to Cuba. Newspapers in BOSTON and JAMAICA warned Cuban authorities that their extreme actions might produce a rebellion like the HAITIAN REVOLUTION and destroy the colony. Foreign merchants complained that the destruction of sugarcane and other agricultural property would compromise Cuban commerce. Cuban officials, however, rejected criticisms and asserted to the international community that the measures were necessary to preserve the island's political and economic security.

To restore Cuba to a stable slave society after the repression, the government implemented new laws designed to bolster white dominance over the African-descended population. New slave regulations permitted SLAVE OWNERS to punish slave insubordination at their own discretion. To curtail the presence, activities, and employment of free blacks, authorities prohibited all free people of color to enter local ports and attempted to expel all foreign-born free blacks. Captain General O'Donnell disbanded Cuba's militia of color, which had been established in the late 16th century. He also suspended issuing freedom papers to former slaves. In addition, the colonial state prohibited free people of color to hold meetings without authorization from local officials. Regulations directed slaveholders to arrest any black person who visited a plantation without written permission. These laws worked to extend the repression for several decades.

During and after 1844, free people of color found ways to resist the repression. Foreign-born free people of color protested expulsion laws. Native Cuban free blacks restricted from their skilled occupations petitioned for reinstatement, while manual laborers protested harsh working conditions. Others restarted schools and initiated new businesses. In 1854, authorities reinstated the MILITIA of color, and although less than enthusiastic about participating given the circumstances of its demise, many free people of color resumed their roles in defense of Cuba. Those in exile petitioned to return, and a general amnesty in 1857 paved the way for their reentry.

The conspiracy and repression of La Escalera intensified tensions associated with poor race relations and slavery in Cuba during the 1850s and 1860s. To increase the number of whites in the colony, and to reduce the threat of black rebellion, Cuban authorities and elites implemented new plans for greater European immigration. As slavery expanded and racial lines hardened, slaves found themselves with fewer opportunities for MANUMISSION, and free people of color confronted reduced civil and economic opportunities. The legacy of La Escalera and tensions over ending slavery and Spanish colonial rule helped set the stage for new conflicts over independence and abolition in the 1860s, 1870s, and 1890s.

Michelle Reid-Vazquez

FURTHER READING
Primary Sources:
Manzano, Juan Francisco. *Autobiography of a Slave.* Translated by Evelyn Picon Garfield. Detroit: Wayne State University Press, 1996.
———. *The Life and Poems of a Cuban Slave: Juan Francisco Manzano, 1797–1854.* Hamden, Conn.: Archon Books, 1981.

Film:
Giral, Sergio, director. *Plácido: The Blood of the Poet.* Albuquerque: Center for Southwest Research, University Libraries, University of New Mexico, 1986 (2007).

Secondary Sources:
Chomsky, Aviva, Barry Carr, and Pamela Maria Smorkaloff, eds. *The Cuba Reader: History, Culture, Politics.* Durham, N.C.: Duke University Press, 2003.
Paquette, Robert L. *Sugar Is Made with Blood: The Conspiracy of La Escalera and the Conflict between Empires over Slavery in Cuba.* Middletown, Conn.: Wesleyan University Press, 1998.
Reid, Michele. "Protesting Service: Free Black Response to Cuba's Reestablished Militia of Color." *Journal of Colonialism and Colonial History* 5, no. 2 (Fall 2004): 1–22.

LANGSTON, JOHN MERCER (1829–1897)
American attorney, educator, congressman, and diplomat
John Mercer Langston was the first African American to hold elective office in the United States. He was an important educator and legal scholar during the antebellum period and played a distinguished role in government during RECONSTRUCTION IN THE UNITED STATES. He served as U.S. consul general and resident minister to Haiti and held other positions in government during a long career of public service. He was one of the best-known African-American politicians of the 19th century.

Son of Ralph Quarles, a white plantation owner, and Lucy Langston, an emancipated slave, John Mercer

An 1882 lithograph of John Mercer Langston (1829–97), the first black American to hold elective office, as clerk of Brownhelm Township in Ohio in 1855. Langston was also one of the last African Americans to hold elective office in the South before the 1970s, as congressman from Virginia from 1889 to 1890, before Jim Crow prevented blacks from participating in politics. *(Library of Congress)*

Langston was born on December 14, 1829, on his father's plantation in Louisa County, Virginia. When his parents died of unrelated illnesses in 1834, he moved to OHIO and was raised in Chillicothe and Cincinnati. Langston attended Oberlin College (1844–49, 1850–52), excelling in debate and oratory and studying theology. Denied entrance to law schools because of his race, he studied (1853–54) under Philemon Bliss, an antislavery attorney and congressman of Elyria, Ohio. As Ohio's first black attorney, Langston was elected clerk of Brownhelm Township (1855), thereby becoming the first African American to hold elective office in the United States. He subsequently became school visitor and secretary of the board of education. Moving to Oberlin, he was elected clerk of Russia Township and became a member of the village council and board of education. He was also active in the Ohio black convention movement, serving on its central committee and lecturing throughout the state about slavery and civil rights (*see* NEGRO CONVENTION MOVEMENT IN THE UNITED STATES).

As the controversy over slavery intensified, Langston became an active supporter of the Free Soil and Republican Parties. During the AMERICAN CIVIL WAR, he recruited volunteers for black regiments, headed the National Equal Rights League, and lectured in favor of African-American suffrage. After the war, he toured Southern and border states on behalf of the freedmen and served as inspector-general of the FREEDMEN'S BUREAU.

Langston joined Howard University's new law department in 1869 and, as a professor and dean, enhanced the department's academic reputation. He also served for a time as vice president and acting president, but in a racially charged controversy, the university's largely white board of trustees refused to award him a permanent appointment as president. Langston resigned in protest at the end of 1875.

In the meantime, President ULYSSES S. GRANT appointed Langston to the Freedmen's Savings and Trust (1872) and to the District of Columbia Board of Health. Langston remained a Republican Party loyalist, campaigning for Grant and participating in national conventions. He had hoped to be appointed commissioner of agriculture but received instead the post of minister resident to Haiti (1877–85). He was considered the dean of the PORT-AU-PRINCE diplomatic corps but left a mixed record by advocating private claims against Haiti and involving himself sometimes too much, sometimes too little, in Haiti's turbulent political situation. American diplomats often played very significant roles in the internal politics of Latin American countries at this time. One accepted role of diplomats during this period was as advocates and even collection agents for debts owed to their country's citizens by foreign governments or private persons. Langston's performance in Haiti was very much in this proconsular mode, but because he was an African American, Haitians and liberals in the United States expected more of him and were disappointed.

After serving as president of Virginia Normal and Collegiate Institute (1885–87), Langston ran for Congress from Virginia's Fourth District (1888) despite opposition from the state Republican leadership. The initial election returns favored the Democratic candidate, but Langston contested the outcome in court, alleging fraud and intimidation of voters. He finally prevailed after 18 months and took his seat for the remainder of the term. He was defeated for reelection in 1890 and declined to run in 1892. He nevertheless continued work on behalf of the Republican Party, retiring in 1894 and publishing his memoirs. He died on November 15, 1897.

Known during his life as a spellbinding orator and supporter of governmental reform, Langston is remembered today for his tireless advocacy of racial justice. He is usually considered one of the two or three most distinguished African-American leaders of the 19th century.

Kenneth Blume

FURTHER READING
Cheek, William F., and Aimee Lee Cheek. *John Mercer Langston and the Fight for Black Freedom, 1829–65.* Urbana: University of Illinois Press, 1996.
———. "John Mercer Langston: Principle and Politics." In *Black Leaders of the Nineteenth Century,* edited by Leon Litwack and August Meier. Urbana: University of Illinois Press, 1998.
Jackson, Wanda Faye. "John Mercer Langston: A Troubled African-American Leader." *Griot* 23 (Spring 2004): 61–72.
Langston, John Mercer. *Freedom and Citizenship: Selected Lectures and Addresses of Hon. John Mercer Langston.* Washington, D.C.: Rufus H. Darby, 1883. Reprint, Miami: Mnemosyne, 1969.
———. *From the Virginia Plantation to the National Capital; or, the First and Only Negro Representative in Congress from the Old Dominion.* Hartford, Conn.: American Publishing, 1894.
———. *John Mercer Langston Personal Papers.* Nashville, Tenn.: Fisk University, Erastus Milo Gravath Library, 1958.

LAS SIETE PARTIDAS

In 1265, King Alfonso X of Castile, one of the Iberian kingdoms that later were combined to create SPAIN, proclaimed a new law code known as Las Siete Partidas. The code was the blueprint for a centralized high medieval kingdom and contained laws controlling everything from the regulation of commerce and manufacturing to the procedures for tax collection. Part of one of the seven sections dealt with the status of slaves and freedmen. The law is noteworthy for the relatively easy procedures it sets up for MANUMISSION. Masters can free their slaves in a wide variety of ways without much oversight by the state, and slaves can sue their master for their freedom if the master commits certain abuses or if the slaves do some important service for the state. This is in keeping with the Roman and Christian roots of medieval Western European legal thinking. However, King Alfonso went further than the Romans and further than other European kings in his desire to see slaves become free people.

When Spain began settling and conquering the Americas in the late 15th and 16th centuries, the Siete Partidas became the fundamental law of its colonies regarding slavery and remained so until the mid-19th century, when those Spanish-American colonies gained their independence. The Siete Partidas was the ancestor of the slave laws of the newly independent countries of Spanish America. While often ignored or undermined in actual practice, this law remained an important tool for people of color seeking to better their situation in the Americas and in Spain itself. Because the other European colonists followed the Spanish to the Americas, their laws were important models, and some elements of the logic of the Siete Partidas entered slave codes throughout the Americas. BRAZIL was especially affected, since PORTUGAL was under the rule of the Spanish Crown for the first century of the Portuguese colonial experience in the Americas.

Interestingly, the law does not mention race or color at all. At the time it was written, most slaves in Spain were North African Moors, with a smaller population of eastern European Slavic people. Only a few sub-Saharan Africans had become slaves in Europe, and slavery was not tied to color at all. Racial tensions began later and complicated the position of people of African descent. The only disability recognized by the legal system was religious—non-Christians were at a significant handicap under the law.

Stewart R. King

FURTHER READING
Peabody, Sue, and Keila Grinberg. *Slavery, Freedom, and the Law in the Atlantic World: A Brief History with Documents.* Boston: Bedford/St. Martin's, 2007.

LAS SIETE PARTIDAS, SPANISH LAW ON RACE AND SLAVERY, 1265

The following is an English translation of the portion of King Alfonso's legal code of 1265 that addressed issues of slavery and liberty. This was the source for all the laws on these subjects throughout the Spanish Empire and served as a model for other colonizers as they followed the Spanish to the Americas.

Title XXIL on Liberty

All creatures of the world naturally love and desire liberty, but men who have reason do so even more than all others, and those of noble heart, the most. . . . We wish in this article to say what liberty is, who can give it, and to whom and how, and what rights the master has in the person and the property of the servant after he has freed him and for what reasons one can lose his liberty.

Law I: What is liberty, and who can give it, and to whom, and in what way?

Liberty is the power that every man naturally has to do as he wishes, unless force or the power of law prevents it. And a master can give this freedom to his servant in the church or outside it, before a judge, or, in some other way, in his will or without a will by letter. He must do this for himself and not through a representative, except by heirs in direct lineage. . . .

Law 3: How the servant can see himself freed for good deeds that he has done even when his master does not wish it.

From time to time, servants will deserve to be freed for the good deeds they have done, despite the fact that their masters do not wish it, and this can happen for four reasons: the first is if a servant makes known to the king or to those who judge for him that a man has raped a virgin; the second is if he identifies a counterfeiter to the authorities; the third is when he reveals that someone who has been placed by the king in command of troops on the frontier deserts his place without orders; the fourth is when he reveals a plot to kill his master or avenges or reveals a plot of treason against the king or the kingdom. But in the first three cases, the king or the authorities to whom the servant reveals the crime must pay the master the value of the slave.

Law 4: How a female servant can become free if her master puts her into prostitution in order to gain money with her.

Whoever puts his servant women into public prostitution, in whichever house or other location where they give themselves to men for money . . . let the master lose his servant women and they shall be free forever. . . .

Law 8: Of how the freedman must honor he who gave him freedom and his wife and his children and in what ways he must give them reverence.

Because liberty is one of the most honorable and highest things in the world, those who receive it owe obedience, honor, and respect to their former masters who set them free. And he wants everyone to know the great gift that he has received and the gratitude he should give . . . since slavery is the most vile thing in the world other than sin . . . and thus liberty is the most dear and precious. And thus the freedman and his children owe great honor and reverence to their former master . . . and his children. . . . And the honor that the former slave owes to the man who freed him is this: he must bow whenever he comes before him or his sons, and if the master comes while the freedman is seated, he must raise himself and receive him very well, speaking good words to him and honoring him in all ways that are possible . . . without asking anything of him. . . .

Sources: Las Siete Partidas del Rey Don Alfonso El Sabio, Cotejadas con varios codices antiguos, por la Real Academia de la Historia. Tomo III, Partida Quarta, Quinta, Sexta, y Septima. Madrid: Imprenta Real, 1807. Available online. http://fama2.us.es/fde/lasSietePartidasEd1807T3.pdf. Accessed July 25, 2011. Translation by Stewart R. King.

LAVEAU, MARIE (1801–1881) *American voodoo practitioner*

Marie Laveau was born on September 10, 1801, in NEW ORLEANS, LOUISIANA, to Charles Laveaux, a white farmer, and Marguerite Darcantel, a free Creole woman of color. Marie Laveau and her daughter were both voodoo priestesses, and accounts of the two women are sometimes confused. Laveau wielded considerable power as a community leader, but little is known definitely about her life: Accounts of her life and acts are contradictory, and scholars' interpretations of events and documents vary widely.

Laveau was raised Catholic under the ministry of Père Antoine, the chaplain at St. Louis Cathedral in New Orleans. On August 4, 1819, Père Antoine married Laveau and Jacques Paris, a free black who had emigrated from SAINT-DOMINGUE (Haiti). Paris disappeared or died around 1820 (the circumstances surrounding his disappearance and/or death were unexplained), and Laveau began calling herself the Widow Paris.

Later, Laveau began a relationship with Louis-Christophe Duminy (or Dumesnil) de Glapion, a white man descended from an aristocratic French family, and gave birth to a daughter, Marie-Héloïse-Euchariste Laveau, in February 1827. Other children followed, but Marie-Héloïse is the daughter with whom Laveau is sometimes confused, and historians generally refer to Laveau's daughter as Marie Laveau II. Laveau II eventually assumed her mother's role as queen of the voodoo practitioners.

Voodoo and other religious traditions of African origin had been practiced in the British colonies of North America that became the United States, as well as in Louisiana since the 1600s, but increased in Louisiana after the slave revolt in Saint-Domingue in the 1790s, as many fled to New Orleans. As with many followers of voodoo, Laveau did not see Catholicism and voodoo as incompatible. Practices and beliefs of the two religions were blended both in New Orleans and elsewhere in the world (CUBA and Haiti, for example; *see also* AFRICAN AND SYNCRETIC RELIGIONS and ROMAN CATHOLIC CHURCH).

When and from whom Laveau learned voodoo are unknown. Some suggest she learned from her mother and/or grandmother (speculating that one or both were priestesses). She also may have learned from Doctor John/ John Bayou or the voodoo queen Marie Saloppé. By the late 1830s, however, Laveau was the preeminent voodoo queen in New Orleans.

In her role as voodoo queen, she led rituals and ceremonies at Congo Square and Lake Pontchartrain. Held on a Sunday after church services, the Congo Square rituals involved dancing and singing, and some accounts suggest that they began with Laveau's dancing with her snake, Zombi. Ceremonies at Lake Pontchartrain often occurred on St. John's Eve, during which participants danced around bonfires and became possessed by spirits. Laveau also made gris-gris (or charms), offered advice, and told fortunes.

Laveau was known for her charity: As a Creole fever nurse, she treated victims of the epidemics and episodes of yellow fever, malaria, and cholera that were common in the 1800s in New Orleans. And beginning in the 1840s, Laveau visited death row prisoners, taking them food and spiritual comforts.

Laveau also bought and sold slaves, although her motives for doing so are unclear. Some sources suggest that Laveau did so in order to aid them in their pursuit of freedom, but the evidence of the transactions is more certain than Laveau's motivations.

Some believe that Laveau's true source of power was not derived from voodoo. They charge that Laveau had developed a network of spies among the black servant class in New Orleans during the time she worked as a hairdresser after Paris's death or disappearance. Her true source of power, then, may have been the secrets revealed to her through this network.

Laveau died on June 15, 1881. Visitors still visit her reputed burial site in St. Louis Cemetery No. 1.

Ultimately, Laveau wielded enormous cultural, political, and religious power among free Creoles of color and other groups, but she is often misunderstood. Some of her contemporaries and, perhaps to an even greater extent, the generations that followed criminalized her and branded her a witch, in part, perhaps, to discredit and disempower her as a powerful African female leader, thereby diminishing and clouding her legacy. This activity occurred against a backdrop of laws in the 1850s and onward that were increasingly restrictive of blacks.

Summer Leibensperger

FURTHER READING

Donaldson, Gary A. "A Window on Slave Culture: Dances at Congo Square in New Orleans, 1800–1862." *Journal of Negro History* 69, no. 2 (Spring 1984): 63–72.

Fandrich, Ina Johanna. *The Mysterious Voodoo Queen, Marie Laveaux: A Study of Powerful Female Leadership in Nineteenth-Century New Orleans.* New York: Routledge, 2005.

Long, Carolyn Morrow. *A New Orleans Voudou Priestess: The Legend and Reality of Marie Laveau.* Gainesville: University Press of Florida, 2006.

Ward, Martha. *Voodoo Queen: The Spirited Lives of Marie Laveau.* Jackson: University Press of Mississippi, 2004.

LAWS OF FREE BIRTH

A very important intermediate step in the abolition of slavery, especially in Iberian America, but also in some Northern states in the United States, was a declaration that all persons born after a certain date would be free. These "free womb" laws, as they were often called, were generally expected to produce a gradual, decades-long abolition of slavery that would not deprive SLAVE OWNERS of their property rights. However, they generally did not function as expected, instead provoking more intensive agitation by slaves, especially those born just before the cutoff date, and leading to political retreat or actual overthrow of governments.

The most famous free womb law was the Rio Branco law of 1871 in BRAZIL. By the provisions of this law, everybody born after a certain date for an unspecified transition period would be an indentured servant until he or she became 21 and then would be free. The status of persons born before the law was passed was not affected. This was an important compromise for the Brazilian government, faced with a powerful abolition movement that had support from the royal family. The law offered a solution that respected two key liberal principles: the freedom and equality of all citizens and respect for private property rights. But given the poor quality of records, it was very easy for masters to pretend that slaves had been born earlier than they actually had been, while slaves were also able to seek false documentation showing that they were younger than they really were. There was little impact beyond some maneuvering for the first several years, but by the 1880s, Brazilian slaves were fleeing slavery by the tens of thousands, state governments were abolishing slavery on their own and welcoming RUNAWAY SLAVES from other states, and the national government could see that the end was in sight. Finally, Princess ISABEL OF BRAGANÇA abolished slavery entirely on her own authority in 1888, and shortly thereafter, the imperial government was overthrown by a republican alliance of military officers and rural landowners who did not, however, reestablish slavery.

CUBA adopted a free womb law, the Moret law, in 1870, in the midst of the TEN YEARS' WAR. Again, this was seen as a concession to the demands of the mostly black rebels in that conflict that would not appear to violate property rights. But the Moret law had little impact on actual practices on the plantations. Those masters who were able to hold on to their slaves while the fighting was going on were not going to release them voluntarily, and the government did not have the resources to force them. Finally, the negotiated end to the war also freed most slaves who had fought on either side, and the final end of slavery in Cuba was the universal abolition decree by the Spanish government in 1880.

Several of the newly independent countries of Spanish America also attempted to implement free womb laws in the 1820s and 1830s. The abolition of slavery was a central theme of the liberal ideology behind most of the rebel movements, and even the more conservative leaders who took over in most countries as the rebellions were triumphant realized that conditions could not continue as they had before. In those areas of Spanish America where plantation slavery had established a foothold in the colonial period, the half-measure of the free womb law did not work out at all. This is especially true of MEXICO. There, a judicial opinion in 1824 declared that all persons born after the effective date of independence were free by virtue of having been born in a free country, and that the government should work with slave owners to purchase the freedom of the remaining slaves. This transitional regime was fragile from the start, with exceptions granted by the conservative government, little funding available for compensation, and many slave owners completely ignoring the law. The Afro-Mexican liberal president VICENTE GUERRERO SALDAÑA declared slavery abolished unconditionally in 1829. In New Granada, which ultimately became the separate nations of VENEZUELA, COLOMBIA, and ECUADOR, a free womb law was adopted under the rule of Simón Bolívar. This law provided for the apprenticeship of the newly freed slave children, and slave owners manipulated the contracts so as to keep people beyond their contracted times. Ultimately, a series of new laws was required in each of these countries in the 1850s to abolish slavery finally.

Several states in the Northern United States had free womb laws in the years after the WAR OF AMERICAN INDEPENDENCE, 1775–83. The first of these was PENNSYLVANIA, which passed a law in 1780 that freed all slaves born after that date at their 28th birthday. Slavery persisted in Pennsylvania until the 1840s. RHODE ISLAND adopted gradual emancipation based on the free womb in 1804. NEW YORK STATE passed a free womb law in 1799, followed by a law in 1817 that indentured all slaves born before 1799 for an additional 10 years. In both cases, these gradual emancipation measures led many masters to sell their slaves to areas farther south that retained slavery. NEW JERSEY adopted a free womb law in 1804 that preserved slavery there until 1846 and explicitly permitted masters to sell their slaves into other states if they wished. The abolition of slavery in the Northern United States was often accompanied by harsher restrictions on free blacks, though Pennsylvania's law bucked this trend and gave the vote and equal legal rights to people of color.

Free womb laws almost always created a transitional status for the people it freed. Children are normally considered to be under the authority of their parents. In the case where the parents are slaves and the children free, the children were held to be under the authority of the master, but an authority limited in scope. The Pennsylvania law explicitly described the newly freed children as indentured servants. Indenture was an institution that existed in colonial America, which was no longer very common by the 19th century. But indentured people had certain legal rights, including the right to a payment in cash or in tools and livestock at the end of their indenture. The theory was that the master gained the right to the person's labor and in return was responsible for caring for the person's basic needs during the period of service and providing the means to become independent citizens at the end. The New Jersey law reimbursed the masters a quite liberal $3.00 per year for this service—the cost of these payments amounted to 40 percent of the state budget in the 1830s, giving masters an important financial stake in seeing the system continue.

Free womb laws offered a promise of fair treatment for slaves, peaceful abolition of slavery, and respect for property rights. However, for the most part, this promise was not realized. Masters retained great powers under the transitional regime the laws created, allowing them to work great injustice on some slaves, cheating them of the freedom the law promised. On the other hand, the laws clearly established the government on the side of freedom, and many slaves took advantage of this looser climate to undermine their status by flight, lawsuit, fraud, or negotiations with their masters. Without the full weight of the government and public opinion behind them, masters were no longer able to maintain their authority as forcefully as they had. The result was that while some slaves gained freedom, and some masters received something in return for the human property they were giving up, the benefits were not distributed equally to either group.

Stewart R. King

FURTHER READING

Harper, Douglas. "Slavery in the North." Available online. URL: http://www.slavenorth.com/. Accessed December 28, 2010.
Klein, Herbert S. *African Slavery in Latin America and the Caribbean.* Oxford: Oxford University Press, 1986.

LECESNE AND ESCOFFERY CASE

The Lecesne and Escoffery case was a cause célèbre of the antislavery movement in Britain in 1825 and arguably played a vital role in the series of events that led the Jamaican legislature to grant civil and political rights to free men of color in 1833. The plaintiffs, Louis Lecesne (1798–1848) and John Escoffery (1795–1875), who were of Haitian descent, were leaders in the campaign launched in 1823 by free men of color in JAMAICA to expand their civil rights. Successful Kingston merchants, Lecesne and Escoffery were members of the Committee of Twenty-One, which was charged with the responsibility of drawing up a petition to delineate the demands of free men of color and of presenting this petition to the House of Assembly, the governing legislative body in Jamaica. Couched diplomatically in the language of request, these demands included the right of free men of color to vote and to serve on juries and the removal of restrictions that prohibited free men of color from working in public offices and in supervisory positions on estates owned by whites. The petition also included a request for repeal of the law that required free men of color to produce testimonials of baptism before they could give evidence in court.

Beset by visions of the HAITIAN REVOLUTION and especially of the role that free men of color in Haiti played in instigating the rebellion, members of the white Jamaican elite were panicked by the unrelenting forward movement of the campaign, and they were determined to thwart the demands of the free men of color to expand their civil rights. As the campaign approached its culmination in November 1823, members of the white elite urged the government to institute a secret committee to investigate the alleged practice of treasonable communication in the island. The investigation, led by Hector Mitchell, representative of the parish of Kingston in the House of Assembly, resulted in the arrest of several people in the island, including Lecesne and Escoffery, under the Alien Law. According to Mitchell's report, Lecesne and Escoffery were both aliens and "persons of a dangerous description." On the strength of this report, the governor of the island, the duke of Manchester, ordered Lecesne and Escoffery to be arrested.

Despite the fact that many witnesses testified that Lecesne and Escoffery had lived in Jamaica since infancy, the fact that they were members of the MILITIA, were freeholders, and had prosperous businesses, they were denied habeas corpus. Left without recourse to the law, Lecense and Escoffery—who were both married and had large families that were entirely dependent on them for their subsistence—were summarily deported to Haiti. In Haiti, Lecesne and Escoffery petitioned Governor Manchester for clemency. However, they were unsuccessful and decided to travel to Britain, where they believed they would be assured a fair hearing. In Britain, they gained the ear of Stephen Lushington, member of Parliament, renowned lawyer, and a prominent member of the Anti-Slavery Society.

The Lecesne-Escoffery case occurred at an opportune moment for the Anti-Slavery Society. In 1823, the society, whose stated intention was the gradual abolition of slavery, achieved a major success when they persuaded the British government to adopt the amelioration of slavery as policy. However, the society quickly lost political capital among its supporters because slave unrest swept through the British West Indies when word of its intention to abolish slavery reached the slaves. Estate owners in the British West Indies blamed the unrest on the society, and when news of the rebellions reached Britain, support among the British public for the antislavery agenda waned. The fortunes of the society plummeted, and it was faced with the dilemma of how simultaneously to keep the pro-abolition attention of the British public on the British West Indies and to continue to press for change without further inflaming the situation in the colonies. The Lecesne and Escoffery case provided the society with the perfect solution. As the historian Gad Heuman argued in *Between Black and White: Race, Politics, and the Free Coloreds in Jamaica, 1792-1865* (1981), society used the case to expose the "injustice inherent" in British West Indian slave societies without the risk of stirring up further slave unrest by focusing not on the unfair treatment of slaves but on unjust treatment of free men of color by the government in Jamaica. Moreover, focusing on Lecesne and Escoffery as free British male subjects and respectable merchants who had been denied rights allowed the society to gain the sympathy of British lower-middle and working-class people, who were struggling to gain their own full civil and political rights.

In June 1825, Lushington presented a petition to the British House of Commons on behalf of Lecesne and Escoffery for redress of their grievances against the government of Jamaica. He charged that the arrest and deportation of Lecesne and Escoffery were a "gross abuse of power, and an utter disregard for all the principles of justice" by the government in Jamaica. Moreover, Lushington accused the governor of complicity in the arrest and deportation of the men, which he asserted was driven by personal malice against Lecesne by Assemblyman Mitchell. Furthermore, Lushington claimed there was no evidence to support the accusation that Lecesne and Escoffery were aliens. Even if they had not been born in Jamaica, he argued that the decision to arrest them using the Alien Law was an abuse of the law, as it was not intended to extend its operations to persons who had resided on the island from their infancy. Finally, Lushington claimed that was there was no evidence to substantiate the charges that Lecesne and Escoffery were dangerous individuals or that they were in secret communication with Haiti for treasonable purposes. Lushington used the Lecesne-Escoffery case to demonstrate forcefully to the British Parliament and the British public that the injustice revealed in the case was symptomatic of the rampant injustice in British West Indian slave-owning societies and of the discrimination and oppression under which free men of color in Jamaica labored.

The Anti-Slavery Society initially supported the Lecesne-Escoffery case as an example of the injustices of colonial slave society: not merely demonstrating the maladministration of justice in general but also the specific injustice of these societies' institutionalized denial of rights to free men of color. However, it seems that the society might well have had another motive for supporting the case. Through direct exposure to Lecesne and Escoffery and other free men of color during the society's advocacy of the case, the members and other influential Britons realized that free people of color were not "low, degraded, or destitute" but instead comprised an exponentially increasing number of wealthy, well-positioned, and influential individuals. By taking their side in the struggle for civil rights, the society hoped to gain the allegiance of free coloreds, who would, in turn, help the society to achieve its agenda of abolition. At the general meeting of the Anti-Slavery Society in 1830, Thomas Babington Macaulay, a leading member of the Anti-Slavery Society, suggested as much. Bemoaning the difficulty that the Anti-Slavery Society had in persuading the white elite–dominated governments in the colonies to enact antislavery legislation, Macaulay claimed that this would change if free coloreds gained political power. Supporting Macaulay's argument, but in somewhat more guarded language, Lushington expressed the belief that the success of the Anti-Slavery society's agenda "lay upon the individual exertions of the free coloreds."

On December 1, 1830, seven years after Lecesne and Escoffery had been deported, a group of prominent free men of color in Jamaica hosted a dinner to celebrate their triumphant return to the island. The free men who met that evening had more than the return of their brethren to celebrate. One month before—October 1830—thanks in no small part to the spotlight shined on the plight of the free coloreds by the Lecesne-Escoffery case in England, the Jamaican legislature had relented and enacted a law that granted to free men of color all the privileges that whites enjoyed. The granting of this law was the first step toward the political emancipation of free men of color in Jamaica. These free men were now poised in a new way to become a significant political force in the colony.

Janette Gayle

FURTHER READING

Campbell, Mavis C. *The Dynamics of Change in a Slave Society: A Sociopolitical History of the Free Coloreds of Jamaica, 1800–1865.* Cranbury, N.J.: Associated University Presses, 1976.

Heuman, Gad. *Between Black and White: Race, Politics, and the Free Coloreds in Jamaica, 1792–1865.* Westport, Conn.: Greenwood Press, 1981.

Holt, Thomas C. *The Problem of Freedom: Race, Labor, and Politics in Jamaica and Britain, 1832–1938.* Baltimore: Johns Hopkins University Press, 1992.

LEE, WILLIAM (ca. 1750–1828) *American artisan, hunter, and servant*

William Lee was a mixed-race enslaved hunter and personal servant to GEORGE WASHINGTON from 1768 until Washington's death in 1799. He was freed by virtue of Washington's will and lived the rest of his life at Mount Vernon as a free artisan. When Washington bought him, he said that his age was 18, but no records exist verifying his life before 1768. Before that time, he was the property of Mary Lee, widow of Colonel John Lee of Westmoreland County, Virginia, and William asserted in later years that the colonel was his father. He said that the colonel had always treated him as a son but that after his death, his widow, embarrassed by his presence, perhaps needing ready cash, decided to sell him.

George Washington was a young planter with a distinguished record from his service on the western frontiers during the SEVEN YEARS' WAR, and he needed a personal servant to take care of him. Washington's wife, Martha Dandridge Custis Washington, was distantly related to the Lees, and she may have been aware of the relationship between William and Colonel Lee. In any case, while the other three slaves Washington purchased along with Lee were sent to work in the fields of Mount Vernon, Lee became Washington's constant companion for the rest of his life. Lee was a remarkably good horseman, much like his master was, and he was responsible for Washington's hunting dogs and for supervising fox and deer hunts.

Lee also accompanied Washington during the WAR OF AMERICAN INDEPENDENCE, 1775–83. While early biographers of Washington, such as Parson Weems, made some fun of Lee's forays onto the battlefield, it is clear from Washington's letters that Lee was untiringly helpful to him under sometimes very difficult circumstances and never failed to go where Washington sent him. Lee was in charge of the servants of the other officers on Washington's staff.

After the war, Lee returned to Mount Vernon with Washington and then accompanied him when he returned to public life in the late 1780s. Before Washington's inauguration in 1789, Lee accompanied Washington on his last call on his dying mother. Washington kept Lee with him throughout his first term as president (1789–93), first in New York City and then in PHILADELPHIA, PENNSYLVANIA, which served as the nation's capitals. Lee was in charge of the servants, both enslaved and free, at Washington's houses in New York and Philadelphia. He married a free colored woman, Margaret Thomas, in Philadelphia, with Washington's reluctant consent. Washington no doubt feared he would lose Lee to free life in Philadelphia, as he had lost others of his enslaved servants during his years in public service in the North. But in fact, Lee, perhaps accompanied by his wife (though

A portrait of the Washington family with William Lee standing at far right. Lee was George Washington's constant companion from 1768 until Washington's death in 1799, after which Lee lived as a free man at Mount Vernon until his own death in 1828. He was an important source for Washington's biographer Charles Willson Peale. *(Library of Congress)*

this is unclear), returned to Mount Vernon, probably in 1796. In the 1780s, the two had gone on a long trip to the Ohio River valley to survey Washington's land claims there. Lee hurt his knee in a fall, an injury that pained him for the rest of his life and contributed to his ongoing alcohol abuse. By the mid-1790s, Lee's alcoholism and the physical disability caused by his injury undermined his effectiveness as a household manager, and Washington reluctantly relieved him of his duties, seeking a replacement during his second term with the same "excellent qualities" and "good appearance."

When Washington died in 1799, his will specified that all slaves whom he owned in his own name should be freed. This was, in fact, done in 1801 by his widow, Martha. But Lee was already free by that time. A special clause in Washington's will independently freed Lee in recognition of his "attachment to me and his faithful services during the Revolutionary War" and gave him an annual pension of $30, the equivalent of about $8,500

today, a respectable living allowance for a single man in rural Virginia. Lee lived quietly in Mount Vernon and worked repairing shoes to supplement his income. He was an important, if unacknowledged, source for early biographers of Washington, talking at length with Charles Willson Peale, among others. He was treated for his alcoholism by a mixed-race informal practitioner who lived nearby, WEST FORD, a man who some people believe was Washington's illegitimate son. Lee died in 1828, either from alcohol-related problems or from excessive bloodletting by Ford.

William Lee epitomizes the life of many free people of color in the Americas. He was one of many faithful retainers, perhaps relatives (though in this case a distant one), who served faithfully all their lives, then were given freedom when no longer very useful as workers but kept on around the plantation, with free housing and maybe rations (perhaps liquid ones, in Lee's case, as the Washington plantation produced grain alcohol in commercial quantities) to show the remaining slaves the reward for hard work and loyalty. He allowed Washington's family and many admirers in early America to have an image of the president as a humane man who cared for his enslaved workforce in a personal way.

Stewart R. King

FURTHER READING

Egerton, Douglas R. *Death or Liberty: African-Americans and Revolutionary America.* Oxford: Oxford University Press, 2009.

Wiencek, Henry. *An Imperfect God: George Washington, His Slaves, and the Creation of America.* New York: Farrar, Straus & Giroux, 2004.

LEGAL DISCRIMINATION ON THE BASIS OF RACE

Race became a reason to discriminate against an individual under law sometime during the period of exploration of the Americas. The process varied from country to country within Europe and from colony to colony within a given country's colonial empire. By the end of the era of slavery in the late 19th century, a legal system of social stratification that had once been based entirely on the status superiority of the ruling class—nobles' being superior to free commoners, who were in turn superior to serfs, foreigners, and slaves—became one based to a large extent on the superiority of race—whites superior to blacks, Indians, and other nonwhites. The process developed along with changing attitudes about race, and along with changing attitudes about the proper justification for social hierarchy and the authority of rulers. In addition, the process was affected by the growing wealth and numbers of free people of color and the challenge they posed to an evolving idea of white superiority.

Medieval Roots

In medieval society, people of color were little different from others of similar social class. If they were subject to discrimination, as Moors were in Spain, it was because they were not Christians or because they were foreigners, subjects of the caliph of Cordoba; or because they were enslaved or serfs. If a person with some Moorish ancestry were a Christian and a nobleman, like the Spanish culture hero El Cid (1044–99), he would have the same social standing as any other Christian nobleman. In the Arthurian epic, Sir Morien, the Black Knight, was a hero, albeit an ambiguous one. Salāḥ ad-Dīn Yūsuf ibn Ayyūb (1137–93), known as Saladin in English, sultan of Egypt, and victor over the Crusaders in 1180, was admittedly a fair-skinned Middle Easterner, a Kurd from what is now Iraq, but was portrayed in Europe as nonwhite and as the epitome of chivalry. Shakespeare could create the character of Othello, the Moor of Venice, and imagine him to be both swarthy and thick-lipped and commander of the armies of Venice, a great European power at the time. Leo Africanus (1488–1544), a North African Muslim with some sub-Saharan African ancestors, was converted and baptized by the pope and became an important papal adviser on relations with the Muslim world.

Medieval law did not generally recognize racial difference, though the LAS SIETE PARTIDAS of Alfonso X (1265) did require that Moors and Jews be separately registered. In this case, however, the reference was to their religion and not any idea of biological origin. It was not until the 15th century in SPAIN, only a few decades before Columbus's voyage to the Americas, that Spanish law created the principle of *limpieza de sangre* (purity of blood) and began to distinguish Christians of "Old Christian" heritage from the descendants of recent converts from Judaism or Islam. Spain was a special case, because of the presence of large numbers of ethnically distinct people living within the borders of the expanding Spanish state. On Europe's other land frontier with the Islamic world, in the Balkans, the fact that Christians were generally retreating until the 17th century meant that similar problems did not arise, and there was no attempt at any time before the 19th century to make any kind of racial distinction between Christians and Muslims. Elsewhere in Europe, the few people who were from Africa were treated as any other foreign merchants, scholars, or wanderers were, that is to say, as appropriate to their social, religious, economic, and political status. It was not that Europeans were blind to the differences in appearance; indeed, they found them interesting. Elizabeth of York, queen of England (1466–1503), had two young black ladies in waiting, Elen and Margaret Moore, and a tournament was held in Elen's honor when she was old enough to be thinking about choosing a husband in 1507.

Period of Settlement of the Americas
Spanish America

Starting with the voyages of discovery of the 1400s, Europeans began to realize that ruling over large populations of people who were ethnically distinct from them posed some challenges. At first, the Catholic world debated the very humanity of non-Europeans they encountered in the various faraway places the explorers and conquistadores were going. The popes consistently proclaimed that every person throughout the world was human, capable of being made a Christian, and once baptized, entitled to all the rights of a European of his or her status. That is, they upheld the traditional social structure of medieval Europe and called for its extension to newly conquered places in such declarations as Sicut Dudum of 1435, which called on the Spanish to treat the Canary Islands natives decently and refrain from enslaving and working them to death. In *Veritas Ipsa* and *Sublimus Dei* of 1537, Pope Paul III extended the same logic to the people of the Americas. The churchmen Bartolomé de Las Casas and Juan Gines de Sepulveda debated these questions before a board of scholars at Valladolid in 1550. The outcome of their debate was the royal proclamation of the New Laws of the Indies.

The New Laws were very important because, while they affirmed the basic humanity of all the residents of the king's domains, they permitted the designation of individuals by race and different treatment of people on the basis of race. The precedent was the concept of *limpieza de sangre,* which was originally created to distinguish between presumably more loyal "Old Christians" and the descendants of recent converts from Islam and Judaism. The "New Christians" were deemed to be at risk of slipping back into their old religions (and, indeed, some had never abandoned their traditional faiths and continued to practice them throughout the period). The same logic applied to Indians in the Americas—however loyal to the ROMAN CATHOLIC CHURCH they appeared, they might secretly, the Spanish believed, be worshipping the devils their ancestors had venerated, and so a special regimen was needed to make sure that they did not contaminate the ruling class. But in this case, the religious deviation was linked to their race, a new concept with some biological implications, distinct from the old concept of religion as identity that was found in the Siete Partidas. Without a certificate of purity of blood or its equivalent, the *CÉDULAS DE GRACIAS AL SACAR,* or royal pardon for those of mixed blood who were to be officially "whitened" (*see* "WHITENING" AND RACIAL PROMOTION), nobody could become a noble, enter the priesthood or a university, buy certain types of land, or hold most official positions.

The New Laws said very little about people of African ancestry. For one thing, blacks were few in number in the Americas at first. Some people of color from Spain had arrived with the conquistadores: JUAN GARRIDO, a free black man from Seville in Spain, accompanied Cortes in the conquest of Tenochtitlan in the early 16th century and was granted urban real estate and an *encomienda* as a reward. Garrido and free people of color of his generation benefited from the medieval rules: They were treated as any free Spaniard was and Garrido was a hero and had the status of a *hidalgo.* But fairly quickly, the Spanish began importing significant numbers of slaves from Africa, mostly as craftsmen or as intermediaries between the new rulers and their Indian subjects. At first, the status of slavery seemed sufficient to keep them in order, but as some among them began to gain their freedom—facilitated by the important jobs they held—the authorities began to see free people of color as a challenge to the racial hierarchy and applied similar rules to free coloreds as had been applied to Indians. Free people of color never benefited from the protections that the New Laws accorded to Indians: immunity to the Inquisition, exemption from most cash taxes (Indians were required to work or provide hired workers instead), limited self-government (for those tribes that had not fought the Spanish when they arrived). But as *PARDOS*, free African Americans were limited in the same way New Christians and Indians were, being prohibited nobility, positions of authority in the government or church, and some professions. Even people of good family were affected including (the future saint) MARTÍN DE PORRES (1579–1639), the son of a Spanish colonial governor and a black woman, who was barred from full membership in the order of DOMINICANS because of his race.

Brazil

In BRAZIL, a somewhat similar set of events unfolded after the beginning of Portuguese settlement in the 1530s. At first, there were only a few Afro-Brazilians, most of them the descendants of Africans who had sailed to southern Portugal with the Moors or who had been taken as slaves in the 15th century. They were joined by a few more Africans from the Portuguese Atlantic islands of São Tomé, Cap Verde, and the Azores. These islands were profitable sugar regions in the 16th century, and about mid-century-SUGAR CULTIVATION began in Brazil as well. At first, the workers in the cane fields were mainly Indians, captured by the *bandeirantes* who ranged throughout the enormous interior of the colony looting and kidnapping. But the supply of Indians was limited, and more and more Africans were imported as time went on.

Portugal did not have a coherent set of regulations like the Siete Partidas and the New Laws of the Indies to govern non-Portuguese within the society. Governmental authority in Brazil was also shared, in the most prosperous and heavily populated sugar-growing regions, between the Crown and the captain-generals, who were the owners of those regions by royal grant. The kings of Portugal did not gain complete control over the government of the colony until after the end of the war with the Netherlands in 1654. Meanwhile, the laws related to free people of color evolved in a patchwork fashion, with social custom in any particular area at least as important as the edicts of the government thousands of miles away in Lisbon. On the whole, however, the outcome was the same: Blacks and Indians were by law human beings, potentially Christians, and citizens of the state. They were potentially subject to status discrimination, if they were slaves. If they were free, they were still limited in some ways in the roles they could take up in society. The greater independence of the Portuguese colonists vis-à-vis their home country government meant that the actual treatment of free people of color varied much more widely in Brazil than in the Spanish colonies. Some free people of color found their way to high positions in society, such as the man whom the British traveler Henry Koster met in 1820. He asked his servant about a particular local official, the Capitão-môr, or port captain. "Was he not a mulatto man?" Yes, said the servant; he was a mulatto but is so no longer. Koster wondered how this could be, and the servant replied, "How could a capitão-môr be a mulatto?" The man in question had escaped the negative consequences of his partially African ancestry by obtaining an official dispensation and by gaining the respect of his white neighbors for his wealth, position, and influence. (*See also* MULATTO.)

French Colonies

The earliest French settlers in the Americas were religious refugees, Huguenots fleeing the Wars of Religion in their home. They were homogenous communities of Europeans, and the political and military pressure they suffered under in the Americas from Catholic Spaniards and Portuguese meant that they had no leisure to gather the wealth to purchase slaves. As the Huguenots morphed into buccaneers, they gathered other disaffected people into their settlements. There were black buccaneers, as well as Indian refugees, and people from all corners of Europe. (*See also* PIRACY.) Buccaneer society was very egalitarian, with the only divisions being those of ability and ruthlessness. The buccaneers of the 17th century were often successful in their war against the Iberians, capturing slaves and treasure from the Spanish colonies and Brazil. The treasure went to buy plantations, and society evolved in much the same way as it had in the Iberian colonies. As the French government, once again united after the Bourbon victory in the Wars of Religion, imposed its authority on the colonies in the Americas, the laws took on a Catholic character. Thus, under the CODE NOIR IN FRENCH LAW (proclaimed in 1685), free people of color were to enjoy all the rights of Frenchmen while being enjoined, if they themselves had once been slaves, to remain respectful to their former masters. As in Brazil, however, these royal edicts were hard to enforce on a population accustomed to being in charge of its own affairs. Free people of color in the French colonies experienced a wide range of treatment, from wealthy planters who integrated themselves almost completely into the white community to poor PEASANTS or laborers who were almost totally excluded and forced to live in the mountains or shantytowns near the colonial towns and accept what few

leavings in the way of land and employment white society would accord them.

North America and the British Caribbean

The British colonies took a very different tack. The first British settlers in the Americas were fishermen along the northern coast of North America. They were followed by a variety of settlers in Virginia and MASSACHUSETTS. All these groups were fairly homogenous. They also shared a model of colonialism that had been developed in Ireland and owed little to Catholic notions of universal humanity. The English went to the Americas to establish "plantations" in the sense used in Ulster, that is, newly implanted shoots from the original tree of English society, complete with all its elements from noble to yeoman free farmer to servant, and without any extraneous elements. It was many years before it became obvious that the supply of English servants was going to be insufficient and some other source of labor would have to be imported to make the new colonies grow profitably. For one thing, in the Northern colonies of North America the white population reproduced itself pretty successfully, after the first or second generation of settlement, ensuring a steady supply of white workers. In the Caribbean colonies, and in the American South, especially GEORGIA, where health conditions were less good, and natural growth started later, colonial governors believed that they could get servant labor from involuntarily transported criminals or political opponents. Although the first Africans were taken to Jamestown, Virginia, in 1619, it was not until the last quarter of the 17th century that significant numbers of Africans were imported to the English colonies.

An important step in this process was England's capture of JAMAICA from Spain in 1655. Such a large island, with such a forbidding disease environment, the English believed, was never going to be successfully settled by Europeans alone. In addition, the Spanish had taken in black slaves and introduced sugar cultivation on a small scale during their rule. So Jamaica rapidly became the destination for many slave-trading voyages. At the same time, sugar cultivation began in earnest in the earlier English colonies in the eastern Caribbean, starting with BARBADOS in 1644. As slave populations grew in the British Caribbean, they provided a market for food exports from British North America, and in return slaves were sold north. The slave populations in Virginia, MARYLAND, and the Carolinas, and later in Georgia, once that colony accepted slave imports, began to grow. Blacks in Virginia increased from about 7 percent of the population in 1680 to about 22 percent in 1700.

The laws regarding slavery and free people of color took some time to settle down. In the Chesapeake Bay until the 1660s, many, though not all, black "servants" had the same rights as white indentured servants, which included freedom after a designated period of service and the right to land and tools from their master. A small population of free black farmers was the result of this policy, which ended in the 1660s and 1670s when the colonial legislature enacted laws making black servants slaves for life and stating that the children of a slave mother were themselves slaves (even if their father were free). Maryland had been the first colony to declare, in 1639, that baptism did not make a slave free, and the other English colonies followed suit. Free people of color retained significant rights under the laws of most colonies, however, until the AMERICAN WAR OF INDEPENDENCE, 1775–83. They could sue and be sued on an equal footing with whites. They could, and did, marry whites. They owned property, including slaves of their own, and served in the MILITIA. Various measures demonstrated, however, that they were not to be considered equal citizens with free Englishmen, and they had status more like that of resident foreigners. They could be baptized in the official Church of England and were required to attend church in most colonies but were not voting members of parishes (though they paid the tithes or taxes to support the church). Naturally, they could not be priests or have other offices in the church. They served in the militia but could not be officers. They could hold no other offices under the government, even as village selectmen in places like Massachusetts that had elected local government. They could not be on juries or be justices of the peace. Their lack of citizenship made the next stage of increasing discrimination easier.

Discrimination Increases: The Eighteenth and Nineteenth Centuries

With the beginning of the Enlightenment in the 18th century, new ideas about the nature of man in society, about science and what it revealed about human nature and specifically about race, and about the role of religious ideas in the structure of society all affected the status of free people of color. In addition, as populations of color, both free and enslaved, grew in many places in the Americas, white leaders grew to fear the black population and reacted with more legal restrictions.

The Enlightenment meant a decrease in the power of religion to shape political ideas and a corresponding increase in secular, scientific ideas. In Catholic countries, the influence of the popes, who had insisted that all people were human beings and should be equal as subjects of Catholic monarchs, declined, to be replaced by more modern notions of the nature of man, sparked in many cases by the growth of the Masons and secular education (*see* FREEMASONRY). In some ways, these ideas were more advanced and egalitarian than what they had replaced. The philosophers of the Enlightenment tended to think

that, as THOMAS JEFFERSON said in the American Declaration of Independence, "all men are created equal, that they are endowed by their Creator with certain unalienable rights, that among these are life, liberty, and the pursuit of happiness."

But Enlightenment political thought was frequently utilitarian; if some group of people did not appear to merit their rights or use them wisely, it was easier to argue that they should not be allowed to enjoy them, because the root of all social rights and laws was the common good of mankind. This is an underlying theme in the thought of the political philosophers who influenced Jefferson, David Hume, John Locke, and Montesquieu, though brought to fruition only in the thought of the 19th-century British liberal thinkers such as Jeremy Bentham. Moreover, the new scientific mind-set of the Enlightenment had explored the condition of slaves on the plantations of the Americas and discovered that they lived under very difficult circumstances, did not appear to work any harder than was needed for survival, and appeared to have great difficulty understanding the commands of their masters. Nobody wondered whether these characteristics had any relation their status as slaves with no stock in the success of their masters' businesses. Instead, a growing racial science, reflected in the *Encyclopedia* of Diderot (published 1751–72), the *Notes on the State of Virginia* (1785) of Jefferson, the *Description . . . de l'Isle de Saint-Domingue* of MÉDÉRIC-LOUIS-ÉLIE MOREAU DE ST.-MÉRY (1797), and a number of lesser-known works, described the black race as naturally barbaric, lazy, violent, and stupid. Furthermore, as the biblical description of humankind's springing forth from a single pair of ancestors lost credibility, scientists began to suggest that perhaps the races of humanity had a number of different ancestral stocks and thus were not really the same species. All this new thought contrasted with the Catholic argument for human rights, which was that everyone was equally the descendant of Adam and thus equally the subject of religion and equally potentially savable though Christ and the church. The Catholic notion of the proper organization of society permitted inequality on the basis of birth or status but insisted on the common humanity of all. This equal humanity came from God and not from nature or any notion of the common good and was truly inalienable. Catholics had had more or less of a monopoly on this line of thinking for several centuries, as Protestants concentrated on reforming church practices in their own countries and began to identify church membership with national citizenship. But as the 18th century dawned, various Protestant groups took up the universal position. As the century continued, the Quakers and Methodists became the leading proponents of a universal humanity and a concept of human rights based on spiritual equality (*see* BAPTISTS AND PIETISTS). Quakers and "dissenting" Protestants led the movement against the slave trade in Britain and welcomed free people of color such as OLAUDAH EQUIANO into their ranks in the 1700s. Thus, the Enlightenment offered an ambiguous legacy to people of color, on the one hand, affirming the fundamental equality of humanity and, on the other, creating the scientific concept of race and suggesting that races had differing abilities to benefit from equal rights.

Changing social and economic conditions also played a role in the deepening legal discrimination against free people of color in this period. Slave numbers increased dramatically throughout the Americas in the 18th and early 19th centuries. This was the period of the height of the slave trade. In addition, slave populations in some places of the Americas, such as the North American colonies, made a demographic turnaround and began to grow naturally, as well as by immigration. At the same time, European immigration to the Americas remained steady or even declined, at least in the early part of the century, as more economic opportunity and political stability in western Europe meant people could live more comfortably there. In those colonies in the Americas where plantation agriculture was becoming more efficient and profitable, the proportion of the population that was enslaved grew dramatically. Free colored populations also grew rapidly, both by manumission and by natural growth. In most places in the Americas, free people of color had the highest fertility rates of any population group.

Economic development in many colonies also made it harder for free people of color to demand equal status with whites. In less-developed colonies and in earlier periods, white elites lived in the colony, on their plantations, beside their free colored neighbors, who in many cases were their relatives, acknowledged or unacknowledged. As the plantation complex became more profitable, many white proprietors became absentees. At the same time, even for resident planters, relationships between masters and slaves became more utilitarian and profit-driven and less feudal and personal. As white elites had fewer relationships with blacks, free or enslaved, it became easier for them to consider discriminatory laws and other forms of harsh treatment.

Free people of color were also growing in their economic importance. Depending on the laws in place in any individual country or colony, free people of color might be restricted in the sorts of professions they could practice. But as a group, they often achieved considerable success within the limited areas open to them. In places where they were permitted to own land and slaves, some free people of color became important planters. In other areas, they were successful large businessmen, respected artists and ARTISANS, plantation managers and technicians, and public servants. The prominence of individual free people of color caused resentment among whites and led to calls for more discriminatory laws from poorer whites, who resented the competition and thought that racial solidarity demanded that they be preferred for these subordinate, but still lucrative, jobs.

The growing population of color, both free and enslaved, posed a threat to the white elites. While whites were able to think of free colored people as free persons like them, they were able to see in them potential allies. To the extent that free people of color were planters or businessmen who benefited from the plantation system, they had an economic stake in its survival. But as white elites began to think of free people of color as different from them because of their race, and similar to the slaves, they started to see them as threats. This change in social and economic conditions, linked to the change in worldview described, led to harsher laws restricting free people of color.

Development of Discriminatory Laws in Spanish America

During the 18th century, the Spanish colonial world remained the one place in the Americas most strongly influenced by Christian notions of universal humanity and a natural structured order of society. The kings of Spain and their viceroys in the Americas took seriously their identity as the "Most Catholic Majesties" and tried to impose Catholic ideas even in the face of increasing secular influences both at home and in the colonies. The Bourbon Reforms of Latin America during the 1750s and 1760s were influenced by Enlightenment ideas, however. In the name of efficiency, governmental centralism, and nationalism, all powerful Enlightenment ideas, people born in the colonies were to have less influence in government there. At the top of society, seats on colonial supreme courts, colonial and city governors and councils, bishops, and other senior positions were increasingly filled by Peninsular Spaniards instead of colonial CREOLES. Lower down in the hierarchy, similar attempts were made to purge people of lower racial castes and replace them with whites, even if those were creoles. Whiteness was seen as superior, and so in the interests of efficiency, inferiors were to be purged from positions of authority. So mixed-race militia officers lost their commissions in MEXICO in the 1760s. There were still some *pardo* priests, such as JOSÉ MARÍA MORELOS, the hero of Mexican independence, but it was harder and harder for mixed-race men who wanted to be priests to obtain the *cédulas de gracias al sacar* they needed to be admitted to seminaries or universities. Creole elites complained that the *gracias al sacar* was being extended to too many *pardos*, weakening the value of the whites' caste privilege, and colonial governments appeased them by issuing fewer and fewer of the "whitening" decrees as the century wore on.

The impact of the revolutions around the turn of the 19th century was dramatic. The HAITIAN REVOLUTION (1791–1804) bred great suspicion of free people of color as well as of slaves. All over the Americas, but particularly in CUBA and PUERTO RICO, the Spanish-American colonies near Haiti, there were fears of rebellion and new discriminatory laws. The rebels in the Cuban plot of 1812 led by the free black man José Antonio Aponte, for example, explicitly referred to the Haitian example. The beginning of the SOUTH AMERICAN WARS OF LIBERATION further deepened the repression of free communities of color by the Spanish authorities. Free people of color, including Morelos and VICENTE GUERRERO SALDAÑA in Mexico and JOSÉ PRUDENCIO PADILLA, Simón Bolívar's naval commander in VENEZUELA, played prominent roles in the rebel armies. Some free people of color remained loyal to Spain, feeling that the local creole elites who were fighting for independence were less likely to grant them equal rights than the Spanish Crown. The famous *llaneros* of the Venezuelan plains were generally of mixed race, and they fought under José Tomás Boves in the "infernal division" of the royalist army, so called because of the many atrocities it was accused of committing.

The liberal, egalitarian spirit of the Enlightenment dominated the first generation of leaders in postindependence Spanish America in the early 19th century. Most countries began to abolish slavery. Official legal restrictions on people of color were generally dropped along with all other legal distinctions of birth and caste. Unofficial discrimination continued, however, and even strengthened, as Simón Bolívar, for example, attacked his mixed-race generals as agents of a *pardocracía* that threatened governmental stability, liberal progress, and national unity.

In Cuba, where the independence movement faltered, repression of free people of color only deepened during the 19th century. Most Cubans were of mixed ancestry in the 1750s, slaves were few, and restrictions on *pardos* would have been impractical. Their situation was actually better on the island than in the mainland Spanish colonies. But starting about the time of the Haitian Revolution, more and more new African slaves were taken into the colony, and the free population of color became suspect. At the same time, the arrival of royalist exiles from the remainder of Spanish America, along with an upsurge of immigration from Europe after the end of the Napoleonic Wars, meant a sharp increase in the white population. Many of the new, very large SUGAR CULTIVATION plantations were owned or managed by North Americans, who had Anglo-American ideas of race rela-

tions. Several attempted slave insurrections, including Aponte's in 1812 and the LA ESCALERA PLOT in 1844, were led by free people of color. In response, legal restrictions on free coloreds grew more and more onerous. Along with the restrictions common throughout Spanish America, limiting admission to university, to the professions, to government jobs, and the like, there were also social regulations requiring segregation of the races in many other public places. These were apparently ideas adopted from North America, since these sorts of laws were more or less unknown elsewhere in Spanish America. When civil war finally began in 1868, the ranks of the rebel armies were overwhelmingly filled by free people of color (some of them RUNAWAY SLAVES and others prewar free people), and one of the most important rebel leaders was ANTONIO MACEO Y GRAJALES, "the Bronze Titan," a free colored man whose father was a planter in the western mountains. Slavery ended in Cuba shortly after the defeat of the rebels, and most formal discriminatory laws were abolished. After Cuba finally achieved its independence in 1898, these laws briefly reappeared under American occupation and then were once again repealed, but informal discrimination against black Cubans continues to this day.

Legal Discrimination Evolves in Brazil
Brazil followed a similar course to Spanish America up to the period of the revolutions of the turn of the 19th century. There were already large numbers of slaves in northeastern Brazil at the beginning of the 18th century, but discrimination against free people of color was not strong because of the feudal nature of society there. The position of any individual was determined much more by family and patronage ties to powerful whites than by color. The 1700s saw the development of gold mining in Minas Gerais and a further renaissance of sugar planting in the Northeast and consequent importation of many slaves. Especially in Minas Gerais, many slaves gained their freedom quickly, either by running away or by ransoming themselves with gold they dug out of the mines. A burgeoning free population of color provoked some resentment among creole whites, but Brazil's white population was much smaller than Spanish America's and much less influential on public policy. PORTUGAL is a small country, and Portuguese migrants in the colonial era were as likely to go to the Asian colonies as to Brazil. As a result, Brazil's ruling class was mostly native and sympathetic to the needs of Afro-Brazilians.

After Brazil gained its independence in 1822, the situation of free people of color under the empire changed little. Various laws, mostly unenforced, imposing legal handicaps on people of color under the Portuguese monarchy were repealed by the Imperial Constitution of

1824, which while conservative in its idea of a monarchist political order was liberal in guaranteeing equality and civil rights to all. Free people of color were citizens and enjoyed the same legal rights as whites. There was considerable informal discrimination, but the liberal legal order persisted up to and after Brazil's abolition of slavery and of the monarchy in the 1880s. Of all the slave societies in the Americas, it was in Brazil that free people of color experienced the fewest legal handicaps.

French Colonies

As SAINT-DOMINGUE became the most important sugar-producing area in the world after 1720, slaves and free people of color outnumbered whites by nine to one. The smaller Caribbean island colonies of Martinique and Guadeloupe and the mainland colony of French Guiana experienced similar, though somewhat less spectacular growth. The racial climate deteriorated as the population changed. Governments adopted the same sorts of laws as seen in other places; free people of color were forbidden to practice the professions, bear arms in public except as part of their militia service, and were no longer granted militia commissions or considered for other official positions. In addition to these measures designed to reserve positions of political power for whites, France adopted a series of social laws, forbidding people of color to use the last names of whites, even those to whom they were related. They were also denied the right to own carriages or wear certain types of clothing. They had to be identified in special, humiliating ways in official documents. All these regulations were more strictly enforced against poorer, urban free people of color, while wealthy planters of color managed to hang on to many of the officially forbidden prerogatives of whiteness. But in an assault on the rural free colored planters, the government in the South Province of Saint-Domingue made a serious effort to root out people of color who had passed as white, in some cases for more than one generation, requiring that they be identified by race in official documents.

Some observers, both at the time and today, see this concerted effort to separate and vilify the free colored population as a "divide and conquer" strategy by the French government to prevent the rise of a creole nationalism among native-born white and free colored planters like what would eventually lead to independence in Spanish America. However, again as in Spanish America, creole whites largely supported these measures, at least in the abstract, even though they might have tried to undermine them as applied to their own free colored relatives.

The FRENCH REVOLUTION abolished all legal discrimination in a series of measures between 1789 and 1794. By so doing, the revolutionaries hoped to gain the support of the free people of color in a violent struggle against British and Spanish enemies throughout the Caribbean and against slave rebels in Haiti. Whites in the colonies violently opposed the granting of civil rights to free people of color, and those who, as did VINCENT OGÉ, demanded their rights met painful ends. The slaves themselves were reconciled to the French Republic by the abolition of slavery in 1794, by which time most colonial whites had joined the royalist opposition or the British invaders. Laws during this transitional period made former free people of color equal to whites, while imposing some restrictions on the newly freed. Most former slaves had to continue working for their former plantations, though they had rights to wages and government regulation of their treatment.

A terrible struggle ultimately destroyed plantation society and racial hierarchy in Saint-Domingue, which became independent as Haiti in 1804. France regained control of its other Caribbean colonies in 1802–03 and tried to turn back the clock to the conditions of the 1780s. Free people of color were once again subject to laws excluding them from many fields of activity as well as subjecting them to humiliating social restrictions and segregation. As in Britain during this period, free people of color, such as CYRILLE-CHARLES BISSETTE, were active in the struggle for the abolition of slavery. There was no serious push for civil rights for free people of color as separate from the movement to free the slaves, though.

Discrimination Increases in the United States and British Colonies

In the British Caribbean colonies after the War of American Independence, whites demonstrated the same growing concern about the role of free people of color that was found in other Caribbean colonies. As the numbers of slaves increased, and therefore the proportion of the population that was of African descent, and as new ideas about race and citizenship took over the (white) public imagination, governments imposed increasingly harsh regulations on the population of color. The Slave Code of Jamaica increasingly penalized free colored owners of slaves with harsh regulations imposing such a financial burden on them that it became almost impossible for a free person of color to own more than a few slaves in the colony. New purchases of slaves by free people of color were effectively banned; as a result, since the slave population was not reproducing itself, the number of slaves owned by free coloreds would naturally decline over time. Free people of color were also limited in their ownership of land, restricted to small plots not in prime agricultural areas. Most free people of color in the British Caribbean lived in towns as a result. There, they were able to be educated and take up skilled trades but were barred from the professions and even from some more prestigious trades, such as jeweler and watchmaker. Naturally, free people of color chafed under these harsh regulations, and there were incidents of unrest as well as peaceful protest. A petition from the free people of color of Jamaica for equal access to the courts was approved by the British House of Lords in 1813. Further protests for civil rights led to the elimination of all discriminatory laws throughout the British Empire in 1830, a few years before the abolition of slavery.

The situation in the newly independent United States began much as in the British Caribbean colonies. The slave populations in the Southern states were large and growing by the 1780s. Slave imports, which had dwindled to almost nothing during the war, rebounded strongly; in addition, unlike in the Caribbean colonies, slave populations in the United States had an excess of births over deaths. Thus, there were plenty of newly arrived Caribbean slaves, as well as native-born slaves in the older established plantation areas of the Chesapeake and Carolinas who could be "sold south" to develop new plantation areas in the Southeast. Free colored populations grew quickly in the older plantation areas as well, both by natural growth and by fairly common MANUMISSION. GEORGE WASHINGTON, first president of the United States, freed all his slaves in his will, and many other SLAVE OWNERS followed his example in the early days of the republic.

However, harsh discriminatory laws in the newer plantation areas ensured that their free colored populations would remain small. Free people of color were mostly forbidden to move to the new states of the Southeast, and anyone who gained freedom in most Southern states was required to leave the region. Free people of color who were already living in these areas, often people who had been there under Spanish and French rule when those areas became part of the United States, were handicapped in their ability to buy land, own slaves, and practice trades and professions. As a result, free colored populations in the Northern states grew rapidly, while those in the Southern states grew slowly or not at all. Even in the older plantation areas, new, harsher laws were passed in the 1820s and 1830s to make manumission more difficult and to encourage free people of color to move out of the South. A Virginia law enacted after the Nat Turner uprising in 1831, for example, made it a crime to teach any black person, free or slave, to read. At the same time, the Northern states were progressively abolishing slavery and for the most part were not replacing it with legal regimes of discrimination against blacks, though many states, including MASSACHUSETTS and CONNECTICUT, maintained separate school systems for blacks. By 1830, almost all slaves north of the Mason-Dixon line had gained their freedom, and free blacks, while not exactly free of informal discrimination, were essential parts of society in the East Coast states. In the Midwest, they were less welcome, as some states passed laws theoretically prohibiting blacks from settling, but these laws were generally unenforced, and free black populations grew throughout the region.

After the abolition of slavery in the United States in 1865, however, discrimination under law gained a new lease on life. The spirit of the era of RECONSTRUCTION IN THE UNITED STATES (1863–77) was hostile to racial discrimination, but Southern states tried nonetheless to impose black codes on their black populations—both the newly freed and the previously free blacks—that limited labor mobility, required special registration, and enforced social segregation (see BLACK CODES IN THE UNITED STATES). Although these laws were struck down by the federal government, after the 1877 compromise and the withdrawal of federal occupation troops, Southern white elites could do as they pleased. Poorer Southern whites were granted privileges on the basis of race, and their alliance with the elites permitted the imposition of harsh new laws. Republican ideals of majority rule and decentralization paradoxically led to the disenfranchisement and oppression of blacks in many places. The new legal and social order in the South, called Jim Crow, imposed harsh social, economic, and political handicaps on blacks. Many Northern states had weaker versions of the same regulations: "Sundown" laws, which were common in many localities in the Midwest and West, required nonwhites to reside outside city limits, and school segregation was almost universal. Blacks resisted these measures as best they could, given that a first step in almost all jurisdictions was to disenfranchise the black. The NEGRO CONVENTION MOVEMENT IN THE UNITED STATES of the late 19th century and the National Association for the Advancement of Colored People, founded after the turn of the 20th century, pursued public protest and legal action against these regulations but, without the support of the federal government, achieved little success.

Conclusion

Legal discrimination against free people of color on the basis of race developed during the period of slavery and became an important tool of white elites in some places by the 19th century. The factors that most influenced this process were, on the one hand, changing ideas about human rights, race as a scientific concept, and the proper roles of government and the church in ensuring social progress and, on the other hand, the changing demographics and economics of slave societies. Discriminatory laws may have been a means for home country governments to divide wealthy free people of color from their white neighbors, but they also functioned to deepen the solidarity of white communities. Faced with black majorities, in many places, whites rallied around each other and put free people of color into a lower place in the social order. This was easier to do because the old Christian idea of universal human solidarity had been undermined, first by the Reformation, among Protestant English and French colonists, and then by the rise of Enlightenment humanism and skepticism. The Enlightenment had its own ideal of universal human solidarity, but it was based not on divine command but ultimately on an idea that equality and freedom were utilitarian, though this notion did not become explicit or dominant in liberal political philosophy until the 19th century. The new governments, both liberal European governments like those in France and Britain and independent American governments, informed by Enlightenment ideas, varied widely in their acceptance of racial equality. Both the British and the French ultimately eliminated discrimination on the basis of race around the time they abolished slavery in their colonies. The former Iberian colonies also generally moderated or eliminated their formal legal discrimination. In the United States, on the other hand, more dedication to republican ideals paradoxically permitted legal discrimination against people of color to outlive the end of slavery by a century.

Stewart R. King

FURTHER READING

Applebaum, Nancy, ed. *Race and Nation in Modern Latin America.* Chapel Hill: University of North Carolina Press, 2003.
Berlin, Ira. *Slaves without Masters: The Free Black in the Antebellum South.* New York: New Press, 1974.
Davis, David Brion. *The Problem of Slavery in the Age of Revolution.* Ithaca, N.Y.: Cornell University Press, 1975.
Foner, Eric. *Reconstruction: America's Unfinished Revolution.* New York: HarperCollins, 1988.
Johnson, Kevin R., ed. *Mixed Race America and the Law: A Reader.* New York: New York University Press, 2003.
Telles, Edward E. *Race in Another America: The Significance of Skin Color in Brazil.* Princeton, N.J.: Princeton University Press, 2006.

LEMBA, SEBASTIÁN (unknown–1547)
rebel leader

Firsts of any kind are important. There were African slaves on Hispaniola, the island now shared by the DOMINICAN REPUBLIC and Republic of Haiti, for several years before 1502, when the first mention of their running away from Spaniards to join isolated Taíno Indian villages appeared in print. Written records reveal that the first mass African slave rebellion on Hispaniola took place on Christmas Day 1521, on a plantation belonging to Christopher Columbus's son Diego. All of those rebellious free blacks in the Americas, however, were unnamed. Sebastián Lemba, who ran away in the late 1520s or early 1530s, is the first free black rebel leader in the Americas whom we know by name.

Scattered documents indicate that Lemba was born in the Congo (*see* CONGO AND ANGOLA), but there is no indication of when he was taken to Hispaniola. We do not even know conclusively that he was a slave on one of the island's sugarcane plantations, but the vast majority of Africans from the 1520s on were taken in for the planting, cutting, and processing of sugarcane. Documents also repeatedly state that Lemba and his men viciously singled out sugarcane plantations, especially the mills and the buildings where the sweet juices were boiled down into raw sugar, indicating that Lemba hated them, probably for the grueling work and abuses that he and other African slaves suffered there.

Lemba became a *cimarrón*, a word that became *maroon* in English, meaning "runaway." He joined the Taíno cacique (chief) Enriquillo, whose successful rebellion against the Spaniards from 1519 through 1534 inspired hundreds of other Taíno and African slaves to run away. When Enriquillo signed a peace treaty with King Charles V, through his representative, Francisco de Barrionuevo, a treaty that offered freedom to Enriquillo and all his Indian and African followers, Captain Lemba refused the deal. In fact, 12 years later, Lemba and Diego de Ocampo, another rebel African slave leader, massacred the remains of Enriquillo's people, supposedly because they had agreed to help the Spanish Crown hunt down other indigenous and African cimarrons, although there is documentary evidence that contradicts this commonly held belief.

At the height of his raiding, Lemba reportedly led up to 400 African warriors. He was "an extraordinarily cunning negro and very knowledgeable about things of war, whom all obey and all fear," wrote two Spanish judges to King Charles V. Lemba was notorious for the many Spaniards he ambushed along the roads and held for large ransoms. And he and his men attacked sugar plantations, stealing arms, ammunition, iron and steel implements, horses, mules, food, clothing, and enslaved women and men. Lemba made sure that the mills and the boiling houses were burned and ordered both Spanish and mestizo plantation managers and their families killed.

Lemba himself was killed in September 1547, after almost 20 years of freedom, by an African slave. As a reward, that unnamed slave was granted his freedom. Decapitated, Lemba's head was stuck on a pike at one of SANTO DOMINGO's main gates. The Spaniards believed this would discourage other African slaves from rebelling. A year later, however, a Spanish colonist warned the Crown, "The island is in terror that the other 12,000 negroes . . . will rise up too." Attacks by the cimarrons, coupled with the Crown's moving the royal fleet to Havana, hit the economy hard. Only one-third of the island's sugarcane plantations were still in operation. The sugar industry on Hispaniola would not recover for more than 300 years.

Lynne A. Guitar

FURTHER READING

Guitar, Lynne. "Boiling It Down: Slavery and Rebellion on the First Commercial Sugarcane Ingenios in the Americas (Hispaniola, 1530–1545)." In *Slaves, Subjects, and Subversives: Blacks in Colonial Latin America*, edited by Jane G. Landers and Barry M. Robinson, 39–82. Albuquerque: University of New Mexico Press, 2006.

LIBERIA

Liberia in West Africa was inhabited by a variety of peoples organized into small political units of a few villages at most, when, in 1625, it was invaded by the Mane, Mandé-speaking soldiers from the fragmenting Songhai Empire to the north. The Mane conquered the region and installed a feudal system, with Mane chieftains ruling over villages and towns and the largest chief elected king and ruling from Grand Cape Mount, in the vicinity of modern Robertsport. Their descendants are now known as the Mandingo, or Malinké, and preserve ethnic ties with Mandingos from Ivory Coast to Gambia. The Mane were Muslims, and they took with them merchants from the North, the Kru, who established towns and trade routes and connected the region to the trans-Saharan trade. European merchants had had little impact on the region because of the lack of good ports, though Kru merchants were in contact with European slave traders and traded on their own account up and down the coast. The area was relatively isolated from the Atlantic slave trade, however, compared to the regions to the north and east.

The relative isolation of Liberia from the slave trade was an important factor leading the AMERICAN COLONIZATION SOCIETY (ACS) to choose it as the location for their African colony in 1821. They knew that the SIERRA LEONE colony, founded by the British in 1787, to the north had had great difficulty with the local slave traders, and some Sierra Leone colonists had been sold into slavery. The first American colonists had settled on Sherbro Island in Sierra Leone but found it unhealthy and met with hostility from the local people. The colony moved to Cape Mesurado, the modern Monrovia, in

1821. Local political leaders sold the colonists a 36-mile stretch of coast, but other local people opposed their presence, and there was intermittent fighting for many years.

The American settlers were mainly free people of color from the Northern states. The American Colonization Society, founded in 1816, raised most of its funds among Southern SLAVE OWNERS, republicans such as THOMAS JEFFERSON, who hoped to create an agrarian society without people of color, free or slave. In the early years of American independence, many slave owners wished to free their slaves, but state legislatures were unwilling to ratify such MANUMISSION because of fear that free people of color would become a disruptive element in society. State laws generally required that people who gained their freedom leave the state. Northern states received some migrants, but white leaders there were also concerned about large free populations of color. Southern free people of color were few in number, because of the legal restrictions, and mostly uninterested in emigrating to Africa, preferring to look north or west for refuge from pervasive racism. Northern free people of color were more likely to be interested in emigration since they experienced racial prejudice in the North and did not have any illusions about being able to fit in there. The evangelical movement among people of color was also stronger in the North at this time, and many Liberian immigrants went hoping to spread

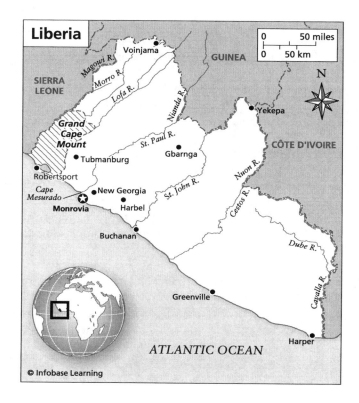

© Infobase Learning

Christianity. PAUL CUFFE, a free shipbuilder of mixed African and Indian ancestry in MASSACHUSETTS and a Quaker, helped encourage New England free people of color to join the colony. Early evangelical preachers in the black community often took up the call, encouraging their parishioners to go to Africa to spread God's word. The first American settlement of Liberia coincided with the Second Great Awakening in Protestantism, and some of the missionary fervor of the religious ferment spread over into the colonization movement.

However, free people of color and Northern white abolitionists soon questioned the motives and effects of colonization. The Liberian colonists suffered enormous losses from disease. As in Sierra Leone, the proponents of colonization had assumed that blackness conferred immunity to the tropical diseases that made West Africa the "white man's grave." In fact, it was birth or long residence in a tropical area that allowed someone of any race to acquire immunity to the strains of tropical disease in that place. Residents of the Tropics moved to a different area also suffered from disease, as slave owners in the tropical Americas were no doubt aware from experiencing the horrendous mortality rates among their own newly imported African slaves. However, the United States had not had any imports of slaves for more than a decade and had never received many Africans, so Americans North and South were not aware of this. The Liberians and their philanthropic promoters back home were horrified at disease death rates approaching 50 percent in the early years of the colony. Moreover, many white supporters of colonization were frankly in favor of ridding America of its black population by sending them to Africa. Some free blacks shared this idea of themselves as Africans rather than Americans, but most saw themselves as Americans, and increasingly, as abolitionism gained traction in the North, they wanted to stay and work for better conditions at home. The ACS was also trying to micromanage the affairs of its colony from across the ocean, with predictable results in the form of corruption and mismanagement. Even the Southern white promoters were increasingly disenchanted with the outcome and lost their ideological reasons for supporting the project. By the 1840s, the impulse to transform Southern society into a racially monolithic society of free small farmers had faded, to be replaced by a proslavery ideology that saw plantations and slave society as an ideal form of life. Southern slave owners thus had less ideological reason to support Liberia. Finally, in 1847, the ACS was unable to continue to support the colony and encouraged the residents to declare their independence. The American settlers duly declared Liberian independence, under President JOSEPH JENKINS ROBERTS, a native of Virginia, who was born free, the son of a black evangelical minister. The American settlers and their descendants continued to rule Liberia until the 1960s.

When the United States joined the antislavery naval patrol in 1820, their West African squadron was based in Monrovia and landed recaptured slaves in Liberia. Most of the recaptured slaves remained in the colony, just as in Sierra Leone, and integrated into the African-American culture they found. A separate colony called New Georgia, near modern Buchanan, was founded by recaptured slaves. The recaptured slaves were much fewer in number than those landed in Sierra Leone and had less of an impact on Liberian culture than did the recaptured slaves landed in Sierra Leone, however. While Sierra Leone Krio is an English Creole with many English loan words, it is manifestly an African language with Mandé grammar and speech patterns. The English spoken in Liberia, on the other hand, is easily comprehensible to a native English speaker from the United States or Britain and is more of a regional dialect than a separate language. Similarly, the culture of the Americo-Liberians, as the descendants of the American immigrants and recaptured slaves are called, is much closer to that of their American forbears than is the culture of the Sierra Leone Krio. Most Americo-Liberians are Protestant Christians, reflecting the evangelical views of their ancestors, while Krio practice a variety of religions, and Islam is probably the dominant faith. Liberians play soccer enthusiastically, as do all West African countries, but Liberia is also the only West African nation with a national baseball team with hopes of participating in the Olympics.

Stewart R. King

FURTHER READING
Boley, G. E. Saigbe. *Liberia: The Rise and Fall of the First Republic*. New York: Macmillan Publishers, 1983.
Shick, Tom W. *Behold the Promised Land: The History of Afro-American Settler Society in Nineteenth-Century Liberia*. Baltimore: Johns Hopkins University Press, 1980.

LINCOLN, ABRAHAM (1809–1865) *sixteenth president of the United States (1861–1865)*

Abraham Lincoln holds a defining place in U.S. history because of the EMANCIPATION PROCLAMATION, which began the formal abolition of slavery. Lincoln, however, had a very complex view of blacks in American society, resulting in mixed historical opinions of his legacy. Yet, Lincoln, president of the United States during the AMERICAN CIVIL WAR from 1861 to 1865, received more blacks in the White House than any other president in the 19th century.

As a young man, Lincoln had limited exposure to free blacks. Though born on February 12, 1809, in KENTUCKY, a slave state, he spent the majority of his early life in the free states of INDIANA and ILLINOIS, where laws limiting immigration kept the number of free blacks low; free blacks had to post large financial bonds insuring proper behavior before being allowed to settle. The individuals who settled in the rural areas where Lincoln lived as a young man were mostly poor whites from the Upper South who were very racist.

Lincoln interacted more often with free blacks after setting up his law practice in Springfield, Illinois, in 1837. In a number of cases, he represented them in legal proceedings, such as divorce cases, or in suits against other blacks. Among his clients was a black Haitian immigrant named William Florville, who later changed his name to William de Fleurville. Also known as Billy the Barber, Florville had met Lincoln in New Salem, Illinois. When both Florville and Lincoln ended up in Springfield, Lincoln helped him build his clientele and frequently spent time visiting the establishment. Lincoln represented Florville in a number of property title cases. The two would continue to correspond until Lincoln's death.

Lincoln could and often did reflect the racial views of his white constituents, however. During the debates that marked his campaign for senator against the Democrat Stephen A. Douglas in 1858, he stated that blacks were perhaps not his equal in "moral or intellectual attainment." In the same sentence, however, he said he felt that they were the equal of any man in the right to "eat the bread, without the leave of anybody else, which his own hand earns." Later in the debates, he said he was not "in favor of bringing about in any way the social and political equality of the white and black races, that I am not nor ever have been in favor of making voters or jurors of negroes, nor of qualifying them to hold office, nor to intermarry with white people; and I will say in addition to this that there is a physical difference between the white and black races which I believe will forever forbid the two races living together on terms of social and political equality." But he once again reiterated that he believed slavery was an evil that harmed the whole country, white as well as black.

The criticism of Lincoln largely stems from his hesitancy to act on abolishing slavery when he became president in 1861. Lincoln's delay of action appears to be rooted in both a desire to appease the South and the dilemma of what should be done about the free blacks. He doubted the ability of blacks and whites to live peaceably with one another. And despite his relationships with some freed blacks, Lincoln, as did most whites, believed that blacks were inferior to whites. For this reason, Lincoln pushed for the removal of blacks. He met with JOSEPH JENKINS ROBERTS, former president of LIBERIA, to discuss the deportation of blacks to Liberia in Africa, but Lincoln was dissuaded by the expense of transporting blacks to Africa. In 1862, he met with a delegation of five free blacks to discuss the possibility of emigration to the South American republic of COLOMBIA. None of the delegates was a leader within the black community; most were newly freed slaves and illiterate. He stressed to the group that blacks and whites would not be able to live together and that blacks would never have the opportunity to live in equality. Lincoln's purpose in meeting with the delegation was to convince them to leave the country. The plan fell through when neighboring Central American countries threatened to use troops to prevent settlement. Not to be discouraged from colonization plans, Lincoln then set his eyes on Île-à-Vache (Cow Island), which is part of Haiti. In April 1863, a group of 453 free blacks left the United States for Cow Island. However, the coordinator of the project had misled Lincoln as to the facilities available on the island. An outbreak of illness, the lack of services for the immigrants, and trouble with the Haitian government forced Lincoln to terminate the project and order that the survivors be taken back. In March 1864, the Cow Island immigrants returned to the United States. Though no other official attempts at colonization were made, Lincoln would continue to support the idea of colonization.

Lincoln's racial attitudes evolved during his presidency toward a more enlightened and modern model of seeing the black as at least a potential equal and a fellow citizen. Much of this evolution was the result of his increased contact with sympathetic African Americans during his time in office. Though he avoided most abolitionists prior to election, Lincoln did meet with many black abolitionists during his presidency. In 1862, when contemplating whether or not to sign the bill that would emancipate blacks in the District of Columbia, he was introduced to Bishop DANIEL A. PAYNE, a bishop in the AFRICAN METHODIST EPISCOPAL CHURCH and president of Wilberforce College. Blunt and to the point, Payne asked Lincoln directly whether he intended to sign the bill. Payne spent 45 minutes with the president but left without an answer.

Lincoln met most frequently with FREDERICK DOUGLASS. Their first meeting occurred when Douglass arrived at the White House unannounced on September 10, 1863. Despite the fact that Douglass had been highly critical of many of Lincoln's actions and policies, he was escorted in to see the president. Douglass's purpose was to convince Lincoln to correct the disparity in pay between black and white soldiers. Lincoln freely discussed this issue, as well as some of his other policies that Douglass had condemned, but was unable to make

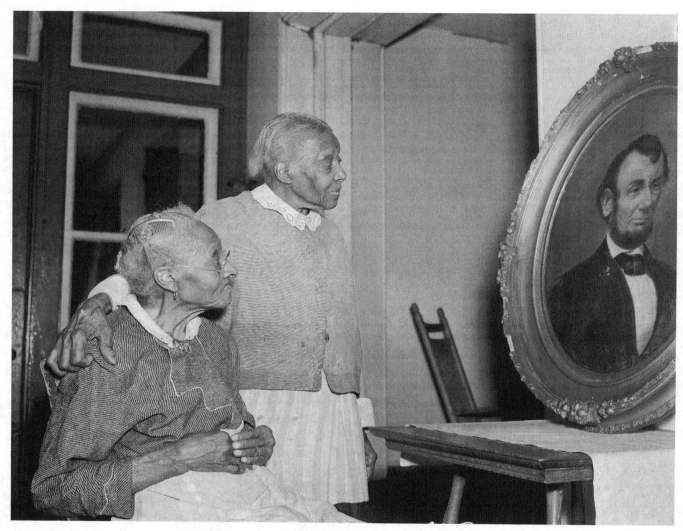

Two elderly black women, one a former slave freed by the Emancipation Proclamation and the other a prewar free woman of color, prepare to celebrate Lincoln's birthday in 1940. The treasured portrait and solemn demeanor of the women indicate the importance of the figure of Lincoln in African-American culture in the years after the American Civil War. *(© Bettmann/CORBIS)*

a concession on the issue of pay. He had only recently agreed to allow blacks to serve in the military, which was still a very controversial issue, and was concerned that authorizing equal pay would be too offensive to many. Lincoln promised, however, that he would be willing to promote blacks to serve as officers if any were recommended by the secretary of war.

The second meeting between Douglass and Lincoln was requested by the president about a year after their initial meeting. Lincoln summoned Douglass to the White House to garner his opinion on a number of issues. One of the matters that Lincoln wanted Douglass's opinion about was an answer Lincoln had prepared to those who criticized him for not seeking a negotiated peace agreement with the South. The concern of both men revolved around what negotiations for peace would mean to emancipation.

Douglass advised Lincoln against issuing the response. Another issue discussed concerned a plan for infiltrating the South with black agents who would inform slaves of the Emancipation Proclamation and aid them in reaching Union lines. Ironically, the plan was similar to one that John Brown, whom Lincoln had reviled as a criminal, had proposed to Douglass at one time.

The third and final meeting between Lincoln and Douglass occurred after Lincoln's reelection. Douglass attended Lincoln's second inauguration ceremony in 1865, as well as the reception. Initially, security officials did not realize who he was and attempted to restrain Douglass. Once admitted, Douglass was received as a friend by Lincoln. Though unable to spend much time with Douglass, Lincoln did ask his opinion of the Inaugural Address. Douglass expressed praise for the document, and it was one of the few public addresses of Lincoln's that Douglass never criticized.

Besides the meeting with Douglass, Lincoln met with a number of other black men to discuss issues surrounding military service. In 1863, Lincoln met with a group of ministers who were seeking permission to work with black soldiers. Representing the American Baptist Missionary Association, they requested from the president the right to provide the soldiers with Bibles. Lincoln readily agreed to let the ministers into the military lines to reach the soldiers as long as their presence did not impede military operations. He granted a letter of introduction to Secretary of War Stanton for a J. H. Putnam, referring him for military service. He also had a meeting of some length with MARTIN DELANY in 1865. Delany proposed a plan whereby a group of black soldiers under a black officer would infiltrate the South for the express purpose of liberating slaves and increasing the number of blacks serving in the military. Noting the similarity to the plan he proposed to Douglass, Lincoln readily agreed and recommended his appointment to Secretary Stanton. Shortly after this recommendation, Delany was commissioned as the first black major in the U.S. Army.

A number of free blacks arranged meetings with Lincoln in order to express their gratitude. One of the black war nurses, Caroline Johnson, met with the president, taking him gifts of wax fruit and a stem table. In 1864, a delegation of five black men representing the city of Baltimore arrived at the White House. They presented Lincoln with an elaborate Bible bound in velvet with gold bands and plating as a token of their appreciation for the abolition of slavery in Washington, D.C. According to several accounts, Lincoln cherished this gift more than any of the others. That same year, SOJOURNER TRUTH traveled to Washington to try to see Lincoln. Admitted, she expressed her admiration of him and gave him a picture of herself. He showed her the Bible he had received, talked with her for several minutes, and signed her autograph book before she left.

Lincoln frequently made the White House grounds available to the black community to host public celebrations. In 1864, a group of three black Catholics who were residents of Washington, D.C., met with the president requesting the use of the White House grounds for a Sunday school picnic. Their spokesman, Gabriel Coakley, informed the president that they wanted to hold the event to raise funds for a Catholic church for blacks. Lincoln agreed, and he and his wife attended the event held on July 4, 1864, which helped ensure its financial success. The White House grounds were used again by blacks a month later in order to observe the national day of prayer. The daylong event included a number of sermons and orations and was well attended.

As for most whites, Lincoln's most intimate relationships with blacks occurred with those in service positions. And Lincoln was known to show his gratitude to those who served. He secured a position as a laborer at the Treasury Department for William Johnson, who accompanied him from Springfield as a valet and personal attendant. Lincoln's intent was to secure employment for Johnson at the White House, but he met resistance from the other staff based on the fact that Johnson was dark-skinned, and generally only light-skinned blacks worked at the White House. Johnson continued to be paid by Lincoln until a position could be found for him, and after Johnson's placement at the Treasury, Lincoln often requested Johnson's service, arranging for time off from his regular employment and paying him directly. After William Johnson's death, Lincoln asked that one of his former bodyguards, Solomon James Johnson, be appointed to the position and later encouraged his promotion. Lincoln also trusted and had an amicable relationship with his White House attendant William Slade, and he had several contacts with Elizabeth Keckley, who was Mary Todd Lincoln's dressmaker and confidante.

Lincoln was killed by an assassin on April 15, 1865. The assassin was part of a group of plotters who hoped to reverse the Confederate defeat but had originally planned to kidnap Lincoln and hold him hostage for the release of Confederate prisoners. He decided to kill Lincoln after hearing him promise in an April 11 speech that he would grant voting rights to blacks.

All blacks who met with Lincoln claimed that the president greeted them wholeheartedly and openly. Even Frederick Douglass, who remained critical of many of Lincoln's deeds and policies, claimed that Lincoln never treated him as anything other than an equal. Despite his personal feelings about blacks and reservations regarding how blacks would fit into American society, Lincoln was known for his kindness and respectfulness to people regardless of color or station.

Amy A. Hatmaker

FURTHER READING

Hudson, Gossie Harold. "William Florville: Lincoln's Barber and Friend." *Negro History Bulletin* 37, no. 5 (1974): 279–281.

Levine, Robert S., ed. *Martin R. Delany: A Documentary Reader.* Chapel Hill: University of North Carolina Press, 2003.

Lockett, James D. "Abraham Lincoln and Colonization: An Episode That Ends in Tragedy at L'lle à Vache, Haiti, 1863–1864." *Journal of Black Studies* 21, no. 4 (June 1991): 428–444.

Mabee, Carleton. "Sojourner Truth and President Lincoln." *New England Quarterly* 61, no. 4 (December 1988): 519–529.

Nelson, Larry E. "Black Leaders and the Presidential Election of 1864." *Journal of Negro History* 63, no. 1 (January 1978): 42–58.

Quarles, Benjamin. *Lincoln and the Negro.* New York: Oxford University Press, 1962.

Sandburg, Carl. *Abraham Lincoln: The War Years.* Vol. 2. New York: Harcourt, Brace, 1939.

Stauffer, John. *Giants: The Parallel Lives of Frederick Douglass and Abraham Lincoln.* New York: Twelve, 2008.

LISBOA, ANTÔNIO (O ALEIJADINHO)
(ca. 1730s–1814) *Brazilian baroque sculptor*

Antônio Lisboa was a Brazilian sculptor and architect who designed and decorated dozens of churches in the mining region of Minas Gerais. He is probably Brazil's most famous artist, and his work, the best surviving example of the South American baroque architectural style. According to historians at the Museum of Aleijadinho, Antônio Lisboa was the son of a Portuguese architect, Manuel Francisco Lisboa, and a slave mother, Izabel. Controversy about his date of birth is based on his supposed baptismal certificate, dated in 1730, which does not show the correct last name for his father. He may also have been born in 1738, as he himself reported in later life, and the 1730 certificate may refer to an older half brother.

Though the illegitimate son of a slave woman, O Aleijadinho, as he later became known, grew up in the home of his father, the carpenter Manuel Francisco de Costa Lisboa, with his two half siblings. His father's people were originally from the Madeira Islands. He learned the trade of carpentry in his father's shop and soon put it to use in the numerous churches that were being built in the rich town of Vila Rica (now known as Ouro Preto). The strength of the ROMAN CATHOLIC CHURCH, population growth, and the affluence of the city were perfect ingredients for the emergence of several religious associations, all of which required their own church.

He began his work under his father's gaze, but he soon took on individual projects of equal complexity to those of his father. The first of these projects would be the Chapel of the Third Order of St. Francis of Assisi in Vila Rica. Lisboa developed his personal style, and in 1769, two years after his father's death, religious associations were already competing for his attention. Having established himself as an architect, Lisboa dedicated himself to what he liked best: sculpture. His images are satirical and playful. The faces of several of his sculptures of religious figures reflect those of people he knew or who had hired him.

By 1777, it is clear that he was sick, suffering from a disease that would slowly consume his body for the rest of his life. Scholars have posthumously diagnosed him with Hansen's disease, or leprosy, which caused him to lose his toes and some fingers, atrophied and curved his hands, and disfigured his facial features. This condition left its sufferers both physically disabled and socially outcast, because of references to Jewish laws that considered lepers especially ritually unclean. It was at this time that he acquired his nickname "O Aleijadinho," "the little cripple." His crippling condition and the inability to walk on his own did not stop him from working. With the help of his three slaves—Januário, Agostinho, and Maurício—he would work at night with long clothes covering his limbs so as not to draw attention to his condition. His slaves would carry him and aid him in holding utensils, sometimes tying them to his hands.

In 1796, Aleijadinho began his masterpiece, the 12 prophets, in the Santuário Senhor Bom Jesus de Matosinhos in the city of Congonhas, close to Vila Rica. The sculptures are all made in the delicate soapstone common in the area. He also sculpted a half-dozen scenes from the Passion of Christ, 60 life-size figures. The project, totaling 78 figures, was finished in nine years with the help of several slaves and students. From 1812 to 1814, his health worsened, and he was taken care of by his daughter-in-law until his death on November 18, 1814.

Ana Janaina Nelson

FURTHER READING
Hogan, James E. "Antônio Francisco Lisboa, 'O Aleijadinho': An Annotated Bibliography." *Latin American Research Review* 9, no. 2 (Summer 1974): 83–94.

Vasconcellos, Sylvio de. *Vida e obra de Antônio Francisco Lisboa, o Aleijadinho.* São Paulo: Companhia Editora Nacional, 1979.

LIVING "AS FREE"

Living "as free" was an alternative to formal MANUMISSION. Masters who could not get government permission to free their slaves or could not afford the manumission tax could simply permit their slaves to go free without any legal certification of their status. The slaves would be armed with a pass or letter from their master to protect them from the authorities. They would remain the property of the master under law. Needless to say, this status was preferable to slavery but still not as good as formal manumission. Both slaves and masters could experience inconveniences. Nonetheless, many people lived under this status, sometimes for fairly short periods while seeking formal manumission and sometimes for their whole lifetimes.

Most governments of slave societies in the Americas placed some sort of restriction on manumission. At a minimum, governments wanted to be sure that newly freed persons would not become a burden on public charity. Governments also wished to limit the growth in numbers of free people of color because they were thought of as disruptive influences on the slaves. And many governments counted on the manumission tax for a substantial part of their revenue. Masters, on the other hand, often had reasons to grant freedom to their slaves, either because the slaves or their free relatives and friends would pay a ransom or because they wished to reward slaves for good service. Many masters thought that granting freedom to a few slaves made the remainder work harder in the hope that their service would also be rewarded. Permitting a slave to live "as free" was a way to achieve some of these goals without the difficulty and expense of formal manumission.

Some slaves paid their master for the right to live "as free," either a share of their crops or wages or a fixed sum. More commonly, many free people would purchase a slave relative and then give that person informal freedom while they sought formal manumission. Many of the people who were living "as free" were in this situation: the "property" of their parents or other relatives, working to accumulate the funds for the manumission tax. White fathers of mixed-race children might well be in this position along with free colored relatives. Whites might be expected to have some more influence with colonial governments, and wealthy white fathers in most places seem to have had little difficulty in having their children's manumissions approved. President THOMAS JEFFERSON, for example, granted freedom to all of the CHILDREN OF SALLY HEMINGS, his lover and slave, without any resistance from the government of Virginia despite the fact that Virginia had fairly harsh restrictions on manumission at the time. Especially in the United States, however, where permission to free one's slaves became increasingly difficult to obtain in the early 19th century, poorer whites could find themselves obliged to settle for informal freedom for their children. Fr. Patrick Healy, S.J., a member of the order of JESUITS, was born a slave in GEORGIA, the child of an Irish immigrant farmer and his mixed-race slave. Father Healy's father lived with his children on their small farm in Georgia throughout their childhood without ever trying to free them formally, finally moving his family to the North only when the children were ready for advanced schooling (see HEALY FAMILY).

It was very common for masters to grant informal liberty to aged slaves, especially if they had given good service. Most places in the plantation Americas had substantial mountainous or wilderness areas where plantation crops could not be grown. Governments offered those lands to planters, sometimes as a package deal with the well-watered, flat land they actually wanted, and expected them to develop the lands, destroying habitat for MAROONS and Indians. These backcountry lands were often converted to provision grounds (see PROVISION GROUND FARMING), growing food for the plantation. These provision grounds could be operated directly by the planter, but this was generally an inefficient use of scarce labor. Sometimes the provision grounds would be given or sold to free coloreds. But a middle course was to give slaves plots in the provision ground and some free time to cultivate them. This way, slaves would provide their own food. It was an easy choice to take the next step, to give a favored elderly slave a larger plot and not require any other plantation work of him or her.

Another common choice for slaves given informal liberty was to allow them to operate a small business. Again, it was not uncommon for slaves to be given free time, especially when the agricultural workload was low, to pursue some trade or business. The surplus produce from provision ground plots could be sold in the market. Slave cooks could make some extra food and sell it in the market or to an inn. Slave maids could take in some other people's washing to do along with the master's laundry. Slaves with valuable job skills such as carpenters or millers often had formal arrangements with their masters permitting them to work a certain number of days on their own account, perhaps in return for a fixed payment. Again, it would not be a big conceptual step for a master wishing to give informal liberty to slaves simply to permit them to spend all their time on whatever kind of paid employment they could find. While Sally Hemings and Thomas Jefferson's children received formal manumission, she herself lived under an informal arrangement of this nature after Jefferson's death. She was 56 when he died in 1826, and she lived the last nine years of her life in nearby Charlottesville with two of her sons while remaining, in a legal sense, the slave of Martha Randolph, Jefferson's youngest daughter and Hemings's childhood companion.

The children and spouses of people granted informal freedom might not be free in any sense, and indeed this was one of the most unfortunate features of the status from the slave's point of view. If a woman gained formal liberty, her children born after her manumission would also be free from birth. But if she was living "as free" and she had a child, that child was the property of her master. Masters could extend the same privilege to children, depending on their relationship with the mother, but there were no guarantees. Also, since the person was still legally a slave, financial catastrophe for the master could lead to a return to forced labor, as the master's property was sold at auction. Masters in SAINT-DOMINGUE created a legal instrument, the irrevocable power of attorney, for slaves to whom they wished to grant informal freedom, permitting any free person (presumably a friend or relative) to apply for permission, pay the tax, and liberate a slave. These irrevocable powers of attorney would presumably protect the slave against RE-ENSLAVEMENT, and there is no record that any such donation was successfully challenged by creditors. In CUBA and Spanish North America, and to a lesser extent elsewhere in Spanish colonies, the custom of COARTACIÓN permitted slaves and masters to reach legally binding agreements for self-purchase that a slave could enforce against any subsequent purchaser. Still, the informality of the status held the possibility that it could be revoked at any time without the slave's having many legal rights to resist.

But informal freedom had some potential pitfalls for the master as well. Under English common law, and by statute in French colonies, a master was responsible for the actions of a slave. If a slave was caught stealing or injured someone else's property, the master would be required to repay the injured party. This was subject to court interpretation, and a master might have been able to defend himself by asserting that the slave was acting independently, but slaves given informal liberty still represented a potential liability for the master.

Governments were aware that these sorts of arrangements existed, and they were not exactly unlawful but they were discouraged and intermittently repressed. The chief problem was that the existence of these informal arrangements provided cover for runaway slaves. If the towns had significant numbers of people who were still slaves under the law but who were allowed to go about their business freely, and the countryside had equally large numbers of people who were legally slaves but nonetheless living unmolested as independent PEASANTS, then a runaway slave could slip in among them and do the same thing. In fact, many did. (*See also* RUNAWAY SLAVES.) In addition, these informal arrangements eroded the control over the free colored population that the laws restricting manumission were supposed to have established. Indeed, by passing laws limiting and taxing manumission, governments had created a perverse incentive to make the line between free and slave even less well defined than it had been. However, governments lacked both the will and the means to curb informal arrangements of this nature effectively. The masters' property rights to do as they saw fit with their slaves were especially strong in the Anglo-American tradition, precisely where laws limiting manumission were the strongest. One can imagine how Jefferson and his social equals, the planters of the Old South, would have responded to a government official, daring to ask them how much work they were assigning their slaves to do. In Spanish and Portuguese colonies, elites might have been somewhat more willing to listen to government suggestions about their treatment of their slaves, but there the governments were not so hostile to manumission. The French colonies saw a lot of what was called there *liberté de savane*, or "bush freedom," because of the heavy taxes on manumission. His biographer, John Vandercook, suggests that Henry Christophe, who became the first king of Northern Haiti (1767–1820, reigned 1807–20), was informally free during the years before the HAITIAN REVOLUTION, though the only records we have on his life before the revolution show him as a slave working in an inn. Madison Smartt Bell, the biographer of Haitian revolutionary TOUSSAINT LOUVERTURE, suggests that his parents may have been *libre de savane* on Bréda Plantation when Toussaint was a boy, and that Toussaint never lived as a slave in the full sense of the term. He was formally freed in the 1760s, when he was about 20 years old.

Because these arrangements were informal, we can give no real statistics on how common they were. Anecdotes abound, from all parts of the plantation Americas. We can guess that prevalence of informal liberty arrangements correlated with harsh manumission laws, and probably also with low profitability in the plantation sector and close, feudal, personal ties between master and slave. Poor race relations per se do not seem to have reduced the practice; it appears to have been very common in the United States, particularly in the longer-settled areas of Virginia, MARYLAND, and the coast of the Carolinas and GEORGIA.

Stewart R. King

FURTHER READING

Bell, Madison Smartt. *Toussaint Louverture: A Life*. New York: Pantheon, 2007.

King, Stewart. *Blue Coat or Powdered Wig: Free People of Color in Pre-Revolutionary Saint-Domingue*. Athens: University of Georgia Press, 2001.

Vandercook, John. *Black Majesty: The Life of Christophe, King of Haiti*. New York: Harper and Brothers, 1928.

LONDON, ENGLAND

BRITAIN's capital and largest city, London is located in southeastern England on the Thames River. It has been a major port since classical times and the center of English life since the Middle Ages. It has had a population of people of color since the early Renaissance. In fact, the nation's earliest relationship with individuals of African descent centered on those who were taken to the metropolis enslaved. Black servants taken by Catherine of Aragon from Spain to London before her marriage to Henry VIII in 1509, are among the first recorded people of African origin in England. Slaving voyages in the mid-16th century carried yet more enslaved Africans to London. Without any positive law on enslavement, however, those forcefully taken to the capital lived in an uncertain legal position. Indeed, it would not be until 1778 in Scotland and 1834 in England and Wales that slavery was legally prohibited in the British Isles. In the meantime, the explosion of British overseas COMMERCE AND TRADE and the rise of the African slave trade sent large numbers of enslaved Africans to London, where many would eventually rise to freedom.

Absences in the law, alongside undeveloped notions of chattel slavery, made life exceedingly complex for blacks in London. Ideologies of racial difference were poorly formed in the early-modern period, and the concept of indefinite slavery tied to race was one that emerged only toward the end of the 17th century. This meant that SLAVE OWNERS in Britain often did not hold blacks in permanent bondage. Not only did Britain lack the climate necessary to make use of enslaved agricultural labor profitable, as its American colonies did, but its large population eliminated the need for chattel slavery at all. Most enslaved individuals, then, worked as servants in the home or with ARTISANS. Masters regularly granted them freedom, either through MANUMISSION or abrogation of service, after several years worked. As the number of slaves grew in the Americas, Britain's colonies began crafting more oppressive legal measures. These targeted all individuals of color by linking those of African descent more strictly with enslavement and therefore stripped them of full civil rights. Britons at home soon began borrowing such repressive measures. In 1677, the King's Bench case of *Butts v. Penny* officially decreed that enslaved Africans were merchandise in England. Therefore, by the end of the 17th century, captive blacks in London more closely resembled chattel slaves in the colonies, drastically curtailing their paths toward freedom.

From the 16th to the 19th centuries, free people of color struggled to form a consolidated community in the British capital. Fractured connections between those of African origin, especially those initially enslaved, and their employers limited the group's cohesion. More damaging was a gender imbalance among people of color that lasted until nearly the 20th century. The disproportionate importation of African men into Britain stymied the formation of black families. This sexual disparity only worsened in the late 17th and early 18th centuries. Many black men cohabited with and married white women instead, sparking heated protest over their presence in London. Geographic separation further discouraged a strong community of color. While large numbers of black and mixed-race individuals lived in the city's poorer East End, records from the various plague outbreaks that struck London in the early-modern period indicate victims of color scattered in both the South and West as well.

Slowly, London's free population of color rose in the 18th century. Estimates have put it as large as 20,000 by mid-century, although most agree that it hovered between 5,000 and 10,000. Such oscillations sprang from the sexual imbalance in the group, as well as spurts in slave imports, which later swelled manumitted numbers in turn. Although it was not a large demographic faction—particularly when London's population reached 1 million by 1800—many in the capital feared its visible presence. Such worry rose to paranoia in 1731 when the lord mayor ordered that "no *Negroes* or other *Blacks* be suffered to be bound Apprentices at any of the Companies of this City." White artisans had little to fear, however, as most of the city's black laborers worked in servile positions or within the military. Under such imagined concerns, racial tensions in the capital started to simmer.

As the 18th century wore on, London's population of color expanded to include a number of different groups and individuals. These new immigrants arrived primarily seeking education. Britain's West Indian colonies held virtually no schools to teach youth, and what institutions did exist banned admission for those of color. Yet the sexual imbalance of the Caribbean's white population, combined with an overwhelming black majority in the islands, produced a rampant culture of MISCEGENATION that resulted in the explosive growth of a mixed-race populace eager for instruction. Many white fathers sent their offspring of color to schools throughout Britain. Indeed, the practice was quite common during the 18th century. Several attended elite institutions such as Oxford and Cambridge, but many more received private tutoring in Britain's large cities. The Jamaican merchant John Morse, for example, sent his five mixed-race children to schools in the capital. Each of his daughters eventually married a white Englishman and entered London's elite metropolitan society.

Merchants along the coast of Africa, engaged in the slave trade, also sent their mixed-race offspring to schools in London, as well as Liverpool (England's slave-trading hub). This was part of a parallel migration of royal African children to British institutions. African kings often sent their descendants abroad to serve as better liaisons to those Europeans who traded within their borders. These royal students served to solemnize the connections between African principalities and European imperialists. The practice became important enough that in 1788 the British Board of Trade began investigating those children entering from Africa, issuing the report, "Conduct of Mulatto and Black African Children, Who Had Been Educated in England." Many who entered London, however, stayed only temporarily. As with a large proportion of the Caribbean students who went to the capital, many African scholars returned home after completing their education. Their transience did little to stabilize the city's free community of color.

The influx of black and mixed-race students into the capital coincided with a rise in prominence of several elite and educated blacks. During the 18th century, black migrants from the colonies carved out a literary niche for themselves through the promotion of their autobiographies. Ukawsaw Gronniosaw and OLAUDAH EQUIANO were both born in Africa, enslaved, and taken to various locations in the Western Hemisphere. Both eventually obtained their freedom and traveled to London, where they published autobiographies of their trials and adventures. British audiences devoured these accounts, particularly as the movement to abolish the slave trade heated. Other freed Africans, including QUOBNA OTTOBAH CUGOANO and IGNATIUS SANCHO, also entered the literary world, publishing on topics as diverse as politics and music. The arts were further encouraged by additional migrants of color into London. PHILLIS WHEATLEY, a freed American slave who visited London in 1772, impressed many British critics with her spirited poetry. George Augustus Polgreen Bridgetower (1780–1860), the mixed-race son of a black man and an eastern European woman, also traveled to England's capital. A violin prodigy, he studied under Europe's great composers and became a close musical colleague of Beethoven. In 1789, he played for King George III at Windsor Castle. Free individuals of color, therefore, operated in many social spaces. Not only did they labor alongside London's white working class, they also circulated in the metropolis's elite ranks.

The city's free population of color increased dramatically in the years immediately after the WAR OF AMERICAN INDEPENDENCE, 1775–83. Having promised freedom to slaves who took up arms against the insurgent Americans, the British government had to relocate those who accepted the challenge. It first sent the group to Nova Scotia, CANADA, before transporting many of those to England. London's black population suddenly swelled, and many whites decried the arrival of so many poor black migrants. Within several years, those cries became louder, and efforts commenced to resettle the group outside Britain's shores. By 1786, the Sierra Leone Company formed to carry London's black poor to Africa in order to establish a free black colony. Some 400 free people of color, most from London, undertook the first voyage to the SIERRA LEONE colony, which was largely unsuccessful. Multiple excursions would take place over the next several decades, transporting more black Britons to the colony, with mixed results.

By the early 19th century, after years of political debate surrounding enslavement and the slave trade, members of London's community of color started to advocate more radical positions. After Parliament officially ended the slave trade in 1807, calls for total slave emancipation increased, growing up alongside white working-class activism. In some instances, both movements merged. Two mixed-race Jamaicans living in the capital became famous for their political radicalism. William Davidson (1781–1820) was hanged in 1820 for his part in the Cato Street Conspiracy to kill British cabinet members. ROBERT WEDDERBURN was arrested several times in the same period for treasonous language, including his calls for a revolution to spread from the slaves of the Caribbean to the poor of Britain. He also demanded revenge for the Peterloo Massacre of 1819, in which parliamentary reformers in Manchester were killed by the military. Both Davidson's and Wedderburn's actions linked white and black working-class political movements. Indeed, London's later black activists, such as William Cuffay (1788–1870), were integral to the Chartist movement of the 1840s, which demanded both British parliamentary reform as well as the equality of all men.

Those who aspired to equal rights were met with hardening racial prejudices in the Victorian period. The 18th century's loose collection of racial ideologies began cohering around scientific notions of biological difference in the 19th century. Victorian attitudes, while not uniform, ascribed innate distinctions between ethnic groups in a much more systematic fashion than ever before. This coincided with the rise of popular minstrelsy in London. Often performed by whites in blackface, and occasionally by black performers as well, minstrel shows in London mimicked those in America, lampooning black figures in their acts. More vehement rhetoric against those of African descent also emerged during this period. Writing from London in 1849, Thomas Carlyle's "Occasional Discourse on the Negro Question" argued that emancipating the slaves in the West Indies had been a mistake because of their lack of intelligence.

Despite these increasingly oppressive attitudes, London hosted several famous figures of color in the Victorian era, as it had in the 18th century. Ira Aldridge (1807–67), a black American, traveled to London in the 1820s and established himself as one of the capital's best theatrical actors. William Darby (1796–1871) (also known as Pablo Fanque), a Norwich-born man of color, took his successful circus act to London in 1847, dazzling audiences before touring the North of England. The Jamaican MARY SEACOLE went to the capital in the mid-19th century, before setting out to work as a nurse in the Crimean War, in which her healing skills gained international recognition. A century after Bridgetower, another mixed-race musician, Samuel Coleridge-Taylor (1875–1912), rose to fame in London. Born in the city's Holborn district, Coleridge-Taylor produced a string of compositions at the end of the 19th century and beginning of the 20th.

By the dawn of the 20th century, London's population of color stayed small but significant. Although colonial migrants continued to repopulate its ranks, a more stable and self-reproducing community developed by the late Victorian era. However, it would not be until the large-scale migration of West Indians and Africans after World War II that London's black population would become a large and established social group. Foreshadowing this demographic influx, Britain's capital hosted the Pan-African Conference in 1900. As a hotbed of both pro- and anti-imperialist sentiment, London was well suited to hold the meeting of black delegates from around the world. As a response to African colonization, as well as the cultural movement of Pan-Africanism, the conference situated London firmly within a global black population. With a history of free black residents dating back hundreds of years, London at the turn of the 20th century was properly poised to become an important node in the black Atlantic.

Daniel Livesay

FURTHER READING
Fryer, Peter. *Staying Power: Black People in Britain since 1504.* Atlantic Highlands, N.J.: Humanities Press, 1984.
Gerzina, Gretchen. *Black London: Life before Emancipation.* London: John Murray, 1995.
Habib, Imtiaz. *Black Lives in the English Archives, 1500–1677: Imprints of the Invisible.* Burlington, Vt.: Ashgate, 2008.
Shyllon, Folarin. *Black People in Britain, 1555–1833.* New York: Oxford University Press, 1977.

LORD DUNMORE   *See* Dunmore, John Murray, earl of.

LOUISIANA
Spaniards led by Pánfilo de Narváez in 1528 were the first group of Europeans to visit what is now the state of Louisiana, but it was the French in the late 17th century who established a lasting foothold in the area. French settlers were not the first to occupy Louisiana, however. Native Americans, including parts of the Choctaw and Caddo tribes, were well entrenched before the arrival of the French.

Indeed, these three groups—Native Americans, French immigrants, and Spaniards—along with peoples from Europe, the Caribbean, Africa, and the United States, developed a culture in Louisiana that is rich and distinctive. While the land Robert Cavelier, sieur de La Salle, claimed for France in 1682 was a vast region that stretched from the Gulf of Mexico to Canada, much of the development of the region centered on New Orleans, Louisiana, located on the banks of the Mississippi River, relatively close to the Gulf of Mexico. It has a subtropical climate with hot and humid summers and mild winters and is often the victim of hurricanes.

Initial Colonization Efforts in Louisiana
The French explorer Robert Cavelier, sieur de La Salle, claimed a vast region for France in 1682, naming it Louisiana in honor of King Louis XIV. The area claimed included land on both sides of the Mississippi River stretching from the Gulf of Mexico to Canada (where French colonists had been established in Quebec since 1608). The Louisiana Territory comprised the present-day states of Arkansas, Illinois, Indiana, Iowa, Kansas, Louisiana, Michigan, Minnesota, Mississippi, Missouri, Nebraska, North Dakota, Oklahoma, South Dakota, and Wisconsin.

After claiming the territory, La Salle journeyed to France to seek the king's support for colonizing the area. Colonization offered several strategic and economic benefits to the French, including confining the British to the lands east of the Appalachians and establishing control of the Mississippi River, guaranteeing an open French trade route from Canada to the Gulf of Mexico. The king hoped to establish a French nation that stretched from the Gulf of Mexico to Canada, making much of the continent French and creating a commercial empire.

France's first permanent settlement in the region, Fort Maurepas (today, Ocean Springs, Mississippi), was founded by Pierre Le Moyne d'Iberville in 1698 with a group numbering 200. A second noteworthy settlement, Natchitoches (located in what is northwest Louisiana today), was established in 1714 by Juchereau de St. Denis. By far the most important settlement to be established, though, was New Orleans, founded a few years after Natchitoches while Louisiana was under the proprietorship of the Company of the Indies. By 1722, New Orleans was the center of civilian and military authority in Louisiana, and the population grew. German immigrants arrived in Louisiana, becoming farmers and increasing food production in Louisiana, although not making the colony self-sufficient. Indeed, the colony was never self-sufficient under France's rule and never generated products that made the colony profitable. Though colonists grew tobacco, for instance, it was inferior in quality to West Indian tobacco and had to be sold for less.

France's control of the colony lasted for 63 years. The venture was considered a failure, both politically and economically. Culturally, however, France had left a footprint in Louisiana, and French culture continued to permeate life in Louisiana even after Spanish rule began.

Spanish Rule and the Growth of Louisiana

In 1754, the French and Indian War began in PENNSYLVANIA, and the hostilities between France and Britain soon spread to Europe, developing into what became known as the SEVEN YEARS' WAR. In the Treaty of Paris, which ended the Seven Years' War in 1763, France ceded most of its territory east of the Mississippi and in Canada to Britain. In the Treaty of Fontainebleau, signed in 1762 but not publicized until 1764, France ceded Louisiana to SPAIN.

Spain's leaders did not believe that Louisiana would be profitable economically but rather looked to Louisiana's strategic position as a way to guard against British expansion farther west, especially into Spanish colonies that existed there. Even after the treaty was made public, Spanish leaders waited some months to take physical possession of Louisiana, and residents continued to fly the French flag over New Orleans into 1769. The first Spanish official to arrive in Louisiana, Governor Antonio de Ulloa, was forced by the population to leave. In 1769, General Alejandro (or Alexander) O' Reilly arrived in New Orleans, punished the rebels, and demanded that residents swear an oath of allegiance to the king of Spain. During his seven months in Louisiana, O'Reilly was effective in establishing Spanish authority, creating the *cabildo* (a town council), establishing Spanish trade regulations, and dividing Louisiana into 21 parishes (a religious distinction that later became political).

During Spanish rule, the population in Louisiana increased dramatically. Early in the French and Indian War, the British expelled from Canada descendants of French immigrants who had settled in Acadia, and many settled in Louisiana, coming to be called the Cajuns. Generous land grants attracted many others, including people from the British colonies (and later people from the United States). Slave insurrections in SAINT-DOMINGUE (Haiti) in the 1790s generated thousands of refugees, including whites, slaves, and free people of color, who traveled to and settled in New Orleans. A concurrent revival of the slave trade in Louisiana caused the number of slaves to increase rapidly.

Louisiana became much more prosperous under Spain, although it was still a financial liability. In the 1790s, the cotton gin and new refining processes helped turn COTTON CULTIVATION and SUGAR CULTIVATION into major industries. These two commodities helped New Orleans became a major trade center.

Spain controlled Louisiana until 1803, although France officially reacquired the region in 1800 in the Treaty of San Ildefonso. Spanish influence in Louisiana never overshadowed French influence in its impact on culture: When the United States purchased Louisiana from France in 1803, many in Louisiana still spoke French and practiced French customs in terms of religion, diet, and so on. Spanish influence, however, had promoted an increase in the total population of the region and in the number of the free people of color who lived there.

The United States and the Louisiana Purchase

In 1783, Great Britain recognized the independence of the United States after the WAR OF AMERICAN INDEPENDENCE, 1775–83. Louisiana's role in the war was relatively minor, although Spanish leaders, motivated more by the desire to weaken Great Britain than to support a colonial revolution, had ordered Louisiana officials to assist American colonists secretly.

The Treaty of Paris of 1783, which officially ended the war, defined the borders of the United States: the Great Lakes, the Mississippi, and the 31st parallel of latitude. Notably, Spain retained all territory, including the Louisiana Territory, to the west and south of the United States as it was defined at the time.

In 1800, however, Napoléon Bonaparte regained Louisiana for France in the Treaty of San Ildefonso. Hoping to develop a colonial empire in the Americas, he was quickly disappointed when his brother-in-law, General Charles Leclerc, failed to put down a rebellion in Saint-Domingue (*see also* HAITIAN REVOLUTION). With the area unsecured, Napoléon was certain that any army sent to Louisiana would be easily captured by British forces, and needing cash, he was receptive when the United States offered to purchase New Orleans. As a result, he offered negotiators not only New Orleans but the entire Louisiana colony, which the United States bought for $15 million in 1803. All free people (including free people of color) were accorded U.S. citizenship in the transfer.

The U.S. Congress divided the area into two territories: the Orleans territory (later the state of Louisiana) and the District of Louisiana. Throughout Louisiana, few residents celebrated their status as a territory of the United States. Two particular issues concerned them: The upper classes were anxious about the imminent ban on importing slaves, to take effect in 1808 (although slave smuggling continued to occur after that date), and the largely Catholic society was apprehensive about religious freedom since the United States was largely Protestant.

In 1803, approximately 50,000 people resided in Louisiana, and again the population grew. American citizens went to Louisiana and settled in increasing numbers, and the Haitian victory in 1804 led thousands of Haitian immigrants, including whites and people of color, to settle in New Orleans.

Louisiana was admitted into the Union as a state in 1812, and by 1840, the city of New Orleans had increased in importance and wealth, becoming the third largest city in the United States. Its role as a major COMMERCE AND TRADE and shipping center grew dramatically as shipping down the Mississippi increased. It also had the largest slave market in the United States.

Free People of Color, Early History

The identity of the first free black or person of color (or *gens de couleur libre*) in Louisiana or when he or she arrived or became free is unknown. But, by 1724, Jean-Baptiste Le Moyne, sieur de Bienville, the French governor of Louisiana, and others had become concerned about the number of blacks and those of mixed parentage in Louisiana, and a set of laws known as the Code Noir was registered. (*See* CODE NOIR IN FRENCH LAW.)

The Code Noir was based on Louis XIV's Black Code, which had governed blacks in France's Caribbean colonies since 1687 and was significantly more liberal than the Louisiana law. Louisiana's Code Noir subjected slaves and free people of color to restrictive legislation. Slaves, for example, were declared movable property, were denied the right to sue, and were required to engage in Catholic baptism and instruction. The code also forbade whites to marry or keep people of color as mistresses, although this restriction was often ignored in the frontier society, where women were scarce.

The Code Noir, however, declared that people of color, once free (whether born free or manumitted), had the same rights as other freeborn persons, including the right to sue; parts of the Code Noir, however, continued to restrict the actions of free blacks, and local regulations further controlled people of color. During French and, to a much greater extent, Spanish rule, the numbers of people of color grew. The refugees from Saint-Domingue, who arrived after the uprisings there in the 1790s, included whites, enslaved Africans, and free people of color. Customs in Louisiana also increased the number of free people of color, as a system known as *plaçage* grew, wherein white males took women of color as mistresses, often supporting them and their children. Because of these relationships, there were an increasing number of native-born people of color, known as Creoles or Creoles of color. (*Creole* is variously defined. At its broadest definition, it includes all people who were descended from the pre-1804 settlers of Louisiana.)

MANUMISSION of slaves was easy under both French and Spanish law. Whites and free persons of color sometimes freed slaves in their wills or after a period of service. Service as a soldier could also lead to a slave's freedom. As a result, people of color served with distinction in the military under both French and Spanish rule in battles with Native Americans, during the American Revolution when the British forts in Baton Rouge and Natchez were captured by Count Bernardo de Galvéz (1746–86), and in the Battle of New Orleans in the War of 1812.

The records from the French period show that many slaves were manumitted for "good and faithful service" (sometimes a euphemism for being a mistress or the master's child by a slave mistress). In the Spanish period, laws were established that provided even more ways that a slave could be freed, including becoming members of a religious order within the ROMAN CATHOLIC CHURCH or performing services to the Crown. It was also possible for a slave to purchase his or her freedom (or that of a relative) during Spanish rule, with or without the master's consent (*see also* COARTACIÓN UNDER SPANISH LAW).

AFRICAN-AMERICANPOPULATION OF LOUISIANA, 1820–1900

Year	Slaves	Free People of Color	Free People of Color as a Percentage of Total Population	Total Population
1820	69,064	10,897	7.1%	153,407
1830	109,583	16,710	7.7%	215,739
1840	168,452	25,502	7.2%	352,411
1850	214,809	17,462	3.4%	517,762
1860	331,726	18,647	2.6%	708,002
1870		364,210	50.1%	726,915
1880		483,655	51.5%	939,946
1890		559,193	50.0%	1,118,587
1900		650,804	47.1%	1,381,625

The slave could petition the court for an appraiser to set a fair price on him or her. Once the slave paid the price, he or she was free, even if the master objected. Slaves also became free in illegal ways—running away and then LIVING "AS FREE."

By the late 1700s, there was a significant population of free people of color in Louisiana and especially in New Orleans. During this time, the people of color began to establish an identity or group consciousness, in effect forming a third social class separate from whites and slaves.

The high point in the development of this third class occurred around 1830. Free people of color could buy, sell, and inherit property at this time, and many free persons of color owned plantations and slaves, owned and ran grocery stores and mercantile shops, and worked in a variety of trades and professions, including tailoring, shoemaking, and cigar making. Free people of color also attended and supported the Catholic Church and created organizations and associations (*see also* CATHOLIC CONFRATERNITIES). Some segments of this group were considered the equal of whites in both sophistication and education, if not fully equal in the eyes of the law.

As the colony grew, officials became concerned about the system of *plaçage* and prohibited concubines. In 1786, the Spanish governor Esteban Miró enacted what came to be known as the tignon law, wherein free colored women who were living as concubines were required to give up their way of life and were threatened with expulsion from the colony if they refused to do so. Women were commanded to wear a tignon (a kerchief worn as a turban) rather than feathers and jewelry in their hair. The tignon law forced free women of color to reveal their status, not as concubines, but as women who had African blood. It was a symbolic law that attempted to disempower women by associating free women of color with slaves in the field by forcing free women of color to adopt the kerchief worn by slaves. Miró's plan failed, as the tignon became a stylish accessory and a mark of boldness and defiance.

During the years of Spanish rule, free people of color made significant gains in terms of population and privilege. After 1803, however, their rights begin to decline significantly.

Rise of Racial Discrimination

The rise of racial discrimination began not long after the United States purchased Louisiana in 1803. The evidence is easily found in the increasingly restrictive laws that usurped the rights of the free people of color.

In 1807, for instance, free blacks or people of color were banned from entering the state in an effort to stop the growth of that segment of the population. In 1812,

free blacks lost the right to vote when voting was limited to free white males only (in 1803, it had been given to all free people). In 1830, blacks' freedom of speech was limited when materials that would engender discontent among either free people of color or slaves were banned from publication. In 1841, free blacks in New Orleans who were not natives of Louisiana could not seek lodging or employment in the city. In 1855, the right to assemble was denied to free blacks, and they were denied the right to form new organizations or societies (e.g., religious, or literary, societies). In 1857, the emancipation of slaves was forbidden. And in 1859, the Louisiana state legislature encouraged free blacks to choose their own masters and become slaves for life. In the end, the civil and political status of the free person of color became very close to the status of the slave.

In addition to these increasing restrictions, free people of color found themselves vilified in the press in numerous ways, perhaps the most offensive of which was the publication of "scientific theories" that suggested that blacks were inherently inferior, animal like, and immoral. Racial discrimination arose from various factors. Some contemporaries believed that free people of color were a challenge to the Southern way of life: To their way of thinking, the institution of slavery was needed for survival. Many were fearful of slave insurrections and believed that free people of color either were directly responsible for slave revolts or helped encourage slaves. The growth of plantation society and the increasing commercialization of products (e.g., sugar and cotton) also led to a kind of distancing between the master and slave, in effect dehumanizing slaves in the eyes of contemporary society.

These restrictive laws had a number of results, and the population of the free people of color failed to grow. In part, this lack of growth can be attributed to masters' being prohibited to free slaves and slaves' being prohibited to buy their freedom. More troubling for the future of the free people of color and for Louisiana itself, a number of free people of color abandoned the restrictive laws and attitudes of Louisiana. Some journeyed to Northern states, but many left the country for France, LIBERIA, and Haiti. This migration meant that Louisiana and the free people of color lost potential leaders and artists, writers, and musicians.

Summary Leibensperger

FURTHER READING

Clinton, Catherine, and Michele Gillespie, eds. *The Devil's Lane: Sex and Race in the Early South.* New York: Oxford University Press, 1997.
Crété, Liliane. *Daily Life in Louisiana, 1815–1830.* Baton Rouge: Louisiana State University Press, 1981.

Domínguez, Virginia R. *White by Definition: Social Classification in Creole Louisiana.* New Brunswick, N.J.: Rutgers University Press, 1997.

Everett, Donald E. "Free Persons of Color in Colonial Louisiana." *Louisiana History* 7, no. 1 (1966): 21–50.

Hanger, Kimberly S. *Bounded Lives, Bounded Places: Free Black Society in New Orleans, 1769–1803.* Durham, N.C.: Duke University Press, 1997.

Moore, John Preston. *Revolt in Louisiana: The Spanish Occupation, 1766–1770.* Baton Rouge: Louisiana State University Press, 1976.

Reinders, Robert C. "The Decline of the New Orleans Free Negro in the Decade before the Civil War." *Journal of Mississippi History* 24 (January–October 1962): 88–99.

Roussève, Charles Barthelemy. *The Negro in Louisiana: Aspects of His History and His Literature.* New Orleans: Xavier University Press, 1937.

Taylor, Joe Gray. *Louisiana: A Bicentennial History.* New York: W. W. Norton, 1976.

LOUVERTURE, TOUSSAINT (ca. 1746–1803)
leader of the Haitian Revolution

The achievements of the man who named himself Toussaint Louverture give him fair claim to be the greatest African-American hero of all time. A self-made man born in slavery around 1746, he capitalized on the liberating trend of the FRENCH REVOLUTION to launch a movement that permanently ended slavery in the French colony of SAINT-DOMINGUE, today's Haiti—outwitting several of Europe's great colonial powers in politics and diplomacy and defeating them on the field of battle along the way. Though he ended his career as a prisoner in FRANCE in 1803, he remains the only black leader in the Western Hemisphere to have laid the foundation of an independent state that still exists today.

Early Years

Little is definitely known of Toussaint Louverture's childhood and youth; uncertainty is complicated by the fact that Louverture rewrote his own story for political purposes. Though he let it be believed that he was a slave when the Haitian Revolution began in 1791, the fact (proved by documents undiscovered until the 1970s) is that he had been a free man since 1776, and perhaps for much longer. By account of his second legitimate son, Isaac Louverture, Toussaint was born on Bréda Plantation, near Saint-Domingue's cultural capital CAP-FRANÇAIS/ CAP-HAÏTIEN, the grandson of an African prince named Gaou-Ginou, who had been captured in war and sold into slavery in the French colony. Though Toussaint's name does not appear on the lists of slaves owned by Bréda Plantation's absentee owners, he may have been the property of the plantation's French manager, Bayon de Libertat—if, in fact, he was not already free from birth or early childhood (*see* LIVING "AS FREE").

According to legend, the boy Toussaint, too frail for fieldwork, was employed as a herdsman. By young adulthood, he had acquired considerable veterinary skills, from both the European and the African traditions, and was reputed as a horse trainer. Isaac reports that Toussaint was taught to read and write by his godfather, Pierre-Baptiste. At the height of his powers, Toussaint liked to claim that he had taught these skills to himself in the late 1780s just before the revolution, but it seems more probable he was literate from childhood. As a young man, he frequented a hospital run by JESUITS and located between Bréda Plantation and Cap-Français, a place that attracted many free blacks, and acquired some basic medical knowledge from working there as a nurse; in later life he would also be known as a *dokte fey*, or herb doctor. A commitment to educating slaves and free blacks was a factor in the Jesuits' expulsion from Saint-Domingue in 1763; it is quite likely these priests played a part in Toussaint's early learning.

Toussaint was a trusted retainer of Bayon de Libertat, perhaps as much companion as servant, but serving Bayon as overseer, livestock manager, veterinarian, coachman, and messenger (*see* PLANTERS AND PLANTER AGENTS). Though never physically prepossessing (he was short and bowlegged and had an outsized head and pronounced underbite), he enjoyed enough success in love to father eight children out of wedlock. He did not marry his wife, Suzanne, till he was in his 40s.

Just how prosperous Toussaint may have become under the slave regime will never be known for certain. At his postrevolutionary peak he owned extensive real estate (most of it very strategically located), and he claimed to have been worth 648,000 French francs before the revolution. Yet if he really was so wealthy, it is strange that his wife and her three sons remained in slavery as late as 1789. No surviving records show that Toussaint owned more than one slave himself (whom he freed in the 1770s). What counted, however, was that as a free black, Toussaint belonged to a very small social class in the colony, for many free people of color were of mixed African and European blood. To put himself at the head of the hundreds of thousands of black slaves he meant to lead to freedom, Toussaint needed to conceal the fact that he was already free.

Dawn of Revolution

The massive slave insurrection that broke out on Saint-Domingue's Northern Plain on August 22, 1791, had been planned ahead at a secret meeting of slaves and enslaved overseers that occurred at a place called Bois

Toussaint Louverture negotiating with British officers, including the commander of the British intervention force, General Thomas Maitland, during the Haitian Revolution. Toussaint defeated all opposing factions in the Haitian Revolution and ruled the entire island of Hispaniola between 1799 and 1802. He was overthrown and imprisoned in France, where he died in 1803, but his lieutenants, including the prewar free people of color Alexandre Sabès Pétion and Jean-Pierre Boyer, went on to defeat the French and establish Haiti's independence in 1804. *(© Bettmann/CORBIS)*

Caiman, several miles outside Cap-Français and a shorter distance from Bréda Plantation. There is no concrete evidence that the man then known as Toussaint Bréda attended this meeting, though many contemporaries claimed that he secretly organized the August insurrection from the start, in cooperation with Bayon de Libertat and other royalist planters and military officers from the Cap-Français area, who believed, however foolishly, that they could use a controlled slave uprising to intimidate a lower class of Saint-Domingue whites whose support of the French Revolution had threatened the ancien régime in the colony since 1789. Most of the plantations of the Northern Plain were destroyed by fire in the first days of the insurrection, and their white inhabitants massacred, but a few, including Bréda, were left unharmed.

Toussaint remained at Bréda until fall 1791, when, after escorting Bayon de Libertat's wife to safety, he went to join the rebel slaves in the mountains. At that point, the situation had become a standoff; the French military was able to protect Cap-Français and other towns on the coast but could not regain any lasting control of the countryside. As the rebel slaves refined guerrilla tactics, Toussaint played a diplomatic role. He saved a party of white prisoners from being slaughtered by their captors and later tried to broker a settlement of the crisis with the Cap-Français Assembly and a group of commissioners sent from France.

When the settlement failed, Toussaint returned to the rebels and discreetly began to develop his own military command. By that time, two of the first rebel slave leaders, Boukman and Jeannot, had been killed, and power in the mountains was divided between Jean-François and Biassou. Nominally Biassou's subordinate, Toussaint began to organize a strategic cordon of small camps under his personal control.

From the start, the rebel slaves had declared themselves to be royalists, supporters of the embattled French king Louis XVI, and they had received covert support from the Spanish colony occupying the eastern two-thirds of Hispaniola, on whose border they were camped. When Louis XVI was guillotined in January 1793, Spain declared war on revolutionary France, and the rebel slaves across the French border were officially enrolled as "auxiliaries" in the Spanish army. Biassou and Jean-François became Spanish generals, while Toussaint was a mere marshal, but Toussaint had a better strategic sense than the other black commanders, and with some help from royalist French officers who found his camps hospitable, he was training a more effective fighting force. He quietly gained control of the Cordon de l'Ouest, a line of posts through the mountain range running west from the Spanish border to Gonaïves, which could isolate Cap-Français and the Northern Plain (where most of the slaves were concentrated) from PORT-AU-PRINCE and the southern two-thirds of the colony.

In 1792, a second commission had arrived from France, led by a lawyer, Léger Félicité Sonthonax. By then, all sorts of factional fighting had begun all over the colony. Racial and class divisions made a jigsaw puzzle of Saint-Domingue's colonial society. The black slaves, of whom more than half had been born free in Africa, were at least half a million strong by 1789. A group of some 30,000 people of mixed European and African blood was recognized in the French system as a third race (gens de couleur); many, though not all, of this group were free, and some people of color were as well educated and as wealthy as their white cousins. For several years, they had been agitating for political rights and in 1789 had sponsored their own unsuccessful armed insurrection (see also VINCENT OGÉ and JEAN-BAPTISTE CHAVANNES). Meanwhile, the outbreak of the French Revolution had split Saint-Domingue's 40,000 whites into radical and royalist factions; some of the latter hoped to make the colony a British protectorate.

An abolitionist in his personal sentiments, Sonthonax had no authority from the French government to end slavery, but he did a great deal to empower the colored class. His official mandate was to enforce a law passed by the French National Assembly on April 4, 1792, giving full political rights to colored people and free blacks (without changing the status of the slaves). Sonthonax and his colleagues struggled, with some success at first, to reassert government control over substantial counterrevolutionary areas in the South and West of Saint-Domingue. His military commander in the North, General Etienne Laveaux, began to secure much of the Northern Plain.

But in summer 1793, Sonthonax was undermined by the arrival of a new royalist military governor, Thomas François Galbaud. On June 20, the competition turned violent. When Galbaud's forces appeared likely to defeat the commissioners in fighting in and around Cap-Français, Sonthonax struck a hasty deal with leaders of rebel slaves nearby, promising freedom for all who fought for his cause. The town was sacked and burned by a storm of some 10,000 blacks; Galbaud and the surviving French royalists fled in a vast flotilla.

Freedom for All

On August 19, 1793, Sonthonax proclaimed the abolition of slavery, hoping to win the loyalty of the rebel slaves, who had abandoned the commissioners after the destruction of Cap-Français. That same day, Toussaint issued his own proclamation from Camp Turel in the mountains, summoning all to join *him* in the struggle for universal liberty. He signed this document *Toussaint Louverture*, a new name with layered implications. The French would understand the word for "opening" in terms of Toussaint's drive for liberation, while the Africans would sense a reference to the *vodun* spirit Legba, opener of crossroads and gates. Toussaint practiced both Catholicism and *vodun* (a common combination in Haiti today), had a foothold in both European and African culture, and knew how to combine the two to his advantage (*see* AFRICAN AND SYNCRETIC RELIGIONS).

Less than a month after Sonthonax's unilateral abolition of slavery, a British invasion began at several points in Saint-Domingue; abetted by French royalists and large landowners, the British gained some important positions without firing a shot. Sonthonax and his cocommissioners made their best effort to defend the colony's capital, Port-au-Prince, but lost a battle there on May 30, 1794, and took refuge with ANDRÉ RIGAUD, a colored commander in the South. Soon afterward, Sonthonax and his colleagues received a dispatch from the French National Assembly, which, while it confirmed the abolition of slavery, called for them to return to France to answer for their conduct.

Their departure left General Etienne Laveaux, now the highest-ranking representative of the French Republic, hemmed in at Port de Paix on the North Atlantic coast by hostile British and Spanish "auxiliary" forces. Cap-Français had become a quasi-independent fief controlled by the colored commander Villatte. Many towns along the coasts were now in the hands of the British and their allies, while the Spanish black auxiliaries controlled the interior.

Toussaint, meanwhile, was increasingly in conflict with the less talented black officers who nevertheless outranked him. Jean-François and Biassou began to dispute control of the posts Toussaint had developed along the Cordon de L'Ouest and to undermine him with the white Spanish commanders. Toussaint could no longer be certain that his wife and children were safe in Spanish territory, where he had tucked them away in fall 1791. One of his closest subordinates, Moyse, was briefly arrested. In March 1794, an ambush laid for Toussaint by the other black leaders took the life of his brother, Pierre. Toussaint retaliated quickly, driving Biassou out of the Cordon de l'Ouest.

Toussaint was always well informed about events all over the colony and was also able to get a certain amount of intelligence from France. By spring 1794, it was clear to him that the three colonial powers vying for control of Saint-Domingue—France, England, and Spain—were all in a precarious position, and that his own force, though still rather small, might be enough to tip the balance.

The British and Spanish colonies remained slave states. The position of Laveaux and the French republicans was the weakest of the three in 1794, but only France had committed to the abolition of slavery. The 1791 slave rising had been meant only to improve the conditions of slavery, not to end it. But since the proclamation of Camp Turel on August 19, 1793, Toussaint was firmly, permanently committed to freedom for all. Sonthonax's unauthorized abolition of slavery had not swayed him. Abolition of slavery by the French National Convention was not officially reported in Saint-Domingue until June 1794, but it is very likely that Toussaint already knew of it in May, when he began negotiating with Etienne Laveaux.

By that time, Toussaint had taken the port town of Gonaïves on behalf of the Spanish. The British invaders may have contacted him there with an effort to win him to their side; if so, they failed. Having reached an understanding with Laveaux, Toussaint conducted a lightning campaign to purge the Cordon de l'Ouest of the Spanish and their black auxiliaries, driving Jean-François east to Fort-Liberté. By May 18, he was able to offer Laveaux a secure line of posts running from Dondon in the interior through Gonaïves all the way up to Limbé and Acul, completely encircling Cap-Français and the Northern Plain, and with 4,000 picked men to protect it.

Black Spartacus

From 1794 to 1796, Toussaint and Laveaux fought a war against multiple enemies on several fronts. Toussaint soon demolished the Spanish threat; Jean-François and Biassou left the island. He fought numerous battles with the British along the west coast and the Artibonite River. Though he preferred to use guile rather than force, his use of both was very sophisticated.

In 1796, Toussaint rescued Laveaux from a coup attempt by the colored commander Villatte at Cap-Français. A grateful Laveaux, proclaiming him a "Black Spartacus," appointed him lieutenant governor of the colony. Soon afterward, Sonthonax returned fully vindicated from France to resume civil leadership of Saint-Domingue. By summer 1797, however, Toussaint had maneuvered both Sonthonax and Laveaux out of the colony (by arranging their election to the French legislature) and was negotiating independently for the departure of the British invaders. Appointed general in chief of the French army by Sonthonax, Toussaint was now the de facto ruler of Saint-Domingue, though there was competition from the colored faction led by André Rigaud, whose strength was in the South.

Concerned by Toussaint's growing autonomy, France sent another representative, Agent Hédouville, who arrived in March 1798. With no real military force to back him, Hédouville could not bring Toussaint to heel; nor could he assert a role in the negotiation of the British withdrawal, which Toussaint accomplished on his own. Hédouville left the colony in October 1798, and Toussaint, who always professed loyalty to France, recruited Roume, a member of the 1791 commission, to assume the agent's post.

Hédouville had been successful enough in setting Toussaint and Rigaud against each other that a civil war erupted in June 1799 between black and colored factions. This bitter and vicious struggle lasted until August of the following year, when Toussaint, with the help of his generals Christophe and Dessalines, crushed the last spark of colored resistance. With the whole colony at peace for the first time in nearly 10 years, Toussaint turned to consolidating his gains.

For several years, he had been encouraging the return of white French planters to manage their property with free labor, though this policy was disputed by both Sonthonax and Hédouville because too many of these returning colonists were royalists. With no further opposition, Toussaint moved more rapidly to restore the plantation economy in 1800 and 1801, intending to prove to France that Saint-Domingue could be profitable without slavery (and to raise money for war, if need be). This effort required a policy of compulsory labor, enforced by the army, which alienated many of the newly freed blacks. In 1801, Toussaint's trusted subordinate and adopted nephew Moïse led a sizable number of discontented workers in a rebellion that ended with his defeat and execution by firing squad.

Later that year, Toussaint sent a force to occupy Spanish SANTO DOMINGO, ceded to France by the Treaty of Basel in 1795—ignoring instructions from France not to do so. Also in 1801, he created a committee to write a new constitution for the colony and, over the protests of trusted advisers, published it before sending it to France for approval. The new constitution proclaimed permanent loyalty to France as well as permanent abolition of slavery in Saint-Domingue; it also appointed Toussaint as governor for life, with the right to name his successor.

Toussaint v. Napoléon

Napoléon Bonaparte and Toussaint Louverture were two self-made men who fueled their extraordinary rise to power with political acumen and military genius. By 1801, First Consul Napoléon had become the de facto ruler of France by means no more nor less legitimate than those that made Toussaint de facto ruler of Saint-Domingue. A degree of sympathy between these two men (who never met) was perhaps as inevitable as their rivalry. Napoléon carefully weighed the question whether he should cooperate with Toussaint's regime or overthrow it and restore the slave system in its place. In the memoir he wrote at the end of his life, he regretted choosing the latter course. The balance was tipped by Toussaint's constitution, his

occupation of Spanish Santo Domingo, and his negotiations with the British, which Napoléon interpreted as steps toward independence.

A fleet carrying a large army commanded by Napoléon's brother-in-law, General Leclerc, arrived on the east coast of Hispaniola at the end of January 1802. Toussaint, while desperately hoping that no invasion would occur, had been furiously preparing to meet it if it did, strengthening fortifications, increasing his army, importing guns from the United States. His strategy—to destroy the coast towns and retreat to the interior—was imperfectly executed because the French invaders (the best-seasoned soldiers from Napoléon's European wars) moved quickly enough to intercept some of Toussaint's communications, and because some of Toussaint's officers were swayed by propaganda messages from Napoléon, claiming that freedom for the blacks would be respected.

In three months of ferocious fighting, Toussaint's and Leclerc's armies practically crippled each other. Toussaint remained strong enough to force a settlement on terms favorable to him and his men. His subordinate generals, notably Dessalines and Christophe, acknowledged the authority of General Leclerc and put their troops under his command. Toussaint retired to his plantations at Ennery, in the mountains just above Gonaïves, taking with him some 2,000 men of his honor guard. His probable plan was to wait till fever season further weakened the French before renewing hostilities. But, with the tacit consent of Dessalines and other high-ranking black officers, Leclerc managed to have Toussaint arrested and deported to France, where he died, after several months' imprisonment in a frosty chateau in the Jura Mountains, on April 7, 1803.

Toussaint's Legacy

Eliminating Toussaint proved to be of no real help to the French cause. One of Toussaint's greatest achievements was to transform a rebellion that could not have continued without someone of his unique gifts into a revolution that no longer needed any particular leader at all. Leclerc effectively acknowledged as much when he informed Napoléon that in order to secure the colony, it would be necessary to destroy every black male above the age of 12. But Leclerc died of yellow fever first, and his successor, Donatien Rochambeau, was driven from the island by Dessalines, who proclaimed the independence of Haiti in 1804. The failure of the French expedition led Napoléon to abandon his ambitions to strengthen the French presence in Louisiana—with an enormous effect on the history of the United States.

Certain aspects of the Louverturian state, notably military dictatorship and leadership for life, have proved persistently problematic for Haiti from Toussaint's day till now. Yet Toussaint's commitment to the declared ideals of the French Revolution—liberty, equality, and brotherhood—was strong and sincere, and his effort to extend these social goods to the black, the white, and the colored races never flagged. At the peak of his career he was closer to achieving these goals than anyone else has been before or since.

Madison Smartt Bell

FURTHER READING

Bell, Madison Smartt. *Toussaint Louverture: A Biography.* New York: Pantheon, 2007.

Dubois, Laurent. *Avengers of the New World: The Story of the Haitian Revolution.* Cambridge, Mass.: Belknap Press of Harvard University Press, 2004.

Fick, Carolyn E. *The Making of Haiti: The Saint Domingue Revolution from Below.* Knoxville: University of Tennessee Press, 1990.

Geggus, David Patrick. *Haitian Revolutionary Studies.* Bloomington: Indiana University Press, 2002.

———. *Slavery, War and Revolution: The British Occupation of Saint Domingue, 1793–1798.* Oxford: Clarendon Press, 1982.

James, C. L. R. *The Black Jacobins: Toussaint L'Ouverture and the San Domingo Revolution.* London: Allison & Busby, 1984.

Parkinson, Wenda. *This Gilded African: Toussaint L'Ouverture.* London: Quartet Books, 1980.

Stein, Robert Louis. *Léger Félicité Sonthonax: The Lost Sentinel of the Republic.* Cranbury, N.J.: Associated University Presses, 1985.

Toussaint-L'Ouverture, Général. *Mémoirs écrits par lui-même, pouvant servir à l'histoire de sa vie.* Edited by Joseph Saint-Rémy. Paris: Pagnerre, 1859.

LYNCHING

Lynching was a form of extrajudicial killing often perpetrated in the American South in the period after the AMERICAN CIVIL WAR, 1861–65, but also found in other countries and times. The motive, at least in part, is to punish some person for a violation or perceived violation of communal mores that cannot for whatever reason be prosecuted as a matter of law. It is distinguished from plain murder or terrorist violence because it is a collective act, carried out by large bodies of people generally representative of a community, as, for example, the white citizens of a U.S. town. The killings often have a ritualistic element, with the erection of gallows, a formalized declaration of the reasons the community has decided to kill the victim, and public torture or humiliation of the victim. Many American lynchings in the 19th and early 20th centuries took place in public gathering places and were attended by hundreds or thousands of people. They were sometimes even advertised in advance in local newspapers. Terrorism is often an additional or indeed principal motive. Thus, a lynching may be intended to strike fear into a larger group that the victim is seen to represent, such as his ethnic group or social class. The killing may use extremely brutal methods in an attempt to heighten this terroristic effect. Communities may use lynching even if the victim could have been prosecuted and punished under law if the terrorist motive is foremost, since extremely brutal public torture and executions were not generally permitted in the Western world from the 19th century. Many lynchings in the South were of locally prominent blacks, often former free people of color or their descendants. Often the victims were economic competitors for white elites who sought to better their own businesses by arranging for the killing of their competitors.

Lynching was an important part of community life in the American South in the period after the Civil War. During the period known as RECONSTRUCTION IN THE UNITED STATES, from 1865 to 1877, the federal government had an important role in local government. Federal officials oversaw a good deal of local law enforcement and legal procedures and insisted on a certain degree of equal justice for blacks accused of crimes. Sometimes white communities would ignore legal processes and kill blacks accused of crimes. After the withdrawal of federal troops, white elites regained control of legal institutions and could use them more or less as they saw fit, but communities continued to perpetrate lynchings, no doubt for the psychological effect on the larger black community. This was a time when legal and political protections for black communities were being dismantled, and perpetrators hoped that lynchings would help to make black communities compliant in their disempowerment.

Lynching of blacks was almost unknown in the pre–Civil War South. Anybody who killed a slave would owe his master a large amount of money—slaves cost more than most workers could earn in many years. In any case, people of the slave-owning class were powerful enough to stop any community effort to destroy their property. Free people of color were very tightly controlled by the law and could also be punished informally by individual whites for perceived slights or crimes without needing to turn to the larger community for validation. On the other hand, lynching of whites and Indians was not uncommon throughout the history of early America, both in colonial times and in the 19th century, particularly in frontier areas. The technique played an important role in solidifying community bonds and validating community leaders through rituals of shared violence. Often, no formal legal systems existed in frontier areas, or community members did not trust those systems that did exist and so resorted to a sort of community self-help law enforcement that could include extrajudicial killings. These killings also often had a terrorist function as they sought to repress excluded groups, including Indians, outlaws, and immigrant workers.

Lynching in its American, communal, ritualistic, brutal form was rare in slave societies in the Americas outside the United States. The repression of slave rebellions was sometimes marked by extrajudicial killings. For example, after the Baptist War in JAMAICA (1831–32), some 340 blacks were killed by the victorious white MILITIA with almost no legal formalities. However, these killings took place in the context of armed resistance to slavery and were often given some formal legal cover by martial law or summary courts-martial. Various armed groups in the SOUTH AMERICAN WARS OF LIBERATION and WAR OF MEXICAN INDEPENDENCE, 1810–21, killed civilians or enemy prisoners with the intent of terrorizing opposing factions, and these acts can be considered lynchings, but again they took place under some sort of official military command structure.

The struggle against lynching in the United States was one of the very earliest stages in the modern civil rights movement. Black journalists, most notably Ida B. Wells (1862–1931), campaigned against lynching. She took up the cause in 1892 after three friends of hers, two of whom were prewar free people of color, were lynched in Memphis, TENNESSEE. The men were accused of rape, but their actual crime was running a grocery store that was taking business away from white storekeepers. Northern white public opinion responded, and bills to federalize investigations and prosecutions of lynchings were regularly passed by the U.S. House of Representatives, only to be blocked by filibuster in the Senate. Black mobilization against lynching helped galvanize a new civil rights movement after 1900 that ultimately led to the successes of the mid-20th century.

Stewart R. King

FURTHER READING
Markovitz, Jonathan. *Legacies of Lynching: Racial Violence and Memory.* Minneapolis: University of Minnesota Press, 2004.
Wells, Ida B. *Southern Horrors: Lynch Law in All Its Phases.* New York: 1892. Project Gutenberg. Available online. URL: http://www.gutenberg.org/etext/14975. Accessed January 1, 2011.

MACEO Y GRAJALES, ANTONIO (1845–1896)
Cuban military leader

Antonio Maceo rose to become the deputy commander of the Cuban independence forces during the TEN YEARS' WAR (1868–78), organized rebel forces in the Little War (1879–80), and was deputy commander again until his death in the Cuban War of Independence (1895–98). His leadership was crucial to the Cuban independence forces, permitting an elite-led movement to connect with ordinary country folk and to pursue an ultimately successful strategy of guerrilla war. He led troops in battle more than 500 times and suffered many wounds. He was finally killed in battle in Punta Brava, CUBA, December 7, 1896, a year and a half before the final Cuban victory.

Antonio Maceo was born on June 14, 1845, the child of two free people of color. His father, Marcos Maceo, was from VENEZUELA. He had fled his home country after the War of Independence there. He owned a small farm in Oriente province, near Santiago de Cuba, an area where there were many free colored farmers. Maceo's mother was a Cuban free colored woman, Mariana Grajales, also from a farm family. Antonio was the eldest of nine children, at least two of whom, in addition to his father and other relatives, would serve along with him in the rebel forces during Cuba's various independence struggles. The family faced many hardships in Antonio's early years, and his mother was an important formative influence during these times. From Mariana, Antonio gained good organizational skills and the tendency to stick to a chosen course of action despite setbacks, a characteristic that was to serve him well in his military career. Marcos Maceo worked as a dealer of agricultural implements and a muleteer in order to supplement the income from his failing farm, and Antonio joined him in this work at the age of 16. The work took him throughout the eastern part of Cuba and put him in contact with many local farmers. He became intimately familiar with the geography and people of this region, which was to be the cockpit of the ensuing struggle for independence.

Cuban society, in a process familiar throughout the Americas, had seen a harshening of racial discrimination during the late 18th and early 19th centuries, as the colony became a leading global producer of sugar. Contributing to this process was accelerating white immigration, both from Europe and from elsewhere in Spanish America. At the end of the 18th century, almost all Cubans had some African ancestry, and free people of color vastly outnumbered enslaved. By the 1850s, when Antonio was a boy, enslaved people were almost half of all people of African origin, and harsh laws meant to control the slaves but expressed in racial terms set free people of African descent apart from a growing class of whites.

White Cubans feared free people of color. They saw the participation of free African-descended people in the HAITIAN REVOLUTION and SOUTH AMERICAN WARS OF LIBERATION as a warning that they could play a similar role in Cuba. Many exiles from Latin America, fierce opponents of independence, had settled in Cuba and helped deepen opposition to independence and liberal reforms there.

However, liberal political ideas had taken hold among the Cuban elite. In the 1860s, discouraged with the pace of reform in the Spanish Empire, Cuban CREOLE nationalists began to think of rebellion and even independence. A group of eastern planters around Francisco Vicente Aguilera (1821–77) and Carlos Manuel de Céspedes (1819–74) launched the Great War of Cuba, also called the TEN YEARS' WAR, October 10, 1868. Céspedes was Marcos Maceo's neighbor and an important patron. On October 12, Céspedes and his men, most of them his former slaves, whom he had freed at the outbreak of the war, stayed at Maceo's farm, and when they left in the morning, Antonio and his younger brother, José, along with Mariana's son by another relationship, Justo Grajales, accompanied them. Marcos Maceo also later joined the rebel forces and served under his son's command.

By the end of October, Céspedes's forces had captured the regional capital of Bayamo. During the battles around Bayamo, Antonio Maceo performed feats of arms that his superiors had considered entirely impossible. At one point, with 37 men under his command, Maceo routed a column of several hundred pro-Spanish militia headed to the besieged city. Maceo realized that the pro-Spanish forces suffered from poor morale and training, and aggressiveness could allow a small force to overcome a larger. In January 1869, he was promoted to colonel in the rebel forces and given an autonomous command in the Guantánamo region. He defeated the Spanish forces in the area on numerous occasions, despite the fact that professional and well-armed troops from Spain had joined the ill-equipped volunteers in the field. Maceo introduced many tactics that have become common in irregular warfare, including the feigned retreat that leads the pursuing enemy into an ambush, heavy reliance on sniping, use of night and forest terrain to shield movement, and effective use of intelligence and reconnaissance. During 1869, Maceo's father, two close friends, and two of the elder Maceo's children by an earlier relationship died as a result of the war.

In June 1870, Maceo joined forces with his most important colleague, General Máximo Gómez (1836–1905), a Dominican-born Spanish army officer who switched sides to support the rebels. Ironically, Gómez had fought on the Spanish side in the DOMINICAN REPUBLIC's War of Independence (1861–65) and had learned from his Haitian and Dominican opponents to appreciate the fighting qualities of black troops. In contrast to the elite Cubans who had led the rebel army up to that point, Gómez was prepared to believe that a person of African ancestry could be a great commander and a dedicated soldier. Gómez and Maceo became close collaborators for the rest of their lives. Together, they developed the strategy of the Cuban rebels in the Ten Years' War. Rather than trying to push westward with organized forces, a strategy that exposed the rebel armies to destruction by the better-armed Spanish in the open terrain of the western plantation zone, they sought to disrupt SUGAR CULTIVATION through irregular warfare while holding the mountainous and forested eastern part of the country with their best forces. Spain could not gain any profit from the colony, and the rebel-held areas were refuges for any slave from the plantation zones who wished to escape. Spanish forces often entered the eastern provinces, by virtue of Spain's monopoly on sea power, but could not move inland. The isolated garrisons in the coastal towns proved to be a drain on Spanish resources, requiring expensive and difficult resupply missions and causing continual casualties that debilitated the Spanish forces. Disease was a very significant threat to troops from Europe, with the result that the military burden of the pro-Spanish side had to be borne by anti-independence conservative Cubans. Few in number, they turned to slaves to man their armies as well, further diminishing the slave workforce and reducing the tax revenues needed to fund the war. With world attention focused on Cuba because of the war, which especially caught the interest of British and Americans opposed to slavery, the illegal slave trade finally ended.

Maceo's forces continued pressure on Spanish garrisons in Guantánamo during 1870 and 1871. Maceo was able to confine the Spanish to a small zone around the city. Under pressure from impatient members of the Cuban Congress, Gómez finally agreed that the time had come for an offensive into the west to try to break the stalemate. This decision led to dissension between the two comrades as Maceo argued that this would mean disaster for the rebels. At first, Céspedes, the provisional president, sided with Maceo, and the rebels continued to wait. In 1874, however, Céspedes was dismissed by the Cuban Congress, which then supported Gómez's plan. Conservative members of Congress attacked Maceo and once again suggested that blacks were incapable of high command responsibilities. In 1874 and 1875, Gómez and Maceo led their troops into the west in two ill-fated expeditions that gained success on the battlefield at great cost in lives but were unable to press on to final victory because of the superior numbers of the Spanish and supply difficulties. The 1875 expedition saw Maceo fighting alongside a volunteer general from the United States, a white man and Civil War veteran named Henry Reeve, and penetrating into Havana province before they were defeated and Reeve was killed. Inconclusive fighting continued for the next two years, and in one incident in 1876, Maceo was severely wounded. The Spanish found out where he was being treated and launched a major expedition to try to capture him. His brother, José Maceo, led the defense and fought a 10-day battle against the Spanish column. Finally, Antonio Maceo got out of his bed, leaped on to his horse, and escaped through enemy lines to a nearby rebel base.

After the Cuban president Tomás Estrada Palma was captured, a group of conservative congressmen led by General Vicente Garcia took control of the rebel movement. They feared that the predominantly black soldiers of the revolution, led by their mixed-race general, might create a black republic in eastern Cuba like that in nearby Haiti. These racial fears, combined with frustration at the slow pace of rebel progress, sparked a fateful decision. They decided to negotiate peace with the Spanish. On February 11, 1878, the Cuban nationalist Congress accepted the Treaty of Zanjón, securing amnesty for all rebels and freedom for all slaves who fought on either side in the war, formally ending the slave trade but preserving the institution of slavery and Spanish rule in the colony.

Maceo disagreed with this decision in his proclamation called the Protest of Baraguá, and he tried to rally his troops for another showdown with the Spanish. However, without the support of the eastern planters, who had accepted the

Cuban independence leader Antonio Maceo (1845–96) was a mixed-race military commander during the Ten Years' War (1868–78) and the War of Cuban Independence (1895–98). He was responsible for many important victories by the rebel forces that helped keep the cause alive. This illustration was published in *Harper's Magazine* in 1896 on the occasion of Maceo's death in battle. As with many 19th-century images of illustrious people of African descent, this image makes the subject significantly lighter in complexion than he appears in photographs. Maceo's Afro-Cuban identity is almost completely concelaed in this drawing, whch was inteded for a primarily white audience in the United States. *(Archives Charmet/The Bridgeman Art Library)*

treaty, he was unable to rekindle the war. He finally agreed to go into exile. Over the next year, he visited Cuban communities in New York, Jamaica, and Haiti, finally settling in the Haitian capital of PORT-AU-PRINCE. From there, he tried to raise forces in coordination with General Calixto García to continue the fight in Cuba. Maceo remained outside Cuba during the Little War of 1879–80, while García invaded, fought, and was eventually captured. The war fizzled out, but the Spanish government was sufficiently concerned at the risk of slave uprising finally to abolish slavery.

Maceo settled in HONDURAS in 1880; there he worked for the government and corresponded with other Cuban nationalists. It was also in this period that he became active in FREEMASONRY, rising to a high rank, though one biographer says he had originally joined the Freemasons as a young man before the outbreak of the Ten Years' War. He adopted the Masonic slogan "God, Reason, Virtue" as his own and was fond of quoting it in letters and proclamations after that time. He helped found the Cuban Revo-

lutionary Party in 1892. The author Jose Martí (1853–95) was the romantic hero of the revolutionary movement, but Maceo and his old comrade Gómez were the military leaders. Maceo became a full-time revolutionary again in 1884, and he urged another invasion at that time. Martí convinced the reluctant military commanders to wait until the groundwork could be laid for a truly national revolution. The tension between Martí and the military men was to pose an ongoing problem for the Cuban revolutionary movement and for Cuban politics after independence. Maceo distrusted the fair-skinned, highly educated Martí because he saw in him the wealthy planters and politicians who he felt had betrayed the movement at the end of the Ten Years' War. Martí saw in Gómez and Maceo the same sort of military men who had betrayed liberal, democratic government in so many places in Spanish America.

After 10 years of these debates, accompanied by political organizing and fund-raising, the moment finally came in January 1895. The U.S. authorities confiscated much of the rebel arsenal as their ships were leaving harbor in Fort Lauderdale, FLORIDA. Nonetheless, a small force of rebels, including Maceo, Gómez, and Martí, landed in Oriente province and began to raise a guerrilla army. Martí, was caught and killed quickly, but Gómez and Maceo built strong forces. Intent on carrying the war to the entire country, Gómez sent Maceo with a column to the farthest western extremity of the country. Crossing the entire country in 96 days, Maceo repeatedly defeated larger Spanish forces sent to intercept him and paralyzed economic activity. This movement was tactically brilliant and achieved the important strategic goals of staking a rebel claim to the entire country and hurting the Spanish economically but ultimately amounted to a raid as the overwhelming Spanish strength obliged Maceo to retreat to the western mountains. In 1896, he was back in the plains near Havana, provoking the Spanish commander Valeriano Weyler (1838–1930) to adopt a strategy of concentration, relocating country dwellers in areas that supported the rebels to concentration camps or slums outside the cities. The camps were administered by plantation managers, and the residents were often people of color. Conditions were terrible: Perhaps as many as a third of all PEASANTS in the camps died during the war. The Cuban concentration camps were to be emulated by many other counterinsurgents during the century ahead, from British fighting the Boers in South Africa (1899–1902) to the American/South Vietnamese forces in the Second Vietnam War (1962–75).

On September 18, 1896, Antonio Maceo won his last great victory, over a large Spanish column in Oriente province. He captured more than 1,000 modern rifles and several pieces of artillery. He was traveling to a meeting with Gómez in western Cuba on December 7, 1896, to decide how to use this windfall when his small headquarters party was intercepted by a roving band of Spanish cavalry. While rallying his men, Maceo was struck in the face and chest by rifle balls and fell dead.

The Cuban War of Independence continued for another year and a half, finally ending when the United States joined the war and American troops captured the Spanish stronghold of Santiago de Cuba. Military men would have a strong influence over Cuban politics, as military dictators ruled the country on several occasions during the 20th century. However, Afro-Cubans continued to suffer from racial discrimination, and Maceo's name was almost forgotten for half a century. Finally, after the Cuban Revolution of 1959, the new government resurrected him as a symbol of racial harmony and national pride. He has often been depicted as an opponent of U.S. presence in the country, although in fact he traveled several times to the United States and was no more anti-American than his wealthier political superiors.

Stewart R. King

FURTHER READING

Ferrer, Ada. *Insurgent Cuba: Race, Nation, and Revolution, 1868–1898.* Chapel Hill: University of North Carolina Press, 1999.

Foner, Philip. *Antonio Maceo: The "Bronze Titan" of Cuba's Struggle for Independence.* New York: Monthly Review Press, 1978.

———. *The Spanish-Cuban-American War and the Birth of American Imperialism.* New York: Monthly Review Press, 1972.

Helg, Aline. *Our Rightful Share: The Afro-Cuban Struggle for Equality, 1886–1912.* Chapel Hill: University of North Carolina Press, 1995.

MACHADO DE ASSIS, JOAQUIM MARÍA
(1839–1908) *Brazilian writer*

Joaquim María Machado de Assis is among Brazil's greatest writers. He did not gain great popularity outside BRAZIL during his life, but writers around the world in the 20th century recognized his genius. The Mexican writer Carlos Fuentes, the Portuguese playwright and Nobel laureate José Saramago, the American poet and activist Susan Sontag, and the American literary critic Harold Bloom have all lauded his work. In his collection of critical biographies *Genius*, Bloom calls him "the supreme black literary artist to date." Interestingly, in America Bloom uncontroversially labeled him "black"; in Brazil, he would have been called a *mulato* or PARDO, and because he was light-skinned and socially prominent, he would have escaped much of the racial discrimination leveled at blacks in that society.

The son of a MULATTO housepainter and an Azorean woman, Joaquim María Machado de Assis was born on June 21, 1839, in Rio de Janeiro. Mostly self-taught, he found work at FRANCISCO DE PAULA BRITO's bookshop and press in 1855 and published his first poem in Brito's *Marmota Fluminense* that same year. Brito secured him a post at the national printing press in 1856. Subsequently, Machado de Assis worked as a proofreader for the *Correio Mercantil.* From 1860 to 1867, he was part of the *Diário do Rio de Janeiro*'s editorial staff, and in 1867, he received a government appointment as assistant to the *Diário Oficial*'s director. In 1873, he received a position in the ministry of agriculture, and for most of the rest of his life, he held a series of mid-level civil service posts that gave him the financial means to devote his time to writing. He married Carolina Augusta Xavier de Novais, a socially prominent Portuguese woman, in 1869, over the objections of her family, who did not want her to marry a mixed-race man. They did not have any children. Social criticism of INTERRACIAL MARRIAGE was the one form of discrimination that this very assimilated free man of color was to experience during his long career.

Machado de Assis was loyal to the monarchy, and his political loyalty and the popularity of his literary work helped him rise in the bureaucracy. He did not become involved in politics and notably refused to speak out against slavery. For this he was criticized by other prominent free people of color, including JOSÉ CARLOS DO PATROCÍNIO. The overthrow of the monarchy on November 15, 1889, was a shock to Machado de Assis, but since he had not been politically active, he was able to keep his job and continue to work on his literary pursuits.

Known today for his great novels, Machado de Assis also wrote poetry, numerous short stories, and regular newspaper columns. His sardonic humor and subtle commentary reveal that he was an astute and critical observer of changes in 19th- and early-20th-century Brazilian society, though he never explicitly addressed questions of race and rarely included slaves and black characters in his work. In this respect, he was fairly typical of successful men of color in 19th-century Brazil who had to adapt to the country's racial etiquette in order to advance in society. His major novels have all been translated into English, including *Quincas Borba* (*Philosopher or Dog?*, 1891), *Dom Casmurro* (1899), *Esaú e Jacó* (*Esau and Jacob*, 1904), and *Memorial de Aires* (*Counselor Ayres' Memoirs*, 1908).

In 1897, Machado de Assis was elected president of the newly established Academia Brasileira das Letras (Brazilian Academy of Letters), a post that he held to the end of his life. He died on September 28, 1908, in Rio.

Hendrik Kraay

FURTHER READING

Caldwell, Helen. *Machado de Assis: The Brazilian Master and His Novels*. Berkeley: University of California Press, 1970.
Graham, Richard, ed. *Machado de Assis: Reflections on a Brazilian Master Writer*. Austin: University of Texas Press, 1999.

MACKANDAL, FRANÇOIS (ca. 1720–1758)
Saint-Domingue maroon leader

François Mackandal (also Macandal or Makandal) was a well-known example of the many slaves who fled to the mountains and threatened the viability of slavery in Saint-Domingue in the middle of the 18th century. Born around 1720, he was originally from West Africa and sold as a slave to the Lernormand plantation in the north of Saint-Domingue in the early 1740s. Not much is known about Mackandal prior to his enslavement, but his execution on a pile of wood on January 20, 1758, on the square of CAP-FRANÇAIS/CAP-HAÏTIEN entered the legend of Haitian history through oral traditions as one of the predecessors of TOUSSAINT LOUVERTURE and Jean-Jacques Dessalines, leaders of the HAITIAN REVOLUTION. According to these traditions and accounts by Haitian historians, Mackandal had been a soldier taken to Saint-Domingue after being made a prisoner of war in his native land. He is believed to have been a Muslim, and some contemporary sources say he spoke Arabic fluently, both of which suggest he was of Fulbe or Fulani origins from SENEGAMBIA (*see also* ISLAM). Other accounts describe him as a *houngan*, or *vodun* priest (*see also* AFRICAN AND SYNCRETIC RELIGIONS). The uncertainty about his religious belief indicates how little solid information on Mackandal exists. However, the significance of these attributes probably placed him in an enviable social standing among his fellow slaves, winning him an influential position on the plantation.

He presented himself to them as a prophet and a sorcerer who could instill respect based on fear. Mackandal, according to the main historical accounts, worked in the plantation's sugar mill; this confirms his relative social standings among the slaves, as this was a position requiring a degree of specialization within the sugar industry. One day, he suffered from an accident at the mill and lost one of his arms. In 1746 or 1747, he fled the plantation to join MAROONS in the northern mountains, where he orchestrated attacks on nearby plantations through his well-established network of allegiance among the slaves and the loyalty of his fellow maroons. Mackandal's weapon of choice to erode slavery in Saint-Domingue was poison; he probably acquired knowledge of poisons through his former days as a soldier and his religious trainings as a *vodun* priest or practitioner, or as a Muslim cleric, a position that may have allowed him to learn about plant medicines. There are no known accounts of how many whites became the victims of Mackandal's schemes, but most accounts suggest that the terror of being poisoned by a servant slave was a real one in the homes of northern Saint-Domingue. Any servant slave could be a secret ally of Mackandal and could easily poison his or her master's food.

Since allegiance to Mackandal was often based on fear, backed by his prophecy that he could not be killed or captured or could transform himself into a fly or a mosquito to return and torture the slave masters, the plantation owners could do little to prevent the intimidated slaves from following his orders. It is important to think of Mackandal's prophecy as a strategic technique to convince the common slave not to be afraid of the consequences of rebellion by transcending his weakness as a human with a material body. Mackandal convinced others he had a supernatural body that could be anywhere at any time, punishing both terrified slaves who did not obey him and whites for their deeds in the colony. For more than 12 years, from 1745 to 1758, Mackandal was the terror of northern Saint-Domingue, and the colonial police known as the *maréchaussée* could not capture him. But his human weaknesses handed him to his enemies. Oral traditions recount that Mackandal was a womanizer and because of his cultural heritage probably practiced polygamy. His uncertain lifestyle as a maroon with no fixed abode made this even more of an imperative. He apparently became involved with the wife of a slave, who in turn revealed his whereabouts to the colonial police while he was attending a slave party. He was drunk and probably did not have a chance to make one of his previously successful escapes and was captured. He was condemned to be burned alive in the central square of Cap-Français, then the capital of the colony. Traditions have it that he broke his chains and escaped from the fire and fulfilled his prophecy of turning into a fly. He probably did break the chains while he was set in fire, which actually may have helped him by burning the cords that bound him. Contemporary accounts by white observers say that after the first attempt to burn him, the square was cleared of black witnesses and then he was tied more carefully and thrown back into the flames.

For the slaves, however, Mackandal continued to live on, and the circumstances of his execution reinforced the effect of his myth. His prophecy and his defiance of the plantation system served as a powerful symbol and possibility of freedom in the minds of the slaves, helping to spark the Haitian Revolution in 1791. The fear of poisoning plots of the white plantocracy gave Mackandal power in the slaves' minds. Whether the plots actually occurred mattered less than the fact that the whites showed fear, demonstrating to the mass of enslaved men and women that the white planter class was not as powerful as it claimed to be. One may extrapolate by saying that when the slave rebels in 1791 launched the plan of killing all whites in Saint-Domingue, the memory of Mackandal's plot could have served to validate their project. Therefore, the significance of Mackandal lies beyond his importance as a definite historical subject with a known past and identity in the history of the fight for freedom in the Americas; rather, it consists of showing possibilities to the slaves and indicating to modern people moments and symbols that redefined slave consciousness from accommodation to revolution in the Atlantic world.

Martine Jean

FURTHER READING

Bell, Madison Smartt. *All Souls' Rising*. New York: Pantheon Books, 1995.

———. *Master of the Crossroads*. New York: Pantheon Books, 2000.

Carpentier, Alejo. *The Kingdom of This World*. Translated by Harriet Onis. New York: Knopf, 1957.

Dubois, Laurent. *Avengers of the New World: The Story of the Haitian Revolution*. Cambridge, Mass.: Belknap Press of Harvard University, 2004.

MADIOU, THOMAS (1814–1884) *Haitian historian*
Thomas Madiou was the first Haitian historian. His master work, *Histoire d'Haïti* (1847), is considered one of the great works of Haitian literature as well as being an invaluable source for the history of the revolutionary and early national periods. His interpretation of the events of this period has become widely accepted among scholars today, thanks in large measure to his careful research.

Madiou was born on April 30, 1814, in PORT-AU-PRINCE, a mere 10 years after the end of the HAITIAN REVOLUTION. He was a child of the middle class; his family were urban ARTISANS and small businesspeople. His mother had been free before 1794, and perhaps other relatives had been as well. His father was a mixed-race artisan who may have been enslaved prior to the revolution but lived with a Frenchman, also named Madiou, who was probably his father. After the revolution, he was a successful civil servant. Madiou himself was rather reticent about his own background aside from a few chance remarks preserved by his descendants and students.

In the 1820s, Madiou's family sent him to study in FRANCE at the Royal College of Angers. He later studied at the university in Rennes and received the bachelor of arts. He then studied law at the University of Paris in order to qualify as a notary. He returned to Haiti to work as a notary in the 1830s. It was then that he began writing *Histoire d'Haïti*, as it is said that after he asked his father for a book on the history of the country, he was told that there were none. He spent the next 15 years writing his masterpiece, in great detail, basing it on study of archival documents now lost to us and many interviews with participants in the events of the period, both the powerful and ordinary people.

Contrary to what the elder Madiou said in 1830, a number of histories of the island during its colonial period existed, including MÉDÉRIC-LOUIS-ÉLIE MOREAU DE ST-MÉRY's three-volume work published in 1798. But there were no histories of Haiti written from a black perspective. Madiou's work *Histoire d'Haïti* is considered one of the most important products of Haitian literature as well as a crucial part of the historiography of the Haitian Revolution and slave societies in general. Today, more than 160 years after its publication, it is still read both for the fine detail and human tone of the events of early

Haitian history and for a deep understanding of the role of race and class in the Caribbean at the turn of the 19th century. His history tried to repair the reputation of the black leaders of the Haitian Revolution, especially Toussaint Louverture, portraying the struggle as a justified rebellion against the terrible oppression of slavery. This placed his work in contrast to another history written by BEAUBRUN ARDOUIN, which appeared at about the same time, which had tried to place the Haitian Revolution in the context of the other independence struggles in Latin America and deny it a class or racial character. Madiou's interpretation is much closer to our modern understanding of slave resistance and post-abolition resolution of tensions in slave societies. Madiou can be seen as the first modern historian of slavery and slave societies.

Madiou was a leading figure in Haitian letters until his death in 1884. He was editor of the national newspaper *Le Moniteur*. As such, he was a very influential voice in debates on the type of education that Haiti was going to give to its young people, as well as other public questions. He was particularly interested in educational issues and encouraged the teaching of literature and the humanities in Haitian schools. In this, his ideas contrasted with the influential arguments of Booker T. Washington (1856–1915), an American educator who argued that black education should focus on practical skills training. As a philosopher of education, he had ideas closer to those of W. E. B. DuBois (1868–1963), and DuBois worked with Madiou's son (also called Thomas) on his *Encyclopedia Africana* project. Madiou brought 19th-century liberal historical thought, the concept of "integral history" taught by Jules Michelet (1798–1874), to bear on the questions of Haitian history, but more important, he gave the Haitian people a history of their own, of which they could be proud.

Stewart R. King

FURTHER READING
Madiou, Thomas. *Histoire d'Haïti.* 7 vols. Port-au-Prince: 1847. Reprint, Port-au-Prince: Éditions Henri Deschamps, 1987.

MADISON, JAMES (1751–1836) *drafter of the Constitution of the United States, fourth president of the United States (1809–1817)*
Born in Port Conway, Virginia, on March 16, 1751, James Madison was a prominent planter in Piedmont, Virginia. He owned more than 100 slaves and several large farms including his main residence at Montpelier. He studied law and was a delegate in the Virginia House of Burgesses. There, he became a protégé of THOMAS JEFFERSON and helped to pass Virginia's Statute of Religious

Liberty. He later served as a representative in Congress (1789–97), U.S. secretary of state (1801–09), and president of the United States (1809–17). As Virginia's representative to Congress under the Articles of Confederation, he first proposed the 3/5 clause, under which states would be charged taxes based on their free population plus 3/5 of their slave population. In 1787, he was Virginia's representative to the convention drafting the Constitution of the United States, and he included the same provision, applying the 3/5 calculation to representation in Congress as well as taxes. The provision was a political compromise between Southern states, which wished their congressional representation to be based on their entire population, and Northern states, which did not wish slaves to be counted at all. Of course, at the time nobody thought that slaves would be allowed to vote. Free people of color, on the other hand, were permitted to vote in some Northern states, and even in those Southern states where they did not have the vote, they still counted as full citizens for the purpose of representation.

As an author of the Constitution, Madison defended it strongly in the *Federalist Papers*, but once elected to Congress in 1789, he proposed 12 amendments, 10 of which passed and became known as the Bill of Rights. As Madison intended them, the amendments prohibited the federal government from interfering with rights that the states might grant, and thus the Bill of Rights permitted states to deprive free people of color (and other oppressed people) of those rights. It was not until 1868—almost a century later, during RECONSTRUCTION IN THE UNITED STATES—when the Fourteenth Amendment provided that Madison's rights applied to individuals and restricted state governments, and it was not until the 1960s that they became fully operational in their application to people of color in the American South. Nonetheless, Madison laid the foundation for the rights that Americans, including people of color, enjoy today.

Madison's views on slavery and race relations mirrored those of other white men of his time and place. As did his mentor, Jefferson, in the abstract, he thought slavery an evil and thought America would be better off without blacks, either slave or free. He supported colonization and gradual, compensated emancipation of slaves in America. He was realistic about colonization, however, and expected that blacks and whites would have to live side by side in America for the foreseeable future. He believed that blacks were inferior by nature and that if treated decently, they would accept their inferiority.

Like any large planter, Madison had free colored neighbors, dependents, and relatives. His personal servant, a slave named Paul Jennings, later worked for the prominent Northern politician Daniel Webster, who sold him his freedom. Jennings wrote a largely sympathetic memoir of his life with Madison. A large family of African Americans claims descent from Madison through a black man named James, son of Madison's slave cook Coreen. James, as were Madison's other slaves, was sold to satisfy the former president's debts when he died, and he lived in KENTUCKY. His children gained their freedom before the AMERICAN CIVIL WAR. Madison died on June 28, 1836.

Stewart R. King

FURTHER READING

Clark, Kenneth M. "James Madison and Slavery." Madison Museum Website. Available online. URL: http://www.jamesmadisonmus.org/textpages/clark.htm. Accessed January 1, 2011.

Jennings, Paul. *A Colored Man's Reminiscences of James Madison.* New York: George C. Beadle, 1865. Available online. URL: http://docsouth.unc.edu/neh/jennings/jennings.html. Accessed January 1, 2011.

MAINE

Maine is a state of the United States. It is located on the Atlantic coast in the far northeastern corner of the country, bordering NEW HAMPSHIRE to the west and CANADA to the north and east. Until 1820, southern and central Maine were a part of MASSACHUSETTS, while the northern county of Aroostook was part of Canada until 1842. The coastline is rocky with many small harbors, while the interior is heavily forested. The climate is cool and damp. The principal economic activities before the 20th century were fishing and timber harvesting.

The native people of Maine were a variety of small groups mostly of the Algonquin language group. They first interacted with Europeans in the 15th century, when European fishermen, explorers, and traders began to pass along the coast, sometimes establishing small camps to salt fish and trade for furs. The arrival of European diseases in the late 16th century resulted in a precipitate population decline, opening the way for European colonization starting in 1604, when the French built a series of small settlements in the northern region, now known as Acadia.

The French settlers had some black slaves, as did the English settlers who began arriving in 1607. Some of the fishermen who visited and established camps along the coast during the 16th and 17th centuries were blacks from PORTUGAL and the Cape Verde Islands. However, Maine was unsuitable for plantation agriculture, and few blacks, either free or enslaved, arrived in the colonial period. Maine was a part of Massachusetts during this period, and most Massachusetts blacks lived in BOSTON,

the colony's largest city. Those who were outside Boston often worked in maritime trades, either as fishermen or as MERCHANT SEAMEN, and could be found when ashore in the port towns. A significant proportion of American merchant seamen in the early 19th century were free blacks. Maine's principal port town was Portland, and by the early 19th century, Portland had a stable black seafaring community of around 100 households. Massachusetts courts decided in 1780, in the case of *Commonwealth v. Jennison*, that slavery was unconstitutional, and all blacks in Maine after that date were declared free.

The black population of Maine grew steadily if unspectacularly during the early 19th century. The growth rate fell behind that of the white community, especially after large numbers of European immigrants began arriving in the 1820s. The table below is based on census figures, which probably undercounted blacks because they were more likely to be poor and often overlooked by the authorities.

The black community grew in 1842 when the portion of northern Maine that now makes up Aroostook County was ceded by Canada. The Maritime Provinces of Canada had significant black populations, many descended from pro-British blacks who had fled the United States at the time of the WAR OF AMERICAN INDEPENDENCE, 1775–83. Two groups of these refugees had settled in Aroostook County, at Marawahoc Plantation and Macwahoc Plantation. These were small towns, with only a few dozen black families each, but they represented a significant

AFRICAN-AMERICAN POPULATION OF MAINE, 1790–1900

Year	Blacks	Blacks as a Percentage of Total Population	Total Population
1790	538	0.6%	96,540
1800	818	0.5%	151,719
1810	969	0.4%	228,705
1820	983	0.3%	298,335
1830	1,171	0.3%	399,431
1840	1,355	0.3%	501,793
1850	1,356	0.2%	583,169
1860	1,327	0.2%	628,279
1870	1,606	0.3%	626,915
1880	1,451	0.2%	648,936
1890	1,190	0.2%	661,086
1900	1,319	0.2%	694,466

reinforcement for the small group of Maine blacks. Most blacks in 19th-century Maine lived in overwhelmingly white communities. There were a few small communities—eight islands off the coast of Maine have *Negro* in their name, indicating the presence of at least some black families. The island of Malaga had a population of several dozen mixed-race families until the state government forced all the inhabitants off in 1912, committing many to the Maine Home for the Feeble-Minded, in order to take their land. This was a low point for race relations in Maine, though. For the most part, blacks were if not welcomed, at least tolerated in the state during the 19th century.

Some prominent individual blacks were Maine residents. Most notable is Bishop James Augustine Healy, the Roman Catholic Church's leader in Portland from 1875 until his death in 1900 (*see* Healy family). Bishop Healy was mixed-race and very light-skinned, but his African ancestry was no secret, and he was accepted as a leader of an important religious community and a very influential figure in Maine's political life. Macon Allen (1816–94) was the first black person in America to be licensed to practice law, joining the Maine Bar in 1844. John Russwurm, a leading black educator, was educated at Bowdoin College in Maine, receiving his bachelor's degree in 1826. He was only the third black person to graduate from a university in the United States.

Maine's small black community contributed to the victory of the United States in the American Civil War. Almost 100 Maine men enrolled in the 54th and 55th Massachusetts Infantry Regiments, a very striking figure given that the total black population of the state was just above 1,300. In addition, Maine was credited with 104 enlistments in the United States Colored Troops, a figure that probably does not count those who joined the Massachusetts regiments as they were state troops.

Union victory in the war made little change in the lives of the black community of Maine. The fishing and shipping industries in the state became less important in the second half of the 19th century. Blacks who had worked in those industries often had to leave the state, and the black population actually fell after the Civil War. The racist climate of late-19th-century America spread as far as Maine, and schools and other public facilities were segregated. Black Down Easters (as citizens of Maine are called) could vote, but they were so few that political participation did not gain them significant power. The black community of Maine, as did that of many other predominantly rural northern states, entered the 20th century as a minority almost too powerless even to spark much resistance or oppression.

Stewart R. King

FURTHER READING
Barry, William David. "The Shameful Story of Malaga Island." *Down East*, November 1980.
Lee, Maureen. *Black Bangor: African-Americans in a Maine Community, 1880–1950.* Durham: University of New Hampshire Press, 2005.
Piersen, William D. *Black Yankees: The Development of an Afro-American Subculture in 18th Century New England.* Amherst: University of Massachusetts Press, 1988.
Price, H. H. "Blacks in 19th-Century Maine," *Maine Archives and Museums (MAM) Newsletter* 4, no. 4 (November 2001).
Price, H. H., and Gerald E. Talbot. *Maine's Visible Black History: The First Chronicle of Its People.* Gardiner, Me.: Tillbury House, 2006.
Stakeman, Randolph. "The Black Population of Maine, 1764–1900." *New England Journal of Black Studies*, no. 8 (1989).

MANUMISSION

Formal manumission—the process of gaining one's freedom—was one way, along with running away, that a slave could become liberated during the era of slavery in the Americas. At the time, white observers assumed that all or at least most free people of color had been formally manumitted, though as a matter of fact most had been born free if slavery had existed in any colony for more than a few decades. The assumption that most free people of color were manumitted also included an assumption that they were the beneficiaries of white generosity, which was also a distortion of the true circumstances even in the case of those people who had been born slaves. Manumission and attitudes toward free people of color were inextricably linked during the period of slavery. The process and impact of manumission varied from place to place and from era to era. Over the centuries, laws and customs related to manumission responded to changing racial attitudes, demographic conditions, the needs of governments for tax income and manpower for the military, and changing economic conditions.

The Process of Manumission

As a general rule, manumission required the permission of two parties, the owner of the slave and the government. Masters could not free their slaves at will in most slave societies in the Atlantic world because governments were interested in limiting manumissions. First, they were concerned that newly freed persons should be able to care for themselves and not become a public charge. Thus, masters wishing to free the elderly and those too young to work always had to show that the newly freed people had free family members to care for them or that the master had provided for them in some way. Some places, especially many American states, required bonds

A document showing the conditions imposed on a Pennsylvania slave who gained his freedom in 1794. This man, Shadrach, was required to work for 11½ years for the man who paid for his manumission. Similar self-purchase agreements are found throughout the Americas, and indeed this sort of arrangement would have been more common outside the United States. Shadrach lived in a state, Pennsylvania, that was beginning the gradual abolition of slavery, and his master may have gambled that this sort of arrangement would be less risky than waiting for the legislature to abolish slavery. *(Photo by Kean Collection/Getty Images)* be posted for any manumission, ensuring that slaves would be cared for in case of disability or that the newly freed people would move out of the state. Next, governments feared that the presence of large numbers of free people of color in a slave society would undermine the subordination of slaves in general. The free person of color was an anomaly in a system based on racial slavery. Neither white nor slave, they demonstrated to slaves that there was an alternative to their situation. They were frequently suspected of receiving property stolen by slaves, of encouraging slaves—their family members and friends, presumably—to run away, and being involved in illegal businesses.

Governments gave their permission for manumission, however, quite regularly in many places throughout the Americas. Many governments saw manumissions as a source of income and placed a tax on them calculated not to discourage the practice but to raise revenue. The colonial government of SAINT-DOMINGUE was gaining about one-third of its domestically produced revenue from the manumission taxes in 1779. Other reasons to grant permission for manumissions were the social status and political influence of the masters requesting it. Powerful white men could often presuade governments to approve manumissions, even despite generally applicable laws against them. GEORGE WASHINGTON, for example, freed all of his slaves in his will. Virginia law specifically forbade general manumissions of an entire slave workforce and required that each individual case of manumission be supported by testimony to the faithful service of the slave. Washington's heirs objected, and many powerful white Virginians thought it set a very bad example, but the manumissions were eventually approved by the Virginia legislature, primarily because Washington was the "father of his country," and refusing his last request was too politically dangerous. One of Washington's neighbors, Robert Carter III, freed hundreds of his slaves upon his death, and the bequest was only approved because Carter had moved in old age to Baltimore, MARYLAND, where the laws were less harsh. Finally, an important reason for governments to grant permission for manumission was to ensure a supply of recruits to the armed forces. The British government purchased slaves to staff garrisons of forts in their Caribbean colonies, promising them their freedom after a term of service. After the end of the slave trade in 1807, all British slave-soldiers received their freedom, though they were still obliged to serve in the military. Even after general abolition of slavery in British colonies in 1833, the British West India Regiment was still enrolling slaves purchased in Africa, granting them their freedom immediately but still requiring some years of service. The French enrolled free people of color in a number of units raised in their Caribbean colonies during the 18th century. One inducement to serve was that the tax on manumission would be waived for soldiers and their family members. Hundreds of people received tax-free manumission in Saint-Domingue during the WAR OF AMERICAN INDEPENDENCE, 1775–83. The French gave tax-free manumission to people in the rural police force during peacetime as well. In one striking case, a man who was actually a runaway slave was serving in the rural police in CAP-FRANÇAIS/CAP-HAÏTIEN when his master arrived looking for him in 1787. His fellow policemen collected enough money to pay his purchase price, and then the government waived his liberty tax. The government would actually grant freedom to slaves in return for exemplary service, purchasing them from their masters and waiving any taxes due. This was commonly used as a reward for betraying plots to rebel but also applied to slaves who cared for the sick (especially sick white people) during epidemics or performed some other signal service to the state. VINCENT OLIVIER of Saint-Domingue, for example, was freed by the French government as a reward for his heroic service in the siege of CARTAGENA de Colombia in 1697.

SLAVE OWNERS might consent to manumission for a number of reasons. Probably the most common was that the prospective freed person was a family member. Sexual relations between masters and slaves were common everywhere, even in those places where they were forbidden by law and social custom such as the United States. The children of a slave woman by her master were much more likely to be freed than the average slave. White observers at the time and later often took for granted that most people who gained their freedom through manumission were the children or sexual partners of their masters. This led to all sorts of misleading gender stereotypes of free people of color. But, in fact, this was not the most common family relationship between master and freed slave. Probably much more common was that a free person of color would purchase an enslaved family member from the master and then grant him or her freedom (see also FAMILY RELATIONSHIPS WITH SLAVES). Governments sometimes disapproved of ransom arrangements (and the similar self-purchase), believing that making the process of manumission commercial encouraged slaves and free people of color to go outside the law in order to accumulate resources and undermined racial subordination. The Spanish government was an exception, however, through its mechanism of COARTACIÓN, under which slaves or their free relatives could demand that a master set a fair price for their liberty. In many cases, however, ransom arrangements had to be concealed in formal declarations, leading to bizarre outcomes such as when a woman in Saint-Domingue in 1783 cited "good and agreeable service" given her by her own godmother during the seven years that the godmother had been her slave between her purchase from her former master and the formal request to the government for permission to grant freedom.

Owners would consent to sell slaves to free family members both because they needed the money and because they wished to reward the slave or free relative for some service. In some cases, we have evidence of both motives in the same act. In 1780, a free colored man bought a young child from a white man, then quickly resold her to another free black in Cap-Français, Saint-Domingue, with the proviso that the sale was conditional on the girl's being granted her freedom within two years. Not stated in the original act of sale, but clear from other evidence, is that the purchaser was the father of the child, and he and the seller had a long-standing business relationship. The purchaser was in financial difficulties because of the economic depression caused by the War of American Independence and was in danger of having his assets seized. The proviso requiring manumission in the act of sale protected the girl against RE-ENSLAVEMENT if the father became bankrupt. But the seller also needed money, and in this case he apparently was paid in cash, perhaps also protecting assets against seizure by less understanding creditors.

Simple self-purchase was another extremely common means of manumission; however, since slaves were officially unable to actually own anything under almost all legal systems in the Americas, some free person would have to be included in the process as a nominal purchaser. It is very difficult to disentangle these sorts of purchases from those in which the assets for the purchase were from the free relative or partner, though sometimes acts of sale or other evidence show that the slave was the source of the funds. Slaves could acquire money in many different ways. Most masters permitted their slaves to have some personal time and land, supposedly for growing crops for their own consumption. This was normally cheaper than buying provisions for them, though in some smaller Caribbean islands where land was very expensive, this was not true. But even there, slaves often had small businesses or worked as ARTISANS to make a little money on the side. And of course, there was always a problem with pilferage. As modern retailers have also discovered, inventory control is difficult when there are many employees who have no particular interest in the success of the business. Slaves who worked as personal servants could also receive gifts;

in many places in the United States and the English colonies, it was customary for guests to tip the servants. Servants also had access to cast-off (or stolen) clothes and personal items that could be sold for cash. Women slaves could exchange sexual favors for cash or valuable gifts (see also PROSTITUTES AND COURTESANS). Many slaves worked significant percentages of the time on their own account. This was particularly true in mining: The gold mining entrepreneurs of Minas Gerais, Brazil, in the 18th century imported thousands of specialized gold miners from present-day SIERRA LEONE and Ghana. These slaves would be sent off into the gold fields to work, expected to report back after weeks or months with a fixed quota of gold. Anything else they found was theirs to keep. Lucky strikes could and did allow many of these men to gain their freedom within a few years. The unlucky ones starved or fell victim to accidents or bandits or Indians, or failed to meet their quotas and were harshly punished. In other fields, though, slaves worked on their own account in many places. Especially in times when agricultural work was not pressing, either because of the season or because of some economic fluctuation, it was very common for masters to arrange with trusted slaves to give them "their time" in return for a regular payment or even gratis. It was never easy for a slave to accumulate enough money to buy freedom, but it was possible and common enough to keep many people working toward this goal. Of course, allowing self-purchase should not be thought of as a form of generosity of the master. Masters were happy to sell slaves their freedom: It might take years to gather the money necessary for self-purchase. By that time, the slave's productivity might be declining, or at least he or she would have few productive years of life left. The price of the self-purchase could be put toward the purchase of a new, younger, and ideally more productive slave.

Sometimes self-purchase would be negotiated between master and slave, with a good deal of tough bargaining involved. The formal manumission of the abolitionist FREDERICK DOUGLASS is an example of this process. Douglass was owned by a white man who may have been a relative. He was relatively well treated until his master ran onto hard economic times and had to rent him to other white men. Douglass fled to the North in 1838, and then, after the FUGITIVE SLAVE ACT OF 1850, to BRITAIN. His Northern friends ultimately negotiated his purchase with his master, who obviously could not hope to recover Douglass as a worker and might well have needed some extra cash.

Masters might also wish to reward slaves by granting them their freedom without demanding payment. This was most likely to occur for aged personal servants who had little economic value, though of course governments needed to be assured that the newly freed person would be supported. It was probably more common for the master's aged nurse or faithful valet simply to be given a small farm and allowed to live "as free," however. But formal manumission was a special, if expensive, mark of the master's favor; allowed masters to think of themselves as generous; and gave other slaves hope that good service would be rewarded. As a leadership tool, it was probably much more effective than any other reward that masters were prepared to give.

There was a difference between white and free colored masters in the reasons why they gave freedom to their slaves. Leaving aside those free colored "masters" who were actually family members who had purchased the slaves with the intention of freeing them, free colored masters also had to decide whether and when to free their slaves. A study of 18th-century Saint-Domingue found that free colored masters were somewhat less likely than white masters to free their slaves. This finding is a little surprising, as contemporary observers and modern attitudes on race would normally assume some sort of racial solidarity between free people of color and slaves that would lead them to be more likely to free their slaves. But the number of slaves owned by any individual free colored master would generally be much lower, meaning that each individual slave freed represented a larger share of the workforce and thus a greater economic loss than for a white planter. Free colored masters were also proportionally much more likely than whites to free male slaves. Though they still freed more women than men, they also owned, on average, more women than men, and the gender ratio of their manumissions was closer to the gender ratio of their slave workforces than was true for whites, who in Saint-Domingue freed twice as many women as men and owned nearly twice as many men as women. Free colored masters were also more likely than whites to free native-born rather than African-born slaves. Manumissions by free colored masters (other than cases of "masters" freeing family members) were much more likely than those of whites to be of unrelated slaves, both in exchange for payment and gratis as a reward for service. This is probably a result of more even gender ratios among free people of color than among whites in the colony, as a result of which sexual relations between free men of color and slaves were either less common or at least less acknowledged and socially acceptable. The relative preference that free colored masters showed for male slaves and for native-born slaves might have been related to racial and gender solidarity or might reflect self-purchase by skilled slaves. There is limited data on this subject from other colonies.

Families of color seeking freedom also had a choice as to which members to prioritize for ransom and self-purchase. It is clear from the data from several colonies that, as did the white masters but for different reasons, they preferred to seek manumission for adult female slaves. Almost everywhere in the Atlantic world, the child of a free woman was free regardless of the status of her husband or partner or other children. Thus, freeing a woman of childbearing age also freed all her subsequent children. Also, women were often in charge of marketing and thus would have access to money. This phenomenon is probably a more significant cause of the generally noted phenomenon of high rates of manumission for women than sexual complaisance by female slaves.

Manumission Laws

Manumission was governed by a variety of different laws and customs throughout the Atlantic world. In general, it became more difficult and expensive to free slaves as slavery became a more important economic institution and as numbers of slaves and free people of color increased in any particular place. In addition to the socioeconomic conditions, cultural and historical traditions of particular countries also affected the relationships between free and slave and black and white in their colonies (see TANNENBAUM HYPOTHESIS).

The origin of manumission laws in most places lies in the Roman legal system. Ancient Rome was a slave society, and the status of slaves and free people was clearly outlined in its laws. Between about 50 B.C.E. and 200 C.E., a majority of the inhabitants of central Italy were either slaves or freed people. Manumission under Roman law imposed formal obligations toward their former masters on freed slaves, which amounted to a patron-client relationship. Generally, masters and former slaves formed a social partnership, with masters, making loans to finance businesses or other activities, while freed people repaid their loans and provided political support. Julius Caesar, for example, received strong support from the freed people of Rome, mostly as a result of the very large number of freed former slave clients he supported. The riot by plebeians, mostly freed people, that broke out when he was assassinated in 44 B.C.E. ended the hopes of the aristocratic party to restore republican government in Rome and gave Augustus Caesar the chance to succeed his uncle as emperor. With the end of imperial expansion and decline of the Western Roman Empire in the 300s and 400s, slavery largely disappeared from Western Europe, to be replaced by serfdom, a form of subordination that attached people to land rather than treating them as property of an individual. Most European countries in the Middle Ages did not have slaves, or if they did, they were few, and the laws governing them drew on Germanic roots. German tribesmen, who conquered Western Europe in the 400s and 500s, introduced a system of personal ties, subordination, and mutual responsibilities that evolved into what we know as feudalism. Even people who were called slaves in these societies had defined places in society—low ones, but with rights as well as duties. And there were no "slave societies" in medieval Europe, in the sense of societies where most or all productive work was done by slaves.

The ROMAN CATHOLIC CHURCH also played an important role in regulating the treatment of slaves in medieval Western Europe. The church's principal interest lay in evangelizing people, especially rural dwellers and newcomers such as slaves, and in protecting the converts and ensuring they could practice their faith. The church also supported a social system based on mutual rights and obligations, with a hierarchical order of subordination, since medieval theology held that this was the divinely inspired order. So the church was not opposed to slavery per se and, in fact, often taught that it was a good thing for foreigners to be enslaved and taken to Europe so they could be exposed to Christianity. But masters had to respect the human rights of their slaves, especially their right to observe church festivals and receive the sacraments. A basic Catholic rule held that Christians could not be enslaved. If a slave became a Christian, this did not mean that he or she would automatically be freed, but it did mean that the strongest valid purpose for the enslavement would have been achieved, from the church's point of view.

The High Middle Ages, from about 1100 on, saw the beginning of European expansion and the arrival of more slaves in areas under Christian control. The Crusades netted Europeans thousands of Arab slaves, and contact with the expanding Turkish states meant that European entrepreneurs could buy slaves originally captured in Eastern Europe, the Middle East, or even Africa. These slaves worked on SUGAR CULTIVATION plantations in the Mediterranean. The Mediterranean islands of Rhodes, Crete, Cyprus, Malta, Sicily, Sardinia, and the Balearics were the first slave societies under Western European rule. In the 1400s, similar colonies were established in the Atlantic islands of the Canaries, the Azores, Cap Verde, and São Tomé. During this period, from the 1100s to the 1400s, most European countries (with the notable exception of England) adopted some variant of Roman law. The Roman practice of patronage as applied to freed slaves was formally a part of most legal codes, though it was weaker as a social institu-

tion. Still, under the early modern European version of Roman law, freedom for a slave was not quite the same as being born free, and even in places where Roman law had never applied, such as the American South, people of color who had been born free made sure their status was recognized.

After 1450, race also became a factor in laws and customs related to manumission. In ancient Rome and medieval Europe, there was no racial difference between masters and slaves. But European navigators opened up the Atlantic after 1450 and began to purchase slaves from sub-Saharan Africa for their plantations. At the same time, the flow of slaves from eastern Europe and the Middle East slowed to a trickle as a result of unending, and relatively fruitless, war between the Ottoman Empire and Western Europe. The conquest of the Americas also led Europeans to equate blackness with slavery. The Catholic Church and the Spanish monarchy both outlawed the enslavement of Indians. Indians were seen as subjects of the monarchs, who were only to be put to forced labor as a punishment for the "crime" of resistance. Even then, this status was not heritable and thus not slavery under the Roman law principle. While Indians were enslaved in BRAZIL, their numbers were few and declined rapidly. English, French, and Dutch colonists followed the Spanish example and defined Indians as subjects with some rights rather than as slaves. White immigrants from Europe, both convicts and indentured servants, were also used as forced labor in the Americas. However, their status only lasted for a fixed number of years and was not heritable under normal circumstances. They also had access to the courts and were clearly considered citizens, although they could be forced to work. Throughout the Americas, then, custom and law came to define slavery as a condition that applied only to blacks and, similarly, blackness as a condition that implied servile status even if a particular individual was not a slave. This affected manumission by making it a step to an intermediate status, and thus something that the state could rightfully control as it also exerted special control over free people in general. The regulation of manumissions by governments became much more intrusive, and manumission itself much less of an individual transaction between master and slave, with this process. The Roman tradition of the male head of household as paterfamilias with the power of life, death, or freedom over his household was replaced by a centralized governmental system that interfered, more or less regularly, in the workings of master-slave relationships in the interests of what governments thought of as the social good.

Manumission in Spanish America

Spanish laws on slavery derive from LAS SIETE PARTIDAS (or Seven Acts) law code of Alfonso X (1265). The fourth *partida* recognized the existence of slavery but held that freedom was the natural state and provided for manumission by gift or purchase with the agreement of the master. A royal decree of 1526 proclaimed that slaves had a right to purchase their freedom even against their masters' will, and many local jurisdictions implemented a process of *coartación*, or court-mediated self-purchase. The system was widespread and generally available to any slave in CUBA, PUERTO RICO, FLORIDA, and LOUISIANA; in other colonies, slaves had to demonstrate some special merit before a court would force their masters into *coartación* agreements. Slave owners naturally disliked the loss of control that this process led to, but the threat to go to court may have impelled masters to negotiate unofficial self-purchase agreements. Certainly in the mainland colonies of Spanish America in the late 18th century, there were higher per capita rates of manumission than in Cuba or the British Caribbean colonies. The Cuban government suspended *coartación* on two occasions during the 19th century, after the LA ESCALERA PLOT (1844) and at the beginning of the TEN YEARS' WAR (1868), but quickly revived the practice. Manumission was culturally important in Spanish America, especially in areas that were outside the plantation zone, such as the highlands of MEXICO and South America or the Rio de la Plata region. The relationship between free blacks and powerful whites, like the patronage relationships in ancient Rome, was important for both parties. It might well have been better for a master to grant freedom to a reliable slave and employ him or her for wages while gaining a useful client.

Manumission in Brazil

Brazil, long a colony of PORTUGAL, had a consistently high level of manumissions throughout its almost four centuries of slavery. One reason for this was the relatively low cost of new slaves. Brazil was close to the sources of supply in Africa, and Portuguese slave traders operated very efficiently and had many slaves available for sale throughout much of the period. A master who allowed a slave to go free was not giving up as much in monetary terms; likewise, a slave who had to purchase his or her own replacement in order to win freedom—a common condition of self-purchase—did not have to make so great an investment as in other colonies in the Americas. Brazilian masters also needed workers to do jobs that could not be entrusted to a slave, and there were very few whites available to do these jobs. Often, a trusted former slave would be the best choice. Also, although Portuguese law did not become fully Romanized until the Pombaline Reforms of the late 18th century, the idea of patronage

and an ongoing relationship between former master and freed slave meant that masters would not lose all economic value from a slave once he or she was freed. Brazilian society remained very feudal in its fundamental structure long after productivity and profit became the primary motives in other slave societies in the Americas. This means that for a Brazilian, personal relationships and popular reputation were much more important than simple income in determining the social worth or influence of any person. Finally, though the colonial government in Brazil did require approval and formal registration of all manumissions starting in the late 17th century, in contrast to most other places in the Americas, permission was rarely refused as long as the government could see that the proper relationship between former master and freed person would be respected. For all these reasons, Brazil was almost unique in the Americas in having a majority of its manumissions be "gracious," or conferred without payment from the slave.

Manumission in the French Colonies

The French had a lower rate of manumission than the Spanish or Portuguese during the 18th century. However, the early French colonists, up until the end of the 17th century, were quite likely to grant freedom to their slaves. Contrary to the Roman law provision, the children of white men and slave women were considered free from birth until the publication of the CODE NOIR IN FRENCH LAW (1685). FRANCE's adoption of Roman law was uneven until the 18th century. Even for almost a century after 1685, it was common for influential free men simply to have their children with slave mothers baptized and record their status as free on the baptismal record, thus avoiding the expense and trouble of formal manumission. The government cracked down on this, beginning in the 1760s, but there were still suspicious cases of mixed-race children with no parents' names recorded in parish registers from the 1780s. Until the end of the 17th century, manumission was a simple gift from the master with no government role at all. France was comparatively late in placing regulations on the practice. Different colonies began regulation at different times: Saint-Domingue required governmental permission from 1710 but only really enforced this law consistently from the 1760s, while Louisiana began to tighten up its laws in 1727. The French were especially interested in gaining revenue from manumissions and imposed a significant tax on the process. The French also consistently granted exemptions from this tax for servicemen to encourage men of color to enlist in the regular army, militia, and police. However, as the colonies grew wealthier and populations of color grew, manumissions became less and less common in the French colonies. During the FRENCH REVOLUTION, the political faction opposed to granting civil rights to free people of color in the colonies argued that free people of color were all freed people and owed the whites a sort of generalized deference that made them incapable of being equal citizens. The free colored activist JULIEN RAIMOND responded that he would be in favor of extending full civil rights only to those who—like him—had been born free. When he first proposed this, in a memorial to the French royal minister of marine in 1787, almost two-thirds of the approximately 25,000 free people of color in Saint-Domingue were born free, and there had been only about 200 manumissions the year before

Manumission in the British Colonies

British laws and practices relating to slavery in general were quite confused in the early years of their colonial experience, and each colony developed its own legal and customary regime with only limited reference to other colonies or the home country government. This was as true of manumission as of any other facet of the period. However, all British colonies were subject to similar socioeconomic pressures and cultural biases, so the outcome was roughly equivalent in each place at any given point in the colony's development. The situation in the early days was similar to that found in France, with the exception that the assumptions of Roman law did not hold. Black forced laborers in Virginia were treated as if they were indentured servants until the late 17th century, with a law specifying the difference between slave and servant not taking effect until 1705. By this time, there were a significant number of free people of color in the colony who had never been formally manumitted because they had never officially been slaves. The colonial government saw these people as potentially disruptive, both because they represented a crack in the increasingly racial subordination of blacks and because their children, as freeborn subjects, were entitled to charity under the poor laws. Starting after 1700, Virginia required that all people gaining their freedom post a £100 bond with the Church of England parish. This was a very significant amount of money and could represent many years' income even for a relatively prosperous small farmer. This and similar measures reduced the rate of manumissions, though some still took place. In JAMAICA, a similar requirement was in place from 1707, but parish poor law councils might accept a mortgage on land or livestock as an alternative to cash, making it easier for slaves or their masters to afford manumission. As in the French and Portuguese colonies, Jamaica and the British Caribbean islands needed free people of color to perform many jobs that could not be entrusted to slaves. The lack of a cultural assumption that there would be an ongoing relationship between master and slave, and

the high profitability of Jamaican plantations in the 18th and early 19th centuries, however, meant that manumissions were rare even there. Jamaica recorded only about 1,300 manumissions for the period 1820–25, and even some of these records referred to liberties granted many years previously. About one-third of these were granted in return for no payment, and in some of the remaining cases, the slave was only required to pay a small tax. In 1824, the colonial government took over poor relief from the church and built a particularly grim workhouse for indigent free people of color. They reduced the cost of manumission from a £100 deposit to 10 shillings, as long as the newly freed person was able to convince the local church authorities that he or she would not be indigent.

The United States

U.S. laws and customs related to manumission derived from British practices but changed in response to American conditions and other cultural practices. The American states disestablished their official churches and had little or no poor relief in the years after the United States declared its independence in 1776. This eliminated the concern that freed slaves would become a burden on public welfare rolls, but governments were still concerned about the implications of manumission for racial hierarchy. As white society in America became more democratic in the 1820s and 1830s, harsher regulations further excluded free people of color from citizenship and equality. Most Southern states made manumission extraordinarily difficult as part of this process, usually requiring that the freed person leave the state within a short period. These regulations were sometimes overlooked or waived if the master was influential and wanted to keep the freed person around, but they nonetheless meant that most parts of the American South had very few free people of color. In the Northern states, the few decades after independence saw the abolition of slavery. In the period before abolition, or during a gradual abolition process like that in NEW YORK STATE, manumission was relatively easy. Slaves had to present a certificate from the city government attesting to their ability to support themselves, along with the permission of the master. These were the only legal requirements for manumission in New York in 1818, looking forward to complete abolition of slavery there in 1824. One sign of how common manumission was in New York at the time is the fact that a special form was printed for the city government to attest to the financial status of the future freedman—with the high cost of printing at the time, it would only make bureaucratic sense to have these letters run off if many were going to be issued. An exception to the general rule that manumission was uncommon and difficult in the South occurred in the former French and Spanish territories: Louisiana and the former territories of Spanish Florida in the states of Florida, MISSISSIPPI, and ALABAMA. The French and Spanish laws were preserved in Louisiana, and even though much harsher laws prevailed in the other states, the Spanish customs in the former Florida territories meant that manumissions remained comparatively high there until the AMERICAN CIVIL WAR. More than half of all manumissions recorded in Alabama throughout the history of slavery in the state were recorded in just one county, Mobile.

Conclusion

Manumission is central to an understanding of the phenomenon of free people of color in the Americas. Most free colored people had either been manumitted themselves or descended from manumitted people (the exceptions include RUNAWAY SLAVES, slave rebels, people who had benefited from general abolition of slavery in some place like the free states in the Northern United States, and a small number of people who arrived as free immigrants). Seeking manumission was enormously expensive: the biggest investment that many free people would make in their lives, especially if they had family members to ransom in addition to themselves. It is important to remember that though manumission almost always took place with the permission of the master, it was rarely an act of pure benevolence, but instead a negotiated transaction between master and slave. Masters gained money, the opportunity to appear benevolent to their neighbors and to their slaves, the opportunity to help family members in a socially acceptable way, and the opportunity to replace an older slave with a younger and perhaps more valuable one. The very existence of such negotiation belied the assumption fundamental to the slave system of the essentially childlike nature of the slave, of his or her incapacity to enter into any sort of contract or negotiation with the master. Family relationships between master and slave were thought, by people at the time, to be behind many manumissions, and indeed manumission itself was attacked during the era of slavery as being the wages of "sinful" relationships between master and slave. But, in fact, most people who were manumitted in most places in the Americas were not related to their masters but instead were either ransoming themselves for money or being rewarded for service. The society both needed manumission to enlarge a class of people who were essential for many social tasks and feared it as potentially undermining white supremacy. As with many other phenomena about free people of color in slave societies, manumission has at its core a fundamental paradox.

Stewart R. King

FURTHER READING
Cohen, David, and Jack Greene, eds. *Neither Slave nor Free: The Freedman of African Descent in the Slave Societies of the New World.* Baltimore, Md.: Johns Hopkins University Press, 1974.
de la Fuente, Alejandro. "Slaves and the Creation of Legal Rights in Cuba: Coartación and Papel." *Hispanic American Historical Review* 87, no. 4 (2007): 659–692.
Kleijwegt, Marc. *The Faces of Freedom: The Manumission and Emancipation of Slaves in Old World and New World Slavery.* Leiden: Brill Academic, 2006.
Schafer, Judith K. *Becoming Free, Remaining Free: Manumission and Enslavement in New Orleans, 1846–1862.* Baton Rouge: Louisiana State University Press, 2003.
Schwartz, Stuart. *Sugar Plantations in the Formation of Brazilian Society: Bahía, 1550–1835.* New York: Cambridge University Press, 1985.
Whitman, T. Stephen. *The Price of Freedom: Slavery and Manumission in Baltimore and Early National Maryland.* Lexington: University of Kentucky Press, 1997.

MAROONS

One group of free people of color who were very important in many areas in the Americas were the maroons. The term *maroon* was used indiscriminately at the time for all RUNAWAY SLAVES, but modern usage reserves the term for slaves who formed organized communities on the outskirts of plantation colonies. In some cases, these communities grew to have thousands of members. The most prominent maroon communities were the *quilombos* of northeastern BRAZIL, founded in the 16th century and wiped out by the end of the 17th; the Bush Negroes of SURINAM, founded in the 17th century and still living a very traditional life today; and the Windward and Cockpit Country maroons of JAMAICA, founded in the late 17th and early 18th centuries and still in existence today. The maroons were always threatened by the colonial governments and often fought desperate wars for survival. Most maroon communities were wiped out in the end, though a few managed to survive the epoch of slavery as organized communities, and some even exist today.

Many slaves sought freedom by running away from their masters. Most runaway slaves sought circumstances similar to what they had left, but without the exploitation and brutality of slavery. Thus, most runaways sought to move to cities or to remain in an agricultural setting, perhaps in an area such as the American North or West where slavery was not permitted in the 19th century, or in areas far from their masters where they could pass for free people (*see* LIVING "AS FREE"). However, most slave societies were located near wilderness areas inhabited, if at all, by scattered populations of native people. If native people were present, they were always significantly less numerous than they had been at the arrival of European and African settlers, and so there were resources to spare for additional inhabitants. In many cases, native populations had been entirely destroyed by the consequences of contact with Europeans and Africans, and the land was empty of inhabitants. Some runaway slaves opted to move into these wilderness areas and try to live as PEASANTS.

Many of the runaways who chose this option were African-born people, in some cases very newly arrived in the colony, who were seeking to reclaim a lifestyle that they had experienced in Africa. The societies they created strongly resembled the African models they had left behind. Many maroon communities preserved African languages or cultural practices. The *vodun* religion and other Afro-Caribbean religious practices were strongest among maroons. FRANÇOIS MACKANDAL, a Haitian maroon and rebel leader, was an important *vodun* practitioner and is worshipped as a powerful spirit by modern *vodun* believers. The Creole languages of Surinam were born in maroon communities and are essentially African languages, though with Dutch, French, English, and Portuguese loan words. African ideas of political organization were also common, as in Palmares in northeastern Brazil, where the rulers were called "kings" but ruled through a confederacy of smaller village chiefs, who in turn were constrained by assemblies of village "big men" in much the same way that many West African polities functioned. These African models persisted even as the communities matured and most of the inhabitants became native-born. A wide variety of people lived in maroon communities, including runaway CREOLE slaves, people of color who were already considered free by the authorities, and even poor whites fleeing indentured servitude or forced military service. The culture of these communities was affected by these new residents and by the surrounding native and European cultures but retained essentially African character in most cases.

Maroons sought to live as peasant farmers. Most had been peasant farmers in Africa and wished to resume that lifestyle. While the vegetation in the Americas was different from what they were accustomed to, the climate was similar. African crops had often been introduced to the Americas, for example, bananas and rice, and were available to the runaways because they were being cultivated on their plantations as food crops. Sometimes the Columbian Exchange worked in the other direction, as African farmers by the late 17th century were accustomed to cultivating crops that had originated in the Americas, such as corn, sweet potatoes, manioc, and chili peppers. When they entered the Americas as forced migrants, they arrived in the homeland of the crops they had been accustomed to cultivating at home, and they readily included them in their diet. The cultivation pattern most maroons adopted was shifting cultivation or swidden, which is commonly found in Africa. In swidden agriculture, the farmer clears most brush from several small plots within a larger area owned by the village or larger lineage group and assigned to him or her temporarily by the chief, while leaving most large trees intact. A variety of different crops are planted in the same field. Since there is no animal traction for plowing, there is no need for organized rows of plants, and different plants existing side by side can often provide nutrients for each other or protect against parasites and disease. After a year or so, when crop yields decline in fragile tropical soils, the farmer abandons the fields to grow up again in brush and restore their fertility naturally and moves to a different plot. It can be hard for the untrained eye to tell the difference between a field and a random forest clearing. Naturally, this form of agriculture is ideal for people who are being hunted—the cultivated landscape is divided up by forest, providing natural defenses and making the settlement hard to detect from a distance. The heavy reliance on root crops, especially manioc, means that even if the enemy occupies the village, the edible part of the crop remains in the ground and can be collected when the rigors of the environment have driven the attacking soldiers back to their barracks. The wide variety of crops in use also ensures that something is always becoming ripe, cushioning the effect of any crop failure.

The maroons often depended on the plantations for tools, seeds, livestock, and, of course, new inhabitants. The planters and their government viewed this as robbery or, worse yet, slave stealing. Helping themselves to a few tools or sacks of seeds was one thing, but encouraging slaves to run away was a significant blow and had the additional effect of undermining the subordination of the remaining slaves. The maroons, thus, were a profound challenge to the entire slave system. The colonial government could have a variety of responses to the presence of maroons, but they almost always attempted violent suppression from time to time.

The problem with waging war against the maroons was that their villages were often located far from colonial power centers. They were protected by distance, challenging terrain, and an equally challenging disease environment. Whenever European troops were sent into the jungles or swamps to hunt down maroons, disease casualties would mount. One way that colonial governments dealt with this problem was to use nonwhite auxiliary forces. In North America and to a lesser extent Brazil, Native American tribes were bribed or coerced into hunting down runaway slaves. This policy was successful in many areas, though in FLORIDA, GEORGIA, and ALABAMA, runaway slaves joined with Creek refugees from American aggression and other native peoples to form the Seminole Nation. The BLACK SEMINOLE band was essentially a maroon community, though one more influenced by native ways of life than most. In other parts of the plantation world, there were fewer native people, and they were not so willing to work with the white authorities. The few surviving Taino Indians in CUBA welcomed runaway slaves, and as a result, maroon communities in Oriente province were strong and were able to withstand pressure from the colonial government until the end of slavery.

A more common measure to combat maroons was to use free colored soldiers. Free coloreds were mostly creoles, and thus they had some immunity against local diseases. Many of them lived on the outskirts of the colony and were familiar with the terrain where the maroons lived. Casualties in their ranks were also not so much of a concern for colonial administrators—if a white militiaman or soldier died of disease or in battle with maroons, he had relatives back in the home country who would complain to the government and have to be paid a pension. If a free colored militiaman died, his white relatives might or might not be saddened, but their relationship, being informal, did not carry any rights to claim reimbursement from the government. In places where there were many free coloreds and no native auxiliaries to call upon, such as the islands of the Caribbean, free coloreds often made up well more than half of the colony's defense forces. In Brazil's Minas Gerais, these two approaches were combined in the Caçadores do Mato, a force composed of Indians, free blacks, and poor whites who worked together against hostile Indians, maroons, and slave rebels.

Generally, the governments of slave societies fought a defensive war against maroons. So long as the maroons kept to their own areas, outside the region of plantation agriculture, the potential advantage to be gained by wiping them out was less than the cost of sending troops to attack them. So colonial MILITIAS and REGULAR ARMY troops patrolled the effective frontiers, and maroons developed their communities. The real problem for the maroons occurred when changes in the global economy, migrant flows, and other outside circumstances combined to make the areas they were living in suddenly useful to the planters. This happened in SAINT-DOMINGUE, the modern Haiti, in the mid-18th century, and in Cuba in the early 19th. In the first case, COFFEE CULTIVATION was introduced into the colony. French people enthusiastically took up coffee drinking, and the mountainous interior of the country went from being a wasteland useless for SUGAR CULTIVATION because of its steep slopes and difficulty of access for bulky cargoes to the site of the Atlantic world's most profitable agrobusiness. Coffee planting rapidly expanded to fill the available space,

and the maroons had to be displaced. A series of difficult campaigns between 1750 and 1779 cleared almost all maroons from the mountains of the North and West provinces, closest to the major ports. A few hung on in the southern mountains, and some made their peace with the government, but most moved across the frontier to the Spanish colony, where they were considered free people of color and were welcomed and given land. In Cuba, sugar planting became much more widespread after the success of the HAITIAN REVOLUTION destroyed the Saint-Domingue sugar industry. Many of the new plantations were in the areas where maroons had once lived, and as a result, again the maroons had to leave, were killed, or managed to make their peace with the authorities.

One method that colonial governments did have to deal with their maroon neighbors was to make peace with them. This was actually quite common, though clearly colonial governments rarely thought of the agreements they signed with maroon leaders as anything but temporary cease-fires. The large and stubborn maroon settlements in the Cockpit Country in Jamaica benefited from several agreements with Jamaican authorities, allowing them to exist in peace for many years. The agreements were always broken, but the costs of suppressing the settlements always led the colonial authorities to sign another peace deal after a period of fighting. These respites actually gained the Cockpit Country people enough time that when slavery finally was ended in the British Empire in 1833, they retained their identity as maroons. The BLACK CARIB in the BRITISH LESSER ANTILLES had similar experiences, preserving a collective identity as a mixed maroon/native society throughout the period of slavery and indeed to this day. The most famous maroon settlement of all, Palmares in Brazil, would have ended its collective existence this way had it not been for some ill-considered double-dealing by the authorities. After a devastating attack in 1676, Gana Zumba, king of Palmares, and many of his followers accepted a peace deal offered by the authorities. The deal ratified their personal liberty but required that they leave the maroon settlement and live in the settled areas nearer the city. A band of more stubborn maroons held out under the leadership of ZUMBI dos Palmares. The government seized on the continuing resistance by this small group to renege on the larger agreement. Gana Zumba himself was poisoned, and his followers found that their liberty was not actually legally ratified as they had hoped. Fearing RE-ENSLAVEMENT, many fled back to the maroon settlement. Zumbi and his people continued to fight the Brazilian government's *bandeirantes* until their final defeat in 1694, made possible only by the use of artillery and the employment of large forces collected from all over the colony.

In popular understanding of the history of slavery, the maroons appear to have been a very romantic and exciting chapter in the story of free people of color in the Americas. Indeed, these were people of color who did not get along by going along with the slave system. They were resisters who provided an important beacon of hope for all people of African descent in their societies. Of course, they could not entirely escape the consequences of living in (or at least near) a slave society. To the extent that they traded their produce with the colonists, as opposed to stealing from them, they were providing support to slavery. Many plantations bought their food supply from nearby small farmers; the surplus food grown by a maroon peasant might well feed a plantation slave.

Some maroon colonies owned their own slaves, as, of course, the African peasants whose lifestyle they emulated had also sometimes owned slaves. This was particularly noted among the Cherokee of OKLAHOMA, NORTH CAROLINA, and GEORGIA in the United States. The Cherokee bands' cultures were influenced more by native roots than were many maroon settlements, but Cherokee culture still had many African elements, especially among those Cherokee who remained in the East after the "Trail of Tears" in 1838 moved most of the tribe to Oklahoma. Cherokee both in the Lower South and in Oklahoma owned slaves before 1865, as did maroons in Surinam and Jamaica. Their model of slavery was not the brutal drudgery of the plantations around them, though, but a somewhat less vicious peasant slavery like that found in West Africa. Children of slaves in Cherokee society were generally almost indistinguishable from other Cherokee, there was no taboo on "race mixing," and manumissions were common. Still, the existence of slavery in their society before the AMERICAN CIVIL WAR and the harsh racial climate in the South afterward created a divide in Cherokee society that persists today, not between people of African and Native American ancestry, because almost all Cherokee have some African ancestry, but between the descendants of slaves and the descendants of free tribal members.

Most importantly, however, most maroons were opposed to being enslaved rather than being opposed to slavery. Or at least if they did oppose slavery on principle, they were willing to sacrifice this principle from time to time in the interests of survival or prosperity. The agreements between the Cockpit Country maroons and the Jamaican government and those between the Haitian maroons and the Saint-Domingue colonial government each specified that the maroons would refuse to receive new runaways. There was a continual tension, even in the absence of formal agreements, between the maroons' desire for population growth (and the desire

of individual maroons to liberate family members) and the need to avoid unwelcome attention from colonial law enforcement. A maroon community was a liminal institution: That is, it existed on the border between legality and illegality and between wilderness and settled colony. Remaining balanced on this border was a tricky business and often required the compromise of principle. Nonetheless, the maroons posed a fundamental challenge to slavery and preserved hope for enslaved people.

Stewart R. King

FURTHER READING

Anderson, Robert. "The Quilombo of Palmares: A New Overview of a Maroon State in Seventeenth-Century Brazil." *Journal of Latin American Studies* 28, no. 3 (October 1996): 545–566.

Corzo, Gabino La Rosa. *Runaway Slave Settlements in Cuba: Resistance and Repression.* Translated by Mary Todd. Chapel Hill: University of North Carolina Press, 2003.

Craton, Michael. "Planters, British Imperial Policy, and the Black Caribs of St. Vincent." In *Empire, Enslavement and Freedom in the British Caribbean.* New York: Markus Weiner, 1998.

Fouchard, Jean. *The Haitian Maroons: Liberty or Death.* New York: Blyden Press, 1981.

Learning, Hugo Prosper. *Hidden Americans: Maroons of Virginia and the Carolinas.* New York: Garland, 1995.

Price, Richard, ed. *Maroon Societies: Rebel Slave Communities in the Americas.* Baltimore, Md.: Johns Hopkins University Press, 1996.

MARRIAGE BETWEEN FREE AND SLAVE

A special case in marriage law in slave societies was a marriage between a free person and a slave (*see* INTERRACIAL MARRIAGE). These relations were treated differently in different places and times, depending on the legal system, the culture of the colonizing country, and their religious practice.

Under Roman law, which was the basis for the legal systems of SPAIN, PORTUGAL, FRANCE, and the Netherlands, a free man who married a slave had to purchase her from her master and free her, but the Code of Justinian permitted and even encouraged such marriages as preferable to concubinage with a slave woman. On the other hand, relationships between free women and enslaved men were not considered valid even if the wife owned and freed her husband. The former was natural, thought the Romans, while the latter was unnatural and disrupted the subordination of women to men.

The ROMAN CATHOLIC CHURCH had a code of canon law in the Middle Ages that gave primacy to the marriage bond over any other social bond, including slavery. When Roman law was adopted by many countries in Europe in the High Middle Ages and Renaissance, the church fought back by insisting that preference be granted to its sacraments. The collision of these two traditions, the Roman and the Catholic, led to compromises that often helped people of color gain freedom and escape social discrimination against unmarried sexual relationships.

The CODE NOIR IN FRENCH LAW (1685) required that free men who fathered children with their slaves marry the women if they were free to marry. The language of the law is gender-specific, and the opposite case, of a free woman pregnant by a male slave, is not discussed. Relations between free men and slaves they did not own were also not discussed, but the common law consensus was the same as the Roman, that the relationship required the permission of the master, and the prospective groom should probably be prepared to purchase his bride. If the prospective husband was already married, said the law, the woman slave and her children would be confiscated by the state. If a master and his slave married, on the other hand, the slave and her children by her husband would be freed without a tax assessed. This proved to be a popular section of the Code Noir. Partial surveys of vital statistics in the 18th-century French Caribbean record dozens of such marriages. Generally, after the middle of the 18th century, these marriages were between free men of color and slaves rather than between white men and their slaves, though in earlier years there were many of both types. There was an overall decline in the number of racially mixed marriages at the time. In addition, the population of free people of color was growing rapidly during this period, providing a larger number of potential free colored grooms. In a half-dozen cases recorded in SAINT-DOMINGUE in the 1770s and 1780s, the groom was the slave and the bride was the free woman. Despite the gender-specific language in the Code Noir, the slave husbands gained their freedom by virtue of the marriages, as the Catholic law demanded, perhaps to some extent justifying the French king's claim to be the "Most Catholic Monarch." The French colonies were charging substantial taxes for MANUMISSION by that time—as much as 2,000 livres (the equivalent of $50,000 in today's money). Avoiding this tax was an important step in ensuring the new family's financial security.

Spain's LAS SIETE PARTIDAS law code (1265) explicitly permitted slaves and free people, of either sex, to marry, even against the wishes of their masters, but did not automatically grant freedom to the slave. However, masters were forbidden to sell married slaves away from their spouses. Masters in the Spanish colonial world greatly resented this part of the law and repeatedly attacked it by routine violations in the field and by political assaults. Local elites controlled law courts, but slaves and free people of color fought back nonetheless. The church was an important ally for them, especially the JESUITS before their expulsion from the Spanish Empire in the 1760s, who were present in many areas where there were many people of color. A royal edict in 1786 reinforced the right of slaves to marry as they wished and empowered priests to intervene with masters to protect slave marriages. Masters were legally liable for actions they took in violation of the code. There was a spate of lawsuits in courts in Mexico City after the public became aware of the 1786 edict, even though it was never officially proclaimed in New Spain. Now in actual practice, few slaves managed to gain their freedom through the court system, but a suit or the intervention of a priest might well convince masters to improve the treatment of slave partners.

In the Dutch colonies, although the Netherlands was Protestant, marriage between free men and slave women resulted in freedom for the slave bride. The Dutch Reformed Church would not perform a marriage unless the minister was convinced of the cultural assimilation of both partners, in keeping with the Calvinist idea of limiting church membership and sacraments to the "elect" (see PROTESTANT MAINLINE CHURCHES). But if a minister could be convinced that a slave was sufficiently assimilated to be able to consider her a church member, then the Roman law principle applied. There were apparently few of these marriages in the Dutch Caribbean colonies or in New Amsterdam (which became the British colony of New York in 1664), but in South Africa, they were known if not exactly common, and many of the Cape Colored families, despite the term commonly applied to them, *baastards*, sprang from officially approved marriages.

The English system was markedly different from that found in Roman law countries. England never adopted Roman law in the Middle Ages, whereas Scotland did. Instead, English common law grew up as a product of German tribal laws and a long trail of precedent. There was very little precedent for servile statuses, though in the early medieval period, England had serfdom and still had indenture in the 16th and 17th centuries. The law of marriage as applied to slaves grew from that applied to indentured servants, which was essentially that they could not marry without their masters' permission. If an indentured servant did become pregnant, the children and mother might well both be bound for a longer indenture to reimburse the master for the expenses of caring for them. Indentured servants, of course, only served for a term of years, and in Renaissance northern Europe, many women worked as servants for some years before marrying. A period of enforced sexual abstinence was supposed to be good for young people, and servants rarely obtained their masters' permission to marry.

Slaves, on the other hand, remained slaves all their lives. But they were not permitted to marry at any time without their masters' permission. If they were married, they might be able to defend their marriage through the Church of England, which had canon law rules derived from those of the Roman Catholic Church. By the 18th century, most British colonies had passed laws that no slave could be freed just because he or she had received sacraments from the Church of England, but masters still feared that the church would criticize their treatment of their slaves. As a result, few masters gave permission. Slaves married each other and free people nonetheless, but those marriages were performed by BAPTIST AND PIETIST ministers, or other unofficial practitioners of religion, often African Americans, and since they were not performed by the established church, they were not officially recognized.

After the United States declared its independence in 1776, state governments wrestled with these problems. Most states disestablished their churches within a few years after independence, depriving them of the convenient expedient of refusing to recognize marriages outside the one official church. But governments in mainland North America were unwilling to interfere in the master-slave relationship even on the grounds of protecting religion. Many states passed slave codes that required a master's permission before a slave could marry. Most states also had MISCEGENATION laws that prevented most interracial marriages. But there were still many marriages of free people of color and slaves. For the most part, these marriages did not have a significant effect on the behavior of masters in selling spouses apart from one another. The early 19th century saw a massive migration of slaves from the Old South, around the Chesapeake Bay and along the coast of the Carolinas and GEORGIA, to the new South, in the COTTON CULTIVATION regions of Georgia, ALABAMA, MISSISSIPPI, LOUISIANA, and TEXAS. Much of this forced migration split up families. Marriage vows in African-American churches in this period often changed the traditional language of the vows to "until death or sale do us part." If both spouses were slaves, there was little they could do. If one partner was free, he or she might follow the other partner to the new lands, but this would mean giving up a farm or a trade and starting over. It might well mean harsh treatment and poverty for the free spouse, and it is not surprising that many people did not choose to make the move. After the end of slavery, in 1865, the FREEDMEN'S BUREAU worked hard to reconnect divided families.

Stewart R. King

FURTHER READING

Collins, Julia C. *The Curse of Caste; or The Slave Bride: A Rediscovered African American Novel.* Edited by William L. Andrews and Mitch Kachun. Oxford: Oxford University Press, 2006.

de la Fuente, Alejandro. "Slave Law and Claims-Making in Cuba: The Tannenbaum Debate Revisited." *Law and History Review* 22, no. 2 (Summer 2004): 339–370.

MARTÍN DE PORRES, SAINT (1579–1639)
church leader and saint

Martín de Porres was a Peruvian free man of mixed race who lived in the 16th and early 17th centuries. He was a junior member of the DOMINICANS religious order and gained a great reputation for sanctity during his life. Subsequently, he has been venerated as a saint by the ROMAN CATHOLIC CHURCH and is the first African-American saint (as opposed to people of African ancestry living in Europe or Africa from antiquity who are considered saints, like St. Augustine of Hippo [354–430] or St. Felicity [181–203]). Martin's life illustrates the role of religion in the lives of African-descended people in Spanish America as well as some of the effects of racial discrimination at this relatively early date.

St. Martín was born in Lima, PERU, on December 9, 1579. He was the illegitimate son of a Spanish gentleman, Juan de Porres, and an Afro-Panamanian free colored woman, Anna Velásquez. Juan de Porres later became governor of the city of PANAMA. He did not do much to help care for his son or have much contact with him when he was young, though after Martín became famous, Juan recognized him as his son. The father may have paid for Martín to be apprenticed to a barber who taught him some medicine—in those days, barbers did minor surgery and dentistry as well as cutting people's hair. Martín worked as a healer in later life and often referred to his early training as a barber. Today, he is venerated by the church as the patron saint of barbers. What became of his mother is unknown, and Martín may have been living on his own by the time he turned 10.

Martín de Porres joined the Dominican friars as a lay servant at the age of 11. Religious orders were very important in the Roman Catholic Church in Latin America in colonial times. Outside the wealthy city centers, where the Spanish and mestizo businessmen and nobles lived, the collections from parishioners at parishes could not support a secular priest. Therefore, most churches in the colonies were led by religious order priests who swore vows of poverty. They often lived lives of poverty, but they were mostly members of the upper classes of the colonies. In the 16th century, the Dominicans had a rule that only whites could become full members of the order. They accepted free black and Indian members, but they were only allowed to be brothers and could not be ordained as priests. A convent in those days might have a dozen full members and as many as a hundred lay servants and non-

A 19th-century devotional portrait of Saint Martín de Porres (1579–1639). No contemporary portraits of Porres exist. Porres was a mixed-race member of the Dominican order who worked as a healer for the poor of Lima, Peru. The image includes several elements of Saint Martín's traditional iconography, including the sickroom behind him, a reference to his profession; animals at his feet, symbols of his care even for homeless animals; and a broom, symbol of his willingness to undertake any work that was necessary. In keeping with racial attitudes of the 19th century, the saint is depicted with a much lighter complexion than he probably had, though he is still identifiable by his appearance as an Afro-Peruvian. *(Rue des Archives/The Granger Collection, New York)*

ordained brothers supporting them. Only priests could vote in the councils of the order, and all the order's property was in their hands. The brothers and lay servants did the heavy physical labor of keeping the order's houses and parish churches functioning.

Porres did not mind hard work and became known for his saying that all forms of work are sacred. In traditional iconography, he is usually depicted with a broom, and he is referred to as the "saint of the broom."

At the age of 24, Porres was promoted from a lay brother to a non-ordained but permanently professed member of the convent. He was assigned to the infirmary. Religious institutions provided most of the health care the majority of the population could hope to receive. Porres is said to have been especially welcoming to the poor, giving one very sick and destitute beggar his own bed. When reproved for his excess of hospitality (presumably outsiders were not allowed in the quarters of the professed members as they are not in most convents today), he responded that with a little water he could clean off the sheets on his bed but there was not enough water in the world to wash away the stain on his soul if he were to be uncharitable.

There were many epidemics in the Americas in the 16th and 17th centuries. Historical demographers estimate that the population of the two continents declined by 90–95 percent between 1492 and the mid-1600s. When one of these lethal epidemics struck Lima, perhaps the 1618 measles epidemic that killed about one in 10 Peruvians, Porres worked tirelessly to heal the sick. In his own convent, there were 60 sick. Some of them were locked away in a room, perhaps to prevent spreading the infection or because they were thought to be beyond help or perhaps because they were not professed members of the order. Regardless, Martín is said to have passed miraculously through the locked door to treat them.

He was also known to be kind to animals and to have kept pets, including dogs, cats, birds, and mice. Tradition holds that he once rid his convent of an infestation of mice by feeding them in the courtyard. Treating animals as companions and showing them kindness were unusual in this period, especially in the Americas, where the native people had had very few domesticated animals until the arrival of the Europeans less than a century earlier.

Another duty that Porres performed in later life was almoner, or chief fund-raiser, for the convent. It is remarkable that the order would have put a free person of color and a non-ordained brother in charge of such an important duty. Perhaps his contact with his father, which he reestablished in later life, helped by giving him connections within the wealthy white community of the city. His reputation for sanctity was also very high, and this may have made people more willing to give donations. He was close to the great Peruvian mystic and fellow Dominican St. Rose of Lima (1586–1617), who may have helped him find donors and gain advancement in the order. In any case, the convent's accounts show that he was able to feed not only the brothers and their servants but also several hundred poor people a day in addition to supporting other good works.

He became quite famous in the Dominican order as well as in Peruvian society. Dominicans who traveled to other colonies, such as the Philippines and Mexico, reported seeing visions of him there, giving rise to the legend that he could bilocate, or travel miraculously, to places where he was needed.

When he died on November 3, 1639, he was venerated at once in Peru as a saint. His body was miraculously preserved, according to pious belief, and people began to make pilgrimages to pray before his tomb. In those days, the Catholic Church did not make formal, centralized proclamations of sainthood as it does today. Martín was officially proclaimed of "heroic" virtue in 1763, beatified in 1836, and proclaimed a saint in 1962. Pope John XXIII said of him:

> Saint Martin, always obedient and inspired by his divine teacher, dealt with his brothers with that profound love which comes from pure faith and humility of spirit. He loved men because he honestly looked on them as God's children and as his own brothers and sisters. Such was his humility that he loved them even more than himself, and considered them to be better and more righteous than he was.
>
> He did not blame others for their shortcomings. Certain that he deserved more severe punishment for his sins than others did, he would overlook their worst offenses. He was tireless in his efforts to reform the criminal, and he would sit up with the sick to bring them comfort. For the poor he would provide food, clothing and medicine. He did all he could to care for poor farmhands, blacks, and mulattoes who were looked down upon as slaves, the dregs of society in their time. Common people responded by calling him, "Martin the charitable."

Porres was not the first black to be proclaimed a saint, but he is among the most important saints for blacks in the Americas today because he experienced the suffering of African peoples in the Americas. Unlike the African saints of antiquity, or saints from Africa during the period of Christian missionary effort there, he lived in a slave society. He was abandoned by his father because of his race. He could not rise to the eminence he clearly deserved within his religious order because of his race.

Yet with the "heroic virtue" of humility, he did not blame his superiors and become bitter; nor did he blame the poor and excluded for their lot; instead, he took the situation he found himself in and worked to make it better in whatever way he could.

Stewart R. King

FURTHER READING
Cavallini, Giuliana. *St. Martin de Porres: Apostle of Charity.* Charlotte, N.C.: T A N Books, 1979.

Fumet, Stanislas. *Life of St. Martin de Porres: Saint of Interracial Justice.* New York: Doubleday, 1964.

Garcia-Rivera, Alex. *St. Martin de Porres: The "Little Stories" and the Semiotics of Culture.* New York: Orbis, 1995.

MARYLAND

Founded as a British colony in North America in 1632, the state of Maryland has three distinct regions. Southern Maryland features the Chesapeake Bay shores, with an economy founded on tobacco farming and fishing. In the central part of the state, a grain farming economy took root. The mountainous western region has always been the least settled. By the turn of the 19th century, Baltimore was emerging as the major urban center on the mid-Atlantic coast.

The southern Chesapeake region was the site of Maryland's earliest colonial settlement, beginning in the 1630s. By the 1740s, the remaining Indian tribes had migrated out of western Maryland. By the 19th century, any remaining individuals of Indian descent in the state had assimilated into the broader population. Today there are no federally or state-recognized Indian tribes in Maryland.

The early colonial economy was based on tobacco farming, which was a labor-intensive process, requiring workers nearly year-round. Africans were imported to Maryland by 1634. For most of the 17th century, agricultural laborers were a mix of African slaves and British indentured servants, but planters preferred English-speaking servants to slaves.

By the turn of the 18th century, the supply of white servants had dwindled significantly for a variety of economic and demographic reasons. The shortage of white labor led the large Maryland planters to place greater reliance on slave labor. While small farmers could grow tobacco on their own, owning slaves became the primary means to wealth, since it increased the amount of tobacco one could produce. Slaves were roughly 3 percent of the colony's total population in the mid-17th century; by 1710, slaves had increased to close to a quarter of the total population. Thus by 1730, slave imports had increased so much that about half of the

A view of a tobacco farm in Maryland. These farms, typically quite small by comparison with most plantations in the Americas, were home to most Maryland slaves and many free people of color as well. *(Library of Congress)*

slave population had arrived within the past 10 years. African imports gradually diminished, and by 1750, only about one-third of the slave population had been born in Africa.

The new Maryland colony in its first decades struggled to define the place of race and class in its social order. In 1663, the Maryland General Assembly determined that any African arriving in the colony was presumed to be a slave, thus linking race and slavery in law for the first time. The next year, Maryland legalized slavery for life based on African ancestry and enslaved free white women who married a slave, as well as the couple's children.

The colonists were uncomfortable with the notion of white immigrants' being held in permanent bondage. Some early laws and customs regulating slavery focused on religion and held that Christians could not be enslaved. This proved unworkable, and so in 1671, the assembly settled on race as the primary marker of eligibility for slavehood and held that conversion to Christianity would not make a slave eligible for freedom.

While slavery was part of the Maryland colony from its earliest decades, free people of color were also prominent members of early colonial society. In 1641, a free African American was elected to the Maryland General Assembly. A handful of free people of color owned substantial plantations, and some owned slaves of their own. In 1820, Maryland had the largest free nonwhite population of any Southern state. By 1860, about half of Maryland's nonwhite population was free. The free population of color in Maryland originated mostly through MISCEGENATION and MANUMISSION.

Miscegenation

The law of descent in the North American colonies held that children's status followed that of their mother. A child of a free woman was legally free; a child of a slave woman was legally enslaved. Race and skin color were not a component of this legal rule. Thus, children of white men and black women were usually slaves, since the majority of black women were slaves. Children of white women and black men were usually free, since very few white women were held in slavery. By 1664, unions between white women and black men had become so common that the state assembly passed a law attempting to regulate them—the first antimiscegenation law passed in North America. The children of such unions formed the basis of Maryland's early free people of color population.

Manumission

After the WAR OF AMERICAN INDEPENDENCE, 1775–83, Maryland SLAVE OWNERS manumitted thousands of slaves in the late 1700s and early 1800s. Many other slaves petitioned to the courts for freedom, claiming descent from a free white ancestress in the maternal line. The postrevolutionary era saw a brief flowering of liberal ideology that favored freedom. The declining market value of slaves in the Chesapeake's depressed tobacco farming economy during that era bolstered the trend toward manumission. This trend was short-lived. By the turn of the 19th century, the market value of slaves was on the rise, driven by new demand in the Deep South cotton-growing regions.

As in other Southern states, many white Marylanders were concerned about the growing free population of color. The Maryland courts began to look less favorably on freedom petitions. Furthermore, a strong EMIGRATION AND COLONIZATION movement emerged in Maryland during the 1830s that encouraged free blacks to migrate out of state to the western territories, to West Africa, or to the Caribbean. In 1831, the state Assembly forbade any freed slave to remain in the state without the permission of the local court.

Legal Status

In 1664, Maryland's assembly deliberated on the problem of "freeborne English women forgettfull of their free Condicon [who] to the disgrace of our Nation doe intermarry with Negro Slaves." The assembly determined that a free woman who married a slave must serve her husband's master as a slave herself for the duration of her husband's lifetime. Children born of such unions prior to the act's passage would serve as indentured servants for 30 years. Children born subsequent to the act's passage would be slaves for life.

Seventeen years later, Marylanders had grown uncomfortable with white women's living in bondage. In 1681, the assembly manumitted the white wives of slaves and their children, but only for marriages contracted after the last day of that assembly session. A woman who was already married to a slave would remain under the provisions of the original act of 1664, still enslaved until the death of her husband. So would her children be slaves—even if they were born after the repeal—for any child born to an enslaved mother inherited her slave status. Many descendants of white female–African male unions who lived as slaves would petition for their free-

dom, into the early 19th century, with varying degrees of success.

The colonial assembly made few laws that specifically pertain only to free people of color, other than restricting the sale and possession of alcohol and firearms by slaves and other people of color. However, certain ostensibly color-blind laws may have been applied more strictly to nonwhites than to whites. For example, an illegitimate child was bound out to a master who would have access to the individual's labor until he or she reached the age of 31. Many of these bound youths of color never experienced freedom, for the master would retain them as slaves for life.

In 1796, the assembly passed its first statute pertaining specifically to free people of color only, stating that any indigent person of color must give a bond or leave the state. Violators could be sold into servitude. This law was liberalized in 1825, mandating that the county must support any aged or infirm person of color.

In 1805, the assembly became concerned that free people of color were fencing stolen farm products obtained from slaves. The assembly held that free people of color could not sell corn, wheat, or tobacco without first obtaining a license documenting their good character. The license had to be renewed every year. In 1825, the assembly imposed a fine on whoever purchased tobacco from an unlicensed free person of color. In 1831, this law was extended to sales of many more products.

In 1824, the assembly required ship captains to keep records of people of color in their employ and prohibited ships to take people of color out of state unless they could document their freedom with official court papers. A decade later, white seamen became concerned about competition from blacks and complained that black-run vessels were participating in helping slaves to escape. The assembly responded by mandating that all ships operating in the state must have a white adult serving as chief navigator. However, black-owned shipping persisted in spite of the new law.

Some Maryland counties passed local laws aimed at reducing black economic competition with whites. Worcester County attempted to restrict black oyster fishermen in 1852. In 1852, three counties excluded people of color from selling liquor altogether and required black merchants to obtain references from 12 respectable neighbors near their shops before receiving a license to engage in trade. Whites were forbidden to partner in trade with a person of color, and white merchants were forbidden to employ a person of color on a shop floor dealing with customers. Charles and Prince George's Counties both attempted to restrict black boating in 1856, by requiring slaves to demonstrate their masters' permission to boat, and by requiring free people of color to document their

AFRICAN-AMERICAN POPULATION OF MARYLAND, 1790–1900

Year	Slaves	Free People of Color	Free People of Color as a Percentage of Total Population	Total Population
1790	103,036	8,043	2.5%	319,728
1800	105,635	19,587	5.7%	341,543
1810	111,502	33,927	8.9%	380,546
1820	107,397	39,700	9.7%	407,350
1830	102,994	52,938	11.8%	447,040
1840	89,495	62,078	13.2%	469,232
1850	96,338	74,723	12.8%	583,034
1860	87,189	83,942	12.2%	687,049
1870		175,391	22.5%	780,894
1880		210,230	22.5%	934,943
1890		215,657	20.7%	1,042,390
1900		284,706	24.0%	1,188,044

freedom with official papers that were backed by two references of good character from reputable landowners. In 1856, the assembly forbade the sale of lottery tickets to free people of color.

To control free black labor, in 1854, the assembly held that any person of color who quit his job before his contract expired was guilty of a misdemeanor. If his contract was written, a judge could compel him to complete it. His new boss could be liable to his old boss for hiring him. In 1856, this was extended to certain oral contract agreements as well. These statutes gave white employers of black labor significant power and the ability to treat their free black employees almost as slaves, with little fear of redress.

SLAVE OWNERS' desire to control RUNAWAY SLAVES led to laws that affected free people of color as well. A 1715 law sanctioned a system of passes for slaves who were traveling away from their masters. Free people of color sometimes felt it necessary to obtain similar passes, so that they could travel without harassment. The 1715 act held that free Negroes could be arrested and sold into servitude if unable to prove their freedom and pay their court costs. More than a century passed before this law was liberalized. In 1796, the assembly imposed special fines on free people of color who assisted a slave in escaping or who provided a freedom certificate to a slave. A decade later, the assembly restricted the issuance of freedom papers to county court clerks and registers of wills.

The ever-present concern over growth in the black population led to additional legal restrictions. An 1807 statute fined any free person of color who entered Maryland from out of state and remained more than two weeks.

Those who could not pay were to be sold into servitude. Exceptions were made for black sailors and transportation workers. In 1831, sojourners were restricted to 10 days in state, and the fine quintupled. In 1839, simply crossing the Maryland border became an offense. Furthermore, Maryland blacks who left the state for more than 30 days should be treated as nonresidents and subjected to the same penalties, with exceptions made for black workers in certain border counties who were traveling on behalf of their white employers. While such laws created significant danger for free people of color, they were not vigilantly enforced.

Political Impact

In the decades before the AMERICAN CIVIL WAR, free people of color in Maryland were nearly equal in number to the slave population. By 1860, there were 11 times as many free blacks as slaves in Baltimore, but the major concern over the free population of color arose from the large slave-owning class in the Chesapeake region. The large free black population created a dual labor system for black agricultural workers. Free people of color had the power of negotiating for wages and terms of employment; slaves did not. This had a major impact on agricultural economics in Maryland and tended to drive labor costs above those in other slave states.

As in other Southern states, Maryland's slave-owning class viewed free people of color as potential insurgents who might lead slaves to revolt. Their preference was either to re-enslave free blacks or to expel them from the state. Non-slave-owning white planters, on the other hand, relied on free black labor to work their fields and were concerned about a potential labor shortage.

By 1858, free blacks could be sold into slavery for crimes that brought only imprisonment for white offenders. In 1860, extremists on the free black question took office in the assembly. The assembly's Committee on Colored Population advocated "the ultimate extinguishment of the free negro element." It proposed outlawing manumission and RE-ENSLAVEMENT of free people of color, forbidding mail delivery to blacks, forbidding any black assemblies, and auctioning off black churches. While these measures did not pass, they fostered public debates that emphasized the serious political differences between those whites who owned slaves and those who did not. This political cleavage between slave owners and nonowners persisted into the Civil War era, as Marylanders sharply divided on loyalty versus secession.

Aftermath

The Civil War led to many changes for free blacks in Maryland. As soon as blacks were authorized to serve in the U.S. Army, black Marylanders began signing up in enormous numbers, even though the Maryland state government was reluctant to make use of them. The 2nd Infantry, U.S. Colored Troops (USCT), though credited to the District of Columbia, was actually composed mostly of Maryland men. Colonel Birney, the white commander of the 2nd USCT, was authorized to raise four additional regiments in Maryland. He established a camp outside Baltimore. His orders restricted him to enrolling men who were already free, but he raided slave pens and took men who had been sent north to avoid military service. Local slave owners protested, but Birney was able to keep his recruits. Ultimately, almost 9,000 blacks were credited to Maryland's total recruits for the U.S. Army during the war. This figure does not count substantial numbers of black Marylanders who served in other states' regiments. Additionally, the black maritime population of Baltimore furnished many recruits to the U.S. Navy, which was not segregated by race at the time.

After the war, since Maryland had not joined the Confederacy, black Marylanders did not have the benefit of Reconstruction supervision of their state government (*see* RECONSTRUCTION IN THE UNITED STATES). Nonetheless, they were able to improve their situation to some extent. Maryland's 1864 constitution abolished slavery. A subsequent constitutional reform, in 1867, gave the vote to black males, well ahead of the U.S. Constitution's Fifteenth Amendment, ratified in 1870. Unlike in most Southern states, Maryland's blacks managed to hold on to the vote throughout the Jim Crow era, and the population rejected proposed disenfranchising amendments in 1905, 1909, and 1910. The

black community of Baltimore in particular remained vibrant, building community institutions including black churches, Morgan College and Coppin College, and a well-run black school system. A product of that school system, whose grandfather was a Baltimore artisan who gained his freedom before the Civil War, Thurgood Marshall (1908–93) was the winning attorney in the first successful court challenge to the *Plessy v. Ferguson* standard of "separate but equal," the case of *Murray v. Pearson* that desegregated the University of Maryland in 1935.

Thomas Brown

FURTHER READING
Brackett, Jeffrey R. *The Negro in Maryland*. Baltimore: Jos. Murphy, 1889.
Brown, Thomas, and Leah Sims. "'To Swear Him Free': Ethnic Memory as Social Capital in 18th Century Freedom Petitions." In *Colonial Chesapeake: New Perspectives*, edited by Debra Meyers and Melanie Perreault. Lanham, Md.: Lexington Books, 2006.
Dorsey, Jennifer Hull. "Free People of Color in Rural Maryland, 1783–1832." Ph.D. diss., Georgetown University, 2002.
Fields, Barbara J. *Slavery and Freedom on the Middle Ground: Maryland during the Nineteenth Century*. New Haven, Conn.: Yale University Press, 1987.
Phillips, Christopher. *Freedom's Port: The African American Community of Baltimore, 1790–1860*. Urbana: University of Illinois Press, 1997.
Wright, James M. *The Free Negro in Maryland, 1634–1860*. Studies in History, Economics and Public Law edited by the Faculty of Political Science of Columbia University, vol. 97. New York: Columbia University Press, 1921.

MASSACHUSETTS

Slavery existed throughout British North America, and Massachusetts, founded in 1629, was no exception. The first blacks taken into the colony, in 1635, were slaves, but by the time of the WAR OF AMERICAN INDEPENDENCE, 1775–83, a strong free black community had emerged in the state, centered mainly in BOSTON and the maritime counties. The coast of Massachusetts hosted the large city of Boston and several smaller port and fishing towns. Employment in seafaring and port occupations was common for people of color (*see also* NAVY and MERCHANT SEAMEN). By the time of the AMERICAN CIVIL WAR, Massachusetts was home to some of the nation's most vibrant free black communities and institutions.

From colonial times, most blacks in Massachusetts resided in clusters, most notably in Boston, the capital. Slaves generally lived with their masters, so the urban clusters were mostly composed of free people of color from an early date. Some urban blacks were still juridically slaves in the 1700s but were permitted "their time" by masters in return for a regular payment—these people, who were LIVING "AS FREE," were treated, for the most part, as free people of color. In 1742, approximately 1,500 blacks, most of whom were free under this definition, lived in Boston, and by 1754, half of the nearly 2,700 adult blacks in Massachusetts lived in the city. More than three-quarters of the remainder lived in the coastal and town centers of Suffolk, Essex, and Plymouth Counties. Indeed, by that year, Boston's population had been about 10 percent black for a decade. Suffolk County was about 4 percent black. Though blacks made up a small overall percentage of the colony's (and later the state's) population, they lived together in clusters that allowed them to form distinct communities. Still, continuing importation of slaves from Africa meant that the black community faced an unbalanced ratio of approximately 1.89 males per female. In addition, poverty meant that there was high infant mortality, which made the growth of black families slow. This situation fostered the preservation of African culture for a couple of generations, but by the turn of the 19th century, with the abolition of slavery in the state, Massachusetts's blacks were beginning the process of acculturation, and before long they became what the historian William Piersen has called "Black Yankees."

According to Piersen, blacks in New England had less influence culturally upon the broader society in which they lived than did blacks in most parts of the United States. First, blacks made up too small a percentage of the population. Also, New England slaves lived and worked within the master's household, and each master owned very few slaves, many of whom were bought as children. This meant that blacks and whites were in closer proximity on a daily basis, and European culture dominated. Given New England's Puritan origins, Protestant Christianity was particularly strong in this region and played a large role in this process. Perhaps the best illustration of the resulting acculturation can be seen in the poetry of PHILLIS WHEATLEY. Wheatley was African-born and had lived as a domestic slave with the Wheatley family from the age of seven. Her masters taught her good English prose style and Protestant Christianity, values reflected in the poetry she wrote after gaining her freedom in 1773.

Even in this atmosphere, New England blacks did manage to retain some African cultural elements and create a unique African-American culture. For example, they mixed into the Christianity of their masters African beliefs in the afterlife and witchcraft (see also AFRICAN AND SYNCRETIC RELIGIONS). They also retained ances-

tral knowledge of herbal medicines. Of course, this often scared white New Englanders, most obviously in the case of the Salem witch trials and the role of the slave Tituba in 1692. Even though the conditions in New England disrupted traditional African extended family ties and made it very difficult to create stable nuclear families, those who were able to achieve economic autonomy created families as soon as they could. They also retained the custom of the African Sunday market, much to the chagrin of their Christian neighbors, and they created their own celebrations and elected black kings and governors on election day, a day of great celebration in the white community. Finally, they introduced African traditions of mimicry and satire to New England, using them as a form of resistance and a safe way to mock white society. By the end of the colonial period, then, black New Englanders had managed to create a unique culture that blended their African roots with their New England surroundings.

Massachusetts blacks played an important role in the War of American Independence. For example, the escaped-slave-turned-seaman Crispus Attucks became famous as the first martyr to the American cause during the Boston Massacre in 1770. Blacks then fought during the war, beginning with the early battles at Lexington and Concord in 1775. PETER SALEM, a man who was freed from slavery so that he could serve in these battles, is one of the most famous examples. He also fought at Bunker Hill, alongside the free black soldiers Salem Poor, Titus Coburn, Alexander Ames, Barzilai Lew, Cato Howe, and many others whose names are unknown. Many blacks hoped that they, too, could gain liberty by fighting for the new country, and in a place like Massachusetts, where a small black population made whites more willing to accept black soldiers, their efforts often proved fruitful, despite efforts by Southern whites including General GEORGE WASHINGTON to block the enlistment of both slaves and free blacks.

As the war for "freedom" and "liberty" raged on, Massachusetts blacks waged a war of their own against slavery. They began by petitioning both the British colonial government (in 1773 and 1774) and then the state government for freedom. If not freedom, they asked at least to be allowed to work for themselves one day each week so that they could earn the money to buy their freedom.

The issue was eventually settled after the war by the QUOCK WALKER CASE. It began with the Massachusetts state constitution in 1780, which included the phrase "all men are created free and equal." Before this constitution was written, a number of slaves had sued for their freedom. One of the first was the slave Adam's successful lawsuit against John Saffin in 1705 that provoked Samuel Sewall's "The Selling of Joseph," a classic early abolitionist work. Saffin had promised Adam his freedom in return for seven years' service but later reneged; his promise was ultimately found by the courts to be binding. Other cases followed in the 1760s and 1770s, and in 1781, Quock Walker sued his master, Nathaniel Jennison, for failing to honor his promise to free Walker. Chief Justice William Cushing not only freed Walker—basing his finding on the long line of decisions dating back to the Saffin case that promises to slaves were legally binding—but ended slavery in the state once and for all when he ruled that slavery was "inconsistent" with the constitution. The state supreme court agreed and outlawed slavery in Massachusetts in 1783.

Free blacks in Massachusetts pushed not only for an end to slavery but for black civil rights as well. PAUL CUFFE, a wealthy black sea captain and shipowner, joined his brother John in applying the revolutionary slogan of "No taxation without representation" to this cause. Because they were denied the vote, they refused to pay taxes on their large landholdings between 1778 and 1780. Though they were eventually forced to pay the back taxes, they gained the support of other blacks in the state and eventually won when the 1780 Massachusetts state constitution removed restrictions against black and Indian voters. The struggle against discrimination led to one of the first major court cases attacking segregation, the case of *Roberts v. Boston* in 1850. The plaintiff, father of a young girl named Sarah Roberts who was a student at the black public school, alleged (as did the plaintiffs in the famous case of *Brown v. Board of Education* that was to end school segregation more than a century later) that separate schools for blacks and whites were inherently unequal and that as a taxpayer he deserved the same standard of education for his children that white children received. The Massachusetts courts disagreed, however, defending segregation in a case that served as a precedent for the U.S. Supreme Court's later *Plessy v. Ferguson* decision in 1896 defending "separate but equal" accommodations in public transportation.

Throughout the early republic and antebellum years, free blacks in Massachusetts continued to strive daily to build a respected community of their own. The basis of the community continued to be the household and family. Revolutionary War veterans returned to settlements like "New Guinea" (also known as "Parting Ways") near Plymouth to create farms of their own in hopes of prospering in their newly won freedom. In their settlements, they incorporated much of their African heritage, from modeling both their homes and the settlements themselves upon African customs to maintaining African burial customs. Freed from bondage, they enjoyed more freedom in choosing marriage partners and could at least hope for more stability in their family lives, though a high rate of mortality made single-parent households increasingly common in the 1820s. Despite these hardships, the black population of Massachusetts grew steadily but unspectacularly during this period. In 1790, the census counted more than 5,000 blacks in the state, and at the outbreak of the American Civil War, this number had increased to more than 9,000. Another common feature of free black family life, in response to the large numbers of single adults and families fractured by premature death or flight to avoid the slave catchers, was the practice of boarding, which developed as families and friends relied upon each other for financial, emotional, and social support.

Despite such efforts to take care of their own community, free blacks faced varying degree of hostility from their white neighbors, who feared that the growing black community would lead to an expanding crime rate and public dole. In 1788, the state legislature passed a vagrancy law that called for all African Americans who were not citizens of the state to be expelled. Then, in 1821, the legislature put together a committee to examine the possibility of banning black migration into the state. It was unsuccessful, and such effort ceased at that point. Even so, many whites continued to complain about high crime statistics among free blacks. Studies have shown that most crimes committed by free blacks were property crimes brought on by poverty endemic to the exclusionary system whereby better jobs were reserved for whites. Among the laboring classes, blacks and whites often competed for jobs, and tensions often resulted. Though there were few black professionals, in the years before the Civil War, a growing middle class consisted of ministers and teachers, along with a few lawyers and doctors. These professionals provided crucial leadership as free blacks built their own social welfare and self-help institutions.

Free blacks in Massachusetts built a number of important community institutions. One of the first resulted from PRINCE HALL's efforts to charter a Masonic order for blacks (*see* FREEMASONRY). After being denied a charter by American Masons, he received approval from British Masons and established the African Masonic Lodge in 1787. Another self-help group in the black community was the African Society of Boston, founded in 1796. Groups of these kind assisted members with burial expenses, built schools for the children of the community, and offered economic and spiritual assistance in times of need. In some cases, they helped raise money to build churches for the community. They also served as a foundation for antislavery and civil rights movements that began to grow, especially after the birth of the AMERICAN COLONIZATION SOCIETY in 1817.

Though one of Massachusetts's first black activists, PAUL CUFFE, dabbled with the idea of African emigration, and some considered various Haitian emigration schemes, most resisted resettlement, and a number of black leaders gained fame through their resistance efforts (see EMIGRATION AND COLONIZATION). One Boston free black who gained prominence and greatly influenced white abolitionists such as William Lloyd Garrison was MARIA W. STEWART (1803–79). Influenced by DAVID WALKER's *Appeal to the Coloured Citizens of the World*, a radical pamphlet published in 1829 calling for immediate emancipation, she became a public speaker and writer, passionately calling upon black Americans to insist upon their rights as citizens, seek more than menial jobs, and avoid vices such as drinking and gambling. She was a leading proponent of both black rights and women's rights.

Antislavery efforts expanded during the period before the Civil War through the work of such agencies as Boston's Massachusetts General Colored Association and the growth of regional, state, and local black conventions (see also NEGRO CONVENTION MOVEMENT IN THE UNITED STATES). Through the work of these groups and the conventions, often held at Boston's Faneuil Hall, as well as a growing black press, African Americans could easily monitor the progress of the civil rights and antislavery crusade throughout the country. They could also spread their message to sympathetic whites such as Garrison, who began publishing the *Liberator* in Boston in 1831 and calling for a new type of abolition known as "immediatism." Immediatists wanted the immediate end of slavery with no compensation to masters, and Boston became the seat of the antislavery movement.

Boston also became an important destination for free blacks and RUNAWAY SLAVES in the 1840s and 1850s. In 1842, a group of free blacks in Boston organized the Freedom Association to aid the fugitives. This group helped secure the passage of a personal liberty law in 1843 and then became part of a new, larger group, the Boston Vigilance Committee, in 1846. The group played an important role in the growth of the Underground Railroad. Famous fugitive slave cases in Boston include those of George Latimer, William and Ellen Craft, Thomas Sims, and Anthony Burns. Efforts to aid fugitives took on an increased significance throughout the 1850s in the face of a growing proslavery climate in the United States in general, as embodied in the FUGITIVE SLAVE ACT OF 1850, which made it much easier for SLAVE OWNERS to reclaim escaped slaves, and the DRED SCOTT decision of 1857, which declared that no black could be an American citizen. The slave catchers did not find a very welcoming climate in Massachusetts, as many whites opposed the return of fugitive slaves and were prepared to break the law to protect them. But the fear of recapture caused many blacks to migrate to CANADA or to leave urban areas where they could be found, contributing to the breakup of black families and the uncertainty of black life in the state before 1861.

When the Civil War began in 1861, Massachusetts free blacks saw an opportunity to build upon their antislavery work and secure freedom throughout the nation. Indeed, blacks from throughout the United States tried immediately to enlist in the army but were refused at first because most whites feared the idea of blacks' being armed. The exigencies of war, however, led to a change in policy, forcing white Americans to accept the aid offered

AFRICAN-AMERICAN POPULATION OF MASSACHUSETTS, 1790–1900

Year	Free People of Color	Free People of Color as a Percentage of Total Population	Total Population
1790	5,463	1.4%	378,787
1800	6,452	1.5%	422,845
1810	6,737	1.4%	472,040
1820	6,585	1.3%	523,287
1830	7,045	1.2%	610,404
1840	8,669	1.2%	737,699
1850	9,064	0.9%	994,514
1860	9,602	0.8%	1,231,065
1870	13,947	1.0%	1,457,351
1880	18,697	1.0%	1,783,085
1890	22,144	1.0%	2,238,943
1900	31,974	1.1%	2,805,346

by free blacks. President ABRAHAM LINCOLN was authorized by Congress to accept blacks in the military in 1862, and one of the most famous results was the creation of the Massachusetts 54th and 55th Infantry Regiments. Forty percent of the black military age men of Boston, or 137 young men, enlisted in one of these two units. Among these men were James H. Gooding (1837–64) of New Bedford, whose moving letters from the front were published in a local newspaper, and William H. Carney (1840–1908), a Medal of Honor winner for his heroism at Fort Wagner.

The African-American population of Massachusetts began to grow steadily after the Civil War. Having increased slowly throughout the prewar years, rising from 5,463 in 1790 to 9,602 in 1860, the population began to climb dramatically, to 13,947 in 1870 and reaching 31,974 by the end of the century. The relatively benign racial climate of Massachusetts must be responsible to some extent for this rapid growth, since the Massachusetts economy was outstripped during this period by New York City and the midwestern cities: The state's total population went from 1.2 million in 1860 to 2.8 million in 1900, somewhat more than doubling, while the African-American population was increasing by a factor of more than three. After the Civil War, some progress was made toward achieving civil rights in the state. For example, Massachusetts became the first state to prohibit racial discrimination in public accommodations in 1865. Also, the Massachusetts senator Charles Sumner also helped lead the Radical Republicans in their quest for greater opportunity for Southern blacks after the war. Indeed, the postwar milieu of Boston led black Bostonians to brag of the city's open racial climate. Important black leaders in Boston between 1890 and 1920 included William Monroe Trotter (1872–1934), editor of the *Guardian* newspaper; Josephine St. Pierre Ruffin (1842–1924), a leader in the black women's club movement; and Butler and Mary Wilson, activists with the National Association for the Advancement of Colored People.

Beverly C. Tomek

FURTHER READING
Horton, James Oliver, and Lois E. Horton. *Black Bostonians.* New York: Holmes & Meier, 1979.
———. *In Hopes of Liberty: Culture, Community and Protest among Northern Free Blacks, 1700–1860.* New York: Oxford University Press, 1997.
Piersen, William D. *Black Yankees: The Development of an Afro-American Subculture in Eighteenth-Century New England.* Amherst: University of Massachusetts Press, 1988.
Schneider, Mark. *Boston Confronts Jim Crow, 1890–1920.* Evanston, Ill.: Northwestern University Press, 1997.
Von Frank, Albert J. *The Trials of Anthony Burns: Freedom and Slavery in Emerson's Boston.* Cambridge, Mass.: Harvard University Press, 1998.

McCABE, EDWIN P. (1850–1920) *American public servant*

Edwin McCabe was born in New York on October 10, 1850. His family was mixed-race, and he himself was very light-complexioned. His family moved several times during the 1850s and 1860s, and for some of this time he may have "passed" as white (*see also* "WHITENING" AND RACIAL PROMOTION). After the AMERICAN CIVIL WAR, he received a legal education in ILLINOIS in the 1860s, at a time when few African Americans were admitted to the bar. He worked on Wall Street as a financial clerk for a time, again when no other African Americans worked there. When he became politically active, however, he made no secret of his racial identity.

McCabe moved to KANSAS in 1878 and became a leader in the EXODUSTER MOVEMENT, a migration of blacks from the South to the West as hopes of racial equality were frustrated (*see also* EMIGRATION AND COLONIZATION and RECONSTRUCTION IN THE UNITED STATES). He was elected court clerk in Graham County, Kansas, the county where the famous Exoduster settlement of Nicodemus was located. He was active in the state Republican Party—at that time most African Americans were Republicans—and sought a state government post after Republicans won the 1888 election. He was frustrated in these hopes and moved to OKLAHOMA at the urging of the Kansas Republican leader Preston Plumb. The Oklahoma Immigration Association encouraged black immigration into Oklahoma, and there was some consideration that Oklahoma could or should be a majority black state. Midwestern Republicans hoped to stem the advance of Southern Democrats into the newly settled territories of the Southwest. Oklahoma had been the Indian Territory until the American Civil War, but when the Indians mostly supported the Confederacy, their land was taken away from them, and the region opened up to settlement. Blacks had been discriminated against in the distribution of land.

McCabe went to Oklahoma by way of Washington, D.C., where he tried to convince the newly elected Republican president Benjamin Harrison to appoint him governor of Oklahoma. Frustrated in this ambition, he arrived in Oklahoma without an official position but nonetheless was quickly recognized as an important leader of the African-American community. He established a newspaper, the *Langston City Herald*, as a voice for African-American Oklahomans. Indians and newly arrived whites from the South both saw McCabe and the organizations that backed him as their enemies. McCabe was also involved in land speculation, and some of his dealings tarnished his image with the public. He was able to make one important contribution to African-American life in Oklahoma by establishing the Colored Agricultural and Normal College (today called Langston University). McCabe also pursued a federal court challenge to segregation in public accommodations in the territories, suing for reversal or modification of the *Plessy v. Ferguson* (1896) decision, but was ultimately defeated. In the end, the Democrats were able to build a coalition of white farmers and rural poor and take control of the territory's politics. The African Americans' only hope lay with the federal government, but that opportunity evaporated when Oklahoma was admitted to the Union as a state in 1907. The Democrat-controlled state legislature immediately adopted segregation laws that lasted until the Civil Rights movement of the 1960s.

After this final defeat, McCabe left Oklahoma for CHICAGO, ILLINOIS, as did many other Southern and Western African Americans at this time of what was called the "Great Migration." He lived the rest of his life in Chicago and died on March 12, 1920.

Stewart R. King

FURTHER READING

Franklin, Jimmie Lewis. *Journey toward Hope: A History of Blacks in Oklahoma*. Norman: University of Oklahoma Press, 1982.
Roberson, Jere W. "Edward P. McCabe and the Langston Experiment." *Chronicles of Oklahoma* 51 (Fall 1973).

MELUNGEON

Melungeon is a term applied to certain mixed-race people who live in southwestern VIRGINIA AND WEST VIRGINIA, western NORTH CAROLINA, and eastern TENNESSEE and KENTUCKY in the United States. Their ancestors include the native people of the area, RUNAWAY SLAVES or those bought by the Indians, and local whites. As mixed-race people, they had a status lower than that of whites, but by stressing their native ancestry, they escaped many of the harshest racial restrictions imposed on blacks during the Jim Crow era of the late 19th and early 20th centuries. Some people described as melungeon have identified a set of surnames and British ancestors for their group, whose ancestry they trace to Tidewater Virginia in the 17th century. Meanwhile, other melungeons deny that the term identifies a cultural group with a common heritage. Other mixed-race groups in the same region, such as the "Brown People of Kentucky" or the Lumbee and Coffee

Indians of North Carolina, reject the label of melungeon and lay greater stress on their African or Native heritage.

Stewart R. King

FURTHER READING

DeMarce, Virginia E. "'Verry Slitly Mixt': Tri-Racial Isolate Families of the Upper South—a Genealogical Study." *National Genealogical Society Quarterly* 80 (March 1992): 5–35.
Forbes, Jack D. *Africans and Native Americans: The Language of Race and the Evolution of Red-Black Peoples*. Champaign-Urbana: University of Illinois Press, 1993.
Kennedy, N. Brent, and Robyn Vaughan Kennedy. *The Melungeons: The Resurrection of a Proud People*. Macon, Ga.: Mercer University Press, 1994.
Melungeon Heritage Association. "Celebrating the Richness of Culture and Diversity of Heritage That Is Appalachia." Availabel online. URL: http://www.melungeon.org/. Accessed March 29, 2010.

MERCHANT SEAMEN

Men of color served as crewmen on merchant ships in every ocean in the world during the epoch of slavery. Nautical employment, both military and civilian, was very open to people of color during this period. (*See also* NAVY.) Because of the unusual nature of society aboard ships, people of color did not suffer under great discrimination, though there were some egregious exceptions. Some captains actually preferred sailors of color for certain types of work.

Black mariners were among the first to crew European ships exploring the Atlantic Ocean in the 15th century. Prince Henry the Navigator of Portugal (1394–1460) sought out African sailors for his exploring ships both because they were skilled with the newly designed caravel sail rig—adopted from an East African model—and because they might be familiar with the languages and cultures that explorers would encounter along the coast of Africa.

Black sailors also served as cultural intermediaries for captains in the slave trade. Many people who were loaded onto slave ships found the presence of a few black faces among the crew at least gave hope that the voyage would not end in certain death. Sailors who spoke African languages were especially valuable to slave ship captains. Slave mortality, insurrections, and suicide were all lower on ships with black crewmen. However, the slave trade paradoxically also saw many incidents of racial discrimination against black sailors, since captains feared racial or even tribal solidarity between free and enslaved Africans. Further, slave ship crewmen were abysmally treated, even by the standards of the time, with murders of crewmen by officers and officers

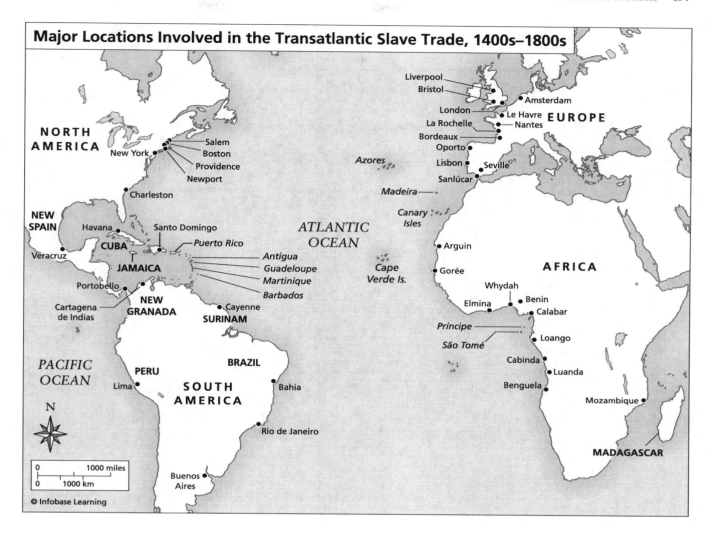

Major Locations Involved in the Transatlantic Slave Trade, 1400s–1800s

by crews both much more common in the slave trade than was usual at sea in those days (*see also* PIRACY).

Black crewmen served in all waters and all types of merchant ships. OLAUDAH EQUIANO was both a merchant seaman and a naval crewman, and he explored the Arctic; sailed to the Americas, Africa, and the Mediterranean; and worked for a short time on a ship hauling coal from northern to southern England. In some places, blacks were more prevalent among sailors than in the general population. In MASSACHUSETTS in the 1770s, there were only a few thousand free men of color, but several hundred of these worked as sailors or fishermen. One was Crispus Attucks, a sailor who was one of the victims of the Boston Massacre in 1770. About 200 others filled the ranks of the Marblehead Regiment, which saved General GEORGE WASHINGTON's army in 1776 during the Battle of Brooklyn in the WAR OF AMERICAN INDEPENDENCE, 1775–83. When the British naval captain Thomas Cochrane, having been fired from his own navy for financial improprieties, joined the Chilean navy in 1818, he found that the merchant ships he was to convert into a navy were crewed almost exclusively by people of color—some of them Indians and mestizos but most blacks, even though CHILE had very few free black inhabitants at the time.

It is clear that blacks were disproportionately drawn to the sea as a profession. Part of the explanation for this lies in the unusual social construction of nautical service. In the navy, sailors were forced into service and hanged if they ran away, so it was no surprise that naval seamen were seen as servile, de facto temporary slaves. Merchant ships were somewhat less coercive than the navy, but once a sailor had signed on to a ship, he was bound for the duration of the voyage and could be physically punished, even killed under some circumstances, by his officers. People serving at sea were, thus, not quite free, and so paradoxically service at sea became a profession that allowed free people of color to liberate themselves, at least a little, from the poverty and discrimination of life on land.

Few blacks became officers on merchant ships, but the intermediate ranks were open to them, and it was

Dockworkers and riverboat workers in St. Louis, Missouri, 1890s. Blacks could often find work on ships and docks, and this was a relatively high-status and well-paid occupation. *(North Wind Picture Archives via Associated Press)*

not unusual to find a black boatswain (responsible for steering the ship and maintaining the ropes), sailmaker, or carpenter's mate. Black cooks were very common. A father-and-son pair of black cooks, Bertrand and Augustin LeMoine, from SAINT-DOMINGUE served on French Royal Navy and merchant ships from the 1740s to the 1790s. The father retired with enough to buy a small farm and several slaves in the vicinity of Fort-Dauphin, near the Spanish border in northern Saint-Domingue. The skilled workers on merchant ships could make a respectable living, as the LeMoines found out. Merchant wages averaged two to three times what naval seamen or soldiers in the REGULAR ARMY were paid.

Fishing and inshore shipping, between ports in the same colony, were very common occupations for blacks. Small boats were fairly inexpensive, offering an opportunity to make a respectable living with small capital. Success in interisland shipping, especially in the plantation zones, could lead to significant wealth. VINCENT OGÉ,

the Saint-Domingue free colored merchant and political activist, started his business with several small merchant ships in the interisland business. Lower down the socioeconomic scale, the free colored militiaman Pierre Simon Zogo owned a 30-ton single-masted vessel, seemingly much like the boats that today carry "boat people" from Haiti to FLORIDA, that carried cargoes between CAP-FRANÇAIS/CAP-HAÏTIEN and smaller ports in Saint-Domingue. The Marblehead, Massachusetts, black fishermen who went as far as the Grand Banks might meet the black crewmen who were common on Portuguese fishing ships in the 18th century.

As the era of slavery ended in the 19th century, paradoxically, it became more difficult for blacks to work on merchant ships. Labor activism among white mariners led to a professionalization of maritime work, with greater protections and rights for seamen. As the work became more respectable, it became less acceptable in the harsh racial climate of the 19th century to hire members of subordinate racial groups. Some maritime unions did accept black members, but others, in the United States in particular, were all-white. Ships trading with Africa and Latin America still had men of color among the crews, and work that involved personal service, including as cooks and stewards on passenger ships, continued to be open to black seamen. Blacks never vanished from the sea, but they became less common and less well rewarded. Only with the Civil Rights movements of the 20th century and the simultaneous move by shipping companies to reflag their ships under the jurisdiction of developing-world "flags of convenience" like LIBERIA and PANAMA did black merchant seamen become common again.

Stewart R. King

FURTHER READING

Linebaugh, Peter, and Marcus Rediker. *The Many-Headed Hydra: Sailors, Slaves, Commoners and the Hidden History of the Revolutionary Atlantic.* Boston: Beacon Press, 2000.

Rediker, Marcus. *The Slave Ship: A Human History.* New York: Viking, 2007.

MEXICAN-AMERICAN WAR (1846–1848)

The Mexican-American War was fought between the United States and MEXICO from 1846 to 1848. The conflict represented a conflagration of issues between the two governments over borders in the American Southwest and a growing push for expansionism by United States leaders and the American public. At the end of the war in February 1848, the United States gained 529,017 square miles of territory from Mexico, including the present-day American states of CALIFORNIA, Nevada, and Utah, and significant parts of Arizona, New Mexico, Colorado, and Wyoming. Also, the United States claimed the border of TEXAS at the Rio Grande, adding 275,000 square miles to the land area Texas originally claimed after the state's independence from Mexico in 1836.

Causes

Multiple causes led to the outbreak of violence between the two nations. First, the annexation of Texas by the United States in 1845 played an important role in the dispute. After the Texas War of Independence (1835–36), Texans gained independence with the signing of the Treaty of Velasco in May 1836. The Mexican government refused to ratify the treaty, however, claiming that the Mexican president Antonio López de Santa Anna had been forced to sign it under duress. In just a short time, Texas politicians such as Sam Houston began to press for annexation of Texas to the United States, but the initiative was stalled for some time by the reluctance of the Whig Party in the U.S. Congress. In 1843, the Mexican Congress

warned that the annexation of Texas to the United States would be viewed as an act of war. The U.S. Congress, by this time controlled by Democrats, ignored the Mexican government and passed a joint resolution for annexation on March 1, 1845. On the same day, the Mexican leaders broke diplomatic ties with the United States.

Another more immediate cause of the war stemmed from the boundary dispute between Mexico and Texas. Since Texan independence, the Mexican government claimed the border at the Nueces River, while Texan and American leaders contended the location of the border was farther south at the Rio Grande. Upon assuming office in 1845, President JAMES POLK sent the diplomat John Slidell to discuss the purchase of California and a monetary settlement of the Texas border issue. Though Slidell proposed sums of money ranging from $5 million to $20 million, Mexican leaders were forced to rebuff the offers for fear of political overthrow by an agitated Mexican public.

The main impetus for American expansion found its expression in the doctrine of Manifest Destiny. Coined by the journalist John L. O'Sullivan, the term embraced the belief that the United States was destined to expand across North America and spread American political, economic, religious, and racial institutions. In the election of 1844, the Democratic presidential candidate James K. Polk's platform embraced these expansionist notions. Though sectional differences over the institution of slavery split North and South, most Americans believed expansion was ordained even if for different reasons. Some Southerners viewed expansion as a way to enlarge the institution of slavery and demonstrate American superiority, while others feared the inclusion of the more than 75,000 nonwhite inhabitants in the American system. Abolitionists from the North opposed the expansion of slavery into the Southwest and Mexico, while some Northern politicians embraced Polk's expansionist motives.

The Spot Resolution and Declaration of War

On May 9, 1846, President Polk readied his war message to Congress after Slidell's failure to reach an agreement with the Mexican government. Later that day, Polk received word Mexican troops had crossed over the Rio Grande and attacked American forces under the command of General ZACHARY TAYLOR. Polk now had his justification for war and revised his message, citing Mexican troop invasion rather than underlying American territorial aggression. A young congressman, ABRAHAM LINCOLN (Whig-ILLINOIS), challenged Polk's assertion of an attack on American soil, arguing that the fighting had occurred on disputed territory. Despite this protest, Congress declared war on Mexico on May 13, 1846, after just a few hours of debate.

The War

The U.S. war plan involved a three-front invasion. General Taylor and his forces crossed the Rio Grande to invade the heart of Mexico. A second unit, the Army of the West under the command of General Stephen Kearny, left Fort Leavenworth in KANSAS and moved toward the Mexican provinces of New Mexico and California, where they encountered little resistance. Taylor's northern campaign won two battles on May 8 and 9, 1846, against Mexican forces at Palo Alto and Resaca de la Palma, respectively.

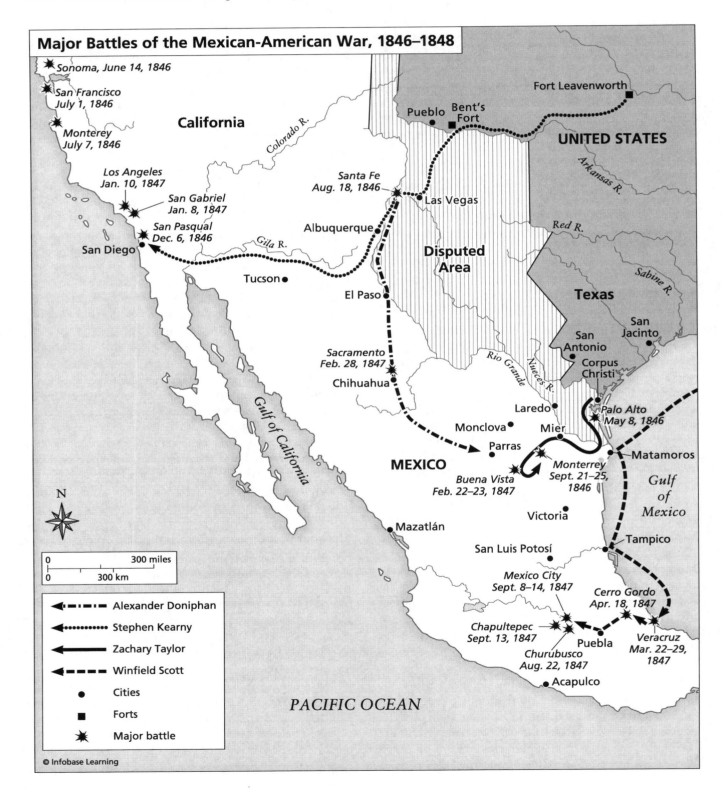

Major Battles of the Mexican-American War, 1846–1848

Sonoma, June 14, 1846
San Francisco July 1, 1846
Monterey July 7, 1846
California
Colorado R.
Fort Leavenworth
Pueblo   Bent's Fort
UNITED STATES
Arkansas R.
Los Angeles Jan. 10, 1847
San Gabriel Jan. 8, 1847
San Pasqual Dec. 6, 1846
Santa Fe Aug. 18, 1846
Las Vegas
Albuquerque
San Diego
Gila R.
Tucson
El Paso
Disputed Area
Red R.
Sabine R.
Texas
San Jacinto
San Antonio
Corpus Christi
Sacramento Feb. 28, 1847
Chihuahua
Rio Grande
Nueces R.
Laredo
Palo Alto May 8, 1846
Gulf of California
Monclova
Parras
Mier
Matamoros
MEXICO
Buena Vista Feb. 22–23, 1847
Monterrey Sept. 21–25, 1846
Gulf of Mexico
Mazatlán
Victoria
Tampico
N
San Luis Potosí
0   300 miles
0   300 km
Mexico City Sept. 8–14, 1847
Cerro Gordo Apr. 18, 1847
Chapultepec Sept. 13, 1847
Puebla
Veracruz Mar. 22–29, 1847
Churubusco Aug. 22, 1847
Acapulco

Alexander Doniphan
Stephen Kearny
Zachary Taylor
Winfield Scott
Cities
Forts
Major battle

PACIFIC OCEAN

© Infobase Learning

After receiving additional supplies, Taylor's forces took the city of Monterey on September 17. President Polk became increasingly angered with what he viewed as Taylor's lack of enthusiasm for the invasion and his reluctance to pursue defeated Mexican forces vigorously. As a result, Polk removed Taylor from leadership after his victory at the Battle of Buena Vista and replaced him with Major General Winfield Scott in winter 1846–47. The third invasion under Scott led to a naval assault and amphibious invasion of Veracruz, on March 27, 1847. After defeating fierce Mexican resistance under the leadership of Santa Anna at Cerro Gordo, Scott's forces slowly advanced on Mexico City. In August 1847, Scott's troops assaulted fortified positions around the city until finally storming the main citadel at Chapultepec on September 13, 1847. The following day, Scott's forces occupied and controlled Mexico City, effectively ending the war.

People of Color in the War

Because of discriminatory practices and slavery in the United States, African Americans were only found in small numbers in the ranks of the U.S. military during the Mexican War. Several NEW YORK STATE regiments that participated in the expedition to Mexico City enlisted free black soldiers from the Northeast. A few light-skinned African Americans secretly served in Southern regiments, and many slaves tried to join the military in order to escape slavery, but very few succeeded. Free men of color served in the U.S. Navy in considerable numbers throughout this period, in menial positions for the most part. The NAVY had never excluded people of color and even promoted them to noncommissioned officer positions. Free people of color mostly served in the U.S. military in hope of personal advancement, either in order to pass as white or to escape slavery, or simply as a form of employment, although some of the New York soldiers also described their service in terms of patriotic duty. Most African Americans who served in the REGULAR ARMY did so as servants to officers. Some servants knew that slavery had been abolished in Mexico and deserted American officers they served to become free men in Mexico. Desertions became so high, many military leaders considered switching to white servants, though they never acted on the idea.

The Mexican military included many people of African ancestry. The ranks of the armies during the WAR OF MEXICAN INDEPENDENCE, 1810–21, had been disproportionately filled by people of African descent, as had the prewar colonial MILITIAS. The descendants of these soldiers still filled the ranks of the regular Mexican armed forces a quarter-century later. This was especially true in the areas where Afro-Mexicans were numerous. In areas attacked by the Americans—in particular the states of Nuevo Leon and Tamulipas along the border with Texas and the region around Veracruz where the American invasion force landed—the local defense forces included many Afro-Mexicans. Afro-Mexicans served in the regular Mexican armed forces as a career, and indeed Mexico was fast developing a separate military class at this time, with an increasing sense of national patriotism and professional pride. The local defense forces were often more motivated by desire to protect their own homes and unwilling to fight in neighboring states. Some of the free colored local militiamen from northern Mexico proved especially difficult for the Americans to overcome at the Battle of Monterey as they were afraid of RE-ENSLAVEMENT. There is no record that Afro-Mexican prisoners were treated in any way differently than other Mexicans captured by the Americans, although Texas masters whose slaves had run away to Mexico apparently took advantage of the American capture of the border region to seek their escaped "property." Unlike the unfortunate case of the San Patricio prisoners, white Catholic Americans who deserted to Mexico and who were hanged on recapture, the few runaways who were recaptured were put back to work as slaves.

The Treaty of Guadalupe Hidalgo and the War's Aftermath

President Polk dispatched Nicholas Trist to Mexico to negotiate the Treaty of Guadalupe Hidalgo. After some setbacks, Trist and the Mexican government agreed on the conditions of the treaty on February 2, 1848. First, the Mexican government ceded the New Mexico Territories and California to the United States, known as the Mexican Cession. Second, the treaty agreed on the border between the two nations as the Rio Grande. In exchange, American leaders paid $15 million for war damages and assumed $3.25 million in damage claims against the Mexican government. Finally, American officials agreed to grant citizenship to Mexican citizens within the Mexican Cession. One consequence of this provision of the treaty was that Afro-Mexicans in the ceded territories also gained citizenship, and subsequently, Afro-Mexicans in California and the Southwest suffered less discrimination than African Americans from other parts of the country. The U.S. Senate ratified the treaty on March 2, 1848, with the Mexican Congress following suit on May 19, 1848. In the United States, the acquisition of the Mexican Cession exacerbated preexisting issues surrounding the institution of slavery. As Americans poured westward into New Mexico, and especially California, disputes over whether or not to expand slavery caused a series of crises, starting in 1850. The resulting Compromise of 1850 failed to address the issues surrounding slavery and expansion, serving only further to divide a sectionalized nation and push the United States closer to civil war.

Robert Little

FURTHER READING

Bardhan-Quallen, Sudipta. *The Mexican-American War.* Detroit: Blackbirch Press, 2005.

Carey, Charles W., Jr. *The Mexican-American War: "Mr. Polk's War."* Berkley Heights, N.J.: Enslow, 2002.

Francavíglia, Richard, and Douglas W. Richmond. *Dueling Eagles: Reinterpreting the Mexican-American War.* Fort Worth: Texas Christian University Press, 2000.

Frazier, Donald S., ed. *The United States and Mexico at War: Nineteenth-Century Expansionism and Conflict.* New York: Macmillan Reference USA, 1998.

Henderson, Timothy J. *A Glorious Defeat: Mexico and Its War with the United States.* New York: Hill & Wang, 2008.

Mahin, Dean B. *Olive Branch and Sword: The United States and Mexico, 1845–1848.* Jefferson, N.C.: McFarland, 1997.

Mills, Bronwyn. *U.S.-Mexican War.* New York: Facts On File, 2003.

Moreno, Luis Gerardo, Jesus Velasco Marques, and Krystyna Libura, eds. *Echoes of the Mexican-American War.* Toronto: Groundwork Books, 2005.

Sylvester, Melvin. "African-American Freedom Fighters: Soldiers for Liberty." C. W. Post Campus of Long Island University, February, 1995. Available online. URL: http://www.liu.edu/cwis/cwp/library/aaffsfl.htm#MEXICAN. Accessed January 3, 2011.

Wheelan, Joseph. *Invading Mexico: America's Continental Dream and the Mexican-American War, 1846–1848.* New York: Public Affairs, 2007.

Winders, Bruce. *Mr. Polk's Army: The American Military Experience in the Mexican-American War.* College Station: Texas A&M University Press, 1997.

MEXICO

The geography of Mexico varies widely from region to region. Before the Spaniards arrived in the early 16th century, there were a wide variety of native cultures. The central-northern region, including modern TEXAS, Arizona, and New Mexico, was populated by nomadic tribes who ranged across the northern tier of states of modern Mexico, from the Atlantic to the Pacific coast. They were hunters and gatherers, called *chichimecas* (barbarians) by their more civilized neighbors. The central fertile lands in the valleys between the two mountain chains were inhabited by ethnic groups organized as kingdoms, and at the time of first contact with Europeans, the Mexica, or Aztecs, influenced or controlled most of this region. The Mexica extended their control to both coasts. In the South, in the humid tropical region of the Yucatán Peninsula and extending into modern GUATEMALA and HONDURAS were found the kingdoms of the Maya that at different stages dominated much of the southern part of the country. Both the Mexica and the Maya were urban civilizations, with dense populations and hierarchical societies.

Conquest (1519–1550)

The encounter of European, African, and American civilizations started on the mainland by 1519, and the results were disastrous for the local inhabitants: war, sickness, and cultural rupture. The population suffered an incalculable loss of lives that took centuries to recover. This defeat led to the growth of a new population descended, at least in part, from people from Europe, Africa, and Asia.

With the Spanish conquering army arrived a number of Africans serving as soldiers and officers' servants, of whom the best known is JUAN GARRIDO, who became one of the first free men of African ancestry to live in North America. His military reputation entitled him to a high position in Mexico City's social hierarchy, as a *vecino*, or citizen, of the city. There were probably few free people of African descent in the early conquest period, but they are distinguishable in other activities not related to the military. For example, ESTÉBAN DE DORANTES was a Moroccan-born black who accompanied Alvar Nuñez Cabeza de Vaca (1490–1559) in his epic voyage from FLORIDA across the future territories of the United States and Mexico to what is now the northwestern state of Sonora, where they met Spanish from Mexico. Without Dorantes's aid, Cabeza de Vaca would surely have died on his voyage. Dorantes then served Francisco Vásquez de Coronado (1510–54) as his chief scout on his exploration of what is now the American West.

Racial lines in the conquest period were very blurred, and many Afro-Mexicans such as Garrido were able to become influential citizens. Even slaves were important people as they were often used as supervisors of Indian laborers. Many of them were able to marry Indian women and head mixed-race families. With growing importation of slaves, however, and the general increase in government control associated with the New Laws of the Indies, racial discrimination increased, and Afro-Mexicans became a distinct, lower racial caste in Mexican colonial society.

Viceregal Period (1550–1810)

Starting in the mid-16th century and continuing until the outbreak of the WAR OF MEXICAN INDEPENDENCE, 1810–21, Portuguese merchants introduced approximately 225,000 African slaves to New Spain. Some of these slaves were forced to work on sugarcane haciendas. Others of these Africans were employed in wealthy Spaniards' houses located in urban areas; there they performed domestic services including the care of the transporta-

Father Miguel Hidalgo y Costilla, Mexican priest and revolutionary. Before the outbreak of the Mexican War of Independence, Hidalgo was rector of a seminary that accepted free colored students who wanted to study for the priesthood. One student was Hidalgo's successor as leader of the pro-independence forces, father José María Morelos. *(The Granger Collection, New York)*

tion facilities such as carriages and horses of the house. Still others worked as ARTISANS or supervisors of Indians employed under the *encomienda* system. The African societies slaves were originally technologically much more advanced than native populations, and they were often used as technical specialists. This environment gave the slaves relative autonomy to move around and the opportunity to socialize and, on occasion, accumulate economic resources to save and buy their freedom. Another important way in which the slaves achieved freedom was to be given it in their masters' wills. With a variety of avenues to become free men or women, judicial appeals were perhaps the most common, with slaves claiming mistreatment, mistakes in registration of their free status, or contracts to grant them their freedom. Slaves did not win very often, but they did sometimes convince courts to grant them their freedom. In addition, it is not rare to find baptismal records where priests, either sympathetic to slaves' desire for freedom or perhaps in return for some payment by the parents or sponsors, recorded the children of slaves as free people—presumably with the

permission of their masters but without fulfilling any of the formalities supposedly required by the government. Frequently in such baptisms the parties in the ceremony were members of the same CASTA, or mixed-race group; endogamy was distinctive in mixed-race groups, especially in their dealings with the religious authorities, as the parochial records show.

These conditions gave a particular tone to the urban population of color during the colonial period. It is important to understand the population distribution in the Spanish city designs. Around the main plaza where the public and religious buildings were located also lived the elites. To think of the cities' populations in concentric circles, the free colored *castas* (mulattoes, PARDOS, etc.) were located in the second of these. The natives and those slaves who were allowed to seek work on their own account, paying a sort of "rent" to their masters (*see also* LIVING "AS FREE"), occupied the outer rings. In cities where manufacturing industries were important and free men of color were employed in them, it is frequent to find "barrios" where the free colored community was more visible. This was the case of the Mexico City neighborhood Calle de Plateros (Silversmith's Street), as free Afro-Mexicans were well represented in this craft. Unlike the natives, free people of color often worked in more specialized trades in industries such as textiles. This landscape can be found in major cities of the period such as Guadalajara, Guanajuato, or Querétaro, all located in Central Mexico. Some other smaller towns also hosted free people of color, in many cases employees in the mining sector that at the time was the most important part of the colony's economy. Commonly among free people of color residing in cities were those who gained their freedom after serving as cowboys in the extensive ranches of the central and northern regions (*see also* RANCHING). In this line of work, many were able to take advantage of their relatively autonomous job assignments to acquire resources and purchase their freedom.

Free people of mixed race living in the predominantly rural areas in Central and northern Mexico often worked in independent activities rather than in commercial or family agriculture. Some of these economic activities were linked to fisheries or salt manufacture and distribution. Another common activity was mule train operation, which carried goods to the cities of the Central region from the Caribbean port city of Veracruz or from the Pacific port city of Acapulco. Veracruz and Acapulco connected Mexico with, respectively, Europe and the Far East and served as crucial links in the Spanish global trade networks. They were the most common workers in this essential trade, which also gave them the opportunity to serve as town criers and give public comic and topical performances in the roads and markets. The trans-Pacific trade was very important to Mexico's economy, and the disproportionately important role that free coloreds played in this sector of the economy magnified their impact on the society as a whole.

Military service was one important way in which a great number of free people of color gained their liberty and a social position within the institutional development of the viceregal state. After the end of the period of conquest in the mid-16th century and the incorporation of former conquistadores in civil life, defense and POLICE activities were sustained by private collaborations that made them a very costly activity that absorbed large amounts of capital. At the early stages of the development of the colony of New Spain, the flight of slaves and the establishment of communities of MAROONS (cimarronaje) were constant problems for merchants and SLAVE OWNERS. The coincidence of these two elements led to a solution convenient to both groups: the pacification of the escaped slaves by recognizing their armed bands as official cavalry regiments of the colony's MILITIA and giving their settlements status as military colonies with special legal rights and responsibilities to provide armed forces to the government at need. This action was similar to steps taken with maroon communities throughout the Americas. It was not uncommon for local officials, overwhelmed by the problem posed by RUNAWAY SLAVES, to use a strategy of divide and conquer, offering freedom and recognition to some in return for their help against other enemies. The pacification and incorporation of the maroon communities allowed the government to establish civil authority in territories where they were settled and, in addition to their military activities against unassimilated maroons and Indians, to allow the government to Christianize them and assimilate them in the society. At the beginning, a white person was named to act as the responsible party for the political activities of the maroon communities, but as time passed, MISCEGENATION with whites and Indians and migration allowed the citizens of these towns to redefine themselves racially as mestizos, or people of mixed Indian and white ancestry, connecting their racial identity to national ideas of assimilation. Villages in today's states of Veracruz, Tabasco, and Guerrero were born of this process. In particular, the mobility of these Afro-Mexicans, equipped with horses and skilled in desert and wilderness life, allowed them to act as cowboys on ranches, as well as temporary agricultural workers on plantations such as the tobacco and COFFEE CULTIVATION plantations in the Veracruz highlands.

In coastal regions of the Gulf of Mexico and south of Veracruz, the tropical climate favors the cultivation of products such as cacao. This product gave employment opportunities to the free people of color of the region both as contract laborers and as farmers. In southern regions, such as the Yucatán Peninsula (contemporary Yucatán and Campeche states), in rural areas they tended to blend into the native population. They were more obvious in the cities of the southern part of the country and ports such as the fortified city of Campeche, where their presence was notable in handicraft manufactures and as general laborers. Free people of color were preferred for dock work and other activities of this nature. Within the city of Veracruz, a fortified city that was perhaps the most important in New Spain because of the volume of the commerce moved through its docks, were a number of businesses dedicated to supplying ships arriving and departing. They needed food supplies for their long journeys, such as preserved bread and chocolates. These two products were manufactured in the city, and accordingly, during the 16th–18th centuries, censuses show that free people of color occupied an important number of positions in those economic establishments.

North beyond the chichimeca frontier, up to CALIFORNIA, Durango, and Chihuahua Provinces, the predominant landform was desert. With modest supplies of water the mining and ranching activities supported a reduced, but always present population of mulattoes, pardos, and other Afro-descended people. To the east, in the territories looking toward the Gulf Coast, the frontier of Spaniards, British, and later North Americans witnessed the growth of a group of free people of color who originated as maroons escaping from plantations and cattle ranches in LOUISIANA and Texas. Spanish law admitted and protected them, granting them freedom and on occasion some land. Spanish authorities thought this a good strategy for an area of low population density, and it was similar to the strategy adopted by the colonial government of SANTO DOMINGO toward runaway slaves from neighboring SAINT-DOMINGUE, and by officials in Spanish FLORIDA toward blacks fleeing the U.S. territories to the north.

Colonial Society and Free People of Color

During the conquest period, through the mid-16th century, miscegenation among Africans, whites, and native people was common because of native population decline and the large percentage of men among the new slaves from Africa and immigrants from Europe. In time, however, as populations stabilized, this profile changed to a more endogamous marriage practice that favored the preservation of an Afro-mestizo grouping. This meant that even though there was a large Indian population, Afro-Mexican families remained a distinct minority. Today the phenomenon is well known, especially in rural areas where native Indian and Afro-descended communities live harmoniously but separated by cultural preferences and personal identification. In the cities, assimilation through race mixing was a stronger cultural value in the colonial period, but the African-descended and European-Indian-descended mestizo populations remained distinct.

According to the accepted principle in many African cultures, women were the culture carriers. Thus, Afro-mestizas formed a feminine culture that, in Hispanic America, left them to face a dilemma between adapting their culture, customs, and even sexuality or shocking Western precepts. This was especially true because many of their cultural values confronted values associated with Christianity and reinforced by the Spanish state that were central to expected moral behavior. From the very beginning, the friars responsible for overseeing the free people of color picture them as having "*licenciosas y desvergonzadas*" (pervasive and licentious) sexual and family practices that Christian teaching opposed (*see also* DOMINICANS). Constant reports from diverse travelers at almost all times during the colonial period draw attention to free coloreds' clothing as an aspect of their violation of colonial mores. For example, Gemelli Carreri, a 17th-century Italian visitor, in a very sharp observation tells us that mulattas, mestizas, and *negras* were forbidden to use Spanish fashion and rejected indigenous costumes; instead, they created a colorful and practical style of skirts and overalls. These styles, because the design and use of the colors recalled African customs, were considered scandalous by opinion leaders in Mexican society. Thomas Gage (1597–1656), an English Dominican friar who visited Mexico and who later converted to Puritan Protestantism, criticized free coloreds' use of jewelry as pretentious and exaggerated. He also described them as lascivious, while recognizing virtues of determination and hard work in their character.

The ROMAN CATHOLIC CHURCH was an important institution that directed and reinforced the social behavior in colonial society. Required religious activities went further than simple Mass attendance to fall into more complex actions such as choosing a patron saint and celebrating processions on the saint's holy day. Organizations called *cofradías* (*see also* CATHOLIC CONFRATERNITIES) went beyond religious activities to plunge into social and economic service. The participants in these groups were commonly free blacks, but slaves were also admitted. The Cofradías de Negros y Mulatos are ancestors of many similar organizations of mutual aid clubs interested in the welfare of Afro-descended people in the Americas. It was not necessary that a church be dedicated to a specific saint, but many of the most popular churches among free people of color venerated saints such as Benito de Palermo (1526–89) a black Italian 16th-century Franciscan friar and saint who was well known and venerated in New Spain. Another well-known saint was Saint MARTÍN DE PORRES, a Peruvian Dominican friar who was the son of a Spaniard and a free black.

As institutions, the religious orders received the benefit of being associated with African-descended saints, but the Mexican provinces never accepted any Mexican free people of color into full membership in their orders during the colonial period. As far as we can tell, the only blacks who were full members of the missions were Europeans or Africans. In the early years, they were from PORTUGAL, which had contacts with Africa going back to the mid-15th century. Some of their missions had integrated natives to preach the gospel more effectively. Some of them reached Hispanic-American territory. Seminaries received and ordained some of them as priests. In the late 18th and early 19th centuries, men of color could more freely join the church as priests and some had distinguished careers.

The Colonial Economy
For free colored children, one common way to learn work skills and enter a trade was to join a craft master's workshop. With an agreement validated by a notary, they were supposed to work for a number of years until they were considered capable of performing the work on their own. Children could sign apprenticeship contracts beginning at age seven, and the agreements typically lasted for about another seven years, sometimes more, depending on the specific occupation. Free colored children could apprentice for all industrial jobs as *obrajeros* (textile workers) and many other manufacturing trades, or in artistic trades (as painters, for example), and those who showed talent were often accepted. Since the law specifically forbade them to hold the same occupational titles as whites, it was the practice to redesignate their positions. Commonly, a worker without a formal occupational title, established independently, served more clients than a white worker who was formally recognized, and thus his or her business was more profitable. The guilds were naturally opposed to this but had trouble finding a way legally to incorporate free people of color in their structures. As many as one-third of free manufacturing workers were of African descent in the 18th century.

Regardless of the legal sanctions that forbade free men of color to obtain titles as masters of the different guilds, they did practice the crafts and in fact their roles were recognized: Free colored silversmiths were a distinctive group in Mexico City, and several painters received orders from church authorities to decorate religious edifices. Sacred art was a favored specialty during the 17th century; JUAN CORREA is perhaps the best known of these artists. Son of a barber and a *flebotómano* (a healing practitioner who extracted blood as a healing procedure), who was a free *MULATTO*, he worked on the altar panels of churches and painted a number of biblical representations considered classic masterpieces of the 17th-century high baroque. Also with the protection of the church, church musicians, choirs, and soloists were recognized because of their abilities.

The free colored MILITIA played a significant social role during the two and a half centuries after the conquest. Free men of color were distinguished not only by military honors but by the social prestige gained through service. After the Bourbon Reforms of the military during the 18th century, a good number of militia regiments (including *pardo* and *moreno* militias) were called into active service in different parts of the viceroyalty because of the British threat after the invasion of Havana. The lancer regiments, many of them descended institutionally from the maroon militia cavalry units created in the previous century, who were sent to defend the city of Veracruz and its vicinity illustrated institutional recognition of the value of free colored soldiers. The rest of the REGULAR ARMY regiments assigned to defend New Spain during the SEVEN YEARS' WAR were racially integrated with Spaniards and white creole Americans serving alongside people of color; an analysis of their personnel has shown that more than half of them were Afro-mestizos. The Spanish NAVY experienced a similar process, as ships assigned for long periods to ports in the Americas often had free men of color disproportionately represented among their crew. Institutions such as the militia, the military, and the church became an important step on a course to a better life because of the immunities they offered to legal discrimination and because of the social prestige they conferred. Members of these institutions benefited from *fueros*, which were legal immunities allowing them special legal protections not offered to ordinary civilians. These legal privileges were sometimes undermined but often served to protect free people of color from legal discrimination.

A very important social development took place at the time of the Bourbon administrative reforms of Charles III (r. 1759–88) and Charles IV (r. 1788–1808) during the last years of the old regime. This was the identification of all Crown subjects according to their phenotype and economic position, what was considered their *"calidad"* (quality). For all African descendants and Afro-mestizos, this definition was made without regard to their legal status (as free or slave). This official racial classification provided the motivation for creative bureaucratic artists who painted the famous *casta* paintings that represent all imagined race mixtures, often with eccentric names that never were used in legal or institutional activities such as censuses or baptismal registers. The moral and psychological traits assigned to these different mixtures, however, give insight into the evolving idea of race in Spanish America. The greater degree and bureaucratization of definitions of racial groups imposed hardships on the Afro-mestizo population and made social promotion more difficult. The Spanish monarchy also offered formal dispensations of *casta* status to light-skinned and upper-class Afro-mestizos through the institution of *cédulas de gracias al sacar* during the Bourbon Reforms, but these were not often granted in New Spain (*see also* "WHITENING" AND RACIAL PROMOTION).

As the colonial period progressed, the demand for slaves in Mexico slackened. Indian populations began to grow again after the end of the 16th century, and Indians were now able to perform the technologically sophisticated tasks that had once been reserved for slaves. One source of the free colored Mexican population during the colonial period was the arrival of servants and some other specialists in the arts. For example, Luis Barreto entered Mexico a slave, became free at the end of the 16th century, and as a free person of color worked as a tenor for the Mexico City cathedral choir. Another source was the migration from the Anglo-American colonies to the north discussed earlier. One famous group who benefited from the Crown policy of encouraging immigration of blacks from the North were the BLACK SEMINOLE, known in Mexico as the Mascogos. This group, driven from Florida to OKLAHOMA because of their Indian heritage, then found themselves discriminated against because of their African ancestry and decided to go to Mexico in 1850. Living in Coahuila, some of their number returned to America after the AMERICAN CIVIL WAR and served as scouts for the U.S. military on the frontier, while others remained in Mexico, where their descendants live to this day. The history of Mexican Texas and the oppression of free blacks there after the territory gained independence from Mexico also helps to explain the presence of free people of color in ranching in northern Mexico. They appear as owners as well as servants.

Independence (1810–1900)

Miguel Hidalgo's (1753–1811) armed uprising of September 1810 in the city of Dolores put forward a demand not only to erase social differences between the races but to abolish the *casta* system and slavery entirely. An important number of slaves, whom the rebels had proclaimed free, and free people of color joined his army. The free colored component of the army increased in number and gained a mulatto identity when the free colored priest JOSÉ MARÍA MORELOS joined the movement in 1811. He led free people of color from the coastal lands of the Pacific where Morelos resided and worked as a muleteer before studying for the priesthood. Free people of color recognized him as one of them. On the side of the royalist army, the *pardo* and mulatto battalions that had

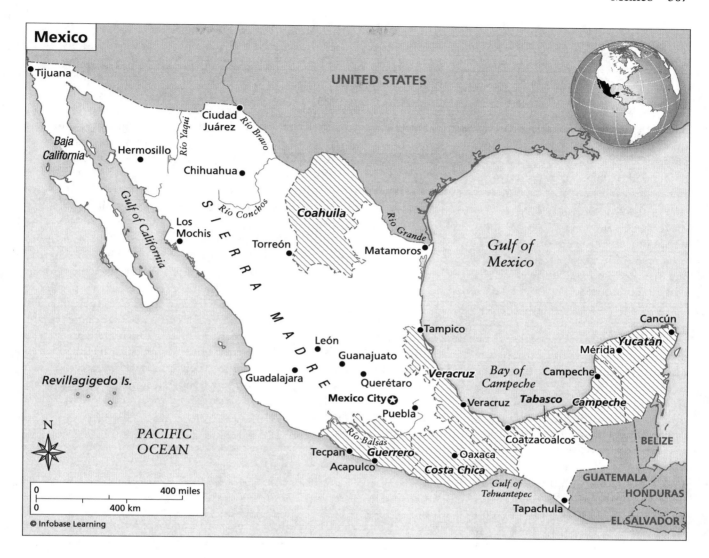

received military training during the Bourbon Reforms were instructed to fight alongside regular army units that also included large numbers of free colored men. As was also common throughout Spanish America, native people never served in important numbers in the structured militias, which were primarily composed of white or mixed-race soldiers. Because of the numerical superiority of Indians, Spaniards generally considered them as a menace to their security and did not wish to rely on them for military service.

At the same time as Hidalgo's rebellion was beginning, delegates from New Spain, elsewhere in the Americas, the Philippines, and other Spanish colonies were meeting with Spanish representatives in the Cortes of Cádiz, which opened September 24, 1810, and governed Spain until 1814. Historians have seen the Cortes as an early step toward liberalism and modern ideas of government in Spain. One of the first matters to be debated was abolition of the African slave trade and slavery. The Mexi-

can representatives offered a plan clearly conciliatory to the interests of all parties. It proposed the end of slave trade and the freedom of the womb, that is, the progressive abolition of slavery by declaring all persons born after a certain date free. Debate was postponed because Spanish and creole Caribbean representatives wanted to protect slavery and because the issue was complicated by the debate over giving political recognition to Afro-descended people citizenship with all its political and social rights and recognition. If the Afro-descended people were granted political recognition, by representation, this would increase the population of the Americas, which would surpass the population in Spain and thus give control of the government of the entire empire to the Americans. The Spanish did not want to cede political control of their empire and saw Spain as the most important part of the empire because of the war against Napoléon. Therefore, the grant of political rights to Afro-descended people was rejected. From the perspective of the majority of Afro-descended Spanish Americans, the 1812 Constitution and the dream of a unified constitutional empire lost all appeal as a result.

The political recognition and rights of African-descended people were then a matter for Americans to resolve and were addressed in the constitution of each one of the newborn countries. In Mexico, the participation of Afro-Mexicans in the independence movement, where all the competing armies integrated African-descended people, led to an Afro-mestizo leadership at the highest levels of the administration and organization of the republic.

The best-known free colored figures of the independence movement are Morelos and VICENTE GUERRERO SALDAÑA. Morelos was in charge of the southern liberation army. He inherited the leadership of the movement when Hidalgo was captured. Imprisoned himself later, he made profound political reflections in the discourse known as "Sentimientos de la Nación" (National feelings), which contain the basis of the egalitarian Mexican constitution of 1824. Born in Tecpan, Vicente Guerrero, also a muleteer, inherited from Morelos the leadership of the southern armies after Morelos was imprisoned in 1816. In 1821, Guerrero joined the loyalist armies and formed the "Ejército Trigarante" (Three Guaranties Army), which took control of Mexico City in 1821 and ended the War of Independence with a qualified victory—Mexico became independent as a monarchy under Emperor Agustín I (1783–1824). Guerrero ultimately cooperated with liberal forces to overthrow the empire in 1823 and establish a constitutional republic. He was elected president of the republic in April 1829 and, as a result of political instability, deposed in December of the same year. During his brief period in power, he decreed the final and immediate abolition of slavery in Mexico. It took some years for this decree to take full effect throughout the national territory, but by the late 1830s, all Afro-Mexicans were free.

As elsewhere in Spanish America, free Afro-Mexicans were mainly integrated over the following century in the larger mestizo population. Many Mexicans have African ancestors today, but few recognize or value this fact. The few identifiable communities of Afro-Mexicans who remain are descended from recent immigrants, such as the Mascogo/black Seminole or others who fled the U.S. Southern states and settled in northern Mexico, and the descendants of slaves imported in the last years of Spanish rule to develop a plantation sector along the Gulf Coast in Veracruz and the Pacific coast in the region known as the Costa Chica. Throughout the 19th century, however, Afro-Mexicans continued to play an important role in the armed forces of the new republic, serving in disproportionate numbers. The Mexican armies that fought the North American invaders in 1845–48 (see also MEXICAN-AMERICAN WAR) had many black soldiers. North American SLAVE OWNERS accompanied the invading armies into northern Mexico, looking for "their" RUNAWAY SLAVES among the Mexican prisoners. Some Afro-Mexicans were sent into slavery in the United States, but the Mexican government did its best to protect its people through the provision of the Treaty of Guadalupe Hidalgo that required the return of prisoners of war.

Africans and their descendants formed along with indigenous people and Europeans the profile of the Mexican nation. Originating from a few hundred thousand immigrants—substantially smaller than the number of blacks imported to CUBA or the United States—they became through miscegenation a definite element of the Mexican identity. Their cultural influence was greater in Mexico because of the wide variety of roles they played in the country's society. When compared with neighboring countries, Afro-Mexicans filled a much greater diversity of social and economic roles. Biological and cultural mixture at once multiplied their impact on Mexican society and diluted it, to the extent that modern Mexicans are only now rediscovering this important element of their national identity.

Juan Manuel de la Serna

FURTHER READING

Benett, Herman. *Africans in Colonial Mexico: Absolutism, Christianity, and Afro-Creole Consciousness, 1570–1640.* Bloomington: Indiana University Press, 2003.

Bethel, Leslie. *The Cambridge History of Latin America.* Vol. 2, *Colonial Latin America.* Cambridge: Cambridge University Press, 1998.

Caroll, Patrick. *Blacks in Colonial Veracruz: Race, Ethnicity, and Regional Development.* Austin: University of Texas Press, 2001.

El Colegio de México. *Historia general de México.* Mexico: El Colegio de México, 2000.

Hernández, Chávez Alicia. *Mexico: A Brief History.* Translated by Andy Klatt. Berkeley: University of California Press, 2006.

MacLachlan, Colin, and William H. Beezley. *El Gran Pueblo: A History of Greater Mexico.* Upper Saddle River, N.J.: Prentice Hall, 2004.

Meyer, Michael C., and William H. Beezley. *The Oxford History of Mexico.* New York: Oxford University Press, 2000.

Vinson, Ben III, and Matthew Restall, eds. *Black Mexico: Race and Society from Colonial to Modern Times.* Albuquerque: University of New Mexico Press, 2009.

Von Germeten, Nicole. *Black Blood Brothers: Confraternities and Social Mobility for Afro-Mexicans.* Gainesville: University Press of Florida, 2006.

POLITICAL ESSAY ON THE KINGDOM OF NEW SPAIN, BY ALEXANDER VON HUMBOLDT, TRANSLATED BY JOHN BLACK (1811)

The document that follows is the viewpoint of an exceptionally talented scientist of the early 19th century on the racial characteristics of the people of Mexico. Born in 1769, Alexander von Humboldt was Prussian and had had almost no actual contact with people of color before embarking on his expedition to the Americas in 1799. Although he had studied under a man who had traveled with Captain Cook, he was unprepared for the great human diversity he would encounter when he arrived in the Western Hemisphere. His point of view was informed by the emerging idea of speciation among animals, that is, that individuals could be assigned to a grouping on the basis of their appearance and behavior. Humboldt's work in classifying the animals of South America was a necessary precursor to Charles Darwin's work, and Darwin himself referred over and over again to Humboldt's work in his On the Origin of Species. *To some extent, Humboldt was fitting what he could observe about human beings into the taxonomic ideas he was developing about animals. In this, he represents the classifying and rationalistic spirit of the Enlightenment. He also reflected to some extent the attitudes of the (mostly) white intellectual class of Spanish America that he worked with during his voyage. He had a fine ear for the prejudice of those he worked with, however, as can be seen in the following selection from his* Political Essay on the Kingdom of New Spain, *written in 1811. In ascribing behavioral characteristics to the mulatto, as he does at one point, he presages the 19th-century field of racial anthropology, a science then in its infancy, which was to become quite influential by the mid-19th century, thanks in part to the contributions of naturalists such as Humboldt.*

To complete the table of the elements of which the Mexican population is composed, it remains for us to point out rapidly the differences of caste which spring from the mixture of the pure races with one another. These castes constitute a mass almost as considerable as the Mexican Indians. We may estimate the total of the individuals of mixed blood at nearly 2,400,000. From a refinement of vanity, the inhabitants of the colonies have enriched their language with terms for the finest shades of the colors which result from the degeneration of the primitive color. It may be useful to explain these denominations because they have been confounded by many travelers and because this confusion frequently causes no small embarrassment to those who read Spanish works on the American possessions.

The son of a white (creole or European) and a native of copper color is called mestizo. His color is almost a pure white, and his skin is of a particular transparency. The small beard and small hands and feet, and a certain obliquity of the eyes, are more frequent indications of the mixture of Indian blood than the nature of the hair. If a mestiza marry a white man, the second generation differs hardly in anything from the European race. As very few Negroes have been introduced into New Spain, the mestizos probably compose 7/8 of the whole castes. They are generally accounted of a much more mild character than the mulattos, descended from whites and Negresses, who are distinguished for the violence of their passions and a singular volubility of tongue. The descendants of Negroes and Indian women bear the strange name of *Chino,* Chinese. On the coast of Caracas and, as appears from the laws, even in New Spain, they ate called zambos. This last denomination is now principally limited to the descendants of a Negro and a female mulatto, or a Negro and a Chinese female. From these common zambos they distinguish the zambos prietos who descend from a Negro and a female zamba. From the mixture of a white man with a mulatto comes the cast of *cuarterón.* When a female *cuarterón* marries a European or creole, her son bears the name of *quinterón.* A new alliance with a white banishes to such a degree the remains of color that the children of a white and a *quinterón* are white also.

In a country governed by whites, the families reputed to have the least mixture of Negro or mulatto blood are also naturally the most honored. In Spain it is almost a title of nobility to descend neither from Jews nor Moors. In America the greater or less degree of whiteness of skin decides the rank which man occupies in society. A white who rides barefooted on horseback thinks he belongs to the nobility of the country. Color establishes even a certain equality among men who, as is universally the case where civilization is either little advanced or in a retrograde state, take a particular pleasure in dwelling on the prerogatives of race and origin. When a commoner is in a dispute with one of the titled lords of the country, he is frequently heard to say, "Do you think me not so white as yourself?" This may serve to characterize the state and source of the actual aristocracy. It becomes, consequently, a very interesting business for the Public vanity to estimate accurately the fractions of European blood which belong to the different castes. It often happens that families suspected of being of mixed blood demand from the high court of justice a declaration that they belong to the whites. These declarations are not always corroborated by the judgment of the senses. We see very swarthy mulattoes who have had the address to get themselves "whitened" (this is the vulgar expression). When the color of the skin is too repugnant to the judgment demanded, the petitioner is contented with an expression somewhat problematical—"that such or such individuals may consider themselves as whites."

Source: http://web.grinnell.edu/courses/HIS/f01/HIS202-01/Documents/HumbSoc.html.

MEXICO, ABOLITION OF SLAVERY IN
(1821–1829)

The abolition of slavery in Mexico occurred in stages. The first was initiated by Miguel Hidalgo's independence proclamation in Dolores (Guanajuato) on September 16, 1810. In that proclamation, Hidalgo called on all SLAVE OWNERS to free their slaves. In a similar document issued in the city of Guadalajara in October of the same year, the order was repeated with the admonition that those who disobeyed it would be shot.

Eleven years later, when Mexico achieved its independence from Spain after a long armed struggle, the movement turned to a political stage. Some of the most prominent and illustrious members of society (some of whom had European and more specifically British experience) were called to prepare a document that was first proclaimed as a judicial advisory opinion. The government established in 1821 was an empire, under Emperor Agustin I, and that is why the text reproduced in the following refers to the imperial government. Drafted on October 24, 1821, this decision looked toward the abolition of slavery, though in a manner intended to assuage proprietor interests. The decision was accepted and ratified by the first Mexican Constitution of 1824.

Judicial Opinion pronounced on diverse dispositions of the life of the slaves in the country of Mexico. Among others things touching the subject of the freedom of the womb favoring newborns, and also for those slaves brought into the national territory. [Date] 24 October, 1821 [Place] Mexico City [Signed] Members in charge of the "Comisión Dictaminadora" (Judicial Council): Juan Francisco de Azcarate, Jose Maria Fagoaga, Francisco Manuel Sanchez de Tagle, Antonio de Gama and Cordoba, The Count of the House of Heras Grove.

First. The introduction of slaves into the Empire is not permitted, either by sea or by land; and in the case of verifying that this has occurred, the subject will be free by virtue of the act: the law in this event does not recognize any right of dominion of the owner.

Second. The foreigner who will bring a slave or slaves for his service into the territory of the Empire, during his residence in it will not treat them as slaves, nor sell them; and if at the departure of the foreign resident the slaves' will is to remain, they will be protected by the law of asylum.

Third. In order to prevent any fraud that can be done [by claiming] that a slave is returning to the country [after being taken out by a Mexican owner] who was a slave at his departure: everyone who owns a slave, must register them and present a list to the City Councils . . . within the term of a month counting

from the publication of this decree. The City Councils will keep record of it in case it is needed.

Fourth. In deference to the property [right] of the owners of slaves who currently reside in the Empire, they will hold these in slavery for the time being. The Provincial Delegations, consulting with the City Councils, and with the intervention of the [national] government will choose advisable means to redeem them from slavery in justice and respect for the laws. Counting on the philanthropy of the owners . . . they should reduce the price in whole or in part in agreement [with the slaves and the local government]. The City Councils should transmit the names of those slaves [gaining freedom] from their respective territories to the Delegations and the Government.

Fifth. The City Councils will try to persuade the redeemed slaves not to abandon the property on which they are located, but voluntarily remain on them [and continue to work for their former owners] until their employers have the necessary laborers to replace them, being pleased with a respectable wage; they should be treated with moderation and benevolence by all other employees and supervisors.

Sixth. Any person born from the 24th of February of the present year [1821] is free, and in this part the law is retroactive. The City Councils should prepare rolls of persons born after this date separately from those born before the date of proclamation of the law, recording the information in accordance with the certainties of the baptismal registers. . . .

Seventh. [Chartered] Manufactures, Tlalpisqueras and offices as well as bakeries, pork butchers and other establishments of this class under whatever name, are abolished [those that operate using indentured or peon labor and claimed that their charters, contracts with workers, or debts by workers permitted them to continue holding people in slavery], and the law will punish those that hold free men in servitude, Even there are persons that do not recognize it, the Empire is the only public office authorized to establish the price of debts and rent services.

Eighth. The personal service of Indian citizens [the *Encomienda*] is abolished even though they [may] want to continue it voluntarily, and those who receive [*Encomienda* service] without distinction of state and condition, will be punished as provided by the laws and will pay to the Indian workers the amount that the service is evaluated at. . . .

The Constitution of 1824, however, was never fully effective throughout the national territory, and slave owners took advantage of delays in implementation, poor records, and weak government, which permitted many to defy the provisions of the judicial decision. Five years later, Mexico's first Afro-Mexican leader, VICENTE GUERRERO SALDAÑA, ended the transitional regime that the judicial decision had instituted. The Mexican Emancipation Declaration of September 15, 1829, definitively abolished slavery in Mexico.

The President of the United States of Mexico: That, desiring to celebrate in the year of 1829 the anniversary of our independence with an act of justice and national benevolence, which might result in the benefit and promotion of a good, so highly to be appreciated, which might cement more and more the public tranquility, which might reinstate an unfortunate portion of its inhabitants in the sacred rights which nature gave them, and which the nation protects by wise and just laws, in conformance with the Thirtieth Article of the Constitution, in which the use of extraordinary powers are ceded to me, I have thought it proper to decree:

1. Slavery is abolished in the republic.
2. Consequently, those who have been until now considered slaves are free.
3. When the circumstances of the treasury may permit, the owners of the slaves will be indemnified in the mode that the laws may provide.

And in order that every part of this decree may be fully complied with, let it be printed, published, and circulated.

Given at the Federal Palace of Mexico, the 15th of September, 1829.

[signed] Vicente Guerrero

Juan Manuel de la Serna

MEXICO, CENTRAL AND NORTHERN

The northern border of Mexico changed during the 19th century as a result of the MEXICAN-AMERICAN WAR of 1846–48. This article will consider the settlement and development of society throughout Mexican territory north of the Valley of Mexico, including those territories that later became part of the United States. This territory is divided first into a central part, the fertile valleys north of Mexico City that still share a climate and geography with "Mesoamerica," which developed a SUGAR CULTIVATION hacienda economy and were heavily populated by sedentary, farming Indians. Second, the far northern areas were scarcely populated, mostly by nomadic Indians accustomed to desert conditions. Mining and cattle-raising were the most important economic activities of this region.

Central Region

Sugar and grain production (maize, wheat) were the most important agricultural activities that slaves of African descent in the central region were involved in, though sugar cultivation became an important activity late in the colonial period. After leaving slavery, free Afro-Mexicans in this region were chiefly integrated into the class of PEASANTS and participated in the independence process along with their Indian or mestizo peasant neighbors in the early 19th century. Queretaro and Guanajuato during the colonial period were two of the most important and heavily populated cities of the region. Priest of orders of the ROMAN CATHOLIC CHURCH (Augustinians, DOMINICANS, and Franciscans) who served there made an intense effort to educate and integrate urban people of color. One step in this process was legalizing marriages. This led to a high degree of MISCEGENATION among Afro-Mexicans, Indians, and Spaniards that gave birth to a free mixed-race class. These mixed-race urban people were heavily involved in textile manufacturing. This was an industry that grew especially strong in the region after Mexico gained its independence in 1821 and during the 19th century and today remains strong. Even though the colonial government formally forbade Afro-Mexicans to enter the craft guilds, the humblest guilds sometimes even accepted them as masters (*see also* ARTISANS). The most common crafts that accepted free people of color were shoemakers, hat manufacturers, silversmiths, and candle makers. This was especially important in peripheral urban areas such as those in the northern region, where Spanish and mestizos were less common and central government oversight laxer.

Free people of color were very important to the textile industry. They operated the weaving machines and worked at dyeing the textiles. Indians were more commonly employed as pieceworkers, spinning the wool at their homes on contract. Even during the colonial period, when regulations theoretically forbade free people of color to work in these craft workshops, they were still an important presence, and after independence when these regulations were abolished, they became dominant in this sphere of activity.

Roman Catholic missionaries, both nuns and secular priests, often employed former slaves for personal services from the earliest days of Spanish presence in the region. Following their example, members of the local elites also employed free Afro-Mexican servants by preference, seeing them as signs of status and gentility. The status of these servants was almost that of junior members of the family, and they would often remain employed for life. These feudal ties did not exist in the same way with the indigenous peoples, who, even though they may have lived in an elite home, maintained familiar and cultural bonds with nearby Indian villages.

Northern Region

The history of Africans and their free progeny in what we consider to be the northern region of New Spain/Mexico may be divided into three areas related, as in the central region, in a socioeconomic landscape. The first zone, close to the central region described earlier, are the areas where the mining industry was strong. The most notable case would be the city of Zacatecas, perhaps the richest gold and silver mines anywhere in the Spanish Empire in the 16th and 17th centuries. There were numerous other gold and silver rushes in the region that had less or temporary success. Mining concentrated a significant amount of African slaves involved in prospecting and extractive digging. Former slaves who gained their freedom sometimes intermingled with sporadic Indian settlements and were socially accepted as part of the Indian or urban mixed-race societies. Similarly, as was true in the central region, the artisan classes in the northern cities had an African legacy mainly among the silversmiths, who manufactured common-use tableware, plates, trays, candleholders, and so on, that were not necessarily luxury items. Their importance was such that the church recognized their brotherhoods (*see* CATHOLIC CONFRATERNITIES), which were dedicated to saints of African descent, for example, the 16th-century Italian Saint Benito de Palermo, who at the time was frequently venerated where mulattoes or other free colored people were concentrated.

The second zone of the northern area is the border region that divided Spanish and North American territories. During the 18th and 19th centuries, it was a porous line that allowed easy population movements. Fugitive slaves of American owners commonly asked for asylum in New Spain, because of the Spanish policy that gave freedom to any slave who escaped from another country. This was, of course, a way to injure the enemies' interests but also resulted in a fairly large free colored population in the region. They were found in towns along the border, on ranches that needed cowboys, and also as part of a community of mixed North American nomadic Indians and African descendants. One well-documented case is of groups of Seminole Indians among whom were RUNAWAY SLAVES, settling in what is now Mexican territory (in the state of Cohuaila) who came to be known as the Mascogo Indians during the late 19th century. In the United States, they would be known as BLACK SEMINOLE, descendants of escaped African slaves who joined the Seminole Indians in FLORIDA to form a new identity. Most of the Mascogo are direct descendants of one group of black Seminole, the Seminole Negro Indian Scouts.

Among the most notorious cases of slave defection to Mexican territory was that of Samuel Houston's escaped slaves, led by Joshua Houston, who ran away and whose resistance helped lead Sam Houston to free the rest of his workforce.

And finally the important zone in the North is the one that developed in the latter half of the 19th century. This was an enormous land located in contemporary Chihuahua and Durango that was home to the biggest and most important RANCHING industry. These ranches employed many free people of color as cowboys and many women of color as domestic laborers at the ranches' main houses. There were also Afro-Mexicans employed as servants and cowboys among the middle-class ranchers who possessed small or medium cattle ranches.

Juan Manuel de la Serna

FURTHER READING

Guevara Sangines, Maria. *Guanajuato diverso: sabores y sinsabores de su ser mestizo, siglos XVI a XVII.* Guanajuato, Mexico: La Rana, 2001.

Schwartz, Rosalie. *Across the Rio to Freedom: U.S. Negroes in Mexico.* El Paso: Western Press, University of Texas at El Paso, 1975.

Tyler, Ronnie C. "Fugitive Slaves in Mexico." *Journal of Negro History* 57, no. 1 (January 1972): 1–12.

Wilkins, Ron. "Mexico's Legacy: A Refuge for Fugitive Slaves and Black Job-Seekers: New Perspectives on the Immigration Debate." *Black Commentator* 182 (May 4, 2006). Available online. URL: http://www.blackcommentator.com/182/182_mexico_black_history.html. Accessed January 3, 2011.

MEXICO, PACIFIC COAST

Since the 16th century, MEXICO's Pacific coast has housed one of the largest populations of Afro-Mexicans. Along the Costa Chica (the south coast from Acapulco to Huatulco), African slaves were assigned to herd cattle and in other labors such as gold mining, SUGAR CULTIVATION, and cacao cultivation.

The Africans mostly settled along the coast close to the sea, alongside Nahua, Mixteco, and Amuzgo native people, with whom they lived closely for centuries. In the 18th century, the free population included descendants of slaves who had intermarried with indigenous people and whites, giving birth to the PARDO and MULATTO castes that were registered in the colonial censuses.

Another stream of the free population was born of the communities of MAROONS who had preserved their freedom through the natural inaccessibility and built defenses of their settlements and the ferocity of their dwellers.

Official figures show that by the end of the Spanish colonial period, in the early 1800s, approximately 85 percent of the coastal population of color was free. Most of them were either small farmers, practicing COTTON CULTIVATION in many cases; or fishermen, cowboys, or domestic servants. Additionally, men were incorporated in provincial MILITIAS, especially the mulatto and *pardo* companies created since the Bourbon Reforms, a period of modernization of government in the mid-1700s. These groups provided the military defenders for the main ports and cities in the colony.

The role of slaves and their free descendants in the independence struggle was important for both sides. The 1810 abolition of slavery proposed by Miguel Hidalgo (1753–1811), the first leader of the independence forces in the WAR OF MEXICAN INDEPENDENCE, 1810–21, was an important factor that drew considerable contingents of people of color, free and slaves, to join revolutionary armies in order to demand freedom and equality. Leaders such as JOSÉ MARÍA MORELOS and VICENTE GUERRERO SALDAÑA—both people of African ancestry—had an enthusiastic reception in the Afro-Mexican community.

Once independence and freedom were gained in 1821, the populations of color sustained their struggle to consolidate their rights, of which land was one of the most important. Ideological currents in the 19th century were against them, however, as Mexico became dominated by positivist ideas. This was a current of liberal thought that placed individual over collective rights and saw traditional systems of landownership as obstacles to progress that needed to be obliterated. The struggle of black farmers to control their land went directly against the policy of liberal governments in the 19th century and led to loss of land and community autonomy. Racial prejudice against Afro-Mexicans also grew worse at this time, as liberal ideology identified progressive values with Western culture and saw indigenous and Afro-Mexican communities as backward and regressive.

At the beginning of the 20th century, the political and economic conditions of la Costa Chica were bumpiest. The most important landowners had accumulated huge estates, compelling the impoverished towns to work on their terms. This was one of the reasons the Afro-Mexican communities supported Zapata's movement during the Mexican Revolution. In the 1930s, the agrarian reform of President Lázaro Cárdenas reduced the landlords' power. The *ejidos* (or rural cooperatives) were created, and the government provided education and health care.

The construction of the coast road uniting Acapulco and Pinotepa finally incorporated the region in the national culture and economy. That gave a new face and more intensity to all aspects of community life. Today, the life of the Costa Chica towns is based in an agriculture and livestock economy. The crops grown in the rich lowlands are sold to external markets: lemons, coconuts, watermelon, and other tropical products. Corn is cultivated for local consumption. Fishing has become an important economic activity on the coast. The *moreno,* as Afro-Mexicans identify themselves, dominate this activity in rivers, lagoons, and sea. Its main products are fish and shrimp, which traditionally they would process with salt that they obtained from the evaporation of the lagoons in the region. Today, however, there are processing plants that are not necessarily controlled by the Afro-Mexican communities.

Over the centuries, this coastal region has given distinctive character to the national culture, not only because of its geography and history, but also in the area of ethnography. In colonial times, the architecture in the region was marked by *redondos*—circular rooms—with conical roofs, probably a sign of African influence. They were built with palms, mud, and other natural products of the region.

Contemporary festivities associated with religious cults are complex and full of symbols. The traditional parties and festivities that are common in the region are noisy and cheerful. Dance, music, and verbal arts—including a particular eloquence and speaking style—are the most distinctive traditions of the *morenos*. Among dances, the *artesa* (in which a couple dances over a hollow log), the *vaqueros* (cowboys), and the *tortuga* (the turtle) are some of the most distinctive. "Los diablitos" (little devils) is the trademark of the communal festivity of All Saints (Día de los Muertos) celebrated throughout Mexico but with distinctive accents in this region. The accompanist musicians play a harp (occasionally replaced by a harmonica), the *cajón* (wooden cube covered with goat leather), a violin, two *ideófonos* (idiophones, percussion and friction), a *charrasca* (horse or donkey jaw), and a *bote* (empty gourd covered with leather patch). These instruments are common to many other African-American populations.

At the turn of the 21st century, Afro-Mexicans have become part of an intense biological and cultural mixing produced by growing migrations to the United States. This allows cultural blending with the traditions of African Americans and with people of African descent from throughout the Americas. This cross-pollination is reflected in changing social and cultural values and modifying racial and cultural traditions in the region.

Araceli Reynoso Medina

FURTHER READING

Aguirre Beltrán, Gonzalo. *Cuijla, Esbozo etnográfico de un pueblo negro.* Col. Lecturas Mexicanas. Mexico: FCE-SEP, 1985.
Campos, Luís Eugenio. "Negros y morenos. La población afromexicana de la Costa Chica de Oaxaca." In *Configuraciones étnicas en Oaxaca. Perspectivas etnográficas para las*

autonomías. Vol. 2. Mexico City: CONACULTA-INAH-NI, 2000.

Moedano, Gabriel. "Notas etnohistóricas sobre la población negra de la Costa Chica." In *Arqueología e etnohistoria del estado de Guerrero*. Mexico: SEP-INAH-Gobierno del estado de Guerrero, 1986.

Vinson, Ben, III. "The Racial Profile of a Rural Mexican Province in the Costa Chica: Igualapa in 1791." *Americas* 57, no. 2 (October 2000): 269–282.

MICHIGAN

Michigan is a state of the United States. It is surrounded on three sides by the Great Lakes and borders INDIANA and OHIO to the south. The province of Ottawa, CANADA, is located across a river to the east. Michigan consists of two main parts: the Lower Peninsula to the south and the Upper Peninsula to the north and west. The Upper Peninsula on the north side of Lake Michigan borders WISCONSIN. The topography is relatively flat, and there are easy water routes throughout the state. The climate is cold in winter, but rainfall is plentiful. The state is well suited to agriculture. The indigenous people were agriculturalists and had a lifestyle like that of other midwestern Indians such as the Shawnee or Huron. They got along well with the first European inhabitants, the French, who traded furs and established missions in the 17th century that converted many of the Indians to the ROMAN CATHOLIC CHURCH. The largest French settlement was a small fort and village at the present site of Detroit. The territory came under British rule after the SEVEN YEARS' WAR ended in 1763. BRITAIN continued the French policy of maintaining trade relations with the Indians and limiting settlement. Although the area was formally ceded to the United States after the end of the WAR OF AMERICAN INDEPENDENCE, 1775–83, British forces remained in possession until after the War of 1812, and the United States did not establish complete control until the defeat of the Shawnee leader Tecumseh (1768–1813) in 1813.

French and British masters took small numbers of slaves into what is now Michigan during their respective colonial periods. Several free blacks lived in Detroit by the end of the 18th century. After U.S. occupation of the region in 1796, a series of conflicting laws and legal decisions began the process of eliminating slavery there. The Northwest Ordinance of 1787 had prohibited slavery north of the Ohio River; nevertheless, officials had to take into account legislation on slavery in Upper Canada (of which Michigan had been a part prior to the U.S. occupation), as well as treaties governing the U.S. occupation, which guaranteed that residents would not lose their existing property rights. Two 1807 cases clarified that slaves born in Michigan before 1793 would remain in slavery, those born between 1793 and 1796 would be free at age 25, and those born after 1796 were immediately free. The 1810 census listed 120 free blacks and 24 slaves in Michigan Territory. By the time Michigan became a state in 1837, there were only three slaves living within its borders. No slaves are listed in the 1840 census.

In the half-century before the AMERICAN CIVIL WAR, Michigan developed a reputation as a beacon of liberty on the Great Lakes. As a result, it attracted hundreds of fugitive slaves seeking freedom from bondage; many free blacks seeking equal rights and economic opportunity also flocked to the territory. In fact, the majority of African-American settlers in antebellum Michigan were free blacks. Some migrated into the region from New England and NEW YORK STATE after the opening of the Erie Canal in 1825. Beginning in the 1830s, free blacks entered in sizeable numbers from the Upper South states of VIRGINIA AND WEST VIRGINIA, NORTH CAROLINA KENTUCKY, and TENNESSEE to escape the tightening enforcement of the black codes in the wake of Nat Turner's rebellion (*see* BLACK CODES IN THE UNITED STATES). On at least one occasion, all of the slaves from a single plantation immigrated to Michigan, having been manumitted in the will of their Virginia master, Sampson Saunders. Some free blacks settled for a time in Ohio, Indiana, or ILLINOIS, before making their way on to Michigan.

Nearly half of these migrants settled in just two counties—Wayne (primarily in Detroit) in the southeast part of the state and rural Cass in the southwest part of the state. Others settled in or near smaller cities along the Territorial Road (now I-94), such as Niles, Saint Joseph, Battle Creek, Marshall, Kalamazoo, Jackson, Adrian, or Ann Arbor. By 1860, eight of 10 blacks in Michigan lived in the two lower tiers of counties in the state, within 50 miles of the border with Indiana and Ohio. Only a few hundred hardy souls ventured farther north into the remainder of Michigan's Lower Peninsula, or into the Upper Peninsula. The black population of Michigan grew rapidly during the antebellum decades, from 293 in the 1830 census, to 707 in 1840, to 2,583 in 1850, to 6,798 in 1860, the year before the American Civil War began.

In spite of the state's reputation, however, it was no racial utopia. In 1827, for example, the territorial council passed an act denying free blacks the right to settle in Michigan unless they registered with the clerk of courts in the county in which they lived and provided a certificate indicating their free status and a $500 surety bond guaranteeing their good behavior. Although this was only enforced once and was not included in Michigan's first revised code, which was authorized in 1838, other black laws were passed by the state legislature or

AFRICAN-AMERICAN POPULATION OF MICHIGAN, 1810–1900

Year	Slaves	Free People of Color	Free People of Color as a Percentage of Total Population	Total Population
1810	24	12	2.3%	5,285
1820		309	3.5%	8,895
1830	32	261	0.8%	31,639
1840		707	0.3%	212,267
1850		2,583	0.6%	367,654
1860		6,798	0.9%	749,113
1870		11,849	1.0%	1,184,059
1880		15,100	0.9%	1,636,937
1890		15,223	0.7%	2,093,889
1900		15,816	0.7%	2,420,982

constitutional conventions in the years that followed. These included a prohibition on black suffrage (which also prevented blacks from serving on juries; *see also* VOTING BEFORE GENERAL ABOLITION, UNITED STATES), a local option law permitting school SEGREGATION, a law against INTERRACIAL MARRIAGE, and another disqualifying African Americans from MILITIA service. Although the law against interracial marriage was rarely enforced, the others proved troubling for Michigan's free blacks. In 1855, the legislature did allow free blacks to vote in local school elections. In addition to these legal inequalities, African Americans in antebellum Michigan faced a range of extralegal discrimination, including denial of service at many restaurants and hotels, confinement to a separate gallery or balcony in many theaters and churches, restriction to crowded and substandard housing, segregation on common carriers, and racial violence. Even so, Michigan blacks faced milder treatment and less rigid enforcement of the black laws than was the case in the Lower Midwest (see BLACK LAWS IN THE MIDWEST).

African Americans and their white allies consistently challenged these racial restrictions. Petition campaigns against disfranchisement were regular features of Michigan politics in the 1840s and 1850s. Hundreds of such petitions reached the legislature, especially from 1843 to 1846, and sparked widespread political debate. Local groups, such as Detroit's Colored Vigilant Committee, led by the free blacks William Lambert and George DeBaptiste, expanded their efforts to aid and protect fugitive slaves into a broad attack on voting restrictions and segregated schools. In 1843, the committee organized a black state convention in Detroit. Affirming their claims as American citizens, delegates reminded the legislature that equal suffrage and education were the first two legs of an "unshackled citizenship." Michigan blacks held simi-

lar state conventions in 1850, 1860, 1863, 1865, and 1884 to protest legal assaults on these claims. The 1863 convention, meeting in the midst of the Civil War, helped prompt the state legislature to overturn the militia law and enlist black soldiers. For many black Michiganians who ultimately enlisted, this, too, was a vehicle for obtaining an "unshackled citizenship" in their state and the nation.

Michigan's black population grew dramatically after the Civil War, more than doubling to 15,816 residents by 1900. So, too, did the rights accorded them, as the legislature and the courts eliminated legal inequalities based on race in the quarter-century after Appomattox. In 1867, the legislature prohibited segregation in public education. Two years later, it approved the Fifteenth Amendment, which prohibited racial inequalities in voting, and submitted it to the voters, who narrowly approved the measure. In 1883, it repealed the ban on interracial marriage. Finally, it approved the Civil Rights Act of 1885, guaranteeing "full and equal privileges of inns, restaurants, eating houses, barber shops, public conveyances, and theatres" without regard to race. This was upheld by the state supreme court in *Ferguson v. Gies* in 1890. Thus, at the very time when Southern states—and the nation as a whole—increasingly upheld segregationist practices and other legal inequalities, Michigan moved in the opposite direction. What remained, according to the black Detroit attorney D. Augustus Straker in 1900, was the task of eliminating the social prejudice that prevented the full enjoyment of those rights.

Roy E. Finkenbine

FURTHER READING

Finkenbine, Roy E. "A Beacon of Liberty on the Great Lakes: Race, Slavery, and the Law in Antebellum Michigan." In *The History of Michigan Law,* edited by Paul Finkelman and

Martin J. Hershock, 83–107. Athens: Ohio University Press, 2006.

Katzman, David. *Before the Ghetto: Black Detroit in the Nineteenth Century.* Urbana: University of Illinois Press, 1973.

McGinnis, Carol. *Michigan Genealogy: Sources and Resources.* 2nd ed. Baltimore: Genealogical Publishing Company, 2005.

Middleton, Stephen, ed. *The Black Laws of the Old Northwest: A Documentary History.* Westport, Conn.: Greenwood Press, 1993.

Smith, Michael O. "Raising a Black Regiment in Michigan: Adversity and Triumph." *Michigan Historical Review* 16, no. 2 (Fall 1990): 22–41.

Walker, Lewis, Benjamin C. Wilson, and Linwood Cousins. *African Americans in Michigan.* East Lansing: Michigan State University Press, 2001.

Wilson, Benjamin C. *The Rural Black Heritage between Chicago and Detroit, 1850–1929: A Photographic Album and Random Thoughts.* Kalamazoo, Mich.: New Issues Press, 1985.

MIDWIVES AND TRADITIONAL HEALERS

Many free people of color, most of them women, provided health care to poor people of any race. Most of these people were not recognized as professionals but were instead informal practitioners, and they sometimes suffered unfortunate consequences of their informality.

Formal certification as a medical doctor was only open to men, and in almost all of the slave societies, to men of high racial status. Men of lower racial status could sometimes slip into the field of healing in a formal way by being recognized as members of lower-status healing professions: apothecaries, such as SAINT MARTÍN DE PORRES, or veterinarians, such as TOUSSAINT LOUVERTURE. But for women of color, there were only the informal healing arts. This was not so much of a handicap, however. European medicine was not very advanced at the time, and often a patient was no better off, or perhaps even at greater risk, under the care of a European-trained physician than with simple nursing care. Traditional healing included a good deal of practical nursing care and added the use of herbs that might well have medicinal value. Women healers could conceivably have had better results than white medical doctors. Doctors were not unaware of this. Some physicians sensibly worked with traditional and informal healers, learning some of their skills and shielding them from the consequences of informality. Other European medical professionals reacted with more jealousy, calling on the authorities to regulate or prosecute their informal competitors. A spate of witchcraft trials before the Inquisition in Mexico in the 1720s started with the arrest of an informal healer whose name has unfortunately not come down to us, then spread to a number of Indian and free colored people, who were suspected of using her magical powers for nefarious purposes.

Before Florence Nightingale, nursing was an occupation for poor, uneducated women of dubious moral character. This meant that, in slave societies in the Americas, it was an occupation ideally suited for women of color. Some hospitals, like that in CAP-FRANÇAIS/CAP-HAÏTIEN, SAINT-DOMINGUE, in the 1780s, employed slaves, but few white people were comfortable entrusting their lives to the hands of a slave they did not know. In any case, most nurses cared for sick people in their homes and thus had to move around freely. This meant that the occupation was less suitable for slaves, because there was always a fear that they would run away if not directly supervised. The profession of nursing blends into that of domestic service, and some of the same considerations of social rank, presumptions about sexual roles and behavior, and racial and class barriers apply to nursing as well (*see also* HOUSEKEEPERS).

A lithograph from Jean-Baptiste Debret's 1839 book *Picturesque and Historic Voyage to Brazil* showing a black surgeon at work in the street above an image of a butcher shop. Surgeons and butchers were both considered artisans and had a similar social status in the 19th century; this is why in Brazil and, frequently, elsewhere in the Americas free people of color were permitted to be surgeons. *(Library of Congress)*

One important medical function that women were uniquely suited to fulfill for social reasons was midwifery. Even many European physicians at the time agreed that obstetrics was women's work. It was not until the 19th century that physicians seized control of matters related to reproduction from midwives. Delivering babies safely was very difficult in the tropical Atlantic in any case. Maternal and infant mortality rates were dismayingly high, especially when there was some obstetrical cutting and sewing to be done with unsterilized tools. Many people thought that mothers and children were better off with midwives. Because of social rules about color lines and occupations, midwives in slave societies were almost exclusively black or mixed-race, and while slave women might help with births on large plantations, the need to be able to move around freely meant that almost all midwives were free women of color. Certainly the most skilled and experienced ones must have been, because even the largest plantation would not have more than a handful of births in a year.

Midwifery had one serious social handicap, however. Abortions and the use of birth control were both fairly common among slave women, as a form of resistance. Free women who were sexually promiscuous, either as PROSTITUTES AND COURTESANS or in informal relationships, often also had need of these services. Naturally, the obvious provider was the midwife, who could logically be expected from her knowledge of how to deliver a baby safely to know how to prevent one's appearance. Informal healers' knowledge of herbs and traditional remedies added to the public assumption that they were behind any covert interference with women's fertility. This made the midwife potentially complicit in sexual deviations by these women, in the eyes of the public, undermining the sexual and gender order of the community. Accusations of witchcraft could also be levied against traditional midwives, as in the case of the slave Tituba during the Salem witch trials.

One further handicap that traditional healers of African ancestry suffered under was the fact that they were operating in a less familiar biogeographic region. The plants that were part of the traditional pharmacopeia in Africa were mostly not also native to the Americas. Sometimes, they might have been transplanted, but mostly informal healers had to learn their new environment. Of course, by the end of the 18th century, people of color had been present in the Americas for three centuries. Jared Diamond, a well-known biogeographer, noted in his fieldwork with New Guinean native people that they would routinely try many different plants that they found in a new area, looking for edible and medically useful ones. Three centuries of this practice would no doubt produce a reasonable familiarity. In addition, studies of witchcraft and traditional healing have demonstrated regular connections between Indians and blacks in this area. Blacks accused of witchcraft would often explain that they had learned their techniques from Indians, and the ZAMBO, a person of mixed African and Indian ancestry, witch was a stock figure in Spanish-American folklore.

The public fear of poisoning was an omnipresent concern for traditional healers and others with some understanding of medicine or reputation for magical powers. Slave societies across the Atlantic world, from North America to Spanish America to BRAZIL, experienced repeated trials and arrests of accused poisoners and public panics about poison. It is unclear how much poisoning of masters by slaves actually occurred and how many accusations were simply scapegoating of an innocent slave by bereaved relatives after a natural death. Certainly the toll of premature deaths among whites in the tropical Americas as a result of disease was appalling. But if anybody was accused of poisoning, the immediate concern of the authorities was to find out where the poison came from. And in many cases, the local midwife or "leaf doctor" found herself on trial along with the accused, often implicated by "evidence" obtained by torture. In all these potential legal problems, a good relationship with local elites, especially those with formal medical training, would be invaluable for the practitioner.

Stewart R. King

FURTHER READING

De Mello e Souza, Laura. *The Devil and the Land of the Holy Cross: Witchcraft, Slavery, and Popular Religion in Colonial Brazil.* Austin: University of Texas Press, 2004.

Lewis, Laura A. *Hall of Mirrors: Power, Witchcraft, and Caste in Colonial Mexico.* Durham, N.C.: Duke University Press, 2003.

MIGRATION

One thing that free people of color were free to do was move around, to change residence or travel freely. This was one of the key characteristics that distinguished their lives from those of slaves. There were substantial limitations on this freedom when compared with that of whites, however, as many states and colonies limited immigration of people of color. Nevertheless, there were several significant mass migrations of people of color in the Americas that changed both the societies they left and the ones where they settled.

Most slave societies were suspicious of free people of color, seeing them as disruptive to the "natural" subordination of blacks to whites and potential sources of rebellious ideas for slaves. They tried to limit the growth in free colored populations through limitations on MANUMISSION, and even by laws requiring newly freed people to leave the territory. Similarly, many places were suspicious of immigrant free people of color and sought to bar them or regulate their entry. For example, many free states in the Midwest of the United States had laws forbidding any person of color to enter the state. These laws were often ignored, but their very existence limited the freedom of free blacks. (*See also* BLACK LAWS IN THE MIDWEST.)

In Spanish America, there were no legal restrictions on moving from one colony to another. However, government and church officials were often suspicious of people who moved from another area. In crackdowns on unorthodox religious practices, such as the persecution of crypto-Jews—members of families who had pretended to convert to the ROMAN CATHOLIC CHURCH from Judaism when it was outlawed in Spain in 1492—in MEXICO in the 1560s, church officials would look first at people who had lived in another colony. Local officials would write to the Inquisition—the church office charged with determining whether people's religious beliefs were acceptable—there to determine whether they had already been suspects. While in Europe the Inquisition mainly targeted Jews and Protestants, in the Americas most people who were investigated were suspected of practicing traditional or syncretic religious customs. Most of these were Indians or African Americans (*see* AFRICAN AND SYNCRETIC RELIGIONS).

BRAZIL began its existence in 1534 as a collection of separate captaincy-generals, each with its own feudal lord. People who wanted to move from one to another had to be accepted as vassals by the captain-general, at least in theory, though in truth the captain-generals had little control over their territories. This system died quickly, though, with only two of 15 captaincies even outliving their first captain. The Portuguese state took over the colony, appointed a governor-general, and unified administration in 1549. People could then move freely from one place to another within Brazil. After this, the administrative system alternated between a more or less unified and a federal system, but there were no longer any limits on internal migration by free people.

Brazil was also the source of an early international migration of Europeans and Africans within the Americas, when the Dutch conquered the northern part of the country in 1630, and then were driven out in 1661. When they left, they took a large number of slaves with them, as well as some free people of color who preferred Dutch rule. The Dutch had tolerated Jewish and Muslim religious practices, and some New Christians who had been practicing their old faiths in secret "came out" during Dutch rule. Their situation was likely to be difficult under reestablished Portuguese rule. They and their free colored relatives, and some hundreds of other free people of color, left Brazil and settled in Curaçao, becoming the core of a creole population speaking a language, Papiamentu, with Portuguese, Hebrew, Arabic, and Dutch roots.

Free people of color from the Dutch Antilles (*see* DUTCH CARIBBEAN ISLANDS) formed a trade diaspora throughout the Caribbean. The Dutch colonies were generally not well suited to plantation agriculture. The Dutch realized this, and their own national dominance in COMMERCE AND TRADE in the 17th century led them naturally toward commerce instead of agriculture as a primary economic activity. The Dutch colonies became entrepôts for the neighboring plantation colonies. Since all other European colonizers practiced mercantilist trade policies to some extent, restricting or forbidding trade between colonies and limiting trade with Europe to their own ships and merchants, this meant that the Dutch were generally smugglers. Dutch merchants could be found throughout the Americas, living quietly, seeming to pursue some legal trade or business, but actually selling smuggled slaves and manufactured goods and buying tropical produce. This sort of borderline life was natural for free people of color. In any case, the white population of the Netherlands colonies was generally quite small. The Netherlands had a small population to start with, and most of their people who wanted to move to the colonies went to Southeast Asia, where there were better chances for profit. In fact, then, many of these "Dutch" merchants were actually free people of color from Curaçao or St. Martin. Many planters in southern SAINT-DOMINGUE, including the free colored activist JULIEN RAIMOND, practiced INDIGO CULTIVATION, growing a crop ideal for smugglers because it combined high value, low bulk, and a legitimate market dominated by national monopoly corporations. These planters had a ready market in a family of Curaçao merchants who were related to Raimond and who made regular voyages to Les Cayes, the major port of the South Province.

A few free people of color in the Spanish colonies migrated along with the conquistadores in the 16th century. The Seville-born free black JUAN GARRIDO was a companion of Hernán Cortés in the conquest of Mexico in 1521. Miguel Ruíz and Juan García, free people of mixed race from Spain, received soldiers' shares of the loot from Cajamarca in 1532, when Francisco Pizarro took the Inca emperor prisoner and extracted a ransom of a room full of gold. Juan Valiente was an African slave with Pizarro in 1532, but by the time the conquistadores arrived in CHILE in 1541, he was free and received a captain's share of the land and Indian slaves. His companion, Juan Beltrán, a free black man originally taken to the Americas as a slave from today's Sénégal, was governor of Villarica in the south of

Chile and died in battle against Araucanian Indians in the 1550s. Free people of color made up a fairly small but still significant percentage of the early "Spanish" immigrants to the Americas. In many cases, they migrated several times during their lives, sometimes from Africa to Spain as slaves, as did Valiente; then from Spain to the Caribbean, as did Garrido; and on to the mainland, and then from one place to another as the path of conquest carried them.

Another important migration of free people of color in Spanish America took place at the time of national independence in the early 19th century. About one-fourth of the armies that liberated South America and Mexico were people of African descent, and the disruption of wartime and the social promotion open to members of the victorious armies allowed people to move far, if they wished. This period saw a good deal of migration from plantation regions to cities, as hope for rapid economic growth led people to seek modern amenities and high-wage jobs.

The migration of RUNAWAY SLAVES and freed slaves in the United States from the South to the North was stimulated by laws in many Southern states requiring freed people to leave the state within a short period after their MANUMISSION was approved. Although some Northern states were reluctant to accept new black immigrants, they nonetheless found ways to enter. Many settled in the cities, as industrialization spread in the Northern states in the first half of the 19th century, providing plenty of economic opportunity. There was a subsequent outmigration of those who had run away from slavery after the adoption of the FUGITIVE SLAVE ACT OF 1850. Some, including FREDERICK DOUGLASS, who had escaped from slavery in MARYLAND in 1838, fled to Europe, but most of these migrants traveled to CANADA, where they joined the descendants of WAR OF AMERICAN INDEPENDENCE black Loyalists as the nucleus of what has become today a significant Afro-Canadian population. There was some migration to the western frontier as well. Black cowboys (see RANCHING) were common, and blacks found jobs in mining, in construction, and as farmhands. Blacks took up land in some frontier regions, especially Colorado and KANSAS, in a movement that continued after the Civil War (see EXODUSTER MOVEMENT).

Brazil saw a very striking migration of people of color as slavery was dying there in the 1880s. Hundreds of thousands of people, some with legal manumission papers, others running away, fled from plantation areas to the cities and to the Southwest as they began to realize that the system did not have the means or the will to keep them at work. ISABEL OF BRAGANÇA, Brazil's princess imperial, officially abolished slavery in 1888, by which time it had nearly been abolished by the slaves.

Brazil's great migration was echoed throughout the Atlantic world by people of color fleeing plantation areas in the immediate aftermath of general abolition of slavery. Planters hoped that they could keep their workforces on the plantation by paying wages and improving conditions. This proved nearly impossible, however. Former slaves did not want to work in plantation labor, even if reasonable wages and treatment could be guaranteed somehow. They wanted to be either PEASANTS or urban workers. Throughout the Americas, vast hordes of blacks moved to unsettled areas in the countryside, to the cities, or at least to different plantation areas where, if they had to work as farmhands, at least they would not work for the same master. Former free people of color headed this migration. They had the resources to set off at once, and in many cases they were already where the newly freed were headed, living in the cities as small businesspeople or in the countryside as free small farmers. They were potential employers, religious leaders, political spokespeople, and role models.

Finally, the resolution of the post-abolition labor crisis often involved significant migrations starting a generation or two after the end of slavery. Blacks migrated from rural areas where plantation agriculture was finally dying to cities or other areas where discrimination might be less and there were jobs for them. These migrations were often led by former free people of color, or their descendants, who had the resources to move first and were welcomed by already-established populations of color descended, for the most part, from pre-abolition free people. The best known of these migrations is the so-called Great Migration of African Americans from the rural South to the northern and midwestern cities in the early 20th century. It was matched in scale by a somewhat earlier migration in the Caribbean to major cities (such as Havana and Kingston and even in Europe) and to the mainland of South and Central America. One major destination for this migration was PANAMA, where French and American investors were offering high wages for construction work on the Panama Canal. Populations of color of Caribbean origin are also found in VENEZUELA's and Mexico's oil fields, in the Yucatán sisal-growing area, and in European cities.

Stewart R. King

FURTHER READING

DuBois, W. E. B. *Black Reconstruction in America: 1863–1880.* 1935. Reprint, New York: Free Press, 1998.

Restall, Matthew. "Black Conquistadores: Armed Africans in Early Spanish America." *Americas* 57, no. 2 (October 2000): 171–205.

MILITIA

In most plantation colonies outside the United States, free people of color played an important role in defending the colony against its enemies, both internal and external.

It is one of the great ironies of the slave societies of the Americas that most of them depended for their security on people who were systematically excluded from many social benefits by RACISM AND RACIAL PREJUDICE. But the militia also served an important purpose for the free men of color who joined, especially the poorest and most vulnerable among them. In many places, militia service was a way for a young man without good MANUMISSION papers to regularize his status. Militia companies also provided social networks for men of color who often did not have access to other social institutions because of their race. And finally, militia service gave men of color contact with powerful whites, both their military superiors and the people they protected and served.

In the early days of the colonization of the Americas, armed service in defense of the colony was the responsibility of all free men but was not organized in any permanent way. The conquistadores of Spanish America and the *bandeirantes* in BRAZIL were private bands of armed men,

organized to attack native people and wrest their wealth from them. After the conquerors settled down in a region, the armed band might reform itself in case of danger. In the French and English Caribbean, the buccaneer crew functioned in similar ways, transitioning into an informal militia when the islands the pirates contested with the Spanish began to settle down into plantation colonies. The people of color among these early immigrants fought alongside the whites without much distinction, even of status. For example, VINCENT OLIVIER of SAINT-DOMINGUE was a teenage slave when he went to CARTAGENA de Colombia in 1695 with his master on the last great pirate raid of the 17th-century Caribbean. Olivier was taken to Europe and given his freedom as a reward for his heroism in the siege. He served in the REGULAR ARMY of King Louis XIV in the German wars and returned to the colony in 1713 after the end of the War of the Spanish Succession.

Olivier became a captain in the militia of Saint-Domingue, a title he held until his death at an advanced

A troop of free black militiamen in Surinam confront three maroons. The Surinam maroon wars ended with treaties that confirmed the independence of the maroons, so long as they refrained from raiding the Dutch plantations and admitting runaway slaves. The free colored militia was an important part of the colony's response to the maroon threat, both in Surinam and throughout the Americas. *(Archives Charmet/The Bridgeman Art Library International)*

age in 1781. By that time, Saint-Domingue and the other colonies of the Americas had developed more regular militias. There were many reasons for this evolution in the colonial defense forces. First, the colonies were growing rapidly, both in population and in wealth. Much of the population growth was in the form of newly imported slaves, who were a serious security threat. The wealth attracted outside threats: All the major colonial nations based large fleets and significant ground forces in their colonies. During the 18th century, there was almost unceasing warfare among FRANCE, the Netherlands, and BRITAIN, and even when there was formal peace in Europe, there were still tension and occasional armed clashes in the Americas. Moreover, the growth of absolute monarchies in Europe meant that kings and governments wanted to exert more control over armed force. In Europe, they progressively took away from their nobles the right to maintain their own private armies and fight their own wars, ultimately even outlawing one-on-one duels. In the colonies, they sought to rein in the private armies of *bandeirantes* and buccaneers and put them on a more professional footing.

The planter class in the colonies was not entirely opposed to this project. Their culture had developed away from its warrior roots. Unlike their grandfathers in the 17th century, they decided they had better things to do than fight. This was especially true when their prospective enemies were either very professional European armies who might well slaughter them or rebel slaves who were numerous and brutal. Even if they defeated rebel slaves or MAROONS, there was no military reputation or loot to be won, just criticism from the abolitionist press. It was best, the colonial elites argued, to leave the business of security to professional soldiers. Professional soldiers, however, had short life expectancies because of the disease environment in the Tropics, and those who did survive, as white men, found that they had much better opportunities in the civilian economy and so they deserted in droves. Some colonies tried to force white civilians to perform active service in militias, but resisted with considerable success. In most places in the tropical Americas, white militia companies were social institutions with little combat power. Occasionally, they might be mustered to face some obvious threat such as an actual slave rebellion or foreign invasion, but if they had to do any actual fighting, they would have some more reliable troops on their flanks and rear. Some colonies considered arming the slaves, but the foolishness of this idea seemed self-evident. Since antiquity, masters had discovered that if they gave a slave a weapon, he ceased fairly shortly to be a slave—either they had to free him or he rebelled. There were some units, such as the British West India Regiment, in which slaves could serve with the permission of their masters and gain their freedom at the end of their term of service, but these are more properly considered part of the regular army. By process of elimination, colonial elites turned to the free people of color for day-to-day security needs.

As the militias were formally organized, one of the first steps was to create separate black, and occasionally also mixed-race, units. In some places, the free colored units had officers from their own racial group. This was normal in the beginning of the process, but placing the militias under central control meant assigning professional military men from the home country, who were, obviously, almost all whites. Captain Vincent Olivier was one of the few black military professionals in Saint-Domingue, and even he lost his position in the 1760s, though he kept the rank as a sign of respect. Mixed-race militias in Mexico and COLOMBIA had a few mixed-race officers throughout the period of slavery, but by the 1770s, most of them were replaced with professional white officers from Spain. The militia in CUBA had free colored officers up until the LA ESCALERA PLOT of 1844, when most of the black militias were disbanded. Militias were generally assigned in small units however, and mortality rates among the immigrant officers were high. The noncommissioned officers, the sergeants and corporals, who actually led the troops in the field, were always men of color. These sergeants and corporals inherited the positions of authority within free colored society that black officers such as Olivier had had in earlier generations.

The militia was an important institution in free colored society. The militia officers and sergeants were high-ranking people, often called upon to guarantee loans, serve as godfathers, or help raise money to free people from slavery. Their opinions on matters of community concern were important. In northern and western Saint-Domingue, they were a true leadership group for the poorer free colored community who were cut off from the free colored planters by social class divisions. In areas where the free colored community was less socially stratified, as in VERACRUZ, MEXICO, the militia leaders often were from wealthy free colored families; younger sons would take up a military career in much the same way, if on a smaller scale, that younger sons of European nobility went into the armed forces.

The free colored militia leaders were also important political voices, speaking on behalf of the free colored community as a whole. Many of the militia sergeants and corporals in Saint-Domingue became officers in the rebel armies during the HAITIAN REVOLUTION. Mexican free colored militiamen were important players in the WAR OF MEXICAN INDEPENDENCE, 1810–21. In 1828, when the Cuban government was tightening legal restrictions on free people of color in the wake of the independence movements in the SOUTH AMERI-CAN WARS OF LIBERATION, free colored militia officers issued a manifesto protesting the changes and claiming equal rights. The free colored militias of Recife and São Paolo were strong supporters of republican, radical policies in Brazil in the 1830s. On the other hand, the conservative military dictator Juan Manuel de Rosas in Argentina used the black militia of Buenos Aires as shock troops to keep the liberal urban opposition in line and to channel benefits to his supporters within the black community.

For poor men, the militia was important primarily because serving in it meant one were a free person. In theory, only free people could serve, and so if a man had questionable status and he could document that he had served in his militia company, that might well be taken as the equivalent of manumission. In most cases, these would be people who were seeking freedom with the permission of their masters: They would have been given "their time" (see LIVING "AS FREE"). Even if the slave was frankly a runaway, however, service in the militia put him in contact with people who could protect him if his master searched for him. Indeed, they might be the very people called upon to look for RUNAWAY SLAVES, leading to the fox's running unobtrusively with the hounds.

In Spanish America, militia companies often coexisted with or sponsored CATHOLIC CONFRATERNITIES. These groups administered burial insurance, ensured admission to hospitals for sick or impoverished members, looked after widows and orphans, and provided other social services.

For poorer men of color, the militia was important as a means of social networking. One's militia comrades were often also the godfathers of one's children, business partners, marriage partners for one's children, and so on. This was especially important for people who had recently gained their freedom. If their family were enslaved, or if they had no family in the colony, the militia company provided a pseudo–kin group. Companionship, reliable occupational associates and employers, and a sense of place and belonging were all benefits of militia service.

Finally, colonial militias served as a feeder for enlistment in the regular military. This might not be seen as a benefit by those better-established free people of color who wanted to remain on their plantations or working in their urban businesses. When, in 1781 during the WAR OF AMERICAN INDEPENDENCE, 1775–83, the French government tried to create a regular army unit composed of conscripts from the free colored militia, the white militia officers and their free colored sergeants both protested the idea. But for those newly freed or poor and down-and-out, the "king's shilling" might have

seemed attractive, just as it did to men similarly placed in Europe. Contact with professional officers through the militia might ensure placement in a good regiment, fair treatment, and advancement, and the skills taught in the militia were valuable to the regular armed forces.

Militia service was not always seen as a benefit. After the La Escalera Plot in CUBA, the government tried to reestablish the black militia. Instead of the proud and empowering force that had existed before, the new militia was to be composed of draftees, employed as laborers on infrastructure projects and systematically denigrated. The Spanish colonial authorities knew they needed black manpower, but having used racism to divide Cuban society and keep Cuba loyal in the 1840s, they could not make militia service a source of honor and prestige for free blacks. Many wealthier free people of color did not see militia service as useful for them and resisted calls to more active service. Free planters in the Southern Province of SAINT-DOMINGUE participated in the white anti-militia demonstrations and riots of the 1760s.

Black militias were almost unknown in the United States. The much larger white population, even in the densest plantation zones, meant that there were more poor whites who would find militia service rewarding for many of the same reasons as poor blacks elsewhere. Militia service remained an important part of white sociability in North America in a way that it did not in most other colonies in the Americas. Even in settled areas where militias almost never saw active service, militia companies were important for sociability and as places where public opinion could be formed and express itself. During the War of American Independence, the importance of militias to white public consciousness was multiplied, even though their military usefulness to the independence movement was limited. For all these reasons, almost every state in the United States banned free blacks from militia service. The exceptions were MASSACHUSETTS, which had free black companies in BOSTON and also a good number of free blacks serving alongside whites in companies from smaller port towns, and LOUISIANA. Louisiana was Spanish and French until 1805, and the French and Spanish pattern of free colored service prevailed. After the United States took the territory with the Louisiana Purchase, most free colored militia units were disbanded. The free people of color of NEW ORLEANS, LOUISIANA, re-formed their militia, the Louisiana Native Guard, at the outbreak of the AMERICAN CIVIL WAR, but the secessionist government of Louisiana quickly disbanded the unit. It later reformed as a pro-Union unit after U.S. forces captured New Orleans and was ultimately incorporated into the regular U.S. Army.

Stewart R. King

FURTHER READING

Hollandsworth, James G. *The Louisiana Native Guards: The Black Military Experience during the Civil War.* Baton Rouge: Louisiana State University Press, 1998.

King, Stewart. *Blue Coat or Powdered Wig: Free People of Color in Pre-Revolutionary Saint-Domingue.* Athens: University of Georgia Press, 2001.

Lokken, Paul. "Useful Enemies: Seventeenth-Century Piracy and the Rise of Pardo Militias in Spanish Central America." *Journal of Colonialism and Colonial History* 5, no. 2 (Fall 2004).

Reid, Michele. "Protesting Service: Free Black Response to Cuba's Reestablished Militia of Color." *Journal of Colonialism and Colonial History* 5, no. 2 (Fall 2004).

Restall, Matthew. "Black Conquistadors: Armed Africans in Early Spanish America." *Americas* 57, no. 2 (2000): 171–205.

Vinson Ben, III. "Articulating Space: The Free-Colored Military Establishment in Colonial Mexico from the Conquest to Independence." *Callaloo* 27, no. 1 (Winter 2004): 150–171.

MINNESOTA

The first free black settlers in the territory that would become Minnesota arrived in the late 18th and early 19th centuries. The first well-known black settler was the fur trader Pierre Bonga (or Bungo), who was probably of mixed African and Ojibwe descent. Pierre's son, George, who was born near the site of Duluth about 1802, also married an Ojibwe woman. The Bonga dynasty in the region lasted well through the 19th century, and several locations in Cass County were named for the family.

As were most other areas of the Northwest Territory, the region that would become Minnesota was also home to a small number of slaves, despite territorial prohibitions on slavery. The military post at Fort Snelling drew slave-owning officers and their slaves to the region during the 1820s and 1830s.

A slave named Rachael spent time at several posts in Minnesota and WISCONSIN between 1831 and 1834 and in 1835 sued for her freedom before the MISSOURI Supreme Court on the grounds that she had been living in free states. In 1836, the Missouri court ruled that Rachael was free and that her owner lost his rights to his property by taking her into a free territory. An opposite conclusion was reached in the famous case of DRED SCOTT and his wife, Harriett, who spent two years at Fort Snelling. In 1857, the U.S. Supreme Court decided that the Scotts' residence in free territories did not lead to de facto freedom.

The Minnesota territorial census of 1850, taken just one year after the region was officially recognized as a territory, counted 39 free black residents, 30 of whom lived in St. Paul. Here, there were seven families headed by men who claimed occupations as barbers and cooks.

During the 1850s, more free blacks and fugitive slaves arrived in the territory, probably traveling north along the Mississippi River, leading to a backlash against the new immigrants. In 1849, 1851, and 1853 the territory followed the lead of ILLINOIS, INDIANA, and IOWA by prohibiting black suffrage at all levels of government, but in 1854, it rejected a law that would have required black immigrants to post bond against becoming a burden on the territory (*see* BLACK LAWS IN THE MIDWEST).

The first Minnesota state constitutional convention in 1857 debated whether to allow black suffrage but ultimately decided against it. A range of personal liberty laws that would have protected RUNAWAY SLAVES seeking asylum in the state were defeated in 1860, but so was an anti-immigration bill. This placed Minnesota considerably in advance of most other midwestern states in the cause of black rights. Although it did not offer them significant protections, neither did the state offer significant roadblocks to eventual free black citizenship.

In 1865 and 1867, Minnesota's voters rejected two black suffrage measures but in 1868 approved the amendment of the state's constitution to allow blacks, "civilized" Indians, and people of mixed heritage to vote. In 1869, the legislature abolished SEGREGATION in the state's public schools, although separate facilities continued to exist in many places.

AFRICAN-AMERICAN POPULATION OF MINNESOTA, 1850–1900

Year	Free People of Color	Free People of Color as a Percentage of Total Population	Total Population
1850	39	0.6%	6,077
1860	259	0.2%	172,023
1870	759	0.2%	439,706
1880	1,564	0.2%	780,773
1890	3,683	0.3%	1,301,826
1900	4,959	0.1%	1,751,394

Because it had gained a relatively benign reputation among the states of the Midwest, Minnesota became a focal point for many black migrants during and immediately after the AMERICAN CIVIL WAR. Unlike the states of the Lower Midwest, Minnesota did not directly border any of the Southern states that allowed slavery, so its black population remained relatively small, even given its rapid growth. Between 1860 and 1870, the state's black population nearly tripled, but even this prodigious growth left the state with a total of only 759 black citizens. Saint Paul was a particular focal point of the wartime migration and received several large groups of so-called contraband fugitive slaves, which swelled the local population literally overnight.

In 1863, Minneapolis blacks formed the St. James AFRICAN METHODIST EPISCOPAL (A.M.E.) CHURCH, and in St. Paul, there were black Baptist and Episcopal congregations by 1870. At different times during the latter 19th century, the black populations of Minneapolis and St. Paul were served by Catholic, Baptist, Methodist, and A.M.E. congregations, which existed under a variety of auspices.

Reasons for the fluctuating fortunes of the religious organizations of Minneapolis and St. Paul were the economic marginalization and residential segregation of the local black population. Although there were many in the community who had significant personal wealth and who worked at skilled occupations, there were many others who had neither the financial resources nor the residential stability to keep religious congregations afloat.

By the 1890s, greater economic opportunities arrived with the railroads, which employed large numbers of black porters and yard workers, as well as the hotel industry, which also employed blacks as waiters, porters, and cooks. Blacks also worked at a range of skilled trades by the turn of the 20th century, including as stonecutters, masons, bricklayers, and cobblers.

As the community diversified during the 1870s, several community leaders took prominent roles in political, social, and religious organizations. James Hilyard arrived in St. Paul in the 1850s and, after traveling to PENNSYLVANIA for military service during the Civil War, returned in 1866 to start a clothing store, sell real estate and insurance, and lead a band of local musicians. Hilyard was also involved in organizing the black Masonic lodges in St. Paul and Minneapolis and was active in the A.M.E. Church (see also FREEMASONRY). Thomas Lyles, who arrived in St. Paul in 1874, worked first as a barber, then as a real estate agent, and finally as a mortician. Lyles was active in Republican Party political clubs during the 1880s and was instrumental in the hiring of the city's first black policeman in 1881. He was also the first grand master of the African Grand Lodge of Minnesota and president of an intellectual society for black citizens.

Both Hilyard and Lyles were involved in publishing St. Paul's black newspaper, the *Western Appeal*, beginning in the mid-1880s. The newspaper helped draw more black professionals to the Minneapolis–St. Paul area, who assisted in the formation of early black advocacy and civil rights organizations. Amanda Lyles, wife of Thomas Lyles, was active in the black mission of the Minnesota Woman's Christian Temperance Union in the mid-1880s. By the later part of the decade, a local Afro-American League was formed under the auspices of the national organization of the same name, and by 1891, there was a Minnesota Citizens Civil Rights Committee.

Thomas Bahde

FURTHER READING
Green, William D. *A Peculiar Imbalance: The Fall and Rise of Racial Equality in Early Minnesota*. St. Paul: Minnesota Historical Society Press, 2007.
Schwalm, Leslie A. *Emancipation's Diaspora: Race and Reconstruction in the Upper Midwest*. Chapel Hill: University of North Carolina Press, 2009.
Taylor, David Vassar. *African Americans in Minnesota*. St. Paul: Minnesota Historical Society Press, 2002.

MIRANDA, FRANCISCO DE (1750–1816)
Venezuelan revolutionary

Francisco de Miranda was one of the most influential figures in the struggle against SPAIN for the independence of Hispanic America. A white man born in VENEZUELA, Miranda had an impact on the free people of color of Spanish America greater than almost any other political leader had at the time. His willingness to use free colored and enslaved soldiers, to grant liberty for military service, and to accept the possibility that blacks could be citizens of a republic helped transform race relations in Spanish South America.

Miranda was born on March 28, 1750, to a Venezuelan merchant family. He was educated in the finest schools but always suffered discrimination because of his CREOLE ancestry. Though his parents were socially defined as white, and he never suffered any formal discrimination for being of a lower racial caste, there were allegations that both sides of his family had some African ancestry—his father was from the Canary Islands, where MISCEGENATION had been common and racial lines blurred since the 15th century, and his mother was from a middle-class Venezuelan family (see RACISM AND RACIAL PREJUDICE). By 1808, when war between FRANCE and Spain began creating an opening for political change in Spanish America, Miranda had been plotting against Spanish rule for more than 20 years. He set up revolutionary projects that he offered to whichever government or ruler was willing to finance them, as he did with Empress Catherine II of Russia in 1787, the British government in 1790, and the French National Convention in 1792. While in France, Miranda became very close to the Gironde Party leader, Jacques-Pierre Brissot, who considered the Venezuelan a key figure to strike Spain's colonial territories overseas. He proposed him as governor for SAINT-DOMINGUE during the HAITIAN REVOLUTION, but Miranda declined the appointment. Miranda did go to the newly independent Haiti, though, gaining support for his revolutionary plans from its president, ALEXANDRE SABÈS PÉTION. In 1806, Miranda sailed from Jacmel, Haiti, to launch his first military expedition against the colonial government in Venezuela. After the failure of this attempt, he returned to LONDON, ENGLAND, where he kept promoting the cause of independence, publishing a newspaper in Spanish entitled *El Colombiano* (Colombian) starting in 1807.

Miranda advocated equality, regardless of skin color. He particularly urged granting citizenship to free people of color, the most numerous group of the Captaincy-General of Venezuela, reaching 44 percent of the population in the early 1800s, a total of some 400,000 individuals. The free colored population was composed mostly of *PARDOS* (a sector composed generally of all mixed-blood categories between black and white) but also contained free blacks. For him, as stated in the republican manifestos he published for Hispanic America from 1801 onward, the new republic he contemplated would suppress the existing distinctions based on skin color or caste groups. The only social distinctions permitted would be based on income and the merits and virtues of each individual. He put into practice this doctrine as soon as he arrived in Caracas, where he returned in December 1810 invited by the autonomous government that had been recently set up there after Napoléon Bonaparte's occupation of Spain. In that city, he counted on the support of the free coloreds and the most radical white politicians. With them he founded a Jacobin-like political club named the Patriotic Society, to which access was allowed not only to *pardos* but also to free blacks and even to women.

Members of this club also exerted strong pressure on the Venezuelan Federal Congress to force a declaration of independence from Spain and on granting full citizenship to free coloreds. The Patriotic Society imposed its point of view in the Federal Constitution sanctioned in December 1810, which eliminated all legal distinctions based on race. Despite this political achievement, outside the city of Caracas most people of color preferred to support the royalist cause. Many people of color saw the Spanish government as their protector against the large landowners, who were mostly strong supporters of the

revolutionary government. A powerful force of former slaves, free coloreds, and Indians from the southeastern part of the country enlisted in the royalist cause and were a key component of their armed forces. These forces were very much feared by the creole elite, and when rumors began to fly that they were committing atrocities against pro-revolutionary forces, there was panic. Despite the frequent exaggeration of the reports, Miranda was convinced that the menace was real. In consequence, considering also the unstoppable advance of the royalist forces from the South and the lack of food, on July 25, 1812, Miranda decided to capitulate to the Spanish general Monteverde.

Miranda would die four years later, on July 14, 1816, in a high-security prison in Cádiz, Spain. His impact on South American society would live on, however. When Simón Bolívar (1783–1830) reestablished the Venezuelan Republic in 1813, he was able to triumph through the support of free colored soldiers who remembered the good treatment they had received under Miranda's rule. The racially diverse *llaneros* of the southeastern plains who had supported the Spanish in 1812 changed sides, under their charismatic leader José Antonio Páez (1790–1873), and the free colored MILITIAS of the cities of Venezuela and the Caribbean coast of COLOMBIA were central elements in his armies. His fleet commander, MANUEL PIAR (1774–1817), and many of the sailors in his fleet were Afro-Venezuelan. Bolívar was more conservative than Miranda and clashed with his free colored generals, but his movement effected considerable progress towards racial equality thanks to the precedent set by Miranda.

Alejandro E. Gomez

FURTHER READING
Racine, Karen. *Francisco de Miranda: A Trans-Atlantic Life in the Age of Revolution.* Wilmington, Del.: Scholarly Resources, 2002.

MISCEGENATION

Miscegenation refers to sexual relations between people of different races. Miscegenation between people considered "black" and "white" was a crime in some places in the Americas at different times, especially in the British colonies and the United States. Punishments were generally mild, especially if the male partner was of European ancestry. Often, the only restriction was on INTERRACIAL MARRIAGE, with informal relationships legally permissible or treated under relatively lax generally applicable laws against sexual activity outside marriage (known as fornication in English law). However, if the African female partner was enslaved, any children would be enslaved as well, according to the almost-universal rule in the Americas. If the male partner was African and the female European, the act was generally punished much more harshly, informally by the public through LYNCH-ING or other forms of mob violence in some cases even if there were no clear laws. Children in such cases, though free from birth, were often subject to severe discrimination and might well be indentured, taken from their parents to be raised in institutions, or otherwise formally punished for the "misdeeds" of their mother.

Stewart R. King

MISSISSIPPI

The state of Mississippi is bordered by the states of TEN-NESSEE to the north and ALABAMA to the east, the Gulf of Mexico and LOUISIANA to the south, and the Missis-sippi River to the west (and the states of Louisiana and ARKANSAS on the other side of the Mississippi River). Much of the state is heavily forested with trees such as pine, elm, oak, and pecan, but the Northwest, referred to as the Mississippi delta, and the Northeast portions of the state have rich, fertile soil. Mississippi has a subtropical climate with hot and humid summers and mild winters, and the coastline includes several large bays. The climate and topography are ideal for plantation crops, especially COTTON CULTIVATION. The Mississippi River offers easy access to a major port at NEW ORLEANS, LOUISIANA, and thus to a global market.

The indigenous inhabitants of Mississippi, the Choc-taw, Chickasaw, and Natchez tribes, were farming peoples who lived in towns and villages. Multi-town chiefdoms existed before the arrival of Europeans, though these large political groupings were devastated by the diseases brought by the Spaniards led by Hernando de Soto, who in 1540 were the first group of Europeans to visit the area. De Soto was accompanied by free and enslaved people of African ancestry, but the Spanish did not settle in the territory. It was the French in the late 17th century who first attempted to settle the area.

Colonial Period

The French explorer René-Robert Cavelier, sieur de La Salle, claimed a vast region for FRANCE in 1682, naming it Louisiana in honor of King Louis XIV. De La Salle's claim included the lower Mississippi River valley. Indeed, the claimed area included land on both sides of the Mis-sissippi stretching from the Gulf of Mexico to CANADA. In today's terms, the territory comprised what would be several U.S. states, including Arkansas, ILLINOIS, INDI-ANA, IOWA, KANSAS, Louisiana, MICHIGAN, MINNESOTA, Mississippi, MISSOURI, NEBRASKA, North Dakota, OKLA-HOMA, South Dakota, and WISCONSIN.

After claiming the territory, La Salle journeyed to France to seek the king's support for developing the area. Colonization offered several strategic and economic benefits to the French, including confining the British to the lands east of the Appalachians and establishing control of the Mississippi River, guaranteeing an open French trade route from Canada to the Gulf of Mexico. The king hoped to establish a French nation that stretched from the gulf to Canada, making much of the continent French and creating a commercial empire.

France's first permanent settlement in the region, Fort Maurepas (today Ocean Springs, Mississippi, near Biloxi), was founded by Pierre Le Moyne d'Iberville in 1699 with a group numbering 200, including soldiers and colonists. The original settlers were from Canada and metropolitan France and do not appear to have included any people of color, either free or enslaved. However, people of color were imported as slaves, and the colony was given its own version of the French Code Noir, or Black Code, in 1724 (*see* CODE NOIR IN FRENCH LAW). The 1718 settlement of New Orleans in what is now the state of Louisiana moved the primary focus of French colonization in the region to the West, and the French settlements in Mississippi remained small. In 1716, however, the French settled in Natchez and built Fort Rosalie. This site had more pro-ductive soil, and the population of the area grew, help-ing it to become the most significant trading post in the area. Settlers grew tobacco and rice and practiced INDIGO CULTIVATION using the labor of African-descended slaves and Native Americans. The colony ultimately declined because of the opposition of the Natchez Indians

Mississippi was formally part of the French colony of Louisiana for 63 years. The venture was considered a failure, both politically and economically. The few set-tlements remaining after the attacks from the Natchez, mostly in the Gulf Coast region, were not as significant as the New Orleans settlement.

In 1754, the French and Indian War began in PENN-SYLVANIA, and the hostilities between France and BRIT-AIN soon spread to Europe, developing into what became known as the SEVEN YEARS' WAR. In the Treaty of Paris of 1763, which ended the Seven Years' War, France ceded most of its territory east of the Mississippi River and its territory in Canada to Britain, so the Mississippi area became British. (Louisiana, on the other hand, ended up in the hands of SPAIN in the 1762 Treaty of Fontainebleau.)

The British referred to their new area as West FLOR-IDA; it stretched from the Mississippi River on the west to the Apalachicola River on the east to the 32°28' north lati-tude line (roughly the location of the Yazoo River). It was largely uninhabited, and the British attempted to increase population through generous land grants. Many arrived and settled in the Natchez area, which had rich soil suited to agriculture.

In 1775, the WAR OF AMERICAN INDEPENDENCE, 1775–83, began. Spanish leaders, motivated more by the desire to weaken Great Britain than to support a colonial revolution, had ordered Louisiana officials to assist American colonists secretly, and in 1779, Spain declared war on Britain. The actions of Governor Don Bernardo de Galvéz enabled the Spanish government to acquire West Florida. In 1779, he directed Spanish troops to victory at Fort Panmure at Natchez, and by 1781, Spain had conquered all of West Florida, including Fort Charlotte at Mobile and Fort George at Pensacola, adding this region to the colony of Spanish Florida they already controlled to the east.

In 1783, Great Britain recognized the independence of the United States after the American Revolutionary War. The Treaty of Paris of 1783 defined the borders of the United States: land south of the Great Lakes, land east of the Mississippi River, and land north of the 31st parallel of latitude (the original northern boundary of West Florida). In 1764, however, the northern boundary of West Florida had been moved to 32°28' north latitude, which was not the latitude specified in the treaty. This land between 31° and 32°28' north latitude line was claimed by both the United States and Spain in the years to follow, in part because this land contained the fertile soil of the Natchez settlement. Notably, Spain retained territory to the west and south of the United States, as it was defined at the time, including Natchez.

In the years that followed, Spanish leaders such as Governor Manuel Louis Gayoso de Lemos y Amorin worked to cultivate the area by attracting U.S. citizens through generous land grants that promoted agriculture (the land reverted to the Crown if it was not improved) and through religious tolerance (Spain was Catholic, while much of the United States was Protestant at the time). Settlers were asked to swear allegiance to Spain and not to practice Protestantism publicly. Those who immigrated from the East included people of color, mostly enslaved, accompanying their masters to this new agricultural colony. The Natchez settlements had few free people of color—the Spanish government did not give them land grants, and the Anglo white colonists from the East did not free many slaves. During this time, settlers grew tobacco primarily but also maintained livestock for their own needs and for profit. South of the 31st parallel, in the Gulf Coast region, the society was more like that found in Spanish America. Free people of color suffered under some legal restrictions but were citizens, had access to the courts, could own any kind of property and pursue most trades, served in the MILITIA, and so on. This predominantly Latin American view of race was to have a profound effect on the free colored population of Mississippi in the future.

In the mid-1790s, the Natchez residents experienced two important changes. In the 1795 Treaty of San Lorenzo, Spain granted the United States free rights to navigate the Mississippi River and to make port at New Orleans. In this treaty, Spain gave up its claim to land between 31st and 32°28' north latitude line: Natchez residents now lived in American lands. Second, planters in Natchez discovered and modified the Whitney cotton gin, and it became widely used in the area, leading to increased cotton growing and increased dependence on slavery.

The United States and Mississippi Statehood
The area that later became the state of Mississippi was organized into the Mississippi Territory on April 7, 1798, by the U.S. Congress, although the territory was later expanded to include disputed land and purchased land (generally from the Choctaw and Chickasaw tribes in treaties that exploited Native Americans).

The first governor of the territory, Winthrop Sargent, faced a number of challenges, ranging from writing laws and policies to dealing with the threat of Native Americans. He was unpopular among the territory's American residents, and his decisions and policies were viewed as anti-Jeffersonian.

Sectionalist tendencies in this period grew stronger. Those in the western part of the territory, including Natchez, relied heavily on cotton and slavery; they were planters beginning to grow wealthy and forming a kind of country gentry. Those in the eastern part of the territory relied on herding and farming for subsistence and small profit. Easterners distrusted westerners, and talk of separation began early.

The population was growing during this time, and the slave population in several counties was more than 50 percent of the total population. The population of free people of color also grew, as children of white masters and slave mistresses were freed, and masters freed slaves in their wills.

The remaining Spanish possessions of West Florida, including the coastal regions of Mississippi and Alabama, were incorporated in the United States between 1810 and 1812, although Spain continued to press its claim to the region until the 1819 Adams-Onís Treaty. Because of the preexisting American claim to the region, this treaty was thought not to give any rights to free people of color living in former Spanish territories, though the cultural distinctiveness of the region did give them a marginally higher status than free coloreds in the remainder of the state. Mississippi was admitted to the Union on December 10, 1817, and Congress divided what was the Mississippi Territory into roughly equal parts along a line west of the city of MOBILE, ALABAMA, that ran north from the Gulf of Mexico. The Alabama Territory was formed from the eastern settlements and included the city of Mobile.

In the 1830s, when Mississippi obtained lands from Native Americans after the Indian Removal Acts, the population again grew dramatically as U.S. citizens arrived and settled in Mississippi. Many of the new settlers grew cotton, and slavery grew and became institutionalized as cotton production increased. Laws that restricted slaves and free people of color increased as a form of social control. As settlers became wealthier in the 1840s and 1850s, notions of white supremacy were strengthened and used to defend and rationalize slavery, and those notions (underlined by economic reliance on slavery) help explain the support for succession before the AMERICAN CIVIL WAR.

Free People of Color, Early History

The French took the first African slaves to Mississippi, and their numbers grew as cotton grew in importance. By 1724, Jean-Baptiste Le Moyne, sieur de Bienville, the French governor of Louisiana, and others had become concerned about the number of blacks and those of mixed parentage in Louisiana, and the Louisiana Code Noir was instituted.

The Code Noir was based on Louis XIV's Black Code, which had governed blacks in France's Caribbean colonies since 1687 and which was significantly more liberal than the Louisiana law. Louisiana's Code Noir subjected slaves and free people of color to restrictive legislation. Slaves, for example, were declared movable property, denied the right to sue, and required to participate in the rites of the ROMAN CATHOLIC CHURCH. The code also forbade whites to marry or keep people of color as mistresses, although this restriction was often ignored in the frontier society, where women were scarce.

The Code Noir, however, declared that people of color, once free (whether born free or manumitted), had the same rights as other freeborn persons, including the right to sue; parts of the Code Noir, however, continued to restrict the activities of free blacks. Local regulations, in addition, could and did restrict people of color further than Code Noir.

During colonial times, the number of free people of color grew through MANUMISSION by white (and later free colored) owners, through self-purchase by slaves, and through other options available to slaves.

In the frontier society, white males took slaves as mistresses, often freeing them and supporting them and their children. Indeed, the records from the French period show that many slaves were manumitted for "good and faithful service" (sometimes a euphemism for being a mistress or the master's child by a slave mistress). Historians argue

that some free women of color and female slaves sought out such arrangements for the improvement in status and the security it afforded them. At this time, free women of color could hold property, including slaves. Additionally, whites and free persons of color sometimes freed slaves in their wills or after a period of service.

It was also possible for a slave to purchase his or her freedom (or that of a relative) during Spanish rule, with or without the master's consent (see COARTACIÓN). The slave could petition the court for an appraiser to set a fair price on him or her. Once the slave paid the price, he or she was free, even if the master objected.

In the Spanish period, laws provided even more ways that a slave could be freed, including taking Holy Orders within the church or performing services to the Crown. Service as a soldier could lead to freedom, and people of color served with distinction in the military under both French and Spanish rule. Slaves also became free in illegal ways—running away and then LIVING "AS FREE".

The population of free people of color was never as large in Mississippi as it was in Louisiana. Fewer than 1,000 free people of color lived in Mississippi before the Civil War, most of whom were settled in Southwest Mississippi, the former French and Spanish West Florida. Free blacks tended to live in urban areas such as Natchez and Vicksburg. Men tended to work in skilled trades (as barbers or blacksmiths, for instance) or as unskilled laborers. Women worked as domestic servants or laundresses. Both men and women worked as agricultural laborers.

The overall population of Mississippi itself was low, and much of the area was still covered in forest—many more settlers would be needed for the state to develop.

Rise of Racial Discrimination

The rise of racial discrimination can be traced most directly to the period after Mississippi became a state in 1817. The number of free people of color was small partly because the overall population was low, but also because increasingly restrictive laws made freedom more difficult to attain. Additionally, laws were created that limited the rights of the free people of color.

In 1819, for instance, free people of color were banned from entering the state, in an effort to stop the growth of that segment of the population. In 1822, slave emancipations had to be approved by the state legislature, and free people of color were again prohibited from immigrating to Mississippi. Also in 1822, free people of color were required to prove their status as free before local courts to receive certificates, and certificates had to be renewed every three years for a fee. If they did not have a certificate, they could be jailed and sold into slavery.

In 1831, after the Nat Turner slave revolt in Virginia, legislators passed a law under which free people of color

AFRICAN-AMERICAN POPULATION OF MISSISSIPPI, 1820–1900

Year	Slaves	Free People of Color	Free People of Color as a Percentage of Total Population	Total Population
1820	32,703	428	0.6%	75,448
1830	65,659	519	0.4%	136,621
1840	195,211	1,366	0.4%	375,651
1850	389,878	930	0.2%	606,526
1860	436,631	773	0.1%	791,305
1870		444,201	53.7%	827,922
1880		650,291	57.5%	1,131,597
1890		742,559	57.6%	1,289,600
1900		907,630	58.5%	1,551,270

between the ages of 16 and 50 were required to leave the state or be sold into slavery; however, the law was not strictly enforced. In 1856, new manumissions were prohibited, and meetings between free people of color and slaves for the purposes of teaching slaves to read were prohibited. Also in 1856, free people of color were prohibited to take abolitionist literature into the state, and any free people of color found planning rebellion against whites would be sentenced to death.

In the end, the civil and political status of the free person of color became very close to the status of the slave, and, indeed, an 1856 statue declared that "for all offenses in the code for which capital punishment or imprisonment in the penitentiary was not prescribed, free blacks would be tried as if they were enslaved."

Racial discrimination arose from various factors. Some white contemporaries believed that the very existence of free people of color was a challenge to the social order: To their way of thinking, the institution of slavery was needed for survival, and free people of color undermined that system. Many were fearful of slave insurrections and believed that free people of color either were directly responsible for slave revolts or helped encourage slaves to rebel. The growth of plantation society and the increasing commercialization of products (primarily cotton) also led to a kind of distancing between the master and slave, in effect dehumanizing slaves in the eyes of contemporary society and making it harder for people to attain manumission.

These restrictive laws had a number of results, and the population of the free people of color failed to grow. In part, this lack of growth can be attributed to masters being prohibited to free slaves and slaves being prohibited to buy their freedom. More troubling for the future of the free people of color and for Mississippi itself, a number of free people of color fled the restrictive laws and attitudes of the state. Some journeyed to Northern states, and

many left the country for France, LIBERIA, and Haiti (*see also* EMIGRATION AND COLONIZATION).

The Civil War and Reconstruction
Mississippi seceded from the Union on January 9, 1861, and joined the Confederate States of America along with the other Southern states that had seceded. As in other Southern states, one of the major motives for secession can be traced to economic reliance on the institution of slavery. A large conspiracy among black Mississippians near Second Creek was suppressed by the militia in summer 1861. About 40 slaves were hanged, and a number of suspects were tortured to death. At least three free people of color and some poor whites were named as suspects, but none was tried because the evidence against them was from slaves, who were not permitted to testify in court against free people. Some of the free colored suspects were lynched, but some seem to have escaped the persecution.

After the American Civil War began in April 1861, the Union opened fronts in Mississippi quickly with the goal of possessing the Mississippi River for its strategic importance. In 1863, the Union successfully captured Vicksburg and Jackson. According to U.S. Army records, 17,869 black Mississippians fought in the Union army, and many others performed noncombatant service, working as servants or providing aid and information to their liberators. The Civil War ended in the Confederacy's defeat in 1865, and Mississippi was crippled in the process—tens of thousands of Mississippians died in combat or from disease; cities, railroads, and factories were destroyed.

What followed was the period of RECONSTRUCTION IN THE UNITED STATES, wherein Southern states that had seceded worked to regain their status as states. Although the U.S. government abolished slavery in 1865 and obliged Mississippi to ratify this decision and guarantee freedom in its own state constitution, it was soon clear that white Mississippians would not willingly create a world where freedmen shared equality with whites or, for that matter, where freedmen had very many rights at all. Legislators in Mississippi soon set to work writing laws that limited the freedmen's rights to own property, defined requirements for labor (and punished those without labor contracts), and restricted black movement.

During Reconstruction, Mississippi and other Southern states were placed under military rule, and Mississippi's attempt at reinstituting a black code, the set of special laws governing the black population, in the postwar environment was thwarted: The military government gave the newly freed blacks the right to vote, and this was confirmed by the new Mississippi State Constitution in 1868 and the Fifteenth Amendment to the U.S. Constitution in 1870. Black males could now vote, and for a brief time, they made some progress, holding positions of power in government. HIRAM REVELS, a freeborn native North Carolinian, became a U.S. senator from Mississippi in 1870, the first African-American member of Congress. Other African Americans, including many from the prewar free colored community, were elected to office in Mississippi. Many of these prewar free colored leaders of Mississippi's black population during the Reconstruction era, including Revels, were from outside the state, since Mississippi had so few free colored inhabitants in 1861.

Democrats in Mississippi who temporarily lost power during military rule began working toward disenfranchising blacks, first using intimidation tactics and then institutionalizing disenfranchisement through literacy tests, residency requirements, and other means. They were successful, and "Jim Crow" laws that resulted in "separate but equal" transportation, schools, and other public services became common throughout the South in the late 19th and early 20th centuries. Sharecropping developed as a system that replaced slavery as a source of agricultural labor, and both blacks and poor whites participated in it.

In the first decades of the 1900s, under the weight of repressive laws and severe poverty, the conditions of most blacks were not improved. Moreover, the state as a whole suffered from the attitudes of its leaders: When faced with opportunities for economic advances that would improve conditions for the entire population (including blacks), leaders fumbled because they feared improving the conditions of blacks.

Hundreds of blacks in Mississippi also were the victims of LYNCHING, often justified by alleged sexual advances made by black men toward white women. Ida B. Wells-Barnett revealed that most lynchings were more focused on reinforcing white hegemony than on punishing the rape of white women.

Even in this repressive environment, art flourished in the form of literature—Mississippi claims William Faulkner, Tennessee Williams, and Eudora Welty, among others, as natives of the state—and music—the blues rose out of the Mississippi Delta. Ironically, little of this art was appreciated in Mississippi.

In the mid-1940s and into the 1970s, economic conditions improved in Mississippi. Leaders finally recognized the need for diversification of crops (until then, cotton was the primary crop grown by most planters). Leaders also began promoting industrialization in the state. Many of these innovations improved the conditions for blacks by ending the sharecropping system, but blacks still faced ongoing RACISM AND RACIAL PREJUDICE. For example, after World War II, Mississippians further restricted laws for voting, worried that blacks who served would vote as blocs, affecting the outcome of elections.

Indeed, disenfranchisement and discrimination lasted well into the 20th century and were reasons for what became known as the First and Second Great Migrations. In the 1920s and 1930s, and again from 1940 to 1970, millions of African Americans migrated from Mississippi and other Southern states to industrial cities, usually in the North, where greater opportunities for education, representation, and advancement could be found.

Summer Leibensperger

FURTHER READING
Berlin, Ira. *Slaves without Masters: The Free Negro in the Antebellum South.* New York: W. W. Norton, 1974.
Bond, Bradley G. *Political Culture in the Nineteenth-Century South.* Baton Rouge: Louisiana State University Press, 1995.
Carson, James Taylor. *Searching for the Bright Path: The Mississippi Choctaws from Prehistory to Removal.* Lincoln: University of Nebraska Press, 1999.
Clinton, Catherine, and Michele Gillespie, eds. *The Devil's Lane: Sex and Race in the Early South.* New York: Oxford University Press, 1997.
Hogan, William, and Edwin Davis, eds. *William Johnson's Natchez: The Diary of a Free Negro in Ante-Bellum Natchez.* Baton Rouge: Louisiana State University Press, 1951.
Hyde, Samuel C., ed. *Plain Folk of the South Revisited.* Baton Rouge: Louisiana State University Press, 1997.
McDermott, John Francis, ed. *The Spanish in the Mississippi Valley, 1762–1804.* Urbana: University of Illinois Press, 1974.
Skates, John Ray. *Mississippi: A Bicentennial History.* New York: W. W. Norton, 1979.

MISSOURI

Missouri is a state of the United States located in the central part of the nation on the west bank of the Mississippi River. The southern border of the state starts approximately where the Ohio River flows in from the east, while the northern border is about 120 miles north of where the Missouri River flows into the Mississippi. The Missouri River traverses the state from northwest to east, and the three largest cities in the state, St. Louis in the east, Kansas City in the west, and the state capital of Jefferson City in the center, are located in the Missouri valley. The state is relatively well watered and fertile. However, distance and climate made plantation agriculture inefficient in the 19th century, and most farms in Missouri were small family operations, perhaps with one or two enslaved or hired farmhands. Eight states border Missouri: ILLINOIS, KENTUCKY, and TENNESSEE are located to the east; ARKANSAS to the south; Nebraska Territory, KANSAS, and OKLAHOMA to the west; and IOWA to the north. Indigenous people practiced agriculture in the river valleys of the state and created the great civilization called the Mississippian culture, whose largest city was at Cahokia, just across the Mississippi River from St. Louis. The western plains of the state were inhabited by nomadic peoples. The southern mountains supported more diverse Indian populations. After horses introduced by Europeans revolutionized Indian society, Missouri marked the frontier between areas dominated by agricultural Indians to the east and the buffalo-hunting plains nomads to the north and west.

The French began exploring the Missouri territory in 1541. The explorers declared the entire region to be under the control of the French after the voyage of Sieur de La Salle in 1682. Spain took control of the territory in 1762 during the SEVEN YEARS' WAR, but French culture remained strong in the region. By 1764 French fur traders had founded St. Louis as a prosperous fur trading post just west of the Mississippi River and just south of the Missouri River. French masters took some slaves into the territory from Louisiana, and some free people of color were employed in the fur trade as boatmen and laborers. There was a small population of color in French and Spanish colonial times, centered on St. Louis. The French temporarily regained Missouri in an 1800 treaty with Spain but never took direct administrative control and sold it to the United States as part of the land sale known as the Louisiana Purchase in 1803. Missouri's location on the west bank of the Mississippi River allowed for the development of important American ports as well as an entryway for westward expansion.

During the colonial period of the Missouri Territory, free people of color lived under the French Code Noir, which specified that they should have the same rights and privileges as any freeborn French citizen (see also CODE NOIR IN FRENCH LAW). Under the same code, however, free people of color were required always to show respect to their former masters, their former masters' widows, and the former masters' children if they had been enslaved. In 1791, there were about 64 free people of color

living in the Missouri Territory. In 1800, there were 75 free people of color living alongside the 1,191 enslaved persons of African descent. Records show that even under American rule in the early 19th century, St. Louis's free people of color often spoke French in preference to English. During this time, free people of color reportedly held jobs such as farming wheat, corn, and tobacco; tending animals, hunting, trapping, and masonry; as boatmen on the Mississippi River; and in mining for lead. By 1817, the territory's free people of color were legally prohibited to travel and gather for meetings.

Missouri became an American state on August 10, 1821. After three years of heated debate in Congress, statehood resulted from the famous Missouri Compromise, that provided that Missouri could enter the United States as a slave-holding state, and then MAINE would enter as a free state. In other territories yet to be incorporated as states, areas south of the southern border of Missouri could be slave territory while those to the west and north would be free. This compromise allowed the balance of slave-holding states and non-slave-holding states within the United States to remain equal. Thus, neither side of the slave issue had the upper hand in the Senate, where every state has equal power. It also meant that Missouri would be an isolated peninsula of slave territory extending north into the zone of free states, surrounded on three sides by free territory. Although it was a slave state, white Missouri citizens were divided about the slavery issue and about the idea of freedom for people of color in their state. In 1820, the proposed Missouri state constitution stated that emancipated slaves were to leave the territory forever. Missouri's black law and treatment of people of color were, thus, a mixture of what was found in slave states to the south and east and that found in other midwestern states that were its neighbors (see also BLACK LAWS IN THE MIDWEST). When the AMERICAN CIVIL WAR began in 1861, Missouri was a critical border state that had substantial public support for the Confederacy. Ultimately, the state remained in the Union while other slave states joined the Confederacy.

During the 19th century, the free black population in Missouri varied, shrinking from 607 in 1810, to 347 in 1820, and then growing to 567 in 1830 and 1,574 in 1840. The 1830 census showed that four free people of color in four different Missouri counties owned slaves. In the 1850s, the census records show that 5.21 percent of Missouri's population consisted of free and enslaved black people, 2,618 of them free people of color. The 1860 census records show a decrease in the overall black population to 2 percent of the total, only 0.3 percent of them free. In 1860, about half of that population lived in the city of St. Louis. The 1850 and 1860 census records show that Missouri's free people of color worked in jobs such as barber,

AFRICAN-AMERICAN POPULATION OF MISSOURI, 1820–1900

Year	Slaves	Free People of Color	Free People of Color as a Percentage of Total Population	Total Population
1820	9,712	347	0.6%	66,586
1830	25,091	567	0.4%	140,455
1840	58,240	1,574	0.4%	383,702
1850	87,422	2,618	0.4%	682,044
1860	114,931	3,572	0.3%	1,182,012
1870		118,071	6.9%	1,721,295
1880		145,350	6.7%	2,168,380
1890		150,184	5.6%	2,679,184
1900		161,234	5.2%	3,106,665

blacksmith, cook, engineer, farm laborer, farmer, laborer, miner, and wood cutter. These jobs were reported even as free people of color were banned from the job of draymen by an 1850 state law. The records also show that the free people of color were not only Missouri born; they hailed from states such as Arkansas, GEORGIA, Illinois, Kentucky, LOUISIANA, MARYLAND, NORTH CAROLINA, Tennessee, and VIRGINIA AND WEST VIRGINIA. Other birthplaces included the District of Columbia and Indian Territory. Thus, not only European settlers found the new state of Missouri to be worth settling, free people of color found it enticing as well, or at least if they were not born in the free class, they found the state worthy of settling for one reason or another. One such reason was that family members were still enslaved in the state.

In the census records, free people of color also were reported to have personal worth ranging in some cases from $15 to $4,500. Even before the 1850 census recordings, Cyprian Clamorgan, a free man of color of some wealth, published a book in 1830 entitled *The Color Aristocracy of St. Louis*. Apparently, he wanted to distinguish the wealthy class of free people of color from all other free people of color. This book describes a number of St. Louis's wealthy families and their households. In a tone that is sometimes informal and discursive, Clamorgan names the heads of households and then details information such as their skin color, their hair texture, their age, their marital status, their birthplace, their occupation, any interesting pieces of personal information, their home interiors, and their economic standings in the city. These passages range from one sentence to three paragraphs. The heads of households include coffeehouse keepers, mistresses, barbers, "chin scrapers," workmen, steamer stewards, farm owners, rental property owners, vegetable dealers, steel and soap dealers, and hotel owners.

White citizens of Missouri passed laws seeking to control the number of free people of color in the state, similar to black laws passed in neighboring Illinois. For example, in 1835, a state law demanded that each free person of color needed a county license in order to live in Missouri. These licenses cost a considerable amount of money, and the person needed to have a good reputation in the county in which he or she lived. The free person of color also could not have committed a crime or own a gaming house. An 1843 law prevented free people of color from moving into the state. Despite these restrictions, the number of recorded free people of color rose in the mid-19th century, possibly the result of unregulated immigration, MANUMISSION, and natural reproduction. Later in 1858, a law was passed stating that no slaveholder could free a slave unless the slaveholder paid a $2,000 bond and affirmed that the newly freed free person of color would leave Missouri within 90 days. This law also stated that in 1860 every free person of color above 18 years old and below 50 years old was to be relegated to slavery. The governor, however, vetoed this law.

Many of the restrictive laws that were passed in Missouri apparently were not adhered to strictly. For example, in 1847, it became illegal to teach free people of color to read and write. The punishment for this crime was a fine of not more than $500 or a prison term of not more than six months or a combination of a fine and prison sentence. The 1850 census, however, reported 40 free people of color attending school in four different counties, and the 1860 census reported 155 free people of color who were students across the state. In 1856, HIRAM REVELS, a free man of color, and the Sisters of Mercy opened separate schools in St. Louis for free people of color. Other schools existed around the state but were especially prevalent in St. Louis. Records also show that some of the wealthier free people of color sent their children to schools in non-slave-holding states.

Three notable free people of color from Missouri are JEAN-BAPTISTE POINTE DU SABLE, JAMES BECKWOURTH, and Elizabeth Keckley. Du Sable, a fur trapper who ultimately settled in Missouri, was the founder of CHICAGO, ILLINOIS. Originally from Virginia, Beckwourth made a name for himself as a part of various western expedition teams, including the 1823 expedition of William H. Ashley and Andrew Henry. He also discovered the lowest pass through the Sierra Nevada in California. He completed dictating his autobiography in 1845; the book was published in 1856 and entitled *The Life and Adventures of James P. Beckwourth, Mountaineer, Scout, and Pioneer, and Chief of the Crow Nation of Indians*. Formerly enslaved in St. Louis, Keckley made a name for herself in Washington, D.C., during the Civil War as the first lady Mary Todd Lincoln's seamstress and confidant some six years after purchasing her own and her son's freedom in 1855. Keckley published her autobiography, *Behind the Scenes: Thirty Years a Slave and Four in the White House*, in 1868. America's first black priest of the ROMAN CATHOLIC CHURCH, Father AUGUSTINE TOLTON, was born in Missouri, although his family moved to Illinois when he was young, and he served throughout his career in Quincy and Chicago, Illinois.

On April 6, 1847, DRED SCOTT, an enslaved man from Missouri, filed a case with the state claiming his freedom because his master had taken him out of Missouri and they lived for seven years in the free states of Illinois and WISCONSIN. Scott's case was strong; the Missouri Supreme Court previously had freed enslaved people who left the state under the charge of their masters. For example, in the 1836 case of *Rachel v. Walker*, Rachel, an enslaved woman, was taken to the same states as Scott, and the court declared her to be a free woman because of this travel. Scott lost his first trial but appealed his case to the Missouri Supreme Court in 1850. This time the court ruled that the previous supreme court judges were more sympathetic to freeing slaves than the current views of the general slaveholding white public. Two of the three judges finally ruled against Scott in 1852. Scott then took his case to the U.S. Circuit Court for the District of Missouri, and in 1854, Scott again lost his case. Scott and his lawyers finally took their case to the U.S. Supreme Court. On March 6, 1857, the judges ruled that Scott was still a slave. The court decided that the owner of any property, slave or other, did not lose his or her property rights if the property was taken from its original place of residence. Enslaved people were like inanimate objects in terms of property rights. The decision overruled the Missouri Compromise, leaving the territories open to slavery. The decision also opened the way to the expansion of slavery into free states, since if taking a slave from Missouri to Illinois did not make that slave free, presumably the slave could be obliged to work in Illinois as in Missouri. White workers in the North feared competition from slave labor, intensifying the conflict between slave and free states.

The American Civil War was a shattering experience for Missourians in general. Missourians of color were affected by the war in many profound ways. The conflict around slavery had deep roots in American history, but the proximate cause appeared in Missouri with the Dred Scott case and the Kansas-Nebraska struggle of the 1850s. Most slaves and most pro-slavery whites lived in the west-central part of the state, along the Missouri River valley. By the end of the decade, a substantial population of antislavery whites and free colored people made up the majority of the population of St. Louis. In cooperation with this population, the commander of the St. Louis federal military arsenal, General Nathaniel Lyon, kept the city loyal to the United States in 1861 when the governor of the state tried to join the Confederacy. Lyon was soon killed in battle, but his troops drove the Confederates from the state and kept it in the Union. Ultimately, almost 100,000 Missourians served in the U.S. military, more than 8,000 of whom were black. Five regiments of U.S. Colored Troops were formed in Missouri. The first combat experience of black troops in the Civil War was a skirmish at Island Mound, Missouri, October 29, 1862, involving the 1st Kansas Colored Infantry. The unit was organized in Kansas, but most of the troops were Missouri or Arkansas free people of color who had left the state to move to free territory in the West in the years before the war. After the U.S. victory on the battlefield in Missouri in 1861–62, Confederate guerrillas continued to keep Southern hopes alive in the state. Confederate guerrillas were especially hostile to black troops, and black soldiers from Missouri, Kansas, and Arkansas were the victims of a massacre in Arkansas, at Poison Springs, in April 1864. The guerrilla band of Bloody Bill Anderson, which included the brothers Jesse and Frank James, raided Centralia, Missouri, on September 27, 1864, and killed 22 U.S. soldiers, including three blacks who had surrendered. Missouri's state legislature abolished slavery in January 1865. After abolition, Missouri continued to discriminate against blacks, and many black Missourians participated in the EXODUSTER MOVEMENT, heading west to escape discrimination and seek a better life. Missouri's prewar free black population does not appear to have maintained a separate identity after the war.

Angela Bickham

FURTHER READING

Beckwourth, James P. *The Life and Adventures of James P. Beckwourth, Mountaineer, Scout, and Pioneer, and*

Chief of the Crow Nation of Indians. New York: Harper, 1856. Available online. URL: http://books.google.com/books?id=6nFNAAAAYAA. Accessed January 3, 2011.

Berlin, Ira. *Slaves without Masters: The Free Negro in the Antebellum South.* New York: New Press, 1992.

Clamorgan, Cyprian. *The Colored Aristocracy of St. Louis.* Columbia: Missouri University Press, 1999.

Keckley, Elizabeth. *Behind the Scenes: Thirty Years a Slave and Four in the White House.* New York: Penguin, 2005.

Kremer, Gary R., and Antonio F. Holland. *Missouri's Black Heritage.* Columbia: University of Missouri Press, 2005.

Reiss, Oscar. *Blacks in Colonial America.* Jefferson, N.C.: McFarland, 2006.

Trexler, Harrison A. *Slavery in Missouri, 1804–1865.* Baltimore: Johns Hopkins University Press, 1914. Available online. URL: http://www.dinsdoc.com/trexler-1-0b.htm. Accessed January 3, 2011.

MOBILE, ALABAMA

Blacks appeared in the Mobile area of present-day ALABAMA as early as 1707, when a priest baptized Jean-Baptiste, a Negro slave of Jean-Baptiste Le Moyne de Bienville. After the Spanish took control of LOUISIANA in 1769, the Code Noir (*see* CODE NOIR IN FRENCH LAW) was adopted in Spanish Louisiana, including the Mobile area. Between 1785 and 1805, the number of free nonwhite inhabitants increased from 61 to 250, free whites from 446 to 673, but the number of slaves decreased slightly from 642 to 612. During the colonial period, free blacks in the Mobile area played an important role in the economy with several involved in cattle raising (*see* RANCHING). Free people of color also participated in the defense of the area, such as Charles Lalande, who commanded a MILITIA of others of his race. The French and Spanish provided the first non-native inhabitants of the Mobile area, in contrast to the rest of Alabama, whose residents migrated from American states east and north of it.

The total population of Mobile County increased from 2,672 in 1820 to 41,131 in 1860. According to federal census figures, 183 free people of color resided in the county in 1820, or about 7 percent of the county's total population. In 1860, the number of free blacks in the county rose to 1,195, which at that time constituted only 3 percent of Mobile's total population. Mobile's free black community, however, represented 44 percent of the total number of free nonwhites in Alabama. Most of Mobile's 1860 free nonwhites were born in Alabama, but others were from such states as VIRGINIA AND WEST VIRGINIA, MARYLAND, and Louisiana, and at least one person reported that she was born in Africa.

The free black community in antebellum Mobile owes its origin to several factors. The most important of these were the offspring produced by relationships between the French and Spanish settlers and their white descendants and African-American women, slave and free. Many times French and Spanish men openly acknowledged their interracial families, but in some cases they did not. However, the records show that they were the parents of the MULATTO children, and usually their relationships were long-term, showing strong family ties and a genuine concern for the well-being of their children.

White fathers generally provided the economic means by which their families could survive, and during the antebellum years, some of these free families of color successfully built upon the resources that were left to them. The French and Spanish had acquired large quantities of land, which they worked with slave labor, and the free people of color frequently inherited both land and slaves. These were important assets for the free people of color, especially for those who had begun their lives in bondage.

One of the more prominent and numerous free families of color in Mobile, the Chastangs, were in Mobile as early as 1760, when two members of the white Chastang family, John, a physician, and his brother Joseph, settled in the Mobile area. They purchased lands in northern Mobile County and present-day Washington County. The Chastangs, as did other Southerners, purchased slaves to work for them. Louison, in 1780, purchased her freedom and that of her four children from Joseph Chastang. Within five years of her MANUMISSION, she began cohabiting with John Chastang. Their relationship produced 10 children and lasted for at least 20 years. Descendants of Joseph's children developed relationships with free women of color.

The origin of other free families of color in Mobile in some respects parallels that of the Chastangs. For instance, Simon Andry, a white inhabitant of the Mobile area, who also purchased land and slaves, maintained a relationship with one of his slaves, named Jane, which began as early as 1782. They had at least seven children who, as did many other free CREOLES of color, were all baptized in the ROMAN CATHOLIC CHURCH. Andry had his children emancipated at their baptismal services inasmuch as the priest recorded that they were "free mulattoes." Another major family of North Mobile County that had ties to the Chastangs and Andrys was the Dubroca family, consisting of three brothers, Maximilian, Hugh, and Hilaire. Each of these white Dubrocas, as did Dr. John Chastang and Simon Andry, had long-term relationships with nonwhite women, two of whom were free women of color. Other families included, for example, the Collinses, Lalands, and Laurendines.

The legislative bodies governing the territory and later the state of Alabama after the territory became part of the United States determined the method by which slaves could be freed. Mobile itself did not become part of the United States until 1812, though the northern counties were organized into the Mississippi Territory in 1802. The Adams-Onís Treaty, signed by the United States and Spain in 1819, confirmed American control of the region and guaranteed that residents, including people of color, would enjoy the benefits of American citizenship. Alabama became a state in 1819. In 1805, the Legislative Council and House of Representatives of the Mississippi Territory had passed a law governing emancipations, which theoretically was to apply in Mobile once it became part of the territory. It was no longer legal to manumit slaves unless they performed a meritorious act for the benefit of either the owner or the territory. The Alabama legislature in 1834 passed an act authorizing the judges of the county courts to manumit slaves. The legislature stipulated that the newly freed slave was required to leave the state within 12 months after the emancipation and not return.

The growth of the black community in Mobile owes its origins to those SLAVE OWNERS who sought the approval of the Alabama legislature after manumission laws became more restrictive as well as to rapid natural growth of this population. Between 1819 and 1845, the Alabama legislature manumitted or confirmed the emancipations of 84 slaves from the Mobile area, of whom only one, Willis Pope, was required to leave the state upon reaching the age of 21. However, he remained in Mobile. The Alabama legislature specifically stated in 13 of the 84 cases that the manumitted slave was not required to leave the state. Although the Alabama Supreme Court ruled in 1830 that owners could not emancipate slaves by wills, many in the state—including some white and nonwhite slave owners in Mobile County—included such provisions in their wills. Some slaves earned enough money to purchase themselves. Another form of manumission was through popular subscription, as in the case of Pierre Chastang, also known as Major Pierre, who does not appear to have been part of the Chastangs of color who were manumitted for familial reasons. For his civic contributions during the War of 1812, some Mobilians took up a subscription for the emancipation of Chastang, who had amassed through hard work real estate worth more than $1,700 when he died.

The rights of some free people of color in the Mobile area were protected by the federal government, and the state confirmed them. The Louisiana Purchase Treaty of 1803 and the Adams-Onís Treaty of 1819 guaranteed to free residents of Louisiana and FLORIDA and their descendants the rights of citizenship. The Alabama legislature sometimes made special provisions for free nonwhites. Prior to 1819, for example, it was illegal for any free black to sell liquor; in 1822, however, the state legislature allowed free people of color who, by the treaty, became citizens of the United States, or their descendants, to sell liquor. The creoles de couleur were also allowed to establish a school.

This relative liberality in the Mobile area, thanks to the French and Spanish influence on the culture and to the legal protections in the treaties of annexation, meant that Mobile's free black community was more accepted by its white neighbors than elsewhere in the state.

Nonetheless, as did other cities in the South, Mobile enacted ordinances to regulate its population. City officials were authorized to pass measures to prohibit nightly meetings or disorderly assemblies of slaves, free blacks, and mulattoes. In 1830, Mobile amended a 10-year-old ordinance concerning free people of color. It was necessary for every free black who resided in the city to register with the mayor's office within 10 days after the passage of the measure. This ordinance did not apply to free people of color born in the city. At least once a year, the names and personal data of free blacks were to be published in the local press. Only one such instance has been found, and that 1830 list contained but 48 names, such as William West, described as black, aged 45, born in PENNSYLVANIA, and a Mobile resident for 14 years. The 1830 census reported 1,532 free people of color living in the state, and on the basis of the estimate that about 45 percent of these people lived in Mobile County, the report understates by a factor of about 15 the actual free population of color in the city. Presumably, only those free blacks who had given the authorities some reason to doubt their bona fides would be listed in the newspaper.

In the wake of the Nat Turner rebellion in 1831, the Alabama legislature, as did some others in the South, enacted restrictive measures regarding nonwhites. Alabama made it unlawful for any free person of color to settle within the state after January 1, 1833. Free blacks who moved to the state after this date were given 30 days to leave or receive 39 lashes. As in other parts of Alabama, this law was disregarded in Mobile, as is documented in federal census records. Matilda Benton, for example, who appears in local records as early as 1853, was born in Virginia in 1835 and thus entered Alabama in violation of the law. Mobile authorities allowed her to reside in the county.

Free people of color in Mobile pursued a variety of economic activities. Some free people of color, particularly the descendants of the French and Spanish, owned land, livestock, and slaves, which allowed them to make a comfortable living (see also PLANTERS AND PLANTER AGENTS). The average farm owned by a free person of color contained about 180 acres, but this figure is misleading since the three largest farms (owned by Zeno Chastang, Sr.; Maximilian Dubroca; and Maximilian Collins) contained about 3,300 acres, or about 80 percent of the total acreage owned by free black farmers.

All other farms owned by free blacks had less than 150 acres. In 1860, the average number of acres per farm operated by free blacks rose to nearly 360 acres, ranging in size from three acres to 2,010 acres. Several members of the Andry family, including Romain, Sylvester, and Jerome, each owned a number of slaves. In 1860, Louise Andry, the largest slave owner of the Andry family, owned 13 slaves. Zeno Chastang, Sr., owned more slaves and land than any other member of the Chastang family—white or nonwhite. According to the 1850 and 1860 federal censuses, he owned 27 and 29 slaves, respectively. This was a quite substantial slave workforce by local standards, qualifying him as a large planter. On the other hand, Zeno Chastang, Jr., in 1860 owned only three slaves. In 1850, Maximilian Dubroca owned 41 slaves and, 10 years later, 40.

Most free nonwhites in Mobile County lived and worked in the city because there were more economic opportunities for them there. During the late 1830s, free African Americans supported themselves in a variety of ways, such as the barber Elam Page, who advertised his services in the Mobile city directory. Polite Collins offered for sale coffee and chocolate at her house, and she and her mother maintained two coffee stands in the public market. One of the free black grocers in Mobile was Clement Joseph, whose success as a businessman is reflected in his urban real estate holdings. Between 1844 and 1861, he and his wife purchased at least 10 lots of land. Carpentry was a popular trade among free people of color, especially members of the Collins family (see also ARTISANS).

In the antebellum South, religion played an important role in the lives of African Americans, both slave and free. Free nonwhites in Mobile were accepted by most major denominations, including Roman Catholic, Baptist, Methodist, Presbyterian, and Episcopalian. For instance, the State Street Colored Church in Mobile chose Jacob Anderson and Cassius Swanson as leaders and stewards. Armstead Saxon, a prominent free person of color in the Good Shepherd Church, acted as baptismal sponsor to numerous slaves owned by whites, indicating that he developed friendships and earned the respect within the white community. BAPTISTS AND PIETISTS had churches in Mobile that also contributed to the religious development of nonwhites. Several Catholic churches served free people of color, who worshipped at St. Vincent de Paul and St. Joseph's Church. But their involvement was greatest in the Church of the Immaculate Conception in Mobile. Many of the free creoles of color were Roman Catholic, and many of their slaves were also baptized. For instance, many of the children and grandchildren of Maximilian Collins were baptized in the Catholic faith. Free people of color served as godparents for others of their race, and in turn some whites did the same for nonwhites, both slave and free.

Free creoles of color operated a fire company and a school, both of which were sanctioned by local and state authorities. These two endeavors helped the creoles *de couleur* to preserve their own class-consciousness, separate from other free blacks and slaves. Membership was limited to those free men of color who had resided a minimum of three years in the city of Mobile. The social event of the year for the fire company occurred in April when it celebrated its anniversary with a torchlight parade, followed by a dance. The Creole Band marched in the parade to entertain the onlookers.

In addition to the fire company, Mobile's creoles of color had their own school. In December 1833, the Alabama legislature empowered the mayor and aldermen of the city of Mobile to license suitable persons to teach the free creole children of color descending from persons living in those areas that were controlled by the French at the time of the Louisiana Purchase. In addition to the creole school in the city, the Mobile School Board organized other such schools in the county. Members of the nonwhite Chastang family served as local trustees.

Christopher A. Nordmann

FURTHER READING

Gould, Virginia. "In Defense of Their Creole Culture: The Free Creoles of Color of New Orleans, Mobile, and Pensacola." *Gulf Coast Historical Review* 9 (Fall 1993): 27–46.

———. "The Free Creoles of Color of the Antebellum Gulf Ports of Mobile and Pensacola: A Struggle for the Middle Ground." In *Creoles of Color of the Gulf South*, edited by James H. Dormon. Knoxville: University of Tennessee Press, 1996.

———. "The Parish Identities of Free Creoles of Color in Pensacola and Mobile, 1698–1860." *U.S. Catholic Historian* 14 (Fall 1996): 1–10.

Holmes, Jack D. L. "The Role of Blacks in Spanish Alabama: The Mobile District, 1780–1813." *Alabama Historical Quarterly* 37 (Spring 1975): 5–18.

Nordmann, Christopher Andrew. "Free Negroes in Mobile County, Alabama." Ph.D. diss., University of Alabama, 1990.

MONROE, JAMES (1758–1831) *fifth president of the United States (1817–1825)*

Unlike the three Virginians who preceded him in the presidency, GEORGE WASHINGTON, THOMAS JEFFERSON, and JAMES MADISON, James Monroe was not a great planter. He was a middle-class professional, a lawyer, who started with very little; ultimately owned a farm, beside Jefferson's much larger plantation, and a couple of dozen slaves; and eventually had to sell the land and his slaves to pay his debts after leaving the presidency in 1825. He made his career in public service and owed very little to family connections. In a way, he represented a new kind of Virginian, and a new kind of leader for the United States. Born on April 28, 1758, Monroe was the son of a small farmer and carpenter, a member of the rural gentry but by no means a wealthy or influential man. He studied law at William and Mary College in Williamsburg. He served in the Continental army during the WAR OF AMERICAN INDEPENDENCE, 1775–83, joining Washington's staff.

In the famous painting *Washington Crossing the Delaware* by Emmanuel Leutze, Monroe is the man standing behind Washington holding the flag. After the war, Monroe returned to his law practice and entered politics. As did many less well-off Americans, he opposed the ratification of the Constitution, but once it was approved, he worked within the system established. He served as senator from Virginia from 1790 to 1794 and then was American ambassador to FRANCE during the Washington administration. He supported the FRENCH REVOLUTION and clashed with Washington and JOHN ADAMS over their foreign policy, which he thought too pro-British. He was governor of Virginia from 1799 to 1802. During his term, a slave named Gabriel Prosser was accused of preparing an uprising. Part of the plan was to kidnap Monroe and his family and hold them hostage. Monroe organized a roundup of several dozen suspects, including both slaves and free people of color. Monroe insisted that all the accused receive trials, and several were found not guilty. All the free people of color who were accused were ultimately released because the only witnesses to their participation in the plot were slaves, and no slave could testify against a free person. Twenty-six slaves were executed.

A close inspection of the painting *Washington Crossing the Delaware* reveals that the man sitting ahead of Washington is black. In fact, free blacks made up about a fifth of the Continental army by the end of the war, and Monroe was aware of their military potential (*see also* REGULAR ARMY and MILITIA). He supported Henry Laurens's proposal to Washington in 1780 that the Continental army form special units of slaves who would gain their freedom by serving. Washington refused, fearing negative reactions from the Southern colonies. Later, when Monroe was governor of Virginia for the second time just before the outbreak of the War of 1812, he tried to include free men of color in the state militia, but the idea was rejected by the slave owner–dominated Virginia government and militia officer corps. While he was secretary of war in Madison's administration in 1813 and 1814, the U.S. Army enlisted men of color. Monroe thought the United States should have a standing army, and he thought blacks suited for service in it.

Monroe was elected president in 1816 and reelected four years later. As president, in 1823, he issued the statement of U.S. foreign policy that has come to be known as the Monroe Doctrine in his State of the Union message to Congress. The Monroe Doctrine stated that the United States would regard any expansion of European colonial rule in the Americas as hostile to its interests and that the United States recognized the independence of the various Latin American countries that had gained independence over the preceding decade (*see* SOUTH AMERICAN WARS OF LIBERATION and WAR OF MEXICAN INDEPENDENCE). Later, this doctrine became a justification for American intervention in Latin America, but at the time it was rightly seen as a defense of the liberal principle of national self-determination. Since these Latin American countries had almost all granted civil and political rights to free people of color, this can be viewed as an important intervention on behalf of Afro-Latinos. At the time, there was some racially oriented criticism of Monroe's stand, both from European diplomats who argued that only European whites could properly govern Latin America and from Monroe's own political opponents in the United States, who thought that he was aligning America too closely with mixed-race governments to the south.

Also unlike the three Virginians who preceded him in the presidency, no evidence suggests that Monroe had any relatives who were people of color. He died on July 4, 1831.

Stewart R. King

FURTHER READING

Ammon, Harry. *James Monroe: The Quest for National Identity.* Charlottesville: University Press of Virginia, 1990.

Egerton, Douglas R. "Gabriel's Conspiracy and the Election of 1800." *Journal of Southern History* 56, no. 2 (May 1990): 191–214.

Scherr, Arthur. "Governor James Monroe and the Southampton Slave Resistance of 1799." *Historian* 61, no. 3 (1999): 557–578.

MONTEZUMA, FRANCISCO GÊ ACAIABA DE (VISCOUNT OF JEQUITINHONHA) (1794–1870)
Brazilian lawyer and politician

The viscount of Jequitinhonha was one of the most influential mixed-race politicians of the Brazilian Empire. He also made important contributions to the development of modern ideas about the law and to the professionalization of lawyers in Brazil.

Born Francisco Gomes Brandão in SALVADOR, BAHÍA, BRAZIL, in 1794, the future viscount of Jequitinhonha was the son of a ship captain involved in the African slave trade. His parents wanted him to enter the Franciscan order, but he had no vocation for this and studied surgery instead. In 1816, he went to Lisbon and, shortly thereafter, matriculated at Coimbra University in PORTUGAL, where he studied law. After graduation, he returned to Bahía, where he became involved in the political questions surrounding Brazilian independence. He wrote for the liberal *Diário Constitucional* and quickly won a seat on the city council. When relations between Brazilian patriots and Portuguese broke down in 1822, Brandão joined the patriots and undertook two important missions to Rio de Janeiro to cement ties between Emperor PEDRO I and Bahíans struggling against the Portuguese troops in Salvador.

On his return from his second mission to Rio de Janeiro, he founded another newspaper, *O Independente Constitucional,* and, in its first issue, announced that he had changed his name to Francisco Gê Acaiaba de Montezuma, a rejection of his Portuguese birth name and a nativist identification with Brazilian indigenous peoples and the Aztec emperor. His growing political prestige secured him election to the new Brazilian Empire's constituent assembly, in which he played an important role in the opposition to Pedro I's authoritarian tendencies. The emperor exiled Montezuma to Europe when he closed the assembly in November 1823. Montezuma traveled widely in Europe, continued his studies in medicine and law, and joined the Masonic order (*see also* FREEMASONRY).

He returned to Brazil in 1831 and resumed his political career, in which he demonstrated a remarkable and sometimes inconsistent independence as a member of the chamber of deputies (1831–33, 1838–41) and a journalist. By the end of the 1830s, he had aligned himself with the future liberal party and briefly served as minister of justice and foreign affairs (1837) and Brazilian representative to Great Britain (1840–41). Upon his return to Brazil, he left politics and devoted his time to his law practice. In 1843, he founded the Instituto da Ordem dos Advogados, the Brazilian bar association, and served as its first president.

Montezuma returned to politics in 1847 as provincial deputy for Rio de Janeiro. His legal reputation earned him an appointment to the council of state, an advisory body to the emperor, in 1850. In 1851, Emperor PEDRO II appointed him to the senate, a lifetime post. Three years later, when Pedro II granted titles of nobility to all of the councilors of state, Montezuma received the title of viscount of Jequitinhonha. In the senate, he gained a reputation as a skilled orator and expert on financial affairs; in 1866, he served as president of the Bank of Brazil. As a senator, he presented various proposals for the gradual ending of slavery, none of which passed. He died in 1870.

The viscount of Jequitinhonha was one of the most successful MULATTO statesmen in imperial Brazil. Periodically during his career, political enemies targeted him with nasty racist invective. While generally liberal in his politics, Jequitinhonha was often inconsistent in his political alliances. His life is an example of how far a person of mixed race could go in Brazilian society, with good family ties, intelligence, good education, and the right choice of political allegiances.

Hendrik Kraay

FURTHER READING
Vianna, Hélio. "Francisco Gê Acaiaba de Montezuma, Visconde de Jequitinhohna." *Revista do Instituto Histórico e Geográfico Brasileiro* 244 (July–September 1959): 104–135.

MOREAU DE ST-MÉRY, MÉDÉRIC-LOUIS-ÉLIE
(1750–1819) *French lawyer and writer*

Médéric-Louis-Élie Moreau de St-Méry was the first historian of SAINT-DOMINGUE and a very important early commentator on race relations and the role of free people of color in the Americas. He was white, born in the French Caribbean colony of Martinique on January 13, 1750 (*see also* FRENCH CARIBBEAN). He studied law in Paris and became a lawyer in the courts of Paris in the 1770s. He was a coffee planter and judge of the regional court in CAP-FRANÇAIS/CAP-HAÏTIEN, in Saint-Domingue from 1780 until 1784, when the court was suppressed in order to concentrate power in the hands of the colonial governor in PORT-AU-PRINCE. Moreau de St-Méry objected to the suppression of the courts, using arguments similar to those of the factions in France supporting the regional *Parlements* courts against the royal prerogative. He returned to France in 1784 and began to compile the laws of the French Caribbean colonies in a coherent form. His six-volume *Loix et Constitutions des Colonies Françaises de l'Amérique Sous le Vent* (Laws and constitutions of the French American leeward colonies) represented an important step not only in the quest of the colonies for a consistent law book but also for the Enlightenment project of positive written law and constitutionalism. He also began the monumental *Description topographique, physique civile, politique et historique de la partie française de l'isle Saint-Domingue* (Topographic, physical, civil, political, and historical description of the French part of the island of Saint-Domingue), intended to be a comprehensive encyclopedia of the colony. The first edition of this work, in three volumes, was published in 1788 in Paris and remains an invaluable resource for historians.

When the FRENCH REVOLUTION began in 1789, Moreau de St-Méry was a deputy in the French National Assembly for the colony of Martinique. He was chosen by the white landowners of the colony, and he represented their interests, fighting against the decision to grant votes to free people of color and against the admission of free colored deputies from Saint-Domingue. He was in danger of arrest during the Terror in 1793, and he fled into exile in the United States. He opened a print shop and bookstore and revised and enlarged his monumental *Description* of the colonies of Saint-Domingue and added one of Spanish Santo Domingo, which came under French control as a result of the Treaty of Basel in 1795, between 1796 and 1798.

In the *Description*, he described the two parts of Saint-Domingue not as they were in 1798, in the throes of the Haitian Revolution, but as they had been before 1789. He expressed the hope that his work would help the French government reconstruct the prerevolutionary society, which he considered preferable to what had replaced it. Unlike many other nostalgic Saint-Domingue exiles, Moreau de St-Méry was willing to acknowledge failures and weaknesses in the old social system. In a moving passage, he described the work of a free man of color, François Jupiter, to establish a hospital for free coloreds in Cap-Haïtien, and he deplored the unwillingness of the colonial government and the Roman Catholic Church to help him. In general, however, his view of the people of color of the colony was that they were incapable of governing themselves and that the only hope of the colony, or any similar colony, was white supremacy. He described free people of color as naturally idle, effeminate, and devoted to physical pleasures and games, although good soldiers and personally brave and honorable. In some ways, he considered the slaves superior to the free coloreds, however, especially some of the African slaves whom he saw as a sort of noble savages, unspoiled by the debilitating effects of modern society, though still entirely unsuited for independence.

He compiled an infamous and widely copied typology of race mixture, defining a large number of shadings of different white and black ancestry, each with a name and each with a personality type that he felt was defined or at least strongly indicated by that degree of mixture. The use of different terms to describe different degrees of race mixture was nothing new; indeed, the CASTA paintings of New Spain predate Moreau de St-Méry's work by almost a century. What was new was the attribution of certain personality characteristics to particular shadings of race mixture. The connection of behavior patterns and race, a staple of 19th- and early 20th-century racial "science," had a very early expression in his work.

His interpretation of Haitian government and society was widely accepted at the time. Indeed, it became the consensus European and North American view of the newly independent Haiti as its government experienced periodic instability during the 19th century. Outside observers following Moreau de St-Méry often argued that Haitians were incapable of governing themselves. The best-known general history of Haiti in English today, first published in 1978, Robert Debs Heinl's *Written in Blood*, largely recreates this conclusion stripped of its racial undertones.

It is easy to dismiss Moreau de St-Méry as another in a long series of nostalgic French exiles after the Haitian Revolution writing about the happy old days on the plantation. However, he was a much more important figure than that. His very careful description of the colony and its people is like a *Domesday Book* for a Caribbean slave colony. Nothing in anything like the same detail exists for any other place in the region. For this alone, his work is valuable for historians. But he also represents a turning point in how the Western world thought about race. Up to that point, the superiority of whites over nonwhites was personal—a white person, the ruler or master, considered himself superior to specific nonwhite persons, the subjects or slaves. Laws had begun to place all whites on a plane of superiority to all nonwhites, but Moreau de St-Méry was one of the first theoretical political commentators to try to portray this superiority as natural, a product of inherent differences between the races that could be described in scientific terms.

Moreau de St-Méry returned to France after the rise of Napoléon Bonaparte. He served in several positions in Napoléon's government and in the restored royal regime after 1814, including as archivist of the French Ministry of Marine (responsible for colonial government). He took advantage of this position to take a large number of papers from the archives into his own files and use them to revise and improve his *Description* and *Loix et Constitutions*. Luckily for historians, after he died on January 28, 1819, his papers went back to the Archives and can be consulted there.

Stewart R. King

FURTHER READING

Moreau de St-Méry, M. L. E. *Description topographique, physique civile, politique et historique de la partie française de l'isle Saint-Domingue.* 3 vols. Paris: printed privately, 1788 [Philadelphia 1796–1797]; reprint of 2nd ed. Blanche Maurel and Etienne Taillemite, eds. Paris: Société de l'Histoire des Colonies Françaises, 1958. Portion of vol. 1 in English translation available as *Civilization That Perished.* Translated by I. D. Spencer. New York: University Press of America, 1986.
Taffin, Dominique, ed. *Moreau de Saint-Méry, ou les ambiguïtés d'un créole des Lumières.* Martinique: Société des amis des archives, 2006.

MORELOS, JOSÉ MARÍA (1765–1815) *Mexican priest and revolutionary leader*

José María Morelos was a Roman Catholic priest and revolutionary leader in Mexico. Born on September 13,

1765, he was a ZAMBO, of mixed African, Native American, and Spanish ancestry. His father was born in an Indian village but passed for Spanish; he may have been a mestizo or a *ladino*, an Indian who had assimilated to Spanish culture. Morelos's mother was dark-skinned and was either black or mixed-race. Morelos's father sent him to school with the intention that he study for the priesthood. Normally, people of color were not allowed to be ordained as priests in the Spanish Americas, but Morelos had been registered as white because of his father's (probably equally assumed) racial status. However, when the father died, the boy had to leave school and go to work as a teamster leading a mule train carrying goods from place to place. It was while he was pursuing this profession that he gained an intimate knowledge of the geography of southern Mexico and of the way of life of working-class Mexicans. Most

mule trains were operated by Afro-Mexicans, and the contacts Morelos made in this business allowed him to raise loyal soldiers later in his life. He also worked as a planter's agent on a sugar plantation in Michoacán (*see also* SUGAR CULTIVATION and PLANTERS AND PLANTER AGENTS).

Morelos did not give up the dream of becoming a priest, however, and at the relatively advanced age of 25, he had saved enough to enter the seminary of San Nicolas at Valladolid. The rector of this seminary was Fr. Manuel Hidalgo (1753–1811), Mexico's other priest-liberator hero, and the friendship that sprang up between the young seminarian and his rector was of great importance for Mexico's future. Morelos was ordained a priest at the age of 33 and assigned to the parish of Carácuro in Michoacán. During his time as a parish priest, he reputedly fathered several illegitimate children, one of whom, Juan

Two portraits of José María Morelos, a mixed-race Catholic priest who was the second leader of the pro-independence forces in Mexico. Morelos was a student of the pioneer of Mexican independence, Father Manuel Hidalgo (1753–1811), and took his place at the head of the independence forces after Hidalgo was captured and executed by the Spanish. Morelos had spent years working as a mule driver in rural west-central Mexico, an area where there were many Afro-Mexicans. His mixed racial identity, similar to that of most Mexicans, and familiarity with the region made him a formidable guerrilla leader. Note the differences in the two images. The one on the left, probably made from life, shows him as dark-complexioned, with a round face, and hair caught up in a scarf or soft hat to conceal its curly texture. The one on the right is from a postindependence engraving used in a patriotic 1825 biography. The later portrait gives him a much sharper nose, thinner face, lighter complexion, and straight or, at most, mildly curly hair, illustrating how Latin American society "whitened" its African-descended national heroes in the 19th century. *(Left: The Granger Collection, New York; right: Library of Congress)*

Nepomuceno Almonte (1803–69), went on to become an important military leader and served briefly as regent of Mexico during the reign of Emperor Maximilian in 1863–64. Morelos was serving as a parish priest when Hidalgo proclaimed the Grito de Dolores, Mexico's declaration of independence, in 1810.

With a small band of followers, Morelos began to wage war against the Spanish colonial government. He began his movement in his parish but quickly moved to the Pacific Coast of Mexico, where he had worked as a muleteer. There, he recruited heavily among Afro-Mexicans, drawing into his movement, among others, VICENTE GUERRERO SALDAÑA, a mixed-race mule driver who later became Mexico's first elected president. Hidalgo was captured and executed in 1811, and Morelos became the leader of the rebel movement. He fought for another four years, gathering other rebel military leaders together in a congress at Chilpancingo in September 1813. This congress proclaimed racial equality in Mexico. Morelos also called for land reform and redistribution of Catholic Church properties, though he was no freethinker and believed that Catholicism should be the state religion of an independent Mexico.

Morelos's movement suffered reverses in 1815, and Morelos and his fellow rebel chieftains began to bicker. The Congress stripped Morelos of some of his powers after he suffered a number of defeats in the field. Finally, he was captured by loyalist cavalry, taken in chains to Mexico City, defrocked by the church, and executed by firing squad on December 22, 1815. By 1828, newly independent Mexico had renamed the city of his birth Morelia in his honor, and a huge statue marked the spot of his execution. He has become Mexico's most popular liberator-hero, mostly because, unlike Hidalgo, he was a man of the people, and also unlike Hidalgo, he was clear and unwavering in his determination that Mexico should be an independent nation built on a foundation of social justice.

Stewart R. King

FURTHER READING

Bethell, Leslie, ed. *The Cambridge History of Latin America.* Vol. 3, *From Independence to c. 1870,* ch. 3. Cambridge: Cambridge University Press, 1985.

Timmons, Wilbert. *Morelos of Mexico: Priest, Soldier, Statesman.* El Paso: Texas Western Press, 1970.

MULATTO

A person of approximately half-African and half-European ancestry. In some places in the Americas, the term was used for all people of mixed race, though more commonly, and less insultingly, the terms colored, brown, and PARDO were used for this purpose. The term is considered insulting in the United States since it derives from the word mule and suggests that the mixing of races is somehow unnatural, as is the interbreeding of a horse and a donkey. Similar terms exist in French (mûlatre) and Spanish (mulato), but these are less offensive in those societies.

Stewart R. King

N

NAVY

Unlike the army, most of the European navies of the 18th and 19th centuries, and the U.S. Navy, were fully integrated at the enlisted and noncommissioned ranks. Even the Confederate States of America navy during the AMERICAN CIVIL WAR had black sailors. Naval service was to a surprising degree free of RACISM AND RACIAL PREJUDICE during this period. One ironic reason for this peculiar lack of racial discrimination was that abuse and mistreatment of naval personnel were common. In most countries, though not the United States, naval servicemen were recruited by force. In Britain, this was the infamous "press" that could conscript almost any man, except those who had high social status or were working in exempted occupations, into the service with no notice whatsoever. "Press gangs" of sailors haunted city streets and even attacked rural villages, hauling men who had never been farther from their home than the nearest market away to serve on ships at the far end of the world. In order to keep these men in the service, navies took extraordinary precautions to prevent desertion, sometimes locking most or all of a crew below decks or in irons when in port. One of the principal causes of the War of 1812 was the British practice of stopping American ships to search among the crew for British deserters. Officers had the power of life and death over their men, as well as physical punishment by whipping and branding. The conditions of naval service were so like slavery that naval service became an occupation that a person of color could take up on equal terms with a white.

Moreover, naval crews were very diverse in all ways, even as armies were becoming less so (see also REGULAR ARMY). The rise of the nation-state and the ideas of the Enlightenment changed the character of service in the army from near-slavery to patriotic duty during the 18th century. However, this change of attitudes lagged behind in the navy. European and North American nations more or less stopped accepting noncitizens (including most men of color) into the ranks of their armies in the early 19th century, but blacks and foreigners continued to serve in navies until the late 19th century in most places. British naval vessels serving in the Caribbean for long periods could have crews that were majority black. Those serving in the Indian Ocean could have large numbers of East Indians, Arabs, East Africans, and East Asians.

Very few people of color were commissioned as officers; one exception was ROBERT SMALLS (1839–1915), who became captain of the USS *Planter*, a vessel he stole May 12, 1862, from the Confederate States navy in which he had served as her pilot. But even without commissions, many blacks were leaders in the world's navies during the age of sail. Naval noncommissioned officers, called petty officers, and technical specialists, called warrant officers, almost all rose from the ranks. Most navies had fewer commissioned officers in proportion to the crew than would be found today, and so warrant and petty officers were entrusted with major responsibilities. Black enlisted sailors probably faced some handicaps in seeking promotion to warrant or petty officer rank, but it was not impossible. As a result, many blacks had the opportunity to become important leaders in the navy. In the Spanish navy, most leadership roles were filled by warrant officers, with only a few commissioned officers on any given ship, and so free colored warrant officers could command large numbers of men. One example is JOSÉ PRUDENCIO PADILLA, who was a navigating officer and third in command on his ship in the Spanish navy, before joining the rebel navies of VENEZUELA and COLOMBIA during the SOUTH AMERICAN WARS OF LIBERATION.

Naval service was important to the men who served as a way to enter a trade that was valuable and at the same time to escape from possible slavery and indeed from slave societies altogether. Many of the black residents of LONDON, ENGLAND, including OLAUDAH EQUIANO, originally entered Britain as naval seamen. Equiano's career shows how important naval service was for him. He first enlisted in the British navy while still a slave, accompanying his master as a servant. He was listed on the ship's manifest, however, and received wages (though perhaps his master took them away from him; at least he signed the ships' books as having received his pay). At several points during his service, he was ashore in Britain for

A group of black sailors on the U.S. Navy warship USS *Vermont* during the American Civil War (1861–65). Black sailors were numerous in the enlisted ranks of many navies in the Americas. Outside the United States, men of color even became officers and some, such as Admiral José Prudencio Padilla in Colombia, held powerful positions. (© Bettmann/CORBIS)

extended periods and thought of himself as a free man. His master thought otherwise and contrived to sell him to a West Indian merchant. Equiano's new master, learning of his nautical experience and skills, put him to work as a traveling merchant's clerk, escorting shipments of the master's goods around the Atlantic world. The second master agreed that Equiano could have his freedom in return for repayment of his original purchase price, and he ultimately was able to save the money and gain his liberty. He worked as a merchant seaman and merchant's agent throughout the rest of his life and earned a respectable living (see MERCHANT SEAMEN). A SAINT-DOMINGUE free man of color, Bertrand LeMoine, was a cook on a French naval vessel during the War of American Independence, then moved over to the merchant service in the 1780s. A man who had served at sea in the navy could easily move into peaceful seafaring and find his skills still useful, and there was little racial discrimination in the merchant service either.

After the American Civil War, the world's navies became increasingly segregated. The sense that military service was a form of citizenship and ought to be restricted to full citizens spread from the army to the navy at this time. In addition, the shift from sail power to steam meant that work on a ship became a technical task, the equivalent in many ways of factory labor, and racial stereotypes, growing in importance at this time, characterized blacks as incapable of such technological knowledge. Black sailors did not entirely disappear, either from the U.S. Navy or from the European navies. But they were increasingly relegated to difficult, dangerous, or menial tasks and denied the opportunity to rise in the ranks. Black sailors in the U.S. Navy were restricted to service as cooks and servants. In the British navy, they could serve in the engine rooms of the new steamships, shoveling coal into the furnaces. The coal dust darkened everybody's skin, and the engine room crew was called the "black gang" and required to eat separately in many ships. The U.S. Navy was actually the last of the American armed services to integrate meaningfully in 1970, under the leadership of Admiral Elmo Zumwalt.

Stewart R. King

FURTHER READING

Bolster, W. Jeffrey. *Black Jacks: African-American Seamen in the Age of Sail.* Cambridge, Mass.: Harvard University Press, 1998.

Equiano, Olaudah. *The Interesting Narrative of the Life of Olaudah Equiano, or Gustavus Vassa, the African.* New York: Penguin, 2003.

Reidy, Joseph P. "Black Men in Navy Blue during the Civil War." *Prologue Magazine* 33, no. 3 (Fall 2001). Washington, D.C. National Archives and Records Administration. Available online. URL: http://www.archives.gov/publications/prologue/2001/fall/black-sailors-1.html. Accessed January 3, 2011.

NEBRASKA

Of the states of the Middle West, Nebraska had one of the smallest free black populations during the 19th century. It became a state in 1867 and is today bordered by South Dakota, IOWA, MISSOURI, KANSAS, Colorado, and Wyoming (*see also* INLAND WEST OF THE UNITED STATES). One of the first black travelers in the territory that would become the state of Nebraska was a slave named York, owned by William Clark of the Lewis and Clark Expedition in 1804–06. By 1819, when the expedition of Maj. Stephen H. Long arrived in the territory, free black pioneers were present at Fort Lisa, and there were several officers' slaves at Camp Missouri.

In 1846, several black members of the Church of Jesus Christ of Latter-day Saints traveled through Nebraska on their way west, including Green Flake, Hark Lay, Elijah Abel, Oscar Crosby, and Jane Manning James. Manning James was born free in CONNECTICUT around 1820 and converted to Mormonism in 1843. She lived in the Mormon settlement at Nauvoo, Illinois, where she worked in the household of Joseph Smith and where she married Issac James. In winter 1846–47, while the couple was camped in Nebraska during their trek west, Manning James gave birth to her first child, a son named Silas, who may have been the first African American born in Nebraska.

In 1854, the Kansas-Nebraska Act established both the Kansas and Nebraska Territories. While the status of slavery in Kansas would be hotly debated during the remainder of the decade, Nebraska's status as a free territory was never seriously questioned. As in Iowa, ILLINOIS, and INDIANA, from which the territory drew many of its migrants, the early statutes of Nebraska were firmly anti-

slavery but were not amenable to the rights of would-be black residents.

Slavery did, in fact, exist in Nebraska during the 1850s, although the extent of its influence was politically negligible. The first territorial census in 1860 listed a total of 15 slaves in Nebraska. In 1859, the territorial legislature approved a law that prohibited the holding of slaves, but slaves were still apparently held in the territory until at least 1860, as permitted by the Supreme Court's decision in the DRED SCOTT case.

Because of its short border with Missouri, eastern Nebraska during the 1850s was a focal point of Underground Railroad activity, and sympathetic Nebraskans helped slaves escape to Iowa and MINNESOTA. Few of these fugitive slaves settled permanently in Nebraska, but in 1913, Henry Daniel Smith of Omaha, born in 1835 in MARYLAND, claimed to have entered the state through the Underground Railroad.

Despite the relatively small numbers of black residents and the antislavery sentiments of many of them, controversy over the rights of slaveholders to their property affected Nebraskans as it did other residents of the Midwest. In 1858, three slaves owned by a Nebraska City merchant named Stephen Nuckolls escaped to Iowa, a free state. Nuckolls launched an aggressive search into Iowa and was ultimately ordered by an Iowa court to pay for damages he had caused in the process. The escaped slaves apparently remained free in Iowa.

During the AMERICAN CIVIL WAR, Nebraskans remained generally opposed to the pro-emancipation policies of the Lincoln administration and joined with other midwestern states in fearing the influx of black migrants from the South that they assumed would result from emancipation. Exclusionary school laws were passed in 1859, and anti–INTERRACIAL MARRIAGE laws were adopted in 1866. In 1867, the public schools were opened to black residents, but they were not mandated to provide equal, integrated educational opportunities.

During the statehood debates of 1867, which coincided with debates over the ratification of the Fourteenth Amendment, the word *white* was stricken from the proposed state constitution. In March 1867, Nebraska was admitted as the first post-emancipation state to join the Union and without exclusionary racial language in its constitution.

Statehood seemed to open the floodgates of immigration to Nebraska during the 1870s, although the majority of this influx was by white settlers. In 1870, the first post-statehood federal census listed the state's total population at 122,993, only 789 of whom (or one-half of 1 percent) were black. By 1890, although their numbers had grown exponentially to nearly 9,000 black residents in the state, black Nebraskans still constituted less than 1 percent of the state's total population.

AFRICAN-AMERICAN POPULATION OF NEBRASKA, 1860–1900

Year	Slaves	Free People of Color	Free People of Color as a Percentage of Total Population	Total population
1860	15	67	0.2%	28,841
1870		789	0.6%	122,993
1880		2,385	0.5%	452,402
1890		8,913	0.8%	1,062,656
1900		6,269	0.6%	1,066,300

Although their numbers remained relatively small, concerns about black citizenship still surfaced through legal challenges to black rights. In 1871, the chief justice of the Nebraska Supreme Court stated that black citizens could not serve on juries, a ruling based on territorial legislative precedents barring black participation in courts of law. The next year, however, a majority of the court dissented from this opinion in *Brittle v. The People*, ruling that one of the conditions for statehood had been that Nebraska could not deny voting or other civil rights to black males, including the right to sit on juries.

In 1879, when Kansas officials began to refuse any more of the so-called Exodusters (black migrants from the South), the riverboats and trains carrying the migrants were sent north to Nebraska, where they received a mixed welcome (*see also* EXODUSTER MOVEMENT). In keeping with the partisanship of RECONSTRUCTION IN THE UNITED STATES, Nebraska Democrats opposed black emigration, while Republicans generally welcomed it. Altogether, despite Democratic worries, probably only about 400 black immigrants entered Nebraska during the Exoduster migration.

Many black Nebraskans lived in towns or cities, where it was easier to find work. Omaha was the center of Nebraska's black population during the late 19th century, with 789 black residents in 1880 and 4,566 in 1890. Lincoln followed with 576 in 1880 and 1,360 in 1890.

The railroad towns of Columbus, Grand Island, and Hastings had small black populations, whose numbers also grew by the end of the 19th century as the region boomed. Between 1880 and 1890, the black population of Hastings soared from just 25 to more than 300. Because of this boom, Hastings developed black Baptist and Methodist (A.M.E.) congregations, a black Masons lodge, social clubs, and a black baseball club (*see* BAPTISTS AND PIETISTS and AFRICAN METHODIST EPISCOPAL CHURCH).

Other black settlers arrived individually and in small groups, establishing short-lived communities in Custer, Dawson, Franklin, Hamilton, and Harlan Counties. Subject to the same hardships as their white neighbors, black Nebraskans were especially hard hit by natural disasters and economic downturns because many of them had established their homesteads with fewer resources. The drought years of the early 1890s, along with financial panics, encouraged many Nebraskans, both black and white, to move on to other areas, so that Nebraska's black population had dropped by more than 2,500, or 30 percent, between 1890 and 1900.

Thomas Bahde

FURTHER READING
Calloway, Bertha W., and Alonzo N. Smith. *Visions of Freedom on the Great Plains: An Illustrated History of African Americans in Nebraska.* Virginia Beach, Va.: Donning, 1998.
Polk, Donna Mays. *Black Men and Women of Nebraska.* Lincoln: Nebraska Black History Preservation Society, 1981.

NEGRO CONVENTION MOVEMENT IN THE UNITED STATES

The "Negro Convention Movement" began in spring 1830 in PHILADELPHIA, PENNSYLVANIA, and continued throughout the 19th century. Free blacks met in these conventions every year from 1830 to 1835 and then sporadically until the late 1800s. In general, the meetings were held at the state and national levels by black leaders seeking a way to better their conditions as free blacks in the North.

The immediate impetus for the first meeting was a series of riots that took place in Cincinnati, OHIO, in August 1829. These riots were part of a general effort throughout the new states of the Northwest to exclude free blacks from the territory in the interest of maintaining "racial purity." Essentially, slavery was barred from this part of the country by the Northwest Ordinance of 1787, and the new states that were carved out of this territory, most notably ILLINOIS, INDIANA, and Ohio, sought to exclude free blacks as well. They used anti-immigration legislation to try to prevent free blacks from settling in their borders, and they used the black codes to try to control those who did manage to move in (*see* BLACK CODES IN THE UNITED STATES).

Ohio provides the most famous example. In 1804 and 1807, the state passed restrictive black laws (see BLACK LAWS IN THE MIDWEST) that required black immigrants to post bonds of $500 to guarantee their good behavior. They also had to furnish court documents to prove that they were legally free and not escaped slaves. Until 1829, these laws were sporadically enforced, but that year authorities in the city of Cincinnati became concerned over the growing free black population and announced that the black laws would be strictly enforced. They ordered black residents to comply or leave within a month. Black leaders managed to convince white leaders to extend the period so that they could send representatives to CANADA to find a location where they could resettle. They also tried to convince the state legislature to repeal the laws. Their white neighbors, however, wanted no such repeal and were impatient to rid the city of black residents, so they began to roam through black neighborhoods in mobs, terrorizing blacks and destroying their property. As a result, as many as 2,200 Cincinnati free blacks left for Canada.

Free blacks faced similar treatment throughout the North and the Northwest. By the 1820s, as more and more blacks were freed (or managed to escape) from slavery, the free black population grew in nonslave states, leading whites to resent job competition or to fear the idea of racial mixing. According to the historian Leon Litwack, in his book *North of Slavery*, "Most northerners, to the extent that they thought about it at all, rebelled at the idea of racial amalgamation or integration. Instead, they favored voluntary colonization, forced expulsion, or legal and social proscription." This sentiment was not confined to new states like Ohio. Older states like MASSACHUSETTS and PENNSYLVANIA also considered barring free black immigration, and many states, including Pennsylvania and NEW YORK STATE, revised their state constitutions to restrict voting rights to white men. Mob action was also widespread throughout the northern regions as whites tried to make free blacks miserable enough to seek asylum in Canada, Africa, or elsewhere. This is the social context that led to the convention movement.

The first convention emerged from the efforts of a 16-year-old free black in Baltimore, Hezekiel Grice. Grice heard about the Cincinnati riots and began to wonder whether others throughout the country should follow the lead of those who had left for Canada. He contacted black leaders throughout the North, calling for a convention to discuss the idea of mass emigration. Black leaders in New York and Philadelphia, were first to respond, and RICHARD ALLEN, a bishop of the AFRICAN METHODIST EPISCOPAL CHURCH (A.M.E.) and respected leader of Philadelphia's free black community, made the official call for the first convention.

Forty free black leaders, from Pennsylvania, NEW JERSEY, New York, CONNECTICUT, RHODE ISLAND, Ohio, MARYLAND, DELAWARE, and VIRGINIA, met at Philadelphia's Bethel Church on September 14, 1830, in Philadelphia. Participants included Allen, Grice, William S. Whipper, Frederick C. Hinton, SAMUEL E. CORNISH, Junius C. Moreal, John Bowers, Austin A. Steward, and Abraham D. Shadd. They chose Allen as president and organized a new organization called the American Society of Free People of Colour for Improving Their Condition in the United States; for Purchasing Lands; and for the Establishment of a Settlement in the Province of Canada. They also issued the "Address to the Free People of Colour of these United States," which stated their purpose to "pursue all legal means for the speedy elevation of ourselves and brethren to the scale and standing of men." They rejected the AMERICAN COLONIZATION SOCIETY's efforts to resettle blacks in Africa, but they supported the creation of a settlement in upper Canada.

Between 1830 and 1835, free blacks met annually in similar conventions. In June 1831, 16 delegates met again in Philadelphia, and they maintained that venue for the 1832 convention, which included 29 delegates, and the 1833 meeting, which included 56. In 1834, 40 delegates met in New York City, and in 1835, they returned to Philadelphia. To further their goal of self-elevation, they founded a network of organizations called Phoenix Societies. Chapters of this group emerged throughout the cities of the North under the leadership of black ministers such as Christopher Rush, Theodore S. Wright, and Peter Williams, Jr.

The historian Philip Foner identified four major issues that were debated at the conventions. First was the initial question of Canadian emigration. Though the first convention supported the idea, by 1833 they had decided against large-scale exodus to any location, instead choosing to focus on improving their conditions "in their native land" and insisting that their rights as Americans be respected. Second, and in a similar vein, the conventions repeatedly spoke out against the American Colonization Society. The third issue involved education. At the 1831 convention, they devised a plan to establish a manual training college for blacks and put Samuel E. Cornish in charge of fund-raising. They secured the assistance of the wealthy white abolitionist Arthur Tappan, who bought land in New Haven, Connecticut, for the campus, but the plan ultimately fell victim to the type of white resistance and violence that had led to the 1831 convention. Finally, the conventions dealt with a number of plans to secure the elevation of free blacks through moral reform. William Whipper, a Pennsylvania temperance leader, led this drive, basically taking control of the 1835 convention and spearheading the founding of the American Moral

Reform Society to push for moral reform through education, temperance, and economy.

After the 1835 convention, disagreements among black leaders led to a lull in convention activity. The main issue was whether or not blacks should fight to build their own institutions or insist on integration into white society. The New York delegates generally favored the former, while the Philadelphia delegates and their supporters advocated the latter. Between 1836 and 1841, annual meetings were held by the American Moral Reform Society, which was dominated by the Philadelphia contingent, and the actual Negro Conventions were not revived until this organization collapsed in the late 1830s. At that point, a younger generation of black leaders, who included HENRY HIGHLAND GARNET, MARTIN DELANY, Samuel Ringgold Ward, Jermain Loguen, James McCune Smith, and FREDERICK DOUGLASS, emerged. Many of this generation had come to resent the way in which white immediate abolitionists such as William Lloyd Garrison had, in some ways, co-opted the black freedom movement, and they began to call for all-black conventions and organizations.

The Negro Conventions resumed in the 1840s. Forty-eight delegates met in 1843 in Buffalo, New York. Delegates participated from New York, Virginia, NORTH CAROLINA, and GEORGIA, but the convention was dominated by the New Yorkers. The most famous of these was a Troy, New York, Presbyterian pastor, Henry Highland Garnet, who issued a famous call for slaves to rise up and overthrow their masters. As had earlier conventions, however, this one focused on the importance of education, mechanical arts, and literary and scientific improvement. In 1847, 68 delegates met in Troy, New York. Though nine states were represented, most of the delegates were from New York or Massachusetts, and the main focus was on the creation of an independent national black press, with no immediate result (see also BLACK PRESS IN THE UNITED STATES). At the next convention, in 1848 in Cleveland, Ohio, the focus was on creating state vigilance committees to "measure arms and assailants without and invaders within." Thanks to Frederick Douglass, this convention was also the first to refer to delegates broadly as "persons" to signal the inclusion of women. After this, the convention movement was dormant once again.

By 1853, the Northern black community was again under the type of assault signaled before by the Cincinnati riots, and this led black leaders to revive the conventions once again. That year, 140 delegates from nine states met in Rochester, New York, in what Foner, in his *History of Black Americans*, calls "the most important of all the National Negro Conventions." The Reverend James W. C. Pennington was chosen as president, and Frederick Douglass, William C. Nell, and John B. Vashon were elected vice presidents. Under Douglass's leadership,

the Committee on Declaration of Sentiments issued an "Address of the Colored Convention to the People of the United States," which called for integration of schools (including colleges), churches, and workplaces. It also called for complete legal equality, unrestricted black voting rights, and the repeal of all discriminatory laws. While some delegates, including Douglass, Pennington, and James McCune Smith, continued to push for the founding of a manual labor college for black youth, others, including Charles L. Remond and George T. Downing, objected to this idea because it would reinforce SEGREGATION. The Douglass group won, and the convention endorsed the project.

The National Council of the Colored People also emerged from this convention. Two delegates to this council were to be elected from 10 different Northern states, and four committees were created. The Committee on a Manual Training School was charged with carrying forth the convention's plans for such a school by raising funds, choosing a location, and establishing the school. The Committee on Business Relationship was created to serve as an employment office, and the Committee on Publication was established to collect and make public records and statistics relevant to black history. Finally, the Committee of Protective Union was formed to establish a cooperative whereby blacks could buy and sell staple products.

Despite enthusiasm for this broad agenda, little was actually achieved, and the last national Negro Convention was held in October 1855 at Franklin Hall in Philadelphia. At this meeting, 124 delegates from six states and Canada reconsidered the manual labor school and concluded that it would only serve to further the segregation of black youth. After this meeting, there continued to be state conventions intermittently until the 1880s.

The main legacies of the Convention Movement included a number of local and state efforts to improve the conditions of free blacks, the emergence of a number of mutual aid and benevolent societies throughout the Northern United States, the advancement of black education, and a legacy of opposing emigration. Importantly, the conventions gave the free black community a sense of pride and self-confidence, giving them a voice from 1830 to the Civil War years. Ultimately, the conventions united free black communities in a civil rights struggle and allowed black leaders to sharpen their leadership techniques and push for political, social, and economic equality.

Beverly C. Tomek

FURTHER READING
Bell, Howard H. *Minutes of the Proceedings of the National Negro Conventions, 1830–1864.* Salem, N.H.: Ayers, 1969.

Foner, Philip S. *History of Black Americans: From the Emergence of the Cotton Kingdom to the Eve of the Compromise of 1850.* Santa Barbara, Calif.: Greenwood Press, 1983.

Gliozzo, Charles A. "John Jones and the Black Convention Movement, 1848–1856." *Journal of Black Studies* 3 no. 2 (December 1972): 227–236.

Litwack, Leon. *North of Slavery: The Negro in the Free States, 1790–1860.* Chicago: University of Chicago Press, 1961.

Middleton, Stephen. *The Black Laws: Race and the Legal Process in Early Ohio.* Athens: Ohio University Press, 2005.

NEW HAMPSHIRE

New Hampshire is a state of the United States. It is located in the northeastern region of New England. It is bordered by Maine to the east, Massachusetts to the south, Vermont to the west, and Canada to the north. In the colonial era, Vermont was a territory in dispute between New Hampshire and New York State, while Maine was a part of Massachusetts until 1820. The state has a short Atlantic seacoast with one large harbor at Portsmouth. A flat coastal plain extends inland from Portsmouth, and the city and its surrounding plains are the home of most of the state's population. The remainder of the state is mountainous and heavily forested. The climate is cool and damp with frequent mountain snow, unsuitable for plantation agriculture.

The indigenous inhabitants of New Hampshire were Algonquin speakers, related to the native peoples of Maine and Massachusetts. They had had contact with Europeans from the 16th century, when a variety of explorers and fishermen camped on the coast for short periods to salt fish and replenish supplies. The Indians resisted long-term European settlement until the early 17th century, when epidemic diseases reduced their numbers drastically.

The first European settlers in what is now New Hampshire were English, people from Massachusetts in 1629. They had an unknown but probably small number of African slaves with them. In 1645, one of these slaves, a newly arrived African owned by a Mr. Williams of Piscataqua, sued for his freedom in the colonial court, alleging that his capture was unjust. The court ordered the slave merchant to return him to his home, though there is no evidence that this was ever done. He may have been re-enslaved in another colony, or he may have remained as a free person. The court decision in this case reveals that, at least at this early date, New Hampshire courts were open to blacks, even enslaved blacks. The black population in Portsmouth was reported to be 187 in a 1767 colonial census, of a total black population throughout the colony of 633. These figures do not differentiate between enslaved and free blacks, and it is pos-

sible that free blacks were counted as "free men" along with poor whites who were not indentured servants. The 1775 census counted 656 slaves but made no mention of free people of color at all, apparently counting them with free whites. The colonial government passed various laws for the governance of slaves during the period, forbidding them to travel without a pass from their master or to purchase alcohol in 1735, for example. By the 18th century, the colony had followed the precedent of the Southern colonies by affirming that children inherited the status of their mother. There were a number of suits during the 18th century in which people sought to prove their titles to freedom, masters won some and free people of color others. In 1760, the courts found in favor of the children of a free black woman, Leisha Webb, ruling that they were all free despite the fact that Webb's husband was a slave. Manumission was a private act in New Hampshire, with slaves gaining freedom through self-purchase, through their master's wills, or as a gift during their master's life without any formal legislation. Free blacks in the colonial period worked mostly in urban occupations, as artisans, dockworkers, retail and merchants; in service trades; and as merchant seamen.

During the War of American Independence, 1775–83, there was no combat in New Hampshire aside from some small raids along the coast by British warships. The New Hampshire militia went to fight in the New England campaign of 1775–76, and three regular army regiments, the 2nd, 5th, and 8th Continental Infantry, under the command of John Sullivan (1740–95) served with distinction in the northern theater throughout the war. As did many of the New England regiments, the 2nd Regiment in particular included soldiers of color, apparently at least 50 of a total unit of around 500 at the time of the Battle of Trois-Rivières (1776), although this figure may include Indians as well as blacks. Among these was Prince Whipple (1750?–96), a slave who accompanied his master, William Whipple, who became commander of the regiment and ultimately a general in the Continental army. After the end of the war, Prince was freed and lived out his life in Portsmouth. Many of his descendants still live in the area today. General George Washington wanted to expel black soldiers from the army in early 1776, but the New England commanders, including Sullivan, opposed his orders, and black soldiers were a significant part of the American army during this war. During the war, a convention of New Hampshire blacks submitted a petition to the state legislature, asking that slavery be outlawed in the state as being inconsistent with the values of freedom and equality that the colonies were fighting for.

New Hampshire's constitution of 1784 contained language about universal freedom and equality similar to that of the Massachusetts Constitution of 1780, which Massachusetts courts held made slavery unconstitutional (*see* Quock Walker case). No similar legal case eliminated slavery in New Hampshire in one stroke. However, over about 15 years after independence, slavery died out in New Hampshire. The state ceased to recognize slaves as taxable property in 1789, but there were some people still considered slaves into the 19th century.

The small numbers of free blacks in New Hampshire did not experience great discrimination when compared to the situation of free people of color elsewhere in the country. They were a tiny minority of the population and must not have seemed very threatening. There was a small black community in the city of Portsmouth, with members working in the usual occupations of urban free people of color—artisans, servants, laborers, merchant seamen, and dockworkers, and in the hospitality industry. Esther Whipple Mullineaux (1840?–96) was a typical example. Granddaughter of the Prince Whipple who fought in the American Revolution, she owned two properties that may have been boardinghouses in Portsmouth, and she ran a laundry business. She enjoyed reasonable comfort and stability. New Hampshire, like the rest of New England, was seen as a place of refuge for African Americans escaping slavery and prejudice in the rest of the country. Ona Judge Staines (ca. 1772–1848), a mixed-race woman who had been enslaved by George Washington's wife, Martha, fled to New Hampshire as Washington's term as president was ending in 1796. She settled in Greenland, New Hampshire, where she lived for the remainder of her life. She worked hard but suffered a number of setbacks and never escaped poverty. When asked, late in life, whether

all the difficulties she had suffered made her wish that she had remained with the Washingtons, she replied, "No, I am free, and have, I trust, been made a child of God [by my] escape to freedom."

Portsmouth blacks created community institutions like those in other Northern cities. The Ladies' Charitable African Society provided poor relief. The first black churches were not founded until after the American Civil War, but there were apparently informal black worship and study groups within white-dominated churches back to the 1840s from which emerged the leaders who established separate black Methodist and Baptist churches in the 1870s.

The Civil War marked a turning point for black New Hampshire, as it did for the rest of the country. New Hampshire blacks had been active in the abolition movement, and Portsmouth was an important nexus in the Underground Railroad moving blacks to Canada to escape the strictures of the Fugitive Slave Act of 1850. Upon the outbreak of war in 1861, New Hampshire blacks were eager to play their part what they hoped would be a revolutionary struggle against slavery and racism. About 50 New Hampshire men enlisted in the famous 54th and 55th Massachusetts Infantry regiments, among the earliest black combat units in the war. In addition, 125 New Hampshire men served in other regiments of the U.S. Colored Troops: Amazingly, more than 25 percent of all black New Hampshire citizens were in uniform at some time during the war.

After the war ended in 1865, New Hampshire experienced, in attenuated fashion, the hopes of Reconstruction (*see* Reconstruction in the United States) and

AFRICAN-AMERICAN POPULATION OF NEW HAMPSHIRE 1790–1900

Year	Slaves	Free People of Color	Free People of Color as a Percentage of Total Population	Total Population
1790	158	630	0.4%	141,885
1800	8	852	0.5%	183,858
1810		970	0.5%	214,460
1820		914	0.3%	344,151
1830	5	602	0.2%	269,328
1840	1	537	0.2%	284,574
1850		520	0.2%	317,976
1860		494	0.2%	326,073
1870		580	0.2%	318,300
1880		685	0.2%	346,991
1890		614	0.2%	376,530
1900		662	0.2%	411,588

the dashed hopes of the post-Reconstruction period. Black citizens experienced discrimination even here, and the KU KLUX KLAN was active in Portsmouth in the 1920s (though their activities were directed primarily at immigrants instead of blacks). New Hampshire blacks emigrated during the postwar era, sometimes to the South during Reconstruction in search of family members who had been taken away by slavery and sometimes in search of economic opportunity in Northern cities. As throughout its history, conditions in New Hampshire were relatively better than those found outside New England, but they were still not ideal.

Stewart R. King

FURTHER READING

Melish, Joanne. *Disowning Slavery: Gradual Emancipation and Race in New England, 1780–1860.* Ithaca, N.Y.: Cornell University Press, 2000.

Piersen, William. *Black Yankees: The Development of an Afro-American Subculture in Eighteenth-Century New England.* Amherst: University of Massachusetts Press, 1998.

Sammons, Mark J., and Valerie Cunningham. *Black Portsmouth: Three Centuries of African-American Heritage.* Lebanon: University of New Hampshire Press, 2004.

NEW JERSEY

New Jersey is a state of the United States of America. It is located along the Atlantic Coast, bordered by NEW YORK STATE on the north and PENNSYLVANIA to the west. The northeastern border is the Hudson River, and the western border is the Delaware River, and these two fertile river valleys defined the early settlement patterns of the state. The northwestern part of the state is mountainous, while the southern part is flat, forested, and relatively barren. The indigenous inhabitants of the area were settled agriculturalists of the Lenape culture group.

The area along the Hudson was part of the Dutch colony of New Amsterdam from 1624. The area along the Delaware was first settled by Sweden and was the colony of New Sweden until 1655, when it was conquered by the Dutch. The Dutch colony was captured in its turn by England in 1664.

The first blacks to live in New Jersey arrived in the northern part of the state in 1630. The Spanish had captured approximately 50 Africans and imported them to the Dutch colony to work on a plantation in Pavonia, which was on the west side of the Hudson River, across from New Amsterdam. Even though Dutch law did not recognize slavery and there were no indentured servitude statutes in the Dutch colonies in the New York and East New Jersey region, most blacks were taken to the area as slaves of the Dutch West India Company. These individuals were the core laborers for the colony, clearing land; building homes, mills, roads, and fences; and performing the rigorous farming tasks.

By the 1640s, the Dutch West India Company emancipated its slaves, either to avoid the expense of caring for aging slaves or to reward loyalty exhibited during Indian attacks. In addition, slaves purchased their own freedom; however, the offspring of the freed blacks were stipulated to be slaves under these emancipation agreements. On occasion, private SLAVE OWNERS also emancipated their slaves, usually with similar provisions regarding the children of the freed slaves.

In the late 17th century, free blacks began migrating from New Amsterdam to New Jersey. John De Vries, Sr., and his son John, Jr., as well as Nicholas Manuels, were three of the original shareholders of Tappan, New Jersey—all were free black farmers who migrated from Manhattan because of rising property taxes. These families passed on their farms to their children; the Van Donck family maintained their small cattle farm into the 19th century. During the 1660s, one of the first freeborn blacks in the colony, Youngham Antonious Roberts, was among the original residents of Hackensack, New Jersey, through his purchase of a large tract of land in the town. A small number of free blacks also settled in Mattawan, Saddle River, and Bergen County, including Roberts, who settled in the Matawan Mountains after leaving Hackensack.

Upon the English conquest of the Dutch colony in 1664, more restrictive laws that affected both slave and free blacks were enacted. Governance of slavery became the purview of the English government through the English Foreign Office, rather than a private matter administered by the Dutch West India Company. However, it was not until the early 18th century that New Jersey had fully developed slave laws.

With English rule came growth in the number of slaves in New Jersey. At the time of the English conquest, there were few slaves working the farms, manors, and plantations of New Jersey; the number climbed from 120 in 1680 to nearly 1,900 by 1730, aiding the area's development. Farmers replaced indentured servants with slaves, generating a rapid expansion of rural slavery, which in turn developed the region's status as a major agricultural center. According to the census of 1726, more than 10 percent of New Jersey residents were black; blacks constituted 18 percent of the population of Bergen County and 8 percent in Middlesex and Essex Counties.

As the Anglican Church in New York began the process of educating and converting black slaves, in New Jersey, the Dutch Reformed Church, the most powerful religion in the rural areas of New Jersey, opposed this practice. (*See also* PROTESTANT MAINLINE CHURCHES.) The Anglican Church was concerned about the number of slaves who were not Christian, and one of its earliest prominent members in the region, Elias Neau, a slave trader and missionary, began holding religious services and teaching the catechism to his slave congregants in New York but did not do the same in New Jersey, where slave owners, who tended to be members of the Dutch Reformed Church, were particularly fearful that the baptism of slaves mandated their emancipation. British laws passed at the time that refuted this baptism-emancipation connection failed to convince slave owners in New Jersey that the British were not attempting to take away their slaves surreptitiously.

New laws increasingly limited civil liberties for blacks, and as the laws became more restrictive, a circular pattern emerged—harsher laws led to an increase in violence and resistance, leading to laws that further restricted blacks' civil liberties and supported bondage, and the cycle repeated, thus leading to further violent reactions and resistance. Statutes enacted in 1712 revoked freed blacks' property rights and required posting of a £200 bond in order to free a slave, which had the effect of making emancipation through the last will and testament of a slaveholder a rare occurrence. The concern was these freed slaves would become a burden on the community, which would then have to support them.

By the 1730s, colonists in New Jersey had become more worried about revolts and the increasing number of violent crimes committed by slaves. White residents were suspicious of slaves imported from the West Indies, whom they perceived to be violent and dangerous, and preferred slaves directly imported from Africa. Slave revolts were averted in 1734 in Somersett County, and in 1741 involving both New York City and New Jersey. The 1734 plot by about 30 slaves involved simultaneously killing their masters while they slept and was only discovered by accident when a man named One Reynolds happened upon a drunken conspirator on the road, who told Reynolds the plan. In 1741, the slave revolt began with the arson of buildings in New York and New Jersey as a prelude to the destruction of New York City and the massacre of its white inhabitants. The plot was uncovered, and the conspirators arrested and executed before it could be carried out, but this did little to calm the white residents of the area. Revolts and violent crime by blacks continued. In 1746 in Bergen County, slaves axed, burned, and poisoned their masters, and news of black violence aboard slave ships reached the colonies. In response, in 1751, the New Jersey assembly enacted laws outlawing gatherings of more than five blacks.

Many New Jersey blacks fought in the War of American Independence on both sides. One of the most important pro-British guerrilla leaders in the colony was COLONEL TYE, a black maroon leader who fought the Americans

for several years until he was killed in 1780. The British promised freedom to any slave who would support their cause. In response, many New Jersey blacks fled to the British positions in New York. The peace treaty that ended the war in 1783 stated that all property should be returned to American owners by the British, but the British commanders refused to recognize owners' property rights in RUNAWAY SLAVES, and the black refugees were taken to Nova Scotia, CANADA, or SIERRA LEONE after the war. The pro-independence New Jersey government also promised freedom under certain limited circumstances to slaves who fought for the rebellion with the permission of their masters, though the U.S. Congress did not support this measure on a national scale. Most blacks who fought in the American forces in New Jersey were prewar free people of color. Most black soldiers in the War of American Independence fought in mixed units. One of the most famous of these was the Marblehead Regiment from Massachusetts, which was about one-third African American, which transported Washington's army across the Delaware River on Christmas Eve, 1776, to attack the Hessians at Trenton, New Jersey. The enemy was taken off-guard because they thought the river was impassable because of the weather and the presence of large floating blocks of ice. But the skilled boatmen of Marblehead conveyed the army across the river, and Washington was able to gain an important small victory and keep rebel hopes alive in New Jersey.

In response to pressure from the state's Quakers, New Jersey's governor, William Livingston, presented a bill for emancipation to the State Assembly, but to no avail. (See also BAPTISTS AND PIETISTS.) In 1786, New Jersey enacted a ban on the importation of slaves from Africa or the West Indies, though slaves could still be imported from other states in the new republic. The law also ended the required £200 bond on MANUMISSIONS, and a later amendment in 1788 required masters to teach slaves to read.

In the late 18th century, states in the North began the process of abolishing slavery. New Jersey, the last Northern state to enact an emancipation law, passed the Act for the Gradual Abolition of Slavery in 1804. Under the act, children born of slaves after the date of its enactment were freed upon reaching the age of 28 for males and 25 for females. However, many slave owners bypassed the 1804 act by selling slaves to a Southern-state slave owner just prior to their emancipation date. A small number of slaves remained in New Jersey into the mid-19th century. In 1846, the state legislature transformed all remaining slaves into indentured servants and required that they be supported for life by their masters. Yet, in spite of the graduated emancipation, prior to the Civil War several laws were enacted that restricted the movement of blacks, such as the 1837 statute requiring the registration of all free blacks, and proof of emancipation

AFRICAN-AMERICAN POPULATION OF NEW JERSEY, 1790–1900

Year	Slaves	Free People of Color	Free People of Color as a Percentage of Total Population	Total population
1790	11,423	2,762	1.5%	184,139
1800	12,422	4,402	2.1%	211,149
1810	10,851	7,843	3.2%	245,562
1820	7,548	12,056	5.3%	227,575
1830	2,254	18,303	5.7%	320,823
1840	674	21,044	5.6%	373,306
1850	236	23,810	4.9%	489,655
1860	18	25,318	3.8%	672,035
1870		30,658	3.4%	906,096
1880		38,853	3.4%	1,131,116
1890		47,638	3.3%	1,444,933
1900		69,844	3.7%	1,883,669

for blacks wishing to reside in the state. Slavery in New Jersey was not completely abolished by law until the end of the Civil War and the enactment of the Thirteenth Amendment in 1865.

Yet while emancipation of slaves during and shortly after the Revolutionary War remained rare, the New Jersey Constitution of July 2, 1776, ignored gender and race barriers in its suffrage clause, granting voting rights to all inhabitants who were at least 21 years of age, owned property worth 50 pounds, and were residents of the county where they were voting for at least one year, including women, aliens, convicts, slaves, and free blacks. However, while the voting rights acts of 1790 and 1797 specifically included the language "he or she" when referring to eligible voters, thus sanctioning women's suffrage, it also restricted voting to free inhabitants, thereby eliminating suffrage for slaves. Opening up suffrage to women and free blacks was a departure from other states in the republic, which while using similarly gender-neutral language in their constitutions did this under the assumption that neither slaves nor women would be eligible to vote. New Jersey state legislators were alone in holding to a different interpretation and acting out of a sense of justice—persuaded by the strong influence of Quakers in the southern part of the state, who held to the philosophy of equality—that, it was the right of every free person who paid taxes to have a vote.

The loss of suffrage for blacks and women in 1807 was tied to political expediency in an effort to unite a split Democratic-Republican Party. The party had divided over an argument regarding voter fraud during a referendum deciding the location of the Essex County seat, and a faction of moderates broke away to form a third party. In New Jersey, political organizations and allegiances were strong and systematized in the state and key to maintaining power. To reunite the party and appear to be addressing widespread voter fraud and reduce political corruption, the new election law enacted in 1807 disenfranchised nontaxpayers to placate the moderate Democratic-Republicans, and aliens were denied suffrage to pacify other factions. To balance out the loss of these voters, blacks and single women, who were traditionally considered Federalist voters, also had their suffrage revoked. Voting was to be restricted to free white males, even though almost all evidence of the corruption prompting the law resided with that group of people. Article II of the state constitution adopted on July 29, 1844, reflected this change, stating that only white male U.S. citizens were entitled to vote. However, a few local election officials viewed this change as unconstitutional and continued to allow women, blacks, and aliens to cast ballots. New Jersey's free black males regained suffrage in 1870 with the ratification of the Fifteenth Amendment to the U.S. Constitution, but black and white women did not regain their voting rights for another 50 years with the passage of the Nineteenth Amendment. The next revision of the New Jersey Constitution, in 1947, reflected the re-enfranchisement of blacks and women.

While there was a small population of second-generation freeborn blacks in New Jersey who owned farms in the early 1700s, their numbers were insufficient to create a viable free black farming class. Free blacks in the urban centers faced poverty and starvation. Mortality rates among urban blacks were high as a result of smallpox, yellow fever, dysentery, and cholera, and other diseases. When facing an outbreak, whites were often able to flee to suburban or country homes, while blacks usually had no such recourse and remained in the city to face the epidemic.

In the 1800s, urban employment for free blacks was usually as domestic servants for women and menial manual labor for black men. Black women performed demanding and poorly paying domestic labor that their white counterparts declined in favor of more lucrative jobs as seamstresses or teachers. Yet even while most free blacks remained in poverty, by the 1850s, some urban black workers had risen to fill middle-class occupations, as small sundry shopkeepers, barbers, and tailors, as well as blacksmiths, carpenters, and shoemakers. Peter Scudder began as a shoe shiner and apple peddler at the College of New Jersey (later Princeton University); by the 1850s, he had become an independent businessman operating a storefront that sold candy and ice cream. Another successful black entrepreneur of that era, Anthony Simmons, used the profits from his catering business and confectionary and oyster shops in Princeton to acquire real estate holdings in the area.

Northern black men and women who were accomplished hairdressers, dressmakers, blacksmiths, carpenters, and the like—who often had learned these trades prior to emancipation—had few opportunities to earn a living at their trade. Northern skilled black workers who either were emancipated or had emigrated from the South were routinely denied licenses as ARTISANS and guild memberships; they were seen as competition by skilled white workers. The typical work found even by artisans during the mid-1800s tended to be low-skilled, manual labor; only a small percentage were entrepreneurs, professionals (such as ministers or teachers), or gainfully employed as artisans and tradesmen.

Yvette Liebesman

FURTHER READING

Berlin, Ira. *Many Thousands Gone: The First Two Centuries of Slavery in North America*. Cambridge, Mass.: Harvard University Press, 1998.

Elmer, Lucius Q. C. *The Constitution and Government of the Province and State of New Jersey, with Biographical Sketches of the Governors from 1776 to 1845*. 1872. Reprint, Memphis, Tenn.: General Books, LLC, 2009.

Hodges, Graham Russell. *Root and Branch: African Americans in New York and East Jersey, 1613–1863*. Chapel Hill: University of North Carolina Press, 1999.

Horton, James Oliver, and Lois E. Horton. *In Hope of Liberty: Culture, Community and Protest among Northern Free Blacks, 1700–1860*. Oxford: Oxford University Press, 1997.

Klinghoffer, Judith Apter, and Lois Elkis. "'The Petticoat Electors': Women's Suffrage in New Jersey, 1776–1807." *Journal of the Early Republic* 159 (Summer 1992): 12.

McCormick, Richard P. *The History of Voting in New Jersey*. Vol. 97. New Brunswick, N.J.: Rutgers University Press, 1953.

Wesley, Charles H. "Negro Suffrage in the Period of Constitution Making, 1787–1865." *Journal of Negro History* 143 (April 1947): 32.

Wiebe, Robert H. *The Opening of American Society*. New York: Alfred A. Knopf, 1984.

NEW ORLEANS, LOUISIANA

New Orleans is a city at the mouth of the Mississippi River, which winds its way through the center of the North American continent. The river begins in an area known today as MINNESOTA and ends its journey more than 2,000 miles away in the Gulf of Mexico. In 1541, Hernando de Soto became the first European to see the river. More than a century would pass before white Europeans began to explore the inland areas of the river. At a crescent-shaped bend in the river, 100 miles north of the Gulf of Mexico, the French established the first European city in 1718. The city was originally called Vieux Carré (meaning the old square). Eventually the city came to be called New Orleans (for the French duc d'Orléans) and acquired the nickname the Crescent City.

New Orleans is a city that is essentially unique in the United States as far as the role free people of color played in its history and the role that the descendants of those free people of color continue to play in its society today. Its background as a French, then Spanish colony meant that the more liberal racial definitions in French and Spanish culture remain important even in the 21st century. French and Spanish law protected the free colored community of New Orleans in some ways during the 19th century. At the same time, Louisiana was a frontier area in the French and Spanish empires, so the cultural and legal protections were not undermined by the pressure of a highly productive plantation sector. For all these reasons, the situation of free people of color in New Orleans and its surrounding area resembles that in Latin America much more than what is found in the Anglo portions of the United States, even in northern Louisiana.

French and Spanish Colonial Period (1718–1803)

From 1718 to 1763, FRANCE maintained control of the vast Louisiana Territory that stretched south from CANADA to the Gulf of Mexico and from the Mississippi River west to the Rocky Mountains. In 1763, in the aftermath of the SEVEN YEARS' WAR, France ceded the territory to SPAIN under provisions of the Treaty of Paris. In 1800, France secretly reacquired the region from Spain but did not exercise administration before turning over the colony to the United States in the Louisiana Purchase treaty of 1803.

UNDER MY WINGS EVERY THING PROSPERS

The city of New Orleans with the main square, later named after Andrew Jackson, in the center. The drawing dates to 1803, when the United States took possession under the terms of the Louisiana Purchase. The oldest neighborhood, home to many of the city's people of color, lies to the right in this view. *(The Granger Collection, New York)*

The city of New Orleans was then, and continues to be, one of the major port cities on the North American continent. Whoever controlled that city controlled the entire Mississippi River. When THOMAS JEFFERSON took office as the third president of the United States in 1801, he was informed that control of the Louisiana Territory would soon transfer back to France. While the territory was under Spanish control, the United States had been guaranteed the right to trade at New Orleans. However, that right would no longer be guaranteed when the French reacquired the city. After much discussion with his advisers, President Jefferson dispatched ambassadors to France with an offer to purchase the city of New Orleans to protect American interests.

Napoléon Bonaparte, ruler of France, lost control of the French Caribbean island of SAINT-DOMINGUE as slaves began their overthrow of the colonial government on that island beginning in 1791 (*see also* HAITIAN REVOLUTION). In 1802, he sent a large expedition to try to restore French fortunes in Haiti, but this force was clearly on the way to defeat by the rebel slaves in spring 1803. In any case, war was about to begin between France and Britain, and Napoléon might well lose New Orleans and his other American territories to British invaders. By the beginning of the 19th century, Napoléon was quickly losing interest in all of his North American holdings because of the financial and military efforts necessary to maintain them. In addition, he needed funds to sustain France's ongoing conflict with the British. When Jefferson offered to buy the city of New Orleans, Napoléon counter-offered. Instead of selling just the city, Napoléon proposed the sale of the entire Louisiana Territory to the United States for $15 million. Although President Jefferson hesitated, he became convinced the purchase was in the best interest of the fledgling nation. When the treaty was signed and the transfer of ownership was complete, the United States instantly doubled in size. The acquisition of this multinational territory, with its diverse cultures and traditions, posed a challenge for Jefferson. When the two nations crafted the treaty that transferred control of Louisiana to the United States, the French demanded the incorporation of provisions that would ensure the rights of free people of color. Despite the guarantees, those rights were never as secure under American rule as they had been under European.

After the United States took possession of New Orleans, the city began to expand geographically beyond its original boundaries. The old part of the city, today located to the northeast of the downtown area, remained home to the French-speaking population and came to be known as the French Quarter. Canal Street, located southwest of the French Quarter, became the dividing line between the French Quarter and the ever-expanding city. On the northeast side of Canal Street, business was conducted in French. Just beyond Canal Street, language of business was English. Canal Street served as a meeting of the two cultures: a bilingual section where all could go to do business of importance to the city.

Colonial Culture and Free People of Color

As an international port, the city of New Orleans had enormous cultural diversity. At the time of the purchase, there were approximately 8,000 people living in and around the city. Of that number, nearly 1,300, or 16 percent, were free people of color. Under the relatively brief period of Spanish rule, prior to the rise of large plantations, slaves experienced greater legal leniency and opportunities for MANUMISSION than they would later under U.S. rule. It became far more difficult for slaves to attain manumission or to buy their freedom once the region fell under American control. Under French and Spanish rule, free people of color enjoyed many more legal rights than free blacks did under American control. The French and Spanish maintained the European tradition of a class-based society. As a result, they did not classify free people of color as one specific racial category; they were seen as a societal class. Conversely, Americans downplayed the notion of a class-based society, choosing instead to focus instead on race as the cultural distinction. This focus on race led to the creation of a term used to describe a new category of race unique to the Americas: Creole.

In the Louisiana context today, some scholars use the term *Creole* to define an ethnic group consisting of those individuals who were, and are, native born to Louisiana. However, the term CREOLE has historically had several definitions, each of which has validity. Creole can refer to the first generation of children born in America to two parents of European birth. It can also mean those children who were born to fathers of European ancestry and mothers who were MULATTO (biracial) and free. There is yet another meaning to the term *creole*: that is, the group consisting of free people of color who spoke the French language and were members of the ROMAN CATHOLIC CHURCH. Some descendents of free people of color living in Louisiana today continue to refer to themselves as Creoles, using the term as a badge of distinction to highlight their French ancestry.

Historically, free people of color were members of a tightly knit, self-sustaining society. Despite the insular nature of their society, there were gradations within the group. The majority of free people of color were laborers and tradesmen; they competed with poor whites and white tradesmen for available employment. However, there was also an elite, highly educated group of free people of color at the pinnacle of their society, who enjoyed a status available to few individuals of any race. This status was recognized in law, as the French-American treaty that sealed the Louisiana Purchase said that all the current inhabitants of the territory would be protected in their rights. Antebellum Louisiana practice honored this provision by granting a somewhat different status to free people of color whose ancestors had lived in the territory before 1803. They could, for example, own land and slaves much more easily than those freed after the treaty, and there was no objection to their institutions of education, though in principle, it was unlawful even to teach blacks to read after 1832 (*see* SLAVE OWNERS and EDUCATION AND LITERACY).

Members of this small group lived in a society closely parallel to that of their white counterparts. In many cases, elite families on both sides of the color line were biologically related because of a well-known Louisiana tradition, the *plaçage* system. *Plaçage* was a system of consensual long-term sexual relationships between wealthy white men and fair-skinned free women of color. The women were usually quadroons (one-quarter African descent) or octoroons (one-eighth, African descent) and entered into interracial relationships of their own free will, sometimes in preference to marriages within their own social group. The wealthy white men who engaged in such relations purchased a home for their chosen mistress and were not allowed to visit without a chaperone until the woman was installed in her own home. Men who participated in these relationships had an acknowledged moral and legal responsibility for their interracial families. From time to time, legislators made feeble attempts to outlaw the *plaçage* system in Louisiana; however, it remained firmly in place until the end of the antebellum era.

The biracial families who resulted from the *plaçage* system added yet another layer to the complexity of social and business relationships in New Orleans. It was not uncommon for white children born to the legal wives of wealthy New Orleanian men to have business dealings with their half siblings who were born of these long-term liaisons with biracial mothers. Occasionally, the Creole children looked very much like their white half brothers and sisters. Although the paternity was apparent, publicly the association was rarely acknowledged (*see also* FAMILY RELATIONSHIPS WITH WHITES).

Privately, some fathers treated their biracial children with as much love and attention as they did their white children. The children born to these unions often received university educations in the North or in Europe; they were commonly fluent in multiple languages, played classical music, and were highly cultured in European-American traditions. Many were educated to take their place in the world of business. Others were trained in the field of the arts or medicine. Louis Charles Roudanez (1823–1890), son of a French man and a free woman of color, went on to achieve success as both a physician and the owner of the biweekly Republican newspaper *L'Union*, which he began in 1862. After the failure of *L'Union*, Roudanez founded the first black-owned daily newspaper in America, *La Tribune de Nouvelle Orleans* (The New Orleans tribune). Both newspapers were French-language publications and were written primarily for an audience of politically militant, free people of color in the city. (*See also* BLACK PRESS IN THE UNITED STATES.)

Other free people of color became extraordinarily wealthy because of wise investments and business acumen. Two such individuals were Thomy Lafon (1810–93) and Aristide Mary. Both men were part of the black citizens' committee fighting for equal rights in the 1880s and were part of the legal struggle that led to the U.S. Supreme Court's *Plessy v. Ferguson* decision in 1896 that sanctioned SEGREGATION. Neither of these men inherited wealth, and both succeeded through diligence and hard work. Both contributed greatly to New Orleans while alive and after death through their bequests. They donated large sums to state institutions, religious organizations, orphanages, and individuals in need with no distinction based on race. They were known throughout the city by people of all races for their demeanor and good works. Before the AMERICAN CIVIL WAR, some free people of color in the New Orleans area were slave owners. At least six families in the region owned more than 65 slaves, putting them in the top 1 percent of all slaveholding units in the United States. As did planters of African descent elsewhere in the Americas, these Louisiana slave owners suffered under some handicaps when compared to their white counterparts. They were required to employ some whites as overseers or managers, at great expense. They were protected against many Louisiana laws designed to keep free blacks down by their status as pre-1803 inhabitants with rights under the Louisiana Purchase treaty. Though most of their slaves lived in rural areas and were involved in agriculture, like the large white planters, these free colored families owned houses in the city and employed slaves there as domestics and craftsmen.

Business relationships were not the only interactions between free people of color and their white counterparts. Relationships across the color line also existed in religious settings. Most of the free people of color in New Orleans were members of the Roman Catholic Church, a vestige of their French and Spanish colonial heritage. Membership in a Catholic parish was determined by location of residence. In antebellum New Orleans, there was no residential segregation. For this reason, Catholic parishes included a wide variety of races and social classes. In the early years after the American acquisition of the Louisiana Territory, status within a Catholic parish was determined more by wealth and family name than it was by race. As a result, those who could afford to purchase a family pew were accorded greater recognition than those relegated to sitting in the distant pews and the balconies.

In keeping with their deeply devout traditions, Catholic free people of color often chose wealthy or important whites to serve as godparents for their children. These relationships based on religious principles bridged the gap between the races. The relationships were technically not social; they generally were patriarchal and created consensual alliances whereby powerful whites served to protect the rights of "worthy" free people of color. Although free people of color within the Catholic Church were far from the bottom of the ladder socially, they were never afforded all the opportunities available to their white counterparts.

American Rule, 1803–1900

Before the Civil War, black Catholic men had virtually no opportunities for service as members of the clergy because white people feared a person of color with the ability to exert any authority over whites. Had a free black man been allowed to serve in the priesthood, he would have access to the confessional and to the decision-making processes that ran the parishes. Free women of color had more opportunities to serve than their male counterparts. In 1842, two free women of color, Henriette Delille and Juliette Gaudin, founded the Sisters of the Holy Family in New Orleans. The mission of the Sisters of the Holy Family was to educate the youth and to care for the poor and the elderly. This religious order served, and continues to serve, a vital need in the community. In addition, it allowed women of color to dedicate their lives to God while offering service to others.

Clearly the city of New Orleans had a substantial Catholic presence, but there were other religious influences as well. One practice that is closely associated with the city of New Orleans is the tradition of Voodoo. Voodoo is a very old religion that has close ties to traditional African religious practices but also incorporates elements of Catholicism (*see also* AFRICAN AND SYNCRETIC RELIGIONS). MARIE LAVEAU, the most famous practitioner of Voodoo in the city of New Orleans, and her daughter, also called Marie Laveau, were two of the most colorful and interesting figures in the city's history. The elder Laveau was born around 1801 in New Orleans. Her mother was a free person of color and her father, a white planter. In 1819, while still in her teens, Laveau married a free man of color, Jacques (or perhaps Santiago) Paris, who had escaped the turmoil in Haiti that followed the slave revolt. Paris died in 1820, and Marie went to work as a hairdresser to some of the wealthiest white families in New Orleans. Later Laveau took a common-law husband, with whom she had numerous children, one of whom she named Marie, after herself. In addition to being a hairdresser, the elder Marie had a second career as the Voodoo queen of New Orleans. It is believed that after her death, her daughter Marie carried on religious activities in her mother's name. The legend of Marie Laveau is so intricately entwined with the history of New Orleans that her fame and power have persisted to the present day. Marie Laveau was purportedly buried in New Orleans at Saint Louis Cemetery Number 1. Her tomb is a tourist destination for visitors to New Orleans. Those who follow the Voodoo faith continue to pray for favors at her tomb. In return for the favors requested, the faithful leave small gifts and offerings of alcohol, tobacco, fruit, and flowers.

The patterns of the lives of free persons of color remained somewhat predictable in New Orleans until Louisiana's secession from the Union in 1861. Soon after the formation of the Confederate States of America, Southern men living within the boundaries of the newly created country began forming militias for the protection of their homeland. The free people of color in New Orleans were no different. It was not the intention of these free men of color to wage war; they simply wanted to defend and preserve their homes, their businesses, and their families. The Civil War was not the first time that free people of color fought side by side with whites in Louisiana. Free blacks fought alongside the French and Spanish when Louisiana belonged to those nations. Free blacks also fought with ANDREW JACKSON at the Battle of New Orleans during the War of 1812. Military service was a long-standing tradition for members of this unique population, who continued to offer their services in defense of their homeland during times of crisis (*see also* MILITIA).

In response to the fears felt by all New Orleanians, several of the more influential members of the free black community decided to convene a meeting and placed a notice announcing it in the *Daily Picayune*. More than 1,000 free people of color attended a rally to discuss the possibility of forming a militia. They quickly organized themselves into regiments and offered their military services to the governor of Louisiana. The governor accepted their offer, and their units were incorporated into the Louisiana State Militia on May 2, 1861. The field level officers for the Louisiana Native Guards were all free men of color. Only the commanding officer was white.

It is somewhat remarkable that white Southerners, who greatly feared the possibility of a slave uprising, were willing to accept the free men of color as armed protectors of their state. Throughout the South, whites had long maintained strict control over the black slave population and continually refused to allow gatherings of African Americans without a strong white presence to circumvent any possibility of insurrection. However, it seemed that as the threat of Northern invasion loomed, many Southern whites, at least in Louisiana, were willing to put aside those fears and to trust the free blacks they knew and with whom they worked on a daily basis.

Despite their initial welcome into the Louisiana militia, the interracial sense of brotherhood quickly faded. The Native Guards were not issued uniforms or supplies. Their services were rebuffed in favor of those of white troops. In January 1862, the state of Louisiana reorganized its state militia and incorporated the conscription of whites in the terms. When the word *whites* was specified, the Native Guards were disbanded and eliminated. They were briefly recalled to service when a Northern fleet commanded by Admiral David Farragut sailed up the Mississippi River, but the Confederate States army at the national level refused to allow the men of color to serve, and they were dismissed once more.

Union troops under the command of Gen. Benjamin F. Butler took control of New Orleans in May 1862, soon after Farragut's conquest. Although the city would remain under Union control for the remainder of the war, Butler feared future Confederate attacks. He petitioned the government in Washington D.C., for additional troops and was refused. Seeing no other alternative, Butler accepted the services of the Native Guards, who were mustered into service in the U.S. military in September 1862, making them the first African-American unit to serve in the Civil War.

During the war years, wealthy Southerners struggled as they dealt with the loss of their property, their wealth, and their slaves. Although whites experienced devastating losses as a result of the war, some of the wealthiest and most powerful free blacks experienced an even more significant loss than their white counterparts. As members of the black elite, they stood as a buffer between the slaves and the whites. After the end of the Civil War when slavery was abolished, the free people of color were no longer seen as a class apart from all other people of color; they no longer occupied a position of privilege. The ratification of the Thirteenth Amendment to the U.S. Constitution in 1865 abolished slavery, and that meant that whites no longer recognized the exclusive social position of wealthy free blacks. As all members of society struggled to accept the changes taking place in America, whites began to view all people of color as a separate racial group rather than separating wealthy free people of color into a category based on social class.

These social and racial changes were not abrupt occurrences; they evolved as all Americans sought to incorporate new elements of society into their existing world. Both whites and blacks struggled to define their places in the new U.S. political system. Some of the men who served in the Louisiana Native Guards went on to serve the nation during Reconstruction (*see* RECONSTRUCTION IN THE UNITED STATES). Caesar Carpetier (C. C.) Antoine, who had actively recruited men to join the Native Guards after Union forces took control of New Orleans in the early years of the war, was not the first member of his family to offer his services to his homeland. His father also served in the U.S. military, fighting around New Orleans during the War of 1812. During Reconstruction, Antoine began a family grocery business in Shreveport, Louisiana. He was present at the Louisiana Constitutional Convention in 1868 as citizens of the state created a new constitution that satisfied the requirements necessary for reincorporation in the United States. After the convention, Antoine was elected to the Louisiana State Senate, serving until 1872. That year, he was elected lieutenant-governor of Louisiana.

Two other prewar free men of color (both born as slaves) also served as Republican lieutenant governors of Louisiana. They were Oscar Dunn and Pinckney Benton Stewart (P. B. S.) Pinchback. Dunn died in office, and Pinchback went on to serve as governor for a short time in 1872–73 after the impeachment of the then-governor Henry Warmouth. Pinchback was the first African-American governor in American history (and the last until 1990).

After his brief tenure as governor, Pinchback continued to serve in a variety of private, state, and federal positions. Some of those included service as a member of the Board of Trustees of Southern University, a member of the Louisiana State Board of Education, and Surveyor of Customs at the Port of New Orleans.

Antoine, Dunn, and Pinchback are only a small sample of the influential individuals who composed the free black population in New Orleans. Talented formerly free people of color continued to serve in numerous capacities throughout Reconstruction and into the first two decades of the 20th century. By the 1920s, the racial barriers had become impenetrable, and there would be few opportunities for African Americans in the American South until the emergence of the modern Civil Rights movement of the 1950s and 1960s.

Kim Carey

FURTHER READING

Blassingame, John W. *Black New Orleans, 1860–1880.* Chicago: University of Chicago Press, 1976.

Everett, Donald E. "Free Persons of Color in Colonial Louisiana." *Louisiana History* 7 (1966).

Gehman, Mary. *The Free People of Color: An Introduction.* New Orleans: Margaret Media, 1994.

Hanger, Kimberly. *Bounded Lives, Bounded Places: Free Black Society in Colonial New Orleans 1769–1803.* Durham, N.C.: Duke University Press, 1997.

Hirsch, Arnold R., and Joseph Logsdon. *Creole New Orleans: Race and Americanization.* Baton Rouge: Louisiana State University Press, 1992.

Hollandsworth, James G. *The Louisiana Native Guards: The Black Military Experience during the Civil War.* Baton Rouge: Louisiana State University Press, 1995.

Kein, Sybil. *Creole: The History and Legacy of Louisiana's Free People of Color.* Baton Rouge: Louisiana State University Press, 2000.

Ochs, Stephen J. *A Black Patriot and a White Priest: Andre Cailloux and Claude Paschal Maistre in Civil War New Orleans.* Baton Rouge: Louisiana State University Press, 2000.

Rousseve, Charles B. *The Negro in Louisiana: Some Aspects of His History and His Literature.* New Orleans: Xavier University Press, 1937.

NEW YORK CITY DRAFT RIOTS (1863)

In the midst of the AMERICAN CIVIL WAR, in July 1863, New York City suffered the most destructive and deadly riots experienced by any city in U.S. history. The original grievance of the rioters was the beginning of conscription of men to fight in the army, but the riot quickly turned into a pogrom against blacks. An unknown number of people died, including many black residents of the city, with the best estimates around 120. Over the course of four days, the rioters destroyed millions of dollars' worth of public and private property. The riot was ultimately suppressed by the military, using live ammunition, artillery fire, and bayonets.

New York City had supported the Union cause at the beginning of the war in 1861, sending many young men as volunteers to join the army. But with the departure of the most committed Union supporters to the front, and the death of many of them in the bloody battles over the next two years, enthusiasm for the war waned. New York City had long been a Democratic Party stronghold, with the large Irish population allying with wealthy financiers. Antiwar Democrat Horatio Seymour managed to win the NEW YORK STATE governor's race in 1862. The city government, known as Tammany Hall, had organized the Irish immigrant community as an important power base. The Irish were of two minds about the war: On the one hand, they saw the Southern SLAVE OWNERS as the American equivalents of the great English landlords who had oppressed them in Ireland. On the other hand, they saw the struggle for abolition of slavery as an elite movement, tied to nativist anti-immigrant sentiment. And they were concerned about the possibility of large numbers of newly freed blacks from the South moving to Northern cities and competing with them for the low-wage jobs that were the only ones they were allowed to hold. The Irish also had a history of rioting as a form of political expression; there had been significant riots in New York's Irish neighborhoods in 1835, on two occasions in the 1850s, and in Philadelphia in 1844. Irish immigrants suffered especially under anti-immigrant sentiment in the 1850s and early 1860s because of both their Catholic faith and the anti-Irish prejudice that pervaded English culture, which was still the dominant culture of mid-19th-century America. Irish resentment of these elite attitudes would also play a role in making the uprising more violent.

In March 1863, Congress passed the Conscription Act to increase the size of the army. The law contained one provision that was especially galling to working-class Northern whites: For a payment of $300, any person called could be exempted for that round of enlistments (though he would be eligible again in six months). In addition, if anybody wanted to avoid service entirely, he could hire a substitute, and as long as the substitute was performing his duties, he was exempt. Substitutes usually cost significantly more than the short-term exemption, sometimes well over $1,000. These sums were well out of reach of the poor—the average daily workingman's wage in 1860 was $1.19.

The riots began in New York City on July 13, 1863, as the federal provost marshal was preparing to draw the second round of names for enlistment. The United States had won a great victory at the Battle of Gettysburg 10 days before, but the casualty lists were long. One regiment, the New York City Fire Zouaves, many of whom were Irishmen, suffered almost 50 percent casualties at Gettysburg. The Irish Brigade, with three of its five regiments from New York City, suffered significant casualties in fighting on the second day of the battle, after having suffered almost 70 percent casualties at the Battle of Fredericksburg in January. Recent Irish immigrants were horrified to discover that having registered to vote for Tammany Hall, they were now subject to conscription. A mob of working-class whites, led by a company of the Fire Department, stormed the provost marshal's office around 10 A.M. on July 13, as the names of the draftees were being drawn. The chief of police attempted to disperse the crowd, but they beat him severely. The police tried to attack the crowd with billy clubs and revolvers, but the mob, larger and better armed, drove them back into their headquarters and then set it on fire. The mob targeted public buildings and the homes of prominent Republican Party politicians at first, but when the Republican newspaper editor Horace Greeley, of the New York Tribune, deployed Gatling machine guns in front of his offices, the crowd turned to softer targets. As night came on, rioters attacked African Americans at random, beating, torturing, and killing throughout the city. A mob attacked the Colored Children's Orphanage, burning it to the ground, although the police were able to escort the children and their caregivers to safety. The next day officials took several steps to try to calm the situation, including a speech by Governor Seymour, in which he contended that the draft was unconstitutional, probably making the crowd angrier. Several more buildings were sacked and numerous blacks lynched. Crowds of black men began fortifying buildings in black neighborhoods and shooting at groups of armed whites from rooftops. Troops began to arrive on the morning of July 15. Ultimately, about 10 regiments of federal and state troops deployed in the city. A mob of armed rioters confronted the federal troops in Gramercy Park, a wealthy neighborhood. The rioters fired on the soldiers, and the soldiers returned fire, with rifles and cannon, breaking up the mob and killing dozens. The rioting finally ended on July 16.

A month later, in August, the draft was conducted peacefully under the supervision of large numbers of federal troops. The black community institutions destroyed during the riots were mostly rebuilt over the coming months and years, thanks to donations from other black communities and from the somewhat chastened city officials of New York. The underlying racial tension, though, was not dispelled, and black and white New Yorkers continued to view one another with suspicion and fear.

The riots were a foretaste for African Americans of the reaction that Northern ethnic and immigrant whites would have to black emancipation. One Northern city after another suffered race riots in the late 19th and early 20th centuries as black populations increased and blacks were seen as competition for jobs. The emotional context of the war and anti-Irish immigrant sentiment made the New York riots especially bloody, but interracial hatreds would be a consistent theme in the decades ahead.

Stewart R. King

FURTHER READING

Bernstein, Iver. *The New York City Draft Riots: Their Significance for American Society and Politics in the Age of the Civil War.* New York: Oxford University Press. 1990.

Harris, Leslie. *In the Shadow of Slavery: African-Americans in New York City, 1626–1863.* Chicago: University of Chicago Press, 2003.

Schecter, Barnet. *The Devil's Own Work: The Civil War Draft Riots and the Fight to Reconstruct America.* New York: Walker, 2005.

NEW YORK STATE

The black communities of New York centered mainly in New York City and the western New York communities of Syracuse and Rochester. New York's first free black, an explorer named Jan Rodrigues, arrived in 1613, a decade before white settlement began. He was a member of the generation the historian Ira Berlin has described as Atlantic creoles—a group of Africans who navigated comfortably throughout the Atlantic world. In 1625, a year after the Dutch settled in New Netherlands, the colony that the English would seize in 1664 and rename New York, the first group of 16 slaves arrived, having been stolen from Spanish ships by pirates and then sold in the colony. Other slaves followed, owned by both the West India Company and private individuals. As the slave trade grew and New Netherlands transformed from a society with slaves to a slave society, bound laborers would be made to serve for life, and it would become harder to gain freedom. The first generation, however, gained their freedom with relative ease and served as the bedrock of the free black community in what would eventually become the state of New York.

Free Blacks in Colonial New York

As the historian Graham Russell Hodges has shown, this community built a solid foundation that enabled future generations to enjoy their freedom, even as slavery became increasingly entrenched in the region, particularly in New Amsterdam, which under English rule would later become New York City. Landownership was crucial. The Dutch West India Company acknowledged black land claims, many of which were in the Bowery area of modern-day New York City, and by the time the English took the colony, at least 30 blacks owned land on Manhattan Island. Land rights were hereditary, so future generations were able to enjoy the self-sufficiency and independence that the first generation had worked hard to obtain. The founding generation also created institutions that would sustain the community for generations. One of the most important was the weekly market, where they sold produce, gathered with friends and family, and held yearly fairs. At the crossroads where travelers to Fort Orange and New England would pass by, this market not only allowed free blacks to trade goods and generate revenue but also gave them a sense of pride and allowed them to trade with outsiders, such as Indians and Dutch, and engage in cultural exchange. Other important fixtures of the community included the "negro burying ground"

at the corner of Broadway and Chambers Street, which provided a sacred ground for the community; taverns throughout the city, which provided places for biracial interaction; and the churches, Reformed and Anglican, which offered rituals and services that served personal and collective functions. Overall, according to Hodges, the black community "governed themselves as an association," tacking such serious issues as child rearing and punishment and serving as a "supportive model for newly arrived, enslaved Africans."

Black rights grew increasingly narrow after the English assumed control of New Amsterdam and New Netherlands, which they renamed New York, in 1664. In 1679, Governor Edmund Andros outlawed the enslavement of Native Americans yet left black slavery intact. Slavery became legally entrenched and racially based for a number of reasons. For one thing, an influx of wealthy planters from BARBADOS in the 1660s led to an increase in black repression as these SLAVE OWNERS, having faced serious slave rebellion in the Caribbean, introduced new and harsher methods of discipline. This trend only increased after the turn of the century. In 1706, the colonial legislature passed laws banning commerce with slaves and restricting black mobility. It also provided for the branding of black thieves with the letter *T* on the face. The slaves responded with violent reprisals, the most famous of which was the 1712 conspiracy to burn New York City on New Year's Day. After setting a house on fire, the conspirators waited in ambush for whites responding to the alarm and managed to kill eight and wound 12. In response, angry white officials held rushed trials, which saw 21 blacks condemned to death and 18 executed. Perhaps even more important, the legislature passed a series of new laws that, according to Hodges, "were the final nails in the coffin of black freedom." The laws restricted the rights of free blacks by ruling, for example, that any who gained their freedom after that point would not be allowed to own property. They also hampered MANUMISSION by requiring that masters post £200 bonds for each slave manumitted and pay £20 each year to ensure the freed person's maintenance and prevent the freed from becoming public charges. These manumission and property restrictions proved to be tremendous hurdles that prevented the free black community from growing and prospering.

This cycle of reprisal and repression continued throughout the first half of the 18th century. Additional slave plots were discovered in 1721, 1734, and 1741, and the unrest continued into the revolutionary years. Hodges attributes the rebelliousness to the lack of avenues for gaining freedom, arguing that emancipations became extremely rare and much of the older generation of free blacks left the colony.

The War of American Independence

The WAR OF AMERICAN INDEPENDENCE, 1775–83, produced unprecedented opportunities to blacks throughout the colonies, including New York. Despite much debate about whether or not blacks should be allowed to serve the Patriot cause directly, they participated in a number of ways, and many gained their freedom as a result. Some fought in place of their masters, while others provided important support services such as building fortifications and other defenses to protect New York City.

Their assistance led to debates over emancipation as compensation. Abolition sentiment spread as state legislatures met to write new constitutions after gaining independence, but New York was not one of the states to free slaves legislatively at this time. At the same time, religious appeals to end slavery weakened. Quakers continued to call for freedom, but their pacifism had cost them much power throughout the country during the war. Most other denominations remained silent about human bondage. Also, despite the revolutionary spirit that caused them to cry out for their own liberty, very few slaveholders felt compelled to emancipate their bondspersons, even by will.

Perhaps as a result, some New York blacks rallied to the side of Lord Dunmore when he arrived at Staten Island in 1776. Dunmore, royal governor of Virginia, had offered freedom to slaves who would fight for the British cause and had led a group, known as his Ethiopian Regiment, in battle for the Redcoats. (*See* DUNMORE, JOHN MURRAY, EARL OF.) After that group's defeat, they traveled to New York, where they were joined by refugees to create a new regiment and met defeat again at the Battle of Long Island. Free blacks as well as escaped slaves assisted the British cause, especially after General Henry Clinton put together a force called the Black Pioneers in 1776. Members of this group played important roles as pilots, spies, guards, drummers, hunters, and interpreters, facilitating communication between the British and Native Americans. Free blacks and escaped slaves also offered informal assistance as guerrilla forces, conducting nighttime raids on the Americans and absconding with livestock and other provisions needed by the English stationed in New York City. Many others served as privateers. (*See* NAVY, PIRACY, and REGULAR ARMY.) Finally, in 1779, Clinton followed Dunmore's lead and offered freedom for blacks who served the British cause. After the war, blacks who answered the call to serve the British were offered an escape and land in Nova Scotia. (*See* CANADA.)

Free Blacks and Abolition

Those who stayed, however, faced uncertainty. In 1790, the first national census counted 3,092 blacks in New York City, 1,036 of whom were free, in a population of 33,131. By 1810, there were 8,137 free blacks and 1,686 slaves.

Free blacks' main ally was the New York Manumission Society, which had been founded in 1785 by Anglicans and Quakers. (*See* BAPTISTS AND PIETISTS and PROTESTANT MAINLINE CHURCHES.) This group tried to convince SLAVE OWNERS to manumit their slaves, sued those who kidnapped blacks to enslave them, and interfered with the sale and recapture of slaves, even when it meant violating the Fugitive Slave Act of 1793. The group also created a repository for free blacks' freedom papers and encouraged and funded a number of anti-slavery activities. Overall, the group claimed to have

AFRICAN-AMERICAN POPULATION OF NEW YORK STATE, 1790–1900

Year	Slaves	Free People of Color	Free People of Color as a Percentage of Total Population	Total Population
1790	21,324	4,654	1.4%	340,120
1800	20,613	10,374	1.8%	586,182
1810	15,017	25,333	2.6%	959,049
1820	9,571	29,980	2.2%	1,372,812
1830	76	44,869	2.3%	1,918,608
1840	4	50,027	2.1%	2,428,921
1850		49,669	1.6%	3,097,394
1860		49,005	1.3%	3,880,735
1870		52,081	1.2%	4,382,759
1880		65,104	1.3%	5,082,871
1890		70,092	1.2%	5,997,853
1900		99,232	1.4%	7,268,894

secured the freedom of 429 slaves between 1792 and 1814. The New York Manumission Society was typical of the gradual emancipation groups of its time, such as the Pennsylvania Abolition Society and the New Jersey Society for the Abolition of Slavery.

As did many Northern states, New York ended slavery through a gradual process that began soon after the Revolution. By 1799, the state legislature had passed gradual emancipation acts through the cooperative efforts of the New York Manumission Society and blacks themselves. Gradual abolition meant that slavery would still exist for decades. The abolition law pertained only to slaves born after July 4, 1799. Those born after that date would gain their freedom after serving their mothers' masters until they were 28, if male, or 25, if female. Through loopholes, the law also provided for compensation to the slave owners. It also allowed people from slaveholding areas to take their slaves to New York for indefinite periods without penalty. Even so, once the law passed, more and more slave owners freed their bondspersons, either by will or outright. Others allowed them to buy their freedom, often with the help of the Manumission Society. This free black population was augmented by the arrival of RUNAWAY SLAVES from other parts of the country.

Free blacks of the post-Revolutionary generation faced a number of challenges. Those in rural areas were generally unable to acquire enough property to provide more than subsistence, thus, they had to accept jobs as farmhands or domestic servants. As a result, many moved to the cities, especially New York City, where most lived in close quarters and worked in various service industries. A growing number, however, were able to rely on skills and provide artisanal services to the growing black community, working as carpenters, cabinetmakers, sailmakers, coopers, bakers, butchers, and barbers. (See ARTISANS.) The high concentration of blacks in certain neighborhoods, as well as an influx of Haitian refugees with their foreign customs fleeing the HAITIAN REVOLUTION, however, gave white New Yorkers a new fear of revolts. Adding to this unease at the growth in the black population was a growth in the number of blacks in almshouses, as some masters freed slaves who were incapable of taking care of themselves, and discrimination prevented others from obtaining good jobs. All in all, however, urban free blacks had more chances to succeed than those in rural areas, partly because they were able to work together to create churches, hold celebrations, and found benevolent societies to help each other with the trials of daily life.

Religion played an important part in the growth of the free black community in New York. From colonial times, the Episcopal Church had gained the most black converts, creating a legacy of black education that cul-minated in the founding of the African Free School in 1789. The Dutch Reformed Church began accepting black members after the Revolution, as did the Presbyterian. The Methodist Church also accepted blacks, beginning at the end of the colonial era, and even went so far as to exclude slaveholders in the postwar years. This church also encouraged black preachers, but it also limited their authority. As a result, blacks formed their own churches.

In 1795, a group of free blacks joined together through the New York City African Society for Mutual Relief, or African Society, and began trying to create an independent place of worship and burial ground. The city of New York granted the group funds to help foster these goals, and fed up with discrimination within the white churches through segregated "black pews," Peter Williams, Sr., led blacks out of the white church and formed the African Methodist Episcopal (A.M.E) Zion Church. Other black churches soon formed, including the Abyssinian Baptist Church, led by the Reverend Thomas Paul. These churches became the centerpieces of the black community, encouraging moral behavior and offering charity as well as playing important roles in the fight against slavery and racism. (See AFRICAN METHODIST EPISCOPAL CHURCH.)

Black benevolent societies also opened important avenues for political and social expression. The African Society played an important role. As a mutual aid society, it provided cash to members who fell ill, provided for the maintenance of widows, and worked to keep members in line by prohibiting such behavior as gambling or visiting prostitutes. Notable members included the first president, William Hamilton; the first secretary, Henry Sipkins; and the members Peter Williams, Jr.; Thomas Paul; SAMUEL E. CORNISH; and Theodore S. Wright, among others. Through groups like this, free blacks were able to train their own leaders, who could then speak out and fight politically for the rights of the overall community.

Free Black Society

By 1825, New York City's blacks had established their own neighborhoods near the landholdings of their 17th-century predecessors, and an urban middle class was beginning to form. According to Hodges, New York's black leaders "began consciously to create an African American intellectual tradition," which by this time included publishing newspapers, writing pamphlets, and "sustaining a cultural enlightenment." Some family incomes in New York City ranged as high as $10,000 as blacks created their own churches, businesses, and entertainment venues while honing a number of skills relevant to middle-class life. They put the city's black schools to great use, sending their children to Anglican Sunday schools or the African Free School, which trained some of the antebellum generation's greatest leaders, including James McCune Smith; Peter Williams, Jr.; ALEXANDER CRUMMELL; and HENRY HIGHLAND GARNET. They also supported the nation's first black-run newspaper, *Freedom's Journal*, which emerged in March 1827. The paper was founded in the home of Boston Crummell (father of Alexander Crummell) and was edited by Samuel E. Cornish, who had grown increasingly incensed at the AMERICAN COLONIZATION SOCIETY's (ACS's) efforts to collect money to "return" blacks to Africa. JOHN RUSSWURM followed Cornish as editor of the paper but eventually changed sides in the debate, agreeing to go to the ACS's colony of LIBERIA and serve as the administrator of schools.

With the growth in the black middle class arose growing class divisions within the community. Those who had less contact with genteel whites, less education, and more contact with slave culture made cultured blacks and whites nervous. The younger generation were known for dressing in a more flashy fashion, wearing extravagant hairstyles, behaving loudly in public, and participating in nighttime entertainment. They set the stage for the Bowery youth culture, described by the historian Christine Stansell, which characterized the Five Points and New York street culture.

Most free blacks were members of the working class. Some worked in various low-paying servant positions. Many were MERCHANT SEAMEN. Others earned their living as street musicians or made their way with odd jobs and petty criminal behavior. The poorest found themselves at odds with immigrants, particularly the Irish, who began arriving in New York in large numbers in the 1830s and 1840s. Those who simply could not overcome the discrimination of the times sought refuge in a lifestyle inspired by slave culture, one in which music, dance, style, and street life figured prominently.

Slavery was finally abolished, once and for all, in New York on July 4, 1827, but the freed still faced a number of hurdles. Most could not vote, and they remained barred from the most lucrative and skilled professions. Perhaps most important, slavery remained intact throughout much of the country, and RACISM AND RACIAL PREJUDICE actually grew throughout the free states once slavery ended. Indeed, it was after 1830 that a number of antiabolition riots broke out throughout the North, including in New York in 1834.

The violence of the 1830s can be attributed largely to the growth of a new antislavery philosophy, known as immediatism. Leaders of this radical abolitionist movement called for an immediate end to slavery throughout the United States, without compensation to slave owners. The movement is often associated with the white reformer and newspaper editor William Lloyd Garrison, who founded the *Liberator* in 1831, but in reality blacks played crucial roles in the switch from the gradual to the immediate emphasis.

Black leaders of New York participated in a number of ways. In the churches, blacks and whites used "pray-ins" to call for desegregation, as blacks occupied white pews and refused to relinquish them. Some even went so far as to leave segregated churches. In the realm of education, some leaders began promoting their own schools, some with a focus on manual labor for the goal of economic self-sufficiency and others with an emphasis on classical education. With the backing of wealthy white abolitionists such as Arthur and Lewis Tappan, black leaders such as Christopher Rush, Thomas Jennings, Theodore Wright, Benjamin Hughes, and Peter Vogelsang founded the Phoenix Society in 1836 to foster the educational needs of the community. Similarly, with the help of the white abolitionist Gerrit Smith, Henry Highland Garnet, William H. Day, and David Ruggles founded the Garrison Literary and Benevolent Association and started a black secondary school. These efforts, along with those of the Reverend Edward Cephas Africanus and his brother, Selah H. Africanus, of Long Island were short-lived. The first broadly successful effort, in the 1840s, was that of the black-led Society of Education among Colored Children. This group founded and operated a number of schools, some of which were secondary.

Abolitionist Movement

Black abolition in New York began to take a more radical turn in 1829. That year saw the release of Robert A. Young's *Ethiopian Manifesto*, which warned in millenarian tones that if slavery did not end soon, a race war might ensue. Less radical than Young's pamphlet, yet radical all the same in its call for direct resistance to slaveholders of the South, was a movement that emerged in 1835 as the black leaders David Ruggles, William Johnson, George Barker, Robert Brown, and J. W. Higgins formed the New York Committee of Vigilance. Sharing many members with the African Society of Mutual Relief, the Vigilance Committee met monthly to protect free blacks and escaped slaves, including FREDERICK DOUGLASS, from kidnappers and slave catchers.

The group played an important part in the Underground Railroad, which emerged in the 1840s through the efforts of black leaders such as Syracuse's Jermain Loguen, an escaped slave from TENNESSEE who helped more than 1,000 fugitives make their way to Canada. Rochester served as one of the last stops on their trek, and black and white Rochesterians, led by Frederick Douglass, who made his home there after escaping along the railroad himself, helped fugitives along the last leg of the journey by donating money, clothing, and other goods and alerting conductors when the authorities were closing in.

Finally, black militants such as J. W. C. Pennington fought SEGREGATION of public transportation facilities and resisted strongly the efforts of the American Colonization Society. They also fought to regain the vote, after a $250 bond placed on the franchise in 1821 left most disenfranchised, through the Political Improvement Association and the Political Association of New York.

Women contributed to New York's black abolition movement in a number of ways. They organized self-help groups such as the African Dorcas Society and the Colored Ladies' Literary Society, and they participated as conductors on the Underground Railroad. One of New York's most famous black women was Isabel Van Wagenen, who later changed her name to SOJOURNER TRUTH.

After the passage of the FUGITIVE SLAVE ACT OF 1850, the lot of free blacks throughout the United States became much worse. In Syracuse, Loguen, the fugitive from Tennessee, appealed to his neighbors to defend the U.S. Constitution by disobeying the act and making their city an "open city" for fugitives. The people of Syracuse voted 395–96 in favor of granting Loguen's request at a town meeting that October. A year later, many made good on that promise by participating in the Jerry Rescue, an action in which a captured fugitive slave was recaptured by a crowd of abolitionists who had gathered in the city for the state convention of the Liberty Party. After successfully securing Jerry's freedom by breaking into his arraignment with a battering ram, abolitionists, including Loguen, managed to help him escape to Canada. They also succeeded in fighting their own indictments for participating in the rescue.

Others became increasingly frustrated with racial discrimination and segregation. Perhaps the best example is that of Elizabeth Jennings, a 24-year-old schoolteacher in New York City, who refused to give up her seat on a city bus, was forcefully expelled, and successfully sued the company in 1854.

Despite small victories like this, conditions became even more dismal in 1857, when the Supreme Court announced through the DRED SCOTT decision that blacks could not be U.S. citizens. In this climate, blacks from across the country emigrated to Canada, and others began to consider such locations as Haiti and Africa. According to Hodges, 144 New York blacks emigrated to the African colony of Liberia in 1859. Famous New York emigrationists include Alexander Crummell, Henry Highland Garnet, and Edward Wilmot Blyden.

The AMERICAN CIVIL WAR, 1861–65, renewed hope among blacks throughout the United States. Even so, racial antagonism continued in New York, manifested most violently in the NEW YORK CITY DRAFT RIOTS 1863. The riots began as a protest of the Union draft, as thousands of white New Yorkers forced suspension of the draft. Rioters, many of whom blamed blacks for the war, soon turned on the city's free blacks, attacking the Colored Orphan Asylum, black homes, and black businesses. Before the rioting ended, at least 105 innocent people had been murdered and 128 wounded. While whites were resisting the draft, however, blacks were volunteering in large numbers. Free blacks throughout the North (and slaves in the South, for that matter) saw the war as a chance to earn their own freedom and were eager to join from the beginning. By the war's end in 1865—the year the United States abolished slavery—4,125 New York blacks had served in the U.S. Army.

Beverly C. Tomek

FURTHER READING
Anbinder, Tyler. *Five Points: The Nineteenth-Century New York City Neighborhood That Invented Tap Dance, Stole Elections and Became the World's Most Notorious Slum.* New York: Free Press, 2001.
Berlin, Ira. *Many Thousands Gone: The First Two Centuries of Slavery in North America.* Cambridge, Mass: Belknap Press, 1998.
Hodges, Graham Russell. *Root and Branch: African Americans in New York and East Jersey, 1613–1863.* Chapel Hill: University of North Carolina Press, 1999.
Horton, James Oliver, and Lois E. Horton. *In Hope of Liberty: Culture, Community and Protest among Northern Free Blacks, 1700–1860.* New York: Oxford University Press, 1997.
Lepore, Jill. *New York Burning: Liberty, Slavery, and Conspiracy in Eighteenth-Century Manhattan.* New York: Alfred A. Knopf, 2005.
Painter, Nell. *Sojourner Truth: A Life, a Symbol.* New York: W. W. Norton, 1996.
Stansell, Christine. *City of Women: Sex and Class in New York, 1789–1860.* New York: Alfred A. Knopf, 1986.
White, Shane. *Somewhat More Independent: The End of Slavery in New York City, 1770–1810.* Athens: University of Georgia Press, 1991.

NICARAGUA

Nicaragua is a nation located on the isthmus of Central America. It is bordered on the northwest by HONDURAS and the south by COSTA RICA. It has a long coastline on the Caribbean Sea and a shorter one on the Pacific Ocean. It is primarily mountainous, with an extensive coastal plain on the Caribbean, or eastern side, and a somewhat shorter and relatively narrow southwestern coastal strip along the Pacific. The Caribbean coastal plain is swampy and heavily forested. The interior is mountainous, but there are several large lakes and river valleys that create fertile plains. The central region is relatively well watered and fertile, and the Pacific

Nicaragua

coastal plain is fertile and ideal for the traditional Central American agricultural staples of corn, beans, and squash.

The indigenous population of Nicaragua before the Spanish conquest in the early 16th century was quite diverse. This area is the border between the Central American and South American indigenous regions. There were a large number of different native groups living here. The Spanish arrived in the highlands, traveling overland from MEXICO, to the north, in 1524, and completed their conquest by 1538, in the process thoroughly destroying native culture. The Caribbean coast remained essentially unexplored and unconquered into the 18th century, when it came under the control of BRITAIN. Unlike areas of Central America farther to the north, western Nicaragua does not have one dominant native culture. Instead, the national culture of the highlands and the Pacific Coast was more mestizo from an earlier point in the colony's existence, with Afro-descended and European-descended Nicaraguans part of a common culture from an earlier time.

Western Nicaragua was part of the Viceroyalty of New Spain, ruled from Mexico City, during the colonial period. All of Central America was organized as the Captaincy-General of GUATEMALA. Nicaragua was a remote and relatively unimportant part of this empire. The early conquistadores established agricultural settlements along the lakes and rivers of the highlands and on the Pacific Coast and did some mining. These Spanish adventurers had some black slaves with them, as domestic servants, technical specialists, and foremen of native work gangs.

A very small slave trade continued throughout the colonial period, introducing no more than a few thousand slaves in all to the national territory before 1800, many of whom were imported from PANAMA or Mexico rather than directly from Africa.

The Afro-Nicaraguan descendants of these slaves were able to gain their freedom in significant numbers. The conditions of their enslavement permitted them access to money and made them valuable to their masters, allowing them to gain the resources to obtain MAN-UMISSION. Likewise, the autonomy they often enjoyed made flight an easier prospect. As did Afro-descended populations everywhere in Spanish America, once free, they came to dominate the urban working class. There were few jobs for them in the countryside, since there were many Indians and mestizos to fill those roles, and in any case their job skills were more marketable in the towns. There are no reliable census data from colonial Nicaragua, but we can estimate that Afro-descended people made up about half the urban population in the late 18th century.

There was some development of plantation agriculture in Nicaragua in the late colonial period, but the difficulty of access to world markets—Nicaragua had no ports on the Caribbean until the 19th century—meant that there was little profit in it. Nicaragua remained an economic backwater until after national independence from Mexico in 1823.

The eastern part of Nicaragua was never actually put under European rule. Britain established settlements at the town of Bluefields and elsewhere along the coast and traded with the lowland Indians. Blacks and Caribbean Indians taken to Nicaragua by the British, along with the local Indians, formed an Afro-Caribbean ethnic community called the Miskito. In addition, a related group called the Garífuna settled northeastern Nicaragua from neighboring Honduras in the 18th century, driving out or absorbing the indigenous people there (*see also* BELIZE for more on the Garífuna). These Afro-Caribbean people were fiercely independent and resisted all efforts by the Spanish or British to exert control over them.

In 1821, Mexico gained its independence from Spain. The WAR OF MEXICAN INDEPENDENCE, 1810–21, had little impact on Central America. The area of the Captaincy-General of Guatemala, including Nicaragua, declared its independence from Mexico in 1823 as the Federal Republic of Central America. The republic was dominated by Liberal politicians, and one key Liberal idea was the abolition of slavery. The Central American constitution of 1824 formally abolished slavery and proclaimed the equality of all races in the new state. The conservative landowners and the ROMAN CATHOLIC CHURCH opposed the republic, at first seeking to return to Spanish rule and then settling for breaking up the federation and creating the independent nations of Nicaragua, Honduras, EL SALVADOR, Guatemala, and Costa Rica out of the various regions of Central America, which were governed under a more conservative set of values. Slavery remained formally outlawed in Nicaragua from 1824 until 1856, but many formerly enslaved blacks continued to work, formally described as peons, under strict labor discipline without the possibility of changing jobs easily. There was a progressive decline in the harshness of the labor regime and increasing integration of Afro-Nicaraguans into the national society, especially under Liberal rule in the 1840s and early 1850s.

In 1855, another round in the seemingly endless power struggle between Liberals and Conservatives produced a strange interlude in Nicaragua. William Walker (1824–60), a native of TENNESSEE in the United States, entered Nicaragua as a mercenary and became president of the republic. He reintroduced slavery in 1856 and hoped to have Nicaragua annexed to the United States as a new slave state. Nicaragua's geography has long made it a good candidate for a transisthmian canal, and Walker and his American businessmen patrons hoped that he would become the leader of a newly prosperous American state. Instead, the people of Nicaragua united to drive him from power after a little more than a year, upon which the old constitution was reestablished and slavery abolished once more.

The government of Nicaragua gained control of the eastern section after 1857. A wave of immigration of blacks from the British Caribbean to this region continued throughout the 19th century, to work in banana plantations and on railroad construction. These new black immigrants and the Afro-Caribbean Miskito and Garífuna people are the ancestors of most of the people who today identify themselves as Afro-Nicaraguans. The older Afro-descended population of the highland and Pacific Coast cities and towns, similar to Afro-descended populations throughout Latin America, tended to disappear into the general population and lose any separate African identity. Many highland and Pacific coastal Nicaraguans have some African ancestry today, but most of them do not self-identify as Afro-Nicaraguans. Nicaragua has the highest proportion of self-identified Afro-descended people of the five Central American countries created out of the old federation, at 9 percent. The predominantly Afro-Caribbean eastern section of the country was organized in 2004 into two autonomous zones to permit the inhabitants to preserve their culture, language, and environment against pressure from the Spanish-speaking mestizo majority from the highlands.

FURTHER READING
Pineda, Baron L. *Shipwrecked Identities: Navigating Race on Nicaragua's Mosquito Coast.* New Brunswick, N.J.: Rutgers University Press, 2006.

NORTH CAROLINA

North Carolina was among the last mid-Atlantic colonies to be settled, primarily by Virginians migrating south from the Tidewater region in the late 1600s. By the first decade of the 1700s, several small towns were established in North Carolina's northeastern quadrant. South Carolinian immigrants settled the southeastern quadrant. Because of North Carolina's later start, the pattern of black slavery and white indentured servitude was already well established in MARYLAND, VIRGINIA AND WEST VIRGINIA, and SOUTH CAROLINA by the time North Carolina was settled. North Carolina's slavery and servitude laws and customs derived from those of its neighbors—Virginia and South Carolina.

Most of the early settlers were pioneers who had few slaves. As the colony grew, slaves were imported from neighboring colonies and from overseas. As in Virginia and South Carolina, slaves were used in labor-intensive industries such as tobacco and rice farming and in manufacturing of naval goods.

The colony's African-American population comprised only about 1,000 people in 1705, 6,000 in 1730, but had begun to grow rapidly by the mid-18th century. African Americans constituted a quarter of the population by the time of the WAR OF AMERICAN INDEPENDENCE, 1775–83, when close to half of the slave population had been born in Africa. Slaveholding was most prominent in the southeastern quadrant, which also featured larger plantations. In the Northeast, slaveholding was nearly as common, but the average owner held fewer slaves. The Piedmont and mountainous regions to the west were still frontier areas, with far fewer large plantations and SLAVE OWNERS.

In antebellum North Carolina, the term "free person of color" described people who were not slaves but who were also not white. North Carolinians made social distinctions between "free negroes" and "free mulattoes" on the basis of skin color. State law treated both groups identically. The free population of color in North Carolina originated from three sources: MIGRATION, MISCEGENATION, and MANUMISSION.

Migration
Free people of color were among the earliest settlers in North Carolina, immigrating from southeastern Virginia and migrating in a southwesterly direction. Many of these immigrants were descended from unions between white women and black men. In 1790, there were fewer

AFRICAN-AMERICAN POPULATION OF NORTH CAROLINA, 1790–1900

Year	Slaves	Free People of Color	Free People of Color as a Percentage of Total Population	Total Population
1790	100,572	4,975	1.3%	393,751
1800	133,296	7,073	1.5%	478,103
1810	168,824	10,266	1.8%	555,500
1820	200,486	14,612	2.7%	538,829
1830	245,601	19,543	2.6%	737,987
1840	245,817	22,732	3.0%	753,419
1850	258,518	27,463	3.2%	869,039
1860	331,059	30,463	3.1%	992,622
1870		391,650	36.6%	1,071,361
1880		531,277	38.0%	1,399,750
1890		561,018	34.7%	1,617,947
1900		624,469	32.9%	1,898,810

than 5,000 free people of color in North Carolina. As early as 1795, the state legislature was alarmed by the free population's increase, requiring free immigrants either to post bond or to face arrest. This law did little to slow the growth rate. By 1810, the free black population had more than doubled. The rate of growth continued to increase over the next decades. In 1826, North Carolina outlawed free black immigration altogether. In 1830, the law was extended to include free black citizens of North Carolina who left the state for 90 days or longer.

Miscegenation

Contrary to popular misconception, the early free black population was, at least in part, not the consequence of manumission but rather of miscegenation. The 1860 census recorded more than two-thirds of the free population as MULATTO. Since slave status was heritable only in the maternal line, descendants of free women were entitled to freedom. Thus, most of the pre–American War of Independence free black population descended from unions between white women and African-American men. These older families tended to be lighter in skin color and in a more advantageous socioeconomic class compared to the free black population descended from 19th-century manumission.

In 1715, the colonial government outlawed INTERRACIAL MARRIAGE of white women and nonwhite men and penalized extramarital childbearing that resulted from such unions. While this law did not stop such unions altogether, the early free black population descended mainly from unions that preceded the law's passage. Unions between white men and black women, on the other hand, typically resulted in slave children, given the rule of maternal descent.

Manumission

While the largest portion of North Carolina's early free black population were born free, the political issues surrounding emancipation and manumission shaped the legal circumstances of all free people of color.

In 1723, North Carolina required that manumitted slaves leave the state within six months. Those who failed to leave—or who left and then returned—were subject to being arrested and sold into slavery for seven years, after which they were again obligated to leave. This law does not appear to have been regularly enforced.

In 1740, the Quaker population in the northeastern region of North Carolina began to discuss and advocate emancipation. In response to the Quaker emancipation movement, North Carolina passed a manumission law in 1741 that forbade owners to free slaves under any circumstances, except for "meritorious service," to be determined by the local authorities.

Quakers continued to flout the law. De facto emancipation increased during the early years of the Revolutionary War. In some cases, local authorities detained illegally emancipated slaves and sold them back into slavery. Quaker abolitionists petitioned on the slaves' behalf, with occasional success. The state legislature responded in 1779 by affirming the legality of selling illegally emancipated persons back into slavery.

Quakers continued to advocate legal emancipation. In 1796, a new law mandated that all free people of color—whether immigrants or freedmen—must post a bond of

£200. In 1801, the legislature made emancipation more difficult by requiring slave owners to post an additional bond of £100 per freed slave.

Nonetheless, manumissions were granted by county courts and by the General Assembly. Petitions were numerous in the early years of the 19th century, from Quakers, from white fathers of slave children, from free blacks attempting to liberate enslaved relatives, and from sympathetic slave owners.

In 1830, a law made it more expensive for a master to liberate a slave and required the slave to leave the state. In 1860, North Carolina outlawed manumission altogether. Motivated owners found ways around the legal obstacles. Slaves could be permitted to escape to the North. Slaves could be willed to trustees or to the Quaker Society of Friends and permitted to live as free people (see LIVING "AS FREE"), even though they were still legally enslaved. The line between freedom and slavery was fuzzy in such situations.

Legal Status
In 1746, North Carolina disallowed court testimony by nonwhites—whether slave or free—against whites. This law remained in place throughout the antebellum era. It effectively removed many civil rights from free people of color, by inhibiting their ability to pursue legal action against whites. It made free people of color vulnerable, given their inability to testify on their own behalf against a white abuser or debtor.

Not until 1826 did North Carolina statutes define the difference between a white person and a free person of color: "All free persons descended from negro ancestors, to the fourth generation inclusive, though one ancestor of each generation may have been a white person." In 1857, the state supreme court held that a person must be of less than one-sixteenth "Negro blood" to be considered white.

The legislature gradually eroded more and more of the free population's legal rights, beginning in 1826, when it placed new restrictions on immigration into the state. It also passed a race-based vagrancy law, placed greater restrictions on associating and trading with slaves, and institutionalized indentured servitude for the illegitimate children of free people. In 1828, the legislature made it illegal for a free person of color to leave the state for more than 90 days, to marry a slave, or to gamble with a slave.

The next year, DAVID WALKER published his *Appeal to the Colored Citizens of the World*, a radical abolitionist pamphlet. White Southerners were alarmed by such insurrectionary rhetoric and became concerned that other free people of color would follow Walker's lead. Nat Turner's slave rebellion in neighboring Virginia in 1831 increased white fear even further. That year, the legislature outlawed free people of color from preaching in public (see also BAPTISTS AND PIETISTS).

During the early national era, free men of color were qualified to vote in North Carolina if they met the property requirements. The North Carolina Constitutional Convention of 1835 disenfranchised all men of color, regardless of economic status.

While the colonial government had banned interracial marriage in 1715, the state legislature again voided and outlawed marriages between whites and free people of color in 1838. In 1840, it barred free people of color from owning guns without permission. In 1844, it forbade them to sell liquor and barred them from public schools. In 1858, it made it illegal to sell liquor to a free person of color. In 1860, free people of color were barred from hiring or supervising slaves.

Threats to Freedom
People of color arriving in North Carolina during the early colonial era entered a frontier society that subjected them to relatively few legal disabilities based on their skin color. Those legal disabilities that were in place were not always enforced. However, in a process that accelerated after national independence, legal rights for free people of color became significantly and increasingly eroded. By the time of the AMERICAN CIVIL WAR in 1861, few civil rights were left for free people of color. As a consequence, a number of free people of color supported the Union during the war, although a large fraction remained loyal to the Confederacy as well.

One consequence of the growing legal disability was that free people of color were often in danger of losing their freedom. This could happen in a number of ways. Free people of color could be kidnapped and sold into slavery in a part of the country where no one knew them, and no one could testify as to their free status. Close to home, illegitimate children of a free woman of color were bound out as indentured servants until they reached adulthood. Some masters retained these people as slaves, even though they were born free. The enslaved person's only recourse was to sue the master in court, which required significant reserves of social and financial capital that were out of reach of many people in such circumstances. A black person could not testify against a white, but legal documents could be introduced and white witnesses presented to testify. During the last 50 years of slavery, the state courts made it more and more difficult for an enslaved petitioner to prevail in a freedom case, although there were still a few victories in such cases.

The North Carolina free black population produced few institutions during the antebellum period to compare with the black churches of South Carolina and Virginia or to the flourishing black business communities, newspapers, and other community institutions of the Northern states. The small town and rural lifestyle of most free people of color made it difficult for them to have the critical mass necessary to form blacks-only community institutions. Instead, especially in poor rural districts, they attended white churches. The contact this fostered between poor whites and free blacks may have contributed to the generally less harsh racial climate in the state.

Demographics and Geography

One of the largest populations of free colored families created by migration and miscegenation was located in what today is Robeson County, along the South Carolina border. This population center emerged as a result of migration from Virginia through the Northeast part of North Carolina, arriving in Robeson County in the second half of the 18th century. Many of these families kept migrating farther into the Deep South. Those who remained in Robeson intermarried with one another, as well as with local blacks and whites alike.

Throughout the South, free people of color preferred to marry other free people instead of slaves, and the number of whites willing to form a union with a person of color was small. Consequently, there was extensive intermarriage within free black families. This resulted in a number of isolated rural free colored communities scattered through the eastern half of the state. These communities were created by constant intermarriage between a small number of free families. Different isolated groups would also exchange marriage partners. These communities tended to accept unions with whites and discourage marriages with slaves.

There was significant skin color prejudice within many of these communities, which discouraged marriages with dark-skinned free people of color. Because of this prejudice, some isolated rural free people of color tended to be lighter in skin color, on average, than more urban free colored communities. Beginning in 1885, and continuing into the 20th century, most of the rural isolated free colored communities in North Carolina began to claim descent from local Indian tribes. While these Indian ancestry stories are often accepted at face value by anthropologists, there is little historical evidence to support them, and most historical evidence contradicts them. There is no question that during the colonial era and throughout the antebellum era, these groups held the legal and social status of free people of color. They were not considered to be Indian tribes, who were treated differently under the law in many ways.

The free colored population originating from manumission tended to be darker in skin color and poorer than the free colored families created by early colonial miscegenation. The largest populations of families created by manumission were located primarily in the Quaker counties found in the Northeast part of the state.

By the time of the last slave era census in 1860, the North Carolina counties with the largest numbers of free people of color tended also to be the counties with the largest slave populations. In 1860, North Carolina enumerated more than 30,000 free people of color, more than any other Southern state save Virginia. In that year, free people of color were 3.3 percent of North Carolina's overall population, and 8.4 percent of the state's black population.

Growing Hostility toward Free People of Color

Compared to other Southern states, North Carolina treated free people of color more liberally. It was the last Southern state to disenfranchise free people of color, passed fewer legal restrictions on them than most other Southern states, and imposed them later than other states did. Part of North Carolina's relative liberalism toward free people of color may have been a residue of Quaker antislavery activism during the late 1700s and early 1800s.

Nonetheless, as the antebellum era progressed, North Carolina's political and intellectual class expressed more and more hostility to the presence of free people of color within the state's borders. Newspapers, politicians—and occasionally citizen petitions—regularly called for increased regulation of free people of color, and even for expulsion of the free population of color to the western territories, or to West Africa or the Caribbean.

However, the majority of North Carolina's white population were rural yeoman farmers, who expressed little animus toward the free people of color in their midst. Thus, while the state legislature passed more and more laws regulating free blacks' activities as the antebellum era progressed, these laws were rarely fully enforced.

Civil War and Aftermath

During the American Civil War, coastal North Carolina was an important battlefield. Union troops occupied the barrier islands and several coastal cities in the northeastern quadrant of the state in 1862 and made several attempts to capture or cut off Wilmington, one of the Confederacy's most important ports. People of color, both free and enslaved, fled to their lines. Approximately 5,000 of these people joined the U.S. Army and were organized into at least seven U.S. Colored Troops regiments. Free people of color in the state, as elsewhere in the Confederacy, faced a quandary. A Union victory promised improvement in their racial situation. However, as did their white neighbors, rural free coloreds in particular thought of the Northern soldiers as foreign invaders and resented their presence. Confederate officials also often behaved badly to the rural poor, both black and white, enforcing ever-increasing taxes and conscripting white men for military service and free colored men for labor duties. Resistance to the Confederacy was strong, especially in western North Carolina, with some cross-racial alliances developing that served as the basis of the postwar alliance of poor whites and blacks in North Carolina politics in the period of Reconstruction (*see* RECONSTRUCTION IN THE UNITED STATES).

The Union victory in the Civil War resulted in big changes for black North Carolinians. Slavery declined with the issuance of the EMANCIPATION PROCLAMATION in 1863, which took effect as federal troops captured an area from the Confederates, and was officially abolished throughout the state by the Thirteenth Amendment to the Constitution in December 1865. The newly freed people relied on the army for the necessities of life, which the War Department provided through the FREEDMEN'S BUREAU. The bureau was run by white military officers, for the most part, but prewar free blacks, both North Carolinians and Northerners, were often employed as agents on the ground, as schoolteachers in bureau-supported schools, and in other administrative roles. This important function cemented the role of prewar free blacks as community leaders. Additionally, Republican Party governments during the Reconstruction era appointed blacks, often drawn from the prewar free colored population, to federal jobs such as customs collector, postmaster, and other professional employment that helped protect their social position.

The towns of the Piedmont region became an important area for North Carolina blacks in the postwar years. The town of Durham was an especially important center, as a tolerant white-dominated city government enabled black businesses and cultural institutions to flourish. The Spaulding family, a free black family that first appeared in the Durham area in the early 18th century, provided one of Durham's most important black business leaders in C. C. Spaulding (1874–1952), founder of an important insurance company and benefactor of churches and schools across the region. Richard B. Fitzgerald (1843–1913) was a free black from DELAWARE, who operated a very profitable brickyard, providing the bricks that built many important buildings in Durham, including several black churches.

Thomas Brown

FURTHER READING

Berlin, Ira. *Slaves without Masters: The Free Negro in the Antebellum South.* New York: Random House, 1974.

DuBois, W. E. B. "The Upbuilding of Black Durham: The Success of the Negroes and Their Value to a Tolerant and Helpful Southern City." Electronic Edition. University of North Carolina at Chapel Hill. Available online. URL: http://docsouth.unc.edu/nc/dubois/dubois.html. Accessed January 4, 2011.

Franklin, John Hope. *The Free Negro in North Carolina, 1790–1860.* Chapel Hill: University of North Carolina Press, 1943.

Taylor, Rosser Howard. *The Free Negro in North Carolina.* James Sprunt Historical Publications, Vol. 17, no. 1. Chapel Hill: University of North Carolina, 1920.

OGÉ, VINCENT (ca. 1750–1791)
Haitian revolutionary

Vincent Ogé is best remembered as the leader of the first armed uprising in the HAITIAN REVOLUTION. A merchant and landowner, he was a prominent free person of mixed race, living in CAP-FRANÇAIS/CAP-HAÏTIEN, SAINT-DOMINGUE, before the outbreak of the war.

Ogé was born about 1750, in Dondon, a farming district outside Cap-Français. He lived under the patronage of a wealthy white man, named Joseph Augé, and his wife, a free woman of mixed race named Angélique Gosse. In official documents in later life, he referred to Gosse as his mother. However, some scholars believe that Augé was his uncle and that his father was Alexandre Augé, a butcher in Cap-Français. He and his brothers and sisters all spelled their name Ogé for most of their lives, probably in deference to a law that prohibited free people of color from using the names of whites, even their own relatives. There were six children who lived to adulthood, Vincent was the third son. Joseph Augé died before 1776.

The Ogé family fortune principally consisted of a small COFFEE plantation, worked by several dozen slaves. Thus, Ogé's family background was in plantation agriculture in the hill country surrounding Cap-Français, similar to that of other reasonably well-off free people of mixed race. Ogé was educated in FRANCE and trained as a goldsmith but upon his return to the island in 1768 went into business as a merchant in the city of Cap-Français. He became probably the most prominent free colored merchant in the city of Cap-Français, and one of the foremost merchants of any color, by the time the FRENCH REVOLUTION began in Paris in 1789.

Cap-Français had a fairly large population of free people of color. Many of these people were free blacks or, if mixed-race, without many white relatives or friends. They formed a tight-knit community, tied together by shared suffering under discriminatory laws. Many of the men of this community served in the colonial MILITIA or as rural constables, giving them contact with white officers as possible patrons but also reinforcing their separation from the wealthier mixed-race free planters, since the units were segregated by race. Ogé, though a city dweller, was closer to the wealthy planter class from which he sprang. He had many white relatives and friends, as well as business associates. He lived in a wealthy neighborhood with mostly white neighbors.

Since his older brothers lived on the plantation, most of Ogé's money seemed to be acquired from urban real estate. In addition to the mansion that he and his mother (or aunt) lived in, worth 42,000 livres or more than a million dollars in today's terms, they also owned or leased and developed other properties in Cap-Français worth hundreds of thousands of livres. In some cases, Ogé was working as an agent for French owners, pocketing a 5 percent commission on each deal. In others, he was the owner in his own right or was acting in his mother's name. One of the properties he leased and then sublet was worth 135,000 livres and was one of the most luxurious residences in the island. It would have been remarkable even among nobles' palaces in Paris for its size, construction standards, and price.

As were many wealthy free people of color in Saint-Domingue, Ogé was a slave owner. He and his family owned more than two dozen slaves, some of whom worked in the coffee groves under difficult circumstances. In 1783, he gave his free colored housekeeper a 12-year-old girl slave, newly imported from what is now Guinea or SIERRA LEONE in Africa, in lieu of cash payment of two years' salary owed her. The following year, he gave her a 28-year-old woman from today's Togo or Benin and her three-year-old daughter to pay the next two years' salary. Ogé was a merchant who participated in transatlantic COMMERCE AND TRADE as well as owning ships trading between ports in the Americas. Though his ships were not slave ships in the sense of carrying hundreds of slaves from African ports to the Americas on the Middle Passage, it is likely that slaves occasionally traveled on his ships from one Caribbean island to another to be sold. His ships also carried the products of slave labor to mainland North American and European markets, closing the third side of the infamous "triangle trade." He was deeply involved in the economy of Saint-

This image from the period of the French Revolution shows Vincent Ogé (ca. 1750–91) rallying free colored rebels near Cap-Français in Saint-Domingue (modern Haiti). This lithograph was probably made in France in the immediate aftermath of his capture, torture, and execution at the hands of colonial authorities. A contemporary image of him drawn from life exists, showing that he was much lighter in complexion than he is depicted here. He was of one-fourth or perhaps one-eighth African ancestry, was free from birth, and sought not to free slaves but to empower a slave-owning wealthy free colored class. However, in a reversal of the usual pattern in 19th-century depictions of mixed-race nationalist heroes, it served the political goals of the revolutionary movement to portray him as a champion of dark-skinned people and as a French patriot. One accurate element in the picture is that he is depicted wearing military uniform. Although, as did many wealthy free colored men, Ogé had avoided service in the militia, when the Revolution began in France in 1789, he obtained a commission as an officer in the National Guard and wore the uniform during his rebellion. *(The Granger Collection, New York)*

Domingue, a slave society. It would have been impossible for anyone of his social status and wealth not to be involved in slavery in some way. He did not appear to have any moral or ethical concerns about slavery.

The Coming of the Revolution

As the political situation heated up in France, Ogé and his fellow wealthy free coloreds saw an opportunity, not to overthrow a system based on racial slavery, but to find a place at the top of that system for themselves. The free colored planters of the South Province of Saint-Domingue had met in 1785 and chosen JULIEN RAIMOND as their spokesman to petition the royal government to relax discriminatory laws against them. Ogé went to Paris to try to resolve a legal dispute related to his family's plantation as the Estates General, an ancient parliament, was being elected in 1788. The meeting of the Estates General became the spark that ignited the French Revolution in 1789, and Ogé could see that the revolutionary climate offered a chance to improve the lot of wealthy free coloreds. As did Raimond, who was also in France at the time, he thought of the free people of color, along with native-born whites, as the natural citizens of the colony. He hoped that a revolution that was calling for more democracy and the end of inherited privilege and unequal treatment of people might allow him and his class more freedom than the royal government was prepared to give them. Ogé had not been elected by any group at home, but he associated himself with Raimond. The two of them first approached the Club Massiac, a group of white planters living in France who had been elected to the parliament. They hoped to forge an alliance among the wealthy native-born citizens of the colony that might lead to greater autonomy and a race-neutral society. The white planters rejected their plan, and Ogé and Raimond turned to the Société des Amis des Noirs, an antislavery group. The Amis des Noirs included several parliament members, who agreed to introduce a proposed law that would give voting rights to wealthy free coloreds. Their proposed law was not passed, but civil rights for free people of color became the central colonial issue debated in the parliament and the French press in 1790. The rules for the election of colonial assemblies that were passed by the parliament did not mention race, specifying instead that all male citizens who paid a certain amount in taxes and were above a certain age were to be permitted to vote. That was enough for Ogé, who returned to Saint-Domingue in October 1790.

First Shots of the Haitian Revolution

Ogé had never served in the militia, as wealthy planters were able to evade service or send substitutes. However, while living in Paris, he had been very much impressed by the fervor of the Parisian revolutionary National Guard. He had befriended the marquis de Lafayette, their commander, and even obtained a commission as colonel in the guard. Upon his return to Saint-Domingue, Ogé began wearing his colonel's uniform and befriended JEAN-BAPTISTE CHAVANNES, a mixed-race planter from the neighboring parish of Limonade, who was also a militia sergeant and veteran of the French army during the WAR OF AMERICAN INDEPENDENCE, 1775–83. He made some attempt to put the demand for free colored voting rights before the government, sending a letter to the governor on October 21, 1790. However, he also began to gather armed free colored men around him on a camp established in a plantation in Grande-Rivière, in the mountains near the border with the Spanish colony of SANTO DOMINGO. The POLICE, who were free people of color, did nothing to stop him, and indeed one of his closest supporters was a constable of the rural police.

On October 27, however, REGULAR ARMY troops from the Cap-Français garrison attempted to arrest Ogé and Chavannes. The soldiers, who numbered only a few dozen, retreated without confronting Ogé's hundreds of armed supporters. The next day, Ogé and his men went to all the neighboring plantations and collected their weapons, handing them out to their supporters. On October 30, a force of about 800 soldiers, militiamen, and constables from Cap-Français, at least half of whom were probably free coloreds, confronted Ogé's 400 free colored soldiers in a battle that lasted most of the morning. The government troops were forced to withdraw to the town.

Ogé's men celebrated, but their leaders knew that the next attack would be even more powerful. Ogé sent messengers to prominent free coloreds across the island but received no response. He built field fortifications at his camp. His followers, including Chavannes, encouraged him to enroll slaves in his army, promising them their liberty in return for their services. Chavannes even enlisted 30 male slaves from his own plantation, it is said, though it is doubtful he actually owned so many slaves at the time; they may have been RUNAWAY SLAVES or the numbers may have been exaggerated. Ogé refused to enroll slaves, however, even with the permission of their masters. He did not want the movement for free colored civil rights to lead to a hugely disruptive slave rebellion, though he had accepted the idea of gradual, compensated emancipation of slaves in discussions with the Amis des Noirs and the Club Massiac in Paris the year before.

When the colonial governor arrived in person the next day with 3,000 men and artillery, the small force at Ogé's command could not resist them. They fled into the hills, and many returned to their homes. Ogé and 24 of his closest supporters, including his four brothers, Chavannes and his two brothers, and two free black militia sergeants, fled across the border to the Spanish side of the island.

The End
In the past, the Spanish had sheltered runaway slaves, and in later years, they would provide refuge for Toussaint Louverture's slave rebel army, but in 1790, they were trying to remain on good terms with the French, and so they extradited Ogé and his men to Cap-Français. Ogé was questioned by the colonial government, tried, and sentenced to death on February 21, 1791. His death sentence ordered that he and his companions

> be led by the high executioner before the principal door of the parish church of this town and there, bare-headed, and wearing [only] a shirt, rope around their neck, on their knees, and each carrying in his hands a two-pound wax candle, to make proper atonement, and to declare in a loud and intelligible voice that he committed these crimes recklessly, with malice and poor judgment, that he is convinced of this and that he repents and asks forgiveness of God, of the king, and of justice; after this, to be led onto the central square of this town on the side opposite from that used for the execution of whites and there, on a scaffold built for this purpose, to have his arms, legs, thighs, and lower back broken while alive and to be placed by the high executioner on the wheel, to remain there as long as it pleases God to maintain his life; after this his head cut off and exposed on stakes; to wit, that of the said Vincent Ogé the younger on the highway that leads to Dondon [his home town], and that of Jean-Baptiste, known as Chavannes, to the road to Grande Rivière, across from the Poisson plantation [where the battle had taken place].

The sentence was carried out the following day, February 22, 1791. Ogé suffered terribly, and his cries gained the sympathy of the onlookers, including the well-known lawyer and Enlightenment figure Médéric-Louis-Élie Moreau de St-Méry.

Aftermath
When the execution became known in France, it provoked outrage. The barbaric and medieval means of execution used, with the public confession reminiscent of the Inquisition beforehand, contrasted with the scientific and reasonably humane guillotine then being introduced in France. The supposed crimes of Ogé and Chavannes did not seem so terrible in retrospect, as by 1792 the slaves had burned most of the sugar cultivation plantations

in the North Province. Ogé's movement did not lead to a colonywide uprising either by free coloreds or by slaves, at least not immediately. The care they took not to involve slaves appealed to moderates. The French parliament responded by passing a law on April 4, 1792, that gave equal citizenship to free people of color. The revolutionary commissioner Léger-Félicité Sonthonax was sent to the island to enforce this decree, and it was he who ultimately declared the abolition of slavery and recruited Toussaint Louverture to lead the colony's armies.

After the end of the Haitian Revolution in 1804, Ogé was recognized as one of the heroes of Haiti's struggle for independence. He was a figure much more popular among the new nation's wealthy mixed-race population than among the black descendants of the slaves he refused to permit to join his movement. He is seen today as an important symbol of the division in Haiti's ruling class that offered the slaves an opening for successful rebellion. His experience also showed other free people of color that they had little to hope for from the white ruling class. In the end, most of the colony's free people of color supported the revolutionary forces rather than the French.

Stewart R. King

FURTHER READING
Garrigus, John. "Vincent Ogé." Available online. URL: thelouvertureproject.org/index.php?title=oge#fn-1. Accessed January 4, 2011.

King, Stewart. *Blue Coat or Powdered Wig: Free Coloreds in Colonial Saint-Domingue.* Athens: University of Georgia Press, 2001.

Rainsford, Marcus. *An Historical Account of the Black Empire of Hayti.* London: 1802. Available online. URL: books. google. com/books?id=EKW-Z44oTrIc. Accessed January 4, 2011.

OHIO
Ohio was the first state carved from part of the landmass known as the Northwest Territory. It is relatively flat, bordered by the Ohio River on the south and east and Lake Erie to the north. In the 19th century, the slave states of Virginia and Kentucky lay on the other side of the Ohio River (*see* Virginia and West Virginia). Ohio is good farming country, and early settlement starting in the 1700s had led to the development of an economy of prosperous small farms. Victories over the Indians in the 1790s permitted rapid settlement of the state by whites and some free blacks from the East. By 1802, the Ohio Territory had met the requirements of the Enabling Act and applied for statehood. As required by the Northwest Ordinance, a law passed in 1787 that organized the Northwest Territory, a delegation of 35 free white men met to draft a constitution. It was approved by Congress

in 1803, allowing Ohio to be admitted as a state. The Constitution of 1803 remained in effect until 1851. As required by the Northwest Ordinance, Ohio was a free state.

Antebellum Period (1803–1861)

In 1804, the General Assembly codified RACISM AND RACIAL PREJUDICE by passing the so-called black laws, which tightly prescribed how blacks would live and interact with whites. (*See* BLACK LAWS IN THE MIDWEST.) The product of southern Ohio legislators who lived in the counties that bordered the slaveholding state of Kentucky, the laws forced blacks and mulattoes moving into the state to produce a certificate of freedom. Those already living in the state were required to register themselves and their children with their respective county clerks before June 1804, at a cost of 12½ cents per name, and to post a bond of $500 within 20 days. In order to be hired by a white person, a certificate of freedom had to be produced. Those whites who hired blacks without the certificate were fined anywhere from $10–$50. Furthermore, whites who aided or abetted RUNAWAY SLAVES could also be fined $10–$50; if the slave owner appeared to claim his slave, he was entitled to be paid by whoever hid the slave 50 cents for every day the slave had been missing. Finally, blacks were barred from attending public schools and testifying against whites in courts of law and receiving any public charity.

In 1807, the black codes were expanded. The new black codes punished whites who harbored runaway slaves. Blacks who had not posted the bond required in 1803 were fined $100; $50 was given to the person who provided the authorities with the information about lack of compliance. This placed free blacks in an especially precarious position; it was not uncommon for them to be trapped into

slavery or claimed as runaways solely because they could not post the required bond. (*See* RE-ENSLAVEMENT.)

Most blacks in Ohio struggled to survive economically. They generally held the most menial jobs, such as day laborers, or worked in the homes of white people as butlers, laundresses, and such. Consequently, they earned little money, could not afford to buy property, and lived in segregated communities, which were often rife with overcrowding, disease, and crime. White laborers, especially Irish immigrants who also faced discrimination, were fearful that blacks might take their jobs as black men were often used to undercut the wages of white men and as strike breakers. The economic competition was such that whites sometimes reacted with mob action, although this was the exception rather than the rule.

By 1830, the black population in Ohio had swelled to almost 10,000 of a total state population of 935,000. The following table shows the evolution of Ohio's black population through the 19th century, as reflected by census figures. We can assume that many people who were runaways, country folk living in isolated settlements, and other marginalized people were not counted.

Some of the blacks counted in the prewar censuses were no doubt runaway slaves. Runaways were increasingly drawn to Ohio as a refuge or as a way station to freedom, and this contributed to the growth in the black population in the prewar years. Ohio teemed with antislavery and abolitionist activities. Chapters of the American Antislavery Society increased around the state. Members of the society were quite involved in the Underground Railroad, the network of safe houses and churches through which escaped slaves passed to freedom. By some estimates, there were more than 300 stations in Ohio, and several

AFRICAN-AMERICAN POPULATION OF OHIO, 1810–1900

Year	Slaves*	Free People of Color	Free People of Color as a Percentage of Total Population	Total Population
1810		1,899	0.8%	230,760
1820		4,901	0.8%	581,434
1830	6	9,567	1.0%	935,884
1840	3	17,342	1.1%	1,519,467
1850		25,279	1.3%	1,980,329
1860		36,673	1.6%	2,339,511
1870		62,313	2.3%	2,685,200
1880		79,900	2.5%	3,198,062
1890		87,113	2.4%	3,672,316
1900		97,341	2.3%	4,157,545

* The persons listed as slaves in the 1830 and 1840 counts could not have been enslaved under state law. It is unclear what their status may have been.

Ohio residents, including John Rankin, Levi Coffin, and the former slave John Parker, were among the most prominent conductors on the Underground Railroad in America. Whites who wanted to rid the state of black citizens countered by forming a local branch of the AMERICAN COLONIZATION SOCIETY with the goal of expatriating blacks to the African country of LIBERIA.

In spite of the prejudice and discrimination, the black population in Ohio increased steadily, and so did their efforts to uplift African Americans as a whole. By the eve of the AMERICAN CIVIL WAR, 1861–65, there were a number of black settlements throughout Ohio that increased black solidarity and institutions of self-help. These included churches; mutual aid societies; women's auxiliaries that were engaged in uplift, temperance, and family sanctity activities; and conventions that were held to discuss the problems facing blacks and their possible solutions. In 1835, Oberlin College in Oberlin, Ohio, became one of the first institutions of higher education to accept blacks as students, and many black leaders in this period were graduates. In 1862, the Ohioan Mary Jane Patterson became the first black woman to receive the bachelor of arts degree in the United States (see HIGHER EDUCATION). One of the earliest black free schools to provide basic education to children and adults was the Harveysburg Free Black School, established in 1831 by Quaker missionaries (see EDUCATION AND LITERACY).

Civil War and Aftermath

Ohio blacks played a crucial role in the American Civil War. The first African-American unit in the North, called the Black Brigade, was formed in Cincinnati. Men in the Black Brigade were drafted and put to work building the infrastructure to support the war effort but were disbanded a month later after the work was completed. In 1863, President ABRAHAM LINCOLN issued the EMANCIPATION PROCLAMATION, authorizing blacks to serve in uniform. The U.S. government also began drafting soldiers, and Ohio began to accept black men in its regiments in order to avoid having to institute the draft in the state. The 5th and 27th U.S. Colored Infantry Regiment were formed in 1864; later, they joined the Army of the Potomac. Black soldiers from Ohio served exclusively under white officers, were poorly equipped, and received half the pay of white soldiers. A total of 5,092 black Ohioans served in the ranks of the U.S. Army during the war, almost 15 percent of the prewar population.

American blacks, through their enthusiastic service in the armed forces, staked a claim to citizenship that was recognized for a time in the postwar years. A variety of federal laws and constitutional amendments confirmed the right of blacks to citizenship in the United States and to certain forms of legal equality (see CIVIL RIGHTS LAWS IN THE UNITED STATES AFTER 1865). Ultimately, though, the failure of Reconstruction in the south (see RECONSTRUCTION IN THE UNITED STATES), the flood of European immigrants moving to Northern and midwestern cities, and a sense of weariness with causes and struggles that spread through the white population in the 1870s and 1880s meant a retreat from this promise of equality. The civil rights laws of the 1870s were unenforced until the revival of the Civil Rights movement in the 1950s.

Economic opportunities for black Ohioans after the Civil War remained blocked by racism and discrimination for decades. As employees, they met with indifference, hostility, and a crushing lack of opportunity. For the most part, they were relegated to low-skill, low-pay jobs in domestic and personal service. Because of racial discrimination and the lack of government land to be homesteaded by the middle of the 19th century, blacks found it hard to get land in Ohio and most lived in the cities. In most cities, blacks were a small part of the population and were in competition with European immigrants for the few low-paid jobs available. Even when blacks managed to obtain jobs, they were rapidly displaced by technological changes in farming and dock work. Often used as strike breakers, they were the first fired when hard times hit their industry. Finally, they were all but left out of the unions and barred from most apprenticeships. There were increased socioeconomic stratification within the black community and increased racial tension between whites and blacks. Between 1876 and 1932, this racial tension resulted in almost two dozen LYNCHINGS and attempted lynchings in various areas of the state.

The first several decades of the 20th century saw a massive population shift in the African-American community. It is estimated that as many as 1.5 million blacks left the rural South for the urban North in what became known as the Great Migration. As in other Northern states, the African-American population in Ohio increased sharply during this time. Blacks found work in the many industrial centers in the North, and in Ohio, they settled in the largest cities: Akron, Cleveland, Columbus, Dayton, Toledo, and Youngstown. The descendants of Ohio's former free black population received these migrants into already-overcrowded black neighborhoods, made room for them in their community institutions, and in many cases led the new, larger black community. While thousands of migrants found higher-paying jobs, they soon discovered that racism existed in the North too. African Americans found difficulty in being promoted and were generally confined to unskilled or semiskilled positions. De facto SEGREGATION also meant that most blacks were confined in densely populated ghettos with virtually no chance of obtaining better housing. Race riots broke out in the cities of Akron and Springfield in 1900, several people died, scores were injured, and hundreds of thousands of dollars in property damage resulted.

Ohio represented a refuge for American blacks, both before and after the Civil War. However, life in the state was not without special hardships for African Americans, some caused by conscious discrimination. African Americans, nonetheless, showed resilience and courage in confronting these hardships and building a self-sufficient community.

Marilyn K. Howard

FURTHER READING

Bigham, David E. *On Jordan's Banks: Emancipation and Its Aftermath in the Ohio Valley.* Lexington: University Press of Kentucky, 2005.

Gerber, David A. *Black Ohio and the Color Line: African Americans and the Color Line in Ohio, 1860–1912.* Champaign: University of Illinois Press, 1976.

Giffin, William W. *African Americans and the Color Line in Ohio, 1915–1930.* Columbus: Ohio State University Press, 2005.

Hagedorn, Ann. *Beyond the River: The Untold Story of the Heroes of the Underground Railroad.* New York: Simon & Schuster, 2002.

Hyde, David. *1968: The Year That Saved Ohio State Football.* Wilmington, Ohio: Orange Frazer Press, 2008.

Knepper, George. *Ohio and Its People.* Kent, Ohio: Kent State University Press, 2003.

Kusmer, Kenneth L. *A Ghetto Takes Shape: Black Cleveland 1870–1930.* Champaign: University of Illinois Press, 1978.

Middleton, Stephen. *Black Laws: Race and the Legal Process in Early Ohio.* Athens: Ohio University Press, 2005.

Moore, Leonard M. *Carl B. Stokes and the Rise of Black Political Power.* Champaign: University of Illinois Press, 2003.

Shannon, Ronald. *Profiles in Ohio: A Legacy of African American Achievement.* Bloomington: University of Indiana Press, 2008.

OKLAHOMA

Oklahoma is a state in the Midwest of the United States, bordered by Texas on the south, New Mexico on the west, Colorado and Kansas on the north, and Missouri and Arkansas on the east. It is generally flat and open country, with relatively low rainfall. Rain-fed agriculture is possible in some river valleys in the eastern part of the state, but prior to the 20th century, for the most part the climate was best suited for ranching. The indigenous people of Oklahoma consisted of populations of farmers by the rivers and hunters and gatherers on the plains. After the introduction of horses in the 1500s, the plains nomads began to hunt buffalo and became dominant. They offered significant resistance to European penetration of the region, and no nation achieved effective control over the area until the United States defeated

them in the 1830s. Up until that time, European presence in the area was intermittent, consisting of exploring, trapping, and trading parties from French Louisiana or Spanish New Mexico. These parties included people of color. It is possible that the explorer Francisco Vasquez de Coronado (1510–54), whose chief scout was the Afro-Spanish conquistador Estéban de Dorantes, passed through the area in 1540 or 1541, though depending on the timing, Dorantes may have been dead by this time. In any case, there has been a feeble and intermittent black presence in Oklahoma at least since the 17th century.

Indian Territory before the Civil War

From 1830 to 1889, during most of the period of slavery and its immediate aftermath, what is now the state of Oklahoma was a special territory set aside for Indians from the eastern states. The Indian Removal Act of 1830 and a series of more-or-less forced treaties with eastern tribes such as the Choctaw, Cherokee, and Seminole, began the process that has become known as the "Trail of Tears," in which tens of thousands of Indians were forcibly moved to Oklahoma. They were given land, and it was hoped that they would become cash-cropping family farmers like the white farmers in Kansas and other midwestern states. However, most of the Indian migrants were from Southern states such as Alabama, Mississippi, Georgia, Florida, and North Carolina, where they had been exposed to the plantation system. Some owned slaves, took their slaves with them to Oklahoma, and aspired to be planters themselves. Slavery among the Indians was a very different institution from that which existed among their white neighbors. Even with the most Westernized masters, slaves were like subordinate family members, living in the same houses and eating the same food as the masters. The sharp racial divisions that characterized non-Indian society in the American South were not found in Indian society in the 19th century. This feature of Indian society frightened Southern whites and contributed to the effort to drive the Indians from their lands in the 1830s.

All the southeastern tribes freely admitted runaway slaves and free blacks as members, though they would sometimes return runaways for a reward. In addition, in keeping with their generally more liberal attitudes toward their slaves, they were quicker to free their slaves than their white neighbors. The Seminole in particular, especially those who remained in Florida longest after the removals began—known as the black Seminole—had so many runaway slaves that their villages can almost be considered communities of maroons. The 1860 federal census of Indian Territory reveals a scattered free black and mixed-race population, with many persons listed as black in race but with the notation *(Seminole)* or *(Cherokee)* after their name indicating that they were tribal members. The occupations of most free blacks were blacksmiths, farmers, and laborers. At the same time, there are some clumps of a dozen or more enslaved blacks listed together, indicating that a few moderately large plantations existed. One of these was owned by Stand Watie (1804–71), a Cherokee leader who had accepted the removal law and had moved to Oklahoma early in the process, thereby gaining access to some of the best land available. Watie and many of the others who agreed with him were of partially European ancestry and are often referred to as the "mixed-race" faction, as opposed to the "pure-blood" Ross faction, led by Watie's enemy John Ross (1790–1866), leader of the National Party, who fought removal. However, Ross also had the support of most part-African Cherokee. Similar divisions existed within most of the eastern tribes, with more Westernized and sometimes part-white members more willing to accept the removal to Oklahoma in the hope that it would permit assimilation into a slave-owning Southern agricultural economy and society, while pure-blood and part-African Indians were more likely to dig in to their traditional land and fight the Americans while any hope of preserving their traditional lifestyle remained. The resistance of the eastern tribes to removal was often in proportion to the number of African-descended people they had in their midst, with the Seminole fighting hardest and longest and still identifying themselves, on their tribal Web site, as the "people who never surrendered."

The Civil War and Reconstruction
The opening of the AMERICAN CIVIL WAR in 1861 coincided with this internal struggle in Indian Territory. Among the Cherokee, Stand Watie was involved in a running feud with John Ross that had led to the murder of three of Ross's top followers and Watie's uncle and cousin before the fighting began in the country as a whole. Watie and his followers signed up with the Confederate States of America in 1861, with Watie ultimately rising to the rank of brigadier general in the Confederate army. Watie raised several thousand Indian cavalrymen to fight alongside the Confederate forces in Missouri and Arkansas. Ross and his followers were driven from the Cherokee lands and took refuge in Kansas, returning to Oklahoma in 1863 accompanied by, among others, a unit of Kansas free colored infantry. The Kansas troops played a crucial role in the Union victory at the Battle of Honey Springs (July 27, 1863), which cemented Union control of eastern Oklahoma. The Creek and Seminole also split into two factions, while most Choctaw and the descendants of the original Oklahoma Indians, the Osage and others, tended to try to avoid the struggle by moving away from the areas where fighting was heaviest. Although racial background was one determining factor in how any individual would

assign his or her loyalty during this struggle, it was only one factor among many. Personal loyalties, class identity, family or band relationships with some of the major contenders, and calculations of self-interest all came into play. Thus, it was that people of partially African descent, such as the Seminole chief and Baptist religious leader John Jumper (1820–85), took Confederate commissions.

The Civil War was a difficult time for most Indians in Oklahoma. Warring armies marched back and forth several times, taking supplies from Indians with even less regard for property rights than Civil War armies generally showed in non-Indian territory. Some hitherto peaceful bands of Indians were driven into the war merely to preserve their livestock and land. In addition, feuds and intertribal violence played into the struggle, with various parties forging shifting alliances with the Union and Confederate forces. The degree of devastation wreaked by the war was comparable to that experienced in the most-affected areas of the South, even though there were only a few large battles in Oklahoma.

Ultimate Union victory in the Civil War in 1865 was hard on the losers but also had a negative impact on the winners. There was no formal Reconstruction period in Oklahoma as there was in Confederate states, but the U.S. military continued to exert authority in the territory much more directly than in other territories or, indeed, than had been the case before the war. (See also RECONSTRUCTION IN THE UNITED STATES.) The postwar U.S. government was suspicious of all Oklahoma Indians because of the support some had given to the Confederacy. Ultimately, this suspicion, along with an ideological commitment to private land tenure and assimilation, led to a profound change in U.S. policy toward Indians, symbolized in the Dawes Act of 1887 (which applied specifically to Oklahoma) and similar acts for the other territories. Under these laws, Indians were to receive individual allotments of land once held collectively by their tribes. The effect of this measure was to handicap smaller and less Westernized Indians further, while helping that small minority who were already practicing cash-crop farming—and white immigrants to the territory—by allowing them to purchase land from their poorer and less well-prepared neighbors. Indians of African descent were generally less well treated than pure-blood or part-white Indians. One provision of these laws required the maintenance of official lists of tribal members, and among the Cherokee, only persons who had been free in 1861 were counted. Many Cherokee freedmen, those freed during the war, were excluded from land distribution and remained as a disadvantaged underclass.

Oklahoma Territory and Statehood
In 1866, the U.S. government declared the lands in Oklahoma that had not yet been taken up by Indian settlers

from the east to be Unassigned Territory. Most of this area was in the arid western part of the state, but in the 1870s and 1880s, North America was experiencing a period of unusually high rainfall, and these areas appeared suitable for rain-fed agriculture. Land promoters began calling these lands Oklahoma and calling for them to be opened to non-Indian settlement. Most prominent among these promoters were whites, but some of the "boomers" or "sooners," as these new settlers were called, were African Americans from Kansas and other states. Most notable among these was EDWIN P. MCCABE, a prewar free mixed-race lawyer from ILLINOIS who had moved to Kansas with the EXODUSTER MOVEMENT in the years after the Civil War and then founded the Oklahoma Immigration Association in 1888 to encourage black settlement in the newly opened territories. He lobbied for more land for black settlers through his political contacts in President Benjamin Harrison's administration. He sought to be named territorial governor of Oklahoma and was apparently seriously considered, though ultimately rejected in favor of a white candidate. Thanks to McCabe's efforts, however, black settlers were treated more or less equally in the distribution of land, and at least 27 black settlements were formed in Oklahoma in the 1880s and 1890s.

Alongside these potential immigrants were black soldiers from the two Buffalo Soldier Regiments of cavalry, the 9th and the 10th, based at Fort Sill and Fort Gibson. Many retiring soldiers and their families wanted to continue living in the area, and many had forged close relationships with the Indians they served among. Some of these retiring soldiers married Indians and lived among them, while others joined non-Indian black settlers in the Oklahoma Territory.

In 1890, blacks made up about 10 percent of the population of the combined territories, a figure that does not take into account those people of African descent who were counted as tribal members. They were mostly poor, but there were substantial numbers of farmers, small businessmen, and professionals. One of the most notable of Oklahoma blacks was Bass Reeves (1838–1910), a former runaway slave from Texas who lived with the Seminole in the 1860s and served as a U.S. deputy marshal from 1875 until 1907. He was said to have arrested more than 3,000 outlaws in the territory during his career. As was the case with Reeves, who owed his position to Republican Party officeholders and the federal civil service system, Oklahoma blacks were protected to some extent from discrimination by the federal control of the territory's politics, though as Oklahoma moved toward statehood, it was granted greater autonomy by the federal government, and discrimination became more prevalent. McCabe and other black Oklahomans fought this process in the courts but were ultimately defeated when statehood was granted

in 1907. The white-controlled legislature immediately passed SEGREGATION laws similar to those found in most Southern states, which persisted until the Civil Rights movement in the 1960s. Blacks generally retired from public life during the Jim Crow era; McCabe moved back to his home in Illinois, and Reeves retired to a farm in Muscogee County, where his family remains prominent in the Oklahoma black community.

Stewart R. King

FURTHER READING
Burton, Art T. *Black Gun, Silver Star: The Life and Legend of Frontier Marshal Bass Reeves.* Lincoln: University of Nebraska Press, 2006.
Franklin, Jimmie Lewis. *Journey toward Hope: A History of Blacks in Oklahoma.* Norman: University of Oklahoma Press, 1982.
Roberson, Jere W. "Edward P. McCabe and the Langston Experiment." *Chronicles of Oklahoma* 51 (Fall 1973): 343–355.

OLIVIER, VINCENT (ca. 1680-1781)
Saint-Domingue farmer and militiaman

Vincent Olivier was a black man who was born a slave but became free in 1697. He served in the French military in various campaigns and battles in the Americas and Europe and lived most of his life in the rural district of Grande-Rivière, in the North Province of the French colony of SAINT-DOMINGUE, the future Haiti. He is an example of a successful free black farmer and militiaman and was especially notable for the fact that his very long life spanned the history of Saint-Domingue, from the pirate days of the 17th century to the eve of the slave rebellion of the late 18th century.

Olivier was born around 1680. He is described as a CREOLE, meaning that he was born somewhere in the colony of Saint-Domingue, but where is unclear. He was a young man when he participated in France's last big pirate raid, on CARTAGENA in COLOMBIA, in 1697 during the War of the Grand Alliance (1688–97). His master was also named Olivier. Apparently Vincent took his master's name when freed as a tribute to him rather than to imply any family relationship. He was very tall and strong, and among the buccaneers of Saint-Domingue, he must have seemed uniquely suited to be a warrior.

We do not know any more about Olivier's master than his name, but since he participated in the attack on Cartagena, he was apparently one of the famous buccaneers who had made the colony a by-word for lawlessness during the 17th century. The French colonial government had tried to impose order but needed the military skills of the pirates to protect the colony against the Spanish. The Cartagena campaign was the pirates' last hurrah, as the

Treaty of Ryswick, signed shortly thereafter, recognized the French claim to Saint-Domingue and meant that the colony was no longer in danger of invasion by the Spanish. The pirates were required to settle down and become farmers, and using the enormous loot of Cartagena, they were able to afford the slaves and machinery needed to do so profitably.

Olivier participated in the pirates' successful attack on the city of Cartagena, but when he was returning to Saint-Domingue, a Spanish cruiser captured his ship. Olivier and his companions were taken as prisoners to SPAIN, where they were released within a few months when the war ended. Olivier went to FRANCE, where, because of his bravery in battle, he was given his freedom. He was also received at court, and his bravery, height, and obvious strength impressed King Louis XIV. Louis gave him a sword and enlisted him in the French army, perhaps in the Royal Guards, who were men of unusual height and strength. It was not unusual for men of color to serve in the REGULAR ARMY in Europe at this time. Olivier fought in Germany and the Low Countries during the War of the Spanish Succession (1701–14). In 1714, he returned to Saint-Domingue with enough money to buy slaves and land and start a small farm.

The colonial government was not about to let an experienced soldier sit idle. Racial discrimination was not strong at this time, but the colony's MILITIA was segregated into free colored and white companies. Olivier was made a captain and put in charge of all the free colored militia units in the North Province. He served in this post for at least 30 years.

By the 1760s, Olivier had had at least three children and perhaps as many as a dozen. His grandchildren and great-grandchildren were too numerous to count. He had a good-sized farm in Grande-Rivière by this time as well as a town house in CAP-FRANÇAIS/CAP-HAÏTIEN. The French government began imposing all sorts of discriminatory and humiliating laws on free people of color, such as prohibiting them to bear arms in public or to serve as officers in the militia or in other professional positions, and requiring them to wear distinctive clothing and to refrain from using the names of whites. This was probably an attempt to encourage racial solidarity among whites of different social classes and a response to the growing size and wealth of Saint-Domingue's free colored population. Olivier is notable for defying almost all of these laws successfully. Of course, he had already grown too old to serve in the militia, but he continued to identify himself by his rank of captain in official documents for the rest of his life. He was never seen in public without the sword that King Louis had given him. He also wore his uniform regularly and continued to use the name of Olivier without bothering to change the spelling as most free coloreds did (for example, VINCENT OGÉ's father spelled his name *Augé*, and JULIEN RAIMOND's father was *Raymond*).

Near the end of his life, Olivier became involved in an attempt to use military service to strengthen the position of free people of color. The colonial government had come to rely more and more on free coloreds to man its defense forces as colonial whites were unwilling to serve and troops from France suffered from diseases. The former colonial governor and French admiral Count d'Estaing wanted to recruit free colored soldiers to fight in support of the Americans during the WAR OF AMERICAN INDEPENDENCE, 1775–83. Men who served were promised wages and a remission of some taxes, but the larger drawing card was hope for greater privileges and recognition of free people of color as equal citizens. Olivier was actively involved in this recruiting effort and sent at least two of his younger relatives. MÉDÉRIC-LOUIS-ÉLIE MOREAU DE ST-MÉRY, the colonial Enlightenment figure who wrote a lengthy description of Olivier's life and merits in his *Description* of the colony's history and people, said that Olivier sent his sons to serve. It is more likely that they were grandsons: His youngest children would have been in their 50s by this time. In any case, he and many other free coloreds had high hopes for this plan, but in the end it came to nothing. The major benefit that free people of color gained from their participation in the expedition was battlefield experience that would serve them in good stead when the HAITIAN REVOLUTION began in the 1790s. Olivier did not live to see this outcome, however, since he died sometime in 1781 before the free colored soldiers returned from the war.

Stewart R. King

FURTHER READING

King, Stewart. *Blue Coat or Powdered Wig: Free Coloreds in Pre-Revolutionary Saint-Domingue.* Athens: University of Georgia Press, 2000.

"ONE DROP RULE" OF RACIAL IDENTITY

The "one drop rule" of racial identity is an idea that took hold in mainland North America that holds that a person who has African ancestry is considered black unless he or she has an alternative nonwhite ancestry, such as Native American, Asian, Arab, or Australian aboriginal. It developed in colonial America out of the culture of institutionalized racially based chattel slavery. After slavery ended in the United States, Southern legislatures employed the one drop rule to codify and strengthen SEGREGATION and disenfranchise African Americans and many poor whites from 1890 to 1910. After the Supreme Court accepted the concept of "separate but equal" in the 1896 case of *Plessy v. Ferguson*, these legislatures enacted

Jim Crow laws to segregate African Americans in public places and accommodations.

As noted, the roots of the one drop rule were in colonial America, a time when the regions had only a few races—whites, blacks, and Native Americans. In the antebellum South, the rule was employed as a method of enlarging the slave population with the children of slaveholders and slaves. Although almost universally throughout slave-owning societies in the Americas, the children of free white men and enslaved black women were slaves, the stronger color line between black and white promoted by the one drop rule helped strengthen slavery in what was otherwise a quite egalitarian society. The rule was designed for the convenience of the slaveholders, who wanted the slave population to grow so they would have a larger workforce. Many of the slave offspring had skin as fair as the slaveholders'. This was the source of the confusion over determining people's racial identity.

But why did the one drop rule develop in North America? In part, it was the result of every slave society's needing a buffer class. In North America, there was a buffer class of poor whites—white working-class people with limited privileges, who would always oppose these Africans. This class of poor whites was smaller in other British slave colonies in the Caribbean, and so there was room for a buffer class of people of mixed race. Thus, the tripartite division into white, brown, and black found in the Caribbean was not followed in North America.

Every person of African descent was considered not only black but a potential slave. Because slavery was generational, the offspring of interracial relationships could then be enslaved. Even if they were free, they would have reduced access to citizenship and democracy. Laws were passed to limit their movement or access to property and privileges.

During the height of the Jim Crow era, TENNESSEE and LOUISIANA adopted a one drop rule statute in 1910, followed in 1911 by TEXAS and ARKANSAS, and by MISSISSIPPI in 1917. Other state legislatures passed one drop statutes in the following two decades: NORTH CAROLINA in 1923, VIRGINIA in 1924, ALABAMA and GEORGIA in 1927 and OKLAHOMA in 1931. Many other states (FLORIDA, INDIANA, KENTUCKY, MARYLAND, MISSOURI, NEBRASKA, North Dakota, and Utah) retained their former "blood fraction" statutes de jure but amended these fractions (one-sixteenth, one-thirty-second) to one drop de facto during this same period.

Persons of mixed European and African ancestry were usually classified as MULATTO before 1930, sometimes as black, sometimes as white, depending on appearance. For Native American descendants with whites, the one drop rule was extended only so far as those with more than one-sixteenth Indian blood. This difference was the result of the "Pocahontas exception," which existed because many influential Virginia families claimed descent from the Native American Pocahontas (ca. 1595–1617) of the colonial era. To avoid classifying such people as nonwhite, the Virginia General Assembly declared that a person could be considered white as long as he or she had no more than one-sixteenth Indian "blood."

Despite the "Pocahontas exception," the one drop rule continues to assert influence in the United States, from both sides of color lines. Multiracial individuals who have visible European and African and/or Native American ancestry are often still considered nonwhite, unless they explicitly declare themselves white or Anglo. Typically, multiracial people are identified instead as mixed-race, biracial, mulatto, or mestizo, or African American or Native American, based on appearance. Latinos, the majority of whom are of mixed ancestry, consider their Latino cultural heritage more important to their ethnic identities than appearance or ancestry. The one drop rule is not generally applied to Latinos or Arab Americans of mixed origin.

The future of the one drop rule in the United States depends on a number of factors, including the way interracial parents label their children on the decennial U.S. censuses, scholarly opinions, and trends in affirmative action cases. Increasingly, people identify themselves as multiracial, biracial, mulatto, or mixed, rather than as black or white, and the Census Bureau has recognized this by permitting respondents to identify themselves as members of more than one race since with the 2000 census. Sixty-nine percent of mixed children identified themselves by more than one racial label in 2000, suggesting that the one drop theory and denial of one's European ancestry are no longer accepted as they used to be.

For the purposes of civil rights laws, minority hiring regulations, and other laws intended to remedy past racial discrimination, ironically, the one drop rule continued to apply to African Americans and to other minority groups recognized in the census. Federal civil rights regulatory agencies reclassified every person who selected white and some minority group (black, Asian, Native American, or Native Hawaiian or Pacific Islander) as a member of the minority group.

Numerous scholars publishing on the topic today (including Naomi Zack, Neil Gotanda, and Michael L. Blakely) affirm that the one drop rule is still strong in American popular culture. Findings in affirmative action court cases, however, when an apparently white person claims entitlement based on invisible black ancestry, are mixed.

The one drop rule does not apply in countries outside the United States, where race is treated much less formally. When people do self-identify racially, they often do so in ways very different from what would be the case in the United States.

Colonial Spanish America had a caste system in which there were fewer barriers to interracial relationships; at the same time, a racial hierarchy was in effect, combined with the Iberian purity of blood rules. (See also CASTA.) As a result, the status of a mixed-race person would be determined by the proportion of "white blood" with an elaborate system of different names classifying the combinations of black, Amerindian, and white. Thus, small drops of white blood were enough to position a person above "pure" nonwhites. Also, racial caste not only depended on ancestry or skin color but also could be raised or lowered by the person's economic and social status. (See also CÉDULAS DE GRACIAS AL SACAR.) After Latin American independence and the abolition of slavery, the caste divisions were blurred into wider groups.

According to Jose Neinstein, a white Brazilian and executive director of the Brazilian-American Cultural Institute in Washington, D.C., in the United States, "If you are not quite white, then you are black." In BRAZIL, however, "If you are not quite black, then you are white." While this is an oversimplification, it gives some idea of the sharply different racial standards of classification in force in Latin America.

Racial culture shock has greeted hundreds of thousands of dark-skinned immigrants to the United States from the Caribbean, Brazil, COLOMBIA, PANAMA, and other Latin American nations. Although most lack the degree of African ancestry required to be considered black in their homelands, in the United States they have often found themselves socially defined as black.

The Brazilian government has attempted to implant the "one drop law" in Brazil, through the Special Secretariat of Policies for the Promotion of Racial Equality, established in 2003 and managed by the Brazilian black civil rights movement. This has generated opposition from the Brazilian mixed-race movement, which accuses the government of not respecting the identity of the mixed descendants of indigenous natives, Africans, and Europeans, or the so-called mestizos, mulattoes, and Caboclos.

As a result of the one drop rule in the United States, there are many light-skinned individuals who are considered African American. In a significant minority of these cases, the person can actually have more white ancestry than African-American. The one drop rule has been explored in various works of popular culture. In the 1927 musical Show Boat, the sheriff chases Steve, a white man who is married to an African-American woman. He plans to arrest Steve and charge him with MISCEGENATION. Steve pricks his wife's finger and swallows some of her blood. When the sheriff arrives, Steve asks him whether he would consider a man to be white if he had "Negro blood" in him. The sheriff answers, "One drop of Negro blood makes you a Negro in these parts." Steve tells the sheriff that he has "more than a drop of Negro blood in [him]." The sheriff leaves without arresting him after being assured by others that Steve is telling the truth.

John McLane

FURTHER READING

Daniel, G. Reginald. *Race and Multiraciality in Brazil and the United States: Converging Paths?* College Station: Pennsylvania State University Press, 2001.

Dominguez, Virginia R. *White by Definition: Social Classification in Creole Louisiana.* New Brunswick, N.J.: Rutgers University Press, 1986.

Grant, Madison. *The Passing of the Great Race.* New York: Charles Scribner's Sons, 1916.

Murray, Pauli, ed. *States Laws on Race and Color.* Athens: University of Georgia Press, 1997.

Smith, J. Douglas. "The Campaign for Racial Purity and the Erosion of Paternalism in Virginia, 1922–1930: 'Nominally White, Biologically Mixed, and Legally Negro.'" *Journal of Southern History* 68, no. 1 (2002): 65–106.

Sweet, Frank W. *Legal History of the Color Line: The Rise and Triumph of the One-Drop Rule.* Palm Coast, Fla.: Backintyme, 2005.

OREGON

Oregon is a state of the United States, located on the Pacific coast between Washington and CALIFORNIA. It became a state in 1859. From 1843 to 1859, it was part of the Oregon Territory of the United States, along with the regions that subsequently became the states of Washington and Idaho. The Nevada Territory bordered Oregon on the southeast. The eastern part of the state is high-altitude scrubland with fertile river valleys, suitable for RANCHING. The western part of the state is the most densely settled part, with the broad valley of the Willamette River especially fertile.

Probably the first African American to set foot in Oregon was a slave, York (1770?–1831), who belonged to Captain William Clark of the Lewis and Clark expedition that explored Oregon in 1804–05. York was enormously useful to the expedition and fascinating to the Indians they met. Clark promised him his freedom upon their return, and he may have been free when he died in MISSOURI. The first nonnative settlers of the region were fur trappers, working for the Astor fur company of New York or the Northwest Company of CANADA, later a part of the Hudson's Bay Company. The Astor company facility at Astoria at the mouth of the Columbia River, established in 1811, is the oldest nonnative settlement in the state. It was located near a large native settlement. The Hudson's Bay facility at Vancouver in what is now Washington State, founded in 1818, was similarly located near a large Native American village. Native American numbers declined precipitously in the decades following the establishment of fur trading posts in the region as European, Asian, and African communicable diseases ravaged the population. By the 1830s, western Oregon was almost uninhabited aside from the small fur company posts, while the more nomadic lifestyle of the Indians of eastern Oregon preserved them somewhat from disease. Western Oregon began to fill up again in the 1830s with migrants from the eastern United States, both whites and blacks.

Some blacks had worked in the fur trade and knew the country well when the migrants began to enter. GEORGE WASHINGTON BUSH was one well-known guide who led a wagon train from Missouri to Vancouver in 1844. He tried to settle near Oregon City, found the racial climate too hostile, and moved north of the river to Washington. Moses Harris (?–1849) was another black guide and trapper of the early days. Very little is known about his life. He may have been a wandering trapper with the Astor Pacific Fur Company in 1823–24. He is also credited with helping to found Fort Laramie in Wyoming in 1836 and with guiding the first wagon train along the Oregon Trail in that year. He settled in The Dalles, at the eastern end of the Columbia Gorge, where he guided wagons across the Cascade mountain pass to Oregon City. He died of disease in 1849.

Most white settlers who entered to Oregon in the 1840s did not want nonwhites living among them. The territorial legislature passed a series of exclusionary laws, in 1844, 1849, and 1851. These laws forbade slavery in the state and required that all slaves taken into the territory be set free but imposed fines, forced labor, or harsh punishments on free blacks in an acknowledged attempt to induce them to leave the territory. The infamous Oregon "Lash Law" of 1844 imposed a punishment of 20–39 lashes on any free black convicted of any crime, in addition to any other punishment the law imposed. Worse, the whipping was to be repeated every six months until the black person left the territory. The law was written in response to fears that blacks and Indians would cooperate against whites in the wake of a confused outbreak of violence in Oregon City in 1843. This law was so harsh that even the Oregon public could not stomach it, and it was repealed in 1845 before it would have gone into effect. The whippings were replaced with forced labor on roads and public works. The exclusion laws were written into Oregon's constitution by referendum when it was adopted in 1857, along with a provision banning blacks from voting, and not removed from the constitution until 1926. In 1853, the territorial courts, administered by federally appointed judges, upheld these laws, paradoxi-

A statue of York, the first African American to enter Oregon. York was a slave of Captain William Clark, who may have freed him after their return from the Lewis and Clark expedition. (©Karl Stelly, Gettysburg, Pa.)

cally using them to declare that a former slave family was free. The court decided that the children of Polly and Robin Holmes, blacks taken in to the area as slaves from Missouri, were free both because of the Oregon laws and because of federal law that did not provide for slavery in the territories.

Many blacks who settled in Oregon in the 1840s left as a result of these laws. Some, such as Bush, or GEORGE WASHINGTON of Centralia, Washington, only moved across the Columbia River to Washington. Hundreds of Oregon blacks, along with many from California, went farther, to British Columbia, Canada, where the governor from 1849 to 1864, a West Indian man of mixed race named SIR JAMES DOUGLAS, was encouraging black immigration and ensuring at least some racial equality.

Despite the harsh laws and social conditions, a few blacks continued to immigrate to Oregon and try to make their lives there. One of Polly Holmes's daughters, named Mary Jane Shipley (1830–1930), married another black man from Missouri, Reuben Shipley (1799–1873). The couple settled on a large farm near Rickreall, about 10 miles west of the state capital of Salem. Mary Jane became

AFRICAN-AMERICAN POPULATION OF OREGON, 1850–1900

Year	People of African descent	People of African Descent as a Percentage of Total Population	Total Population
1850	207	1.6%	13,234
1860	128	0.2%	52,465
1870	346	0.4%	90,923
1880	487	0.3%	174,768
1890	1,186	0.4%	313,767
1900	1,105	0.3%	413,536

a teacher in a school for black children and was an influential elder figure in the community after the turn of the century. She helped attract the Oregon Teacher's College, now Western Oregon University, to nearby Monmouth. Louis Southworth (1830–1917); his wife, Maria (?–1901); and her son, Alvin McCleary (1862–1951), lived in the Willamette Valley into the 1870s. They moved to Waldport, on the Pacific Coast, in 1879, and McCleary went on to become a respected fisherman, businessman, and city councillor.

As in many of the places in the Midwest where the settlers emigrated from, many Oregon towns adopted "sundown" laws, or informal codes that forbade blacks to settle inside the city limits (see BLACK LAWS IN THE MIDWEST). The largest city of Portland and the college towns of Monmouth and Corvallis (home of the Oregon Agricultural College, now Oregon State University) were exceptions. Blacks tended to concentrate in those towns, or in smaller communities, unincorporated at the time, such as Waldport or The Dalles. Still, the harsh racial climate, as well as the great distance that separated Oregon from the areas of dense black population in the South, meant that few blacks settled in the state during the 19th century. The census bureau counted only 1,105 blacks in 1900, of a total population of almost 450,000. Neighboring Washington State had more than 2,500 at that time of a state population of just above 500,000.

The story of Oregon's early black settlers is one of perseverance against high odds. The few black pioneers faced the same challenges as their white neighbors, as well as official RACISM AND RACIAL PREJUDICE that placed further hurdles in their path. Because there was no single black community, black pioneers were obliged to rely on support from their white neighbors. This paradoxically meant that individuals might be respected in their communities at the same time that their neighbors were voting for laws excluding other blacks. Peter Burnett, an author of the 1844 "Lash Law," was also the former master and patron of a black farmer, James Burnett, who lived near him and maintained good relations with him. Ultimately, blacks made homes in Oregon despite hardships and welcomed the arrival of large groups of migrants during the Great Migration of the 20th century.

Stewart R. King

FURTHER READING

Katz, William Loren. *The Black West.* 3rd ed. Seattle: Open Hand, 1987.

McClintock, Thomas C. "James Saules, Peter Burnett, and the Oregon Black Exclusion Law of June 1844." *Pacific Northwest Quarterly* 86 (1995): 121–130.

McLagen, Elizabeth. "A Peculiar Paradise: A History of Blacks in Oregon." The Oregon Black History Project. Available online. URL: http://gesswhoto.com/paradise-index.html. Accessed October 1, 2009.

Richard, K. Keith. "Unwelcome Settlers: Black and Mulatto Oregon Pioneers." *Oregon Historical Quarterly* 84 (1983): Part 1, 29–55; Part 2, 172–205.

P

PADILLA, JOSÉ PRUDENCIO (1784–1828)
Colombian admiral

José Prudencio Padilla was a PARDO, or free person of mixed ancestry, born on March 19, 1784, in the Colombian town of Río Hacha. After working for a while in merchant vessels, he enrolled in the Spanish Royal Navy as cabin boy in the late 1790s. He was promoted to a junior navigating officer, and in 1805, he was part of the crew of one of the Spanish ships that took part in the Battle of Trafalgar, during which he was taken prisoner by the British. He was released three years later and returned to SPAIN, where he was appointed director of the armory at CARTAGENA in COLOMBIA. In this city, he participated in the popular movement (composed mainly of people of color) that forced the local autonomous assembly to form an independent government in November 1811. Afterward, he joined the naval forces of the new Carthaginian state, participating in several battles, among which stands out his victory over the Spanish fleet at Lake Maracaibo in 1823, for which the revolutionary leader Simón Bolívar called him "the Nelson of Colombia" in allusion to the famous British admiral. His performance during the war of independence gained him many promotions, until he reached the rank of rear admiral and brigadier general.

In 1825, he was elected member of the Electoral College of the province of Cartagena, and the following year as senator represented the department of Magdalena at the National Senate in Bogotá. In early 1828, Padilla supported an uprising in Cartagena against what he considered Bolívar's attempt to become dictator. For this reason, he was accused of sedition, arrested, and sent to Bogotá to be tried. While in prison there, he became entangled in a conspiracy to murder Bolívar. Although Padilla had nothing to do with it, the conspirators set him free and named him their leader. Once the coup failed, all the implicated were accused of treason and sentenced to death. On October 2, 1828, Padilla was executed along with the real conspirators. Later on, the Granadian Convention of 1832, in an attempt to clean his memory, exculpated him of the crime that had put him on the scaffold.

Alejandro E. Gomez

FURTHER READING
Helg, Aline. "Simón Bolívar and the Spectre of Pardocracia: Jose Padilla in Post-Independence Cartagena." *Journal of Latin American Studies* 35 (2003): 447–471.

PANAMA

The contemporary country of Panama is located on the narrowest part of the American continent. It has an S shape from west to east, and its coasts are bathed by the Pacific Ocean and the Caribbean Sea. COSTA RICA is to the northwest, and COLOMBIA to the southeast. The country is very mountainous and receives heavy rainfall. The resulting mountainous jungle is nearly impassable, especially in the southern part of the country. Narrow coastal plains provide some possibility for plantation agriculture, but the economic heart of the country is the corridor between the modern cities of PANAMA CITY and Colon, which provides a relatively low-altitude path between the Caribbean and Pacific. This passageway was crucial to the economy of Spanish America from the 16th century and has remained economically important to this day.

Historical Overview

The Spaniards first explored the Caribbean coast of Panama in 1501. After several unsuccessful attempts to establish a colony on the coast, in 1510, they founded the first permanent settlement in mainland America, Santa María la Antigua, located in the eastern region of Darién (in present-day Colombia). Vasco Núñez de Balboa crossed the Isthmus of Panama with the help of the Indians and in 1513 reached the Pacific Ocean, which was originally named the South Sea. In 1519, the Spaniards founded Panama City on the Pacific coast and immediately afterword Nombre de Dios on the Caribbean coast and built a path between the two coasts, creating the transisthmian way. In 1522, the town of Natá was founded inland as a center of agricultural activities, and later on, other inland cities were established. Santa María la Antigua was abandoned in 1524 along with the Darién region, which, despite Spanish attempts, remained under Indian control

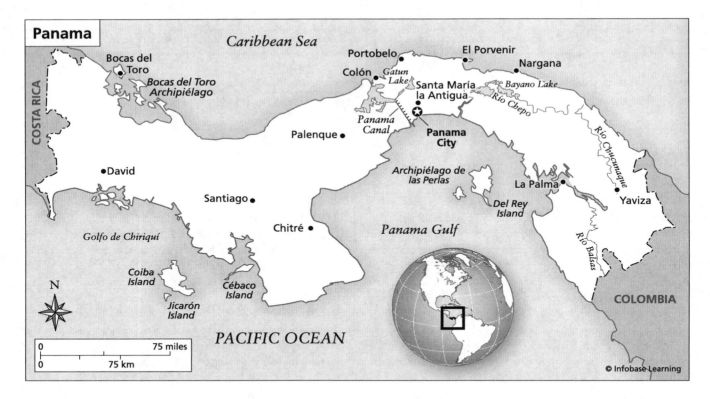

during most of the colonial period. Indeed, today's Kuna Indians of the Darién region are a paradigmatic example, since they maintained their autonomy throughout the centuries. However, the Spanish also decimated indigenous people and used them as a labor force. *Pueblos de Indios* (Indian villages) were created close to Spanish towns, and Indians were forced to live in them and work for the Spaniards.

Included in the Viceroyalty of Peru since 1542, the region of Panama was fundamental to the Spanish Empire for its strategic position. Panama City quickly became the departure point for exploratory voyages to Central and South America, and the Isthmus of Panama became a place of transit where people, goods, and treasures arrived, met, and departed. The trade system established by the Spanish Empire was based on the fleet system and fairs; one of the most important was held in Nombre de Dios (until 1597) and later in Portobelo (from 1597), both on the Caribbean coast of Panama. These periodic fairs not only attracted merchants from Spain and the Viceroyalty of Perú but also reunited in the Isthmus most of the treasure that the southern Spanish-American colonies sent to the king in Spain. This trade system was in place until 1739, when Portobelo was destroyed by the British. Without the protection of defenses, with the rising preference for the route around Cape Horn at the southern tip of South America, and the difficulties occasioned by the international economic and political situations, the fleet system to Portobelo was abandoned, and

the transisthmian route lost its relevance. The region of Panama passed under the Viceroyalty of Nueva Granada, and the Audiencia of Panama (High Court), which had existed nearly uninterrupted since 1539, was suppressed in 1751. From then onward, the region entered a period of economic stagnation only saved by contraband, intra-American and regional trade, and slave trading. With the turn of the century, the region experienced an economic recovery that lasted until the early 1820s and was then only reactivated with the CALIFORNIA gold rush in 1849. During the independence wars, Panama's regions were divided in their support for Spain or for independence. The region finally declared its independence from Spain in 1821 and decided to become part of Colombia—whose territory and name would change throughout the 19th century. Despite some failed attempts at independence during the 19th century, it was not until 1903 that Panama became an independent country with the support of the United States, which then oversaw construction of the Panama Canal.

Slaves and Maroons

African slavery was present in the isthmus from the late 1520s. Given Panama's location at the crossroads of the empire, many slaves were taken to and transported through the isthmus. The exact number of slaves who actually remained in the isthmus is unknown, but they were the main workforce from the 16th century until the mid-18th century. Afterward, although slaves were still taken to Panama, it has been suggested that the unfavorable economic situation and the high percentage of free people of color available to work might have reduced the need for buying slaves. In 1778, free people of color were 57.3 percent of the population of Panama (37,540 people); slaves, 10.3 percent (6,808 people); whites, 13.8 percent (9,054 people); and Indians, 18.4 percent (12,083 people). These figures are approximate and do not include people living outside Spanish jurisdiction or the territory they did not control, for instance, the northwestern Caribbean coast and the eastern region of today's Panama.

In contrast with other colonies in America, Panama did not have an economy based on plantations. Instead, the focus was on COMMERCE AND TRADE–related activities in the route from Nombre de Dios/Portobelo to Panama City, and on other urban and rural activities. Slaves worked as carriers, sailors (in the small boats transporting goods up the river to cross the isthmus), domestic servants, cooks, carpenters, seamstresses, vendors, and as the public workforce, among other occupations. Other slaves worked as miners, wood cutters, and laborers in agriculture in the interior areas, mainly in the regions of Veragua and Coclé, where the suppression of the encomienda created a demand for slaves as the main labor force from 1558 onward.

Slaves frequently escaped from their owners and went to the forests or big cities where they would not be captured or identified. They were called MAROONS (from the Spanish *cimarrón,* which described escaped cattle) and presented a danger for the Spanish colonial system, not only for the raids, attacks, and damage they caused to the transisthmian trade, but also because of the encouragement they gave other slaves to escape and join them. They frequently settled in *palenques* (maroon communities), which were inhabited by both men and women, and frequently included people of mixed ancestry and Indians. The *palenques* appeared in Panama from the early days and caused problems for the local authorities, who dealt with them in two ways: making war against them or reaching peace treaties that included freedom for the maroons. In 1549, the maroon community led by Felipillo was destroyed. Felipillo was a slave working in the Pearl Islands who ran away, sailed to the mainland with some other slaves, and created a *palenque.* When the *palenque* was defeated, Felipillo was killed, and the *palenque* was destroyed. In 1553–55, Bayano and his approximately 300 maroon supporters were pacified: The maroons were allowed to settle near Nombre de Dios, but Bayano was sent to PERU to be put on trial and apparently ended his days in Spain. In 1575, the Crown ordered freedom for those who agreed to integrate themselves in the empire and remained peaceful and allowed them to settle in villages. In 1579, the group led by Luis de Mozambique

agreed to peace with the Spaniards, who recognized their freedom and allowed them to found the village of Santiago del Príncipe, near the future town of Portobelo. As slaves continued to escape, the 17th and 18th centuries also registered conflicts between maroons and the local authorities. For instance, in 1691, a group of maroons were given freedom and created the village of Palenque in the outskirts of Portobelo, with the specific condition that they would fight the Kuna Indians and protect Spanish territory.

Free People of Color during the Colonial Period

Alongside the maroons, there were other free people of color in Panama. A few of them entered the region as conquerors, and a very well-known case is that of Ñuflo de Olano, who was with Balboa when he first arrived at the Pacific Ocean. Many others were freed slaves or descendants of Africans who had been taken to the region as slaves and obtained freedom by receiving pardons or by paying for freedom. The population of free people of color increased through the centuries, and by 1778, they were the main population group of the region. Some free colored people lived on small villages on the Caribbean coast, and their isolated location has preserved some traces of their Afro-Hispanic culture until today, as seen in the *congo* ceremonies during the Carnaval. However, most free coloreds integrated completely into Spanish society and culture. Many free women and men continued to work in the same occupations as the slaves, and some of them managed to have plots of land in the outskirts of the city or in the rural areas that they cultivated for their own profit. Other free coloreds became craftsmen as tailors, barbers, and carpenters with their own businesses and employed other people as officials and apprentices. Most free men of color formed part of the colored MILITIA of Panama, and there are accounts of their existence from the early 17th century. They had an important role in the defense of the isthmus from indigenous people, maroons, and European attacks and contributed to the protection of Crown interests in the isthmus.

Despite their slave ancestors and restrictive legislation, some free people of color managed to improve their socioeconomic situation. For instance, when in 1622 the king asked for economic aid, free people of color willingly contributed: 86 colored people donated money in Panama City, 42 in Portobelo, and 25 in Santiago del Príncipe (the village created in 1579 from a maroon community). Of the 86 contributors for Panama City, 61 were women, showing that women were also heads of household, successful entrepreneurs, and integrated in the society. Some free people of color dedicated themselves to retail trade, although they were temporarily banned from this activity in the 18th century, and a few Afro-Panamanians traveled to other cities in the Spanish colonies and established themselves as traders. A very successful small group of free colored people managed to occupy minor bureaucratic positions in the colonial administration. Indeed, from the mid-17th century and possibly before, free men of mixed African ancestry became notaries and scribes in several cities of the region, even though these were posts reserved for whites in many other cities of colonial Spanish America. Colored families and single mothers not only put their sons into apprenticeship but had previously arranged for their education and possibly paid for the official title after they finished their training.

The End of Slavery, the Nineteenth Century, and the Panama Canal

After Panama became part of the New Republic of Colombia in 1821, the Ley de Vientres (free womb law) was also applied in the isthmus. This law stated that from 1821 onward, anyone born of a slave mother would be free, although the person would be under the control of the mother's owner until he or she had reached 18 years of age. Alongside this law, a MANUMISSION Junta (body) was established in every canton with the purpose of freeing slaves by lottery on December 25, 26, and 27 of each year. Some statistics of the period state that by 1843, Panama had some 119,697 inhabitants, and there were only 1,286 slaves (about 1 percent of the total). Slavery was finally abolished in Colombia and Panama in 1851, and the manumission Junta of Panama created to free all the remaining slaves had finished its work by December 1852.

From the 1880s, African descendants from the Antilles were imported as a labor force to build the Panama Canal. First the French imported workers from the French and British Antilles. The French attempt to build the canal failed, many workers died, and the few remaining either returned home or stayed in Panama. When in 1904 the United States initiated their project for the canal, thousands of West Indians of African descent were again taken to Panama, along with many workers from other American and European countries, and many remained in Panama afterward. This migrant labor force modified the existing race relations in Panama for many reasons, among them that West Indian migrants did not speak Spanish and the United States introduced to the Panama Canal a racist SEGREGATION of the workforce.

Silvia Espelt Bombín

FURTHER READING

Castillero Calvo, Alfredo. *Historia General de Panamá*. Vol. 1, T. 1 and 2. Panama: Comité Nacional del Centenario, 2004.
Gallup-Díaz, Ignacio. "'Haven't We Come to Kill the Spaniards?' The Tule Upheaval in Eastern Panama, 1727–1728." *Colonial Latin American Review* 10, no. 2 (2001): 251–271.
Jaén Suárez, Omar. *La población del Istmo de Panama del siglo XVI al siglo XX*. Panama: Instituto Nacional de Cultura, 1979.
Lipski, John M. "The Negros Congos of Panama: Afro-Hispanic Creole Language and Culture." *Journal of Black Studies* 16, no. 14 (June 1986): 409–428.
Newton, Velma. *The Silver Men: West Indian Labour Migration to Panama, 1850–1914*. Kingston, Jamaica: Ian Randle, 2004.
Pike, Ruth. "Black Rebels: The Cimarrons of Sixteenth-Century Panama." *Americas* 64, no. 2 (October 2007): 243–266.

PANAMA CITY (PANAMÁ CITY)

Panama City was founded in 1519 on the Pacific coast and became the capital of the Audiencia, Capitanía, and later on Departamento and country of PANAMA. Due to the lack of defenses, the city was destroyed and burned during the attack by the English Pirate Henry Morgan in 1671. Instead of rebuilding the city, a new one was founded on a nearby peninsula and protected with a wall. Since there was not enough space for all the inhabitants of the old city, a suburb appeared some meters outside the city wall: the *arrabal* of Santa Ana.

As centuries passed, free people of color became the main group of inhabitants in Panama City. In 1575, Panama City's population was composed of 800 whites, 2,809 slaves, 300 free people of color, and more than 2,500 MAROONS in the surroundings. The city census of 1610 lists 1,267 whites, 3,696 slaves, 246 free mulattoes, 313 free blacks, 79 quadroons, 64 octoroons, and 27 Indians and ZAMBOS. In 1794, the city counted 862 whites, 118 ecclesiastics, 1,676 slaves, 5,112 free people of color, and 63 Indians. These figures show that free people of color made up approximately 65 percent of the city population by 1794, that MISCEGENATION made difficult the identification of people's origins, and that there were fewer slaves. It is known that slaves acquired freedom by paying for it or through pardon, but the process was not always easy. When the mulatta slave Damiana Pérez, who was a highly reputed seamstress, earned money with her work, wore fine clothes, and bought her own food, asked her owner, also a woman, the cost of her freedom, the owner fixed an abusive amount. When the owner refused to give her freedom and punished her, Damiana complained to the authorities, who forced the owner to grant her freedom and fixed a lower price. She paid it and became free at 22 years of age in 1745. (*See also* ARTISANS; MULATTO.)

Free people of color had different occupations and attained different levels of success. Many of them lived in huts made of straw, worked in occupations related to transisthmian transport, cultivated small plots of land in the surrounding areas, later sold the products to the inhabitants of the city, and occupied themselves in different crafts. Most of them earned enough to maintain themselves and their families and even to have some savings. Free men of color also had an important role in the MILITIA, which became a nearly full-time prestigious occupation for some of them. For instance, three different generations of the Meneses Rivas family of Panama City made a career in the militias of the city. The grandfather was captain of the company of slaves and free blacks. The father, who had served under the grandfather, asked permission from the king to create a company exclusively of free blacks at his own expense in 1692. He was granted permission and became captain of the company, which still existed in 1736, when the son presented his credentials to become its captain.

As the free colored population grew in number, a small group became relatively wealthy and moved upward socially. Among them were those who occupied minor bureaucratic posts as scribes, notaries, and receptors in the city from the mid-17th century. There was also a group of silversmiths, tailors, barbers, and other craftsmen that had the economic potential and interest to become involved in trade in the mid-18th century. Although trade had once been open to colored people, during the first half of the 18th century, legal measures were initiated to ban them from retail trade in the streets and from shops (see also COMMERCE AND TRADE). Consequently, these craftsmen formed a colored guild in 1759 to fight for their right to trade in Panama City. After an arduous legal process, the Consejo de Indias (the highest court for the Spanish colonies) granted them the right to trade in 1765, although the decision only applied to people of mixed race and did not extend to free blacks. Also, some free colored families sent their sons to universities elsewhere in Spanish America, although colored people were forbidden by law to obtain university degrees. This was the case for Nicolás de Uselay, who obtained a degree in medicine in Lima and served for one year as doctor of the garrison battalion of Panama in 1757 before moving back to Lima. Nicolás's father was a tailor who became part of the colored guild, and Nicolás's godparents were members of Panama City's white elite, which illustrates how free coloreds fought to increase their rights at the same time that their social networks included well-off whites. The case of the colored student José Ponciano de Ayarza is also interesting, as he petitioned the king to be granted a degree in philosophy from the University of Santa Fé in Bogotá in 1794–95. His petition, along with the documents presented by his father, captain of the militias of Portobelo, José de Ayarza, became one of the applications that fell within the Gracias al Sacar decree of 1795. This decree meant that colored people all over Spanish America could pay a fee to have their mixed-ancestry origins erased and be considered white. The young Ayarza was granted the degree and was officially recognized as white in 1797; later, his brothers would have the same luck.

After the turn of the century and independence from Spain, there is the case of General José Domingo de Espinar (1791–1864), a mulatto born in the *arrabal* of Santa Ana in Panama City who fought in the independence wars, was a general in the army, was elected twice senator for the Department of Panama to the Gran Colombia congress, and was the doctor of Simón Bolívar, among other posts. When in 1830 Espinar was given the job of general commandant of the Isthmian Department, he proclaimed the independence of Panama from COLOMBIA. It lasted less than a year because it was quickly suppressed by the whites in fear of a race war, as Espinar had the support of the colored people of the city.

Silvia Espelt Bombín

FURTHER READING

Castillero Calvo, Alfredo. *Historia General de Panamá*. Vol. 1, T. 1 and 2. Panama: Comité Nacional del Centenario, 2004.

Figueroa Navarro, Alfredo. *Sociología del Arrabal de Santa Ana en Panamá (1750–1850)*. Panama: Impresora de Panama, 1978.

King, James F. "The Case of Jose Ponciano de Ayarza: A Document on Gracias al Sacar." *Hispanic American Historical Review* 31, no. 4 (November 1951): 640–647.

Mena García, María del Carmen. *La Ciudad de Panamá en el s. XVIII. Trazado urbano y técnica constructiva*. Panama: Editorial Portobelo, 1997.

PARAGUAY

Paraguay is a nation in South America, located along the Paraguay and Paraná Rivers in the interior. It borders BRAZIL on the north and ARGENTINA on the south and east. To the west, across the Chaco region, which was almost uninhabited in colonial times, lies BOLIVIA. Paraguay was inhabited by the Guaraní Indians in precolonial times, and these Indians survived contact with Europeans to become the dominant population group in modern Paraguay.

Several groups of Europeans, including Portuguese, English, and Spanish, explored the Paraguay region between 1509 and 1524 but did not settle there. The Portuguese explorer Alexio García lived in the vicinity of modern Asunción, Paraguay, for two years in 1524–25 gathering supplies and recruiting Indian allies for an attack, ultimately unsuccessful, on the Inca domains to the west. His settlement was abandoned after his defeat by Huyana Inca Capac but was reoccupied in 1527 by Sebastian Cabot (1474–1556), an Italian explorer working for the English, who built a fort there. In 1537, the Spanish settlers at Buenos Aires, Argentina, under Gonzalo

de Mendoza, facing hostile natives and harsh weather, discovered that Cabot had abandoned his settlement, so they decided to move upriver to the more welcoming Paraguay. They gave the settlement its modern name of Asunción. It is unclear whether any of the early conquistadores were black. There are no notable early colonists who were black or Afro-mestizo. However, within a half-century, the colony had a small number of blacks and mulattoes, both free and enslaved. Slave imports began in small numbers in the 1560s, mostly intended as personal servants of high-ranking Spaniards or skilled workmen in urban trades. Labor on farms or in the small mining sector was provided by the large Indian population. The Jesuits established a series of missions along the Paraná River, and they introduced black slaves with them as servants and skilled workers. The Jesuit villages were the most economically successful European installations in the colony, and they were able to import as many as a thousand Africans; some entered directly from Africa as slaves, and some were taken from neighboring Brazil as free people. The Jesuits were ejected from the Spanish Empire in 1767. While some of the Jesuit villages also disappeared at this time, and many of the Indian inhabitants left, a core of Afro-mestizo inhabitants remained at some villages, and at least one of these, Kamba Kokué, retains a cultural connection with the Jesuit mission.

As Brazil's economy grew, and Brazilian settlement moved west toward the border with Paraguay, more people of color emigrated from there to Paraguay. The Brazilian settlement of Colonia dô Sacramento in modern URUGUAY was an important slave-trading port. Slaves from there were sent up the Paraguay River to Bolivia and Peru to work in the mines, but some were sold in Paraguay. Many more Afro-Brazilians entered Paraguay as RUNAWAY SLAVES in the late 17th and early 18th centuries. Relations between PORTUGAL and SPAIN were strained after 1645, and the Spanish colonial governor obtained permission to grant freedom to any Brazilian runaway who arrived on Paraguayan soil. The government established a chain of towns for these free blacks in order to strengthen the defense of the border region with Brazil and pacify local Indians. The best known of these, today a town of 13,500 people that has preserved a PARDO identity among at least some of its citizens, is San Agustín de la Emboscada, founded in 1740 by settlers from an earlier black settlement.

The Afro-Paraguayan population grew through the 17th and 18th centuries. By 1682, fragmentary census figures and estimates of local officials suggest that about 6 percent of the total population of the colony were of African descent (blacks or *mulatos*), with the total rising to 11 percent in Asunción. A reasonably reliable census a century later, in 1782, found 10,838 blacks and *mulatos*, both enslaved and free, compared with 82,400 whites, mestizos, and *ladinos*, or Indians living under the authority of the colonial government.

A revolt in 1721 marked the beginning of a long decline for Paraguay and especially for poor Paraguayan country people, such as the free colored villagers. The rebellion was originally led by large farmers opposed to the Jesuits because of the egalitarian society they had set up on their mission farms. However, the original rebel leaders lost control of their movement to small farmers who protested increasing poverty and economic dislocation in the country. Trade routes had shifted, and economic and political power was drifting to Buenos Aires and away from Asunción. The rebels included many free people of color, but the recently established colonies of runaways generally remained loyal to the colonial government. The ultimate success of the government in this rebellion encouraged the creation of more free colored settlements, including Emboscada.

Paraguay gained its independence in 1811. Buenos Aires had gained its independence in 1810, and an army from Buenos Aires attempted to incorporate the Paraguay area into their rebellion. The Paraguayans at first fought the Argentine invaders but ultimately decided that becoming separately independent was a better choice than remaining loyal to Spain while isolated in the interior of the continent. Dr. José Francia (1766–1840) became the first president, ruling for the remainder of his life. Francia styled himself "El Supremo" (the Almighty) and tried to remake Paraguay into a racially mixed, socially egalitarian society. He forbade whites to marry other whites, encouraging INTERRACIAL MARRIAGE. He welcomed rebels and exiles from neighboring countries, including the Uruguayan nationalist leader José Artigas (1764–1850), who took with him a unit of 250 black gaucho lancers from the pampas of Uruguay. Most of these men settled in two free black villages, called Camba Cua and Laurelty, now suburbs of Asunción, which, like Emboscada, retain their *pardo* and revolutionary identity.

Francia believed strongly in the idea that racial mixing would create an integrated country without racial discrimination. His authoritarian and idealistic rule went a long way toward destroying Afro-Paraguayan identity. His successors, the father and son presidents Carlos López (1790–1862) and Francisco Solano López (1826–70), who ruled from 1840 to 1870, maintained this process by asserting strongly that there were no blacks in Paraguay. Carlos López conducted a careful census in 1846, which revealed that there were 17,212 Afro-descended people in the country, making up 7.19 percent of the population. The census was part of an attempt to extinguish black identity by encouraging intermarriage. Carlos López's son, Solano López, also plunged Paraguay into the terrible War of the Triple Alliance (1862–70) against Argentina, Brazil, and Uruguay, which cost him his life and killed almost two-thirds of Paraguay's population. The enormous devastation associated with this brutal war destroyed many communities and thoroughly mixed the surviving population so that traditional identities were submerged in a common painful victimhood. Paraguay's leaders attributed the defeat to the "negro hordes" of Brazil's army, and indeed free colored soldiers played a very important role in Brazil's triumph. Paradoxically, Solano López had a division of several thousand Afro-Paraguayan soldiers who were his shock troops, always put in the toughest situations in battles and winning many victories. These men constituted a significant fraction of the entire Afro-Paraguayan population, and they were killed almost to the last man in the final battles of the war in 1870. Hostility to Brazilian blacks translated easily into hostility to blackness in general, and so Afro-Paraguayans did their best to forget, and make others forget, their black ancestry. Thus it is that Paraguay's African heritage was almost completely lost until the late 20th century.

After the fall of the dictator Alfredo Stroessner (1912–2006) in 1989, researchers and poor Afro-descended Paraguayans worked together to recapture this heritage. The post-1989 Paraguayan government has been friendly to these efforts, and the country has at last begun to value its black cultural heritage.

Stewart R. King

FURTHER READING

Crockett, Lawrence. "Neighborly Lessons: From Afro-Brazil to Afro-Paraguay." January 22, 2009. Available online. URL: http://lanic.utexas.edu/project/etext/llilas/ilassa/2009/crockett.pdf. Accessed April 15, 2010.

Durbin, Paula. "Afro-Paraguayans: Identity, Synergy, Census." *Grassroots Development: Journal of the Inter-American Development Foundation*, no. 2 (2007): 26–29.

Lipski, John M. "Afro-Paraguayan Spanish: The Negation of Non-Existence." *Journal of Pan-African Studies*, no. 7:2 (2008): 2–37.

Lopez, Adalberto. *The Colonial History of Paraguay: The Revolt of the Communeros, 1721–1725*. New Brunswick, N.J.: Transaction, 2005.

PARDO

Pardo is a term used in Spanish America for free people of mixed race if one of the parents was of African descent. It was a general term that was socially constructed and thus could also include people of entirely African ancestry if they were well-off, educated, and incorporated in colonial life. *Pardo* also implies relatively high social status, wealth, education, and political influence. The term was especially important in COLOMBIA and VENEZUELA, where the *pardos* played an important role in the independence struggle (*see also* SOUTH AMERICAN WARS OF LIBERATION).

Stewart R. King

PATROCÍNIO, JOSÉ CARLOS DO (1853–1905)
Brazilian abolitionist

The political activist, writer, and journalist José Carlos do Patrocínio was an influential African-Brazilian abolitionist and member of the intellectual community of Rio de Janeiro, BRAZIL, in the late 19th and early 20th centuries. He was an important participant in the struggle to end slavery and to transform Brazilian society after the end of the monarchy. His life reveals the handicaps and possibilities open to people of mixed race in 19th-century Brazil.

Patrocínio was born in Campo Goytacazes in the state of Rio de Janeiro on October 9, 1853. His father was a priest, and his mother, a slave. Although under law he was a slave, because of his mother's status, he grew up being treated as a free person of color among the slaves on his father's property (*see* LIVING "AS FREE"). The daily contact with slavery and perhaps his own dubious status may have been important parts of the motivation behind his work as an abolitionist. In 1868, he moved to the city of Rio de Janeiro, where he decided to pursue a career as a pharmacist. Unable to pay for rent after he finished his

A photograph of José Carlos do Patrocínio taken about 1900. He was a prominent Afro-Brazilian journalist and abolitionist. *(Photograph in* História dò literatura Brasileira *by José Veríssimo, 1916)*

degree in pharmacy, he moved into the house of Emiliano Rosa Sena, a white man, who offered board in exchange for the tutoring of his children. The move would mark Patrocínio's personal and professional life. Despite Sena's initial opposition to the idea of mixed-race relationships, Patrocínio courted and married Maria Henriqueta, Sena's daughter. While at Sena's residence Patrocínio also became acquainted with the Republican Club of Rio de Janeiro, which met regularly at the house. Patrocínio became a member of the club and met prominent political activists such as Quintino Bocaiúva.

Patrocínio's involvement in the abolitionist movement began in 1877, when he joined the ranks of political journalists. Two years earlier, he had begun his career with a self-published satirical fortnightly paper. In 1877, he moved to *Gazeta de Noticias*, an abolitionist newspaper, and in 1881, he bought the *Gazeta da Tarde,* making it an important newspaper in the abolitionist campaign. He was one of the founding members of the Brazilian

National Anti-Slavery Society in 1879 and soon became its most active supporter, fund-raising and organizing slave escapes. He drafted the manifesto of the confederation of antislavery societies in 1883, which drew together his national society and many local groups and liberal supporters, and signed the manifesto along with ANDRÉ REBOUÇAS and Aristides Lobo.

Brazilian abolitionists gained new ground when in 1885 the sexagenary law, which freed all elderly slaves, was enacted, and in 1886, Patrocínio was elected to the chamber of representatives of Rio de Janeiro state. In 1887, Patrocínio closed *Gazeta da Tarde* and opened a new abolitionist newspaper, *Cidade do Rio.* In 1888, Princess ISABEL OF BRAGANÇA, a strong abolitionist, abolished slavery in Brazil. After the ruling, Patrocínio, along with other free persons of color, adopted the monarchist cause in honor of the princess. Patrocínio joined the Guarda Negra, a black promonarchic group, and expounded promonarchic ideas in the *Cidade do Rio.* After the installation of the republican regime in 1889, Patrocínio supported the opposition by publishing a manifesto of one of the leaders of the Armada Revolt (1893–94), an uprising of the Brazilian NAVY against the new republican government. He was exiled by the regime to the Amazon region in 1892 to prevent him from working with the dissident officers. After his return in 1893, he was unable to continue working as a journalist; that led him to turn his attention to supporting the work of Brazil's aviation pioneer, Alberto Santos Dumont (1873–1932). Patrocínio died of tuberculosis on January 29, 1905, three days after an outbreak of bleeding from the lungs that occurred while he was giving a speech in honor of Santos Dumont.

Ana Janaina Nelson

FURTHER READING

Junior, R. Magalhães. *A Vida Turbulenta de José do Patrocínio.* São Pualo: Lisa-Livros Irradiantes, SP, 1969.
Silva, Eduardo. "Black Abolitionists in the Quilombo of Leblon, Rio de Janeiro: Symbols, Organizers and Revolutionaries." In *Beyond Slavery: The Multilayered Legacy of Africans in Latin America and the Caribbean,* edited by Darin J. Davis. New York: Rowman & Littlefield, 2006.

PAULA BRITO, FRANCISCO DE (1809–1861)
Brazilian journalist, poet, and publisher

Francisco de Paula Brito was a publisher and author who supported the work of many important literary figures in 19th-century BRAZIL, both blacks and whites. In addition to his being an important figure himself, his life illustrates the role that journalism and literature played in the creation of a free colored identity and the building of the free colored community. His outspoken support for the monarchy is an example of the deep feelings of loyalty that Dom PEDRO II and Princess Imperial ISABEL OF BRAGANÇA inspired in many free people of color, especially among the educated elite.

Born in Rio de Janeiro on December 2, 1809, the son of a free mixed-race carpenter and his free black wife, Francisco de Paula Brito grew up in the nearby town of Suruí. In 1824, he returned to Rio de Janeiro, by then the capital of the independent empire of Brazil, and apprenticed at the government-owned national printing press. Three years later, he was employed as a typesetter by the new *Jornal do Comércio*, and he quickly rose to head its print shop. In 1830, he struck out on his own and took over a bindery and bookshop from a cousin.

Over the next three decades, his bookshop and the presses associated with it became the center of Brazilian literary culture. The first generation of romantics gathered at the informal and nonpolitical salon that Brito hosted, dubbed the Sociedade Petalógica, and published their work at his presses, the Tipografia Imparcial de Brito (1833–50s), the Tipografia Dois de Dezembro (1850–57), and the Tipografia de Paula Brito (1840s–67). Major mid-19th-century Brazilian writers such as Joaquim Manuel de Macedo, Domingos José Gonçalves de Magalhães (the viscount of Araguaia), Luiz Carlos Martins Pena, and ANTÔNIO GONÇALVES TEIXEIRA E SOUSA (Paula Brito's close friend) published with him and benefited from Paula Brito's support. JOAQUIM MARÍA MACHADO DE ASSIS, Brazil's greatest writer, published his first poem in Paula Brito's *A Marmota*, briefly worked on this newspaper, and, in 1861, published his first two books with the Tipografia de Paula Brito.

Paula Brito was the publisher and principal writer for two major popular newspapers, *A Mulher do Simplício ou A Fluminense Exaltada* (1835–43) (The wife of simplicity or the exalted woman of Rio) and *A Marmota na Corte* (A groundhog in the courtyard), later published under the titles of *A Marmota Fluminense* and *A Marmota* (1849–61). More important for Brazil's literary development, Paula Brito published the country's first major literary magazine, *Guanabara* (1849–55), as well as many other periodicals.

As a writer, Paula Brito produced much poetry, some of it collected in a posthumous work, *Poesias de Francisco de Paula Brito* (1863), prepared by his friends and admirers. He also wrote several plays, none of which has survived, and actively supported the development of drama and opera in Brazil.

Deeply monarchist, Paula Brito benefited from the moral support and financial patronage of Emperor Pedro II. His press regularly produced adulatory and patriotic flyers and pamphlets for distribution on national holidays.

Despite their literary and cultural importance, Paula Brito's presses struggled financially; the 1857 bankruptcy of the Tipografia Dois de Dezembro cost him considerable personal losses, and he died poor on December 1, 1861. Journalism and literature offered men of color such as Paula Brito an opportunity for social mobility (*see*, for instance, JOSÉ CARLOS DO PATROCÍNIO), but as a somewhat marginal profession, it was not a route to great wealth.

Hendrik Kraay

FURTHER READING
Gondim, Eunice Ribeiro. *Vida e obra de Paula Brito*. Rio de Janeiro: Livraria Brasiliana Editora, 1965.
Hallewell, L. *Books in Brazil: A History of the Publishing Trade*. Metuchen, N.J.: Scarecrow Press, 1982.

PAYNE, DANIEL A. (1811–1893) *American educator, clergyman, abolitionist, and historian*
Daniel A. Payne was active in the Lutheran church and AFRICAN METHODIST EPISCOPAL CHURCH, but he is perhaps best known for his role as president of Wilberforce University. Indeed, he was the first African American chosen to lead an American college.

Payne was born to free black parents, London and Martha Payne, in CHARLESTON, SOUTH CAROLINA, on February 24, 1811. He received his early education at a school in Charleston established by the free black community, and he later operated a similar school of his own there, until the state legislature outlawed the teaching of blacks—free or enslaved—in 1834. He also studied in Gettysburg, PENNSYLVANIA, at the Lutheran Theological Seminary, and he worked to persuade the Lutheran Church in NEW YORK STATE to join the antislavery movement in the United States. (*See also* PROTESTANT MAINLINE CHURCHES.) He became the first black ordained by the Franckean Evangelical Lutheran Synod in 1839 and briefly served a white Presbyterian congregation in Troy, New York, where he founded the Mental and Moral Improvement Society of Troy. In 1840, he moved to PHILADELPHIA, PENNSYLVANIA, to open a coeducational school. In 1863, he was chosen as president of Wilberforce, an OHIO university established for blacks in 1856. He greatly enhanced the reputation of this institution by attracting high-quality educators and students and making it financially solvent. He served as president of the university until 1877, overcoming financial crises and rebuilding after a fire set by a disgruntled Southern sympathizer.

Payne also served in a number of important roles in the abolition movement. He addressed the American Anti-Slavery Society, the country's leading immediate abolition group, in 1837. The "immediatists," unlike the older antislavery groups such as the Quaker-led Pennsylvania Abolition Society, called for more direct action to push for the immediate (rather than gradual) end of slavery in the United States, and his involvement with these abolitionists led him to assist RUNAWAY SLAVES through the city's Vigilant Committee. He also raised funds for the *Colored American* newspaper.

In addition to his work as an educator and abolitionist, Payne was a Lutheran preacher and an African Methodist Episcopal (A.M.E.) Church bishop. His affiliation with the A.M.E. Church began in 1826. Though he studied at the Lutheran Seminary and was ordained an elder in that church in 1837, he returned to the A.M.E. in 1841 and was elected the sixth bishop of that denomination in 1852. He was known for giving the A.M.E. church a more formal and standardized style of worship, and he helped the church expand its foreign missionary work, as well as its post–Civil War efforts in the South. Under his leadership, the church also revived its journal, the *Christian Recorder*. He also became a historian for the A.M.E. Church in 1848. His books, including his 1891 *History of the African Methodist Episcopal Church*, and an 1888 memoir, *Recollections of Seventy Years*, chronicle the first 75 years of that organization.

Payne was married to Eliza Clark Payne, and together they raised five children: Julia, John, Laura, Augusta, and Peter. Only one of the children was his biological child. He died on November 2, 1893.

Beverly C. Tomek

FURTHER READING

McMickle, Marvin Andrew. *An Encyclopedia of African American Christian Heritage*. Valley Forge, Pa.: Judson Press, 2002.

Payne, Daniel. *History of the African Methodist Episcopal Church*. Nashville, Tenn.: A.M.E. Sunday School Union, 1891. Reprint, New York: 1968.

———. "Slavery Brutalizes Man." *Lutheran Herald and Journal of the Fort Plain, New York, Franckean Synod* 1, no. 15 (August 1, 1839), 113–114.

PEASANTS

In many parts of the tropical Americas, free people of color lived as peasants, farmers who produced primarily for their own consumption. MAROONS were peasants, or they aspired to be, if they could avoid the colonial militia and slave catchers. Many people who were LIVING "AS FREE," that is, who were legally considered to be slaves but who were living independently either with the permission of their masters or as RUNAWAYS SLAVES, also lived as peasants. Finally, the ranks of the peasantry included many people of color who were legally considered free but who were unable to accumulate the resources necessary to advance themselves economically. There were also white peasants in some areas, especially in North America, but they were not common. Where the plantation sector was well developed, poor whites could generally find some sort of paid employment that was preferable to peasant farming.

It was relatively easy to begin peasant farming in many places in the plantation societies of the Americas. Governments often awarded undesirable plots of land to prospective planters along with the land they wanted in order to encourage development of remote or difficult country. For the colonial government, this was a way to close off areas to maroons or Native Americans and encourage the spread of settlement. For the white planter, these plots were an embarrassment, because under many legal systems if a planter did not develop a grant of land, it could be taken away. An easy solution to this quandary was to give the backcountry plots to free colored relatives or sell to free coloreds who would develop them.

Peasant farmers could cultivate the standard food crops of the plantation Americas: potatoes, cassava, maize, and other grains. Small amounts of livestock and hunting would provide needed protein. Any surpluses could easily find a market in the plantation zones, as plantations were always short of food. The temptation to put more land into cultivation of the staple crop was too much for almost any planter, especially if he or she knew PROVISION GROUND FARMING could supplement any shortages.

Peasant farming could prove to be a profitable business. Demand was always strong for the product, and prices did not fluctuate nearly as much as for the staple crops (sugar cultivation, cotton cultivation, and the like). The peasant had few expenses, especially if he or she owned land. Rents, if there were any, were generally not burdensome since the land was by definition not useful for staple crop production, and in most colonies, there was plenty of undeveloped backcountry land. This was especially true on the continents of North and South America, where there were open frontier zones inhabited, if at all, by small numbers of Native Americans and sometimes a few maroons. On island colonies, however, there were also often substantial areas that were almost uninhabited. Most of the islands of the Caribbean have high mountains that are ideal for peasant producers. In the islands, geography gave peasants an advantage that their counterparts on the mainland did not have since the islanders' potential market, the plantation, was often only a few hours away by mountain trail. Some peasant producers actually managed to move up the income scale by taking up staple production and relying to a much greater degree on selling to an international market. (*See also* COTTON CULTIVATION; SUGAR CULTIVATION.)

Some of these free colored peasants owned slaves. People who wanted to move up from the peasantry to the ranks of small cash crop farmers would first have to have

The Cotton Pickers, an 1876 painting by Winslow Homer, depicts two young African-American women working in a cotton field. Cotton was a cash crop that many African-descended peasants in the Americas cultivated in order to earn cash or pay rent in kind (known as sharecropping). This could trap people in a cycle of dependency on landlords or commodity purchasers but could also offer the resources needed for an escape from peasant life. *(Art Resource, NY)*

enough laborers to take advantage of economies of scale. Free colored families were often large, but acquiring slaves might well be the first step toward profitability and participation in a larger market. If the free colored peasant was a relative of a white person who had given him or her a small amount of land, the peasant might also have received a slave or two. And free colored peasants might also have bought their own relatives and "own" them as slaves, as a first step toward MANUMISSION. It was not easy to free a slave in most places in the Americas—one needed the permission of the government or a court, and often there was a substantial tax. So along with peasant farming, peasant slavery grew up in many places. (*See also* SLAVE OWNERS.)

In some places, especially in North America, there were restrictions on the right of free people of color to own land. These restrictions hampered but did not eliminate the practice of peasant farming among free people of color. In some cases, free colored peasants would be renters or sharecroppers on white-owned land. In other cases, they might be considered Indians and might well have some native ancestry. In many cases, as with small-scale white farmers on the frontier, they simply occupied

land without the formality of registering their claim with a government. These "squatter" land claims proved a problem when development entered the area. Squatting white farmers often benefited from government recognition of their claims, extended by state land reform laws in most of the Southern and midwestern states during political reforms of the 1830s and 1880s. However, black farmers often found it difficult to take advantage of these reforms because of pervasive RACISM AND RACIAL PREJUDICE, sometimes written into the laws and sometimes in their application by local judges, and had to move farther west. Free colored "squatter" farmers driven off land in the Upper South were among the first settlers of KANSAS and Colorado in what became known as the EXODUSTER MOVEMENT of the 1870s and 1880s.

In much of the Americas outside the United States, there were few laws that prevented free people of color from owning land, but the application of supposedly equal laws often worked against farmers of color. Especially where positivist ideas influenced government policy, as in MEXICO and BRAZIL after independence, governments favored large landowners who were supposedly better able to care for the land and make it productive. Small farmers were driven from their land throughout the Iberian Americas in the 19th and early 20th centuries, which was also the era of the end of slavery and the transition to a free labor regime. Black (and Indian) peasants suffered inordinately during this process, and it is not surprising that black farming communities in Mexico were strong supporters of the agrarian rebel movements of Pancho Villa and Emiliano Zapata at the beginning of the 20th century.

Once black plantation workers gained their freedom, either individually as runaways, though self-purchase, or by general abolition, many turned to peasant farming as an alternative to continuing as landless agricultural workers or going to the cities. This phenomenon was especially marked in post-abolition societies in the Caribbean, where sugar plantations became bankrupt for lack of labor while their former slave workforces were growing maize and herding pigs in the nearby hills. In the post–AMERICAN CIVIL WAR South, many blacks tried peasant farming, though many found themselves compelled by landlords to grow cotton on a sharecropping basis. In Brazil, the Sertão filled up with former slaves living as peasants in the late 19th and early 20th centuries.

In conclusion, peasant farming was a common way of life for free blacks and people of mixed race throughout the Americas. It was a good alternative to urban life or plantation farming for people who had few alternatives. People without good liberty papers, people with little capital, or those free colored populations suffering under especially discriminatory legal regimes often turned to peasant farming. Land was usually fairly easy to come by, either to purchase or to rent, or, in the worst case, to squat on informally. Methods of agriculture were sufficiently productive to ensure most people enough to eat and a surplus for sale to nearby plantations. The plantations always needed to buy food, and so prices were generally good for the producer. In the post-abolition period, peasant farming became the preferred alternative for most populations of color, though hostile racial climates and positivist attempts to reform agriculture by consolidating landholdings often worked against black peasant populations in this period.

Stewart R. King

FURTHER READING

Schwartz, Stuart. *Slaves, Peasants, and Rebels: Reconsidering Brazilian Slavery.* Champaign-Urbana: University of Illinois Press, 1992.

PEDRO I (1798–1834) *king of Portugal and first emperor of Brazil (r. 1822–1831)*

Son of King John VI of Portugal (1767–1826), Pedro de Alcântara de Bragança e Bourbon I became the first emperor of Brazil after declaring independence from Portugal in 1822.

Born in Portugal on October 12, 1798, Pedro moved to Rio de Janeiro, Brazil, with his family in 1807 during Napoléon Bonaparte's invasion of Portugal. While the royal family was in Brazil, the British armed forces protected Portugal. In exchange, Pedro's father, King João, signed two treaties with Britain, in which he granted trade preferences with Brazil to Britain and agreed to abolish the slave trade gradually. In 1818, Pedro married the Austrian princess Maria Leopoldina Habsburg. In 1821, his father returned to Portugal to secure the throne. Pedro remained behind as viceroy of Brazil. Centralizing liberal politicians in Portugal wanted to reduce the autonomy of Brazil and the other colonies, and resistance began in Brazil. Within a year, as a result of domestic pressure, Pedro declared Brazilian independence from Portugal and instituted the Brazilian monarchy.

Foreign recognition of Brazilian independence would not come easily. The newly independent Latin American states were wary of the Brazilian monarchist option, and European countries that were members of the Holy Alliance resisted recognizing the independence of their former colonies. Negotiations with Portugal took three years and were mediated by Britain, which would only recognize Brazilian independence after Portugal had. Among the conditions established by Britain for the recognition were the continuity of the trade preferences and the assurance that slave trafficking would be abolished by 1830. This agreement created tensions with the agrarian elite in Brazil, who believed that the government was acting against the best interests of Brazil. Rural rebellions, by both conservatives and those calling for more liberal reforms, paralyzed the government of Brazil. In addition, a war with Argentina (1825–28) consumed many state resources.

Pedro was generally liberal in his political views. His politics were similar to those of other liberals of the Iberian Americas in the early 19th century. He sought national unity, free trade, the abolition of distinctive social statuses including slavery and racial discrimination, and an activist government supporting national development. Free people of color generally supported his cause, including the Bahían rebel leader FRANCISCO SABINO ÁLVARES DA ROCHA VIEIRA. Ultimately, he was unable to bring about the liberal reforms he sought, either in Brazil or in Portugal, and the abolition of slavery and advances in legal equality for people of color had to await the rule of his son, PEDRO II.

In 1826, after his father's death, Pedro returned to Portugal and tried to establish a liberal constitution there. Facing resistance from absolutist forces led by his brother Miguel, he fought an eight-year civil war. In 1831, preoccupied with Portuguese matters and facing resistance from his Brazilian subjects, he abdicated the Brazilian throne in favor of his son, Pedro II. He died on September 24, 1834, in Lisbon.

Ana Janaina Nelson

FURTHER READING
Costa, Sergio Correa da. *Every Inch a King: A Biography of Dom Pedro I, First Emperor of Brazil*. New York: Macmillan, 1950.
Macaulay, Neill. *Dom Pedro: The Struggle for Liberty in Brazil and Portugal, 1798–1834*. Durham, N.C.: Duke University Press, 1986.

PEDRO II (1825–1891) *emperor of Brazil (r. 1831–1889)*

Son of Dom PEDRO I, Pedro de Alcântara de Bragança e Habsburgo, as emperor of Brazil for 48 years, Pedro II ruled over the gradual process of abolition of slavery in Brazil.

The seventh child of Emperor Pedro I of Brazil, he was born heir to the throne on December 2, 1825. His father abdicated the throne when Pedro II was five years old in order to fight for the throne of PORTUGAL. Pedro II was only crowned when he was 14 years old, after the legal age of majority was reduced to accommodate him. He was an enlightened monarch with great intellectual and cultural curiosity. He attempted to learn Guaraní, an indigenous language in Brazil; extinguished several archaic royal adoration customs; and publicly declared his opposition to slavery. He did not, however, take a very active role in the abolitionist struggle, leaving Congress to enact the laws at its own pace. He was supported by and friends with several free colored abolitionists such as ANDRÉ REBOUÇAS and JOSÉ CARLOS DO PATROCÍNIO. In general, wealthy and socially prominent free people of color supported him, seeing in his enlightened rule the best chance for civil rights and racial justice. Some more radical free people of color supported a republican system of government, but most republicans were regional white elites and military leaders who tended to support slavery and racially discriminatory laws. Under Pedro's rule, slave trafficking was abolished in 1850, and children of slaves were considered free after a 1871 law as well as slaves older than 60 years after 1885. Free people of color made significant advances in Brazilian society, gaining economic equality; admission on an equal basis to a wide variety of state institutions, including the military, universities, and public employment; and cultural respect. A major turning point was the War of the Triple Alliance (1864–70), in which free colored soldiers played an important role in saving Brazil from humiliating defeat at the hands of tiny Paraguay. In 1888, Pedro left for his third trip to Europe for health reasons, and in

his name his daughter, Princess Imperial ISABEL OF BRAGANÇA, abolished slavery. When the republic was declared, Emperor Pedro II and his family left for exile in France, where he died three years later on December 5, 1891.

Ana Janaina Nelson

FURTHER READING
Brown, Rose. *American Emperor: Dom Pedro II of Brazil*. New York: Viking Press, 1945.
Schwarcz, Lilia Moritz. *The Emperor's Beard: Dom Pedro II and His Tropical Monarchy in Brazil*. New York: Hill & Wang, 2003.

PÉLAGE, MAGLOIRE (ca. 1766–1813) *Guadeloupean military officer*

Magloire Pélage was a prominent military and political leader in the revolutionary French Caribbean, who played a central role in the events that led to the reestablishment of slavery in Guadeloupe in 1802. He was probably born a free man of color in Martinique around 1766, and little is known about Pélage's early life; it is even a matter of debate whether he was born free or gained his freedom as an adult, though most contemporary scholars accept his own affirmation as an adult, after the FRENCH REVOLUTION, that he was born in freedom. In 1789, he joined the republican camp on the island as the French Revolution began (*see also* FRENCH CARIBBEAN). He distinguished himself during armed conflicts with antirepublican groups on the island and was promoted to the rank of lieutenant in 1793. When the British took over the island in 1793, he was captured and deported to Europe. Returned to metropolitan FRANCE as part of a prisoner exchange, he became part of the Bataillon des Antilles formed in 1794 and was made a captain in the unit. In early 1794, the French reconquered Guadeloupe, which had also been captured by the British the preceding year. They were aided in their struggle by the large enslaved population, who saw France as their ally since the French National Assembly had abolished slavery on February 4, 1794. They were unable to take back Martinique, which remained in British hands. With the Bataillon des Antilles, Pélage was sent to Guadeloupe, which became the French military stronghold in the eastern Caribbean in the 1790s, as war raged between the British and the French.

In 1795, VICTOR HUGUES, who was in command of Guadeloupe, launched an invasion of nearby British Saint-Lucia, and Pélage was sent to fight there. On the battlefield there, he was once again promoted, this time to *chef de bataillon* (a rank equivalent to lieutenant colonel in the U.S. military). The French were briefly able to capture all of Saint-Lucia, but a large British counterattack retook the island, and Pélage was captured for a second time and sent across the Atlantic as a prisoner again. The British again released Pélage to metropolitan France, and there he briefly became part of an all-black Compagnie des Hommes de Couleur in the metropolitan French army formed in 1798 and then spent time in Paris. In 1800, a set of new commissioners were sent to Guadeloupe, and they were accompanied by a military force that included Pélage, now a *chef de brigade* (the equivalent of a brigadier general). He became the second-ranked officer in Guadeloupe on his arrival. He was well respected in the colony, notably among the many men of African descent (including a large number of formerly enslaved individuals) who served in the REGULAR ARMY under his command.

In Guadeloupe as in SAINT-DOMINGUE in the early 1800s, many people of African descent were increasingly concerned that the French government under Napoleón Bonaparte was planning to reverse emancipation. It was in this context that, in September 1801, the white commander in Guadeloupe, General Jean-Baptiste Raymond de Lacrosse, infuriated many soldiers in Guadeloupe by passing over Magloire Pélage for a promotion. The highest-ranked officer on the island, a white Frenchman, had just died, and Pélage merited promotion; Lacrosse placed himself in charge instead. Some prominent officers protested the decision, and Lacrosse imprisoned several of them, inciting more resistance. On October 21, 1801, Lacrosse ordered the arrest of Pélage, whose influence he clearly feared. Pélage, however, pushed his way past the white officers who were trying to arrest him. Other officers of African descent had already mobilized their troops as they heard about what was happening. As soldiers began to square off against one another, and laborers from the surrounding countryside joined in the fray, Pélage took control of the situation. Pushed by more radical officers, he expelled Lacrosse from the island and became the de facto governor of the colony. Pélage's coup was more than just a power grab by a disappointed office-seeker—he was trying to find a way to preserve freedom and nondiscriminatory racial policies within the French revolutionary system. In Saint-Domingue, the prerevolutionary free black leader TOUSSAINT LOUVERTURE had the same goal and finally created a quasi-independent state with himself as "governor-general for life." Pélage was not prepared to go as far as Toussaint, and ultimately he preserved the unity of Guadeloupe with France at the cost of the reestablishment of racial discrimination.

For the next six months, Pélage oversaw a relatively conservative regime in Guadeloupe, working closely with merchants and property owners and intervening directly to punish insurgents who rose up on some plantations. He also wrote to Bonaparte to explain his actions against Lacrosse and request that a new governor be sent from France. Lacrosse (who was captured by the British and taken to Dominica) and other French officials, however, represented Pélage as a dangerous radical who was leading an insurrection against white rule on the island. One newspaper in France smeared Pélage by publishing a false story claiming he had won his freedom years ago by killing the white woman who owned him as a slave.

When French troops under the command of General Antoine Richepanse arrived in Guadeloupe in May 1802, Pélage greeted them warmly. Richepanse, however, ordered that all soldiers of African descent be disarmed. While Pélage followed the orders, many refused, and resistance to French troops coalesced around the figure of one of Pélage's officers, the Martiniquan-born LOUIS DELGRÈS. The insurgents gathered in the colonial capital of Basse-Terre and fought the French with some success, aided by bands of laborers from throughout the island who feared the restoration of slavery. Pélage was imprisoned, along with many of his troops, in the holds of French ships. As the battles continued, however, he offered to help the French troops suppress the insurrection, and they accepted. He led a large number of soldiers, many of them of African descent, in the fight against Delgrès, helping to seal his defeat at the hand of the French.

Despite his service to the French, Pélage was arrested and deported and accused of being an enemy of the republic. After a lengthy trial in 1804, he and others who had fought against Delgrès in Guadeloupe were ultimately freed. Pélage continued to serve as an officer in the French army, fighting in the Napoleonic Wars in Europe, until his death in combat during the Russian campaign in 1813. Today, he is remembered both for his role in the uprising against Lacrosse—in 2009, a pro-independence group in Guadeloupe spray-painted walls with the date "21 October 1801" as a way of recalling his uprising against French authority—and for the role he played in defeating Delgrès and therefore helping the French in the brutal reestablishment of slavery they instituted in 1802 and 1803 on the island.

Laurent Dubois

FURTHER READING
Dubois, Laurent. *A Colony of Citizens: Revolution and Slave Emancipation in the French Caribbean, 1787–1804*. Chapel Hill: University of North Carolina Press, 2004.

PENNSYLVANIA
Pennsylvania is a state of the United States. It is located in the Mid-Atlantic region, west of NEW JERSEY, south of NEW YORK STATE, east of OHIO, and north of West Virginia, MARYLAND, and DELAWARE. The Mason-Dixon

line marks the southern border with Maryland and Delaware and is the traditional border between slave and free states, though slavery existed in Pennsylvania and other Northern areas in the early 19th century. The state has important river ports at PHILADELPHIA, PENNSYLVANIA, on the Delaware, and at PITTSBURGH, PENNSYLVANIA, on the Ohio. The state has a relatively harsh climate that made plantation agriculture impossible in the colonial period. Instead, most farms were small family operations. There are many mineral resources; east-west transportation links and manufacturing were important aspects of the economy from a very early time. However, the workforce in these activities was primarily composed of free or indentured whites.

The history of free African Americans in Pennsylvania followed a complicated trajectory. Pennsylvania was one of the first states to abolish slavery. Yet Pennsylvania's free blacks experienced great hardship and suffered attacks on their rights, property, institutions, and bodies. At every step, they struggled against whites and among themselves to create stable communities and claim their place in a hostile society. Pennsylvania's free blacks endured fluctuations in their rights and status, but their resistance and internal debates created a vibrant history of social, economic, and political development.

Slavery in Colonial Pennsylvania

In colonial Pennsylvania slavery never achieved dominance as a labor source, but it shaped the historical relationship between European and African descendants. Fewer slaves lived in Pennsylvania than in NEW JERSEY or New York, and the slave population relative to the European never approached SOUTH CAROLINA's 2 to 1 ratio. Between 1700 and 1750, the slave population rose from about 1,000 to 6,000. Imports spiked during the SEVEN YEARS' WAR (1756–63) as a result of a shortage of European laborers, but even by 1775, when the WAR OF AMERICAN INDEPENDENCE, 1775–83, began, slaves accounted for only 5 percent of the total population (12,000 people). Most of these slaves lived in Philadelphia and its surrounding counties. Despite comparatively low slave populations, slavery circumscribed African life. In his "Frame of Government" (1682), the Pennsylvania founder, William Penn, promised settlers they would be "governed by laws of your own making. . . . I shall not usurp the right of any." This affirmation of individual rights did not include Africans or their descendants. By the 1720s, the Pennsylvania General Assembly had enacted a series of "black codes" limiting African-Americans' rights to travel freely, consume liquor, and jury trials (see BLACK CODES IN THE UNITED STATES). It also limited the ability of masters to manumit their slaves.

Slavery framed the working and social aspects of African-American life. Men and women worked at different tasks. Women often labored as domestic servants, learning skills such as spinning, weaving, and sewing. Men learned a more diverse set of skills. Their masters ranged from ARTISANS to merchants and gentlemen farmers to ship captains. This variety of owners allowed some men to learn specialized tasks, which made it possible to work in semiskilled or skilled jobs if they were freed. Moreover, the General Assembly allowed black property ownership, and even some single women and widows accumulated comfortable amounts of personal and real property. Black family life depended to some degree on location. Enslaved couples and families lived together more often in rural areas than in Philadelphia. Colonial Philadelphia probate records show only 3 percent of enslaved women living with men listed as their husbands. Fewer than 50 percent of slaves lived with a member of the opposite sex, and even fewer lived with children who could have been theirs. Nevertheless, family members often did live near one another. Interestingly, rates of black and white unions also differed between country and city. In the country, 15 percent of children were born to interracial couples compared to 5 percent in Philadelphia.

The presence of slavery in Penn's colony created a moral quandary for some white Pennsylvanians. In the late 17th and 18th centuries, Quakers, who settled in larger numbers in Pennsylvania than the other colonies, began to question slavery. In 1688, Daniel Francis Pastorius (1651–1720), a German Quaker living in Pennsylvania, argued that slavery contradicted the golden rule. Beginning in the 1730s, Benjamin Lay (1681–1760) led efforts to confront slaveholding Quakers. By midcentury, Anthony Benezet (1713–84) and John Woolman (1720–72) were writing antislavery tracts and imploring fellow Quakers to free their slaves. Benezet even opened his home as a black school. Despite these efforts, Quakers proved slow to embrace antislavery principles as a group. Not until in 1776 did they move to bar slaveholders from their meetings. A related antislavery effort emerged in Philadelphia before the American Revolution. Before the war, the notable Philadelphians Benjamin Franklin (1706–90) and the physician Benjamin Rush (1745–1813) founded the Pennsylvania Abolition Society (PAS) to aid free blacks against kidnappers. After waning during the war, the society revived in 1784. The PAS worked through legal channels to protect free blacks from kidnappers, sue masters for freedom, and lobby state and federal governments for abolition of the slave trade and slavery. Though effective, the white leadership of the PAS often looked condescendingly on free black leadership.

Gradual Emancipation and the Growth of Free Black Communities in Revolutionary and Early National Pennsylvania

Antislavery sentiments produced tangible results during the American Revolution. The most important was the Gradual Emancipation Act, passed by the General Assembly on March 1, 1780. The act worked by freeing all slaves born after March 1 at the age of 28, but slaves born before this date remained enslaved for life. The act required slaveholders to register slaves with local authorities, and it imposed a $1,000 fine for slave trading. (Slaveholders beyond Philadelphia sometimes succeeded in ignoring these rules.) It also repealed many of the "black codes," though new restrictions on free African Americans soon took their place. As a result of the act, the slave population declined steadily. In 1790, 3,737 slaves lived in Pennsylvania; that number fell to 1,706 in 1800, 795 in 1810, 211 in 1820, and 64 in 1840, after which census data reported no slaves.

Gradual emancipation stimulated the growth of African-American communities throughout Pennsylvania. The state's free black population at the turn of the 19th century was still relatively small, numbering only about 6,500 in 1790. It was a diverse population, however, including freeborn blacks, manumitted slaves, and RUNAWAY SLAVES from Pennsylvania and nearby states. In addition, a significant number of displaced people fleeing a bloody slave revolt in SAINT-DOMINGUE migrated to Philadelphia in the 1790s and 1800s (see also HAITIAN REVOLUTION). The heaviest concentration of free blacks lived in Philadelphia, and there African Americans formed some of the earliest black churches and assistance organizations. RICHARD ALLEN and ABSALOM JONES, for example, split from St. George's Methodist Episcopal Church in 1787, after being removed from the church for praying on the main floor, a space reserved for white worshippers. They soon organized the Free African Society, which provided religious instruction as well as assistance to widows, orphans, and the sick. They went on to lead the effort to combat a yellow fever epidemic in 1793. Allen eventually founded (Mother) Bethel AFRICAN METHODIST EPISCOPAL CHURCH, the first fully independent black church in the United States, and Jones founded St. Thomas' African Episcopal Church. Beyond Philadelphia, other black communities grew. Harrisburg's population increased nearly 400 percent between 1790 and 1830. Other important locales included Lancaster and Columbia, located in the southern part of the state near the Susquehanna River. Columbia's population numbered only about 1,100 people, but 300 of them were African Americans. Black Columbians amassed considerable wealth and welcomed runaway slaves crossing the Mason-Dixon line. Pittsburgh's black population, which constituted 6 percent of the city's population by 1837, was crucial to the vitality of black life in western Pennsylvania. The black Pittsburghers MARTIN DELANY, LEWIS WOODSON, and John Vashon (see also VASHON FAMILY), among others, published antislavery materials and founded mutual assistance, educational, and antislavery societies.

An important element of free black population growth lay in FAMILY life. Regardless of past status, free blacks formed stable families in Pennsylvania. To be sure, families were not initially secure. Particularly early in the

AFRICAN-AMERICANPOPULATION OF PENNSYLVANIA, 1790–1900

Year	Slaves	Free People of Color	Free People of Color as a Percentage of Total Population	Total Population
1790	3,737	6,537	1.5%	434,373
1800	1,706	14,564	2.4%	602,365
1810	795	22,492	2.8%	810,019
1820	211	32,155	3.1%	1,049,398
1830	403	37,930	2.8%	1,348,233
1840	64	47,854	2.8%	1,724,033
1850		53,626	2.3%	2,311,786
1860		56,949	2.0%	2,806,215
1870		65,294	1.9%	3,521,951
1880		85,535	2.0%	4,282,891
1890		107,596	2.1%	5,258,014
1900		156,845	2.3%	6,802,115

19th century, poverty sometimes forced black parents to hire out their children. The PAS reported 39 such cases between the years 1779 and 1790. After 1780, state authorities supported indenturing children of manumitted slaves. In the decades before the AMERICAN CIVIL WAR, however, two-parent households accounted for 80 percent of former-slave-headed households and 77 percent of freeborn-headed households in Philadelphia. Other parts of the state exhibited similar statistics. Harrisburg, for example, maintained numbers above 75 percent.

As the number of free blacks increased, their socioeconomic status grew more tenuous and their communities more stratified than during the colonial period. Manumitted slaves were often forced into indentured labor or a cottage system that exchanged lodging for work. Most free men worked in unskilled positions (for example, gravediggers, dockworkers, bootblacks, porters, waiters, ashmen) and were largely excluded from the developing factory system. Women worked as domestic servants, washerwomen, and cooks. Some opportunities for social mobility did exist. In Philadelphia, perhaps 10 percent of free blacks enjoyed upward mobility due to the city's large labor market. Some amassed substantial wealth. James Forten, a freeborn Philadelphia sailmaker, became one of the richest men in the city (see also FORTEN FAMILY). William Whipper and Stephen Smith of Columbia accumulated wealth through a variety of ventures, and Benjamin Richards reportedly became one of the wealthiest men in Pittsburgh in the late 18th century. Of course, the vast majority of free African Americans did not accumulate such wealth, and many relied on some form of public assistance, including local almshouses.

Setbacks and Opportunities: Free Blacks in Antebellum Pennsylvania
Population growth created problems for free blacks. In 1830, Pennsylvania's black population stood around 38,000, and by 1860, it had jumped to 57,000. In reaction, white people segregated schools, cemeteries, and churches. White riots against black people, black property, and symbols of black community such as churches and meeting places erupted in the 1830s and 1840s throughout the state. Seven major riots occurred in Philadelphia alone between 1830 and 1849. This violence had multiple causes. Some white workers and European immigrants resented competition with black laborers, while others reacted to black attempts to exercise political and civil rights. At the same time, Democratic Party politicians moved to restrict black voting after they charged that African Americans had influenced their losses in a Bucks County election. In 1838, a constitu-

tional convention extended suffrage to all white men and formally banned black voting. African Americans across the state showered the capital with petitions protesting the action.

Believing that self-improvement and virtuous behavior could soften white RACISM AND RACIAL PREJUDICE, black leaders sought to cultivate the intellectual and moral life of their communities. Black churches flourished and gave spiritual direction to local neighborhoods. African Americans organized numerous moral reform societies, including the Colored Temperance Society (formed in Philadelphia in 1831) and the American Moral Reform Society (a national group formed by an African-American convention in Philadelphia in 1835). Finding educational opportunities lacking, African Americans formed literacy and debating societies for men and women such as the Theban Literary Society (Pittsburgh, 1831), the Philadelphia Library Company for Colored Persons (1833), and the Female Literary Society (Philadelphia, 1836). Three formal schools and colleges were also established: the Quaker-administered Institute for Colored Youth in Philadelphia (1832), the Ashmun Institute in nearby Chester County (1854), and Avery College in Pittsburgh (1849).

Blacks further consolidated their communities by offering assistance to runaway slaves. Pennsylvania's location on the Mason-Dixon line made it the first destination for runaways from Maryland, Delaware, and Virginia. The state legislature further enacted so-called PERSONAL LIBERTY LAWS in 1820 and 1826 that excused Pennsylvanians from enforcing the federal fugitive slave act of 1793, which required locals to help slaveholders reclaim runaways. Free blacks in Philadelphia, Lancaster, Columbia, and York in the southeastern part of the state and places like Washington and Pittsburgh in the west were especially active in helping runaway slaves. People such as Martin Delany in Pittsburgh, Lancaster County's William Parker, and the Philadelphian William Still led in these efforts. Events in Pennsylvania were of national importance. In 1842, the U.S. Supreme Court ruled Pennsylvania's 1826 personal liberty law unconstitutional after Pennsylvania tried a Maryland slaveholder who forcibly removed his slaves from York. In 1851, Parker led local blacks against a slaveholder trying to reclaim four slaves in Christiana, east of Lancaster (see also CHRISTIANA RIOT). The slaveholder died in the violent clash, but Parker and the runaways escaped. The event heightened sectional animosity between North and South, further contributing to the tensions leading to the Civil War.

More formally, African Americans participated in the national abolitionist movement. In 1833, two black Philadelphians attended the inaugural meeting of the

American Antislavery Society. Auxiliaries emerged across Pennsylvania with biracial membership. In 1833, the Philadelphia Female Antislavery Society formed and included the leadership of important black women such as Harriet Forten Purvis and Sarah and Margaretta Forten (James Forten's daughters). Other antislavery societies emerged in the southeastern and western parts of the state, where abolitionist sentiment was strongest. Black Pennsylvanians were instrumental in the development of African-American journalism. In Pittsburgh, Delany published an antislavery newspaper called the *Mystery*. Mother Bethel took over Delany's paper in 1852 and renamed it the *Christian Recorder*. William Whipper, a wealthy black businessman from Columbia, edited the *National Reformer*, the official organ of the American Moral Reform Society.

Though African Americans worked hard to strengthen their communities and resist political, economic, and social marginalization, they did not always speak with one voice. Tensions existed among elites and between elite leaders and poorer blacks. The role of women in black communities created one source of division. Beyond the antislavery movement, some women formed their own societies, including the Daughters of Africa, a Philadelphia mutual aid society. Women also assumed de facto leadership roles in churches, where they handled disputes among congregants. This public work sometimes alienated conservative men and women who believed women should remain in a domestic sphere. Black leaders also divided over the issue of emigrating to Africa, a movement propagated by the white-led AMERICAN COLONIZATION SOCIETY beginning in 1817 (*see also* EMIGRATION AND COLONIZATION and MIGRATION). Some, including Delany and Woodson, believed in the merits of voluntary colonization, while others, such as those attending an 1817 meeting at Mother Bethel, denounced the idea. Finally, the moral uplift ideology represented by reform societies created class conflict among African Americans. Uplift ideology hinged on the belief that working-class blacks lived debased moral lives. In response, poorer blacks questioned the moral superiority of black elites. In one instance, Richard Allen quashed dissent against his leadership of Mother Bethel in the 1830s after members of decidedly less affluence tried to found their own church. Allen publicly derided the dissidents' morals and behavior and claimed authority based on his presumed superior character.

The Civil War and the Black Struggle for Equality

The American Civil War (1861–65) provided an opportunity for African Americans to reassert their rights and move beyond internal divisions. African Americans answered President ABRAHAM LINCOLN's call for black enlistments in 1863. Eight thousand black Pennsylvanians served in the conflict. Many early Pennsylvania soldiers enlisted in the famed 54th Massachusetts Infantry. Some black men served in other ways. Thomas Morris Chester of Harrisburg worked as a war correspondent, and Delany served as a major and later worked for the FREEDMEN'S BUREAU in South Carolina, assisting newly freed slaves. Black women contributed to the war effort by raising money, making bandages, and sending packages to men in the field. Influential black women also took on a leading role in the Philadelphia Port Royal Relief Association, which sent aid to South Carolina blacks.

The war rejuvenated African-American efforts to lobby state and federal authorities, but it did not necessarily improve lawmakers' views of blacks. In Philadelphia, the desegregation of streetcars became an important cause in the latter years of the war. Black organizations such as the Pennsylvania State Equal Rights League protested the SEGREGATION of railcars after families complained they were unable to find transportation to visit wounded relatives in military hospitals. The Equal Rights League lobbied state authorities to overturn railroad policies, but it was not until 1867 that legislators banned the practice. After the war, the Equal Rights League also pushed for the extension of black voting rights, but state politicians resisted discussing black suffrage. Only in 1870, when Pennsylvania ratified the Fifteenth Amendment—banning racial discrimination at the polls—did black males regain the right to vote. Ratification did not mark total success. Women still lacked voting rights, and whites routinely threatened black voters with violence, sometimes following through. During an election in 1871, Octavius V. Catto, a vocal black civil rights advocate who had been a free person before the war, was shot in Philadelphia in broad daylight.

Catto's death underscores other problems faced by black Pennsylvanians in the late 19th century. Despite the railcar victory, segregation continued in schools and other public facilities. Racial separation in public schools dated from 1854, when the General Assembly required separate black public schools for areas in which more than 20 black students lived. National efforts succeeded in outlawing segregation in public facilities such as hotels and theaters in 1875, but schools remained racially separated. Pennsylvania did not begin to desegregate schools until 1881, when the state supreme court ruled the 1854 law unconstitutional. Another law, in 1887, required fines for racial discrimination in all public places. Regardless of this legislation, increased residential and de facto segregation in the next century rendered these developments unresolved.

The situation for black workers grew more complicated after the Civil War. Opportunities expanded after the war for both men and women. African Americans worked in factories in greater numbers than before the war. Interestingly, newcomers from the South accounted for many of these employees rather than Pennsylvania-born blacks, probably because Southern-born blacks lacked the skills to work in other positions. But expanding industries such as iron and steel witnessed significant increases in black workers only after 1900. In the 1880s and 1890s, African Americans held more semiskilled jobs than "new" immigrants arriving from southern and eastern Europe in industrial towns like Steelton near the state capital, but this trend reversed by the early decades of the 1900s. A growing number of black workers were taking positions as domestic workers in the homes of whites as well. In Philadelphia, this trend resulted in a decline in two-parent households. Between 1850 and 1880, the number of blacks living outside traditional two-parent families doubled. Usually this resulted from parents' taking positions in white households as domestic workers.

Faced with these problems, African Americans continued to rely on internal efforts to develop their communities. Black leaders built more schools and colleges focused on industrial and agricultural education. Pittsburgh leaders expanded Avery College into the Avery Institute, and Philadelphians established the Berean Industrial School. In nearby Chester County, the Downingtown School also provided industrial education. In addition, black business enterprises and other associations flourished throughout the state as African Americans depended on each other against solidifying white racism. Black building associations and savings and loan associations reached out to business owners and other residents. Churches, the bedrock of black communities, continued to grow in every town and city with black populations. Finally, social and athletic clubs helped to bind communities together through recreation and entertainment.

Conclusion

The situation at the end of the 19th century was complex for African Americans in Pennsylvania. The scholars George Washington Williams and Gertrude Mossell published important histories of black achievements in the state and beyond. Artists such as John G. Chaplin of Huntingdon and Henry Ossawa Tanner of Pittsburgh promoted black cultural life. Newspapers such as the Pittsburgh *Courier* and Philadelphia *Tribune* continued the work of their antebellum predecessors by disseminating information and engaging in political activism. Most blacks, however, shared the instability and poverty of previous generations, and many faced the reality of cheap housing, poor sanitation, and ingrained racism. Through their labor, families, and protest, African Americans created a multilayered culture characterized by conflict and compromise. By the dawn of the 20th century, Pennsylvania's African Americans had lived a history of oppression and resistance, disappointment and success.

Thomas H. Sheeler

FURTHER READING

Dunbar, Erica Armstrong. *A Fragile Freedom: African American Women and Emancipation in the Antebellum City.* New Haven, Conn.: Yale University Press, 2008.

Lapsansky-Werner, Emma J. *The Black Presence in Pennsylvania: "Making It Home."* 2nd ed. University Park: Pennsylvania Historical Association, 2001.

Nash, Gary B. *Forging Freedom: The Formation of Philadelphia's Black Community, 1720–1840.* Cambridge, Mass.: Harvard University Press, 1988.

Nash, Gary B., and Jean R. Soderlund. *Freedom by Degrees: Emancipation in Pennsylvania and Its Aftermath.* New York: Oxford University Press, 1991.

Newman, Richard S. *Freedom's Prophet: Bishop Richard Allen, the AME Church, and the Black Founding Fathers.* New York: New York University Press, 2008.

Trotter, Joe William, Jr., and Eric Ledell Smith, eds. *African Americans in Pennsylvania: Shifting Historical Perspectives.* University Park: Pennsylvania State University Press, 1997.

Turner, Edward Raymond. *The Negro in Pennsylvania: Slavery, Servitude, Freedom, 1639–1861.* Washington, D.C.: American Historical Association, 1911.

Winch, Julie. *A Gentleman of Color: The Life of James Forten.* New York: Oxford University Press, 2002.

——. *Philadelphia's Black Elite: Activism, Accommodation, and the Struggle for Autonomy, 1787–1848.* Philadelphia: Temple University Press, 1988.

Wright, Richard R. *The Negro in Pennsylvania: A Study in Economic History.* New York: Arno Press, 1969.

PERSONAL LIBERTY LAWS

Although some midwestern states of the United States enacted laws in the 19th century that restricted the rights of free blacks (*see* BLACK LAWS IN THE MIDWEST), others passed laws that were meant to provide them with some protection. Many Northern states passed so-called personal liberty laws between the Fugitive Slave Act of 1793 and the outbreak of the AMERICAN CIVIL WAR in 1861. Most of these laws, including those in VERMONT, NEW HAMPSHIRE, MAINE, MASSACHUSETTS, CONNECTICUT, RHODE ISLAND, NEW JERSEY, NEW YORK, PENNSYLVANIA, INDIANA, ILLINOIS, OHIO, MICHIGAN, and WISCONSIN, were passed before 1830 and were generally concerned with preventing private individuals from kidnapping others on the pretext that they were debtors or owed service in some way. In British law, the master of an apprentice or someone who was owed a debt could send private agents to kidnap and extort money from his debtor. Most of these laws also prevented the capture of fugitive slaves or the kidnapping of free blacks within the states. Although preventing the capture of blacks was the main objective, some personal liberty laws also attempted to extend some basic civil rights to blacks, including the right to file habeas corpus (or wrongful imprisonment) petitions, the right to trial by jury, the right to testify in court, and the right to be considered citizens of the states in which they resided. In many of these states, these laws were subsequently strengthened in response to attacks on the legal status of free people of color under national law in the 1850s.

Pennsylvania's personal liberty law of 1824, like many of the earlier laws, simply accorded citizenship to immigrants (including RUNAWAY SLAVES) and declared that anybody who set foot in Pennsylvania thereby became free under Pennsylvania law. This statute was overruled by the U.S. Supreme Court in 1842 in the case of *Prigg v. Pennsylvania.* The Court said that states could not eliminate the property right of a slave owner in his slave but were not obliged to assist him in any way in exercising that right. A new wave of personal liberty laws in the 1840s and 1850s were designed to avoid the unconstitutional elements of the Pennsylvania law by withholding any government assistance from SLAVE OWNERS seeking to reclaim their property and by offering protections under state law to permit purported slaves to argue against their RE-ENSLAVEMENT in court. The FUGITIVE SLAVE ACT OF 1850 overruled some of these actions by compelling state aid in some circumstances and requiring that all claims to freedom be adjudicated in federal courts under an abbreviated process. The personal liberty laws of the late 1850s, in turn, either defied the restrictions of the Fugitive Slave Act or looked for inventive ways to continue to protect the runaway slaves.

Of all the midwestern states, Ohio established the most significant personal liberty laws. Before the 1850s, the personal liberty laws of Ohio were largely concerned with preventing kidnapping generally and bore little relevance to most free blacks. However, in 1857, when the U.S. Supreme Court decision *Dred Scott v. Sandford* held that slaves did not become free merely by residing in a free state, many states, including Ohio, tried to resist the decision by strengthening their own personal liberty laws to protect free blacks and fugitive slaves. In 1857, Ohio passed "An Act to Prohibit the Confinement of Fugitives from Slavery in the Jails of Ohio," as well as "An Act to Prevent Slaveholding and Kidnapping in Ohio" and "An Act to Prevent Kidnapping." These laws intentionally made it difficult under state law to recapture fugitive slaves effectively.

Wisconsin and Michigan also passed laws in the 1850s that were meant to undermine the Fugitive Slave Act of 1850. Michigan's 1855 law, "An Act to Protect the Rights and Liberties of the Inhabitants of This State," and Wisconsin's 1857 law, "Of the Writ of Habeas Corpus Relative to Fugitive Slaves," were specifically designed to allow alleged fugitives to appear before courts of law to appeal their confinement. Although it did not carry the force of law, in 1859, the Wisconsin legislature even passed a resolution declaring the Fugitive Slave Act unconstitutional.

Although Ohio, Michigan, and Wisconsin seemed to favor greater rights for free blacks and fugitive slaves, both Indiana and Illinois failed to pass any new personal liberty laws after the 1830s. In fact, both states actively strengthened their black laws during the same period when other states in the region adopted or strengthened personal liberty laws. In Indiana, only two personal liberty laws were passed in 1824 and 1831; in Illinois, only one section of an 1833 law, entitled "Offenses against the Persons of Individuals," dealt with the problem of kidnapping in a general sense. The failure of Indiana and Illinois to adopt measures protecting free blacks and fugitives from kidnapping or recapture was significant because both states were gateways into the Midwest from the slave states of the Upper South, the region from which fugitive slaves were most likely to enter.

The personal liberty laws were a major irritant to the South. In much the same way as Southern states tried to impede the effect of federal laws they did not like, as in the nullification crisis of 1832, when SOUTH CAROLINA tried to overrule a federal tariff, the Northern states were trying to overrule federal laws on race and slavery. Southern slave owners believed that the Northern state governments were trying to deprive them of their property. When talk in the South turned to secession in the political crisis of 1860–61, these laws were frequently cited as impediments to continued union, and peace proposals, including that by the former president JOHN TYLER in February 1861, proposed that the seceded states would rejoin the Union if personal liberty laws in the North were effectively overturned.

Tom Bahde

FURTHER READING

Morris, Thomas D. *Free Men All: The Personal Liberty Laws of the North, 1780–1861.* Baltimore: Johns Hopkins University Press, 1974.

PERU

Peru is located on the Pacific coast of South America south of ECUADOR and north of CHILE and BOLIVIA. BRAZIL is to the east. The country is located along the

Andes Mountain chain, and most of the population lives in the high mountain plateaus and valleys. The eastern region of the country is heavily forested and was lightly inhabited until the 20th century. The coastal plains are mostly desert, though rivers flowing down from the mountains offer the possibility of irrigation. This region was used for plantation agriculture in colonial times.

The highlands of Peru were the heartland of the Inca Empire. This was an enormous Indian political entity that stretched across 40 degrees of latitude from modern COLOMBIA in the north to Chile in the south. The Inca imperial government was well organized, with a rich tax base and labor service obligations owed by millions of subjects.

Free people of color in Peru shared the same general experience as free blacks elsewhere in the Americas. However, important differences arose as a result of the societies in which they and their descendants were to live and work. The social, economic, demographic, political, geographical, and cultural characteristics of Peru influenced the living and working conditions of Peruvian free people of color and marked them for centuries. Peru did

not develop into an isolated slave society with a plantation economy, and hence, both free and slave Afro-Peruvians shared with local population the geographical and cultural environment.

The Colonial Period (1532–1834): Arrival of Blacks and Creation of a Free Colored Class

African blacks arrived in Peru with Spanish conquerors and settlers early in the 16th century. Most of them were slaves who accompanied the Spanish conquerors as personal servants, including female concubines of North African Muslim origins, but some were free African- or Iberian-born blacks, carrying with them both slave and free labor systems in force at that time in SPAIN. Slavery was a labor system in Spain that complemented the more prevalent free labor; slaves and free blacks both served in roles as sharecroppers or peons on rural estates, as servants in urban households, and as employees in artisanal shops (see also PEASANTS and ARTISANS). Spanish slavery was also a multiracial phenomenon, with Muslim Mediterranean and even some eastern European slaves, and hence very different from the racial slavery created by the Atlantic slave economy.

The Spaniards took Africans to Peru with no specific large economic activity in mind. Blacks just accompanied the Spanish as part of their households since the Spaniards found in Peru a large and politically organized population sufficient for the extractive activities developed in the country during the first decades after the conquest. In fact, blacks were then more valuable for their loyalty and technical skills than for their labor power. Indeed, from the very first, they participated as combatants in the wars against native peoples, and then in civil wars between factions of Spanish conquerors. They also served in subordinate positions as members of the households of encomenderos, or rural landholders, and, increasingly, those of merchants and urban landlords as well. Initially, large lords had huge households with blacks, Indians, and Spanish servants and Muslim concubine women. With time, however, as the Indian population declined through diseases introduced by Europeans and Africans, even large lords had to reduce their households and put their extra hands to work.

African slaves were taken to Peru to work on agricultural enterprises, including SUGAR CULTIVATION and COTTON CULTIVATION plantations on the coast at different times throughout the colonial and national periods, and to perform domestic service in towns and cities. Demographically important along the coastal valleys, blacks concentrated in the capital city of Lima, where around three-quarters of Peru's slaves and free blacks lived. Although Peruvian slavery was indeed a coastal and urban phenomenon, slaves and free blacks lived also in the highlands, where land and mines were worked mostly by Indians and mestizos.

As scholars such as James Lockhart and Frederick Bowser have demonstrated, European and African settlers in early Peru were disproportionately male. With the MISCEGENATION of the three principal races (Indian, white, and black), mestizo, mulattoes, and ZAMBOS (mixture of blacks and Indians), coastal Peru was populated by different categories of persons that constituted a potential source of free workers for urban and rural economic activities. These new ethnic categories were called CASTAS in Spanish America. Since *castas* were more likely to be manumitted, over time this term became increasingly a synonym for free black and, correspondingly, to be referred to as black was connected almost always with slavery. Certainly, the majority of free people of color in Peru were mulattoes, zambos, and persons of mixed race; in a caste society; racial background had great implications for their social and cultural status for, it was said, *castas* inherited the worst of all races. *Casta* situation was reversible, however. A person who had just a small part of African or Indian blood could be considered white by social convention or official proclamation. Economic success played a role in this ethnic transformation, since money "whitened" people with dark skin (*see* "WHITENING" AND RACIAL PROMOTION).

Local conditions remarkably influence social, economic, and demographic conditions of the free Afro-Peruvian population. Strictly speaking, colonial Peru did not need a larger workforce to fill the labor requirements of its rural, urban, and extractive activities. Indeed, although diminishing through exploitation and diseases, the Indian population still was sufficient for assuming that responsibility. However, it proved difficult and even impossible to put Indians to work outside their rural communities since the Spanish colonial administration preferred not to eliminate pre-Hispanic communal and Incan labor relationships but adapt them to the circumstances. Destitute half-self-sufficient Indian communities were obliged to work by turns in mines, agricultural enterprises, public works, and communications. In addition, tribute payment to the Spanish Crown obligated Indians to work outside their poor lands to get some cash. The Incan mita (a rotating collective forced labor obligation similar to the encomienda of MEXICO) and *yanaconaje* (individual service by Indians who tied themselves to white patrons) led to the development of colonial mita and peonage, respectively. However, this was not enough to fulfill labor requirements, especially for those Spanish and mestizo entrepreneurs who had no rights to forced mita Indian labor, and this gap was increasingly filled by slave and free black people. In an environment with so much servile labor, it is not surprising that free black labor was far from being free in a modern sense.

It is well known that the Spanish colonial society was divided into two "republics": one of Spaniards and the other of the Indians, separated by two different legal corpuses in force for these ethnic groups. Free people of color were placed with the Spaniards in a subordinate status.

This is the social, working, and legal context in which slave and free persons of African descent became part of the Peruvian colonial society. It is difficult to state with any accuracy the numbers of Africans arriving in Peru during the time in which the slave trade was in force. It is pertinent, however, that by the first half of the 17th century, Peru was, along with Mexico, the principal destination of the Atlantic slave trade. Then, as slave requirements were fulfilled by the human trade, free people of African descent ceased to immigrate to Peru in important numbers. In fact, the Peruvian free colored population was a result of MANUMISSION or birth in Peru. In a sense, it was a freed population, usually called *liberto* or *horro*.

Iberian slavery was strongly influenced by Roman, Mediterranean, and Muslim norms and practice that permitted slaves to obtain their freedom in different ways. To begin with, the *esclavitud de vientre* (the womb principle) in force in almost all the slave societies of the Americas made the offspring of a free woman free no matter whether the father was a freeman or a slave. With the prevalence of interracial sexual relations, the emergence of zambos (also called in Peru *chino*) and other mixed categories who were free due to the free status of their Indian, mestizo, MULATTO, or zambo mothers should not be surprising. In addition, sexual unions between masters and their female slaves were common, and the resulting mulatto children were often freed by the masters as a tacit recognition of their paternity. Another way to liberty was manumission for good and loyal service or through self-purchase. In the first case, masters freed their slaves after a long term of loyal and efficient service, but one can expect that the slave was by that time too old to be an active worker. In fact, in such cases, the master freed him or herself from taking care of a person who had natural difficulty in making a living. Another situation was the common practice of freeing slaves (or their offspring) by will, for this could also apply to young slaves. In some cases, however, gratuitous manumission was made conditional on serving until the master or a relative died.

Another route to freedom consisted of paying the market price. Since normally a slave would be too old by the time he or she was able to gather the resources needed to become free, ransom payments were often directed to free the children of a slave, especially their daughters. Young children were, obviously, cheaper, and correspondingly raising money for their freedom was less difficult, but preference for daughters had a special connotation, since in freeing them before they achieved sexual maturity, slave parents were conscious that their grandchildren would be free. If this practice was far from a challenge to slavery as a system, at least it was useful as a FAMILY strategy. Self-purchase was possible because of the ancient Roman right of peculium, which enabled some slaves to have the benefit of at least part of the fruits of their labor if they could make specific arrangements with their masters. Many slaves worked under a regime of self-employment with the obligation of paying a constant sum of money to the masters. In Peru, in contrast to other places, these payments (called *jornales*), because they were to be paid daily, were established at one real for every 100 pesos of the market price of the slave. Hence, if the slave cost 400 pesos, he or she must give his or her master four reales a day for the partial freedom that these arrangements created. If this was theoretically a possibility, in reality achieving this goal meant that slaves had to work hard for most of their lives in a labor market where they had to compete with free people of color, Indians, and other casual laborers. (*See also* COARTACíON UNDER SPANISH LAW and LIVING "AS FREE.")

At any rate, numerous slaves achieved freedom through this thorny pathway to form part of the multiethnic and multicultural world of freemen in the Peruvian society. Actually, free persons of African descent had an important presence in Peruvian history, a situation that only in the recent past has begun to be recognized by Peruvian society.

The fact that their numbers were important is reflected in the numerous attempts at regulating the activities, habits, and behavior of freedmen, both in colonial and in independent Peru. Since manumission was historically an urban phenomenon, it was in cities and towns where freedmen mainly concentrated. Although most lived in coastal cities, following the demographic patterns of geographical distribution of slaves, presence of freedmen was not unusual in highland urban centers and even in rural areas as well.

The presence of freedmen was promoted by entrepreneurs who lacked Indian workers for their businesses and trades, and at the same time, it was feared by those who considered that free people of color were more numerous than was really necessary in the workforce and that actually freedmen constituted a threat to security and good social customs. Urban elites saw in the increasing numbers of freedmen an additional source of labor, and in their turn, rural and mining proprietors sought to use freedmen as supplementary to the traditional well-established Indian labor systems to prevent shortages and other difficulties in obtaining and assuring workers. In particular, freedmen were very useful as skilled workers on estates, in shops, and in mines. However much necessity owners experienced, they were generally reluctant to attract free workers through cash incentives in an economy where coercive labor and state intervention were the rule. This circumstance may explain the fact that a good share of black, mulatto, and zambo freedmen preferred to work independently rather than to enter direct subordinated labor relations with employers who could prove abusive.

As a result of racial and cultural prejudices, free blacks had generally limited rights to work in trades as artisans, and although this measure was systematically avoided, some trades that were considered "noble arts" (such as embroidering, goldsmithing, and silversmithing) succeeded in forbidding blacks to become masters. However, numerous free blacks did acquire the status of artisan masters (especially in the construction trades, clothing, and blacksmithing) and became surgeons and veterinary surgeons, musicians, and painters.

Many of the principal occupations of free blacks were independent: That is, they often got by as day laborers in domestic service, general labor, transport, or agriculture. In all these activities, free blacks found that they faced competition from slaves who were allowed to work on their own account, as well as from workers of the other *castas*. Domestic service in the cities was often restricted to Indians, but the other occupations were open to all. Free people of color were the majority of the workforce in construction and were well-represented in such artisanal activities as shoemaking and tailoring, which were the two principal artisanal activities of the cities. On the other hand, free women of color sold vegetables, meat, fish, baked goods, and general merchandise in the streets, in competition with Indian and mestizo market women. In the countryside, free people of color of both sexes worked as peons on farms, often in competition with slaves, mestizo PEASANTS, or Indian dependents (yanaconas). They played a very important role in transportation among the highland cities, the countryside, and the port cities. Specialized roles for free blacks were as town criers and executioners. One sign of the social and economic situation of free people of color was that the great majority of free blacks lived in rented rooms in alleyways in the poorer barrios of the cities.

In some cases, nevertheless, free people of color reached relatively high positions in the economy. Thus, some free people achieved the status of master artisans, dentists, artists, merchants on a small or medium scale, moneylenders, operators of mule trains, or plantation managers. It is important to note that ownership of slaves was very widespread among the free population. It would not be good, nonetheless, to exaggerate the levels of wealth achieved by free people of color because for the most part even these relatively wealthy figures managed relatively small amounts of money.

There were a few free blacks who really managed to gain great success in economic, professional, or cultural activities. James Lockhart recorded the case of the free black woman Catalina de Zorita, who owned a bakery in the 1540s. She married a white man, and when her mulatto daughter was to marry, she gave her a dowry of 3,000 pesos, a quite significant sum. In another case, Lockhart discusses Juan de Fregenal, who made a fortune in urban and rural real estate. The French scholar Jean-Pierre Tardieu noted an even more striking case in Cuzco, that of the mulatto Baltasar de los Reyes, who, soon after gaining his freedom, in 1627 owned a hacienda with livestock in the valley of Ichobamba. Tardieu also counted 24 free blacks who were owners of mule trains in the region of Cuzco.

Several Peruvians of African descent were distinguished in science, letters, and art or are held up as examples of piety and sanctity. Perhaps the most outstanding colonial Peruvian person of color was the mulatto SAINT MARTÍN DE PORRES, who became one of the few saints of Spanish America. Another was a mulatto, too, José Manuel Valdés (1767–1843), who besides being a medical doctor graduated in 1806 was at the same time a historian, writer, poet, and, after independence, a congressman. Colonial and republican painting have had several black representatives, among others Andrés de Liébana, a black painter of Black Virgins in Cuzco; José Gil de Castro (1783–1841), a mulatto portrayer of the leaders of Peruvian independence; and especially Pancho Fierro (Francisco Fierro Palas, 1809–79), a watercolor painter of everyday life in mid-19th-century Lima. Ricardo Palma, one of 19th-century Peru's most influential CREOLE writers, was a mulatto, as was Enrique López Albújar, a 20th-century novelist, author of the celebrated *Matalaché*.

Religion, which in Peru was dominated by the ROMAN CATHOLIC CHURCH, played an important role in free colored life. *Cofradías* were CATHOLIC CONFRATERNITIES that brought blacks into the church but at the same time may have protected syncretic religious practices (*see* AFRICAN AND SYNCRETIC RELIGIONS). Two examples of this overlapping devotion are Señor de los Milagros, a Limeño cult related perhaps to the Bantu god Zambi, and Santa Efigenia in Cañete. Both cults now include people of all races and social conditions. The church both supported a hierarchical order of society that placed the Afro-descended in a lower position and insisted, sometimes more emphatically than others, that white elites respect the human dignity of the blacks.

National Period (1824–1900): Assimilation and Decline of Peruvian Free People of Color

The figures for Lima may serve as indicators of the demographic importance of free people of color in Peru. Lima and its environs concentrated most of the free people of color in Peru, who constituted half of its population during most of the colonial period. By the end of Spanish rule in Peru in the early 1820s, blacks composed one-third of Lima's population, and it was still a quarter by the mid-19th century, when slavery was formally abolished in the country. These figures reflect both the gradual increase of other ethnic components of the population and, on the other hand, the fact that free people of color who with successive generation of race-mixing became less dark could hide themselves and merge with the white population, avoiding social and racial prejudices. This was even more possible when, after independence, the caste society had only a weak presence in big cities where free blacks used to live and work.

Other studied cases are Cuzco and Potosí, important cities in highland Peru. Cuzco and Potosí held free blacks in significant numbers, especially if taking into

A formal photo of a young Afro-Peruvian woman with an incense burner. The portrait may have been taken to commemorate her first communion or confirmation in the Roman Catholic Church. African-descended people in Spanish America were often noted for their religious devotion. *(Library of Congress)*

consideration that their Indian and mestizo populations were particularly numerous. Perhaps because of this circumstance, blacks in highland cities were especially noteworthy. As in coastal areas, they lived in smaller numbers in the countryside and performed highly skilled tasks. Thus, Tardieu has found free blacks working as foremen on Cuzco rural estates and even as owners of small farms.

Concentration in cities allowed freed blacks, mulattoes, and zambos to establish economic webs to ease their living and working conditions and, on the other hand, to create and preserve cultural and social ties. This same multicultural environment had a negative influence on their cultural expression. Living together with persons of other cultural backgrounds is reflected in the mixed character of Afro-Peruvian culture through the present day.

A recent demographic study of an Indian district of Lima at the close of the colonial period shows marriage patterns that may explain the slow but permanent tendency of blacks in Peru to "disappear." Jesús Cosamalón found that the majority of free blacks practiced endogamy; but 12 percent of males married Indian and mestizo women, and females married Indian males in 16 percent of the cases. In addition, female free blacks married white males 15 percent of the time. Informal interracial sexual relations were much more common than INTERRACIAL MARRIAGE in Peruvian cities and towns. After a few generations, the relatively small free black population became vanishingly small, and the mixed-race population became increasingly Indian and/or white instead of African in ancestry. At some point, mixed-race people would be identified as mestizo rather than zambo or mulatto, or even as white, if they were light-skinned and high-status enough.

The free black population was considered a permanent threat to security in cities. From the very beginning, all the city councils passed laws to restrict free blacks' mobility to live and work in an independent manner. Blacks were prohibited from being outside their homes after nine o'clock in the evening, owning offensive weapons, or wearing certain garments and jewels. In fact, judicial records show that most persons accused in crimes in cities were actually free people of color.

Assimilation was greatly accelerated by the final abolition of slavery in 1854. The formal restrictions on free coloreds' occupational choice, access to education, and other economic activities had been either formally abolished or ignored since the time of national independence. But when slavery was abolished, people of color who were wealthy or light-skinned found it easier to move into the ranks of the white population. Although racial discrimination and slavery are two different phe-

A watercolor by an anonymous painter depicting an Afro-Peruvian couple dancing. The image was painted in the 1830s as Peru was in the process of gradually abolishing slavery and integrating Afro-Peruvians into the larger mestizo culture. *(Library of Congress)*

nomena, they reinforce each other, and weakening one can weaken the other as well.

One of the main concerns of both colonial and independent authorities, especially after 1854, was to compel blacks to work for white employers in order to preserve plantations and other productive enterprises. In fact, more than once during colonial times, free blacks were ordered to leave the country. Since this and other measures were not effective, authorities made attempts, equally fruitless, at concentrating blacks in special towns just as Indians were settled or at sending them to work in silver and gold mines. More effective, though temporary in its effect, was the 17th-century attempt to collect tribute from free blacks. These and other measures failed through the lack of means to impose them, the interests of proprietors in free blacks' labor, and their resistance.

Perhaps the only successful measure along these lines was the late colonial era decision to impose on urban free blacks the obligation to clean streets and squares periodically. To fulfill the specific tasks, city councils used the guild institutions of some trades to impose on free colored cart drivers, porters, and water carriers the duty of cleaning dunghills or killing street dogs throughout the town. After independence, the job of cleaning up the city became a profession, one exercised disproportionately by blacks. For example, the duty of killing stray dogs became a cultural phenomenon and created an entire profession of *mataperros*, or dog killers, who were almost always Afro-Peruvians in the 19th century.

Political independence from Spain in 1821–24 opened more possibilities to blacks and people of color in Peru. However, to succeed, blacks and coloreds had to incorporate themselves at least to a certain degree in the Spanish and creole cultures, a trend that began with the very inception of the colony back in the 16th century.

Several Peruvian traditional foods are of African origin. Among them are *anticuchos*, *mondongos*, and *choncholíes*, which are said to have slave origins; northern *natillas*; and central coastal *frejol colado*, *melcocha*, *sango*, *arroz zambito*, *champuz*, *turrón*, *revolución caliente*, *humitas*, *concolón*, and *cau-cau*.

Black Peruvian music has a legacy of percussion instruments (especially the famous *cajón*, a simple wooden box with a hole in its back; the *quijada*, the jawbone of an ass, mule, or horse struck with a hand; and hand clapping) and dances (from the Bantu samba to the mestizo *zamacueca*, to the *penalivio*, to the *festejo* and *landó*, *tondero*, and *marinera*). In fact, there is no longer a pure African legacy in black Peruvian dance and music. The blending of black, white, and indigenous traditions began in the 18th century, and even the *vals criollo*, a popular waltz style, has evident black influence due to black composers, singers, and dancers.

Conclusion

The official and semiofficial versions of Peruvian history reduce Africa's contribution mainly to some folkloric manifestations, such as food, and specific outstanding persons in the arts, academy, and sports. African legacy is more than that. It is present in a wider sense in every aspect of Peruvian history and present. Yet, the African legacy is hardly pure. Instead, it was modified by the centuries of biological and cultural mixture. Ultimately, as Afro-Peruvians disappeared through intermarriage into the general population, their cultural contributions were also adopted by the population as a whole as part of their culture and ceased to be distinctively Afro-Peruvian. The last groups of blacks to be assimilated were the descendants of enslaved agricultural laborers on the coast, and it is in this area where the majority of people who today identify themselves as Afro-Peruvians have their roots. The descendants of pre-1854 free people of color found assimilation the easiest, given their advantages in wealth and education over the newly freed. Thus, very few former free colored families are still today considered Afro-Peruvian.

Francisco Quiroz

FURTHER READING

Bowser, Fredrick. "The Free Person of Color in Mexico City and Lima: Manumission and Opportunity." In *Race and Slavery in the Western Hemisphere: Quantitative Studies*, edited by Stanley Engerman and Eugene Genovese, 331–368. Princeton, N.J.: Princeton University Press, 1975.

Busto Duthurburu, José Antonio del. *Breve historia de los negros del Perú*. Lima: Congreso de la República, 2000.

Keith, Robert G. *Conquest and Agrarian Change: The Emergence of the Hacienda System on the Peruvian Coast*. Cambridge, Mass.: Harvard University Press, 1976.

Lockhart, James. *El mundo hispano-peruano*. México: Fondo de Cultura Económica, 1982.

Quiroz, Francisco. *Artesanos y manufactureros en Lima colonial*. Lima: Instituto de Estudios Peruanos, 2008.

Tardieu, Jean-Pierre. *El negro en el Cuzco: Los caminos de la alienación en la segunda mitad del siglo XVII*. Lima: Pontificia Universidad Católica del Perú, Banco Central de Reserva del Perú, 1998.

Walker, Sheila S., ed. *African Roots/American Cultures: Africa in the Creation of the Americas*. Lanham, Md.: Rowman & Littlefield, 2001.

PÉTION, ALEXANDRE SABÈS (1770–1818)
Haitian military leader and president

Alexandre Sabès Pétion was the first president of independent Haiti and an important military leader in the HAITIAN REVOLUTION. He represented the free colored elite in Haitian politics but forged an alliance with poor rural newly freed blacks that allowed him to dominate Haitian politics.

Born in PORT-AU-PRINCE, SAINT-DOMINGUE, on April 2, 1770, Pétion was named Alexandre Sabès at birth and was the son of a French colonist named Pascal Sabès and a free mixed-race woman named Ursule. The colonial government issued regulations in 1773 that forbade free people of color to use the names of white people, even if they were related, and so at some point Alexandre took the name Pétion in honor of the French abolitionist Pétion de Villeneuve, though he used Sabès as a middle name throughout his life. His father supported him and, when Pétion was old enough for higher education in 1788, sent him to the Military Academy in Brienne, FRANCE. There, Pétion learned to be an artilleryman, just as Napoléon Bonaparte had between 1779 and 1783. As with Napoléon, Pétion could not rise very high in rank in the old Royal Army because he lacked noble birth, but he was prepared for a career as a junior officer in the French REGULAR ARMY.

In 1789, the FRENCH REVOLUTION began. Pétion appears to have fought for some years in the French armies in Europe, gaining valuable experience as an artillery officer and more promotions than he would have had before the Revolution. He was in the most advanced and scientific branch of service, one that the French revolutionary armies and especially Napoléon favored and supported. At some point, he returned to Saint-Domingue, probably with one of the various reinforcement groups sent to the garrison during the 1790s. The Haitian Revolution had begun in 1791, unleashing a decade of efforts both to free the colony's slaves and to protect the colony from foreign invasion. Pétion was certainly present by 1797, when he commanded the forces under the Haitian general and former slave TOUSSAINT LOUVERTURE besieging the British garrison of Port-au-Prince. Fighting alongside him was a younger officer, JEAN-PIERRE BOYER, who was to become a lifelong companion and his successor as president of Haiti. The campaign to expel the British invaders ended with victory in 1799, and shortly thereafter the "War of the Knives" between the southern army and the forces under Toussaint Louverture broke out. Pétion and Boyer supported the southern leader, ANDRÉ RIGAUD. Pétion commanded the garrison of Jacmel, a strategic town on the southern coast that was the linchpin of the southern forces' defenses. The town was besieged by troops under Jean-Jacques Dessalines, Toussaint's chief lieutenant. Finally, in March 1800, the defenders were overcome, with the help of U.S. warships that bombarded the fortifications. Pétion and the other mixed-race leaders of the southern faction went into exile in France. Dessalines's capture of the South was marked by terrible atrocities against the mostly mixed-race southerners that built up a store of resentment between the regions and the racial groups.

Pétion and Rigaud returned to Saint-Domingue in 1802 with the French expeditionary force commanded by Charles Leclerc, Napoléon's brother-in-law. Many of the former free people of color supported the invasion, convinced that Toussaint Louverture wanted radical social revolution that would undermine the privileged place in society that they had managed to win. Pétion played an important role in Leclerc's quick victory over Toussaint, commanding the artillery that finally defeated Toussaint's stronghold at La Crête à Pierrot. Toussaint was arrested and sent off to prison and death in France, and at the same time, Pétion's old commander André Rigaud was treacherously sent back to exile in France. Pétion and the other black officers finally realized that Leclerc and Napoléon intended to restore the old system, including slavery and racial discrimination against free people of color. Leclerc owned plantations in Saint-Domingue and had a personal interest in restoring the old ways. Napoléon may have thought it worth giving up the support of the free people of color in order to court the old plantation interest and was also concerned that the colony could not produce its customary enormous revenues for France without slavery and racial discrimination. Leclerc had secret orders from Napoléon to arrest all black and mixed-race officers and to restore slavery as soon as he thought it feasible. As the black and mixed-race officers slowly realized the French government's plans, the French expeditionary force grew to rely more and more on soldiers of color as French soldiers became ill with tropical diseases, including yellow fever. Finally Pétion, along with Dessalines, Boyer, and the rest of the Afro-Dominguan military leaders, went over to the resistance and drove the French out of the colony. Pétion commanded the artillery in Dessalines's army at the decisive battle of Vertières in November 1803. He was one of the signatories of the Haitian Declaration of Independence on January 1, 1804.

Shortly after independence was achieved, Dessalines declared himself emperor of Haiti. His officers went along, for a while. Many poor blacks in the colony saw a royal title as a form of legitimacy and thought of a king or emperor as a better guarantor of their rights than a mere governor-general for life, which had been Toussaint's title. Dessalines, as had Toussaint, wanted to restore plantation agriculture under a system of wage labor, which would become a common concern of governments throughout the plantation zone after the abolition of slavery. Dessalines forced former slaves to go back to work on their plantations, suppressing strikes and rounding up RUNAWAY SLAVES with harsh measures that almost matched those of the old plantation system. The workers objected, some of them using the guns that Toussaint and the other leaders had distributed widely throughout the society. Finally, Pétion and Henry Christophe, another general from the Northern Department, decided to take matters into their own hands. They assassinated Dessalines in October 1806 as he was leaving Port-au-Prince with his troops to put down yet another labor uprising.

There was a sharp contrast between Pétion and Christophe on almost all levels. Pétion had been born free, a mixed-race son of a French planter, raised in relative privilege and educated in France. He was also from the relatively relaxed environment of the West Department, where racial barriers were not so strong as in the North. Christophe, on the other hand, was black, had been taken to the colony as a slave, and had lived his whole life up to the revolution in the North Province. He may have been LIVING "AS FREE" before the revolution, but he had never been formally manumitted. Christophe wanted to preserve the plantation system, with a modified form of the labor organization championed by Dessalines. Pétion, on the other hand, wanted to break up the plantations into small farms and distribute them to war veterans. The two tried to govern together. Christophe was elected president in 1806 but refused to take office because he thought the constitution excessively limited the powers of the president. Pétion, who had been elected vice president, took office in his place as Haiti's first president. Ultimately, civil war broke out and raged from 1807 to 1810. Christophe's forces retreated to the North, where he declared himself the king of Haiti. Pétion remained in Port-au-Prince as the president of the Republic of Haiti from 1806 to 1818.

Pétion implemented his program in the South, and although tax revenues and exports fell dramatically, he had the loyalty of his people, who called him Papa Bon Kè, Kreyol for "Father Goodheart." He supported education and COMMERCE AND TRADE and encouraged the shift of the country's mixed-race elite, mostly former free people of color, to the cities and especially to Port-au-Prince. Many of them settled in a hillside suburb that today bears his name, Pétionville. He supported independence movements outside the country, giving refuge to Simón Bolívar and several of his lieutenants after the second Venezuelan Republic was defeated by the Spanish in 1815 (see also VENEZUELA). Haitian troops, money, and weapons supported Bolívar's triumphant return to Venezuela in 1817.

Pétion died on March 29, 1818, ironically of yellow fever, the disease that had killed so many of his French enemies in 1802 and 1803. His 12 years in office laid the foundation for Haitian society in the 19th and 20th centuries, with its urban mixed-race elite, free landholding peasantry, and relatively decentralized economy and government. Boyer, his successor, carried on his accomplishments, uniting the entire island and putting a definitive end to the plantation system in Hispaniola.

Stewart R. King

FURTHER READING
Dubois, Laurent. *Avengers of the New World: The Story of the Haitian Revolution.* New York: Belknap, 2005.

PHILADELPHIA, PENNSYLVANIA
Colonial Period (1684–1775)
In November 1684, three years after the colony of PENNSYLVANIA was founded, 150 African slaves arrived on an English ship. They joined a population of about 1,000 settlers. Over the next century, slavery would continue to grow in Pennsylvania and in its largest city, Philadelphia. Fifty years after the first arrival of slaves, Philadelphia alone had 8,000 residents. This rapid population growth was largely driven by white immigration, but by 1750, half of all those with recorded wills had slaves. Slaves were 15 percent of all male laborers in the 1740s, but by the early 1760s, this proportion had increased to 20 percent. Throughout the colonial period, slavery rose and fell with economic and political changes. Slaves were frequently

drawn from the Caribbean or other mainland colonies, but in the midst of the SEVEN YEARS' WAR (1754–63), many were imported directly from West Africa. The slave trade peaked in the waning years of the war, when 50 slaves arrived in 1762 alone. Only a few years later, there were about 1,400 slaves in a city of about 18,000.

After the war, white labor became preferable, for economic reasons, because more white immigrants arrived and because of increasing moral objections to slavery, and by 1770, fewer than 30 slaves a year were imported into Philadelphia. Not long thereafter, one citizen noted that more slaves were being exported than imported. Though most white Philadelphians owned one or two slaves, they seldom owned more than four. These slaves usually worked alongside whites. There were nearly as many in skilled artisanal labor as in domestic service. Despite notable difficulties, these slaves formed bonds of community, including religious and burial groups. Slave marriages often involved partners owned by a different master.

Some whites did make an effort to reach out to enslaved people. The early efforts were led by the Church of England and instigated by the preacher George Whitefield in 1739, leading to the first opportunity for blacks to receive formal schooling. From 1745 to 1776, more than 250 African Americans, about 20 percent of them free, were baptized at the largest Anglican church, Christ Church. In addition, 45 couples were married there. A much smaller number were members of other, non-Anglican churches. These early efforts would be subsumed in a much broader effort by the Society of Friends, or Quakers, but the Anglican Church would long prove attractive to African Americans in Philadelphia (see also PROTESTANT MAINLINE CHURCHES and BAPTISTS AND PIETISTS).

In the late 1700s, there was growing antislavery sentiment among Quakers, though most shared the larger society's discomfort with free blacks. Driven by a few activists and reformers, such as Anthony Benezet (1713–84), who began a 20-year career of teaching African Americans in 1750, the Quakers finally voted to exclude all slave-owning members on the eve of the WAR OF AMERICAN INDEPENDENCE, 1775–83. Benezet and others published antislavery pamphlets and even argued for full equality. Their efforts led to the opening of the African School in 1773. They educated more than 250 students in the ensuing six years, including future leaders of the free black community such as James Forten (see also FORTEN FAMILY). Though Quakers never sought to include blacks in their worship, their early activism would give Philadelphia a reputation as the best and friendliest home for African Americans in early America.

There was a notable growth in the free black population during this period, mostly through posthumous

MANUMISSION. This practice, freeing one's slaves upon one's death, was negligible before 1730. In the 1730s, one in seven Quakers did so, but in the 1740s, more than one in three Quakers did so. By the 1760s, 43 percent of Quakers did so. An economic slump in the 1760s also made slave owning less profitable and, therefore, less desirable. By this time, one-third of members of other religious groups were also freeing slaves in their wills. In 1767, there were 1,400 slaves in a city population above 18,000. Eight years later, there were only 700 slaves in a population of 25,000. The rapid growth in the free black population is attributable to manumission and in-migration. The growing free black community also occasioned white concerns and racial laws.

Revolutionary and Early National Period (1775–1800)

During the revolutionary period, Philadelphia was the largest city in the United States. In 1775, a group of concerned white Philadelphians created the Society for the Relief of Free Negroes Unlawfully Held in Bondage. Though originally intended only to help the illegally kidnapped, it would become the first English-speaking antislavery group. It handled only four legal cases before it disbanded in the midst of the American Revolution, but when it reformed in 1784, it would be with a much broader mandate.

During the British occupation of Philadelphia in the late 1770s, many local slaves escaped to the British and assisted them in the war effort. Local free blacks and some slaves assisted the Americans as well. They mainly served at sea, as James Forten did. A few did serve in the Continental army and local MILITIA, though RACISM AND RACIAL PREJUDICE usually excluded them until desperation necessitated their inclusion. In 1778, numerous former slaves left with the retreating British.

In 1780, the new state government met to consider emancipation. The explicit causes were the example of slave action during the British occupation as well as revolutionary ideals, but implicitly the declining economic benefits and rebelliousness of slaves no doubt contributed as well. Under the new law, those slaves born after March 1, 1780, would remain in servitude until age 28, when they would be free. This gradual abolition law was the first in America, though VERMONT had earlier forbidden slavery within its borders, and MASSACHUSETTS was pursuing abolition through the courts. Masters were required to register their slaves within eight months of the bill's passage. Those who did not were frequently taken to court by their slaves, where the slaves gained their immediate freedom. This law and the history of Philadelphia made it home to the largest free black community in early America, though total abolition did not happen until 1847.

Freedom and Community in the Early Republic

By the end of the Revolutionary War in 1783, about 400 Philadelphians remained in slavery. More than twice that number of newly freed people had arrived in the city during the Revolution. They petitioned the government to protect their rights and began to organize as a community. Aside from a few notable white individuals, the only groups actively interested in abolition were the Society of Friends and the Pennsylvania Society for the Abolition of Slavery, revived in 1784. At least 269 slaves were freed from 1781 to 1790, and by the latter date, 5 percent of Philadelphia was black. Some of this increase was due the to the Abolition Society, but most was due to recent arrivals from the surrounding countryside and neighboring Chesapeake area. This occasioned a dramatic increase in marriages, but a much smaller increase in independent black households. Many families lived separately, unable to afford a home, and were forced to sign indentures for their children. This form of servitude was common among poor whites, as well, but black children were almost always indentured for longer terms of service, usually serving until age 28.

RICHARD ALLEN and ABSALOM JONES represent this period of growth and in-migration. Both were former slaves drawn to Philadelphia by economic opportunity and religious fervor. In 1787, they established the Free African Society for mutual aid and support. In Philadelphia that same year, the deliberations of the Constitutional Convention took place alongside debates about an early plan for colonizing Africa with Africans. The Free African Society sent a representative, Henry Stewart, to New England to meet with other African Americans about colonization. Ultimately, black Philadelphians decided against African colonization, in part because of the local support they received.

The Abolition Society was renamed the Pennsylvania Society for Promoting the Abolition of Slavery and for the Relief of Free Negroes Unlawfully Held in Bondage and for Improving the Condition of the African Race. This longer, more descriptive name symbolized a new, more ambitious mission and a larger and more active group. Notable white members of this group also supported African-Americans' efforts at equality and autonomy. Benjamin Rush (1745–1813) especially lent his support to efforts to build an African church. After Richard Allen's exit from the Free African Society, due in part to its Quaker leanings, Absalom Jones assumed sole leadership. Before an African Church could be built, however, events intervened.

When a yellow fever epidemic struck Philadelphia in late summer 1793, carried to the city by ships fleeing the rebellion on SAINT-DOMINGUE, Benjamin Rush called on African Americans for help. Rush, along with many other scientists of the period, mistakenly believed they were immune to the disease. Absalom Jones and Richard Allen answered his call and organized African-American porters, nurses, and burial crews. Rush's theories were quickly disproved as almost 10 percent of African Americans died in the outbreak, and Allen himself became very ill. Despite their good work, the local publisher and author Mathew Carey attacked African Americans for poor conduct and profiteering. In January 1794, Jones and Allen responded with the first federally copyrighted pamphlet by African Americans. Jones and Allen refuted the allegations. Letting no opportunity go to waste, they also added an "Address to Those Who Keep Slaves and Uphold the Practice." Probably authored by Allen alone, this coda attacked slavery and racial prejudice. If the oppression of slavery were removed, they argued, African Americans could and would succeed.

A few years before these events, white citizens accosted African-American worshippers at St. George's Methodist Church and demanded they remove themselves to a newly constructed balcony. Insulted and aggrieved, Absalom Jones and Richard Allen led their followers from the church, never to return. Though there is some debate about the timing and sequence of the event, in March 1793, Allen broke ground on an African Church on Fifth Street between Walnut Street and Locust Street in Philadelphia. After some delay, the church opened in early 1794. Despite the early unanimity, some African Americans refused to be associated with Methodism because of their treatment at St. George's. Thus, this first black church became St. Thomas's African Episcopal Church, and Absalom Jones, its minister. Allen still believed in Methodism and led others to a plot he purchased years earlier, in 1791, at Sixth and Lombard Streets. In summer 1794, a pack of mules dragged a converted blacksmith shop to the site. It was dedicated on July 29, 1794. This church would become known as Mother Bethel, the first of what became the independent AFRICAN METHODIST EPISCOPAL CHURCH (A.M.E) in 1817. In 1794, St. Thomas had 246 members, and Bethel had 108. One year later, the membership had grown to 427 and 121, respectively. This growth was mirrored in baptisms and marriages as well.

Most of the new African Americans in Philadelphia were drawn from the surrounding countryside of Pennsylvania and NEW JERSEY, though others were newly freed from MARYLAND and VIRGINIA, while a smaller group arrived from Caribbean plantations as well as Saint-Domingue. Before 1820, this immigration was largely male, and for this reason, the population had a slow rate of natural growth in the early years and maintained its numbers through immigration. Their numbers grew from 1,100 in 1780 to more than 2,000 in 1790 and almost 6,500 in 1800. The population would continue to rise over the next 20 years, exceeding 12,000 in 1820. Though the numbers would continue to increase throughout the century, 1820 represents the peak of African Americans as a percentage of the population. In 1780, they were only 3.6 percent, but the percentage hovered around 10 percent from 1790 onward until reaching 10.7 percent in 1820. Thereafter, there would be a steady decline as the white population of Philadelphia grew more quickly.

African Americans frequently had difficulty in finding good jobs, through a combination of lack of skills, lack of opportunity, and broader economic conditions. Despite some notable success—the sailmaker James Forten was one of the richest Philadelphians, black or white—most worked in manual labor or domestic service (see also ARTISANS). The other major source of employment were maritime jobs; usually around 20 percent of sailors were African American (see also MERCHANT SEAMEN). Though maritime work offered decent wages, the absence of husbands and sons at sea helped account for a growing predominance of female African Americans in the community in Philadelphia after the beginning of the 19th century. The Abolition Society continued to assist families in finding positions and indentures for their children as a way to learn a trade.

African Americans moved from a dispersed pattern of settlement in the commercial center to cluster in two main areas: one to the north of Center City crossing into the Northern Liberties, the other to the southern and southwestern areas of Southwark. Though this increasing racial exclusivity in neighborhoods was driven by class as much as race, over the ensuing decades a greater and greater percentage of black households moved to the Southwark and Cedar Street corridor south of Center City. Not coincidentally, this was also the location of the independent black churches. This area was mixed by occupation as well as race; whites still outnumbered blacks by 2 to 1 even in these neighborhoods.

The Antebellum Period and the Civil War (1800–1865)

Increasingly, the hopes of interracial harmony represented by men like Anthony Benezet and Benjamin Rush were replaced by increasing racial tension and sporadic violence. After 1800, the largely poor black immigrants lacked the skills and social networks of earlier African Americans. This, coupled with white fears and sparked periodic attacks on the black community. An attack on free blacks on July 4, 1834, is symbolic of this larger hostility. Five times, from 1805 to 1814, the Pennsylvania legislature debated discriminatory laws ranging from outlawing black immigration to a special tax. Petitions from free blacks and the support of white friends helped defeat each of these proposals. In the midst of the War of 1812, as African Americans were organizing to assist in the defense of Philadelphia, the legislature again considered special regulations and prohibitions on its black residents. James Forten published a series of letters in the local newspaper decrying this proposal and reminding Philadelphia of its Revolutionary heritage.

This growing tension encouraged black Philadelphians to reconsider African colonization (see also EMIGRATION AND COLONIZATION). They were among the leaders of PAUL CUFFE's emigration plans, though only four residents sailed with Cuffe to Africa in 1815. With the founding of the AMERICAN COLONIZATION SOCIETY in late 1816, the possibility of a national colonization movement was now a reality. On January 15, 1817, nearly 3,000 African Americans met at Mother Bethel to consider colonization. Though the leaders of the meeting, Jones, Allen, and Forten among them, evidently were open to the plan, the people completely rejected the idea. Only 22 left from Philadelphia on the first ACS ships in 1820. In 1822, another 12 went to LIBERIA, and 20 more left a year later. For the rest of the century, black Philadelphians would remain staunch opponents of colonization, instead focusing their energies on abolition and moral reform.

Beginning in 1808, after years of petitions and activism, African Americans could celebrate the end of the slave trade. In what would become an annual tradition, African-American ministers gave thanksgiving sermons of January 1 each year. Absalom Jones's church had leveled off with about 500 members during this period. Allen's church had grown more slowly, but by the early 1800s, it had more annual baptisms and by 1813 had more than 1,200 members, more than twice that of St. Thomas. The personal appeal of Allen and the more emotional form of Methodist worship proved overwhelming. Nearby, John Gloucester's African Presbyterian Church and Henry Simmon's African Baptist Church were small but growing. Despite the growth in church membership, schooling proved more difficult. Quakers, as well as most churches, offered evening classes, but children often had to work during the day. In addition, they were excluded from most white schools. There was also a rapid growth in groups and associations, including several lodges of African Masons (see also FREEMASONRY).

The 1820 census reveals that more than 11 percent of black Philadelphians were firmly middle class, owning property, working in the professions, or owning respected businesses. There were growing class divisions within the black community. Many black laborers seemed more interested in colorful clothes, public parties, and drinking than moral uplift. Their social betters took every opportunity to reprimand and upbraid them, especially since white authors and cartoonists lampooned and mocked all

African Americans for the social foibles of a few. Leading African Americans had formed the Society for the Suppression of Vice and Immorality in 1809, as well as various insurance companies and cultural societies over the years. This effort at moral reform and uplift would culminate in a national Convention Movement.

During the 1820s, the African-American population of New York City was growing. Though Philadelphia had long been prominent, black New Yorkers sought to assume leadership of a national convention (see also NEGRO CONVENTION MOVEMENT IN THE UNITED STATES). Hearing this, Philadelphians, led by Richard Allen, planned and hosted the first National Convention in 1830. Though ostensibly called to consider a plan for Canadian emigration, the meeting also considered plans for agricultural and mechanical education. Conventions would meet annually until 1834, though Philadelphia would take less of a leadership role, and the convention finally met in New York City in 1834. Though there were plans to continue meeting, the newly formed American Moral Reform Society would take its place. The planned 1842 Philadelphia convention never took place amid an outbreak of racial violence, and the movement was increasingly sidelined amid the new more radical conventions of the 1840s and 1850s.

In the 1820s, a movement to create an African Fire Association in Philadelphia was quickly quashed by black leaders fearful of white reactions—fire protection at the time was the province of private clubs of firemen, which were seen as quasi-military and not suitable for black service. Black churches were increasingly targets for vandalism. Worsening conditions locally and nationally after 1820 caused a reconsideration of African Americans' place in America. In the mid-1820s, black Philadelphians looked at Haiti as a possible place of opportunity. JEAN-PIERRE BOYER, the president of Haiti, sent an emissary to Philadelphia, and in 1824, 60 free blacks sailed for the island republic. Hundreds more left a few months later, including members of the free black elite such as Richard Allen's son. Eventually, some 6,000–7,000 arrived, but by 1825, many had returned because of inhospitable climate, unmet expectations, and religious differences.

Throughout the 1820s and 1830s, black Philadelphians met increasing white hostility and violence with resistance and new institutions. In 1832, there were 50 benevolent societies. Five years later, this number had nearly doubled, and more than 80 percent of black adults belonged to one of them. A riot in 1834 burned many black businesses and homes, especially targeting the most prosperous. One man, Stephen James, was beaten to death. The next year, an angry white crowd threw boxes of abolitionist literature into the Delaware River. An 1838 rally with members of the American Anti-Slavery Society, formed in Philadelphia five years earlier, again drew the ire of local whites. They besieged the meeting at the newly constructed Pennsylvania Hall and, as city authorities refused to act, burned the building to the ground. The crowd moved on to attack a shelter for colored orphans and a black church.

Though leaders of the abolition movement frequently traveled to Philadelphia and sought the support of the local black community, black involvement in the leadership of the movement was rather limited. James McCrummill, ROBERT PURVIS, and James G. Barbadoes were three of the founders of the American Anti-Slavery Society, and James Forten served as a vice president, but their role was mostly symbolic. There was more direct involvement in the Pennsylvania Anti-Slavery Society, which elected Robert Purvis as its president in 1845. The Philadelphia Young Men's Anti-Slavery Society, founded in 1836, had many black elites among its members. The Philadelphia Female Anti-Slavery Society, founded soon after the national society, had the wives, sisters, and daughters of the free black elite among its members. However, as the elite became increasingly freeborn, their overt commitment to abolition lessened as they faced other more pressing personal concerns, both economic and political.

The Pennsylvania legislature officially disenfranchised blacks during this period, and wealthy blacks remained a target of white violence. By 1848, there were 19 churches and a network of schools, societies, and institutions. There were nearly 20,000 black Philadelphians, the second largest community behind only Baltimore, but they were only 5 percent of the city's population. There was a renewed interest in abolition as well as focus on racial solidarity as the interracial goals of the Moral Reform movement had clearly foundered. Though they continued to organize and petition throughout the 1850s, black Philadelphians would not regain the right to vote until the passage of Fifteenth Amendment.

This new leadership rallied the city in support of the Union cause and enlisted African Americans to fight in the AMERICAN CIVIL WAR, 1861–65. Pennsylvania had the largest contingent of black recruits for the Union army of any free state, with almost 9,000 young Pennsylvanians of color serving in the ranks of the U.S. Colored Troops (USCT). The 8th Infantry, USCT, a unit of about 1,000 men, was recruited at Camp William Penn, near Philadelphia, in December 1863, and contained a large proportion of Philadelphia residents. Some were native Pennsylvanians, but many were runaways from as far away as JAMAICA. As did any other soldiers, these men signed up out of a variety of motives, including patriotism, hatred of slavery and the Southern slave-owning class, desire for steady pay, and the enlistment bonuses being offered. Still largely untrained, the 8th was sent into action during the Battle of Olustee, FLORIDA, February 20, 1864. The Union forces were outmaneuvered by the Confederate defenders, and the 8th was put in at the point where the Confederate pressure was the strongest. The regiment suffered about 330 casualties. By the end of the war, its cumulative battle casualties made it the third hardest hit of all USCT regiments.

Reconstruction and After

The African-American population of Philadelphia grew from almost 21,000 in 1860 to nearly 63,000 by 1900, increasing from 3.7 percent to 4.8 percent of the total population. In the immediate postwar period, there were a series of legal advances, led by the Fourteenth and Fifteenth Amendments (see also CIVIL RIGHTS LAWS IN THE UNITED STATES AFTER 1865). In 1881, school discrimination was made illegal, though de facto SEGREGATION persisted as whites often rioted when blacks attempted to attend schools that had historically been all-white. An 1887 state law made discrimination in pubic business illegal. Despite the fact that thousands of African Americans from Pennsylvania fought in the Civil War, they were excluded, marginalized, or attacked in annual postwar celebrations.

On the afternoon of October 10, 1871, Octavius Catto (1839–1871), the principal of the Institute for Colored Youth and a leading member of the African-American community, was shot and killed in the midst of an election day riot in Philadelphia. Catto had long been active in seeking political and legal equality for African Americans, and he was mourned by both blacks and whites. In the run-up to the election, Democrats appealed to white prejudices since the black voters would, for the first time, play an important role in the election. The local POLICE force, home to many Democrats, did not provide much protection for African-American voters, and violence began two days before the election and continued throughout the voting. White vigilantes killed the African Americans Isaac Chase and Jacob Gordon before killing Catto. Despite witnesses and evidence, no one was punished for the murders. The riots of 1871 were the last widespread attacks on blacks in their homes, though sporadic violence did continue.

Despite the lack of formal segregation, there was an ongoing lack of opportunity and real equality. There were some jobs in the professions of medicine and the law, but only for a select token few. White opposition continued to limit manual labor opportunities. When two black men were hired as motormen for Philadelphia streetcars, a two-week strike by the other workers quickly ended the experiment. Other businesses used the existence of willing black workers to threaten their white workers with replacements if they made too many demands.

An increasing concentration in housing continued, but not total segregation. A small percentage of blacks could patronize some white businesses and churches, and the ROMAN CATHOLIC CHURCH especially made an effort to be catholic in its appeal and outreach.

Over the 19th century, Philadelphia had gone from being the center of black America to being one black city among many. Baltimore and, later, New York City surpassed it in both population and cultural importance. By the 20th century, the black scholar W. E. B. DuBois could describe it as past its prime and its citizens as too removed from African-American life and culture. Despite this, it remained the home of many important institutions, including the African Methodist Episcopal Church and its newspaper the *Christian Recorder*. Unfortunately, the early hope of equality in America, represented by the free black community of Philadelphia, remained an unfulfilled promise for years to come.

Matthew J. Hudock

FURTHER READING

DuBois, W. E. B. *The Philadelphia Negro: A Social Study*. Philadelphia: University of Pennsylvania Press, 1899.

Dunbar, Erica Armstrong. *A Fragile Freedom: African American Women and Emancipation in the Antebellum City*. New Haven, Conn.: Yale University Press, 2008.

George, Carol. *Segregated Sabbaths: Richard Allen and the Emergence of Independent Black Churches, 1760–1840*. New York: Oxford University Press, 1973.

Lane, Roger. *Roots of Violence in Black Philadelphia*. Cambridge, Mass.: Harvard University Press, 1986.

Melton, J. Gordon. *A Will to Choose: The Origins of African American Methodism*. Lanham, Md.: Roman & Littlefield, 2007.

Nash, Gary. *Forging Freedom: The Formation of Philadelphia's Free Black Community, 1720–1840*. Cambridge, Mass.: Harvard University Press, 2003.

Newman, Richard S. *Freedom's Prophet: Bishop Richard Allen, the AME Church, and the Black Founding Fathers*. New York: New York University Press, 2008.

Winch, Julie. *A Gentleman of Color: The Life of James Forten*. Oxford: Oxford University Press, 2002.

———. *Philadelphia's Black Elite: Activism, Accommodation, and the Struggle for Autonomy, 1787–1848*. Philadelphia: Temple University Press, 1988.

PIAR, MANUEL (1774–1817) *Venezuelan general*

Manuel Piar was a senior commander of the Venezuelan forces in the early stages of the independence struggle there (*see also* SOUTH AMERICAN WARS OF LIBERATION). He was a member of the *PARDO*, or mixed-race middle class, and he represented its interests not only against the Spanish Crown but also against the pro-independence white elite led by Simón Bolívar.

Piar was born on April 28, 1774, in Willemstad, Curaçao, in the Dutch Antilles (*see* DUTCH CARIBBEAN ISLANDS). He was the son of a Curaçao free woman of mixed race named María Isabel and her white Spanish sailor companion Fernando Piar Lottyn. Although a Dutch colony, Curaçao was economically and culturally tied to Venezuela, and the family split its time between Willemstad and the town of Santa Ana in Venezuela, where Piar was baptized shortly after his birth. Piar lived a middle-class life, mostly in Venezuela, suffering discrimination against people of color but managing to get an education. By the age of 23, when he began his revolutionary career, he had managed to learn Spanish, Dutch, Portuguese, the Papiamentu language of Curaçao, and Latin. He was also a skilled merchant sailor, following the sea as his father and many free men of color in the Americas did (*see* MERCHANT SEAMEN).

In 1797, he participated in the Gual y España conspiracy in Venezuela, an early attempt to seek independence inspired by the WAR OF AMERICAN INDEPENDENCE, 1775–83, and HAITIAN REVOLUTION. Many of the movement's supporters were free people of color. After the conspiracy was exposed, Piar fled to Haiti, where he served in the navy of Jean-Jacques Dessalines and his successor, the president of southern Haiti, ALEXANDRE SABÈS PÉTION. It is unknown whether he was involved in the conspiracy launched by FRANCISCO DE MIRANDA, based in southern Haiti, in 1806, but he clearly knew Miranda and worked well with him later. In January 1807, Piar was made captain of one of Haiti's small warships. In April 1810, after the beginning of the Venezuelan struggle for independence, he left the Haitian service and joined the Venezuelan armed forces, serving under the command of Miranda. At first, he was commander of a ship in Venezuela's small NAVY. On March 26, 1812, he participated in the naval Battle of Solinas. Venezuelan victory there cut off royalist forces under General José Tomás Boves along the Orinoco from their seaborne lines of communication and limited their ability to attack pro-independence forces farther north and west. Nonetheless, at the end of 1812, the royalists were victorious, and Miranda surrendered. Piar and the other Venezuelan leaders took refuge on the island of Trinidad, by then a British colony (*see* TRINIDAD AND TOBAGO). In 1813, they returned to the country to renew the struggle. Piar took command of pro-independence forces ashore in the Orinoco region and captured several cities. He then organized a small squadron of ships to blockade Puerto Cabello, to the west of Caracas, cooperating directly with the forces of Simón Bolívar. From 1814 to 1817, he fought in several battles against the royalist forces, becoming one of the most important military commanders of the pro-independence army. He concentrated his efforts in the northeast of the country, where he was well known and where there were a large number of *pardos*.

In one of the most dishonorable acts of Simón Bolívar's career, the famed liberator turned against Piar after his April 11, 1817, victory over the royalist forces led by Miguel de la Torre at the Battle of San Felix. With a force of ill-equipped and half-trained *pardo* and Indian soldiers, Piar overcame 1,600 Spanish professionals with almost no loss to his own men. Piar had always pushed for equality for people of color and an end to slavery in the new republic. Bolívar was not prepared to overturn the old racial system completely, though he was open to some reforms. Friction over these issues and the fear that Piar would become a threat to his own leadership led Bolívar to remove Piar from direct command of troops, while promoting him to the rank of general in chief. Piar continued his agitation and public criticism of Bolívar's racial policies, and so finally Bolívar had him court-martialed for insubordination and treason to the revolution. He was convicted and executed by firing squad on October 16, 1817, against the wall of the cathedral in Angostura. It is said that Bolívar wept when he heard the shots and cried out, "I have shed my own blood."

Piar demonstrated the heights that revolutionary disruptions permitted free people of color to attain in Spanish America. At the same time, his fate reminds us that color prejudice remained strong even among revolutionaries. His chief enemy among the Spanish officers, General de la Torre, said that he was the one rebel officer the Spanish feared most, because he could ignite a racial war that would sweep SPAIN from the Americas. Ultimately, his own superiors feared the same thing. Bolívar repeated his persecution of Piar, with somewhat more justification, in the case of the Colombian admiral JOSÉ PRUDENCIO PADILLA, whom he also had executed in 1825 after accusing him of plotting to overthrow the state. Bolívar feared *"pardocracía,"* or the rule of mixed-race people

Stewart R. King

FURTHER READING
Harvey, Robert. *Liberators: Latin America's Struggle for Independence.* Woodstock, N.Y.: Overlook Press, 2000.
Lynch, John. *Simon Bolivar: A Life.* New Haven, Conn.: Yale University Press, 2006.

PIERCE, FRANKLIN (1804–1869) *fourteenth president of the United States (1853–1857)*
Like his predecessor in office MILLARD FILLMORE, Franklin Pierce was a Northerner who never owned slaves, and like Fillmore, he was quite sympathetic to Southern positions during a politically charged time. Serving as president of the United States from 1853 to 1857, Pierce took several positions that caused or could have caused great hardship to free people of color. He is generally considered one of the least successful American presidents.

Pierce was born in Hillsborough, NEW HAMPSHIRE, on November 23, 1804. His father, Benjamin Pierce (1757–1839), served as governor of the state and commanded New Hampshire's troops in the WAR OF AMERICAN INDEPENDENCE, 1775–83. Pierce descended from an old Puritan family whose forebears had settled MASSACHUSETTS Bay Colony in the 1630s. Pierce was well educated, graduating from Phillips Exeter Academy and Bowdoin College, where the writers Nathaniel Hawthorne and Henry Wadsworth Longfellow were fellow students. As did his father, Franklin Pierce served in the state's MILITIA, rising to the rank of general and commanding a brigade during the MEXICAN-AMERICAN WAR, 1846–48. He was wounded during the capture of Mexico City by the American army under the command of Winfield Scott, who was to be his opponent in his race in the presidential election of 1852.

Pierce married Jane Appleton, the daughter of the president of Bowdoin College, in 1837; they had three children, who all died before reaching adulthood. The tragic deaths of their children pushed Jane into depression, and Pierce drank heavily for the rest of his life. His problems with alcohol and his wife's illness may have influenced his judgment, but he was still able to win the Democratic Party nomination for president in 1852. He was a compromise figure, who was not identified with either the Southern or Northern factions within the Democratic Party. He was hopeful for compromise on the issue of slavery and handily defeated the Whig candidate, his former commander, Scott.

Pierce's presidency was marked by continuing and increasing division over the issue of slavery and its expansion into the western territories. With Pierce's support, the ILLINOIS senator Stephen Douglas pushed through the Kansas-Nebraska Act in 1854. This law repealed the Missouri Compromise of 1820 and opened all the West not yet organized into states to slavery, if the white male inhabitants wished to have the institution. The proponents hoped that this policy would defuse debates at the national level over slavery by transferring those debates to territorial legislatures in the West, but instead national factions began competing for control of those legislatures. KANSAS had two competing state constitutions for much of the 1850s, one that opposed slavery and one that permitted it. Each constitution had a slate of proposed representatives and senators seeking to be seated in Washington, D.C., and in Kansas each had armed men fighting for it. Northern abolitionists funneled arms and volunteers to the Free State faction, while Southerners, especially from the neighboring slave state of MISSOURI, conducted damaging raids into the territory. "Bleeding Kansas" rapidly became a security threat to the United States and a foretaste of the AMERICAN CIVIL WAR. The Kansas-Nebraska Act and the violence that followed had a serious impact on free people of color. Both sides saw blacks as the cause of the problem. Some Northern abolitionists, such as John Brown (1800–59), were friendly to free blacks, but most of the Free State support was from Northern whites who wanted no blacks around, either enslaved or free. Proslavery Southerners saw free blacks as their natural opponents, and in fact many free people of color were involved with the Underground Railroad and other forms of direct action against the interests of SLAVE OWNERS. Violent repression of free blacks living in the West was often the result of this debate.

During the crisis in Kansas, Pierce's administration faced and took part in a concerted effort by Southern slave owners to expand U.S. territory to the south. In 1854, Pierce's diplomats, led by the future president JAMES BUCHANAN, threatened war with SPAIN to gain CUBA for the United States. Although many Northerners and the newly formed Republican Party blocked the move, it showed the world how serious Americans were about finding new territory for slavery to expand. An American adventurer, William Walker (1824–60), invaded MEXICO in 1853 to establish a U.S.-dominated puppet state in Sonora and Baja California, where slavery would be permitted with the support of a rebel conservative faction in Mexican politics. Walker's allies failed to go to his aid, and the liberal Mexican government was able to defeat his invasion force. He was put on trial in U.S. courts in order to satisfy diplomatic proprieties but was rapidly acquitted. Then, Walker raised a larger force and invaded NICARAGUA, briefly becoming its president and restoring slavery before being overthrown by the combined forces of the other Central American republics. The U.S. government never officially sanctioned Walker's exploits, but under the Pierce administration, the U.S. military twice went to his rescue when outraged Latin Americans defeated his plots. Had any of these moves been successful, it is clear that the situation of free people of color in those countries would have worsened. In his "Republic of Sonora," Walker proclaimed the law code of LOUISIANA in force. Of all the slave states, Louisiana provided the most protection for free people of color, permitting landownership and even slave ownership, but still its provisions were less even than those found in Mexico before independence from Spain. By the 1850s, Mexico had had liberal, formally race-neutral laws that had been enforced for more than 20 years. Walker's brief tenure as president of Nicaragua also saw the introduction of harsh American-style repressive laws

against people of color and even the RE-ENSLAVEMENT of some Afro-Nicaraguans. An official American purchase of Cuba would have proved disastrous for that island's large and increasingly influential free population of color, who were about to play a large role in the half-century struggle for national independence.

After leaving office in 1857, Pierce continued to be a supporter of the Southern Democrats. He declined to run for office in 1860 and 1864 but spoke in favor of the Democratic nominees and against abolitionism. He had a harsh exchange of letters with Secretary of State William Seward in 1862, in which each accused the other of disloyalty—Seward accusing Pierce of working with the Confederate enemy to undermine the war effort and Pierce accusing Seward, and by extension President ABRAHAM LINCOLN, of subverting the Constitution. Pierce continued a friendly correspondence throughout the Civil War with his former secretary of war and close political ally, Jefferson Davis, who served as president of the Confederate States of America. Unlike the former president John Tyler, Pierce did not play any active role in the Confederate government and remained in the North, so avoiding any formal accusations of treason, but made no secret of the fact that he opposed the war. Pierce died on October 8, 1869, in New Hampshire.

Stewart R. King

FURTHER READING

Hawthorne, Nathaniel. *The Life of Franklin Pierce*. Gloucester, Mass.: Dodo Press, 2009.

Taylor, Michael J. C. "Governing the Devil in Hell: 'Bleeding Kansas' and the Destruction of the Franklin Pierce Presidency (1854–1856)." *White House Studies* 1 (2001): 185–205.

PINTO DA GAMA, LUIS GONZAGA (1830–1882)
Brazilian abolitionist attorney

Acting as a lawyer, without a degree, Luis Gonzaga Pinto da Gama gained the freedom of more than 500 slaves and is considered a pioneer of the abolitionist movement in BRAZIL.

The son of a free black mother and of an upper-class white Portuguese father, Gama was born in Bahía on June 21, 1830. Gama's mother, Luiza Mahin, was an important participant in the Revolta dos Malês, an Arab-African slave revolt, and of the Sabinada, a movement for the independence of Bahía. She disappeared in 1837. When Gama was 10 years of age, he was sold by his father to a slave trafficker from São Paulo. The transaction was illegal because Gama had been born of a free mother and had never been registered as a slave by his father.

In São Paulo, Gama worked on the property of a noncommissioned officer of the Brazilian REGULAR ARMY. When he 17 years old, he was taught to read and write by a law student who lived with the officer. A year later, he ran away and enlisted in the army after proving the illegality of his status as a slave. While in the army, he worked part-time in a private law firm. In 1850, he attempted to audit classes in the University of São Paulo's law school but gave up because of the reaction of other students and professors. In 1854, six years after entering, he was discharged from the army for insubordination and sent to work for the secretary of police, from which he was fired two years later for advocating the rights of slaves.

After leaving public service, Gama dedicated himself to JOURNALISM and political activism. He became an accomplished poet and mainly criticized the Europeanization of successful members of society of African descent. He advocated pride in their ethnicity and help for slaves and poor blacks. Gama also joined the Republican movement in Brazil. Along with Rui Barbosa, he created the radical *Republicano* newspaper and help found the Republican Party in 1873.

Gama is considered a pioneer of the abolitionist movement for his work as a lawyer for those in condition of illegal slavery. On the basis of the Lei Eusébio de Queiros (the Queiros Law), which made the importation of slaves unlawful, he was able to free more than 500 slaves. He argued that the law, by citing earlier prohibitions dating back to 1831, actually freed everybody imported in violation of those earlier regulations. He practiced law without a degree with the knowledge he had acquired over the years of personal interest in law. Among his controversial arguments were that a slave who killed his or her owner was acting under the principle of self-defense. He also helped slaves who, even though they had the ability to pay for their own MANUMISSION, were prevented from doing so by their owner. In 1880, Gama also led a group called Young Republicans and Abolitionists. After his death on August 24, 1882, Gama's example inspired the creation of a group called Caifazes, which adopted a strategy of attrition against slavery. They financed collective slave escapes or stole slaves from their owners.

Gama was also a noted neoromantic poet. Many of his poetic works had themes drawn from the simple life of rural Brazil, and he helped spark a turn toward a more domestic style in Brazilian literature. His life illustrates the relative flexibility of the Brazilian slave system, since he was able to succeed in so many freedom suits, and at the same time the difficulties faced by free people of color in the country. His support for an end to the monarchy put him on the other side of this issue from many free people of color, who thought of Emperor Dom PEDRO II as their protector against the planter class, who were mostly Republicans.

Ana Janaina Nelson

FURTHER READING

Azevedo, Elciene. *Orfeu de Carapinha: A trajetória de Luiz Gama na imeprial cidade de São Paulo.* Vol. 1. 2nd ed. Campinas: Editora da Unicamp, 1999.
Mennucci, Sud. *O precursor do Abolicionismo no Brasil—Luiz Gama.* Coleção Brasileira. Série 5. V. 119. São Paulo: Companhia Editora Nacional, 1938.

PIRACY

The pirates of the late 17th and early 18th centuries in the Atlantic world were, like the MERCHANT SEAMEN most of them had been before they turned to crime, racially integrated to a surprising degree. Pirates were people who lived beyond the frontiers of civilized European life. Those frontiers marked the limits of required social behavior, including the evolving racial SEGREGATION, religious discrimination, social class and property rights, or political loyalties. They even ignored gender rules, as women, though greatly outnumbered by men, nonetheless played an important role in their society, as equals or even in some cases as leaders. As were all trans-frontiersmen, the pirates were useful to the states that sponsored them and protected them and tried to make use of them. However, when those states became powerful enough to exert their authority over the places the pirates had conquered, they moved to stop the transgressions of racial, political, religious, and social lines. These transgressions made it easier for the newly dominant state to define the pirates as creatures outside the nation and suppress them by force. Nonetheless, piracy offered an opportunity for some people to enter into the national community with status and wealth. A very few of these successful, assimilated pirates were people of color.

The era of piracy in the Atlantic basin started in the late 16th century with the English-Spanish wars (1577–1604) and the Dutch war of independence from Spain (1568–1648). Dutch and English ships attacked Spanish commerce, first along the European coast and then in the Caribbean basin and the Americas. French pirates joined the fray during the French Wars of Religion (1562–98). The Spanish invaded FRANCE in support of the Catholic faction in the 1580s, and the ultimately victorious Bourbon faction retaliated by supporting privateers to attack Spanish possessions in the Americas and Africa. The war widened further in 1580, when the Portuguese and Spanish Crowns were united and the northern European enemies could attack BRAZIL and Portuguese possessions in Africa and Asia.

The first generation of northern European pirates were based in European ports, and their crewmen were of a variety of European nationalities, but a few were people of color. However, most of the European corsairs became

A contemporary illustration of Henry Morgan's attack on Panama in 1671. The illustration appeared in the 1678 Dutch edition of Exquemelin's biography of Morgan. As with Exquemelin's text, the illustration does not show the racial diversity of Morgan's followers. *(The Bridgeman Art Library)*

involved in the Atlantic slave trade to some extent. The most famous of the early English seafarers, John Hawkins and Francis Drake, got their start shipping slaves to Spanish America in violation of the Spanish import restrictions. The slave traders all hired many African and American black sailors because their presence helped control the slaves. Basing themselves in small northern European ports in the Caribbean and West Africa, the 16th- and 17th-century corsairs gathered more and more sailors of color around them. A century after Hawkins's defeat at Veracruz in 1567, the most famous 17th-century British buccaneer, Henry Morgan, captured PANAMA in 1667 with a crew that was more than half nonwhite. A number of his men were MAROONS from the Caribbean coast of Central America, who were of mixed African and Indian ancestry, including a band who lived near Panama and who helped him find a hidden way through the jungle of Darien from the Caribbean coast to Panama on the Pacific. Others were free men of color from JAMAICA and BARBADOS.

Morgan and his men and the other corsairs of the 16th and 17th centuries were privateers: That is, they sailed with the authorization of a national government as part of its war effort. As a result, they were free to use the ports controlled by that power, sell their loot there, and recruit new crewmen. Therefore, their crews resembled the populations of those colonies, which is to say, they were in large measure black. The most famous British pirate haven was Port Royal, in Jamaica, established in 1655. When the British conquered Jamaica, the population was almost entirely black or mixed-race, and even the few people socially defined as white Spaniards had significant African ancestry. The political situation changed for private sea rovers at the end of the 17th century. The European governments of the 18th century were increasingly interested in reining in private armies of all sorts. The buccaneers of the Caribbean met the same sort of resistance as noble armed forces or municipal MILITIAS in Europe. Those who could have some military usefulness for the new regime were integrated into its armed forces, while those who could not fit into the system's conception of a properly organized society were forced to change occupation or be defined as criminals and hunted down. Black pirates generally fit into the latter category.

The pirates of the 17th century were private adventurers serving their king and lining their own pockets. The pirates of the 18th century were working-class rebels, fighting back against mistreatment by sea captains and merchant companies and hostile to all national governments almost by definition. Many of them were people of color. When the Welsh pirate Bartholomew Roberts captured a number of slave ships at Ouidah in 1722, he took men out of the slave cargo and enrolled them in his crew so as to have enough men to be able to sail the captured ships but only awarded them one-quarter shares in the loot, not because they were black, but because they were landsmen. He gave the same limited shares to European soldiers he captured off a transport ship in 1721 who wanted to join his crew. The freed slaves joined dozens of men of color who already served in Roberts's crew. When the British pirate Edward Teach, known as "Blackbeard," was finally defeated in Ocracoke, NORTH CAROLINA, in 1718, his last crew consisted of "thirteen crackers and six negroes," according to the Royal Navy lieutenant who led the attacking party. The pirate utopia of Libertalia, on the

A contemporary drawing of Bartholomew Roberts, a Welsh pirate who had served as an officer on slave ships and had liberated slaves among the crews of his pirate ships *(Art Resource, N.Y.)*

northeast coast of Madagascar, had as citizens both African inhabitants of the region and European and American pirates and lasted for about 30 years in the early 18th century. The actual details of this settlement are unclear, and some research suggests that it was an urban legend, but smaller village ports along the coast of West and Central Africa permitted pirates to live alongside Africans for shorter period. Africans certainly joined pirate crews; one "Coast Negro" was hanged along with the British pirate "Calico Jack" Rackham in 1720 in Jamaica.

The black pirates of the 18th century can be thought of as seagoing maroons. In many cases, they were actual RUNAWAY SLAVES or slaves liberated by the pirates, as were the men Roberts took into his crew. In other cases, they were merchant or naval seamen who had run away from or rebelled against a bad work situation. The systematic abuse of sailors by their officers and merchant companies was a feature of nautical life in this period. Ironically, one of the reasons that public opinion accepted blacks as crewmen with equal status to whites on merchant ships was that all seamen were in some sense servile. They were obliged to work for the duration of the voyage, they often were cheated of their wages and worked essentially for nothing other than their living, they could be whipped and tortured by their employers if they resisted, and if they tried to run away, the government could arrest them and take them back. Black sailors' treatment was equal, but in many ways equally degrading. That both white and black sailors rebelled should surprise no one, and that, having rebelled, the pirates mostly rejected racial divisions and worked together against their oppressors is also unsurprising.

The contemporary observers of the pirates were generally at least somewhat sympathetic to their cause. Writers such as Alexandre Exquemelin and Daniel Defoe in the late 17th and early 18th centuries chronicled the lives of pirate chieftains in such a way as to make them romantic and sympathetic figures to European readers. In so doing, they mostly erased the black faces from the picture of piracy that they portrayed, in keeping with evolving European ideas of color lines and stereotyped roles for blacks. Exquemelin acknowledges to some extent the role maroons and black sailors played in the work of his hero, Morgan, in his 1678 work *The Buccaneers of America*. Writing half a century later, Defoe (under the pen name of Charles Johnson) was more thorough in removing any mention of the race of most of the people he profiled in his *Account* (1724). Popular culture followed the lead of these contemporary writers by portraying pirates as exclusively white in such works as Robert Louis Stevenson's *Treasure Island* (1883) and Rafael Sabatini's *Captain Blood* (1922), strongly based on Exquemelin's work. It is only with the development of modern social history that the role of people of color in piracy has been recaptured, in Marcus Rediker's *Villains of All Nations* (2004), for example. Popular culture has followed the scholars: The hugely popular *Pirates of the Caribbean* movie franchise has one character, a white man, whose crew is largely black—the blacks are the villains, perhaps showing that popular culture has not come completely to terms with racial equality.

Stewart R. King

FURTHER READING
Exquemelin, Alexandre. *The Buccaneers of America*. Translated by Alexia Brown. Originally published in Dutch *De Americaensche Zee-Roovers* (Amsterdam, 1678). American edition, New York: Dover, 2000.
Johnson, Charles [Daniel Defoe]. *A General History of the Robberies and Murders of the Most Notorious Pirates*. London, 1724. Modern edition, New York: Carroll and Graf, 1999.
Rediker, Marcus. *Villains of All Nations: Atlantic Pirates in the Golden Age*. Boston: Beacon Press, 2004.

PITTSBURGH, PENNSYLVANIA

Pittsburgh is a city located in southwestern PENNSYLVANIA, a state of the United States. The city lies at the confluence of the Allegheny and Monongahela Rivers, where they form the Ohio River, which flows into the Mississippi River. In the 1740s, a British fur trading post operated at the river junction, but the French took control of the area in 1754 and erected Fort Duquesne. During the SEVEN YEARS' WAR, 1756–63, the British destroyed Fort Duquesne and replaced it with Fort Pitt, named in honor of the British statesman William Pitt; the surrounding area became known as Pittsburgh. In the 19th century, Pittsburgh's riverside location made it a major trading and manufacturing center, and the city's business elite developed ties to southern and western merchants, traders, and slaveholders. Despite Pennsylvania's status as a free state, Pittsburgh's black community experienced a combination of hardship and success in the 19th century.

Black Pittsburgh from the Seven Years' War to the Civil War

Slavery existed in southwestern Pennsylvania from at least the mid-18th century. During the Seven Years' War, British officers used enslaved Africans as laborers, servants, and soldiers. The small size of most farm holdings in the region and the high cost of slaves relative to those of other North American colonies limited the prevalence of slavery in the area. Slaves were subject to various restrictions under colonial Pennsylvania law, including limits on their rights to travel, consume liquor, and own firearms. Slaves in Pittsburgh and its environs began to see a shift in their status during the WAR OF AMERICAN INDEPENDENCE, 1775–83, when the new state government passed the Gradual Emancipation Act (1780). It freed all

slaves born after March 1, 1780, at the age of 28, and it required slaveholders to register their slaves with local authorities.

Gradual emancipation increased the number of free blacks in the Pittsburgh area, but the overall population remained relatively small through the early 19th century. In 1790, 150 slaves lived in Pittsburgh and surrounding Allegheny County. In 1830, only 27 slaves lived in Allegheny County. That same year, census records indicate a total of 1,193 African Americans in Allegheny, with 472 living in Pittsburgh. By 1850, Allegheny County's free black total reached 3,431, and of these, approximately 2,000 lived in Pittsburgh (5 percent of total population). African Americans settled in distinct neighborhoods. Most important were a section of the city known as "Hayti" and several outlying towns, including Arthursville to the east and Allegheny City, located across the Allegheny River.

Several fundamental problems circumscribed black life in Pittsburgh in the 1800s. RACISM AND RACIAL PREJUDICE excluded black men from many jobs in the city's growing industrial sector. As a result, most men worked as day laborers, coachmen, waiters, stewards, porters, and stevedores. Women held a smaller range of jobs, working mostly as cooks, spinners, and domestic servants. A minimal degree of class stratification developed among African Americans in early Pittsburgh. Some men worked as shoemakers, barbers, and wigmakers, occupations that, because of their largely white clientele, ranked among the most prestigious jobs blacks could hold. One man, Benjamin Richards, accumulated considerable wealth by serving the local military post through his butcher shop, and by 1800, he had become one of the wealthiest men in Pittsburgh. John B. Vashon, a leading figure in Pittsburgh's antislavery movement, also amassed wealth by running a barbershop and public baths (*see also* VASHON FAMILY). Most blacks, however, did not enjoy such success. In 1860, only 12 blacks in Pittsburgh owned more than $2,000 worth of property (little more than 1 percent of the black population). In addition to job discrimination, racial SEGREGATION marked most public and private facilities. Churches were segregated, and businesses such as hotels and restaurants would often employ blacks but not serve them. Furthermore, though Pittsburgh was spared the degree of racial violence that other cities experienced, two notable riots did target the black population, in 1834 and 1839.

As in other Northern U.S. cities, African Americans in Pittsburgh sought to counter discrimination by constructing autonomous institutions. By the 1840s, African Americans had organized four benevolent societies, a temperance association, a MILITIA company, and their own cemetery. Churches emerged as the bedrock of the community. Bethel AFRICAN METHODIST EPISCOPAL

CHURCH (A.M.E.), the first black church in western Pennsylvania, opened its doors in 1822. By 1841, four black churches existed in Pittsburgh and neighboring Allegheny City: Two were Methodist, one Episcopalian, and one Presbyterian (*see also* PROTESTANT MAINLINE CHURCHES). Additionally, two Sunday Schools served the city's black children. Efforts to improve education constituted another main element of community building. Public schools in the city were segregated, and white officials generally neglected black schools. To rectify this situation, black leaders including Vashon and LEWIS WOODSON, a Methodist minister, formed the African Education Society in 1832 to purchase books and property for a school. The school opened in 1837, and a second school in Allegheny City was built around the same time. A white abolitionist, the Reverend Charles Avery, expanded educational opportunities for black students in 1849, when he contributed stocks and ground for the Avery Mission Institute. Vashon's son, George, served as president for a time, and HENRY HIGHLAND GARNET, a black New England abolitionist, briefly worked as the school's principal.

Pittsburgh's black leaders also participated in state and national politics as means of improving their condition. Some of the earliest black residents, including Richards, included their names in a petition calling for the creation of Allegheny County in the 1780s. Later, after a state constitutional convention prohibited black suffrage in 1838, black activists from the city organized conventions and issued petitions, such as the *Memorial of the Free Citizens of Color in Pittsburgh and Its Vicinity, Relative to the Rights of Suffrage*, protesting the move. Nationally, several Pittsburghers played important roles in the antislavery movement. MARTIN DELANY, one of the most visible black leaders in the United States, published one of the first black newspapers, the *Mystery*, from 1844 to 1848. Vashon organized abolition societies and distributed copies of the abolitionist William Lloyd Garrison's newspaper, the *Liberator*. Moreover, black Pittsburghers attended the national black conventions (*see* NEGRO CONVENTION MOVEMENT IN THE UNITED STATES) that began in the 1830s to debate the AMERICAN COLONIZATION SOCIETY's mission of resettling African Americans outside the United States (*see also* EMIGRATION AND COLONIZATION.) These forms of mobilization put black leaders into direct interaction with white politicians, making them prominent obstacles to white political power.

Pittsburgh's black community was especially active in assisting RUNAWAY SLAVES. A network developed in the 1840s and 1850s that used aggressive tactics to help runaway slaves secure their freedom. Local African Americans often "kidnapped" suspected runaways before slave catchers could find them. In 1854, for example, black Pittsburghers took a woman and her three children from a man claiming to be her husband. He could offer no proof of his relationship, and the four went free. One year later, however, these tactics backfired, after locals took a free black servant working for a man from out of state. The incident caused considerable distress to local businessmen concerned that such acts would alienate Southern clients. After passage of the FUGITIVE SLAVE ACT OF 1850—requiring residents of Northern states to assist slaveholders in reclaiming slaves—a large portion of Pittsburgh's black population fled the state rather than resist emboldened slave catchers. More than 800 African Americans fled the city in the 1850s, reducing the population from nearly 2,000 a little more than 1,100. Population growth stagnated for the next decade.

Black Pittsburgh from the Civil War to the Twentieth Century

The AMERICAN CIVIL WAR, 1861–65, provided African Americans in Pittsburgh a hopeful view of the future. Blacks celebrated in the streets after President ABRAHAM LINCOLN issued the EMANCIPATION PROCLAMATION on January 1, 1863. Some blacks joined the federal cause; Delany served as a major before working in SOUTH CAROLINA for the FREEDMEN's BUREAU, an organization dedicated to helping newly freed slaves. In the years after the war, the city's black population grew exponentially, aided by migrants from Virginia and MARYLAND. Between 1870 and 1900, the black population grew from 1,162 to 20,355, making Pittsburgh's black community the sixth-largest in the United States.

In the late 19th century, blacks continued to face major challenges. Residential segregation grew more extreme than before the Civil War, particularly as growing numbers of European immigrants moved to the city and began to create ethnic neighborhoods. Regarding segregation in public places, Pennsylvania's government passed laws in 1867, 1881, and 1887 that desegregated everything from railcars to schools and theaters. Legal challenges to desegregation in 1887, however, resulted in the implementation of so-called separate but equal public facilities for blacks. Moreover, Pittsburgh grew rapidly as an industrial center, but it was also one of the dirtiest cities in the country. African Americans often lived in cramped conditions, and they faced a constant threat of diseases spreading through their tenement buildings.

Despite the explosive growth of Pittsburgh's industrial sector, blacks continued to work at a narrow range of jobs. As did antebellum workers, African Americans operated in a two-tiered system. The top tier included barbers, porters, butlers, maids, and waiters. The bottom tier—the majority of black workers—included teamsters, refuse collectors, janitors, and laundresses. In 1907, 58 percent of male workers labored in domestic and personal services (compared with 90 percent of women). Additionally, blacks competed with waves of immigrants from southern and eastern Europe, and white employers usually favored the immigrants. In 1910, one-third of employed black men worked in manufacturing and mechanical jobs, and most of these were general laborers, janitors, or wait staff. Only 2 percent of steelworkers in 1908 were black. Labor unions usually excluded blacks from joining, leaving strikebreaking as black workers' greatest potential for work. Nearly every strike in Pittsburgh during the 1870s and 1880s resulted in the use of blacks as strikebreakers. In some cases, companies went into the South to recruit nonunion black workers. This trend continued well into the 20th century.

Pittsburgh's black community continued to shore itself up against discrimination and racism. One key element of community organization was the press. The black press resurged in the 1890s after waning for much of the late 19th century. Papers like the *Meteor* and the *Western Enterprise* gave the black community a needed public forum for discussion and debate. The *Pittsburgh Courier*, established in 1910, had the greatest impact. It became one of the most prominent black newspapers in the country, reaching a readership of 70,000 in 1930. (*See also* BLACK PRESS IN THE UNITED STATES.) Business organizations also helped to stabilize the black business class. The central irony of segregation was that it created opportunities for black entrepreneurs to serve the black community where whites refused to do so. For instance, the Diamond Coke and Coal Company, established in 1890, became the largest black business in Pittsburgh, employing about 1,000 people. Additionally, several black-owned building and loan associations provided financial support to African-American residents.

Churches and benevolent associations provided the most important anchor for black neighborhoods. Baptist congregations grew most rapidly after the Civil War, owing to large numbers of Southern black migrants. Some 30 Baptist existed in Pittsburgh before 1914. The earliest of these were Metropolitan, established in 1868, and Ebenezer, founded in 1875. Both had more than 1,000 members in the early 1910s. Other denominations experiencing growth during this period were Presbyterians, who founded Grace Memorial Church in 1868, and Catholics, who established St. Benedict's in 1890. As churches did, a number of benevolent institutions aided Pittsburgh's black community. Perhaps most important were institutions such as the Home for the Aged and Infirm Colored Women and the Colored Orphans' Home. Together, churches and benevolent institutions helped to provide a public and moral center to black life.

Finally, numerous social, literary, and cultural endeavors served black Pittsburghers' intellectual and artistic interests. Among the oldest social clubs were the GRAND UNITED ORDER OF ODD FELLOWS and Masonic lodges (*see also* FREEMASONRY) founded before the Civil War. Others included literary groups like the Aurora Reading Club and social clubs like the Goldenrod and White Rose clubs. Many of these clubs catered to specific groups such as professional men, university students, and busy women. The turn of the century was a time of artistic growth as well. The music and theater scenes expanded in the early 20th century. Churches traditionally had hosted performances, but after the turn of the century, private clubs began to promote secular styles like ragtime, jazz, and even orchestral music. Black Pittsburgh also became a center for sports in the early 20th century. The Homestead Grays, organized in the early 1900s, counted among the earliest and most celebrated black baseball teams.

Conclusion

Throughout the city's history, Pittsburgh's black population worked to resist racial prejudice. From the colonial-era black residents who petitioned the General Assembly to late 19th-century Southern migrants who established Baptist churches, African Americans in the city balanced their hardships with active involvement in the development of their neighborhoods. The 20th century introduced new challenges and opportunities, particularly during the Great Migration, a mass movement of Southern blacks to Northern cities during World War I. Blacks arriving in Pittsburgh found increased chances to participate in the city's continuing industrialization but also hostility from white workers. More important, they found a vibrant black community into which they could move and try to prosper.

Thomas H. Sheeler

FURTHER READING

Blackett, R. J. M. "Freedom, or the Martyr's Grave: Black Pittsburgh's Aid to the Fugitive Slave." In *African Americans in Pennsylvania: Shifting Historical Perspectives*, edited by Joe William Trotter, Jr., and Eric Ledell Smith. University Park: Pennsylvania State University Press, 1997.

Brown, Eliza Smith, ed. *African American Historic Sites Survey of Allegheny County*. Harrisburg: Pennsylvania Historical and Museum Commission, 1994.

Glasco, Laurence, ed. *The WPA History of the Negro in Pittsburgh*. Pittsburgh: University of Pittsburgh Press, 2004.

A Legacy in Bricks and Mortar: African American Landmarks in Allegheny County. Pittsburgh: Pittsburgh History and Landmarks Commission, 1995.

PLANTERS AND PLANTER AGENTS

The plantation was the basic social and economic unit of the slave societies of the Americas from the 16th to the 19th century. They varied widely in many ways, but they shared some basic characteristics: (1) They were operated by slave labor, generally African or of African descent. (2) They produced large staple crops for distant markets, selling into a global marketplace dominated by capitalist values. (3) They were feudal in their internal management, as the planter exercised some quasi-governmental functions, such as law enforcement and jurisdiction over family structure. (4) They were generally demographically impoverished. That is, they had lower birthrates and higher death rates than the surrounding society or the societies from which their enslaved workers or owners originated. (5) Most plantations were owned and operated by white proprietors, who ruled over black slaves. However, there were a surprising number of free blacks who were either owners or managers of plantations in many areas throughout the Americas.

In addition to the owner and family members, most plantations had a good-sized staff of free employees. Free people often managed the plantation, marketed the products, did some of the skilled labor, and may also have been the direct supervisors of slaves in the field. Masters might have preferred to assign some of these jobs to slaves, in order to avoid having to pay wages. However, many states and colonies had laws requiring a minimal level of staffing by free persons, both to protect jobs and to ensure that slaves would be kept confined and disciplined. Many of these laws were overtly discriminatory against free people of color.

White elites and colonial governments were very suspicious of giving free blacks direct supervisory authority over slaves. Putting a black in charge represented a violation of the basic nature of racial hierarchy in these societies. Whites also worried that free blacks might be lenient or sympathetic to their slaves and might even help them escape slavery. The Deficiency Acts in JAMAICA dating from the late 17th century are an example of these laws that tried to limit the role free blacks could play in supervising slaves by imposing extra taxes on planters who employed free blacks in supervisory positions. The CODE NOIR IN FRENCH LAW and subsequent statutes in the FRENCH CARIBBEAN made a free black employee cost the planter exactly twice as much as a white in taxes. Nevertheless, planters persisted in using free colored managers, for a variety of reasons.

The main reason was that the free people of color employed were related to the planter. Sexual relationships between male masters and female slaves were common in every slave society. Many of these male masters wanted to provide for their children in some way, though there were

sharp cultural and individual differences in how much they did or could do for their enslaved children. In all societies before the Industrial Revolution, however, family ties mattered greatly, and white fathers and free colored children both tended to feel they could rely on each other. One common role assigned to mixed-race children of planters was on plantation management.

In addition, planters often preferred free blacks, even those not related to them, as employees because they often cost less than white employees and because they were more familiar with the culture of the slaves. Generally, white professional plantation managers were new immigrants from Europe who had business skills but needed interpreters to understand the slaves' languages and required years to understand their cultures. Native-born whites might know the slave culture, but in many places there were few of these as white birthrates were low. Enslaved or free black "drivers," or gang foremen, were very common, even in places like the American South, where there were plenty of native-born whites. Foremen who gained their freedom might want to work at higher levels of the internal hierarchy of the plantation, as bookkeepers, managers, or attorneys. Because of laws and customs, there were fewer blacks in these jobs, but occasional cases are found almost everywhere.

Another way planters could help their colored children was to give them some of their plantations' land and slaves and set them up as planters for themselves. This was also a choice frowned upon by governments and societies. In many British colonies and American states, there were laws against the practice that were fairly efficiently enforced, though even so there were free black masters who figured out how to get around the laws. And in French, Portuguese, and Spanish colonies, there were numerous free black farmers who owned slaves and grew cash crops, though they might not rate some of the formal marks of status that white planters had.

Free black farmers may well have had an easier situation than urban free blacks, as far as RACISM AND RACIAL PREJUDICE were concerned. In rural areas, they were far from the machinery of official racial discrimination, and laws might be overlooked in their favor if they were accepted as members of their community by the white majority. If they were the relatives of locally powerful white people, this connection protected them against the harsher effects of racism. Even if they were not related, they might well have powerful white patrons. TOUSSAINT LOUVERTURE, the liberator of Haiti, is an example of this: Although he was not related to them in any way and was in fact the child of two black slaves, he gained his freedom through the friendship and support of Bayon de Libertat, his former master, and the count de Noé, Bayon de Libertat's employer. He came to own land adjacent to

Noé's plantation. He worked his land himself at first, but after he earned enough money, he bought some slaves and leased others, slowly acquiring more land as conditions permitted. He claimed later that by 1791, when the HAITIAN REVOLUTION began, his assets were worth as much as 100,000 livres (more than $2 million today). His was an unusual but by no means unheard-of success story in the Atlantic world. Free black planter classes lived under a variety of conditions in different regions of the Americas.

The United States

Most American states were very reluctant to allow free blacks to own or exercise authority over slaves. However, bedrock principles of Southern political culture were respect for property rights and a very limited role for government. The collision between these two principles created a certain amount of wiggle room for a few free black planters to succeed. They were clearly the exceptions, however, as most rural free blacks in the South were peasants or very low-level employees on larger white-owned farms.

The free black Metoyer family of LOUISIANA owned hundreds of thousands of dollars' worth of land and slaves in the Nachitoches area before the AMERICAN CIVIL WAR. They were the descendants of a French man and his slave who began their relationship in the 1760s, when the territory was owned by SPAIN. Thanks to the Spanish and French heritage of Louisiana, there were more free black planters there than anywhere else in the United States. The Metoyers were one of 472 black families in the state to own more than $10,000 worth of rural property in the 1860 census, a sum that could buy a small farm and a half-dozen slaves. Although not a big operation by the standards of the Caribbean or BRAZIL, it was sizable for the United States, where most slaveholdings were small. Thus, these free blacks were the peers, in economic terms, of most white planters in the state at the time.

The next largest population of free black planters in the United States was in SOUTH CAROLINA, where there were only 162 free blacks who owned more than $10,000 in rural property in 1860. The other Southern states lagged far behind. The cultural resistance of whites to the idea of blacks in economically prominent roles was too strong in most places for a large free black planter class to grow up in the United States.

State Black Codes generally prohibited entrusting a free black with the management of a plantation for an extended period (see BLACK CODES IN THE UNITED STATES). However, most Southern planters lived away from their plantations for at least part of each year. This meant that there was some room for free blacks to work as overseers and managers. Nevertheless, deeply entrenched social prejudices held that the management of slave workforces was a white man's job, at least at the top level, so slave foremen or drivers who gained their freedom could rarely advance to more senior positions. INTERRACIAL MARRIAGE of whites and blacks was forbidden in slave states, and white fathers of illegitimate mixed-race children in America were generally prohibited by social rules from recognizing their children or doing very much to help them. Even MANUMISSION became difficult in the 19th century, to say nothing of gifts of property and slaves. Some fathers made use of their illegitimate children as plantation supervisors or managers on an informal basis, though this, too, was very difficult and rare outside Louisiana and the Carolina and GEORGIA low country.

The British Caribbean

In the British Caribbean, the situation was much as in the United States, with the exception that there were fewer poor whites to take the management positions and more plantation owners were absentee proprietors, living in BRITAIN or in the large colonial cities. This meant that some free black men gained employment as planters' agents, though this was rare. White employers preferred immigrants from Scotland or Northern Ireland as plantation agents, thinking them more reliable than free blacks and better able to handle the business side of the manager's job. The British plantation system had its origin in Northern Ireland in the 17th century, and so Irish Protestant immigrants to the Caribbean in the 18th century might have been at least somewhat acquainted with the leadership skills necessary to manage a plantation.

Deficiency laws imposed taxes on free coloreds who owned more than a few slaves unless they employed a white manager, as well as on white planters who failed to maintain a sufficiently large staff of white employees. Since these laws were an important source of income for the colonial government, they were strictly enforced. As a result, most free colored farmers stayed small, and few of their farms could be called plantations. White fathers still wanted to help their mixed-race children but were more likely to do so by setting them up in business or training them for a craft than by trying to establish a plantation for them.

The French Caribbean

There were no laws against free colored land ownership in the French colonies, and although there were special taxes on free colored SLAVE OWNERS and plantation managers, these taxes were low and often not collected in remote areas. The children of masters and their slaves could and often did receive agricultural land and slaves from their fathers. The colony of SAINT-DOMINGUE, the future Haiti, experienced a major economic boom in the 1750s and 1760s, when mountainous areas were developed as COFFEE CULTIVATION plantations and the colony became Europe's principal source for coffee. Free coloreds were very prominent as coffee planters and controlled many other small plantations growing secondary crops such as food and practicing COTTON CULTIVATION and INDIGO CULTIVATION. There were a few free colored sugar planters, such as Julie Dahey near PORT-AU-PRINCE, who owned about 60 slaves and a large sugar mill, but SUGAR CULTIVATION required considerable investment capital to become established. As a result of all these factors, free coloreds owned about one-fourth of the arable land and slaves in Saint-Domingue, and lesser but still significant amounts in the other FRENCH CARIBBEAN colonies.

Many white planters in the French Caribbean were absentee owners, living in France or in the colonial cities. Those who had free colored relatives often entrusted their plantations to them rather than to white immigrants. Whites born in the colony were preferred, but they were few in number, and many of them also wanted to move to the cities or to France. Free coloreds were prohibited by law from moving to France (though many managed it despite the law), and they preferred to stay out of the colonial cities because of their discriminatory laws and unwelcoming social climate. For those without plantations of their own, managing a white-owned plantation could provide a good living. There is little evidence of wage discrimination in French colonies, and a free colored plantation manager or professional employee could make decent wages.

Most of the leading members of the free colored community in Saint-Domingue were planters, as were many leaders of the Haitian forces in the HAITIAN REVOLUTION, including the early rebel JEAN-BAPTISTE CHAVANNES, the free colored political activist JULIEN RAIMOND, and the rebel governor-general Toussaint Louverture. The rebel generals ALEXANDRE SABÈS PÉTION and ANDRÉ RIGAUD were children of white planters who helped manage their fathers' plantations. LOUIS DELGRÈS, the leader of resistance to slavery in Guadeloupe, was also a farmer before 1789, though his fairly meager holdings of a couple of slaves and a small amount of land might not qualify him for the title of planter.

The Spanish Caribbean

As in the French colonies, there were no laws preventing free blacks from owning slaves, and many did. As sugar cultivation became widespread in CUBA after the turn of the 19th century, however, free coloreds faced increasing discrimination in rural areas and often moved to the cities. This is why, in contrast to those in the Haitian Revolution, the free black leaders of the various Cuban struggles against slavery and for independence were mostly urban. SANTO DOMINGO, the future DOMINICAN REPUBLIC, did not experience the same sugar revolution as Cuba, and there the most prominent free colored person involved in the independence movement, FRANCISCO DEL ROSARIO SÁNCHEZ, was a well-off farmer. He cannot, strictly speaking, be called a planter since Haiti had abolished slavery in the Spanish part of the colony during its administration, from 1821 to 1844.

Brazil

In Brazil, as in Spanish America, there were no laws restricting free black land ownership. The rate of interracial marriage and recognized informal interracial couplings was even higher there, and many Brazilian free people of color became important planters. The coffee region of Vassouras, developed as slavery was dying in Brazil, had an important free black planting class, though its economy collapsed in the end, leaving many of them impoverished. Earlier, the British merchant Henry Koster encountered a prominent local official and planter in Recife who was clearly of African ancestry. When he questioned the fact that this man held a government role supposedly reserved for whites, he was informed that the man in question "had once been mulatto, but was no longer. For how can a mulatto man be *capitaõ-mor*?" To a North American, as to the British Koster, this was an incomprehensible blurring of racial lines. The flexibility of these lines in Brazil helped free people of color ascend the social hierarchy to the highest positions.

Conclusion

It is a strange paradox that black people, the principal victims of the slave system and the racism and racial prejudice it engendered, could also be found among the ranks of the oppressors. Yet plantations were the principal sources of wealth in the slave societies of the Americas, and that wealth was liberating. People of color who wanted to be liberated could choose this road, and some did. In any case, their loyalties were frequently not determined by their race. Family was all-important in this age, and as planters or planter agents they might well be showing loyalty to their fathers and half brothers while oppressing strangers who had entered from a foreign land.

Stewart R. King

FURTHER READING

King, Stewart R. *Blue Coat or Powdered Wig: Free People of Color in Pre-Revolutionary Saint-Domingue*. Athens: University of Georgia Press, 2001, esp. chap. 10.
Spivey, Christine. "Early Success of the Metoyer *Gens de Coleur Libre*." *Loyola University of New Orleans Student Historical Journal* 27 (1995–96).

POLICE

The 18th century saw the organization of police forces in the Atlantic world, first in the major cities of the European colonial powers, and then in their colonies and the newly independent nations of the Americas. In many places, free people of color served as policemen, and police duty gave them many of the same advantages as MILITIA service. Also, because of the RACISM AND RACIAL PREJUDICE against them, they were frequently the targets of unfair treatment by the police. This conflicted relationship with the police has become a part of the black experience throughout the Americas.

Rapidly growing cities and wide disparities in wealth in the 18th century created severe crime problems. This period was the "age of gin," as distilled beverages became widely available, and alcoholism created its own set of social problems, with which that society was ill equipped to deal. There were no organized police in the Western world at the beginning of the 18th century. FRANCE had its *maréchaussée*, or rural police, the ancestors of today's gendarmes, but they were few in number and originated through feudal service obligations by rural gentry. During the 17th century, the absolutist monarchy in France slowly eroded feudal service obligations, and the *maréchaussée* was all but eliminated by the 1710s. Urban businessmen sometimes hired watchmen, who could protect property but had no formal law enforcement powers. Wealthy men had private bodyguards and carried weapons, and poor people were armed with simple weapons and looked out for themselves. In BRITAIN, there were town watches and parish constables, again organized on a feudal basis by urban corporations and church parishes, and again the feudal form of organization and obligation to serve was increasingly a dead letter by the beginning of 18th century. In addition, the town watches had been strong supporters of Parliament during the civil wars of the 17th century in England and had mostly been dissolved as politically suspect during the Restoration of Charles II. In SPAIN, again, the municipal corporations had had their own armed forces in the 16th century, but by the 18th century, these independent armed detachments were increasingly suspect for political reasons, after many *comumero* revolts calling for greater power for local governments. They were slowly being dissolved or converted into ceremonial units.

The newly assertive central governments realized that they had a problem with social order, however. One by one, during the 18th century, they created organized police forces. France was first, with the *maréchaussée* reform act of 1720, which turned the intermittently patrolling rural notable into a professional force assigned to both city and countryside. The Bourbon Reforms in Spain and the Pombaline Reforms in PORTUGAL after 1750 established central control over the municipal council and then established city watch forces. The British were the last to join the reform; the establishment of the London Metropolitan Police had to wait until 1829, when London had more than a million people.

The new system spread rapidly to the colonies. The duties of the colonial police force and the militias overlapped much more in the Americas than in Europe. Colonial police forces in plantation zones had to maintain social order in the same way that metropolitan police departments did, suppressing criminals and exuberant spirits in the port cities, protecting dignitaries, investigating thefts, enforcing regulations about street maintenance or tavern closing hours, and the like. In addition, they were the colony's first line of defense against its most important security threat, the slave population. The normal violence of making slaves work and preventing them from running away or rebelling was in the hands of the master. However, the degree of harm masters were permitted to inflict on slaves was at least theoretically limited by law and practically limited by the fact that the master and a small professional staff were significantly outnumbered by their workforce. For backup, masters turned to the police. Nobody wanted to do this, because if a slave's misconduct became an official matter, the master risked losing property rights. Slaves were recognized as human if they violated laws, no matter what theories about chattel were put forward to justify slavery in other circumstances. If a slave committed a crime, he or she might well be killed or punished so severely as to be no longer useful as a worker. But the police were the ultimate threat. The form of misconduct most commonly reported to the police was flight. Chasing RUNAWAY SLAVES was a principal duty for the *maréchausée* in the French colonies and the *caçadores* in BRAZIL.

The French colonies had had *maréchaussée* detachments since their inception, composed originally of planters and their dependents, mostly men of color. They were formally established by the act of 1720, further revised throughout the 18th century. Each town or parish had a professional armed force of up to a couple of dozen horsemen. Throughout the plantation zone, these were exclusively men of color, with white officers, who were professional military men from the metropole. Budgets were never sufficient to maintain the large numbers of men necessary for really effective law enforcement, so the *maréchaussée* took on supernumerary assistants. These were generally young men with deficient liberty papers who served in return for tax-free MANUMISSION, potentially beneficial contacts with influential patrons, and, of course, any bribes they could extract from lawbreakers and the citizens they protected.

The Spanish colonies received formal town watch detachments in the Bourbon Reforms of the 1750s and

1760s, but the creation of rural police forces had to await the independence period in the early 19th century. The rural police proved to be important bulwarks for centralizing national governments, as in MEXICO under the mid-19th-century liberal regimes and in ARGENTINA under Juan Manuel de Rosas. People of color played an important role in both of these forces. Brazil's Minas Gerais province had regiments of *caçadores do mato*, or "bush hunters," from the 1720s on, who hunted runaway slaves, disciplined slaves, chased away Indians, and enforced mining regulations. Almost all the *caçadores*, even the officers, were people of African or Indian ancestry. Portugal also created intendants of police in Brazilian cities in the 1750s who were responsible for urban policing as well as keeping order on the surrounding plantations. Most line officers in the urban police forces were recruited from the free black militia companies.

Police service in the tropical colonies was attractive for many of the same reasons militia service was. Policemen were socially important: They were frequently godfathers; they helped people in trouble and gained clients and supporters; they expressed community values politically on occasion. Policemen, unlike militiamen, also were paid regularly and had access to informal sources of income ranging from off-duty guard jobs and gratuities to out-and-out bribes. Policemen looked out for each other, and the white officers in many units were important patrons for their free colored subordinates.

Thus, in these countries, Spanish America, Brazil, and the French colonies, there was an ambiguous relationship between the police and poor blacks. On the one hand, the police represented an avenue out of poverty, a way to meet potential white patrons, to gain respect within black society, and to earn one's living. On the other hand, the black policeman was the face of repression for slaves, MAROONS, and people of color whose manumission papers were not in order. Any contact with the police for someone living on the margins of free black society might have a disagreeable or even violent ending.

The British colonies lagged behind other places in the Americas in creating organized police forces. Patrols of militiamen chased runaway slaves in JAMAICA, with the assistance of maroon groups with whom the government had made deals. Masters were permitted a greater degree of violence against their slaves—in practice, their power was unlimited—and were required to maintain comparatively large groups of armed white employees. They were also civilly responsible for the misconduct of their slaves—this is part of the legal theory of chattel. If a person's horse escaped and ate a neighbor's crops, the person was responsible. In the same way, under British law, if a slave did some harm to someone's property, the master was responsible. It is unclear, however, how often a master was

successfully sued to recover property stolen by a runaway. Putting more responsibility and authority in the hands of the business owner and permitting him or her informally to externalize some of the business's costs while keeping government's role very minor are very much in keeping with Anglo-American practice at the time.

In the United States, the establishment of formal police organizations dates to the same period as the beginning of massive immigration from Europe. European immigrant groups dominated the newly established police forces, leaving no room for free people of color. Black policemen in the United States were extremely rare until the 1960s and 1970s.

Stewart R. King

FURTHER READING
Dantas, Mariana L. R. "'For the Benefit of the Common Good': Regiments of Cacadores do Mato in Minas Gerais, Brazil." *Journal of Colonialism and Colonial History* 5 no. 2 (Fall 2004).
King, Stewart R. "The Maréchaussée of Saint-Domingue: Balancing the Ancien Regime and Modernity," *Journal of Colonialism and Colonial History* 5, no. 2 (Fall 2004).

POLK, JAMES (1795–1849) *eleventh president of the United States (1845–1849)*
President of the United States from 1845 to 1849, James Polk was responsible for greatly enlarging the territory of the United States, in ways that ultimately would lead to the AMERICAN CIVIL WAR. He was a large planter and slave owner and lived around people of color, both free and enslaved, for his entire life. Many of his decisions as president had enormous impact on the lives of free people of color in the United States and MEXICO.

James Polk was born on November 2, 1795, near Charlotte, NORTH CAROLINA. His father was a landowner who owned several slaves, but he was not part of the wealthy planter elite. Instead, Polk's ancestors were small farmers, descended from Scots-Irish immigrants who settled in the mountains of the Southern United States. Polk became quite wealthy in later years, owning plantations in both TENNESSEE and MISSISSIPPI. However, like his political patron and hero ANDREW JACKSON, he retained a class identity with small white farmers and immigrants. The leadership of Polk, Jackson, and the New Yorker MARTIN VAN BUREN helped create the Democratic Party coalition of poor Southern whites, Northern urban immigrants, and newly wealthy planters from the Lower South that made it politically powerful in the mid-19th century. Since much of the Democrats' political appeal resulted from populism, they tended to recognize and encourage white RACISM AND RACIAL PREJUDICE against nonwhites in both the North and the South. Polk was a supporter of the expansion of slavery in part because it was good for planters like himself, permitting expansion of COTTON CULTIVATION plantations to the west and south, but also because, he argued, it opened a road to wealth for working-class whites, who could only afford land and slaves if territorial expansion, and expansion of the area of the country open to slavery, kept them both cheap.

Polk won the presidency in 1844, succeeding his ally JOHN TYLER. He pledged to serve only one term and stressed territorial expansion as his principal policy objective. The first step in this process was to use a combination of threats and clever negotiations to acquire the Oregon Territory, governed up until that point in a loose codominion with CANADA, a colony of Great Britain. The British government agreed to divide the territory at the 49th parallel, and Polk accepted, even though his original position had been "54-40 or fight," that is, that the northern border of the U.S. Oregon Territory should be at 54 degrees 40 minutes north, taking in most of what is today British Columbia. This turned out to be a good outcome for the free people of color of Oregon. When white settlers passed harsh antiblack laws in the 1840s, including the infamous "lash law" of 1845, which required that all free blacks be publicly whipped if they refused to leave the territory, British Columbia under its mixed-race governor SIR JAMES DOUGLAS offered a refuge, and thousands of western blacks moved there.

The next step in Polk's territorial expansion scheme was to firm up his predecessor Tyler's agreement to annex TEXAS. Overcoming French and British attempts to mediate between Texas and Mexico, Democrats in Texas gained public support for annexation, and Texas joined the Union as a state in December 1845. The border between Mexico and Texas had never been determined, and this uncertainty was to lead to war, but first Polk made another effort to expand the country by attempting to purchase CUBA from SPAIN. Many American investors owned plantations in Cuba. Cuba had continued an illegal slave trade into the 1840s, and in addition, the CREOLE slave population was growing naturally, so there were plenty of slaves in Cuba who could potentially be reexported to the United States if Cuba joined the Union. The island was one of the world's largest areas of SUGAR CULTIVATION and also a major exporter of tobacco. Polk's diplomats were empowered to offer up to $100 million for the island, but the Spanish government refused, and Polk did not feel strong enough to threaten war. American acquisition of Cuba would certainly have meant hardship for the island's large free colored population. Under Spanish rule, they had almost equal economic rights with whites and significant civil and social rights. They were becoming politically active and would play an important role in the long independence struggle of the late 19th century.

The final and most controversial step in Polk's expansionist agenda was the conquest of northwestern Mexico. CALIFORNIA had attracted a significant number of American settlers, both white and black, by 1845. The military officer John Frémont (1813–90) had led an exploratory mission to California, and he encouraged the American settlers there to rebel against Mexico. At the same time, Polk had sent troops into the disputed region along the Texas-Mexico border, and they clashed with Mexican army units. There was considerable opposition to the war, especially in the Northern states. Congress was slow to respond to Polk's demand for a declaration of war but ultimately, on May 13, 1846, declared what became known as the MEXICAN-AMERICAN WAR. Fighting lasted for two more years before the Americans subjugated the Mexicans and took what are now the Southwest and California and the disputed border region from Mexico. Mexican citizens in the occupied territory were supposed to be protected in their rights and property. Afro-Mexicans were often able to gain recognition as Mexican Americans rather than as blacks, giving them some protection against discrimination. However, for English-speaking free people of color in the captured territories, annexation was a step backward. Texas passed restrictions on free people of color similar to those elsewhere in the Lower South, limiting MANUMISSION, hindering free blacks' access to the courts, and requiring immigrant free blacks to post a large bond. California entered the Union as a free state in 1850 but passed laws hostile to free blacks including its own Fugitive Slave Act, which encouraged kidnapping and the transportation of blacks out of the state as slaves. Undoubtedly, the acquisition of these territories by the United States was a hardship to free people of color living there.

Polk fulfilled his pledge to serve only one term, leaving office in March 1849. While on a tour of the South, he contracted cholera and died on June 15, 1849. He was one of the most influential of pre–Civil War presidents, but his legacy is controversial. His expansionist policies had at their core the desire to expand the territory open to slavery. His success in expanding the territory of the country led to more than a decade of political controversy and finally to the American Civil War. His populism and democratic values only applied to white people. He was a man of his times, of course, and shared these characteristics with many other American leaders. He was an effective politician and helped build an institution, the Democratic Party, which survived the Civil War and played an important role in subjugating the newly freed slaves in the postwar era of RECONSTRUCTION IN THE UNITED STATES.

Stewart R. King

FURTHER READING

Borneman, Walter R. *Polk: The Man Who Transformed the Presidency and America*. New York: Random House, 2008.

Dusinberre, William. *Slavemaster President: The Double Career of James Polk*. New York: Oxford University Press, 2003.

Merry, Robert. *A Country of Vast Designs: James K. Polk, the Mexican War and the Conquest of the American Continent*. New York: Simon & Schuster, 2009.

PORT-AU-PRINCE

Founded in the 1740s, Port-au-Prince was the capital of the French colony of SAINT-DOMINGUE on the island of Hispaniola. It became the capital of Haiti when the country gained its independence in 1804 and has remained the capital ever since. In the late 18th century, when Saint-Domingue was the wealthiest colony in the French Empire, Port-au-Prince had the second-largest population of free people of color on Hispaniola. Of the city's population of 1,509 free civilian inhabitants in 1780, 587, or 39 percent, were free people of color, and 922 were white. The city also harbored a large population of slaves, ranging from 5,000 to 8,000, depending on the season, and as many as 2,000 soldiers and 2,500 sailors at any time. During the HAITIAN REVOLUTION (1791–1804), the city changed hands many times and was partially burned twice. The free colored inhabitants of the region were very active politically and formed their own political faction in the early stages of the revolution. ALEXANDRE SABÈS PÉTION, the postwar president of the Republic of Haiti, was a free man of color from Port-au-Prince, and it was he who concentrated the economic and political life of the new country in the city in the years after 1804.

Geography

Port-au-Prince is located where the northern slopes of Morne de l'Hôpital, one of the many mountains that make up the spine of the southern peninsula of the island of Hispaniola, meet the sea. To the north is the Plaine de la Cul de Sac, a rather dry plain spotted with saline lakes and marshes. To the east is the Spanish part of the island, today's DOMINICAN REPUBLIC. To the west and northwest is the Bay of Port-au-Prince, giving on to the Caribbean Sea. The harbor is quite large and protected by the Isle de la Gonâve, a large island. The port is somewhat exposed to winds from the west, but the most damaging storms in the Caribbean come from the south and east, and in those directions, Port-au-Prince is protected by mountains that reach more than 7,000 feet. There are some coral heads and difficult channels, but for the most part, it is an excellent port. However, direct sailings from Port-au-Prince to FRANCE were not common in the 18th century because they required a long beat to windward to round the northern tip of the island, and then a dangerous passage through the Bahamas. The port mostly received interisland shipping within the Caribbean. The produce of the hinterland of Port-au-Prince made its way by small boats to the city of CAP-FRANÇAIS/CAP-HAÏTIEN on the northern part of the island, where it was transshipped into large merchantmen for the Atlantic crossing. As a result, the Port-au-Prince commercial sector was weak in the 18th century.

The mountains often receive extremely heavy rains, and there are several rivers that make their way to the sea at or near the city. An especially fine spring rises just above the town, in the modern fashionable neighborhood of Turgeau, providing good clean drinking water. The mountains also produce a regular alternation of sea and land breezes, which make the heat more bearable and keep down mosquitoes. The city's location is relatively healthful and pleasant.

The site of modern Port-au-Prince was inhabited in precolonial times, and after the Spanish conquest in the early 1500s, a small port developed there. When the Spanish colony declined in the 17th century, the colonial government withdrew the garrison and the port was almost abandoned. When French settlers entered the region after 1650 and established the colony of Saint-Domingue, they built a city down the coast about 12 miles at Léogane, where the soils are more fertile. A rest camp for French buccaneers occupied the Turgeau spring site for many years in the early 17th century. Port-au-Prince was a rural district until the 1740s, however. Much of the land was still owned by the French government, but considerable parcels had been given to rather marginal tenants, including many free people of color. The farmers in the area either ran cattle on their land, selling salt beef and hides to plantations in more settled areas, or grew small amounts of foodstuffs. (*See also* PROVISION GROUND FARMING and RANCHING.)

Founding of the City

In 1740, the French Ministry of Marine, the agency responsible for governing the colonies, decided to establish a new colonial capital. They wanted a location that was more central than Cap-Français, the old capital, and they wanted to encourage development of SUGAR CULTIVATION in the Plaine de la Cul de Sac. The city was founded, thus, by government fiat rather than natural growth, and government became and remains its most important business.

The city was laid out on a strict grid pattern of streets, and there was a careful allocation of space. Central lots were reserved for the wealthy, while poorer and less influential persons were forced to live on the outskirts. Many free people of color were allocated lots in areas south and east up the hill from the main square by the cathedral, but as the city grew in that direction, these lots turned out to be very valuable, and many early free colored settlers made substantial fortunes in land speculation. The hinterland of the city also flourished, as investments in waterworks allowed the rather dry land in the Plaine de la Cul de Sac to be irrigated. With water, these areas proved to be very productive, and soon sugar cultivation began to produce enormous profits. Sugar cultivation requires large capital investment, especially if irrigation is needed, and most free colored people did not have the resources to make a profit as planters, but they were able to sell their meat, hides, and food crops in a better market or work as professional managers for the white planters.

At the same time, COFFEE CULTIVATION began in the colony, and the heights to the south of the city proved ideal for this crop. The mountains were home to substantial populations of MAROONS, or RUNAWAY SLAVES, but the MILITIA and rural POLICE suppressed many maroon bands, and the government came to terms with the more stubborn ones. Many of the militia sergeants and rural police constables, most of whom were free men of color, took up land in the mountains and became coffee planters. Sugar and coffee made Saint-Domingue the wealthiest colony in the Americas and in the French Empire.

In 1751, a great earthquake devastated the new city, but the colonial government rushed in money to help with rebuilding. Port-au-Prince required many important public buildings consonant with its status as the capital of France's wealthiest colony. The growing prosperity of the sugar plantations and the beginnings of coffee cultivation also meant that there was plenty of private money to redevelop. The earthquake caused many stone buildings to collapse, crushing their inhabitants, so when rebuilding the city, the inhabitants primarily used wooden construction. Port-au-Prince is known to this day for its exceptionally beautiful "gingerbread" wooden architecture, used in public as well as private buildings.

The Free People of Color under Colonial Rule
The city grew rapidly despite the setback, and by 1780, its population exceeded 10,000, and about 40 percent of the free inhabitants were free people of color, making this city the second-largest concentration of free coloreds in the colony after Cap-Français. The urban population of Port-au-Prince was not as wealthy as that of Cap-Français. The commercial sector of the city's economy was weak, offering fewer opportunities for free colored businesspeople. Real estate speculation was the foundation of many free colored fortunes in Port-au-Prince, as it was in Cap-Français, but in the capital the real estate market was driven more by government decision making and less by the more predictable needs of the marketplace. There

was a certain amount of cronyism in all sectors of the old regime French economy, but this was more marked in the government sphere.

Nonetheless, there were opportunities for enterprising free people of color, and some of the region's inhabitants were among the wealthiest free colored planters in the colony. The Turgeau family, descended from the French buccaneer who gave his name to the spring, but entirely mixed-race by the 1780s, owned hundreds of acres planted in coffee bushes and foodstuffs. The Barbancourt family, with a white patriarch still living alongside his free colored wife and children, owned almost 100 acres of sugarcane in the plain as well as some coffee properties higher up. Their descendants still produce fine rum in the mountains behind Port-au-Prince.

As in Cap-Français and throughout the Caribbean plantation colonies, the urban and rural populations of free people of color in the Port-au-Prince area were quite different. The countryside had planters like the Turgeau and Barbancourt families, similar to the wealthy northern planters. In addition, and unlike the Cap-Français region, there was a fairly large free colored peasantry in the West. There were large areas near Port-au-Prince that had only recently been settled, or reclaimed from maroon bands, and the now-pacified maroons and other liminal blacks—recent runaways, poor freed people, ambitious would-be coffee planters—established small farms in these areas. In the city, there was a population of free ARTISANS, as in Cap-Français, but this group was less self-aware and confident than in the northern capital. As a result, the free colored population in the Port-au-Prince region was less internally divided. Free blacks and free people of mixed race were more likely to intermarry. There were fewer blacks-only or mixed-race-only militia companies and more mixed units. When the Haitian Revolution began in 1791, the free people of Port-au-Prince were less likely to find themselves on different sides.

Port-au-Prince's Free People of Color during the Revolution
The FRENCH REVOLUTION began in 1789 as a struggle among the French king Louis XVI, his nobles, and the non-noble middle class. The problems of colonial people and even the rural poor in France were not really taken into consideration until rebellions in those places called them to the attention of the central government. A delegation of free people of color from the southern and western parts of the colony, led by JULIEN RAIMOND, had gone to plead with the royal government for more rights for free coloreds in 1787, and the minister of marine had promised reforms. Prompted by this free colored civil rights campaign, the French revolutionaries debated the question of

race relations and slavery but did not reach any conclusion until events in the colonies overtook them.

The Haitian Revolution spared Port-au-Prince at first. The free colored uprising in the North did not attract much support around the capital in the West at first. The great slave uprising of 1791 was confined to the northern plain around Cap-Français. But war did come to Port-au-Prince. The first outbreak of violence was between whites in 1791, as the colonial assembly, controlled by white craftsmen and plantation managers who thought of themselves as the revolutionary "third estate," as did the middle-class faction back home in France, fought the governor's troops. The assembly was ultimately dissolved, but not before changing the name of the city temporarily to Port Républicain. Most of its members were driven into exile, and the city was governed by supporters of the king. Free people of color in the area tended to support the government, because the poor whites had shown RACISM AND RACIAL PREJUDICE toward them, and there had been a number of incidents of mob violence and even LYNCHING in response to the free coloreds' civil rights campaign. Free coloreds thought they had more to gain from the king than from the revolutionary process, which, at least in their immediate experience, did not see people of color as citizens with rights. Poorer free people of color were more likely to support the slave rebels, however, just as in the North Province.

Late in 1791, however, the revolution finally spread to the Port-au-Prince area, and for the rest of the decade-long struggle, Port-au-Prince was deeply involved. Free colored activists in the hill town of Mirebalais, to the north of the city, formed an assembly and demanded civil rights. When the radical white-controlled city government in Port-au-Prince refused, they took up arms. Unlike VINCENT OGÉ in the North Province, the Mirebalais free coloreds were not too proud to arm slaves, and they allied themselves with a group of slave rebels called the "Swiss" after the French king's elite mercenary guards. The Swiss and the Mirebalais free coloreds defeated the Port-au-Prince forces in battle in the field and besieged the city. Léger-Félicité Sonthonax and his colleagues, the first civil commissioners appointed in Paris by the National Assembly that now ruled France, arrived in the colony in Cap-Français in December 1792 and imposed a new, more radical revolutionary policy. Sonthonax's initial focus was on civil rights for free people of color, which the National Assembly had decreed in April 1792. The powerful whites of the colony opposed almost everything Sonthonax wanted to do, and their resistance was strong in the West. Sonthonax allied himself with the Mirebalais free people of color and captured Port-au-Prince, but the area was always restive under his control. In one uprising in August 1793, royalist whites temporarily recaptured Port-au-Prince, and some 800 buildings were burned in a conflagration that broke out during the fighting.

British forces landed at Jérémie, at the tip of the southern peninsula, in fall 1793, and in June 1794, they landed at Port-au-Prince. After a short struggle, the French revolutionary forces abandoned the city and retreated to the mountains to the north and south. The British had royalist white émigrés with them and enlisted people of color in their army. For the most part, the British were content to hold the city and the surrounding sugar fields. They left the French revolutionary army, by this time headed by TOUSSAINT LOUVERTURE, leader of the slave rebels from the North who had rallied to the republican cause once the French abolished slavery, and ANDRÉ RIGAUD, leader of the free people of color of the South and West, to hold the mountains and the interior. This was the time-honored strategy used to deal with the maroon threat. But Toussaint and Rigaud were not maroon chieftains trying to preserve their lifestyle in a remote camp: They were revolutionaries trying to remake a whole society. They held military officers' commissions from the French government, and they had a mission to drive the enemies of France from the soil of its most valuable colony. The French forces carried out guerrilla war against the British occupiers while consolidating their control over those parts of the colony that remained unoccupied. In the area around Port-au-Prince, the remaining independent bands of slave rebels and free colored militiamen were incorporated in the national army. French forces still controlled the port of Jacmel, Rigaud's main base, just 25 miles from Port-au-Prince over the mountains. Privateers based in Jacmel attacked British shipping, and neutral ships from the United States could dock there, buying sugar and coffee and selling needed supplies.

French attacks in the Port-au-Prince region devastated agriculture in the plains, particularly focusing on the destruction of irrigation infrastructure, much of it located in the mountains, where they were masters. The destruction of the sugar plantations was further accelerated by the attrition of their labor force, as both sides recruited slaves into their armies while other slaves ran away to live quietly in the hills. The British had hoped that their occupation would pay for itself by exploiting the rich resources of the plains, but in fact they needed continual resupply and reinforcement from Britain. In the end, the Saint-Domingue expedition was more costly to the British government, both in monetary terms and in terms of lives lost, than Wellington's campaign in Spain (1808–14).

Finally, in 1798, the British withdrew. As they left Port-au-Prince, Rigaud and Toussaint began to fight over the spoils. Toussaint's general in the West, Jean-Jacques Dessalines, seized the city, but outlying areas to the South, including the cities of Léogane, Grand Gôave, and Petit Gôave, were in dispute. Fruitless negotiations ended in a sudden outburst of violence in which the pro-Dessalines garrison of Petit Gôave was slaughtered to the last man by Rigaud's forces. Once again, fighting damaged the infrastructure that permitted the prosperity of the region, this time in the plains extending southward from the city. The "War of the Knives," as it was called, lasted a year and ended when Rigaud's forces were driven out of Jacmel. Dessalines then methodically slaughtered the wealthy free people of color of the South Province, killing between 2,000 and 10,000 people over a period of a week in March 1800. The city of Port-au-Prince was not directly affected by this massacre, but many refugees fled there because the garrison was not under Dessalines's command, and they hoped they would be protected.

The last stage of the revolution was the arrival of the military expedition under Charles-Victor-Emmanuel Leclerc (1772–1802), Napoléon Bonaparte's brother-in-law. This French force took control of the colony fairly rapidly, as most of Toussaint's forces did not put up much resistance. The garrison of Port-au-Prince evacuated the city and joined with Toussaint in his defense of the interior. Unlike the British, Leclerc was not content to sit in the cities, and he had the support of many soldiers of color, including Rigaud and his talented subordinate, Alexandre Sabès Pétion, a native of Port-au-Prince. Toussaint's forces were pursued, brought to battle, and, after a tough fight, defeated. Toussaint was ultimately arrested and sent to prison in France, where he died. In Port-au-Prince, conditions seemed calm at first. But Leclerc's black soldiers, including especially Pétion, grew more and more aware of Leclerc's ultimate objective: the reestablishment of slavery and white supremacy. Pétion conspired with his old adversary Dessalines, the northern leader Henry Christophe, and other black generals and launched a second uprising in 1802.

The chieftains met at Archaïe, on the coast north of Port-au-Prince, on November 2, 1802, and agreed that their goal would be independence. On the same day, Leclerc died of yellow fever. He was followed in death by a majority of the French soldiers, leaving the French army dependent on its few remaining loyal black soldiers, mostly prerevolutionary free people of color still hoping for a revival of the old system, but with equal rights for them. The new commander, Rochambeau, still held the major cities, but the Haitian forces dug in for sieges. The siege of Port-au-Prince lasted until June 1803, when tens of thousands of reinforcements landed from Europe, and the Haitians withdrew once again into the mountains. The new French reinforcements rapidly followed their predecessors into the hospitals and graveyards, thanks to the difficult disease environment of the colony. In addi-

tion, many of the reinforcements sent to Port-au-Prince were not French but from other parts of the empire and were not very enthusiastic. A group of as many as a few hundred Polish soldiers actually defected and joined the Haitian side, where they were welcomed and made much of. Their descendants still live in a pair of mountain villages northwest of Port-au-Prince. These were the last reinforcements that Rochambeau was to receive, as France and Britain went to war in May 1803, and British fleets rapidly blockaded the few ports the French still controlled on the island.

Pétion captured Port-au-Prince from its French garrison in September 1803, seizing the fortress and rest camp near the town that now bears his name, Pétionville, in the hills overlooking the city, and then allowing the garrison and a few loyal civilians to surrender to the British and depart on their ships. The final act of the War of Independence took place to the North, at Vertières, in November 1803, on the outskirts of Cap-Français.

Aftermath

On January 1, 1804, Dessalines became "governor-general for life" of Haiti and in September became the nation's first emperor, a title he took to emulate Napoléon and to ensure that everyone understood that Haiti intended to be sovereign. The ruthlessness he had learned during the terrible years of war did not desert him as peace arrived. When he took Cap-Français, he changed its name to Cap-Haïtien and decreed that no whites were to live there. Most had already left, but the majority of those who were still there were marched out to the graveyard and slaughtered. In Port-au-Prince, which Dessalines gave back its prerevolutionary name after the French radicals who had called it Port Républicain were gone, potential victims went into hiding. But the military commander of Port-au-Prince was Pétion, and he had no intention of massacring anyone. There were no mass killings in Port-au-Prince.

Dessalines did not target people of mixed race as a class. In fact, his stated policy was to seek racial reconciliation between mixed-race and black and between prewar free people of color and former slaves. However, his behavior during the War of the Knives and his open suspicion of wealthy landowners led many of those who had been planters and merchants before the revolution to seek refuge in Port-au-Prince. Dessalines finally fell victim to a military plot led by Pétion and Christophe. He was murdered October 17, 1806, at Pont-Rouge, the northern gate of the city.

Christophe and Pétion immediately began to fight, and Christophe retreated to his northern stronghold. Soon, a de facto partition of the country left the Republic of Haiti, in the South and West, to Pétion, with his capital at Port-au-Prince. While Christophe tried to reestablish plantation agriculture with wage labor for sugar workers in his northern Kingdom of Haiti, Pétion distributed state lands in small plots to his former soldiers and concentrated the economic activity of the country in the capital. Port-au-Prince grew, and after the reunification of the country under Pétion's successor, JEAN-PIERRE BOYER, in 1820, it became the cultural and economic heart of the entire country. Before the 2010 earthquake, wealth and economic opportunity were so concentrated in Port-au-Prince that it was often referred to as a different country, the Republic of Port-au-Prince, as if one had to cross a border to go to the rest of Haiti. The surviving descendants of the great prerevolutionary free families of color are mostly to be found in Port-au-Prince as the country's educational and economic leaders.

Stewart R. King

FURTHER READING

King, Stewart R. *Blue Coat or Powdered Wig: Free People of Color in Pre-Revolutionary Saint-Domingue.* Athens: University of Georgia Press, 2001.

Nicholls, David. *From Dessalines to Duvalier: Race, Colour, and National Independence in Haiti.* New Brunswick, N.J.: Rutgers University Press, 1995.

Trouble, Michel-Rolph. *Haiti: State against Nation: The Origins and Legacy of Duvalierism.* New York: Monthly Review, 1989.

PORTUGAL

Portugal is located on the southwestern tip of the continent of Europe, along the Atlantic coast of the Iberian Peninsula. The northern and central part of the country is mountainous, with broad river valleys providing good farmland. An enormous natural harbor at the mouth of the Tejo River is the site of the capital and largest city, Lisbon. The southern part of the country is largely plains, and the climate in this region is marginally suitable for plantation cultivation of tropical produce. To the north and east lies SPAIN, which ruled Portugal during parts of the last millennium.

Medieval Period (868–1415)

The Iberian Peninsula was conquered in the early 700s by Muslim Africans who crossed the Straits of Gibraltar and occupied most of the peninsula. All the area that is now Portugal was under the rule of the Muslim Moorish caliph by the year 800. In 868, Count Vímana Peres (820–73) captured the Douro River valley from the Moors and established the County of Portugal, with its capital at Oporto. The country was nominally a part of the Kingdom of León, based in Galicia in what is now Spain. The counts of Portugal were effectively independent from the

1000s on, and in 1128, the country gained full independence. Over the next century, the Portuguese conquered the remainder of what now constitutes the national territory from the Moors. The final territory to be captured was the Algarve, the southern plains, in 1249–50. This region was already home to large slave-worked plantations when the Portuguese gained control of it, and they continued to operate those plantations using slaves captured or bought from the Moors. The kings of Portugal also forged close relationships with Italian merchants, benefiting from their contacts with the Ottoman Empire and access to Asian trade routes to import crops and techniques. The Algarve was an important source of SUGAR CULTIVATION for the European market from the 1300s on.

Medieval Portugal was, like neighboring Spain, a multireligious, multiethnic society. The national religion was Catholic Christianity (*see also* ROMAN CATHOLIC CHURCH), but substantial Muslim and Jewish minority populations were present (*see also* ISLAM). Many of the people of African descent living in Portugal during the 15th century were either Muslims or recent converts to Christianity. Only members of the Catholic faith could hold high positions in society, but the minority religions did not suffer under the very severe discrimination that was found in neighboring Spain. Spain developed religious discrimination because Moors and their Jewish allies were threats to security—a Moorish state existed in southern Spain until 1492. Portugal did not have this security threat to worry about and could preserve a more tolerant society. Even in the 17th century, when the two countries were temporarily united and the Spanish Inquisition pursued Muslims and Jews, the Portuguese were more tolerant of diversity than the Spanish and the Inquisition much less effective there.

Portuguese tolerance for religious diversity also extended to a tolerance for ethnic and racial diversity. In any medieval society, ancestry was all-important. Descent from aristocrats who arrived with the conquerors from Léon was the most important criterion for social advancement. Legitimate descent was best, but children born in informal unions who were recognized by their fathers were not at a great disadvantage. People who had Portuguese fathers and Moorish or African mothers could rise in society, and influential people of mixed race could gain recognition as whites much more easily in Portugal than in any other European society (*see also* "WHITENING" AND RACIAL PROMOTION).

Age of Discovery (1415–1640)

Portugal began to explore the Atlantic Ocean intensively in the reign of John I (1358–1433, r. 1385–1433). The Moors still opposed them, carrying out raids on the Iberian coast and maintaining enclaves in Spain.

On the other side of the Muslim-controlled territory, in central Africa, there might be enemies of the Muslims who could be allies for the Portuguese. Beyond Africa lay the Indian Ocean, source of spices and home to great non-Muslim empires. John's youngest son, Henry the Navigator (1394–1460), established a school for navigators and gathered all the information known in Europe at the time about the world's oceans. He sponsored voyages down the coast of Africa and into the open ocean. Portuguese navigators explored the Madeira Islands (1420), the Azores (1427), SENEGAMBIA (1444), the Cape Verde Islands (1456), São Tomé Island (1458), and finally the Cape of Good Hope at the southern end of Africa in 1490. As the Portuguese ships moved south along the coast of Africa, they entered into contact with African kingdoms. These kingdoms were eager to trade for goods the Portuguese offered, especially when the Portuguese explorers finally reached India in 1498 and had a consistent supply of Asian goods to sell. The Africans had gold to spend—there are extensive deposits in modern Ghana, Guinea, and Mali—but one commodity that became increasingly important was slaves. The Kingdom of Kongo in modern Angola (see CONGO AND ANGOLA) was expanding rapidly in the late 15th century and was friendly to the Portuguese. King Nzinga a Nkuwu was baptized in 1491, taking the name João in honor of King John of Portugal. Congo took many prisoners in its wars of expansion, and those who could not be incorporated in Congo's economy were often sold to the foreigners. Portugal imported slaves to expand plantations in the Algarve throughout the 15th century. By 1550, as much as 10 percent of the population of Portugal had some African ancestry, counting both the descendants of the medieval Moors and the newcomers. Although many of these were slaves working in the Algarve, there were thousands of free people of color. Portugal had no formal census at the time, and city records give only a fragmentary view of the size of the population since they record only citizens—those who owned enough property or paid enough taxes to have some privileges. Portugal also developed plantation colonies on the Atlantic islands it discovered. São Tomé became the Western world's largest sugar producer in 1500. These colonies also employed many slaves, and some of them became free. Portugal also established valuable colonies in Asia, such as Goa in India, Malacca, and Timor, and by the 16th century had become a global empire. The ships carrying goods and slaves around the Portuguese empire often employed black sailors. Towns where Portuguese ships traded, from Europe to East Asia, gained African-descended populations as sailors took temporary partners and fathered children or left the sea and settled.

One of the secrets of successful navigation of the African coast that Henry's navigators discovered was that strong northward currents made travel directly down the coast very difficult south of the equator. Going far out to sea, ships could pick up south-flowing currents that would speed them on their way toward the southern tip of Africa. Going north, as a ship passed the equator, it was best to go far out to sea to pick up northeast-flowing winds and currents. Some of these ships probably sighted the coast of South America in the late 15th century, though the first expedition to the continent did not arrive until 1500, when a fleet led by Pedro Álvares Cabral landed in BRAZIL. For the first 50 years of Portuguese presence in the new colony, Brazil was merely a resupply base for ships traveling between the Indian Ocean and Europe. Small groups of colonists, divided into more than a dozen small colonies, produced food and traded with the Indians for small cargoes to send back to Portugal. But demand for sugar in Europe outstripped the productive capacity of the Portuguese Atlantic islands by the mid-1500s. The Brazilian colony of Pernambuco began sugar cultivation in 1542. At first, the labor force was almost entirely composed of Indian slaves, but as Indian populations declined, the labor shortage led the colonial leaders to turn to more expensive African slaves. Portugal played a major role in establishing and creating the transatlantic slave trade, and by 1600, the same process that had already transformed the Algarve and the Atlantic islands took place in northeastern Brazil: A large population of enslaved people of African descent was under the supervision of a small group of free people, some wholly European but many—a majority in some Brazilian states—of wholly or partially African ancestry. Free people of color filled many roles in society, from laborers to powerful and wealthy planters and businessmen. The wealthy were free to travel to Portugal, and many did. They took slaves and free colored employees with them, further enlarging the free colored population of the mother country.

From 1580 to 1640, Portugal was under Spanish rule. Spain was involved in a global war at the time, and among its enemies were BRITAIN and the Netherlands. Dutch invaders seized northern Brazil and many of Portugal's African and Asian bases. The Brazilians were able to drive out the invaders, thanks to the vigorous support of Brazil's free people of color, who quickly realized that the northern Europeans were much less tolerant of racial diversity than the Portuguese. The resistance to the invaders helped forge a unified Brazilian consciousness. In turn, Portugal focused its colonial efforts much more intensely on the development of Brazil. Gold was discovered in the southern part of the country in the 1670s, leading to a rapid expansion of settlement in that region. Brazil was a slave society in the sense that most productive work was done by slaves. Some free people were small farmers or ARTISANS, but generally whites and the large free colored population directed the work of slaves.

Mature Colonial Period and Revolution (1640–1821)

As was the case with Spain, Portugal became increasingly weak and peripheral in European affairs after the mid-17th century. Many colonies had been lost to the Dutch. Portuguese dominance of Indian Ocean trade was lost forever. A terrible earthquake in 1755 destroyed Lisbon, the capital, and caused economic disruption throughout the empire. The one global market the Portuguese still played an important role in during the late 18th and early 19th centuries was the Atlantic slave trade, though in the course of the 18th century, British competitors passed them in total numbers of people carried. Portuguese merchants controlled the interface between slave shippers and African sellers at the ports on the African coast. In many cases, these were people of partially African and partially Portuguese ancestry, who considered themselves Portuguese (see also SLAVE COAST, BENIN, AND THE BIGHT OF BIAFRA). Even in colonies under the formal rule of other countries, these Portuguese-descended merchant families played an indispensable role facilitating the trade. Brazil was by far the most important remaining Portuguese colony, with a larger economy and population than Portugal and the rest of the empire combined, and the other territories focused on serving its needs.

In an attempt to revive the fortunes of the country, the marquis de Pombal (1699–1782), prime minister from 1750 to 1777, initiated a series of reforms in government and society. Many of these reforms were progressive, including an expansion in public education, technological modernization in manufacturing and transportation, and increased efficiency and transparency in the courts and government. Portugal abolished slavery in the home country and in its Asian colonies in 1761. But the reforms also strengthened social and racial divisions. As in other European countries that abolished slavery, regulations formalizing special statuses for people of color were enacted at this time. Portugal's small black population gained freedom but suffered under discriminatory laws, and the result was that over a period of several generations, they began to assimilate into the white majority. The effect of the Pombaline Reforms on the colonies was dramatic, however. The similar Bourbon Reforms in Spanish America were even more transformative, but the effect in Brazil was similar. Middle-class free people of color in Brazil saw avenues of social advancement closed. They began to see the relationship with Portugal as harmful for their country and for themselves personally.

At the same time, the fundamental weakness of Portugal and its dependence on Brazil did not disappear.

As Napoléon Bonaparte's armies overran Portugal in 1807, Brazil became the center of the empire. Queen Maria (1734–1816) and Prince-Regnant João de Brangança (1767–1826, later to rule as João VI, 1816–26) moved the imperial capital from Lisbon to Rio de Janeiro, Brazil. From 1807 until 1822, the empire was administered from Brazil. Brazilians became accustomed to being essentially no longer a colony but instead the capital of an empire. In 1821, a liberal army revolt broke out in Portugal. A revolutionary legislature met, wrote a constitution for the united kingdom, and insisted that King João return to Portugal. The empire was henceforth to be ruled from Lisbon, as a centralized state, with the colonies granted some freedoms but in a subordinate position to the mother country. King João left his son, Prince Pedro de Alcantara (1798–1834), to administer Brazil. The young Prince Pedro I had liberal sympathies but also supported the unity and autonomy of Brazil. When the revolutionaries back in Lisbon tried to impose the new order by force, Pedro led the Brazilians in rebellion. A complex series of political maneuvers and some fighting over the following five years resulted in full independence for Brazil as an empire, under the rule of Pedro, who was succeeded by his son, Dom PEDRO II. The liberal revolutionaries in Portugal and the rebels in Brazil both enjoyed broad support among free people of color. Essentially, they had similar ideas about equality and progress.

Aftermath

After the independence of Brazil, Portugal continued to rule a number of colonies in Africa. Angola, in particular, became quite prosperous, as the slave trade with Brazil continued into the 1850s. The free colored merchants of Angola had close relations with their counterparts in Brazil and little connection to Portugal. Some did travel to Portugal for education or other purposes. Portuguese African subjects continued to work as merchant seamen, and some did settle in the mother country. However, the decline of Portugal's globe-spanning commercial empire meant that fewer and fewer new people of color went to Portugal. Intermarriage and consequent whitening meant a decline in the number of people identified as free people of color in Portugal, starting at the end of the 17th century. By the early 19th century, residents of the southern part of the country might well sometimes have African-looking features, but they were almost all considered white. The population of Portugal today has a small number of people identified as blacks, mostly recent immigrants from sub-Saharan Africa and their descendants. However, at least 7 percent of all Portuguese carry a genetic marker indicating that they have female ancestors from sub-Saharan Africa.

Portugal's generally more tolerant attitude toward diversity of all kinds had a profound impact on the lives of free people of color. Throughout the Portuguese empire, during the colonial period, free people of color generally found less discrimination and more opportunity than were prevalent in other countries' colonies. In Portugal itself, tolerance of INTERRACIAL MARRIAGE, the end of slavery, and a decline in immigration of people of color led to the disappearance of free people of color as a distinct group.

Stewart R. King

FURTHER READING

Miller, Joseph C. *Way of Death: Merchant Capitalism and the Angolan Slave Trade, 1730–1830.* Madison: University of Wisconsin Press, 1996.

Nafafe, José Lingna. *Colonial Encounters: Issues of Culture, Hybridity and Creolisation, Portuguese Mercantile Settlers in West Africa.* Bern: Peter Lang, 2007.

Naro, Nancy Priscilla. *Cultures of the Lusophone Black Atlantic.* Studies of the Americas. New York: Palgrave Macmillan, 2007.

Saunders, A. C. de C. M. *A Social History of Black Slaves and Freedmen in Portugal, 1441–1555.* Cambridge: Cambridge University Press, 2010.

PROSTITUTES AND COURTESANS

Providing sexual services in exchange for pay is a common resort for poor women. In the slave societies of the Americas, these services were often provided by free women of color. Their services were in great demand for a number of social, cultural, and demographic reasons, and there was little competition in this line of work from slaves or white women. Simple fee-for-service arrangements, prostitution properly so called, were quite common, but many women and men aspired to longer-term relationships. These relationships may or may not have been to some degree commercial transactions, but society often saw almost any woman of color in a relationship with a white man as a paid courtesan. This social prejudice colored public attitudes toward all women of color throughout the Americas even after the end of the era of slavery.

In most places in the Americas, except the United States, wherever there were many slaves and free people of color, white women were uncommon. In the tropical plantation zones, a significant proportion of the white population, in some areas a majority, were European-born young men. These men either were single or immigrated without their wives and families in order to work as plantation managers, skilled craftsmen, government officials, or soldiers. As with young men everywhere, these men were not strongly constrained by their culture's prevailing sexual mores. This was especially true in the absence of the white female relatives, wives and mothers, who would normally be the enforcers of cultural values. So they were looking for sexual outlet. They were interested in sex with women of color, both because white women were unavailable and because there was a cultural stereotype that women of color were both sexually interested and naturally more pleasurable sexual partners. (*See* GENDER ATTITUDES.)

The easiest target for men of the master class interested in sex with women of color would have been the slave population. Certainly the most celebrated relationships between white men and women of color were with slave women, like that between THOMAS JEFFERSON and his slave Sally Hemings (*see* HEMINGS, SALLY, CHILDREN OF). However, there were reasons why making sexual advances on a slave might not be the best solution. Men without slaves, of course, did not have the option, or at least had to resort to other people's slaves with attendant cost or risk of giving offense to another, more powerful white. In many cases, SLAVE OWNERS represented a minority of the white population. Even for those with potential targets among their own slaves, the disruption caused to normal family and community life among their slaves by their sexual predation and the consequent loss of productivity, in addition to damage to their reputation among their peers that might result from a scandal, were enough to deter them. One who was not deterred was Thomas Thistlewood (1721–86), a British plantation manager in JAMAICA who kept detailed records of his sexual molestation of his employer's and neighbors' slaves. But Thistlewood was roundly condemned by his neighbors, not for being brutal per se, which they considered normal and even desirable, but for damaging their property and being too obvious about breaking the color line. And even Thistlewood generally had sex with women in exchange for money rather than coercing slaves. Finally, a man who, unlike Thistlewood and many of his Jamaican white peers, had a white woman present in the household to exercise moral restraint might often find that keeping his informal sexual behavior outside the home was better for family harmony. Some prostitutes *were* slaves, owned by keepers of houses of prostitution. This was a particularly brutal business with masters regularly searching and taking money from their slaves. Nonetheless, as did any slaves who worked around valuable objects or worked directly for free people who were not their masters, they often found a way to get money. Stealing the customers' property or getting cash tips were two possible sources of funds that were open to them. These women could

Rachel Pringle, Proprietress of a Bridgetown Brothel, 1796, a caricature by the British artist Thomas Rowlandson. This image reflects the public image of free women of color as sexually provocative, disconnected from patriarchal norms, and contributing to the degeneracy of colonial white men. Pringle was born a slave in 1753, gained her freedom, and became the first free colored innkeeper in Barbados in the 1770s. She died a wealthy woman in 1793. *(The Bridgeman Art Library)*

frequently buy their freedom or find a way to escape (often with the aid of a client) after a relatively short though certainly unpleasant period of service. This form of slavery still exists today, and masters still find that the slaves can escape fairly rapidly once they acquire cultural knowledge.

We have referred consistently here to the behavior of white men. Of course, there were also free men of color who had property and who might have been interested in sexual relations with a variety of women. There is some evidence of prostitution in the United States that suggests that it, as with many other elements of American life, was racially segregated. Some prostitutes, women of color, were only for whites, while others were available to men of color. However, it was much less common for men of color to have long-term relationships with courtesans, probably because free populations of color were gender-balanced (or even skewed in favor of women), and thus, suggest a number of demographic surveys in different colonies, most adult free men of color were married. While Mediterranean cultures, under the influence of machismo, might have tolerated married men's having outside relationships or making occasional visits to prostitutes, even the loosest of cultural moral codes would have disapproved of married men's keeping paid courtesans. In fact, free men of color were more constrained by conventional morality than were white men, at least from the mid-18th century on. Church attendance, marriage rates, illegitimacy and fertility rates, and many other indices from many countries show that throughout the Americas the tighter moral codes of the 19th century arrived earlier among populations of color and held them much more tightly than they constrained white men.

Therefore, generally the customers for prostitutes and the men seeking long-term relationships with women who might be characterized as courtesans were overwhelmingly white. The women who were providing these services were generally free women of color. The relationships themselves, as already demonstrated, ran the gamut from simple fee-for-service contacts to long-term arrangements. The longer-term arrangements are the ones that actually caused the greater harm to the reputation of women of color in general, because they fed the cultural assumption that all relationships between white men and women of color were commercial in nature and that free people of color as a class owed their freedom and prosperity to the sexual misconduct of their women.

The complicated tangle of emotions and expectations that make up any relationship are hard enough for the participants to untangle, and in these cases, where there was such an imbalance of social standing and power between the parties, it is harder for observers either at the time or 200 years later to understand what was occurring. But this did not stop people at the time from making assumptions that were in general very prejudicial to people of color. The near-universal condemnation of these sorts of relationships and the tendency of white society to ascribe all or almost all informal sexual unions between white men and women of color to prostitution had a profound effect on gender attitudes toward free people of color.

Stewart R. King

FURTHER READING
Beckles, Hilary McD. *Centering Woman: Gender Discourses in Caribbean Slave Society.* New York: Markus Wiener, 1998.
——. "Freeing Slavery: Gender Paradigms in the Social History of Caribbean Slavery." In *Slavery, Freedom and Gender: The Dynamics of Caribbean Society,* edited by Brian L. Moore, B. W. Higman, Carl Campbell, and Patrick Bryan. 197–231. Mona: University of the West Indies Press, 2003.

LETTER FROM CHATEAUNEUF TO ROSETTE, FEBRUARY 22, 1782

This letter was sent on February 22, 1782, by a white planter named Chateauneuf to his housekeeper and presumed sexual partner, a free woman of color named Rosette. She lived on his plantation, near Port-au-Prince, Saint-Domingue (modern Haiti), and he was in the colony's commercial center of Cap-Français/Cap-Haïtien on an extended business trip. There was clearly an emotional connection between Chateauneuf and Rosette. He misses her and feels bereft that he has not received a letter from her. He knows her family, both her mother and some other relatives in Cap-Français. There is also a commercial connection. He is either selling or renting out some of her slaves, and her creditor is refusing to pay. He wants to make sure that she will get paid. The sum mentioned, 1,200 livres a year, would have been a modest though respectable salary for a professional plantation employee. So was Rosette a courtesan? The emotional content of the letter suggests that they were having a sexual relationship, and it is clear that he was giving her money. In any relationship between the sexes, especially one like this marked by an imbalance of social standing and education, the connection between the two will never be completely clear.

I do not recognize you my dear Rosette. Three mail deliveries have not seen a letter from you. Capes has given to me the buckles of Peter's shoes but no single letter from you, please let me know if you are ill. There doesn't appear to be any possibility that I will go at once to Port-au-Prince. I received a letter from Victoire Duvivier who made me some foolish propositions about the slaves. I replied to her letter and ordered her to give you back the slaves and to pay you what she owes on the rental. You will be able to find out how much she owes by means of the receipts that she has from me and what I have received over three years of the 1200 livres a year she owes. You will put these together with the four slaves coming from Saint Lucia and see monsieur Ponce to whom I will write so that he will do me the favor of putting them up for rent through the court. Get your money from Mamant [*sic*] Victoire and if she will not pay, then issue a summons for her. The money I gave you when I left Môle Saint-Nicolas must be gone by now. My intention was never to let you lack for anything. To tell you the truth, I didn't expect that my voyage would take so long. Here it is almost three months that I have been separated from you. It seems that Port-au-Prince amuses you since you don't have the time to write to me. From Cap, Mari Louise and Marie-jane greet you. Write to me, I beg you, if you have found your papers, because I cannot conceive what may have become of them. Give my best to your mother, Adieu . . . . three months

always the best of your friends,
(signed) Chateauneuf

Make sure to see Giliobel for me, I shall write to him a second time. Make sure he sends me what I asked him for.

Source: Archives Nationales Françaises, Centre des Archives d'Outremer, Notariat de Saint-Domingue, Vol. 876, power of attorney dated February 22, 1782, annex to act no. 163. Translation by Dominique Rogers, in Dominique Rogers and Stewart King, "Housekeepers, Merchants, *Rentières*: Free Women of Color in the Port Cities of Colonial Saint-Domingue, 1750–1790." In *Women in Port: Gendering Communities, Economies and Social Networks in Atlantic Port Cities, 1500–1800,* edited by Jodi Campbell and Douglas Catterall. Leiden: Brill, forthcoming.

PROTESTANT MAINLINE CHURCHES

The Protestant movement had not consistently opposed slavery from its foundation in the 16th century up to the late 18th century. However, at that time, some of the most forceful opponents of slavery, including most notably William Wilberforce (1759–1833) and his allies, had that religious perspective and clearly felt motivated by their faith. Wilberforce was part of a new movement in mainline Protestantism, called the evangelical movement, which ultimately became very important in the lives of people of color in the Americas and their struggle for justice. (*See also* BAPTISTS AND PIETISTS.) To understand this evolution of Protestantism and its attitude toward people of color, however, it is necessary to look back to the period before the beginning of the Protestant movement in the 16th century.

Christianity had been torn between two visions of mankind and the church ever since the time it became accepted as the official religion of the Roman Empire in the fourth century. The original Christian idea about human nature was summed up by the apostle Paul in his letters to the Galatians and Colossians when he told them that in Christ there was no free or slave, and no Jew or Greek—and thus that racial, ethnic, and status distinctions were meaningless between Christians. This radical egalitarianism was easier to practice when Christianity was countercultural, and indeed unlawful, but when Christianity became the official religion of the Roman Empire, it became harder. For one thing, to be Roman after 380 was to be Christian. Also, the Christian Church included everyone, including both masters and slaves, and because it was the official religion of the state, Christian leaders found it difficult to criticize the social order. After the fall of the Western Roman Empire in the 400s, the identity of state and religion became diluted. People could be Christians even though they served many different political leaders. Indeed, a common identity as Christians united Western Europeans and the few Eastern Christians who visited the remote and backward Western

Europe during the Middle Ages. Christianity underlay and supported feudalism, a social structure that was far from egalitarian but did include all orders of society in a common humanity and insisted on the mutual obligations of the different orders.

The Reformation (Sixteenth–Seventeenth Centuries)
This social structure was under siege in the early 1500s, however. The knightly class and the churches they supported were in a financial crisis due to both a long-term decline in feudal revenues and the rise of the business class of the cities. To fill the gap, the ROMAN CATHOLIC CHURCH had been looking for new sources of revenue in the new ways of the business class and of the bureaucratic royal governments that were springing up. These methods were extremely unpopular, especially with the rural poor. At the same time, the Catholic Church was giving unprecedented power to the rulers of Catholic countries to govern church affairs in their own way. As a result, the Catholic Churches in the various countries were becoming agents of the state and in some way diluting the ideal of universal humanity.

The Reformation that gave rise to Protestantism in the 16th century was sparked by the writings of Martin Luther (1483–1546), a German monk and university theologian who began by criticizing Catholic Church fund-raising methods. His criticisms went to the root of the Catholic idea of legitimate authority. One of Luther's most significant conclusions was that God had not authorized the church to have a universal authority over secular society as well as religious matters, as the Catholic Church had taught since the fall of the Western Roman Empire. Instead, God chose secular rulers who were "sovereign" over all matters within their own country, worldly as well as religious. This meant that the church structures that grew out of Luther's movement were closely tied to the state. As in the late Roman Empire, to be a member of the nation in a Lutheran country was to be a member of the national religion, and vice versa. Joining the national religion was tantamount to pledging allegiance to the state. In fact, Lutheran (and Lutheran-inspired) churches often included pledges of allegiance in their orders of services. In practice, similar ties between church and state grew up in Catholic Europe at the same time, especially in FRANCE, SPAIN, and PORTUGAL, the Catholic powers most involved in the colonization of the Americas. However, these Catholic countries observed the official Catholic teaching that all people were at least potentially Catholics and thus citizens. For the northwestern European countries with Lutheran churches, the identity of church, state, and nation meant that they were somewhat reluctant to accept converts from outside. Established in the 1530s and 1540s as England's King Henry VIII drew away from Catholicism, the Church of England, the state religion of England, while somewhat more Catholic in its theology and practice, shared this Lutheran idea of what the church was. To be a member of the Church of England was to be English, whereas people who followed variant faiths, such as Catholics and Separatist Puritans, were in some ways un-English. People who were not English ethnically but who lived in English territory were only permitted to become part of the church if they became English in their way of life at the same time. The Church of England maintained a creative ambiguity in its doctrines until the end of the 17th century, permitting people with predominantly Catholic beliefs, so long as they did not insist on the rule of the pope, and those with strong Calvinist beliefs, so long as they were willing to accept the authority of bishops and the king, to remain formally within the church. After the Glorious Revolution (1688–89), the Church of England began to fragment, with Calvinist believers instituting separate denominations.

A variant strand of Reformation thought arose from the writing and preaching of John Calvin (1500–64), a French legal scholar and theologian. Calvin accepted the arguments of Luther but went further in his definition of the church as really being composed only of those persons God has called to salvation, presumably a minority of all people in any society. Nobody sitting in a pew in a Calvinist church on Sunday could be sure that he or she was among the "elect" whom God would save, nor could he or she be sure that somebody outside, even somebody entirely different in race, nationality, class, or other characteristics, was *not* among the elect. Paradoxically, though Calvin limited the possible circle of those who could be part of the church even more than Luther had, he opened up the possibility that people from outside the nation could be among the saved. This potential did not actually cause many people of color to join Calvinist curches in the beginning, but ultimately Calvin's idea was to have profound effects on the inclusion of non-Europeans in Christianity. Calvin's ideas were popular among minority groups in Catholic Europe, such as the Huguenots in France and the Puritans in England, and dominant in only a few small corners of Europe: Switzerland, the Netherlands, and Scotland. Many of these were very wealthy groups or places, however, entrepreneurial populations who were involved in world COMMERCE AND TRADE and were shortly to launch the Industrial Revolution. Their entrepreneurial attitudes tended to exclude them from the traditional European social system, while Calvin taught them that their wealth and hard work were signs of God's favor of them. Calvinism's appeal to excluded minorities was also to be very important for populations of color in the Americas.

The most important Calvinist Churches in regard to the treatment of people of color in the Americas were the Dutch Reformed, the French Huguenots, the English Puritan, and the Scots Presbyterian. The Dutch Reformed Church was Calvinist; indeed, it was the touchstone for Calvinist orthodoxy, with the decisions of their Synod of Dort (1619) forming the fundamental theological creed of Calvinism. However, it was also a state church in the 17th century, and membership in the church in the colonial context functioned as a method of staking a claim to citizenship. Dutch cultural ideas about race were similar to those held by English and America: That is, from a relatively early moment, they saw race as an invariable characteristic of the person and thought of nonwhite races as inferior, but colonial subjects of other races who adopted the religion and culture of the Netherlands were nonetheless much better treated. They were not as insistent on a bivalued racial structure as were the British in North America, recognizing mixed-race groups as different from entirely nonwhite ones and typically granting them higher status. In general, however, Calvinists during the Reformation period made it difficult to take up church membership. One could not simply begin attending, perhaps with some sort of sacramental initiation through baptism that was open to everybody, as in Lutheran or Catholic Churches. Potential new members had to convince the current members of a church community that they were among the "elect" whom God had predestined for salvation before they were permitted to describe themselves as members. This acceptance often required adopting cultural characteristics such as Western clothing and Dutch language, family patterns, cultural tastes, and so on. But some free people of African ancestry did overcome this barrier. Most notable were the *baastards* or Cape Coloreds of South Africa, many of whom were people of mixed race who were descended from Dutch settlers and Khoi-San Africans.

The French Huguenot, or French Reformed Church, was a Calvinist movement that was very strong among urban merchants along France's Atlantic Coast. In fact, the major slave and colonial trade ports of La Rochelle, Nantes, and Bordeaux were all Huguenot strongholds during the 17th century. Not surprisingly, the French colonies in the Americas were first settled by people from these cities, many of them Huguenots, and the Calvinist idea became strong in France's Caribbean colonies. After King Louis XIV revoked the Edict of Nantes in 1685, making Protestantism at least theoretically unlawful in France, many Huguenots converted to Catholicism. However, the form of Catholicism that was dominant in France up until the 19th century was Jansenist and Gallican. Jansenism and its companion idea, Gallicanism, combined to strengthen the identity between nation and church in France in a way similar to what was found in northern European Protestant countries. The Catholic concept of universal humanity and an all-inclusive ordered hierarchy in society was associated with ultramontanism, or a belief in the supremacy of the pope over the king. The most powerful spokesmen for ultramontanism in France were the Jesuits, and it is not surprising that they were also the most energetic in evangelizing blacks and Indians in France's American colonies. Protestant Frenchmen and Catholic Frenchmen influenced by Protestant ideas were more likely to adopt a Dutch or English attitude to people of color, being unwilling to accept them as fully human unless they fully adopted French cultural ways and proved their faith in a difficult personal way.

The English and Scottish Calvinists, like the French, predominated in the cities and social groups most involved in relations between the British and people of color. The English merchant class had a disproportionate number of Puritans. London, England, the largest port in the slave and colonial trades, was an important center for Puritans. The largest groups of settlers to immigrate to the Americas in the 17th and 18th centuries were from Puritan eastern England and Presbyterian Scotland and Northern Ireland. Both groups had ideas about the relationships among state, nation, and church that were compromises between the Calvinist and state church ideas. Puritans were trying to remain inside the Church of England while purifying it of Catholic ideas. The Presbyterians were the state Church of Scotland. Both groups thus found it difficult to welcome members who were not British or to include people of color in the universe of people who were potentially Christian and thus fully human.

Protestants in the Americas (Sixteenth–Seventeenth Centuries)

For its first century, the Reformation was basically a European phenomenon, spreading primarily across the northern and western parts of the continent. Protestants lived in Germany, Scandinavia, the Low Countries, and Britain, and in scattered hunted groups in Catholic Europe. Europe's overseas expansion from the 1400s to 1600 was conducted chiefly by Catholics from Spain and Portugal. The early relationship between Europeans and Africans in the Americas did not include Protestants until the end of the 16th century. But at that time, Protestant colonies began to spring up in the Americas.

Protestant Frenchmen had established various short-lived colonies in the Americas that were generally homogeneous and poor. However, after the end of the French Wars of Religion in 1598, they were integrated into the general French colonization drive and played a role there out of proportion to their numbers at home. Many of the early French buccaneers, planters, and merchants were practicing Protestants, and others were recent converts from Huguenot families who continued to hold some Calvinist ideas through the Catholic Jansenist movement. The French colonists, as a result, had an easier time justifying the exclusion of people of color than did Catholics from Spain and Portugal. The French colonies became better organized by the end of the 17th century, however, after the Treaty of Ryswick (1685) gave France clear title to the Caribbean islands of Martinique, Guadeloupe, and SAINT-DOMINGUE. Colonial governors and royal edicts, including especially the CODE NOIR IN FRENCH LAW (1685), reaffirmed the Catholic identity of these colonies and stressed Catholic ideas about the inclusion of people of color who were properly Catholic in the social order. But the FRENCH CARIBBEAN colonies continued to have an ambiguous set of religious beliefs and equally ambiguous racial values throughout their existence.

The Dutch moved into the colonial game in a big way at the end of the 16th century, attacking Spanish interests in the Americas and conquering a number of Portuguese colonies during the 17th century. The Dutch learned about plantation slavery and SUGAR CULTIVATION from the Portuguese during their occupation of northern Brazil (1630–61). Their Brazilian plantations were inherited from the Portuguese, along with the system of labor organization and cultural attitudes, and often even the employees, both slave and free. Therefore, Dutch plantations were hardly distinguishable from Portuguese ones at first. When the Dutch were driven out, they took the concept of the plantation with them, transplanting it to British colonies in the Caribbean since they had no suitable territories for sugar growing. The Dutch had little time to work out how their religion and culture required them to treat people of color before they lost their role as major planters, but they nonetheless had a strong influence on British planters after them.

The Dutch taught the British about plantations and, in addition, influenced some elements of their national religious makeup and reaction to people of color. The British had their first big sugar colony in BARBADOS in the 17th century, and from there, the idea of the plantation mode of production spread throughout the English Caribbean, to British North America, and beyond. The British were responsible for creating a system of slavery that was compatible with Protestant ideas about the nature of humanity and the nation. At first, the British treated their African servants much the same as European indentured servants, requiring them to work for a set period of time and then freeing them. But fairly quickly, they decided, in a series of court cases and colonial legislative actions, that black people were different, that they were slaves for life, and that their children inherited their status.

Ultimately, the British evolved the legal term *chattel slavery* to express the concept that the slave was not a person under law but shared the status of a domestic animal, though as a matter of fact they never carried this concept to its natural conclusion, instead holding slaves responsible for their actions under the criminal law and at least theoretically regulating their treatment. This system was not fully developed until the 18th century, when a number of new ideas began to change the religious mind-set of Britons. One important element of this system was reluctance, even refusal, to extend the sacraments of the Church of England to slaves. In the end, the universal message of Christianity was strong enough that the Church of England had to accept people of color as members, though most colonies passed laws that made it clear that baptism did not make one free. This debate was to have important repercussions in the 18th century as the Protestant mainline churches began to reach out beyond their national constituencies.

The Enlightenment and the Evangelical Movement (Eighteenth–Nineteenth Centuries)

The Enlightenment was a very powerful movement in Europe, especially in Protestant Britain and the Netherlands. The central idea of the Enlightenment was, at least at first glance, a positive one from the point of view of people of color in the Americas. As THOMAS JEFFERSON of Virginia, one of the Enlightenment's key spokespeople, wrote in the Declaration of Independence in 1776, "All men are created equal, and endowed by their creator with certain unalienable rights, and that among these rights are life, liberty, and the pursuit of happiness." In short, arbitrary inborn distinctions between people were no longer acceptable, and every person had an inherent freedom to control his own body and make use of his own time for his own benefit. How was such a radical reimagining of the meaning of humanity to be made consistent with a social system based on slavery?

Northern European Protestants proposed several answers to that question. The first was the same one that many southern European Catholics used—denial of the ideas of the Enlightenment and a firmer attachment to what was seen as a divinely inspired social structure that placed slaves at the bottom. Of course, assigning slaves to the bottom meant at least that they had to be included, that they were not mere domestic animals with human shape. The conservative reaction to the Enlightenment had the paradoxical effect of encouraging paternalism toward slaves or at least a public pretense of paternalism. The proslavery ideology of American Southerners, and some British Caribbean SLAVE OWNERS, at least pretended to be arguing for the interests of the slaves as well as the masters. In this way, conservative Christian responses to the problem of slavery had the effect of including everyone in an imagined community that was hierarchical but at least had a place for the slave. These conservative arguments relied on scripture and Christian religious tradition for much of their ideological support. They often saw blacks as the descendants of Ham, cursed by Noah, or otherwise assigned them a lower position, but within the human family. Part of the paternalistic agenda of conservative defenders of slavery was the conversion of slaves to Christianity, and by including them in the church, they further buttressed an implicit claim by blacks to humanity and some form of citizenship. These paternalistic arguments were convincing enough that they made up a great deal of the antiabolition discourse in Britain in the 1820s and in the United States in the 1840s and 1850s.

The strongest current of the Enlightenment, however, was liberal and secular. Within a liberal, secular, modern state, slavery could only be tolerated if it could be shown to be temporary or scientifically based and, in any case, necessary for the greater good. During the 18th century, most Enlightenment liberals, including Jefferson and his fellow Virginian GEORGE WASHINGTON, thought that slavery would die out soon. Washington freed his slaves in his will and called on his fellow Virginia planters to do the same. Jefferson thought that Virginia would be better off without blacks of any condition and supported colonization schemes to send American blacks to live in Africa or the Caribbean (see AMERICAN COLONIZATION SOCIETY). Utilitarian arguments, that is, that slavery was no doubt bad for the slave but necessary for the improvement of the colonies and produced a greater good, were also an important part of the Enlightenment defense of slavery and figured in Jefferson's analysis of the situation in his *Notes on the State of Virginia* (1785). Importantly, while Washington was a member of the Episcopal Church, neither man was an orthodox Christian believer, a characteristic they shared with many slave owners and political leaders in the Protestant Americas at the time. They were Masons (see FREEMASONRY) and deists, who believed in a generally benevolent God but did not have conventional Christian ideas about the nature of humanity or the proper social order.

In fact, the ideological conviction that all human beings were fundamentally equal that Christianity had taught from its very beginning was under siege during the Enlightenment. New concepts suggested that humans originated in a number of different stocks; that each race was like a different species of animal. Under the banner of scientific racism, many scientists advanced these theories, further arguing that blacks were suited by biology to slavery or a subordinate position in society. Many northern Europeans subscribed to some variant of the idea of

multiple origins of mankind, called polygenesis, though some rooted it in scripture, pointing out that the book of Genesis in the Christian and Jewish Bibles has two stories of creation. For the religious polygenists, the first story told of the creation of nonwhites, while the second was the creation of whites. Only the progeny of Adam, the second creation, were subject, some argued, to the Fall of Man and the Redemption of Jesus. These conclusions were not orthodox according to the mainline Protestant denominations, but these denominations and their centralized teaching authority were under attack at this time, especially in Britain.

Conservative Britons had clung to the Church of England as the only legitimate religion since the Glorious Revolution of 1688–89. However, by the 18th century, Protestant groups that did not want to belong to the state church were growing more powerful. The evangelical movement first appeared in the 1720s with the preaching of the Methodist founders Charles Wesley and George Whitefield. Methodism was not just Puritanism remodeled for a new era; it laid great stress on personal emotional commitment to Christianity and on at least the possibility that Redemption might be open to everyone. The evangelical movement essentially made the potential benefits of the Calvinist idea that God could choose anyone for salvation actually available to people of color and other minority groups. Some Methodists went their own way, leaving the Church of England and setting up independent Protestant denominations alongside those already established by separatist Puritans (the Congregational Church) and by Pietists (Quakers, Moravians, and various forms of Baptists). Though many English people remained in the Church of England, that church would never regain the comfortable identity with English ethnicity and government policy that it had once had. By the 19th century, the Church of England and the various Nonconformist Protestant denominations had established missionary societies devoted to evangelizing nonwhites throughout the world.

One important element of evangelical thought was an idea that was actually even more important to Baptists, scriptural fundamentalism. Ever since Martin Luther proclaimed his famous doctrine of *sola scriptura*—that the Bible contained everything that a Christian needed to know about religion and that it was a sure guide to salvation—the Protestant movement had focused heavily on the study of the Bible. Different Protestant groups understood this doctrine differently, however. The state churches of the Reformation generally thought that it meant that church teaching, by priests and bishops, needed to be based on scripture rather than on "tradition" and the writings of theologians, on which they said the Roman Catholics were overly reliant. On the other hand, evangelicals generally shared with Baptists the belief that scripture was literally inerrant and absolutely true and could be interpreted by any believer to provide sure guidance in matters of faith. This meant that individuals could quote even very short passages from scripture and use them to give powerful support to arguments without much consideration of their historical context, stylistic elements, or any other more subtle elements of interpretation. The Bible refers many times to slavery, and a selective culling of these references permitted some mainline evangelicals, as well as some Baptists, to support a conservative approach to slavery.

In addition to converting people of color to their religion, a goal shared by all evangelicals, liberal evangelicals and their allies were also interested in bettering their lot in more worldly ways. They worked in the Americas and in Britain to end the slave trade, slavery, and discrimination against people of color.

The Mainline Protestant Movement, Free Blacks, and Abolition (Eighteenth–Nineteenth Centuries)

The most important black abolitionists in Britain, OLAUDAH EQUIANO, QUOBNA OTTOBAH CUGOANO, and Mary Prince, were members of Baptist or Pietist groups, as were most free blacks in Britain and its colonies. However, black abolitionists worked with white evangelical members of the Church of England, such as Wilberforce. The mass opposition in Britain to slavery was a result of this cooperation. The British evangelical community almost universally opposed slavery, with converts even coming from the ranks of the slave traders themselves, such as the evangelical Church of England priest John Newton (1725–1807), a former slave ship captain. Supporters of slavery in Britain were from the nonevangelical wing of the Church of England or were secular Enlightenment deists, such as the Jamaican Bryan Edwards (1743–1800), who used racist and utilitarian arguments to advance the idea that slavery, however unfortunate in the abstract, was necessary for the time being and would remain so for a long time.

In the British colonies in the Caribbean, free people of mixed race were more likely than slaves and free blacks to join the Church of England rather than Baptist groups. Even this was rare, however, until after the end of slavery when the Church Mission Society (founded by Wilberforce in 1799) began to develop active missions in British colonies in the Americas. Both evangelical mainline Protestant and Baptist groups, though, insisted on a considerable degree of cultural conversion as well as a new religious vision for their African converts. The degree of syncretism that Catholics tolerated was entirely unacceptable for all varieties of Protestants, many of whom even criticized European Catholics for hanging on to traditions from Western Europe's pagan past such as Christmas trees and maypoles. (*See* AFRICAN AND SYNCRETIC RELIGIONS.)

In the United States, the evangelical movement was not so uniformly effective in turning public opinion against slavery. Many abolitionists, both black and white, were evangelicals. Samuel Sewall (1652–1730), the first white American to speak out against slavery, was a Puritan minister. Theodore Weld (1803–95) had been a seminarian and minister before becoming a journalist, and Henry Ward Beecher (1813–87) was a Congregationalist minister. But many Southern evangelical churches taught that slavery was acceptable, relying on conservative arguments and a selection of Bible passages that they argued justified slavery. The split in the American evangelical movement persisted in some cases up to the modern day. There are still forms of American Protestantism that are divided into Southern and Northern denominations, though only the most isolated and reactionary religious groups still try to justify slavery.

Mainline denominations in the South, nonetheless, attracted African-American members. Some of these were the slaves of masters who had taken the paternalistic, conservative idea about slavery to heart. But for the most part, slaves in the South, like slaves in the British colonies, were drawn to Baptist groups, often single-race groups that might have preserved some elements of African spirituality, more than in the British Caribbean, since these groups were often entirely informal and outside the control of masters or governments. Free people of color were more likely to join mainline denominations. In Virginia and MARYLAND in particular, the Episcopal Church drew many older free families of color into its orbit. The conservative idea of a hierarchical structure of society was strong in these groups, so black members had to sit in the back or in special lofts, were not permitted to be ministers or assistants, and otherwise experienced discrimination.

In the North, mainline denominations attracted free people of color in similar ways: Established families of color and the slaves of more pious masters were more likely to join mainline churches while newly freed or poorer free people of color were more likely to be Baptists. SOJOURNER TRUTH, for example, was raised in the Dutch Reformed faith of her master, and she joined a Baptist group after she gained her freedom. The best-known African-American church, the AFRICAN METHODIST EPISCOPAL CHURCH, was founded in Philadelphia by RICHARD ALLEN in 1816. Allen had been born in slavery, and his master was a Quaker. Absalom Jones, Allen's friend, follwed a similar path when he sought and obtained ordination in the Episcopal Church, the first African American to do so, then founded an African-

American Episcopal parish in Philadelphia. Allen and Jones had both been free for a long time and had achieved considerable material success when they formed these churches for free blacks.

Conclusion

The Protestant faith provided northern Europeans with a number of ideas that helped form their attitude toward free people of color. As people of color joined Protestant groups, these ideas also affected their struggle for respect, inclusion, and freedom. The most important of these concepts was ecclesiological: What was the church, who could be a member, how did one qualify, and what were the benefits of membership? Under state churches like the Church of England, the Dutch Reformed Church, or the Lutheran Churches of northern Europe, membership in the church was like membership in the nation, at least at first. People of color had a very difficult task convincing these groups that they ought to be permitted to join. Even when they did join, the churches limited the benefits that they could receive, separating the concept of church membership from that of citizenship.

By the middle of the 18th century, the state churches were affected by the evangelical movement, which put new emphasis on the Calvinist idea that God could choose anyone for salvation. People of color were included in the potential promise. Evangelical ideas especially affected the Church of England, creating a powerful mass movement among Britons for the abolition of slavery and at least some inclusion of people of color in a Christian community by the beginning of the 19th century. Evangelicals also created new denominations, some of which also supported the inclusion of people of color while others used unorthodox interpretation of scripture to defend slavery. Even the religious defenders of slavery, however, were forced by the logic of their arguments to adopt a paternalistic attitude, or at least a paternalistic rhetoric, toward people of color, including them implicitly in the human family and undermining the idea that they were "chattel."

Stewart R. King

FURTHER READING

Frey, Sylvia R., and Betty Wood. *Come Shouting to Zion: African American Protestantism in the American South and British Caribbean to 1830.* Chapel Hill, N.C.: Duke University Press, 1998.

Juster, Susan, and Lisa McFarlane, eds. *A Mighty Baptism: Race, Gender, and the Creation of American Protestantism.* Ithaca, N.Y.: Cornell University Press, 1996.

Kidd, Colin. *The Forging of Races: Race and Scripture in the Protestant Atlantic World, 1600–2000.* Cambridge: Cambridge University Press, 2006.

Sidbury, James. *Becoming African in America: Race and Nation in the Early Black Atlantic.* New York: Oxford University Press, 2007, especially chap. 6, "African Churches in the Atlantic World."

PROTTEN, REBECCA (ca. 1718–ca. 1779)
Afro-Caribbean Christian minister

Rebecca Protten was an important pietistic Christian preacher in the Danish Virgin Islands in the 18th century. She is notable as one of the earliest ordained female leaders in any Christian denomination since the days of the early church. She was able to forge important cross-status and cross-racial alliances and build a denomination that remains one of the largest religious groups in the islands.

Protten was born around 1718 in the British colony of Antigua. She was of mixed race, and nothing is known of her parentage. She claimed that she was born free and was subsequently kidnapped into slavery, though there are no records in Antigua that mention her at all (*see also* RE-ENSLAVEMENT). She was sold to Lucas van Beverhout, a large planter in St. Thomas, in the DANISH VIRGIN ISLANDS, in 1725 or 1726. She worked as a domestic servant in the Beverhout household, gaining her freedom in the early 1730s, perhaps at the time of Lucas's death. The Beverhout family was friendly to the Moravian missionaries working in the colony, and Rebecca became a member of the Moravian Church at about the same time as her MANUMISSION (*see also* BAPTISTS AND PIETISTS). She remained close to the Beverhout family for many years and became the housekeeper for Adrien van Beverhout, the son and heir of the family plantations (*see also* HOUSEKEEPERS).

She also began working actively as a missionary in the late 1730s, traveling widely throughout the colony preaching and converting slaves and free people of color. She was also renowned as a healer, treating slaves and free people with success. The Moravian congregation on the island grew rapidly and began attracting unfavorable attention from the established Lutheran Church. Powerful white planters and the colonial government they controlled also were suspicious of the Moravians, fearing that their egalitarian preaching would lead to unrest among the slaves. Rebecca married at this time, about 1739, to a white Moravian missionary named Matthäus Freundlich. INTERRACIAL MARRIAGE was not unlawful in the Danish colonies, but it was quite unusual and especially scandalous for a minister of religion. Since they had not been married in the official Lutheran Church, Rebecca and Matthäus were accused of fornication, and she was sentenced to be re-enslaved but was spared on the intercession of aristocratic patrons of the missionaries. Persecution of the congregation continued, however. Rebecca and her husband, exhausted, finally left the colony for Germany, where he died in 1742. Rebecca and their daughter, born about this time, lived in Germany for several years.

In 1745, she met Christian Protten, a Moravian minister from what is today Ghana, in West Africa. He was a man of mixed race, the child of a Danish soldier in the colony's garrison and an African woman. They were part of a small Afro-German population living in the Moravian community of Marienborn. The pair were married in 1746, and after her marriage, she was ordained as a deacon. Christian Protten was sent as a missionary to Christianborg, today's Accra, in Ghana, in 1757. Rebecca Protten stayed in Germany until 1762, when she and their daughter joined him in Africa. Their mission was difficult, and they had strained relations with church authorities back in Germany. Christian Protten died in 1769. Church authorities offered to send Rebecca back to St. Thomas, but she declined and spent the rest of her life in Ghana. She died around 1779.

There are several features of Protten's life that make her a very striking figure in Afro-Caribbean religious history. She was apparently one of the first two women of any race ordained in the Moravian Brethren and indeed one of the first women to be ordained a minister in any Christian group in modern times. Her role as a preacher and missionary in St. Thomas illustrates the unusual autonomy and authority that women had in free colored communities. Slaves sometimes argued that her free status made her different and prevented her from being an effective minister, but no Afro-Caribbean converts suggested that women should not preach. Even her German and Danish coreligionists accepted her as a preacher. The tension between her and the church in her later years was caused by her second husband, Christian Protten, who had some personal qualities that irritated his superiors. After his death, she would have been welcome to return to mission work in the Caribbean, had she desired it.

Another interesting feature of Rebecca Protten's life is the persecution she and the other Moravian Brethren experienced at the hands of the Lutheran and Dutch Reformed Churches. The theological differences between the Moravians and the official churches were small, and they coexisted fairly harmoniously in Germany and the Baltic by the 18th century. But the Moravians stressed the egalitarian values of Christianity. They tended to live together in community, like the better-known Pietists the Amish and Mennonites. This lifestyle appeared dangerous in a slave society. The Moravian mission on St. Thomas was actually a plantation, which the Moravians operated, practicing COTTON CULTIVATION and growing other crops to provide an income and owning slaves,

who were members of the church. But the seemingly "normal" structure of their operation did not placate the neighboring planters. As with the similar establishments of the JESUITS in Catholic colonies, the very existence of financially successful large cash-crop farms that were not run on a basis of harsh oppression of the slave workforce was a standing criticism of the slave system. The system reacted by official oppression, such as the arrest and trial of Protten and her first husband, and even more commonly by unofficial mob violence against missionaries and converts. Since Pietists are pacifists, the white thugs ran no risk, but the oppression encouraged conversions. In particular, Protten's sentence to re-enslavement and her behavior during her trial and imprisonment caused many slaves to join the church. After Protten left the colony, King Frederick V of Denmark wrote a series of letters to the colonial government that finally led to official toleration of the Moravian church by the 1750s. The Moravian church remains the oldest and largest black congregation in the islands.

Stewart R. King

FURTHER READING
Sensbach, Jon. *Rebecca's Revival: Creating Black Christianity in the Atlantic World*. Cambridge, Mass.: Harvard University Press, 2005.

PROVISION GROUND FARMING

Provision ground farming is the cultivation of food crops for sale in a market, usually local. The term originated in the practice by a number of plantations of maintaining separate farms, often on marginal or frontier land, to grow food crops to feed the slaves. Some planters, including GEORGE WASHINGTON in his operation at Mount Vernon, managed their own provision ground farms. Washington made more money from his food crops than he did from tobacco and ultimately converted most of his operation to grain production. However, because of the difficulty of managing separate operations, the provision ground farms would often be sold, given away, or leased, in some cases to free people of color.

The land grant system in many colonies awarded distant plots in frontier areas to planters in the hope that they would develop them and expand the effective area of the colony. Often, developing the remote plots was made a condition of the entire grant, as was commonly the case in French and Spanish colonies and in LOUISIANA. These distant plots were often unsuitable for production of the staple crop of the plantation (SUGAR CULTIVATION or COTTON CULTIVATION, for example) because of difficulties of transportation, forest patterns, or relief. Many plantation owners wanted to get rid of these plots, and they were popular as gifts to free colored children. They were also often sold to free colored buyers. For free people of color, moving to distant territories was one way to escape discriminatory laws and social norms. Some white people also moved to frontier areas, especially in colonies like those in North America with large populations of poor whites. Provision ground farming was a common practice among both groups of settlers.

To be profitable, provision ground farming required easy access to markets. In the Caribbean Islands, with their high mountains often very near the seashore, the provision ground farms could be located only a few miles from the sugar plantations. On the mainland, and in some of the larger Caribbean islands, provision ground farmers had to rely on water transportation or roads to take their food to market. Pieces of land distant from transportation were often condemned to pure peasant production, though one alternative, which started in the 18th century, was to grow grain and distill it into liquor, leading to the growth of famous whiskey-producing areas in western Virginia, Tennessee, and Kentucky.

But straightforward provision ground farms were found throughout the Americas wherever the geography was favorable. Blacks were farmers in many places. Where the legal or social climate was not favorable to blacks owning land, small black-owned provision ground operations were often acceptable even if larger plantations would have been seen as disruptive to the racial hierarchy. The black "butter and egg man" is almost as much a stock figure of antediluvian stereotype in the Old South as the kind, self-sacrificing black cook or nanny.

Many of these small operations were almost peasant holdings, with most of the produce of the farm consumed by the farmer and only a small surplus going to a larger market, often a local one. Drawing the line between the two is hard to do, and perhaps individuals would have moved back and forth across this line, depending on their life circumstances and the success of the year's crop. Other provision ground farms were very large, with slave workforces equivalent to those on a staple crop plantation. In some cases, they served distant markets (though generally markets within the plantation Americas), such as Mount Vernon or the many rice plantations in the Carolina and Georgia low country, and the food crop can be thought of as another plantation staple. Between these extremes were many farms that can be thought of as the nucleus of a family farming community within the plantation complex.

The provision ground farmer was respectable to the extent that he or she made a profit and was connected to larger markets. Thus, Washington or his colleagues who owned Carolina low country rice plantations were members of the plantocracy. A small grain farmer in the Shenandoah Valley of Virginia or the upper Artibonite Valley in Saint-Domingue could aspire to some status, though not what a bigger planter might have. In Virginia, these middling farmers were called the "yeomanry," a reference to the small independent English farmers of the Middle Ages; the term was redolent of English archers who slaughtered French knights in the Hundred Years' War, a tradition familiar to every American through the works of Shakespeare. Free blacks had more difficulty being yeomen, because racism and racial prejudice meant that even a successful black farmer would not be thought of in those terms by society. However, the term is sometimes used to describe comfortable black farmers in the postabolition period, and occasionally before the American Civil War in the Upper South. This being said, however, all else being equal, food production conferred less status on a farmer than production of the staple crop—sugar, tobacco, cotton, or coffee—and this was a further reason for white planters to avoid provision ground farming while free people of color, who had little status to lose, could take it up more easily without causing scandal by "getting above themselves."

In conclusion, the chief advantage of provision ground farming was that it did not require many inputs that came from off the farm, thus reducing debt loads. The product could also be eaten by the farmer and family if not successfully marketed. This gave provision ground farmers valuable protection against fluctuations in the markets for commodities and capital, which were the cause of a great many bankruptcies among planters. The plantation was erected on a foundation of debt, and low prices for the staple commodity from one year to the next could ruin a planter. The provision ground farmer, especially one who was a free person of color, owed little. There was always a market for food, as plantation regions by their very nature tended to be net food importers. These advantages meant that food production was an excellent, low-risk choice for small free black farmers.

Stewart R. King

FURTHER READING

Dalzell, Robert F., Jr., and Lee Baldwin Dalzell. *George Washington's Mount Vernon: At Home in Revolutionary America.* New York: Oxford University Press, 1998.
Kennedy, Roger G. *Mr. Jefferson's Lost Cause: Land, Farmers, Slavery, and the Louisiana Purchase.* New York: Oxford University Press, 2003.

PUERTO RICO

Puerto Rico is the easternmost island of the Greater Antilles islands in the northern Caribbean. It is mountainous but well watered and has coastal plains suitable for plantation agriculture. The history of the free blacks and free people of color on the island is closely related to its long colonial history, first under Spanish sovereignty, from 1508 to 1898, and second under U.S. rule, from 1898 to the present. Free blacks and free people of color have been, since the beginning, at the center of all the important events and processes in the social, cultural, and political history of the island.

The history of free blacks and free people of color in Puerto Rico started in southern SPAIN. First during Moorish rule of the Iberian Peninsula (711–1492) and later through PORTUGAL's slave trade with West Africa (starting in the 1400s), people of African descent became part of Spanish life and culture. This process created the basis of the MULATTO culture of southern Spain, where most of the people in the first wave of the conquest and settlement in the Antilles originated.

Juan Ponce de León was appointed governor of the first Spanish settlement of Puerto Rico in 1508. The island's original name was Borikén, the name given by the Taino, the native inhabitants of the island, and it was renamed San Juan Bautista (St. John the Baptist) by the Spaniards. Today we know that among that first group of Spanish settlers were free blacks and free colored families from southern Spain. For example, Francisco Mexias; his wife, Violante Mexias; and his son Antón Mexias, as were JUAN GARRIDO and Francisco Piñón, were among the island's first landholders and were owners of blacks and Taino slaves in the island. Other free blacks and *PARDOS* were part of that society: Francisco Gallego was a merchant, Diego Hernández was a domestic servant, Juan Medina a miner, and Juan Blanco a pirate.

During the late 17th and early 18th centuries, the lives of MIGUEL ENRÍQUEZ and his lover, Ana Muriel, both mulattoes, illustrate the color line in 18th-century Puerto

Rico. Enríquez was a shoemaker, belonging to one of many of the city guilds dominated by mulattoes. During the Spanish-British hostilities during the first decade of the 18th century, he became a member of the coast guard, at that time, a private armed naval MILITIA licensed by the Spanish Crown to intercept British ships. In the process, he received highly distinguished military and civilian titles, as well as a significant fortune. Enríquez became a rich person in San Juan; from the one armed merchant ship he started with, he increased his fleet to 25, he had a store where he sold what he captured in his raids, and he owned a sugar mill with 60 slaves. He required society to accept the presence of his lover, Ana Muriel, in public settings, including at Mass.

Enríquez's economic activities positioned him as an important moneylender; in one instance, the government borrowed from him to pay the salaries for the entire San Juan military garrison. However, the white-male-dominated Puerto Rican society of his time could not tolerate for long a *pardo*, or person of mixed race, who had such financial and social success. By 1735, Enríquez's former legitimate activities, which helped him to achieve noblelike status, became his ruin. His former high-class patrons, prominent government and church officials, friends, and debtors ultimately could not tolerate him. In his dire hour of need, he was treated as any other low-class *pardo*. His political opponents and the public prosecutor accused him of being a "man of inferior category, a poor mulatto shoemaker, and member of that despicable race, seeking to place himself among the honorable men of the first class of this city." Ultimately, he was accused of fraud in connection with his moneylending, lost all his wealth and power, and died a poor man.

Free people of color and black slaves composed a significant part of the workforce in the island. Slaves could hold important positions and do jobs requiring significant skills: For example, El Sancú and El Negro were slaves owned by the mayor of the city of San Juan, who leased them as chief cooks for a formal dinner celebrating the inauguration of Don Marcos Vergara de Lupe as governor general on March 13, 1766. However, free colored people dominated a wider spectrum of trades and could use their work to attain social mobility. In urban areas, mainly San Juan, mulattoes dominated trades such as masonry, shoemaking, cigar making, and carpentry, as well as unskilled labor. In Miguel Enríquez's case, we can see that he pursued a combination of trades: He was a shoemaker but maritime activities generated his fortune.

From the early 16th through the late 18th centuries, free blacks and free *pardos* were central to the service economy of Puerto Rico. Their services covered a wide

Puerto Rico

ATLANTIC OCEAN

Arecibo
San Juan
Aguadilla
Río Guajataca
Río Grande de Arecibo
Río Grande de Manatí
Río de la Plata
Bayamón
Loiza Aldea
L. Loiza
Río Grande de Loiza
Fajardo
Culebra I.
Mayagüez
Río Grande de Añasco
Utuado
Caguas
Vieques Passage
Ponce
Guayama
Vieques I.

Caribbean Sea

N

0   30 miles
0   30 km

© Infobase Learning

array of occupations and trades, ranging from organists and musicians in the Cathedral Church to silversmiths, shoemakers, masons, and carpenters, among others. In addition to Enríquez, there are also the examples of the silversmith and organist of the cathedral Domingo De Andino (1737–1820) and the painter and music professor, José de Rivafrecha Jordán (1751–1809).

Popular religiosity was a cultural practice in which unfree and free blacks and *pardos* left a deep footprint. Bishops incessantly complained, from the 17th through the late 18th centuries, of popular expression of religiosity and public festivities such as the dances and plays in the city of Ponce in 1712, the celebration of secular and religious activities in 1729, presence of priests at parties called *saraos* (parties with music and dancing) in 1760, the popularity of the fandango (an African-influenced dance genre) in 1763, and the *rosarios cantados* (chanted rosaries, popular religious gatherings) in 1789. The 18th century saw the development of popular cultural practices in which poor whites, free colored people, the lower clergy, and even slaves danced, played music, and participated in theatrical representations together.

At the beginning of the 19th century, two events provoked a hardening of the Spanish colonial rule over the island. First were the wars of independence in the Americas, and the second was the triumph of the HAITIAN REVOLUTION—the slave revolt in the French colony of SAINT-DOMINGUE through which the first black independent republic was born in 1804. The specter of the slave revolt in Saint-Domingue shed a shadow of suspicion over the SLAVE OWNERS who migrated from the French colony to Puerto Rico.

The rapid increase in the number of slaves taken to the island was a response to the growth of the sugar market in the world economy. The slave population grew from 17,500 slaves in 1794 to 31,874 slaves in 1827, and to 51,216 slaves by 1846. The immediate results were a rise in the overall racial tensions in the island and an increase in POLICE attention to the activities of unfree and free blacks and *pardos*. Between 1795 and 1848, slave revolts of various sizes and levels of success broke out across the island. A series of laws regulating the lives of unfree and free blacks and *pardos* were created, from the bylaws of 1826 for slave owners, on how to treat and educate slaves, to a law criminalizing any act of an unfree black or *pardo* against a white person established in 1842, culminating in an all-encompassing law, which applied to both unfree and free blacks and *pardos* alike, called the Black Edict, in 1848.

During the 19th century, two African-based and -influenced musical practices and genres emerged. In both genres unfree and free blacks and *pardos* were the main creators: The text-based dance genre called *bomba* and an instrumental dance music called *danza*.

A statue of the Afro–Puerto Rican composer Juan Morel Campos (1857–96). Born free just as slavery was ending, Campos went on to become the most famous composer of *danzas*, turning this traditional Puerto Rican musical style into high art that became popular around the world. (© *Macduff Everton/ CORBIS*)

The *bomba* is deeply rooted in the Puerto Rican drumming tradition. The word encompasses the drums, the dance, and the genre. Throughout the 19th century, it was closely related to slave revolts, and it was practiced in the slaves' barracks in the plantations and the poor neighborhoods outside the cities and towns and was an urban practice within the walled city of San Juan.

The *danza* was a dance music created in the Americas as an outgrowth of the European country dance. From the 1840s to the early years of the 20th century, this genre was sung, played, and danced by the majority of Puerto Ricans of many different social backgrounds. There were *danzas* of popular origin that a small stringed ensemble could perform with traditional instruments such as the Puerto Rican *cuatro*, the *bordonúa*, the *violarina*, and the guitar, as well as *danzas* for full ballroom dance orchestras. However, it was during the last two decades of the

19th century that a new kind of *danza* took hold in the repertoire as a piano form. Because of its widespread usage, the *danza* became an identity marker.

The *danzas* for piano solo, as songs without lyrics, became a showcase for Puerto Rican composers. Afro–Puerto Rican musicians, descendants of free blacks and *pardos*, were the composers who created the Puerto Rican version of this pan-American genre. Among the most important are Julián Andino (1845–1926), Juan Morel Campos (1857–96), the brothers Heraclio (1837–91) and Federico (1857–1927) Ramos, José Ignacio Quintón (1881–1925), José María Rodríguez Arreson (1875–1947), Simón Madera (1875–1957), and Rafael Duchesne (1890–1986). The very presence and influence of these people created the basis for an identity debate that looked with suspicion at the heavily African rhythm that propelled this musical form.

Slavery officially ended in Puerto Rico on March 22, 1873. Government records show that by 1873 there were 29,335 slaves in the island. Puerto Rico, under Spanish sovereignty, was a society in which race and class were closely related. New freed blacks and *pardos* were part of a marginalized class in a clear contrast with the descendants of the pre-abolition free blacks and *pardos* who formed the core of the classes of ARTISANS and professionals. These artisans and professionals became the organizational base of the labor movement in the 20th century.

By 1898, Spanish race politics, with the acquiescence of the white CREOLE people, turned the attention of blacks and *pardos* to race politics in the United States as an alternate path of social negotiation. The results were mixed. On one hand, José Celso Barbosa (1857–1921) became the leader of the political movement that had as a goal the annexation of Puerto Rico to the United States as a state. Barbosa was an admirer of the African-American educator Booker T. Washington and of the Tuskegee Institute, which Washington led from 1881 to 1915. Arturo (Arthur) Alfonso Schomburg (1874–1938), on the other hand, represents the blacks and *pardos* who focused on the inequities of RACISM AND RACIAL PREJUDICE and discrimination; he identified himself with W. E. B. DuBois and the National Association for the Advancement of Colored People (NAACP).

U.S. Rule, 1898 to the Present

Racial prejudice became a central issue when the new United States gained possession of Puerto Rico in 1898. The island's population was a shock for U.S. colonizers at the turn of the century. For military and civil government officials and visitors, including Henry K. Carrol, Trumbull White, James D. Dewell, L. S. Rowe, R. A. Van Middledyk, and Victor S. Clark, the problem was not the people who

were clearly blacks but the majority of the population, which was classified as half-caste or of mixed blood.

Their reports to Washington, D.C., are full of cautionary notes to the newcomers that black teachers not only taught white children but did so in racially integrated classrooms. The U.S. policy toward Puerto Rico was based on the idea that Puerto Ricans were racially and politically immature, and unready for the responsibilities of self-government.

The U.S. colonial occupation and public policy toward Puerto Rico created the right circumstances for a decades-long debate among Puerto Ricans about national identity. This identity debate shaped the articulation of ideologies, collective cultural self-identification, and politics in Puerto Rico for the rest of the 20th century.

From 1898 to 1930, the colony's Department of Education implemented a deliberate and systematic process of Americanization through the public schools. All classes other than Spanish-language courses were to be taught in English, and the department's policy was to have a fully English-speaking faculty in the least time possible. This Americanization program brought about a fierce reaction from a sector of the Puerto Rican society who wanted to develop a sense of nationhood for self-determination.

Race was crucial in this process. From 1929 to 1940, an identity debate worked as the catalyst for ideas that were born under Spanish sovereignty that could be recast to fit the new colonial situation. The view of race based on appearance used during Spanish rule was retooled in the idea of the *three root races* from which the Puerto Rican identity was formed: the Taino, the African, and the Spanish. However, the dominance of the Spanish civilization over the Taino and the African cultures was explained in terms of racial superiority of the former over the latter.

Tomás Blanco (1900–75), Antonio S. Pedreira (1899–1959), Vicente Géigel Polanco (1904–79), Samuel R. Quiñones (1904–76), and Alfredo Collado Martell (1900–30) were the leaders and representatives of the white Puerto Rican intellectuals who created the ideological bases for a Puerto Rican identity that collapsed in itself every other category of identity. Afro–Puerto Ricans such as Arturo Schomburg, Rafael Hernández, Julia De Burgos, and Carmen María Colón Pellot could not identify themselves openly as such without infringing the essentialism of a Puerto Ricanness defined mainly as an offshoot of the Spanish culture.

Afro–Puerto Ricans did express openly their Afro-diasporic identity. African descendants celebrated festivities as their identity markers from the 19th century through the mid-20th century. Instances of such activities were the coronations of the king and queen of the

Congo people on Saint Michael's Day in San Juan City, Three Kings Day on January 6, and Saint James's Day on July 25 at the black and *pardos* town of Loiza Aldea.

Poets who included Julia De Burgos, Carmen María Colón Pellot, Fortunato Vizcarrondo (1895–1977), and Juan Boria (1905–95) wrote about blackness, race politics in Puerto Rico's everyday life, and Afro–Puerto Rican black pride. Racial prejudice and discrimination were dealt with ingeniously in popular music. In Félix Manuel "Bobby" Rodríguez Capó's (1922–89) *Mataron al negro bembón* (Somebody killed the big-fat-lip negro), Catalino "Tite" Curet Alonso's (1926–2003) *Las caras lindas de mi gente negra* (My black people's beautiful faces), and Roberto Angleró's (1929–) *Si Dios fuera negro* (If only God were black), the struggle and hopes of Puerto Ricans of African descent are sung and danced in a constant renewal of black selfhood and identity.

Noel Allende-Goitía

FURTHER READING
Allende-Goitía, Noel. "The Mulatta, the Bishop, and Dances in the Cathedral: Race, Music, and Power Relations in Seventeenth-Century Puerto Rico." *Black Music Research Journal* 26, no. 2 (Fall 2006): 137–164.

———. *Por la encendida calle Antillana: Cultura musical y discurso histórico en la sociedad puertorriqueña en la década del treinta, 1929–1939.* Master's thesis, University of Puerto Rico, 1992.

Alvarez Nazario, Manuel. *El Elemento Afronegroide en el español de Puerto Rico.* San Juan, Puerto Rico: Instituto de Cultura Puertorriqueña, 1961.

Diaz Soler, Luis Manuel. *Historia de la Esclavitud Negra en Puerto Rico.* 4th ed. Río Piedras, Puerto Rico: Editorial Universitaria, 1974.

———. *Puerto Rico: desde sus orígenes hasta el cese de la dominación española.* Río Piedras, Puerto Rico: Editorial de la Universidad de Puerto Rico, 1996.

Fernández Méndez, Eugenio. *Historia cultural de Puerto Rico, 1493–1968.* Río Piedras, Puerto Rico: Editorial Universitaria, 1980.

Malavet Vega, Pedro. *De las bandas al Trío Borinquen, 1900–1927.* Ponce, Puerto Rico: Ediciones Lorena, 2002.

Mayo Santana, Raíl, Mariano Negrón Portillo, and Manuel Mayo López. *Cadenas de esclavitud . . . y de solidaridad: Esclavos y libertos en San Juan, siglo XIX.* Río Piedras, Puerto Rico: Centro de Investigaciones Sociales, Universidad de Puerto Rico Recinto de Río Piedras, 1997.

Piñero de Rivera, Flor. *Arturo Schomburg un puertorriqueño descubre el legado histórico del negro.* San Juan, Puerto Rico: Centro de Estudios Avanzados de Puerto Rico y el Caribe, 2004.

Ramos Rosado, Marie. *La mujer negra en la literatura puertorriqueña.* Río Piedras, Puerto Rico: Editorial de la Universidad de Puerto Rico, Instituto de Cultura Puertorriqueña and Editorial Cultural, 2003.

Scarano, Francisco A. *Puerto Rico: Cinco siglos de historia.* San Juan, Puerto Rico: McGraw-Hill, 1993.

Zenón Cruz, Isabelo. *Narciso descubre su trasero: El negro en la cultura puertorriqueña.* 2 vols. Humacao, Puerto Rico: Editorial Furidi, 1974 and 1975.

PURVIS, ROBERT (1810–1898) *American businessman, abolitionist, and reformer*

Robert Purvis was one of the most important African-American leaders during the mid-19th century. He was nationally known and was successful in forging cross-race and cross-class alliances to support a broad range of reform proposals including abolition of slavery, civil rights, women's rights, and justice for oppressed people around the world.

Robert Purvis was born on August 4, 1810, in CHARLESTON, SOUTH CAROLINA. His father, William Purvis, was white and English. His mother, Harriet Judah, was of mixed race but free. Robert was the middle of three sons born to the couple. Later in life, Robert claimed an early antislavery education, either ignoring or forgetting the fact that both his parents bought and sold slaves—or illustrating a paradox of human nature, that somebody could be opposed to a system in which he or she participated. Robert and his younger brother, Joseph, were sent to PHILADELPHIA, PENNSYLVANIA, in 1820, seeking better opportunities in the country's largest free black community. They quickly became acquainted with the local free black elite through church and school, especially the family of the local businessman James Forten (*see* FORTEN FAMILY). Robert and Joseph attended Amherst College in MASSACHUSETTS. After their father's death in 1826, they inherited his sizable fortune and returned to Philadelphia. Robert lived in the city for most of his life and married Harriet Forten, daughter of James, on September 3, 1831.

Though Robert was often mistaken for white and some of his father's friends advised him to seize the opportunity (*see also* "WHITENING" AND RACIAL PROMOTION), he chose to continue to identify himself as an African American and became an outspoken advocate of abolition of slavery and racial equality. Robert and Harriet lived in the Forten home for the first months of their marriage but soon purchased a new home nearby. Robert was a founding member of the American Anti-Slavery Society, alongside William Lloyd Garrison (1805–79), in 1833 (*see also* ABOLITIONISM AND RESISTANCE TO SLAVERY). Purvis frequently supported Garrison's antislavery efforts, even siding with Garrison in his disagreement with FREDERICK DOUGLASS over the best tactics to further the abolitionist cause. Garrison was harsher in his language while Douglass tried to employ reasoned debate. However, when Garrison disbanded the American Anti-Slavery Society after the AMERICAN CIVIL WAR, Purvis opposed him, arguing that equality had not yet been achieved. He only reconciled with Garrison and Douglass late in life. When James Forten was elected president of the National Convention Movement in 1835 (*see also* NEGRO CONVENTION MOVEMENT IN THE UNITED STATES), Purvis served alongside his father-in-law and helped reshape and refocus the group as the avowedly interracial American Moral Reform Society. Purvis protested the 1838 disenfranchisement of black Pennsylvanians in print, accusing white legislators of betraying their history and their people. When Forten died in 1842, Purvis eulogized him, and the proceeds from the sale of the printed tribute benefited the abolition movement.

After Purvis defended his home during a Philadelphia race riot in 1843, he, Harriet, and their five children moved to a mansion outside the city. At this new home, they raised their children and their niece, Charlotte Forten Grimké. They entertained guests of all colors and legal statuses; a hidden room was added for RUNAWAY SLAVES. Purvis had organized the Vigilant Committee in 1837 and continued to help slaves escape, including the future author HARRIET JACOBS. Purvis served as president of the Pennsylvania Anti-Slavery Society in the late 1840s, supported in all his activities by his wife. Their marriage was a true partnership, as both worked fervently for abolition and equality. Though they briefly considered immigration to Britain after the decision in the DRED SCOTT case in 1857, they remained in America to continue the struggle. During the Civil War, she raised funds while he worked to recruit black troops. Harriet died in 1875, and Purvis married Tacie Townsend, an old family friend of European descent, three years later.

For the rest of his life, Purvis worked for universal equality, supporting Native Americans, Irish home rule, and women's rights. When there was a split over the wording and the goal of the proposed Fifteenth Amendment in 1869, Purvis was the only black leader to side with Susan B. Anthony and Elizabeth Cady Stanton, who were calling for the amendment to grant votes to women as well as black men. He said he would prefer that his son never voted if his daughter could not vote as well. By the time of his death, several states had already begun allowing women to vote, and the success of the suffrage movement was less than 20 years away. When Purvis died on April 15, 1898, he was eulogized by the *New York Times* as the president of the Underground Railroad and by Elizabeth Cady Stanton for his support of women's rights. His life's work had been freedom and full equality for all people.

Beverly C. Tomek

FURTHER READING

Bacon, Margaret Hope. *But One Race: The Life of Robert Purvis.* Albany: State University of New York Press, 2007.

Nash, Gary. *Forging Freedom: The Formation of Philadelphia's Free Black Community, 1720–1840.* Cambridge, Mass.: Harvard University Press, 2003.

Winch, Julie. *A Gentleman of Color: The Life of James Forten.* Oxford: Oxford University Press, 2002.

———. *Philadelphia's Black Elite: Activism, Accommodation, and the Struggle for Autonomy, 1787–1848.* Philadelphia: Temple University Press, 1988.

QUOCK WALKER CASE (*COMMONWEALTH V. JENNISON*)

The Quock Walker case, which was actually a series of cases, is best known as the catalyst for ending slavery in the state of MASSACHUSETTS during the WAR OF AMERICAN INDEPENDENCE, 1775–83. The 1780 Massachusetts state constitution opened the door for this case by including the declaration that "all men are born free and equal" and have "the right of enjoying and defending their lives and liberty." The case came about after a slave named Quock Walker (sometimes referred to by different variations of the name, such as Quok, Quacks, Quork, and Quaco) sued his owner, Nathaniel Jennison, for assault.

The drama unfolded when Walker escaped from Jennison in 1781 and hid on a nearby farm owned by John and Seth Caldwell, the brothers of his former owner. Walker's owner, who had reportedly promised him his freedom at the age of 25, had died, and his widow had married Jennison. Since Walker had passed the age at which he had been promised freedom, he left the Jennisons and asked the younger Caldwell brothers for employment. Captured by Jennison and his friends, Walker was beaten severely. He responded by filing suit against his new owner for assault and battery, and Jennison in turn sued the Caldwells for allegedly trying to entice his slave away. The Caldwells turned to Levi Lincoln, a highly regarded local attorney, who would later become lieutenant governor of Massachusetts and attorney general for Massachusetts and the United States. The focal point of the case was whether or not Walker was a slave and as such could be disciplined by his master, or whether he was a free man. If he was a free man, then Jennison had committed assault. This case, *Quock Walker v. Jennison*, ended June 12, 1781, with the jury declaring that Walker was free and awarding him $50 of the $300 for which he had sued.

The second case, *Jennison v. Caldwell*, dealt with Jennison's accusation that the Caldwells had "seduced" Walker away to work for them and thus deprived Jennison of the labor of his slave. In this case, the jury contradicted the ruling of the previous case by siding with Jennison and ordering the Caldwells to pay him £25. The Supreme Judicial Court, however, overturned this ruling on appeal after Lincoln and another attorney, Caleb Strong, argued that Walker had not been "seduced" away and that, more importantly, Walker was not Jennison's legal property. Despite the apparent antislavery wording of the state constitution, Lincoln did not rely on that document. Instead, he focused on the broader idea that slavery violated natural rights guaranteed to all humans by the laws of God and nature. As a result, he insisted, any constitution that did authorize slavery conflicted with natural law.

The third and final case, *Commonwealth v. Jennison*, saw Jennison indicted for assault and battery upon Walker. The attorney general argued that when Jennison attacked Walker, he had attacked a free man. This assertion was based upon testimony that Walker's former masters, Caldwell and his wife, had both promised Walker that they would free him when he turned 25 and that Jennison was aware of this promise. Although Jennison's lawyer correctly insisted that the 1780 constitution did not prohibit slavery outright, Chief Justice William Cushing instructed the jury that even if the constitution never expressly forbade slavery, "slavery is in my judgment as effectively abolished as it can be by the granting of rights and privileges wholly incompatible and repugnant to its existence." Although the constitution did not, and was never amended to, prohibit slavery, the jury in this case ruled against Jennison, convicting him of assault and battery on a free man. The premise that the state constitution made slavery incompatible with Massachusetts law lived on in future rulings, so this is seen as the case that led to the end of slavery in the state.

Beverly C. Tomek

FURTHER READING

Egerton, Douglas R. *Death or Liberty: African Americans and Revolutionary America*. New York: Oxford University Press, 2009.

Higginbotham, Leon. *In the Matter of Color: Race and the American Legal Process: The Colonial Period*. New York: Oxford University Press, 1978.

Zilversmit, Arthur. "Quok Walker, Mumbet, and the Abolition of Slavery in Massachusetts." *William and Mary Quarterly* 3rd ser., 25, no. 4 (October 1968): 614–624.

RACE AND CAPITALISM

In Marxist theory, either classical, as created by Karl Marx and Friederich Engels in the 19th century, or neo-Marxism, as ably put forward by Eugene Genovese, the slave societies of the Americas were a phase in the pre-history of the capitalist system. Capitalism, Marxists argued, needs to grow if it is to live. As the transformation from feudalism to capitalism moved forward toward the Industrial Revolution in Europe, increasingly large segments of the European workforce were drawn into capitalism. Capitalists needed new markets and preferential access to products. They could not incorporate the Americas directly into their system because of distance, the difficulty of transport and communication, and their own lack of capital. So they developed the Americas as protected colonial markets under mercantilism and developed the plantation sector to ensure access to raw materials for their developing industries. The colonial systems were not truly capitalist; indeed, in many ways, they were feudal. The white master class, whether or not officials of the state, ruled over their slaves as if they were governments, duplicating in some fashion the power of the "low, middle, and high justice" exercised by feudal barons. Feudal classes had been divided by birth and "blood" as well as serf and noble status, and in a similar fashion the class structure in the colonies of the Americas was divided by "blood," that is, European or non-European ancestry, and status, as slave or free. But the plantation system was capitalist in that its primary function was to produce a good for sale in a market, and the master class gained status based on monetary gains rather than ancestry or "honor." Slave property was not like capitalist property: The slave was in one sense a capital good, like a tractor or farm animal—at least, that is the way the SLAVE OWNERS often treated them. But slaves were in fact people, and this stubborn fact kept preventing the slave system from becoming more capitalist.

The development of plantations and the long-distance trade in slaves and plantation products permitted the accumulation of capital that allowed businessmen in Europe to become capitalists. Finally, as capitalism became fully mature, it was able to incorporate the plantation areas of the Americas directly into its system without the need for the transitional regime of slavery. European countries abolished the slave trade and slavery in their colonies in the 19th century as their own capitalist systems became mature, the more enthusiastically because slave labor is incompatible with the basic idea of capitalism, which is freedom. Some of the former slaves were converted into capitalist workers, either as hired agricultural laborers or as migrants to cities where they could become factory workers. Others became PEASANTS, especially in those former plantation areas that ceased to be important parts of the economy of the home country as capitalism began to rely less and less on protected markets in colonial empires.

Race remained important as a way to divide people in the newly capitalist societies, both the former colonies, or pseudo-colonies like the American South, and the industrial heartlands of Western Europe and the northeastern United States. Race was not essential to the functioning of the system, and indeed, capitalists ignored racial differences when it suited them; for example, the meat-packing houses of CHICAGO, ILLINOIS, imported black workers to break a major strike in 1903. To their detriment, the mostly eastern European immigrant workers had not allowed blacks to join their union. Racial divisions were a form of "false consciousness," Marxists argued, an idea that was very useful to the capitalists because it divided the working class. The machinery of formal racial discrimination in the United States and the European colonies of the Caribbean, and the informal but no less pervasive discrimination in Spanish America, served the interests of the ruling class and were encouraged by institutions they supported. University schools of "racial science" or "ethnography," "white citizen's councils," and "neighborhood associations," as well as groups engaged in direct action such as the American KU KLUX KLAN terrorists all benefited from support from business people who might sneer at their prejudices behind closed doors but thought it useful to support public RACISM AND RACIAL PREJUDICE.

But where, in all this theory, do the free people of color fit? They turn out to be as ambiguous in this view of the plantation world as they were in the eyes of their contemporaries. The best explanation, found in the work of the historian Ira Berlin, is that they constitute an "intermediate class." That is, they are a group that illustrates the contradictions inherent in the system and bears within itself the seeds of a new order that will emerge after a revolutionary change. The parallel group in the medieval feudal order would be the city dwellers. The medieval cities contained a group of people who were neither serfs nor nobles but who provided goods and services that the noble-serf system could neither bring itself to do without nor provide itself. Nobles desired manufactured goods and luxury products from faraway places. The people of the cities made or acquired the goods for them. The nobles also desired supervisors and managers to help them run their estates, and the ordinary people desired educated priests to provide religious services and demanded manufactured and imported goods. The city people also provided an outlet for surplus production from the peasants, slowly incorporating them into the new, money-dominated order. The free people of color filled an analogous role in the plantation societies of the Americas. They would do jobs that whites did not want: low-status ones like artisanal manufacturing, direct supervision of slave labor, small retail commerce, or innkeeping, or dangerous ones like slave catcher or MILITIA member. (See also ARTISANS, COMMERCE AND TRADE, PLANTERS AND PLANTER AGENTS, and POLICE.) These were jobs that could not be entrusted to slaves or, at least, represented more profound challenges to the social order when performed by slaves. The system needed these things done. Thus, by default, they were done by free people of color. In addition, the white master class desired sexual access to women of color, and a mixed-race group of FAMILY members were the natural result. Unacknowledged though they may have been, they had a family claim to the assistance of their white relatives, one that colonial whites were often still sensitive to, given their incomplete incorporation into the "money-is-all" spirit of capitalism. To the extent that they still valued family ties, their mixed-race relatives had a legitimate claim to their support, and they could also trust their free colored relatives ahead of other people of color because of the same family ties.

The free colored civil rights activist JULIEN RAIMOND of SAINT-DOMINGUE called the free mixed-race planter class to which he belonged the "natural bourgeoisie of the islands." By this he meant that they valued family relationships, especially marriage, highly; kept control over their women in traditional patriarchal families; and were good stewards of their capital. Raimond died in 1802, 16 years before Karl Marx was born, but had he read Marx,

he would have seen a deeper meaning to his argument: The free people of color were the new class of the plantation areas, especially those with very small white populations. In Raimond's own Haiti, they became the ruling class, and in much of the rest of Latin America, they became the leaders of the African-descended population after the abolition of slavery. Even in the United States, where their numbers were relatively small and racial discrimination pervasive after the end of slavery, former free people of color are the ancestors of many successful black families and preserved a class identity in some areas up to the 20th century.

Stewart R. King

FURTHER READING
Berlin, Ira. *Generations of Captivity: A History of African American Slaves.* Cambridge, Mass.: Harvard University Press, 2003.
———. *Slaves without Masters: The Free Negro in the Antebellum South.* New York: New Press, 1974.
Blackburn, Robin. *The Making of New World Slavery: From the Baroque to the Modern, 1492–1800.* New York: Verso, 1997.
Fox-Genovese, Elizabeth, and Eugene Genovese. *Fruits of Merchant Capital: Slavery and Bourgeois Property in the Rise and Expansion of Capitalism.* New York and Oxford: Oxford University Press, 1983.
Genovese, Eugene. *The Political Economy of Slavery: Studies in the Economy and Society of the Slave South.* 1965. Reprint, Middletown, Conn.: Wesleyan University Press, 1988.
Marx, Karl. "The Genesis of Industrial Capital." *Das Kapital,* chap. 31, first English edition 1887. Available online. URL: http://www.marxists.org/archive/marx/works/1867-c1/ch31.htm. Accessed January 7, 2011.
Williams, Eric. *Capitalism and Slavery.* London: Andre Deutsch, 1964.

RACISM AND RACIAL PREJUDICE
Racism is defined as racial prejudice backed up by power. Someone who is racist dislikes a group of people because of their race and has the power as a result of his or her social position or privilege to do harm to members of that racial group. Racism took two forms in the period of slavery in the Americas (*see* LEGAL DISCRIMINATION ON THE BASIS OF RACE), which included legal restrictions limiting the activities free people of color could engage in and informal racial discrimination against people of color, in economic, cultural, or personal relations, such as restrictions on INTERRACIAL MARRIAGE and informal sexual relations. This article examines the origins and effects of informal racial discrimination by people acting in their private economic or cultural capacity against people of African ancestry.

The Origins of Racial Prejudice

There is a great deal of debate about the origins of racial prejudice in European and American culture. Racial theorists in the 19th and early 20th centuries argued that the races were biologically distinct and that people naturally feared and were disgusted by the other. They were especially upset about interracial marriage, although somewhat less so by informal interracial sexual relations, holding them to undermine the biological distinctions between the races. They also often argued that the races should remain as separate as possible in all matters, in order to prevent the risk of interracial mating and to permit each race to work out its biological destiny in isolation. Modern sociobiologists have argued that restrictions on interracial sex and other cultural codes recognizing racial differences are just one part of a standard human strategy to preserve and reproduce one's own genes. This analysis has the advantage of explaining why white men in colonial societies passed laws restricting sexual activity between people of different races and then notoriously violated those laws in their own personal behavior. Sociobiologists would argue that the laws were intended to ensure that the children borne by women of the dominant group would all have fathers from the dominant group, while the men of the dominant group would be free to father children with women of the subordinate group. Sociobiology does not explain other forms of discrimination against people of color other than sexual isolation of dominant group women, except in that they preserve the dominance of the leading group males and thus their ability to control the sexuality of women of both groups. A larger problem with the sociobiological analysis is that racial prejudice in European culture is of relatively recent origin.

Medieval Roots

Five or six hundred years ago, people of African ancestry living in Europe did not suffer under any unusual handicap associated with their race. There were few people of African descent in Europe in the Middle Ages, but those who did live there did not experience great discrimination on the basis of race. For example, Elizabeth of York, queen of England (1486–1503), the wife of Henry Tudor, had two black ladies in waiting, Elen and Margaret Moore, sisters whose origin is unclear but who may have come from West Africa by way of PORTUGAL. Elen Moore lived through the reign of Elizabeth's son, Henry VIII (r. 1509–47), and was in her old age a favorite companion of Elizabeth of York's granddaughter, Queen Elizabeth I (r. 1558–1603). Blacks and North African Muslims were both called "Moors" in England at the time, but the Moore sisters were described by contemporaries as striking because of their dark skin and curly hair. Elen was considered a great beauty, and a tournament was organized in her honor by Elizabeth's husband, Henry VII (r. 1485–1509), in 1507, at which English noblemen fought for her favor with sword and lance. English men do not seem to have been repulsed by her unusual appearance, and she wielded some political power in a mode appropriate for a woman of the upper classes.

Late medieval British culture, as demonstrated by its greatest playwright, William Shakespeare (1564–1616), accepted people of African ancestry as members of society on an equal basis. Shakespeare's great hero Othello, the Moor of Venice, could at the same time have "swarthy skin," "thick lips," and "wooly hair" and command the armed forces of Venice, one of the most powerful European states of the period. Some literary critics have argued that Shakespeare saw Othello's race as one of the causes of his tragedy because it made him more hot-blooded or impetuous in his personal decisions, but this is by no means explicit in the play and may represent a later reinterpretation of the character by critics influenced by more modern racial ideas. Othello was, nonetheless, for Shakespeare and his audiences, a man equal to any other, and better than some, noble in character and feeling, somebody the audience could identify with as a tragic hero.

In other parts of Europe, people of color might experience discrimination, but on the basis of religion or ancestry rather than race. In SPAIN, actual "Moors" from Morocco were barely tolerated in the Middle Ages and finally expelled from the country after the Christian conquest was complete in 1492 if they refused to convert to Christianity. On the other hand, in the early Middle Ages, the Spanish culture hero El Cid (1044–99) apparently had some Moorish ancestry, but because he was also descended from noble Spaniards, was a Christian, and fought most of the time against the Almoravid conquerors of Muslim Spain (though also occasionally against Christian opponents), he was one of the most respected Spanish noblemen. The difference appears to have been religious rather than racial. Even when the Spanish government began issuing certificates of *limpieza de sangre*, or "purity of blood," after 1492 to people of "old Christian" ancestry, a person of Jewish or North African ancestry could also receive a certificate if he or she were especially heroic in religious orthodoxy and cultural assimilation.

Slavery in medieval Europe was not linked to color at all. Western Europe did not have many slaves after about 1000 C.E., and those few who arrive on the Continent were mostly light-skinned people from eastern Europe or the Middle East. The Crusaders enslaved Palestinian Muslims captured in battle and began to develop plantations using slave labor. After they were driven out of the Holy

Land, they transported plantation slavery to the islands of the Mediterranean, staffing them with slaves purchased from the Islamic world. Many of these slaves were Christian Europeans, from Russia and the Balkans, while others were Middle Easterners. There were slaves from black Africa among them—the famous "Moor" of Peter the Great, ABRAM PETROVICH GANNIBAL (1696–1781), originally from the modern nation of Chad, was enslaved by Ottoman Turks and then sent to Russia, where he gained his freedom and became a nobleman. But blackness and slavery were not equated in any way, and blackness, for Europeans before the 1600s, did not mark one out for special discrimination.

The Birth of Racial Discrimination

As the Atlantic slave trade grew in the 1500s and 1600s, Europeans developed a justification for enslaving millions of people. No racial arguments were made at first. African slaves were seen in the same light as European or Middle Eastern slaves, that is, as people who had been justly imprisoned as a result of war and were obliged to work for their conquerors. African slaves worked alongside European and Arab slaves on the islands of the Mediterranean and in southern Spain and Portugal in the 1500s. By that time, however, the supply of slaves from the eastern Mediterranean was tapering. The Ottoman Empire had a growing economy and needed slave labor, and the ancient eastern slave markets of Bari and Constantinople and the Italian Black Sea ports fell into Turkish hands in the 1400s and 1500s and were closed to Western merchants. The early conquistadores in Spanish America and BRAZIL enslaved Indians, but the New Laws of the Indies in Spain, declining Indian populations, and papal decrees all but eliminated Indian slavery by the 1600s. By 1650, almost all the slaves in the Atlantic basin were of African origin. Europeans began to associate blackness and slavery.

This was also the beginning of the Enlightenment, when Europeans began to look for scientific explanations for the way the world worked. The first "scientific" division of humanity into races was François Bernier's (1625–88) *Nouvelle division de la terre*, published in FRANCE in 1684. Bernier sought to define the characteristics of each race, though it is notable that he did not ascribe to Africans many of the negative characteristics used by later biological thinkers. Bernier's relatively liberal ideas about race may have been affected by his long residence in India, where he was court physician to the Moghul emperor Aurangzeb, but he was also a product of his times. Carl Linnaeus (1707–88), a Swedish biologist and the father of modern taxonomy, or the division of animals into species, saw humans as divided into five taxonomically undefined subdivisions. Linnaeus

described *Homo sapiens africanus* as phlegmatic, black, slow, relaxed, and negligent. The progression from Bernier to Linnaeus parallels the progression in public attitudes about racial differences. From conceiving of racial differences as intrinsic and immutable in the 1600s, Europeans progressed to a belief in the unchanging inferiority of the African race by the 1700s.

Racial attitudes also changed with changing religious beliefs during this period. The medieval Christian Church taught the unity and fundamental equality of humankind within a society ordered by birth and status (*see* ROMAN CATHOLIC CHURCH). In the early days of the Protestant Reformation, the new faith preserved this teaching (*see* PROTESTANT MAINLINE CHURCHES). Many Protestant groups continue to argue that God calls on people to treat each other equally and refrain from discrimination. The Quakers were early supporters of this idea, but many others of the new Protestant groups of the 1700s and 1800s also worked for racial justice (*see* BAPTISTS AND PIETISTS). But in this period, new interpretations of scripture and declining authority for established churches meant that those who felt racial prejudice could find religious thinkers who supported their ideas. Some Protestant thinkers, especially in the United States, developed the concept of polygenesis, that God had created human beings twice, or more often, relying on the fact that Genesis, the first book of the Bible, contains two creation stories. Some, though not all, polygenists argued that the salvation story laid out in the Bible only applied to descendants of the second genesis, that of Adam and Eve, and that other humans not descended from the first couple, usually defined as nonwhites, were not really among those who could be saved through Christianity. Another religious explanation common at this time, the Hamite hypothesis, preserved a single creation of mankind, while still permitting racial discrimination. Under this reading of the story of the Flood, the descendants of Noah's son Ham, cursed by God for disrespect toward his father, were the nonwhite peoples of the world. While they could be Christians and be saved, they were condemned to be the servants of the descendants of the two good brothers, defined as whites and Semites. British Israelitism, or the belief that the British were the descendants of the 10 lost tribes of Israel, was another white supremacist quasi-religious idea common at this time. This belief held that the promises of God to the Israelites were to be fulfilled for the British and their white American descendants, seen as the "true" Israelites. All of these beliefs were at their height in the early 1800s, and they had some impact on general public racial attitudes among whites, especially in North America. However, the influence of religion on culture was declining during this period. The fervor of the religious wars of the 1500s and 1600s was replaced by an attitude of toleration, especially among cultural and political elites in Western Europe, and many intellectual leaders of the Enlightenment were deists or agnostics. Even for religious believers, by the mid-1800s, it had become common to say that religious ideas should not be permitted to influence public policy. We think of this as a liberal idea, as indeed it was, but it also served to permit racial prejudice to survive in the Western world unchecked by the fundamentally egalitarian and universal message of Christianity, still the religion of the vast majority of whites in the Americas.

Negative racial attitudes, now supported to some extent by the emerging science of the Enlightenment and by new religious ideas, became widespread among whites in the Americas in the 1700s and 1800s. It became unexceptionable, routine, even for those who supported greater justice for blacks to affirm that they still considered whites superior beings. For example, in his debates with Stephen Douglas during the senatorial election in ILLINOIS in 1858, ABRAHAM LINCOLN said, "There is a physical difference between the white and black races which I believe will forever forbid the two races living together on terms of social and political equality." William Lloyd Garrison, the abolitionist publisher of the *Liberator*, was almost unique among U.S. white abolitionists in his uniform condemnation of all forms of racial discrimination, not just slavery. Public opposition to slavery in the Northern states of the United States often centered on the threat slavery posed to Northern jobs, especially after the DRED SCOTT decision of 1857 opened the possibility that Southern SLAVE OWNERS could take their "property" to the North with them. Antislavery lawmaking was often linked with restrictions on free people of color, as in OHIO, where the first legislature of the state in 1803 both outlawed slavery in its constitution and placed harsh restrictions on free colored immigration. In the private sector, opponents of slavery often thought that abolition could mean a society entirely free of black presence. This was behind the strong support among whites throughout the United States for the AMERICAN COLONIZATION SOCIETY, founded in 1816, which sought to help free people of color emigrate to Africa (*see* EMIGRATION AND COLONIZATION).

The Effect of Racial Prejudice

Informal racism affected all kinds of decisions made by whites during the period of slavery. It was even more important as a brake on the progress of people of color after the end of slavery and led to stagnation in many areas for decades, even persisting to the present day in many places. The racial attitudes that lead to racism are much harder to eradicate than are formal laws, and they may prove to be the most dangerous legacies of slavery for the modern world.

During the epoch of slavery in the Americas, even in the absence of laws preventing free blacks from holding high-status jobs, entering universities, or otherwise taking up high positions in society, there were still few black people fulfilling any of these roles. The reasons were informal racism, often quite frankly expressed. When Harvard admitted its first black student, Beverly Garnett Williams, in 1847, the student body responded with violent protests that finally forced the institution to withdraw its offer of admission. Harvard did not award its first degree to an African American, Richard Greener, until 1870. Free people of color in the Southern states of the United States before the AMERICAN CIVIL WAR were legally prohibited from pursuing certain occupations. In the North, there were fewer of these sorts of laws, but black physicians, lawyers, and other professionals were rare. The first black lawyer admitted to the bar in the United States was Macon Allen, in MAINE, in 1844, but he was one of only a handful of colleagues before the Civil War. Bar associations refused to admit black candidates even if they had completed apprenticeships or law school. Even lower-level occupations were restricted to certain races: In the railroad industry in the United States, the roles of conductor, brakeman, and engineer were reserved for whites, while porters, waiters, and firemen were blacks. Trade unions respected these rules, although after the Civil War some radical industrial unions accepted black members. Black-owned businesses could deal with white clients, as long as they were in a limited set of occupations such as shoemakers and blacksmiths.

In Latin America during the epoch of slavery, access to the high-status professions and higher education was a little easier to gain for free people of color, if they had high social standing. In general, racial standards were more flexible and less tied to ancestry in Spanish and Portuguese America. By redefining the individual as white, society found a way to permit people of partially African ancestry to achieve high social rank. The Peruvian physician JOSÉ MANUEL VALDÉS was able to enter the university to study medicine in 1806 through the patronage of his Spanish godparents and a famous white physician, who obtained a *cédula de gracias al sacar*, or royal pardon of blackness, even though his parents were of quite humble social standing (*See* CEDULAS DE GRACIAS AL SACAR).

After independence in the early 19th century, most Latin American countries abolished formal legal prohibitions to entering the professions, attending university, or working in any sort of business of free people of color. But racial prejudice continued and even strengthened in many places. CUBA, still a Spanish colony until 1898, had a relatively open racial climate in the early 1700s. By the middle of the 1800s, Cuba was passing laws prohibiting free blacks to get an education or perform certain types of work. Plantation managers, many of whom were free people of color in the 1700s, were almost exclusively white by 1858. Cuba is an exception to the general trend, in part because of the continuing Spanish rule and persistence of the slave trade there, and also because of the influence of expatriate North American investors and managers on the plantation industry. Rapidly growing slave populations led to increases in racism against free people of color in many places in the 1700s; the unusual aspect of Cuba is that this was happening in the 1800s. But in Brazil, often seen as having a relatively benign racial climate in the 1800s, racial prejudice after the abolition of slavery in 1888 led to reverses in advances that people of color had made up to that point. Black sailors in the Brazilian NAVY rebelled in 1910 against what they saw as a retreat on principles of racial equality, which included the use of the lash as a form of punishment. Brazil had many prominent black intellectuals, journalists, and businessmen in the 1880s. However, by the 1920s, when the Brazilian social scientist GILBERTO FREYRE was lauding Brazil's racial democracy and acceptance of MISCEGENATION, blacks had largely disappeared from the professions and the higher levels of the business community. In many cases, as a result of miscegenation, they had been replaced by a population socially defined as white even though they might well have had a few African ancestors. But people who could be identified as Afro-Brazilian by their skin color paradoxically found it more difficult to advance in society. As did the United States in the 1960s and 1970s, Brazil needed a civil rights movement, in Brazil's case starting in the 1980s, to restore blacks to a less unequal position in society.

In the United States after the end of slavery in 1865, there was a brief moment when legal restrictions on people of color were mostly dismantled, in the North as well as the South. Informal racism remained strong, however, and indeed grew stronger during the period of RECONSTRUCTION IN THE UNITED STATES, 1865–77. Southern whites sought to recoup their prewar dominant position through conscious use of racial solidarity and separation of the races. Meanwhile, Northern whites reacted to the growing competition for jobs from blacks moving to Northern cities by excluding blacks from most unions, business and professional associations, and, in large measure, higher education. A few blacks broke through the wall of prejudice, thanks in some cases to black-only educational institutions set up during Reconstruction, but most black professionals and businesspeople in the late 1800s served predominantly black clienteles.

The new aspect of racism, the racial separation called Jim Crow imposed in the United States after the end of Reconstruction, was a product both of law and of social custom. Southern states generally enshrined the principles of SEGREGATION in law, but many of the daily injustices of Jim Crow, such as separate dining facilities or washrooms or limitations on types of jobs blacks could hold, were a product of informal decisions made by white businesspeople and others. Especially in the North, no law required real estate agents to refuse to show houses in "white" neighborhoods to blacks, but their own preferences and those of their white peers and customers meant that almost all complied with an unwritten rule. Bankers, restaurant and bar owners, hoteliers, and principals of private schools all met the same pressure, and few overcame it. Even large institutions with formal nondiscrimination policies often had to struggle with informal racism among their employees and members: The Roman Catholic Church in the United States had to threaten to excommunicate Catholic school directors and staff before they would admit black students in many dioceses. Job discrimination was rife throughout the United States from the 1880s to the 1970s, and even institutions and employers who thought of themselves as enlightened merely practiced tokenism by employing a few blacks, in numbers greatly disproportionate to their population. It took a law, the Civil Rights Act of 1964, and decades of struggle to enforce it, to achieve even the limited equal access to employment that American blacks enjoy at the beginning of the 21st century.

Stewart R. King

FURTHER READING
Dain, Bruce. *A Hideous Monster of the Mind: American Race Theory in the Early Republic.* Cambridge, Mass.: Harvard University Press, 2002.
Levi-Strauss, Claude. *Race and History.* New York: UNESCO, 1952.
West, Cornel. *Race Matters.* New York: Vintage, 1993.

RAIMOND, JULIEN (1744–1801) *Saint-Domingue planter, civil rights activist, and political leader*
Julien Raimond was an indefatigable campaigner for the rights of free people of color within the French colonial system. He protested the rising tide of anti–free colored racial laws in the 1780s, and after the outbreak of the FRENCH REVOLUTION, he urged the new French government to create a race-neutral system in its American colonies. He went as a representative of the government to SAINT-DOMINGUE to implement such a system in 1796, in the midst of the HAITIAN REVOLUTION, and became a convert to TOUSSAINT LOUVERTURE's vision of an autonomous or independent Haitian state as the only route to defeat RACISM AND RACIAL PREJUDICE. He was one of the authors of the first Haitian Constitution of 1800.

Born in Bainet, in the South Province of Saint-Domingue, on October 16, 1744, Raimond was the son of a French planter, Pierre Raymond, and his mixed-race wife, Marie Bégasse. In 1726, when they married, INTERRACIAL MARRIAGE was common, and the elder Raymond profited handsomely from his relationship with Bégasse, gaining lands and slaves worth tens of thousands of livres, or colonial pounds, and contacts with the province's wealthiest families. Julien Raimond and his seven brothers and sisters were trained to fill the same role in society as their parents—as planters and local notables. By the time Pierre Raymond died in 1772, the family had two plantations in Bainet and the neighboring parish of Aquin and owned dozens of slaves.

In the wake of a rebellion against increased MILITIA service that took place in the South Province in March–June 1769, the government feared that cooperation between white and free colored planters might lead to an independence movement. Thus, starting in the 1770s, the French government introduced a series of laws that redefined the acceptable roles of free people of color in colonial society. While the right to own land and slaves was never challenged, a variety of humiliating measures were intended to divide the free colored planting class from their white neighbors. Among these was a requirement that free blacks could not bear the same surnames as whites, even if they were legitimate children. Free blacks, the law stated, had to have names "drawn from the African idiom." Raimond and his family simply changed the spelling of their father's name, observing the letter but not the spirit of the law. Laws also made it almost obligatory for free black planters to hire white plantation managers, and Raimond's mother hired a white man to oversee her lands after her children married. Julien Raimond and his brother had a physical altercation with this man in 1775, accusing him of poor management of their mother's money. Had the laws been fully enforced, the two Raimond brothers could have had their hands cut off for the crime of striking a white man. Luckily for them, their neighbors protected them, perhaps believing their accusations well founded, and nothing more came of the matter—but a less well-connected free colored person might have been in serious trouble for the sort of violent disagreement that would have been entirely unremarkable between white men in that society.

In 1771, Julien Raimond married a wealthy free colored cousin named Marie-Marthe Vincent. She died after two years, leaving him a substantial landowner with property that, by 1782, would be worth more than 300,000 livres. In 1784, he married again, to Françoise Dasmard, the mixed-race daughter of a white neighbor and widow of another white planter who had bought a noble title in France (apparently violating or predating the 1770s rule that whites married to people of color were ineligible for noble status). Their extensive landholdings proved to be more than they could manage, especially the lands in FRANCE that Françoise had inherited from her previous husband. In an attempt to sell the excess and establish commercial contacts, Julien and his wife traveled to France in 1784. Before he left, he gathered his free colored neighbors together and persuaded them to ratify a petition he planned to submit to the minister of marine, the French government official charged with overseeing colonial governments. The petition asked that free mixed-race people who were legitimately born should have equal rights with whites. Raimond claimed that two-thirds of all free coloreds in the colony fit this description, and in his own social class this was generally true. Raimond himself was legitimate, as were his first wife and many other local planters. His second wife was illegitimate but recognized by her father. Almost all of his social circle were of mixed race. For the colony as a whole, this was an overestimate, but still the reform he called for would have given civil rights to tens of thousands of people in the French colonies. He argued that it would have a progressive effect—that free blacks would seek relationships with mixed-race or white people, leading to "WHITENING" AND RACIAL PROMOTION, and that marriage, legitimacy, and landholding would create a stable and growing middle class in the colonies.

He presented his petition to the minister on May 24, 1784, and followed it up with three other communications over the next three years. The minister, Charles de Castries (1727–1801), was sympathetic to the appeal. During his term in office, he issued several regulations improving the conditions of slaves and making MANUMISSION easier. Raimond's own proposals were never acted on, however. Raimond and his family remained in France until 1795. In 1789, the FRENCH REVOLUTION began. Raimond maintained a salon in Paris where the Société des Amis des Noirs, or the Friends of the Blacks, the principal abolitionist group, often met. He was friendly with Jacques Pierre Brissot de Warville (1754–93), an important leader in the revolutionary legislature. Raimond joined the Jacobin club, the center of power in the revolutionary legislature. Between 1790 and 1793, Raimond was very influential in the revolutionary debates on the subject of race and slavery. The Amis des Noirs, on his urging, added opposition to racial discrimination to their core issue of the abolition of slavery. Raimond himself, who still owned more than 100 slaves, accepted the Amis des Noirs's goal of the ultimate abolition of slavery. Raimond's friendship with Abbé HENRI GRÉGOIRE, a Catholic priest who became France's foremost abolitionist, was an important step in drawing Grégoire into the abolitionist movement. On

May 13, 1791, Raimond addressed the Jacobin club, calling for racial equality. Two days later, the Jacobin vote was crucial when the National Assembly granted the vote to free people of color who were of legitimate birth and who met the property qualifications. On April 4, 1792, the new Legislative Assembly passed a law granting full civil equality to free people of color. Raimond, along with Grégoire, had been key players in the committee that drafted this law. Raimond was an adviser to the Civil Commission, headed by Léger-Félicité Sonthonax (1763–1813), that was sent to Saint-Domingue to implement this order and ultimately abolished slavery there. He engaged in an exchange of pamphlets with MÉDÉRIC-LOUIS-ÉLIE MOREAU DE ST-MÉRY, the colonial philosopher and writer, on the proper role of free people of color in the colonies, which produced the clearest explanation of the civil rights argument offered during the Revolution. In his *Observations on the Origin . . . of Prejudice*, published in book form in 1791, Raimond argued that the Revolution can and should bring about freedom for all the people of the colonies. The abolition of slavery should not take place overnight, because that would cause chaos. Instead, the groundwork should be laid by making free people of color equal citizens, introducing gradual emancipation of slaves, and taking measures to lessen the burden of slavery. In essence, the course he recommended was adopted in many Spanish-American countries after they gained independence in the early 19th century. Reducing prejudice against blacks would build a society where freed slaves could become equal citizens without suffering prejudice.

Brissot, Raimond's patron, fell out with the more radical revolutionary leadership in June 1793. Their debates had centered on the question of what to do with deposed King Louis XVI but turned into a broader debate about the course of the Revolution, which the more moderate faction of Brissot lost. Brissot and his more moderate Girondin faction had preferred to keep the former king as a hostage, but the radical majority prevailed, and he was put on trial and executed in January 1793. After this, the Brissot supporters were portrayed as supporters of the monarchy, and Julien Raimond, a close Brissot ally, could not escape suspicion. In addition, the white representatives from Saint-Domingue were important allies of the radicals. Therefore, Raimond was arrested in June 1793 and spent more than a year in prison.

Upon his release and political rehabilitation after the fall of the radical faction, Raimond began to campaign for a new government job. He was rewarded in February 1796, when he was named Sonthonax's assistant on the Third Civil Commission sent to Saint-Domingue. He found that the colony had changed beyond measure during his 12 years' absence. The Haitian Revolution had yielded freedom for all the slaves but economic disaster for the planters. Those who remained in the country, such as Raimond, were able to work the land using the labor of *cultivateurs,* or agricultural laborers, former slaves who served under semi-military discipline but had to be paid wages and could protest their treatment to local commissioners. Toussaint Louverture, the leader of the black rebels who now controlled the colony, was trying to create a race-neutral society where plantation SUGAR CULTIVATION and growing of other crops were carried out by free labor. He was also trying to wage war against numerous opponents, ranging from Spanish and British invaders to rebel *cultivateurs* who saw little difference between their status and their former slavery. Sonthonax fell out with Toussaint and was ultimately sent home. Napoléon Bonaparte, now in control back in France, was increasingly unhappy with the black rebels and their too-independent leader and would ultimately reverse the abolition of slavery and send an army to force the people of Saint-Domingue back into their old ways of life. Raimond, scenting this change in the wind, in failing health after years of prison and struggle, worked devotedly for the success of Toussaint's system. Among his last contributions to the cause of racial equality in Saint-Domingue was his work to draft Toussaint's colonial constitution, which provided that no "distinction other than those based on virtue and talent" should exist among citizens of Saint-Domingue. Raimond lived to see the constitution promulgated on July 8, 1801, and died a few weeks later.

Raimond remains a controversial figure in the Haitian Revolution. An early supporter of equal rights for his own wealthy free mixed-race planter class, he never abandoned the dream of plantation wealth. He campaigned for the abolition of slavery but supported, and made use of, Toussaint's oppressive labor code that subjected the *cultivateurs* to harsh discipline. He was one of the first blacks ever to address a European legislature and was a successful lobbyist for the free colored cause. Ultimately, faced with the success of the black rebel movement, however, he made his peace with Toussaint and supported him even against Napoléon. He realized, long before other mixed-race leaders such as ANDRÉ RIGAUD or ALEXANDRE SABÈS PÉTION, that Saint-Domingue's wealthy mixed-race and black former slaves would have to work together to oppose resurgent French colonialism and protect a society of racial equality and freedom on the island.

Stewart R. King

FURTHER READING

Dubois, Laurent. *Avengers of the New World: The Story of the Haitian Revolution.* Cambridge, Mass.: Harvard University Press, 2005.

Garrigus, John. "Opportunist or Patriot: Julien Raimond (1744–1801) and the Haitian Revolution." *Slavery and Abolition* 28, no. 1 (April 2007): 1–21.

Raimond, Julien. *Observations sur l'origine et les progrès du préjugé des colons blancs contre les hommes de couleur.* Paris: Belin, Desenne, Bailly, 1791.

RANCHING

A boom in cattle ranching in the United States took place in the 1870s and 1880s after the AMERICAN CIVIL WAR, when railroad lines were extended into the Great Plains, permitting cattle ranchers to take their animals to market. Elsewhere in the Americas, cattle ranching was an important activity during the era of slavery, and many blacks worked on ranches. Some free people of color were ranch owners or managers, owned packing plants or butcher shops, or were otherwise involved in the business at a higher level. Ranching was an important economic activity for free people of color for a number of reasons.

The most important reason was that cattle ranching required a relatively small initial investment of capital. A beginning rancher could often use land for grazing in the backcountry without the formality of actually getting title to it, round up feral cattle that effectively belonged to nobody, and start a business for little more than the cost of feeding and housing himself and his crew. Of course, established interests might take a dim view of this, and struggles over title to wild land and livestock were common in cattle country. Small operators often were squeezed out by bigger ones who had preferential access to markets and support from governments. But at least in theory, there was opportunity in ranching for people of color.

Most plantation colonies had significant interior areas where plantation farming was difficult and not very profitable. These backcountry areas were state property, but gaining title to them was fairly easy. Most colonies wanted these areas put into production in order to reduce the chance that Indians or communities of MAROONS would inhabit them. They generally had some sort of legal mechanism to grant title to these lands to owners who would make some pretence of using them for productive purposes. Sometimes these were leases and sometimes outright grants. Often people of color found it harder to get these grants, but there was also the possibility of buying the lands from white grantees. Backcountry lands were also convenient gifts for free colored children or clients, costing a planter little and providing preferential access to the produce of those lands if the free colored recipient could put them into production. In plantation areas, the produce of ranching found a ready market on the plantations. Meats, both fresh and salted, and leather were both important products, and the plantations also purchased oxen for motive power. (*See also* PROVISION GROUND FARMING.)

When the Spanish first explored the Americas, they had a practice of releasing livestock into the wild. Eurasian grazing species such as cattle, horses, pigs, and goats had no natural predators or disease threats in the Americas. While local predators did adapt their hunting behavior, the nonnative species still squeezed out native grazing animals throughout their ranges. The first European settlers, sometimes arriving as much as a century after the first Spanish explorers passed through, found enormous numbers of cattle, especially, grazing on the plains of MEXICO and South America and the larger Antillean islands. These "breakout populations" were ripe for exploitation, and early settlers treated them as a free good, not even bothering to claim title to individual animals but only to the right to exploit animals found in particular places.

In many of these areas, there were significant numbers of free people of color. This is especially true of the Spanish Antilles, the pampas of ARGENTINA and URUGUAY, the *llanos* of VENEZUELA, and northern Mexico. The *boucaniers* of SAINT-DOMINGUE, the vaqueros of northern Mexico, the gauchos of the Pampas, and the *llaneros* of Venezuela all had significant numbers of blacks in their ranks alongside Indians and people of mixed race. Mostly, the managers and organizers of these activities were white, and the blacks, Indians, and mestizos were the employees. White managers often preferred blacks as employees because, in the early days, they were more likely to be familiar with horses and the care of cattle than were Indians. In the 16th century, the Spanish regularly imported slaves from African regions where cattle were kept in order to supervise groups of Indian workers. In Uruguay and Argentina in the 18th century, white managers benefited from the low cost of slaves, a product of proximity to the CONGO AND ANGOLA and the flourishing smuggling trade of slaves from BRAZIL, mostly heading for the mines of Bolivia, but enough stopping in Uruguay that its population was more than half African or MULATTO in the 18th century. When the port of Buenos Aires was opened in 1776, this generated a further flood of cheap slaves and further growth in the black population of the Southern Cone colonies.

But using slaves in ranching was dangerous. The nature of the work required that the employees be left to their own devices for weeks or months at a time. Without supervision, nothing prevented a slave from running away, maybe taking a valuable horse and tack, weapons, and equipment, and maybe even some livestock.

The wide open spaces of northern Mexico or Patagonia offered plenty of hiding places for RUNAWAY SLAVES, even if they did not blend into the free population and continue working as cowboys. In any case, the working life of a cowboy was short, and in the slave systems of the Americas, masters were required to take care of their slaves for life. In Spanish America, there were courts and government officials responsible for making sure that owners fulfilled this responsibility. Buying a slave cost a good deal of initial cash outlay, while a free employee could often be paid his wages at the end of the season, after the cattle had been sold. In general, hiring free colored employees was cheaper and more flexible than using slaves.

Some of these free people of color who worked as cowboys managed to rise to owners. There were free mixed-race ranchers in the *llanos* of Venezuela, enough that when José Antonio Páez organized the *llaneros* into an army to fight for Venezuelan independence after 1810, three of his seven cavalry regimental commanders were men of mixed race. Three black families were ranching near Carson City, Nevada, in the late 1850s, just before the American Civil War. Ancillary businesses including meatpacking or salting facilities; feed store, corral, and feedlot operators; and skilled tradesmen were also niches where free people of color could find economic independence. (*See also* ARTISANS.)

Stewart R. King

FURTHER READING

Slatta, Richard. *Cowboys of the Americas.* New Haven, Conn.: Yale University Press, 1990.

RAPIER, JAMES T. (1837–1883) *American lawyer, labor organizer, and public servant*

James Thomas Rapier served as a U.S. representative from 1873 to 1875. One of ALABAMA's three African-American congressmen during RECONSTRUCTION IN THE UNITED STATES, Rapier was born on November 13, 1837, to John H. and Susan Rapier in Florence, Alabama. He had three older brothers: Richard, John, Jr., and Henry. His father, a freed slave, became wealthy by building a prosperous business as a barber.

When Rapier's mother died in 1841 during childbirth, John Rapier sent James and his older brother, John, Jr., to live with their paternal grandmother, Sally Thomas, in Nashville, TENNESSEE. Thomas, an enslaved laundress, raised Rapier from 1841 to 1856, during which he attended a secret school for African-American children in Nashville. In 1856, Rapier's father learned that Rapier had spent time drinking and gambling on riverboats. Deciding that his son needed more direction, he sent

James to live in the experimental African-American community of Buxton, Ontario, where John Rapier's brother had property. All of Buxton's residents were RUNAWAY SLAVES who had escaped to CANADA via the Underground Railroad.

Once in Buxton, Rapier attended the Buxton Mission School. He next attended Montreal College, studied law, and was admitted to the bar. While in Buxton, Rapier experienced a religious conversion and decided to devote the rest of his life to helping African Americans. He attended school in Toronto, received a teaching certificate in 1863, and returned to Buxton as an instructor. In late 1864, Rapier returned to Nashville, where he worked as a reporter for a Northern newspaper for a short time. With the help of his father, Rapier bought 200 acres of land in Maury County, Tennessee, and became a successful cotton planter.

After the AMERICAN CIVIL WAR, Rapier entered politics. A keynote address Rapier delivered at the Tennessee Negro Suffrage Convention in Nashville in 1865 marked his first political experience. Rapier worked for African-American voting rights but became disillusioned with the restoration of former Confederates to power in the state government. That, coupled with his father's illness, made him decide to return to Florence, where he rented 550 acres along the Tennessee River in Alabama. Rapier's success as a planter allowed him to hire black tenant farmers and finance sharecroppers with low-interest loans.

In March 1867, when freedmen could vote, Rapier called a local meeting to elect a black registrar. His father won the election, and James Rapier was chosen unanimously to represent the county at the Alabama Republican Convention. Rapier served as the convention's vice-chairman and directed the platform committee. In October 1867, Rapier served as a delegate to the Alabama constitutional convention.

Two years later, in 1869, Rapier attended the founding convention of the National Negro Labor Union in Washington, D.C. The union organized to protect African-American laborers, to assist sharecroppers, and to improve educational and economic opportunities for freedmen. In 1870, the union selected Rapier as its vice president. A year later, he opened an Alabama office, serving as president and executive chairman.

Rapier ran for Alabama secretary of state in 1870 and lost. He secured appointment as a federal Internal Revenue assessor with the assistance of the African-American Alabama representative Benjamin Turner. Rapier became one of the most powerful African-American politicians in Alabama. He began the state's first African-American–owned and –operated newspaper, the Montgomery *Republican State Sentinel,* to crusade for the Republican

Party, freedmen's rights, and the reelection of President ULYSSES S. GRANT in 1872.

That same year he was elected to the U.S. Congress. His effort was aided by congressionally enacted federal enforcement acts (the KU KLUX KLAN bills) that temporarily quelled Klan violence and enabled a peaceful election. Before he went to Washington, D.C., he traveled to Vienna, Austria, as Alabama's commissioner to the Fifth International Exposition. In the 43rd Congress, Rapier introduced legislation to designate Montgomery, Alabama, a federal collections site. The measure, signed into law by President Grant on June 20, 1874, would boost the city's economy.

During the remainder of his term, Rapier worked for other improvement projects for Alabama, served on the Committee on Education and Labor, and sought to advance the Civil Rights Bill. The House passed a weakened version of the bill at the end of the 43rd Congress.

Rapier's bid for reelection in 1874 was stymied by threats and voter intimidation. The Ku Klux Klan often disrupted his campaign appearances. He pleaded with federal authorities to ensure a peaceful election, but they took no action. More than 100 people were killed, and many African Americans stayed away from the polls. Rapier lost to the former Confederate army major Jeremiah Williams, who ran as a conservative Democrat.

In 1876, Rapier moved to Lowndes County, near Montgomery, so he could run for the only remaining district with an African-American majority (65 percent) after gerrymandering by the Democratic legislature. Rapier lost the general election. The Republican Party recognized Rapier's service by appointing him as a collector for the Internal Revenue Service in July 1878. That same year, he transformed the *Republican State Sentinel* into the *Haynesville Times* and began a call for black emigration to the West—a movement he supported financially and by testifying before a Senate committee. (*See also* EXODUSTER MOVEMENT and MIGRATION.)

In 1882 and 1883, political opponents attempted to remove him from his post. While he successfully rebuffed those efforts, failing health forced him to resign. Rapier was appointed a disbursing officer for a federal building in Montgomery just before he died of pulmonary tuberculosis on May 31, 1883.

John McLane

FURTHER READING

Feldman, Eugene Pieter Romany. *Black Power in Old Alabama: The Life and Stirring Times of James T. Rapier, Afro-American Congressman from Alabama, 1839–1883*. Chicago: Museum of African-American History, 1968.

Foner, Eric. *Freedom's Lawmakers*. Baton Rouge: Louisiana State University Press, 1996.

"James Thomas Rapier." In *Black Americans in Congress, 1870–2007*. Prepared under the direction of the Committee on House Administration by the Office of History & Preservation, U.S. House of Representatives. Washington, D.C.: Government Printing Office, 2008.

Rabinowitz, Howard N., ed. *Southern Black Leaders of the Reconstruction Era*. Champaign: University of Illinois Press, 1982.

Schweninger, Loren. "James Rapier and the Negro Labor Movement, 1869–1872." *Alabama Review* 28 (July 1975): 185–201.

———. *James T. Rapier and Reconstruction*. Chicago: University of Chicago Press, 1978.

RAYNAL, GUILLAUME (1711–1796) *French philosopher and abolitionist*

Guillaume Raynal was a French man of letters. He was born on April 17, 1711, in south-central FRANCE. He was ordained a priest in the order of JESUITS in 1743. Although he subsequently left the order and did not work as a priest after 1748, he shared the attitude of most Jesuits that people of color should be treated fairly. The ROMAN CATHOLIC CHURCH had taught that white and nonwhite people were spiritually equal, but many Catholic countries nonetheless were leaders in slavery and the slave trade. Raynal pointed out this contradiction in his writings and ultimately called for the complete abolition of slavery.

Raynal sold his sermons to other priests while serving at the Parisian church of Saint-Sulpice. Although this was a common practice in the Protestant world in the 18th century—books of sermons by famous preachers were best sellers in BRITAIN, Germany, and the Thirteen Colonies, not only to other religious leaders, but to the laity as well—it was unknown in the Catholic Church and somewhat scandalous and contributed to the Jesuit order's decision to fire him. Raynal then abandoned active ministry and began to frequent the salons of Enlightenment Paris, discussing philosophy and ultimately publishing his ideas. His most influential work was the *Histoire philosophique et politique des établissements & du commerce des européens dans les deux Indes* (Philosophical and political history of the colonies and commerce of Europeans in the two Indies), first published in 1770 and reissued in 1774 and 1780 after earlier editions were banned by the censors. This work is not groundbreaking history or geography, mainly collecting and repeating research done by other observers.

It is Raynal's analysis and argument that were revolutionary. He criticized the very idea of monarchy, which led to so much trouble that he had to leave France in the 1780s, spending time in Switzerland, Prussia, and Russia before returning shortly before the

FRENCH REVOLUTION. Most radical, though, were his ideas about slavery. He argued, as other philosophers had, that human beings were free by nature, and he systematically and logically rejected the wide variety of arguments that had been made to justify the existence of slavery—that slaves had consented to their condition by being captured in wars or sentenced as criminals, that slaves as individuals were naturally suited to slavery, or that some races were naturally inferior. His commitment to democratic equality of all people was far ahead of the thinking of other philosophers of the day.

A portrait of Guillaume Raynal (1711–96) from his famous book, *Histoire philosophique et politique des établissements & du commerce des européens dans les deux Indes.* Born in France, Raynal was a supporter of the rights of free people of color and an opponent of slavery. He was not an active participant in the politics of the French Revolution, but his philosophical vision of democratic equality of people regardless of race became the consensus of the modern age. His call for a "black Spartacus" to overthrow colonial slavery was a rallying call for Toussaint Louverture and the other rebels of the 1790s and 1800s. *(Library of Congress)*

His works gained wide circulation, and such important leaders as THOMAS JEFFERSON, Simón Bolívar, and TOUSSAINT LOUVERTURE had copies in their libraries. In the 1780 version of his *Histoire,* he wrote his most inspiring lines:

> Where is this great man, whom nature owes to her afflicted, oppressed, and tormented children? Where is this new Spartacus who will not find a Crassus? Where is he? He will undoubtedly appear, he will show himself, he will lift up the sacred standard of liberty. This venerable signal will collect around him the companions of his misfortunes. They will rush on with more impetuosity than torrents; they will leave behind them, in all parts, indelible traces of their just resentment. Spaniards, Portuguese, English, French, Dutch, all their tyrants will become the victims of fire and sword. The plains of America will suck up with transport the blood which they have so long expected, and the bones of so many wretches, heaped upon one another, during the course of so many centuries, will bound for joy. The Old World will join its plaudits to those of the New. In all parts the name of the hero, who shall have restored the rights of the human species will be blest; in all parts trophies will be erected to his glory.

This call for a new Spartacus to overthrow colonial slavery resonated for free black resistance leaders in the Americas. Toussaint Louverture referred to himself as a "child of Raynal" on several occasions. JEAN-BAPTISTE BELLEY, a free black man who was elected representative of SAINT-DOMINGUE to the French National Assembly in 1793, had his portrait painted with a bust of Raynal. James Forten (*see also* FORTEN FAMILY) included Raynal among the benefactors of the Negro race in the constitution of the PENNSYLVANIA black convention in 1817 (*see also* NEGRO CONVENTION MOVEMENT IN THE UNITED STATES).

Raynal's vision of democratic equality has become the dominant view in Western civilization today, thanks to the efforts of the practical politicians he influenced. He himself engaged in little practical politics. He was friendly with many of the important figures of the French Revolution. Jacques-Pierre Brissot (1754–93) and Abbé HENRI GRÉGOIRE, both leading abolitionists, were friends, but he did not become an active member of their society, the Amis des Noirs. He knew Robespierre, leader of the radicals, but was not very close to him and did not suffer when his regime fell in 1794. In 1795, the new government asked him to become a member of the Institut de France, but he declined the honor because of his failing health. At his death, on March 6, 1796, a very diverse collection of world figures mourned, and he was almost immediately recognized as a leading figure in democratic philosophy.

Stewart R. King

FURTHER READING

Raynal, Guillaume. *Histoire philosophique et politique des établissements & du commerce des européens dans les deux Indes.* Available online in English translation from Google Books. URL: http://books.google.com/books?id=HnYIAAAAQAAJ. Accessed January 7, 2011.

Raynal, Guillaume, and Peter Jimack. *A History of the Two Indies: A Translated Selection of Writings from Raynal's* Histoire philosophique et politique des établissements & du commerce des européens dans les deux Indes. Farnham, U.K.: Ashgate, 2006.

REASON, CHARLES L. (1818–1893) *American mathematician and educator*

Charles Reason was born free in 1818 in New York City, of free colored parents who fled Haiti during the HAITIAN REVOLUTION. He was educated at the African Free School and had his first paying job in education at the age of 14 when he became a mathematics teacher at the school at a salary of $25 a month. He pursued further education, both through tutors and by attending one of the few institutions of higher education open to blacks, McGrawville College, now New York Central College, a Baptist institution. Reason felt he had a calling to the priesthood, and as he had been raised Anglican, he sought admission to an Episcopal seminary. He was refused because of his race, and he left the Episcopal Church (*see* PROTESTANT MAINLINE CHURCHES).

Reason continued to be interested in mathematics, but his primary work was improving the quality of education for blacks in New York. In 1840, he established a normal school to train black teachers, and in 1847, he was founding director of an organization approved by the state legislature to oversee black schools in the city. In 1848, he became the superintendant of P.S. 2, a New York City public school for free blacks, which he turned into a highly respected institution.

In 1849, Charles Reason, George Vashon (*see also* VASHON FAMILY), and William G. Allen were appointed professors at New York Central College. They were the first African Americans to hold professorships at a predominantly white U.S. college. Reason resigned his post in 1852, when he was appointed to head the Institute for Colored Youth in PHILADELPHIA, PENNSYLVANIA (now Cheyney State University). Reason built the school into an important institution in Philadelphia free colored life during the three years he served there. In 1855, he

returned to the New York City public school system, where he served for the remainder of his career. He retired in 1892 after 60 years of service. While employed in the school system, he worked successfully for desegregation of New York's schools in 1873.

Reason was also active in politics throughout his life. In the 1840s and 1850s, he was active in the Negro Convention Movement (*see* NEGRO CONVENTION MOVEMENT IN THE UNITED STATES) and worked with HENRY HIGHLAND GARNET for votes for blacks. He also worked to get fugitive slaves the right to a jury trial, in response to the FUGITIVE SLAVE ACT OF 1850. He was opposed to the movement to resettle free blacks in Africa (*see also* AMERICAN COLONIZATION SOCIETY) and organized a demonstration, along with FREDERICK DOUGLASS, opposing Garnet's African Civilization Society. He supported black civil rights during and after the AMERICAN CIVIL WAR, including the successful campaign for school desegregation. He was also active in the labor movement after the Civil War. He died on August 16, 1893.

Charles Reason's life illustrates the importance of the educational system and HIGHER EDUCATION in the lives of free people of color. Reason's education permitted him to advance in society, and hence, he was able to support the black community through developing black educational institutions. Educators were and are very important figures in the black community in the United States. For many years, few opportunities in the professions were open to blacks, no matter how high their skills. Reason did work in predominantly white institutions, but people of color in such jobs were very few in the 19th century. Education, because it was delivered in segregated institutions, created opportunities for black professionals. School principals, in particular, dealt with everybody in the black community and were very influential figures. Reason is a prototype for similar figures throughout the 19th and 20th centuries.

Stewart R. King

FURTHER READING

"Charles L. Reason: African-American Mathematician, 1818–1893." Available online. URL: http://www.math.buffalo.edu/mad/special/reason_charles_l.html. Accessed January 7, 2011.

Mayo, Anthony R. "Charles Lewis Reason." *Negro History Bulletin* 5 (June 1942): 212–215.

REBOUÇAS, ANDRÉ (1838–1898) *Brazilian military engineer, abolitionist*

Involved in the abolitionist campaign in BRAZIL during the mid-19th century, André Rebouças was an engineer and a leading liberal intellectual of African descent loyal to the Brazilian monarchy and monarch.

Although the lesser known of the three, his intellectual contribution to the abolitionist effort should be considered together with that of Joaquim Nabuco (1849–1910) and Alfredo Maria Adriano d'Escragnolle Taunay (visconde de Taunay) (1843–99). They were liberal monarchists who believed that republicanism would lead the country in the ways of the Latin American *caudillos* rather than that of the "civilized" European nations. While Nabuco's written contributions were to historiography and Taunay's to literature, Rebouças preferred an economic approach, based on his engineering and agricultural knowledge, to analyzing the political context of Brazil. Additionally, while Nabuco was a member of the liberal party and favored the English political tradition and Taunay was a member of the conservative party and favored the French tradition, Rebouças was not party-affiliated and favored the U.S. political tradition, minus the republicanism.

Son of ANTÔNIO PEREIRA REBOUÇAS, a black activist and lawyer, André Rebouças was born in 1838 in Cachoeira in the state of Bahía and moved to Rio de Janeiro in 1846; there, he studied in the Escola Militar of Rio de Janeiro. He spent two years in Europe studying engineering and traveling with his brother Antônio Pereira Rebouças. While in the military school in Rio and during the Paraguayan war, in which he served at the rank of lieutenant in the engineering corps, he became acquainted and involved with the positivist tradition of liberal thought. His tendency toward positivism appears contradictory in the face of his strong relationship with the emperor and his family, as well as his defense of the empire. Several prominent positivists in Brazil, such as Benjamin Constant, who were also members of the armed forces, would later inaugurate the republican era.

Rebouças's life was a series of contradictory political and economic beliefs and frustrated personal projects. As an engineer, he was known for having revolutionized techniques of port construction in Brazil and for solving water supply problems in Rio de Janeiro, but he worked on very few construction projects. Like the great Brazilian entrepreneur the barão de Mauá, Rebouças was very industrious and started several companies with both domestic and foreign private investments, but unlike Mauá, Rebouças never prospered. Rebouças's work in the abolitionist campaign is best represented by his penning of the manifesto of the Confederação Abolicionista together with JOSÉ CARLOS DO PATROCÍNIO and Aristides Lobo. Rebouças was also a member of the Brazilian Society against Slavery, which he founded with Nabuco, and of the Central Immigration Society, of which Taunay was also a part. Rebouças's strategy in his abolitionist efforts was to convince SLAVE OWNERS of the larger economic benefits of both an agrarian reform and the abolition of slavery.

In 1889, with the fall of the empire and the inauguration of the republic, Rebouças went into exile with Emperor Dom PEDRO II. From exile in Europe, he supported the monarchists in Brazil and dedicated himself to the restoration of the dethroned emperor. He moved to Africa after the emperor died. In 1898, he committed suicide off the coast of the island of Madeira, "half way between Africa and America."

Ana Janaina Nelson

FURTHER READING
Carvalho, M. A. R. *O quinto século: André Rebouças e a construção do Brasil.* Rio de Janeiro: Revan, 1998.
Silva, S. M. G. dos. *André Rebouças e seu Tempo.* Petrópolis-RJ: Vozes, 1985.
Veríssimo, J. I. *André Rebouças através de sua auto-biografia.* Rio de Janeiro: Documentos Brasileiros, 1939.

REBOUÇAS, ANTÔNIO PEREIRA (1798–1880)
Brazilian lawyer and politician

Antônio Pereira Rebouças was an important liberal political leader in the early imperial period of BRAZIL's history. He was also the father of the important abolitionist and military engineer ANDRÉ REBOUÇAS and the engineer Antônio Pereira Rebouças filho (1839–74). His life illustrates many of the conditions that affected socially prominent free people of color in 19th-century Brazil.

The son of a Portuguese tailor and a freedwoman, Antônio Pereira Rebouças was born sometime in 1798, in Maragogipe, Bahia, Brazil, where he received his primary education. In 1814, he moved to SALVADOR, BAHIA, BRAZIL, capital of the province, and apprenticed in a notary's office where he taught himself law, for he could not afford to attend university. He was so successful that, in 1821, the regional supreme court licensed him to practice law in the province (in 1847, by a special act of parliament, this license was extended to all of Brazil).

Rebouças rose to prominence in the Brazilian struggle for independence and served as secretary to the patriot junta that led the struggle against the Portuguese in Bahia (1822–23). After Brazil gained its independence in 1822, he was appointed secretary to the government of the neighboring province of Sergipe, the start of a lengthy political career in which he served several times in the provincial legislature and three terms in the national chamber of deputies (1830–33, 1834–37, 1843–44). In 1848, he retired from politics to devote his time to his legal practice in Rio de Janeiro and to jurisprudence, for which he was highly regarded. Blindness forced him into retirement in 1870. He died some time in 1880.

The elder Rebouças faced many of the obstacles that dogged upwardly mobile mulattoes in the Brazilian empire. Early in his political career, he was considered something of a radical, and in 1824, his political enemies falsely accused him of seeking to foment a Haitian-style revolution in Sergipe. Rebouças identified closely with the liberal promises of equality embodied in the Brazilian constitution of 1824 and regularly denounced anything that smacked of RACISM AND RACIAL PREJUDICE among the free, including the provisions that barred freedmen from serving as officers in the national guard. While he proposed measures to facilitate the MANUMISSION of slaves, he nevertheless owned slaves himself by virtue of his marriage to the daughter of a merchant. Rebouças was deeply committed to working within the established order and rejected the Sabinada Rebellion of 1837–38, which mobilized many men of color against a new conservative government. Moderate in his politics, yet radical in his jurisprudence, Rebouças sought to enact social change through law by extending equal rights to all of the free and freed.

Hendrik Kraay

FURTHER READING

Grinberg, Keila. *O fiador dos brasileiros: Cidadania, escravidão e direito civil no tempo de Antonio Pereira Rebouças*. Rio de Janeiro: Civilização Brasileira, 2002.

Spitzer, Leo. *Lives in Between: Assimilation and Marginality in Austria, Brazil, West Africa, 1780–1945*. Cambridge: Cambridge University Press, 1989.

RECONSTRUCTION IN THE UNITED STATES

Prewar free people of color played an important role in the immediate aftermath of slavery in the United States, the period known as Reconstruction. Both as activists working from Northern states to push the federal government and Northern public opinion toward greater racial justice and as leaders of black communities in the South, prewar free people of color were disproportionately important in this period. The Reconstruction era ended sadly for African Americans, and at the same time, prewar free people of color began to assimilate into the larger black community.

First Steps: The War and the End of Slavery

The Reconstruction era began while the AMERICAN CIVIL WAR, 1861–65, still raged. Four slave states, MISSOURI, KENTUCKY, MARYLAND, and DELAWARE, remained loyal to the United States in 1861 when the remaining Southern states seceded and created the Confederate States of America. In addition, a substantial portion of western Virginia rejected the state's decision to secede and formed a loyal government, which ultimately was admitted to the Union as the separate state of West Virginia. The Civil War began as a struggle over national unity, with the issue of slavery lying beneath the surface. The governments of the loyal slave states started out hoping that they could preserve slavery within the Union. However, the logic of the struggle and changing public attitudes in the North meant that they had to adjust to a new order even while the war was continuing.

The loyal states were not forced to abolish slavery, but Maryland, West Virginia, and Missouri nonetheless did by changing their own state constitutions during the course of the war. Kentucky and Delaware waited until the ratification of the Thirteenth Amendment to the U.S. Constitution in fall 1865, just after the end of the war. In each case, the formal end of slavery was preceded by a slow erosion of the institution as slaves ran away from their masters, in many cases to join or follow the Union army. The FUGITIVE SLAVE ACT OF 1850 was still theoretically in effect, requiring federal officials to assist masters in recovering their escaped slaves. But the SLAVE OWNERS in the border states had often been supporters of secession. Many of them were actually serving in Confederate army units. Many were loyal, or at worst neutral, but few Union officers were prepared to try to sort out the loyal from disloyal ones. Especially after the beginning of 1863, when President ABRAHAM LINCOLN's EMANCIPATION PROCLAMATION permitted blacks to enlist in the U.S. Army (*see* REGULAR ARMY), blacks began to be essential to the Union war effort.

Brigadier General William Birney (1819–1907), a white Army officer and abolitionist from ALABAMA, gave a particularly marked example of the process. Named commander of the 2nd U.S. Colored Troops in the District of Columbia in spring 1863, he realized quickly that there was a vast pool of potential black recruits just across the district line in Maryland. The state government of Maryland did not want to recruit black soldiers—although they had done so in the WAR OF AMERICAN INDEPENDENCE, 1775–83, the century before—because they feared disruption of racial hierarchies. Birney also wanted to disrupt racial hierarchies, and he knew the regular army needed the manpower, so he established a camp near Baltimore in May 1863. He accepted any recruits who entered, without inquiring as to their status. When local whites complained that their runaway slaves were at the camp, Birney's men put bureaucratic obstacles in their way. Birney's men also raided slave barracks in Baltimore that were full of slaves sent to the city to remove them from potential conflict areas, claiming that they were looking for the slaves of disloyal masters but in fact taking anyone who wanted

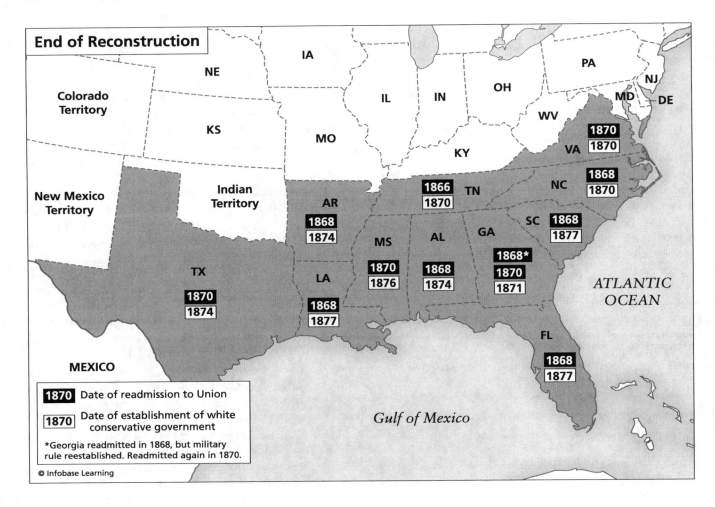

End of Reconstruction

Colorado Territory

New Mexico Territory

MEXICO

NE

KS

Indian Territory

TX

1870
1874

IA

IL   IN

MO

AR

1868
1874

LA

1868
1877

MS

1870
1876

OH

KY

TN

AL

1868
1874

1866
1870

GA

1868*
1870
1871

PA

WV

VA

1870
1870

NC

1868
1870

SC

1868
1877

FL

1868
1877

Gulf of Mexico

ATLANTIC OCEAN

MD   DE
NJ

| 1870 | Date of readmission to Union |
| 1870 | Date of establishment of white conservative government |

*Georgia readmitted in 1868, but military rule reestablished. Readmitted again in 1870.

© Infobase Learning

to leave. Ultimately, Birney raised seven regiments, more than 1,000 men each, from Maryland.

Joining these territories in making this early adjustment were extensive parts of the Confederate states that were occupied by U.S. troops—parts of the states of Virginia, GEORGIA, SOUTH CAROLINA, LOUISIANA, and most of TENNESSEE before the end of 1863. The Emancipation Proclamation applied in some of these territories and not in others, but the hostility of the U.S. Army to the institution of slavery was even stronger. This hostility gained some legal force with the passage of Confiscation Acts in 1861 and 1862 that declared the property of rebels, including land and slaves, forfeit to the government if it could be used for military purposes. Almost any slave who could run away and reach areas controlled by Union forces could be free, or at least enter a sort of limbo known as "contraband" status, where in effect he or she became the property of the army. Many slaves in occupied areas were happy to exchange slavery to a single master for servitude to the army, which they saw as working for the freedom of all.

In particular, the South Carolina and Georgia low country, occupied by federal troops in fall 1862, was

an early laboratory for a comprehensive reconstruction policy that pursued racial justice. The Union commander of the region, General David Hunter (1801–86), a career army officer and devoted abolitionist from New York, anticipated Lincoln's proclamation by more than six months with his General Order no. 11 of May 9, 1862, freeing all slaves in his district and enrolling black men in local MILITIA regiments. Many of his moves were overruled by higher headquarters in 1862, but by 1863, he was writing the plan for military-led reconstruction throughout the South in areas covered by the Emancipation Proclamation. Plantations that had been abandoned by their pro-Confederate white proprietors were confiscated by military authorities and distributed to their black former workforces. Black men were encouraged to enlist in the army, and very large percentages did. Former slaves in the coastal regions of Georgia and the Carolinas controlled by the Union were promised "forty acres and a mule" by General Hunter, a rallying cry that spread across the South and continued to be quoted for decades. Hunter intended to carry out significant land reform, though only slaves who served in the military were destined to receive land. But the newly freed and poorer prewar free people of color, saw land reform as an essential element of freedom and rallied to the Union because of this promise as much as anything else.

Prewar free people of color were among the earliest recruits to the Union forces and often served as the sergeants and corporals of these new units and the civilian leaders of the new communities created. In Louisiana, the military governor, General Benjamin Butler (1818–93), enrolled an entire regiment of Louisiana free people of color as one of the first black regiments to serve in the U.S. Army during the war. A number of famous black leaders in the U.S. Colored Troops were prewar free people of color, including Sergeant Major CHRISTIAN ABRAHAM FLEETWOOD, from Maryland; Sergeant Major Thomas Hawkins, from PENNSYLVANIA; First Sergeant Alexander Kelly, from Pennsylvania; and Sergeant William Carney, from MASSACHUSETTS. All four won the Medal of Honor for their battlefield heroism.

The Immediate Postwar Period: Presidential Reconstruction

The period from the end of the war between April and June 1865 until the middle of 1866 marked the period known as Presidential Reconstruction, thanks to the influence of President ANDREW JOHNSON (1808–75, served 1865–69) on the process. President Johnson was a Tennessee Democrat, one of the few elected officials from the South who remained loyal to the United States when the Southern states seceded. President Abraham Lincoln sought to draw Southern white opponents of the Confederate government into his coalition by selecting Johnson as vice president when he ran for reelection in 1864. Lincoln was assassinated on April 14, 1865, only five days after the surrender of the Southern army in Virginia, and Johnson found himself in the presidency with an administration and Congress controlled by fervent Republicans, his erstwhile political opponents. Although a strong supporter of national reunification, and an opponent of slavery, Johnson did not favor racial equality. He was prepared to allow Southerners to reconstitute their prewar society as much as possible, so long as they did not attempt to reestablish slavery. He opposed all sorts of federal interventions in the government of the South. He was especially opposed to the FREEDMEN'S BUREAU, an agency set up by the federal government to administer confiscated lands, deliver relief supplies to displaced people of all races, and ensure some measure of economic security and racial justice for newly freed slaves. Johnson quickly realized that he could not enforce his ideas through federal lawmaking, since Congress passed civil rights laws and renewed funding for the Freedmen's Bureau over his veto (*see* ALSO CIVIL RIGHTS LAWS IN THE UNITED STATES AFTER 1865).

He also could not control the various departments of the administration, because of a law called the Tenure of Office Act, which required Senate approval before firing any administration official who had required Senate confirmation for his appointment.

Instead, Johnson used his power of pardon and his power as commander in chief of the army to recreate Southern governments led by former Confederate officials who swore oaths of loyalty to the United States. Southern whites quickly reestablished state governments under a plan that had been put forward by Abraham Lincoln called the Ten Percent Plan, which provided that any state in which 10 percent of the prewar voters took oaths of allegiance could regain its status as a member of the Union. The southern state governments passed black codes (*see* BLACK CODES IN THE UNITED STATES) that largely restored prewar restrictions on free people of color and applied them to all blacks. Blacks were required to work on long-term labor contracts, and refusing a contract could lead to prosecution for "vagrancy," the crime of being black and unemployed. Blacks were denied equal access to the courts, prohibited to vote or in any way participate in politics, and were subject to other harassing regulations that reinforced their second-class status in the public mind.

Congressional Reconstruction

Although Republicans in Congress opposed Johnson's plans as soon as they became apparent, Congress strongly reacted in late 1866, after the congressional elections of that year. The congressmen and senators elected by the new state governments were refused their seats, and then Congress subjected most of the former Confederacy to martial law. In states where blacks did not have equal access to the courts, Freedmen's Bureau adjudication tribunals, composed of military officers and often containing black judges, heard blacks' lawsuits against white employers or neighbors. The Freedmen's Bureau also sought to increase the number of independent black farmers by distributing confiscated land as small farms, but Johnson's pardons partially foiled this strategy by allowing pardoned landowners to reclaim their confiscated land from the government. Nonetheless, a certain number of blacks, many of whom were prewar free people of color, were able to gain title to land and become small farmers. Despite harassment by public officials and terrorist attacks in many areas, a substantial community of black small farmers grew up. This group was especially important in areas where blacks were in a majority, as in the "black belt" of Georgia, Alabama, and MISSISSIPPI. Many in this group endured the discrimination and economic hardships of the late 19th century and persisted, often forming the nucleus of a black middle class in the

Southern countryside. They were the black school board members, the vestrymen of the black churches, and the "responsible negroes" whom white elites turned to when trying to control the black community.

Alongside the group of small independent farmers, a much larger group of black tenant farmers came into being. Blacks consistently refused to work on long-term contracts as agricultural laborers, considering the conditions little short of slavery, especially given the corruption often inherent in the system of making and enforcing labor contracts. In any case, plantation owners often found that they could not afford to hire agricultural laborers even at very low salaries. The Southern economy was so devastated in the late 1860s that sharecropping proved to be the only viable system to ensure agricultural labor. Black farmers gained a measure of independence as tenant farmers, and as long as governments and courts protected them, they had a chance to prosper.

The period of congressional Reconstruction, from 1866 to 1877, also saw the development of black institutions in the South. The Freedmen's Bureau contributed land and some financial support for black schools. Northern free blacks and white abolitionists had begun offering schooling to Southern blacks even during the war. A school was founded on St. Simon's Island in Georgia in 1863, led by the Georgia free black SUSIE BAKER KING TAYLOR. Taylor received some support from the Union forces under General Hunter, though she never received any support from the Freedmen's Bureau and had to close her school in the late 1860s. Hundreds of other schools received support, however, and flourished and grew. Ultimately, 10 black colleges and universities were founded, along with hundreds of secondary and elementary schools. Blacks were eager for education—many Southern states had forbidden it before the Civil War, and although there were literate blacks, like Taylor, in the South before the war, they were few in number. Large numbers of adults entered school, and significant percentages of school-aged black children were enrolled in Southern states. By 1880, 37 percent of all blacks aged five to 19 in the South were enrolled in school, a proportion 23 percent lower than the comparable figure for whites but still an enormous increase over the prewar figures. Adult literacy rates for blacks rose from 20 percent in 1870 to 65 percent in 1900.

Black churches played an important role in all community-building initiatives, offering education and poor relief, providing a forum for communities to gather, and cautiously leading efforts for greater civil rights. The leadership of the hundreds of black churches formed in the postwar years had a variety of sources: Northern black religious leaders from the AFRICAN METHODIST EPISCOPAL CHURCH, black Baptist congregations, predominantly white denominations, Southern black "bush preachers," and some white evangelists. The majority of these groups were Baptist in ecclesiological orientation, meaning that individual congregations were independent, though linked in voluntary federations that operated seminaries and organized mission activities (see also BAPTISTS AND PIETISTS). Although the level of education required for ordination in these groups was not very high, at least some theological study was necessary, meaning that the very few blacks who had received university educations before the war were very much in demand. These were, of course, all free people of color, and in fact, Southern black churches were almost all led by prewar free people of color in the first decades after 1865. All the black church groups created seminaries and worked hard to train young men for ministry, and the second generation of pastors was more diverse in terms of social origin. The white-dominated PROTESTANT MAINLINE CHURCHES and the ROMAN CATHOLIC CHURCH tried to reach out to the newly freed Southern blacks as well. There were small numbers of black clergy in some of these denominations—the Episcopal Church had ordained its first black priest, ABSALOM JONES, in 1804. The Catholics had several mixed-race clergymen at the time of the Civil War (see HEALY FAMILY) but did not ordain its first unambiguously black man, AUGUSTINE TOLTON, to the priesthood in the United States until 1886. Clergy in these denominations were almost always prewar free men of color.

Congress made some attempts to move toward a society of formal racial justice in the Reconstruction era (see CIVIL RIGHTS LAWS IN THE UNITED STATES AFTER 1865). The Civil Rights Act of 1875 prohibited discrimination in "public accommodations," building on the Fourteenth (1868) and Fifteenth (1870) Amendments to the U.S. Constitution, all of which committed the country to racial nondiscrimination. The continuing occupation of most of the former Confederate states by federal troops provided the government the tools it needed to force racial equality on unwilling Southern whites. To some extent this was done. Northern public opinion was not prepared to treat Southern whites mercifully in the immediate wake of the war. Generals Ulysses S. Grant and William T. Sherman were widely criticized for their relatively mild treatment of Confederate prisoners captured in the final collapse of the Southern armies in spring 1865. Most Southern officers, even top leaders, were allowed to go home with the "honors of war," and only a few serious war criminals were arrested. Even Gen. Nathan Bedford Forrest (1821–77), commander of the Confederate troops who massacred hundreds of black prisoners at Fort Pillow (April 12–13, 1864), was allowed to return home unmolested. Many Northerners hoped that Southern leaders, whom they saw as traitors responsible for the deaths of more than half a million of their fellow countrymen, would hang for their crimes. When President Johnson's pardons made this impossible, Northerners were not reluctant to force their former enemies to accommodate a black community with some economic and political power. Northern whites, however, generally harbored racist attitudes, if perhaps less virulently than Southern whites, and showed increasingly less sympathy and support for black claims to justice. When the spirit of revenge began to be replaced with a more generous spirit of reconciliation, it was easy for Northern white public opinion to forget about the blacks, leaving them to rely on their own strength to protect their position.

One of the most important innovations of congressional Reconstruction was the attempt to give black men in the South the vote. The Fourteenth and Fifteenth Amendments both addressed the issue: the Fourteenth threatening to deprive states of seats in Congress if they prevented citizens from voting on racial grounds and the Fifteenth unambiguously prohibiting racial discrimination in voting. Black voter participation rates in the South shot up in response. White elites recognized this as a direct assault on their power and retaliated in a variety of ways. The terrorism of the KU KLUX KLAN was a direct response to black political participation. The army and Congress perceived the Klan's violent assault on black voters and Northern supporters as a continuation of Southern armed resistance and responded with violence. The Klan was suppressed in the early 1870s, though other groups continued violent resistance.

States where Democrats managed to gain political power tried to pass laws restricting the franchise in apparently nondiscriminatory ways—for example, by imposing a poll tax that would be paid for white voters by candidates but was high enough to deter most poor blacks from voting, or by imposing literacy tests or other registration requirements that were administered in a discriminatory way by local officials. As long as Northern military governments remained in place, however, local governments effectively could not prevent blacks from voting. Blacks were able to gain elected office in many areas in the South. Many of these Reconstruction era black politicians were prewar free people of color, though they were joined by significant numbers of the newly freed who had risen to leadership through the disruption of the war years. Among prewar free people of color who held high office were HIRAM REVELS, senator from Mississippi; Robert B. Elliott (1842–84), congressman from South Carolina; ROBERT SMALLS, congressman from South Carolina; and JOHN MERCER LANGSTON (1829–1907), congressman from Virginia. Most former Confederate states were governed for at least part of the second half of the 19th century

by Republicans, consisting of a coalition of poor rural whites and blacks.

The End of Reconstruction and the Birth of Jim Crow

The collapse of this Republican coalition was the immediate cause of the failure of Reconstruction. In 1876, the Republican candidate for president, the former Union general Rutherford B. Hayes (1822–93), received fewer popular votes—and seemingly fewer electoral votes—than the Democratic candidate, Samuel J. Tilden (1814–86) of New York. However, the Republicans who held power in FLORIDA, South Carolina, and Louisiana managed to deliver their states' electoral votes to Hayes, giving him a one-vote edge in the electoral college. Southern Democrats were outraged, and a constitutional crisis over the presidency emerged. The tacit compromise that resulted allowed Hayes to take office, on the condition that he withdrew the army from the South and permitted Southern state governments to regulate racial matters without interference.

The election results in Florida were clearly fraudulent, and those in Louisiana and South Carolina only slightly less clearly so. The taint of corruption reduced the ability of Southern Republicans to draw votes from poor whites, although blacks remained loyal to the end. However, terrorism reduced black voter participation after 1872. The Reconstruction era Republican governments had not, actually, been notably corrupt or mismanaged. America was going through a period of serious corruption in public life, and the Southern governments had some remarkable successes in rebuilding infrastructure, education, public health, and simple restoration of public order. Poor whites in the South were convinced by the 1870s that they could have a populist alliance with white elites, however, and they fell away from the Republicans. Without a substantial white vote, blacks could not win many elections. Without substantial political power, advances for blacks in voting rights were wiped out, property rights were endangered, funding for institutions was withdrawn, and social SEGREGATION was established. The era of Jim Crow had begun.

Stewart R. King

FURTHER READING

DuBois, W. E. B. *Black Reconstruction in America, 1860–1880.* New York: Free Press, 1998.

Fitzgerald, Michael W. *Splendid Failure: Postwar Reconstruction in the American South.* Lanham, Md.: Ivan Dee, 2008.

Foner, Eric. *Nothing but Freedom: Emancipation and Its Legacy.* Baton Rouge: Louisiana State University Press, 2007.

———. *Reconstruction: America's Unfinished Revolution, 1863–1877.* New York: Harper Perennial, 2002.

Litwack, Leon. *Been in the Storm So Long.* New York: Vintage Books, 1980.

Stalcup, Brenda, ed. *Reconstruction: Opposing Viewpoints.* San Diego, Calif.: Greenhaven Press, 1995.

RE-ENSLAVEMENT

One of the greatest fears of free people of color was that they would be relegated once again to the status of slaves. Because of the association between blackness and slavery, this was always a risk in the Americas. The danger was especially high for people who were not well integrated into their communities: either the newly freed, migrants who had traveled to an urban area from the rural place where they had been slaves, the poor in general, and RUNAWAY SLAVES and others whose legal status was in doubt. But even some wealthy and powerful people of color still faced the danger of re-enslavement. One important factor was the access that free people of color had to the courts. If their testimony was not acceptable or the system was stacked against them in other ways, it might be difficult for them to prove their right to their liberty. Re-enslavement was rare, in truth, but still enough of a threat that it dominated discussion of laws on racial matters within the free colored community in most places.

The best-known cases of re-enslavement or threatened re-enslavement in the United States resulted from the FUGITIVE SLAVE ACT OF 1850. This law was part of the Compromise of 1850, which temporarily resolved sectional differences and delayed the AMERICAN CIVIL WAR by a decade. The price paid by the free states for this interlude of peace was this law, which provided that Southern SLAVE OWNERS could reclaim their "property" in the form of runaway slaves, with the assistance of local or even federal forces. Several notorious cases arose in which free people who had been living in Northern states for many years were suddenly arrested, to the scandal and outrage of the community, and conveyed back to Southern owners. Local law enforcement officers or citizens who refused to help or actively hindered the re-enslavement process were subject to large fines and even prison terms. These threatened penalties did not prevent antislavery Northerners from helping their neighbors resist re-enslavement, by hiding runaway slaves or even applying mob justice to rescue prisoners. The Underground Railroad had some of its greatest successes smuggling Northern free blacks threatened with re-enslavement to CANADA. Fugitive slaves and their supporters in Christiana, Pennsylvania, killed a MARYLAND slave owner and wounded members of his posse in a gun battle that broke out when the owner attempted to reclaim them from the home of a prominent abolitionist (*see* CHRISTIANA RIOT). Joshua Glover, a runaway slave from MISSOURI, broke out of jail in Milwaukee, WISCONSIN, after his former owner caught up with him and, with the aid of local abolitionists, was smuggled to Canada. One of his helpers was indicted under the Fugitive Slave Act, and the Wisconsin courts found the act unconstitutional and released the prisoner. Similar reactions by state courts in the North were not uncommon—although today the principle in the American legal system that states cannot overturn federal laws is unchallenged; before the Civil War, both Northern and Southern states took the position that they could prevent the implementation of federal laws with which they disagreed. Indeed, the federal government had little power to enforce its laws against the united opposition of the local authorities. Anthony Burns, a runaway slave and Baptist preacher from Virginia, was recaptured in BOSTON in 1854. The MASSACHUSETTS authorities refused to cooperate, and President FRANKLIN PIERCE sent in U.S. marshals and military forces to remove him. They were successful, at the cost of the life of one of the U.S. marshals, but the effort strained both the federal government's resources and the relationship between the Northern states and the federal government. Clearly, all the runaway slaves in the North could not be recaptured in this way. The Fugitive Slave Act resulted in the return of a significant number of people to slavery, but its largest effect was to convince white Northerners that slavery affected them as well and make war more likely.

One of the elements of the Fugitive Slave Act of 1850 that made it effective was that it almost completely denied the person of color who was claimed as a slave the right to contest his re-enslavement in the courts. Gaining access to the court system was always difficult for blacks in the United States, even in the Northern states. But Northern states' courts did generally defend the liberty of their black citizens, and legislatures passed PERSONAL LIBERTY LAWS in many places, giving them the legal tools to do so. Before 1850, re-enslavement of blacks in the North through legal means was almost unheard-of. Even President GEORGE WASHINGTON had regretfully given up an attempt to recover his slave who had run away to RHODE ISLAND in 1789 when he realized that local courts and law enforcement would not cooperate. Pure kidnapping was the only recourse open to masters, and if they or their agents were caught, substantial fines and even prison time were likely punishments. The Fugitive Slave Act took jurisdiction away from state courts and offered the purported slave very little recourse in federal court. Almost no grounds for a defense other than erroneous identification were acceptable. This meant that runaways and other free people of color whose title to liberty might be challenged had to leave. The fear of re-enslavement after 1850

Entitled *Kidnapping*, this 1834 woodcut from the book *Pictures of Slavery* depicts a black being taken by slave catchers. Free blacks in the North feared capture by slave catchers, either because they were actually runaway slaves or because they feared being unable to prove they had been born free or manumitted. Northern states passed personal liberty laws after 1793 to protect black citizens against arbitrary capture, but these laws were overturned by the Fugitive Slave Act of 1850. *(© CORBIS)*

led to a significant MIGRATION of Northern free blacks to Canada, LIBERIA, and other foreign countries.

Elsewhere in the Americas, re-enslavement was a common fear among people of color, though not common in actual practice for those who were juridically free. Free people of color who had formal legal MANU-MISSION had full access to the courts in French, Spanish, and Portuguese colonies, and even in the British, Dutch, and Danish Caribbean, they had considerable if not entirely equal legal rights to whites. But runaway slaves, MAROONS, and those LIVING "AS FREE" were always in fear of the slave catcher. These intermediate statuses were much more common in Latin America and the Caribbean than in mainland North America, as a manifestation of the more flexible racial hierarchy and generally more hierarchical "society of orders" found there. In the FRENCH CARIBBEAN, for example, formal manumission was a grant from the state, not the owner. It was not unusual for a master who wished to free a slave to give that person the right to seek formal manumission

from the government, making the slave responsible for paying the often-substantial taxes and lawyers' fees. If a person living as free under such a status did not manage to raise the money for his or her liberty tax before the master died, an unsympathetic heir, a difficult judge, or a mistake in the wording of a legal document could relegate an entire family to slavery. In SAINT-DOMINGUE, Paul Carenan, a wealthy free colored planter, and his family found themselves hauled into court in the 1770s and threatened with re-enslavement because their ancestor a half-century earlier had not formally registered her manumission. If the family were children and grandchildren of a supposed slave, the French heirs of their ancestor's former master argued, they were their slaves, and all the substantial property the free colored family had accumulated belonged to them too. The colored family retained its liberty, but only at the cost of a substantial payment and years of legal disputes. In another case in northern Saint-Domingue, a young man named Pierre living as free in the large city of CAP-FRANÇAIS/CAP-

HAÏTIEN in the 1770 and working, ironically, as a member of the rural POLICE, which was charged with chasing down runaway slaves, was arrested at the behest of his owner. It is unclear whether he was a true runaway himself or whether he had failed to live up to an agreement to pay for his freedom. In any case, his fellow policemen and white commander collected enough money to purchase his freedom from his owner, after a few days of uncertainty.

In the Spanish colonies, especially CUBA, the institution of COARTACIÓN led to distressing outcomes for some free people of color. Relying on a master's promise to grant them their freedom in return for a stated payment, these people went about their affairs, saving for the eventual day of formal manumission. But if the contract was not properly framed or some provision was not fulfilled, people who had lived as free for many years could find themselves returned to active slavery or required to pay much more for their freedom than they had thought.

In BRAZIL, coartaçaõ was an institution similar to that found in the Spanish colonies. Defining the precise rights and responsibilities of the slave who had signed a contract of coartaçaõ was among the many confusing features of the law of race and slavery that prevented Brazil from creating a modern civil law code for a century after independence, until 1916. Brazilian state governments, like North American ones, varied widely in the degree of justice accorded to people of color.

In most cases, re-enslavement was more of a threat than a reality. While few people ever actually experienced what might seem the ultimate horror, the fact that it was a possibility meant that free people of color had to take steps to prevent it. Many people throughout the plantation Americas carried manumission documents at all times, like talismans to protect them from the slave catcher. People who had dubious titles of liberty had to move to safer areas or spend money and time confirming their manumission. Some people found themselves in court, paying for lawyers and in fear for their freedom. The lack of predictability this introduced into the lives of free people of color probably hampered economic success and deterred free people of color from entering professions or fields of activity that were very visible. The very nebulous nature of the threat played a role in the pervasive climate of fear that reinforced the racial subordination of free people of color.

Stewart R. King

FURTHER READING

de la Fuente, Alejandro. "Slave Law and Claims-Making in Cuba: The Tannenbaum Debate Revisited." *Law and History Review* 22, no. 2 (2004): 339–370.

França Paiva, Eduardo. "Revendications de droit coutumiers et actions en justice des esclaves dans le Minas Gerais du 18° s." *Cahiers du Brésil Contemporaine* 53/54.

Gross, Ariela J. *Double Character: Slavery and Mastery in the Antebellum Southern Courtroom.* Princeton, N.J.: Princeton University Press, 2000. Available online. URL: http://ssrn.com/abstract=246411. Accessed June 1, 2011.

REGULAR ARMY

It is a little-known fact that the armies of the 17th and 18th centuries, especially in the Americas but also in Europe and around the world, included significant numbers of men of color. These early armies were professional forces, not the national armies that only came into being as a result of the FRENCH REVOLUTION. Enlisted soldiers were mostly poor men, serving for the pay and not emotionally invested in the struggle. Their officers were mostly noblemen who saw military service as an honorable career rather than a form of service to a nation that was only vaguely defined anyway. It was not at all unusual for foreigners to serve in a country's army, and soldiers might well serve in several different armies in the course of a career. At the higher ranks, officers moved from place to place as they saw a chance for better pay and professional advancement, though they would generally refrain from serving against their own home country. GEORGE WASHINGTON had many foreign officers serving under him, some for personal and ideological reasons such as the French marquis de Lafayette or the Polish Kazimierz Pułaski but others out of strictly professional motives, such as the German baron von Steuben. Some countries included large numbers of foreign enlisted men in their armies. Prussia was especially notable for this; during the reign of Frederick the Great (1740–86), as many as 75 percent of Prussian soldiers were not native Prussians. France enlisted foreigners in special units, such as the Swiss regiments, which were often used to keep order where national troops might be unwilling to use force against their own compatriots. The British used Scots and Irish troops for the same purpose. Enlisted soldiers were under strict discipline, and they were often treated as somewhat less than free people. Enlisting in the army was like entering into an indenture: The employer could force the person to work for the duration of his term, hunt him down if he ran away, and whip or torture him for disobedience.

When these countries acquired colonies in the Americas, their generals saw colonial subjects in much the same way as they saw the other foreigners who served them. They were a source of manpower to be exploited. For most colonial militaries, the color of their new recruits was unimportant. All soldiers were of lower status than the free people around them. Military service was not a way to serve one's country for enlisted men until the late 18th century, when the political ideas of the liberal Enlightenment began to take hold. Militaries preferred black soldiers for some duties, especially as bandsmen or drummers. It is unclear whether this was based on a cultural perception that blacks were especially musically gifted or because being a drummer was a particularly dangerous job. The drummers and musicians wore distinctive uniforms, made a lot of noise, and stood beside the flag, all in the interests of being seen and heard so that soldiers separated from the unit could find their places on a noisy, smoky battlefield. Of course, it meant that the enemy could see them and shoot at them too. The French army enlisted slaves as drummers, and seven years of service entitled one to MANUMISSION, tax-free. Spanish colonial armies had special detachments of black soldiers as headquarters guards, again, perhaps because they were thought to be willing to use force against their compatriots, in this case, possible mutinous soldiers, and because protecting the commander was a post of special danger when generals still led from the front.

For colonial blacks, the army offered a way out, not only of slavery, but even of the slave society itself. Enlisting in a regular regiment generally meant serving in Europe. When a soldier finished a term of service, if he had saved his pay, he might be able to take up a trade or open a business and live comfortably in Europe. Many of the free blacks of LONDON, ENGLAND, had arrived after serving a term in the Royal Navy (see also NAVY), but quite a few were army veterans. VINCENT OLIVIER, a young black man from SAINT-DOMINGUE, started his military career as a buccaneer in 1695 (see PIRACY), but after he was taken to Europe, he was presented at the court of Louis XIV. King Louis was impressed by his size and good looks and enlisted him in the Royal Guards regiment, and he fought for about 20 years in Europe. He returned to the colony after finishing his service and became a planter and MILITIA officer, but many of his colleagues stayed. ABRAM PETROVICH GANNIBAL, the grandfather of the Russian writer Alexander Pushkin, went even further and rose higher in military rank. He was bought by Peter the Great of Russia, who freed him and enrolled him in his guards, then sent him to France to be educated as a military engineer. Gannibal rose to the rank of general and became a nobleman under Peter's daughter, Empress Elizabeth.

Some of the colonial powers tried to enlist blacks as regular soldiers for duty in the colonies. Of course, most of the armed forces of the colonies were composed of free colored militiamen. But regular troops were much more effective militarily than part-time soldiers because they had more time to train and develop esprit de corps.

A photograph of black soldiers in the U.S. army, taken during the Spanish-American War (1898), which was the last act of the long struggle for Cuban independence from Spain. American black soldiers played an important part in this struggle. In the decisive battle for Santiago, Cuba, the black troopers of the 10th Cavalry led the way for Theodore Roosevelt's "Rough Riders" up Kettle Hill, while San Juan Hill was captured by the black 24th and 25th Infantry regiments. *(Library of Congress)*

Regular troops from Europe suffered appallingly high mortality rates in the challenging disease environment of the Tropics, and their transport and supplies were costly. Using blacks as regular soldiers was a possible solution. BRITAIN raised the West India Regiment in 1795, staffing it with RUNAWAY SLAVES from North America like those who had served in Dunmore's regiment and West Indian slaves whose masters were willing to give them their freedom. The men served for seven years, at the end of which those who started as slaves received their freedom tax-free and a small amount of wages. In order to keep numbers up, the West India Regiment ultimately brought a certain number of slaves, an expense that reduced the cost-effectiveness of the policy, but the unit was a valuable military asset. The French tried to create a similar unit to staff the defenses of Saint-Domingue and their other Caribbean colonies, requiring all men gaining their freedom to serve, but the potential recruits and their masters objected, and the idea was dropped.

When nationalism became an important force in drawing people into military service, toward the end of the 18th century, the role of blacks in the regular army changed. All sides in the WAR OF AMERICAN INDEPENDENCE, 1775–83, recruited black soldiers. Like Lord Dunmore, generally the governments promised slaves their freedom as a reward, but they also urged free people of color to sign up out of patriotic motives and to help stake a claim to citizenship. The equation of citizenship and military service was becoming established, and blacks and whites alike took advantage of it. The French recruited a force of more than 1,000 free men of color from Saint-Domingue to fight in North America—a large proportion of the colony's estimated population of 7,000 free adult men of color. After tough fighting in the siege of Savannah in 1779, the unit was split up into companies and assigned to defend various French and American posts around the Atlantic. Some of them did not return home until 1783. When the free people of color were demanding civil rights in the 1780s, they cited the service of these men as a sign that they were prepared to serve the common good. Pro-British loyalists in GEORGIA and SOUTH CAROLINA formed ranger units staffed with men of color at the enlisted ranks. The Georgia Rangers were responsible for almost completely reconquering the inland areas of the colony for Britain between 1779 and 1783. The rangers and other black loyalists who fled the country after the American victory became the leaders of black communities in SIERRA LEONE, Britain, and CANADA. The Americans recruited Northern blacks to fill the ranks of the Continental army, though their use was controversial. The Marblehead Regiment that saved the main American army after the defeat at the Battle of Brooklyn in 1776 was almost one-third black, mostly MERCHANT SEAMEN and fishermen from the port towns of MASSACHUSETTS. The Continental army was about one-fourth black in 1781–83. Henry Laurens, a prominent rebel leader from South Carolina, urged Washington and the Congress to enroll slaves with a promise of manumission, but they refused. The use of black troops in the American army was never completely acceptable for Southern leaders such as Washington. His own thinking evolved over time, from a shocked and hasty order to get all black soldiers out of camp when he took command of the army in 1776 to an ultimate acceptance that black troops were effective and necessary to the cause by 1779. Black veterans of the Continental army received some benefits in Northern states, but generally their service was not rewarded to the same degree as was that of whites. Black veterans did play a leading role in black communities in the North, as with the prominent FREEMASONRY organizer PRINCE HALL and the AFRICAN METHODIST EPISCOPAL CHURCH cofounder RICHARD ALLEN. In the South, black veterans were almost entirely forgotten by white society, though many black Southerners had gained their freedom through their service. The ideology of America as a white man's country was so strong, especially among the Jeffersonian Democrats who dominated the South, that it

was almost impossible to conceive of black men who had fought for America's independence.

After the United States gained its independence, the ideological character of warfare and military service only grew. The French armies of the Revolution and the era of Napoléon Bonaparte depended on people of color as an important source of manpower. In Europe, many blacks served in the French revolutionary armies, including the sons of TOUSSAINT LOUVERTURE, Placide and Issac Louverture, who were enrolled in Napoléon's Consular Guard (though they never saw active service, many other French free blacks did). THOMAS-ALEXANDRE DUMAS, father of the French popular author Alexandre Dumas, enlisted in the French army before the revolution and rose to the rank of general under Napoléon. In the Americas, the French armies of Saint-Domingue and the Lesser Antilles were chiefly composed of black soldiers. In Saint-Domingue, the rebel forces under Toussaint Louverture were incorporated into the regular French army in 1794. Even after the French invasion force arrived to restore the old regime in 1802, the black soldiers who were willing to cooperate with the invaders kept their ranks. By the end of the HAITIAN REVOLUTION in 1803, the French forces under General Rochambeau were about two-thirds black. In the Lesser Antilles, VICTOR HUGUES captured Guadeloupe in 1794 by sparking a rebellion against the British by free people of color. He then proclaimed the end of slavery, rallied a large army of former slaves, and captured a number of other islands for France.

Black soldiers also played an important role in the independence struggles of the Spanish Americas. When the wars of independence began in the early 19th century, many of the Spanish soldiers fighting against the rebels were people of color (see SOUTH AMERICAN WARS OF LIBERATION, VENEZUELAN WAR OF INDEPENDENCE, and WAR OF MEXICAN INDEPENDENCE). Some of these men remained loyal to the Spanish Crown, and some other free colored communities rallied to Spain against independence movements dominated by white CREOLES. Many people of color in the Americas saw the local white population as hostile to their interests and thought of the king as their protector, thanks to the fairly liberal laws of the late colonial era and the spotty enforcement of those laws by local elites. For example, the free colored militia of CARTAGENA in COLOMBIA supported the Crown at first, as did the *llaneros* of the Venezuelan plains. For the most part, however, free people of color in the Spanish Americas tended to support independence, and many of the regular soldiers of the liberation armies were men of color. Several leaders of the pro-independence armies were of African ancestry, including JOSÉ MARÍA MORELOS and VINCENTE GUERRERO SALDAÑA in MEXICO,

An 18th-century image of a black regular soldier, from John Singleton Copley's painting *The Death of Major Peirson, 6 January 1781*. The battle depicted took place on the Isle of Jersey in the English Channel between British defenders, many of whom were Virginia blacks who had served in Lord Dunmore's Ethiopian Legion, and French invaders. *(Tate, London/Art Resource, NY)*

JOSÉ PRUDENCIO PADILLA in Colombia, MANUEL PIAR in Venezuela, ANTONIO MACEO Y GRAJALES in CUBA, and BERNARDINO RIVADAVIA in ARGENTINA. Rivadavia was a military officer before the outbreak of the independence struggle, holding the rank of captain during the struggle against the British invaders in 1806–07. Padilla was a noncommissioned technical specialist in the Spanish navy.

In the postindependence period, there was an increasing reluctance almost everywhere to permit men of color to serve in the army. In the United States, blacks were accepted as recruits in the army for some years, but under increasingly harsh restrictions. American public opinion opposed having a standing army at all, and soldiers of color were increasingly seen as inconsistent with racial and nationalist ideology. They were limited to stereotyped roles as servants, bandsmen, or labor troops or forced to serve in segregated units that were assigned the least pleasant duties. After the War of 1812, in which some black soldiers served in regiments raised by Northern states, the regular

army formally ceased to accept black recruits except as bandsmen and drummers. A few blacks served in regiments raised "for the duration" of the MEXICAN-AMERICAN WAR, over the objections of Southern officers, but the army was again all-white until the AMERICAN CIVIL WAR. After the Civil War, even though slavery had ended in 1865, blacks were again mostly demobilized, though a few black regular army regiments remained, assigned to tough duty fighting Indians in the West. Strangely enough, throughout this period, the U.S. Navy had black sailors, who served in all capacities until after the Civil War, when they were restricted to menial roles, a restriction that did not end until after World War II.

Events in Latin America followed a similar pattern. The newly independent states often purged their armed forces of people of color. Simón Bolívar attacked the *pardocracía* of free colored officers in Colombia, executing several, including José Prudencio Padilla. Black soldiers did not disappear in Latin America as thoroughly as they had in North America, but they were much less visible than they had been during the wars of independence. Once again, the concept of nationhood became associated with color in many places, and military service with membership in the nation, so the service of blacks became less and less acceptable to elite public opinion. Mexico continued to employ black soldiers during the 19th century, but as in North America, they served in remote areas of the North against hostile Indians. The Juarez and Diaz administrations established military colonies in the North, including some for black soldiers, and many of the descendants of the black Mexicans who defeated the Apache and the Yaqui fought for Pancho Villa in the Mexican Revolution. A number of these Mexican BLACK SEMINOLE also served in the U.S. Army during the Indian Wars of the West.

Stewart R. King

FURTHER READING

Holton, Woody. *Forced Founders: Indians, Debtors, Slaves, and the Making of the American Revolution in Virginia*. Chapel Hill: University of North Carolina Press, 1999, esp. chap. 5.

Restall, Matthew. "Black Conquistadors: Armed Africans in Early Spanish America." *Americas* 57, no. 2 (2000): 171–205.

Voelz, Peter. *Slave and Soldier: The Military Impact of Blacks in the Colonial Americas*. New York: Routledge, 1993.

Weincek, Henry. *An Imperfect God: George Washington, His Slaves, and the Creation of America*. New York: Farrar, Straus & Giroux, 2003, esp. chaps. 6 and 7.

REIS, MARIA FIRMINA DOS (1825–1917) *author of the first Brazilian antislavery novel*

A schoolteacher and accomplished author, Maria Firmina dos Reis, a mulatta from the northern state of Maranhão, wrote BRAZIL's first antislavery novel in 1859. Born in the state capital of São Luis in 1825, dos Reis moved with her family to the township of Guimarães, located in the interior of the state, when she was just five years old. In 1847, at the age of 22, dos Reis was hired as a primary-school teacher in Guimarães. She educated generations of young boys, holding the post until she retired several decades later. In 1880, however, Maria Firmina dos Reis opened a school for both boys and girls, the first of its kind in the state of Maranhão, perhaps in all of Brazil. Public pressure, wrote one biographer, forced her to abandon the project within two years, however. Maria Firmina dos Reis died in Guimarães, blind and poor, some time in 1917. She neither married nor had any children.

Maria Firmina dos Reis's antislavery novel, *Ursula*, was first published in São Luis, Maranhão, in 1859. Two years later, she published in a local newspaper, *Gupeva*, a novel that explored indigenous themes. Dos

Reis also wrote articles for a host of newspapers, some literary, others dailies, but her ideas usually circulated only in northern Brazil. In 1887, she published "The Slave Woman," a short story with an explicit abolitionist message. Distance and a modest background prevented Maria Firmina dos Reis from gaining greater access to the more prestigious literary circles in Rio de Janeiro, the Brazilian capital.

Published only seven years after Harriet Beecher Stowe's famous *Uncle Tom's Cabin* (1852) in the United States, Maria Firmina dos Reis's *Ursula* conveyed an antislavery perspective that had been absent from Brazilian letters. Although *Ursula* is fundamentally a love story between a wealthy young man and Ursula, a young woman of humble origins, neither of whom is black, the plot hinges on the pivotal roles of a number of slaves. For example, the slave Túlio rescued the young man from death and later put him in contact with Ursula. Dos Reis's representation of slaves as resilient and humane provides a different angle on a group of people who were largely just thought of as property. She develops the slave characters to significant depth, portraying them as complex and compassionate people whose "spirit" remained untouched by the evils of slavery. Maria Firmina dos Reis reveals information about the slaves' lives through reminiscences of their days in "Africa," a place that she evokes with a storied, albeit romanticized, heritage. Maria Firmina nevertheless eschews contemporary views of Africa as "savage" and "uncivilized." Her account of the transatlantic slave trade, for instance, impels readers to feel the deprivation and separation embedded in the experience, a theme that was certainly not prevalent in Brazil at the time. It had only been nine years prior to *Ursula* that Brazil had outlawed the transatlantic slave trade in 1850.

A courageous woman, one whose career and writings called attention to the powerless, to women and slaves, Maria Firmina dos Reis remains a figure sorely underappreciated by the Brazilian and North American academy. The release of a third edition of *Ursula* in 2004 is promising, yet much remains to be discovered about Maria Firmina dos Reis's teaching career, her political writings, and her literary pieces.

Celso T. Castilho

FURTHER READING

Filho, José Nascimento Morais. *Maria Firmina dos Reis: Fragmentos de Uma Vida*. São Luis, Maranhão: Estado do Maranhão, 1975.

Marfo. Florence. "Marks of the Slave Lash: Black Women's Writing of the 19th Century Anti-Slavery Novel." *Diáspora: Journal of the Annual Afro-Hispanic Literature and Culture Conference* 11 (2001): 80–86.

Muzart, Zahidé Lupinacci. "Maria Firmina dos Reis." In *Escritoras Brasileiras do Século XIX*. Florianópolis, Santa Catarina, Brazil: Editora Mulheres, 1999.

Reis, Maria Firmina dos. "A escrava." *Revista Maranhense* 3 (1887).

———. *Ursula*. São Luis, Maranhão: Typografia Progresso, 1859. Reprint, Barcaren, Portugal: Presença, 1988

REVELS, HIRAM (1827–1901) *U.S. senator, religious leader, educator, and public servant*

Hiram Rhodes Revels was the first African American to serve in the U.S. Congress. Revels was born on September 27, 1827, into a free family in Fayetteville, NORTH CAROLINA. While some biographers claim that Revels had Scottish and American Indian ancestry, this has never been documented.

Revels moved to the Midwest in his teens, studying at seminaries and Knox College in Galesburg, ILLINOIS. He was ordained a minister in the AFRICAN METHODIST EPISCOPAL CHURCH in Baltimore in 1845 and then returned to serve as a pastor in the Midwest. Revels reported being imprisoned in MISSOURI in 1854 "for preaching the gospel to Negroes," even though, he claimed, he had "sedulously refrained from doing anything that would incite slaves to run away from their masters." After his release, Revels returned to Baltimore. There, at the onset of the AMERICAN CIVIL WAR in 1861, Revels helped recruit black soldiers and became a chaplain for black Union regiments in MISSISSIPPI. After the war ended in 1865, Revels stayed on in the South and organized black churches and schools.

Revels began his political career in Natchez, Mississippi. He was elected alderman in 1868 and state senator in 1869. In 1870, the legislature elected Revels to fill Mississippi's vacant seat in the U.S. Senate for the remainder of the term.

Revels took his seat in February 1870. During his year in Congress, his positions on race were moderate and occasionally timid. Revels believed that race-neutral public laws and policies were the best strategy for reducing RACISM AND RACIAL PREJUDICE. Revels sided with the radical Republicans in opposition to school segregation in Washington, D.C. However, he did not advocate full equality among the races. Revels's moderation was also apparent in his support for amnesty for former Confederates who were willing to take a loyalty oath.

After Revels's Senate term expired in 1871, he became president of Alcorn State University in Mississippi. In 1873, Revels took a leave of absence to become Mississippi's interim secretary of state. After Revels feuded with the Republican governor, he lost his position at Alcorn in 1874.

Revels switched his support to Democratic candidates in the controversial 1875 election. In 1876, he testified to the U.S. Senate that, to his knowledge, the Mississippi elections had been conducted without any violent intimidation of black voters. The state Democrats rewarded Revels by reappointing him to the presidency of Alcorn.

Revels's tactics drew opprobrium. In a letter to the Republican former president ULYSSES S. GRANT, Revels cited Republican corruption to justify switching his support to the Democratic Party, even though it supported segregation. At the time, Revels's turnabout was met with dismay by black Mississippians and by national civil rights advocates. Revels was not alone among black leaders in trying to find room for compromise with Democrats, however. ROBERT SMALLS, a member of the House of Representatives from SOUTH CAROLINA and a Civil War naval hero, worked with the Democrat and former Confederate general Wade Hampton in the 1890s to create a ticket that balanced the interests of blacks and poor whites. In many ways, Revels prefigured the arguments of the educator Booker T. Washington (1856–1915) in his Atlanta Compromise speech of 1895, which called

Hiram Revels (1827–1901), American political leader. Revels was the first African American to serve in the U.S. Congress, as senator from Mississippi from 1870 to 1871. He was also president of Alcorn State College, a historically black college in Mississippi, and urged blacks to accommodate the white supremacist leadership of the state after the end of Reconstruction. *(Library of Congress)*

on blacks to accommodate a climate of racial segregation while working to improve themselves through education and hard work.

Revels withdrew from electoral politics but continued publicly to advocate an accommodationist stance toward Jim Crow. He edited the A.M.E. Church's *Southwestern Christian Advocate* newspaper. After retiring from Alcorn in 1882, he taught theology at Rust University in Mississippi and returned to preaching. He died on January 16, 1901.

Thomas Brown

FURTHER READING

Borome, Joseph, ed. "The Autobiography of Hiram Rhodes Revels Together with Some Letters by and about Him." *Midwest Journal* 5 (Winter 1952–1953): 79–92.

Lawson, Elizabeth. *The Gentleman from Mississippi: Our First Negro Senator*. New York: University of Chicago Library, 1960.

Thompson, Julius Eric. *Hiram R. Revels, 1827–1901: A Biography*. New York: Arno Press, 1982.

———. "Hiram Rhodes Revels, 1827–1901: A Reappraisal." *Journal of Negro History* 79 (Summer 1994): 297–303.

Wheeler, Gerald E. "Hiram R. Revels: Negro Educator and Statesman." M.A. thesis, University of California at Berkeley, 1949.

RHODE ISLAND

Rhode Island is the smallest state of the United States geographically. It is located on the Atlantic coast of New England, south of MASSACHUSETTS and east of CONNECTICUT. Although formally named "Rhode Island and Providence Plantations," it was not in fact a strongly agricultural area and was only peripherally a part of the Atlantic plantation world, with a small agricultural zone with some large slave-worked farms. Instead, the colony, founded in 1636, and later state was primarily urban, centered around the towns of Newport and Providence. The harbor is excellent, and Rhode Islanders developed important trading links with Europe, Africa, and the tropical Americas that strongly influenced black life there.

The story of African slaves in Rhode Island shows that slavery in the United States was not only a Southern way of life but was also the social and economic foundation of life in the North. While slavery became mainly a Southern institution by the 19th century, the North, particularly in Rhode Island, as the historians Anne Farrow, Joel Lang, and Jenifer Frank have argued, "promoted, prolonged, and profited from slavery." Rhode Islanders dominated the North American share of the African slave trade, mounting more than a thousand slaving voyages

in the century before the abolition of the trade in 1807. As the most active Northern colony in importing slaves, this smallest of states competed heavily with the "big three" European slave-exporting nations (BRITAIN, PORTUGAL, and SPAIN) in the transatlantic trade. In the century from 1709 and 1807, Rhode Island merchants sponsored at least 934 slaving voyages to the coast of Africa, carrying an estimated 106,544 Africans from their homeland to the Americas. And from 1732 to 1764, Rhode Islanders sent annually 18 ships, bearing 1,800 hogsheads of rum, to West Africa to trade for slaves, earning £40,000 annually. Newport, the colony's leading slave port, transported an estimated 59,070 slaves to the Americas before the WAR OF AMERICAN INDEPENDENCE, 1775–83. In the years after the revolution, Rhode Island merchants controlled 60–90 percent of the U.S. trade in African slaves. The Rhode Island historian Jay Coughtry concluded: "All together, 204 different Rhode Island citizens owned a share or more in a slave voyage at one time or another. It is evident that the involvement of R.I. citizens in the slave trade was widespread and abundant. For Rhode Islanders, slavery had provided a major new profit sector and an engine for trade in the West Indies." Slavery endured in Rhode Island for nearly 200 years. It was such an integral part of the developing economy of colonial and postrevolutionary Rhode Island that two of America's most determined slave merchants, John Brown of Providence and Captain James Dewolf of Bristol, joined forces with the state government to protect the trade and its slaves. For example, the runaway law of 1714 severely penalized ferrymen who carried any slaves out of the colony without a certificate from their masters. The entrenched position of the slaveholders is clearly seen in this law, for all public officers of the colony and all citizens, as well, were charged with arresting, securing the slave, and notifying the master. A law against thefts by slaves, the most severe in New England, carried a sentence that could be 15 lashes or even banishment from the colony. Also, masters had the right to search any ship they suspected of harboring RUNAWAY SLAVES.

The first enslaved Africans arrived in Rhode Island sometime after 1638, and by the end of the 17th century, Rhode Island had become the only New England colony to use African slaves for both labor and trade. After overtaking BOSTON, Newport and Bristol became the major slave markets in the American colonies. At the outbreak of the American Revolution in 1775, Rhode Island controlled two-thirds or more of the colonies' slave trade with Africa. When the trade resumed after the war, Rhode Island had a virtual monopoly, shipping nearly 50,000 new slaves in less than 20 years. Samuel Hopkins, an early opponent of American slavery, observed that "Rhode Island has been more deeply interested in the slave-trade, and has enslaved more Africans than any other colony in New England." He later wrote in 1787 that "the inhabitants of Rhode Island, especially those of Newport, have had by far the greater share in this traffic, of all these United States. This trade in human species has been the first wheel of commerce in Newport, on which every other movement in business has chiefly depended. That town has been built up, and flourished in times past, at the expense of the blood, the liberty, and happiness of the poor Africans; and the inhabitants have lived on this, and by it have gotten most of their wealth and riches."

Rhode Island's blacks made up a higher percentage of the colony's population than anywhere else in New England, and the state had the highest proportion of slaves to whites in the region. The greatest concentration of slaves lived in Newport, the colony's major port, and in Narragansett County (also known as "South Country"), which was home to a small but prosperous plantation economy. The most famous plantation region were the Narragansett plantations, described as looking "like the Southern plantation economies."

Although the chief growth in Rhode Island's free black population took place after the revolution, there were a substantial number of free blacks in Rhode Island's cities before 1784. Many of these free blacks were, as in Massachusetts, fishermen, boatmen, dockworkers, and sailors. The slave trade with Africa in particular employed many black sailors, because their color and possible cultural connections (including language skills, in some cases) helped calm the slaves and keep them under surveillance (see also MERCHANT SEAMEN). In addition, Rhode Island free blacks worked as domestic servants and ARTISANS, particularly in trades associated with shipping; as sailmakers, marine carpenters, and metalworkers.

In 1700, the total population of New England was about 90,000, with only 1,000 blacks, no more than half of whom were free. However, with the increased importation of African slaves, the growth in the region's black population was quite rapid during the mid-18th century, with the largest percentage of blacks to be found in Rhode Island. From 5.9 percent in 1708, black slaves rose to account for 11.5 percent of the colony's population by 1755. By 1774, Rhode Island had 3,761 black residents, of whom at least 2,000 were free. Depending on the setting, the enslaved blacks in colonial Rhode Island served in various functions. They worked alongside free people of color as house servants in Newport; worked as shoemakers, blacksmiths, carpenters, seamen, and house servants in Providence; and hired themselves out to work for employers other than their masters, earning money that some used to secure their own freedom (see also

LIVING "AS FREE"). In Narragansett County, conditions favored large-scale farming, and well-known planters like William Robinson and the Stantons of Narragansett and Robert Hazard of South Kingstown used their slaves both as laborers and as domestic servants. Robinson owned an estate that was more than four miles long and two miles wide, and he kept about 40 slaves there; Hazard owned 12,000 acres and had 24 slave women just to work in his dairy; Stanton had at least 40 slaves. This black workforce was one-third of the population of the county by the mid-18th century, making this small area of Rhode Island comparable demographically to states in the South. In keeping with the usual pattern, a higher percentage of blacks meant a more strict control mechanism. South Kingstown had perhaps the harshest local slave control laws in New England. A county ordinance passed in 1718 stated that if any black slave were caught in the cottage of a free black person, both would be whipped. After 1750, anyone who sold so much as a cup of hard cider to a black slave faced a costly fine of £30.

The colonial period also saw the beginnings of a movement to abolish the slave trade. Thanks in part to the abolitionist movement and the Society of Friends, or Quakers, powerful leaders like Hopkins denounced the transatlantic trade "not simply as cruel and impolitic but as criminal, a violation of the fundamental laws of man." (See also BAPTISTS AND PIETISTS.) The influence of the abolitionist movement was particularly felt in Rhode Island. Here, it needs pointing out that there were some initial attempts to restrict or outlaw slavery in Rhode Island, but to no avail. As early as 1652, Rhode Island passed a law abolishing African slavery. According to the statute, which was never enforced, "no black mankinde" could be forced to serve a master for "longer than ten years," after which they would be "free, as the manner is with English servants." The colony passed another law in 1659 to ban the further importation of African captives, which was also not enforced. More than a century later, in 1784, Rhode Island again enacted a Gradual Emancipation Act, which also made the slave trade illegal. Echoing the Declaration of Independence, the law, "An Act Authorizing the Manumission of Negroes, Mulattos & Others, and for the Gradual Abolition of Slavery," declared that "all Men are entitled to Life, Liberty and the Pursuit of Happiness, yet the holding Mankind in a State of Slavery, as private property, which has gradually obtained by unrestrained custom and the Permission of the Laws, is repugnant to this Principle and Subversive of the Happiness of Mankind." This 1784 law made MANUMISSION much easier and provided for gradual emancipation, similarly to laws enacted at about this time in PENNSYLVANIA, NEW JERSEY, and NEW YORK STATE. But all these laws did not change anything for Rhode Island's slave traders. The U.S. abolition of the slave trade in 1808 was a more dramatic event, although Rhode Island shippers continued to provide support to the Portuguese and Spanish illegal slave trade for decades. The law of 1784 showed considerable deference to SLAVE OWNERS. For example, it allowed some slaveholders to sell their slaves out of state, some held supposedly freed slaves in forced servitude, others simply ignored the legislation, and some slaves were transformed into "slaves of the community," indentured municipally by local town councils. The law also did nothing to alter the status of those born before the date of enactment and who continued to serve their masters for life. Nor did it immediately change the circumstances of freeborn children, who were forced to serve their mother's owners for some 21 years before assuming their promised status. As did gradual emancipation laws elsewhere in the Americas, however, this law undermined the automatic assumption that blackness equaled slavery and laid the groundwork for the disappearance of the institution. The census of 1850 counted no slaves whatsoever in the state.

Perhaps it was the conversion in the early 1770s of Moses Brown that advanced the cause of black freedom in Rhode Island. Brown and his brothers, Nicholas, John, and Joseph, were partners in Nicholas Brown & Company, one of the biggest slave-trading businesses in New England for more than half a century. The company reaped huge profits, which laid the foundation for the Brown fortune (their donations to Rhode Island College were so generous that the name was changed to Brown University). One of the deadliest slave voyages in the his-

tory of Rhode Island was taken on behalf of the Brown brothers. In 1764, Essek Hopkins, who later became the first commander in chief of the U. S. Navy, sailed to West Africa in command of the slave ship *Sally*, owned by the Brown brothers. After sailing from Providence, it landed in Africa and purchased 196 Africans. At least 109 of them died on the ocean voyage through disease, suicide, and starvation. Such a terrible incident might have caused Moses Brown to have second thoughts, and in time he withdrew from the family business. Indeed, upon the illness and death of his wife, Anna, in 1773, he deepened his involvement with the antislavery movement. He became a Quaker and renounced slavery. In 1819, near the end of his life, he recalled, "I saw my slaves with my spiritual eyes as plainly as I see you now, and it was given to me as clearly to understand that the sacrifice that was called for of my hand was to give them liberty." On November 10, 1773, he gathered family and friends together and read a formal deed of manumission: "Whereas I am clearly convinced that the buying and selling of men of what color soever is contrary to the Divine Mind manifest in the conscience of all men however some may smother and neglect its reprovings, and being also made sensible that the holding of negroes in slavery however kindly treated has a tendency to encourage the iniquitous practice of importing them from their native country and is contrary to that justice, mercy, and humanity enjoined as the duty of every Christian, I do therefore by these presents for myself, my heirs etc. manumit and set free the following negroes being all I am possessed of or any ways interested in." In 1785, the

AFRICAN-AMERICAN POPULATION OF RHODE ISLAND, 1790–1900

Year	Slaves	Free People of Color	Free People of Color as a Percentage of Total Population	Total Population
1790	948	3,407	5.0%	68,825
1800	380	3,304	4.8%	69,122
1810	108	3,609	4.7%	76,931
1820	48	3,548	4.3%	83,038
1830	14	3,564	3.7%	97,185
1840	5	3,238	3.0%	108,830
1850		3,670	2.5%	147,545
1860		3,953	2.3%	174,626
1870		4,980	2.3%	217,353
1880		6,488	2.3%	276,531
1890		7,393	2.1%	345,506
1900		9,092	2.1%	428,556

Rhode Island Society for Abolishing the Slave Trade was founded in Providence. Its purpose was to organize anti-slavery activities, assist free blacks in finding employment, provide education, register deeds of manumission, and discourage the slave trade.

Few slaves waited for their owners to act on their behalf. Seizing the moment brought about by the American War of Independence, blacks throughout the Thirteen Colonies fled bondage by the thousands, both during the war and afterward. Blacks from Rhode Island generally headed for British-controlled territory during the war. After the war, they went north-ward to New England states that had abolished slavery, especially Massachusetts and VERMONT. In 1775, JOHN MURRAY, EARL OF DUNMORE, Virginia's royal governor, had promised liberty to fugitive slaves who reached his camp. Other British commanders followed Dunmore's lead, and many blacks who reached British lines were welcomed and declared free. British forces occupied part of Rhode Island on several occasions during the war, facilitating the voyage of any blacks from the state who wanted to join them. Seeking their freedom, these slaves chose to serve the British, others served rebellious Americans, and by the end of the war, black men, slave and free, enlisted in several Northern states. At one time or another, almost every state counted some black men under arms, mostly serving in racially mixed units like the famous Massachusetts Marblehead Regiment. In Rhode Island, some slaves gained their freedom by enlisting in the Black Regiment of Rhode Island when it formed in 1778. An entirely black force of about 300, it was organized by General Nathanael Greene and said to be the first black army unit in American history. The regiment came into being after the Rhode Island General Assembly of the colony approved manumission for any slave who enlisted in the Continental army. This black army unit proved its bravery in the battle of August 29, 1778, the only battle of the Revolution fought in Rhode Island, holding the line against three times as many British at Newport for almost four hours, enough time to allow the American army to escape a trap. This engagement, known as the Battle of Rhode Island, led General Lafayette to describe the bravery of this black regiment as the "best fought action of the war." Rhode Island blacks served under Lafayette's command in the 1781 Virginia campaign and made the decisive assault at Yorktown, along with a veteran unit of French regulars, that seized the redoubts guarding the harbor and forced the surrender of Cornwallis's army to end the war.

These developments still did not make conditions easy for Rhode Island's blacks. Having begun the abolition of slavery with the gradual emancipation act in 1774, the state sought to make it difficult for blacks to remain in Rhode Island or move there. It turned to the old New England custom of "warning out" strangers, exiling them from the community, to "purify" the state racially. Although the aim was the removal of poor and undesirable strangers from a community, the custom increasingly targeted blacks out of proportion to their numbers and without regard to whether they were long-term residents or not. For example, a study of Rhode Island records showed that only 5 percent of the transients warned out in the 1750s were identifiable as black, but as slavery was disappearing, the figure rose sharply, to 22 percent by the 1790s and 50 percent by 1800.

RACISM AND RACIAL PREJUDICE often manifested themselves in more violent and destructive ways. In the 1820s, the black population of Providence had grown to 7.2 percent of the total, more than 1,000 people in all. Two-thirds lived in their own homes, and many owned their own businesses. Racial tensions escalated and resulted in a four-day race riot in the "Hard Scrabble" district of Providence, the first separate black neighborhood, in October 1824. More than 400 whites attacked black residents to protest the employment of blacks while whites were unemployed. The white mob alleged that blacks were working at "white jobs." Many homes and businesses were destroyed, but apparently nobody was killed. A subsequent riot in 1831 in the same area resulted in the deaths of four or five white rioters (sources differ on the exact number) at the hands of the state MILITIA.

Free blacks who were longtime residents and chose to remain in Rhode Island despite the riots and official discrimination led several successful movements of resistance. Blacks were stripped of voting rights and segregated in schools from the 1820s. Free blacks sought to address their political powerlessness and led numerous systematic attempts to win or regain the franchise. Despite overwhelming and repeated rejections of their claims by white voters, judges, and legislators, free blacks persisted. For example, a convention of free Negroes petitioned in 1831 for full voting rights or an exemption from taxes (see also NEGRO CONVENTION MOVEMENT IN THE UNITED STATES). The Dorr Rebellion of the early 1840s also led the Legal Party, dominant in state politics at the time, to approve a new constitution, which gave voting privileges to all native-born males who met a three-year residency requirement. Rhode Island thus was one of the few states that allowed blacks to vote before 1868. Stations of the Underground Railroad, a clandestine escape route for slaves moving from the South to CANADA, were also developed. Elizabeth Buffum Chace (1806–99) opened her home as an active station. As elsewhere in the North, Rhode Island free blacks worked actively in the abolition movement. Other black community institutions helped unite blacks for self-help and political activism. The second American Negro Masonic Lodge, established by PRINCE HALL as a black self-help fraternal institution in the United States, was established in Providence in 1797 (*see also* FREEMASONRY). And as the black community became established, other organizations were formed to enhance the social fabric and provide services to a community that was largely unserved by the government. These included the African Union Society, the African Benevolent Society, the AMERICAN COLONIZATION SOCIETY, and several churches and schools, including the Shelter for Colored Children. Finally, shortly after the AMERICAN CIVIL WAR, George Downing, a wealthy black caterer in Newport, was able, after a short campaign mobilizing the black population and sympathetic whites, to gain public approval for integrated schools in Rhode Island in 1866. Later, the John Hope Settlement, named in honor of Dr. John Hope (1868–1936), an 1894 graduate of Brown University and a former president of Atlanta University, was created to meet the social and recreational needs of black people and anyone else wanting to participate. Blacks in the community also began to gain some worthwhile recognition. Notable were Edward Bannister (1828–1901), a landscape artist and winner of the bronze medal in the 1876 Centennial in PHILADELPHIA, PENNSYLVANIA, and cofounder of the Providence Art Club, which formed part of the founding of the Rhode Island School of Design, and Sissieretta Jones (1869–1933), a premier black singer, who performed for President Benjamin Harrison and for Europe's royalty and trained at the Providence Academy of Music.

Henry Codjoe

FURTHER READING
Berlin, Ira. *Many Thousands Gone: The First Two Centuries of Slavery in North America.* Boston: Belknap Press, 1998.
Berry, Frances B., and John W. Blassingame. *Long Memory: The Black Experience in America.* New York: Oxford University Press, 1982.
Christian, Charles M. *Black Saga: The African American Experience.* Boston: Houghton Mifflin, 1995.
Coughtry, Jay. *The Notorious Triangle: Rhode Island and the African Slave Trade, 1700–1807.* Philadelphia: Temple University Press, 1981.
DuBois, W. E. B. *The Suppression of the African Slave Trade to the United States, 1638–1870.* New York: Dover, 1970.
Farrow, Anne, Joel Lang, and Jenifer Frank. *How the North Promoted, Prolonged, and Profited from Slavery.* New York: Ballantine Books, 2005.
Franklin, John Hope, and Alfred A. Moss, Jr. *From Slavery to Freedom: A History of Negro Americans.* 6th ed. New York: Alfred A. Knopf, 1985.
Greene, Lorenzo J. *The Negro in Colonial New England, 1620–1776.* New York: Columbia University Press, 1942.
James, Sydney V. *Colonial Rhode Island—A History.* New York: Charles Scribner's Sons, 1975.
Melish, Joanne. *Disowning Slavery: Gradual Emancipation and "Race" in New England, 1780–1860.* Ithaca, N.Y.: Cornell University Press, 1998.

RIGAUD, ANDRÉ (1761–1811) *Haitian general*
André Rigaud was born in Les Cayes, in southern SAINT-DOMINGUE, in 1761, the son of a French planter named Benoit Rigaud and his free black companion, Rose Bossy. Rigaud was trained as a goldsmith, but free people of color were forbidden to practice this trade after 1774, and he became a small planter. He owned about a dozen slaves and practiced COFFEE CULTIVATION.

He was apparently not involved with the civil rights movement of free people of color in the South Province of Saint-Domingue that sent JULIEN RAIMOND to Paris in 1787. But when the HAITIAN REVOLUTION began in 1790, Rigaud quickly became involved. He was a supporter of the civil rights movement championed by VINCENT OGÉ and JEAN-BAPTISTE CHAVANNES, though he did not participate in their armed uprising. When the assembly of PORT-AU-PRINCE, dominated by poor whites, began to persecute people of color, he joined the free colored movement based in Mirebalais that opposed them. It was at this time that he began his association with ALEXANDRE SABÈS PÉTION, who remained his loyal subordinate throughout most of what followed.

In 1792, the French National Assembly abolished racial discrimination and made the free people of color full citizens. A Civil Commission, with executive powers, headed by Léger-Félicité Sonthonax (1763–1813), traveled to Saint-Domingue to impose the new law on the unwilling white authorities. Rigaud and his comrades enthusiastically rallied to the republican cause. They were less enthusiastic when Sonthonax made overtures to the black slave rebels, led by TOUSSAINT LOUVERTURE. Still, when in 1793, the British invaded the South, the free colored planters remained loyal to FRANCE. Rigaud rose to command the southern army, with the same rank of general held by Toussaint and the leader of the northern free colored army, Jean-Louis Villatte. The overall commander of French forces on the island was a white general, Etienne Laveaux, who worked closely with Toussaint. Villatte and Rigaud conspired to overthrow Toussaint and Laveaux and launched a coup in 1796. The coup was unsuccessful because of the spontaneous support of the black workers and soldiers for Toussaint in CAP-FRANÇAIS/CAP-HAÏTIEN. Toussaint became governor-general as a result of the coup, and Villatte was arrested. Rigaud was able to keep his position after the coup, however, mainly because he had a powerful army behind him in the South, while Villatte's men remained loyal to Toussaint and the colonial government.

Rigaud became almost completely autonomous as the leader of the South Province after this. He instituted similar reforms to those put in place by Toussaint in the North and West, requiring former slaves to return to work on their former plantations if they did not have land or were not serving in the REGULAR ARMY. The southern blacks resisted, and there was heavy fighting in the Platons mountains, but Rigaud was generally more successful than Toussaint in increasing sugar and coffee production.

Rigaud's turn to confront Toussaint occurred in 1799, in the "War of the Knives." The French sent a special political agent, Thomas Hédouville (1755–1825), to work with Rigaud to undermine the authority of Toussaint. When Toussaint discovered their plot, he sent Jean-Jacques Dessalines with a powerful army to the South. Rigaud and Pétion's forces fought them to a standstill at Grand Gôave, but then Dessalines attacked their flank at Jacmel, an important port and the source of much of the MULATTO generals' political support. Jacmel had also served as a base for French privateers attacking U.S. shipping during the Quasi-War of the late 1790s. When Toussaint promised the U.S. government that he would not allow French ships to use ports he controlled as bases, the U.S. Navy closed the ports controlled by Rigaud. Without resupply by sea and cut off by Dessalines's forces by land, the garrison at Jacmel was obliged to surrender. Rigaud and Pétion fled the colony for France.

In 1802, they returned with the expedition led by General Charles Leclerc (1777–1802). It was at this time that Pétion broke with Rigaud. Rigaud remained loyal to Leclerc and his successor Rochambeau until the French decided to arrest all the free colored officers. Rigaud was deported to France, where he was held a prisoner in the same castle as Toussaint Louverture. He was released after a few years and lived quietly in France until returning to now-independent Haiti in 1810.

By that time, Pétion had been president of southern Haiti for four years. He welcomed his old comrade back and made him military commander of the Southern Department. But Rigaud's loyalty to his former subordinate was not strong: He rose up in rebellion and proclaimed himself president of the Southern Department. He died on September 18, 1811, and the department returned to Pétion's authority without bloodshed.

Stewart R. King

FURTHER READING
Dubois, Laurent. *Avengers of the New World: The Story of the Haitian Revolution.* New York: Belknap, 2005.

RIVADAVIA, BERNARDINO (1780–1845)
Argentine military officer and president (1826–1827)

Bernardino Rivadavia was a military officer and served as president of ARGENTINA from 1826 to 1827. He was the first free person of color to hold this position.

Bernardino Rivadavia was born on May 20, 1780, into a middle-class Buenos Aires family. Some of his ancestors were African, and although the family had acquired a government exemption from the status of free person of color, either in his father's or grandfather's generation, the fact of his African ancestry was known and used against him by political and social rivals during his career. (*See* CEDULAS DE GRACIAS AL SACAR.) The fact that he was legitimate and of reasonably high social rank meant that he was able to overcome many obstacles that would have hindered a person of African ancestry without those advantages.

He was educated at the military academy and had achieved the rank of captain in the Viceroyalty of Rio de la Plata's MILITIA when, in 1806, the British invaded the Spanish colony during the Napoleonic Wars. The viceroy and the REGULAR ARMY forces of the colony fled to the interior, but the militia of Rio de Janeiro under its commander Santiago Liniers decided to resist. The young captain played a gallant role in the successful fight that led to the British surrender in 1806 and in a subsequent campaign against another British force in 1807–08. By the end of the struggle in 1810, the Argentine militias were battle-tested and their leaders self-confident and uninterested in submitting themselves to Spanish authority. Liniers was named viceroy by the Spanish government, but fairly soon Argentina declared its independence. Rivadavia married the daughter of a popular former viceroy, Juana del Pino y Vera, in 1809 and became an important member of the new government in 1810. The government sought to unify the entire territory of the viceroyalty under a centralized government that could defend against British and Spanish invaders and implement liberal reforms efficiently. Rivadavia was devoted to the liberal cause and served as secretary of the treasury and secretary for war between 1811 and 1812. His political fortunes took a turn for the worse in October 1812, when the government fell and was replaced by a looser association of regional military commanders with a more conservative agenda. It was during this period that his ethnic identity became a political issue, as federalist opponents referred to him as "Doctor Chocolate." Rivadavia was then sent on a diplomatic mission to Europe, where he managed to gain grudging acceptance of Argentina's independence and searched unsuccessfully for a European prince to become Argentina's king.

Rivadavia returned to Argentina in 1821 and played a number of roles in the government of Buenos Aires, the capital city and province. His policy was to develop Buenos Aires and to centralize government and the economy of the country in the city. He led the Unitario faction in Argentine politics, which opposed the federalists, who wanted to decentralize power and develop the provinces alongside the capital. A Constitutional Convention of regional leaders elected him president of Argentina in 1826. He made a serious effort to implement liberal policies drawn from British utilitarianism and political economy, though his understanding of these ideas as well as his power to put them into effect may have been limited. His term was marked by the establishment of many cultural and educational institutions, including the national museum, which today bears his name; a national library; and the expansion of the University of Buenos Aires. He also faced a stubborn war with BRAZIL in which Argentine armies were often victorious but could never finish off the larger Brazilian forces. The Argentine rural population, weary of war and high taxes to support expensive development projects, ultimately rebelled and forced him from office in 1827. He fled into exile in Europe and died in Spain on September 2, 1845.

Rivadavia's life illustrates many important points about free people of color in the Spanish Americas. First was the degree to which he was integrated in the white population. He was light-skinned and of high social status, he married a white woman, and so the African side of his identity was almost lost. In 1830, as many as one in three people of Buenos Aires were socially identified as black or MULATTO, in contrast to today's figure of less than 5 percent. The Afro-Argentines did not die or fail to reproduce or vanish mysteriously; rather, they became integrated in the larger population and ceased to be identified as black or mulatto. Another important theme in Rivadavia's life is the role that he played as a free colored military officer. More than half of the Argentine armed forces were men of color during the war of independence. The soldiers who defended Buenos Aires and Montevideo and those who liberated CHILE and PERU included many free blacks. Another important theme in Rivadavia's life is that he took complex political positions focused on an ideal of modernization. He supported national unity and an activist government. In this, he was in tune with European utilitarian and positivist liberal thought, and with some early leaders in the Americas such as

Simón Bolívar and the North American Whigs but not the political spirit of the Americas in the 19th century, which was more focused on decentralization and weak government.

Stewart R. King

FURTHER READING
Bushnell, David. *Reform and Reaction in the Platine Provinces, 1810–1852.* Gainesville: University of Florida Press, 1983.
De Ganda, Enrique. *Historia Politica Argentina.* Tomo 8, *Rivadavia y su tiempo.* Buenos Aires: Claridad, 1998.
Harris, Jonathan. "Bernardino Rivadavia and Benthamite 'discipleship.'" *Latin American Research Review* 33, no. 1 (1998): 129–150.

ROBERTS, JOSEPH JENKINS (1809–1876)
first president of Liberia (1848–1856, 1872–1876)

A native of Norfolk, Virginia, Joseph Jenkins Roberts gained fame in 1848 by becoming the first president of the independent African republic of LIBERIA. By this point, he had already made a name for himself in the colony of Liberia, first as a merchant and then, in 1833, as high sheriff; in 1839 as vice governor; and in 1841 as the first nonwhite governor. Liberia had been founded by the AMERICAN COLONIZATION SOCIETY, an organization led by whites in the United States that sought to remove free people of color from the country by sending them "back" to Africa. Of course, almost all free black Americans in the 1800s were born in the United States, and many perceived the emigration movement as antiblack (*see also* EMIGRATION AND COLONIZATION). However, some, including the Roberts family, saw Liberia as a potential refuge, especially if they could establish a relationship of equality and respect with their white patrons in the mother country. In 1846, Roberts led the drive for independence of the colony, pledging continued good relations with the Colonization Society, and on July 26, 1847, he declared Liberia independent and won the first presidential election that October. He was then sworn in on January 3, 1848.

Roberts gained respect throughout the international black community as the leader of one of only two independent black republics (the other was Haiti), but as with many American free blacks, he was actually of mixed ancestry. He was born on March 15, 1809, in Norfolk, Virginia. His mother, Amelia, was a slave who had gained her own freedom and managed to put herself on a comfortable footing. She married James Roberts, a free black who owned a successful boating business in Norfolk, and though controversy surrounds Joseph's paternity, the couple raised him together. They had two other sons, John

A photograph of Joseph Jenkins Roberts (1809–76), taken while he was serving his first term as president of Liberia, about 1851. Roberts was the best-known and most effective African-American supporter of emigration from the United States to Liberia. He worked for the independence of Liberia from the political control of the American Colonization Society and was a dominant figure in the new nation's politics for a generation. *(Library of Congress)*

and Henry. Joseph Roberts's portrait supports a claim made by his biographer C. W. Tazewell that whoever his biological father was, he could have easily "passed" for white but instead took pride in his position as a leader of the black community. Roberts followed in his father's footsteps in the family business but was also trained as a barber under the tutelage of William Colson, a respected free black from Petersburg, Virginia.

In 1829, Roberts and his family left for Liberia and opened a store in the capital city of Monrovia. The store quickly became successful, and each of the Roberts brothers played important roles in the colony. John W. Roberts eventually became a bishop of the Liberia Methodist Church, Henry Roberts earned a medical degree in the United States and opened a practice in Liberia, and Joseph Roberts entered politics.

Roberts was elected four times and served eight years in his first term as Liberian president from 1848 to 1856. During his first term, he worked to gain diplomatic recognition for Liberia throughout the world. He met with suc-

cess in BRITAIN, FRANCE, PORTUGAL, BRAZIL, Sardinia, the Austrian Empire, Norway, Sweden, Haiti, Denmark, and a handful of German cities. Despite his efforts, he failed to gain recognition from the United States because the racial climate precluded official acceptance of a black republic. U.S. recognition did not occur until 1862, during the AMERICAN CIVIL WAR. He also tried to reach out to indigenous groups and managed to extend Liberian boundaries by negotiating with African leaders. He is known for his diplomatic skills as well as his support for agriculture and his efforts to raise money for Liberia College, where he served as a professor of law. In addition to teaching, he served in the Liberian army, attaining the rank of major general. In 1872 he was elected to the presidency again, serving as the country's seventh president in 1872–76. He died shortly after his final term ended, on February 24, 1876, leaving much of his estate to fund Liberian education.

Beverly C. Tomek

FURTHER READING

Matthews, Pat. *Joseph Jenkins Roberts, the Father of Liberia.* Richmond: Virginia State Library, 1973.

Tazewell, C. W. *Virginia's Ninth President, Joseph Jenkins Roberts.* Virginia Beach, Va.: W. S. Dawson, 1992.

ROCHA VIEIRA, FRANCISCO SABINO ÁLVARES DA (1796–1846) *Brazilian medical doctor, journalist, and rebel leader*

Francisco Sabino Álvares da Rocha Vieira was an important participant in liberal agitation in BRAZIL in the early imperial period. He led a rebellion in SALVADOR, BAHÍA, BRAZIL, in 1837–38 that is called the "Sabinada." His life gives us an example of the important role that free people of color could play in politics in Brazil, even those who, as he did, sprang from relatively humble origins.

Little is known about Sabino's early life. He was born into a free colored family in Bahía sometime in 1796. His family was not wealthy, but they were able to apprentice him to a surgeon for training. At the time, surgery was considered a skilled trade rather than a profession, and thus a suitable employment for a free man of color who did not have powerful white patrons. (*See also* ARTISANS and MIDWIVES AND TRADITIONAL HEALERS.) At the time of Brazilian independence in 1822, he had completed his training as a surgeon, and he served in one of the patriot battalions that fought in the war to expel the Portuguese troops from Salvador. Sabino gained a reputation for radical liberalism. Liberalism in the 19th-century Brazilian context means a general commitment to freedom: the abolition of slavery, the equality of all citizens before the law, freedom of speech, universal or at least expanded suffrage, federalism, and an end to official racial discrimination. Sabino was dismissed from the REGULAR ARMY in 1824 for his involvement in the conspiracies that led to the revolt of the Periquitos battalion (1824), an early armed uprising against aristocratic rule and the slave system in Brazil.

Late in the 1820s, after independence from Portugal had been obtained, Sabino sought to resume his medical career, but his reputation as a radical liberal and his penchant for violence prevented him from obtaining an appointment as director of the military hospital in Salvador. Instead, he turned to journalism, publishing a radical liberal newspaper, *O Investigador Brasileiro* (1829–33). In 1833, he was charged with killing his wife after she discovered him in bed with a black man. Acquitted in this trial, Sabino soon fell into additional legal difficulties. A conservative newspaper had attacked Sabino, and in 1834, he murdered the publisher's brother, allegedly in self-defense. Sabino served one year of a six-year sentence and after his release, remarkably, won a professorial appointment at Salvador's Medical School in early 1837 on the strength of a brilliant thesis.

In November 1837, Sabino played a leading role in the Sabinada rebellion. This radical liberal and federalist revolt rejected a conservative government that had come to power in September 1837 and announced Bahía's separation from the rest of Brazil. Sabino served as secretary of the rebel government and published its official organ, the *Novo Diário da Bahia*. The rebellion drew strong support from Salvador's free black and MULATTO population and eventually began to enlist Brazilian-born slaves in its forces. Sabino's newspaper railed against the "puffed-up aristocrats" of the SUGAR CULTIVATION plantation hinterland (the center of opposition to the Sabinada) and declared that "they are warring against us, because they are white, and in Bahía there must be no blacks and mulattos, especially in office, unless they are rich and change their liberal opinions." The rebellion's defeat in March 1838 led to a massacre of more than 1,000 rebel soldiers and supporters, most of them black men.

Sabino was sentenced to death for inciting slaves to rebellion and homicide, but in 1840, Emperor PEDRO II granted amnesty to all those involved in the rebellions of the 1830s. Sabino's amnesty was, however, conditional on his exile from Salvador. He was sentenced to reside in remote Mato Grosso, in the southwestern part of the country, where he respected the terms of his amnesty and refrained from writing for publication and political activism. He appears to have worked as a surgeon for the remainder of his life. He died sometime in 1846; the date and circumstances are unknown.

Hendrik Kraay

FURTHER READING

Kraay, Hendrik. "'As Terrifying as Unexpected': The Bahían Sabinada, 1837–1838." *Hispanic American Historical Review* 72, no. 4 (November 1992): 501–527.

Reis, João José, and Hendrik Kraay. "'The Tyrant Is Dead!' The Revolt of the Periquitos in Bahía, 1824." *Hispanic American Historical Review* 89, no. 3 (2009): 399–434.

Souza, Paulo Cesar. *A Sabinada: A revolta separatista da Bahía (1837)*. São Paulo: Brasiliense, 1987.

ROMAN CATHOLIC CHURCH

Christianity has at its root a strongly egalitarian social message. This message is also universalistic, that is, the equality that must exist between people applies to everyone regardless of where they originate. Christianity has functioned, however, since its inception in a world with sharp social divisions including slavery and, more recently, racial division as well. The church has struggled to reconcile the real differentiated social existence of its believers with its theology, which insists on their absolute equality. The result of this struggle has been a series of teachings from the authorities of the church that recognize the reality of social divisions but call on Christians to transcend them as much as possible. Christian theology and practice from earlier times have always had a great impact, especially in the Roman Catholic Church, and so in order to understand how Catholic thinkers and leaders dealt with slavery in the early modern age, it is necessary first to understand what happened more than 1,000 years earlier.

Early Christianity (First–Fifth Centuries)

In the early days of the church, before the conversion of the Roman emperor Constantine and the subsequent adoption of Christianity as the official religion of the Roman Empire in the fourth century, it was easy to reconcile social reality and egalitarian Christian theology because being a Christian was an unlawful activity. The very illegality of the faith permitted all sorts of other countercultural behavior, such as treating slaves, free people, and even Roman aristocrats as equals. The early history of Christianity is full of aristocratic martyrs who went to their death alongside their slaves, such as Perpetua and Felicity, a noble Roman matron and her African slave, who refused to give up their faith during one of the many persecutions and were duly fed to wild animals in the arena of Carthage. The apostle Paul intervened in an argument between Philemon and his slave Onesimus, both of whom were Christians. His letter to Philemon is part of the New Testament of the Christian Bible. Onesimus had fled to Paul for protection, and Paul urged him to return, at the same time directing Philemon to treat him as a brother rather than as a slave. Paul urged Christian congregations to integrate, not only ethnically (Jews and non-Jews) but also socially (slave and free). At the same time, Paul urged slaves to remain obedient to their masters, even if those masters were pagans, as part of a teaching that true spiritual progress could not be achieved by violently breaking social bonds. Christian congregations and leaders during the following two centuries condemned slavery and the slave trade over and over again, and indeed many of the early followers of Christianity were slaves and newly freed people. Christian converts routinely freed their slaves in these early days.

After Christianity became legal within the Roman Empire in 313, then the official religion in 380, maintaining the balance became somewhat more difficult. The Roman Empire was a slave society. In the first century, much of the productive labor in the empire had been done by slaves. Most slaves were war captives, taken during the wars of conquest that established the Roman Empire, or their descendants. As the era of expansion ended, the proportion of the population that was enslaved fell, and client relationships between freedmen and aristocratic patrons began to replace slavery as the principal social bond between producers and rulers. This tendency accelerated as the social order disintegrated, especially in the Western Empire, under the pressure of disease, economic decline, and barbarian invasion. However, there were still many slaves in the fourth century, and any religion that aspired to universality had to accommodate both slaves and SLAVE OWNERS as members. Some alternative Christian groups, especially the Manicheans, preached radical social leveling, and this led the official church to assert specifically, in a formal way, in 340, that owning slaves was consistent with Christianity and that Christians who were slaves were obliged to obey their masters.

Christian leaders continued to teach, however, that all people were the same in a spiritual sense, and specifically that there was no fundamental difference between ethnic groups. In early Christianity, this was a way to contrast themselves with Pharisaic Jews, who argued that God chose the Jews and that to achieve salvation a non-Jew would have to convert ethnically as well as religiously. The great attraction of Christianity for the multiethnic Roman Empire was that one could become a Christian without changing ethnicity. As Christianity became predominantly the religion of Europeans and Mediterranean people in the fourth and fifth centuries, it continued to assert that it ought to be the religion of all people. The result of the partial closing off of Europe from the world, however, was that Christianity became more and more an ethnic religion of Europeans. This was particularly true of the Western variant of Christianity, which grew into the Catholic Church.

The Middle Ages (Fifth–Fifteenth Centuries)

Christianity divided into two cultural entities as the Roman Empire fell apart, though the Eastern Churches (which are now known as Eastern Orthodox) and the Western (the ancestors of today's Catholics and Protestants) did not formally divide until 1054. The Eastern Churches remained tied to the political organizations they worked with, the Eastern Roman Empire and, after its fall, the Russian Empire and other national governments. In the West, though the church attempted to reestablish an empire through the Holy Roman Empire, there was no direct linkage between church and state and a sense that a common identity as Christian transcended nationality. This idea had important implications for the role of ethnic outsiders in the society. If someone of a non-European ethnic group traveled to backward, remote Europe, if he or she were Christian, acceptance as part of the social group was smooth. There are examples of black Africans as well as other people of color who lived in Europe during this time. The best known is Leo Africanus, who was born in the late 15th century in Islamic Spain of black African parents, was enslaved by Christian sea raiders, but was converted to Christianity and freed by the pope. He was a respected papal adviser on international affairs and wrote an influential geography of sub-Saharan Africa.

Slavery still existed in Catholic Europe during the Middle Ages, though it was in decline as an institution. In SPAIN and PORTUGAL, prisoners captured in the War of Reconquest against the Muslims could be enslaved, and many were. The Crusaders kept war prisoners and their descendants as slaves both in their territories in the Middle East and, when they were driven out of those lands, in the Mediterranean islands. The Turkish conquerors in the 1400s had war prisoners from eastern Europe and the Middle East to sell, while German conquerors enslaved and marketed eastern Europeans. Indeed, the modern English word *slave* is derived from *Slav*, indicating the origin of the slaves who were living around English-speaking people as the language developed. The Latin word for slave was *servus*, the origin of the English *servant*. The Catholic Church was ambiguous about these activities. The first general principle was that prisoners taken in a just war could justly be enslaved. Thus, Pope Nicholas V, in Dum Diversas (1453), authorized the kings of Spain and Portugal to enslave Moors. However, his predecessor, Eugene IV, in Sicut Dudum (1435), had judged a Spanish war of conquest against the Canary Islands insufficiently moral to justify making the Canarians slaves, and he ordered all of them who had been enslaved released on pain of excommunication for the possessor. In addition to the justice of the war, another contrasting element between these two cases was the religion of the slave. The Canarians had been evangelized; and at least some had been baptized before the war began. A second basic principle of Catholic ideas about slavery in the Middle Ages, evolving gradually throughout the period, was that Christians could not be made slaves, though slaves who became Christians, such as Onesimus, did not have to be freed.

The notion that there were some people who were naturally suited for slavery entered Catholic Christian thought toward the end of the Middle Ages when Thomas Aquinas adapted the work of Aristotle to Christian ideas in the 13th century. Aquinas's ideas were considered, if not exactly heretical, at least questionable while he was alive, but by the late 14th century, his ideas had become central to Catholic philosophy and anthropology. The acceptance of social differences, including slavery, as natural and part of God's plan for mankind, always implicit in Western Christianity, became explicit just as Western Europeans were beginning to reach out into the world's oceans and develop the tools they would need to become dominant for centuries. Aquinas had no sense that there were different races of mankind, however, and there is no idea of racial superiority in his work. But his idea that slavery was "natural" and that there were "natural" slaves was to provide important intellectual support to ideas of racial differences.

The Age of Discovery and Colonization of the Americas (Fifteenth–Seventeenth Centuries)

As Europeans explored the world's oceans and conquered some parts of the world they found, they began to need and rely on slavery and ideas of racial difference (and of white superiority) as never before. At the same time, the Western Christian Church was divided by the Reformation, creating two very different religious traditions and challenging the Catholic side's idea of universality.

The Portuguese and Spanish had been exploring the Atlantic and conquering islands, such as the Canaries, even while still fighting the Muslims in their own countries, but after the final victory of the War of Reconquest in 1492, Iberian expansion into the wider world grew more rapid. The Spanish conquistadores in the Americas rapidly adapted their ideology of rule over Muslims and Jews at home to permit them to rule over Indians in the Americas. The institutions of rule in the Iberian Peninsula, the Inquisition, the encomienda, and a society of castes, were transplanted to the Americas. However, the castes in Spain—Old Christian (descended from people who had been Christian before the 1100s), New Christian (descended from recent converts from Judaism or ISLAM), *morisco* (descended from Moorish Muslims)—were based on religion though expressed in terms of blood relationships. The religious choices of

one's ancestors were said to make the children unreliable, allowing differential treatment of those descended from Muslims and Jews. But although similar logic was used to establish a racial caste order in the Americas, it subtly developed into a fundamentally new concept, that there were groups of people—those with Indian or African ancestors—who were naturally suited for a subordinate role in society. When the Spanish and Portuguese began transporting people from Africa to the Americas, they fit them into this racial order. Blacks rated below Indians in the racial hierarchy (though often above them in a functional hierarchy of productivity and integration into social structures) because they were tied to slavery, while at least in Spanish America enslaving Indians was almost completely unlawful.

The Catholic Church contributed to this development in two ways. The first was in its role as the principal source of education and scholarship in the regions where it was dominant, the institution of philosophers who were interested in the human condition and beginning to study what in our day would be called anthropology. Frey Bernardino de Sahagún, a Spanish Franciscan missionary to Mexico, collected and translated the Aztec historical documents and wrote extensive commentaries that modern scholars still use to help them understand Mesoamerican civilization. This intellectual development helped lead to the rise of a theory of the division of mankind into races, which paralleled the growth of racial divisions in society and provided some intellectual justification for it.

On the other hand, the Catholic Church also provided a home for people of color, a place where they could feel they were on common ground with their white conquerors and masters. Since religious conversion was the moral and religious justification for the conquest, all Catholic rulers in the Americas insisted on the full participation of blacks and Indians in religious services. Of course, whites found ways to enhance their status even through worship. For example, Catholic churches did not have seats for the worshippers at this time; everybody stood through the services. People sometimes took in something to kneel on, but only white people were so privileged in the churches of Mexico. A great persecution of purported secret Jews in Mexico in the 1630s was sparked when some poorer white women complained that a prominent New Christian woman was permitted to use a rug to kneel upon during Mass. White babies of good family could be baptized in special masses, while poorer children had to make do with a sort of assembly-line process on a special day once a month. Even though some such marks of social distinction might be open to whites, the fact that everyone was part of the same congregation and the church gave the same sacraments to everyone emphasized their common humanity to everyone. This common humanity was reflected in laws, which in Catholic countries were governed by religious strictures to a great extent. The CODE NOIR IN FRENCH LAW (1697) begins by requiring masters to include slaves in religious services and goes on to protect (to some extent) FAMILY bonds among slaves and even their right to a certain limited standard of living, basing these requirements on church laws.

Many blacks became Catholics after arriving in the Americas, but it is important to note that some slaves were already Catholics when they left Africa. Portuguese missionaries had been working in the Kingdom of Kongo since the early 16th century, and many Congolese had become Catholic. The Congo was the source of many of the slaves imported to the Americas in the late 17th and 18th centuries, during a period of political strife in the kingdom. (*See also* CONGO AND ANGOLA.) The Congolese believers practiced a somewhat modified form of Catholicism, influenced by African spiritual ideas and practices and reflecting the lack of priests. Many black Catholics in the Americas also had somewhat syncretic practices, also caused by the lack of priests to give them careful training in Catholic ideas and by the persistence of African cultural values. (*See also* AFRICAN AND SYNCRETIC RELIGIONS.) Catholicism was more open to this sort of syncretism, especially if the differences from Catholic practices did not touch central theological ideas. The Catholic Church in the Middle Ages in Europe had adopted and Christianized many pagan religious practices, rededicating pagan festivals to Christian purposes and blending the names and characteristic symbology of pagan deities with those of saints. Protestantism was much less open to syncretism, criticizing the Catholics for their flexibility and themselves insisting that all converts in the Americas give up any African cultural or spiritual practices.

Another intellectual current that affected the Catholic Church in its relationship to people of color at this time was the Reformation. In northern Europe in the 16th century, a new branch of Christianity, Protestantism (*see also* PROTESTANT MAINLINE CHURCHES), had sprung up that was more accepting of individual rights and initiative but was also more willing to associate church membership with the state and the nation, and thus to exclude from the church and from common humanity those people who did not belong. The Catholic Church reaffirmed its Catholicity, that is, what it applied to all people everywhere, but in practice it became more deeply committed to states and nations in its effort to defend itself against the new movement. Popes granted great powers to Catholic monarchs to control the church in their lands. National Catholic Churches began to think and teach that being French or Spanish or Portuguese meant being

Catholic and that being Catholic automatically conferred at least some of the rights of a citizen. In Europe, this was a period of great persecution of Jews, and in the colonies, similar questions arose about the status of the blacks and Indians. If they were Catholics, did that mean they were Spaniards? If not Spaniards, perhaps they were not really Catholics, and if not Catholics, perhaps they were even not deserving of human rights.

The Spanish and Portuguese church and government, however, took the catholic part of the Catholic Church's mission very seriously. Bartolomé de Las Casas, a missionary of the order of DOMINICANS, is often held up as a singular example of humane behavior for his defense of the Indians and blacks against the conquistadores and the colonial state. However, there were many such churchmen in Spanish America who tried to defend the people of color. The JESUITS' missionaries in ARGENTINA and PARAGUAY defended the Guaraní Indians against the Brazilian *paulistas* who wanted to enslave them. The archbishop of Mexico City was under arrest in 1624 when he was rescued by mob action against the viceroy. The riot arose because of a conflict with the viceroy over the actions of the *corregidor,* a local official responsible for overseeing the Indians. There were many issues in the conflict; one important component of the crisis was the belief of the poor, mostly people of color, that the archbishop was their defender and the government their enemy.

In both Spanish and Portuguese America, the Catholic Church provided blacks, both slave and free, with ways to organize themselves. The CATHOLIC CONFRATERNITIES, or brotherhoods, allowed people of color to work together for spiritual direction and education, organizing community festivals and community self-help measures such as burial insurance and microcredit. The Catholic Church was initially reluctant to permit people of color to rise in the organization. The famous early Afro-Peruvian SAINT MARTÍN DE PORRES was not permitted to become a priest, or even a full brother in the Dominican order until rather late in life, and he was the son of a colonial governor. By the 18th century, people of mixed race were being accepted as priests and religious brothers, however, and the mixed-race priest JOSÉ MARÍA MORELOS was an early supporter of independence for Mexico. Free people of color in Spanish America were notably pious, even in a very Catholic and pious place and time. Pope Paul III cited the notable religious fervor of Indians and blacks in *Sublimus Dei,* and the German voyager Alexander von Humboldt noted the many dark faces at Mass in several cities he visited in the 18th century.

The Catholic Church in FRANCE was very much under the authority of the king, even more so than in Spain and Portugal. Therefore, Catholic authorities were generally more willing to support the social order in the colonies. Parishes in the FRENCH CARIBBEAN colonies were run as missions: That is, they were under the nominal supervision of a bishop at home rather than having a local bishop, who would have represented a power center separate from the government. The bishop was far away, but the colonial government and local elites were close and were in charge of parish finances. Thus, parish priests were under the control of local white elites and had no alternative chain of command on which to rely. They were very unlikely to upset matters by pushing for fair and equal treatment for people of color. The chief exceptions were the religious orders, especially the Jesuits but to a lesser extent the Capuchins and Franciscans. Religious order priests had their superiors within their order to rely upon, and those superiors often had strong views about the importance of evangelizing and supporting people of color. The Jesuits in SAINT-DOMINGUE (the modern Haiti) were so energetic at evangelizing and teaching the blacks, slaves as well as free people, that finally the local authorities expelled them all from the colony in 1763. Paradoxically, while almost every white person owned at least some slaves in Saint-Domingue, the Jesuits were known for their financially successful plantations, which owned hundreds of slaves, who in many cases worked under conditions not markedly better than those of slaves of secular masters.

Mature Plantation Societies (Seventeenth–Nineteenth Centuries)

This expulsion occurred as the plantations of Saint-Domingue were becoming the most productive in the Americas and Saint-Domingue was on its way to becoming the wealthiest spot on earth. As a general rule, as the plantation became a more and more important part of any colony's economy, conditions for blacks, both free and slave, became worse. This was true in Catholic as well as Protestant countries' colonies.

The wealth of the plantations allowed their owners to relocate to the cities, and often to the home country. Absentee masters did not have the feudal, personal ties to workers that resident proprietors did. These personal ties went a long way toward softening the harshness of any slave regime, though they had their own potential for abuse in the form of favoritism, sexual harassment of the weaker party, and so forth. But as the relationships among master, slave, and free employee became to entirely based on cash and labor power, the racial divide deepened. Old structures, like the Catholic Church, which called for different groups to treat each other as fellow human beings, weakened.

In any case, this was the age of Enlightenment, and the influence of the Catholic Church was waning throughout its range. The Masonic movement (*see* FREEMASONRY) was growing in strength; many plantation owners, colonial officials, and even a few free people of color were members. Freemasonry in particular and Enlightenment free thought in general taught that divine commands were no sure guide to moral behavior, which could only be based on reason. At the same time, European thinkers were creating the modern concept of science, which held that true knowledge can only be discovered by observing natural phenomena and conducting experiments, and not by listening to religious authorities. At the same time, the new scientists said that they could not determine what was good from empirical data, just what was true, but that the question of good was meaningless anyway. This is because, they said, if you based your behavior on what was true, matters would turn out for the best since progress was scientifically inevitable. A new system of thinking about social relations based on these ideas, known as liberalism, was coming into being. The liberal Enlightenment started out by accepting the notion of the nation-state that had been growing for the preceding few hundred years as the primary unit of analysis. The members of the nation-state, the "people," were the sources of "sovereignty," which meant that collectively they could make any sorts of decisions they considered best about how society within the territory under their control should be structured. Membership in the nationstate did not include every person living within its boundaries. Significant groups of people were excluded: Women and children were only partially included, for example. Additionally, in almost all places, only those people who were descended from an imagined set of ancestors who were believed to have inhabited the particular patch of European soil that was seen as the cradle of the nation at some time in the past were considered true citizens. Thus, to be a Frenchmen was not to be a Catholic living under the sovereign rule of the king of France, as in the past, but to be a descendant of Vercingetorix the Gaul, Caesar the Roman, Clovis the Frank, or one of their followers. That is, only white people could be true citizens of European countries under the consensus liberal idea of the late 18th and 19th centuries. Those liberal thinkers who thought out the universalist implications of their scientifically based ideas about society tended to argue that black people or Indians ought to have their own national identity and their own state structures, at least someday. This line of thinking was not prominent until the 20th century, however. The result of all this new thought was that the Catholic idea of a universal humanity was generally abandoned by intellectual leaders. Indeed, some scientists began to argue (as some Protestant theologians had for some time) that humanity was not one but several different entities: that the "races" of mankind were actually different species.

In the Catholic world, the opponents of the new liberal scientific progressive consensus fought on the ground of the established church, aristocratic privilege, and the sovereign authority of monarchs. These ideas were thought of by both sides as being linked. One could not be truly Catholic without supporting king and aristocracy and a society of orders; one could also not be truly royalist without also supporting Catholicism and, at least to some extent, accepting the Catholic idea of common humanity. Catholics continued to uphold this idea in the late 18th and early 19th centuries. Most notably, Pope Gregory XVI issued *In Supremo Apostolatus* in 1839, condemning the slave trade, still operating at that time in Cuba and Brazil, and declared that slavery was fundamentally unjust.

Antiliberal forces gained some people of color as their supporters: In the early stages of the HAITIAN REVOLUTION in the 1790s, TOUSSAINT LOUVERTURE and the slave rebels fought for the French king against the forces loyal to the FRENCH REVOLUTION. Before the revolution, the most obviously pious people in Saint-Domingue were the free people of color. Toussaint himself was notably pious throughout his life. In the WAR OF MEXICAN INDEPENDENCE, 1810–21, the black and Indian soldiers of Hidalgo, Morelos, and VICENTE GUERRERO SALDAÑA carried the banner of Our Lady of Guadalupe and claimed to be fighting for the real king and true religion against liberal, Masonic Bourbon forces. In Brazil, many free colored activists in the 19th century supported Dom PEDRO II and Princess Imperial ISABEL OF BRAGANÇA, seeing their rule as offering a better hope for inclusion to people of color than their liberal opponents.

For the most part, however, people of color were or became supporters of the liberal consensus as it evolved. The logic of the liberal idea of the nation-state required that if the nation was in the Americas, then American people had to be considered members, at least provisionally or in part. People of African descent had a harder time than Indians or mestizos in this regard, but outside the United States, most of the new nations of the Americas would accept free African Americans as citizens at least in some measure. Liberalism left room for the possibility that while everyone might be a citizen, some people could not exercise their citizenship actively, that is, vote and participate in public debate, because of some inborn incapacity. In many places, people of color had to overcome this hurdle and demonstrate their capacity, but at least some would be accepted in most places in the Catholic Americas. Additionally, and very important in this regard, free labor was a central idea of liberalism. Most liberal regimes in the Americas abolished slavery within a generation after they were established, again with the exception of

the United States. The abolitionist movements provided important opportunities for free people of color and liberal whites to work together. This collaboration drew free people of color into support for other liberal ideas, though not in all cases: In 1852, FREDERICK DOUGLASS famously questioned the idea of nationalism in his speech "What Is the Fourth of July to a Slave?"

In the former colonies of Catholic America, the growing liberal consensus and the growing adherence of people of color to it did not mean that the Catholic Church lost its central place in the lives of free people of color. Afro-Mexicans in Veracruz and the American Southwest remained stubbornly Catholic even as their mestizo neighbors moved toward modern secularism. But the Catholic Church of Latin America, under attack from liberal nationalists, reacted by retreating from even the limited active social criticism it had been willing to make in the colonial period. For the most part, the Catholic Church became the supporter of a new conservative opposition in Latin America in the 19th century, with the military and landowners replacing the aristocracy and the state replacing the monarch in the new ruling trinity. It would not be until the 20th century that liberation theology would reaffirm universalist Catholic ideas opposed to racism and social inequality in the region.

In the United States, the Catholic Church only became important as slavery was dying there. There were small numbers of Catholic Englishmen among the early settlers of MARYLAND, and some of their slaves and free black neighbors had adopted Catholicism, urged by the masters who followed Catholic teaching. The priests who served Maryland were Jesuits, and as did the Jesuits in Haiti, they financed their activities by owning plantations that were worked by slaves. When LOUISIANA became part of the United States in 1804, a larger but still fairly small number of Catholic blacks became Americans. But it was not until the 1840s when large numbers of Catholic immigrants from Ireland and Germany began to arrive that the Catholic Church became an important part of America's religious makeup. The English Catholic Church was the source of the national character of American Catholicism, at least up to the late 19th century, and the Catholic Church in England had been conditioned by persecution during the Reformation to avoid open political criticism of the government at any cost. The Catholic Church in the United States before the Civil War refrained almost without exception from criticizing slavery, though individual Catholics did play a role in the struggle against slavery. Daniel O'Connell, the Irish nationalist leader, called for the abolition of slavery in the British Empire and America. But for the most part, the Catholic Church in the United States, even more than the Catholic Churches in Latin America, viewed abolitionism and the quest for black civil rights in the 19th century as projects of liberalism and thus inherently suspect.

Nonetheless, the Catholic Church in America continued to serve black Catholics and created an avenue, however small, for blacks to rise in society and organize. Father AUGUSTINE TOLTON, a free black from MISSOURI, was the first black Catholic priest ordained in the United States in 1886. The church created a religious order, the Josephites, in 1871 to evangelize blacks after the Civil War, and by the end of the century, many of their priests were black. The Catholic school system, very strong in the United States in the 19th century, was a way for blacks in northern and midwestern cities to obtain an education, although there were significant SEGREGATION and discrimination even here. It was not until the mid-20th century that the last Catholic schools in the United States were desegregated, by order of the Vatican and in some cases under threat of excommunication of white Catholics who resisted.

Throughout centuries of European and African presence in the Americas, the Roman Catholic Church has had a great influence on the lives of free people of color. Most importantly, by continually insisting on the essential humanity of people of African descent, the church assured some minimal standard of human dignity and racial justice. Although the church did not, until quite late, oppose slavery, Catholic teaching did help protect the weak and perhaps opened the door to MANUMISSION a little wider in places where it had influence. By allowing some people of color to serve the church as priests, religious brothers, and nuns, the church provided an avenue for advancement and a set of potential leaders for the larger black community.

Stewart R. King

FURTHER READING

Congar, Yves, O. P. *The Catholic Church and the Race Question.* Geneva: UNESCO, 1953.

LaFarge, John. *The Race Question and the Negro: A Study of the Catholic Doctrine on Interracial Justice.* Toronto: Longman's, 1943.

Peabody, Sue. "A Dangerous Zeal: Catholic Missions to Slaves in the French Antilles, 1635–1800." *French Historical Studies* 25, no. 1 (2002): 53–90.

SUBLIMUS DEI BY POPE PAUL III (1537)

The Roman Catholic Church had taken an equivocal position on the legitimacy of racial differences and racially based slavery during the 15th century. In 1435, Pope Eugene IV called the enslavement of Canary Islanders by the Spanish unjust and ordered all Canarians released on pain of excommunication. On the other hand, in 1453, Pope Nicholas V authorized Spain and Portugal to enslave Moors captured during the reconquest of the Iberian Peninsula. In both cases, the Catholic Church emphasized that slavery was only justified by "just war" and did not grant the master unlimited powers. Masters were responsible for the religious education of their slaves and had to treat them humanely.

The conquest of the Americas gave Spain and Portugal access to a vast new pool of potential slaves. Moreover, the very humanity of the people of the Americas was open to question, because of theological speculation that they might not be descended from Adam and Eve. This meant that the restrictions on the treatment of slaves in earlier Papal documents might not apply to Native Americans. And already by the 1530s, slaves of African origin were beginning to arrive in the Americas. Their treatment was also affected by decisions made about the proper status of the native peoples of the Americas because those decisions became embedded in generally applicable law codes for the colonies such as the New Laws of the Indies (1542).

Pope Paul III issued Sublimus Dei on May 29, 1537, on the request of the Spanish bishops, who wanted to be able to guide King Charles of Spain in the preparation of the New Laws of the Indies. A serious debate had been going on in Spain for some years on this topic, which was to culminate in the famous Valladolid debates (1550-51) between Bishop Bartolomé de Las Casas and Juan Ginés de Sepúlveda.

Pope Paul's declaration in Sublimus Dei goes beyond merely criticizing the treatment of Indians in the Americas to assert the fundamental unity and dignity of all humanity. It refutes the argument put forward by the Spanish conquistadores that native people in the Americas were not truly human and had a separate origin, and it was taken by later interpreters and formal Church teaching by later Popes as also refuting similar arguments made about other racial groups, including Africans. The debate about separate origins of mankind, which continued in Protestant (and secular scientific) circles into the 19th century, was settled definitively in Roman Catholic thought by this document. In addition, it commands that the Indians and other non-European peoples should be converted by preaching and the good example of missionaries—not, therefore, by force or violence. Furthermore, it links their human character, susceptibility to conversion to Catholic Christianity, and human rights to life and property. This document is rightly considered a foundational assertion of generalized human rights that apply to all people everywhere.

Sublimus Dei
Pope Paul III

To all faithful Christians to whom this writing may come, health in Christ our Lord and the apostolic benediction.

The sublime God so loved the human race that He created man in such wise that he might participate, not only in the good that other creatures enjoy, but endowed him with capacity to attain to the inaccessible and invisible Supreme Good and behold it face to face; and since man, according to the testimony of the sacred scriptures, has been created to enjoy eternal life and happiness, which none may obtain save through faith in our Lord Jesus Christ, it is necessary that he should possess the nature and faculties enabling him to receive that faith; and that whoever is thus endowed should be capable of receiving that same faith. Nor is it credible that any one should possess so little understanding as to desire the faith and yet be destitute of the most necessary faculty to enable him to receive it. Hence Christ, who is the Truth itself, that has never failed and can never fail, said to the preachers of the faith whom He chose for that office "Go ye and teach all nations." He said all, without exception, for all are capable of receiving the doctrines of the faith.

The enemy of the human race, who opposes all good deeds in order to bring men to destruction, beholding and envying this, invented a means never before heard of, by which he might hinder the preaching of God's word of Salvation to the people: he inspired his satellites who, to please him, have not hesitated to publish abroad that the Indians of the West and the South, and other people of whom We have recent knowledge should be treated as dumb brutes created for our service, pretending that they are incapable of receiving the Catholic Faith.

We, who, though unworthy, exercise on earth the power of our Lord and seek with all our might to bring those sheep of His flock who are outside into the fold committed to our charge, consider, however, that the Indians are truly men and that they are not only capable of understanding the Catholic Faith but, according to our information, they desire exceedingly to receive it. Desiring to provide ample remedy for these evils, We define and declare by these Our letters, or by any translation thereof signed by any notary public and sealed with the seal of any ecclesiastical dignitary, to which the same credit shall be given as to the originals, that, notwithstanding whatever may have been or may be said to the contrary, the said Indians and all other people who may later be discovered by Christians, are by no means to be deprived of their liberty or the possession of their property, even though they be outside the faith of Jesus Christ; and that they may and should, freely and legitimately, enjoy their liberty and the possession of their property; nor should they be in any way enslaved; should the contrary happen, it shall be null and have no effect.

By virtue of Our apostolic authority We define and declare by these present letters, or by any translation thereof signed by any notary public and sealed with the seal of any ecclesiastical dignitary, which shall thus command the same obedience as the originals, that the said Indians and other peoples should be converted to the faith of Jesus Christ by preaching the word of God and by the example of good and holy living.

IN SUPREMO APOSTOLATUS
BY POPE GREGORY XVI (1839)

The following letter, written by Pope Gregory XVI, was first sent to the national Catholic bishops' meeting at Baltimore, Maryland, on December 3, 1839, but was intended as a general instruction to all Catholics around the world. Though principally addressing the trade in slaves, it makes no distinction between the international and domestic slave trade, condemning the resale of people already enslaved, and thus, as the American bishops recognized as soon as the letter was read, essentially makes slavery itself a violation of church law. It also describes countries that have abolished slavery as having escaped from "barbarous" practices. It condemns slavery as harming the church by turning the targeted peoples away from Christianity. Finally, it reaffirms longstanding Catholic teaching that, even if one could argue that it was just to hold a person as a slave, all people of whatever color have basic human rights. Although Catholic countries continued to permit slavery for another 50 years (Brazil was the last to abolish slavery in 1889), this document spelled the end of the contradictory policy of the Catholic Church toward the institution.

In Supremo Apostolatus
Pope Gregory XVI

Placed at the summit of the Apostolic power and, although lacking in merits, holding the place of Jesus Christ, the Son of God, Who, being made Man through utmost Charity, deigned to die for the Redemption of the World, We have judged that it belonged to Our pastoral solicitude to exert Ourselves to turn away the Faithful from the inhuman slave trade in Negroes and all other men. Assuredly, since there was spread abroad, first of all amongst the Christians, the light of the Gospel, these miserable people, who in such great numbers, and chiefly through the effects of wars, fell into very cruel slavery, experienced an alleviation of their lot. Inspired in fact by the Divine Spirit, the Apostles, it is true, exhorted the slaves themselves to obey their masters, according to the flesh, as though obeying Christ, and sincerely to accomplish the Will of God; but they ordered the masters to act well towards slaves, to give them what was just and equitable, and to abstain from menaces, knowing that the common Master both of themselves and of the slaves is in Heaven, and that with Him there is no distinction of persons.

But as the law of the Gospel universally and earnestly enjoined a sincere charity towards all, and considering that Our Lord Jesus Christ had declared that He considered as done or refused to Himself everything kind and merciful done or refused to the small and needy, it naturally follows, not only that Christians should regard as their brothers their slaves and, above all, their Christian slaves, but that they should be more inclined to set free those who merited it; which it was the custom to do chiefly upon the occasion of the Easter Feast as Gregory of Nyssa tells us. There were not lacking Christians, who, moved by an ardent charity "cast themselves into bondage in order to redeem others," many instances of which our predecessor, Clement I, of very holy memory, declares to have come to his knowledge. In the process of time, the fog of pagan superstition being more completely dissipated and the manners of barbarous people having been softened, thanks to Faith operating by Charity, it at last comes about that, since several centuries, there are no more slaves in the greater number of Christian nations. But—We say with profound sorrow—there were to be found afterwards among the Faithful men who, shamefully blinded by the desire of sordid gain, in lonely and distant countries, did not hesitate to reduce to slavery Indians, negroes and other wretched peoples, or else, by instituting or developing the trade in those who had been made slaves by others, to favor their unworthy practice. Certainly many Roman Pontiffs of glorious memory, Our Predecessors, did not fail, according to the duties of their charge, to blame severely this way of acting as dangerous for the spiritual welfare of those engaged in the traffic and a shame to the Christian name; they foresaw that as a result of this, the infidel peoples would be more and more strengthened in their hatred of the true Religion.

It is at these practices that are aimed the Letter Apostolic of Paul III, given on May 29, 1537, under the seal of the Fisherman, and addressed to the Cardinal Archbishop of Toledo, and afterwards another Letter, more detailed, addressed by Urban VIII on April 22, 1639 to the Collector Jurium of the Apostolic Chamber of Portugal. In the latter are severely and particularly condemned those who should dare "to reduce to slavery the Indians of the Eastern and Southern Indies," to sell them, buy them, exchange them or give them, separate them from their wives and children, despoil them of their goods and properties, conduct or transport them into other regions, or deprive them of liberty in any way whatsoever, retain them in servitude, or lend counsel, succor, favor and co-operation to those so acting, under no matter what pretext or excuse, or who proclaim and teach that this way of acting is allowable and co-operate in any manner whatever in the practices indicated.

Benedict XIV confirmed and renewed the penalties of the Popes above mentioned in a new Apostolic Letter addressed on December 20, 1741, to the Bishops of Brazil and some other regions, in which he stimulated, to the same end, the solicitude of the Governors themselves. Another of Our Predecessors, anterior to Benedict XIV, Pius II, as during his life the power of the Portuguese was extending itself over New Guinea, sent on October 7, 1462, to a Bishop who was leaving for that country, a Letter in which he not only gives the Bishop himself the means of exercising there the sacred ministry with more fruit, but on the same occasion, addresses grave warnings with regard to Christians who should reduce neophytes to slavery.

In our time Pius VII, moved by the same religious and charitable spirit as his Predecessors, intervened zealously with those in possession of power to secure that the slave trade should at least cease amongst the Christians. The penalties imposed and the care given by Our Predecessors contributed in no small measure, with the help of God, to protect the Indians and the other people mentioned against the cruelty of the invaders or the cupidity of Christian merchants, without however carrying success to such a point that the Holy See could rejoice over the complete success of its efforts in this direction; for the slave trade, although it has diminished in more than one district, is still practiced by numerous Christians. This is why, desiring to remove such a shame from all the Christian nations, having fully reflected over the whole question and having taken the advice of many of Our Venerable Brothers the Cardinals of the Holy Roman Church, and walking in the footsteps of Our Predecessors, We warn and adjure earnestly in the Lord faithful Christians of every condition that no one in the future dare to vex anyone, despoil him of his possessions, reduce to servitude, or lend aid and favour to those who give themselves up to these practices, or exercise that inhuman traffic by which the Blacks, as if they were not men but rather animals, having been brought into servitude, in no matter what way, are, without any distinction, in contempt of the rights of justice and humanity, bought, sold, and devoted sometimes to the hardest labor. Further, in the hope of gain, propositions of purchase being made to the first owners of the Blacks, dissensions and almost perpetual conflicts are aroused in these regions.

We reprove, then, by virtue of Our Apostolic Authority, all the practices abovementioned as absolutely unworthy of the Christian name. By the same Authority We prohibit and strictly forbid any Ecclesiastic or lay person from presuming to defend as permissible this traffic in Blacks under no matter what pretext or excuse, or from publishing or teaching in any manner whatsoever, in public or privately, opinions contrary to what We have set forth in this Apostolic Letter.

Source: Papal Encyclicals Web site. Available online. URL: http://www.papalencyclicals.net/Greg16/g16sup.htm. Accessed January 9, 2011.

ROSSIGNOL, ANNE (flourished 1770–1790)
Senegalese and Saint-Domingue merchant

Anne Rossignol was born in Gorée, Sénégal, sometime before 1750. Her mother was African and her father was a white man, a citizen of the French community of Gorée. Her parents were married, and thus she benefited from the status of citizen. Sénégalese national legend holds that Gorée was a major slave trading port, but this is not actually true. Only a few hundred slaves were ever embarked at Gorée. The chief slave trading ports in the region were on the Sénégal River, at St.-Louis, and on the Gambia River. By the middle of the 18th century, these ports were declining as sources of slaves, and a "legitimate" trade in African products, especially peanut oil, woven mats, fibers, simple clothing, and shoes, was growing. Gorée was an important source for this legitimate trade, and Rossignol's family apparently played major role.

Sometime about 1770, Rossignol traveled to SAINT-DOMINGUE, accompanied by her young daughter, Marie-Adelaide. Marie-Adelaide was a *quarteron*, of one-fourth African and three-fourths European ancestry, so her father must have been white. However, it is unclear who he was. Rossignol never described herself as married or widowed in any official documents, and Marie-Adelaide's marriage contract did not mention a father.

Rossignol went into business as an importer of a variety of African goods. Oil, presumably peanut oil, was her principal product. She did business with small retailers run by free people of color or poor whites and appears once in the notarial records as a successful plaintiff in a lawsuit asking for payment for a shipment she made to a white merchant. She also maintained a network of business contacts across the Atlantic and around the Caribbean. On one occasion, she forwarded a slave to a relative, Jean-Charles Floissac, an artisan also from Gorée, who had lived in Saint-Domingue for a while before 1778 and then, after a period of service in the French army, had settled in the colony of St-Lucia. She also sent a younger relative to be Floissac's apprentice, strengthening ties between the branches of the family and perhaps grooming someone to be her business agent in that colony.

We do not know what happened to Rossignol after the outbreak of the HAITIAN REVOLUTION in 1791. Many free people of color participated in the revolution and became leaders of Haitian society after independence. Others fled to France or to other colonies in the Americas. Rossignol could also have returned to Sénégal, where she was a citizen. Her daughter, Marie-Adelaide, moved to CHARLESTON, SOUTH CAROLINA, where she was a prominent businesswoman. Anne may have lived quietly with her, though no record exists of her being there.

Rossignol's life is remarkable for several reasons. One is that she was a woman who was an important actor in her own right in international commerce. Almost all the large businesspeople of Saint-Domingue, those who bought and sold products in overseas markets, were men. The fact that she was able to break into this trade without the aid of any obvious white husband or companion is unusual. She was almost unique as a person of color in this rarefied economic sphere. Only one of the other major merchants of Saint-Domingue that we know of was a free person of color, VINCENT OGÉ. Even though she broke color and gender lines in her occupational choice, she apparently had very conventional social goals. Her largest recorded transaction was the gift of some 66,000 livres of property—a very substantial sum worth at least $825,000 in today's money—to her daughter as a dowry to permit her to marry a successful white businessman. Promoting one's family by "marrying up" in color and class was a preoccupation of the old regime, and the fact that Rossignol put such value on it makes her anything but a revolutionary.

Stewart R. King

FURTHER READING
King, Stewart. *Blue Coat or Powdered Wig: Free People of Color in Pre-Revolutionary Saint-Domingue*. Athens: University of Georgia Press, 2001, chap. 5.
King, Stewart, and Dominique Rogers. "Housekeepers, Merchants, *Rentières*: Free Women of Color in the Port Cities of Colonial Saint-Domingue." In *Women in Port: Gendering Communities, Economics, and Social Networks in Atlantic Port Cities, 1500–1800*, edited by Douglas Catterall and Jodi Campbell. Leiden, Brill, forthcoming.

RUNAWAY SLAVES

Along with seeking formal MANUMISSION and LIVING "AS FREE," or arranging informal liberty with a master, running away was a method of gaining freedom from slavery. Many people who ran away were seeking to leave slavery forever, either by joining settlements of MAROONS, fleeing to an area where their enslavement would not be recognized, or hiding among free people of color within the slave society. Other incidents of running away were intended to be temporary, either as tactical moves in a dispute with the master or for visiting friends or family, and the runaways were willing to return on under certain conditions. This article is primarily concerned with those incidents of flight when the goal was to gain freedom. Of course, free people of color who owned slaves might find themselves hunting their own runaway slaves.

The most common destination for runaway slaves in most places in the Atlantic world was somewhere within the same colony where they could blend into the free population. Traveling long distances to other colonies or states was difficult, and many people would have little geographical knowledge to help them find the way. People of color in slave societies were always subject to questioning by POLICE and even random white people, so travel was dangerous. Better to find someplace nearby to settle down, so long as the master was unlikely to look there. This was especially true for CREOLE slaves, that is, those born in the colony, since they could more convincingly pass for free people of color. Big cities, with their anonymous multitudes of people, were common choices. A study in SAINT-DOMINGUE (present-day Haiti) of runaway slaves found that more than half of those caught were living in the three largest cities in the colony, while a significant proportion of the remainder were living very near their native plantations. Of course, this tells us nothing about those who avoided being caught; perhaps they chose better hiding places.

We tend to think of running away to wilderness areas to live as a maroon as an attractive option, and for some slaves at some times it was. Maroon communities suffered as the plantation complex grew in wealth and power in any particular place, however. Many maroon communities made treaties with colonial authorities that forbade them to accept new runaways. While these agreements might be ignored in certain cases, they led maroons to be less welcoming of runaways after the start of the 18th century. And while maroon communities would often accept a very diverse group of new residents, including creole slaves, Indians, and even whites, most newcomers to maroon communities were African-born slaves. They had both the military skills and the backgrounds as PEASANTS that were necessary for successful life as a maroon. Often maroon communities used African languages or Creole languages with African roots, making acculturation difficult for slaves born in the colony. An alternative in some areas, particularly the United States and BRAZIL, was to run away to native communities (see also BLACK SEMINOLE). Like the maroons, the Indians often had deals with governments that made them less willing to accept runaways, and the lifestyle of even the most settled native community would be very different from the creole slaves' familiar lifestyle. For these slaves, more settled areas would have been a better choice in most cases.

Some runaway slaves tried to make their way to other colonies or places where their slavery would not be recognized. This is well known in the case of the United States, where within a generation after independence the Northern states had all abolished slavery. The U.S. Constitution provided that slaves who ran away to other states had to be returned, but free states generally ignored this provision until the FUGITIVE SLAVE ACT OF 1850 was passed. Many of the slaves who ran away to the North, including FREDERICK DOUGLASS and HARRIET TUBMAN, were among the most famous free people of color in antebellum America. It was much easier, of course, to escape from MARYLAND, as Douglass and Tubman did, than from the Deep South states of ALABAMA or GEOR-

The people depicted here are intended to be blacks from the Southern United States fleeing to areas protected by the Union army during the American Civil War, but the painting could represent any of the many groups of African Americans throughout the hemisphere who migrated to seek better living conditions. *(Theodore Kaufmann/Getty Images)*

GIA. While FLORIDA was in Spanish hands, up until 1818, it served as an alternative destination for slaves fleeing the Deep South. Although SPAIN had slavery, and there were slaves in Florida, if any runaways arrived there and were willing to become a Catholic, the Florida colonial government would accept them as free people. The rebels in the Stono Conspiracy in SOUTH CAROLINA in 1739, for example, may have meant to seek refuge in Florida. Many runaway slaves in Saint-Domingue sought to cross the frontier to the Spanish colony of SANTO DOMINGO (present-day DOMINICAN REPUBLIC), as did the western Saint-Domingue maroons after their treaty with the government proved unreliable. Both Florida and Santo Domingo were sparsely populated, and their governments wanted to settle them in order to prevent neighboring colonies from swallowing them. The black population of the border regions of Santo Domingo became quite dense, and the most densely settled area, the central plateau, became part of independent Haiti. The northern region remained part of the Spanish colony, and some of the descendants of these 18th-century runaways were victims of the Dominican Republic dictator Rafael Trujillo's 1935 pogrom against dark-skinned people.

In the United States, the Underground Railroad is famous for having smuggled thousands of slaves to freedom. Most of these were freed during the AMERICAN CIVIL WAR, 1861–65, after the Northern states stopped returning runaways, for the most part, even to those slave states that remained loyal to the Union, and after radical antislavery generals and finally the U.S. government officially began to encourage slaves to run away to join the armed forces. Before 1861, the Underground Railroad was more of a political threat to slave society than an actual possible route to freedom for the average slave. Still, its activities were widely known and offered hope to people in slave states who dreamed of freedom. Many Underground Railroad "conductors" were evangelical or Baptist ministers, and this reinforced the sense of abolitionism as a religious crusade (see also BAPTISTS AND PIETISTS and PROTESTANT MAINLINE CHURCHES).

Nonetheless, most attempts to run away ended unhappily for the slave. Even though most slaves were recaptured, running away posed a significant threat to the slave system. It was a form of resistance that struck directly at the SLAVE OWNERS' interest in extracting labor from their slaves. It demonstrated the slaves' continuing resistance, and it did provide a few lucky individuals with a chance for true freedom. Recaptures were common, however. Official police stood to gain significant bounties, set by law in Saint-Domingue at 10 percent of the value of the slave and in some Southern states at one-quarter. There were also private slave catchers, especially in the United States, where governments were generally weak and in some cases uncooperative. Northern states offered little or no assistance to slave catchers and even obstructed their activities with PERSONAL LIBERTY LAWS that threatened them with prison for kidnapping. Nonetheless, they did manage to re-enslave some runaways from Northern states, especially after the Fugitive Slave Act required federal officials to assist them. The seminal antislavery novel *Uncle Tom's Cabin* (1852) portrays a slave catcher as one of its most important white characters, who is ultimately redeemed by the faith of the protagonist, Eliza.

In Latin America, many slave catchers and policemen were free people of color. Additionally, some free people of color owned slaves themselves, and those slaves sometimes ran away. Many white slave owners and contemporary observers believed that free colored people were much harsher on their slaves and so those slaves ran away more frequently. There is no statistical evidence for this belief. In the historian Jean Fouchard's study of runaways in Saint-Domingue, slaves owned by free people of color were featured in about one-fifth of the advertisements for runaway slaves, while free people of color owned between one-fourth and one-third of all slaves in the colony. A runaway would be a more serious blow to a free colored masters, since on average they owned fewer slaves than did whites. In one case in Saint-Domingue in the 1780s, a poor free colored woman was in danger of having to give up her only slave to the government because she could not afford the 10 percent bounty for the police. She tried after the fact to withdraw her accusation that the slave had run away, apparently unsuccessfully.

Stewart R. King

FURTHER READING
Fouchard, Jean. *The Haitian Maroons: Liberty or Death*. Translation of *Les Marrons de la Liberté*. Translated by A. Faulkner Watts. New York: Blyden, 1981.
Franklin, John Hope, and Lauren Schweniger. *Runaway Slaves: Rebels on the Plantation*. Oxford: Oxford University Press, 1999.

RUSSWURM, JOHN (1799–1851) *U.S. educator, newspaperman, and politician*
John Brown Russwurm was one of America's earliest and most prominent black journalists. He went on to have a very influential role in the colonization of LIBERIA.

Russwurm was born in JAMAICA on October 1, 1799, to a black woman and a white man who was a plantation owner and merchant. It is unclear whether his mother was free or enslaved; in any case, it was customary in Jamaica for favored mixed-race children to live in their father's house without a doing chores and to receive a better education. Beginning in 1807, Russwurm attended boarding school in Quebec, CANADA, for three years. He then lived with his father in MAINE, beginning at age 13. He was evidently close to his father, who proudly introduced his son around the community. Russwurm attended private school in Maine, the Hebron Academy, and graduated in 1819. His father died in 1815, but his stepmother continued to support him and consider him part of her family. Russwurm moved to BOSTON, MASSACHUSETTS, in 1821 and taught at two African-American schools, Abiel Smith and Primus Hall. In 1824, Russwurm was admitted as the first African-American student at Bowdoin College in Maine. There, he joined the Athenaean Society, a literary fraternity that had Nathanial Hawthorne as its president. Upon his graduation in 1826, as only the third African-American college graduate in the United States, Russwurm planned to study medicine in Boston and practice in Haiti. He spoke at his commencement on "The Conditions and Prospects of Haiti." Russwurm saw strong inspiration in the example of Haiti as the first independent black republic (see also SAINT-DOMINGUE).

After graduating from Bowdoin, Russwurm was offered a position in Liberia by the AMERICAN COLONIZATION SOCIETY after expressing his interest (see also EMIGRATION AND COLONIZATION). He politely declined the offer in February 1827 and moved to New York City, where with SAMUEL E. CORNISH he coedited *Freedom's Journal*, the first African-American newspaper in the United States. The newspaper had a goal of serving the African-descended community throughout North America and was distributed in the Caribbean as well as in many states of the United States and in CANADA. It published four articles by DAVID WALKER, including an early version of his famous "Appeal to the Colored Citizens of the World." In these articles, Walker called for active resistance to slavery and said that a slave would be justified in killing his master.

In spring 1829, Russwurm was the sole editor of the *Journal* when he publicly expressed his support for African colonization. His position was widely seen as a rejection of the African-American community, and Russwurm was burned in effigy in PHILADELPHIA, PENNSYLVANIA. The free colored community in the North was generally hostile to plans to settle them in Liberia. They thought of America as their country, and few had any desire to "return" to a continent almost none had ever seen. The controversy finally forced Russwurm to resign from the editorship of *Freedom's Journal*.

He then agreed to emigrate and arrived in Liberia in November 1829. From Liberia, he published letters in the *African Repository and Colonial Journal* advocating colonization and expressing his excitement about the prospects and opportunities for blacks in Liberia. Russwurm became the superintendent of schools and revived the

Liberia Herald in March 1830, serving as its editor. He was elected colonial secretary and married Sarah E. McGill, daughter of the most prominent family in Liberia, in 1833. They had four children together. In his private correspondence Russwurm expressed disappointment with the white leadership of the colonization movement and their RACISM AND RACIAL PREJUDICE. He also acknowledged that tropical illnesses were taking their toll and that business was slow as a result of tribal conflicts, but publicly his paper continued to publish glowing reports and commentary in support of colonization. In America, James Forten (see FORTEN FAMILY) and William Lloyd Garrison, among others, complained about the accuracy of Russwurm's reports. In Liberia, other settlers noted the *Liberia Herald's* sympathy with official American Colonization Society policies and positions. When Russwurm reluctantly printed a declaration by opponents of the Colonization Society's government in 1835, he was removed as both colonial secretary and editor by the society. Russwurm left the territory claimed by Liberia and moved farther down the African coast to a separate colony, established by the state of MARYLAND at Cape Palmas. There, he was appointed governor in October 1836. Despite numerous difficulties with food supplies, other officials, and indigenous people, he served as governor for 15 years. He was strongly encouraged by Liberian independence in 1847 and hoped Maryland-in-Africa could also become independent. Russwurm died on June 17, 1851, before the Maryland colony achieved independence in 1854, followed by annexation to Liberia in 1857.

Matthew J. Hudock

FURTHER READING

Alexander, Leslie M. *African or American? Black Identity and Political Activism in New York City, 1784–1861*. Urbana: University of Illinois Press, 2008.

Bacon, Jacqueline. Freedom's Journal: *The First African-American Newspaper*. Lanham, Md.: Lexington Books, 2007.

Beyan, Amos J. *African American Settlements in West Africa: John Brown Russwurm and the American Civilizing Efforts*. New York: Palgrave Macmillan, 2005.

Harris, Leslie M. *In the Shadow of Slavery: African Americans in New York City, 1626–1863*. Chicago: University of Chicago Press, 2003.

Tripp, Bernell. *Origins of the Black Press: New York, 1827–1847*. Northport, Ala.: Vision Press, 1992.

Young, Sandra Sandiford. "John Brown Russwurm's Dilemma: Citizenship or Emigration?" In *Prophets of Protest: Reconsidering the History of American Abolitionism,* edited by Timothy Patrick McCarthy and John Stauffer. New York: New Press, 2006.

S

SAINT-DOMINGUE (HAITI)

The French colony of Saint-Domingue was located on the western third of the island of Hispaniola. The colony's territory makes up the largest part of the modern nation of Haiti. The colony was the third largest in the Caribbean (after CUBA and the Spanish part of Hispaniola, called SANTO DOMINGO), at 9,500 square miles. Most of the territory was mountainous, and it was covered with thick forests when the French began to settle there in the 17th century. Only the limited coastal plains were suitable for agriculture in the beginning, and at first settlement focused there.

The colony was geographically divided into three regions: the North, the West, and the South. In the North, a series of broad coastal plains, well watered, face the Atlantic Ocean. There are a number of good ports including the bay of CAP-FRANÇAIS/CAP-HAÏTIEN, the commercial center of the colony and its largest city. This is the area best suited for settlement. It is also the area most open to invasion from the Spanish side of the island and thus strategically significant. Around the Bay of PORT-AU-PRINCE is the region called the West Province. It also has a large coastal plain, running from St-Marc in the North to Port-au-Prince in the South and eastward as far as the border with the Spanish colony. There are also smaller coastal plains around Léogane in the West and Gonaïves in the North. The bay is sheltered from storms but also suffers from drought. Intensive agriculture on these plains would require extensive investment in irrigation infrastructure. The southern peninsula is quite mountainous and was the last area to be heavily settled by Europeans and Africans.

Early History

The colony was the site of the first settlement established by Christopher Columbus in the Americas in 1492, near Limonade in northern Haiti. At that time, the island had a dense population of native people, estimated at between 800,000 and four million for the whole island (perhaps a third of these lived in the western part, which became Saint-Domingue). The native people attacked and destroyed Columbus's first settlement, and when he returned on his second voyage in 1493, he planted a new settlement in what is now the Dominican Republic. Through disease and conquest, the Spanish settlers wiped out the native people of the island within a few generations. Then many Spaniards departed to the mainland when they heard stories of the fabulous wealth of MEXICO and PERU in the 16th century. The western part of the island was never much settled by the Spanish. In the 17th century, French hunters established small settlements along the coast and on the island of Tortuga, just off the north coast. Many of these early French settlers were Huguenots, Protestants fleeing religious strife in France. As such, they were doubly anathema to the Spanish, who were staunch Catholics and reluctant to allow any foreigners in what they considered their territory, much less those they considered religious heretics. So there was intermittent war between the French and Spanish throughout the century. The French settlers developed good military skills, built or stole boats, and became powerful enemies. They were known as *boucaniers,* because as hunters they had used *boucans,* or barbecues, to smoke and preserve meat. As buccaneers, they became famous. Tortuga was the greatest pirate haven of the mid-17th century, ahead of even Port Royal in neighboring JAMAICA, in terms of the number of sailings and value of merchandise landed there.

Early populations were quite low: When the first royal governor of the colony, Bertrand d'Ogeron, arrived in 1665, he estimated that the French population was about 800 (presumably he meant permanent settlers and was not counting the pirates, who came and went). He and his successors encouraged immigration and the importation of slaves, but as France was enjoying a period of prosperity, it was hard to convince people to immigrate, and the monopoly company that dominated French transatlantic trade was inefficient and could not deliver many slaves. War also hindered immigration and trade in the late 17th century. There were about 12,000 whites and about 2,000 blacks, most of them slaves, in the colony in 1697.

The Old Regime and Plantation Society in Saint-Domingue

The French government in the late 17th century, under the leadership of King Louis XIV, wanted to impose order and stability on the colonies. Especially after Spain and France made peace, in the Treaty of Ryswick of 1697, then became allies, in the War of the Spanish Succession (1701–14), France could no longer tolerate PIRACY in its Caribbean possessions. A number of French governors encouraged the pirates to settle down and take up farming. D'Ogeron, who was governor from 1665 to 1675, encouraged the development of tobacco planting and INDIGO CULTIVATION while also organizing the pirates into an auxiliary force for the French military. Later governors encouraged SUGAR CULTIVATION.

The sugar revolution in the island really dates from the formal legal establishment of the colony of Saint-Domingue in 1697 with the Treaty of Ryswick and the return, the year before, of a pirate force that had raided and looted CARTAGENA in COLOMBIA. Cartagena was the principal port for the gold and silver of Colombia and Peru and had never before been captured. The loot was fabulous, and much of it went to buy slaves and build infrastructure to establish plantations.

Sugar cultivation is very labor-intensive, even today. In the 18th century, growing sugar profitably in Saint-Domingue required several hundred acres of well-watered flat land, an expensive mill, and highly trained staff of millers (some of whom could be slaves), and at least 70 or 80 field slaves. The total cost of such an establishment could easily exceed a quarter of a million livres, worth five million to 10 million dollars in modern terms. Profit margins could be high, however, for those with the capital to establish such a plantation. Many sugar planters became rich enough to go back to France and become nobles, and the "sugar interest" had become quite powerful in French politics as the FRENCH REVOLUTION loomed.

The plantation economy was further strengthened in the mid-18th century by the introduction of COFFEE CULTIVATION. The mountainous interior of the colony had been, up to that time, generally abandoned by the French and Spanish settlers. Communities of MAROONS and a scattering of PEASANTS, hunters, and ranchers lived there. But when coffee became profitable, the colony quickly conquered the interior. Maroons either were driven out, often into the Spanish side of the island, or made their peace with the government and became free black peasants. The forests were cleared and coffee bushes planted. A dense population began to grow up in the backcountry. Coffee growing was still the second-biggest industry in the colony in 1791, but it was closing in on sugar. It was certainly the most dynamic sector of the economy. Coffee growing is a less labor- and capital-intensive industry

than sugar growing. A profitable coffee farm could be as small as a dozen or so acres of land employing just a handful of workers (who could be slaves or even family members). Bigger was better but not so much better that smaller operators were pushed out of the market, especially since the market was growing as more and more Europeans took up coffee drinking. There were other crops grown in the mountains—indigo, for example, had many of the advantages of coffee, and the product was very easily transported. A year's production from a good-sized farm could be carried by a few mules. Therefore, indigo plantations were found in even more remote places than coffee farms. Many backcountry farms grew food crops to be sold to sugar planters, who had much more profitable uses for their flat, irrigated fields than growing yams or corn.

By the 1780s, Saint-Domingue was the wealthiest colony in the Americas. France had elected to invest in Saint-Domingue before the SEVEN YEARS' WAR, 1756–63, but after the loss of the North American colonies of Canada and LOUISIANA, Saint-Domingue became France's most important colony. With easy access to Continental markets, Saint-Domingue produced about half of all the sugar sold in Europe, and well over half its coffee. It also received as many as a third of all slaves imported into the Americas.

The colony's population grew rapidly during the 18th century. Slave imports shot up from 2,000 to 3,000 a year at the turn of the 18th century to at least 25,000 a year in the 1780s. Numbers are unclear because France's strict commercial regulations limited legal imports, so smuggling was common and the volume of the illegal trade can only be estimated. White immigration was slow until the 1760s, when France's loss of Canada meant that prospective migrants had fewer choices. Both the white and slave populations experienced natural decline, with more deaths than births. This was because at least a third of all immigrants died in their first five years in the colony. In addition, men outnumbered women by as much as two to one in both groups of immigrants. More white women entered as immigrants and more enslaved women were taken in as the century wore on, but overall, immigrant populations of both colors remained dominated by males and thus incapable of high birthrates. CREOLE, or native-born, populations were more resistant to diseases, having grown up around them, and obviously were gender-balanced, so they tended to increase at normal rates. However, many young white creoles emigrated from the colony to France or mainland North America. Creole slaves were much more likely than the African-born to gain their freedom, and harsh living conditions on plantations hindered fertility of all slaves. The only racial group that had an excess of births over deaths were free people of color. The colony's population in 1791 was between 500,000 and 600,000 people, of whom about 90 percent were slaves. Five to 7 percent were free people of color. Numbers are uncertain because although the government carried out censuses, there were plenty of reasons for both the government and private SLAVE OWNERS to falsify the statistics on slaves, and many free people of color and poorer whites lived in marginal areas where census takers might miss them.

Free People of Color, Early History
The first free colored person to set foot in Saint-Domingue was Diego, a servant on Columbus's ship the *Santa Maria*, in 1492, about whom we know very little other than that he was African. Spanish settlers took in African slaves very early, before 1503, and some of them managed to run away or otherwise gain their freedom. In various ways, the Spanish colony of Santo Domingo developed a flourishing free colored population during the 16th century.

The French settlers in the western part of the island were a wild group of frontiersmen in the first decades after their arrival in 1629. Racial lines are often rather loosely drawn in frontier areas, and this was true of the people living in Saint-Domingue during the 17th century. The children of free men and slave women were free until the adoption of the CODE NOIR IN FRENCH LAW in 1685, which resulted in the growth of a small free population of color. The missionaries Jean-Baptiste Du Tertre (1610–87) and Jean-Baptiste Labat (1663–1738) of the order of Dominicans both described a society in which blacks and whites mixed freely and either or both could be slaves, free citizens, or leaders at different times in their lives. Labat, who was active in the colony just as social rules about race were hardening, noted that quite a few people of color ended up on the white side of the racial lines, "passing" as white, at least for a while, though later, when conditions worsened for people of color in the colony, some supposed whites were redesignated as people of color. This process of identifying as free colored people who had previously been thought of as white may have added thousands to the recorded numbers of free coloreds in the colony during the period 1770–90. Those afraid of being caught might have numbered many more. According to Labat, many of the planting families of the southern peninsula had some African ancestors. One that we know of is the family of the free colored activist JULIEN RAIMOND. Raimond's father was a white Frenchman who immigrated to the colony in the 1720s, while Labat was there. He got a job as a plantation manager and then married his employer's mixed-race daughter. Raimond's mother was not identified as a person of color in official documents until regulations became more stringent in the 1770s.

Rise of Racial Discrimination
People of mixed race could sometimes pass as white, but even blacks could aspire to high positions in society in the early days. One early prominent free black citizen was VINCENT OLIVIER, who was born a slave in the colony about 1680. He accompanied his master on the pirate expedition to Cartagena in 1696, when he fought so valiantly that he was granted his freedom. He served in the French military as a commissioned officer for years, both in Europe and in Saint-Domingue. He ended his career as the commander of all the black MILITIA troops in the province. He finally settled down as a planter near Cap-Français and lived past 100 years old.

In the early days of the colony, people of color, both free and enslaved, were few. The racial mixture in the colony began to change in the 1730s, as more and more slaves were imported. Free people of color were a minority in the free population until about 1780, when their numbers probably overtook those of whites. At the same time, free people of color were becoming wealthier, with the assets of some individuals equaling those of the white sugar planters. Colonial governments reacted to what they saw as a threat to the established racial order by imposing a series of discriminatory laws on free coloreds. Free coloreds were prohibited to work in the professions, to be officers in the military, or hold many government jobs, even to wear European-style clothes or ride in coaches. Free colored children of white men were forbidden to use their fathers' last names, and even the wealthy and powerful Julien Raimond had to change the spelling of his last name (his father spelled it Raymond). Some historians have argued that fostering divisions between white and free colored planters served to divide the colony's elite and made whites more reliant on French colonial rule at a time when native-born elites throughout the Americas were beginning to think about independence. France supported the independence of the United States as part of a global struggle against British colonial ambitions. However, the Americans were a terrible example for French colonial elites since they showed that a slave society could become independent of its European colonial master and still preserve slavery.

The discriminatory laws did not slow the growth of the free colored population, nor its increasing wealth. Indeed, the laws were more thoroughly enforced in the cities, thus driving economically successful free coloreds into the countryside, where they became planters. Free coloreds resisted the laws, both passively by avoiding them and actively by petitioning the government in France. Various French colonial governors had proposed schemes under which free people of mixed race would be allowed to "whiten" themselves under various conditions (*see* "WHITENING" AND RACIAL PROMOTION). The count d'Estaing, governor in the 1760s, had proposed that people who had one-fourth African ancestry or less who were of legitimate birth and who had served in the colonial militia would be considered white. Both local whites and the French government at home rejected d'Estaing's plan. Those free coloreds who would have been affected, the planter class, sent Julien Raimond to France in 1785 to appeal. He wrote two "memorials" to the government, asking for equal rights for free coloreds. These memorials are among the first proposed laws calling for equal rights for blacks in the Americas. The minister responsible for the colonies, Maréchal Charles de Castries, was sympathetic but unable to pass the laws before the FRENCH REVOLUTION began in 1789. Raimond subsequently worked with the French Revolutionary assemblies to gain equal rights for free coloreds, though many of his reforms were abolished by Napoléon Bonaparte.

Free Colored Society

The effect of discriminatory laws and hardening racial attitudes among whites was to divide free society on the basis of color. The division was strongest where the laws were the most harshly enforced, which is to say, in the wealthy and densely populated North Province and in the cities. In the South and West, and in the countryside, the old system where class counted for more than race persisted longer, though even there conditions worsened for free coloreds. Whites and blacks had married and raised families together and had participated together in church parishes, public works projects, military adventures, and social life up until the middle of the 18th century. By the 1780s, however, marriages of whites and people of color became rare—only very occasionally would a wealthy free colored family find a white husband for one of their daughters, and at the lower levels of society, marriages of immigrant white men and free black women were even more rare. Marriages of free colored men and white women were almost entirely unheard of, both because of the opposition of white society and because of the scarcity of white women living in the colony. Social events, religious services, and the like were increasingly segregated. Even executions were segregated: When the free colored rebels VINCENT OGÉ and JEAN-BAPTISTE CHAVANNES were executed, their scaffold was set up on the opposite side of the town square from the side used for the executions of whites. Whites still had close relationships with free colored relatives, and there were still many long-term informal sexual relationships between white men and free colored women, but these family relationships increasingly were unacknowledged. A white man might have half a dozen children with his free colored mistress, but in his will, he would declare that he was a bachelor and childless—while leaving significant legacies to the children. A white family might find a place as a plantation manager for a free colored relative or pay for his training as a craftsman, but they would not announce the relationship and would instead present their actions as simple disinterested benevolence.

Free coloreds were also increasingly divided among themselves, especially in areas like the North Province where the economy was strong and the plantation system powerful. At the time, people looked at it in terms of color: Free people of mixed race (called generically *mûlatres*, or mulattoes) contrasted with free blacks. In some areas, government addressed the two groups separately, providing separate militia companies, separate areas for burials in churchyards, and so forth. The two groups did not interact much socially, and there was limited intermarriage. They also tended to have different politics when the revolution began, as many mulattoes supported continuation of slavery and French rule, except with equal rights for them, while the free blacks tended to support the end of slavery and independence. In fact, though there was a racial component to the division, there were also other factors in play. The entirely black mistress of a wealthy white plantation owner who had gained her freedom and a substantial donation of land and slaves for her mixed-race children would count as a member of the mixed-race group. On the other hand, a mixed-race person who had no white family, had no father in evidence, and who worked as an artisan or small businessman in the cities would be thought of as one of the blacks. He might even serve in a black militia company. In Haiti today, the division between black and MULATTO still exists, and in Haitian Kreyol, they say *nèg riche sè mulat, mulat pov sè nèg* (a rich black is a mulatto and a poor mulatto is black).

The division between the two groups was not entirely one of wealth either. The wealthiest free colored planters were among the mulatto group, even if, as suggested previously, they were entirely African in ancestry. But some free blacks also became planters, including Vincent Olivier and TOUSSAINT LOUVERTURE. Most mulattoes lived in the countryside; Vincent Ogé, the great merchant and early rebel leader, however, was a city dweller. There were also many young mulattoes who lived in the cities and pursued a lively social life. Many free blacks split their time between city and country as well, if they could afford to do so, while many of the poorest of the free blacks were small farmers.

The division was not so strong in the West and especially in the South Province, where free blacks and free people of mixed race intermarried much more frequently than in the North and did not maintain separate social worlds. The well-known free mixed-race revolutionary leaders were from the West and South: ALEXANDRE SABÈS

PÉTION from Port-au-Prince, ANDRÉ RIGAUD from Les Cayes, Louis Boisrond Tonnerre, author of the Haitian Declaration of Independence, from Torbeck in the South.

A third group of free people of color were those living on the margins of society. In the early days of the colony, there were many maroons, or runaway slaves, living as peasants or hunters in the mountainous areas of Saint-Domingue. These areas were increasingly put under government authority from the 1750s onward, and the maroons either moved to the Spanish side of the colony, fought and were wiped out by the militia, or made peace with the colonial authorities. One famous maroon was FRANÇOIS MACKANDAL, who led a poisoning plot and was caught and executed in 1757. The traditional Haitian national origin story gives a big role to maroons in the making of the revolution, but evidence from government sources suggests that by the time the revolution began, there were only a few unassimilated maroon groups left, most in the South Province. The virtual destruction of the maroons in the other two provinces did not deter slaves from running away, however. Most slaves who ran away did not intend to leave for good but wanted to visit family or protest conditions. These stayed fairly close to their homes and returned to work, sometimes after negotiating with their master for remission of punishment or better working conditions. Other slaves who ran away intended to remain free, and they generally went farther. Traveling across the border to the Spanish part of the island was an attractive option if the slave could avoid the border patrols, because the Spanish colony was lightly populated and their government welcomed runaways. If a runaway slave preferred to remain in the colony, the colonial cities often beckoned, especially after 1770, when populations grew rapidly. They could blend into the urban population of free coloreds and often live undisturbed for years.

Another marginal group were those who had provisional or unratified liberty papers. Starting in the 1770s, colonial governments began to impose a tax on MANUMISSION. The tax became quite significant, amounting to as much as 2,000 livres, or $50,000 in today's terms. Masters did not want to pay if they did not have to, and so they would neglect to go through the formal process of manumitting a slave. The slave would then have what was called *liberté de savane*, or "bush freedom." If the freed person could then accumulate enough money to pay the tax, so much the better, but it sometimes took years to save that much money, and some people never managed to do so. Additionally, many owners would allow slaves to work on their own account, paying a regular rent for the privilege. Again, these would be people who were allowed to go about their business freely but who were not, legally speaking, free. The confused status of so many people made it easier for runaways to slip between the cracks.

The government realized this was a problem and made laws to address it, but those laws never solved the problem. Some authorities believe that the future king of (North) Haiti, Henry Christophe, was *libre de savane* before the revolution, though there is no documentation relating to his life before the revolution. In fact, these marginal peoples were not very well documented, for good reason: They avoided the authorities as best they could. So there is little we can say for certain about them, even how many there were. Between those with unclear liberty papers, though, and runaways, there must have been thousands of people in addition to the officially recognized number of free people of color.

Stewart R. King

FURTHER READING

Garrigus, John. *Before Haiti: Race, Class, and Citizenship in Colonial Saint-Domingue.* New York: Palgrave Macmillan, 2006.

Geggus, David. "Slave and Free Colored Women in Saint-Domingue." In *More than Chattel: Black Women and Slavery in the Americas,* edited by David B. Gaspar and Darlene C. Hine, 259–278. Bloomington: Indiana University Press, 1996.

King, Stewart R. *Blue Coat or Powdered Wig: Free Coloreds in Pre-Revolutionary Saint-Domingue.* Athens: University of Georgia Press, 2000.

Socolow, Susan. "Economic Roles of the Free Women of Color of Cap Francais." In *More than Chattel: Black Women and Slavery in the Americas*, edited by David B. Gaspar and Darlene C. Hine, 279–297. Bloomington: Indiana University Press, 1996.

Trouillot, Michel-Rolph. "Motion in the System: Coffee, Color, and Slavery in Eighteenth-Century Saint-Domingue." *Review* 3 (Winter 1982): 331–388.

SAINT-GEORGES, JOSEPH BOLOGNE, CHEVALIER DE (1745–1799) *French musician, composer, and competitive fencer*

Joseph Bologne was born on December 25, 1745, in Baillif, Guadeloupe, the son of an African-born slave named Nanon and her white French master, Georges Bologne de Saint-Georges. Bologne's father cared for him and took him to France in 1747 when he had to flee the colony because of legal troubles. At that time, the legal status of slaves taken to France from the colonies was unclear, but increasingly they were treated as free, especially in Paris, where the *parlement*, or superior court, refused to register the various edicts of Police des Noirs that sought to preserve masters' property rights in their slaves. Therefore, Bologne was never formally manumitted, but there was no question of his being a slave after his move to France.

Young Joseph was mainly raised in France, where he was privately educated and studied with leading musicians and fencing masters.

He first became famous as a competitive fencer when, at the age of 18, he defeated a well-known French fencing master who had mocked him for his race. He became a gentleman of the Garde du Roi, the personal bodyguard of King Louis XVI, at the age of 19 and received the courtesy title of chevalier, a title that he continued to use throughout his life. He fought a number of celebrated duels and was thought of as the finest swordsman in Europe in his prime.

The chevalier de Saint-Georges, as he became known, had also studied music, and he began to compose and lead orchestras in the 1760s. He worked for the marquise de Montesson, a noted hostess and central figure in the salons of the Enlightenment. He was also director of the Concert de la Loge Olympique, the largest orchestra of its time, and directed it when it premiered the Paris Symphonies of Haydn, performances that were very well received by the public and represent the pinnacle of the chevalier's musical career. He was thwarted in his ambition to become the director of the royal orchestra, though whether this was the result of racial prejudice or simple artistic politics is unclear. His first composition, Sonata for Harp and Flute, Opus 1, was performed in 1772. He wrote a musical comedy entitled *Ernestine*, which was first performed in 1777 at the Comédie Italienne in Paris. He wrote at least four sonatas and 10 concertos. He was a gifted instrumentalist, often playing the principal violin part as well as directing his orchestra.

Saint-Georges was interested in the struggle of free people of color in the colonies for equal rights. He helped form the Société des Amis des Noirs, the French abolitionist organization. He supported JULIEN RAIMOND of Saint-Domingue in his petition to the government for equal rights for free people of color. When the French Revolution began in 1789, Saint-Georges organized a unit of people of color living in France. The Légion Saint-Georges, as it was called, participated in fighting in Belgium against the Austrians and French Royalist forces. Saint-Georges chose as his second-in-command THOMAS ALEXANDRE DUMAS, father of the author of *The Three Musketeers*. Dumas ultimately superseded Saint-Georges in command, as Saint-Georges became involved in the complicated political maneuverings around the defection of the French general Dumouriez to the Austrians in 1793. Originally a hero for seemingly preventing the general's treason, he was denounced, arrested, and, while ultimately freed, not permitted to serve in the military any longer. He returned to his musical career,

leading a not especially successful orchestra in Paris for the rest of his life. He died on June 10, 1799.

The chevalier de Saint-Georges rose higher than almost any other person of color in France before the Revolution. He held a quasi-noble title, he guarded the person of the king, he was a colonel in the revolutionary armies, and he was both a popular musician and a sports hero. He experienced racism, but at the same time he had a remarkable ability to escape its effects. He was an important player in the cultural life of the Enlightenment, meeting central figures such as Diderot, Rousseau, and Voltaire. He is a living example of the ambiguous position of the mixed-race children of powerful white men in French society in the old regime.

Stewart R. King

FURTHER READING
Guédé, Alain. *Monsieur de Saint-George: Virtuoso, Swordsman, Revolutionary*. New York: Picador, 2003.
"Le Chevalier de Saint-Georges (1745–1799), Afro-French Composer, Violinist and Conductor, France's Best Fencer and Colonel of Black Legion." Available online. URL: http://chevalierdesaintgeorges.homestead.com/page1.html#33. Accessed December 18, 2010.
"Le Mozart Noir." Audio CD on CDc Audio, 2003.

SALEM, PETER (1750–1816) *American soldier*
Peter Salem was one of the thousands of African Americans who served in the WAR OF AMERICAN INDEPENDENCE, 1775–83. He gained fame for his exploits at the Battle of Bunker Hill on June 17, 1775, outside BOSTON, MASSACHUSETTS. He was only a minor participant, a soldier in the ranks, but his bravery and loyalty to the cause of independence won him renown.

Salem was born into slavery in 1750 in Framingham, Massachusetts. Captain Jeremiah Belknap originally owned Salem and later sold him to Major Lawson Buckminster. Little is known about Salem's life prior to his enlistment in the Continental army. Blacks had not served in Massachusetts's MILITIA before the outbreak of the Revolution, but there were black members of some of the revolutionary groups. When the fighting began in spring 1775, blacks were recruited into many New England units. Major Buckminster, a leader in the Massachusetts militia, freed Salem so that he might join the militia. Salem enlisted and joined Captain Simon Edgell's company. He fought bravely for seven years, until his discharge in 1780.

Salem played an important role in the early battles against the British in Massachusetts. His unit participated in the Battles of Lexington and Concord on April 19, 1775. Salem's company soon faced the same British troops again, led by the British marine major John Pitcairn (1722–75), in

June 1775 on Bunker Hill. The Battle of Bunker Hill was the first major battle of the American Revolution. At this time, Salem was a member of Captain Drury's company, serving in Colonel Nixon's 6th Massachusetts Regiment. Approximately 15,000 American troops from Massachusetts, CONNECTICUT, RHODE ISLAND, and NEW HAMPSHIRE had concentrated around Boston, held by the most powerful British force in North America, 6,000 soldiers and marines and dozens of ships of the British NAVY. The British forces sought to expand the area they controlled by taking and fortifying a series of hills surrounding the city. Key to their plans was the low summit of Breed's Hill outside Charlestown, Massachusetts. The American commander, William Prescott (1726–95), anticipated the British movement and established a small earthwork fortification on Breed's Hill manned by 1,200 soldiers, including Salem. The British crossed the bay in small boats and stormed the fort. The British charged three times, each time suffering heavy losses from American fire. The third assault was led by the British marines, under Major Pitcairn. The Americans were running low on ammunition, and Pitcairn's men were able to gain control of the fort. As they were entering the fort, Pitcairn was shot. A soldier named Salem in Drury's company was reported to have fired the fatal shot. This could have referred to another African-American soldier named Salem Poor (1748–1802), but Peter Salem received the credit at the time. Salem's fellow soldiers honored him by taking up a monetary collection for him. Moreover, Salem's deeds earned him a visit with General GEORGE WASHINGTON. Most historians have credited Salem with shooting Pitcairn. Peter Salem's musket is now on display at the Bunker Hill Monument. He is visible in the foreground of John Trumbull's famous painting of the climactic moments of the Battle of Bunker Hill.

Salem also fought in the Battles of Stony Point and Saratoga in 1777. The surrender of the British major general Burgoyne at the Battle of Saratoga proved a major victory and turning point for the Americans. Despite the bravery and loyalty of an estimated 5,000 African-American soldiers serving in serving on the American side, their presence in the REGULAR ARMY remained a source of controversy. Contemporary white leaders, especially in the South, resisted the idea of allowing blacks to serve. Some feared that blacks would not be able to fight effectively, while others feared that allowing them to serve would encourage slave rebellion. The British offered freedom to slaves who would serve in their cause, and many did—probably more African Americans served in the pro-British forces during the war than on the pro-independence side. Shortly after the Battle of Bunker Hill, General Washington issued an edict forbidding recruiters to enlist blacks in the Continental army. Those already enlisted were not affected by the new order. Peter Salem, LEMUEL HAYNES, Sampson Talbert, and other black veterans protested the new order. Faced with manpower shortages, the protests of New England officers who did not want to lose their black soldiers, and the evidence of black loyalty and courage given by Salem and other New England black soldiers, Washington rescinded his order and permitted blacks to serve. By the end of the war, entire regiments of the Continental army were composed exclusively of black soldiers.

Salem resided in Leicester, Massachusetts, after his discharge from the army in 1780. He made a meager living weaving baskets and cane bottom chairs. He married Katy Benson in 1783 and died sometime in 1816. In death, Salem received the honor of burial in the Old Burial Ground of Framingham. Traditionally, neither African Americans nor former slaves were buried there. In 1882, the town erected a grave monument in his honor. Despite this honor, the historical memory of the role blacks played in America's war for independence slowly faded away. Salem was edited out of the popular mid-19th-century reproduction of Trumbull's painting.

Caroline Castellanos

FURTHER READING

Frey, Sylvia R. *Water from the Rock: Black Resistance in a Revolutionary Age.* Princeton, N.J.: Princeton University Press, 1991.

Selig, Robert A. "The Revolution's Black Soldiers." Available online. URL: http://www.americanrevolution.org/blk.html. Accessed December 9, 2009.

Wiencek, Henry. *An Imperfect God: Washington, His Slaves, and the Creation of America.* New York: Farrar, Straus & Giroux, 2003.

SALVADOR, BAHIA, BRAZIL

The capital of the state of Bahia, in northeastern BRAZIL, Salvador today is the third-largest city in the country, with nearly three million inhabitants. Its current residents are mostly descendants of indigenous peoples, European settlers, and, predominantly, former African slaves. These groups coexist in a city marked by enormous contrasts between its dynamic economy and social inequality, the intense ethnic mixing of the population and the continuing practice of racial discrimination, the vibrant culture and the high rates of urban violence. Some of these current paradoxes of Salvador are better understood by studying the slave background and struggles for freedom that marked the entire history of this city.

The city was officially founded in 1549; the current area of Salvador was traditionally occupied by the Tupinambá, one of more than a thousand indigenous groups who spoke Tupi-Guaraní in every part of the territory of Brazil. Attracted by the abundance of fish of the tropical Atlantic Ocean and by the abundant rain forest that covered the landscape, thousands of Tupinambá were living in this area at the time when the first Portuguese landed in 1500 at the warm waters of the so-called Kirimurê, renamed Bay of All Saints by the European colonists.

Portuguese colonization was based on the supposed superiority of European civilization. As a result, the Tupi were persecuted, captured, and forced to work, initially in the lucrative trade of Pau-Brasil wood, later in the sugarcane plantations.

The intense Tupi resistance to forced labor, as well as the significant number of deaths due to epidemics of diseases introduced by the Europeans, led the Portuguese to search in Africa for an alternative workforce. Thus, at the beginning of the 16th century, the first Africans were forcibly transported to Bahia to work as slaves.

Slavery and Resistance

The city of Salvador was both the first capital of the Portuguese Empire in America, an urban center in the middle of an important slavery-plantation region, and one of the ports through which most Africans entered Brazil. These factors explain why it is a key location from which to understand not only the various faces and phases of the slave system, but also the strategies to defeat it promoted by slaves and free people.

Perhaps the first and best known resistance to slavery was the organization of *quilombos*, communities of MAROONS. Although normally associated with an image of isolation, many *quilombos* were established very near to cities. Around Salvador, for example, many *quilombos* established complex networks with free people of color, other slaves, and whites, guaranteeing them supplies of food, weapons, and, especially, information and solidarity from many people living inside the city.

The *quilombos* around Salvador were the first to indicate how important associations between slaves and free people of color would be in challenging the existing slave order throughout Brazilian history. None of these alliances would have more radical goals than the one that hit Salvador in the late 18th century: the Tailors' Revolt.

The Tailors' Revolt

The Tailors' Revolt of 1798 was a revolt by urban blacks in Bahia, both free and slave, calling for the liberation of slaves, democracy, national liberation, and racial equality. The ARTISANS planned to call on the plantation slaves of the nearby *reconcavo* district to join them, but quick action by the local MILITIA forestalled their plans. The rebels of 1798 did not share the elitist profile of previous anticolonial conspiracies, consisting instead of slaves and, notably, many free mulattoes and blacks.

The rebels were inspired by North American and French Revolutionary ideals. The free colored participants were usually lower-class workers such as soldiers, goldsmiths, sailors, barbers, and, especially, tailors, from whom was derived the name of the rebellion. Anticipating by nearly one century what would in fact occur throughout Brazil, they promised not only to abolish the monarchy in favor of a republic but also to liberate all slaves.

Before that, however, an internal betrayal brutally ended the movement. Thirty-two people were convicted, most sentenced to imprisonment in Brazil, some to exile in Africa. Only four were sentenced to death, two soldiers and two tailors. Not coincidentally, all of them were free blacks and mulattoes. Although their names were declared "cursed" until the third generation by the colonial administrators, today those free people of color continue to inspire struggles among Afro-descended people not only in Salvador but throughout Brazil.

The Parakeet's Battalion

The Tailors' Revolt was only one of many that would strike Salvador during a period of urban crisis that lasted until 1838. The instability of those years can be partly explained by looking at the city's internal tensions and disputes among its various social groups.

Most of the inhabitants of Salvador in the early 19th century were of African descent: 37.3 percent slaves and 41.8 percent free people of color. The remaining whites were subdivided between those from PORTUGAL and those born in Brazil. As in other parts of Latin America, Europeans enjoyed considerably more privileges than those born in the colony, such as access to the most prestigious public jobs. Generally dissatisfied with their status as "inferior" citizens, many whites born in the colony joined the army as a way to gain social status and authority.

For different reasons, service in the army was also a common fate for many free people of color. Inside the relatively diversified economy of 19th-century Salvador, free people of color formed a mass of workers having varied (yet less prestigious) urban occupations. A significant proportion of these workers, however, were gradually incorporated into the military services, often by force. For many free mulattoes and blacks, then, army recruitment became a de facto form of slavery (*see also* REGULAR ARMY). This was because they were subjected to strict military discipline, including corporal punishment; they suffered from nonpayment of salaries; and they often were so poor that they starved from lack of food.

Although poorly paid, humiliated, and punished in public, these men worked daily with guns in their hands.

It was not surprising that it was among these soldiers that many of the rebellions that shook Salvador during the 19th century began. Battalions of free black and mulatto soldiers, together with disgruntled native-born white officers, gradually became agents of destabilization of the political system that they were supposed to maintain.

In 1823, although the rest of Brazil had officially gained its independence from Portugal, people in Bahia continued fighting against Portuguese attempts to reconquer the colony and against conservative local elites. With the promise of MANUMISSION at the end of the conflict, many slaves joined the war. Usually fighting side by side with free people of color, they exhibited bravery and patriotism that were widely recognized as crucial to helping defeat the Portuguese forces.

After the war, many slaves were, in fact, declared free. But once more, the tensions of Bahian society became evident as these former slaves, now free people and war veterans, would try to live in the midst of a society still extremely racist and hierarchical. These contradictions, along with the permanent fear that these free mulattoes and black soldiers would support other struggles for freedom, encouraged the city's administration to relocate many of them forcibly out of Salvador.

Although most Brazilian historical textbooks still highlight the bravery of another group of soldiers, the "Independence Dragoons" (an elite troop that followed Brazil's first emperor, PEDRO I [1798–1834, r. 1822–31]), the "Parakeet's Battalion," as this military body formed by free people of color and slaves was known, helped both to consolidate Brazil's formal independence in 1823 and to inspire democratic struggles among Afro-Brazilian militants.

But not only black and mulatto soldiers represented a threat to the city's local authorities. Free people of color of many professions played important roles in organizing and encouraging social movements in Salvador. As was seen with the Tailors' Revolt, free blacks and mulattoes were often skilled workers. Because of their lower-middle-class position, they were normally the most vulnerable group in economic crises. Not surprisingly, during the first decades of the 19th century, as the economy fluctuated wildly during European wars and independence struggles, they participated actively in several riots and protests against the shortage of food, especially of manioc flour.

The Malês Revolt

Concerns about alliances between free people of color and slaves would reach their peak in the year 1835, with the Malês Revolt. Most of those involved in this street rebellion were Muslim slaves, known as Malês, but they were joined by slaves from several other African nations, as well as many free people of color.

As in previous riots, the alliance between free people of color and slaves during the Malês Revolt can be partly explained by the peculiar characteristics of urban slavery in comparison to that in rural areas. Slaves living in Salvador often had traveled widely in the city and had vast knowledge of its streets and dynamics. By transporting their masters, carrying goods, selling foods, and performing countless other urban activities, these slaves had intimate contact with the city's daily life, including many of its inhabitants.

Because of deep-seated RACISM AND RACIAL PREJUDICE, freed blacks and mulattoes normally had to work with others of the same color. Thus, free people of color and slaves often worked together. Feelings of solidarity and indignation often emerged from these daily interactions, culminating in the Malês Revolt.

Among these complex networks of workers and slaves in the Malês Revolt, a free black woman had a distinguished role. Luiza Mahim was a candy manufacturer who obtained her manumission in 1812. Her *tabuleiro* (street food court) was accused of being a central location where people left and received information about the revolt. Many scholars claim she would have been declared queen had the Malês been victorious.

The Malês Revolt broke out January 25, 1835, during the Muslim month of Ramadan (*see* ISLAM). A large conspiracy had been formed over the preceding weeks. The conspiracy was known to the Brazilian officials, but security precautions were not complete when the fighting began. The rebels seized many strategic locations in the heart of the city but were unable to overcome the garrison or to make contact with columns of slaves coming from the countryside. Communications through RUNAWAY SLAVES had been disrupted by the POLICE presence on the roads leading out of the city. Reinforcements rushed to the city from neighboring towns, including cavalry, succeeded in crushing resistance by the next day. A dozen slaves and free people of color were executed and more than 100 deported to Portuguese settlements in Africa. Despite being quickly smothered, the Malês Revolt unleashed a subversive power through the alliance between slaves and free people of color, which once again scared SLAVE OWNERS and local authorities. After 1835, repressive actions would become more severe and extensive not only in Salvador but throughout Brazil; all of them trying to protect Brazil from a successful black and mulatto revolution like the one witnessed in Haiti in the 1790s and early 1800s (*see also* HAITIAN REVOLUTION).

Coincidently or not, apart from a mostly peaceful, liberal-led republican movement in 1837 known as Sabinada, which would again rely large and active participation of free people of color, the city of Salvador would not experience significant uprisings from that point on. This in no way meant that struggles against slavery and social inequality ended in the city of Salvador. During this period, another kind of struggle emerged, the move for abolition.

The Abolition Movement

One of the largest sociopolitical movements in Brazil, the abolitionist struggle, tried by legal means to influence public opinion and courts of law both to free slaves and to abolish the slave system in Brazil formally. As in previous cases, the abolitionist movement would not have been successful without the active engagement of the free people of color in the city of Salvador. This work took many forms, from denouncing holding slaves illegally under the laws that prohibited the slave trade in 1831 and 1850 to providing legal services and support to slaves and opening their homes to abolitionist debates and meetings; from sheltering runaway slaves to promoting public debates in the press and raising money to buy manumissions. The intense and constant abolitionist agitation by free people of color would contribute to forcing the Brazilian government to abolish slavery officially in 1888.

In spite of these facts, until at least the 1980s, many Brazilian history textbooks explained the end of slavery in Brazil as an almost natural event, which would inevitably have happened because of the liberal ideas that became predominant by the end of the 19th century and resulted from the self-awareness and generosity of white men (*see* GILBERTO FREYRE). Through this interpretation, blacks and mulattoes usually were depicted as passive victims.

The abolition of slavery in Salvador, and in Brazil as a whole, was to a great extent the result of intense engagement in the struggle by Bahian free people of color. Contrary to the image of passivity, struggles for freedom began the moment slavery began. Both slaves and free people fought, fled, boycotted, and helped stop captivity in Brazil from the first century of colonization. Whether by strengthening networks between *quilombos* and cities or plotting and participating in rebellious movements, fighting in the wars of independence of Brazil and Bahia, or campaigning for abolitionism, free people of color had an indispensable participation in all phases of this process.

Genaro Vilanova Miranda de Oliveira

FURTHER READING
Kraay, Hendrik. *Afro-Brazilian Culture and Politics: Bahía, 1790s to 1990s.* Armonk, N.Y.: M. E. Sharpe, 1998
Nishida, Mieko. *Slavery and Identity: Ethnicity, Gender and Race in Salvador, Brazil, 1808–1888.* Bloomington: Indiana University Press, 2003.
Reis, João José. *Death Is a Festival: Funeral Rites and Rebellion in Nineteenth-Century Brazil.* Chapel Hill: University of North Carolina Press, 2003.
———. *Slave Rebellion in Brazil: The Muslim Uprising of 1835 in Bahía.* Baltimore: Johns Hopkins University Press, 1995.

SÁNCHEZ, FRANCISCO DEL ROSARIO
(1817–1861) *fighter for Dominican independence*
Francisco del Rosario Sánchez was one of the most important political leaders of the independence struggle in the DOMINICAN REPUBLIC. He died a heroic martyr to the cause of freedom and is today considered the father of the Dominican nation.

As were many residents on the Spanish side of the island of Hispaniola—which would one day become the Dominican Republic, in great part because of his efforts—Francisco del Rosario Sánchez was dark-skinned, and his mother, Olaya del Rosario, was not married to his father, Narciso Sánchez, at the time of his birth in San Juan de la Maguana on March 9, 1817. His mother's birth certificate lists her as a *pardo libre*, a free person of color, and his father was also known to be of African descent. Sánchez showed a high level of intelligence as a child, and his father was determined to provide for his education. He came of age during what Dominicans call the Haitian Occupation of 1822–44, a period when the island of the Hispaniola was united under the rule of the Haitian strongman and former free man of color JEAN-PIERRE BOYER (1776–1850).

The Haitian occupation of "Spanish Haiti" had both positive and negative effects. Haitians laid claim to many of the rural estates and elegant urban homes that belonged to Spanish elites and took over the government islandwide, causing extensive resentment, for the Spanish "whites" (most of whom were mixed-blood peoples) considered themselves superior to the Haitians, most of whom were black. On the positive side, however, slavery, which had been abolished by the Haitian leader TOUSSAINT LOUVERTURE across the island in 1801 but reinstated when Spanish Haiti again briefly became a colony under the protection of the Spanish Crown (1809–21), was abolished once and for all by the Haitian government in 1822.

Since 1812, for the first time in its history, both free people of color and whites had been allowed to enroll in the university in the capital of SANTO DOMINGO. By the time he was in his 20s, Sánchez had graduated from law school, and his associates were the young educated elites of the capital. He joined a group called the Trinitarians, headed by Juan Pablo Duarte (1813–76) and composed of patriots whose goal was to overthrow Haitian rule and establish an enlightened Spanish republic—the Dominican Republic.

Pursuing and persecuting the group for their rebellious activities, Haitians caught and jailed the Trinitarian leader Ramón Mella (1816–64). Other Trinitarians fled the island, including Duarte. Sánchez hid out. Seriously ill, he escaped capture by feigning death, but he remained in secret communication with Duarte, the movement's exiled intellectual leader. Inspired by Duarte, Sánchez reorganized the Trinitarians. Together with Mella, who was released from jail, and the Haitian reformer Charles Hérard (1789–1850), Sánchez led the fight for freedom that resulted in the signing of the Declaration of Independence on February 27, 1844, and the establishment of the Dominican Republic.

Only 27 years old, Sánchez was elected commander in arms and chief of the government junta of the fledgling republic. He held the position less than two months, for there was a clash of goals between the Trinitarian liberals and Dominican conservatives, led by Pedro Santana (1801–64), who wanted to reannex the republic to Spain. The clash split Dominicans into two warring sides. Exiled for four years, Sánchez returned to find the annexationist forces in control. Sánchez refused to play along and fought for his liberal ideals for many long bloody years that severely damaged the country's already bad economy. In 1861, he was captured by Santana's forces and executed on July 4.

It is because of his lifelong battle for liberal republican ideals and the many times that he risked his life for them that many consider Sánchez to be the real founder of the Dominican Republic among the three patriots who are so honored: Juan Pablo Duarte, Francisco del Rosario Sánchez, and Ramón Mella.

Lynne A. Guitar

FURTHER READING

Moya Pons, Frank. *The Dominican Republic: A National History.* New Rochelle, N.Y.: New Rochelle Books, Hispaniola Books, 1995.

SANCHO, IGNATIUS (1729–1780) *author in 18th-century Britain*

Ignatius Sancho was born in 1729 on a slave ship sailing from Guinea to the Spanish West Indies. His mother died of a fever shortly after his birth, and his father killed himself rather than live the remainder of his life as a slave. Sancho was two years old when his master took him from Grenada to Britain and sold him to three sisters living in Greenwich near LONDON, ENGLAND. The sisters refused to give Sancho an education because they believed keeping slaves ignorant was the way to maintain obedience. Sancho, however, had the good fortune to meet John Montagu, the second duke of Montagu, and his wife, Lady Mary Churchill, the youngest daughter of the duke

Ignatius Sancho (1729–80), British author. This painting, entitled *Portrait of a Negro Man*, by Joshua Reynolds, was previously thought to depict Olaudah Equiano, but the subject is probably Sancho. Sancho was a poet, composer, and actor and was the first black Briton to vote in a British election. *(The Bridgeman Art Library International)*

and duchess of Marlborough. The duke and duchess lived nearby and upon visiting the sisters immediately recognized that the young Sancho was eager to learn.

The duke often invited Sancho into his home, where he taught him to read and write. When he was 20, feeling that he could no longer tolerate the life of a slave, Sancho ran off to live with the Montagus. Soon after the duke died, the widowed duchess told Sancho that she had to send him back to the sisters, but when Sancho exclaimed that he would rather die, the duchess agreed to hire Sancho as her butler. In his new position, he was able to read books on many subjects. In later life, he became particularly fond of the works of PHILLIS WHEATLEY, the black poet and former slave from BOSTON, MASSACHUSETTS. When the duchess died in 1751, she left Sancho £70 and an annuity of £30. From the time when he went to live with the Montagu family, he was always considered free. There was never any formal act of MANUMISSION but a series of legal cases in England between 1702 and 1772, ending in the famous SOMERSET V. STEWART case of 1772, had increasingly limited the rights of SLAVE OWNERS to pursue or constrain their "property." In any case, with the protection of a powerful noble family, Sancho was in little danger of RE-ENSLAVEMENT. The sisters who claimed ownership of Sancho never pursued him.

After the duchess's death, Sancho left the Montagu residence and went to London, seeking work in the theater. But he spent unwisely and gambled and soon fell upon hard times. He swallowed his pride and returned to the country, becoming the personal attendant to the new duke of Montagu, George Brudenell. Shortly after taking up his new post, Sancho married a Caribbean woman named Anne, with whom he had six children. In 1773, Sancho had to retire as Brudenell's attendant after repeated attacks of gout, but with the new duke's assistance, Sancho and his wife were able to open a grocery store in Westminster.

In addition to running his own business, Sancho pursued his interests in music, painting, and literature. He wrote several poems and two plays and composed a collection of minuets and country dances. His art reviews appeared in magazines, and his opinion was treated with great respect. Through these interests, Sancho became acquainted with well-known people in London's literary and artistic circles such as the sculptor Joseph Nollekens, the violinist Felice Giardini, the novelist Laurence Sterne, and the painter John Hamilton Mortimer. Most of his work was not explicitly political. He wrote a book-length *Theory of Music*, which was his best-known work at the time. He did speak out in favor of the British position during the WAR OF AMERICAN INDEPENDENCE (1775–83), motivated both by experience of gaining freedom in Britain and by the support the British cause received from American blacks. In 1780, the year of his death, as a property holder Sancho was able to vote in the parliamentary elections. A collection of Ignatius Sancho's letters was published two years after his death and offers insight into his life, revealing a man of not only culture and learning but also compassion. His letters show that he was concerned with the treatment of slaves and the problems faced by black people in Britain.

Carole Levin

FURTHER READING

Carretta, Vincent, ed. *Ignatius Sancho: Letters of the Late Ignatius Sancho, an African.* New York: Penguin Books, 1998.
———. "Sancho, (Charles) Ignatius (1729?–1780)." In *Oxford Dictionary of National Biography*, edited by H. C. G. Matthew and Brian Harrison. Oxford: Oxford University Press, 2004.
Edwards, Paul, and James Walvin. *Black Personalities in the Era of the Slave Trade.* Baton Rouge: Louisiana State University Press, 1983.
Fryer, Peter. *Staying Power: The History of Black People in Britain.* London: Pluto Press, 1984.
Levin, Carole. "Backgrounds and Echoes of Othello: From Leo Africanus to Ignatius Sancho." *Lamar Journal of the Humanities* 22, no. 2 (Fall 1996): 45–68.
Scobie, Edward. *Black Britannia: A History of Blacks in Britain.* Chicago: Johnson, 1972.

SANTANA, JOAQUIM FELIX DE (unknown–1814)
Brazilian militia captain

All that is known of the MILITIA captain Joaquim Felix de Santana has been discovered through the very detailed will he left in the files of the local notary on October 30, 1809. Not an enormously important individual in himself, he led a life that illustrates many important circumstances in the lives of free people of color in colonial BRAZIL at the end of the colonial era.

The will makes no mention of his date or place of birth or any of the circumstances of his life other than what is recounted here. As with many free people of color in the Americas, his life is not well documented.

We do know that he was a barber and a musician, he owned slaves himself, and was a respectable member of the society of SALVADOR; BAHIA, BRAZIL. One source of his respectability was his position as a captain in the local militia. Free men of color were permitted to serve as officers under certain circumstances in Brazil, and holding such a position was a significant mark of social success. He had been born a slave and apparently purchased his own freedom in or before 1790. Under certain conditions, he allowed his own slaves to do the same.

According to his will, Santana had five different owners before buying his freedom for 135,000 Brazilian reis, the equivalent of about $250 in the United States at a time when a skilled workman could not count on earning even one dollar a day. He was also a member of one of the CATHOLIC CONFRATERNITIES, that of Our Lady of the Rosary of Vitória, an entity that allowed freed slaves some social status in Brazilian society. As did many other freed people, Santana owned slaves himself, possibly in part to indicate to others his own state of freedom.

Santana's will declared all his worldly possessions, from kitchenware to his 12 slaves, and describes the manner in which he came to possess some of them. He also described transactions and legal negotiations over ownership of slaves. Possibly because of inheritance laws in Brazil, Santana listed his kin and marriages. He married twice but had no children with either wife. He did have one child out of wedlock, a girl born in captivity, previous to his two marriages. Santana's will indicated that this girl was to be freed and given a dowry with money from his inheritance. He also granted freedom to his personal slaves, upon his death, which apparently took place on December 25, 1814.

Santana served in the black militia regiment under Colonel Manoel Pereira da Silva and, as did the colonel, left his will to be read by a notary. He was an officer in this regiment. People of African ancestry who were mixed-race or born free could become officers, but it was unusual for someone who had been born a slave to rise to such a height. Joaquim became a barber and a musician and taught these trades to the four Angolan slaves of Manuel Salgado, for which he received payment. (*See also* ARTISANS.)

Service in the militia was very important to his social status, and his relationship with his commanding officer, suggested by their use of the same notary, could have been an important source of patronage for him. His tangled personal relationships, with enslaved and free kin needing to be cared for, were typical of the circumstances of many a family of color. He is an example of the prevalence of skilled tradespeople among the newly freed in colonial times. And the importance of the religious brotherhoods in his life, both as a source of spiritual solace and as a way to build networks with other free people of color, illustrates aspects of the relationship between people of color and the ROMAN CATHOLIC CHURCH.

Ana Janaina Nelson

FURTHER READING

Boyer, Richard, and Geoffrey Spurling. *Colonial Lives: Documents on Latin American History, 1550–1850*. New York: Oxford University Press, 1999.

Kraay, Hendrik. *Afro-Brazilian Culture and Politics: Bahía, 1790–1990s*. Latin American Realities. Armonk, N.Y.: M. E. Sharpe, 1998.

Reis, João José. *Death Is a Festival: Funeral Rites and Rebellion in Nineteenth-Century Brazil*. Chapel Hill: University of North Carolina Press, 2003.

SANTO DOMINGO

We will never know certainly the number of African slaves shipped to Santo Domingo (founded in 1496), much less the number of free people of color who lived there. The reasons are multifold, including the scarcity of records, the illegal (therefore, unreported) importation of slaves, the unimportance to Spaniards of distinguishing the color of a free person—although they carefully distinguished between free and enslaved—and the inexactness of census information, among other factors. Note that the entire island, and later the part that became the DOMINICAN REPUBLIC, was called Santo Domingo, and still is by many Dominicans today, because of the capital city's centrality and its vital importance to Dominican history, economics, and politics.

Free persons of color were not at all rare in 15th-century Spain or in the new American colonies. Not only was there little to no stigma attached to color, but Spain's slave laws, promulgated in the mid-13th century by King Alfonso "The Wise," followed the old Roman laws that recognized the humanity of all slaves, unlike the later Carolinian black codes. Slaves could be manumitted by their owners or freed through COARTACIÓN, meaning they could earn their own money through the sale of their labor, skills, or artisanry, money they could use to purchase their freedom or that of their children.

Various documents from Santo Domingo mention free people of color who entered as the *criados* (loyal men or retainers) of Spanish officials, including church officials. They were members of the officials' domestic or administrative staffs or worked as their mining and sugar plantation managers and military attachés. Many loyal slaves were freed because of these positions and the services they provided, while many females were freed because of the particular services that they, too, provided—some of which meant being loving concubines as well as mothers to the Spaniards' mixed-blood children.

Three other peculiarities of the early Spanish laws and customs were that the child of a slave was not born into slavery; second, if the child were recognized by his or her father, and if the father were free to marry at the time of the child's birth (even if he did not marry the child's mother), the child was not considered illegitimate; finally, if the child were baptized Catholic, spoke Castilian, and was educated and raised as a Spaniard, then he or she was considered to be a Spaniard. Thus there were many criollos (American-born people) who were people of color via their indigenous or African mothers but who were accepted as free Spaniards. In fact, by the mid-1500s, this was the norm rather than the exception to the rule across the island.

Indeed, by the late 17th century, with the extermination of the native population and the mass departure of the white elite to the mainland colonies, almost every citizen of the colony had some African ancestry. In a sense, the history of free people of color is the history of the colony of Santo Domingo.

In the city of Santo Domingo, however, there were far more whites—rich and powerful Spanish administrators—than in the smaller cities and towns, and certainly more than in the *campo* (countryside). The criollo sons of these elite Spaniards were often sent to their fathers' ranches and sugar plantations as managers or were given military command positions to maintain the security of the city and the island. With the profits earned in mining, SUGAR CULTIVATION, shipping, and imports/exports,

A painting of the cloth market in Santo Domingo dating from the 18th century. As in other Caribbean colonies, sellers in the market-places of Santo Domingo were overwhelmingly free people of color, or those living "as free," mostly women. *(Photo © Christie's Images/The Bridgeman Art Library)*

elite Spaniards built vast mansions in Santo Domingo, which required large domestic staffs. Both free people of color and slaves filled these domestic and administrative positions in the capital. They also both worked in the city's warehouses, as porters, dockworkers, boatmen; in construction; as butchers, bakers, and candle makers; and in trades such as gold and iron smithing, as well as in military positions. Spaniards had to grant free people of color the right to bear arms and appoint them to military positions because there were not enough whites to protect the city and because white elites did not like the risks involved in leading military patrols—although this gave members of the PARDOS and *morenos* battalions a level of social status that the Spaniards would have preferred they not have. Among other things, military officers benefited from the *fuero militar,* or immunity from civil law. It is important to realize, however, that free people of color helped defend the city from the invasions

of the English generals Penn and Venable in 1655, but a free person of color from Seibo, 11 leagues north of Santo Domingo, helped the English soldiers to plan and carry out their unsuccessful attacks. Both free and enslaved people of color conspired with Haitians in the 1820s to help them take over "Spanish Haiti."

Women of color dominated as vendors in Santo Domingo. Many of these women were not technically free but enjoyed freedom of movement during the day to sell fruits, vegetables, eggs, crafts, and other products that they produced for their owners and for themselves. While the slaves among them had to turn over most of the profits to their owners, they were allowed to keep a small percentage. Spaniards of the era complained (probably an exaggeration) that these female vendors spent most of their money trying to elevate their perceived social status by buying clothing of satin and brocade, jewelry, and other adornments.

Free people of color in Santo Domingo had their own churches and *cofradías* (CATHOLIC CONFRATERNITIES), their own cultural fiestas, and their own markets and homes, although for most of them, home was a shack in a neighborhood adjacent to the mansions of the Spanish elites, along the shores of the Ozama River, or just on the other side of the river, where Los Minas is located. Los Minas was a town founded by former slaves of the French, who were freed by the Spaniards in exchange for promising to fight the French, should the need arise. These neighborhoods of free people of color provided inexpensive labor for the elite of the capital. They also, however, provided temporary safe refuge for slaves who fled the island's plantations and sugar mills. For this reason, in 1768, a law was promulgated decreeing that no free people of color would henceforth be allowed to buy or rent houses in Santo Domingo unless the house were beside their "[last] known owner."

Colonial Santo Domingo, with its large multicolored population, offered more opportunities for economic and social gain to the free and enslaved alike, no matter their color or gender. During the Haitian Occupation (1822–44), slaves on the Spanish side of the island were declared free, and dark-skinned peoples were given preference over lighter-skinned peoples in both Santo Domingo and across the island. Trujillo, the dictator who ruled the Dominican Republic from 1930 through 1961, tried his best to deny the percentage of people of color who formed the popular masses. He attempted, unsuccessfully, to convince the world that Dominicans were "white," or at least "Indian colored," and he did not allow PEASANTS to move to the city.

Since Trujillo's assassination in 1961, metropolitan Santo Domingo has become home to more than two and a half million Dominicans and immigrants of all colors and hues. Do they all get along? Sometimes, sometimes not, and darker-skinned people have to struggle harder to be successful. As in other modern cities in the developing world, Santo Domingo is a hustling, bustling, crowded place, where it is as easy to starve as it is to become it rich, and where color is not as important, socially or politically, as the amount of money you earn, where you live, what kind of car you drive, what position you hold, and whom you know.

Lynne A. Guitar

FURTHER READING

Deive, Carlos Esteban. *La esclavitud del negro en Santo Domingo (1492–1844)*. Santo Domingo: Museo del Hombre Dominicano, 1980.

Ferguson, James. *Dominican Republic: Beyond the Lighthouse*. London: Latin America Books, 1992.

Moya Pons, Frank. *The Dominican Republic, a National History*. New Rochelle, N.Y.: Hispaniola Books, 1995.

SCOTT, DRED (1799–1858) *plaintiff in U.S. Supreme Court case* Scott v. Sandford *(1857)*

Dred Scott was born a slave in Virginia in 1799. He later lived in MISSOURI, and his owner took him to the free territories of ILLINOIS, MINNESOTA, and WISCONSIN in the 1830s. Scott sued for his freedom and became the plaintiff in *Scott v. Sandford* (1857), one of the most significant cases ever decided by the U.S. Supreme Court. Scott argued that because he had lived on free soil, he was entitled to freedom. In rejecting his argument, the Supreme Court declared that Congress had no power to outlaw slavery in the territories. The decision outraged antislavery advocates in the North, fueled sectional tensions, and contributed to the AMERICAN CIVIL WAR, which began four years later.

Scott was born in Virginia and was a slave of the Peter Blow family. Blow moved his family and slaves from Virginia to ALABAMA in the 1830s, then on to St. Louis,

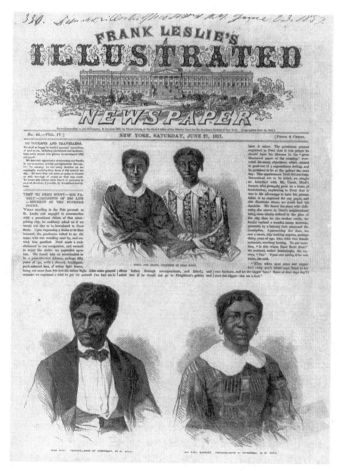

The front page of *Frank Leslie's Illustrated Newspaper* reporting on the outcome of the Dred Scott case in 1857. The portraits at the bottom are of Dred Scott (1799–1858) and his wife, Harriet Robinson (1815–1876). Despite losing their case before the U.S. Supreme Court, Scott and Robinson were granted their freedom by their former masters. *(Library of Congress)*

Missouri, at the time. There, he sold Scott in the 1830s to Dr. John Emerson, a military surgeon who also lived in St. Louis. Scott traveled with Emerson to different posts, including parts of Illinois and the Wisconsin Territory. Slavery had been prohibited in Illinois by its own state constitution. The territories north of the Ohio River and east of the Mississippi River, including Wisconsin, were part of the old Northwest Territory, which had been established as free territory by the Northwest Ordinance in 1787 and then reaffirmed as such under the new Constitution in 1789. This rule was extended to all the territories north of the southern border of Missouri, including part of Minnesota, by the 1820 Missouri Compromise. So Emerson and Scott lived in territories that had been declared free by the Articles of Confederation government of the United States before the adoption of the Constitution, by the Congress in two laws 30 years apart, and by the framers of the Illinois state constitution.

During this time, Scott married Harriet Robinson, a slave; they had two children. The Emersons and Scott and his family eventually returned to St. Louis. Dr. Emerson died in 1843, and later Mrs. Emerson's brother, John F. A. Sanford, became the administrator of her property. (Sanford was the defendant in the U.S. Supreme Court case, but his name was misspelled *Sandford* by Court clerks.)

On April 6, 1846, Scott and his wife sued for their freedom in St. Louis Circuit Courts, arguing that since they had lived in places where slavery was prohibited, they should be considered free. A number of such cases had been tried in Missouri, and judges in prior cases had generally ruled that once slaves were taken into free territories or states they were free.

On March 6, 1857, more than 10 years later and after a number of trials and appeals, *Scott v. Sandford* was decided by the Supreme Court. In a 7 to 2 decision, the Court ruled that slaves and their descendents were not U.S. citizens and did not have the rights granted to U.S. citizens, including the right to sue in a federal court. As a slave, the Court argued, Scott was personal property and had never been free. Further, the Court declared unconstitutional the provision in the Missouri Compromise of 1820 that had prohibited slavery in the territories, indicating that the prohibition violated the Fifth Amendment of the Constitution, prohibiting the federal government from taking property from a citizen without due process of law. Finally, and most importantly for free people of color in the United States, the Dred Scott decision found that blacks, free or slave, were not and could not be citizens of the United States, because the founders at the time of the adoption of the Constitution in 1787 had not considered them to be citizens. In the words of Chief Justice Roger Taney, blacks "had

no rights which the white man was bound to respect." The court did not directly hold that Illinois's provision outlawing slavery on its territory was unconstitutional, but the logic of the decision certainly implied this and invited SLAVE OWNERS who wished to take their slaves into free states to use the same arguments that Scott's owners had used to permit this.

The effect of the Dred Scott decision was to increase further tensions between the North and South, since many saw the decision as the Supreme Court's giving constitutional sanction to slavery. The Court was heavily criticized by many for its decision, and critics charged the Court with bias, forsaking justice for partisan politics. Additionally, the case gave the fledgling Republican Party an issue to rally around. The controversial decision was an important point of contention in the Lincoln-Douglas senatorial debates of 1858 and probably contributed to ABRAHAM LINCOLN's nomination as the presidential candidate of the Republican Party in 1860. Lincoln's victory in 1860 led to the South's secession from the Union and then to the Civil War. By placing limits on Congress's power, the Dred Scott decision inflamed pro- and antislavery advocates and further divided South and North.

Mrs. Emerson remarried and later returned the Scotts to the Blow family, who granted the Scotts freedom in May 1857. Dred Scott died of tuberculosis on September 17, 1858.

Summer Leibensperger

FURTHER READING

Ehrlich, Walter. *They Have No Rights: Dred Scott's Struggle for Freedom.* Westport, Conn.: Greenwood Press, 1979.

Fehrenbacher, Don E. *The Dred Scott Case: Its Significance in American Law and Politics.* New York: Oxford University Press, 1978.

Kutler, Stanley I. *The Dred Scott Decision: Law or Politics?* Boston: Houston Mifflin, 1967.

Potter, David M., and Don E. Fehrenbacher. *The Impending Crisis, 1848–1861.* New York: Harper & Row, 1976.

SEACOLE, MARY (1805–1881) *Jamaican nurse*

"Mother" Mary Seacole (née Grant) was a prominent nurse and public health campaigner in BRITAIN during the Crimean War (1854–56). Less well known than Florence Nightingale (1820–1910), she may have had as great an influence on the well-being of British soldiers during that conflict. She is one of the pioneers of modern nursing.

Mary Grant was a woman of mixed race born sometime in 1805 in JAMAICA. Her father was a Scottish soldier in the garrison, and her mother was a free black tradi-

A contemporary drawing of "Mother" Mary Seacole (1805–81). Seacole was a pioneer in nursing, serving during the great cholera epidemic of the 1850s in Latin America and the Caribbean and during the Crimean War. She also operated a hospital for the poor in her native island of Jamaica in the 1850s and 1860s. She was very popular among British veterans of the Crimean War and was received by Queen Victoria. *(The Bridgeman Art Library International)*

tional healer and innkeeper. Mary's mother arranged for her to be educated, first in Kingston, the capital of Jamaica, and then in LONDON, ENGLAND. She cared for sick soldiers in the garrison in Kingston and traveled in the region during her early life. Shortly after the abolition of slavery in Jamaica, in 1836, she married a white man, a naval officer named Thomas Seacole, who was the godson of Horatio Nelson, the British naval hero of the Napoleonic Wars. Her husband and mother both died in 1844, and she took over her mother's businesses.

As a healer, Mary Seacole treated many patients with a variety of tropical diseases, including many victims of an 1850 cholera epidemic that took 30,000 lives in Jamaica. She traveled to PANAMA in 1851, accompanying her brother, and worked as a nurse when the cholera epidemic began there. When the news of the outbreak of the Crimean War arrived in the Caribbean in 1854, she immediately went to London to offer her services to Florence Nightingale's nursing corps. Nightingale rejected her, probably because of her social class as well as RACISM AND RACIAL PREJUDICE, as one of Nightingale's objectives was to redefine nursing as work that a "lady," a member of the upper classes, could do. Undeterred, Seacole went to the Crimea on her own and set up an "English hotel" with accommodations for convalescent soldiers. She charged officers but took care of enlisted men without charge. She also prepared and sold meals and had the assistance of a famous French chef de cuisine who was interested in improving the nutritional standards of the allied armies. She visited the army camps and was present on the battlefield in two of the war's most desperate encounters, the crossings of the Tchernaya River (August 16, 1855) and the Battle of the Redan outside Sevastopol (August 27, 1855). After the fall of Sevastopol in September 1855, she was the first woman from the victorious side to enter the city and cared for Russian wounded whose hospital had been damaged by fire during the siege.

The revenues from her "hotel" never equaled the expenses, and she ended the war destitute. She was declared bankrupt in Britain, but former British officers in the Crimea, including Lord George Paget (1818–80), the commander of the famous Light Brigade, worked to raise money to restore her finances. An important step was the publication in 1857 of her memoirs, *The Wonderful Adventures of Mrs. Seacole in Many Lands,* which proved popular in Britain and went through two editions. She returned to Jamaica in the 1860s, joined the ROMAN CATHOLIC CHURCH, and continued to work for better health care for the poor. In the 1870s, she returned to London, where she was again turned away by the British medical establishment. Florence Nightingale wrote a letter accusing her of having run a brothel in the Crimea. Nonetheless, she was very popular in Britain and was received by Queen Victoria. She died in London on May 14, 1881.

Stewart R. King

FURTHER READING

"Mary Seacole." Thames Valley University. Available online URL: http://www.maryseacole.com/maryseacole/pages/. Accessed January 9, 2011.

Seacole, Mary. *The Wonderful Adventures of Mrs. Seacole in Many Lands.* 1857. Reprint, London: Penguin, 2005.

SEGREGATION

Segregation is the separation, by custom or law, of people for whatever reason, but typically by race or ethnic grouping. Under segregation, various sorts of sanctions, ranging from social disapproval through fines and imprisonment to mob violence and LYNCHING, are imposed on members of one race who associate in prohibited ways with members of the other. Generally, persons of a subordinate group are more harshly punished, while members of the dominant group who seek prohibited forms of contact with members of the lower-ranking group are at worst met with social disapproval by their peers. Most groups in a multiethnic society practice some form of customary segregation, which can be as innocuous as ethnic pride organizations and clubs or as potentially harmful as restrictions on access to educational or cultural institutions or different categories of service offered by businesses.

Throughout the Americas, there was informal segregation of people perceived as "white" from those perceived as "black," "colored," or "Indian." This informal segregation was found in almost all areas except those very far beyond the frontiers and was generally stronger where there were large populations of free people of African descent. Indians were segregated in villages, on reservations, or beyond the frontier of settlement, and thus white

society felt less need to push them away, though in places where there were large numbers of acculturated Indians, such as in the Andes or Central MEXICO, there was (and remains) a certain amount of informal segregation in relation to them.

In the United States, however, and to a lesser extent in other places in the Americas, regimes of formal segregation between white and black, required or at least protected by law, sprang up in the wake of the end of slavery after the AMERICAN CIVIL WAR. This system was known as Jim Crow in the United States, after a black stock comedic figure. Under Jim Crow, as codified after the U.S. Supreme Court's *Plessy v. Ferguson* decision in 1896, government services were provided in different places, times, or conditions to members of the different races. There were often two school systems, especially in Southern states. Courtrooms and public libraries had separate entrances and seating areas for patrons of different races. Public transportation had separate seating areas. Although these services were supposed to be equal, the provisions for blacks were generally distinctly inferior. In

One of the many manifestations of segregation in the United States was the provision of separate public amenities, such as water fountains and rest rooms. The principle of "separate but equal" held by the Supreme Court in its 1896 decision *Plessy v. Ferguson* permitted this, and governments required it in many cases, reinforcing the subordination of people of color. *(Library of Congress)*

addition to these official forms of segregation, businesses were encouraged or required to provide separate accommodations. Real estate brokers and lenders encouraged residential segregation. Restaurants would only serve blacks food for take-out. Hotels had separate rooms or were for the use of one race only. Private schools and colleges were encouraged to preserve single-race policies. Finally, strict rules discouraged MISCEGENATION and INTERRACIAL MARRIAGE, with harsh official and unofficial penalties. The Civil Rights movement of the 1950s and 1960s overturned the legal regime of segregation in the United States, though informal segregation continues in an attenuated form. The most persistent form of segregation in the United States today is residential, as many neighborhoods are overwhelmingly black, white, or Latino. Informal restrictions on interracial sex and marriage also persist, with some members of all racial groups opposed in principle to interracial unions.

Stewart R. King

SENEGAMBIA

The people of Senegambia in West Africa were Muslims and subjects of the Empire of Songhai when that kingdom was at the height of its power. After the collapse of Songhai in 1591, the people of this region created a number of small kingdoms that ruled over the area throughout the era of the slave trade. This area was connected to the trans-Saharan trade, and kings and scholars from here made the pilgrimage to Mecca (*see also* ISLAM) on many occasions during the early modern period. Europeans arrived on the Senegambian coast in the middle of the 15th century, and explorers from PORTUGAL established a permanent settlement on Gorée Island off the coast of the modern city of Dakar in the 1450s. The Portuguese gave way to the Dutch in the 17th century, and then the French and British established posts along the coast late in the 17th century.

Senegambia was an important source of slaves for the Atlantic slave trade from the late 17th to the mid-18th century, a period coinciding with the Fulani jihad in the Fouta Djallon Mountains and upper Sénégal River basin. The most important ports for this trade were at the mouth of the two rivers, the Sénégal in the North and the Gambia in the South. Saint-Louis, at the mouth of the Sénégal, was controlled by the French from 1659. The French strengthened their control over the trade on the Sénégal River by establishing several smaller forts upriver and gaining the support of the Wolof kings. They also established several other posts along the coast, including the famous island base at Gorée; however, none of these was a particularly important source of slaves. At the mouth of the Gambia, the local rulers permitted several European

powers to establish slave trading posts, including British and Polish merchants at James Island and French traders at Albreda on the north bank. The rulers authorized villages of Mandingo merchants near the foreign trading posts on the Gambia River to trade with the outsiders, giving them a monopoly over trade and facilitating tax collection; Jufureh, the place where Alex Haley, the American author of the novel/memoir *Roots*, said his ancestor Kunta Kinte was from, is one such village, located only a few miles from James Island and Albreda. It is more likely that Kunta Kinte was from the Fouta Djallon, a 100 miles or more upstream and was merely loaded onto the slave ship at Jufureh—the name *Kinte* is a variant of *Kante*, a common family name in Upper Guinea and the Fouta Djallon.

The high period of the slave trade in Senegambia was the first half of the 18th century. By 1750, the jihad in the Fouta Djallon had died down, and the new rulers were not disposed to expand their territory beyond the mountains. The slave traders turned their attention to Central Africa, where a new civil war had broken out in Kongo. Only about 3 percent of slaves imported into the Americas from 1750 to 1850 were Senegambian. In place of slaves, European merchants on the Senegambian coast began exporting other commodities. These included peanuts and peanut oil, woven mats, gum arabic, and cotton. This "legitimate" trade was much heralded by opponents of the slave trade to show that profitable African trade was possible without slavery. In some cases, however, the "legitimate" trade was in products made in Africa by using slave labor. Slavery was common in Senegambia, particularly in those areas where the Fulani jihad had been active, but this was not plantation slavery like that found in the Americas. Slaves were tied to their land and could not be sold and were owned by governments or villages rather than by individuals. In any case, much of the produce of Senegambia was grown by PEASANTS in Wolof lands.

The merchants of the European trading posts along the coast, especially the French "communes," were to a great extent people of mixed race. European merchants found the disease environment very challenging, were often sick, and generally either died or had to go home quickly. Often, if they were lucky, they could marry local women and establish families of color who could carry on their business after them. Women were particularly important as merchants in the French ports. The signares, as they were called, of Saint-Louis and Gorée were active participants in transatlantic trade in the 18th century. There was one Gorée merchant, ANNE ROSSIGNOL, living in SAINT-DOMINGUE in the 1780s before the HAITIAN REVOLUTION. She had commercial contacts in FRANCE and in other Caribbean islands. She appeared to be primarily involved in the oil trade, though she did receive a slave on one occasion sent to her by a relative in Africa to be forwarded to another contact in Saint-Lucia.

The French colonies in Senegambia were also the home of the formidable French African army unit called the Tirailleurs Sénégalais. The Tirailleurs were first formed in the mid-19th century, succeeding local MILITIA forces that had been raised in the communes. The French originally recruited for their local forces in Sénégal by purchasing slaves, as slavery was not abolished in France's African colonies until the mid-20th century, then freeing them in return for a 20-year enlistment in the French army. This practice was similar to proposals that had been made in the Caribbean colonies in the years before the FRENCH REVOLUTION, proposals that were always rejected because of the threat to the racial order that armed slaves would have posed. (*See also* REGULAR ARMY.) By the 19th century, attitudes had changed enough that this measure was possible, even as slavery was abolished in France's few remaining colonies in the Americas.

Stewart R. King

FURTHER READING
Curtin, Philip. *Economic Change in Precolonial Africa: Senegambia in the Era of the Slave Trade.* Madison: University of Wisconsin Press, 1975.

SEVEN YEARS' WAR (1756–1763)
The Seven Years' War, known in the United States as the French and Indian War, began in North America on May 28, 1754, when a mixed British-Indian force under GEORGE WASHINGTON attacked a French construction party near the modern PITTSBURGH, PENNSYLVANIA. Washington's troops killed a number of French and their Indian allies, but the French counterattack drove him back to Virginia. French-Indian forces also confronted NEW YORK STATE MILITIA and Iroquois Indians in what is now northwestern PENNSYLVANIA. Two years later, the war merged with a European conflict between Prussia, Britain's ally, and its Continental neighbors and became a global war between two great alliances centered on FRANCE and BRITAIN. The war ended with the Treaty of Paris in 1763, which confirmed Prussia's great power status, placed Britain in control of CANADA and India, and more or less restored the prewar situation in the Caribbean. As a result of the war, France lost all its territory in mainland North America.

The Americas were a central theater of this war, both the mainland of North America and the Caribbean Islands. Both sides used nonwhite troops extensively in this struggle. In North America, native people fought on both sides, though the French had more native allies. In the Caribbean, both sides made extensive use of black troops and noncombatant auxiliaries.

The Caribbean was the site of active privateering and jockeying for position but only became an active theater of war in 1759. In that year, a British expedition attacked the French colony in Martinique but was driven off by gunfire from the island's forts manned in part by the locally raised free colored militia and supported by slave laborers who took up guns during the crisis. At least a dozen slaves gained their freedom after this battle. The British then went on to Guadeloupe, a less heavily defended French island colony. After a siege of four months, the French garrison surrendered only days before the arrival of a large French relief force. Sixty survivors from among the slaves who had fought with the garrison were purchased by the government after the war and freed. During the campaign in Martinique, both sides suffered enormous casualties from disease among their European troops. Locally raised troops would have higher resistance to diseases, it was thought, and both sides began recruiting. The French in SAINT-DOMINGUE raised a free colored unit to defend the most vulnerable part of the island, the northern plains, though in the end the British never invaded Saint-Domingue, and the unit never saw combat. The governor of Saint-Domingue, the comte d'Estaing, was so impressed with the enthusiasm of free colored soldiers, however, that he proposed an abortive militia reform at the end of the war that would have created a sort of standing national guard of soldiers of color, who could either gain their freedom through seven years service or gain the right to free FAMILY members without paying the large MANUMISSION tax. This reform was not adopted because of white resistance to changes in their militia service, but D'Estaing revived the idea of free colored armed service in the WAR OF AMERICAN INDEPENDENCE (1775–83), and more than 1,000 black Dominguans signed up to fight for America's freedom in 1779.

SPAIN joined the war, belatedly, as France's ally in 1761. The British responded by attacking Havana, CUBA, the main Spanish base in the Caribbean. A British force of almost 25,000 men confronted a Spanish garrison of a few thousand REGULAR ARMY troops plus the Havana militia. The militia was composed of free colored and white units, and both groups performed with distinction. A free colored company was involved in an important sortie from the defenses on June 29, 1762, that damaged the British guns and slowed the progress of the siege. Free colored pioneers set the British breastworks afire during the night of July 1–2, destroying much of the work that had been done over the preceding two months. White and free colored militiamen participated in a last-ditch sortie on July 20 that failed to prevent the British engineers from blowing a hole in the wall of the critical Morro fortress.

Ultimately, British firepower and some miscalculations by the Spanish commanders led to the city's surrender on August 14. Once again, the British suffered terrible losses from disease, and the resilience of the Spanish defense resulted in part from their general good health.

The Seven Years' War demonstrated the growing importance of black troops for the defense of the tropical Americas. Free colored numbers were growing at this time and would almost double in many places in the Caribbean and the tropical mainland of Central and South America by the time the next major war, the American Revolution, began in the 1770s. The lessons learned about disease casualties and the fighting quality of black militias were to be remembered, as French, British, and even North American factions in the War of Independence were to turn to blacks as soldiers. The link between military service and more equal citizenship was made explicit in the comte d'Estaing's plan for Saint-Domingue, but the lesson was not lost elsewhere. White elites feared black military participation, so much so that in SOUTH CAROLINA in the coming American war, patriotic white planters were to say they would rather lose the war than win it with blacks as soldiers. But most colonial governments made the opposite choice, giving free blacks a chance to prove their loyalty to the system by armed service.

Stewart R. King

FURTHER READING

Anderson, Fred. *Crucible of War: The Seven Years War and the Fate of Empire in British North America, 1754–1766.* New York: Alfred A. Knopf, 2000.

Brown, Christopher, and Philip Morgan. *Arming Slaves: From Classical Times to the Modern Age.* New Haven, Conn.: Yale University Press, 2006.

SHARP, GRANVILLE (1735–1813) *British abolitionist*

Born into a family of Anglican clergy in Durham, England, on November 10, 1735, Granville Sharp would become the leading abolitionist of the late 18th century and a strong advocate for civil liberties and parliamentary reform in Great BRITAIN. His early education was constrained by family financial troubles, and Sharp was apprenticed at the age of 15 to a linen draper in LONDON, ENGLAND, who was a Quaker. (*See also* BAPTISTS AND PIETISTS.) He became a freeman, or voting citizen, of the City of London upon completing his apprenticeship in 1757 and ultimately obtained a position as clerk-in-ordinary, or civil servant, at the Tower of London. In London, he also encountered Presbyterians, Catholics, and even agnostics, among others, developing a lifelong interest in theological matters that led to his mastering Greek and Hebrew by his own efforts. His passionate interests in linguistics, antiquarianism, and biblical studies would lead to the printing of his first published works, including *A Short Treatise on the English Tongue* in 1767, in multiple editions. The success of these early works led to his being offered an Anglican clergy benefice by his uncle, which he declined, having been drawn by a chance encounter with an escaped slave in 1765 into an abiding engagement with the abolition movement and constitutional reform.

Granville Sharp's brother, William, was a well-regarded surgeon in London. After a visit to his brother's East End house in 1765, Sharp noticed an emaciated, bruised, and nearly crippled African boy about 16 years old waiting with the other ill poor for William's free medical services. The boy, Jonathan Strong, had been beaten so severely by his master that he could barely walk, he was almost blind, and his head was badly swollen. Having been taken to England from BARBADOS as a slave by David Lisle, a JAMAICA plantation owner and lawyer, Strong had been discarded into the streets of London as valueless after being physically broken by Lisle's abuses. After four months in the hospital, courtesy of the Sharp brothers, Strong beseeched them for further help, having no one else to whom to turn. They found him employment with a local apothecary, in which position Strong thrived. Two years later, fully healed and grown into a fine young man, Strong had the misfortune to be seen by his former master. Lisle subsequently resold Strong without his knowledge to James Kerr and arranged to have slave hunters capture Strong in order to have him shipped to Kerr's Jamaica plantation.

Held captive in the Poultry Compter, a small London prison, until he could be put on board a Jamaica-bound ship, Strong appealed to Granville Sharp for rescue. After initially being lied to by the prison keeper that Strong was not there, Sharp was allowed to see Strong, immediately remembering him and promising his aid. Sharp brought an action for false imprisonment in the Lord Mayor's Court, which released Strong because he had committed no legal offence. Several days later, Sharp was sued by Kerr for trespassing against his property rights in Strong and unsuccessfully challenged to a duel by Lisle (Sharp refused to fight, saying that Lisle could have his satisfaction from the law if he could get it). Sharp was advised by his lawyers that under British law, neither baptism nor residence in Britain freed a slave and that any slaveholder could forcibly take his slave out of the country. Advised to settle with Kerr and leave Strong to his own devices, Sharp instead chose to make a study of the law himself. Showing the same dedication and aptitude with which he had mastered ancient languages and theology, he produced an answer to Kerr's suit and managed to have at least 20 manuscript copies circulated in London's legal community. Sharp's self-taught legal argument that habeas corpus applied even to slaves and that an action for false imprisonment was indeed the proper remedy was ultimately enough to deter Kerr's lawyers from pursuing the case further, though they dragged matters out for eight years. Sharp subsequently published his manuscript in 1769 as *A Representation of the Injustice and Dangerous Tendency of Tolerating Slavery; or of Admitting the Least Claim of Private Property in the Persons of Men, in England.*

Finding inspiration from his success in releasing Jonathan Strong from the shackles of slavery, Sharp then set upon a personal quest to help other slaves in Britain obtain their liberty, with the ultimate goal of having slavery abolished under the laws of Britain. After several partially successful cases, including that of Thomas Lewis in *Rex v. Stapylton*, which resulted in the individual slaves' being freed but failed to produce a ruling on the law that would apply to all slaves in Britain, Sharp was alerted to the plight of James Somersett in November 1771. In the case of SOMERSET V. STEWART, Sharp nearly achieved his goal. Lord Mansfield crafted a ruling in 1772 that prohibited slaveholders from using British law or calling upon English officials either to capture escaped slaves or to compel their slaves forcibly to leave Britain against their will. The opinion in *Somerset* failed, however, to address the issue of whether a slaveholder retained a right in property or contract to the life service of a slave and had specifically stated that British law would enforce a contract for sale of a slave. Undeterred by the narrow nature of his victory in freeing Somerset, Sharp promptly proceeded to publicize the practical effect of Lord Mansfield's opinion through the abolition movement and Britain's growing community of free persons of color. Thanks to his efforts, as of summer 1772, any slave taken to or living in Britain who could escape from his or her master's custody was effectively freed from slavery. The *Somerset* case quickly became known as holding that any slave setting foot on British soil was immediately set free.

Sharp would not live to see the rule of the *Somerset* case given full statutory force by section 3 of the 1833 act of Parliament abolishing slavery in the British colonies. He had, however been integral in the movement that led to Great Britain's abolishing the African slave trade by act of Parliament in 1807. When the Society for the Abolition of the Slave Trade had been established in 1787, he was among the 12 original members. Sharp also helped to sponsor and direct the establishment of SIERRA LEONE as a colony for freed slaves in the 1780s and 1790s. Sharp cooperated with OLAUDAH EQUIANO in the case of the slave ship *Zong* (1783), whose owners were claiming insurance payments for the cost of slaves thrown overboard during an epidemic. He also continued to write abolitionist works, including *The Just Limitation of Slavery in the Laws of God, Compared with the Unbounded Claims of the African Traders and British American Slaveholders* and *The Law of Liberty, or, Royal Law, by Which All Mankind Will Certainly Be Judged! Earnestly Recommended to the Serious Consideration of All Slave Holders and Slave Dealers* in 1776, and his 1805 publication *Serious Reflections of the Slave Trade and Slavery Wrote in March 1797.* Sharp was also active in other reform movements, supporting attempts to democratize the British election system, prison reform, and evangelical missionary work. Sharp died on July 6, 1813, revered as a hero of the abolition movements in Britain and abroad and a respected advocate of civil liberties and political reform.

Emily M. Brewer

FURTHER READING

Blackburn, Robin. *The Overthrow of Colonial Slavery, 1776–1848.* London: Verso, 1988.

Brown, Christopher Leslie. *Moral Capital: Foundations of British Abolitionism.* Chapel Hill: University of North Carolina Press, 2006.

Ditchfield, G. M. "Granville Sharp." In *Oxford Dictionary of National Biography,* vol. 50, 15–18. Oxford: Oxford University Press, 2004.

Drescher, Seymour. *From Slavery to Freedom: Comparative Studies in the Rise and Fall of Atlantic Slavery.* New York: New York University Press, 1999.

Gerzina, Gretchen. *Black England: Life before Emancipation.* London: John Murray, 1995.

Jennings, Judith, ed. *The Business of Abolishing the British Slave Trade, 1783–1807.* London: F. Cass, 1997.

Lascelles, E. C. P. *Granville Sharp and the Freedom of Slaves in England.* New York: Negro University Press, 1969.

Oldham, James. "New Light on Mansfield and Slavery." *Journal of British Studies* 27 (1988): 45–68.

Prince, Hoare. *Memoirs of Granville Sharp, Esq. Composed from His Own Manuscripts, and Other Authentic Documents.* London: Henry Colburn, 1820.

Shyllon, F. O. *Black Slaves in Britain.* New York: Oxford University Press, 1974.

Turley, David. *The Culture of English Antislavery, 1780–1860.* New York: Routledge, 1991.

Wise, Steven M. *Though the Heavens May Fall: The Landmark Trial That Led to the End of Human Slavery.* New York: Da Capo Press, 2005.

SIERRA LEONE

The region in West Africa now known as Sierra Leone was inhabited by Mande-speaking people in the South and Temne speakers in the North when, in 1787, British ships landed the first shiploads of black poor people from LONDON, ENGLAND, near the site of modern Freetown, establishing the colony that became the modern Sierra Leone.

For about a century before this time, Sierra Leone had been a secondary source of slaves for export to the Americas. The Mende of Sierra Leone had paid tribute to the Empire of Songhai in the 15th century, and when that empire fell apart after the Moroccan invasion of 1591, the Mende formed a number of small states. One of those states gave permission to the Royal African Company to establish a factory (so called not because it was engaged in manufacturing but because it was the residence of a "factor," as commercial agents were called in those days) at Bunce Island about 20 miles up the Sierra Leone River from modern Freetown. The Royal African Company was mismanaged, and their operation in Sierra Leone was unprofitable, but in 1750, the factory was taken over by a British private firm with an important connection to the port of CHARLESTON, SOUTH CAROLINA. American planters establishing rice farms along the Carolina and GEORGIA low country specifically requested slaves from this region, since rice was the staple crop there and the slaves would have needed skills. As a result, this is one of the few areas in the modern United States with any recognizable cultural links to a particular place in Africa. Sea Island Gullah, a language spoken in low country Georgia and SOUTH CAROLINA, is very similar to Sierra Leone Krio. About 1,000 slaves a year were taken from Sierra Leone directly to South Carolina and Georgia between 1750 and 1808 (the year the United States abolished the slave trade). This represents more than 10 percent of all slaves imported into British North America and the United States.

The British settlement of Freetown was an effort by wealthy Britons to remove the large numbers of black poor people of London from the charity rolls. Many of these people were veterans of the British Navy or REGULAR ARMY from the time of the WAR OF AMERICAN INDEPENDENCE (1775–83), while others were former MERCHANT SEAMEN or servants who had been discharged in the city. The laws of Britain required that people who needed charity be taken care of by the Church of England parish nearest their birthplace. In the case of freed slaves, this meant the parish closest where they were living when they gained their freedom. Since any black person who set foot in Britain became free as a result of SOMERSET V. STEWART, there were many free blacks living in British port cities. The people responsible for the Poor Law in London decided that their native-born poor and the church finances would be better off if the blacks were sent to Africa.

Some of those who went to Sierra Leone in the first fleet were Africans, but most had been born in the Americas

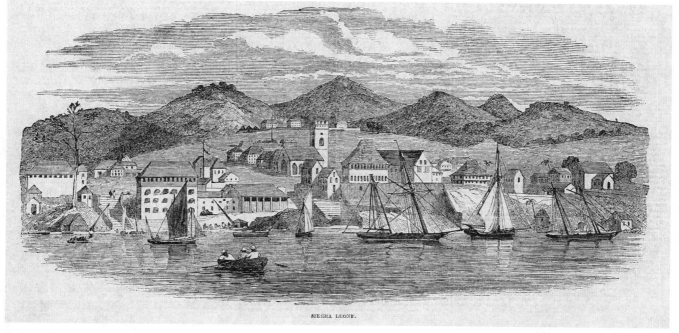

SIERRA LEONE.

A view of the harbor of Freetown, Sierra Leone, in the 1850s. The first settlers of the British colony of Sierra Leone were free blacks from London, who were followed by a number of American-born blacks who had fled by way of Canada after the War of American Independence. Later settlers included Jamaican maroons and people liberated from slave ships captured by the British navy. The descendants of these colonists are the ancestors of the Krio ethnic group, which remains influential in the economy of modern Sierra Leone. (© Bettmann/CORBIS) or Britain. The contributors to the expedition, and perhaps the black colonists themselves, believed that blackness conferred immunity to tropical diseases, but in fact it is birth or long residence in a tropical area that allows someone to acquire immunity to the particular strains of tropical diseases found in that place. Even moving from one place to another in the Tropics can expose a person to diseases for which he or she has no immunity, as slave traders and SLAVE OWNERS knew from experiencing the enormous mortality rates of slaves newly arrived in the Americas. But the Sierra Leone colonists were surprised when almost all of them fell sick within a year or so of their arrival in the colony. They were victims not only of disease but also of the hostility of the local people, egged on by the slave traders at Bunce Island who did not want an abolitionist settlement only a few miles away. Some of the early Sierra Leone colonists were even kidnapped and sold into slavery. The colony was poorly supplied and not well organized politically, and few of the colonists had the skills needed for farming in the Tropics. Almost two-thirds of the first settlers died within a few years. The second group of settlers arrived in 1791: almost 1,000 free black North Americans led by Thomas Peters, a North Carolinian who gained his freedom by fighting for Britain during the War of American Independence. Peters had enlisted the support of the white abolitionist GRANVILLE SHARP, and the reformed Sierra Leone Company

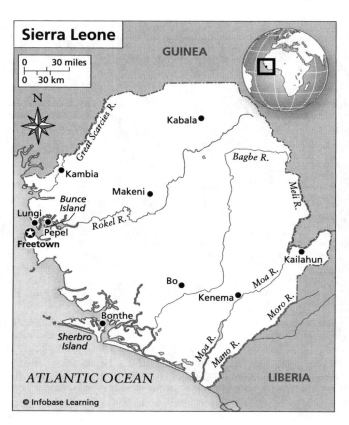

had better financing, diplomacy, and organization than the earlier effort. The new company also had a philanthropic goal of establishing a homeland for blacks where they would be treated justly and could introduce Western Christian ideas and beliefs to Africa. Most of the colonists were, like Peters, veterans of the American war and with their families, had been living in Nova Scotia and feeling rather unwelcome since the British lost that war. Peters himself died shortly after his arrival, as did many of his fellow immigrants, but enough survived, thanks to plentiful supplies and more careful diplomacy with the local people, that the colony began to flourish.

The Sierra Leone Company hoped to develop local resources, including gum, oil, and ivory, for a "legitimate" export trade but expected to make most of its money from land rents. The settlers of Sierra Leone expected to become independent landowning farmers as many of them had hoped to be in North America in the case of a British victory in the Revolution. These contrasting ambitions came into conflict, inevitably, and there was a rebellion against the company in 1799. The company could not convince the government to send any troops to intervene—the Napoleonic Wars were raging in Europe, and British troops had just ended an occupation of SAINT-DOMINGUE that had cost thousands of troops their lives through tropical diseases. So the company enlisted a MILITIA of MAROONS from JAMAICA, who at least were experienced in irregular warfare in the Tropics if not in the Sierra Leone disease environment. The maroons crushed the rebellion and stayed on as settlers.

The abolition of the British slave trade in 1807, the end of the Napoleonic Wars in 1815, and various treaties with other slave-trading countries during the first quarter of the 19th century ushered in a new era for Sierra Leone. The British government based a squadron of frigates there that patrolled the coast of Africa looking for slave traders. This was a lucrative business for the Royal Navy captains and crews, who were paid "prize money" for each slave liberated. They searched enthusiastically, recaptured many thousands of slaves, and greatly hampered the illegal slave trade in the North Atlantic. Paradoxically, one of the toughest illegal slave-trading ports to eradicate was Gallinas, near modern Sulima, only 150 miles from Freetown near the modern border with LIBERIA. Gallinas was protected by the local authorities and located up a river that was difficult for warships to navigate. The "governor" of Gallinas was a Spanish citizen, possibly of mixed racial heritage, who had some diplomatic protection from SPAIN. For all these reasons, Gallinas was able to keep functioning as a slave trade port until 1849, when the British navy finally closed it down. Some years before that time, it was the port at which the slaves of the *Amistad* were embarked. These slaves overwhelmed the crew of their slave ship and sailed it to CONNECTICUT, where they launched an important legal case that confirmed their freedom and the end of the slave trade in America.

The recaptured Africans were landed at Sierra Leone. The Sierra Leone Company and British philanthropists made some effort to return them to their homes, but in fact this proved almost impossible. Even those of the *Amistad* survivors who accepted repatriation, most of whom were from within a few hundred miles of Freetown, were generally unable to return to their original home villages and had to settle in the Freetown area. The recaptured African slaves, along with the American-born settlers, created a mixed culture called Krio, with its own language, an English Creole. As in many post-emancipation societies, the descendants of the former free people of color, the American, British, and Jamaican early settlers, went on to be the ruling class of the new society. Under colonial rule, the Krio were the most important group in business and the civil service. When Sierra Leone gained independence in the 1960s, the politics of the new country were dominated by people from the more numerous Mende tribe, but the economy of the country was dominated by Krio businesspeople. The rebel forces during the Sierra Leone Civil War (1991–2002) targeted Krio businesses, but the peace settlement seems to have restored Krios to their earlier dominance in the economy, the professions, and education.

Stewart R. King

FURTHER READING

Alie, Joe A. D. *A New History of Sierra Leone.* New York: St. Martin's Press, 1990.

White, E. Frances. *Sierra Leone's Settler Women Traders: Women on the Afro-European Frontier.* Ann Arbor: University of Michigan Press, 1987.

SILVA, CHICA DA (ca. 1730–1796) *wealthy Brazilian freedwoman*

Chica da Silva was an outstanding example of a free colored businesswoman in BRAZIL in the 18th century. Her life illustrates some of the choices open to women of color and some of the constraints on their choices.

The daughter of an African slave woman and a Portuguese militia officer, Francisca da Silva de Oliveira, better known as Chica da Silva, was born around 1730 and gained her freedom in 1753, in the Brazilian town of Tejuco (today Diamantina), Minas Gerais. Her last owner, João Fernandes de Oliveira, a Portuguese man and the regional diamond contractor, had purchased her only a few months before freeing her, suggesting that they had already established a relationship. Over the next 17 years,

Chica and João Fernandes had 13 children, all of whom were recognized by João Fernandes.

Through to her relationship with the wealthy diamond contractor, Chica gained considerable wealth, owned slaves, and entered into Tejuco high society. She had her daughters educated in the best ROMAN CATHOLIC CHURCH school in Minas Gerais; she and her children were members of the principal lay brotherhoods of the town (*see also* CATHOLIC CONFRATERNITIES). João Fernandes was obliged to return to PORTUGAL in 1770 but continued to look after Chica and their children. He arranged for their oldest son to inherit an entailed estate in Portugal, the Morgado do Grijó. Another son became a priest and acquired the post of MILITIA lieutenant-colonel in Minas Gerais. Chica da Silva died in 1796 and was buried in Tejuco's Saint Francis of Assisi church.

Though more successful than most, Chica da Silva followed strategies common to many colonial Brazilian freedwomen, who sought to rise socially through connections to the white elite and thereby distance themselves from their slave background. Thanks to a brief mention of her in an 1868 local history of Tejuco, Chica da Silva entered regional folklore and literature as an emblematic figure of the mulatta who rises in society through her sexuality. She is today best known inside and outside Brazil through Carlos Diegues's 1975 film *Xica da Silva*, which portrayed her as a lascivious and sensual mulatta, although there are no contemporary sources to support this interpretation of her character.

Hendrik Kraay

FURTHER READING

Furtado, Júnia Ferreira. *Chica da Silva: A Brazilian Slave of the Eighteenth Century.* Cambridge: Cambridge University Press, 2009.

SLAVE COAST, BENIN, AND THE BIGHT OF BIAFRA

The region from the Gold Coast to Fernando Po Island in Africa was the principal source of slaves in the Atlantic slave trade from the 16th to the early 18th century. Even though superseded by the Congo region in the late 18th and early 19th centuries, this region remained an important source of slaves up until the end of the legal slave trade and continued to export a few slaves illegally till the end of slavery in the Americas. People of color from the Americas and their descendants were important intermediaries and employees for slave traders across this region, and their descendants are still an important group in the economies and societies of Ghana, Togo, Benin, and Nigeria, the modern nations that make up this area.

Portuguese merchants arrived on the coast in 1471, as part of the great exploratory drive that ultimately led to the discovery of trade routes to the Far East. The Portuguese very early realized that they did not have the skills to trade successfully with the Africans. They lacked knowledge of the languages, of course, but also cultural familiarity, legal rights, and knowledge of the local market. Portuguese merchants began by leaving "factors," or commercial agents, behind on one voyage, and then picking them up on the way back from Asia or on a subsequent voyage. These "stay-over" factors settled down with the African merchant communities, often marrying local women and fathering families. However, the mortality rate was very high because of harsh disease environment, and often the African partners, wives, and children did not have time to learn the skills necessary to trade with Europeans.

In 1482, the Portuguese built their first permanent settlement, São Jorge da Mina, or Elmina, in what is today Ghana, staffing it with "stay-over" factors and their families. The Portuguese actually began their presence in Elmina as slave importers, selling slaves acquired farther south to the growing Asante kingdom in the interior in return for gold that the Asante mined, using slave labor, in the Volta gold fields. They carried the gold to India and China to pay for Asian products that they carried to the Americas and Europe. But fairly rapidly the expansionist Asante captured enough slaves for their own needs, and shortly thereafter, they had a surplus to sell to the Portuguese. Portugal had settled several Atlantic islands including the Cap Verdes and São Tomé and was practicing SUGAR CULTIVATION there. By the middle of the 16th century, Portuguese planters were also growing sugar in BRAZIL, just a short distance by sea across the South Atlantic Ocean from the Gold Coast. SPAIN and Portugal were also united under one ruler from 1580 to 1640, during which time MEXICO and other places in Spanish America were losing population rapidly and demanding new sources of labor. Slaves from the Gold Coast formed the first black populations of the Americas.

The Portuguese continued their development of the West African slave trade, establishing "factories" (so called not because they were engaged in manufacturing but because they were the offices of factors) throughout the region. The pattern of settlement was similar in most cases: Purchase a bit of land and establish a settlement near a growing African political entity that would have slaves for sale and provide a market for Asian, American, or European goods that the Portuguese ships could transport. The settlements were fortified mainly to exclude other Europeans, as Portugal's empire was under siege from Dutch and English attackers throughout the 17th century. They relied on the support of local rulers and

had no interest at all in exerting sovereignty across most of the region. One condition that disrupted their business was African political disorder. The decline of the Kingdom of Benin put a flood of slaves onto the market, but the Portuguese traders with their tight relationships with the ruling faction were poorly placed to take advantage. Their colleagues in Central Africa met a similar challenge when the Kingdom of Kongo was falling apart by expanding their own sovereignty and creating a territorial colony, but the Portuguese slave traders north of the equator did not have the resources to emulate them. As a result, the Portuguese share of the trade in the region declined, and ultimately Portugal lost most of its West African colonies.

As black populations in the Americas grew, and as free populations of color began to appear in Brazil, the Portuguese realized that they were a potential resource for development of trade on the African coast. The top positions in most of the Portuguese factories were reserved for actual Peninsular Portuguese governors or commercial chiefs. But many of the representatives of the various merchant houses, individual traders, and the skilled employees in the factories were people from the Americas or their descendants. The African partners of the merchants were also often descended in part from Portuguese merchants as a result of many marriages and informal liaisons of African women and Portuguese factors. These Afro-Brazilian-Portuguese people became a self-aware group, the Coast Traders, throughout the region.

Elmina fell to Dutch attackers in 1637, and the remainder of the Slave Coast settlements had been captured by the Dutch by 1642. The Dutch themselves were ousted from many of these places by the British or French during the wars of the 18th century. Even though Portugal's European enemies flew their flags in these places and appointed the governors, the Coast Trader merchants continued to play an important role in business, both the slave trade and in the "legitimate" trade that succeeded it (see also COMMERCE AND TRADE). They also became the dominant commercial culture in the region up through the 20th century. As late as the early 19th century, merchants and envoys of the new wave of European colonialism found that Portuguese was the language of trade and diplomacy all along this coast. The people of the powerful empire of Benin used Portuguese to communicate with outsiders and had exchanged ambassadors with the king of Portugal as early as the 1400s. These families remain important in the political, cultural, and economic life of this area to this day. The first president of independent Togo, Sylvanus Olympio, was a descendant of an Afro-Brazilian family. He was killed in a coup in 1963, but his sons are still important political figures in the country today.

The Slave Coast was also the destination of some groups of African-American colonists during the 19th century. Bishop SAMUEL AJAYI CROWTHER, from Sierra Leone, established a mission settlement in Yorubaland in modern Nigeria. Crowther's role was important both in increasing British influence in the area and in encouraging the British government to treat their African colonial subjects decently. He remains a national hero of Nigeria today. The British Gold Coast colony, which included the old Portuguese Elmina settlement after 1880, received many people of color from the Americas as immigrants. Among these were the famous American writer and political activist W. E. B. DuBois, who became a citizen of newly independent Ghana shortly before his death in 1963.

Stewart R. King

FURTHER READING
Curto, Jose C., and Renee Soulodre-La France, eds. *Africa and the Americas: Interconnections during the Slave Trade.* Trenton, N.J.: Africa World Press, 2004.

SLAVE OWNERS
One of the most surprising facts about free people of color is that significant numbers of them owned slaves themselves. In some cases, their slaves were their FAMILY members, whom they had ransomed from other owners and who were destined for MANUMISSION, but it was also not uncommon for free people of color to employ dozens of slaves in their farms and businesses. This fact presented a challenge to the racial hierarchy at the time, because blacks were not supposed to be able to exercise leadership. It also challenges our ideas about race and slavery today because we assume that there should have been racial solidarity between free and enslaved blacks that would prevent the one from oppressing the other. White observers and commentators on the colonial scene at the time suggested that free people of color were harsher in their treatment of their slaves than were white masters. Today, we suspect these commentators of having a bias, but it is hard to find the evidence to prove them wrong. Paradoxically, white elites often opposed permitting free people of color to own slaves because it was felt that the free people of color would help the enslaved out of feelings of racial solidarity.

Acquiring Slaves
Free people of color who were the children of wealthy white men often received slaves as gifts or legacies from their fathers. The young MULATTO men James and Charles Hérivaux, for example, inherited hundreds of slaves when their father died in SAINT-DOMINGUE in the 1770s, though they were not able to take possession until after a long lawsuit against more distant white kin in FRANCE. They were

not alone: In Virginia, John Custis, father-in-law of Martha Dandridge Custis, later GEORGE WASHINGTON's wife, had a mixed-race son, Jack Custis, to whom he left half of his estate, including dozens of slaves. The boy died within a few years of his father, without having any children of his own; Martha inherited the property, and the land and slaves finally came into the hands of George Washington. Part of this estate was the farm that is now Arlington National Cemetery outside Washington D.C.

Free people of color could also acquire slaves on their own, by purchase or as a reward from the government. JUAN GARRIDO, an African man who accompanied Cortéz to MEXICO in the early 1500s, was awarded a large hacienda in Michoacán, where he employed several black overseers who were apparently slaves. We do not know whether they were part of the grant of the plantation or he purchased them separately. Pierre-Guillaume Provoyeur, a mason and urban real estate developer in CAP FRANÇAIS/CAP-HAÏTIEN, SAINT-DOMINGUE, bought several slaves off slave ships and trained them in building trades to help him in his business. The use of slave labor was common in ARTISANS' workshops throughout the Americas. African slaves with needed skills could sometimes be bought, or, if not, the craft master could train slaves as his apprentices. Training other people's slaves was a source of income for free colored artisans. Pierre Toussaint, of Saint-Domingue and New York, was sent to be an apprentice by his master, a white planter, to a master hairdresser while still a slave and then gained his freedom and became a prominent free black artisan in his turn.

Free people of color participated in the Atlantic slave trade as buyers and resellers of imported slaves. ZABEAU BELLANTON, a professional cook in Cap-Français, Saint-Domingue, was an active buyer and seller of imported slaves. She was apparently selling slaves imported to the colony by English smugglers violating the French mercantilist restrictions on free trade. The slave ships often had many sailors of color; indeed, slave ship captains sometimes sought out black seamen because their presence on the ship served to reassure the African slaves (*see also* MERCHANT SEAMEN).

Rental of slaves was an option for those without the capital to purchase then outright. TOUSSAINT LOUVERTURE, the liberator hero of Haiti, rented half a dozen slaves from his son-in-law in 1779 in order to start work on a new farm. Renting slaves could prove to be very costly over the long run, but for somebody just starting up, especially a free person of color who might have limited access to credit, it was an option.

Restrictions on Slave Ownership
Placing free blacks in charge of slaves was a challenge to racial stereotypes, and laws or social customs often put

obstacles in the way. In JAMAICA, for example, the law required a fixed ratio of free supervisors to slave workers, on pain of payment of a fine. White people were allowed under this law to supervise twice as many slaves as free people of color. In theory, free colored masters were thereby obliged to hire white managers, but in fact many of them, as well as many white-owned plantations, simply paid the fine, and the government grew to depend on the fines as a source of revenue and kept them affordable. In many states in the Southern United States, especially in the Lower South, slave codes explicitly forbade free blacks to own slaves (see BLACK CODES IN THE UNITED STATES). However, these laws were mainly passed in the 1830s and 1840s, and free blacks could generally keep slaves they already owned. The mixed-race Metoyer family of LOUISIANA, along with some hundreds of other free black Louisianans, Floridians, and South Carolinians, managed to keep large slave workforces until the AMERICAN CIVIL WAR. In Louisiana and FLORIDA, which had once been French or Spanish colonies, blacks whose ancestors had been free before the Americans conquered the territory benefited from treaty provisions that protected their rights to own slaves. In the French, Spanish, and Portuguese colonies one finds the fewest legal restrictions on slave ownership by free people of color. In these colonies, free people of color owned significant proportions of all slaves in the colony. This total reached approximately one-quarter of all slaves in Saint-Domingue, or about 125,000 by 1789. We do not have as good a statistical picture for BRAZIL, but anecdotal evidence suggests that the situation there was about the same. In the COFFEE CULTIVATION region of Vassouras in northern Brazil, there was a large class of free black and mixed-race planters who owned a total of thousands of slaves at the height of the region's prosperity. Free black planters and owners of workshops in Mexico in the 16th and 17th centuries owned many slaves, but most of the very large slave-worked plantations that sprang up there in the 18th century were owned by whites. The proportion of slaves owned by free coloreds in Spanish America probably declined significantly after 1750, not because of legal restrictions, but because of the difficulty free people of color had getting access to capital to participate in a more vibrant international market after the Bourbon Reforms. In the British and Dutch Caribbean, there were few free black planters, but artisans and small businessmen in the cities frequently owned a few slaves.

Treatment of Slaves

Writers on colonial affairs in the 18th and 19th centuries, when they took note of the phenomenon that free people of color owned slaves, generally argued that slaves preferred white masters because masters of color were harsher and more arbitrary. For example, MÉDÉRIC-LOUIS-ÉLIE MOREAU DE ST-MÉRY, the Martiniquan lawyer and encyclopedist, argued that free colored women punished their slaves more harshly than white women. Girod de Chantrans, a Swiss visitor to Saint-Domingue and Guadeloupe in the 18th century, thought that most brothel keepers were free colored women, who often forced their slaves to work as prostitutes (see PROSTITUTES AND COURTESANS). It is easy to dismiss these arguments as propaganda for a racially stratified social hierarchy. There are plenty of anecdotes of good relationships of free colored masters and their slaves—as, of course, there are of white masters and their slaves. This anecdotal evidence does not really tell us much about the conditions for slaves in general. In Saint-Domingue, historical demographers working on mortality rates of slaves concluded that slaves owned by free people of color had lower mortality rates than those owned by whites, but this may be entirely due to the dominance of free people of color in COFFEE cultivation, while SUGAR CULTIVATION plantations in the colony were mostly owned by whites. Sugar cultivation is much more difficult and dangerous work than coffee growing. No similar work on slave mortality rates in other colonies has been published.

Paradoxically, governments justified the regulations in many colonies that prevented free people of color from owning slaves or taxed them more heavily with the claim that free people of color would induce the slaves to rebel. To the extent that this belief was based on a presumption of racial solidarity between free and enslaved people of color, this is obviously a contradictory belief. However, it was probably true that slaves were encouraged to think of their condition as not entirely absolute and changeless if they could see people of color around them who were free. In this sense, the free person of color was a subversive influence by his or her mere existence. Moreover, RUNAWAY SLAVES could "pass" more easily where there were large free populations of color. In fact, most runaway slaves in the Caribbean did not join settlements of MAROONS, but instead were LIVING "AS FREE" in towns.

In one ironic case of this nature, in Saint-Domingue, a free colored master found his runaway slave living in a distant city, working, of all things, as a slave catcher with the rural POLICE. The runaway slave was able to borrow enough money from his comrades and his white officer to buy his freedom and keep his job. This case illustrates the many paradoxes of the situation of free people of color: The white authorities needed free men of color to serve in the colonial defense forces. At the same time, the free population of color served as a cloak for a large, unregulated population of people living "as free." Finally, the master in this case, also a free man of color, needed his slaves to work just as the white masters did. The colony needed free people of color to be successful as masters of slaves and plantations since they owned much of the productive land in the colony and were responsible for what was, by the 1780s, its most profitable agricultural sector, coffee.

Peasant and Transitional Slavery

While plantation slavery was the most common situation for slaves, whether owned by free people of color or by whites, some slaves owned by free people of color were not exploited in the same way as plantation slaves but were more like subordinate family members. In this sense, the free people of color were "easier" masters than were whites, who were much less likely to live as PEASANTS in most parts of the Americas. Peasant slavery was similar to the pattern of slavery found in the West and Central African societies where the slaves and the ancestors of the free people of color had lived. In some cases, as in the maroon settlements in many colonies, the masters were consciously reproducing the model of slave ownership they knew from Africa. In other cases, we can assume that similar conditions produced similar outcomes without much conscious intent.

Free people of color who acquired land in the plantation colonies of the Americas were often relegated to poorer plots. Often, colonial governments allocated marginal land far from ports or roads to prospective planters along with the more productive plots they actually wanted in order to encourage development of remote areas. For the white planters, these remote plots were obvious choices when giving or selling land to free people of color. The location and productivity of these plots made commercial farming on them difficult anyway, and in addition free people of color had more difficulty borrowing money to buy the slaves, machinery, and livestock necessary for successful cash-crop farming. Peasant farming was an alternative, if not an entirely comfortable one. The slaves who belonged to peasant farmers were peasants themselves: Master and slave lived and worked side by side.

As an example of this way of life, the two sisters (or possibly daughters) of the free black captain VINCENT OLIVIER lived on a small farm in the Saint-Suzanne canton in Saint-Domingue. This was a mountainous and heavily forested region where many poor people of color lived. Captain Olivier was approximately 100 years old when he died in 1781; the two women could not have been much younger. The two owned one male slave, aged 78 in 1787, and a little girl, aged nine. The four of them shared a 30-square-meter house with their livestock. They owned a few very simple pieces of furniture, a few plates, and not much else. The women earned cash from time to time by renting out their young slave as a house servant, while the old man and the two old ladies grew food on several small plots of land, totaling in all less than four hectares. When the old ladies died, their land was sold, with the condition that the old slave be allowed to live on it for the remainder of his life.

Many of the "slaves" of peasant farmers were their own kinsfolk, though this does not appear to have been the case in the Olivier household. Most slave societies placed substantial restrictions on manumission, in the form of taxes or the requirement that masters seek the approval of courts or legislatures. These restrictions were especially onerous for free people of color, since they generally had fewer resources than whites—indeed, it was the intent of these laws to hinder self-purchase and ransom of slaves, seen as disruptive to the discipline of the slave population. If one member of a family were able to become free, that person might well become the titular "master" of the remainder of the family, as he or she was able to purchase relatives but not to obtain the requisite permissions or pay the required taxes. Since all the disposable income of the family was going toward purchase and manumission of family members, there would be little left over to capitalize a farm, and thus peasant farming would be a common default option. Additionally, in the remote frontier areas where peasant holdings were often found, the lack of legal manumission papers for some family members would be less of a hardship for them.

Stewart R. King

FURTHER READING

Berlin, Ira. *Slaves without Masters: The Free Negro in the Antebellum South*. New York: New Press, 2007.

Stein, Stanley L. *Vassouras: A Brazilian Coffee County, 1850–1900: The Roles of Planter and Slave in a Plantation Society*. Princeton, N.J.: Princeton University Press, 1986.

SMALLS, ROBERT (1839–1915) *American naval officer and politician*

Robert Smalls gained fame with a daring escape during the AMERICAN CIVIL WAR and went on to become one of the nation's first black statesmen and an important figure in the political history of RECONSTRUCTION IN THE UNITED STATES in SOUTH CAROLINA. Born on April 5, 1839, in Beaufort, South Carolina, to the slaves Robert and Lydia Smalls, he grew up a slave in CHARLESTON, SOUTH CAROLINA, where he was forced to work in a number of jobs. He taught himself to read and write and developed the seafaring skills that would enable his escape.

Smalls became famous on May 13, 1862, when, while working as a pilot in the port of Charleston, he delivered the Confederate NAVY ship *Planter* to the Union navy. He began by smuggling his wife and three children onto the

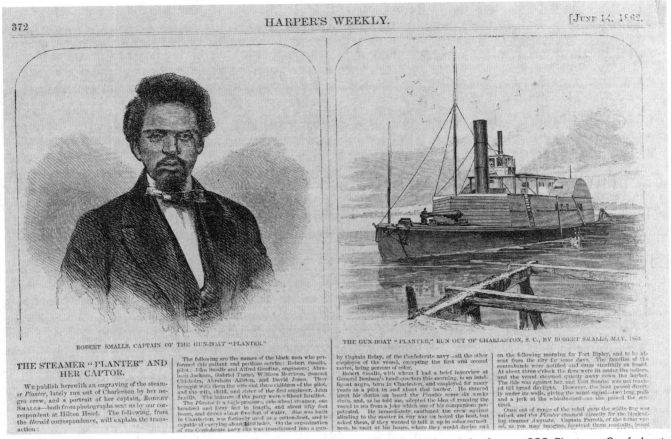

ROBERT SMALLS, CAPTAIN OF THE GUN-BOAT "PLANTER."

THE GUN-BOAT "PLANTER," RUN OUT OF CHARLESTON, S. C., BY ROBERT SMALLS, MAY, 1862.

Illustrations from an 1862 issue of *Harper's Weekly* of Robert Smalls (1839–1915) and the former CSS *Planter,* a Confederate navy gunboat that he took over and delivered to the Union side. Smalls became commander of the *Planter* in Union service, thus becoming the first African American to command a U.S. Navy warship. After the American Civil War, he became a civil servant, served as a member of Congress, and was a major general in the South Carolina militia. *(Library of Congress)*

ship, hoisting the Confederate flag, and boldly sailing past other Confederate ships. As soon as he was past the range of Confederate gunfire, he replaced the flag with a flag of surrender and presented the ship to the Union commander. The U.S. government happily accepted the "contraband" ship and manpower and rewarded Smalls and his crew. Smalls was later made the official commander of the ship, as well as ultimately holding the rank of captain in the U.S. Navy. He served in that role throughout the remainder of the war.

Smalls also used his fame to help gain support for an important project that was to set the stage for Reconstruction—the Port Royal Experiment. This project, which began in December 1861, was an effort to prove black worthiness for freedom by preparing abandoned slaves in Port Royal and the Sea Islands off the coast of South Carolina to support themselves after the war. It was, as the historian Willie Lee Rose describes, a "Rehearsal for Reconstruction." Smalls contributed to this project by appealing to New Yorkers for books, schools, and clothing for the freed persons. He also provided an important

symbol to Sea Islanders, who used his legacy of bravery to support their local efforts to raise funds. Finally, he contributed a great deal to education efforts by buying and donating an eight-room, two-story building to be used as a school for black children in Beaufort.

After the war, Smalls played a prominent role in South Carolina's Reconstruction efforts. He served in the state senate in 1868–70 and was elected to the U.S. House of Representatives in 1875. He served in Congress for five terms; there he worked for the legal protection of mixed-race children and against SEGREGATION, especially through his fight for equal travel accommodations for African Americans. In 1895, he participated in the South Carolina constitutional convention, as one of six black representatives. After his congressional career, he served as a major general in the South Carolina MILITIA and as a customs collector for the port of Beaufort. In Beaufort, he bought the house in which he had once lived as a slave, and it was there that he died on February 23, 1915.

Beverly C. Tomek

FURTHER READING

Miller, Edward A. *Gullah Statesman: Robert Smalls from Slavery to Congress, 1839–1915.* Columbia: University of South Carolina Press, 1995.

Rose, Willie Lee. *Rehearsal for Reconstruction: The Port Royal Experiment.* New York: Vintage Books, 1964.

Quay, Okon Edet. *From Slavery to Public Service: Robert Smalls (1839–1915).* New York: Oxford University Press, 1971.

SMITH, VENTURE (1729–1805) *American farmer and author*

Born in 1729 and said to be the son of a prince, Venture Smith was captured in Africa as a child and taken to America. In 1765, he purchased his freedom and began working to purchase freedom for his entire family. We know details of his life because he gave a narrative of that life to a CONNECTICUT schoolteacher, Elisha Mays, who compiled the information and published it in 1798 under the title *A Narrative of the Life and Adventures of Venture, a Native of Africa, but Resident above Sixty Years in the United States of America, Related by Himself.*

Venture Smith was born Broteer Furro in West Africa. According to the narrative, he was from the savannah region of the continent, descended from ancestors much larger than the average height and weight of the time. When he was about seven years old, he was kidnapped by a tribe of Africans who worked for slave dealers and forced to march to the western coast of Africa. In 1736 or 1737, Robertson Mumford purchased Smith for four gallons of rum and a piece of calico and renamed him *Venture*, because he considered the purchase a business venture. Smith's sale at the modern seaport of Anomabu, in modern Ghana, makes it likely that he was from somewhere in modern Ghana, Togo, or Benin. (*See also* SLAVE COAST, BENIN, AND THE BIGHT OF BIAFRA.)

The ship with Smith and 260 other slaves set sail for BARBADOS. According to Smith's narrative, by the time of the ship's arrival, more than 60 of the original 260 slaves on board had died of smallpox. Many of the survivors were sold to planters on Barbados, but Smith and some of the other slaves were sent to RHODE ISLAND, where they arrived in 1737. Smith went to Mumford's residence on Fishers Island in Connecticut, where he remained until 1752. Growing up, he worked in the residence. As Smith grew older, Mumford switched him to harder tasks and administered more severe punishments.

Smith married another slave, named Meg, when he was 22. A short time later, he and an Irish indentured servant named Heddy attempted to escape Mumford. They headed south to Long Island, New York. Heddy stole provisions and clothing from Smith, and Smith turned him in to the authorities, who returned him to Mumford.

Venture and Meg had their first child, Hannah, in 1752. Mumford separated Smith from his family less than a month later by selling him to Thomas Stanton in Stonington, Connecticut. Stanton bought Meg and Hannah in 1753, reuniting the family. Smith began saving money, which he earned by selling produce he grew and by performing outside jobs, so he could purchase freedom for himself and his family.

Two more children joined the family—Solomon in 1756 and Cuff in 1758. Smith was sold twice more, finally to Colonel Oliver Smith in 1760 in Stonington. He agreed to let Venture Smith work for money when he did not need him at home. Venture showed his appreciation by taking Smith's last name for himself and his family. Around 1765, Venture Smith purchased his freedom for 71 pounds and two shillings, the equivalent of more than $10,000 today.

Now a free man, Smith moved to Long Island and began working to free his family. He earned enough money from cutting wood for four years to purchase the freedom of his sons, Solomon and Cuff, in 1769. Solomon died of scurvy in 1773, while on a whaling expedition (*see also* MERCHANT SEAMEN). Cuff fought in the WAR OF AMERICAN INDEPENDENCE, 1775–83, serving as a Continental soldier in 1781–83. After he purchased freedom for his sons, Smith purchased the freedom of an unrelated slave for £60.

In 1773, four years after purchasing his sons' freedom, he purchased his wife, Meg, who was pregnant, from Thomas Stanton. The couple had a boy, whom they named Solomon in honor of his deceased brother. When Smith purchased his daughter, Hannah, in 1775, he had freed his entire family.

A year later, Smith purchased a farm in Haddam Neck, Connecticut. He made a living by fishing, whaling, farming his land, and trading on the Solomon River, located near his residence. He became well known in New England, renowned for his size (more than six feet tall and 300 pounds) and strength. One legend had Smith wielding a nine-foot ax to cut wood. In 1798, he relayed his story to Elisha Mays. Smith's story is one of inspiration and perseverance.

Venture Smith died on September 19, 1805. Meg died four years later. The narrative of Smith's life was reprinted numerous times in the 19th and 20th centuries. In 2006, with the permission of more than a dozen of Smith's living descendants, scientists dug up Smith's grave to look for artifacts and take DNA samples from him and his wife. Unfortunately, the soil was so acidic that almost no bones remained. The scientists were able to obtain some DNA samples from the forearm bones of Meg Smith. The DNA obtained was damaged and results were inconclusive.

John McLane

FURTHER READING

Africans in America/Part 2/Venture Smith. Available online. URL: http://www.pbs.org./wgbh/aia/part2/2p80.html. Accessed January 10, 2011.

A Narrative of the Life and Adventures of Venture, a Native of Africa, but Resident above Sixty Years in the United States of America, Related by Himself. Middletown, Conn.: J. S. Stewart, 1897. Available online. URL: http://docsouth.unc. edu/neh/venture2/menu.html. Accessed January 10, 2011.

Works by Venture Smith. Available online. URL: http://www. gutenberg.org/author/Venture+Smith at Project Gutenberg. Accessed January 10, 2011.

SOMERSET V. STEWART (SOMERSETT V. STEUART)

The case of *Somerset v. Stewart* has long occupied a near-mythic place in the history of the British-American law of slavery as establishing the rule that slavery was per se contrary to the common law of BRITAIN and therefore any slave setting foot on British soil was immediately set free. Abolition movements in recent scholarship has conclusively proven that this was in fact not the holding reached by Lord Mansfield, chief justice of King's Bench, that set James Somerset (or Somersett) free in 1772. Lord Mansfield's opinion held only that slaveholders could not call upon British law or officials either to capture escaped slaves or to compel their slaves forcibly to leave Britain against their will.

In November 1769, James Somerset had been taken to Britain as the slave of Charles Stewart (or Steuart), the cashier and paymaster of customs for the British colonies in North America. Stewart had temporarily returned to Britain to tend to his business affairs and obligations in London. Two years later, in October 1771, Somerset decided he had had enough of slavery and escaped into the community of freed persons of color of LONDON, ENGLAND. Having tracked down Somerset by late November, Stewart seized him and turned him over to the captain of the JAMAICA-bound ship *Ann and Mary*, John Knowles, in order to have Somerset taken there and sold on behalf of Stewart. Alerted to his plight, Somerset's friends sought out the leading abolitionist of the day, GRANVILLE SHARP, who prevailed upon Lord Mansfield to issue a writ of habeas corpus on November 28 against Captain Knowles, ordering him to take Somerset before the chief justice to justify his detention of Somerset aboard the *Ann and Mary*. Knowles brought Somerset before Lord Mansfield the first week of December, which was nearly the end of the court's current term. The chief justice, having heard Knowles's explanation that Somerset had been given into his custody by his owner, Charles Stewart, in order to be sold in the Jamaica slave market, referred the case for a full hearing before the Court of King's Bench at the start of the next term, in February 1772. Somerset was temporarily released on a bond of surety for his appearance then.

After both sides had obtained some of the best barristers then practicing in Britain to argue their cause, King's Bench began hearing arguments on February 7, 1772. On four different days between then and the end of May, they presented their arguments. Somerset's lawyers argued forcefully "that no man at this day is, or can be, a Slave in England." Because slavery undeniably violated the law of nature, the lawyers contended, it could only be supported by a local law explicitly establishing and supporting it. Since slavery was not so established by either the common law or statute law of Britain, Charles Stewart, therefore, had no rights over Somerset, and Somerset must be set free. Several precedents in British law were cited for support, including an earlier assertion by the lord chancellor of England in the 1726 case of *Shanley v. Harvey* that "as soon as a slave enters England he becomes free." The fact that slavery was established by law in the colonies could have no relevance to Stewart's claims over Somersett in the absence of any specific British law recognizing such rights within Britain. Furthermore, to uphold Stewart's claim would leave Britain at the mercy of slavery "in all its various forms, in all the gradations of inventive cruelty," and would transform Britain, "so famous for public liberty," into "the chief seat of private tyranny."

Stewart's lawyers asserted to the contrary that the fact that slavery was established by the colonial laws of Virginia and Jamaica meant British courts should give deference to a slaveholder's rights while in Britain through the principle of judicial comity. Not to give force to such foreign or colonial laws would unjustly deprive slaveholders of their rightful property interests merely because they had traveled from a British colony to Britain itself. In addition, the right of Britain's Royal Africa Company to procure slaves in Africa and then sell them in the American colonies was acknowledged by British law, and this legal commerce had led to at least 14,000 slaves' being taken into Britain by British subjects who had bought them in the colonies. All of this, Somerset's lawyers argued, raised "very strong and particular grounds of apprehension, if the relation in which they stand to their masters is utterly to be dissolved on the instant of their coming into England." A final argument was raised that since contracts for "service for life" by indentured servants were in fact recognized by British law, then the British courts were in fact "authorized to enforce a service for life in the slave, that being a part of his situation before his coming hither; which, as not incompatible, but agreeing with our laws, may justly subsist here."

On June 22, 1772, Lord Mansfield delivered his ruling in *Somerset v. Stewart*, stating that "so high an act of dominion" as holding an escaped slave captive for the purpose of resale abroad is of such a nature that it can only be upheld if expressly "recognized by the law of the country where it is used." In setting Somerset free, Lord Mansfield held that the institution of slavery is "so odious, that nothing can be suffered to support it, but positive law. Whatever inconveniences, therefore, may follow from a decision, I cannot say this case is allowed or approved by the law of England; and therefore the black must be discharged." However, this ruling only applied to Somersett; it did not in itself free every slave then held in Britain. At the close of the last day of arguments in May, Lord Mansfield had purposely left aside the question of whether a slaveholder had a legally enforceable right to the slave's service while in Britain and expressly stated that "contract for sale of a slave is good here; the sale is a matter to which the law properly and readily attaches, and will maintain the price according to the agreement." He had further stated that "the setting 14,000 to 15,000 men at once free loose by a solemn opinion, is much disagreeable in the effects it threatens."

Notwithstanding the narrow nature of Lord Mansfield's opinion in *Somerset v. Stewart*, the popular perception that it did in fact free every slave within Britain almost immediately spread through the British abolition movement and the growing community of escaped slaves and freed persons of color in Britain. Within a month, James Somersett was writing to other slaves in Britain that they had been set free. In a letter dated July 10, 1772 (found by the historian James Oldham among Charles Stewart's personal papers in the late 20th century), "an acquaintance named John Riddell" informed Stewart that his slave "Mr. Dublin [had] run away [having] told the Servants that he had rec'd a letter from his Uncle Sommerset acquainting him that Lord Mansfield had given them their freedom." Six years later in 1778, the Scottish case of *Knight v. Wedderburn* would be brought by Joseph Knight, a slave who had been bought in Jamaica and then taken to Scotland in 1769 by John Wedderburn. Knight, with the help of others, learned to read and eventually came across a newspaper article about the *Somerset* case. Resolved to assert his freedom, Knight refused to continue in Wedderburn's service. Apprehended and taken before the local justice of the peace, Knight was informed that he had no right to leave Wedderburn's service. Knight then applied by petition to the local Sheriff's Court, which ruled that slavery was against the laws of Scotland. On appeal to Scotland's highest civil court, the Courts of Session, the sheriff's ruling was upheld, the Courts of Session holding that Wedderburn "had no right to the Negro's service for any space of time, nor to send him out of the country against his consent."

The cases of *Somerset v. Stewart* and *Knight v. Wedderburn* significantly influenced the eventual success of the abolition movement within Great Britain and abroad.

They would be printed in tandem in *Howell's State Trials* in 1809, and American courts would later cite the *State Trials* joint report to support judicial efforts to free slaves there, including the MASSACHUSETTS case of *Commonwealth v. Aves* in 1836 (also known as *Med's case*). Finally, in 1833, the British Act of Parliament abolishing colonial slavery would legislatively establish the broader rule of freedom throughout Britain and Ireland, providing "that all Slaves who may at any Time previous to the passing of this Act have been brought with the Consent of their Possessors, and all apprenticed Labourers who may hereafter . . . be brought, into any part of the United Kingdom of Great Britain and Ireland, shall from and after the passing of this Act be absolutely free to all Intents and Purposes whatsoever" (3 & 4 Wm.4 c. 73).

Note: Unless otherwise noted, all quotes from *Somerset v. Stewart,* Lofft 1–20 , 98 Eng. Rep. 499-510 (1772) and *Knight v. Wedderburn,* 33 Morison's Dict. Dec. 14545–14549 (1778).

Erin Rahne Kidwell

FURTHER READING

Brown, Christopher Leslie. *Moral Capital: Foundations of British Abolitionism.* Chapell Hill: University of North Carolina Press, 2006.

Byrd, Alexander X. *Captives and Voyagers: Black Migrants across the Eighteenth-Century British Atlantic World.* Baton Rouge: Louisiana State University Press, 2008.

Drescher, Seymour. *From Slavery to Freedom: Comparative Studies in the Rise and Fall of Atlantic Slavery.* New York: New York University Press, 1999.

Gerzina, Gretchen. *Black England: Life before Emancipation.* London: John Murray, 1995.

Lascelles, E. C. P. *Granville Sharp and the Freedom of Slaves in England.* New York: Negro University Press, 1969.

Oldham, James. *The Mansfield Manuscripts and the Growth of English Law in the Eighteenth Century.* Chapel Hill: University of North Carolina Press, 1992.

———. "New Light on Mansfield and Slavery." *Journal of British Studies* 27 (1988): 45–68.

Shyllon, F. O. *Black Slaves in Britain.* Oxford: Oxford University Press, 1974.

Weiner, M. S. "Notes and Documents: New Biographical Evidence on Somersett's Case." *Slavery and Abolition* 23 (2002): 121–136.

Wise, Steven M. *Though the Heavens May Fall: The Landmark Trial That Led to the End of Human Slavery.* Cambridge, Mass.: Da Capo Press, 2005.

SOUTH AMERICAN WARS OF LIBERATION
(1809–1824)

The Spanish colonies of South America gained their independence between 1809 and 1824 as the result of a series of bloody wars against SPAIN and among factions within each colony. Each colony has its own history, but there are significant common elements, the most important of which is the participation in other liberation struggles of armies from the places where the struggle was first victorious, especially ARGENTINA and VENEZUELA (for comparison, *see also* MEXICAN WAR OF INDEPENDENCE. The Argentine army of liberation, led by José de San Martín (1778–1850), and the Venezuelan army, led by Simón Bolívar (1783–1830) and José Antonio Páez (1790–1873), included many men of color. Free people of color served in disproportionate numbers in all the liberating armies, but also in the armies raised by Spain and by conservative forces in the colonies trying to prevent independence.

Free colored soldiers joined the various armies of the Wars of Liberation for a variety of reasons. Soldiers were paid, though irregularly, and provided food and housing. They also had opportunities to loot and in some cases preferential access to government grants of land, government jobs after the end of their service, and MANUMISSION for those who were enslaved at the beginning of their service. These material motivations were the main reasons that people of color joined the armed forces during the colonial period (*see also* REGULAR ARMY) in disproportionate numbers in keeping with their general poverty. They still were powerful motivators of enlistment during the revolutionary period, the more so because economic dislocation caused by war meant that people were in greater need. A bonus paid for enlistment might prevent a refugee family from starving.

But free people of color also responded to important ideological appeals from both sides. The rebel forces were generally organized around a liberal idea of nationalism that grew out of the FRENCH REVOLUTION, which began in 1789. The French revolutionaries had a conflicted relationship with people of color, but the logic of their beliefs in the fundamental equality of all human beings and the importance of the broadest possible participation of all citizens in the nation's economy and politics clearly appealed to free people of color. They were systematically excluded from some of the benefits of society under the colonial regime, and although some individuals could gain access to higher levels of society, this was an exception to a generalized system of racial inequality. The leaders of the Spanish American independence forces were wealthy locally born whites, the criollos, many of whom were SLAVE OWNERS, but they espoused the liberal Enlightenment values of THOMAS JEFFERSON and Jean-Jacques Rousseau. Educated and socially prominent free people of color often shared economic status with wealthy whites, owning slaves and land themselves, and thus shared their resentment of Spanish mercantilist rules and the political dominance of Spanish-born whites. For all these reasons, the free colored elite, as, for example, the *pardos bienméritos* of Venezuela, generally supported the independence movement.

On the other hand, slaves and poorer free people of color often saw local prominent whites as their enemies. Whites and wealthy free people of mixed race were the owners, the master class, who had supported the system that so oppressed the majority of blacks. The institutions of Spanish colonial rule were seen, by many poorer or more excluded blacks, as potential allies. The Spanish, through both the ROMAN CATHOLIC CHURCH and the government administration, had set up various systems over the years to oversee the treatment of slaves and to allow some sort of inclusion for free people of color (for example, *see also* CÉDULAS DE GRACIAS AL SACAR and CATHOLIC CONFRATERNITIES). Many slaves saw the king and the church as their protectors. Persistent rumors, common throughout the slave societies of the Americas, held that the king had decreed regulations limiting the work hours or punishments of slaves and that the masters were conspiring to prevent these laws from taking force. These rumors had some basis in fact—many regulations ameliorating the slave regime in the Americas were never enforced because of the resistance of slave owners. So when the master class rebelled against the king, slaves and poor free coloreds thought they knew on which side their interests lay and many opposed independence. The Venezuelan royalist army headed by José Tomás Boves (1782–1814) included many soldiers of color, especially slaves who had run away from pro-independence masters. Boves's forces conducted a particularly bloody campaign against pro-independence elites in eastern Venezuela. His forces sought out and killed prominent whites and committed several general massacres of white civilians. His campaign culminated in the Battle of Urica (1814), in which Boves himself was killed, but his forces, triumphant, destroyed the troops of the Second Venezuelan Republic and drove Simón Bolívar into exile in Haiti.

Bolívar and his men were ultimately triumphant, however. One reason was that the llaneros, or cowboys of the southern plains, many of whom were free people of color, who had been a source of strength for Boves before 1814, became, under the leadership of Páez, a strong component of the new republican army. Poor people in Spanish America, both the Afro-descended and those descended from Indians and whites, often chose sides based on personal or patronage relationships, rather than ideology. If the *patrón* changed sides, his clients changed sides too. When Boves was replaced by Páez, it was the ideology of the leader that was important.

The southern independence armies were also ultimately successful. Three campaigns in the region of the Río de la Plata between 1811 and 1813 cleared the modern

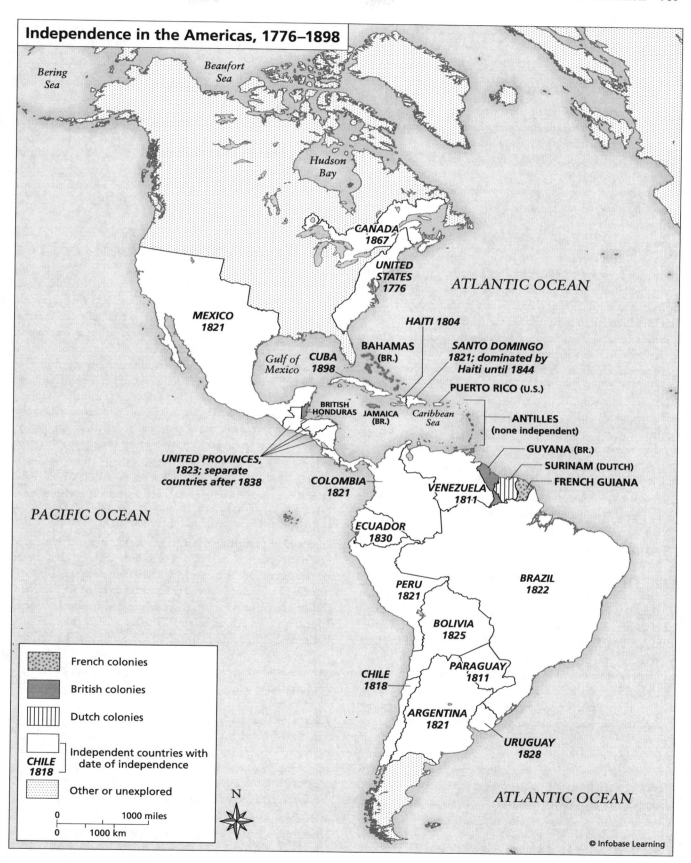

Independence in the Americas, 1776–1898

Bering Sea

Beaufort Sea

Hudson Bay

CANADA 1867

UNITED STATES 1776

ATLANTIC OCEAN

MEXICO 1821

Gulf of Mexico

CUBA 1898

BAHAMAS (BR.)

HAITI 1804

SANTO DOMINGO 1821; dominated by Haiti until 1844

PUERTO RICO (U.S.)

BRITISH HONDURAS

JAMAICA (BR.)

Caribbean Sea

ANTILLES (none independent)

UNITED PROVINCES, 1823; separate countries after 1838

COLOMBIA 1821

VENEZUELA 1811

GUYANA (BR.)

SURINAM (DUTCH)

FRENCH GUIANA

PACIFIC OCEAN

ECUADOR 1830

PERU 1821

BRAZIL 1822

BOLIVIA 1825

PARAGUAY 1811

CHILE 1818

ARGENTINA 1821

URUGUAY 1828

ATLANTIC OCEAN

N

French colonies

British colonies

Dutch colonies

Independent countries with date of independence

CHILE 1818

Other or unexplored

0   1000 miles

0   1000 km

© Infobase Learning

nations of Argentina, URUGUAY, and PARAGUAY of Spanish supporters. Many Argentines were happy to settle down and enjoy their independence, but General José de San Martín convinced the governments of the liberated territories to support an expedition ultimately aimed at driving the Spanish from PERU. Peru was the center of Spanish power in South America, and San Martín knew that he could not leave a refuge anywhere on the mainland, or there would be a risk the Spanish would return and recapture the peripheral areas, including Argentina, that had already become independent. He formed an army of the most professional units from all the various proindependence forces in the region, centered on his own Army of the North, which had fought on the frontiers of BOLIVIA against the main Spanish forces. Many of his men were free coloreds from Buenos Aires or Uruguay. The major port cities on both sides of the mouth of the Río de la Plata, Buenos Aires in Argentina and Montevideo in Uruguay, had relatively large free colored populations since they had been major transshipment points for African slaves heading to Peru in the 16th and 17th centuries. These urban populations of people of color were relatively well educated and aware of world events, and so they responded ideologically to San Martín's call to liberate all the people of South America. Moreover, as in Venezuela, economic disruption caused by the war and an unsettled political situation meant that the stability and (somewhat) regular pay in the military were very attractive. San Martín's armies crossed the Andes into CHILE, where they linked up with forces led by his old school friend Bernardo O'Higgins (1778–1842) and defeated the pro-Spanish forces there. Then, the Chilean and Argentine troops moved on to Peru, linking up with Bolívar's Venezuelans and Colombians for the final campaign, with ultimate victory occurring in 1824.

Service in the victorious armies generally had a positive effect on the lives of free men of color who survived the experience. Governments of the postindependence period valued war veterans. Occasional efforts to disarm by liberal governments were short-lived, and armies remained large throughout Latin America during the 19th century. There were many subsequent wars between the newly independent countries, and military coups and rebellions were also common. The skills of free colored veterans were necessary to the new state, and many held high military rank. The Venezuelan free colored general MANUEL PIAR and the Colombian admiral JOSÉ PRUDENCIO PADILLA both ultimately were accused of coup plotting and executed by Bolívar, but not before they had reached high rank and made great contributions to the cause of independence. Other, somewhat less prominent leaders were able to stay alive and profit from their experience. Many ordinary soldiers received land grants, loot, and pay to finance businesses or to purchase the freedom of relatives still in slavery, and other benefits.

Stewart R. King

FURTHER READING

Blanchard, Peter. *Under the Flags of Freedom: Slave Soldiers and the Wars of Independence in Spanish South America.* Pittsburgh: University of Pittsburgh Press, 2008.
Lynch, John. *The Spanish American Revolution, 1808–1826.* New York: W. W. Norton, 1986.

SOUTH CAROLINA

South Carolina is a state of the United States, located along the Atlantic coast between NORTH CAROLINA and GEORGIA. Unlike those two states, South Carolina has only a very small mountainous area. Most of the state consists of coastal islands, low-lying coastal plains, and a "piedmont" area of rolling hills. The climate is warm and damp. The entire state is well watered and reasonably flat, characteristics that made it a good region for plantations. The coastline has many inlets and bays, providing easy access to the ocean. For these reasons, South Carolina was an important part of the plantation zone from the early 18th century onward. The largest city, CHARLESTON, SOUTH CAROLINA, was an important center for Atlantic trade and was the only port where ships in the Atlantic slave trade could deliver their cargoes after the WAR OF AMERICAN INDEPENDENCE (1775–83). Charleston developed a significant population of free people of color in the 18th and early 19th centuries.

Most of the indigenous inhabitants of South Carolina were speakers of languages in the Souian family. There were some Cherokee and Chickasaw living in the state, but most of those larger confederacies lived to the west. South Carolina's Indians were defeated by the colonists in the Yamasee War (1715–17), after which they no longer posed a threat to colonists. Surviving small groups of native people, however, proved welcoming to RUNAWAY SLAVES, and modern South Carolina Indians have a large proportion of African ancestry.

Colonial Period (1526–1775)

The first European explorer to enter what is now South Carolina was Lucas Vázquez de Ayllón (1475–1526), who landed near Georgetown, South Carolina, in 1526 before establishing a short-lived colony in Georgia. Vázquez de Ayllón was accompanied by African slaves whom he took with him from SANTO DOMINGO (*see also* DOMINICAN REPUBLIC). There is no record that he was accompanied by any free Africans or Afro-Spanish, though it is likely, given the fact that Santo Domingo had many free people of color. The next major Spanish incursion into the state, the expedition of Hernando de Soto (1496–1542) in 1539, included several free Afro-Cubans and Afro-Spaniards, along with 50 slaves.

The Spanish made little impact on the region, however, and the first sustained presence of Europeans and Africans began in 1670, when immigrants from BARBADOS arrived in Charleston to create a new colony. Barbados was

The South Carolina legislature, including black representatives, at work in 1873. During much of Reconstruction from 1869 to 1876, the majority of the members of the South Carolina legislature were men of color, the first time a legislature in the Americas had been majority black. *(North Wind Picture Archives via Associated Press)*

the earliest of the British plantation colonies in the Caribbean, and by 1670, land usable for SUGAR CULTIVATION was becoming scarce. The colonists hoped to reproduce their success in the new region. They quickly discovered that, though South Carolina is warm by North American standards, the winters are still too cold for sugar cultivation. The proprietors, the large planters who had financed the original venture and theoretically owned the entire colony, lost a good deal of money trying to figure out a way to make a profit. Finally, they lost control of the colony in 1719, and it was ruled from that point on directly by the British Crown. Smaller producers increasingly took over land and imported slaves, developing a variety of crops, including especially rice. Rice grows very well in the coastal lowlands. The planters imported slaves from SIERRA LEONE, a rice-growing region in West Africa, to teach them the needed technical skills and sold their crops to the island colonies in the Caribbean.

The Barbados immigrants apparently did not include any free people of color from that island, but Caribbean ideas about racial lines and family relationships with people of color persisted in the colony for some time. Under these more relaxed standards, people of mixed race were a separate group from blacks with somewhat higher social status. Fathers were somewhat responsible for their illegitimate children. Therefore, as in many places in the British Caribbean and in LOUISIANA and West FLORIDA—French and Spanish possessions during the 18th century—but unlike any place else in the future United States, South Carolina acquired a small but significant "brown" group of mixed-race free people of color. Later called the "CREOLES," these people filled a similar niche to that filled by mixed-race free coloreds in the British Caribbean. They married within their own group, but women of this caste often had informal unions with white men. They were mainly ARTISANS, though some were small farmers or retail merchants (see also COMMERCE AND TRADE and PROVISION GROUND FARMING). They were few in number—census records in 1770 counted only 53 households in Charleston and 871 in the entire colony. This census counted households that were taxable and certainly overlooked many poorer free people of color (and poorer whites). The census of 1790, somewhat more systematic than the colonial census, counted 1,801 "other free persons" in the state, 350 of them in Charleston. This census was supposed to count every person no matter who he or she was, but many poorer people and those whose titles to liberty were questionable certainly were uncounted. Later censuses were more comprehensive, though there are always questions that marginal people were left out, even in today's census.

Nonetheless, South Carolina was often unwelcoming to free people of color in the colonial period. The Stono Rebellion of 1739, although it was carried out exclusively by slaves, resulted in the colonial legislature's restricting manumissions. Subsequently, and throughout the period of slavery, MANUMISSION was increasingly difficult to obtain. Even if a master wanted to free his or her slaves, permission from the governor or legislature was required and was not always granted. Often large fees or bonds would be required, or the newly freed person would be required to leave the state. These laws changed frequently, normally for the worse, though enforcement was often inconsistent. They did not stop the development of a free colored community, but they did slow it, and as a result South Carolina never did have the large free colored community found in others of the original Thirteen Colonies where slavery existed.

Independence and Early National Period (1776–1822)

The outbreak of the War of American Independence in 1775 led to great changes for free people of color, indeed for all residents, in South Carolina. At first, the South was spared the direct effect of war. South Carolinian white supporters of independence went off to fight in the Continental army in New England and the middle colonies. At home, the colony declared its own independence from Britain some months before the country as a whole did and created a state government. There were many dissidents, however, especially among the population of color. As was common throughout the plantation Americas, slaves and poorer free people of color often saw the king as their protector against local elites, who were their direct oppressors. The rebellion removed any protections that the royal government might actually have been providing to blacks in the colony, minor as they were. The mixed-race people who were legally defined as Indians were actually protected by the royal government, and most Indians saw the independence movement as a threat. Wealthier free people of color, on the other hand, were more likely to share the attitudes of the wealthy whites, who generally supported independence because they thought it would allow free trade, higher profits, and local autonomy. One wealthy free colored man, Thomas Jeremiah, was caught between British authority and rebel white aristocrats and was hanged for organizing a rebel plot on very skimpy evidence in 1775. Ironically, his principal accuser was Henry Laurens (1723–92), a prominent Patriot whose son, John, became an advocate of using free black soldiers to help the rebel cause.

The war came to South Carolina in June 1776 with an abortive British attempt to capture Charleston. The harbor defenses withstood the British seaborne attack, and the small landing party was withdrawn. The British did not return for two and a half years. In February 1779, British

AFRICAN-AMERICAN POPULATION OF SOUTH CAROLINA, 1790–1900

Year	Slaves	Free People of Color	Free People of Color as a Percentage of Total Population	Total Population
1790	107,094	1,801	0.7%	249,073
1800	146,151	3,185	0.9%	345,591
1810	196,365	4,554	1.1%	415,115
1820	291,973	6,712	1.4%	490,309
1830	315,401	7,921	1.4%	581,185
1840	327,038	8,276	1.6%	594,398
1850	384,984	8,960	1.3%	668,507
1860	402,506	9,914	1.4%	703,708
1870		415,814	58.9%	705,606
1880		604,332	60.7%	995,577
1890		688,934	59.8%	1,151,149
1900		782,321	58.4%	1,340,316

forces advancing from their bases in Florida through Georgia captured Port Royal and fought an inconclusive battle. This second invasion ushered in a lasting British presence in the area and had a profound impact on the life of people of color. The British, following up on the 1775 proclamation of JOHN MURRAY, EARL OF DUNMORE in Virginia offering freedom to all slaves who would agree to fight in their armies. They enrolled thousands of black soldiers by the end of the war. Banastre Tarleton (1754–1833), leader of a loyalist dragoon regiment that was the bane of pro-independence forces in the Carolinas, had both blacks and whites in his regiment. As many as half of his soldiers were black at some points in the campaign. In Georgia, a group of loyalist frontiersmen called the King's Rangers included some free blacks from Florida and many people of mixed Indian and African ancestry from the Seminole and Creek tribes (see also BLACK SEMINOLE). The Rangers fought in South Carolina during the 1780 campaign that led to the British capture of Charleston. The British recruited troops from the German states that were part of King George's European domains, who were collectively called Hessians. As disease and battle casualties reduced the strength of Hessian regiments, they were quick to recruit black soldiers into their ranks—the German armies had always been multinational professional forces rather than units composed exclusively of citizens of their own small states, and the Germans had little racial prejudice when compared to British or Americans. The "black Hessians" were famous in the Carolinas as tough troops who struck fear into the hearts of their pro-independence countrymen.

The British captured almost the entire state in 1780. Their American opponents turned to irregular warfare to resist them, and they also enrolled black soldiers in their cause. One prominent South Carolina white leader, John Laurens (1754–82), urged the state legislature to adopt a formal policy of offering freedom to slaves who would fight for the duration of the conflict, but the lawmakers refused. One member of the state Privy Council is reported to have replied that the step was "impolitic" and "disgusting." Laurens, nonetheless, enrolled black soldiers, both slaves whose masters agreed to their service and free blacks, in his irregular unit. Other white guerrilla leaders also employed blacks, though in some cases for noncombatant labor and without a promise of emancipation. Wealthier free blacks were more likely to support the independence movement, though after the fall of Charleston in 1780, their homes and families were hostage to the British, and few continued serving the independence cause.

Ultimately, the British were forced to leave and agree to American independence. The decisive struggle was in Virginia, where the British southern army, under Lord Cornwallis, was forced to surrender at Yorktown in October 1781. In a tragic episode during that battle, General Cornwallis, running short on supplies, decided to expel all the black noncombatants from his camp, and GEORGE WASHINGTON, the American commander, refused to let them through his lines. So many Southern black loyalists starved between the lines, while others were recaptured and hauled back into slavery. The war continued on in a desultory fashion for another two years after Yorktown, however, and the British still controlled Charleston and much of South Carolina. By the end of the war, about one-quarter of the people of color who had lived in South Carolina at the beginning of the war had left for

British-controlled territory. Some immigrated to Nova Scotia, CANADA, with the Northern black loyalists, and many then went on to SIERRA LEONE. Among these was David George (1760?–1832), a black Baptist preacher from rural South Carolina. Others went to the Caribbean, and many settled in the Bahamas (see also BRITISH LESSER ANTILLES).

The black population of South Carolina, free as well as enslaved, grew rapidly after the end of the war, however. The port remained open to slave imports, while other states mainly decided to end the slave trade through their own ports. From 1791 to 1808, when the slave trade was abolished by federal law, Charleston was the only port in the United States that accepted international imports of slaves.

Antebellum Period (1823–1860)
The booming South Carolina economy began to slow in the 1830s. The rapid development of the Deep South states, with their own ports and access to the sea, reduced the importance of Charleston as a port city. The market for South Carolina rice did not disappear, but with the abolition of slavery in the British and French Caribbean (in 1834 and 1848, respectively), the most important bloc of customers, the Caribbean planters, left the marketplace. Slave exports to other states grew from the 1820s on and, of course, after 1808 were not offset by significant numbers of new imports. The rapid increase of COTTON CULTIVATION meant that the inland piedmont region could develop economically, and this did something to offset the relative decline of the coastal region. The cotton boom proved to be a good opportunity for some free people of color. WILLIAM "APRIL" ELLISON, a mixed-race freedman who had been trained as a cotton gin mechanic by his presumed father, a white man also named William Ellison, became one of the largest equipment dealers in South Carolina, owned a large cotton plantation, and bought and sold approximately 900 slaves during his life. In the cities, the free colored community continued to grow. The free mixed-race religious leader JEHU JONES, JR., lived in South Carolina as a young man. He was the first African American ordained a minister in the Lutheran Church, after he studied in a seminary in PHILADELPHIA, PENNSYLVANIA. He attempted to return to Charleston after his ordination in 1832 but was turned away because of a state law that forbade free blacks to immigrate into the state, which also applied to returning residents like Jones.

By this time, the state had begun to place severe restrictions on the rights of free people of color. In part, this was a consequence of the general trend in slave societies, as they mature demographically and economically, to restrict the activities of free people

of color. In South Carolina, this trend took a particularly savage turn after the DENMARK VESEY case of 1821–22. Vesey was a free man of color, originally from the DANISH VIRGIN ISLANDS, who had worked as one of the large class of black MERCHANT SEAMEN and ARTISANS in the port city. He was also active as a lay leader in the AFRICAN METHODIST EPISCOPAL (A.M.E.) CHURCH. In 1821, he was accused of being the leader of a plot among slaves and free people of color in Charleston to rebel against the slave system, burn the city, steal ships, and run away to Haiti. Historians are divided about how real the plot was, but at the time, white South Carolinians took it very seriously. In addition to executing Vesey and some of his alleged coconspirators, the government of South Carolina outlawed the A.M.E. Church, exiled many leading free coloreds, forbade immigration of new free coloreds, and even prevented South Carolinians who had left the state, such as Jehu Jones, Jr., from returning to their homes. Educating blacks, both free and slave, was outlawed, although this particular law was often not enforced against black churches that quietly ran schools for their parishioners. Still, although the free colored community was able to preserve some economic status and some freedom within a repressive system, in general they went backward between 1830 and 1860.

The Civil War (1861–1865)
The first shots of the AMERICAN CIVIL WAR were fired in Charleston harbor, when South Carolina troops bombarded the United States–held Fort Sumter on April 12–13, 1861. South Carolina had been the first state to proclaim its secession from the Union in December 1860. White South Carolinians were early and enthusiastic supporters of the independence of the Confederate States of America. Some black South Carolinians were ambivalent, but most were strong supporters of the Union.

U.S. troops arrived on the South Carolina coast relatively early in the conflict, with an expedition capturing Port Royal, South Carolina, in November 1861. General David Hunter was assigned command of the force, increased in strength to a full army corps, in March 1862. Hunter was an abolitionist and strong supporter of President ABRAHAM LINCOLN, and he put his political clout on the line to work for the elimination of slavery. His forces captured most of the coastal islands and freed the slaves there. He enrolled black men in local self-defense units, which later became among the first regiments of the U.S. Colored Troops (see REGULAR ARMY). The first black armed unit to join the U.S. Army during the conflict was raised in South Carolina, in summer 1862, though it was not officially accepted by the War Department until January 1863, along with other regiments of what became the U.S. Colored Troops. Other black regiments raised in the North, including the 54th MASSACHUSETTS, were assigned to Hunter's command. The Massachusetts men charged the walls of Battery Wagner on Morris Island near Charleston in one of the most famous Civil War actions by black troops on July 18, 1863. The siege of Charleston was ultimately unsuccessful, and the city was finally taken from the landward side by the troops of General William Sherman after his "march through Georgia" in 1864.

The most prominent South Carolina free black, and a leading figure in the postwar black community, was a war hero thanks to his actions during the siege of Charleston. ROBERT SMALLS was legally a slave but was working on his own account, almost LIVING "AS FREE," in Charleston before the war. Smalls was a ship's pilot, a very demanding and technically skilled job essential to the functioning of the port. His family, however, were enslaved, and when the war began, he secretly sympathized with the U.S. cause. He was required by his job to work with the Confederate forces defending the city, however, and he gained an encyclopedic knowledge of the harbor defenses, secret codes used by the Confederates, and other crucial military knowledge. On May 13, 1862, he loaded his family and some other slaves aboard a Confederate NAVY ship, *Planter*, which he was responsible for piloting, and took them out to the blockading Union fleet. He continued to work as the pilot of the ship in U.S. naval service and was ultimately confirmed as its captain, becoming the first African-American commissioned officer in the U.S. Navy. After the war, he went on to become an important businessman and political leader in South Carolina, representing the city in the U.S. House of Representatives for nine years.

Reconstruction and Jim Crow Era (1866–1900)
Smalls is a good example of the important role played by prewar free people of color in the black community of Charleston. Though a tiny fraction of the black population, the South Carolinian prewar free people, along with blacks from the North such as Charlotte Forten (*see also* FORTEN FAMILY), helped create a period of relatively equal rights for blacks and to preserve the community after this period ended in renewed repression. The South Carolina state government almost immediately adopted a new state constitution that did not provide any meaningful rights for blacks aside from the end of slavery. Many Southern states created such black codes in the immediate aftermath of the Civil War (*see also* BLACK CODES IN THE UNITED STATES), but South Carolina's is notable in how similar its provisions were to laws restricting the behavior of free people of color in the antebellum period. The black

codes were quickly overturned by Congress, controlled by Northern radical Republicans, who imposed military government on the Southern states. Under the auspices of the military, a new constitutional convention met in 1868, this time with many black members. The state constitution of 1868 provided for equal rights. Many whites were disenfranchised if they had served the Confederate government. Blacks were an absolute majority in the state's population and controlled politics in the late 1860s and 1870s.

As a result, whites turned to terrorism to achieve their political goals. The KU KLUX KLAN joined locally based groups with similar methods, the most notable of which was called the Red Shirts, to suppress the black vote and intimidate Republican Party leaders. The elections of 1876 and 1882 saw the return to leadership of Democrats, many of whom were former Confederates. The governor, Wade Hampton (1818–1902), a former Confederate army officer, promoted populist policies, mostly aimed at whites, but with provision of at least some social services to blacks as a way to reconcile them to their loss of political power. Overt political violence against blacks was reduced, as paramilitary groups demobilized, turned to peaceful political organizing, or were suppressed by law enforcement. The POLICE, now under the control of the white-dominated government, took on the role of controlling blacks and making sure they stayed "in their place," if necessary by violence. Governor Ben Tillman (1847–1918), who succeeded Hampton, was more overtly racist, and the 1895 constitution passed under his leadership completed the process of disenfranchisement of blacks. His administration also codified SEGREGATION and heightened control of black community institutions by the government. But segregation offered at least some opportunities to blacks. There were black schools, including a public state college to train teachers and agronomists. Other black community institutions such as churches and fraternal groups could function without much interference so long as they did not become involved in politics. Accepting this sort of compromise was the policy advocated by the African-American leader Booker T. Washington (1856–1915) in his famous Atlanta Exposition speech of 1895. Black South Carolina began to pursue its own independent course of economic and social development. It also created its own indigenous group of leaders, progressively reducing the distinctive role of the prewar free people. By 1900, there was very little to distinguish the descendants of the prewar free people from other middle-class blacks, and from then on South Carolina's black community began more and more to resemble those found in other Southern states.

Stewart R. King

FURTHER READING

Harris, J. William. *The Hanging of Thomas Jeremiah: A Free Black Man's Encounter with Liberty.* New Haven, Conn.: Yale University Press, 2009.

Higginson, Thomas. *Black Soldiers/Blue Uniforms: The Story of the First South Carolina Volunteers.* Tuscon, Ariz.: Fireship Press, 2009, originally published 1870 as *Army Life in a Black Regiment.*

Johnson, Michael P., and James L. Roark. *Black Masters: A Free Family of Color in the Old South.* New York: W. W. Norton, 1984.

Jones, George Fenwick. "The Black Hessians: Negroes Recruited by the Hessians in South Carolina and Other Colonies." *South Carolina History Magazine* 83 (October 1982): 287–302.

Koger, Larry. *Free Black Slave Masters in South Carolina, 1790–1860.* Jefferson, N.C.: McFarland, 1985.

Sciway.net, The South Carolina Information Highway. "South Carolina African Americans, 1525–1865." Available online. URL: http://www.sciway.net/afam/slavery/indexs.html. Accessed January 10, 2011.

Wilkramangrake, Marina. *A World in Shadow—the Free Black in Antebellum South Carolina.* Columbia: University of South Carolina Press, 1989.

SPAIN

Spain ruled the largest colonial empire in the Americas from 1492 until most of its colonies gained their independence in the 1810s and 1820s, with the last territories leaving Spanish rule in 1898. The modern nations of ARGENTINA, BOLIVIA, CHILE, COLOMBIA, COSTA RICA, CUBA, the DOMINICAN REPUBLIC, ECUADOR, EL SALVADOR, GUATEMALA, HONDURAS, JAMAICA, MEXICO, NICARAGUA, PANAMA, PARAGUAY, PERU, PUERTO RICO, TRINIDAD AND TOBAGO, URUGUAY, and VENEZUELA, as well as the American states of Arizona, coastal ALABAMA and MISSISSIPPI, CALIFORNIA, Colorado, Nevada, New Mexico, TEXAS, Utah, and the territories that made up the LOUISIANA Purchase were under Spanish rule at some point. Spanish America was one of the largest importers of slaves in the Americas, especially in the 16th and 17th centuries, and Spain itself had many enslaved African inhabitants. Because of elements of Spanish culture, and because of the special economic conditions in the Spanish colonies, many African-born people were able to gain their freedom. The Spanish colonies had large populations of free people of color, as did the homeland in Europe.

Medieval and Renaissance Period (1200–1492)

Spain was finally unified as a nation the same year as the colonial project in the Americas began, 1492. Prior to that time, it had been divided into a number of small kingdoms. However, in 1492 the queen of Castile, Isabel I (1451–1504), and her husband, the king of Aragon, Ferdinand II (1452–1516), conquered the last Muslim kingdom on the Iberian Peninsula, the Emirate of Grenada. Isabel paid for Christopher Columbus's (1451–1506) four voyages across the Atlantic, and the colonies established there were Castilian, ruled by the laws of Castile. Castile had spent hundreds of years locked in war with Muslim Spain. (*See also* ISLAM.) As a result of the successful struggle during the 15th century, much of Castile's territory was inhabited by Muslims or recent converts to Christianity whose ancestors had originated in Africa. The original Muslim conquerors of Spain in the eighth century had been Arabs from southwestern Asia, but for centuries the Moorish kingdoms had been largely cut off from their Arab roots and connected more strongly to sub-Saharan Africa. The Moors ruled the bend of the Niger, the modern nations of Mali and Sénégal, for much of the High Middle Ages, and many Moors were black Africans. Many of the lower class in Castile, especially in the southern provinces along the coast, were African-descended. Castile's laws reflected the ambivalence of Christian, Western European Castilians toward their diverse subject population. Castile's great medieval ruler Alfonso X had published a new law code, LAS SIETE PARTIDAS, in 1265. In this code, he laid out liberal policies for MANUMISSION of slaves and expressed the basic principle that freedom was man's natural state. He also expressed the ROMAN CATHOLIC CHURCH's basic conviction that all human souls were equal and all could achieve salvation and benefit from the "one true faith." On the other hand, he imposed restrictions on people who had converted to Christianity from Islam or Judaism. Race was not an important concern at that time, however. The term *Moor* applied to all Muslims, regardless of skin color. The issue for Castilians was religious affiliation or presumed loyalty to Christianity among recent converts. The fear of false conversions haunted Castilian lawmakers throughout the 15th century. Several revolts by Moriscos, or Moorish workers, took place in the 15th and 16th centuries. The government's reaction was to drive out all who were not willing to convert to Christianity and to impose increasing restrictions on New Christians, as converts and their descendants for several generations were called. These restrictions ultimately led to the establishment of the Spanish Inquisition in 1478. The Roman Catholic Church gave the Spanish Crown unprecedented independence to enable the state to prevent religiously based uprisings. The special supervision by the Inquisition and the limitations on types of employment, access to noble status, admission to university, and even such seemingly trivial matters as dress created a separate, subordinate caste based on ancestry in Spanish society. The treatment of

A 1728 Spanish illustration of the first arrival of Christopher Columbus in the Americas in 1492. Columbus was accompanied by at least one and probably several free people of African descent from southern Spain, and it is at this moment that the history of free people of color in the Americas begins. The Spanish claim to be legitimate owners of their American territories sprang in part from Columbus's actions. He met with Indians, visited and charted islands, set up crosses and other symbolic markers, and proclaimed the sovereignty of the Castilian monarch, Queen Isabella. *(Scala/White Images/Art Resource, NY)*

Spanish and Portuguese Settlements in the Americas, 1600

Santa Fe

NEW SPAIN

ATLANTIC OCEAN

Gulf of Mexico

Florida

Mexico City

Acapulco

Cuba

Jamaica

Hispaniola

Puerto Rico

Santo Domingo

San Juan

Caribbean Sea

NEW SPAIN

Panama

Cartagena

Bogotá

BRAZIL

Lima

PACIFIC OCEAN

PERU

N

Santiago

Buenos Aires

0   600 miles
0   600 km

© Infobase Learning

Spanish claims
Portuguese claims
Viceroyalty borders

New Christians set the model for the treatment of non-whites in the Americas.

While Spain was fighting for national unity, PORTUGAL was expanding down the African coast. The Portuguese established several enclaves along the North African coast and sent expeditions down the Atlantic coast of Africa starting in the mid-1400s. These explorers took back slaves, who, along with slaves purchased from Moorish traders and those captured by the Spanish in their wars, permitted the growth of plantations in southern Portugal. Some of these slaves were sold to Spaniards, and some plantations were established in southern Spain, as well, before 1492. Aragon and the Italian merchants who were their allies had operated plantations on the Mediterranean islands since the time of the Crusades (1100s–1300s). The slaves there were a very diverse group, most of them from eastern Europe or the Middle East, but the techniques transferred easily to these new plantation zones worked by African slaves.

The relatively liberal Castilian laws on manumission meant that at least some of these slaves were able to gain their freedom. They joined the very diverse Castilian working class, alongside ethnically North African Moors and African-descended Moors. Many of these free people of color worked in maritime occupations as MERCHANT SEAMEN, dockworkers, dockside innkeepers, or fishermen. The Portuguese sought out black African sailors for their voyages of discovery as cultural interpreters. When the Spanish began their own voyages of exploration with Columbus's voyages, they followed the same pattern, and many African-descended Castilians participated in the exploration and conquest of the Americas.

The Age of Exploration (1492–1700)

The first groups of explorers and conquerors to go forth from Spain to the Americas were mainly from the southern port cities, home to many free people of color. Among these were JUAN GARRIDO, who had been a slave in Seville, gained his freedom either there or in Hispaniola, and subsequently became a householder of Mexico City. Another case is that of Juan Valiente (1505–33), a free black man from Cádiz who was one of the leaders of the first expedition to Chile. ESTÉBAN DE DORANTES was a slave in Spain and during his decadelong voyage with Álvar Núñez Cabeza de Vaca (1490–1559), only gaining his freedom after the expedition finally arrived in Mexico City in 1537. Subsequently, the colonial project recruited more widely, and there were many white Western European conquistadores and early settlers from Extremadura, Old Castile, Leon, the Basque country, and throughout the Habsburg domains from Belgium to Austria.

After the initial phase of exploration ended and the densely settled areas of central Mexico and the Andean highlands were conquered in the 16th century, the Spanish government sought to impose religious unity on the colonies by forbidding New Christians to settle there under most circumstances. This kept out a lot of Spanish people of color, those whose ancestors had been Moors and had converted from Islam. However, the early arriving Spanish free people of color, mostly men, often married to Indian women, fathered a growing Afro-mestizo population. They were joined by slaves imported from Africa, some of whom similarly found ways to gain their freedom. The newly arrived slaves were often taken in as technical specialists and work supervisors and were in positions of authority over Indians. There were few plantations in early Spanish America, and those that were

established generally obtained the mass of their workforce from among the large Indian population. It was the same way in the mining industry; the technical specialists and work supervisors were often free or enslaved people of African ancestry, while the heavy labor was done by Indians. The African workers' daily contact with Indians and their relatively superior position in the functional hierarchy of the workplace made it easy for them to find Indian partners and father Afro-mestizos. The children, born of Indian mothers, were free from birth. By the mid-1600s, the African-descended population of many cities outnumbered that of whites, with a large and increasing percentage free people of color.

An important development during the postconquest phase was Spain's attempt to reassert control over its new colonies. Spain imposed a common set of laws, the New Laws of the Indies, between 1542 and 1553. Facing significant opposition from colonists, especially in South America, the Spanish Crown imposed its rule and reined in local elites. One part of the strategy was to sharpen the lines dividing white colonists from nonwhites. It was at this time that the rules limiting access to the professions, university, and other social benefits of New Christians were generalized to apply to all nonwhites. As with many aspects of Spanish law, there were always exceptions. People who had small amounts of non-European ancestry could apply for certificates of *limpieza de sangre* (purity of blood) attesting to their whiteness (*see also* "WHITENING" AND RACIAL PROMOTION), a process that had been created for the descendants of Jewish and Muslim converts whose devotion to Catholic orthodoxy was unquestioned. Even without the formal certificate, the children of important men could attain some social benefits unavailable to the general nonwhite community. For example, SAINT MARTÍN DE PORRES, a Peruvian mixed-race free man, could become a full member of the DOMINICANS, a position usually reserved for whites, after his father, the governor-general of PANAMA, recognized him.

Free people of color continued to play an important role in the Spanish colonial empire during this period. One important role that was open to them was military service. In the Caribbean port cities, especially threatened by English and French pirates during this period, the most stalwart defenders were often the free colored MILITIA units. During the Battle of San Juan de Ulua (1568), off the Mexican harbor of Veracruz, the English pirate and slave trader John Hawkins (1532–95) saw his ships nearly destroyed by a large Spanish fleet. The Spanish were able to defeat Hawkins's forces with to landing party of Veracruz militiamen, mostly men of color, who recaptured the fortress guarding the harbor mouth in a daring raid. In the Spanish NAVY, an increasing number of ships were built in the Americas and manned with racially mixed crews. Those ships that were permanently assigned to the defense of the Americas often had crews that were largely nonwhite, although the officers were almost always whites. But even Spanish navy ships stationed in Europe often had many nonwhites among their crews, and the ports they frequented, from the Mediterranean to the Netherlands and Germany, began to have small African-descended populations as crewmen left the sea and settled down.

This tendency was especially marked in Spain itself, where the southern port cities had had significant black populations since the 1400s and blacks settled the northern ports in the 1500s and 1600s. On the other hand, plantation agriculture declined in southern Spain after contact with the Americas. The climate was not really suitable for tropical crops, and the costs of production were much lower in the Americas. During the late 16th and early 17th centuries, Portugal and its colony BRAZIL were under the rule of the Spanish Crown, and the Brazilian SUGAR CULTIVATION plantations were able to drive the Spanish from the market. In the countryside, African-descended people blended into the larger population of PEASANTS, especially after their families had lived in Spain and practiced Christianity long enough that they were no longer considered New Christians (there was no formal limit on how long a family would remain New Christian, and some people were still discriminated against into the 18th century). Generally, these people would no longer have been identified as nonwhite in any official documents. Thus, the reported populations of color in the few censuses that were taken in early modern Spain cannot be relied upon as a guide to the real percentage of the population who had African ancestry. Anecdotal reports show the growing presence of African-descended people in large numbers in Spanish seaports throughout the 17th century.

Mature Colonial Period (1700–1825)

The 18th century saw significant changes in the relationship between the Spanish government and its colonial peoples that would lead ultimately to the independence of most of Spanish America. In 1700, the last Habsburg king of Spain, Charles II, died; he was succeeded, after a long struggle, by Phillip V, grandson of France's King Louis XIV. The War of the Spanish Succession (1700–14) was mainly fought in Europe, but the threat to the Spanish colonies in the Americas led to substantial changes in government and society there. Reforms continued even after the end of the war, as the threat from the northern European invaders remained strong and the government at home hoped for more resources from their colonies. The British and French colonies had grown from tiny enclaves of half-starved pioneers in the early 17th century to substantial settlements with their own large militias

and naval bases for large squadrons by the beginning of the 18th. Most of the fighting in the Americas in the wars of the 18th century was between the French and the British, in North America and the Caribbean, but the Spanish suffered raids by British privateers, and several important port cities, including Veracruz, Havana in CUBA, and Maracaibo in Venezuela, were attacked by British fleets. Havana was captured in 1762 and held by the British for several years. Spain did not have the resources to base large land forces in the Americas and instead relied on local militia and imposing fortifications to protect them. The militiamen were often free people of color, especially in the coastal cities most threatened by the British. The Spanish authorities feared their increasing reliance on free coloreds, however, especially as their overall numbers continued to grow. In any case, one part of the Spanish project to improve governance in the colonies was to place all their public institutions more under the control of the central government by placing *peninsulares*, or Spanish-born whites, in charge to the greatest extent possible. The old expedient of divide and conquer was also part of the Spanish calculation, as they attempted to divide the free colored military leaders from upper-class colonial whites. The militias in the Americas were regularly purged of their free colored officers during the 18th century—though colored enlisted men continued to predominate in the Caribbean coastal cities, and colonial governors sometimes found themselves forced to rely on elite free colored men to lead their black troops. White CREOLE officers kept their positions in the militia but were hampered in seeking promotions. Instead of dividing the two groups, however, the common experience of discrimination often meant that wealthy free coloreds were ready to listen to the arguments of pro-independence creole elites.

The free colored population of Spain itself stagnated during this period. In France and Britain, this was a time of rapid growth in black populations, both free and enslaved, as the colonies matured and black servants and sailors moved from the Americas to the home country. As free mixed-race populations grew in the French and British colonies, wealthy white fathers sent their children to school or to learn a trade in the home country. In Spain, which had experienced a similar population boom in the 17th century, the 18th century was a time of slow growth in the colonies. At the same time, the more mature colonial society in Spanish America had created schools and businesses that could train young people, making the trip across the Atlantic less necessary. The Afro-mestizo elite leader of the Mexican independence movement JOSÉ MARÍA MORELOS, for example, was educated at a seminary in Mexico. The MULATTO general of the South American independence movement, MANUEL PIAR, was educated in Venezuela.

The independence struggle in the Americas was preceded by a great struggle for national liberation in Spain. Napoléon Bonaparte invaded Spain in 1808, holding the king and crown prince hostage in a French jail. The Spanish people fought back ferociously, using guerrilla tactics and rallying their people with promises of liberal reforms. The 1812 constitution promised civil equality to free people of color and made the colonies equal to the homeland in political rights. People of color fought for Spain out of nationalism, from devotion to the liberal principles of the constitution, and for a wide variety of other reasons. In the colonies, the liberal constitution also gained adherents. Middle- and working-class free coloreds especially saw the combination of racial justice and democratic reforms as an important step in the right direction. In addition, while the leaders of the Venezuelan independence struggle, Miranda (1750–1816) and Simón Bolívar (1783–1830), were personally liberal and sought racial equality, many elite white Venezuelans hoped to preserve a racially stratified society under an independent government. Many free coloreds in Venezuela fought for the royalist forces until 1818.

After Napoléon was defeated in 1813, however, the situation in Spain changed dramatically. The exiled King Ferdinand VII (1784–1833) had liberal ideas as a youth, but after six years in Napoléon's jails, he was not ready to accept anything but the absolute rule of his predecessors. He abolished the Constitution of 1812, ruled by decree, and refused to call the parliament. A series of revolts against his rule, suppressed with the help of the new royalist government in France, only made matters worse, preventing the Spanish from offering more than token aid to royalist forces in the Americas. Ferdinand's abandonment of the liberal constitution turned most free people of color, in Spain as well as in the Americas, against royal rule. The American independence movements saw their first success in 1810 in Argentina, but most of Spanish America did not finally throw off European rule until the 1820s. From 1820 to 1823, liberal forces controlled the government, and Ferdinand was a prisoner, but the reforms they were able to implement were achieved too late to save the royalist cause on the mainland of the Americas. The last Spanish possession there, Bolivia, gained its independence on August 6, 1825. By that time, Ferdinand was back in charge and busy executing or exiling his liberal opponents. Only Cuba and Puerto Rico remained of the Spanish Empire in the Americas.

The Nineteenth Century

Cuba, however, had become an important colony by the 1820s. In the 1770s, it had been a sleepy colonial backwater important only because it was a stopover for the fleets going to and from the mainland colonies. Free people of color were almost half of the total African-born population in 1775, and there was little discrimination against them. In the next 50 years, however, sugar production in principal producers SAINT-DOMINGUE and Jamaica, collapsed. Saint-Domingue had experienced a revolution (*see also* HAITIAN REVOLUTION) that freed the slaves and established an independent black republic but destroyed the sugar plantations. Many Saint-Domingue planters had fled to Cuba, only a short distance away across the Windward Passage, with their slaves and their technical expertise. Sugar and COFFEE CULTIVATION in Cuba boomed with their help. Jamaica had lost new slave imports as the result of the 1807 decision by the British Parliament to end Britain's role in the Atlantic slave trade. Jamaican production was stagnant or declining by the 1820s, and slavery itself was approaching its end in the British Empire. Cuba produced most of the cane sugar consumed in Europe from 1815 to 1850. Spain had agreed to end its slave trade in 1817, but in fact the trade continued illegally, but with the full support of Cuban local officials, until the 1860s. Because the trade was illegal after 1817, the exact numbers are unclear, but most scholars estimate that somewhere around 15,000 slaves were landed in the colony each year through the 1840s, and a smaller number, not fewer than 8,000 a year, until 1862. Official prohibition in 1862, combined with the effects of the TEN YEARS' WAR (1868–78), reduced new slave imports to a negligible amount by the 1870s.

But the massive infusion of new African slaves, along with the new wealth of the plantation sector, had already had a great negative effect on the lives and status of free people of color in Cuba and throughout the Spanish Empire. As slave numbers grew, the color line became more and more important to local elites as a way of ensuring control. The great wealth the plantations produced allowed planters to remain apart from their slave workforces, reducing the human interaction that somewhat softened the system and encouraged the growth of a free population of color. The participation of so many free people of color in revolutionary movements on the mainland and in neighboring Saint-Domingue did not help matters. Free people of color were automatically suspects in early 19th-century Cuba. The Aponte Revolt in 1812 and the ESCALERA PLOT in 1844 were two movements in which free coloreds made common cause with slaves seeking to overthrow the system, though in the Escalera crisis it is unclear how many people were really involved and how many were innocent victims of hysteria. The government and white elites responded with harsh repression of free people of color, preventing free colored men from serving in the militia, holding various government jobs, entering universities, and working in various occupations. The level of discrimination never equaled that found in North America, but it was strikingly greater than had prevailed on the mainland before the turn of the century. Free people of color in Cuba finally unified and fought back against the system during the Ten Years' War, led by their charismatic general ANTONIO MACEO Y GRAJALES. Cuba finally gained its national independence in 1898, thanks in part to the intervention of the United States. American racial attitudes were at their worst at that particular time, and Afro-Cubans found the transition to U.S. supremacy did not improve their situation markedly.

The growing phenomenon of nationalism added a further element to the mix in metropolitan Spain. Resistance to Napoléon and to the reactionary forces during the 19th century used Spanish nationalism as a unifying ideal. The Spanish nation was redefined to some extent, excluding nonwhite people from the colonies as well as other Europeans. By this time, many of the pre-1492 African-descended people, the descendants of the medieval Moors, had disappeared into the general population, and there was no tendency to discriminate against dark-skinned people from Spain. But if someone had recent colonial ancestors, especially dark-skinned ones, the growing consensus in Spain was that he or she was not truly Spanish.

Stewart R. King

FURTHER READING

Knight, Franklin. *Slave Society in Cuba in the Nineteenth Century.* Madison: University of Wisconsin Press, 1970.
Lane-Poole, Stanley. *The Story of the Moors in Spain.* 1886. Reprint, Baltimore, Md.: Black Classic Press, 1996.
Peabody, Sue, and Keila Grinberg. *Slavery, Freedom, and the Law in the Atlantic World: A Brief History with Documents.* Boston: Bedford/St. Martin's, 2007.
Sweet, James. "The Iberian Roots of American Racist Thought." *William and Mary Quarterly* 54 (1997): 143–166. Reprinted in Colin A. Palmer, ed. *The Worlds of Unfree Labour from Indentured Servitude to Slavery.* Aldershot, England: Ashgate, 1998, 1–24.

STEWART, MARIA W. (1803–1879) *American abolitionist lecturer, writer*

Maria W. Stewart (née Miller) was a pathbreaking advocate for abolition of slavery and women's rights. She also had a long career in education and demonstrated the importance of free people of color in the field of education.

Born to free black parents in Hartford, CONNECTICUT, in 1803, Maria Miller was an orphan by the time she was five years old. She was then sent to live with the family of a minister until she was 15 years old. In her young adulthood, she learned how to read and write at Sabbath

schools. She paid for her studies at the Sabbath school by working as a domestic servant.

In August 1826, Maria was 23 years old and married James W. Stewart in BOSTON. James W. Stewart was a veteran of the War of 1812 who then worked as a shipping agent. Besides her husband's surname, she adopted his middle *W.* After her husband's death three years later, Stewart was left destitute, after some white businessmen cheated her and took the money her husband had left her. A childless widow, Stewart worked as a teacher in the public school systems of New York City, Baltimore, and Washington, D.C., throughout her life. It was in Washington, D.C., that Maria W. Stewart started a Sunday school for children. Together with her educational work, Stewart supported herself with the speeches she gave in favor of ABOLITIONISM and women's rights. She was deeply influenced by the African-American abolitionist DAVID WALKER.

In 1831, Stewart published a short pamphlet entitled *Religion and the Pure Principles of Morality, the Sure Foundation on Which We Build.* One year later, she published another religious-oriented text, *The Meditation from the Pen of Mrs. Maria Stewart.* Her writings and lectures had as their central theme the egalitarian nature of Christian teachings and their application to the question of the status of women and people of color in society (*see also* BAPTISTS AND PIETISTS). Her career as a public speaker lasted for three years, and although some of her speeches provoked opposition both because she was a woman and because of her support for abolition, William Lloyd Garrison published them all in his abolitionist newspaper the *Liberator.* She is remembered as the first American-born woman to give a lecture to an audience of men and women. This groundbreaking lecture took place in the New England Anti-Slavery Society in 1832. Her farewell address took place in the African Meeting House on September 21, 1833. She published her collected works in 1835: *Productions of Mrs. Maria Stewart.*

Although she had given up her career as a public speaker, Stewart never gave up her activism and involvement in social matters. She joined the Female Literary Society of New York in 1834 and attended the Anti-Slavery Convention in 1837 (*see also* NEGRO CONVENTION MOVEMENT IN THE UNITED STATES). Stewart became deeply involved with education after the end of her career as a public advocate of abolitionism. In her last years, she worked at the Freedmen's Hospital that was part of Howard University in Washington, D.C. She applied for a war widow's pension, which she eventually received. She died on December 17, 1879, in Washington, D.C. Maria W. Stewart became an example to other African-American women such as Elizabeth Keckley and Ellen Watkins Harper.

Laura Gimeno-Pahissa

FURTHER READING

Foster, Francis Smith. *Written by Herself: Literary Production by African American Women, 1746–1892.* Bloomington: Indiana University Press, 1993.

Richardson, M. *Maria Stewart: America's First Black Woman Political Writer: Essays and Speeches.* Bloomington: Indiana University Press, 1987.

Rycenga, J. "A Greater Awakening: Women's Intellect as a Factor in Early Abolitionist Movements, 1824–1834." *Journal of Feminist Studies in Religion* 21, no. 2 (Fall 2005): 31–59.

Stewart, Maria. "An Address Delivered at the African Masonic Hall" and "A Lecture Given at Franklin Hall." In *Early Negro Writing, 1760–1837*, edited by Dorothy Porter, 129–140. Baltimore, Md.: Black Classic Press, 1995.

STRONG, JONATHAN (ca. 1747/8–1773) *British laborer and antislavery plaintiff*

Jonathan Strong was at the center of a legal case that helped define the status of people of color under British law. His defense of his rights in this prominent court case was an important element in turning public opinion against slavery in BRITAIN. Strong was born a slave, probably in 1747 or 1748, in BARBADOS. His master, David Lisle, took him to Britain, in the early 1760s. They resided in LONDON, ENGLAND, where the majority of Britain's people of African ancestry lived, and Strong worked, as did many of his fellow black Britons, as a servant.

In 1765, after receiving a brutal beating from Lisle, who left him for dead, the teenaged Strong made his way to Mincing Lane, London, where he sought treatment from William Sharp, a noted surgeon. Strong's face was a mass of mangled, raw, red flesh. In this, the most recent abuse in a string of violent incidents, his master had inflicted a pistol-whipping upon Strong so forceful that the gun had separated from its handle.

Assisted by William Sharp and his brother, GRANVILLE SHARP, a noted abolitionist, Strong immediately received medical care and money for food. The next day, he entered Bart's Hospital, where he remained for more than four months. Upon release, Strong found work running errands and acting as a servant for William Sharp's apothecary, a man named Brown. While accompanying Brown's wife on an errand two years later, in 1767, Strong encountered Lisle, his abusive former master. Believing that strong had died as a result of his beating, Lisle was enraged to discover that he had been dispossessed of his discarded human property.

Once aware of Strong's survival, Lisle sold Strong to James Kerr, a planter, at the price of £30, well under the going rate for a healthy male slave at the time. Lisle then arranged to have Strong detained by officers of the city government of London so that Strong could be consigned to a slave ship. But Strong was a baptized Christian, literate, and resourceful, and so he applied for help to his employer, Brown, and eventually to Granville Sharp. In previous cases argued in British courts, judges had ordered slaves returned to their masters, but Sharp decided to pursue the case, basing his arguments on the common law presumption of freedom for citizens of the city of London dating back to the Middle Ages. Sharp appealed his case to the lord mayor's court, responsible for the City of London. On September 18, 1767, Sir Robert Kite, the lord mayor, ruled that Strong had not committed any offense and was free to go. At that, Captain Laird, commander of the ship that would have carried Strong across the Atlantic again, lunged at Strong, apparently in an attempt to gain physical possession of him and defy the court and was only deterred by Sharp, who charged Laird with assault. Lisle challenged Sharp to a duel but Sharp refused to meet him.

Strong was free, but Kerr and Lisle now sued Granville Sharp for £200 for detaining their property. Sharp's anxiety about the case spurred him to begin to research and conduct a monumental antislavery campaign. After almost two years of court action, Lisle and Kerr dropped their case against Sharp and were fined triple the court costs for wasting the court's time. Strong built a network among runaway slaves and other free people of color in London. He was able to alert Sharp to other cases of mistreatment of RUNAWAY SLAVES. Strong's example inspired the tiny community of people of color in London, and the dramatic nature of the legal proceedings, covered by the fledgling newspaper industry of London, helped spark broader public interest in the status of enslaved black servants. Strong's premature death, in his mid-20s, on April 19, 1773, could not diminish the spectacle of his resolute sufferings, which would empower antislavery campaigns for years to come.

Myron C. Noonkester

FURTHER READING

Fryer, Peter. *Staying Power: The History of Black People in Britain.* Alberta, Canada: University of Alberta Press, 1987.

Schama, Simon. *Rough Crossings: Britain, the Slaves and the American Revolution.* New York: HarperCollins, 2006.

Weiner, Mark S. *Black Trials: Citizenship from the Beginnings of Slavery to the End of Caste.* New York: Vintage, 2004.

SUGAR CULTIVATION

For more than two centuries, sugar was the most valuable crop of the plantation complex in the Americas. It was the engine that remade the Atlantic economy in the 1600s and fueled the rapid expansion in the slave trade in the 1700s. Millions of slaves sweated their lives out in the cane fields in places like northeastern BRAZIL; GUYANA; the Antilles; Oaxaca and Chiapas, MEXICO; the coasts of PERU, ECUADOR, and COLOMBIA; and LOUISIANA. Most of those slaves were owned by white people, but there were some free people of color who were sugar planters (*see* PLANTERS AND PLANTER AGENTS).

Sugar was a crop that required a good deal of startup capital. The machinery and labor forces required to transform sugarcane into sugar crystals were expensive. The cane first had to be harvested and moved into processing very quickly to reduce spoilage. Using many horses or oxen sped this process. Moreover, this meant that many laborers needed to be employed both in the fields and in the processing at the same time. The same crew could not do both jobs because each required its own set of rather difficult skills, and in any case, they had to be done at the same time for maximal efficiency. Then, the equipment itself was complicated and always evolving, requiring continuous reinvestment to keep the sugar mill competitive. Finally, only very flat, well-watered land where temperatures never dip below freezing is appropriate for sugarcane cultivation. The tropical regions of the Americas are generally fairly mountainous, leaving only very small areas where sugar cultivation is possible. This made land values universally high, with the land costs on the smaller islands of the Lesser Antilles the highest. Water supply is also an issue in many parts of the tropical Americas. The Pacific Coast of tropical South America was a profitable sugar cultivating region, but only after investors paid for extensive irrigation works, since these regions receive almost no rain naturally.

Sugar was originally cultivated in India. It was introduced to Europe through the Middle East and grown on the islands of the Mediterranean and Atlantic in the Middle Ages. Columbus introduced sugar into the Americas in the first decade of the 1500s, but the Spanish system could provide neither the labor nor the financial capital to make sugar plantations profitable at that time. It was left to the Portuguese in Brazil to make sugar cultivation in the Americas profitable, importing business techniques and agricultural technologies from their successful sugar colonies in the Atlantic islands of Saõ Tomé, Principe,

An engraving of the refining process on a sugar plantation, from the Dominican father Jean-Baptiste Du Tertre's *General History of the Antilles*, 1667. Almost all of the heavy labor on sugar plantations in the Americas was performed by slaves, but skilled laborers such as millers and refiners were frequently free people of color, especially when sugar cultivation became better established in any particular colony. *(New York Public Library/Art Resource, NY)*

and Cap Verde in the early 16th century. The Portuguese also had access to African slave labor through their relationship with the Kingdom of Kongo in Central Africa and their slave trading posts on the coast of West Africa.

The Brazilians instituted a racial system that permitted free people of color to advance under some circumstances. Colonial Brazil was not the racial democracy portrayed by 19th-century Brazilian patriots, but free people of color were permitted to own land and slaves. Whites and people of color could marry, and even if they did not marry, children of mixed race who were acknowledged by their fathers were an accepted part of society with rights of inheritance. Mixed-race children of wealthy white men could inherit their fathers' plantations, and some did. Additionally, northeastern Brazil had a good supply of land suitable for sugar cultivation. Brazilians developed the *engheno* system. Large planters invested in the machinery and livestock needed for an efficient sugar processing operation. Small plots of land around their mills were owned by *lavradores do cana*, or cane workers, who grew sugar on their own account, milling their crops at the planter's mill and selling them through his contacts. This could be an exploitative system, but it also offered an avenue for people of lower status to enter sugar cultivation cheaply. Many did, and some rose to be independent planters.

When the sugar revolution moved to islands in the Antilles after 1650, beginning in BARBADOS and then spreading throughout the Caribbean region, there were not so many opportunities open to free blacks at first, and there were no large black landowners in Barbados. The British were reluctant for cultural reasons to permit free blacks to own large amounts of land or supervise slaves. In the French colonies, there were no such restrictions. As the French began to dominate global sugar production in the 1750s and SAINT-DOMINGUE became the wealthiest Caribbean colony, there were openings for free blacks to enter the sugar market. Julie Dahey, the companion of a wealthy white man named Peignanan, became a sugar planter in the parish of Croix des Bouquets, near PORT-AU-PRINCE, in 1780, upon the death of her companion. She was actually not the owner of the plantation he willed her; she had to pay rent to a white heir in France. But she was in control of dozens of slaves, hundreds of acres of prime land, and a large mill, as well as owning some less-valuable land in her own right. But she was in a minority, even in the French Antilles, as most free black planters practiced COFFEE CULTIVATION or grew other crops that required less capital outlay.

The sugar revolution moved from the French Antilles to the Spanish colonies, especially CUBA, but also the coastal regions of Colombia, Mexico, Peru, and Ecuador. These sugar plantations were huge. Even Spaniards and Spanish-American whites did not have enough capital in most cases—they needed investors from the Anglo-American world. Free blacks had no real chance to participate, and in fact, most Cuban free blacks who achieved economic success did so as ARTISANS or merchants in the cities.

Throughout the 17th, 18th, and early 19th centuries, sugar was the route to the largest fortunes in the slave societies of the America and, as such, was the economic sector most difficult for free blacks to enter. In most places, the capital necessary for sugar production exceeded what they could save or borrow on their own. Legal prohibitions, discriminatory taxes, or informal restrictions on their land and slave ownership also made it difficult for them to enter into the sugar industry in most areas. Brazil was an exception, because of the structure of the sugar industry there, with its small farmers dependent on a central mill.

The fact that there were few free black sugar planters, however, did not mean that free people of color were excluded entirely from the wealth of the sugar sector. Many free blacks worked as skilled artisans in the sugar business, as millers, for example. Other free blacks were planter agents in sugar plantations, especially those of their white relatives. As salaried management talent, or as wage-earning free labor, free people of color were able to participate in this important sector of the economy, even if ownership was denied to them.

Stewart R. King

FURTHER READING
Mintz, Sidney. *Sweetness and Power: The Place of Sugar in Modern History*. New York: Viking Penguin, 1985.

SURINAM

The modern nation of Suriname, known throughout most of its history as Surinam, is located on the north coast of South America, between GUYANA and French Guyana. The nation borders BRAZIL to the south. The main area of settlement is along the Suriname River; the capital, Paramaribo, is located at the mouth of the river. Most of the national territory is covered with dense forests, with extensive mangrove swamps along the Atlantic coast.

The indigenous inhabitants of Surinam were Arawak and Carib, related to the native people of the Caribbean islands. They were farmers and lived in villages, and a good deal of the northern coastal plain was cleared and under cultivation when European settlers arrived in the 17th century. The native inhabitants were decimated by diseases, both those imported from Europe such as smallpox and measles and those introduced from Africa such as malaria and yellow fever. The Indians of the coastal plains were almost all killed by disease and European conquerors, but the Indians of the forested regions in the interior, aided by RUNAWAY SLAVES, preserved their independence and their culture until modern times.

The first European colonists arrived in 1630 from BARBADOS. They were Englishmen, led by Major Anthony Rowse. The colony slowly grew, and by 1663, there were more than 1,000 European inhabitants, about 3,000 African slaves, and about 1,000 Indian slaves. Many of the Europeans were refugees from Dutch Brazil, which had been reconquered by the Portuguese in the 1650s. They introduced techniques for SUGAR CULTIVATION with slave labor and also for reclaiming land from the ocean and coastal swamps, permitting the creation of plantations. The colony was conquered by the Dutch in 1667, and their rule was formalized by a treaty in 1674, which incidentally granted the small

Houses built by free people of color in the 19th century in the capital city of Paramaribo, Surinam. A fire in 1821 destroyed the neighborhood where most of the city's free people of color lived, and these houses were probably built at that time. (akg–images)

Dutch colony at New Amsterdam at the mouth of the Hudson River in North America, today's New York, to the British. Surinam was the poor neighbor to the much wealthier Guyana, also under Dutch rule, throughout the 18th century. Slave ships docked first in Guyana, so Surinamese planters had to take the leftover slaves. Shipping prices were higher, so Surinamese sugar was less profitable. As a result, the colony grew slowly.

The more resistant slaves who were rejected in Guyana and taken to Surinam, and the problems Surinamese planters had in buying enough food for their slaves, as well as typically harsh treatment on plantations, caused many slaves to run away. In the jungles, they joined remnant Indian groups to create the Surinamese MAROONS, called the "bush negroes." The "bush negroes" were famous throughout the region for their size and aggressiveness. They were the largest and most important group of free people of color in the colony. They effectively controlled the interior of the colony into the 20th century. They conducted regular raids on the plantation zone, both to capture slaves, supplies, and tools for themselves and to liberate family members and friends. They also had extensive trade networks with Indians farther into the interior and with colonists, especially in French Guyana. In 1760, after a number of expeditions, the Saramaka maroons negotiated the treaty of Ouca, under which they were granted their freedom and control over the lands they held in the interior, while they agreed not to attack plantations and to help capture other rebel or runaway slaves. Hostility among different groups of maroons offered the government a chance to have more influence in the region. A subsequent expedition against other groups of maroons, lasting from 1772 to 1778, supported by troops from Europe, finally resulted in similar treaties with all the maroon bands. Surinamese maroon warriors helped put down the Berbice slave uprising in neighboring Guyana in the 1760s. Maroon society in Surinam was similar to that found in other slave colonies in the Americas. Maroons followed Afro-Caribbean religions that were very strongly influenced by African ideas and much less by Christianity (see AFRICAN AND SYNCRETIC RELIGIONS). One feature of these religions was the existence of secret societies that could cross tribal lines. These societies were similar to those found among the people of southeastern Nigeria, the home of many of the slaves taken to Surinam in the 18th century. Members of the societies were supposed to consider each other as brothers or sisters, and the societies often formed the glue that held maroon tribes together. Maroon towns were governed by oligarchies of influential elder men, with a fairly high degree of social mobility. Age, military prowess, and status within traditional religious societies were more important determinants of social standing than wealth. Tribes had chiefs, or *granmans*, who were selected by the village oligarchies but had limited powers to intervene in village affairs. Newcomers to maroon communities could be accepted as members or held as slaves depending on whether they had been captured on raids or entered voluntarily and what relationships they had with people already members of the community. The form of slavery practiced among the maroons was unlike that in the plantations; maroons' slaves were more like subordinate kinsmen than mere fieldhands.

The coastal strip remained a peripheral part of the plantation zone until after the turn of the 19th century. Society there was similar to that found in nearby Guyana or in the DUTCH CARIBBEAN ISLANDS. The Dutch attitude toward free people of color lay somewhere between the inflexible racial lines of the British and the more subtle shadings and racial transformations possible in Spanish and Portuguese colonies. Many of the early European settlers of Surinam were Brazilians. The Dutch themselves had been under Spanish rule for centuries before they began their colonial expansion. They never adopted a "ONE DROP RULE" OF RACIAL IDENTITY and instead saw mixed-race people as a separate group. Even free blacks could be treated as citizens, perhaps second-class citizens but at least members of the community. Membership in the established Dutch Reformed Church; acculturation in language, dress, and family life; wealth; and service to the community could all earn a person of color respect and inclusion. Elisabeth Samson, a free black woman, was the wealthiest woman in Surinam in the 1770s. She already owned several plantations when as a young woman in 1764 she and a young white man newly arrived from the Netherlands sought permission to marry in the church despite the general laws against MISCEGENATION. After a great struggle, which included arrest for violation of the miscegenation laws, the state was finally forced to accept their marriage. For every Samson, though, there were dozens of poor black families existing on the margins of colonial society, as small farmers in remote areas or as laborers or small shopkeepers in the towns. As in the British colonies, much of the small retail sector in Surinam's economy was controlled by women of color, both free and enslaved.

British troops captured Guyana in 1798 and Surinam in 1799. British rule in Guyana was formalized in 1814, while Surinam was returned to the Dutch. After that time, the Netherlands began to provide more resources to Surinam. The slave trade was ending, and Netherlands agreed to a general abolition of the trade in 1816. Dutch colonies along the coast of West Africa had in any case been lost to the British during the wars of the FRENCH REVOLUTION, and so there was little supply of slaves for Dutch colonists. Slave populations had never been very high in Surinam, and there were few other Dutch colonies in the Americas to export slaves to Surinam. Therefore, Surinam, as did the nearby colonies of Guyana and Trinidad, began importing plantation laborers from the East Indies. Most of the new arrivals in Surinam were from the Dutch East Indies, the modern nation of Indonesia, though there were also some immigrants from China, India, and Sri Lanka. The population of slaves diminished from the 1790s on, and by the 1860s, free people of African descent outnumbered slaves by an estimated three to one. The Netherlands preserved the institution of slavery for a much longer time than Britain or France, only passing an abolition law in 1863, the same year that President ABRAHAM LINCOLN issued the EMANCIPATION PROCLAMATION in the United States. This was a gradual abolition law, and the last slaves in Surinam were not freed until 1873. By this time, almost all the plantation workforce consisted of indentured East Indians supplemented by free Afro-Surinamese day laborers in the harvest season. During the 19th century, the Afro-Surinamese of the coastal strip and the cities began to identify themselves as a people distinct from East Indians and the maroon and Indian inhabitants of the interior regions. Mixed-race people, often descended from former free people of color, provided a leadership class for the black community during the 19th and 20th centuries. Both Henck Arron (1936–2000), the first leader of independent Surinam, and his longtime rival Desi Bouterse (1945–) were members of this group.

In conclusion, although a colony with plantation production of sugar, Surinam was not so strongly controlled by the plantation sector as other European colonies in the region. As a result, there was more space in the society for liminal people like free coloreds, maroons, and Native Americans. The role of northern European Dutch culture, which might have been expected to have created a very harsh racial climate, was tempered by the presence of Brazilian immigrants and by the general poverty of the area. As a result, Surinam developed a more open and racially mixed society than that found in British or Dutch colonies elsewhere in the Americas.

Stewart R. King

FURTHER READING

King, Johannes. "Guerilla Warfare: A Bush Negro's View." In *Maroon Societies: Rebel Slave Communities in the Americas*, edited by Richard Price, 298–304. Baltimore: Johns Hopkins University Press, 1996.

McLeod, Cynthia. *The Free Negress Elisabeth: Prisoner of Color.* London: Waterfront Press, 2004.

Stedman, John Gabriel, and Richard Price, eds. *Stedman's Surinam: Life in an Eighteenth-Century Slave Society. An Abridged, Modernized Edition of Narrative of a Five Years Expedition against the Revolted Negroes of Surinam.* Baltimore: Johns Hopkins University Press, 1992.

TANNENBAUM HYPOTHESIS

As the Civil Rights movement developed in the years after World War II, scholars sought to understand the origins of the struggle for equality. In trying to get to the root of American racial ideology, they began to study both the origins of slavery and the role of African Americans in creating the United States. Historians of the 1940s onward sought to understand American RACISM AND RACIAL PREJUDICE by asking why it developed, and many tried to combat it by showing that blacks had played a valuable role in the creation of American societies.

Frank Tannenbaum led the way toward a deeper understanding of slavery in the Western Hemisphere with his short but intriguing book *Slave and Citizen: The Negro in the Americas*. Published in 1946, this volume grew out of the first of a series of interdisciplinary seminars at Columbia University and was an attempt to understand "the historical experience of different cultures," as well as the institution of slavery. Not only did Tannenbaum call for a "reconsideration of the role of the African people in this hemisphere," he also compared slavery in Latin America and British America. In tracing the development of modern racial thought in each area, he sought to explain the racial animosity he saw in the United States.

A member of the National Association for the Advancement of Colored People and the American Civil Liberties Union, Tannenbaum began his work by providing a forceful argument for black agency in the settlement of the Americas. He maintained that "African participation in the New World adventure began early," and that "the Negro . . . was just as important as his master." He then celebrated the post-emancipation achievements of blacks in CUBA and BRAZIL and lamented the failure of Americans to accept blacks as equals in the 20th-century United States. According to Tannenbaum, the black man had "become culturally a European, . . . a white man with a black face," but "in spite of his adaptability, his willingness, and his competence, in spite of his complete identification with the *mores* of the United States, he is excluded and denied." Insisting that emancipation legally freed

blacks in the United States but denied them "the moral status requisite for effective legal freedom," Tannenbaum went on to compare slavery in different societies to show how alterations in the system "shaped the political and ethical biases that have manifestly separated the United States from the other parts of the New World."

According to Tannenbaum, slavery in the Iberian colonies was milder, and three factors prevented the Spanish and Portuguese from developing theories of racial inferiority. To begin with, Iberians were familiar with slavery. Though the system had "long since died out in the rest of western Europe," it had survived in PORTUGAL and SPAIN largely as a result of wars with the Moors. This continuity preserved not only the system but its laws as well, and Tannenbaum insisted that Roman law protected the enslaved from physical abuse, offered freedom for accepting Christianity, provided legal protection for slave marriages, and allowed opportunities for freedom by permitting the slave to appeal to the court and to buy himself or herself. Thus, legal codification made Iberian slavery a "contractual arrangement between the master and his bondsman" and prevented the master class from using the system as evidence of moral or biological inferiority. The ROMAN CATHOLIC CHURCH served as the final inhibitor of racism in Latin America. Because the church saw the slave and the master as equal under God, slaves were taken to church and allowed to participate in communion and other sacraments such as marriage.

When the British adopted the system of slavery, however, they did not have prior experience. As they struggled to find a place for slaves in their existing laws, the fact that they had a different skin color "merely added to the confusion; it did not create it." According to Tannenbaum, the lack of legal precedent was worsened by the position of the Protestant churches. Without legal or religious protection for the slave, it was easy for the planter to assume full control, and whites developed theories of racial inferiority that differentiated slavery in the United States from ancient and Iberian systems. These ideas of inferiority also made it hard to see blacks as "moral beings." This attitude created a disgust for racial mixing that did not exist in the Iberian world. Slavery, then, created racism in the United States, and when it ended, the adjustment was difficult since blacks were considered slaves by nature.

Tannenbaum's arguments set the tone for the next two decades and spawned a number of institutional, intellectual, and social histories of colonial slavery. While his stress on black contributions to the Americas would not be expanded sufficiently until the rise of social history in the 1960s, his immediate successors used institutional history to develop further his comparison of slavery in the Americas. For these historians, the primary task involved examining the relationship between slavery and racism in the United States.

The historians Oscar and Mary Handlin contributed to this strain of inquiry four years after Tannenbaum's study. Also blaming the institution of slavery for the development of racial ideology, they extended Tannenbaum's examination of the lack of legal precedent in North America. According to the Handlins, the system "emerged . . . from the adjustment to American conditions of traditional European institutions." Citing the traditions of villeinage, apprenticeship, and indentured servitude, they argued that the English were familiar with "several gradations of 'unfreedom'" and sought to fit blacks into their existing framework. They also followed Tannenbaum's lead by focusing on laws and statutes to argue for the mildness of Iberian slavery.

Unlike Tannenbaum, who devoted much of his career to the study of Latin America, the Handlins focus more heavily on the development of slavery in the English mainland colonies. They portrayed the system as mild in the early years, and they insisted that chattel slavery did not develop immediately, was not modeled on other slave systems, and was not a "response to any unique qualities in the Negro himself." According to the Handlins, the absence of an institutional structure proved that blacks started out much as indentured servants in the colonies. They maintain that this was true until the 1660s and that when the term *slave* appeared in the documents prior to that time, it simply meant "a low form of service." The change in status after that point, they claimed, was due to the colonists' reaction to the "rudeness of the Negroes' manners, the strangeness of their languages, the difficulty of communicating to them English notions of morality and proper behavior." Therefore, they contended that it was "not necessary to resort to racialist assumptions to account for" the legal codification of slavery. Finally, blacks were only taken into the colonies in large number when attempts to make indentured servitude more appealing failed to attract more white laborers.

Once blacks began to arrive in large numbers, however, their status as chattel slaves began to evolve. To begin with, the absence of laws limiting their time of service left them vulnerable to permanent enslavement. As their terms became life sentences, their children were enslaved in order to repay the planter for the loss of time while the mother was pregnant and for the care of the children. Racial mixing was prohibited early on because the mixed offspring complicated the legal status. After the 1680s, however, it became a matter of racial control as the trade in slaves directly from Africa rather than the West Indies caused regulation against blacks to grow harsher as fears of plots and conspiracies grew. Also at this time, the master's power of discipline grew, and "the emerging difference in treatment was calculated to create a real division of interest between Negroes on the one hand and whites on the other." As this division grew, 18th-century Southerners could argue that blacks did not share in natural rights because they "were not fully men."

Carl Degler challenged the assumptions shared by Tannenbaum and the Handlins in his 1959 article "Slavery and the Genesis of American Race Prejudice." According to Degler, who also relied heavily on laws and statutes, the lack of codification before 1660 did not necessarily mean that blacks were not chattel slaves earlier. Arguing that racism preceded slavery, he explained that the laws were created to put into writing that which had already been accepted practice. He insisted that the Handlins' assertion that white servants' status was improving after the 1660s was not supported by clear evidence. For Degler, the lack of precedent left the English able to create a status for the slave that was "worked out within a framework of discrimination," and he argued that blacks were treated as inferiors "from the outset." As evidence, he cited the inferior treatment of pagans, whether black or Native American, and he added that blacks never enjoyed fixed terms and were prevented from owning firearms. Furthermore, black women, unlike white women, were classed as tithables. That is, their husbands (if free), owners, or contractors (if enslaved or indentured) were obliged to pay taxes on them, showing that they were seen as capital goods. All of this occurred during the time in which blacks were still generally referred to as servants rather than slaves. Finally, he contended that "the supposition that . . . slavery long antedated the law is strengthened by the tangential manner in which recognition of Negro slavery first appeared in the Virginia statutes." He concluded that discrimination preceded slavery in both the Northern and Southern mainland colonies. Therefore, "instead of slavery being the root of discrimination visited upon the Negro in America, slavery was itself molded by the early colonists' discrimination against the outlander."

While Degler's refutation of the Handlins made sense, it did not resolve the issue, and the debate continued throughout the next decade. An overall shift from institutional to intellectual history altered the nature of the argument in the late 1960s, and historians began to consult new sources for a more thorough explanation. Two major studies, David Brion Davis's 1967 Pulitzer Prize–winning *The Problem of Slavery in Western Culture* and Winthrop Jordan's 1969 National Book Award winner *White over Black: American Attitudes toward the Negro, 1550–1812*, expanded upon Tannenbaum's conclusions on American racism. While these authors examined many of the same laws as their predecessors, they also drew upon a wider range of sources, including philosophical tracts, literature, journalism, histories, and travel narratives from their focal periods to create a more comprehensive explanation of the genesis of race prejudice in the United States.

Agreeing with Degler that practice did not depend upon existing law, Davis called for "a clear distinction between slavery as an abstract legal status, and as an actual institution involving economic functions and interpersonal relationships." While he conceded that North American slavery was different, he insisted that "we simply do not know enough about the actual treatment of bondsmen in different societies to warrant precise generalizations on the relative severity of slave systems." He then emphasized the continuity between ancient and modern slavery, agreeing with the Handlins that villeinage "was the vehicle . . . which served to transmit legal notions of total subordination to the early modern era." Claiming that "the basic characteristics of chattel slavery were clearly established in antiquity," and that Spain and Portugal provided the "transitional link" between the systems, he added that slavery, which had always depended upon "real or simulated ethnic barriers," took on unique characteristics in America, where black skin came to mean "slave." He disagreed with Tannenbaum's emphasis on ease of MANUMISSION as a measure of harshness, insisting that the ideal embodied in law was not necessarily followed in practice.

In looking for the origins of race-based slavery, Davis pointed to the Bible and ancient philosophy. He argued that these sources "connected slavery with ideas of sin, subordination, and the divine order of the world." He cited the doctrine of original sin and the belief in enslaving foreigners and infidels as crucial, and he traced the process by which the basis shifted from "religious difference to ethnic origin." To many Europeans, he maintained, slavery was a civilizing force that prevented African war captives from being put to death. Because they saw most Africans as Moors, Europeans believed that they had been introduced to Christianity but had rejected it and were "infidels." Native Americans, on the other hand, were simply considered heathen since they had not yet made such a decision. This reason, and the need to secure trade with

peaceful Indians, made Europeans more willing to enslave Africans. Davis added that both Protestants and Catholics failed to question the system as long as the slaves were obtained legitimately through war.

In his comparison of slavery in the Latin American and British colonies, Davis challenged two historical assumptions. First, he insisted that slavery varied as much within these two regions as between them, and he claimed that there were more similarities than differences throughout the Americas in general. More important, he argued that physical treatment is as important in gauging the systems as legal statutes are. He pointed out that slaves in both societies could earn freedom through loyalty or self-purchase. Furthermore, he argued that racial mixing in Latin America was a product of the scarcity of European women rather than a lack of prejudice.

Jordan agreed with Davis that the survival of villeinage in English law and a tendency to use controlling measures in dealing with the poor provided a vague tradition for what would become slavery, but he emphasized the role of science over religion in the creation of racial ideology. He cited the unfortunate coincidence that the English encountered anthropoid apes and black people at the same time and in the same place, but he insisted that most did not see blacks literally as animals. According to Jordan, the English saw black "savagery" as a temporary characteristic that could be overcome. Black skin, however, was permanent, and many began to see it as the visible marking of the "curse of Ham"—a biblical reference to the curse that Noah put on his disobedient son Ham that cursed Ham's children to be slaves to their uncles' progeny. The Israelites saw the story as referring to the original inhabitants of Palestine, the Canaanites, but in 19th-century Protestant Europe and America the story was thought to refer to blacks, and blacks were even called "Hamites" in early anthropological writing (*see* PROTESTANT MAINLINE CHURCHES). He added that enslaved blacks were war captives and were "strangers" as well as non-Christians. The English drew upon Portuguese experience and enslaved these blacks partly out of social and economic necessities in the Americas "which called for some sort of bound, controlled labor."

Jordan insisted, however, that economic necessity alone was not sufficient to justify racial differentiation. He argued that prejudice against blacks and the institution of slavery "seem . . . to have generated each other" and were both "twin aspects of a general debasement of the Negro." He maintained that "the colonists' initial sense of difference from the Negro was founded not on a single characteristic but on . . . qualities which, taken as a whole, seemed to set the Negro apart," and he claimed that the two most striking of these, "his heathenism and his appearance were probably prerequisite to his complete debasement."

Agreeing with Degler, Jordan claimed that the institutionalization of slavery occurred after the practice developed, and as Davis did, he compared the treatment of blacks with that of Native Americans. Jordan concluded that Indians were not enslaved as systematically because of different work habits. He also cites their ability to fight back by raiding and the need to deal with them as nations rather than individuals. In addition, he stressed the distinction between friendly and unfriendly tribes and the fact that Indians came to symbolize "America" to most Europeans.

While the works of Davis and Jordan reveal new trends in the historiography by stressing ideology over legal policy, they were simply part of an expanding methodology during the 1960s. Other historians built upon various new techniques to address the Tannenbaum thesis. Philip D. Curtin's 1969 book *The Atlantic Slave Trade: A Census* illustrates another development in historical scholarship. Part of the move toward the treatment of history as a science, this work uses quantitative methods to refute Tannenbaum's claims for a milder Latin American slavery. According to Curtin, Tannenbaum's assertion that Latin American slavery was milder "may have been true at some times and in some places," but he pointed out that "one measure of well-being is the ability to survive and to multiply," and he used population figures to show that North American slaves did just that.

Curtin relied heavily on secondary sources to compare the number of slaves imported into the different colonies. Introducing his work as an "attempt at an intermediate level of synthesis," he drew upon existing estimates to support his claims. He concluded that of 9,566,000 slaves imported into the Americas, 1,552,000 went to Spanish America and 3,646,800 went to Brazil. The total imports for English North America were 399,000, and the remainder went to French, Dutch, and other colonies. Curtin warned that his numbers serve as a range rather than as set figures, but he argued that their principal value was "not in being correct, but in being correct enough to point out contradictions in present hypotheses and to raise new questions for comparative demography and social history." Most importantly, his numbers show that "the United States was only a marginal recipient of slaves from Africa," and they support his claim that the region was unique in its pattern of natural growth among the enslaved population.

Curtin used the methods of hard science to frame his challenge, and Peter H. Wood employed the techniques of social history to answer it. His 1974 *Black Majority: Negroes in Colonial South Carolina from 1670 through the Stono Rebellion* considers the laws and statutes of the late 17th and early 18th centuries, but its significance lies in the pioneering effort to understand the role of the enslaved in American history by looking at human relationships and specific contributions. Wood's sources included colonial records, parish transcripts, public records, contemporary newspapers, and plantation diaries, as well as less traditional sources such as land records, inventories, and wills. He also employed a multidisciplinary approach by relying on statistics as well as modern medical and linguistic theory.

According to Wood, Africans played a significant role in the development of SOUTH CAROLINA. He claimed that while planters were familiar with the process of enslaving blacks, the difference between lifelong slavery and limited servitude were not clear during the initial settlement. The move to an African workforce, he explained, depended in part on variables concerning the Africans themselves. He argued that not only did a number of Africans possess prior knowledge of rice cultivation, but many also had retained a sickle-cell trait that gave them some resistance to malaria.

Wood also portrayed the development of slavery in South Carolina as part of a larger shift from a frontier to a market-oriented society. The settlement was unique among mainland colonies because it emerged from Barbados rather than directly from England. Its initial role was to raise cattle and provide meat for Barbados, but the settlers sought a cash crop of their own. According to Wood, blacks were imported during the first 25 years in small numbers, mostly from Barbados, and they played a large role in the early success through their familiarity with open grazing. Initially, "the conditions of life and labor did not yet vary greatly between servant and slave, free and unfree," and slaves "simply shared the calling of the white households to which they were annexed, participating fully in the colony's growing number of specialized trades."

The shift to full-scale African slavery involved a number of factors. White laborers served for a limited time and earned freedom dues. While planters could use creative means to extend the terms of white workers, such action would cause fewer white workers to leave Britain as word of such treatment spread. Proprietors could not enslave large numbers of Indians because they did not wish to arouse hostilities with local tribes, and they wanted to protect their trade in deerskins. Initially, the high price, limited supply, and high mortality rates of Africans discouraged planters, and many were tempted to sell them for a profit rather than keep large numbers and risk a loss. As rice cultivation became more important, however, African skill "was one factor which made black labor attractive to the English colonists." Thus, Wood argued that blacks were taken to the colonies as skilled rather than unskilled laborers. Also, he drew upon medical theories of "epidemiologic regionalism" and "balanced polymorphisms" to explain that, as the English soon learned, Africans contracted malaria less often because of inherited and acquired immunities.

After explaining how blacks became the majority in South Carolina, Wood described what life was like for them there. During the early years of diversification, planter absenteeism was low, and "though racial lines were growing and sometimes brutal . . . servants and masters shared the crude and egalitarian intimacies inevitable on a frontier . . . as common hardships and the continuing shortage of hands put the different races. . . upon a more equal footing than they would see in subsequent generations." He pointed to fairly frequent racial mixing until the growth of the black population, especially "unseasoned" laborers from Africa, caused the government to place restrictions against manumission, INTERRACIAL MARRIAGE, and the rights of free blacks in general.

By describing the evolution of racial distinction as well as the contributions of blacks in the development of American society, Wood addressed both major themes of Tannenbaum's work while answering Davis's call for a distinction between the prescriptions of laws and the reality of practical, everyday life. His book serves as a major transition in the field of colonial slavery, linking the early studies of the institution and its relationship to American racism and the current emphasis on the enslaved population and black agency in creating the Americas.

Beverly C. Tomek

FURTHER READING

Curtin, Philip D. *The Atlantic Slave Trade: A Census*. Madison: University of Wisconsin Press, 1969.

Davis, David Brion. *The Problem of Slavery in Western Culture*. Ithaca, N.Y.: Cornell University Press, 1966.

Degler, Carl. "Slavery and the Genesis of American Race Prejudice." *Comparative Studies in Society and History* 2 (1959): 49–66. Reprinted in James Kirby Martin, ed., *Interpreting Colonial America: Selected Readings*. New York: Harper & Row, 1978, 124–139.

Handlin, Oscar, and Mary F. Handlin. "Origins of the Southern Labor System." *William & Mary Quarterly*, 3rd *ser* 7 (1950): 199–222.

Jordan, Winthrop. *White over Black: American Attitudes toward the Negro, 1550–1812*. Chapel Hill: University of North Carolina Press, 1968.

Tannenbaum, Frank. *Slave and Citizen: The Negro in the Americas*. New York: Vintage Books, 1946.

Wood, Peter. *Black Majority: Negroes in Colonial South Carolina from 1670 through the Stono Rebellion*. New York: W. W. Norton, 1974.

TAYLOR, SUSIE BAKER KING (1848–1912)
American educator

Susie Baker King Taylor is an outstanding example of the role played by free people of color in the reconstruction of the South after the AMERICAN CIVIL WAR (*see also* RECONSTRUCTION IN THE UNITED STATES). As a child, she was able to obtain an education, in part because she was free and in part because local whites subverted regulations to help her. She put her education to work supporting the newly freed people during and after the war and later wrote an autobiography.

A photograph of Susie Baker King Taylor (1848–1912) in her later years, published as the frontispiece to her memoirs in 1902. As a teenager, living "as free" in Georgia, Taylor joined a large group of African Americans who lived under the protection of Union soldiers near Port Royal, South Carolina. Since she had managed to learn to read, she worked as a literacy teacher for her compatriots, as well as working as a laundress and cook for black Union soldiers. She became friends with the regimental commander, the poet Thomas Wentworth Higginson. She married a soldier, ran a school in Georgia after the Civil War, and then moved to Massachusetts, where Higginson and the other officers of her regiment encouraged her to publish her memoirs. (*Art Resource, NY*)

She was born Susie Baker, a slave in Liberty County, GEORGIA, on August 6, 1848. At the age of seven, she was informally freed by her owner and went to Savannah to live with her free grandmother (*see also* LIVING "AS FREE"). She lived there until the outbreak of the American Civil War in 1861. During this time, she attended a secret school for children of color and learned to read and write (*see also* EDUCATION AND LITERACY). In her autobiography, she explains that the school pretended to be a place where children of color were taught manual trades, but it in fact also offered literacy training; it was against Georgia law at the time even for free blacks to learn to read.

Baker moved to St. Simon's Island in SOUTH CAROLINA, an area under the control of Union forces, along with many other people of color from the Savannah area. In April 1862, Union forces under command of General David Hunter (1802–86) occupied many islands along the coast of South Carolina and Georgia. Hunter was a committed abolitionist and immediately sought to encourage blacks to flee to his lines and enrolled black men first in a locally created MILITIA and then in the REGULAR ARMY. Only 13 years old, Taylor opened a school to teach literacy to both children and adults. Confederate raiders attacked them there in summer 1862, and many of the men of the community took up arms to defend themselves. A Union officer, Colonel Thomas Wentworth Higginson, organized the community self-defense force into what was officially designated the 1st South Carolina Colored Volunteers on January 31, 1863, shortly after President ABRAHAM LINCOLN issued the EMANCIPATION PROCLAMATION, which permitted blacks to serve in the Union army. This was the first African-American unit in the Union army, although it was not formally organized as a regiment until after a few other black units, including the New Orleans Native Guards and 54th MASSACHUSETTS regiments, were accepted into the Union army. Higginson was later to be famous for describing the Gullah culture of the coastal islands of Georgia and South Carolina and preparing a dictionary of their language. The 1st South Carolina ultimately was redesignated the 33rd U.S. Colored Troops regiment.

Taylor married Edward King, a black sergeant in the unit, in 1863 and enrolled as laundress of his company. She took care of the uniforms and clothing of the men of her unit, nursed them when sick or injured, and taught reading and writing to many of the men of the regiment. She had good relations with the regiment's white officers, most of whom were abolitionists from Massachusetts.

Taylor continued with the unit throughout the war, during several campaigns. The unit participated in the Union attempt to capture Jacksonville, FLORIDA, in February 1864; in the siege of CHARLESTON, SOUTH CAROLINA, in summer 1864; and in campaigning along the coast of Georgia. Taylor was present when Charleston fell in February 1865. The regiment participated in the occupation of South Carolina, being finally disbanded in February 1866.

Taylor returned to Georgia after the war, but tragedy struck when her husband died in fall 1866 just before the birth of their child, a girl. She opened a school for freedmen, supporting herself through small tuition charges. She was never able to receive any support from the FREEDMEN'S BUREAU or other organizations assisting the newly freed. She finally took a job as a personal servant to a wealthy Northern woman and moved to Massachusetts in 1870. She remarried, to Russell Taylor, and had one more child, a son. In Massachusetts, she reestablished contact with a number of the officers whom she had served under during the war, and they encouraged her to write her story. Her autobiography, *Reminiscences of My Life in Camp,* was published in 1902. She lived in Massachusetts until her death sometime in 1912.

Stewart R. King

FURTHER READING
Higginson, Thomas Wentworth. *Army Life in a Black Regiment.* Boston: Fields, Osgood, 1870. Available online. URL: http://www.gutenberg.org/ebooks/6764. Accessed January 12, 2011.
Taylor, Susie King. *Reminiscences of My Life in Camp.* Boston: privately published, 1902. In *Collected Black Women's Narratives,* edited by Anthony Barthelemy. Oxford: Oxford University Press, 1988.

TAYLOR, ZACHARY (1784–1850) *military officer and 12th president of the United States (1849–1850)*
Zachary Taylor was one of the two principal American military leaders in the MEXICAN-AMERICAN WAR, which increased the size of the United States by almost a third. His short term as president from 1849 to 1850 was marked by the debate over what was to be done with these new territories, and especially over the question of slavery. Taylor reaffirmed the position that presidents including the Democratic Party hero ANDREW JACKSON had taken against secession and states' power to overrule federal laws.

Taylor was born on November 24, 1784, in Virginia. He was descended from a family of large planters. As a boy, he moved with his family to KENTUCKY, near Louisville, where they were large landowners and also owned a number of slaves. He grew up surrounded by people of color, both free and enslaved. Louisville had a large population of free people of color, and he must have seen them in the streets, done business with free colored ARTISANS and shopkeepers, and employed free colored laborers as a young man. In 1808, he joined the REGULAR ARMY and served until 1847, rising to the rank of general. During his military career, he acquired a large plantation in LOUISIANA. He was the last U.S. president to have owned slaves while in office.

As with most military officers, Taylor had no formal political affiliation, but he was close to Kentucky's best-known politician, Senator Henry Clay, leader of the Whig Party. As were most of the Whigs, Taylor was personally opposed to war with MEXICO, but when the Democratic president JAMES POLK ordered him to take his troops into the disputed border region in April 1845 and seek battle with Mexican army units based there, he obeyed. The fighting that broke out led to the Mexican-American War, declared by Congress, after a bitter political battle, in May 1846. Taylor led his men into northern Mexico, capturing the large city of Monterey. After this victory, President Polk diverted many of his soldiers to the more politically reliable General Winfield Scott's expedition to Mexico City, and the weakened army under Taylor was attacked by the main Mexican army. Taylor's victory over the Mexicans at the Battle of Buena Vista (February 23, 1847) made him a national hero. While serving as commander of the American forces, Taylor fought against a unit of the Mexican army, the San Patricio Battalion, composed of American deserters and African Americans who had fled to Mexico to escape slavery. The San Patricios caused the American forces many casualties, especially at Buena Vista, where their artillery fire was key to ensuring the safe escape of the main body of the Mexican army. However, unlike General Scott in the Mexico City region, Taylor treated prisoners taken from the San Patricio unit the same as other Mexican prisoners of war, releasing them on parole awaiting exchange. Scott, on the other hand, hanged 30 San Patricio soldiers as traitors when he captured them after the Battle of Churubusco (August 20, 1847). Taylor did more than almost any other American leader to gain victory in the Mexican War, even though he opposed it on principle. The victory over the Mexicans caused considerable hardship for the free people of color of the captured territories, substituting a harsh Anglo-American racial climate for the more nuanced and flexible Hispanic approach.

Resenting his treatment by the Democratic leadership, Taylor left the military and ran for president as a Whig in the 1848 election. Antislavery Northerners put forward a third-party challenge, the Free Soil Party, with the former president MARTIN VAN BUREN as their standard bearer. Van Buren drew immigrant and Northern votes away from the Democrats, and Taylor cruised to victory.

The great issue of Taylor's presidency was the question of the status of the new territories acquired from Mexico. President Polk had suggested that the MISSOURI Compromise line should be extended to the Pacific, putting most of the newly conquered lands in slave territory. Northern abolitionists put forward the Wilmot Proviso, which would have prohibited slavery in all the territories. Southern state governments threatened secession if the proviso became law. Taylor announced that he would personally lead the army against any state that tried to leave the Union. In January 1850, Senator Clay proposed a set of compromises that would ultimately defuse the crisis. Among these compromises was the FUGITIVE SLAVE ACT OF 1850, a measure that had a profoundly negative impact on free blacks living in the North. Taylor was opposed to further extension of the lands open to slavery. He had served in the West and realized that plantation agriculture was impossible there, and he agreed with the Northern Whig position that the tradition of the United States, dating back to the Northwest Ordinance, opposed the expansion of slavery. However, he favored reconciliation and probably would have signed the measure had it come to his desk. However, before Clay and the ILLINOIS senator Stephen Douglas could guide these proposals through Congress, Taylor died suddenly on July 9, 1850.

Taylor's 16-month tenure as president limited his impact on free people of color. Although a Southerner and a slave owner, he sought compromise on the expansion of slavery into the newly conquered territories. He supported the power of the federal government against the states. He was more humane as a military leader than his colleague, Scott. Premature death robbed him of the chance to confront the issue of slavery head on in the crisis of 1850.

Stewart R. King

FURTHER READING

Bauer, K. Jack. *Zachary Taylor: Soldier, Planter, Statesman of the Old Southwest*. Baton Rouge: Louisiana State University Press, 1993.

Smith, Elbert B. *The Presidencies of Zachary Taylor and Millard Fillmore*. Lawrence: University Press of Kansas, 1988.

TENNESSEE

Tennessee is a state in the United States bordered on the north by the states of KENTUCKY and Virginia; on the east by NORTH CAROLINA; on the south by GEORGIA, ALABAMA, and MISSISSIPPI; and on the west by the Mississippi River, beyond which lie ARKANSAS and MISSOURI. Tennessee is divided into three regions: East Tennessee, Middle Tennessee, and West Tennessee. Much of East Tennessee is mountainous (containing parts of the Smoky Mountains), while Middle Tennessee has the foothills of these mountains and fertile countryside, and West Tennessee comprises low hills and plains. Three major rivers also run along or through the state—the Mississippi, Tennessee, and Cumberland—contributing to the fertile soil of the state and providing transportation and fuel.

Colonial History

Spaniards led by Hernando de Soto in 1540 were the first group of Europeans to visit what is now the state of

Tennessee. As with many other Spanish *entradas*, or exploratory missions, in the 16th century, he was accompanied by people of African ancestry, both free and enslaved. De Soto was accompanied by at least 34 slaves from CUBA, and some of his free recruits from Cuba must have been mulattoes or blacks, given the racial makeup of the Cuban people at that time, though no detailed listing with racial identifiers survives. De Soto and other explorers found Native American farming communities and fortified villages in the 16th century. Indeed, modern researchers have discovered evidence of humans in the Tennessee area as early as 7,500 B.C., and Tennessee has numerous artifacts from the prehistoric Mound Builder culture. The state's name is taken from the Tennessee River, which was derived from the name of a Cherokee village.

Despite the early exploration by the Spanish, the area was claimed by the French in the 17th century. While traveling down the Mississippi River in 1682, the French explorer Robert Cavelier, sieur de La Salle, claimed for FRANCE a vast region of land on both sides of the Mississippi River, stretching from the Gulf of Mexico to CANADA and including Tennessee. The French established some trading forts in the area, including Fort Prudhomme on the Mississippi River north of Memphis, the first settlement by Europeans in West Tennessee.

But the French claim to the area was never secure: English frontiersmen who traveled regularly over the mountains from Virginia and the Carolinas had also been exploring and hunting in the area and trading with Indians (Choctaw, Shawnee, Chickasaw, and Cherokee Indians lived and hunted in what is today Tennessee). In 1763, the French permanently lost their claim to the land in the peace settlements after the French and Indian War (known in Europe as the SEVEN YEARS' WAR).

By the early 1770s, dozens of British families had settled in the valleys of the Watauga, Holston, and Nolichucky Rivers in Eastern Tennessee. And settlers kept coming, from Virginia, North Carolina, and PENNSYLVANIA. Largely ignored by colonial authorities, these settlers formed the Watauga Association, which established an independent government and adopted the first constitution in America in 1772. The association continued until the outbreak of the WAR OF AMERICAN INDEPENDENCE (1775–83), when the settlements were annexed to North Carolina. In 1779, James Robertson, known as the "Father of Tennessee," led a group that settled Nashboro (later called Nashville). These immigrants, from slaveholding areas for the most part, included some free African Americans and more numerous enslaved people. Slavery and black life in Tennessee in the 18th century were, as in many frontier zones throughout the Americas, looser and more nuanced than in the plantation zones.

The presence of large numbers of native people in Tennessee also affected the racial climate. The Cherokee, in particular, were well organized, and many operated large farms, grew cash crops, and owned African-American slaves. Native people, however, were more willing than whites to grant equal treatment to at least some African Americans, and between the arrival of people from the eastern colonies in the territory in the 1770s and the expulsion of the Cherokee in the Trail of Tears in the 1830s, many African Americans went to live among the Cherokee as equals.

Tennessee Statehood

The state of Tennessee was eventually organized out of western lands that North Carolina ceded to the United States in 1785. In 1785, however, Tennesseans, angered at the cession of lands made without their consent, briefly formed an unrecognized independent government known as the State of Franklin—named after Benjamin Franklin—which lasted until 1789. Tennesseeans also negotiated with the Spanish authorities, then in control of NEW ORLEANS, LOUISIANA, leaving open the possibility of the area's joining the Spanish colonial empire. The racial climate found in Spanish territory was much different from even the relatively loose rules observed in Tennessee, and this may have been one of the reasons Tennessee ultimately elected to remain part of the United States. In 1789, the federal government created what became known as the Southwest Territory, with Tennessee part of it.

By 1795, the Tennessee area had a population large enough to apply for statehood, and the state legislature elected senators (William Blount and William Cocke) and a representative (the future U.S. president ANDREW JACKSON) before the state was even admitted to the Union. After a close vote in the U.S. Congress, Tennessee was admitted as the 16th state of the Union on June 1, 1796. Tennessee entered the Union as a slave state, but its constitution provided free blacks with the right to vote if they met residency and property requirements. Free people of color made up barely 1 percent of the population of the territory in 1790, but the formal acceptance by Tennessee of their citizenship demonstrates that the relatively looser racial climate of the colonial days still persisted.

In the post–Revolutionary War era, veterans who had been awarded land grants for their service and speculators arrived in Tennessee. Some land had been gained by a series of treaties with Indians, and in other cases, land was captured as a result of wars. Ultimately, many Indians and the free and enslaved blacks who lived among them were removed by force and marched on foot to the Oklahoma Territory in the 1830s in what became known as the Trail of Tears.

AFRICAN-AMERICAN POPULATION OF TENNESSEE, 1790–1900

Year	Slaves	Free People of Color (not counting those living among Indians)	Free People of Color as a Percentage of Total Population	Total Population
1790	3,417	361	1.0%	35,691
1800	13,584	309	0.3%	105,602
1810	44,535	1,317	0.5%	261,727
1820	78,896	2,149	0.5%	422,813
1830	141,603	4,555	0.7%	681,903
1840	183,059	5,524	0.7%	829,210
1850	239,459	6,422	0.6%	1,002,717
1860	275,719	7,300	0.7%	1,109,801
1870		322,331	25.6%	1,258,520
1880		403,151	26.1%	1,542,359
1890		430,678	24.4%	1,767,518
1900		480,248	23.8%	2,020,616

The number of blacks in the state grew dramatically in the early 19th century, exceeding 145,000 in 1830 though only 4,555 of them, or 3 percent, were free. Tennessee's status as a frontier state led to its becoming one of the leading states in slave trading: Its economic dependence on COTTON CULTIVATION, as elsewhere in the South, supported its reliance on slavery.

The slave population in Tennessee was highest in West Tennessee, where large cotton plantations developed in the rich soil area of the Mississippi Delta. Middle Tennessee was also home to many slaves, but planters there had smaller operations where they raised horses and developed mixed crops, so fewer slaves were required to support their efforts. East Tennessee had the fewest slaves; generally, farmers in the mountainous East were subsistence or small cash-crop, or "yeoman," farmers. By the time of the AMERICAN CIVIL WAR, there were more than 275,000 slaves in Tennessee, almost one-quarter of the population.

Free People of Color and the Rise of Racial Discrimination

After statehood, Tennessee adopted many of North Carolina's stringent laws governing MANUMISSION, but settlers did not always follow them and freed slaves for service or merit, in wills, and for other reasons. Indeed, notions of slavery did not sit well with some early Tennesseans, especially those in the East. Dependence on slavery seemed to contradict the Tennessee frontier or pioneer spirit and conflict with the revolutionary ideas of liberty and independence.

Free people of color could own property and vote in early Tennessee. Although free people of color did not have the same degree of personal freedom as whites, social roles were flexible, in part because of the small total number of settlers. By 1870, there were approximately 2,100 free people of color in Tennessee, less than 1 percent of the state's population.

As early as the 1790s, Thomas Embree and other white citizens of Tennessee, especially Presbyterian clergymen and Quakers, desired to establish an abolition society. Charles Osborn, with support from Quakers, was eventually successful in establishing the Tennessee Society for Promoting the Manumission of Slaves in 1815. The society argued that slavery was counter to Christian teachings and advocated freeing individual slaves on the basis of their merit (as the idea of universal and immediate emancipation seemed too radical). It was partly due to this group's efforts that Tennessee banned the importation of slaves from other states in 1826. Free people of color were also working toward emancipation, notably Elihu Embry of Jonesboro, who began publishing the weekly *Manumission Intelligencer* in 1819 and the monthly *Emancipator* in 1820. These small, intermittently published newspapers predate what has long been thought of as the first black newspaper in the United States, New York's *Freedom's Journal*, which began publication in 1827. (*See also* BLACK PRESS IN THE UNITED STATES.) The latter paper was much more important because it gained national attention for the cause of abolition and for its free black publisher, JOHN RUSSWURM.

As cotton growing became more firmly entrenched in the early 19th century, slavery grew dramatically in Middle and West Tennessee. The size of the free black community also grew, but far more slowly. East Tennessee held the most free blacks and the fewest slaves, while West Tennessee held the most slaves and the fewest free blacks.

In West and Middle Tennessee, most free people of color resided in urban areas. The largest free black population in the state was found in Nashville, the state capital and largest city, where almost 1,000 of the total statewide population of around 6,500 lived in 1850. The trades and professions that free people of color could enter were limited. Generally, men worked as skilled or unskilled laborers. Women often worked as cooks or seamstresses. A few of these free people of color were landowners and had slaves of their own. Tennessee's wealthiest black slave owner was Sherrod Bryant, who owned 700 acres in Middle Tennessee. In East Tennessee, free blacks lived in the countryside.

Some of these free people of color in rural East Tennessee came to be known as MELUNGEONS (a term with negative connotations until the 20th century). Modern scholars speculate that Melungeons were freed slaves who intermarried with British settlers and Cherokee Indians who were in the area. The Indian identity of these groups, as with similar groups in western North Carolina, may have been adopted as a way to evade the harsher racial strictures on African Americans in the post–Civil War period, as DNA analysis shows that most individuals have little native ancestry.

Despite the work of abolitionists, after the bloody Nat Turner slave revolt in Virginia in 1831, legislators enacted several laws that limited the rights of free blacks and attempted to decrease their number. In 1834, delegates met to revise the 1796 state constitution. While delegates were faced with several petitions that called for the abolition of slavery (these were primarily from East Tennessee), the revised constitution changed the laws so that free people of color could not vote and further required that manumission occur only with the consent of the slave's owner and not on the initiative of the state government or local community. In 1853, the Tennessee legislature required that manumission by will be accompanied by the slave's removal from the state. In 1855, the legislature repealed its 1826 law prohibiting the interstate slave trade. While this law had never been enforced systematically, its repeal was a declaration of the government's new sympathy toward slavery. Finally in 1858, the legislature passed a law that permitted free people of color to choose to become slaves—again, not something very likely to happen, but a sign that slavery was beginning to be seen in a more positive light by Tennessee white opinion leaders. (See also BLACK CODES IN THE UNITED STATES.)

The Civil War and Reconstruction

When the American Civil War approached in 1861, Tennessee was divided between joining the Confederacy and remaining with the Union. Support for secession was concentrated in Franklin County in Middle Tennessee, while much of the rest of the state desired to remain part of the United States. But after the attack on Fort Sumter and President Lincoln's call for volunteers in April 1861, Tennesseans in both West and Middle Tennessee supported secession. East Tennesseans disagreed with the rest of the state and attempted to secede from Tennessee, as their neighbors to the north had seceded from Virginia to create West Virginia, but were suppressed by force. On June 8, 1861, Tennessee withdrew from the Union and soon joined the Confederacy. As in other Southern states, one of the motives for secession can be traced to economic reliance on the institution of slavery.

Second only to Virginia in the number of battles fought within its borders, Tennessee was a bloody battleground during the Civil War. Gaining control of Tennessee's rivers and railroads was an important part of the Union's strategy. Nashville in 1862 became the first Confederate state capital to fall. ANDREW JOHNSON, from Eastern Tennessee a serving U.S. senator from Tennessee, and the only Southern member of the 1860 Congress to remain loyal to the United States, was appointed the state's military governor.

In 1861, free blacks in Tennessee were drafted into the Confederate army by an act of the Tennessee legislature. Enforcement of the draft was inconsistent. Southern commanders did not want blacks carrying weapons. Some individual blacks served in the Confederate forces as servants or laborers, often accompanying former masters. After the state was occupied by Union soldiers in 1862–63, many blacks in Tennessee and elsewhere contributed to the Union side.

Thousands of fugitive slaves fled to Union armies in Tennessee. The federal government established refugee camps for these people, calling them "contraband of war," comparable to confiscated horses or wagons. That is, slaves were at first treated as was any other form of enemy property, confiscated to prevent it from being used for military ends. The refugees nonetheless saw that a Union victory was in their interest. Some of these fugitives worked for the Union army as skilled and unskilled laborers and eventually were recruited to fight for the Union. More than 20,000 black Tennesseans served as soldiers in regiments such as the 14th U.S. Colored Infantry Regiment, organized at Gallatin, Tennessee, after the Battle of Chickamauga in 1863. This regiment and other U.S. Colored Troops units engaged in battles in Alabama, ARKANSAS, Louisiana, Mississippi, and Georgia. Free people of color served as community leaders in this early phase. As leaders of black churches, teachers in schools in the refugee encampments, and noncommissioned officers in the black army units, they helped their fellow blacks adjust to their new status of freedom and concentrate their efforts for the overthrow of the slave system.

The Civil War ended in the Confederacy's defeat in 1865; Union soldiers had occupied Tennessee for much of the war, and its resources were depleted as a result. What followed the war was the period known as RECONSTRUCTION IN THE UNITED STATES, wherein Southern states that had seceded worked to regain their status, and slavery was abolished. Tennessee abolished slavery in a state constitutional amendment on February 22, 1865, and ratified the Fourteenth Amendment to the U.S. Constitution on July 18, 1866. Partly because of these actions, it was the first former Confederate state to be readmitted to the Union on July 24, 1866, and was spared the military rule common in other Southern states.

The lack of military rule might imply that conditions for blacks were better in Tennessee than in other states, but conditions were poor in the cities, and sharecropping developed in rural areas. In May 1866, the Memphis Race Riot erupted, the result of a bitter political and social situation. The riot broke out because of local whites' hostility to the black soldiers who guarded the city. When the commanding officer of the military post disarmed his black troops, at the insistence of local officials, mobs led by white policemen and firefighters rampaged through the black districts, killing, burning, and raping for two days. When the riot ended, two white and 46 black residents had died. Black schools, churches, and homes were burned and destroyed.

Blacks did make some headway in serving as state and city officers. For instance, Ed Shaw was elected Shelby County commissioner in 1867, and the first black legislator, Sampson W. Keeble, a former free black pressman for the Murfreesboro newspaper, was elected in 1872 and served one term.

Blacks made some gains in education, especially before 1870, with the financial assistance of the FREEDMEN'S BUREAU. When the grants from the Freedmen's Bureau ended, the students of Fisk University, a black college in Nashville, developed the Fisk Jubilee Singers group as a way to raise money to ensure the survival of the college. Singing slave spirituals, the group was successful and traveled throughout the United States and abroad. Many black schools, however, closed because of lack of funding.

Blacks made other kinds of progress in the state as well. William B. Scott (1821–55), a prewar free black from North Carolina, published the newspaper the *Colored Tennessean* in Nashville. In Maryville, in 1868, he published the *Maryville Republican,* later called the *Maryville Democrat.* Scott served as mayor in Maryville in 1879 and helped found a school for blacks, the Freedman's Normal Institute.

Blacks often organized themselves through churches. The First Baptist Church in Nashville originally had a mixed membership of whites, free blacks, and slaves, but a separate mission for blacks developed in the 1840s. Nelson Merry (1824–84), born a slave but freed before the Civil War, led the mission from 1853 to 1884, expanding its membership dramatically. The mission became the First Colored Baptist Church in 1865.

By the 1870s, however, the prewar white leaders were working to regain power and disenfranchise blacks, and they were ultimately successful. Voting rights for blacks were limited after the passage of a poll tax, and former Confederates regained their right to vote. Intimidation techniques to prevent blacks from voting were also common. In 1866, the KU KLUX KLAN was organized in Pulaski, Tennessee, and the organization grew throughout the South as members intimidated, harassed, and killed blacks.

In the years that followed, white elite Democrats gained control over both houses of Tennessee's legislature. Jim Crow laws that resulted in "separate but equal" transportation, schools, and other public services were passed in Tennessee and throughout the South.

These provisions for SEGREGATION and disfranchisement lasted into the 20th century, although they were challenged by such leaders as the journalist Ida B. Wells (1862–1931) and the politician and educator James C. Napier (1845–1940), who was a prewar free black, and through such events as the 1905 boycott of streetcars in Nashville, organized in part by Wells.

Summer Leibensperger

FURTHER READING
Alexander, Thomas B. *Political Reconstruction in Tennessee.* New York: Russell & Russell, 1968.
Dykeman, Wilma. *Tennessee: A Bicentennial History.* New York: W. W. Norton, 1975.
Goodstein, Anita S. "Black History on the Nashville Frontier, 1780–1810." In *Trial and Triumph: Essays in Tennessee's African American History,* edited by Carroll Van West. Knoxville: University of Tennessee Press, 2002.
Hahn, Steven. *A Nation under Our Feet: Black Political Struggles in the Rural South from Slavery to the Great Migration.* Cambridge, Mass.: Belknap Press of Harvard University Press, 2003.
Lamon, Lester C. *Blacks in Tennessee, 1791–1970.* Knoxville: University of Tennessee Press, 1981.
Van West, Carroll, ed. *Trial and Triumph: Essays in Tennessee's African American History.* Knoxville: University of Tennessee Press, 2002.

TEN YEARS' WAR (GREAT WAR OF CUBA)

The Ten Years' War, also known as the Great War of CUBA and the first Cuban War of Independence, was fought between 1868 and 1878. The Spanish government, inter-

TYPES OF THE CUBAN PATRIOT SOLDIERS.—[SEE PAGE 674.]

A contemporary illustration showing a number of Cuban soldiers from the Ten Year's War. The racial diversity and social egalitarianism of the Cuban rebel army is visible, as the light-skinned soldier is holding the dark-skinned officer's horse. *(The Granger Collection, New York)*

mittently distracted by rebellion at home, aided by conservative Cubans, fought against liberal CREOLE nationalists, who had the support of most of Cuba's people of color, both free and enslaved. The war resulted in a military stalemate and a set of political compromises that met some of the demands of the rebels, including the abolition of the slave trade, while preserving the political tie between SPAIN and Cuba and the existence of the institution of slavery. The war was immediately followed by the Little War (1879–80), which led to the abolition of slavery, and, 15 years later, the Cuban War of Independence (1895–98), which was connected to the Spanish-American War in 1898 and led ultimately to the independence of Cuba. Free people of color were important members of the liberal, pro-independence coalition, and their position in Cuban society was profoundly affected by the struggle.

In the decades before the war, Cuba had become the wealthiest part of the plantation world. Almost 2 million slaves worked in Cuba by 1868. Many of them had been taken to the island from Africa, despite Spain's formal agreement to end the slave trade to Cuba in 1817. The illegal trade to Cuba was financed by capital from Europe

and North America and was a very profitable business. Cuba was a world leader in both SUGAR CULTIVATION and tobacco production in the 1860s. The continuing strength of the plantation system meant that the relative racial harmony that had existed in Cuba in the 17th and early 18th centuries had sharply eroded. Cuba's slaves worked under increasingly harsh conditions on huge, factorylike plantations, especially in the western part of the country around Havana. In the East, there were plantations, but they were smaller, and work regimes and personal relationships were more like those of pre-sugar Cuba, with masters who cared more about the social value of large slaveholdings than about extracting every last dollar of work from them. Free people of color were increasingly excluded from social positions and public institutions that had accepted them a century before. For example, the free colored MILITIA, an important social institution and means of social advancement for Afro-Cuban men, had been dissolved after the LA ESCALERA PLOT conspiracy of 1843. It was reestablished in 1857, but few free colored men received leadership positions, and the militia was often assigned to menial tasks. The professions were increasingly difficult for free men of color to enter, though there were still some free black journalists, authors, and medical professionals. The *cabildos*, or fraternal organizations, organized along African tribal lines, which had been important social avenues for free colored men, were shut down or restricted to people born in Africa, and they were under increasing surveillance and suspicion. Similarly, the AMERICAN CIVIL WAR caused an economic downturn in Cuba after 1862, as the United States had always been an important trading partner for Cuba. Nonetheless, the situation of free people of color in Cuba in the mid-19th century was considerably better than that of free blacks in the United States at the same time. There were Afro-Cubans who had real political influence, significant wealth, and social respectability, though their numbers were small. Poor and middle-class free blacks made up a significant proportion of the free population, especially in the eastern part of the country, where the plantation sector was weaker.

The various concerns of Cuba's elites were addressed by a series of reforms implemented by the liberal Spanish government during the early 1850s. These included some movement toward local self-government, relaxation of harsh regulations against free people of color, limited enforcement of the prohibition on importation of slaves from Africa, and economic reforms. However, political deadlock in Spain meant that these reforms were short-lived, with conservative governments rolling back progressive reforms only to be overthrown in their turn by liberals who would try to implement change again. The rapid changes succeeded only in irritating Cuban conservatives without actually improving the situation of the Cuban people.

Cuba's rebel movement was led at first by elite whites from eastern Cuba, such as Francisco Vicente Aguilera (1821–77), owner of one of the region's largest plantations, with hundreds of slaves. At the outbreak of the rebellion, he freed 500 of his slaves, armed them, and marched on the regional capital of Bayamo. Similar was Carlos Manuel de Céspedes (1819–74), provisional president of the rebel movement until 1873, who was also a large landowner in the eastern region and also freed his slaves when the fighting began. Another important early leader was the Spanish cavalry officer Máximo Gómez (1836–1905), who had been born in the DOMINICAN REPUBLIC. Ironically, he had fought for Spain in the Dominican War of Independence in 1864 and moved to Cuba, where he took up the cause of independence. He learned from his adversaries in the Dominican war, Haitians and Dominican irregular troops, to trust the fighting qualities of black soldiers, and it was he who encouraged the rebels to enroll people of color in their ranks and promote the most capable to the ranks of commanding officers. His

longtime second in command and closest collaborator throughout all the terrible struggles for freedom in the Antilles was ANTONIO MACEO Y GRAJALES, the "Bronze Titan," a free colored entrepreneur and planter from the vicinity of Santiago de Cuba. Another important black leader was Guillermo Moncada (1841–1905), a free black carpenter known as "Guillermón" because of his huge size, who rose to the rank of general and also fought alongside Maceo in the War of Independence.

The rebels began their movement with an aggressive attempt to seize control of the capital, Havana, and the surrounding plantation areas. However, this ambition was foiled by the few REGULAR ARMY troops in the colony and by militias raised by western landowners. The Spanish army's counterattack into eastern Cuba was foiled in its turn. The next several years saw the reduction of the few remaining loyalist strongholds in the East, in Santiago and Guantánamo, and one more rebel attempt to invade the western part of the country, in 1874. The coffee planters of Guantánamo were especially fervent in their resistance as many of their ancestors had immigrated from Haiti after the HAITIAN REVOLUTION. In the faces of the Afro-Cuban soldiers, they saw their ancestral enemies, the Haitian slave rebels, and both sides fought a war without mercy in that region. Spain sent troops as they could spare them, but most of the Spanish army was occupied at home fighting a liberal military uprising (1868) and then the Second Carlist War (1872–76). The Cuban forces were internally divided. The wealthy liberal creole elites who sought national unification and racial harmony lost power within the movement—Céspedes was removed as provisional president and killed, by Spanish forces but perhaps with the complicity of his enemies within the Cuban leadership. Military leaders such as Gómez and Maceo remained powerful through their control of troops, but political leadership of the movement drifted into the hands of people less devoted to the cause of independence and racial justice.

After the moderate victory in the Carlist War, Spain was able to send a quarter-million battle-tested troops to Cuba, and the rebels' position began to decline. Spain offered a political compromise to the rebel commanders that resulted in the Pact of Zanjón on February 8, 1878. This agreement, not signed by Maceo and several other important free colored leaders, gave freedom to all slaves who had fought in the rebel army, proclaimed amnesty for the rebels, finally ended the slave trade, and established local representative institutions and administrative reforms that went some way toward the democracy the rebels had initially demanded. The free colored leadership went into exile for the most part, and Maceo launched another rebellion in 1879 from his refuge in New York. This rebellion was easily crushed, but one important repercussion was that the Spanish government finally agreed to end slavery definitively, as they finally did in 1886 after a short-lived experiment with an apprenticeship system called *patronato* in which slaves were to continue to work for their masters as indentured servants with government supervision.

The Ten Years' War devastated Cuba, especially the eastern provinces, and profoundly affected the lives of every Cuban, white or black. The western part of the island was not much affected by the war in a direct sense, but occasional rebel attacks combined with risk-averse capital markets, unwilling in any case to be associated with one of the few remaining strongholds of slavery, meant that the rapid growth of the plantation sector was interrupted. Both sides drew on the slave population for soldiers and noncombatant auxiliaries such as construction troops, porters, and servants. Slaves who left the plantation, even if they were not formally freed by the provisions of the treaty ending the war, had a much better chance to gain their freedom either by running away or by manumission. Slave importation was effectively stopped by the war, since the main slave port for the island had always been Santiago, and it was in rebel hands for most of the time. Even when reoccupied by loyalist forces, Santiago was still closed to civilian shipping. In any case, the war attracted world attention that made ignoring the laws against the slave trade harder to conceal. Shortly after the end of the war, slavery was replaced with a system of indenture, which was itself abolished six years later. With rapid manumission, frequent flight, and no new imports, the slave population of Cuba fell by more than half during the struggle. After the war, Asian indentured workers were imported to work on the plantations, but without an easy source for these laborers, planters also turned to local free blacks as field hands much more enthusiastically than in other sugar plantation regions. Cuba also began to encourage immigration from southern Europe. These two migrant streams, from South Asia and the Mediterranean, created a wave of immigration that, by the 20th century, profoundly changed the racial makeup of Cuba's population. Ultimately, the plantation sector in Cuba was able to remain profitable without slave labor through a combination of immigrant and free black labor.

The outcome of the war for free people of color was mixed. On the one hand, the end of the slave trade and the limited relaxation in regulations meant a somewhat enhanced social standing for people of color on the island. At the same time, many free colored men had enhanced their personal status and wealth through military service. However, small farms across the eastern part of the island were ruined by passing armies, and many of the small independent free colored farmers of the region found themselves driven either to the cities as workers or into the migrant farm labor population. The wealthy and powerful were better able to survive these changes, and of course most free people of color were poor and excluded. The war offered opportunity as well as danger. Soldiers needed services, and the armies needed goods, and businesspeople could provide them. A few black entrepreneurs were able to join Cuba's new urban business class. Most of the wartime leadership was in exile, but there were some influential free coloreds working for abolition of slavery and full inclusion of people of color in Cuban society. Most notable among these was Juan Gualberto Gómez, a free mixed-race businessman and journalist. Gómez organized a colored political party to agitate for equal civil rights and abolition, then went on to command troops in the War of Independence and after the war continued the struggle against racist laws and U.S. domination.

The war was only a single step in the long history of Afro-Cubans' struggle for freedom and justice. It was an important step, but the high hopes that many had at the outset were dashed, and the outcome, especially with the similarly somewhat disappointing outcome of the American Civil War and RECONSTRUCTION IN THE UNITED STATES and of abolition in BRAZIL, happening at roughly the same time, showed the people of color in the Americas that they still had a long way to go to achieve full civil rights and equality. However, what was achieved during the Ten Years' War could only have been achieved by the efforts of free colored soldiers, leaders, and workers. The elite white rebels who cared about racial justice were driven from leadership, and slaves were rarely in a position to have much impact on events.

Stewart R. King

FURTHER READING

Ferrer, Ada. *Insurgent Cuba: Race, Nation, and Revolution, 1868–1898.* Chapel Hill: University of North Carolina Press, 1999.

Pérez, Louis A., Jr. *Cuba: Between Reform and Revolution.* 3rd ed. New York: Oxford University Press, 2006.

Prados-Torreira, Teresa. *Mambisas: Rebel Women in Nineteenth-Century Cuba.* Gainesville: University Press of Florida, 2005.

Scott, Rebecca J. *Slave Emancipation in Cuba: The Transition to Free Labor, 1860–1899.* Princeton, N.J.: Princeton University Press, 1985.

TEXAS *(TEJAS, LONE STAR STATE)*

Texas is a state of the United States. It is bordered by MEXICO to the southwest, the Gulf of Mexico to the southeast, LOUISIANA and ARKANSAS on the east, OKLAHOMA on the north, and New Mexico on the west (and north). It is a large and diverse place, with the southeastern and eastern sections relatively well watered and having a mild climate, making them suitable for plantation agriculture for COTTON CULTIVATION and planting of other crops, while the West and North are more arid and have a harsher climate, making them more suitable for natural resource extraction or RANCHING. The indigenous inhabitants of Texas were equally diverse, with southwestern and plains Indians who relied on horses and buffalo hunting after the 1500s found in the West and North while settled agriculturalists inhabited the eastern part of the state.

The earliest European visitors were Spaniards, including Álvar Núñez Cabeza de Vaca (1490–1559) and his Afro-Spanish companion ESTÉBAN DE DORANTES, who explored the region from 1529 to 1532. SPAIN claimed Texas as part of the colony of New Spain, but Spanish settlement did not begin until the 17th century. French settlers established a short-lived colony at Matagorda in 1682, and Spanish colonists arrived in the next century to establish a sparse presence. Some of the Spanish settlers had African roots or took Afro-Mexican slaves with them, but Texas was not a plantation region under Spanish rule. Instead, the few hundred Afro-Texans during Spanish colonial times were domestic servants, ARTISANS, technical specialists working in mining or manufacturing, or supervisors of Indian workers, as in CENTRAL AND NORTHERN MEXICO. Of these, most were free.

Anglo and African-American settlers from the United States began to enter in the 1810s, with the permission of the Spanish colonial government. They began to establish plantations and grow cotton and other commodities, for sale to the world market through Louisiana or Texas ports. The movement accelerated after the Mexican victory in the WAR OF MEXICAN INDEPENDENCE, 1810–21. It is estimated that by 1834, there were about 34,000 American settlers (whites and blacks combined) as against around 7,000 Mexicans (not counting Indians native to Texas). The Mexican government was changing its policy about slavery rapidly during this period. Three different proclamations of abolition were published, in 1810, 1821, and 1829. The first was the product of a rebel group and had no effect in Texas, where the Spanish government kept control. The 1821 proclamation was ignored in Texas with respect to slaves imported by North American settlers, and until 1834, in general the structure of Mexico allowed the states wide latitude to govern their own affairs (see MEXICO, ABOLITION OF SLAVERY IN). The 1829 emancipation proclamation by Afro-Mexican president VICENTE GUERRERO SALDAÑA was intended to affect the entire country and abolish slavery immediately, but in fact it was almost four years before it was enforced in any meaningful way in Texas. The government of Mexico

from the late 1820s on was controlled by centralizing liberals who wanted to abolish the separate autonomy of the states, and conservative leaders in many peripheral areas, including Central America and the northwestern territories, considered rebellion. Texas's rebellion was successful in 1836, resulting in the creation of an independent government that was not, however, internationally recognized. Texas attempted to join the United States but was rebuffed for several years. Finally in 1845, Democrats pushed an annexation bill through the U.S. Congress, which eventually led to the MEXICAN-AMERICAN WAR (1846–48).

For African Americans in Texas, the struggle for social, political, and economic equality proved to be long and difficult. From their arrival in the area starting in the 16th century, they fought to overcome the institution of slavery, seething racial hatreds, harsh economic hardships, and the passage of laws explicitly designed along racial lines. White Southern slaveholders traveling to Texas took them there as chattel slaves beginning in the 1810s, expanding enslaved African-American numbers until the AMERICAN CIVIL WAR, 1861–65. When the war ended in 1865 and the United States abolished slavery, African Americans, now freed, faced a litany of violence and oppression as white Texans fought to hold on to old social and political hierarchies. Many African Americans left the state for more promising opportunities, while others stayed behind, attempting to carve out a decent life and fight the various forms of repression imposed upon them.

African-American Origins in Texas

The African-American experience in Texas reflected the unique influence of the Spanish and then Mexican governments, along with expansive trends occurring in the Deep South of the United States. After Mexico gained independence from Spain in 1821, Mexican officials formally abolished the institution of slavery while still allowing American settlers to import "indentured servants." Free blacks who immigrated from the United States were offered equal citizenship in Mexico. American settlers continued to pour into Texas in large numbers in the 1820s, eventually outnumbering the native Mexican population by more than 20,000 people. A suspicious Mexican government then attempted to exert more control over the Texan population in the 1830s, including the enforcement of the federal law prohibiting slavery. By 1836, African-American slaves in Texas numbered 5,000, whereas free blacks numbered only a few hundred. Angered by this more centralized policy of Mexican rule, many Texans began to push for separation between this Mexican state and its federal government. During the ensuing Texas War of Independence (1835–36), Texan forces emerged victorious against Mexican troops, gaining their independence. Free Afro-Texans mostly supported the Texas independence movement, either because they shared American attitudes toward the Mexican government or because they felt pressure from their American neighbors. Notable among these was William Goyens or Goings (1794–1856), a blacksmith and innkeeper in Nacogdoches, who helped Sam Houston negotiate a treaty with the Cherokee Indians of Oklahoma to support the republic during the war against Mexico. Samuel McCullough, a free mixed-race immigrant from NORTH CAROLINA, was wounded when Texan troops took the fort at Goliad at the beginning of the rebellion. However, the Republic of Texas, established in 1836, did not extend citizenship to free blacks and passed laws to exclude new free black immigrants unless they had special permission from the legislature.

Nine years later, in 1845, the United States formally annexed Texas into the Union. SLAVE OWNERS continued to transport enslaved African Americans into the state in large numbers, increasing their population in 1860 to more than 180,000 to work the vast cotton and sugarcane plantations.

After joining the United States, Texas laws relative to free people of color were similar to those found in other places in the Lower South: That is, they were fundamentally hostile to the existence of free people of color as a class. MANUMISSION required legislative permission, and an 1840 law required that all free people of color leave the state within two years or face RE-ENSLAVEMENT unless they had special, individual permission to remain from the legislature. This provision was widely ignored but led to the creation of an indeterminate, but large group of people of color whose legal claim to freedom was unclear. Local prominent whites, in some cases even the same people who, in their capacity as legislators, had voted for these laws, then protected their free black neighbors from their effects. The existence of such a large group of people of unclear status was actually not uncommon in the slave societies of the Americas (see LIVING "AS FREE"), though

it was unusual in the slave states of the United States. In addition, the looser racial categories active in the Spanish-American world continued to function to some degree in Texas, at least for Spanish speakers, known as Tejanos. People of African descent who could claim to be descended from pre-1821 residents were socially defined as Mexican American rather than black.

Many free blacks also migrated out of Texas to the West or South during the period before the Civil War. Mexico continued to offer a greatly superior environment for American blacks, and both free and enslaved black Texans took advantage of this. A substantial population of Afro-Mexicans can still be found in Nuevo León and Tamaulipas states, including the famous BLACK SEMINOLE, descended in many cases from immigrants from Texas. After 1848, the United States controlled New Mexico and Arizona, and both of these places attracted black immigrants from Texas.

For all of these reasons, the population of free people of color in Texas stagnated. While the last Spanish census in 1792 had counted almost 450 blacks and mulattoes, the U.S. Census counted only 355 free colored individuals in 1860. Undoubtedly, there were thousands more people of African ancestry who were not slaves but who were not counted by the census. However, they were a tiny fraction of the total Afro-Texan population of 180,000.

Texas during the Civil War
During the American Civil War, 1861–65, enslaved Afro-Texans urgently hoped the conflict would end their condition as slaves. Texas was not strongly affected by the war; unlike in much of the South, U.S. armies did not occupy much of the territory of the state before the end of the war. Relatively secure Confederate control limited the role that people of color, free or enslaved, could play in the struggle. A few slaves escaped aboard Union ships along the Texas coast or with Union armies. As slave owners throughout Texas responded to the Confederate call to aid the war effort by fighting in other Southern states, enslaved African Americans benefited from their

AFRICAN-AMERICAN POPULATION OF TEXAS, 1850–1900

Year	Slaves	Free People of Color	Free People of Color as a Percentage of Total Population	Total Population
1850	58,558	397	0.2%	212,592
1860	182,921	355	0.1%	604,215
1870		253,475	31.0%	818,579
1880		393,384	24.7%	1,591,749
1890		488,171	21.8%	2,235,527
1900		620,722	20.4%	3,048,710

absence, while others formulated plans of escape across the Mexican border or to Union-controlled Louisiana. Only 47 Texans are counted among the U.S. Colored Troops, although more may have joined Louisiana regiments and counted in Louisiana's recruitment quota. Emancipation for the enslaved Texans finally arrived on June 19, 1865, as the Confederate troops in the state became almost the last Southern army to surrender to the Union. This date, also known as Juneteenth, has become a holiday for African Americans throughout the United States to celebrate the end of slavery. Though African Americans in Texas had gained their freedom, they now faced many challenges in their search for economic, political, and social justice against the same forces that had fought to hold them in the chains of bondage.

Texas and Reconstruction

In the period of RECONSTRUCTION IN THE UNITED STATES (1865–76) that followed the Civil War, African Americans in Texas began the long and difficult process of rebuilding their lives out of the ashes of war while trying to realize the freedom they had gained. Disputes over the process of Reconstruction during the ABRAHAM LINCOLN and ANDREW JOHNSON administrations allowed former supporters of the Confederacy in the Texas government to remain in power until 1868. At almost every level, white politicians and others, opposed to Republican Party policies, attempted to maintain control of newly freed African Americans through black codes and violence (*see* BLACK CODES IN THE UNITED STATES). The codes, targeted at newly freed blacks, were created to curb their rights, promote SEGREGATION in public areas, and force them back to the plantations. Other white Texans utilized terrorism and mob violence to reestablish the racial social order, committing more than 1,500 acts of violence against African Americans, including more than 350 murders, between 1865 and 1868. Finally in 1868, radical Republicans in Congress imposed "radical reconstruction" in parts of the South, including Texas. This plan placed Southern states under military rule in order to ensure the physical and legal protection of African Americans. While the radical Republicans pushed through citizenship and voting rights for African Americans, their suffrage proved limited, lasting only until U.S. troops were withdrawn after the U.S. ELECTION OF 1876. Despite this, African Americans in Texas played a vital role in political Reconstruction. From 1868 to 1900, 43 African Americans served in the state legislature. Among them, George T. Ruby (1841–82), Matt Gaines (1840–1900), Walter Burton (1829–1913), and Norris Wright Cuney (1846–89), all of whom were either free or living as free before the Civil War, contributed significantly to the political and social landscape of Texas. Reconstruction only lasted for a short

time in Texas, and by the 1870s, Democrats and former supporters of the Confederacy wrested control of the Texas state government away from Republicans.

African Americans remained on the margins of Texan society and never very far out of the reach of white oppression and violence. Most African Americans in the state resided on farms as sharecroppers. Though these farmers were no longer bound to the land, the practice of sharecropping limited their ability to grow economically or own acreage. Thus, this system represented more a return to European feudalism rather than economic independence for African Americans in Texas. In an attempt to avoid the terror of the newly formed KU KLUX KLAN and seek out economic opportunities, some free blacks in Texas migrated to cities such as Houston, San Antonio, Austin, and Dallas between 1865 and 1870, doubling the urban black population. The efforts of many of these African Americans helped tremendously in the transition from agriculture to industry in the state. A significant portion of African Americans found work during the postwar cattle boom (1865–85). The Texas Longhorn provided the food necessary to sustain a poor and hungry postwar country. African-American and Hispanic vaqueros, or cowboys, accounted for more than half of the cowhands during the period of the long drive. Other African Americans left Texas, venturing to KANSAS as Exodusters to gain workable farmlands of their own (*see also* EXODUSTER MOVEMENT). With the opening of Oklahoma to settlement in the 1890s, some African Americans left to stake their claims to free farmland as "boomers" or "sooners." Most African Americans, however, chose to remain in Texas during the postwar period, courageously facing challenging economic situations and closed legal systems, violent RACISM and RACIAL PREJUDICE, and vindictive communities.

African Americans at the Turn of the Twentieth Century

With the start of the 20th century, African Americans in Texas faced renewed efforts by whites to discriminate against them in the voting booth, public facilities, and the workplace. In 1902, the state adopted a law requiring a poll tax for voters, and by 1904, the "lily white" Republicans embraced the prevailing trend in the South of "white only" primaries, thereby abandoning their long-standing support of political rights for African Americans. These actions effectively reduced the number of African-American voters by more than 95,000 between the 1890s and 1906. Terrorist violence continued to plague black Texans during the first half of the century, leading to more than 370 known LYNCHINGS between 1882 and 1927. Aside from violent vigilante groups, African Americans faced legal exclusion from public facilities under the Jim Crow laws prevalent throughout the South and this state. Local governments in urban areas such as Dallas, Houston, and San Antonio passed laws segregating black Texans in public transportation, lodgings, restaurants, parks, libraries, schools, and even residential neighborhoods. Although their 1916 effort proved successful in overturning the law separating neighborhoods by race in Dallas, most African Americans remained disenfranchised and were treated as second-class citizens with little recourse. Black Texan workers faced discrimination that often limited job opportunities for them as whites fought to hold jobs in traditional industries and to keep wages high. More traditional jobs such as sharecropping supported the largest number of black laborers, while others expanded their numbers in jobs as longshoremen, railroad workers, and oil "roughnecks" throughout the state.

Robert Little

FURTHER READING

Abernathy, Francis Edward, ed. *Juneteenth Texas: Essays in African American Folklore.* Denton: University of North Texas Press, 1996.

Barr, Alwyn. *The African Texans.* College Station: Texas A&M University Press, 2004.

———. *Black Texans: A History of African Americans in Texas, 1528–1995.* Norman: University of Oklahoma Press, 1996.

Crouch, Barry A. *The Dance of Freedom: African Americans during Reconstruction.* Austin: University of Texas Press, 2007.

———. *The Freedmen's Bureau and Black Texans.* Austin: University of Texas Press, 1992.

"Free Blacks." The Handbook of Texas Online. Available online. URL: http://www.tshaonline.org/handbook/online/articles/FF/pkfbs.html. Accessed January 12, 2011.

Glasrud, Bruce A., and James M. Smallwood, eds. *The African American Experience in Texas: An Anthology.* Lubbock: Texas Tech University Press, 1999.

Hales, Douglas. *A Southern Family in White and Black: The Cuneys of Texas.* College Station: Texas A&M University Press, 2003.

McDonald, Archie. "William Goyens." TexasEscapes.com Online Magazine. Available online. URL: http://www.texasescapes.com/DEPARTMENTS/Guest_Columnists/East_Texas_all_things_historical/WilliamGoyensamd102.htm. Accessed January 12, 2011.

Schoen, Harold. "The Free Negro in the Republic of Texas." *Southwestern Historical Quarterly* 39, no. 4 (April 1936): 292–308; 40, no. 1 (July 1936): 26–34: 41, no. 1 (July 1936): 83–108.

Williams, David. *Bricks without Straw: A Comprehensive History of African Americans in Texas.* Austin, Tex.: Eakin Press, 1997.

Winegarten, Ruth. *Black Texas Women: 150 Years of Trial and Triumph.* Austin: University of Texas Press, 1995.

TOLTON, AUGUSTINE (1854–1897) *American religious leader*

Although not the first person of African ancestry to serve as a Catholic priest in North America, Augustine John Tolton was the first who was socially defined as black to serve in the United States after its independence. He faced racial exclusion and persecution, and his humility and hard work helped lay the groundwork for Catholic missionary efforts among urban blacks in the North and Midwest. His life illustrates the difficulty the American Catholic Church had in reconciling its universal Catholic teachings and its American cultural roots, so deeply permeated with racial consciousness.

Tolton was born on April 1, 1854, in northern MISSOURI, near Hannibal. His parents were slaves of a Catholic master, who ensured that the boy and all his other slaves participated in the ROMAN CATHOLIC CHURCH. When the AMERICAN CIVIL WAR began in 1861, Tolton's father, Peter Paul Tolton, served in the Union army. It is unclear whether he ran away or was released by his master. The remainder of the family moved to Quincy, ILLINOIS, in 1862 with the assistance of sympathetic Union army soldiers. Tolton's recollection in later years was that their departure was a flight from slavery, though their former masters later claimed that they gave Tolton's mother permission to leave as an informal form of MANUMISSION. In any case, slavery was abolished in Missouri in January 1865, when Tolton was 10 years old, and in the United States as a whole later that year.

Tolton's father died in the Civil War, and the family lived under difficult circumstances in Illinois. Augustine Tolton had to begin work in a cigar factory at the age of nine. He attempted to go to school but was rejected because of his race. His parish priest, an Irish immigrant named Peter McGirr, encouraged him to go to the parish school when the factory was not open. Tolton attended the school, over the objections of white parishioners, and then was tutored privately by Father McGirr and other priests. Tolton was a regular churchgoer and assisted at Mass. Several of the priests encouraged him to think about a vocation to the priesthood.

Tolton first contacted the Franciscans, and then the Josephite fathers, a missionary order created especially to serve people of color in North America, but these negotiations fell through. For several years in the 1870s, Tolton was a lay brother of the Franciscan order. With the assistance of the Franciscan order, Tolton was admitted to the Pontifical Urban College in Rome in 1880. The Urban College, also known as the Propaganda, was a special seminary for missionary priests. Tolton expected that he would be sent to Africa to serve as a priest. He completed his studies and was ordained at St. John Lateran basilica in Rome on April 24, 1886, Holy Saturday. He celebrated

Mass for the first time the following day, Easter Sunday. He was the first U.S. black man ordained a priest in the Catholic Church (three men of mixed race, Patrick, Alexander, and James Healy, were ordained in the 1860s; *see also* HEALY FAMILY).

After graduation, Tolton was told that he would be assigned to serve in the diocese of Alton, Illinois, his home diocese. He returned home in 1886 and was assigned as the pastor of St. Joseph's parish in Quincy. St. Joseph's was conceived as a black parish, part of the Catholic Church's attempt in the United States in the 19th century to serve each "national" grouping in parishes of their own, led by priests drawn from their homeland or community. This system led to the creation of Irish Catholic churches served by Irish priests, German Catholic churches served by Germans, Polish churches with Polish priests, and so forth. Blacks were treated as another group comparable to the immigrant communities, but they did not have the linguistic issues that immigrants had. They were racially excluded but mostly shared a culture with native-born whites, and there was no religiously valid reason why blacks and native-born whites should be served separately. There also were few black Catholics, especially outside LOUISIANA, and very few black priests. Therefore, as in other black "national" parishes in Illinois, St. Joseph's actually had many parishioners from outside its "national" group, and there was racial tension in the parish community and with the majority white parish, St. Boniface's, only a few blocks away. After an appeal from the priest of the "white" parish, a German who apparently had racial hostility to him and to American blacks in general, Tolton was forbidden to raise funds among white parishioners and finally even to minister to them in any way. He performed a marriage between a young white woman from a prominent family and a socially "unacceptable" person. Exactly why the groom was "unacceptable" is unclear from the sources; he may have been of the wrong social class or personally unacceptable to the bride's parents, but Tolton's biographer hints that it may have been a case of INTERRACIAL MARRIAGE, very strictly forbidden by commonly accepted cultural norms (though acceptable under Catholic canon law) at the time. In any case, all the church regulations were observed, but white elites in Quincy were outraged. After this incident, Tolton had to leave the diocese of Quincy, and his parish and school were closed.

He went to the archdiocese of CHICAGO, ILLINOIS, in 1889, where he was assigned as pastor of St. Augustine's, later known as St. Monica's, the black national parish there. Chicago was beginning to experience the rapid migration of Southern blacks to the city that was later to be called the Great Migration. In 1889, there were more than 25,000 blacks living in the city, where only about 6,000 had lived at the end of the Civil War. Tolton's missionary efforts to this community were supported by St. Katherine Drexel (1858–1955), founder of the Sisters of the Blessed Sacrament and a strong supporter of missionary outreach and social justice for blacks and Indians in the United States. The effort was successful; a beautiful parish church and a strong organization still exist today. The international missionary organization of the Catholic Church, observing the success of Tolton's work, gave official support to a special religious order, the Josephites, founded in 1870, to minister to American blacks. Tolton became famous for his devoted service to his parish. He died on July 9, 1897, at the age of 43.

Stewart R. King

FURTHER READING

Bauer, Fr. Roy. "They Called Him Father Gus." Available online. URL: http://www.cospq.org/Parish%20History/Tolton%20Biography.htm. Accessed January 12, 2011.
Hemsath, Sr. Caroline. *From Slave to Priest: A Biography of the Reverend Augustine Tolton (1854–1897): First Black American Priest of the United States*. Chicago: Ignatius Press, 2006.

TRINIDAD AND TOBAGO

Trinidad and Tobago and a number of smaller nearby islands in the Caribbean now form an independent nation, located off the coast of South America near eastern VENEZUELA. At different times during the colonial period, these islands were ruled by a variety of European countries, though from the time of the FRENCH REVOLUTION in the 1790s until national independence in 1962, the islands were colonies of BRITAIN.

Trinidad is the largest island; with an area of more than 1,800 square miles, it is larger than any of the other Lesser Antilles. It has high mountains in its interior and had extensive areas of wilderness during the colonial period. There are some fertile coastal plains suitable for plantation agriculture, and COFFEE CULTIVATION and cacao growing are possible in the hills. Cacao may have been originally domesticated by Native Americans in Trinidad, or on the nearby coast of South America. Tobago, though smaller than Trinidad, had a more significant plantation sector in the 18th century. Geography favored plantation development as the coastal plain on the leeward (northwestern) side of the island was broad and well watered, very suitable for SUGAR CULTIVATION on plantations.

Tobago was originally settled by the Dutch in the 1660s after the defeat of their Brazilian colony. It was at this time that sugar was first cultivated and slaves began to be imported. The Dutch colony was not very successful, and so the colony was turned over to settlers

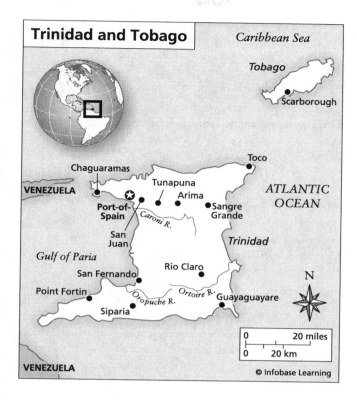

Trinidad and Tobago

from modern Latvia, known then as Courland. Most of the Courlanders died of tropical diseases, but enough survived to make the plantation sector successful. The island changed hands 22 times during the various wars of the 18th century, finally being captured by Britain from FRANCE in 1798 and officially joined to the British Empire in 1802. By that time, the population of the island was about 15,000, of whom more than 13,000 were slaves and about 500 were free people of color. The free colored people of Tobago were, like those in many other British Caribbean colonies, mostly urban and worked as ARTISANS or laborers. There were few landowners or SLAVE OWNERS in their ranks.

Trinidad was very lightly inhabited until the turn of the 19th century. It remained part of the Spanish Empire throughout the 17th and 18th centuries, and the Spanish focused their development efforts on their mainland colonies. Trinidad was a base for pearl fishing and a minor naval port with no plantation sector. The island's population in 1783 was 2,713, of whom 295 were free people of African descent. The island still had a substantial Native American population at that time, comprising more than 2,000 people. In 1783, the Spanish government, as part of the Bourbon Reforms, decided to encourage settlement and offered land grants to any Catholic immigrant who agreed to settle and develop the land for agriculture. The size of the grant depended on the number of slaves the grantee took to the island, and so the plantation sector and the slave population expanded rapidly. Thousands

of people, including many free coloreds from French islands as well as Spanish colonies, moved to Trinidad, and the island's population exceeded 17,000 by 1797. Of these, about 4,500 were free people of color and almost 9,000 were slaves. Many of these settlers were from the French islands of Guadeloupe, Martinique, and SAINT-DOMINGUE, all of which were experiencing great disorder at the time as a result of both the FRENCH REVOLUTION and the HAITIAN REVOLUTION. The French were very influential in Trinidad; a French-based patois became the dominant tongue throughout the 19th century and is still heard to this day on the island.

Britain captured Trinidad from the Spanish in 1802, and it became a formal part of the British Empire with the Treaty of Paris ending the Napoleonic Wars in 1814. Britain ended its participation in the Atlantic slave trade in 1807, and Trinidad's plantation sector was especially hard-hit by this cutoff in supply, since it was still expanding rapidly at that point. Trinidadian planters adopted a number of strategies to address this problem. One was to lease small farms to black soldiers whom Britain had recruited during the various recent wars. A contingent of about 600 black Royal Marines settled the highlands of Trinidad, starting in 1819, forming villages based on the companies they had served in during the war. Many of these veterans were people who had fled slavery in the United States during the WAR OF AMERICAN INDEPENDENCE, 1775–83, or their children. These men were not interested in being plantation laborers, but many did grow coffee on small farms, which they would then market through existing coffee plantations. There were attempts to put Native Americans to work or to import slaves from Tobago or BARBADOS, but the ultimately successful expedient was the importation of South Asians as indentured servants. There were small numbers of South Asian workers from the 1810s, but the pace of importation did not increase until after the end of slavery in 1834 and the practice was formalized by a government subsidy in 1844.

The status of free people of color in Trinidad declined under British rule. An early sign of this development was the case of Louisa Calderon (1782?–?), a free woman of color who was accused in 1801 of theft by her Spanish employer and, presumably, lover. She was arrested on the orders of the military governor, General Thomas Picton (1758–1815), and tortured in the jail of Port of Spain, the colonial capital, ultimately being confined in irons in a half-crouching position in a nearly lightless cell for almost eight months. The fact that Picton treated Calderon and several free colored men with impurity for so long was a sign that the British colonial authorities and the Trinidadian ruling class were unwilling to protect the rights of free nonwhites in the colony. Finally, however, an investigation of Picton's behavior was mounted from Britain, spearheaded by British abolitionists, and he was tried and convicted of mistreating Calderon, though he never served time in jail. By the 1820s, conditions had reached a low point. Dr. Jean-Baptiste Philippe (1796–1829), a free man of mixed race and a physician, was an important free colored activist. He wrote a petition to the governor, Lord Woodward, in 1824 in which he argued for civil rights for free people of color and criticized the institution of slavery. His appeal was based on the terms of the Spanish surrender of the colony to Britain, in which the rights that inhabitants had had under Spanish law were not to be violated, but he made a more general argument for racial equality even for black slaves.

The abolition movement in Trinidad was a fruitful example of cooperation between free people of color and slaves. The large free colored population generally supported the nonviolent protest movement against slavery and the "apprenticeship" system that replaced it in the 1830s. Under "apprenticeship," former slaves were legally free after 1833 but still bound to serve their former masters for six years. Even though many free coloreds in Trinidad owned slaves and were planters, they nonetheless had learned that under British rule, at least, blacks were second-class citizens. By working to abolish slavery, many realized, they were also improving their own position. A mixed group of "apprentices"—former slaves bound to serve their former masters for six years—and free people of color besieged the governor's mansion in August 1834, calling out, "Pas de six ans" (No to six years), demanding an absolute end to slavery. The relative wealth and established social position of free people of color in Trinidad helped the cause, and the apprenticeship system was always weaker there than in other British colonies in the Caribbean. Many apprentices left their plantations and rented or squatted on mountain land, while others insisted on wages in order to remain. Many planters, whites as well as free coloreds, agreed to pay wages and looked for other sources of labor.

There is little evidence that Trinidad's black population was subdivided into former free people of color and the newly freed in the years after the end of slavery. For one thing, many Trinidadian free coloreds lived in rural areas, as did most of the former slaves, while in other British colonies the free colored population had been urban. The experience of working together against slavery and the apprenticeship system also helped unify the black community. The fact that both slaves and free people of color spoke the French-based patois, in contrast to most whites, who spoke English or Spanish, also helped cement blacks together. And finally, the arrival of South Asian indentured servants helped forge a black community by creating an "other" against which the community could measure itself. The South Asians, once their indentures were complete, tended to move to urban areas and become workers and small businessmen, filling a niche occupied by free people of color in other colonies. The South Asian population grew rapidly, nearing 100,000 by 1900. Trinidad's black population was of comparable size, and the two communities were often rivals. Trinidad's complex ethnic makeup today, and its byzantine ethnic politics, are products of this rivalry.

Stewart R. King

FURTHER READING

Anthony, Michael. *Historical Dictionary of Trinidad and Tobago.* Lanham, Md.: Scarecrow Press, 1997.
Cudjoe, Selwin. *Beyond Boundaries: The Intellectual Tradition of Trinidad and Tobago in the Nineteenth Century.* Amherst: University of Massachusetts Press, 2003.
Philippe, Jean-Baptiste. *A Free Mulatto.* Port of Spain: Paria, 1987.
Williams, Eric. *History of the People of Trinidad and Tobago.* London: Andre Deutsch, 1964.

TRUTH, SOJOURNER (ca. 1797–1883)
American abolitionist and feminist

Sojourner Truth was born a slave in Ulster County, New York, before slavery was outlawed there, probably before 1800 (the most commonly accepted date of birth for her is 1797). Her masters at birth were the Hardenburgh family, descendents of Dutch "patroon" planters. She was named Isabella Baumfree at birth. She grew up speaking Dutch at home, only learning English as a teenager when she was sold to an English-speaking master. Her English was always somewhat accented, though she became a powerful preacher and speaker in later life. During her time as a slave she was sold several times. She married Thomas Dumont, another slave on her plantation, and had at least four children with him. She had five children in all; the father of her first child may have been another slave living on a nearby plantation. In 1827, New York freed all remaining slaves, but Isabella had already left her owner, John Dumont, after he reneged on a promise to free her. After the abolition of slavery, she successfully sued the Dumont family to obtain the freedom of her son Peter, whom they had transferred to ALABAMA.

The 1820s and 1830s were a time of great religious ferment in the United States, a period known as the Second Great Awakening. Isabella was caught up in the movement, and she traveled around the Northeast and settled in several religious communes. She was supported by Quakers in her legal struggle for the freedom of her family, but her religious vocation centered on evangelical Protestantism. She was deeply influenced by the ideas of

Sojourner Truth (ca. 1797–1883), American abolitionist, religious leader, and women's rights leader. Born Isabella Baumfree in New York, she gained her freedom, took the new name by which she is known today, and became an evangelist. Her most famous speech, "Ain't I a Woman?" combined calls for racial and gender equality. *(MPI/Getty Images)*

the Union military and against SEGREGATION in Northern cities. After the war, she called for the establishment of a "Negro state" in the West, and supported the EXO-DUSTER MOVEMENT. She also supported the FREEDMEN'S BUREAU and tried to help black war refugees and the newly freed people in the South find jobs and housing. She continued to work for women's rights, civil rights for blacks, and temperance (laws restricting alcohol consumption) until her death on November 26, 1883.

Sojourner Truth helped set the terms of reference for the debate over slavery, civil rights for blacks after the Civil War, and women's rights in the United States in the mid-19th century. She is probably as important a figure as any of the other well-known abolitionists she worked with—Douglass, Garrison, and Stowe—especially because as a black woman she had inherent credibility on both black and woman's issues. She is also important as an example of a little-appreciated phenomenon, the links among Protestant evangelical Christianity, abolitionism, and women's liberation. Finally, she deserves attention because of her lively speaking style. There is a reason that she stood out as a speaker and sold many books in that era, so well provided with great speakers and writers.

Stewart R. King

FURTHER READING

Painter, Nell Irvin. *Sojourner Truth: A Life, a Symbol.* New York: W. W. Norton, 1996.

Truth, Sojourner. *The Narrative of Sojourner Truth.* New York: Penguin Classics, 1998.

Elijah Pierson, a religious reformer who urged converts to abide by Old Testament law. It was about this time that she began calling herself Sojourner Truth and became an itinerant preacher.

In the 1840s, she became active in the abolitionist movement, and she worked with many abolitionist leaders such as FREDERICK DOUGLASS and William Lloyd Garrison. She was in great demand as a speaker, and her memoir *The Narrative of Sojourner Truth, a Northern Slave* (1850) was dictated to and edited by the abolitionist author Harriet Beecher Stowe.

Sojourner Truth also became involved in women's rights issues. As did many abolitionists, she saw a connection between the issues of women's liberation and freedom for blacks. Her most famous speech, "Ain't I a Woman?" was delivered at a women's rights conference in 1851. When the AMERICAN CIVIL WAR, 1861–65, began, Truth worked for better conditions for blacks in

"AIN'T I A WOMAN?" SPEECH BY SOJOURNER TRUTH, MAY 28, 1851

Sojourner Truth spoke to the Ohio Women's Rights Conference in Akron on May 28, 1851. There were a number of hostile people in the audience, and she encountered a good bit of heckling. The following is what she is reported to have said in response to hecklers. It is unclear whether it was totally impromptu or whether portions of it were what she was planning to say anyway. Oratorical traditions at the held that speakers should say their piece without notes, and it is unclear how literate Truth was. In any case, no original text has ever been discovered.

The speech was transcribed by another abolitionist, Frances Gage, who published it almost 30 years later. Gage's text is the only record of Sojourner Truth's oratorical style, and it is written in nonstandard English. It is unclear whether that is really the way Truth spoke. Contemporaries, both black and white, always described her as a riveting speaker. She was a native Dutch speaker and learned English as a teenager, but no one who heard her ever suggested that her English was poor or difficult to understand. Nonetheless, the speech as transcribed shows some of the power of Truth's oratory: the biblical or theological arguments mixed with homely, rural simile, the chatty tone, the repetition of "and ain't I a woman?" and other rhetorical elements that have made this speech a classic of early feminism.

What we have here is probably a fragment of a longer speech. Oratory and preaching at the time were intended to be savored, and no speaker would sit down after only a few paragraphs. This might have been the peroration, in which many speakers spoke off the cuff. Perhaps that is why Gage copied only it down, assuming that the rest of the speech was made from a prepared text and would survive.

"Ain't I a Woman?"
Delivered 1851 at the
Women's Rights Conference in
Akron, Ohio

Well, children, where there is so much racket there must be something out of kilter. I think that 'twixt the Negroes of the South and the women at the North, all talking about rights, the white men will be in a fix pretty soon. But what's all this here talking about?

That man over there says that women need to be helped into carriages, and lifted over ditches, and to have the best place everywhere. Nobody ever helps me into carriages, or over mud-puddles, or gives me any best place! And ain't I a woman? Look at me! Look at my arm! I have ploughed and planted, and gathered into barns, and no man could head me! And ain't I a woman? I could work as much and eat as much as a man—when I could get it—and bear the lash as well! And ain't I a woman? I have borne thirteen children, and seen most all sold off to slavery, and when I cried out with my mother's grief, none but Jesus heard me! And ain't I a woman?

Then they talk about this thing in the head; what's this they call it? [member of audience whispers, "intellect"] That's it, honey. What's that got to do with women's rights or Negroes' rights? If my cup won't hold but a pint, and yours holds a quart, wouldn't you be mean not to let me have my little half measure full?

Then that little man in black there, he says women can't have as much rights as men, 'cause Christ wasn't a woman! Where did your Christ come from? Where did your Christ come from? From God and a woman! Man had nothing to do with Him.

If the first woman God ever made was strong enough to turn the world upside down all alone, these women together ought to be able to turn it back, and get it right side up again! And now they is asking to do it, the men better let them. Obliged to you for hearing me, and now old Sojourner ain't got nothing more to say.

Source: Internet Modern History Sourcebook. Available online. URL: http://www.fordham.edu/halsall/mod/sojtruth-woman.html. Accessed January 12, 2011.

TUBMAN, HARRIET (ARAMINTA ROSS)
(ca. 1822–1913) *American abolitionist, spy, and political activist*

Harriet Tubman was born Araminta "Minty" Ross sometime in the early 1820s to enslaved parents in Dorchester County, on the Eastern Shore of MARYLAND. Tubman's master owned a large plantation, but as were many planters in Maryland at the time, he was oversupplied with labor as his profits from tobacco cultivation declined. As a result, he sold several members of Tubman's family to buyers in the Deep South and leased Tubman herself out as a servant to several local men as soon as she was old enough to work. Tubman was resistant and gained a reputation as a troublesome slave. On one occasion, when she refused to help a white man from a neighboring plantation capture a runaway in a store, he hit her in the head with a two-pound lead weight from the counter. The blow gave her a severe concussion and almost killed her. It also caused seizures that recurred throughout her life. She was becoming very interested in Christianity at that time, and she interpreted the seizures as religious experiences. This was a period called the Second Great Awakening, when evangelical Christianity emerged as a powerful force in the United States, and many African Americans converted. In many cases, these were people who had been only marginally Christianized before, and the emotionalism, spiritual focus, and egalitarianism of the Baptist movement appealed to African-American cultural values (*see also* BAPTISTS AND PIETISTS). Tubman's religious conversion was part of this pattern, and her seizures gave her an aura of sanctity among other believers. As did many African-American Baptists, she paid great attention to scriptural promises of equality and freedom and had a special devotion to the figure of Moses, who led the Israelites out of captivity in Egypt. She occasionally acted as a preacher for the rest of her life and recounted visions that she had experienced while having her seizures.

Her father, who had been the property of another master, gained his freedom in 1840, through a provision in his former master's will that freed all his slaves when they reached the age of 45. Tubman believed that her mother should also have benefited from this provision, which would have freed Tubman herself, but her master refused. This was a point of contention between them, but Tubman remained in bondage for another nine years. In 1845, she married a free black man named John Tub-

Harriet Tubman (far left) with a group of slaves she helped during the American Civil War. Tubman is most famous for leading many slaves to freedom in the 1850s and 1860s and working as a nurse, guide, and spy during the Civil War. She was also an important spokesperson for abolition before the war and for the rights of the newly freed in the years after the end of slavery. *(© Bettmann/CORBIS)*

man and changed her name to Harriet, either at the time of her wedding or a few years later, when she decided to run away. Her master died in 1849, and faced with the possibility that she might be sold away from her husband to settle the debts of the estate, she decided to run away definitively. She had fled for short periods before, to protest poor treatment or avoid punishment, but on this occasion she clearly intended to stay away. She made one abortive attempt in September 1849, accompanied by her brothers, and then left again by herself just before New Year's, arriving in PHILADELPHIA, PENNSYLVANIA, in January 1850.

In Philadelphia, she began working as a servant and laborer. The U.S. government had just enacted the FUGI-TIVE SLAVE ACT OF 1850 as part of the Compromise of 1850. Under this law, state governments were required to assist SLAVE OWNERS who were looking for their runaway "property." This made life dangerous for fugitives like Tubman. But she had a more serious problem—her fam-

ily, with the exception of her husband, remained enslaved, and the slaves belonging to her former master were in danger of being sold. This would have meant that they would have been moved to the Deep South, probably to work as fieldhands on cotton plantations. Tubman was not willing to allow that to happen. First, in December 1850, Tubman went in disguise back to Maryland. She helped move her free brother-in-law's enslaved family to Philadelphia. Then, in spring 1851, she returned to Maryland again to help her brother Moses and two other men from her former plantation to freedom. On this second trip, she had financial help from Thomas Garrett (1789–1871), a DELAWARE Quaker abolitionist who ultimately helped an estimated 2,700 slaves to freedom. Each trip gave her more skills in clandestine work and more confidence in her abilities. She also continued to experience visions that she interpreted as messages from God encouraging her in her work and promising divine protection. This gave her great self-confidence and gave her clients confidence in her. The very harsh racial lines in antebellum Southern society made blacks effectively invisible to Southern whites. They were just unable to conceive of a black person, especially a woman, as a potential antagonist, and so Tubman was able to slip in and out of slave territory over and over again without arousing suspicion. She worked with an extensive network of agents including some of the best-known "conductors" of the Underground Railroad, many of whom were also free blacks. William Still (1819–1902), a New Jersey free black known as the "father of the Underground Railroad," worked closely with her. By the time Tubman went back to Dorchester County in 1851 to get her husband, he had remarried and refused to go with her. As a free black, he was under less threat, and their marriage, as with many among blacks in the antebellum South, may have been promised to last "till death or distance you part." The Fugitive Slave Act began to put pressure on the black community of Philadelphia, and Tubman and the other conductors of the Underground Railroad turned to the task of escorting runaways farther North, to safety in CANADA. She moved her own family to St. Catherine's, Ontario, where many other American blacks settled. She also continued to make trips to southern Maryland for eight years, escorting some 70 slaves to freedom as well as a much larger number from Philadelphia to Canada. In what was probably her last trip to Maryland, in 1859, she took out her own parents, by this time both free but suspected of having harbored RUNAWAY SLAVES.

In 1858, she met the abolitionist leader John Brown (1800–59), who advocated the violent overthrow of slavery. Most abolitionists, especially the pacifist Quakers, opposed Brown's plans, but Tubman gave him her support. Tubman put him in contact with clandestine networks in the border states who might be willing to provide intelligence to Brown's forces in the event of a successful uprising and helped recruit former runaways to join his band. At this time, Tubman also began to travel in the North, speaking to abolitionist audiences. These public appearances made her clandestine activities harder, and she appears to have stopped traveling to the South in 1859 or 1860—there is a disputed story that she tried and failed to rescue some family members in that year. She also bought a farm in 1859 near Auburn, New York, from the abolitionist New York senator William Seward (1801–72). She moved her family from Canada to this farm and began to live a more settled life. She did not accompany Brown on his raid at Harpers Ferry, where he and his men were killed or captured.

With the outbreak of the AMERICAN CIVIL WAR in 1861, Tubman immediately saw that this event might mean the end of slavery. When Union forces captured territory along the coast of GEORGIA and SOUTH CAR-OLINA in 1862, Tubman was one of a number of black abolitionists who accompanied the Union general David Hunter (1802–86) to the newly captured territory. Hunter wanted to recruit black soldiers and encourage resistance among the dense slave population of the area, and Tubman and her companions worked to implement his plan. Hunter's efforts were often undermined by higher authorities in Washington, D.C. His order abolishing slavery in his district anticipated the EMANCIPATION PROCLAMATION by six months but was overruled by President ABRAHAM LINCOLN. His first attempt to raise black soldiers, in spring 1862, was also overruled, and only later did South Carolina and Georgia blacks get the right to fight for their freedom. Tubman was incensed by these roadblocks but continued to work for the cause. She served as a nurse in army hospitals and, after the Emancipation Proclamation in 1863, organized a group of scouts. She guided Union naval forces through Confederate river fortifications, she guided troops through the swamps on routes unknown even to the Confederate defenders, and she passed on information from blacks living behind rebel lines. At one point, she traveled to Jacksonville, FLORIDA, then in rebel hands, to gather information on the defenses that helped Union forces capture the city in 1864.

After the war, Tubman returned to Auburn, New York. She did not receive any pay for her work during the war, and not until 1899 did the U.S. government grant her a pension for her services during the war. She married a black Civil War veteran named Nelson Davis in 1869, they had one daughter. The family experienced financial hardship in later years, becoming victim of a financial con and almost losing their farm. A pair of biographies by the suffrage leader Sarah Bradford sold fairly well in the postwar years and helped keep Tubman solvent. She traveled the country speaking on behalf of votes for women, working with the prominent suffragist Susan B. Anthony (1820–1906). She was a founding member of the National Federation of Afro-American Women in 1896. As her religious views moderated somewhat from the independent evangelical Baptist approach of her youth, she also became active in the AFRICAN METHODIST EPISCOPAL CHURCH. In 1908, she established a home for elderly blacks associated with the church in Auburn, and in 1911, she retired to this home. It was there that she died on March 10, 1913.

Harriet Tubman was one of the most effective African-American leaders of the 19th century. Her story of unrelenting resistance to slavery, self-sacrificing service to her country during war, and activism in a variety of causes after the war made her a national figure. Many white Americans recognized her heroism and valued her services even as they failed to support equal rights for blacks in general. She is also a good and fairly well-documented example of the hardships free blacks experienced in the North during this period. Despite her fame, she was always in financial difficulty, and she had to work in a variety of low-status occupations to support herself. She confronted racial discrimination in housing and transportation even while she was playing a major role in political debates. The government refused to pay her for her service for decades, despite promises from prominent military leaders and politicians.

Stewart R. King

FURTHER READING

Bradford, Sarah. *Harriet Tubman: The Moses of Her People.* 1881. Reprint, New York: Corinth Books, 1961.

——. *Scenes in the Life of Harriet Tubman.* 1867. Reprint, Freeport, N.Y.: Books for Libraries Press, 1971.

Clinton, Catherine. *Harriet Tubman: The Road to Freedom.* New York: Little, Brown, 2004.

Larson, Kate Clifford. *Bound for the Promised Land: Harriet Tubman, Portrait of an American Hero.* New York: Ballantine Books, 2004.

TYE, COLONEL (TITUS CORNELIUS) (1753–1780) *American guerrilla leader*

Born Titus Cornelius in 1753, Colonel Tye was a slave of a Monmouth County, NEW JERSEY, master named John Corlies. Cornelius suffered abuse from his master, especially when he demanded his freedom under the principles of Corlies's Quaker faith (*see also* BAPTISTS AND PIETISTS). It is not known whether Cornelius was also a Quaker, but he certainly knew that the elders of the church had remonstrated with Corlies about his refusal to emancipate his five slaves. In November 1775, shortly after the outbreak of the WAR OF AMERICAN INDEPENDENCE (1775–83), the 22-year-old Cornelius heard about the proclamation issued by JOHN MURRAY, EARL OF DUNMORE, the pro-British governor of Virginia that promised freedom to any slave of a pro-independence master who ran away to join the British forces. He ran away and made his way to Virginia, enlisting in Lord Dunmore's Ethiopian Regiment. His activities during the ensuing two years are not documented, but he survived the disease and battle deaths that felled so many of Dunmore's soldiers, and in 1778, he was present in British-held New York, serving in a loyalist unit. On June 28 of that year, he fought at the Battle of Monmouth, during which he single-handedly captured an American officer. The British referred to him as "Colonel" Tye, a courtesy rank rather than an actual king's commission but still a significant mark of respect.

During the remainder of 1778 and 1779, Colonel Tye led a group of black loyalist partisans out of a base on Sandy Hook, New Jersey. They raided throughout northern New Jersey, paying special attention to SLAVE OWNERS. Since many of Tye's men were locals who had also run away from slavery, these raids often had an element of personal vengeance. Seizing wealthy white farmers and hauling them off to New York in chains gave Tye and his men great satisfaction, as well as spreading terror among New Jersey's American Patriots. Capturing their livestock and food supplies provided important support for the British forces in New York, who otherwise would have to transport supplies by sea from CANADA or the Southern colonies they controlled. The farmers of the region appealed to the government, describing Tye's band in apocalyptic terms. New Jersey state troops and Continental soldiers from General GEORGE WASHINGTON's army in the western part of the state hunted for Tye's band without success through 1779 and 1780.

On September 1, 1780, Tye's men, in cooperation with the Queen's Rangers, a white loyalist band, attacked the Tom's Neck farmhouse of Josiah Huddy. Huddy had been responsible for the killings of several local loyalists, and the attackers sought revenge as well as the destruction of a Patriot underground network in the vicinity. Huddy was captured, but his companions ambushed the loyalist party and freed him. During the struggle, Tye was shot, receiving a pistol ball through the wrist. The wound did not seem dangerous at first, but tetanus set in, and he died some time later that year.

Tye's career demonstrates the importance of military service for blacks in the revolutionary period. He might well have had a chance of gaining his freedom in any case, given the sustained campaign against slavery waged by the Quakers. Indeed, the local meeting ultimately disciplined Tye's former master for his persistent violation of their rules. But Tye's rise to social respectability and posthumous heroic reputation were a result of his military service. At the same time, the kind of warfare he waged was the nightmare of the slave system, and the fact that he was able to wage it in a place so far from the plantation complex was an indictment of that system that New Jersey's citizens took to heart when they considered the abolition of slavery in 1804.

Stewart R. King

FURTHER READING

Egerton, Douglas R. *Death or Liberty: African Americans and Revolutionary America.* New York: Oxford University Press, 2009.

TYLER, JOHN (1790–1862) *tenth president of the United States (1841–1845)*

President of the United States from 1841 to 1845, John Tyler was a member of the Virginia planter aristocracy.

His father was a close friend of the former president THOMAS JEFFERSON, and Tyler shared Jefferson's dream that America should evolve into a white agrarian republic without blacks, either enslaved or free. As did Jefferson, Tyler owned slaves throughout his life and lived among people of color, both enslaved and free.

Tyler was born on March 29, 1790, in Virginia, only a few miles from the birthplace of his running mate and predecessor in office WILLIAM HENRY HARRISON. This was one of the most highly developed plantation regions in the country. Tyler remained a loyal Democrat during the 1820s, serving as a member of Congress and governor of Virginia. He broke with them during the presidency of ANDREW JACKSON over the Nullification Crisis in the early 1830s, when Jackson threatened to use federal troops to force SOUTH CAROLINA's government to enforce federal tariff laws. Although unenthusiastic about the KENTUCKY senator Henry Clay's plan to use the federal government's resources to spark economic development, Tyler aligned with the Whigs and ran for vice president on the Whig ticket in 1836 and 1840. Tyler also supported the AMERICAN COLONIZATION SOCIETY (ACS), of which Clay was a founding member. The ACS planned to help American free blacks emigrate to LIBERIA. Many free blacks opposed this, thinking of themselves as Americans rather than Africans.

In 1840, Tyler was elected vice president with William Henry Harrison. Harrison died after only a few weeks in office, and Tyler assumed the presidency on April 4, 1841, serving out the remainder of Harrison's term. Tyler almost immediately broke with the Whigs over banking policy and was expelled from the party. He had no party affiliation for the remainder of his life, the only American president other than Washington not to belong to a political party. In fact, Tyler's presidency was marked by growing tensions between North and South. He was clearly on the Southern side, though that side would only become firmly associated with the Democrats in the term of his successor, JAMES POLK. Tyler's most momentous

decision that affected free people of color while he was president was to admit TEXAS to the United States. The racial climate in Texas had been relatively benign under Spanish and, later, Mexican rule, but upon admission to the United States, Texas adopted harsh restrictions on MANUMISSION and free black immigration similar to those found in the other states of the Lower South. A treaty between the independent Republic of Texas and MEXICO in 1836 gave Spanish-speaking Texans some protection, and many free blacks who had been living in the state before 1845 could claim to be Mexican American. Tyler made no effort to protect free people of color in Texas in the negotiations that led to the annexation of the state.

After leaving office, Tyler retired to a plantation in Virginia. As the AMERICAN CIVIL WAR approached in 1861, Tyler came out of retirement to lead a peace initiative. His proposal would have strengthened provisions of the FUGITIVE SLAVE ACT OF 1850, forcing Northern states to assist Southerners who claimed to be the owners of RUNAWAY SLAVES. The act had already led to increases in kidnapping and violence in the North, with negative impacts on Northern free blacks, and Tyler's proposal would no doubt have made conditions worse for them, had it been accepted by the president-elect ABRAHAM LINCOLN. With the failure of the peace initiative, Tyler accepted election to the Confederate States Congress; he died of a stroke on January 18, 1862, before he could be sworn in. Because by joining the Confederates he was considered to have committed treason, he is the only American president whose death was not followed by official mourning.

Stewart R. King

FURTHER READING

Crapol, Edward P. *John Tyler, the Accidental President*. Chapel Hill: University of North Carolina Press, 2006.

Peterson, Norma Lois. *The Presidencies of William Henry Harrison and John Tyler*. Lawrence: University Press of Kansas, 1989.

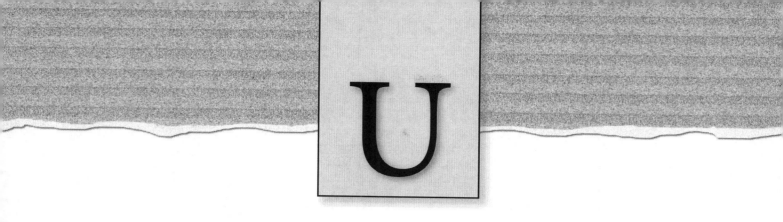

U

UNITED STATES, ABOLITION MOVEMENTS IN

African Americans played important roles in every phase of the American antislavery movement. Throughout U.S. history, slaves resisted bondage by surviving day to day, running away, and, rarely, revolting. Many who managed to escape joined free black communities in the Northern United States, and free blacks worked from the revolutionary period onward to create a vibrant abolition and civil rights movement that eventually led to the end of slavery.

Some of the earliest black abolition and civil rights efforts occurred in the period around the WAR OF AMERICAN INDEPENDENCE, 1775–83. In MASSACHUSETTS, slaves and free blacks used the rhetoric of the American Revolution to present their own pleas for liberty. In 1777, PRINCE HALL (1735–1807) and a number of his associates sent a petition to the Massachusetts General Court citing their natural and inalienable rights to freedom, in language that sounded much like the Declaration of Independence. In an even more famous instance, a slave named Quock Walker (1753–unknown) sued for his freedom in 1780 by using the language in the Constitution of Massachusetts to insist that he, as were all men, was born free and equal (see QUOCK WALKER CASE). Similarly, PAUL CUFFE (1759–1817) led an effort to petition the state government to grant blacks and Native Americans the right to vote or to exempt them from taxation.

PHILADELPHIA, PENNSYLVANIA, blacks were equally active during this period, influenced by the antislavery culture that the Pennsylvania Abolition Society (PAS) had cultivated since the colonial period. Made up primarily of Quakers, the PAS had fought to convince SLAVE OWNERS of the evil of human bondage, to provide education for free blacks, and to secure the gradual emancipation of all slaves through court cases and other legal means (see BAPTISTS AND PIETISTS). Indeed, the main characteristic of most antislavery agitation during this period is that it focused on gradual, rather than immediate, abolition.

While the PAS did not recruit black members, Philadelphia black leaders fought their own campaign to end slavery and gain civil rights, and their work often dovetailed with that of the PAS. Among Philadelphia's leaders was James Forten (1766–1842), a free black sailmaker who served as a privateer during the Revolution; he was captured and refused a chance at freedom in Britain, choosing instead to remain a prisoner of war until he could return to his home after the war (see FORTEN FAMILY). Other black leaders of this generation were RICHARD ALLEN (1760–1831), a bishop in the AFRICAN METHODIST EPISCOPAL CHURCH, and ABSALOM JONES (1746–1818), the first African American to be ordained a priest in the Episcopal Church. These leaders created independent black churches and mutual aid societies to help their fellow African Americans as they fought for the emancipation of slaves and civil rights for free blacks. They successfully led the drive against proposed legislation that would have excluded free blacks from entering PENNSYLVANIA, and they unsuccessfully fought to resist efforts of the state legislature to revoke black voting rights in 1837. After helping to push for freedom in their own state and prevailing in 1870, when the state passed the first gradual abolition bill in the new nation, they continued to fight slavery nationwide.

Thanks primarily to the PAS, Pennsylvania is known as the leader in the gradual abolition movement, which dominated the American antislavery scene from colonial times to the 1830s. Though the gradual movement lived on after that period, it faced two challenges, one from the colonization movement and one from a new movement that was born in response to black resistance to colonization and was much more receptive to free black participation—the immediatist movement calling for immediate and unconditional abolition. Pennsylvania had strong chapters of both of these movements, and so did many other states.

The colonization movement, led by the AMERICAN COLONIZATION SOCIETY (ACS), had some free black participation, but its main function in the antislavery movement of the United States was to awaken more and more free blacks to the need to resist colonization and fight for the immediate release of all bondspersons without compensation to their masters. Though at first interested in African coloni-

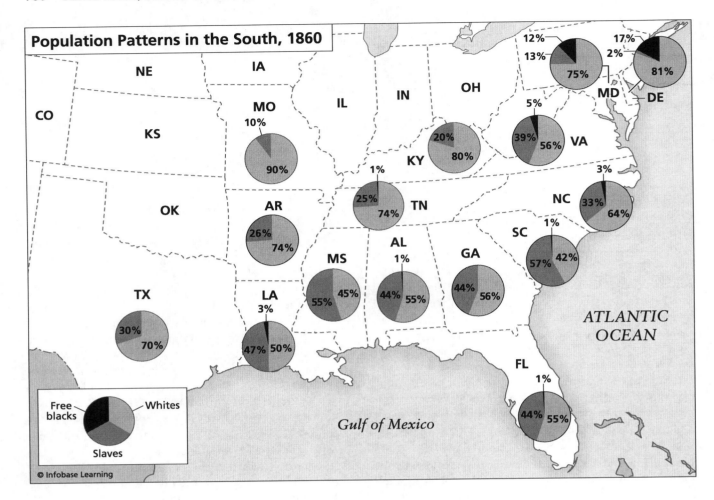

Population Patterns in the South, 1860

NE

IA

CO

KS

MO
10%
90%

IL

IN

OH
12%
13%
75%

17%
2%
81%
MD
DE

KY
20%
80%

5%
39% 56% VA

OK

AR
26%
74%

TN
1%
25%
74%

NC
3%
33% 64%

TX
30%
70%

LA
3%
47% 50%

MS
55% 45%

AL
1%
44% 55%

GA
44% 56%

SC
1%
57% 42%

ATLANTIC OCEAN

FL
1%
44% 55%

Gulf of Mexico

Free blacks — Whites
Slaves

© Infobase Learning

zation, Forten helped lead the drive against the ACS and in so doing attracted the attention of a number of key white opponents of slavery who had supported colonization. The most famous of these white supporters was William Lloyd Garrison (1805–79), who in 1831 began a newspaper, the *Liberator*, that was based in Boston, Massachusetts. He also played an important role in starting the immediatist American Anti-Slavery Society (AASS) in 1833.

Once Garrison entered the scene, antislavery became a much more radical movement that refused to compromise with slaveholders in any way, and the focus moved beyond the courthouse to the street as Garrisonians worked diligently to win grassroots support of whites as well as blacks, men as well as women. While gradualists generally fought *for* black Americans rather than *alongside* them, immediatists built a biracial movement that directly challenged the American racial system. They used the innovations of the American market revolution, such as the penny press and improved transportation methods, as well as the evangelical religious climate of the time to spread their message.

The economic and social climate of industrialization shaped the antislavery movement in many ways. Among

the most obvious and most important were innovations in printing. These innovations made pamphlet literature cheaper to produce and distribute. Even more importantly, the rotary press opened the door to much cheaper newspapers, and this led to a vibrant antislavery press that included newspapers operated by blacks as well as whites. The first black abolitionist newspaper, *Freedom's Journal*, was established in 1827 by John Russwurm (1799–1851) and Samuel E. Cornish (1795–1858), and Cornish later founded the *Colored American*. Another important paper, the *North Star*, was founded by Frederick Douglass (1818–95) and Martin Delany (1812–85) (*see* black press in the United States).

It also became easier to distribute pamphlets and newspapers as transportation innovations such as improved roads, canals and railroads began to spread. These same transportation changes also made it easier for speakers to go on antislavery lecture tours and spread the word verbally. This was particularly important to former slaves such as Douglass, Henry "Box" Brown (1815–79?), and William (1824–1900) and Ellen Craft (1826–91), who toured the Atlantic world, from North America to England, sharing the stories of their lives in bondage and their dramatic escapes from slavery to freedom. These tours not only exposed listeners to the evils of slavery but also provided a chance for speakers to earn money, either in speaking fees or in sales of their memoirs and pamphlets. In many cases, the speakers used the proceeds to buy their family members' freedom.

The evangelical religion of the time also played an important role in the antislavery movement, primarily through the revivals of the Second Great Awakening. The logic of this "awakening" posited that every human being, no matter how "lowly," should strive to live a life of perfection and thus influence society overall to strive for the same goal. Central to this idea was the concept of "moral suasion," which essentially meant that individuals had to want to participate in this perfectionist drive and could not be forced to do so. Thus, the goal of reformers was to enlighten people as to the errors of their ways and encourage them to repent and seek to live better lives.

Releasing humans in bondage was an important goal for most of these perfectionists, and the evangelical movement was crucial to the black abolition movement. First, evangelicalism attracted a number of black leaders, most notably SOJOURNER TRUTH (1797–1883), because it focused on the egalitarian idea that anyone could seek perfection, even those who had been in bondage and had thus been denied education most of their lives. Despite the efforts of former masters to make blacks feel inferior, evangelical Protestantism gave them confidence to participate publicly in the antislavery movement. Indeed, blacks of both sexes and women of both races were drawn to the movement through the evangelical emphasis on the inherent equality of all humans.

A central component of the black abolitionist movement was the "self-help" concept. This idea held that free blacks had a duty to live exemplary lives so that whites could no longer justify slavery on the basis of racial inequality and would no longer argue that the best place for free blacks was "back" in Africa. Important to this overall drive were the creation and operation of independent black schools, churches, and businesses. Mutual aid societies figured prominently in the self-help crusade because it was through these societies that black leaders collected money and pooled together resources so that they could help members of the black community in times of need. This was important because it kept black Americans off public relief rolls and thus helped to counter arguments that free blacks would drain American society of its resources. Self-help was also crucial in making the distinction between blacks' earning their freedom through their own efforts rather than being "given" freedom through the efforts of white leaders.

It was important for blacks to lead the antislavery and civil rights fight, but the extent to which black and white antislavery leaders cooperated effectively is still debated by historians. The historian Paul Goodman has insisted that abolitionists like Garrison challenged the American social order by calling for full human equality rather than just an end to slavery. This is true but also easily overstated. Contemporary accounts by black leaders like Douglass and Delany describe a great deal of paternalism among white abolitionists. Though working with black leaders and including them in the AASS, most white leaders failed to share important offices with blacks. For example, William Still (1821–1902) and William Cooper Nell (1816–74) both devoted decades to the AASS but never rose above the position of clerk in the organization.

By the 1840s, many black leaders had become disenchanted with infighting among white leaders over such issues as the role of women, churches, and politics in the movement, and the lack of true black leadership. One result was a more radical thread of abolitionism in general, and black abolition in particular. This side of the movement gained greater support as Americans debated the fate of slavery in the western territories and more and more slaves began to liberate themselves by escaping. In the tradition of the black abolitionist DAVID WALKER (1785–1830), more and more antislavery leaders at this time began to appeal to slaves rather than masters. The most famous example of this was HENRY HIGHLAND GARNET's (1815–82) appeal to American slaves to, except all-out revolt, "USE EVERY MEANS, BOTH MORAL, INTELLECTUAL, AND PHYSICAL, THAT PROMISES SUCCESS."

Another example of more radical abolition activity involved slave rescues and work on the Underground Railroad. Both black and white abolitionists participated in these endeavors and thus strengthened the overall abolition movement by showcasing biracial cooperation and making abolitionists appear to Southerners as a unified, very active, and quite formidable opponent. The most famous former slave affiliated with Underground Railroad activity was HARRIET TUBMAN (ca. 1822–1913), who gained the nickname "The Moses of Her People." She, Josiah Henson (1789–1883), and John P. Parker (1827–1900) were all former slaves who went back South to lead slaves northward to freedom. Perhaps the most famous free black who helped assist escaped slaves along their way to freedom was William Still, the leader of Philadelphia's vigilant association.

This type of activity became even more important to black leaders after national events such as the Compromise of 1850, the Kansas-Nebraska Act (1854), and the DRED SCOTT court decision (1857) posed a substantial threat to free blacks. Many black leaders began to focus on political action as an important goal. Henry Bibb (1815–54), Samuel Ringgold Ward (1817–ca. 1866), and many others joined the Liberty Party, a new political party dedicated to fighting slavery. Others, including black clergy leaders such Cornish, Theodore S. Wright (1797–1847), and Garnet, were attracted to the American and Foreign Anti-Slavery Society (AFASS), founded by the white leader Arthur Tappan (1786–1865). Many, however, began to call for black independence from white leadership. According to the historian C. Peter Ripley, white and black abolitionists had distinct movements by the 1840s, whites choosing to focus on the more abstract and ideological aspects of antislavery, and blacks defining both slavery and freedom in more concrete terms based on their day-to-day experiences, seeking practical changes, and more concerned with results than tactics.

The events of the antebellum years highlighted the connection between free blacks and slaves in the United States. The FUGITIVE SLAVE ACT OF 1850, which was part of the Compromise of 1850, perfectly illustrates this. It threatened the security of all free blacks by denying them the right to trial by jury if accused of being a fugitive slave and placing the burden of proof on the accused. For those who had never been enslaved and thus did not have freedom papers, this was a tremendous burden indeed. Compounding the problem, the law created a bounty system that awarded commissioners $10 for each case in which a slave was returned to his or her master, but only five dollars for each case in which the accused fugitive was released. Most Northerners disagreed with the law in principle but recognized the danger to the federal union of disobeying the law, so they reluctantly accepted the law and their role in its execution.

Black abolitionists, of course, knew what was at stake, and their resistance to the law led to one of the most militant periods in antislavery history. Forced to watch fugitive slaves such as Anthony Burns (1834–62) returned to slavery despite public outcries, many free blacks began to encourage civil disobedience. Many even began to consider emigration to a number of different places. Some supported the idea of emigrating to MEXICO, but many more chose CANADA. Others left for Great Britain, and still others, most famously Delany, Garnet, and ALEXANDER CRUMMELL (1819–98), supported African emigration. These

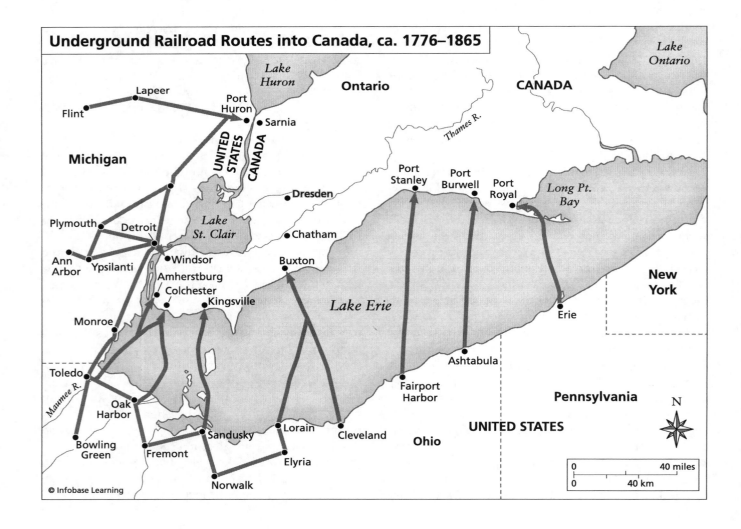

Underground Railroad Routes into Canada, ca. 1776–1865

emigration schemes gained popularity after the Fugitive Slave Law; the Kansas-Nebraska Act, which threatened to allow slavery to spread into the western territories; and the *Dred Scott* decision, which resulted in the declaration that blacks would never be citizens of the United States and thus enjoyed no protection under the federal Constitution. One very important distinction must be made, however, between the resettlement plans of the ACS and the emigration plans of men like Delany. While the ACS sought to resettle blacks under white guidance, Delany planned a settlement that would be led by blacks, away from the stifling atmosphere of white prejudice.

Before plans like the one Delany offered could be seriously considered, however, the AMERICAN CIVIL WAR began in 1861, and most free blacks saw it right away as an opportunity to fight for black freedom and civil rights throughout the nation. Indeed, when the war first erupted, white leaders and politicians insisted upon maintaining the focus on preserving the Union, but free blacks had a different agenda. They saw the potential for the war to lead to a permanent solution to the slavery issue, and they began immediately to volunteer to serve the Union. Rejected at first, they finally gained acceptance through President ABRAHAM LINCOLN's EMANCIPATION PROCLAMATION in 1863. The president issued this statement only after free blacks, among them Sojourner Truth, Douglass, and Delany, had approached him personally with plans for black participation in the war. The proclamation opened the door for the eventual end of slavery, but just as importantly, the president agreed to allow African Americans to serve in the Union army and fight actively for their own freedom. This was crucial so that emancipation could be seen as something earned by black Americans rather than a gift given to them by whites.

Beverly C. Tomek

FURTHER READING

Goodman, Paul. *Of One Blood: Abolitionism and the Origins of Racial Equality.* Los Angeles: University of California Press, 1998.

Harrold, Stanley. *American Abolitionists.* Essex: Pearson Education, 2001.

Johnson, Reinhard O. *The Liberty Party, 1840–1848: Antislavery Third-Party Politics in the United States.* Baton Rouge: Louisiana State University Press, 2009.

Mayer, Henry. *All on Fire: William Lloyd Garrison and the Abolition of Slavery.* New York: St. Martin's Press, 1998.

Nash, Gary. *Forging Freedom: The Formation of Philadelphia's Black Community, 1720–1840.* Cambridge, Mass.: Harvard University Press, 1988.

Newman, Richard. *Freedom's Prophet: Bishop Richard Allen, the AME Church, and the Black Founding Fathers.* New York: New York University Press, 2008.

———. *The Transformation of American Abolitionism: Fighting Slavery in the Early Republic.* Chapel Hill: University of North Carolina Press, 2002.

Ripley, C. Peter, ed. *The Black Abolitionist Papers.* 5 vols. Chapel Hill: University of North Carolina Press, 1986–1992.

Winch, Julie. *A Gentleman of Color: The Life of James Forten.* New York: Oxford University Press, 2002.

URUGUAY

Uruguay is positioned on the east coast of South America surrounded by BRAZIL to the north and ARGENTINA to the south and west. It is the smallest Spanish-speaking country on the continent in terms of land size and population. In 1534, Pedro Mendoza began exploring the region, known during the colonial period as the Banda Oriental. Permanent Spanish settlements did not appear until 1726, when the Spanish Crown established Montevideo as a key Spanish military outpost.

The key population centers are located along the bank of the Rio de la Plata, in fertile soil and a relatively flat topography. The vegetation and climate are well suited to RANCHING, which was the primary economic activity in the colonial and early national periods. The access to the ocean along the wide and navigable Rio de la Plata is good, and Uruguay has several fine ports including the capital, Montevideo, and Colonia, the site of an early Portuguese settlement.

Uruguay's status as a buffer state between Brazil and Argentina has deeply influenced its history. Its proximity to Brazil, a Portuguese colony, threatened Spanish interests in the region as the Portuguese Crown attempted to secure a rival garrison in Colonia do Sacramento. The Portuguese also turned into a formidable economic competitor as they took control of the region's slave trade. Uruguay also fought against Brazilian encroachment and formally declared independence in 1825. During the wars of independence in the Platine region, political leaders in Buenos Aires attempted to incorporate Uruguay into the Argentine Republic, but Uruguay successfully repelled these efforts.

Colonial History and Slavery

In 1534, the first people of color arrived in Uruguay as *ladino* (or acculturated) servants, accompanying Mendoza on his conquest of eastern South America. Some of these were slaves, but many were free people. After the Spaniards settled the region, they imported thousands more African-born slaves, a total of almost 13,000 by 1630. Colonial administrators relied heavily on African slave labor in establishing settlements. The very survival of these colonies depended on enslaved people of color as soldiers, fieldworkers, miners, and household servants. The demand for slaves encouraged large-scale smuggling operations, which explain why it is so difficult to count with any precision the number of slaves imported into the region.

People of color in colonial Uruguay labored in a wide array of occupations under diverse conditions. Most were employed as domestic slaves and day laborers in Montevideo's meat-salting plants, slaughterhouses, workshops, bakeries, and *pulperías* (general stores). Female slaves, in particular, tended to work as seamstresses, cooks, laundresses, and wet nurses, while males often engaged in artisan work, tailoring, shoemaking, pest control, and various jobs at Montevideo's ports. Some urban SLAVE OWNERS allowed their slaves to contract themselves out and earn a free wage, which allowed many to buy their freedom (*see also* LIVING "AS FREE"). As a consequence, the urban slavery of Montevideo is often described as relatively benign compared to that of other regions of the Americas. In the hinterlands, the JESUITS actively bought African slaves to work in their missions and SUGAR CULTIVATION plantations throughout the Platine region, although there were relatively few of these operations in existence. Still, the Jesuits eventually became the largest slave owners in the region. People of color not owned by Christian missionary groups on the frontier were often employed as peons and gauchos on large cattle ranches, lucrative businesses at the time. By the early 19th century,

some free blacks had achieved the status of foreman and even chief administrator.

Although a few African slaves achieved freedom and some upward social mobility, this does not mean that slaves were content with their condition. Enslaved and free people of color engaged in various forms of resistance. They would, for example, steal cattle in order to earn income and subsistence. African slaves also resisted culturally as they preserved their own mixed forms of ancestral rites, music, and dance. Some met together and formed their own "nations" based on ethnic heritage from Africa. Sometimes, this ethnic identity was acceptable, if organized through the ROMAN CATHOLIC CHURCH's religiou's Cofradías (*see* CATHOLIC CONFRATERNITIES). More violent expressions of resistance, such as those of the size and scope of Haiti, Brazil, or the southern United States, were not common in the River Plate. However, in 1803, a slave rebellion in Montevideo occurred when almost two dozen people of color, both enslaved and free, conspired to escape and establish their own runaway settlement (*see also* MAROONS). The Spanish governor responded by quickly attacking the rebels, and the rebellion was ultimately defeated.

The Spanish and Portuguese competed over who would control the regional slave trade in the Platine region. The Spanish Crown had adopted a strict mercantilism, which tightly regulated the purchase and sale of goods within its colonies. From Buenos Aires, the royal government attempted to monopolize the supply of slaves transported into inland Spanish settlements, including Córdoba, Salta, Tucumán, Mendoza, and Montevideo. In particular, increasing demand for slaves to work in the silver mines of Alto Perú, in present-day BOLIVIA, meant that many passed through this region. Portuguese slave traders, based in Colonia do Sacramento, a colony situated directly west of Montevideo, provided an available yet expensive supply of African slaves to the region in spite of the Spanish Crown's best efforts to end this practice. Contraband slave trade continued well into the 17th and 18th centuries as the Dutch and the British established a greater military and commercial presence in the region. In 1611, the Spanish Crown discovered that more than 15 Dutch and English ships had smuggled hundreds of African slaves into Buenos Aires. By the late 18th century, the Spanish Crown granted *asientos*, or permits to trade slaves, to other European powers, including the British, French, and Portuguese. Montevideo evolved as a key center for the slave trade, and between 1751 and 1810, more than 20,000 slaves were sold legally in the port city. While slaves were transported to other regions, many remained in the area, altering the country's demographic character. By 1810, the number of people of color, free and slave, in Montevideo grew to above 2,500. Hundreds more settled as free people of color within Uruguay's interior.

Uruguay

BRAZIL

ARGENTINA

Artigas
Embalse Salto Grande
Río Cuareim
Rivera
Río Arapey Grande
Salto
Río Uruguay
Tacuarembó
Río Tacuarembó
Lago Artificial de Rincón del Bonete
Río Negro
Río Yaguarón
Melo
Paysandú
Lago Artificial de Paso del Palmar
Río Tacuarí
Lagoa Mirím
Fray Bentos
Río Negro
Paso de los Toros
Mercedes
Río Yí
Durazno
Río Cebollatí
N
Colonia
Minas
Rocha
Río de la Plata
Montevideo
ATLANTIC OCEAN

0   100 miles
0   100 km

© Infobase Learning

Slavery ended gradually in Uruguay. Under Spanish colonial law, slaves could become free through MANUMISSION, a process whereby slave owners could grant freedom to their slaves or allow slaves to purchase their freedom. Slavery also declined with the establishment of so-called free womb laws during the 1810s. These decrees declared that subsequent generations of people of color in Uruguay would be born free and only remain slaves until the age of 21; however, slavery and slave trading persisted into the 1840s and 1850s despite lawmakers' attempts to pass laws to end these practices. In 1842, for example, Joaquín Suárez, president of Uruguay, issued a formal declaration abolishing slavery. However, lawmakers extended the period of servitude for slaves born under free womb legislation until the age of 25. In 1853, all Uruguayan slaves were finally given their freedom when abolitionist language was incorporated the national constitution. By the 1850s, slavery in the region had all but ended in practice.

Independence and Marginalization

After independence and the abolition of slavery in the first half of the 19th century, people of color were gradually assimilated in Uruguayan society. Many joined the ranks of the colonial and national militaries (*see also* REGULAR ARMY and MILITIA). Indeed, they had fought in the Spanish armies against indigenous groups, such as the Guaraní and Charruas. Military service provided a viable yet risky path to freedom, especially since the region was constantly embroiled in a variety of civil wars and foreign invasions during the early 19th century. Between 1816 and 1820, when Uruguay began to fight for its independence from Spain, people of color tended to favor independence. As evidence of this, many fought alongside José Gervasio Artigas (1764–1850), one of the heroes of Uruguay's independence movement and founders of the Uruguayan nation. Starting in 1821, people of color in Uruguay also served in Uruguay's armies against Brazil when it occupied the Banda Oriental. By 1825, Uruguayan insurgent leaders, the so-called Immortal 33, accomplished a key victory against the Brazilian invaders, and several Afro-Uruguayans were among this group, though the precise number is unclear since racial lines were blurred for people of high social status, as was common in Spanish America. Many other lower-ranked free people of color fought heroically as soldiers. (*See also* SOUTH AMERICAN WARS OF LIBERATION.)

People of color made tremendous sacrifices in the wars of independence, yet their socioeconomic conditions did not improve greatly. Although legal restrictions of the colonial period and slavery had been dismantled by the mid-19th century, people of color continued to face various degrees of alienation and discrimination. They were prevented from holding certain jobs or having access to education. If they lived in Montevideo, they tended to live in *conventillos*, or poor tenement houses. The slums of Medio Mundo, Palermo, Reus, and Sur are a testament to the impoverished conditions that Uruguay's people of color currently live in today. The arrival of European immigrants at the end of the 19th and early 20th centuries also added to their socioeconomic marginalization.

Assimilation and Contributions

Despite this marginalization, African Uruguayan leaders began to form their own institutions. In 1917, a number of intellectuals founded the journal *Nuestra Raza*, which was published widely, and it continued in print until the middle of the 20th century. In 1937, prominent intellectuals, such as Ventura Barrios, Elemo Cabral, and Salvador Betervide, founded the Partido Autóctono Negro (PAN). Considered more a movement than a political party, PAN never developed a specific political program nor was able to mobilize its base among people of color. As a result, they never voted for the party as a bloc and more often had no choice but from the traditional Colorado or Blanco parties. By 1944, PAN disbanded amid divisions over the direction of the party. In 1950, the playwright Andrés Castillo founded the Teatro Negro Independiente, a notable African Uruguayan cultural institution, which survived until it closed down in 1982. The company sought to celebrate the achievements of people of color in Uruguay.

As elsewhere in Spanish America, many people of partial African ancestry assimilated into the larger population and ceased to be identified as Afro-Uruguayans. Thus, Afro-Uruguayans as a percentage of the population continues to fall. Today, persons identified as being of African ancestry constitute only about 6 percent of the total population of Uruguay. Nonetheless, they have profoundly influenced Uruguay's language and culture. Linguists have noted African influences in the nation's speech patterns. Words such as *cacunda, mandinga,* and *quilombo* have been incorporated the everyday Spanish language of the country. Beyond language, however, their influence is deeply embedded within Uruguayan culture. In music, African influences are also evident in the *payada*, a form of music common among black communities throughout the Americas. Prominent artists of the 20th century included Ildefonso Pereda Valdés, Juan Julio Arrascaeta, Carlos Cardoso Ferreira, Cristina Rodríguez Cabral, José Emilio Cardoso, and Julio Guadalupe. Black Uruguayans either created or helped shape Platine forms of music and dance, especially the *candombe*, the *milonga*, and the tango. Music and popular religion intersect in Montevideo during particular holidays, especially during Carnival and the festival of San Baltasar. Furthermore, folklore also reflects uniquely African elements. The legend of Mandinga is common to the River Plate's folklore: A devil, usually represented as a black cowboy or gaucho, roams the Platine frontier in search of souls to steal. Prominent black writers have written on the African experience, including Pilar Barrios, who authored a powerful drama about racism in *Piel morena* (1947), and Virginia Brindis de Salas, who, in her work, stressed black pride, liberation, and accomplishment in *Pregón de Marimorena* (1974). People of color have also been the important subjects for visual artists. The 19th-century "impressionist" Pedro Figari, a white painter, was enamored with the culture of the *conventillo* and the *candombe*. Furthermore, Afro-Uruguayan entertainers such as Rey Charol and Rubén Rada and athletes, especially soccer players, have proudly represented the Uruguayan nation on the world stage. People of color throughout Uruguay have been assimilated in the general population, but the slow but steady influx of Afro-Brazilians into the country means the constant presence of African-descended peoples.

Jesse Hingson

FURTHER READING

Chasteen, John C. *Heroes on Horseback: A Life and Times of the Last Gaucho Caudillos.* Albuquerque: University of New Mexico Press, 1995.

Montaño, Oscar D. *Umkhonto: La lanza negra. Historia del aporte negro-africano en la formación del Uruguay.* Montevideo, Uruguay: Rosebud Ediciones, 1997.

Pereda Valdés, Ildefonso. *El negro en el Uruguay: Pasado y presente.* Montevideo, Uruguay: Revista del Instituto Histórico y Geográfico del Uruguay, 1965.

Rama, Carlos M. *Los afrouruguayos.* 3rd ed. Montevideo, Uruguay: Editorial El Siglo Ilustrado, 1969.

Williams, John H. "Observations on Blacks and Bondage in Uruguay." *Americas* 43 (1987): 410–428.

U.S. ELECTION OF 1876

Though the year 1876 represented America's centennial celebration, the social and economic climate had remained relatively unchanged for free African Americans since the signing of the Declaration of Independence. Slaves had gained their freedom, but in 1876, it was beginning to be apparent that freedom was not going to translate quickly into socioeconomic advancement. A new system was emerging that combined racial oppression with political and social exclusion. The temporary advancement in political status of blacks during the period of RECONSTRUCTION IN THE UNITED STATES, which had offered significant opportunities to the prewar free colored population, was nearly at an end. The prewar free black population might actually be experiencing a step backward: Slaves had at least gained freedom, although with racial discrimination, while the formerly free were in danger of losing what rights they may have had before the war.

Radical Republicans had imposed Southern Reconstruction after the AMERICAN CIVIL WAR, 1861–65, by excluding former Confederates from political office and placing several Southern states under military control. In response, Southern Democrats looked for new ways to regain political and social power. For many white Southerners, the desire to overthrow Republican domination of their states became a crusade. By 1876, Republicans retained control of only three Southern states: SOUTH CAROLINA, FLORIDA, and LOUISIANA. Additionally, the creation of the KU KLUX KLAN in the late 1860s and its campaigns of terror against thousands of African Americans in the South aided Democratic efforts to regain local hegemony.

The approaching end of ULYSSES S. GRANT's presidency (1869–77), stained with corruption and mired by economic hardship, set the stage for the 1876 election. In June 1876, Republicans met to choose a viable candidate to run for president. The early choice fell to James G. Blaine of MAINE, but soon reports of possible corruption spread regarding his dealings with an ARKANSAS railroad, and he was dropped. In order to remove any hint of graft from the party, the Republicans nominated the politically untarnished governor of OHIO, Rutherford B. Hayes. Democratic delegates nominated the well-known NEW YORK governor and reformer Samuel J. Tilden. Both candidates adopted similar platforms on key issues such as civil service reform, hard currency, and the end of military rule in the South. As the election results came in, Tilden commanded a quarter of a million popular vote lead over Hayes and led him in the electoral college 184 to 165 votes. Twenty additional electoral votes remained in dispute. If Tilden could win just one of them, he would claim a majority of the electoral votes and win the presidency.

Almost immediately, the Republican Party disputed the electoral returns of four states: South Carolina, Louisiana, Florida, and one electoral vote in OREGON. The Oregon dispute was quickly resolved in the Republicans' favor, and the Republican leadership centered its efforts on the other three states. They claimed Democrats utilized voter intimidation to limit African-American turnout, while Democrats countered that Republicans employed voter fraud to boost their vote totals. Since control of Congress remained divided between the parties, lawmakers established a bipartisan commission composed of seven Democrats and seven Republicans to determine the election's outcome. A 15th member, the U.S. Supreme Court justice Joseph Bradley, was to serve as the independent swing vote of the committee. The commission eventually sided eight to seven with Hayes on all electoral votes in the disputed states, ensuring him the presidency. The decision of the commission itself was questioned by Democratic members of Congress, who at first threatened to prevent the election results from being certified. But at last they gave in. Rumors spread of a backroom deal between the parties that guaranteed Hayes's victory in return for the removal of federal troops from the South, increased money for Southern internal improvements, and better Southern representation in Washington, D.C.

Ultimately, the election of 1876 brought an end to Reconstruction. Northern Republicans sacrificed most of their long-term political goals for African Americans in order to retain short-term political control of the nation. For African Americans, the promises of civil rights and suffrage made during Reconstruction would lie unfulfilled for nearly a century. The era that followed, from 1877 until after the turn of the century, was called "Redemption" in the South. Southern white elites recaptured political power through a strategy of excluding blacks from the political process through terror and legal barriers, co-opting poor whites with public services to which only whites had access, and terrorizing the few remaining liberal whites. The resulting SEGREGATION of the black community in the South paradoxically encouraged the growth of a black middle class, to run black-only businesses and provide professional services that blacks could not obtain from whites. Many members of this new class, though by no means all, were from the ranks of the prewar free black population, who in many cases had a head start on the newly freed with education, capital formation, and contacts that they had obtained in the years before the war.

Robert Little

FURTHER READING

Boller, Paul, Jr. *Presidential Elections: From George Washington to George W. Bush.* New York: Oxford Press, 2004.

Holt, Michael. *By One Vote: The Disputed Election of 1876.* Lawrence: University Press of Kansas, 2008.

Morris, Roy. *Fraud of the Century: Rutherford B. Hayes, Samuel Tilden, and the Stolen Election of 1876.* New York: Simon & Schuster, 2003.

Rehnquist, William H. *Centennial Crisis: The Disputed Election of 1876.* New York: Knopf, 2004.

Robinson, Lloyd. *The Stolen Election: Hayes versus Tilden, 1876.* New York: Tom Doherty Associates, 2001.

Trefousse, Hans L. *Rutherford B. Hayes.* New York: Times Books, 2002.

U.S. PRESIDENTS AND FREE BLACKS

The president of the United States, as the head of the executive department of the federal government, and as commander in chief of the nation's armed forces, is the ultimate superior of almost all government employees and ultimately responsible for the implementation of federal laws. In addition, the president of the United States is the political leader of his party, and many presidents were also political thinkers and writers of the greatest importance. In each of these capacities, as leader of government, political organizer, and thinker or public advocate for policy, the president had a great impact on the lives of free people of color in the era of slavery.

The U.S. federal government in the late 18th and early 19th centuries was not the enormous entity familiar to people in the 21st century. In the era of GEORGE WASHINGTON and THOMAS JEFFERSON, the federal government employed only a few hundred civilians, and Jefferson's staff as secretary of state in the first Washington administration in the early 1790s numbered seven (several U.S. ministers and consuls also worked in foreign policy, but it was unclear at the time whether they worked for the secretary of state or directly for the president). In fact, senators and congressmen and their staffs, the employees of the legislative branch of government, might even have outnumbered the executive branch in the first years of the republic. Even by the time of the AMERICAN CIVIL WAR, the executive branch numbered only about 10,000 civilian employees, the largest contingent of these scattered around the country as postmasters. The Postal Service, at the time an integral part of the federal government, was the only federal agency that most people encountered in their daily lives.

People of color were employed by the federal government before the Civil War. The federal government never owned slaves but did employ slaves owned by others on a wide variety of construction projects, from the U.S. Capitol building to military facilities and other public buildings throughout the South, paying their wages to their masters. The eight presidents who owned slaves during their term in office (Washington, Jefferson, JAMES MADISON, JAMES MONROE, ANDREW JACKSON, JOHN TYLER, JAMES POLK, ZACHARY TAYLOR) took their domestic servants with them to the White House, as did many Southern congressmen and civil servants. One reason the Southerners wanted the national capital to be located in slave territory was so that they could continue to have their accustomed lifestyle while serving as federal officials. While the capital was located in PHILADELPHIA, PENNSYLVANIA, Washington's cook Hercules and one of his wife's maids ran away, and the president found it impossible to recapture them without creating a scandal. But in addition to slaves, free people of color also worked for the government and for the presidents directly. JOHN ADAMS employed a free black couple, who worked on his farm and took care of his house in MASSACHUSETTS while he was away on various government missions. He gave them his old house when he bought a newer, bigger one while he was vice president. When the husband died, Abigail Adams provided the widow with a pension for the rest of her life. During the Washington and Adams administrations in the 1790s, the federal government employed the free African-American surveyor Benjamin Banneker to help lay out the plan for the new national capital's streets in Washington, D.C. Banneker collaborated with two Pennsylvania Quaker brothers, Andrew and Joseph Ellicott, to revise the plan originally submitted by the French architect Pierre L'Enfant.

Almost all the states adopted rules barring free blacks from voting during the first 30 years of the country's existence. Prior to this, free blacks who owned enough property to qualify for the franchise, a very small number given the pervasive poverty of American free people of color, could vote in PENNSYLVANIA, RHODE ISLAND, and Massachusetts, though few did, for fear of sparking public hostility. By the outbreak of the Civil War, only WISCONSIN explicitly permitted blacks to vote. Because blacks had no political power, presidents and other politicians did not need to court them or include them in political organizations. However, antiblack rhetoric was an important element of the political formula of many Northern politicians, especially Democrats. Immigrant groups that began to settle in Northern cities after 1840, such as the Irish, saw the free black communities as competitors for jobs and used their right to vote to pressure their politicians to do something about it. Discriminatory laws were unusual, but social exclusion was fairly strong, especially in the cities, and many free blacks found business more difficult during this period. Whites who were not members of recent immigrant communities often were suspicious of the immigrants, and this became an important political divide in the North in the decades before the Civil War. New immigrants were strong supporters of the Democrats, while the descendants of older immigrant groups supported various opposition parties, including, finally, the Republican Party after 1854. The Republicans incorporated the American, or Know-Nothing Party, when they formed. The Know-Nothings opposed both more immigration and the inclusion of free blacks, though most were antislavery. Republican political leaders were generally favorable to free blacks, or at least neutral towards them, opposing exclusionary laws in the northwestern states and calling for the incorporation of blacks in the army after the outbreak of the Civil War. ABRAHAM LINCOLN supported colonization efforts and Illinois's exclusionary law in the 1840s but changed his mind by the time he became president in 1861 and worked fairly consistently for the inclusion of blacks in his political coalition and American society as a whole during his presidency. The only president during this period to be strongly identified with

antiblack political rhetoric was JAMES BUCHANAN, a Pennsylvania Democrat who relied on the support of Philadelphia's immigrant community.

Aside from transient political rhetoric and political team building, several presidents had deeply held beliefs about the proper role of free people of color in American society and put forward concrete proposals. The most important figures in this regard are Lincoln, ANDREW JOHNSON, and ULYSSES S. GRANT, because when they were president, during and after the Civil War, they had a chance to put their ideas into practice during the period of RECONSTRUCTION IN THE UNITED STATES. Lincoln moved toward a position more favorable to blacks as he gained more experience in national affairs. By the time of his service as president, he included blacks in the U.S. Army, urging Northern states to abolish their exclusionary laws and to free slaves where slavery still existed. He remained ambivalent on voting by blacks, however, arguing, as was constitutionally correct at the time, that states had the right to decide who was eligible to vote. Johnson does not appear to have had any particular philosophical objection to free blacks, and he used black soldiers in TENNESSEE units while military governor of the state during the Civil War. But as president he opposed measures to include blacks more fully in American society for political reasons. Grant, who succeeded Johnson in 1869, presided over the period of radical Reconstruction in the South. He appears to have been convinced that blacks should be full citizens of the United States and worked hard toward this end, sending federal troops to attack antiblack terrorist groups and pushing for full implementation of the Reconstruction amendments. His memoirs are the place where he explains his ideas about the world most fully. They were written in the closing days of his life, in the 1880s, after blacks were already being put back under subjection by Jim Crow laws in the South. Grant speaks over and over again of his admiration for black troops and the important role black agents played in his intelligence operation.

Presidents before the Civil War were often constrained in what they could do for people of color by the political power of the South and by the South's insistence that the federal government had no role legislating on matters of race and slavery. There were "gag rules" in place in Congress from the 1790s on that forbade even the discussion of slavery and rights for blacks. During his years in the House of Representatives in the 1830s and 1840s after his one term as president, JOHN QUINCY ADAMS took great pleasure in defying these rules every chance he could and spoke openly of his support for more rights for blacks. Thomas Jefferson epitomized the attitude of many enlightened Southerners, especially in the early years of American independence, when he wrote in his *Notes on the State of Virginia* that he abhorred slavery but did not feel that blacks and whites could live together as equals. He thought slavery was a sadly necessary intermediate stage but looked forward to a time when all American blacks had left the country, for Africa or elsewhere, and the country was a republic of white small farmers. His Southern fellow presidents, Madison and Monroe in particular, supported these ideas, though in his will, George Washington famously freed all his slaves and urged his fellow Virginia planters to do the same. Later presidents began to take up the defense of slavery as a positive good, for Southern blacks as well as whites. The most notable defender of this pro-slavery ideology was Vice President John C. Calhoun.

Stewart R. King

FURTHER READING

Berlin, Ira. *Slaves without Masters: The Free Negro in the Antebellum South*. New York: New Press, 2007.
Sinkler, George. *The Racial Attitudes of American Presidents from Lincoln to Theodore Roosevelt*. New York: Doubleday, 1971.

V

VALDÉS, JOSÉ MANUEL (1767–1843) *Peruvian physician*

José Manuel Valdés was a distinguished Afro-Peruvian doctor and writer born in Lima, PERU, sometime in 1767 in very humble conditions. He was the illegitimate son of a poor free black or MULATTO laundress and an Indian musician. Thanks to his willingness to work hard at his studies, and with the aid of his Spanish godparents, Valdés could attend elementary school and, later, the Lima Augustinian College, where he studied Latin, philosophy, mathematics, and theology.

People of color in colonial Peru could not expect to rise very high in society. At 21, Valdés became a surgeon, which at the time was a low-status medical trade, similar to a barber, and thus open to free people of color (*see also* MIDWIVES AND TRADITIONAL HEALERS). However, his determination to succeed in the medical profession led him to continue studying. Thanks to references from the hospital where he worked, he entered the university and received the bachelor's degree in 1797. He was under the patronage of Hipólito Unanue, a very influential CREOLE (Peruvian-born white) physician of the time. Valdés's own reputation and the protection of Unanue allowed him to petition the Lima High Court and the Town Council to ask the Spanish Crown for a special royal pardon of his color and birth (*see CÉDULAS DE GRACIAS AL SACAR*). A special royal decree of June 11, 1806, permitted him to receive the doctoral degree one year later. By the end of the colonial period in the early 19th century, formal restrictions notwithstanding, some mulattoes and Indians became physicians.

As a free colored physician, Valdés represents the contributions of the American, the creole, and in particular the Afro-Peruvian elements of colonial society. Two other contemporary free colored physicians we know of made similar contributions: José Manuel Dávalos (who studied in SPAIN and FRANCE) and, especially, José Pastor de Larrinaga, author of a special treatise published in 1793 in favor of Peruvian surgeons and opposed to government and social preference for European-trained physicians. Valdés also wrote and published several reports on local diseases and their healing linked to climate, pleading for a truly Peruvian medicine.

However, Valdés's goal was to incorporate himself in white Peruvian medicine, as he ultimately did. Soon, he became one of the favorite physicians of the Lima social elite and one of the leading professors of Lima's San Fernando College of Medicine, where he worked to vindicate surgery as a university subject and thus eliminate its negative connotation as a trade for people of color. The Royal Medical Academy of Madrid enrolled Valdés as an honorary member in 1816.

His house was a center of literary discussion, and he himself was an important writer. As a poet, he wrote odes to San Martín and Bolívar, but in general, he preferred religious compositions. He wrote a translation of the book of Psalms from the Christian Bible, with commentary on their cultural significance, entitled *Peruvian Psalter or Paraphrases of the 150 Psalms of David and Some Sacred Canticles*. His most famous and important work in prose is his biography of SAINT MARTÍN DE PORRES, entitled *The Admirable Life of the Fortunate Frey Martín de Porres, Native of Lima and Professed Member of the Convent of Rosario of That City*. Martín was a mulatto brother in the order of Dominicans and health care worker of the 17th century beatified by the ROMAN CATHOLIC CHURCH in 1837. In the 1840 edition, Valdés declared that he wrote this biography as a racial and social obligation because he and Porres were fellow countrymen and of the same "lowest class and birth."

Valdés was a patriot and a liberal. Together with other physicians, he participated in protests against the Inquisition in 1812 and supported the independence of Peru in 1821. Ten years later, Valdés was elected to the Peruvian Parliament. In 1836, he was designated protomédico general (the highest position for a physician in the country), and in 1840, he became director of the Lima College of Medicine. He died on July 29, 1843, at the age of 76.

Valdés's life is an important milestone in the process of incorporation of Peruvians of African descent into the national life because he succeeded in challenging social and racial prejudices of his time.

Francisco Quiroz

FURTHER READING

Lavalle, J. A. de. *El doctor José Manuel Valdés, (Capuentes sobre suvida y su sobres)*. Lima: Torres Aquirrer 1886.

López Martínez, Héctor. *El protomédico limeño José Manuel Valdés*. Lima: Dirección de Intereses Marítimos, 1993.

Paz Soldán, Carlos Enrique. *José Manuel Valdés, 1767–1843*. Lima: Imprenta Lux, 1942.

Valdés, José Manuel. *Salterio peruano o paráfrasis de los ciento cincuenta salmos de David y algunos cánticos sagrados*. Lima: Masias, 1833.

———. *Vida admirable del bienaventurado fray Martín de Porres, natural de Lima y donado profeso en el convento del Rosario del orden de predicadores de esta ciudad*. Lima: Masias, 1840.

VAN BUREN, MARTIN (1782–1862) *eighth president of the United States (1837–1841)*

Martin Van Buren served as eighth president of the United States from 1837 to 1841. He was born on December 5, 1782, in Kinderhook, New York, in a Dutch family whose ancestors had immigrated to New York before 1666. He is the only U.S. president who was not a native English speaker; he grew up speaking Dutch. His father was a farmer and tavern keeper and owned several slaves. He studied law, entered public service, and rose through the DeWitt Clinton (1769–1828) and Tammany Hall political organizations in New York. His primary skill was as a political organizer, and although his predecessor in office, ANDREW JACKSON, is ordinarily thought of as the founder of the Democratic Party, Van Buren probably deserves the most credit. He welded a disparate coalition of frontier agrarian populists; urban, often immigrant-based political machines, aristocratic planters from the old South, and big-city financial interests into a tightly functioning political organization that dominated American politics in the mid-19th century. Van Buren did his most important organizing work during the administration of his patron and political model Andrew Jackson. As leader of the "Albany Regency," one of the first political machines in American history, he controlled politics in New York in the 1820s and provided key Northern support for Jackson's campaigns in 1824, 1828, and 1832. He served as Jackson's secretary of state during his first term and was vice president in Jackson's second term. Democrats saw Van Buren as Jackson's heir, and he won election in 1836.

The Democrats ultimately supported slavery during the period before the AMERICAN CIVIL WAR. Van Buren himself defended the Spanish government's right to reclaim the slaves who had captured the slave ship AMISTAD in 1839. But Van Buren preferred peace between North and South, refusing to annex TEXAS into the United States after it declared its independence from MEXICO and opposing other attempts to conquer new territory for slave states. Defeated in 1840 by the Whig candidate WILLIAM HENRY HARRISON, Van Buren attempted several times to return to the White House. In the 1844 presidential election, he opposed JAMES POLK for the Democratic nomination, and the biggest issue was Polk's intention to invade Mexico. After Polk became president and fought and won the MEXICAN-AMERICAN WAR, Van Buren ran for president a fourth time in 1848 on the Free Soil ticket, calling for the exclusion of slavery from the territories conquered from Mexico.

The *Amistad* case is the one major public act Van Buren took while president that directly affected the status of free people of color. His campaign for president as a Free Soiler represented opposition to slavery but not necessarily support for equality for people of color. Indeed, much of the motivation for the Free Soil movement was resistance by western whites to the idea of black presence in any form, and many midwestern states passed laws prohibiting free blacks to settle there. (*See* BLACK LAWS IN THE MIDWEST.) However, in his private life, Van Buren seems to have been a consistent opponent of racial discrimination. He never owned slaves himself as an adult, freeing or selling his father's slaves when he inherited them in 1817 (slavery in New York did not end until 1824). As a Democrat, Van Buren supported the Democratic presidents of the 1850s but was horrified by JAMES BUCHANAN's failure to respond to the secession of the Southern states in 1860–61. Van Buren gave critical Democratic support to ABRAHAM LINCOLN's war measures in the early months of the American Civil War, before falling ill with pneumonia in fall 1861; he died on July 24, 1862.

FURTHER READING

Widmer, Ted. *Martin Van Buren*. New York: Holt, 2005.

VASHON FAMILY *John Bathan (1792–1853) and George Boyer (1824-1878), American educators and abolitionists*

The Vashon family is a prominent example of a free mixed-race family in the North of the United States. For four generations spanning the first century of America's existence as an independent country, the Vashons built black PITTSBURGH, PENNSYLVANIA, and blazed trails for black leaders of succeeding generations. Freedom was, for them, only the beginning of substantial social advancement possible even within the racially polarized society of 19th-century America.

The War of 1812 veteran John Bathan Vashon was one of Pittsburgh's leading free blacks and Underground

Railroad agents in the 19th century. His father, George Vashon—who also served in the War of 1812—was white, and his mother, Fanny, was of mixed ancestry. The couple was not married, and at one point Fanny was owned by George's father, Simon Vashon, a veteran of the WAR OF AMERICAN INDEPENDENCE (1775–83), but there is evidence that the couple shared a caring relationship, and Fanny was free by the time of John's birth in 1792. John's son, George Boyer Vashon, was born on July 25, 1824, in Carlisle, Pennsylvania. He was also a noted essayist and poet and became the first black graduate of Oberlin College and the first black lawyer in NEW YORK STATE. As a young man, George was one of the first students to attend the school founded by his father, the Pittsburgh African Educational Society. The education he received as a student of the Reverend LEWIS WOODSON at this school, combined with lessons his father taught him at home, served as the bedrock of his early education. He also followed their example in joining the black abolitionist movement at an early age, helping to establish and serving as secretary of the Pittsburgh Juvenile Anti-Slavery Society.

During his service in the War of 1812, John Vashon was captured by the British and, like James Forten (see FORTEN FAMILY), was held prisoner on a British prison ship, the *Jersey*. He was eventually released in exchange for a British soldier, a symbolic equality that he talked about throughout his life. After his release, he settled in Leesburg, Virginia. While there, he married Anne Smith,

a free black, and started a family. They moved to Carlisle, Pennsylvania, in 1822 seeking a community with fewer racial restrictions. In Carlisle, he became a successful barber, but in 1829, the family decided to move to Pittsburgh, where they became well respected among both whites and blacks.

In Pittsburgh, John Vashon worked with Lewis Woodson in founding the Pittsburgh African Education Society and the Anti-Slavery Society of Pittsburgh. He served as president of the school. A successful barber and owner of the first public bathhouse in western Pennsylvania, he was a mentor to MARTIN DELANY. He was also one of William Lloyd Garrison's main benefactors and gave large contributions to help establish the *Liberator*, an abolitionist newspaper that began publication in 1831. He was named to the board of managers, of the American Anti-Slavery Society, founded in PHILADELPHIA, PENNSYLVANIA, on December 4, 1833. He also contributed in a number of cases to purchasing the freedom of individual slaves and allowed his home and businesses to serve as stations on the Underground Railroad from the 1830s to the 1850s.

At age 16, John's son, George Boyer Vashon, was enrolled in Oberlin College, one of the few institutions of HIGHER EDUCATION in the country to admit black students on equal footing with whites. While there, he joined the prestigious men's literary Union Society and volunteered as a teacher and tutor at local schools, teaching future leaders such as JOHN MERCER LANGSTON, who would later become the first African American elected to Congress. In 1844, Vashon graduated as valedictorian from Oberlin. In 1849, he was awarded a master of arts from Oberlin.

Upon his return to Pittsburgh, George Vashon studied law under Walter Forward, the future U.S. secretary of the treasury. He then applied for admission to the Allegheny County bar so that he could practice law in Pennsylvania but was rejected because of his race under the provision of the 1838 state constitution that barred blacks from practicing law. In disgust, he left for Haiti, the world's first black republic and a nation he had long admired. He stayed there until 1850, at which point he moved to Syracuse, New York, where he had been admitted to the bar.

In Syracuse, George Vashon became a leader of a local vigilance committee that had formed in response to the FUGITIVE SLAVE LAW OF 1850. Along with his father, he also served as a conductor on the Underground Railroad and developed close bonds with white abolitionists such as Gerrit Smith. Through Smith he became involved with the Liberty Party, which chose him as the candidate for New York attorney general and thus the first black to run for office in that state. Along with his father, George

Born in 1824, George Boyer Vashon became the first African American to graduate from Oberlin College in Ohio, the first African-American lawyer in New York, and the first African-American professor at Howard University in Washington, D.C. *(Keith Srakocic/Associated Press)*

Vashon held a number of important roles in the black abolitionist movement. Both men signed the call for the Colored National Convention in Rochester, New York, organized by Frederick Douglass (*see also* Negro Convention Movement in the United States).

George Boyer Vashon, who had been given his middle name in honor of the former Haitian president Jean-Pierre Boyer (1776–1850), is also known for his literary and academic achievements. His first great poetic work, "Vincent Ogé," an epic celebration of the Haitian Revolution, appeared in 1853, and he became professor of belles-letters at New York Central College. (*See also* Vincent Ogé.)He also contributed to Frederick Douglass's newspaper. Beginning in 1857, he served as principal of the Colored Public Schools of Pittsburgh.

Though not accepted during his lifetime to the Pennsylvania bar, Vashon was admitted to practice by the U.S. Supreme Court. He was posthumously admitted to the Pennsylvania bar in 2010. He also worked in the Solicitor's Office of the Freedmen's Bureau after the American Civil War and became the first black professor at Howard University. He also served as professor of ancient and modern languages at Alcorn University in Mississippi and was admitted to the bar of that state. He died during a yellow fever outbreak on October 5, 1878.

Beverly C. Tomek

FURTHER READING

Quarles, Benjamin. *Black Abolitionists.* New York: Oxford University Press, 1969.
Switala, William J. *Underground Railroad in Pennsylvania.* Mechanicsburg, Pa.: Stackpole Books, 2001.
Thornell, Paul N. D. "The Absent Ones and the Providers: A Biography of the Vashons." *Journal of Negro History* 83, no. 4 (Autumn 1998): 284–301.

VENEZUELA

Venezuela is a nation in South America, located along the Caribbean/Atlantic coast between Colombia and Guyana. In the far interior, in territory unsettled in colonial times, Venezuela also has a border with Brazil. Lying nearby off the coast are a number of small island colonies, notably the Dutch Caribbean Islands and Trinidad and Tobago. The country is divided into four main geographical regions. In the West, along the Colombian border, broad plains surround Lake Maracaibo, backed by tall mountains leading up to the border with Colombia. This region was suitable for plantation agriculture and was a major producer of cacao into the 19th century, as well as home to large Sugar cultivation plantations. Today it is a major oil-producing region. In the center of the country, high mountains line the coast. An interior plain and

a narrow coastal plain are home to a dense population. In the central region is found the national capital, Caracas, along with other important cities. The northeastern region is the delta of the Orinoco River, a swampy region but one offering good access to the interior along a great river and also protected harbors on the Atlantic Ocean. The northeastern region was also home to some plantations growing sugar and cacao. In the southern interior lie the llanos, or plains. Enormous near-wild herds of cattle and horses roam these plains, and a herding culture grew up in the 18th century that had many similarities to cowboy societies in the North American West and the pampas of Argentina and Uruguay. The Indians of Venezuela were related to those found in the islands of the Lesser Antilles and Guyana. They were farmers, lived in villages and towns, and had a decentralized political structure. Diseases introduced from Europe and Africa decimated the native population. In the highlands along the Colombian border and in the deep interior, Indian populations survived contact as distinct groups, while in the central and northeastern regions, the few surviving Indians assimilated into the African and European population, creating an Afro-mestizo population.

Colonial Period (1508–1810)

The first African-descended people to visit Venezuela arrived with Columbus on his third voyage, when in August 1498 his ships passed along the northeastern coast. The first enslaved Africans taken to the South American mainland were pearl divers, exploiting rich oyster beds around the islands of Margarita. Spanish colonists settled on the mainland in 1522, in the city of Cumaná in the central region, and regular importations of slaves for agricultural work were taking place as early as 1528. As native populations declined throughout the 16th century, they were replaced as a source of labor by enslaved Africans. Venezuela was always a peripheral area in the Spanish Empire, however, and it imported a grand total of about 130,000 slaves between 1508 and 1810. As in many peripheral areas of Spanish America, many of those slaves, or their descendants, managed to become free, and free Afro-Venezuelans constituted the largest part of the population of the colony by the end of the 18th century.

Some Afro-Venezuelans became free not through MANUMISSION but instead by flight. Settlements of MAROONS first appeared in the 16th century, and by the late 17th century, several had become large enough to challenge the colony's authority in remote regions. The maroon community of Ocoyta, in Barlovento in the mountains near Caracas, was one of the last and most successful of these settlements, surviving until 1770 under the leadership of the charismatic runaway Guillermo Rivas.

The French voyager François Depons, who visited the Captaincy-General of Venezuela in 1797, in a book he published afterward to recount his experience in the Caribbean, wrote of the human landscape he observed when visiting the city of Caracas, "In proportion to other social classes, probably there is not in the West Indies a city with as many emancipated or descendents of emancipated." This description accurately reflects the racial profile of the population in that territory by the late 18th century, since free people of color there were the most numerous racial group, reaching nearly 45 percent of the total population (some 190,000 individuals), almost double the number of the whites (25 percent) and triple that of the slaves (16 percent). More than two-thirds of the free people of color were PARDOS, mixed-blood descendants of Euro-African ancestry (mulattoes, ZAMBOS, quadroons, tercerones, quinterones, etc.), while the free blacks only made up a small fraction of the total population (7 percent). It is important to point out that in Spanish America, from the perspective of the local whites, the word pardo was used in a pejorative way, meaning the same as free people of color and, at times, even as a synonym of CASTA. From the perspective of the pardos, on the other hand, its use was more restricted, only including individuals who had both African and European ancestry.

As had happened in other parts of the Hispanic Caribbean, the extraordinary growth in free colored populations during the colonial period in Venezuela was the product mainly of two factors: on the one hand, the elevated level of racial MISCEGENATION between conquistado-

res and their female African servants, facilitated by the absence of European women; and, on the other hand, that Spanish law authorized Spaniards to emancipate their mixed-blood offspring. In the province of Caracas, this phenomenon grew as the introduction of African slaves increased from the mid-17th century onward, the result of a boom in the cultivation of cacao. Normally, most free people of color performed manual occupations considered not worthy of whites (especially craftsmanship of all sorts). They also ran small retail stores (pulperías) in cities and worked smallholdings (conucos) in which they grew vegetables for local consumption. From the beginning of the 18th century, many pardos became very wealthy, becoming hacienda owners (hacendados) in the southern plains or llanos, and owning houses in the cities that they used or rented as retail stores. One example is the case of Diego Ignacio Mejía Landaeta, who probably was one of the wealthiest pardos of Caracas: By 1807, his estate included 26 houses and 9,700 pesos in assets. Other members of this elite had enough money to celebrate fancy parties, to make generous donations to their church in Caracas (the Temple of Altagracia), and to acquire the very expensive royal dispensations from the penalties attached to free colored status.

Those wealthy pardos were also often the most light-skinned of the people of mixed race (the quadroons and quinterones), as their economic status had allowed them to marry their daughters to lower-class, or "lesser-quality," whites (Blancos de Orilla). Similar to whites, members of the pardo elite tried to preserve their racial and economic status by carefully controlling marriages. They did this by seeking marriages with whites that would advance their children's racial status, but also by opposing unions between their children and persons of lower racial rank. From 1778 on, they could count on the support of the Spanish king, who approved the application in the Americas of a royal edict on weddings (Real Pragmática de Matrimonios), in an attempt to prevent the "confusion of classes and races." According to this legislation, a person could not marry without the authorization of the head of his or her family, and if the elder did not consider the intended spouse of his relative his or her equal, he could oppose the marriage (Disenso Matrimonial). The edict applied to military officers, including pardo officers from the MILITIA, in effect, most male members of the pardo elite. The section of the Venezuelan National Archives dealing with marriage law is filled with hundreds of this kind of declaration of opposition to a proposed marriage, denoting how strongly the local population was aware of the importance of keeping their lineages "clean."

Members of the pardo elite also had the conviction that they possessed special credentials or "esteem" (*estima*), because of their superior level of education and the services they had loyally performed for the king in the militia. All these aspects made them believe they were at the summit of the free colored socioracial pyramid. At times they called themselves the "worthy pardos" (*pardos beneméritos*), despising those who were below. By the end of the colonial period in the early 19th century, they had developed a strong sociopolitical identity, as shown by the unsuccessful efforts they carried out in 1806 to convince the Cabildo, or city government of Caracas, to allow them to create a special school for their children, and in the first stages of the Revolution of Caracas (1810–12), during which they founded a political club reserved for themselves, in a parallel to the one created by most radical white republicans. Perhaps the most emblematic document that exposes this self-identity is a letter addressed to Venezuela's governor in 1774, by the officers of the *pardo* Battalion of Caracas, in which they demanded the highest authority of the colony to expel from that force one of its members, arguing that this individual had a lesser racial "quality": They suspected he was a "Held-in-the-Air" (Tente en el Aire: a person whose parents were both MULATTO) or, "worse," a *zambo* (Indian and black parents), or a "Jump-Back" (Salto Atrás: a *pardo* parent and a black parent).

This reaction reflected a wider behavioral pattern that had originated in late medieval times in Spain, where, after the Reconquest (1492), thousands of Jews and Muslims who had converted to Catholicism (New Christians) attempted to merge with Spaniards. As many privileges and public functions were reserved to Old Christians, it was crucial to prove that one's ancestry had no "stains" of Muslim or Jew. This could be accomplished with the application of a legal mechanism known as a blood cleanliness test (Limpieza de Sangre), through which the authorities checked the ancestors as far as three generations back. In Hispanic America, particularly in places where mixed-blood people of African descent were numerous and where light-skinned *pardos* were visually indistinguishable from whites, that mechanism was also applied, not aiming to rule out heretic ancestors, but rather to look for African "stains" in one's ancestry. At times this mechanism proved to be ineffective, as many wealthy *pardos* managed to bribe priests to modify the baptism registers, moving the names of their ancestors from the free people of color book to the whites' book. The very arguments "worthy *pardos*" used to stand out among the free people of color were the same they made use of to acquire a "color dispensation" that became available in the mid-1790s, through the legal mechanism of the *cedulas de gracias al sacar*.

This measure was introduced as part of a series of enlightened measures known altogether as the Bourbon Reforms, which intended to increase the productivity of the Spanish colonies in the Americas. In the case of the *cedulas de gracias al sacar*, it also aimed to put an end to the hegemony of the local white aristocracies over the *pardo* elite, or at least counterbalance its power by allowing the latter legally to remove their "African stigma." To accomplish this, *pardos* had to prove that they were highly "esteemed" in the society they lived in; then, if their application was approved by the king, they would need to pay a very expensive dispensation fee. As far as we know, only two such dispensations were granted in Venezuela, mainly because of the strong opposition of white creoles. Using the local Cabildo, they made an address to the king urging him to reconsider his decision. Notwithstanding the qualities members of the *pardo* elite insisted they had, from the perspective of white creoles—in particular for those belonging to the local aristocracy, the so-called Mantuanos (a term used because their women were the only ones allowed to take carpets, or *mantos*, into Churches to kneel upon)—the *pardos* were all the same: the result of the worst of all human mixtures, as they were not only marked by the stigma of slavery, but also because they had "illegitimate" origin. The white creole perception of the *pardos* also had an aesthetic side, as they regarded them, following the priest Juan Antonio Navarrete in the 1780s, as "the ugliest and most abominable race, and even extraordinary."

As the numbers of free people of color in the Americas increased, the white elites managed to introduce a series of measures to keep them checked, some of which were inspired by the restrictive measures applied to New Christians in Spain: prohibitions of going out during the night, of using of luxurious articles, of using the honorific form of address *Don*, of attending schools and universities, bearing arms, holding public positions, receiving appointment as officers in their militias beyond the grade of captain, visiting churches reserved to whites, marrying white persons, walking by whites in the streets, and being invited by the latter to enter their houses.

On the eve of the war of independence, the conflict between *pardos beneméritos* and Mantuanos reached its peak: In 1806, the *pardos'* request for a special school for their children was not considered by the Cabildo, and in 1808, when this assembly attempted to form an autonomous government, after the arrival of the news of the occupation of Spain by Napoléon Bonaparte, the officers of the *pardo* battalions reacted violently, offering their services to the Spanish authorities for crushing the conspiracy.

War of Independence (1810–1823)
The VENEZUELAN WAR OF INDEPENDENCE was a terrible 12-year struggle that profoundly changed the lives of all

Venezuelans. Several armed factions supporting independence fought against the Spanish and occasionally against each other. The Spanish also had the support of Venezuelan armed groups. The majority of Venezuelans were people of African descent, and they fought on both sides. In a seesaw struggle, pro-independence forces three times captured the cities of the central region and proclaimed independence, first in 1810–12, then again in 1813–14, and finally after 1821. After the first and second rebel successes, Spanish troops and Venezuelan royalists were able to retake the capital but not to extinguish the insurgency.

The leaders of the independence movement were mostly powerful white creoles with generally liberal political attitudes, like the first leader, Francisco de Miranda, and his successor, Simón Bolívar. Colonial whites had lost power during the Bourbon Reforms. Spanish whites had been appointed to many important roles in government under the reforms. Although these immigrants often married the daughters of local elite families, they still formed a separate class of *peninsulares*, or European-born Spaniards, and monopolized power. At the same time, Spanish government measures to improve the status of the *pardos beneméritos* reduced the superiority of whites over nonwhites. Racial tensions were high in all of these groups. At first, therefore, nonwhites were suspicious of the rebel movement. Urban free people of color in Caracas generally joined the rebellion of 1810 when it began, however. The local white leaders of the movement promised racial equality in the new state, and their liberal principles appealed to the urban free people of color, who were generally better educated than rural people of any race. Free blacks and Afro-mestizos in the countryside, however, generally opposed the independence movement, at least at first. Miranda's first independent government fell in 1812, in part because slaves in the plantation regions rebelled against their pro-independence masters, pledging loyalty to the Spanish. The racially mixed community of *llaneros,* the cowboys of the southern plains, under their military leader, or caudillo, José Tomas Boves, fought stubbornly for the Spanish king against the second republic. The struggles between Boves and Bolívar often had overtones of race and class struggle, as Boves's troops slaughtered whites and wealthy people indiscriminately in captured cities. The independence movement had its own army of free people of color, a quasi-autonomous force operating the northeastern region led by the Dutch Antillean–born general MANUEL PIAR. Piar's forces included many free colored veterans of the French Revolutionary and Napoleonic Wars, including many who had fought in the Antilles for the French in the 1790s.

The second republic was destroyed by Boves and his men, although Boves himself was killed at the decisive Battle of Urica, December 5, 1814. Bolívar fled into exile and recruited a new army, which included troops from Haiti, BRITAIN and the British Caribbean, and Colombia. Bolívar established himself in the South, this time allying with the *llaneros* under their new caudillo, José Antonio Páez. The *llaneros* had left the Spanish side after new regulations undermined the authority of the caudillos, while Bolívar was happy to permit at least some of his generals to have their own fiefdoms. This tolerance did not extend to Piar, however, who was shot on Bolívar's orders in October 1817, after he had become too popular and successful and threatened Bolívar's position as the supreme military commander of the revolution. Piar's soldiers became an integral part of the army of liberation and fought in Colombia and Ecuador before returning to Venezuela for the closing campaign of the war there. Bolívar won an important battlefield victory at Carabobo on June 24, 1821. At the same time, he was unifying northern South America politically under his control. The congress of Cucutá ratified a constitution for the united Gran Colombia, composed of today's Venezuela, Colombia, and ECUADOR, October 21, 1821. This constitution called for racial equality and provided for compensated MANUMISSION and free birth laws as the means for gradual abolition of slavery. The last act of the military struggle took place on July 24, 1823, when the Gran Colombia NAVY, under the command of the Afro-Colombian admiral JOSÉ PRUDENCIO PADILLA, defeated the Spanish navy at the Battle of Lake Maracaibo. This naval victory cut off the last hope of reinforcement or resupply for the isolated Spanish garrisons of the cities of the northwestern region, and those cities fell.

National Period (1823–1900)

The end of the war and the adoption of the new constitution put an end to the caste system. It also gave birth to new forms of racial and political discrimination. Perhaps the most evident manifestation of the latter was the attitude many members of the political elite showed toward the new colored citizens. Among them stood out the president, Bolívar, who despised what he described as *pardocracia,* or government of the *pardos.* Although he held generally liberal ideas about the basic equality of all human beings, he shared a belief common among educated whites at the time that whites were superior morally and intellectually, mostly for inborn reasons. Governmental authority should be entrusted to the fittest persons, not because of RACISM AND RACIAL PREJUDICE but in the interest of the best outcome for everybody. This relatively mild form of white supremacy theory, nonetheless, meant that Bolívar was uncomfortable whenever he had to work with people of color as equals. When the free Afro-descended people of the northern coast of Colombia protested continuing prejudice and unequal treatment by the government and plotted either to separate from Gran Colombia or to overthrow the central government, Bolívar had their political leader, his admiral Padilla, shot in 1825.

Back in Venezuela, Afro-Venezuelans were confronting new challenges but also enjoying new opportunities. Gran Colombia disintegrated into its component parts in 1830. José Antonio Páez became president of the restored Venezuela, and although in and out of office, he continued to wield enormous power in the country until his final exile in 1863. He was popular with the Afro-Venezuelan masses, who saw him as the protector of their rights against the wealthy white oligarchs. The relatively light-skinned *pardos beneméritos* disappeared quickly into the white population, and vice versa. They were followed by the children of mulatto-white relationships, as a growing number of European immigrants entered the country, attracted by relative political calm and prosperity. The ideology of "WHITENING" AND RACIAL PROMOTION remained an important part of the Venezuelan cultural mind-set in the 19th century, and beyond. Today it still works as a sort of endoracism, hidden behind a social myth that highlights the light-colored skin of the population in appealing terms, such as *color canela* (cinnamon) or *café con leche* (coffee with milk).

Alejandro E. Gomez

FURTHER READING
Andrews, George Reid. *Afro-Latin America, 1800–2000.* Oxford: Oxford University Press, 2004.
Bushnell, David. "The Independence of Spanish South America." In *The Independence of Spanish America,* edited by David Bushnell. Cambridge: University of Cambridge Press, 1987.
Helg, Aline. "Simon Bolívar and the Spectre of *Pardocracia*: Jose Padilla in Post-Independence Cartagena." *Journal of Latin American Studies* 35 (2003): 447–471.
McKinley, P. Michael. *Pre-Revolutionary Caracas: Politics, Economy and Society, 1777–1811.* New York: Cambridge University Press, 1997.
Thibaud, Clément. *Républiques en armes. Les armées de Bolívar dans la guerre d'Indépendance en Colombie et au Venezuela.* Rennes: Presses Universitaires de Rennes, 2006.
Wright, Winthrop R. *Café con Leche: Race, Class, and National Image in Venezuela.* Austin: University of Texas Press, 1990.

VENEZUELAN WAR OF INDEPENDENCE

The Venezuelan War of Independence (1808–21) was a crucial phase in the SOUTH AMERICAN WARS OF LIBERATION. VENEZUELA and ARGENTINA were the first Spanish colonies to rebel. The role of free Afro-Venezuelans was especially important, both because they constituted such a large proportion of the population of Venezuela and because both sides called upon them for military support.

The war passed through three phases. In the first, pro-independence leaders, most of them from the white CREOLE elite, began an uprising against Spanish rule in April 1810. This move was generally opposed by the free population of color, though the rebel leader Francisco de Miranda was able to rally free Afro-Venezuelans from the eastern portion of the country to his cause. Ultimately, local royalists were able to crush this rebellion with some support from metropolitan SPAIN in July 1812. One of Miranda's followers, Simón Bolívar, returned to the fray with troops from COLOMBIA in July 1813, raising the standard of revolt in the western part of the colony and ultimately controlling much of the coast. This Second Venezuelan Republic was crushed once again, this time with the help of free nonwhite cowboys from the southern plains called *llaneros.* Undeterred, Bolívar retreated to Haiti, raised troops and funds, and returned to Venezuela in 1816. This time with the cooperation of the *llaneros,* under the command of José Antonio Paez, and of a coastal army led by the free colored general MANUEL PIAR, Bolivar was able to preserve Venezuelan independence. A Venezuelan expeditionary force went to Colombia and routed the royalists there, then the Colombian forces repaid the favor by assisting the Venezuelans in their final assault on the royalist strongholds. The decisive battle at Carabobo (June 24, 1821), marked by a stirring charge by Paez's *llaneros,* defeated the royalist field armies, though the last royalist cities did not fall until 1823.

The ambiguous role that free people of color played in the Venezuelan war sprang from their ambiguous place in colonial society. People of African descent were very numerous in Venezuela when compared to the other mainland South American colonies. There was a class of reasonably wealthy and socially acceptable (to the whites) mixed-race people known as the *pardos beneméritos.* Beneath them in the social order were free blacks and mulattoes in the cities, often working as ARTISANS and small businesspeople, and many free colored farmers and farmworkers in the countryside. Racial tensions were high, especially as the upper-class whites saw their influence decline during the period of the Bourbon Reforms (1770–1810). The tensions between free coloreds and whites erupted in violence in November 1808, after the news of the overthrow of the Spanish Crown by Napoléon Bonaparte and the establishment of a provisional assembly in the Spanish city of Cádiz. Members of the white elite attempted to set up an autonomous government in Venezuela. When the PARDO MILITIA officers became aware of this project, they become alarmed and without delay sent a very emotional letter to the captain-general offering their services to fight like "a brown beast" *(parda fiera),* to restore the king's authority over the territory.

This initiative was soon supported by many "islanders" (immigrants from the Canary Islands) and by individuals from "all classes" *(de todas las clases)*, generating a popular turmoil that would only be controlled when most of those implicated in the conspiracy were arrested.

Two years later, after the fall of Andalucía to the French and the establishment of the Regency Council (Consejo de Regencia) in Spain, lower-class white creoles, who so far had been reluctant to support any attempt to become autonomous because of the aristocratic profile of the pro-independence leaders, joined them in a new effort to establish an autonomous—though not completely independent—government. As a result, a local assembly was formed on April 19, 1810. More plural in its social composition than its predecessor, it counted not only on the support of other nonaristocratic whites but also on the *pardo* elites. *Pardo* militiamen (most of them from the Aragua Valley garrison) under the command of the colored officer Pedro Arévalo were the first unit to offer military support to the white rebels. Once the Conservative Assembly (Junta Suprema Conservadora de los Derechos de Fernando Séptimo) was formally established, its members introduced several measures in order to keep the *pardo* militias faithful to the autonomist cause: They allowed them to have a representative in the assembly (the white creole José Félix Ribas); increased their salaries; promoted some of them beyond the grade of captain, thus contravening colonial laws; and decorated those who had taken part in the events of April 19. Arévalo was given a medal engraved with the words "Virtue and patriotism." The Conservative Assembly also took measures in the area of traditions that had segregated *pardos* in everyday life: In November 1810, it gave permission to the wife of a *pardo* (Félix Salinas) who lived in the southern town of Calabozo to make use of a carpet at the church (a privilege reserved to white women), under the very "enlightened" argument of "preserving the hygiene and cleanness of her clothes."

An even more significant signal of the Conservative Assembly's determination to grant equality to the *pardo* elite can be found in the electoral code published in parts from mid-June 1810. It was addressed to "all classes of free men" *(clases de hombres libres)* for the election of the members who would comprise the first General Congress of Venezuela. However, for eligibility to vote, it established very demanding property qualifications (owning at least 2,000 pesos in property), which most of the colored population of lesser racial and economic status could not meet. The usage of materially based principles to exclude the vast majority of "lesser-quality" free coloreds from voting turned out to be the spark that would introduce an element of class struggle into the debate around *pardo* citizenship. Poorer people of color had developed great enthusiasm for

and awareness of the process they were living. In November 1810, during the public acts honoring the victims of a massacre of white creole deputies of the assembly of the city of Quito, ECUADOR, by royalist forces, a multiclass mass of free coloreds gathered in the surroundings of the Temple of Altagracia (traditionally the *pardos'* church) to cry out their discontent against Spain and its monarchy. This behavior was apparently encouraged by J. F. Ribas, a young white creole who had become an important patron and community leader for the city's free coloreds. The noisy demonstration frightened the wealthy white creole political leaders of the movement, and Ribas was expelled from the province, along with many of his white and *pardo* collaborators. The most radical sectors of the autonomist movement profited from the agitation that reigned among "lesser-quality" free coloreds later, particularly after the arrival of FRANCISCO DE MIRANDA. This Caracas-born white creole had been promoting the independence of Hispanic America in Europe and the United States, showing himself to be particularly keen on granting full citizenship to free coloreds.

From his arrival in Caracas in December 1810, Miranda aroused the enthusiasm of free coloreds, who cheered him as he entered for the first time through that city's main gate. Once there, he made use of his huge prestige in order to gain the support of those who represented the most radical wing of the revolution. Many of them were the young sons of local white aristocratic families, such as Bolívar, Montilla, and Ribas. They joined to form a Jacobin-inspired club they named the Patriotic Society (La Sociedad Patriotica), which almost immediately became a public forum for those whose interests had not been considered by the local autonomist leadership. According to one of its members, the words of "equality and liberty among men" were regularly spoken there, and men from "all the classes, status and conditions" and even women were admitted to the sessions. For this reason, its numbers quickly began to rise and eventually exceeded 100 members.

The members of the Patriotic Society also encouraged political actions in the streets, reacting against the commands of those Miranda referred to as "patriot aristocrats": On March 2, 1811, the same day the first General Congress of Venezuela was installed, six *pardos* were arrested for their participation in a discussion of topics related to government and equality. Their leader was in possession of a forbidden "subversive text," to which Miranda apparently had added a "flattering apostrophe." The prosecution of these men, guilty of no more than political debate and speculation, inflamed free colored public opinion against the autonomist government. This political posture made them clash with more conservative white and *pardo* sectors, who, from early 1811, began to accuse Miranda and his followers of promoting *sansculotism*—or dangerous political radicalism—among "lesser-quality" free coloreds. According to the testimony of the Scottish officer Gregor McGregor, who traveled to Caracas to support its revolution in 1811, by the end of that year, a "mulatto party" was starting to take shape. This development was regarded with growing fear by white creoles, republicans and royalists alike, whose political differences were starting to narrow because of this situation.

By mid-1811, the members of the Patriotic Society who had been elected as deputies to the General Congress of Venezuela were pushing to accomplish another of their political objectives: a declaration of total independence from Spain. That moment occurred on the session of July 5, after which the members of the society were joined by colored people to celebrate this achievement in the streets of Caracas. In the beginning of the session, they proposed that previous to any debate on independence the deputies should discuss "the fate and condition of the *pardos*." They all eventually agreed on putting off this matter under the condition that it should be "the first thing to be considered after Independence." The debate took place on July 31 in a private session specially held to discuss this matter. When it began, it became clear that it was not going to be a discussion merely of *pardo* rights but rather about the aspiration of some provinces other than Caracas to maintain some autonomy within the newly born Venezuelan Federation. Mirandinian radicals, on the other hand, as well as other independent representatives who also supported the cause of the *pardos*, pointed out the advantages of granting them legal equality and of demonstrating that they were as qualified as whites to exercise citizenship. At the end of the session, because of their differences, deputies had not been able to reach an agreement, as a result of which the voting on any resolution concerning the *pardo* question was postponed. Nonetheless, from what happened later, we know that the pro-*pardo* deputies ultimately imposed their position, as can be seen in the Federal Constitution adopted in December 1811, through which the "laws that imposed civil degradation to a fraction of the free population of Venezuela known until now by the denomination of *pardos*" were suppressed.

The declaration of independence provoked brutal reactions from free coloreds on both sides. In Caracas, summary executions of white royalists began to take place, while in Valencia royalist *pardos* were hunting down white republicans in the name of the Spanish Crown. Widespread violence against whites did not seem to respond to ideological principles but to a rather older hatred of this racial group for so long oppressed under the colonial rule and the white creoles. This became clearer in Valencia (a city that embraced the royalists' cause after

Congress sanctioned independence), where when *pardo* royalist fighters heard the news that white Valencians had reached an agreement with Miranda to surrender the city, they turned against the whites and their properties without asking who was for or against the monarchy. Then they turned their anger against churches to tear up the acts of baptism stored there, which represented a symbol of their oppression as they contained the evidence of their African and illegitimate origin.

Although the insurrection in Valencia was defeated, from then on, it was clear that free coloreds outside the city of Caracas and its immediate surroundings were not willing to fight for the republic. This attitude was due to many reasons: the hatred *pardos* felt for the white aristocracy, the preaching of some bishops against the Jacobinism of Miranda and his followers, and the fact that the royalists were also introducing liberal measures, especially after news arrived of the Spanish constitution sanctioned in Cádiz in 1812, which granted a higher sociopolitical status to American CASTAS, including free coloreds. But the royalists went even further, being the first to offer emancipation to slaves if they joined their forces. This measure was apparently very successful in the region of Barlovento, located on the northeastern coast of Venezuela, where most of the cacao plantations were located. Although there was no solid evidence that slaves and MAROONS from Barlovento had joined the royalist army, Miranda (who had been appointed general in chief of the republican army) decided to take no chances and in mid-July 1812 made public a Conscription Act (Acto sobre la Conscripción de los Esclavos), through which he expected not only to avoid the risk of a black royalist army's marching to Caracas but also to reinforce his own by "conscripting a thousand slaves, who the State would buy, paying for them when possible." A message was also published during that time, in a desperate attempt to enlist the *pardos* in the republican cause, by reminding them of the despicable way they were treated under the former system and the countless achievements they had made during the two years of republican rule.

These efforts were fruitless as bad news kept on arriving, especially from the eastern front. Once Miranda realized he could not count on the support of the colored people (free or enslaved) beyond the limits of Caracas, and when he became convinced that there was a massive slave insurrection taking place in Barlovento, and probably bearing in mind the devastation of the HAITIAN REVOLUTION, he made the decision to surrender. Consequently, on July 25, 1810, he surrendered to the Spanish general, Domingo de Monteverde, at the town of La Victoria. Once again under Spanish rule, many free coloreds in Caracas kept demonstrating their support for the fallen republic. During nighttime, cries could be heard calling for independence, while royalist patrols were ambushed. Toward the south of the city, a region that had been "a seedbed of the revolution," two conspiracies in which free coloreds took part were discovered.

In 1813, Simón Bolívar carried out a successful campaign reestablishing a republic in Caracas. This so-called Admirable Campaign featured Colombian troops, many of them raised in the coastal region around CARTAGENA, where free people of color were numerous. Bolívar issued his manifesto from the city of Cartagena, and by invoking the name of that place where free colored patriots had established a republican government, he sent a message to Venezuela's *pardos*. Between January and August 1813, Bolivar's forces conquered the North-Central region of Venezuela and established an independent government in Venezuela. At the same time, a rebel force under the command of the *pardo* general Manuel Piar invaded the northeastern region from TRINIDAD AND TOBAGO. Piar was operating in the delta of the Orinoco, and small boats manned by Trinidadian and French and Dutch Antillean sailors were an important part of his force. His ships were able to cut off supplies and reinforcements bound for the only remaining royalist army, the *llaneros* of the southern plain, led by José Tomás Boves, but failed again one year later, when a large royalist army, composed mostly of *llaneros,* stormed the city.

Although this new defeat meant the end of the Venezuelan second republic, the war of independence continued until 1821. For as long as it lasted, free coloreds would fight for both sides, but at the end of the conflict, for many reasons (the death of the royalist chieftain José Tomás Boves, the appearance of new pro-*pardo* republican leaders, and increased political awareness), most of those who were still fighting had joined the republican forces. Many of them would keep fighting after Venezuelan independence was accomplished, in the southern campaigns Greater Colombia carried out against royalist rule in Ecuador and PERU. The end of the war, although it put an end to the caste system, gave birth to new forms of racial and political discrimination. Perhaps the most evident manifestation of the latter was the attitude many members of the political elite showed toward the new colored citizens. Among them stood out the president, Simón Bolívar, who despised what he described as "pardocracy" (*pardocracia),* or government of the *pardos*, having executed two of the most illustrious free colored military representatives, General Manuel Piar and Admiral José Prudencio Padilla.

Alejandro E. Gomez

FURTHER READING

Bushnell, David. "The Independence of Spanish South America." In *The Independence of Spanish America*, edited by David Bushnell. Cambridge: University of Cambridge Press, 1987.

Helg, Aline. "Simon Bolivar and the Spectre of Pardocracia: Jose Padilla in Post-Independence Cartagena." *Journal of Latin American Studies* 35 (2003): 447–471.

VERACRUZ, MEXICO

Veracruz was the major port city of colonial MEXICO, located on the coast of the Gulf of Mexico. It has a fine harbor, which Spanish settlers heavily fortified from the 16th century. A major road runs from Veracruz to Puebla and Mexico City in the interior. It is near the spot where Spanish conquistadores landed in 1520 and was the first Spanish municipality founded in Mexico. In the 18th century, it had a population that fluctuated between 2,500 and 3,000, rising when the fleet carrying goods and treasure back to Spain was in port and then declining after the fleet departed as merchants from interior cities and farmers returned to their homes. Of the permanent urban population, about 25 percent were free people of color. In addition, the surrounding countryside had a substantial population of free people of color, both those of urban origin who had bought land and become farmers and freedmen from the many plantations in the area.

During the late 18th century, urban society in Veracruz was organized along racial lines similar to those in all Spanish settlements. Jalapa, Orizaba, and the port city of Veracruz were organized spatially with concentric bands of neighborhoods of residents who were progressively more non-Hispanic on the edges, and an urban core population with heavy Peninsular Spanish and white CREOLE representation. Peoples socially subordinate to Spanish commonly resided in barrios, or outer neighborhoods (outside the city walls). *PARDOS,* mulattoes, and mestizos ranked below Spaniards. This lower rank relegated them to residences on the fringes of the urban core. Hispanicized Indians represented a second subordinate group, and they made their homes in the most distant barrios.

In rural Jalapa, Córdoba, Orizaba, and Veracruz, Spaniards and CASTAS, or mixed-race free people, commonly lived in a select number of pueblos closest to the district capitals. All groups were represented in small and large agricultural units. In the large plantations in the Córdoba region, Afro-mestizo slaves accounted for two-thirds of the plantation population. In the rural zones, spatial distribution of population apparently followed ethnic rather than racial lines. This resulted from the dominance of native peoples in the countryside. There was much racial mixture over the centuries of Spanish rule, and people of mixed ancestry lived among Indian villagers. However, within the Indian world, "social race"—the degree to which any person had adopted European ways—seems to have counted more than biological race in shaping socioeconomic patterns.

Socioeconomic status was indicated by occupation. Commercial elites and sugar planters composed the top ranks, which also included manufacturing entrepreneurs, high government officials, and professionals. The middle ranks of society encompassed medium and small commercial farmers such as ranchers and produce farmers. It also included estate administrators, small merchant clerks, and other salaried employees. The lower ranks included common urban and rural workers, servants, bearers, muleteers, and common soldiers. *Castas* including all kinds of free Afro-mestizos were most strongly represented in the middle and lower levels in the most important cities: Córdoba, Jalapa, Orizaba, and Veracruz. This held true in both urban and rural sectors.

Studies of the Veracruz population based on analysis of parish registers of marriages show that race was associated with social rank. As was common but not frequent (it was a very expensive procedure) in Spanish colonies, a person of mixed ancestry but high social rank might well have been able to be socially promoted in racial rank as well. In addition, families sought to promote their children in racial status by seeking marriage partners of higher racial status. (*See also* "WHITENING" AND RACIAL PROMOTION and *CÉDULAS DE GRACIAS AL SACAR*.) Godparenting and marriage witnessing were other ways free people of color could build social linkages if they lacked close kin who were not enslaved; between 1645 and 1715, free people of color in Jalapa were more likely to be godparents and witnesses at marriages with members of other racial groups than any other segment of the population. Most of their interracial contacts took place with other groups of African descent. People of mixed race served as godparents or marriage witnesses for blacks, and vice versa. This strengthened the internal coherence of the Afro-Mexican population, as well as demonstrating how people of color sought social promotion through FAMILY strategies.

Free people of color had important population representation inside and outside the city. Inside the fortified walls, a good deal of them worked as bakers and chocolate manufacturers, among other manufacturing jobs, but also played an important role on the docks, loading and unloading ships, especially at the times of arrival and departure of fleets. They also had an important role as part of the local MILITIA, who also acted as POLICE forces inside the city walls. The city was a port with bureaucratic and economic activities, and a source of services and amusements for sailors and MERCHANT SEAMEN (some legal, others not). Free people of color were important in these activities as well. In this regard, over the years, the local authorities issued a number of regulations to maintain social control, some of which noted especially the role of free people of color in questionable activities. There were also military barracks and a artillery school that placed further demands on the urban economy for services and entertainment.

Outside the city walls, to a distance of approximately 100 miles around, the economic activities concentrated on agriculture and cattle RANCHING to serve the city and the foreign market. In the big haciendas, the *pardos* and mulattoes (free people of color) were employed as cowboys, often living isolated from the ranch's main houses. Using a long spear called a *jarrucha* to drive the cattle, they soon received the nickname of *jarocho*, which has the connotations of race and job occupation described.

During the WAR OF MEXICAN INDEPENDENCE, 1810–21, colored militias in the region fought on both sides. The mulatto and *pardo* regiments from the city fought on the royalist side as disciplined soldiers. The rebel army in the region was in part formed by hacienda owners who went to war leading the slaves they had previously freed, tied to them through patron-client links. The cavalry forces composed of *jarochos* were an important element of the pro-independence armies. Although this has not been studied in depth, evidence suggests that many Veracruz slaves escaped during the war, seeking individual freedom and social advancement by supporting the independence movement.

Juan Manuel de la Serna

FURTHER READING

Carroll, Patrick. *Blacks in Colonial Veracruz: Race, Ethnicity and Regional Development.* Austin: University of Texas Press, 1991.

VERMONT

Today, Vermont is often referred to as the whitest state in the Union with a black population of just 0.5 percent. These data hide a rich history of black MIGRATION and settlement as far back as the 17th century. Although Vermont never had large communities of people of color compared to other New England states, many blacks have lived among the native Abenaki and migrant populations of French, Dutch, and English as they conquered and settled the Green Mountains. Many have lived in small biracial communities and black neighborhoods, and some rose to national and international prominence. Despite the small numbers, during the 18th and 19th centuries, the percentages of blacks living in the state were higher than they are today. In some towns, the black population reached 7–12 percent.

In 1609, a group of Algonquian from Quebec showed Samuel de Champlain the lake that would later bear his name (*see also* CANADA). Subsequently, the French claimed what is now Vermont and started creating small outposts along the Champlain Valley. There is evidence that blacks accompanied the soldiers, priests, and French "habitants" who spearheaded movement into the area. The Dutch, including many blacks, claimed the southern part of the Champlain Valley. Men of color performed the hard labor needed to carve out pioneer communities, and women generally served within the households and tended gardens and small animals.

As the numbers of native peoples in Vermont dwindled through warfare with Europeans and the contraction of white diseases, including smallpox, Abenaki welcomed blacks escaping slavery into their midst in order to increase their numbers. So many enslaved blacks freed themselves by escaping to northern tribes that British colonial governors grew alarmed, especially since many escaped slaves wanted to join the French and their Indian allies to fight the British. Officials offered rewards to local tribes and met with local sachems, or tribal elders, to convince them to return fugitives. In 1705 (and 1715 and 1745), New York (see NEW YORK STATE), which claimed what is now Vermont, passed a law that any enslaved person found more than a mile from home without a pass would be shot on sight. This deadly activity was intended to prevent fugitives from reaching New France or Ndakinna, the Abenaki homeland in Vermont.

Vermont became an important corridor for war parties and kidnapped British settlers who were taken to Quebec during the SEVEN YEARS' WAR, 1756–63. Blacks fought on both the French and British sides. After the British defeated the French in 1763, many soldiers who saw Vermont during the war decided to settle there after-ward. Jeffrey Brace, an enslaved soldier on the British side, later wrote a memoir about his experiences including his kidnapping in Africa, service in British and American armies, and settlement in Vermont.

After the Seven Years' War, British and Africans from the lower colonies began moving north. At that time, there still was no "Vermont" because the area was considered part of New York. A conflict emerged, however, when the governor of NEW HAMPSHIRE granted townships in the land between the Champlain Valley and the Connecticut River, along with the New York governor. This caused the contested land to be called the "grants."

Both British and Africans flowed into these grants. Many black migrants were enslaved or indentured, but many also were free British citizens. The regions known as Castleton and Hungerford (later Sheldon) represent the typical experiences of those enslaved. In 1767, a black man accompanied Colonels Amos Bird and Noah Lee to explore and survey the town of Castleton and to build a cabin for winter. It was an especially bitter winter, and the men were reduced to chasing down game on their snowshoes. The 19th-century Vermont historian Abby Hemenway reported that the black man's feet were badly frozen. Two years later, three families arrived to begin permanent settlement and take advantage of the work done by Bird, Lee, and a black man whose name is unknown.

The first non-Indians arrived in Hungerford in spring 1790. The group included George Sheldon, a Scottish couple, and several black servants. We know little about them, but surely among these servants were men who helped chop trees, hew logs, and build the cabin. There is no doubt that there were black women who helped with the household chores. Hemenway reported that the first

AFRICAN-AMERICAN POPULATION OF VERMONT, 1790–1900

Year	Slaves	Free People of Color	Free People of Color as a Percentage of Total Population	Total Population
1790	16	255	0.3%	85,559
1800		557	0.4%	154,465
1810		750	0.3%	217,913
1820		916	0.4%	235,764
1830		881	0.3%	280,657
1840		730	0.3%	291,948
1850		718	0.2%	314,120
1860		709	0.2%	315,098
1870		924	0.3%	330,551
1880		1,057	0.3%	332,286
1890		937	0.3%	332,422
1900		826	0.2%	343,641

child born to this group was the child of "Old Mary . . . a servant of Colonel Sheldon, who bought her in Connecticut where she was sold for the commission of some crime." Her child was the first non-Indian born in the town. In 1790, these black servants represented 12.5 percent of the town's population.

In the first U.S. Census conducted in 1790, a year before Vermont joined the Union, Vermont had a free black population of 255 representing 0.31 percent of its total population. Blacks did not live evenly throughout Vermont, however, and certain towns had a much higher black percentage. The black population in Vergennes totaled 7 percent, three other towns were more than 1 percent black.

Free blacks also moved to the grants. Many of those can be named, especially the ones who gained prominence, such as Lucy Terry Prince and LEMUEL HAYNES. In 1775, Lucy Terry and Abijah Prince, both formerly enslaved, and their six children moved to Guilford from Deerfield, MASSACHUSETTS. Like their neighbors, they were farmers. Lucy Terry is known for her poem "Bars Fight," about a 1746 raid on Deerfield by French and Indian soldiers. This is the first known poem by a person of color in North America.

During the revolutionary era, there were black "Green Mountain Boys" among the soldiers who took Fort Ticonderoga in the early days of the WAR OF AMERICAN INDEPENDENCE (1775–83). Lemuel Haynes, a former indentured servant from Massachusetts, volunteered as a Minuteman and served under Ethan Allen and Benedict Arnold at the fort. In 1776, he wrote a theological reflection entitled *The Battle of Lexington,* explaining why he fought: "Much better those in Death consign Than a Surviving Slave." After the war, he became a teacher and in 1785 became the first African American ordained as a Protestant minister in the United States. He became a Congregational minister in West Rutland in 1788 and led his parish there for 30 years.

By 1777, the people of the grants had grown tired of the quarrels between New York and New Hampshire over who governed them, and they declared themselves the free republic of Vermont. The state constitution they drafted outlawed adult slavery, the first in the nation to do so. However, young blacks could still be enslaved until they were adults, and many whites sold their slaves out of state as they reached the age of majority. The legislature passed a law in 1786 outlawing the practice, but it continued. Many whites ignored the Constitution altogether and kept people enslaved well past early adulthood.

The difficulty of being enslaved in a state that outlawed slavery was illustrated by the case of *The Town of Windsor v. Judge Stephen Jacob.* Jacob, a white man, freed his slave, Dinah Mason White, in 1800 when she was blind and too old to work. The town of Windsor, located in east-central Vermont, took up her expenses but sued Jacob for reimbursement. The case eventually went to the Vermont Supreme Court. The judgment declared that her bill of sale to Jacob could not be admitted as evidence, because adult slavery was outlawed in the state. She was banished from the town, but the government nevertheless continued to pay her expenses until she died in 1809.

In 1810, Jeffrey Brace from Georgia, Vermont, who had been kidnapped from Africa as a young man and fought in the American Revolution, published his memoirs so "that all may see how poor Africans have been abused by a Christian and enlightened people." Another Revolutionary war veteran, Charles Bowles of New Hampshire (1761–1851), became a traveling missionary in Vermont for 20 years, holding Free Will Baptist revivals all over the state. His home was in Huntington, a northern Vermont town, which he said was to him "as Jerusalem was to the Jews." Huntington was the site of his first church and the spiritual source of all the other churches he founded in the state. His biographer, John Lewis, wrote that he had many friends all over the state but also experienced RACISM AND RACIAL PREJUDICE because of his color.

Many people of color sought for victories against slavery, prejudice, and discrimination and were inspired by the HAITIAN REVOLUTION, which led to the first black republic in history in 1804. There were thousands of American blacks who viewed Haiti as a place to escape prejudice and migrated there. One of the earliest was Prince Saunders (1775–1839), a former indentured servant from Thetford, Vermont, who eventually became the first attorney general of the new Republic of Haiti. As hope for equality in Vermont turned to disappointment, he thought of Haiti as a paradise for African Americans and lived out his life there along with thousands of other blacks from the United States. In 1816, he published the "Haytian Papers," the first English translation of Haitian laws. In it, he declared that his purpose was to prove to a world that believed in black inferiority that blacks could write laws for themselves and that they were equal to the citizens of white nations.

Research on one black neighborhood in Hinesburgh, a town in northern Vermont not far from Burlington, shows that some black pioneers escaped the ideology of the inferiority of blacks, which grew during the 19th century. In this Vermont farming community, blacks and whites attended the Baptist Church together, Shubael and Violet Clark became leaders in the church, and the men voted on election day. The women participated in the farm economy by selling their butter and other products to local stores. Between the Revolution and the AMERICAN CIVIL WAR, their numbers increased, and they lived a middle-class life as independent farmers. Some of their hill farms were more than 100 acres, and later generations sold the hill acreage and bought new farms nearby in the valley.

Despite the fact that some people of color thrived, the occupational data from the federal census reports show that inequality existed in the state. From 1840 to 1870, the majority of blacks were employed as farm laborers, day laborers, or servants. The majority of whites owned their own farms or were farm laborers. Only whites entered the professional or merchant classes. In 1870, 27 percent of African-American women were domestic servants compared to 7 percent of European women. One trade that was open to blacks was barbering, a job held exclusively by blacks that could provide a good living. An example was George T. Williams, who owned a barber shop for 40 years across from the city hall in Burlington, the largest city in the state.

There were, of course, exceptions. Alexander Twilight was born on a farm in Bradford, Vermont, and worked as an indentured farm laborer but managed to become the first African American in the United States to graduate from college when he graduated Middlebury College in 1823. He became a Congregational minister in Vergennes and Brownington and became the headmaster of the Orleans County Grammar School. In 1836, he was elected to the Vermont General Assembly, the first African American to serve in a state legislature in the United States.

As the century advanced, however, some decided that emigration to Canada, Haiti, or LIBERIA was the only way to thrive and escape growing racism. This movement, referred to as COLONIZATION, was principally put forward by white elites and focused on sending blacks to Liberia in Africa to start new communities. Martin Freeman, a black man from Rutland, was a colonizationist. He attended Middlebury College, where he was salutatorian and voted by his class to give the commencement address, which he gave in Latin. In 1850, he moved to PITTSBURGH, PENNSYLVANIA, to become the first black college professor in the nation at Allegheny Institute—later renamed Avery College. He and his family later emigrated to Liberia to farm, and Freeman also taught at the university there. They moved because he became convinced that Africa was the only place where people of color could "attain the full stature of manhood, and bring up their children to be men and not creeping things."

Other people of color despised colonizationist ideas and chose instead to live in the land of their birth and fight for equality there. One example is Loudon Langley from Hinesburgh, who wrote in 1854, "The writer should warn all people whose color is identified with his own, to resist, with more than usual energy, the extraordinary efforts now made by the Colonizationists, inasmuch as they are founded on the most unjust prejudice against all the men of our race."

Langley and his comrades later fought in the famous all-black 54th Massachusetts Infantry during the American Civil War, along with more than 150 other men of color from the state. Vermont African Americans enlisted at a rate above 21 percent, as compared to 10 percent for whites across the North in the Civil War. Their wives and children worked the farms and otherwise supported themselves, at the same time making clothes and maple sugar to send to their husbands in the field. Langley later transferred to the SOUTH CAROLINA 33rd U.S. Colored Troops, attained the rank of sergeant major, and stayed in South Carolina with his family during RECONSTRUCTION IN THE UNITED STATES. He represented Beaufort at the 1868 Constitutional Convention and became one of the leading supporters of radical Republicanism in the South.

In the post–Civil War United States, many black people migrated to Vermont, and the state's black population jumped 30 percent to almost 1,000. One migrant, George Washington Henderson, was born enslaved in Virginia and graduated from the University of Vermont as valedictorian and a member of Phi Beta Kappa in 1877. Another migrant, William Anderson, bought a farm in Shoreham and hired out his sleigh, horse, and wagon to earn extra money. He married Philomen Langwire of French Canadian and Indian heritage, and the couple had two children. Their son, William John, became an apple orchardist and later became the second black man to serve in the Vermont legislature. Their daughter, Mary Annette, graduated from Middlebury College as valedictorian and the first black woman to achieve Phi Beta Kappa in 1899. She later taught at Howard University.

Another daughter of Civil War–era migrants was Daisy Turner, who lived to 105 of the time of her death in 1988. She earned fame in Grafton by her remarkable memory of stories from her formerly enslaved parents and her life experiences. Her recorded stories about the Civil War appeared in *The Civil War, a Film by Ken Burns* in 1990.

The experiences of the general population of blacks between 1870 and 1920 are best understood within the larger migration of many ethnic groups to the state. By the turn of the 20th century, Vermont's foreign-born population had swelled to 14 percent, only slightly lower than the national average of 15 percent. In the 1910s and 1920s, Vermont's African Americans represented 0.5 percent of the population, the highest in the history of the state. The total percentage, however, conceals sections of higher density in urban areas, where people were more likely to find jobs. One example is Burlington, the largest city, where blacks lived together in distinct neighborhoods and generally found jobs as laborers, servants, and barbers. Others in the rural area outside the city owned their own land and survived as farmers through the turn of the century. Competition from Canadian and European immigrants, however, made it increasingly difficult for many landless blacks to find work. Largely laborers and domestic servants, they were even edged out of these menial positions. As the former abolitionist FREDERICK DOUGLASS lamented, "Every hour sees the black(s) elbowed out of employment by some newly arrived immigrant whose hunger and whose color are thought to give him better title."

One new job for black men that appeared on the 1870 census for Vermont was caring for horses at private stables or inns. Many enslaved black men had been experts at caring for and breeding horses on Southern plantations. Some of those freed found paying jobs in the same area through the turn of the century. Black women continued to be employed, in much larger percentages than white women, as domestic servants, laundresses, and HOUSEKEEPERS, sometimes in inns as they helped usher in the state's tourist trade era.

The history of Vermont shows that there are multiple stories of people of color in the state. The pathbreaking 1777 Constitution outlawing adult slavery gave people hope. As a result, some towns developed pockets of relatively high-density free black neighborhoods. Regardless, some remained enslaved. Some blacks were highly educated; others were not. Some owned land and farmed it for generations; others worked as laborers for their neighbors. Some achieved middle-class status and respect in their communities, while others lived out their lives on the margins. Some emigrated out of the country to achieve prominence; others stayed in the land of their birth. These diverse experiences add depth and complexity to the history of the Green Mountain State.

Elise A. Guyette

FURTHER READING
Brace, Jeffrey. *The Blind African Slave, or Memoirs of Boyrereau Brinch, Nick-Named Jeffrey Brace.* Chapel Hill: University of North Carolina Press, 1810. Available online. URL: http://docsouth.unc.edu/neh/brinch/brinch.html. Accessed June 4, 2001.
Foner, Philip S., and Robert James Branham, eds. *Lift Every Voice: African American Oratory, 1787–1900.* Tuscaloosa: University of Alabama Press, 1998.
Fuller, James. *Men of Color, to Arms! Vermont African Americans in the Civil War.* Lincoln.: University of Nebraska Press, 2001.
Gerzina, Gretchen Holbrook. *Mr. and Mrs. Prince.* New York: HarperCollins, 2008.
Guyette, Elise A. *Discovering Black Vermont: African-American Farmers in Hinesburgh, Vermont, 1790–1890.* Burlington, Vt.: University of Vermont Press, 2000.
———. "The Working Lives of African Vermonters in Census and Literature, 1790–1870." *Vermont History* 61, no. 2 (1993): 69–84.
Hemenway, Abby, ed. *Vermont Historical Gazetteer, a Local History of All the Towns in the State, Civil, Educational, Biographical, Religious and Military.* Vol. 2. Burlington: n.p., 1871.
Irvine, Russell W. "Martin H. Freeman of Rutland, America's First Black College Professor and Pioneering Black Social Activist." *Rutland Historical Society Quarterly* 26, no. 3 (1996): 71–98.
Langley, Loudon's Letters to Editors. Vermont Civil War Database. Available online. URL: http://vermontcivilwar.org/units/afam. Accessed January 13, 2010.
Lewis, John W. *The Life, Labors and Travels of Elder Charles Bowles of the Free Will Baptist Denomination.* Watertown, N.Y.: Ingalls and Stowell's Steam Press, 1852.
McManus, E. J. *Black Bondage in the North.* Syracuse, N.Y.: Syracuse University Press, 1973.
Saillant, J. *Black Puritan, Black Republican: The Life and Thought of Lemuel Haynes, 1753–1833.* New York: Oxford University Press, 2003.
Williamson, Jane. "'I Don't Get Fair Play Here': A Black Vermonter Writes Home." *Vermont History* 75, no. 1 (2007): 35–38.
White, A. O. "Prince Sauders: An Instance of Social Mobility among Antebellum New England Blacks." *Journal of Negro History* 60, no. 4 (1975): 526–535.
Whitfield, Harvey Amani. "African Americans in Burlington, 1880–1900." *Vermont History* 75, no. 2 (2007): 101–123.
Vermont Folklife Center Media. "Journey's End: The Memories and Traditions of Daisy Turner and Her Family." Available online. URL: http://www.prx.org/series/16101. Accessed January 13, 2010.

VESEY, DENMARK (TELEMAQUE) (1767–1822)
American artisan and freedom fighter

Denmark Vesey was an American free man of color who was accused of leading the largest conspiracy of blacks in the United States during the 19th century. He was executed as a punishment, though it remains unclear whether there ever was a conspiracy or, if so, who was involved.

Much of Denmark Vesey's early life remains a mystery. Historians agree he was born in 1767, but it is more difficult to ascertain the place of birth. Denmark's place of origin was either in the African country of Guinea or on the Caribbean island of St. Thomas. Originally called Telemaque, this young African first encountered the institution of slavery on the Danish-controlled island of St. Thomas (*see also* DANISH VIRGIN ISLANDS).

Vesey entered the historical record in 1781 on a cargo manifest, when he crossed paths with the captain of the slave ship *Prospect*, Joseph Vesey. The captain delivered his young human cargo to the French-controlled island of SAINT-DOMINGUE, a rum and sugar producer in the Caribbean. Sold as a plantation worker, Telemaque spent only six months there. His owner complained to Captain Vesey that Denmark suffered from epileptic seizures, though it is not known whether this condition was legitimate or manufactured as a form of resistance.

As a result, Captain Vesey reclaimed the slave, who became his personal servant aboard the *Prospect* (*see also* MERCHANT SEAMEN) and was henceforth known as Denmark Vesey. For the next two years, he sailed throughout the Atlantic, transporting enslaved Africans to the Caribbean and the American South. By summer 1783, Captain Vesey retired from the slave ship trade, making a permanent home for the two in CHARLESTON, SOUTH CAROLINA. Though Denmark remained enslaved to Joseph, he enjoyed the relative mobility in the community that skilled craftsmen and ARTISANS had. He had married twice, the second time to a slave woman named Susan, who was owned by a different master, and fathered at least two sons with her.

In 1800, Denmark Vesey purchased his freedom for $1,600 with money he won in a lottery. Lotteries were common methods of fund-raising, for both private interests and governments, in late 18th- and 19th-century America. Vesey no doubt bought his ticket with his earnings from his work as an artisan. With the rest of his winnings, he opened a carpentry shop and gained acclaim for his work. Despite his relative success and his newly acquired freedom, Vesey loathed slavery and those who profited from it. He became well versed in the arguments made in the limited amounts of abolitionist literature that made its way to SOUTH CAROLINA and began to speak out about its injustices. Though a free man, Vesey turned his attention to the effects of slavery on his own children, who remained in perpetual bondage.

In spring 1822, testimony at his later trial alleged, Vesey organized a plot to overthrow slavery in Charleston and enlisted the help of many within the African-American community. As a class leader in the local AFRICAN METHODIST EPISCOPAL CHURCH (A.M.E.), he utilized passages in the Old Testament concerning the liberation of slaves to inspire African Americans, both slave and free, to take part in the fight. With the help of five lieutenants, Vesey was accused of recruiting more than 9,000 African Americans to aid in the plot.

The plotters set the rebellion date for Sunday, July 14, 1822, but it was not to be. George Wilson, an African-American servant, betrayed the plot by informing his owners of the planned events. Rumors of rebellion and panic spread throughout Charleston, forcing Vesey to revise the date to June 16. As word of the plot again leaked, government officials gathered a MILITIA to arrest anyone thought to be connected with the upcoming rebellion. Authorities rounded up hundreds of African Americans and a few poor whites, while Vesey evaded capture for 22 days. The trial that followed resembled little in the way of justice.

On June 27, 1822, Vesey and the others stood accused of fomenting rebellion. The magistrates who presided over the case, Lionel H. Kennedy and Thomas Parker, allowed tortured confessions of Vesey's lieutenants in the record and refused to let him confront some of his accusers, who testified privately to the court. The judges quickly convicted Vesey and 66 others of conspiracy. On July 2, 1822, Vesey and five other men were hanged on crudely constructed gallows near the courthouse. Vesey bravely and quietly faced his execution, becoming by his death a martyr and inspiration for later opponents of slavery. By August 9, the total number of executions reached 35. Hundreds of slaves were sold to other colonies, including Vesey's own son, Sandy. Vesey's wife, Susan, and older son, Robert, escaped punishment—Susan emigrated to LIBERIA and Robert remained in Charleston, reestablishing the A.M.E. Church there in 1865.

The conspiracy in Charleston generated fears of slave rebellion throughout the South. The fear of rebellion sparked by this event, along with the 1831 uprising led by Nat Turner in Virginia, led Southern governments to deepen repression of free blacks and slaves. It also encouraged Northern opponents of slavery by showing them that Southern blacks, contrary to what proslavery ideology asserted, hated their status and were willing to give up their lives to end slavery. The chasm between the two regions and between black and white Southerners deepened as a result of Vesey's actions.

The injustice of his trial was apparent to outside observers at the time, but only recently have scholars begun to consider the possibility that Vesey and his accused coconspirators were actually innocent. A 2001 article by the historian Michael Johnson argues that factions within South Carolina white politics used a false accusation of rebellion to discredit opponents and permit a military buildup. This interpretation remains controversial; for example, the noted historian Douglas Egerton wrote a biography of Vesey in 2004 that accepts the idea that Vesey was engaged in a serious conspiracy when he was arrested.

Robert Little

FURTHER READING
Egerton, Douglas. *He Shall Go Out Free: The Lives of Denmark Vesey.* New York: Rowman & Littlefield, 2004.

Johnson, Michael P. "Denmark Vesey and His Co-Conspirators." *William and Mary Quarterly* 58, no. 4. (October 2001): 915–976.

Johnson, Michael P., et al. Responses in "Forum." *William and Mary Quarterly* 59, no. 1 (January 2002), 123–202.

Paquette, Robert L. "From Rebellion to Revisionism: The Continuing Debate about the Denmark Vesey Affair." *Journal of the Historical Society* 4 (Fall 2004): 291–334.

Pearson, Edward, ed. *Designs against Charleston: The Trial Record of the Denmark Vesey Conspiracy of 1822.* Chapel Hill: University of North Carolina Press, 1999.

Robinson, David. *Denmark Vesey: The Buried History of America's Largest Slave Rebellion and the Man Who Led It.* New York: Alfred A. Knopf, 1999.

Starobin, Robert, ed. *Denmark Vesey: The Slave Conspiracy of 1822.* Englewood Cliffs, N.J.: Prentice Hall, 1970.

VIRGINIA AND WEST VIRGINIA

Virginia and West Virginia are states of the United States. Virginia is located on the Atlantic Ocean on the western shore of the Chesapeake Bay. Until the outbreak of the AMERICAN CIVIL WAR, its western boundary was the Ohio River; after 1863, most of the mountainous western region became the state of West Virginia. Virginia was bordered on the north by MARYLAND, on the south by TENNESSEE and NORTH CAROLINA, and on the west by KENTUCKY and OHIO. A small portion of the eastern shore of the Chesapeake is part of Virginia. The state is divided geographically into three regions. Along the Chesapeake shore is the region known as Tidewater. Tidewater Virginia is characterized by a large number of broad, slow-moving rivers, which divide the area into a number of peninsulas. The rivers were navigable by the oceangoing vessels of the 17th and 18th centuries, allowing Tidewater plantations direct access to overseas markets without passing through market towns. Towns in the Tidewater region, therefore, were small, focusing on governmental and religious instead of economic functions. A line of waterfalls or rapids ends the estuaries of these rivers and marks the eastward border of the region known as the Piedmont. This region is marked by rolling hills and generally well watered and fertile soils. The towns in the Piedmont are larger and are often located at the heads of navigation on the rivers; good examples are Richmond, the capital of the state from the time of the WAR OF AMERICAN INDEPENDENCE, 1775–83, and Petersburg, home to one of the largest free black populations during the 19th century. Travel by road and later railroad was important in this area as the rivers were not navigable except by very small craft. The Blue Ridge Mountains mark the beginning of the Appalachians. Alternating high ridges and valleys mark this region. The valleys are suitable for farming, indeed quite fertile, but communication

with the rest of the state is difficult since the ridges run northeast-southwest, right across the route of travel. A few important "gaps," or passes, connect these valleys to the rest of the state. One important relatively flat route runs to the southwestern part of the state and on to Kentucky and Tennessee; another important route runs along the Potomac River at the northern border of the state.

The indigenous inhabitants of Tidewater and Piedmont Virginia were the Powhatan, a group of eastern woodland Indians, agriculturalists who lived in large villages. The first European visitors to this area were Spanish JESUIT priests, who established a small mission along the shores of the Chesapeake in 1570–72. This little-known expedition lasted only a couple of years, but this was long enough to transmit European diseases to the Indians and to introduce the Indians to European ways. Opechancanough, who became chief of the Powhatan in 1618, may have traveled to Havana, CUBA, as a young man with the Jesuits. He was implacably hostile to the English. The Powhatan fought several wars against the English during the 17th century and ultimately were exterminated or driven onto reservations. The Indians of the interior mountains were Siouan people, who lived a more nomadic lifestyle and did not have a centralized political organization. They also suffered from European diseases and were driven from their lands during the 18th century. Unlike the larger and more-centralized Indian groups to the south, the Virginia Indians did not offer a great deal of refuge for RUNAWAY SLAVES, and the small Indian groups that still survive in Virginia do not have as strong an African component in their culture and ancestry as those found in North Carolina and Tennessee.

Colonial Period (1607–1775)

Virginia was the site of the first permanent English settlement in the Americas (other small temporary settlements had been set up in North Carolina and New England). English settlers established Jamestown in 1607. The first settlers were all white English people, mostly young men from the southwestern part of England. Very soon, however, they were joined by Africans. The first recorded landing of blacks in Virginia was in 1619, when approximately 20 arrived on a Dutch ship, possibly from Dutch BRAZIL rather than directly from Africa. In the very early days, blacks were treated the same way as white indentured servants; that is, they had to serve for a certain period and then were freed, with some resources to help them establish an independent farm or enter a trade. However, quite rapidly, the Virginia colonists developed a theory of slavery, under which blacks were servants for life and slavery became heritable from mother to child. This coincided with the introduction of tobacco as a cash crop, which rapidly became the dominant economic product of the colony by the mid-1600s. Tobacco demands a specialized and stable labor force. At the same time, the supply of white Britons willing to indenture themselves was decreasing. After 1660, Britain's civil wars generally ended, and peace and increasing prosperity meant that poor whites saw opportunity for themselves at home. In 1640, a court declared that the newly arrived black John Punch was to be considered a servant for life—he was the first person in Virginia to be explicitly designated a slave. Other documents from this period suggest that this had become the default status of newly arrived blacks. Slave imports increased from the 1650s on and reached an annual total of more than 2,000 by the early 1770s.

Black slaves managed to gain their freedom for various reasons, and these people, combined with those who had arrived before the imposition of special status for black servants, made up a small but growing free black community by the middle of the 17th century. The rapid growth of this group concerned colonial lawmakers. As elsewhere in the plantation Americas, free people of color constituted a contradiction to the racial ideology—neither white nor slaves. Masters wanted to free their slaves for various reasons: as a reward for faithful service, in return for money payments, because they were their own children, or because of discomfort with the institution of slavery. As elsewhere, this contradiction between private generosity (at least in some cases) and public concern led to a host of confusing and often-unenforced laws. In 1662, children of a free man and an enslaved woman were declared to be slaves. Of course, as it turned out, there were plenty of children born of enslaved fathers and free mothers, and these could not be considered slaves. By this time, there were white women as well as men coming to the colony as indentured servants, often from Ireland or the Continent of Europe, who harbored little racial prejudice. Indentured servants often worked alongside black slaves and suffered similar abuse and discrimination. Naturally there was fellow feeling, and relationships began between them, even though the prevailing racial prejudice held that white women would never be attracted to black men. The black men involved in these relationships, if discovered, were often punished very harshly; they were frequently accused of rape, and their actions profoundly undermined the racial assumptions of the day. Society punished the mothers as well, often with extended periods of indenture, and the children suffered discrimination, but they provided an important component of the growth of the free colored population. In 1667, it was declared that the baptizsm in the established Anglican Church did not make someone free (*see also* PROTESTANT MAINLINE CHURCHES). In 1691, Virginia passed what was apparently the first law against INTERRACIAL MARRIAGE in the English empire. This law did not stop informal interracial unions, and the population of free mixed-race people continued to grow. Also in 1691, the legislature passed the first of many laws that supposedly required newly freed people of color to leave the colony. These laws were broadly and continually violated in Virginia, as demonstrated by the frequency with which the colonial and state governments reenacted them: People of color who were freed had to have an important patron, their former master, who might well protect them if they chose to remain in the area. Since law enforcement in Virginia was in the hands of local elites, anyone who had the support of a local planter could ignore this and other similar legislation against blacks' owning firearms, or horses, or other high-status or economically important goods. However, during the late 17th century, Virginia did generate a long list of quite harsh restrictions on free black life. These laws served as the model for restrictions imposed in other territories as they were settled. In those places, particularly the plantation zones of the Deep South settled in the early 19th century, these laws were more efficiently enforced, and free blacks found it very hard to live in those places. (*See* BLACK CODES IN THE UNITED STATES.)

In Virginia, however, the free black population evolved in much the same way as in other mature plantation societies, doubling about every 20 years throughout the 18th and early 19th centuries. The total black population increased much more rapidly as a result of continued importation of slaves. However, the relatively mild disease environment and plentiful food supplies meant that populations could increase dramatically by natural growth. In addition, though increasingly difficult, MANUMISSION remained a possibility. And MISCEGENATION between black men and white women continued to occur, with the children born of these unions free from birth. By 1775, at the outbreak of the American Revolution, there were 190,000 blacks in the colony, the majority of whom were native-born, and about 12,000 of whom were free, roughly 6 percent of the total black population. The numbers of blacks in these early censuses are uncertain and probably understate the actual population, because poor people and those with uncertain titles to liberty would have avoided the census taker. The Federal Census of 1790, probably more reliable, counted 12,866 free people of color.

Independence and Early National Period (1775–1830)

The War of American Independence had a very significant effect on black life in Virginia, despite the fact that relatively little military activity actually took place there. In the early stages of the war, the colonial governor, JOHN

MURRAY, EARL OF DUNMORE, rallied loyalists at the colonial capital, WILLIAMSBURG, VIRGINIA. Murray realized that many of his most prominent opponents owned large plantations in the Tidewater region near the capital, and so he invited any slave who belonged to a pro-independence master to rally to his camp to fight for the king and gain freedom. He soon was forced to move his camp to the vicinity of Norfolk, but thousands of slaves joined him nonetheless. He organized a regiment of 800 black soldiers, "Lord Dunmore's Ethiopians," who embroidered "Liberty to Slaves" on their battle flag. Among their ranks was the future COLONEL TYE, an important black loyalist leader from NEW JERSEY. The regiment fought only one major battle, at Great Neck, Virginia, on December 9, 1775. Pro-independence forces defeated the loyalists and drove them onto their ships. There, smallpox broke out and devastated the regiment. Only 300 of the original 800 soldiers survived to reach New York, where they were assigned to a variety of loyalist units as the regiment was disbanded. Among these men, or departing shortly thereafter, was HARRY WASHINGTON, one of GEORGE WASHINGTON's slaves. Washington joined the Royal Artillery in New York and served throughout the war, around New York and in the Carolina/GEORGIA campaign.

With Dunmore's departure, Virginia was left in relative peace for several years. Occasional loyalist or British naval raiding parties passed through, offering opportunities for slaves to make a break for freedom. One British ship stopped at Mount Vernon, George Washington's plantation on the Potomac River, and took away about a dozen slaves who wanted their freedom. But unlike in the Carolinas and Georgia, where both slave and free

colored numbers plunged during the war, there was no permanent presence of loyalist forces to provide a nucleus around which Virginia blacks could rally. As a result, slave numbers actually rose in the state during the war, as masters from farther south arrived as refugees with their slaves. However, the disruption caused by the British blockade and occasional raids still dealt a significant blow to the Tidewater region's economic dominance and to the tobacco industry. Many SLAVE OWNERS moved their slaves to inland farms and began growing grain. This was an acceleration of a trend that had existed at least since the 1760s—George Washington's plantation at Mount Vernon had been growing grain as its principal cash crop since 1768. Grain could be sold to consumers in North American cities, though there were also important overseas markets in the SUGAR CULTIVATION islands of the Caribbean and in Continental Europe. (See PROVISION GROUND FARMING.) Grain could also be converted fairly easily into alcohol, which was a low-bulk, high-value commodity that held its value well in poor economic times. Mount Vernon had a large and commercially successful distillery.

British forces eventually did arrive in Virginia in considerable numbers. Lord Cornwallis (1738–1805), commander of the British southern army, entered the state in 1781. However, American forces under the French marquis de Lafayette (1757–1834) bottled him up in Yorktown, the site of the final major battle of the Revolution. Lafayette employed a black man, James Armistead (1760–1830), a Virginia slave, as an intelligence operative. Armistead infiltrated Cornwallis's lines and sent back valuable intelligence. After the war, Armistead gained his

AFRICAN-AMERICAN POPULATION OF VIRGINIA, 1790–1900

Year	Slaves	Free People of Color	Free People of Color as a Percentage of Total Population	Total Population
1790	292,627	12,866	1.7%	747,610
1800	346,671	20,493	2.3%	885,171
1810	392,518	30,570	3.1%	974,622
1820	425,303	37,339	3.5%	1,065,365
1830	469,757	47,348	3.9%	1,211,405
1840	449,087	49,852	4.0%	1,239,797
1850	472,598	54,333	3.8%	1,421,661
1860	490,865	58,042	3.7%	1,586,318
1870		512,841	41.9%	1,225,163
1880		631,616	41.8%	1,512,565
1890		635,438	38.4%	1,655,980
1900		660,772	35.6%	1,854,184

AFRICAN-AMERICAN POPULATION OF WEST VIRGINIA, 1870–1900

Year	Free People of Color	Free People of Color as a Percentage of Total Population	Total Population
1870	17,980	4.0%	442,014
1880	25,886	4.2%	618,457
1890	32,690	4.3%	762,794
1900	43,499	4.5%	958,800

freedom with Lafayette's intervention and took Lafayette as his last name. Many other blacks went to Cornwallis seeking their freedom, but he was less friendly to them than Dunmore had been. He sent runaways back to their masters unless the masters were notoriously supporters of independence. And when the main American-British army arrived and supplies began to run short, he sent all blacks out of his lines, even those who had been freed by the British army earlier in the Carolinas and Georgia. On the American side of the lines, free black soldiers from RHODE ISLAND played an important role in the defeat of Cornwallis, as a regiment that was more than 50 percent black led the final assault on the British fortifications that forced their surrender in October 1781. Virginia enrolled black soldiers; slaves gained their freedom through service, and some free blacks served for pay and bonuses as white soldiers did.

After independence was achieved in 1783, Virginia temporarily regained its place as the most important plantation region in the new country. Slave imports boomed, and the economy was strong. But Virginians had been among the foremost leaders of the rebel movement against Britain. The early U.S. Presidents George Washington, THOMAS JEFFERSON, JAMES MADISON, and JAMES MONROE were all Virginians, as was the firebrand orator Patrick Henry. Ideas of universal liberty and human rights were in the air in the late 18th century. The state government unilaterally freed all blacks who had served in the army during the war. The Democratic-Republican Party, dominant in national politics after 1800, energetically expressed an ideology of universal freedom and equality, at least as applied to whites. Blacks took these ideas as their own. Gabriel, a Virginia slave, appropriated these ideas as he prepared for a rebellion in 1800. The motto on the rebels' banner was "Death or liberty," drawn directly from Patrick Henry's famous speech at the Virginia Convention in Richmond in March 1775. Gabriel was literate and had read reports of the Revolution and its ideology. When he was on trial after the rebellion failed, he is said to have told the court, "I have nothing more to offer than what General Washington would have had to offer, had he been taken by the British and put to trial by them. I have adventured my life in endeavoring to obtain the liberty of

my countrymen, and am a willing sacrifice in their cause." The historian Douglas Egerton suggests that Gabriel had white coconspirators; he may also have had unindicted free black coconspirators. Gabriel himself was a blacksmith who was allowed to work on his own account, making regular payments to a master, a system that was common in Virginia and Maryland at the time. Of course, this meant that he and others like him were almost LIVING "AS FREE," and the mobility this allowed gave him the ability to organize an uprising. After this rebellion, the state legislature tried to limit masters' freedom to make these sorts of arrangements with their slaves, but the cash income was too attractive to masters in hard economic times, and the practice continued.

Not only blacks, but also elite whites were becoming uncomfortable with the institution of slavery during this period. In his will, George Washington freed all his slaves upon his death in 1799, though in fact more than half of the slaves who worked for him actually belonged to his wife, and they generally remained enslaved. The Virginia legislature debated gradual emancipation bills, similar to those passed in Northern states, in 1803 and again in 1831–32. The laws and culture of Virginia were friendlier toward free people of color during the early national period. There were few effective restrictions on manumission, and although laws requiring permission from county courts and deposits remained on the books, these rules seem to have been only occasionally enforced. A remarkable change for the worse in these relatively benign conditions became apparent after 1830.

The End of Slavery (1830–1865)

Hard economic times affected Virginia in the 1830s, as increasing areas of the Tidewater became unsuitable for tobacco cultivation because of loss of soil nutrients. Tobacco was cheaper to produce in the new areas in Kentucky, North Carolina, and Piedmont Virginia. Through the expulsion of the Indians and the purchase of lands from FRANCE and SPAIN, huge new areas were open to plantation development in the Deep South. Masters often sent their slaves to these new areas to develop plantations, either selling them through dealers or sending them with family members. A great migration from the Chesapeake region meant that populations stagnated or even declined in many counties. Slavery seemed on the verge of extinction in the Chesapeake region at this time as it was disappearing in DELAWARE and farther north. One reaction to these events was a greater willingness of cash-strapped masters to agree to take money for their slaves' freedom. New laws restricting manumission made this more difficult if the newly freed person wished to remain in the state. But if he or she was willing to move, the northeastern states were entirely open and almost completely free of slavery by this time, and the Midwest, though mostly theoretically closed to black immigration by state laws, was still attainable with little difficulty (see BLACK LAWS IN THE MIDWEST). For example, of the CHILDREN OF SALLY HEMINGS, thought to be fathered by Thomas Jefferson, two settled in Ohio and ILLINOIS after Jefferson's death in 1826.

Many of the new, harsh restrictions on black life in Virginia were the result of the Nat Turner rebellion of 1831. Turner (1800–31) was a slave from rural Southampton County. He gathered a group of fellow slaves around him and attacked neighboring plantations, killing as many whites as he could before he was finally captured, tried, and hanged. Unlike Gabriel's Rebellion 31 years before, Turner's uprising was not clearly connected with the ideals of the Revolution and the Enlightenment. Turner and his men were interested in taking revenge for mistreatment under slavery and were motivated by strong religious beliefs.

This was a period of religious ferment, called the Second Great Awakening. BAPTISTS AND PIETISTS were very important in this movement. In the American South, Baptists did not work against slavery so uniformly as they did in other places, but nonetheless the radical egalitarian message of dissenting Protestantism appealed strongly to blacks. It was during this period that the mass of Virginia slaves became regular practicing Christians. Turner and many other black rebels of this period from JAMAICA to SOUTH CAROLINA to the African coast of SIERRA LEONE were motivated by this message. Among free blacks in Virginia, Baptist churches were important community institutions. The First Baptist Church of Richmond had had black congregants since its foundation in 1780. The congregation had black leaders, including Lott Carey (1780–1828), who later emigrated to LIBERIA as a missionary. However, racial tensions in the 1830s led to the separation of the black and white congregations and the establishment of the First African Baptist Church in 1841. The First Baptist Church in Petersburg started as a meeting of slaves on a nearby plantation in 1774. In 1820, some of these early congregants, now freed, moved to Petersburg and set up one of the first black churches in the United States. After Nat Turner's rebellion, black churches were required to have a white pastor, but many churches skirted this requirement by having a number of black deacons or assistant pastors who actually led religious services, while a sympathetic local white clergyman preached occasionally and lent his name to the institution. This was actually a common situation in Protestant churches throughout the plantation Americas—the egalitarian message of radical Protestantism affected many white Christians as well as blacks, and cross-racial alliances were found in Jamaica, GUYANA, and elsewhere.

Free black populations continued to grow throughout this period, though mostly now by natural growth since manumissions had become more difficult after Turner's rebellion. Petersburg, which had been home to 390 free blacks in 1790, boasted more than 3,270 by 1860. Similarly, Richmond grew from a mere 83 in 1790 to 3,590 in 1860. The total free colored population of the state in 1860 was 58,042 of a total free population of 1,105,453, or a little more then 5 percent. There were 490,865 slaves, so free people of color constituted more than 10 percent of the black population, a very high proportion when compared to that of other Southern states. Free blacks in Virginia lived in both rural and urban environments. The greatest concentration lived in the southeastern quarter of the state, from the Rappahannock south to the North Carolina border, from the Richmond-Petersburg area east, and on the eastern shore of the Chesapeake. The western mountains had only around ten thousand blacks, either free or slave, though there were about 1,000 free blacks living in Winchester, Virginia, the largest town in the Shenandoah Valley. The Southside counties, west and south of Richmond, had many slaves but few free blacks; their society was more like that of the newer plantation areas in the Deep South. Northern Virginia had a few old free black settlements, such as that at Gum Springs (now in Alexandria, Virginia), where WEST FORD, thought by some to be George Washington's illegitimate son, had a farm. There was also a substantial population of at least 1,000 free blacks in Leesburg, Virginia, near the Potomac.

The beginning of the American Civil War in 1861 had a huge impact on black life in Virginia, even before the formal issuance of the EMANCIPATION PROCLAMATION in 1863. After some hesitation, Virginia joined the Confederate States of America in May 1861. Most of the western mountain region refused to go along and organized themselves separately, inviting in federal troops and ultimately joining the United States as the state of West Virginia. Some mountain counties remained part of the state of Virginia, especially those along the Shenandoah Valley and in the far Southwest of the state, mainly because these areas remained under Confederate military control until 1864. The counties east of the mountains in the Piedmont and Tidewater areas all voted for secession, and most whites in those areas remained loyal to the Confederacy throughout the war. However, much of this territory was occupied by U.S. troops at a fairly early date. Northern Virginia down to the Rappahannock River was occupied by summer 1862 and remained in U.S. hands, with the exception of occasional Confederate raids, for the rest of the war. The southeastern corner of the state, around Norfolk and at the tip of the James Peninsula, was also under Union control from spring 1862 on. In summer 1864, the United States occupied all of north-central Virginia down to Richmond—the Confederate capital—and the Shenandoah Valley. Occupied territories were refuges for slaves who wished to gain their freedom. At the very beginning of the war, there was some confusion in the Union ranks about what to do about runaway slaves. Some Southern masters applied to U.S. Army commanders for return of their property under the FUGITIVE SLAVE ACT OF 1850, and some slaves actually were returned. But fairly quickly, within a few months after the outbreak of the war, the United States adopted the policy that runaway slaves were "contraband of war," that is, like war supplies and weapons, property with a military use that allowed the conqueror rightfully to take possession of it. Southern masters were informed that since they claimed to have left the United States, the Fugitive Slave Act no longer protected them. By fall 1862, the ABRAHAM LINCOLN administration announced that all slaves in rebel territory as of January 1, 1863, would be considered free and also called for the enlistment of black soldiers in the U.S. armed forces.

Black Virginians responded to these initiatives with enthusiasm. The Union-controlled bases in Norfolk and Fort Monroe were close to the densest area of free black settlement, and black Virginians free and enslaved flocked to the Union lines. The U.S. commander at Fort Monroe, Benjamin Franklin Butler (1818–93), though a Democrat, was sympathetic to the plight of black Virginians and gave them shelter and work. Many U.S. military officers were opposed to actually enrolling blacks in the armed forces, as opposed to using them as labor troops, as Butler had. Nevertheless, starting in 1863, black Virginians were allowed to enlist in the U.S. Army. The first to enroll were probably in the 1st Infantry, U.S. Colored Troops, which was credited to the District of Columbia's recruitment total but included many men from both Virginia and Maryland. The 2nd, 10th, 23rd, 36th, and 37th Infantry; 1st and 2nd U.S. Colored Cavalry; and Battery B, 2nd U.S. Colored Heavy Artillery were all organized in Virginia. Some 6,000 black Virginians served in the U.S. armed forces during the Civil War.

Black Virginians also helped Union forces by passing them information. A white Richmond Quaker woman named Elizabeth Van Lew was one of the most important Union spies in the city. She could move easily in high Richmond society. Her fellow spy, MARY ELIZABETH BOWSER (1839–?), a free colored woman who had been a slave of Van Lew's husband, could gather information from servants while Elizabeth was visiting her powerful white friends. Bowser took a job for a while as a servant in the home of the Confederate president, Jefferson Davis, where she picked up all sorts of useful information, which she passed on to General ULYSSES S. GRANT, the commander of U.S. forces outside the city.

The Civil War devastated Virginia. Large armies crisscrossed the state, taking or destroying civilian property as they went. Guerrilla bands and simple bandits proliferated. In Confederate-controlled areas, especially in the mountainous western region, harsh military rule enforced conscription and the collection of supplies for the Confederate army. Free blacks in rural areas suffered especially under this repression, as they were always suspected of pro-Union leanings. Confederate patrols could impose harsh punishments on blacks on their own initiative and often beat and robbed or even killed unfortunate people they suspected of spying or trading with the enemy. Tens of thousands of civilians, blacks as well as whites, were driven from their homes by the competing armies. Northern Virginia west of Arlington and Alexandria was almost completely abandoned by its civilian population. The important north-central Virginia market town of Fredericksburg, home to a small free colored population of about 500, was completely destroyed by the battle fought there in December 1862. The third-largest city, Petersburg, home of a vibrant free black community of more than 3,000, was heavily damaged by U.S. artillery during the siege, which lasted from June 1864 to April 1865. When U.S. forces were on the verge of finally capturing Richmond, in April 1865, the retreating Confederates set fire to accumulated military supplies at the railroad station, and the conflagration spread, destroying most buildings in the downtown area, the area of the city where most free blacks lived and had their businesses. Urban blacks, and especially the prewar free population, suffered disproportionately from these disasters. Without the resources to restore their position or even a rural homestead where they could retreat to practice subsistence farming, as many impoverished whites did, they faced severe poverty at the end of the war.

Aftermath (1865–1900)

The FREEDMEN'S BUREAU, an agency established by the federal government to assist former slaves, played an important role in the Reconstruction of Virginia's shattered black community in the years after the war. (*See* RECONSTRUCTION IN THE UNITED STATES.) Bureau agents helped unite families who had been separated by slavery, supported schools for the newly freed, and helped connect people with work and resources to start businesses. Prewar free people of color could also benefit from the bureau's support, and the War Department officials who ran the bureau often relied on the prewar free population as a liaison to the newly freed. As the bureau began to hire civilian staff to supplement, and eventually replace, its original military personnel, many of the new employees were prewar free blacks.

Virginia had a state government when the war ended, unlike the Confederate states of the Deep South. This state government was composed of white Unionists from northern Virginia, who had organized in those areas under U.S. control starting in 1862. As did other Southern white Unionists, however, Virginia's leaders in the immediate postwar period were not interested in giving blacks meaningful political rights. They readmitted conservative whites to the political process if they would renounce their loyalty to the Confederacy, and they were adamantly opposed to votes for blacks or any other sort of civil rights measure. Virginia passed black codes (see BLACK CODES IN THE UNITED STATES), which imposed severe restrictions on blacks, both the newly freed and prewar free people of color. Blacks were required to work, subject to arrest if not employed or if they left their employer, limited in their mobility, and completely barred from public employment or political participation. Congress forced black suffrage on Virginia, the black codes were repealed, and the 1867 Constitutional Convention included 24 blacks among its 88 delegates. This was the high point for black political participation in Virginia, as congressional Reconstruction ended in 1870 and white conservatives rapidly regained control of state government.

Nevertheless, blacks in Virginia made significant gains in economic standing and community organization during the Reconstruction period. Virginia blacks adjusted to the political dominance of conservative whites where they had to and resisted when they could. The black churches remained an important means of community organization for mutual aid and resistance. Some formerly enslaved pastors established churches in the wake of abolition, but most black churches continued to be led by prewar free coloreds for a generation, as they had the necessary education. Mass meetings organized at black churches in Richmond and Petersburg in April and May 1865 to welcome the arrival of the U.S. Army and freedom created interchurch groups that worked for mutual aid and political empowerment for the rest of the Reconstruction era.

The Republican Party proved to be an important institution to Virginia blacks throughout the 19th century,

and even into the first half of the 20th. Virginia black Republicans managed to create a cross-racial alliance with some whites, led by a former Confederate general, William Mahone (1826–95), which kept control of state politics until 1883. This movement, called the "Readjusters," was organized around issues of public debt and finance but provided important benefits for their black constituents. Finally, they lost power because they appointed two blacks to the state school board in the face of growing support for segregated schools. The opposition Conservative Democrats also supported laws against interracial marriage and against so-called common-law marriages that affected many freedmen. Even after the fall of the Readjusters, the prewar free black JOHN MERCER LANGSTON, Virginia-born but living in Ohio before the war, managed to gain election to the U.S. House of Representatives in 1891, the last black Virginian to serve in national office until the 1970s. Langston was an educator, the president of Virginia Normal College (now Virginia State University) in Petersburg, an important historically black college.

The black educational system was another important community institution after the Civil War. Most newly freed people eagerly sought educational opportunity, if not for themselves, then for their children. The Virginia Constitution of 1870 was the first to mandate public education for all children. The schools established were segregated, although some remote western counties without many blacks or the resources to establish two school systems redefined their black children as Indians so they could attend the white schools. But in those counties where there were a large number of black children, at least some public funds were made available to educate them in segregated institutions. These institutions were poorly funded, even when compared with the rather poor white schools. But black communities around the state rallied around their schools, providing teachers with housing and other support in addition to their meager state salaries and giving them great social prestige. Alongside the preacher at the local black church, the principal of the black school was a natural community leader. The first generation of teachers in these schools, in the 1870s and 1880s, were often from the North. Many were white Quakers or liberal reformers, while others were Northern free people of color. The State Normal College in Petersburg, Langston's institution, was the pinnacle of the educational establishment, because it was there that black teachers were trained. By the turn of the 20th century, most teachers in black schools were black Virginians, and the difference between the descendants of the prewar free people and those freed by the war was hard to distinguish.

Stewart R. King

FURTHER READING

Breen, T. H., and Stephen Innes. *"Myne Own Ground": Race and Freedom on Virginia's Eastern Shore, 1640–1676*. New York: Oxford University Press, 1980.

Dickinson, Richard B. *Entitled! Free Papers in Appalachia Concerning Antebellum Freeborn Negroes and Emancipated Blacks in Montgomery County, Virginia*. Washington, D.C.: National Geographic Society, 1981.

Egerton, Douglas. *Gabriel's Rebellion: The Virginia Slave Conspiracies of 1800 and 1802*. Chapel Hill: University of North Carolina Press, 1993.

Eldridge, Carrie. *Cabell County's Empire for Freedom: The Manumission of Sampson Sanders' Slaves*. Huntington, W.Va.: John Deaver Drinko Academy, Marshall University, 1999.

Engs, Robert. *Freedom's First Generation: Black Hampton, Virginia, 1861–1890*. New York: Fordham University Press, 2004.

Hashaw, Tim. *The Birth of Black America: The First African Americans and the Pursuit of Freedom at Jamestown*. New York: Caroll & Graff, 2007.

Holton, Woody. *Forced Founders: Indians, Debtors, Slaves, and the Making of the American Revolution in Virginia*. Chapel Hill: University of North Carolina Press, 1999.

McDonnell, Michael. *The Politics of War: Race, Class, and Conflict in Revolutionary Virginia*. Chapel Hill: University of North Carolina Press, 2007.

McLeroy, Sherrie. *Strangers in Their Midst: The Free Black Population of Amherst County, Virginia*. Bowie, Md.: Heritage Books, 1993.

Morgan, Edmund. *American Slavery American Freedom: The Ordeal of Colonial Virginia*. New York: W. W. Norton, 1995.

Wolf, Eva. *Race and Liberty in the New Nation: Emancipation in Virginia from the Revolution to Nat Turner's Rebellion*. Baton Rouge: Louisiana State University Press, 2006.

VOTING BEFORE GENERAL ABOLITION, UNITED STATES

The right to vote and participate in the political life of a country is a fundamental component of citizenship in any republican system of government. Most of the countries in the Americas with substantial black populations wrestled with whether to grant this right to people of color once they gained independence from their European colonizers. The most serious denial of voting rights to people of color took place in the United States, where blacks were frequently denied the right to vote until the middle of the 20th century, 100 years after the end of slavery.

During the era of the early republic, in the late 18th and early 19th centuries, racial boundaries were still being set in the new country, and African Americans were allowed to vote in many places. The climate soon began to change, however, and every state that entered the Union after 1819 excluded free blacks from the franchise. By the time the AMERICAN CIVIL WAR erupted in 1861, racial boundaries had hardened drastically, and many states that had previously allowed free blacks to vote had disenfranchised African Americans. This was a product of many factors.

Ironically, voting restrictions were being loosened throughout the first half of the 19th century for most white male Americans, even as they were being tightened for black Americans. Indeed, between 1790 and 1850, the number of states that excluded free black voters increased significantly. NEW JERSEY, MARYLAND, and CONNECTICUT led the drive, taking the franchise from free blacks before 1820. In NEW YORK STATE, property requirements were abolished and residence requirements amended in the same revised state constitution that excluded blacks from the franchise in 1821. NORTH CAROLINA and PENNSYLVANIA followed suit by adding the word *white* to their voting requirements in revised state constitutions in 1835 and 1838, respectively. Many states, including WISCONSIN, OHIO, INDIANA, and New York, reiterated this disenfranchisement in the following decades, and by 1855, only MASSACHUSETTS, VERMONT, NEW HAMPSHIRE, MAINE, and RHODE ISLAND (which collectively held only 4 percent of the country's free blacks) did not prohibit blacks from voting. The federal government also excluded free blacks from voting in the national territories, and the U.S. Supreme Court officially ended black voting in its ruling in the 1857 DRED SCOTT case, which denied citizenship, and, by extension, the vote, to all blacks, free or enslaved.

Blacks were not excluded in the beginning of the American republic because most blacks were slaves and thus their voting was not an issue. As the free black population grew, concern was raised over their capabilities to participate in the nation's experiment in republican government, especially as some free blacks, such as James Forten (*see* FORTEN FAMILY) and PAUL CUFFE, managed to acquire enough property to gain eligibility. By the mid-19th century, there was a general trend to loosen property requirements and allow for a broader electorate, but this raised the specter of poor, uneducated black voters, many of whom were newly freed. Also, some state leaders feared that allowing blacks to participate fully in civic life would encourage more free blacks and RUNAWAY SLAVES from the South to seek a new life within their borders. As a result, most of the same state legislators who called for a broadened franchise also called for the insertion of the word *white* in state constitutions.

Finally, as the historian Alexander Keyssar has pointed out, there was a general growth in RACISM AND RACIAL PREJUDICE in the North during this period. Part of the reason was the growing abolitionist sentiment among some sectors of the white population. As more whites began to question slavery, it created a backlash, leading others to resist antislavery and racial justice measures even more strongly. Some hoped somehow to prove to their Southern neighbors that they respected their property rights, and others hoped to prevent the level of tension that would lead to civil war. Still others simply resented the presence of free blacks in their state and neighborhood and hoped to make their lives so miserable that they would leave.

This exclusion met a number of challenges by free blacks and sympathetic whites. Perhaps the most famous case was the groundswell of resistance in PHILADELPHIA, PENNSYLVANIA, where black leaders issued the *Appeal of Forty Thousand Citizens, Threatened with Disfranchisement, to the People of Pennsylvania* (1838). New York blacks, as did their counterparts in Philadelphia, protested to no avail, but blacks in Providence, Rhode Island, succeeded in preventing their disenfranchisement during electoral reforms in 1840–41. Sympathetic whites in several states such as Ohio, New York, Pennsylvania, and WISCONSIN also spoke out against the injustice. One Pennsylvania attorney tried to use the state's abolitionist legacy to convince his fellow delegates that whites had a duty to assist free blacks in their efforts at moral and mental improvement, elevating and improving their condition rather than "cutting them off." Others questioned what exactly the word *white* meant and who exactly would be excluded for not fitting this category. Finally, some pointed out that many blacks had fought in American wars and should thus be allowed to participate in the nation's government.

The right to vote without discrimination on the basis of race was formally guaranteed in the Fifteenth Amendment to the U.S. Constitution (*see* CIVIL RIGHTS LAWS IN THE UNITED STATES AFTER 1865), ratified in 1870. This right was respected for a few years, but once again denied after the end of Reconstruction in many states, especially in the South (*see also* RECONSTRUCTION IN THE UNITED STATES). Blacks did not finally gain the right to vote in all of the United States until the 1960s.

Beverly C. Tomek

FURTHER READING

Keyssar, Alexander. *The Right to Vote: The Contested History of Democracy in the United States.* New York: Basic Books, 2000.

Winch, Julie. *A Gentleman of Color: The Life of James Forten.* New York: Oxford University Press, 2002.

W

WALKER, DAVID (1785–1830) *American journalist*
David Walker was a journalist and writer best known for his 1829 *Appeal to the Coloured Citizens of the World*, a militant abolitionist pamphlet that called for immediate emancipation, by violence if necessary. David Walker was born in Wilmington, NORTH CAROLINA, on September 28, 1785, to an enslaved father and a free mother. Following the condition of his mother, as prescribed by law, he was born free. Even so, he witnessed firsthand the horrors of slavery, including an incident in which a young man was forced to whip his own mother until she died. After traveling throughout the United States, he settled in BOSTON, MASSACHUSETTS, and became an important journalist and leader of the free black community, gaining the respect of many blacks and the hatred of many whites after his 1829 *Appeal.*

Though he made his living by operating a used clothing store, Walker began a journalism career in the 1820s and by the end of the decade had become Boston's leading free black activist. He began by writing for the New York–based *Freedom's Journal*, the nation's first African-American newspaper, and in September 1829, he published the first edition of his *Appeal.* This antislavery pamphlet gained immediate notoriety throughout the United States by calling upon the enslaved to rise up against their masters if the chance presented itself.

Walker's pamphlet was important in the black abolitionist movement for a number of reasons. First, it attacked notions of racial inferiority head on by taking on THOMAS JEFFERSON's assertions that blacks were of a different, inferior species. It also refuted colonizationist notions that blacks could not succeed in the United States (*see also* EMIGRATION AND COLONIZATION). Unlike supporters of the AMERICAN COLONIZATION SOCIETY, Walker was unwilling to give up on the dreams of a biracial America and claimed that blacks were as fully American as whites. Instead, he presented a hope that Christian principles would lead the country to fulfill its promise of equality. If it failed, however, he preferred racial warfare to continued RACISM AND RACIAL PREJUDICE and servility. It is this final idea, the

argument that if condition would not change peacefully, then blacks should rise up, that gained Walker notoriety as a dangerous and vengeful leader. Perhaps most importantly, Walker's work inspired the growth of a new current of antislavery known as immediatism by influencing the young editor and former colonizationist William Lloyd Garrison, who launched his newspaper, the *Liberator*, in 1831. He also influenced the next generation of black abolitionists, most notably HENRY HIGHLAND GARNET.

Walker's *Appeal* terrified white Southerners, who tried to prevent slaves and free blacks from reading it. To support such efforts, they passed laws that forbade blacks to learn to read and write and made the distribution of antislavery literature in the South illegal. In response, Walker used his experience as a used clothing merchant to ensure its circulation by sending copies south with MERCHANT SEAMEN who bought clothing from him and even sewing copies into the lining of sailors' clothes. As a result, slaveholders offered a bounty of $3,000 for Walker's head and an award of $10,000 to anyone who could produce him alive in the South.

By the time Walker died on June 28, 1830, his pamphlet had gone through three editions. Suspicion and speculation have always surrounded his death, as rumors of poisoning gained much attention. More recent scholarship, however, suggests that he died of tuberculosis. *See also* BLACK PRESS IN THE UNITED STATES; EDUCATION AND LITERACY; UNITED STATES, ABOLITION MOVEMENTS IN.

Beverly C. Tomek

FURTHER READING
Hinks, Peter P., ed. *David Walker's Appeal to the Coloured Citizens of the World.* University Park: Pennsylvania State University Press, 2000.

WAR OF AMERICAN INDEPENDENCE
(1775–1783)
The War of American Independence, 1775–83, also known as the American Revolution, between the Thirteen Colonies in mainland North America and Great

Britain was an important event in the lives of free people of color, not only in what became the United States, but also in CANADA, the BRITISH LESSER ANTILLES, and the FRENCH CARIBBEAN. The movement for independence in the United States was primarily driven by native-born upper-class whites who were seeking more control over their societies, but their movement was presented and justified in terms of liberal principles that "all men are created equal," as the Declaration of Independence stated in 1776, and many poor and excluded people drew hope from those principles. Many of the American rebel leaders, including SLAVE OWNERS such as GEORGE WASHINGTON and THOMAS JEFFERSON, used the rhetoric of resistance to slavery to justify their opposition to the British government. They were portraying themselves, the native-born white landed aristocracy, as the slaves of the British government because local government's autonomy was being undermined and commercial relations were unfavorable. But real slaves and other subjugated people took these arguments literally. At the same time, the disruption caused by the war permitted slaves to gain their freedom and other poor and excluded people to better their situation. Drafted in 1787, the U.S. Constitution that ultimately grew out of the revolutionary movement created a system of government that again suffered from a clash of values—on the one hand, it was hierarchical in action and protected property rights, including rights over slaves. On the other hand, it enshrined egalitarian principles and was implicitly based on the right of people to resist tyranny.

The Northern States

The earliest steps in the movement for independence took place in the North, especially in MASSACHUSETTS. There were significant numbers of free people of color among the early rebels. The first man killed during the Boston Massacre on March 5, 1770, Crispus Attucks, was a free mixed-race sailor. As open warfare broke out between British soldiers and rebel Massachusetts men five years later at Lexington on April 19, 1775, four African Americans stood among the militiamen and fired the "shot heard 'round the world": Prince Estabrook of Lexington, Pompey of Braintree, Cato Wood of Arlington, and PETER SALEM. Two months later, on June 17, 1775, Salem shot and killed a British senior officer, Major Pitcairn, at the Battle of Bunker Hill. The rebel army that assembled around Boston after these battles included many men of color, some sources say as many as one-fifth of all its manpower. When the Continental Congress appointed a commanding general, George Washington, from Virginia, he was at first horrified by the number of armed black men he saw in the ranks of his army. He attempted to ban

all blacks from the Continental army. He was supported by prominent Southern politicians, including Edward Rutledge of SOUTH CAROLINA, who in September 1775 introduced a resolution in Congress demanding that all blacks be expelled from the army. The resolution did not pass, but Washington tried in October to persuade the army commanders to agree not to reenlist any blacks whose time expired or to admit any new blacks into the ranks. Even as he was pressing these measures, however, blacks continued to join the army. Massachusetts pension records contain the statement of a Jacob Francis, a NEW JERSEY black man who had moved to Massachusetts after gaining his freedom, who enlisted in October just as Washington's new regulation was supposedly taking effect. New England officers such as Israel Putnam of CONNECTICUT, Francis's commander, apparently simply ignored Washington's prejudices. Finally, in December, Washington gave in and agreed to permit free blacks to enlist, pending a decision by Congress, which never resolved the issue decisively.

Nonetheless, the Northern colonies enlisted thousands of black soldiers in their state regiments. One of the most famous units was the Marblehead Regiment, or 14th Continental, raised by organizing the MILITIA units of the port towns around Marblehead, Massachusetts. Many of the militiamen were MERCHANT SEAMEN or dockworkers, who had been thrown out of work by the Intolerable Acts that closed the ports of Massachusetts in 1774, and then by the British blockade once the war began. Many of these sailors and stevedores were black. The Marblehead Regiment enlisted for one year and fought in the New York campaign and the Battles of Trenton and Princeton. They played a very important role in the survival of the rebel army after its defeat in the Battle of Long Island (July 11–August 28, 1776) and in the rebel victory at Trenton (December 25, 1776), through their skill with small boats. Marblehead soldiers manned the boats that helped Washington's army escape across the East River after their defeat in Brooklyn, and then advance across the Delaware River to take the Hessian garrison in Trenton by surprise. In Emmanuel Leutze's famous 1851 painting *Washington Crossing the Delaware*, the soldiers paddling the boat are Marblehead Regiment soldiers, and the one sitting just behind Washington's upraised leg is a black man.

Another prominent black unit was the 1st RHODE ISLAND Regiment, the only Revolutionary War unit to be segregated by race. Several companies of this regiment were composed of black soldiers; at the time of its most important battle, at Yorktown, Virginia, in October 1781, the regiment was about 75 percent black. Rhode Island had many free blacks because of its important role as

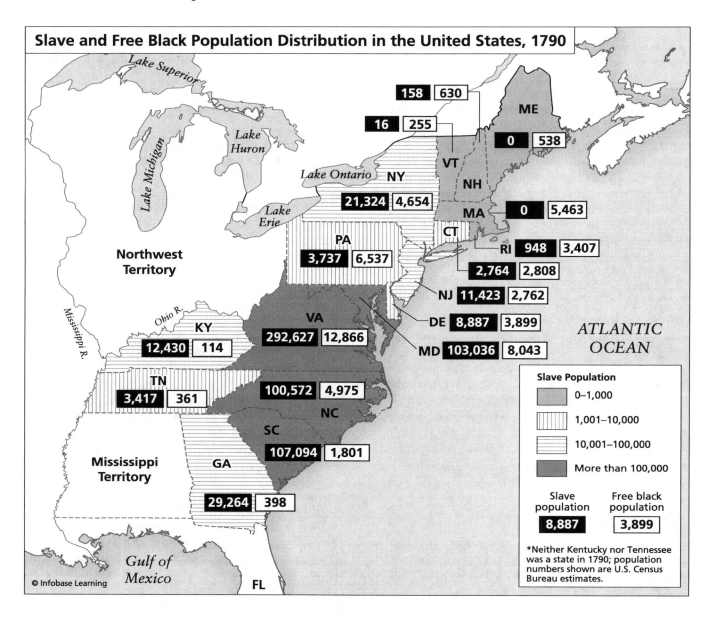

Slave and Free Black Population Distribution in the United States, 1790

Lake Superior

Lake Huron

Lake Michigan

Lake Ontario

Lake Erie

ME

158 | 630

16 | 255

0 | 538

VT

NH

NY

21,324 | 4,654

MA

0 | 5,463

CT

RI   948 | 3,407

2,764 | 2,808

Northwest Territory

PA

3,737 | 6,537

NJ   11,423 | 2,762

DE   8,887 | 3,899

MD   103,036 | 8,043

ATLANTIC OCEAN

Ohio R.

Mississippi R.

KY

12,430 | 114

VA

292,627 | 12,866

TN

3,417 | 361

100,572 | 4,975

NC

SC

107,094 | 1,801

Mississippi Territory

GA

29,264 | 398

Gulf of Mexico

FL

© Infobase Learning

Slave Population

	0–1,000
	1,001–10,000
	10,001–100,000
	More than 100,000

Slave population   8,887

Free black population   3,899

*Neither Kentucky nor Tennessee was a state in 1790; population numbers shown are U.S. Census Bureau estimates.

a slave trading port. Many of these men were sailors or dockworkers, and as were the Marblehead men they were out of work because of the British navy's blockade of the American ports. At Yorktown, this unit, under the personal command of Alexander Hamilton (1755–1804), stormed the British Redoubt No. 10. Their success and that of an elite French regular regiment that took adjoining Redoubt No. 9 were the decisive blows that led directly to the British surrender. Major von Clausen, a Prussian officer attached to Washington's staff, said that they were the most professional unit in the rebel army and deserved to be chosen for this crucial and dangerous mission.

Not all Northern blacks supported independence, however. Britain pursued a consistent policy of encourag-

ing slaves owned by pro-independence masters to desert to areas they controlled. Many of these RUNAWAY SLAVES and some free blacks in the cities controlled by British troops, joined loyalist units. One famous Northerner who fought for Britain was COLONEL TYE, a New Jersey man, who led a loyalist guerrilla unit that fought out of a base on Sandy Hook from 1778 until his death in 1780. The British did not give him a formal commission as an officer but accorded him the courtesy rank of colonel, a sign of the respect he had gained for his many daring raids against the rebels. Blacks who supported King George were promised their freedom and freedom for their families, and for the most part they received it. When the British evacuated their bases along the American coast at the end of the war, they took along any blacks who wished to go with them. These black loyalists were mainly resettled in Canada, while others went on to a career in the British REGULAR ARMY or navy or to settle in BRITAIN. A large contingent of veterans settled in SIERRA LEONE, in West Africa.

Northern blacks who served in the American armies received pay, qualified for pensions and land grants, and were generally treated more or less as well or badly as other Revolutionary War veterans. Military service had an impact on their lives, but less of an impact on the racial climate of their communities. The next time these states needed a large number of soldiers, during the AMERICAN CIVIL WAR, the debate about the legitimacy of putting blacks in uniform was not so easily settled in the North. It was not until early 1863, almost two years after the conflict began, that Massachusetts organized its first black regiments, the famous 54th and 55th Massachusetts.

Southern States

The black experience of war in the Southern states was much more diverse than in the North. At first, there was little fighting in the Southern colonies. Rebels seized control of the colonial governments very quickly in most states, and loyalist opponents had to keep quiet. The British regular forces were mostly committed to the North in the period 1775–78, with only occasional raids at the Chesapeake and southward.

One exception to this general rule was the attempt by the royal governor of VIRGINIA, JOHN MURRAY, EARL OF DUNMORE, to rally loyalist support. Ejected from the colonial capital of WILLIAMSBURG, VIRGINIA, in spring 1775, Dunmore took refuge on a British ship in the York River. A small group of loyalists, whites and their black slaves and dependents, rallied around him. Hearing of Washington's initiative to expel black soldiers from the rebel army, in November 1775, he issued a proclamation promising freedom to all slaves belonging to rebel masters who would join his forces. Thousands of enslaved Americans flocked to his camp at Kemp's Landing, near today's Norfolk. The young men were organized into the "Ethiopian Regiment." This force defeated a militia column that attacked their camp in mid-November but then were defeated in December at the Battle of Great Bridge. After this defeat, the loyalists were besieged in their camp, where smallpox and other diseases caused a high mortality rate. Finally, in January 1776, Dunmore evacuated Virginia and took the remnant of his troops to New York. Colonel Tye is said to have been among the survivors of the Ethiopian Regiment. The unit was disbanded in 1776, but some of the survivors were incorporated in another unit, the Black Pioneers, who served with British forces until 1783. When New York was evacuated at the end of the war in 1783, these men, about 172 in number by

that point, were transported by the British to Nova Scotia, Canada, where the unit was disbanded and many settled.

Also among the Southern blacks who supported Britain were around 10 slaves of George Washington's, who fled Mount Vernon to a British ship in 1776. One of Washington's slaves, HARRY WASHINGTON, fought alongside the British throughout the war, was evacuated to Canada at the end of the war, and then went on to help found the British colony of Sierra Leone.

Not all Southern blacks supported the British. George Washington was accompanied throughout the war by his faithful servant, WILLIAM LEE, who later gained his freedom and helped to preserve Mount Vernon as a park and legacy of his former master. Lee was more than just the person who washed Washington's uniform and prepared his food—he rode into battle alongside his master, organized supplies and living quarters for Washington's officers, and is credited with rallying other black noncombatants to take ammunition to the front at a crucial moment in the Battle of Monmouth (June 28, 1778). Lee was probably a relative of Washington's—probably a distant relative, by marriage—as was commonly the case with mixed-race personal servants in many slave societies in the Americas. But many Southern blacks served the cause of the American rebels in the hope of personal advancement or even advancement of black people as a whole. John Laurens (1754–82), of South Carolina, a prominent white military leader and close friend of Alexander Hamilton's, proposed to Washington that Southern slaves be enlisted in the Continental army with the permission of their masters, and that they gain their liberty and a land grant for successful completion of a term of service. This idea was rejected, but Laurens nonetheless enlisted free blacks and runaway slaves in an irregular unit that he commanded around CHARLESTON, SOUTH CAROLINA, in 1782. He was killed at the head of his men in a skirmish August 27, 1782, only a few days before the British evacuated Charleston.

MARYLAND independently took up Laurens's suggestion in October 1780, when the state legislature agreed to accept slaves offered by their masters in the Maryland Line regiments, which were among the most reliable regiments of Washington's army and had suffered heavy losses during the British victory at the Battle of Camden, South Carolina (August 16, 1780). Maryland state records suggest that about 10 percent of the 1st and 3rd Maryland regiments were people of color by the end of the war.

The war in the Deep South was shattering to black life in many ways. Unlike the situation in most parts of the North, where armies faced each other in the open field and civilians were mostly held harmless unless they were directly in the way of the warring troops, in the South the war was more irregular and pervasive (eastern New Jersey, where Colonel Tye fought, was an exception to this rule in the North and suffered enormous devastation). Civilians of all social ranks were at risk from raiding parties, which were often hard to distinguish from common bandits. Free blacks were in particular peril since they could be considered a form of booty if sold into slavery. At the same time, both sides appealed to blacks, either free or enslaved, to serve them as spies, laborers, or even armed soldiers in some cases. Black men could protect their families by signing up with one of the warring parties, but if their side suffered a defeat, they might be in an even worse situation than when they started. For example, during the siege of Yorktown in 1781, the British commander Lord Cornwallis drove black camp followers, including the families of black men who had fought for the British, into the no-mans-land that separated the two armies. The American-French force was no better able to care for them, and many of these poor refugees sat between the competing forces and starved.

Southern blacks who served in American armies sometimes qualified for benefits similar to those awarded to Northern black soldiers. The Maryland registers were used as evidence to grant pensions and land grants to black Marylanders in the early 1800s. Black veterans in GEORGIA also qualified for land grants alongside white former comrades. But the payoff for service was much less consistent in the Southern states, given the opposition of important political leaders to the very concept of black military service. Some Southern black loyalists escaped to Sierra Leone or Canada, but the large contingent with Cornwallis was either killed or recaptured.

International Ramifications
After the Continental army achieved notable victories, FRANCE (1778), SPAIN (1779), and the Netherlands (1780) joined the war on America's side, although both Spain and the Netherlands fought as France's ally and offered half-hearted support to the American rebels. All three countries had colonies in the Americas with large black populations, both free and enslaved. The issues around white CREOLE nationalism, liberal principles, and black resistance were also very much present in these colonies, and the war had profound impacts on the whole European colonial endeavor in the Americas.

France called on the free people of color of its American colonies to fight for American independence. About 1,500 free colored men from Martinique, Guadeloupe, and SAINT-DOMINGUE enlisted in the French army during the course of the struggle. Nine hundred of these men made up the Chasseurs-Volontaires de Saint-Domingue, who participated in the Georgia and South Carolina campaigns of 1779–80. The Chasseurs-Volontaires were the only fresh troops left in the combined French-American army after the defeat of the assault on Savannah, Georgia, on October 18, 1779. When the besieged British counterattacked, the Chasseurs-Volontaires held the line and allowed the French forces to return to their ships. Chasseurs-Volontaires companies then served in the defense of Charleston against British forces in 1780, and in the defense of French-held islands in the Caribbean. The Chasseurs-Volontaires were free men of color, though at least one famous slave, the future king Henry Christophe (1767–1820) of independent Haiti, is said to have served in the regiment. He may have been LIVING "AS FREE," as he was the manager of an inn near CAP-FRANÇAIS/CAP-HAÏTIEN after the war.

The Spanish and British both appealed to the free blacks and MAROONS of FLORIDA for support during the campaign there in 1781. The BLACK SEMINOLE generally fought for Spain, participating in the Battle of Pensacola (March–May 1781) alongside black militiamen from CUBA.

Dutch land forces did not participate in the war, but Dutch warships and privateers operating out of St. Eustatius were very active in support of the American cause, and the island was an important source for arms smuggled into North America. Many Dutch sailors were black, and indeed blacks served in all the navies of the various warring powers during the struggle. In fact, naval and merchant marine service was a common experience for free blacks during this period. Since naval enlisted men were very much constrained in their liberty, subject to the arbitrary jurisdiction of their captains, subject to whippings and capital punishment almost without appeal, and otherwise unfree at least for the duration of their enlistments, society did not think it unusual that blacks might do this work. Some blacks even rose to the rank of warrant officers, as for example, Bertrand LeMoine of Fort-Dauphin, Saint-Domingue, who served in the French navy as a purser, or ship's supply officer, during the American war.

The British also enlisted free black soldiers in their militias in their colonies in the Caribbean, though none of these men participated in campaigns outside the islands during the war. The Jamaican maroons, however, were used as mercenaries by the British during this period. They were sent to suppress resistance by the early settlers of Sierra Leone in the 1780s and many remained there.

The impact of the war on black servicemen in the Caribbean was profound. In the French colonies, many who, perhaps like Christophe, had been living "as free," gained legal title to liberty. Others were able to have relatives freed and acquire through military pay the resources to purchase a farm or start a business. They also gained valuable experience of combat that would serve them well during the ensuing HAITIAN REVOLUTION. The American war can be seen as a continuation of the century-long struggle between France and Britain for global colonial dominance, which had created many opportunities for people of color and other poor and excluded people.

However, the impact of the American War for Independence on the peoples of the Americas, Afro-descended as well as Indian and white, was even more shattering. The American victory ratified the creole nationalism, liberal ideals of democracy, and belief in human progress for which the Americans had fought. The American Revolution also altered the balance of power in the global struggle—paradoxically, although Britain had lost an important part of its empire, it was nonetheless able to cement its power in the rest of the world, thanks to its naval victories in the Caribbean and Indian Ocean. The defeat of France in this struggle helped launch the FRENCH REVOLUTION in 1789, which in turn led to the independence movements in Latin America (see SOUTH AMERICAN WARS OF LIBERATION) in the early 19th century. The American war and the subsequent establishment of constitutional government in the united American states also provided a somewhat deceptive model to creole elites elsewhere in the Americas. The United States they saw was a country that appeared to have solved the problem of having a locally governed republican state that nonetheless preserved property and slavery. This model led many Latin American and Caribbean elites to attempt rebellion from 1789 to 1825. The most successful rebellion was the Haitian Revolution. In this struggle, early attempts by white elites to lead a transition to independence that preserved slavery were foiled by a vigorous slave uprising that finally resulted in black majority rule and universal abolition. This experience showed slave-owning elites throughout the region that the American model was not applicable to the slave societies of the tropical Americas, but some still clung to the American inspiration as late as the TEN YEARS' WAR in Cuba (1868–78). Cuban independence leader Carlos Manuel de Céspedes drew on the American Declaration of Independence to justify his rebellion. Elites were similarly, though not quite so thoroughly, disappointed in MEXICO, where a liberal mixed-race president, VICENTE GUERRERO SALDAÑA, abolished slavery in 1829 and society developed toward a less racially stratified state much earlier than in the United States. Elsewhere in the plantation Americas, the liberal principles of the American Revolution helped justify creole-led movements, some of which managed to find a place for free people of color and even to abolish slavery. The one part of the plantation Americas not strongly influenced by the American example was the British Caribbean. Many pro-British whites from the American South moved to the Caribbean after their defeat. The earl of Dunmore became governor of the Bahamas after the war. Some black loyalists settled there, along with black Seminole who did not want to stay in Florida under American rule after 1817. Having seen what independence meant for American blacks, people of color in the British Caribbean were somewhat cool to the idea, and the disturbances in the British Caribbean in this period were tied more to ideas of universal British citizenship and the British abolition movement than to the North American example.

Stewart R. King

FURTHER READING
Egerton, Douglas R. *Death or Liberty: African-Americans and Revolutionary America*. New York: Oxford University Press, 2009.

Malcom, Joyce Lee. *Peter's War: A New England Slave Boy and the American Revolution*. New Haven, Conn.: Yale University Press, 2009.

Wiencek, Henry. *An Imperfect God: George Washington, His Slaves, and the Creation of America*. New York: Farrar, Strauss & Giroux, 2004.

WAR OF MEXICAN INDEPENDENCE (1810–1821)

A mural on the wall of the National History Museum in Mexico City places the leaders of the independence struggle at the center of the panoply of MEXICO's national heroes. In the very center of the image is Miguel Hidalgo, the "father of Mexico," who started the independence struggle. On both sides of him are his two chief lieutenants: to the left, in civilian clothes and holding a banner but without clerical garb, is JOSÉ MARÍA MORELOS, his former student in the seminary and a fellow Catholic priest, and facing away from him some distance to the right wearing a brilliant military uniform in red and gold and holding a sword is VICENTE GUERRERO SALDAÑA, the first Afro-Mexican president of Mexico. Hidalgo was white, and Morelos and Guerrero were free people of African ancestry.

The importance of Afro-Mexicans to Mexico's independence struggle was not limited to these two leaders. As many as one-third of the soldiers in Mexico's liberation army were black or of mixed race. Many of the soldiers in the army of the Spanish viceroy were black too, but free blacks tended to support Mexican independence. They hoped for a better situation for Afro-Mexicans from an independent government, and to some extent their hopes were realized as one of their own came to lead the new nation. Slavery and artificial racial caste laws against free people of color were abolished, but in some ways society did not realize the dream of equal treatment.

A detail of a 20th-century mural by Juan O'Gorman in Mexico's Chapultepec Castle illustrating the outbreak of the Mexican independence struggle. In the foreground is the father of Mexican independence, the white Catholic priest Miguel Hidalgo, reading the declaration of independence. The figures surrounding him represent the first army of independent Mexico, and the racial and class diversity of this force is obvious. Many Afro-Mexicans are depicted, along with Indians, mestizos, and zambos; upper-class white and mixed-race people; and peasants. The figure on the left holding a banner is intended to represent José María Morelos, and the man in uniform standing in the foreground on the right holding a sword is Vicente Guerrero Saldaña. *(The Granger Collection, New York)*

The 11-year Mexican War of Independence (1810–21) was a terrible and chaotic struggle, with several factions and a dizzying series of triumphs, betrayals, and bitter battles before independence was finally won. Father Hidalgo started the struggle with his Grito, or "cry," of Dolores, on September 16, 1810. Hidalgo was priest of a rural parish, and he immediately gained support from the local Indians and poor mestizos. Within a week, on September 22, he announced that there were to be no slaves in Mexico, and supporters of the independence movement had to liberate their slaves. He was also generally opposed to any sort of caste laws or special privileges for whites. His forces were defeated, and he was captured on March 21, 1811, before he could make any sort of legal formulation of his intentions. Leadership of the movement fell to the Afro-Mexican priest José María Morelos, who led the movement until his capture and execution in December 1815. He was able to codify the abolition of slavery and legal discrimination against blacks in the Convention of Chilpancingo, September 13, 1813. After Morelos's death, several rebel chieftains took up the struggle; foremost among them was the Afro-Mexican former mule-train entrepreneur Vicente Guerrero Saldãna. Finally, Guerrero and the pro-Spanish leader Agustín de Iturbide joined to lead Mexico to independence on September 27, 1821. Guerrero and the liberal revolutionaries ultimately fell out with Iturbide, overthrowing him on March 18, 1823. Guerrero held power as president briefly in 1829, serving long enough to abolish slavery and racial discrimination formally and definitively under law with his proclamation of September 15, 1829.

The war had its origins in an elite conspiracy among whites born in Mexico, or criollos. This group, once dominant in Mexican colonial institutions, had been eased from power by Spanish-born whites during the reforms of the 1760s–90s. After the invasion of Spain by Napoléon Bonaparte in 1808, Mexican whites saw an opportunity to regain the power they had once had. In addition, they saw in the liberal reforms of Spain's government a chance for greater democracy for themselves. They did not really want to start a social revolution and modeled themselves on the North American revolutionaries in the AMERICAN WAR OF INDEPENDENCE, 1775–83. Miguel Hidalgo was one of the plotters, and when his fellow conspirators were arrested on September 15, 1810, the next day he issued the call for an uprising from his rural church in what is now Dolores Hidalgo, Guanajuato, north of Mexico City. The local Indian and mestizo people flocked to his movement, both because they were personally loyal to him as a beloved parish priest and because they saw in his movement a chance to overturn a social order that kept them down. The liberal principles of the revolution included an end to caste laws that lim-

ited the social roles that people of color could fill and a promise of education and economic development that would confer prosperity on the countryside.

Hidalgo had a broad-based coalition behind him. Many urban whites were aghast at the racial and social character of his revolutionary movement, but some continued to support him. Indians were of two minds about the independence movement, because in some ways the old regime's laws protected them and their traditional ways. But many Indians also supported Hidalgo, especially those outside the core areas around Mexico City, who did not have recognized rights to the soil and autonomous villages. He also had contact with the Afro-Mexican population through a former student, José María Morelos, who was a village priest in the modern state of Morelos, south of Mexico City. Hidalgo made Morelos his commander in the southern part of the country, and Morelos in turn recruited Vicente Guerrero Saldaña to the cause. Guerrero was a teamster from the modern state of Guerrero. Teamsters, most of whom were Afro-Mexicans, were an important occupational group both because they had contacts throughout the country, especially with the small business community, and because they had an intimate knowledge of the roads and of transport conditions. Hidalgo scored some early successes against the colonial government's troops but was fairly quickly defeated. Morelos, and then Guerrero after his death in 1815, managed to keep the independence movement alive for 10 years against local loyalist troops and REGULAR ARMY units from Spain. They waged guerrilla war against the government and slowly gained the support of the rural population. The areas where Afro-Mexicans were numerous in the Costa Chica, south of Acapulco and in VERACRUZ, MEXICO, on the Gulf of Mexico coast, were crucial areas of support for the rebels. Finally, in September 1821, the rebel chieftains including Guerrero agreed on a compromise with the loyalist commander, Agustín de Iturbide, calling for independence, constitutional monarchy, and an end to caste laws and racial discrimination.

The Mexican War of Independence had a variety of ideological roots. First was the Enlightenment liberalism of the original criollo plotters. Though many liberal whites were frightened away from the revolutionary movement, enough of this faction remained active that their ideas were never abandoned, and in many ways they were the agenda of the Guerrero administration. They wanted, as Hidalgo had said in his original Grito, "good government, true religion, and death to the *gachupines* (Peninsular Spaniards)." That is, they were fighting for modern, organized, efficient, relatively uncorrupt, and somewhat democratic government. They also wanted national sovereignty, free of the increasingly intrusive Spanish administrators. Good government and nationalism were cornerstone ideas of the Enlightenment. By true religion, they meant the religion of the people, a heartfelt Catholicism with popular overtones instead of the formalized and sterile state Catholic faith of the Enlightenment era, influenced as they saw it by Masonic ideas (see also FREEMASONRY and ROMAN CATHOLIC CHURCH). The rebels carried the banner of Our Lady of Guadalupe to show that they were fighting for a different idea of religion from the loyalists, who fought under the banner of Our Lady of Sorrows. The liberals of Europe mainly treated religion with disdain, but in very Catholic Spanish America that would not have worked very well, and so rebels there looked for an authentic emotional and nationalistic religion. In this they embodied a new current in religion and thought just coming to the fore in the early 19th century, romanticism.

This concept of popular religion as a glue that could hold the movement and the nation together was very appealing to people of color, both Indians and Afro-Mexicans. The Roman Catholic Church in Mexico in the days of the Habsburgs, before the Bourbon Reforms, had been a paternalistic organization with a certain amount of room for people of color. CATHOLIC CONFRATERNITIES provided health care and insurance as well as sociability and networks with high-status individuals. People of lower racial status could rise to some degree within the church: Morelos, for example, entered a seminary and became a priest, even though his father was a poor mestizo artisan and his mother a free black woman. But the church was increasingly a creature of the state in the 18th century. After what were known as the Bourbon Reforms for the ruling family that took power in Spain in 1701, this was especially true after the expulsion of the JESUITS in the 1760s. The connection between popular religion and national sentiment is visible in Mexico and among Mexican Americans to this day, and the image of Guadalupe has become as much a Mexican symbol as the national flag. Rural people, predominantly Indians, who supported the movement for Mexican independence were not really liberals, however. They looked back to a past, often an imagined one, when they felt a national community had existed, one based on the Catholic Church, local criollo notables, and a king who wanted the best for his subjects. The cult of Guadalupe was a way for these two ideologies to merge.

The idea of nationhood was appealing to people of African ancestry as well, insofar as it meant a national community that transcended race. They had been most strongly affected by the caste laws, more than the Indians, who had some protection from the autonomy of their village governments and their special status under the old laws. The Afro-Mexicans were more likely to be urban and educated and in contact with ideas from Europe than the Indians, and on the other hand, they were more likely to be affected by legal discrimination. As a result, they responded to both liberal and traditionalist arguments for independence.

Good government could mean many things. If it meant more equitable government, with "careers open to talent" without regard to race or class origin, that was something that free people of color could support. The examples of Afro-Mexicans like Guerrero who rose to the very top of society were testimony that the liberal ideal could mean better things. But good government could also mean greater integration of the country in the world economy. Liberalism was strongly associated with ideas of free trade, thanks to Adam Smith and his successors, the political economists of the 19th century. Free trade was suspect for Afro-Mexicans, many of whom had worked in the artisanal manufacturing sector before the 1760s, when Spanish America's ports were opened to foreign manufactured goods and the manufacturing sector in Mexico was crushed. Of course, more imports meant more jobs for muleteers like Vicente Guerrero Saldaña, but many free people of color had no reason to welcome liberal economic reforms. Finally, good government meant impersonal, bureaucratic government, a "rule of law" unmediated by personal contacts and clientage. For free people of color in the old regime, clientage, either from former masters or other powerful whites, often took the place of the special protections extended to Indians by the laws. Clientage ensured free people of color a place in society. With the liberal "government of laws, not men" as yet untested, many Afro-Mexicans proved reluctant to adopt the ideal of good government very enthusiastically. Nonetheless, even with mixed emotions, most Afro-Mexicans supported the independence struggle.

Afro-Mexican soldiers gave the pro-independence forces needed combat skills and organization. Especially along the Gulf of Mexico coast, but also inland, where they were numerous, the colonial government had made extensive use of men of color in the MILITIA before the war. There was reluctance to have Afro-Mexicans in leadership roles, and a purge had removed most officers of color from command positions in the 1780s. But the black soldiers were too useful for the government to dispense with their services. White and high-status mestizo men did not want to serve actively in the militia—they considered the militia more of a social club and believed that active duty should be limited to actual foreign invasions. Some Indian villages provided fighters, but the government did not trust them. The free blacks could be persuaded to serve. They were poorer and of lower status and could be attracted more easily by pay or coerced into serving. Militia units were generally committed to fight Indians or RUNAWAY SLAVES in small detachments. The leaders in the field were noncommissioned officers, who were also Afro-Mexicans.

This meant that when war began, the black militiamen had plenty of experience, as well as skilled leaders whom they were accustomed to following.

The consequences of the war for Afro-Mexicans were mixed. The Guerrero administration abolished slavery as one of its first acts. It also abolished any remnants of the caste laws that had existed under the Spanish. Henceforth, in principle, all Mexicans were to have equal opportunity to hold government jobs and attend schools and were to be equal before the law. As a matter of fact, however, RACISM AND RACIAL PREJUDICE remained strong. Institutions were reluctant to employ blacks. Schools were reluctant to admit them. One result of this, given the flexible nature of the color line in Spanish America, was that Afro-Mexicans began to be integrated in the larger population. A country that had received more African than European immigrants before 1810 somehow became a country with only about 3 percent of citizens who identify themselves as Afro-Mexicans today.

FURTHER READING

Guedea, Virginia. "The Process of Mexican Independence." *American Historical Review* 105, no. 1 (February 2000): 116–130.

Rodriguez, Jaime, ed. *The Independence of Mexico and the Creation of the New Nation.* Los Angeles: UCLA Latin American Center Publications, 1989.

Van Young, Eric. *The Other Rebellion: Popular Violence, Ideology, and the Mexican Struggle for Independence, 1810–1821.* Palo Alto, Calif.: Stanford University Press, 2001.

WASHINGTON, D.C. (DISTRICT OF COLUMBIA, UNITED STATES TERRITORY)

The District of Columbia is a small territory in the United States, which is the home of the national capital, Washington. It lies along the Potomac River between the states of MARYLAND and Virginia. The heart of the city of Washington is a low-lying, swampy region between the Potomac and its small tributary, the Anacostia. The land rises gradually to low, rolling hills to the northwest, northeast, and southeast. When originally established by the first U.S. Congress in 1791, the District of Columbia was a 10-mile square, stretching from the small Virginia port of Alexandria in the south to the small Maryland port of Georgetown in the north. In 1847, the west bank of the Potomac was retroceded and became Arlington County and Alexandria City, Virginia.

During the colonial period, and up until 1791, this was a farming region at the edge of the plantation zone in Maryland and Virginia. Farmers here grew some tobacco, but the more important products were food crops, for sale to the more prosperous plantations to the south and east (*see* PROVISION GROUND FARMING). The small ports were centers for trade, both locally and up the Potomac River to western Maryland and Virginia. GEORGE WASHINGTON, America's first president, lived just south of the district line in Virginia at Mount Vernon, and he was involved in a project to build a canal along the Potomac River that would connect with the Ohio River, making the region an important terminus for trade with the western frontier. The canal was never completed all the way to its destination, though it did help develop the interior of VIRGINIA AND WEST VIRGINIA, Maryland, and PENNSYLVANIA. Commercial activity in Maryland was centered in Baltimore, especially after the construction of roads and railroads across the state and on to the Ohio River valley.

People of color, both free and enslaved, lived in the region from colonial times onward. Prince George's County, in Maryland, which gave up about one-third of its territory to create the district, had 164 free people of color (0.8 percent of the total population) and 11,176 slaves (52.4 percent) among its 21,344 inhabitants in 1790. The town of Alexandria, Virginia, had 52 free people of color (1.9 percent) and 543 slaves (19.8 percent) among its 2,748 inhabitants in 1790. Most of these people would have been town-dwelling ARTISANS in Alexandria and Georgetown, though there were also some small farmers. One town dweller was Yarrow Mamout (1731?–ca. 1820), a practicing Muslim (*see* ISLAM), who was a brick maker by profession and owned a house in Georgetown. A rural provision ground farmer was Tobias Henson, who bought his freedom in 1813 and owned more than 100 acres in what became the Anacostia neighborhood, a historically black neighborhood in southeastern D.C. Members of his family were important landowners in the neighborhood at least through the 1940s.

Even after the establishment of Washington as the seat of the U.S. federal government, substantial rural areas remained inside the district, and white and free black farmers continued to work there. However, the population became increasingly urbanized as the federal government grew in size and complexity. The black population reflected this change, taking on characteristics similar to those found in other mid-Atlantic cities such as Baltimore and Richmond. By 1830, the majority of the black population of the district was free. Most slaves were domestic servants, many employed by public officials living in the city temporarily. Much of the commercial activity of the city was driven by the federal government, with hotels, restaurants, retailers, and wholesalers all seeing the government and federal officials as their principal market. Many free people of color worked for federal officials. Elizabeth Keckly (1818–1907) was one such. She was born a slave in Virginia, gained her freedom, and worked as a dressmaker in Washington, serving the wives of high government

AFRICAN-AMERICAN POPULATION OF WASHINGTON, D.C., 1800–1900

Year	Slaves	Free People of Color	Free People of Color as a Percentage of Total Population	Total Population
1800	2,072	400	4.9%	8,144
1810	unavailable, as records were destroyed by British forces in 1814			
1820	6,380	4,048	12.3%	33,039
1830	6,119	6,152	15.4%	39,834
1840	4,685	8,361	19.1%	43,712
1850	3,687	10,059	19.5%	51,687
1860	3,185	11,131	14.8%	75,189
1870		43,404	33.0%	131,700
1880		59,596	33.6%	177,624
1890		75,572	32.8%	230,267
1900		86,702	31.1%	278,718

officials. She became a friend and confidante of Mary Todd Lincoln (1818–82), wife of President ABRAHAM LINCOLN.

Free people of color found Washington a relatively comfortable environment, compared to other Southern cities, but life was not entirely free of RACISM AND RACIAL PREJUDICE. In 1808, Congress, acting as the government of the district, enacted black codes based on those in the neighboring states (see BLACK CODES IN THE UNITED STATES). Free colored immigrants from states other than Maryland and Virginia had to post bonds. There was a curfew for free coloreds and slaves that was enforced by the new urban police force, created in 1802 and one of the first in the country. Gambling and sale of alcohol were prohibited, though there is plenty of evidence of bars and gambling houses operated by people of color. One of these, operated by free black Beverly Snow, sparked a race riot in 1835 when Snow allegedly insulted the wives of white Navy Yard employees. White mobs smashed Snow's restaurant and a number of other black-owned businesses, and Congress reacted by increasing the bonds new free black residents had to post and cracking down on enforcement of the bonding requirement. Despite these handicaps, however, Washington's free colored community became one of the largest and wealthiest in the South during the years before the AMERICAN CIVIL WAR, 1861–65. Newly freed blacks from the Upper South continued to move to the city, including, in 1822, Beverly and Harriet Hemings, the oldest surviving CHILDREN OF SALLY HEMINGS and THOMAS JEFFERSON, who, however, were so light-skinned that they were able to pass as white (see also "WHITENING" AND RACIAL PROMOTION).

Policy toward race and slavery in the district, like all laws there in the 19th century, was made by the federal Congress instead of a local legislative body. As such, it reflected a national position on these issues. In response to the abolition movement (see UNITED STATES, ABOLITION MOVEMENTS IN), Congress took steps to limit slavery in the district. As part of the Compromise of 1850, importation of new slaves for sale was prohibited in 1850, though owners who were going to live temporarily in the city (as federal officials) could still bring their slaves with them. At this time, some of the harsher elements of the black codes were also lifted, although the FUGITIVE SLAVE ACT OF 1850 was also fully enforced here and RUNAWAY SLAVES found Washington a dangerous place in the 1850s. A group of 77 runaways on a ship was recaptured in 1848, thanks to a tip from a free colored taxi operator who delivered a number of them to the dock and became suspicious.

With the outbreak of the American Civil War in 1861, life changed dramatically for Washington's blacks. Congress abolished slavery in all federal territories, including the district, in 1862. By that time, any slave who wanted to leave had already had a chance, as the U.S. Army, encamped in enormous numbers in and around the city, took in all runaway slaves as "contraband of war" without inquiring too carefully whether their owners were supporters of the Confederacy or not. White Washingtonians were, like whites in southern Maryland and northern Virginia, mostly supporters of the Confederacy in any case. Many whites left the city in 1861 to go south and were replaced by enormous numbers of employees in the rapidly expanding federal government. Washington did not lose its southern character entirely during the war, but its race relations became a mixture of what was found in the South and what was found in Pennsylvania or New York at this time.

The Republican Party, which dominated the federal government almost uninterruptedly in the late 19th century, saw blacks as an important part of their electoral coalition. Before civil service reform in the 1880s, political parties filled the ranks of government employees with their supporters, and blacks benefited from these circumstances to gain a foothold in the federal workforce. John F. Cook, a prewar free black, was chairman of the D.C. Republican Party from 1866 to 1880 and an important power broker in the city. One beneficiary of black political power in the Republican Party was CHRISTIAN ABRAHAM FLEETWOOD, a black Marylander who moved to the district after a spectacular career in the army during the Civil War, working at the War Department from 1867 until retirement in 1891. The most famous black in America, abolitionist FREDERICK DOUGLASS, lived in the Anacostia neighborhood in the district from 1874 until his death in 1895 and worked for the federal government as a U.S. marshal and as a diplomat. He was also an employee of the district government as recorder of deeds.

After the end of the period of RECONSTRUCTION IN THE UNITED STATES, with the adoption of civil service reform, and with the return of Democrats to power with Woodrow Wilson (1856–1924, served 1913–21), this door for blacks began to close. By 1921, only 25 blacks were working in the government of the district. An unknown, but larger, number were working in federal government offices in the district, but President Wilson signed an order in 1915 that imposed SEGREGATION in federal workplaces. In July, 1919, an outbreak of racial violence left 15 dead in the city, and fighting only stopped when federal troops arrived from nearby military bases.

Despite the discrimination they faced, Washington's blacks were able to build a strong, self-reliant community during the period after the end of Reconstruction. The city was a principal early destination for blacks fleeing harsher oppression farther to the South in what became known as the Great Migration. By the 1960s, the city was overwhelmingly black, and it remains so to this day.

FURTHER READING

Borchert, James. *Alley Life in Washington: Family, Community, Religion, and Folklife in the City, 1850–1970.* Champaign-Urbana: University of Illinois Press, 1980.

Clark-Lewis, Elizabeth, ed. *First Freed: Washington, D.C., in the Emancipation Era.* Washington, D.C.: Howard University Press, 2002.

Laprade, William T. "The Domestic Slave Trade in the District of Columbia." *Journal of Negro History* 11 (January 1926): 17–34.

Snethen, Worthington. *The Black Code of the District of Columbia: in Force September 1st, 1848.* New York: A&F Anti-Slavery Society, 1848. Available online. URL: http://books.google.com/books?vid=OCLC43590918&id=GWINAAAA IAAJ. Accessed January 12, 2011.

Tremain, Mary. *Slavery in the District of Columbia.* New York: Putnam, 1892. Available online. URL: http://books.google.com/books?vid=OCLC05202324&id=kcYkM9M-4XgC. Accessed January 12, 2011.

WASHINGTON, GEORGE (1732–1799) *planter, general, first president of the United States (1789–1797)*

General of the Continental army during the WAR OF AMERICAN INDEPENDENCE (1775–83), and first president of the United States (1789–97), George Washington was a planter in Virginia. He was related by marriage to the Custis and Dandridge families, who were among the wealthiest planters in the colony. He owned more than 100 slaves in his own name and in addition managed more than 100 more who belonged to his wife, Martha. He was a prominent military leader in the SEVEN YEARS' WAR against FRANCE, organizing Virginia's western defenses against the Indian allies of the French and actually sparking the first fighting of the war near the modern city of PITTSBURGH, PENNSYLVANIA. In the 1770s, he was a Virginia delegate to the Continental Congress, a supporter of American independence, and was appointed the commander of America's army in 1775. He led the American colonial forces during the War of American Independence and was elected president of the United States after America adopted its Constitution in 1789.

Washington was born on February 22, 1732, and had numerous free colored relatives and neighbors. His wife's first husband, Daniel Custis, had had a mixed-race half brother who was to have received half their father's estate except that he died young, under the care of his half siblings. Washington had a slave companion, WEST FORD, who was of mixed race and was a relative, though the precise relationship is unclear. Some people, including West Ford's descendants, have suggested that he was Washington's son, though Washington's biographers have generally concluded that Washington was not fertile as the result of a childhood infection. Ford may have been the son of one of Washington's nephews or his adopted son. In any case, Ford was freed after Washington's death in 1799 and willed a 160-acre farm by Washington's brother. His descendants continue to live in Virginia to this day.

During his time as commander of the Continental army in the War of American Independence, Washington's views on black military service underwent a transformation. When he first took command of the Continental army on July 3, 1775, during the siege of BOSTON, MASSACHUSETTS, he was horrified to discover that many blacks were serving as soldiers in New England regiments. One of them, PETER SALEM, had gained fame as the man who killed the British marine commander,

Major Pitcairn, at the Battle of Bunker Hill (June 17, 1775). Washington ordered that no further blacks be enrolled in Continental units and that those currently serving be mustered out as soon as practicable. In this, he was demonstrating the views commonly held by Southern whites that blacks were either too cowardly or too impulsive to be disciplined soldiers. The New England officers mostly ignored this order, and we know of several blacks who enrolled during the period this order was in effect and can assume that there were hundreds more. The order was rescinded, but Washington still distrusted the black troops. The prowess of the black soldiers in combat, however, especially at the retreat from Long Island (August 27, 1776), where the mixed-race Marblehead Regiment saved the Continental army from destruction at the hands of a greatly superior British force, led Washington to revise his opinion. By the Battle of Yorktown (October 14, 1781), he was ready to entrust the crucial assault on the fortification that led to the British surrender to a mixed-race unit, the Rhode Island "Black Regiment."

A number of Washington's slaves ran away during the War of American Independence, and one of them, HARRY WASHINGTON, was one of the first British settlers of SIERRA LEONE. Washington's slave cook, Hercules, ran away when Washington left PHILADELPHIA, PENNSYLVANIA, at the end of his term as president. Hercules lived in Philadelphia "as free," so famous that nobody dared arrest him (see LIVING "AS FREE"). He was formally freed by Washington's will.

While president, Washington made several decisions that were harmful to free people of color. He provided assistance to the French colonial government in SAINT-DOMINGUE during the early stages of the HAITIAN REVOLUTION (1791–1804). Free people of color served on both sides in this struggle. He signed the Fugitive Slave Act of 1793, which permitted slave catchers to travel to other states searching for RUNAWAY SLAVES. However, this law gave the states a role in deciding the status of people within their boundaries, so people accused of being runaways could appeal to state courts. RE-ENSLAVEMENT under this law proved to be so difficult that a half-century later, Southern SLAVE OWNERS insisted on the much tougher FUGITIVE SLAVE ACT OF 1850. Finally, Washington signed the Naturalization Act of 1790, which allowed only white persons to become citizens of the United States. This law was one of the precedents that the Supreme Court relied upon in its decision in the case of DRED SCOTT in 1857, in which the court said the founders never intended that blacks, whether free or slave, should be citizens.

Washington freed all the slaves he owned personally upon his death on December 14, 1799, and urged his wife and her heirs to follow his example. He argued that slavery was unjust and incompatible with republican government, though he appears to have shared the racial ideas of other white Virginians of his period.

Stewart R. King

FURTHER READING
Weincek, Henry. *An Imperfect God: George Washington, His Slaves, and the Creation of America.* New York: Farrar, Straus & Giroux, 2004.

WASHINGTON, GEORGE (OF CENTRALIA, WASHINGTON) (1818–1905) *American pioneer*

George Washington was born free in 1818 in Frederick County, Virginia, the son of a white mother and an enslaved black father. His father was sold away from the family, and his mother disappeared when George was very young. He was adopted by a white couple, James and Anna Cochran. As a mixed-race family, the Cochrans were unwelcome in Virginia, so they moved west, first to OHIO and then to MISSOURI. George learned the skills of a backwoods farmer, including distilling whiskey. He attempted to open a distillery in ILLINOIS when he became an adult, but people of color were not permitted to pursue this trade. He also tried to cut and sell lumber, and when a white customer refused to pay him, he was unable to sue, as blacks had no standing in Missouri state courts. His adoptive parents requested and obtained a special legislative grant of citizenship for George, the only one accorded to a free person of color in Missouri at that time, but he was still unable to do business because of pervasive discrimination. Therefore, the Cochrans and George traveled west along the OREGON Trail in 1850.

They first settled at Oregon City, then moved across the Columbia River into what is now the state of Washington (see also WASHINGTON TERRITORY). George settled at the junction of the Skookumchuk and Chehalis Rivers, where the town of Centralia now stands. His adoptive parents filed for a 640-acre land claim for him because African Americans were barred from participation in the Oregon Donation Land Claims Act. After the Cochrans died, George married a mixed-race widow, Mary Jane Cooness, who also owned land in the vicinity. The couple and their neighbor, a Jewish storekeeper named Wiengard, founded the town of Centralia in 1875 as the Northern Pacific Railroad built its Portland-Seattle line through their land. They sold lots for $10 and founded a Baptist Church, parks, and a school. The town grew steadily, and by 1891, Washington had sold 3,000 lots and become a wealthy man.

Washington remained active in community affairs throughout his life. During the economic crisis of 1893–94, he organized relief efforts at his own expense. He also loaned money at no interest for settlers to buy lots to keep the town growing. He died on August 25, 1905.

Washington is an outstanding example of the role of African Americans in the settlement of the Far West. He overcame pervasive discrimination in order to be successful as a land developer and businessman. Many early white settlers in the Pacific Northwest were from New England and New York State, where racial discrimination was not so profound in the early 19th century, and this may have made the region less hostile to Washington and other black pioneers in the area. Even so, the Oregon territorial legislature passed several antiblack measures before Oregon became a state in 1859. After the AMERICAN CIVIL WAR, many Southern whites migrated to the West and took their unreconstructed racial attitudes with them. Many blacks in the Northwest found Washington, or indeed even British Columbia, more accommodating and moved north during the second half of the 19th century. As were many other free blacks, Washington was active in spreading evangelical Protestant Christianity (see also BAPTISTS AND PIETISTS). The role of this group, with a strong tradition of lay leadership and nondogmatic beliefs, was an important one among both populations of color and poor whites throughout the West.

One feature of Washington's biography that attracted notice at the time and also strikes modern readers as unusual was his parentage: A surprising number of mixed-race people were the children of black men and white women, usually poor and marginalized servants. Unlike the almost complete separation of the races that prevailed during the era of Jim Crow, in the old South during the period of slavery, blacks and poor whites actually lived and worked side by side, separated by the status of slavery but often doing the same work and experiencing comparable social exclusion. Slaves had a worse time of it, of course, but natural human attraction could still function even in this perverted environment to lead to births that elites and opinion molders considered even more monstrous than the more "conventional" mixed-race offspring of a white father and a black mother. And, of course, the children were free from birth, even if their fathers were slaves, because children in almost all legal codes in the Americas followed the condition of their mother. So Washington and others like him were, if anything, even more of a destabilizing force within slavery than most free blacks.

Stewart R. King

FURTHER READING

Katz, William. *The Black West: A Documentary and Pictoral History of the African American Role in the Westward Expansion of the United States.* New York: Harlem Moon, 2005.

Oldham, Kit. "George and Mary Jane Washington Found the Town of Centerville (Now Centralia) on January 8, 1875." HistoryLink.org Essay 5276. Available online. URL: http://www.historylink.org/index.cfm?DisplayPage=output.cfm&File_Id=5276. Accessed January 13, 2011.

WASHINGTON, HARRY (dates of birth and death unknown, active 1763–1800) *American soldier, Sierra Leone pioneer*

Harry Washington was born somewhere in SENEGAMBIA, probably in about 1740, as he was fully adult when sold to GEORGE WASHINGTON in 1763. He worked in the Dismal Swamp on Washington's rice plantation and married a woman named Nan. In 1766, George Washington moved Harry to Mount Vernon, leaving his wife behind, and Harry tried to run away. He was recaptured and lived at Mount Vernon, laboring on irrigation works and clearing fields, until 1776. In that year, a British warship sailed up the Potomac River, and Harry was one of 10 Mount Vernon slaves who scrambled aboard. In 1777, he was a corporal in the Black Pioneers, a combat engineer unit attached to the Royal Artillery in New York (see also WAR OF AMERICAN INDEPENDENCE. He fought in the northern theater until 1780, when the Black Pioneers were transferred to SOUTH CAROLINA. He became famous among black loyalists and British officers who led them both as George Washington's slave and for his heroism in battle. His unit saw action against Francis Marion's famous guerrilla force in an especially bloody struggle in the Carolina low country. In 1782, the British evacuated CHARLESTON, SOUTH CAROLINA, and Washington again traveled north to New York. In 1783, as the British commander Henry Clinton negotiated the evacuation of the city, George Washington was very concerned that blacks who had been enslaved by rebel masters and freed by the British be returned. He was aware of Harry's presence in the city and referred to him several times in his correspondence. But the British kept faith with their black soldiers and their families, and Harry and his new wife, Sarah Washington, traveled to Nova Scotia, CANADA, in July 1783. The blacks in Nova Scotia did not receive the land grants that they had been promised and found the community unwelcoming. Harry lived in Nova Scotia until January 1791, when he and his wife joined 1,196 black emigrants who sailed from Nova Scotia to SIERRA LEONE. The Sierra Leone colony was very chaotically administered, and local government was hostile to them. The colony suffered from disease and starvation, and finally in 1799, the settlers rebelled and overthrew the colonial government. A resupply and reinforcement convoy, carrying 500 Jamaican MAROONS, arrived, and the maroons crushed the rebels. A number of the rebels were executed, but Harry was sentenced to exile. The last we know of his story was the moment when he, at the age of 60, left the colony and headed north toward the land of his birth, 500 miles away.

Stewart R. King

FURTHER READING

Egerton, Douglas. *Death or Liberty: African-Americans and Revolutionary America.* New York: Oxford University Press, 2009.

Frey, Sylvia. *Water from the Rock: Black Resistance in a Revolutionary Age.* Princeton, N.J.: Princeton University Press, 1991.

Pybus, Cassandra. *Epic Journeys of Freedom: Runaway Slaves of the American Revolution and Their Global Quest for Liberty.* Boston: Beacon Press, 2007.

WASHINGTON TERRITORY

The Washington Territory of the United States was formed in 1853 when the OREGON territory was split. At first, the Washington Territory consisted of the modern states of Idaho and Washington. In 1863, Idaho became a separate territory (*see* INLAND WEST OF THE UNITED STATES). Most settlement was concentrated in western Washington, around Puget Sound and along the road south to Vancouver, Washington, across the river from Portland, Oregon. Vancouver was the first place in the territory settled by whites and blacks, as the Canadian Hudson's Bay Company (HBC) fort there was established in 1824. An early free colored fur trapper who worked occasionally for the HBC and more often as an independent was GEORGE WASHINGTON BUSH, who finally settled in what is now Tumwater, on the Puget Sound in Washington. Another early Washington resident of African ancestry was Sir James Douglas, later governor of British Columbia, who served at Fort Vancouver from 1828 to 1846. Between 1818 and 1846, all the territory from the California border to Alaska was under the joint sovereignty of BRITAIN and the United States. In 1846, the Oregon Treaty divided the territory into Canadian British Columbia and American Oregon. The territorial government of Oregon was formed south of the Columbia River at Oregon City, and the Hudson's Bay Company continued to manage the area north of the river under American sovereignty.

The white settlers who immigrated to Oregon in the 1840s were generally not very welcoming to nonwhites. Even Dr. John McLoughlin (1784–1857), the Hudson's Bay Company manager who helped the early settlers and retired to live in Oregon City, found that his Indian wife and half-Indian children faced significant discrimination. While Oregon was a federally administered territory, federal officials enforced at least minimally equal justice, but when Oregon became a state, McLoughlin's children lost much of their land in Oregon at the hands of prejudiced local courts. Blacks were especially unwelcome, and many black settlers who traveled the Oregon Trail in the years before the AMERICAN CIVIL WAR decided to locate north of the river. Federal law, for example, protected Bush and his neighbors and relatives, who had been granted land under the British regulations, when Oregon's territorial government tried to void their claims. Farther south, the pioneer GEORGE WASHINGTON established the town of Centralia. His land claims had originally been filed on his behalf by his white adoptive parents and so were not challenged, and he carefully picked sites where the railroad line would pass. As did Bush, Washington helped his neighbors and became the leading citizen of a substantial town.

Ultimately, as elsewhere in the Far West of the United States, blacks were few in number in Washington. The 1860 Census found only 38 in a total population of 11,594. Racial definitions were a little looser on the frontier, and many people of color escaped the notice of the census taker. For example, George Washington and his wife were both living in Lewis County in 1860, but the census takers only managed to find one free colored in that county—perhaps because Mary Jane Washington née Cooness was of mixed race and may have been counted as white by the census.

Nevertheless, blacks were few, and their very scarcity may have helped weaken prejudice against them. The white populist movements of the late 19th and early 20th centuries in the Northwest were directed against other targets: Asians, Indians, and southern European Catholic immigrants. Even these movements were weaker in Washington than in Oregon; the Washington KU KLUX KLAN in the 1920s never achieved the degree of political control over the state government that the Oregon Klan did, and the Washington Klan's ballot measures were all resoundingly defeated. Many smaller towns in Washington adopted formal or informal "sundown laws" that prohibited people of color from living there or staying after dark, but others, especially those with rail company ties, avoided formal discrimination. The rail companies insisted that their multiracial workforce needed places to live near the station or yards and would not accept forcing them into unincorporated slums on the outskirts of town. Sometimes, as in Seattle, racial SEGREGATION would follow the communities of color into the city limits, but at least they were closer to jobs and services they needed.

Thus Washington, while no paradise of racial equality, nonetheless offered a tolerable environment to black pioneers during the 19th century. Many settlers preferred Washington to Oregon, and the small black community there made significant contributions to the development of the state and of a more tolerant society.

Janet McClellan

FURTHER READING

Black Heritage Society of Washington State. Available online. URL: http://www.blackheritagewa.org/. Accessed January 13, 2011.

Katz, William. *The Black West: A Documentary and Pictoral History of the African American Role in the Westward Expansion of the United States.* New York: Harlem Moon, 2005.

Oldham, Kit. "George and Mary Jane Washington Found the Town of Centerville (now Centralia) on January 8, 1875." HistoryLink.org Essay 5276. Available online. URL: http://www.historylink.org/index.cfm?DisplayPage=output.cfm&File_Id=5276. Accessed January 13, 2011.

Washington State University, Manuscripts, Archives, and Special Collections Division. "Black Oral History Collection." Available online. URL: http://www.wsulibs.wsu.edu/cdm-5985. Accessed January 13, 2011.

WEDDERBURN, ROBERT (1762–1835) *British religious leader*

One of BRITAIN's earliest radicals of color, Robert Wedderburn was born in JAMAICA in 1762 to an enslaved black woman named Rosanna and her owner, James Wedderburn, originally of Inveresk, Scotland. While Rosanna was still pregnant with his son, James sold her to the Kingston resident Lady Douglas, stipulating that Robert be freed upon birth. Wedderburn later claimed that his father had two other mixed-race sons while in Jamaica, whom he sent to Scotland. Raised primarily by his enslaved grandmother, "Talkee Amy," in Kingston, Wedderburn left the island in 1778 aboard a warship. He soon arrived in LONDON, ENGLAND, where he took up the tailoring trade near St. Martin-in-the-Fields and lived on Great Windmill Street. (*See also* ARTISANS.)

Finding little success in the capital, Wedderburn labored in poverty and sought refuge in radical branches of Christianity. After hearing a fiery sermon by a Wesleyan preacher, he devoted himself to religious and political matters. Later ordained a Unitarian minister, Wedderburn had a brand of theology that was unconventional, particularly in its denial of the Trinity. He also embraced the teachings of Thomas Spence, a protocommunist advocate of the eradication of private property.

Wedderburn's ideological conversions pushed him to campaign for revolutionary change. Beginning in 1817, he started publishing a pamphlet entitled *The Axe Laid to the Root*, which he sold at his tailoring stall. In it, Wedderburn called for the dissolution of both the monarchy and noble titles, emancipation of the enslaved, and revolution in Jamaica. To illustrate abuse experienced by slaves, Wedderburn told of his own experiences witnessing his grandmother's beating after she was labeled a witch.

After Manchester's Peterloo Massacre in August 1819, Wedderburn began drawing a straight line between the struggles of working-class Britons and those of the enslaved in the West Indies. He opened a meetinghouse in Soho and invited like-minded radicals to attend. Wedderburn's sermons in fall 1819 were even more politically combative, this time assigning responsibility for slave deaths to Parliament in its attempt to feed the textile industries of the North. At a meeting of some 80–90 people, including several black men from the Caribbean, he also argued that the enslaved were justified in killing their masters, and that the prince regent should die for failing to enforce scriptural law. Urging retribution for Peterloo, he called for a revolution in London that might engulf the country. His theology took a sharp turn as well: citing inconsistencies in Jesus's teachings, petitioning for the end of clerical positions, and condemning Wesleyan missionaries for preaching passive obedience to slaves while extorting tithes from them.

Spies sent by the Home Office infiltrated Wedderburn's meeting and soon arrested him. He pleaded innocent to charges of blasphemy and seditious language in spring 1820, but a jury found him guilty and sentenced him to two years in Dorchester prison. After leaving jail, Wedderburn wrote *The Horrors of Slavery* in 1824, which he dedicated to the antislavery crusader William Wilberforce. The tract was largely autobiographical but also contained an extended condemnation of enslavement. Closing the gap yet further between enslaved and working-class people, Wedderburn highlighted his own roots as a mixed-race man, noting with pride his Scottish grandfather, who fought alongside the Jacobites against the government. Prominent within British popular radicalism, Wedderburn was an instrumental figure in the development of working-class activism in 19th-century Britain.

Wedderburn returned to prison in 1831 for involvement with a brothel and died four years later in 1835. He was survived by two sons, Jabez (ca. 1798–1880) and Jacob (1806–41), fathers of Wedderburn's 15 British grandchildren.

Daniel Livesay

FURTHER READING

Fryer, Peter. *Staying Power: Black People in Britain since 1504.* Atlantic Highlands, N.J.: Humanities Press, 1984.

Hoyles, Asher, and Martin Hoyles. *Remember Me: Achievements of Mixed Race People Past and Present.* London: Hansib Publications and Ethos Publishing, 1999.

McCalman, I. D. *Radical Underworld: Prophets, Revolutionaries and Pornographers in London, 1795–1840.* Cambridge: Cambridge University Press, 1988.

WEST VIRGINIA   *See* VIRGINIA AND WEST VIRGINIA.

WHEATLEY, PHILLIS (1753–1784) *American poet*
Phillis Wheatley was the first published black American poet. She was also a participant in an important religious revival movement in America and BRITAIN that led ultimately to the Second Great Awakening.

Phillis Wheatley was born in 1753 in Senegal, Africa (*see also* SENEGAMBIA). She was transported to BOSTON, MASSACHUSETTS, in 1761 abroad a slave ship and purchased by John and Susannah Wheatley. Presumably, Susannah purchased Phillis to aid her in household duties. Mary Wheatley, the 18-year-old daughter of John and Susannah, quickly took Phillis under her wing and guided her in not only domestic duties but also a classical education. Phillis studied English literature, Latin, and the Bible. Her three favorite books were the Bible, a collection of classical mythologies, and Pope's translation of Homer. At the age of 13, Phillis began writing her own poetry. The Wheatleys were so impressed with her verse that they boasted about and shared her writings with friends, family, and the Boston elite. Phillis soon became a lively addition to literary circles.

Phillis published her first poem, "On the Death of the Reverend Mr. George Whitfield," in 1770. George Whitfield (1716–70) had been an important leader in the Protestant revival movement of the 1740s and 1750s called the First Great Awakening, which led ultimately to the creation of the Baptist and Methodist branches of Christianity (*see also* BAPTISTS AND PIETISTS and PROTESTANT MAINLINE CHURCHES). This elegy to Whitfield places Phillis in the mainstream of Protestant Christian reform at the time. She was only able to publish one book in her short lifetime, *Poems on Various Subjects.* Much of her poetry was influenced by the writing of Alexander Pope. The influence of Pope is seen in the use of elegy and an impersonal and artificial tone, quite common in the 18th-century ideal of objectivity. Religion was also a prominent theme in her verse, demonstrating Calvinist and Methodist beliefs. Phillis Wheatley's work was published both in the United States and in Britain. Even Voltaire complimented her poetry.

In 1773, Phillis sailed to LONDON, ENGLAND, for medical treatment but ultimately discovered a new patron, Selina Hastings, the countess of Huntingdon (1707–91). Huntingdon, like Whitfield, was an important early leader in the Protestant revival movement that led to the creation

Image of Phillis Wheatley from the 1773 edition of her book, *Poems on Various Subjects*, the first book of poetry published by an African American in the United States. (*Library of Congress*)

of the Methodist Church and to what became known as the Second Great Awakening of the 1830s and 1840s. The Wheatleys' son, Nathaniel, escorted Phillis to London, where she won the support of the countess. Phillis dedicated her only book, a collection of 39 poems, to the countess of Huntingdon in 1773. Phillis was quickly called back to Boston as Mrs. Wheatley's health began to fail. After the death of Mrs. Wheatley in March 1774, Phillis turned her attention not only to communicating with friends via letter and verse but also to the WAR OF AMERICAN INDEPENDENCE (1775–83). Phillis wrote a letter and poem to General GEORGE WASHINGTON on October 26, 1775. The general was so pleased that he invited her for a visit at his military headquarters. Soon afterward, Mr. Wheatley passed away in 1778. Historians disagree as to whether Phillis was granted her freedom with the death of Mrs. Wheatley or later Mr. Wheatley. Nevertheless, after the deaths of the Wheatley's, Phillis embarked upon a new direction in her life. She married a black businessman living in Boston named John Peters. They moved to Wilmington, Massachusetts, during the War of American Independence and later returned to Boston. During the war, many suffered economic hardship, and John and Phillis were not spared.

Records note that John Peters was temporarily imprisoned for debt shortly after the end of the war in 1784.

Hard times or not, Phillis remained in the literary circle, and several of her poems were published in the *Evening Post and General Advertiser* on October 30, 1779. Phillis and John also wished to have a family, but unfortunately their two children died in early infancy. Soon afterward, Phillis herself died in childbirth on December 5, 1784, at the age of 31. Phillis Wheatley was mourned by the literary elite of Boston and many friends. She is celebrated and remembered as the first black American to publish poetry.

Caroline Castellanos

FURTHER READING:

Applegate, Anne. "Phillis Wheatley: Her Critics and Her Contribution." *Negro American Literature Forum* 9 no. 4 (Winter 1975): 123–126.

Renfro, Herbert G. *Life and Works of Phillis Wheatley.* Salem, Mass.: Ayer, 1993.

"WHITENING" AND RACIAL PROMOTION

"Whitening" is the term used to describe a process of racial promotion by which people of color improved their status in society by adopting a different racial identity. There are two different ways in which this could occur. First, in some places, a free person of color could apply to some authority for official recognition of a new racial status for which he or she qualified through a combination of social attributes, appearance, and ancestry. Second, a person could simply begin to assert a new racial status, and if this was accepted by the community, especially influential local whites, within a generation it would be accepted. This process was sometimes aided by putting a geographical distance between oneself and the place where one had been known as a member of another racial group, but not always.

These transformations were strongly conditioned by the ideas about race held by the dominant culture in that place, and by the role that free people of color played in the society. But there was no place in the Americas in which some sort of racial promotion did not take place.

Official Racial Promotion

In the Iberian colonies, colonial governments could and frequently did issue certificates, called CÉDULAS DE GRACAS AL SACAR in Spanish America and in Brazil, *limpieza de sangue* (in Portuguese). The concept of *limpieza de sangre* (in Spanish) was formally defined during the period of the Reconquista, when Spanish Christians were warring against Muslims, while Jews were common within both communities. In order to preserve the higher ranks in society for members of their own community, in the 15th century, the victorious Christians created a formal process to recognize the Spanish Christian ancestry of an individual and make him or her eligible for nobility, admission to the priesthood, and the like. The official certificates of *limpieza de sangre* were carefully researched and as accurate as the records of the time permitted. People whose ancestry was somewhat tainted could still be granted the *cédula,* or dispensation of their racial status, in recognition of their own personal piety, devotion to the cause, contributions to the state, and the like.

In the Iberian Americas, certificates were occasionally issued to people who wished to avoid the taint of Jewish or Muslim ancestry, but for the most part, *limpieza de sangre* in the American context meant lack of nonwhite ancestry. Just as any person born in the parts of SPAIN and PORTUGAL that had been ruled by the Muslims and reputed to be an Old Christian was suspected of MISCEGENATION and needed a certificate, so any person born in the Indies and reputed to be white was suspect and needed a certificate. Colonial governments in the Americas issued many of them. The *cédulas* that stood in for the certificates in the case of people of known African ancestry, the PARDOS and *quinterónes,* cost money. They proved to be a minor but significant source of revenue for colonial governments. People paid because once possessed of a *cédula,* the person of color and all his or her descendants could be admitted to university, own certain classes of land in Spain, hold official positions at any rank, become nobles, and refer to themselves as Don. Once promoted, one could not subsequently be demoted, even though one's ancestry might be known or even visible. The British traveler Henry Koster remarked on this phenomenon in 1820. He asked his servant about a particular local official, the capitão-môr, or port captain. "Was he not a mulatto man?" Yes, said the servant, he was a MULATTO but is so no longer. Koster wondered how this could be, and the servant replied, "How could a capitão-môr be a mulatto?" The man in question had obtained the Portuguese equivalent of a *cédula* for his great success in business, his unquestioned piety, and his support for the monarchy. His appearance, and his known African ancestry, were of no importance next to the official declaration.

Courts in French and English colonies sometimes pronounced themselves on the racial status of individuals. Sometimes these pronouncements were accepted, and in some cases they were not. The colonial encyclopedist and legal scholar MÉDÉRIC-LOUIS-ÉLIE MOREAU DE ST-MÉRY served as the attorney of a man in SAINT-DOMINGUE, the future Haiti, who was reputed to be white but suspected by the public of having some African ancestry. The man had served as an officer in the French army in Europe, and when he moved to Saint-Domingue, the colonial government put him in charge of his local MILITIA. The white militiamen refused to serve with him because he was, they said, a man of color and should serve in the colored militia. By making him an officer, the royal government back in France had implicitly accepted him as white, since no nonwhites were granted commissions in the French army after 1770. The colonial government decided not to award him his command, and so he sued. The case went all the way to the Royal Council in France, which pronounced him officially white, deciding that his nonwhite ancestress was a Native American woman from the Lesser Antilles whose people had been given the status of whites by virtue of a treaty. The decision was ineffective, however, as the man was never accepted as an officer by the other Saint-Domingue militiamen.

British and American courts were even less willing than French ones to become involved in deciding what race anyone was. For the most part, law had little part in assigning racial status, and thus the courts had little role in reviewing such decisions. People's racial status was assigned informally by their neighbors in the British Americas. LOUISIANA was one of the few places in the United States that had a formal process of defining a person's race, inherited from the Spanish and French who ruled there before the Louisiana Purchase. Louisiana also had a three-valued racial system, with white, colored, and black classifications, unlike the rest of the United States, which had a two-valued system. Louisiana had an office in the state government's Bureau of Vital Statistics until the 1980s that determined what racial identifier to put on birth certificates, based almost exclusively on the status recorded for the person's ancestors. A lawsuit in 1983 finally led the state to end the system.

Informal Racial Promotion

The United States has many people who are socially accepted as white but who have African ancestors. One famous case is that of two brothers, Paul and Philip Malone, who were hired as BOSTON, MASSACHUSETTS, firefighters in the 1970s through an affirmative action program because they self-identified as blacks, even though they appeared to be and were considered by their peers to be white. When challenged, they presented a photo of an ancestor who appeared to be black. In the case, the courts decided that since they had never been thought of as nonwhite before applying for the fire department jobs, the important factor was the social construction of their identity and not their apparently mixed ancestry. The Malones were fired for fraud. In another famous case, the descendants of the CHILDREN OF SALLY HEMINGS, the mixed-race companion of THOMAS JEFFERSON, are about equally split between those identified as black and those identified as white. Hemings herself was very fair-skinned, and several of her even more light-skinned free colored children, presumably fathered by Jefferson, moved to the Midwest. There, some of them identified themselves as white, and others as black; their descendents also had various opportunities to redefine their racial status.

In the case of the Hemings descendants, and the presumed ancestor of the Malones, the "passing" was done secretly. The black person moved to another city or neighborhood, broke connections with black friends and family, and adopted a new identity as a white person. This is the most common pattern in the United States, but alternatives were not unknown. Among the Louisiana Creoles, descendants of white French or Spanish planters and their colored companions or wives, some passing was almost automatic and socially accepted by all concerned. The woman who sued Louisiana in 1983 to have her birth certificate reflect her white social identity, Susie Phipps, was always aware that she was descended from a French planter and a woman of color. It is just that she thought of herself as a white person, as did all of her friends and family, and she thought that her microscopic quantaum of African ancestry should not change that.

This phenomenon of light-skinned people of color who "pass" as white has led to white populations in areas of the American South, Louisiana, for example, that have a significant percentage of African ancestry, when measured by modern genetic analysis. White populations in other parts of the Americas are even more likely to have mixed origins because of the possibility of official racial promotion that existed there, as well as a generally more liberal attitude toward race mixing and the flexibility of color lines that exist outside this country.

There were many marks of white status in various areas of the Americas, and individual people of color might qualify for some but not for others. In the French colonial world, free people of color were heavy users of the notarial system because before a notary would notarize a document, he had to affirm that all the actors were free people. Possession of a notarized document meant that you had proof you were a free person. Additionally, notarized deeds and sales contracts established title to property, and free people of color often felt in danger from a legal system stacked against them. But when the notary checked the free status of a person of color, he noted the MANUMISSION papers or other proof in the notarized document, referring to the person of color as "the named person," a formula used in legal documents in France for criminals. So free people of high status persuaded their notaries to omit the attestation to their free status, so that they could be referred to as "Sieur" or "Dame," the terms used for nobles in France and for any white person in the colonies. Similarly, in Spanish colonies, free men of color who were the sons of high-status white men would attempt to style themselves "Don," though colonial governments were careful to prevent this if the person did not have a *cédula*. In the French colonial world, free people of color were not supposed to bear arms in public except when they were performing militia service. But a medium-sized planter in CAP-FRANÇAIS/CAP HAÏTIEN, SAINT-DOMINGUE, Captain VINCENT OLIVIER, had received a sword from King Louis XIV as a reward for valor long before, and even in 1779 he was never seen in public without it. Olivier was a free black, with no European ancestors and no pretentions to whiteness, but he could adopt a characteristic of white maleness because of his service to the state.

Racial Demotion
It was also possible to assume a lower racial status, typically as a result of discovering or revealing a previously concealed African ancestry. In a sense, the Malone brothers in Boston did this, though they were not exposed to any of the negative consequences of blackness in American society of the 1970s. But in the period under study in this encyclopedia, the time of slavery and its immediate aftermath, for a person considered to be white to be discovered to have African ancestors would be a social catastrophe of the first order. Some white people who lived near the social margins anyway were willing to demote themselves, for example, if they wished to marry a person of color without confronting informal or formal prohibitions on MISCEGENATION. Sometimes people who had successfully "passed" as white for a time would resume a black identity in order to reconnect with their families. But much more controversial were the occasional cases when a descendant of someone who had successfully "passed" would be involuntarily revealed to be of partially African ancestry. The French Dominican missionary Jean-Baptiste Labat noted, after visiting the South Province of Saint-Domingue in 1700, that many of the white families of the region had some hidden black ancestors, and occasionally a child would be born in these families with noticeably black features, sometimes causing a serious scandal. In the 1760s in the same region, a stricter enforcement of royal edicts led to the official designation of a number of families as being of color. The social damage was serious, although they did not suffer in their property at all.

In conclusion, racial status was not fixed at birth; nor did it always correspond to the individual's ancestry or physical appearance. Even in the United States and the British colonies in the Americas, where the immutable nature of race was a truism, plenty of people crossed racial lines unofficially. In the Spanish, Portuguese, Dutch,

and French Americas, there were official means of racial promotion and demotion, while the unofficial methods also worked with greater speed and efficiency than in the American colonies. Racial status bore some relationship to ancestry and appearance everywhere, however. A person of predominantly European ancestry could manage to overcome some African background to become officially recognized as white, while someone with mainly African ancestry could manage to promote himself or herself to a "brown" or intermediate status. Some of the attributes of whiteness were easier to obtain than others. As were many other aspect of the world of the free people of color in the Americas, race itself was a borderline experience, sometimes one thing and sometimes another, and always a field where advances and retreats were possible.

FURTHER READING
Aubert, Guillaume. "'The Blood of France': Race and Purity of Blood in the French Atlantic World." *William and Mary Quarterly* 61, no. 3 (July 2004): 439–478.
Dominguez, Virginia. *White by Definition: Social Classification in Creole Louisiana*. New Brunswick, N.J.: Rutgers University Press, 1993.
Martinez, Maria Elena. "The Black Blood of New Spain: *Limpieza de Sangre*, Racial Violence, and Gendered Power in Early Colonial Mexico." *William and Mary Quarterly* 61, no. 3 (July 2004): 479–520.

WILLIAMSBURG, VIRGINIA
Hard information about the free black population of Williamsburg is difficult to come by: There is no surviving census prior to 1775, and Virginia censuses did not, as a general rule, differentiate between enslaved and free blacks until 1790. More general information about the place of free African Americans in antebellum Virginia can help to expand our understanding, but much remains unknown.

Colonial records indicate that five Williamsburg slaves gained their freedom between 1723 and 1792, and the register of Bruton Parish Church records the births or baptisms of 74 free children of color between 1744 and 1790. Of those children, a little more than half were born to free parents—details of the other children's parentage are unclear. Some may have been born to a free black mother and enslaved father; others may have had a white or biracial mother. Though some black families in Virginia had been free for several generations, most free blacks had a white mother or grandmother and could attribute their free status to that lineage.

The 1782 Williamsburg census records the presence of four female heads of households, with the designation "free" after their names; since white women would not be so described, it can be inferred that they were free women of color. On the basis of these women, the number of people listed in their households, and property records, it has been suggested that free blacks may have accounted for as much as 4–5 percent of the Williamsburg population in the early 1780s.

Throughout the antebellum period, free African Americans were disproportionately urban. Their skills and ways of supporting themselves varied widely; some were ARTISANS, but it seems likely that most plied a variety of trades and took what work was available. Women commonly worked as domestics, and children of both sexes were usually bound out for long periods of indenture, often until the age of 31—substantially longer than their white counterparts.

Religion, particularly the Baptist faith, was a prominent force in the lives of Williamsburg's free black men and women. Some belonged to mixed congregations but were subjected to frequent discrimination. Informal religious communities of both free blacks and their enslaved brethren had a long, if obscure history in 18th-century Williamsburg, but when these groups tried to organize formally, they encountered fierce opposition from the white community. In 1793, after a protracted struggle, a group of 500 black men and women—headed by Williamsburg's noted black preacher, Gowan Pamphlet—were recognized as a formal congregation by the Dover, Virginia, Baptist Association

Williamsburg's free black community, as with others throughout Virginia, did not exist in a vacuum; it had close connections to the slave population. Given the small size of the free community and the official ban on INTERRACIAL MARRIAGE, free people of color frequently found their spouses among the slave population. As a result, black families often consisted of both free and enslaved members. Some men and women managed to purchase relatives and free them—through either formal or informal means.

In a society where the overwhelming majority of black men and women were enslaved, free African Americans all over Virginia occupied a curious and increasingly tenuous position. Representing as they did an alternate way of life for Southern blacks, they were viewed by white Virginians as a threat to the slave system. Free black communities were a natural source of aid and refuge for RUNAWAY SLAVES, especially in light of their frequent familial ties. No doubt their actual subversive activities were greatly exaggerated by their white neighbors, and individuals often lived in genuine amity with local whites; nevertheless, as the slavery debate intensified in Virginia throughout the antebellum period, free blacks as a whole faced growing suspicion and persecution.

In the wake of the WAR OF AMERICAN INDEPENDENCE (1775–83), and a flurry of revolutionary emancipations, Virginia's ruling class took steps to limit the size of the

state's free African-American population. In 1793, the state government passed a law prohibiting free people of color from immigrating to Virginia. Thirteen years later, in 1806, another law was passed, mandating that all newly emancipated black men and women leave the slate within 12 months or risk RE-ENSLAVEMENT. While it appears that neither of these laws was enforced rigidly, the simple fact of their existence testifies to the vulnerability of free black men and women throughout Virginia.

The African colonization movement—which advocated the removal of African Americans to LIBERIA—represented another attempt to decrease the number of Virginia's free people of color. Colonization fervor had its heyday in Virginia between approximately 1820 and 1840, and Williamsburg's free black population, as would their counterparts throughout the state, would have been subjected to significant pressure to emigrate (see EMIGRATION AND COLONIZATION). A series of slave rebellions—particularly Nat Turner's in 1831—added outright persecution to this pressure. What few civil rights enjoyed by free blacks were under increasing attack. In some counties, white mobs preyed on the free black population; Williamsburg's hard-won Baptist church was dissolved within a year of the revolt, and many free blacks fled the state and even the country to avoid fearful worsening conditions.

In spite of Virginia's efforts—both legal and extralegal—to limit the number of African Americans within its borders, the free black population actually increased throughout the antebellum period. But while these growing numbers may have helped free black communities to sustain themselves, they also contributed to the steady erosion of their civil rights and left them ever more vulnerable to persecution.

Caroline Hasenyager

FURTHER READING
Berlin, Ira. *Slaves without Masters: The Free Negro in the Antebellum South.* New York: Pantheon Books, 1974.

Ely, Melvin P. *Israel on the Appomattox: A Southern Experiment in Black Freedom from the 1790s to the Civil War.* New York: Knopf, 2005.

The Network, a Colonial Williamsburg Publication. Williamsburg, Va.: John D. Rockefeller Library, Colonial Williamsburg Foundation, 1999.

WISCONSIN

Free black trappers, traders, boatmen, and guides traversed the Wisconsin region in the late 18th century, including two free black traders who opened a post in the early 1790s at Marinette, near the mouth of the Menominee River. There were also French slaves in the territory

AFRICAN-AMERICAN POPULATION OF WISCONSIN, 1835–1900

Year	Slaves	Free People of Color	Free People of Color as a Percentage of Total Population	Total Population
1835	27	64	0.5%	11,683
1840	11	185	0.6%	30,945
1850		635	0.2%	305,391
1860		1,171	0.2%	775,881
1870		2,113	0.2%	1,054,670
1880		2,702	0.2%	1,315,497
1890		2,444	0.1%	1,686,880
1900		2,542	0.1%	2,069,042

of Wisconsin when the French ceded the territory to the British in 1760. The peace provisions allowed French residents to retain their "negro and Pawnee" slaves, who may have numbered as many as 500.

The growth of the lead mining industry in the Wisconsin territory drew greater numbers of white settlers in the 1820s and 1830s, many of whom were Southerners who took slaves with them. Some of these slaves were freed in Wisconsin, while others were sent or sold back into slavery in the South. In 1835, the territorial census of the Wisconsin region counted 27 slaves in a total black population of 91. By 1840, there were 11 slaves, but 185 free black residents. In 1850, there were 635 free blacks listed in the census, and no slaves. On the eve of the AMERICAN CIVIL WAR, the 1860 census listed 1,171 free black residents of the state, many of whom were probably RUNAWAY SLAVES who had arrived via the Underground Railroad.

Milwaukee and Racine had the largest black populations in the state in 1860, but in both cities, there were fewer than 100 black residents. In 1870, Racine's black population had risen only to 141, and Milwaukee's to just 176.

Although the urban centers remained relatively small, black settlers also arrived in rural counties, where they established communities of some size. The largest was in the Cheyenne Valley, Forest Township, Vernon County, which was first settled in 1855 by Walden Stewart, who was freeborn in SOUTH CAROLINA. By 1870, the population had grown to 62. Although the black families of Forest Township probably considered themselves part of a common community, their settlements were also interspersed with those of Norwegian, Irish, and Bohemian immigrants, with whom they shared equipment and labor and even intermarried. There was another focal point of black settlement in Grant County, where the 1860 census found 35 free blacks, 15 of them in the community of Pleasant Ridge.

Of all the midwestern states, Wisconsin during the 19th century developed probably the least negative reputation in its dealings with free blacks. (See BLACK LAWS IN THE MID-

WEST.) Although a black suffrage measure was proposed by the framers of the state's constitution, it was rejected by Wisconsin's voters in 1846. The right of black suffrage was not acknowledged until 1866, when a Milwaukee activist named Ezekiel Gillespie sued for the right to vote and carried his case to the Wisconsin Supreme Court, simply introducing the measure placed Wisconsin well ahead of other states in the Midwest before 1865 (see also VOTING BEFORE GENERAL ABOLITION, UNITED STATES).

As in other states in the region, the antebellum black population of Wisconsin was relatively small but did experience some growth in the decade preceding the Civil War. In 1840, only 200 free blacks lived in Wisconsin, but by 1860, that number had increased to roughly 1,200. This growth, although not massive, was encouraged by several factors that gave Wisconsin a reputation as a haven for black migrants. Although it generally did not represent the will of the entire populace, vigorous antebellum antislavery activism of both abolitionists and the state's supreme court gave blacks in Wisconsin a greater degree of freedom than they could hope for in other midwestern states.

The most famous antislavery incident in antebellum Wisconsin involved the fugitive slave Joshua Glover, who escaped a Milwaukee jail in 1854 with the assistance of an abolitionist mob. When the prosecuted leader of the breakout took his case to the Wisconsin Supreme Court, justices declared the federal FUGITIVE SLAVE ACT OF 1850 unconstitutional. The state supreme court's decision in the Joshua Glover case lent precedent to Wisconsin's 1857 law, "Of the Writ of Habeas Corpus Relative to Fugitive Slaves," which was specifically designed to allow alleged fugitives to appear before courts of law to appeal their confinement.

This generally liberal attitude toward fugitive slaves and hostility to slavery did not necessarily mean that Wisconsin residents welcomed all black settlers. In 1861, a black man accused of murder was dragged from the Milwaukee jail by a white mob and lynched, and in 1863, the state assembly considered petitions that would have outlawed further black immigration into Wisconsin. These measures were in keeping with the widespread anti-black sentiments of the Midwest as a region and were due in large part to fears that black migrants from the South would undermine white wage labor and cause social disruption by exciting prejudice and discrimination.

Despite the broader negative trends, however, Wisconsin remained a relatively welcoming state for blacks during the period after RECONSTRUCTION IN THE UNITED STATES. Milwaukee's black population rose from 304 in 1880 to 980 in 1910, and along with the growing population grew black churches, social organizations, and economic opportunities. But even with a relatively small black population, and a relatively liberal popular attitude toward them, Wisconsin's black population continued to experience SEGREGATION and unequal access to public facilities in the postwar era, an unpleasant reminder of the recent past. In December 1889, Milwaukee black leaders called a state convention that demanded an end to legal segregation in public places and state employment, a demand that was not realized for decades (*see also* NEGRO CONVENTION MOVEMENT IN THE UNITED STATES).

By the early decades of the 20th century, Wisconsin's black population remained small, segregated, and under-employed. The state experienced the revival of white supremacist ideologies in the 1920s, and it was not until the Civil Rights movement of the mid-20th century that Wisconsin's blacks finally began to realize the promise of the state's relatively liberal 19th-century beginnings.

Thomas Bahde

FURTHER READING

Baker, H. Robert. *The Rescue of Joshua Glover: A Fugitive Slave, the Constitution, and the Coming of the Civil War.* Athens: Ohio University Press, 2006.

Cooper, Zachary. *Black Settlers in Rural Wisconsin.* Madison: State Historical Society of Wisconsin, 1977.

Schwalm, Leslie A. *Emancipation's Diaspora: Race and Reconstruction in the Upper Midwest.* Chapel Hill: University of North Carolina Press, 2009.

WOODSON, LEWIS (1806–1878) *American minister and abolitionist*

A leader in the AFRICAN METHODIST EPISCOPAL CHURCH, Lewis Woodson was a prominent free black in OHIO and western PENNSYLVANIA. One of the most dedicated early black abolitionists and an original trustee and founder of Wilberforce University, he was also a writer and educator. He was born in January 1806 to Thomas and Jemima Woodson in Greenbrier County, Virginia, and lived in Chillicothe, Ohio, and PITTS-BURGH, PENNSYLVANIA. He is perhaps most famous for a colonization scheme he outlined in *Freedom's Journal* in 1829 and expanded under the pen name Augustine between December 1837 and February 1838 in the *Colored American.* (*See also* EMIGRATION AND COLONIZATION and MIGRATION.)

Woodson's plan involved settlement in the American West, where he hoped a select group of black pioneers could create an independent colony, the success of which would prove their equality. He insisted that, whether they liked it or not, blacks formed a "distinct class" in America, and it was up to them to better their own condition. He compared the situation of black Americans to that of the Irish, Spanish, Turkish, and Russian people, who were stereotyped as "low, ignorant and degraded" even though "there may be found in all these countries, many who excel in whatever is elegant, polite and refined." As with African Americans, "the few who have risen above the condition of the many, are not regarded [and] . . . their virtues and attainments will never be fully appreciated, until the majority of the class with whom they are identified, have risen to something like a level with themselves." One of the most challenging obstacles was the need for "union and concert of action," which was impossible to achieve with a population that was "scattered over a vast surface of country, and settled in small communities at a great distance form each other, knowing little of each other, and feeling but little interest in each other's welfare." A black western settlement plan would solve the dilemma of unity. His idea set off a debate with SAMUEL E. CORNISH, the editor of the paper. Both men agreed that westward migration could serve as a vehicle for securing black independence, but Cornish disagreed with the idea of creating exclusive black settlements.

Woodson responded by defending separate black settlements. First, he pointed out that, given the racial climate in many eastern cities, "contact" must not necessarily foster friendship. Next, he insisted that groups like the Quakers had separated to form their own settlements within the larger communities they sought to influence. He insisted that there was a clear difference between black-led colonization in the western United States and white-led "Back to Africa" movements such as that advocated by the AMERICAN COLONIZATION SOCIETY. Finally, he pointed out that he was not advocating mass exodus of all blacks to the West. Instead, what he wanted to create was an asylum where a group of American blacks could succeed independently and prove their worth to white Americans, themselves, and their fellow African Americans. Woodson was a mentor to MARTIN DELANY, and much of his plan can be seen in Delany's later scheme for an African settlement, though Woodson himself never advocated African emigration.

Woodson also participated in the first Negro Convention in Philadelphia, Pennsylvania, in 1830 (*see* Negro Convention Movement in the United States), helped John B. Vashon (*see* Vashon family) to establish the African Education Society in Pittsburgh, and advocated black education efforts in Pennsylvania and Ohio in the 1830s. He also helped to establish the Ohio District of the African Methodist Episcopal (A.M.E.) Church, as well as that organization's Union Seminary. He served as secretary for the group of black leaders who fought in vain to help black Pennsylvanians retain the vote, issuing a document called the Pittsburgh Memorial,

and he joined the Western District of the Pennsylvania Anti-Slavery Society. He died on January 14, 1878.

See also Black Press in the United States.

Beverly C. Tomek

FURTHER READING

Miller, Floyd L. *The Search for a Black Nationality: Black Colonization and Emigration, 1787–1863.* Urbana: University of Illinois Press, 1975.

Ripley, C. Peter, ed. *The Black Abolitionist Papers.* Vol. 3, *The United States, 1830–1846.* Chapel Hill: University of North Carolina Press, 1991.

Smith, Eric Ledell. "The Pittsburgh Memorial." *Pittsburgh History* 80 no. 3 (Fall 1997): 106–107.

ZAMBO

In Spanish America, a person of mixed African and Indian ancestry. African slaves in Spanish America in the 16th and 17th centuries were often imported to work as supervisors and technical advisers of primarily Indian workforces. The African slaves, as were the Spanish conquistadores, were almost exclusively male, and naturally, relations developed between them and Indian women. The children of these relationships were often just raised as and thought of as Indians, but if the couple married—more common if the African male partner was free, and thus more common later in the colonial period—then their offspring would be officially referred to as a zambo/a. To the extent that the couple lived in the larger society, outside the largely separate world of the Indian villages, their zambo children would develop a separate racial identity as another part of the CASTA group.

Stewart R. King

ZUMBI (ca. 1655–1695) *Brazilian rebel slave leader*

Little is known about Zumbi, the last leader of Palmares, the long-lived 17th-century *quilombo*, or community of MAROONS, located in the modern-day Brazilian state of Alagoas (*see also* BRAZILIAN MAROONS). Zumbi may, in fact, have been a title rather than his name. The Angolan slave of a Brazilian priest, he had run away as a teenager. After the time of the 1678 treaty signed by Ganga Zumba and the governor of Pernambuco, Zumbi emerged as leader of the faction within Palmares that rejected peace with the Portuguese. When hostilities resumed in the 1680s, Zumbi was the undisputed leader of Palmares. He rejected peace overtures that included offers of freedom for himself and his family and was killed on November 20, 1695, by the São Paulo backwoodsmen who led the final assault on Palmares.

In the late 20th century, Zumbi became a symbol of the Brazilian black movement, for whom he is a hero in the struggle against slavery, although there is no evidence that the fugitives in Palmares sought to end slavery. The date of his death is today commemorated as the national

A 20th-century statue of Zumbi, leader of the maroon community of Palmares during its final confrontation with the Brazilian authorities in 1695. The anniversary of his death, November 20, is now celebrated in Brazil as Zumbi Day, a day to recognize and celebrate Afro-Brazilian heritage. (© *Jenny Matthews/Alamy*)

day of black consciousness and is a holiday in some parts of the country. In 1986, a monument to Zumbi was raised in Rio de Janeiro.

Hendrik Kraay

FURTHER READING

Schwartz, Stuart B. "Rethinking Palmares: Slave Resistance in Colonial Brazil." In *Slaves, Peasants, and Rebels: Reconsidering Brazilian Slavery*, 103–136. Urbana: University of Illinois Press, 1992.

Bibliography

Abernathy, Francis Edward, ed. *Juneteenth Texas: Essays in African American Folklore.* Denton: University of North Texas Press, 1996.

Ackerson Wayne. *The African Institution (1807–1827) and the Antislavery Movement in Great Britain.* Lewiston, N.Y.: Mellen Press, 2005.

Acuña, María de los Ángeles, and Doriam Chavarría. *El mestizaje: la sociedad multirracial en la ciudad de Cartago (1738–1821).* Master's thesis, Universidad de Costa Rica, 1991.

Adams, John. *Old Square-Toes and His Lady: The Life of James and Amelia Douglas.* Victoria, Canada: Horsdal & Schubert, 2001.

Adams, John Quincy. *Amistad Argument.* New York: S. W. Benedict, 1841. Reprint, Whitefish, Mont.: Kessinger, 2004.

Ade-Ajayi, J. F. *A Patriot to the Core: Bishop Ajayi Crowther.* Santa Rosa, Calif.: Spectrum Books, 2002.

Adeleke, Tunde. *UnAfrican Americans: Nineteenth-Century Black Nationalists and the Civilizing Mission.* Lexington: University of Kentucky Press, 1998.

———. *Without Regard to Race: The Other Martin Robinson Delany.* Jackson: University Press of Mississippi, 2003.

Aguilar Bulgarelli, Oscar. *La esclavitud negra en Costa Rica. Origen de la oligarquía económica y política nacional.* San José: Editorial Progreso, 1997.

Aguirre Beltrán, Gonzalo. *Cuijla, Esbozo etnográfico de un pueblo negro.* México: FCE-SEP, 1985. (Col. Lecturas Mexicanas).

Alegría, Ricardo E. *Juan Garrido, El Conquistador Negro en las Antillas, Florida, México y California c. 1503–1540.* San Juan, P.R.: Centro Estudios Avanzados de Puerto Rico y el Caribe, 1990.

Alexander, Leslie M. *African or American? Black Identity and Political Activism in New York City, 1784–1861.* Urbana: University of Illinois Press, 2008.

Alexander, Thomas B. *Political Reconstruction in Tennessee.* New York: Russell & Russell, 1968.

Alford, Terry. *Prince among Slaves: The True Story of an African Prince Sold into Slavery in the American South.* New York: Harcourt Brace Jovanovich, 1977.

Alie, Joe A. D. *A New History of Sierra Leone.* New York: St. Martin's Press, 1990.

Allen, Rose Mary. *Di Ki Manera: A Social History of Afro-Curaçaoans, 1863–1917.* Amsterdam, Netherlands: SWP, 2007.

Allende-Goitía, Noel. "The Mulatta, the Bishop, and Dances in the Cathedral: Race, Music, and Power Relations in Seventeenth-Century Puerto Rico." *Black Music Research Journal* 26, no. 2 (Fall 2006): 137–164.

Alves, Castro. *The Major Abolitionist Poems of Castro Alves.* Translated by James J. Wilhelm. London: Routledge, 1990.

Amistad: Martin Van Buren and John Quincy Adams: Original Manuscripts from the Gilder Lehrman Collection. Introduction by David Brion Davis. New York: Gilder Lehrman Institute of American History, 1998.

Ammon, Harry. *James Monroe: The Quest For National Identity.* Charlottesville: University Press of Virginia, 1990.

Anbinder, Tyler. *Five Points: The Nineteenth-Century New York City Neighborhood That Invented Tap Dance, Stole Elections and Became the World's Most Notorious Slum.* New York: Free Press, 2001.

Anderson, Eric. "Black Émigrés: The Emergence of Nineteenth-Century United States Black Nationalism in Response to Haitian Emigration, 1816–1840." *49th Parallel: An Interdisciplinary Journal of North American Studies* 1 (Winter 1999).

Anderson, Robert. "The Quilombo of Palmares: A New Overview of a Maroon State in Seventeenth-Century Brazil." *Journal of Latin American Studies* 28, no. 3 (October 1996): 545–566.

Andrews, George Reid. "The Afro-Argentine Officers of Buenos Aires Province, 1800–1860." *Journal of Negro History* 64, no. 2 (1979): 85–100.

———. *The Afro-Argentines of Buenos Aires, 1800–1900.* Madison: University of Wisconsin Press, 1980.

———. *Afro-Latin America, 1800–2000.* New York: Oxford University Press, 2004.

———. *The Methodists and Revolutionary America, 1760–1800: The Shaping of an Evangelical Culture.* Princeton, N.J.: Princeton University Press, 2002.

———. "Race versus Class Association: The Afro-Argentines of Buenos Aires, 1850–1900." *Journal of Latin American Studies* 11, no. 1 (1979): 19–39.

Andrews, William L. *To Tell a Free Story: The First Century of Afro-American Autobiography, 1760–1865.* Urbana: University of Illinois Press, 1986.

Angola Maconde, Juan. "Los afrodescendientes bolivianos." *Journal of Latin American and Caribbean Anthropology* 12, no. 1 (April 2007): 246–253.

Angrand, Jean-Luc. *Céleste ou le temps des signares.* Paris: Éditions Anne Pépin, 2006.

Anthony, Michael. *Historical Dictionary of Trinidad and Tobago.* Lanham, Md.: Scarecrow Press, 1997.

Antoin, F. D. *Lantamentu di katibu na Boneiru.* Bonaire, Netherlands Antilles: National Printing Bonaire, 1997.

Antón Sánchez, John. *Sistema de indicadores sociales del pueblo Afroecuatoriano.* Santiago de Chile: CEPAL, 2005.

Applebaum, Nancy, ed. *Race and Nation in Modern Latin America.* Chapel Hill: University of North Carolina Press, 2003.

Applegate, Anne. "Phillis Wheatley: Her Critics and Her Contribution." *Negro American Literature Forum* 9, no. 4 (Winter 1975): 123–126.

Archivo General de la Nación. "El sentimiento patriótico de Francisco del Rosario Sánchez." Available online. URL: http://www.agn.gov.do/departamentos-agn-dominicana/dep-hemeroteca-biblioteca/historia-dominicana/596-el-sentimiento-patriotico-de-francisco-del-rosario-sanchez.html. Accessed October 30, 2008.

Ardouin, Beaubrun. *Etudes sur l'histoire d'Haiti* followed by *La vie du général J.-M. Borgella.* 11 Vols. Paris: Dezobry et E. Magdeleine, 1853–1860.

Ashmore, Harry S. *Arkansas: A Bicentennial History.* New York: W. W. Norton, 1978.

Atkins, John. *A Voyage to Guinea, Brasil, and the West Indies.* London: C. Ward & R. Chandler, 1735.

Austin, Allen. *African Muslims in Antebellum America: Transatlantic Stories and Spiritual Struggles.* London: Routledge, 1997.

Azevedo, Célia Maria Marinho de. *Abolitionism in the United States and Brazil: A Comparative Perspective.* New York: Garland, 1995.

Azevedo, Elciene. *Orfeu de Carapinha. A trajetória de Luiz Gama na imeprial cidade de São Paulo.* Vol. 1, 2nd ed. Campinas: Editora da Unicamp, 1999.

Bacon, Jacqueline. *Freedom's Journal: The First African-American Newspaper.* Lanham, Md.: Lexington Books, 2007.

———. *The Humblest May Stand Forth: Rhetoric, Empowerment, and Abolition.* Columbia: University of South Carolina Press, 2002.

Bacon, Margaret Hope. *But One Race: The Life of Robert Purvis.* Albany: State University of New York Press, 2007.

Bailey, Anne J., and Daniel E. Sutherland, eds. *Civil War Arkansas: Beyond Battles and Leaders.* Fayetteville: University of Arkansas Press, 2000.

Baker, H. Robert. *The Rescue of Joshua Glover: A Fugitive Slave, the Constitution, and the Coming of the Civil War.* Athens: Ohio University Press, 2006.

Baker, Jean. *James Buchanan.* New York: Times Books, 2004.

Ballew, Christopher Brent. *The Impact of African-American Antecedents on the Baptist Foreign Missionary Movement, 1782–1825.* New York: Edwin Mellen Press, 2004.

Barber, John Warner, comp. *A History of the Amistad Captives.* New Haven, Conn.: E. L. & J. W. Barber, 1840. Reprint, New York: Arno Press, 1969.

Barman, Roderick. *Brazil: The Forging of a Nation, 1798–1852.* Palo Alto, Calif.: Stanford University Press, 1988.

———. *Princess Isabel of Brazil: Gender and Power in the Nineteenth Century.* Wilmington, Del.: SR Books, 2002.

Barnes, Hugh. *The Stolen Prince: Gannibal, Adopted Son of Peter the Great, Great-Grandfather of Alexander Pushkin, and Europe's First Black Intellectual.* New York: Ecco, 2006.

———. *Brazil: The Forging of A Nation, 1798–1852.* Palo Alto, Calif.: Stanford University Press, 1988.

Barr, Alwyn. *The African Texans.* College Station: Texas A&M University Press, 2004.

———. *Black Texans: A History of African Americans in Texas, 1528–1995.* Norman: University of Oklahoma Press, 1996.

———. *The Freedmen's Bureau and Black Texans.* Austin: University of Texas Press, 1992.

Barry, William David. "The Shameful Story of Malaga Island." *Down East,* November 1980.

Bauer, Fr. Roy. "They Called Him Father Gus." Available online. URL: http://www.cospq.org/Parish%20History/Tolton%20Biography.htm. Accessed May 7, 2010.

Baumann, Roland. *Constructing Black Education at Oberlin College: A Documentary History.* Athens: Ohio University Press, 2010.

Bayley, Frederic William Naylor. *Four Years' Residence in the West Indies: During the Years 1826, 7, 8, and 9.* London: William Kidd, 1833. Available online. URL: http://books.google.com/books?id=AiljAAAAMAAJ&source=gbs_navlinks_s. Accessed March 10, 2010.

Beckles, Hilary McD. *Centering Woman: Gender Discourses in Caribbean Slave Society.* New York: Markus Wiener, 1998.

———. "Freeing Slavery: Gender Paradigms in the Social History of Caribbean Slavery." In *Slavery, Freedom and Gender: The Dynamics of Caribbean Society,* edited by Brian L. Moore, B. W. Higman, Carl Campbell, and Patrick Bryan, 197–231. Mona: University of the West Indies Press, 2003.

———. *A History of Barbados: From Amerindian Settlement to Nation State.* New York: Cambridge University Press, 2007.

Beckwourth, James Pierson. *The Life and Adventures of James P. Beckwourth as Told to Thomas D. Bonner.* 1856. Reprint, Lincoln: University of Nebraska Press, 1972.

Bell, Howard H. *Minutes of the Proceedings of the National Negro Conventions, 1830–1864.* Manchester, N.H.: Ayers, 1969.

Bell, Madison Smartt. *All Souls' Rising.* New York: Pantheon Books, 1995.

———. *Master of the Crossroads.* New York: Pantheon Books, 2000.

————. *Toussaint Louverture: A Biography*. New York: Pantheon, 2007.

Bellamy, Donnie D. "The Legal Status of Black Georgians during the Colonial and Revolutionary Eras." *Journal for Negro History* 74, no. 1 (Winter–Autumn, 1989): 1–10.

Benett, Herman. *Africans in Colonial Mexico: Absolutism, Christianity, and Afro-Creole Consciousness, 1570–1640*. Bloomington: Indiana University Press, 2003.

Bentley, George R. *A History of the Freedmen's Bureau*. Philadelphia: University of Pennsylvania, 1955.

Bergad, Laird W. *The Comparative Histories of Slavery in Brazil, Cuba, and the United States*. Cambridge: Cambridge University Press, 2007.

Berlin, Ira. *Many Thousands Gone: The First Two Centuries of Slavery in America*. Cambridge, Mass.: Harvard University Press, 1998.

————. *Slaves without Masters: The Free Negro in the Antebellum South*. New York: W. W. Norton, 1974.

Berlin, Ira, Barbara J. Fields, and Steven F. Miller, eds. *Free at Last: A Documentary History of Slavery, Freedom, and the Civil War*. New York: New Press, 1995.

Bernasconi, Robert, and Tommy Lee Lott, eds. *The Idea of Race*. New York: Hackett, 2000.

Bernstein, Iver. *The New York City Draft Riots: Their Significance for American Society and Politics in the Age of the Civil War*. New York: Oxford University Press, 1990.

Berry, Frances B., and John W. Blassingame. *Long Memory: The Black Experience in America*. New York: Oxford University Press, 1982.

Berry, Mary Francis. *My Face Is Black Is True: Callie House and the Struggle for Ex-Slave Reparations*. New York: Alfred A. Knopf, 2005.

Bethel, Leslie, ed. *The Cambridge History of Latin America*. Vol. 2, *Colonial Latin America*. Cambridge University Press, 1998.

————, ed. *The Cambridge History of Latin America*. Vol. 3, *From Independence to c. 1870*. Cambridge: Cambridge University Press, 1985, chap. 3.

————, ed. *Colonial Brazil*. Cambridge: Cambridge University Press, 1987.

————. "The Independence of Spanish South America." In *The Independence of Spanish America*, edited by Leslie Bethell. New York: Cambridge University Press, 1991.

Beyan, Amos J. *African American Settlements in West Africa: John Brown Russwurm and the American Civilizing Efforts*. New York: Palgrave Macmillan, 2005.

Bigham, David E. *On Jordan's Banks: Emancipation and Its Aftermath in the Ohio Valley*. Lexington: University Press of Kentucky, 2005.

Billington, Monroe Lee, and Roger D. Hardaway, eds. *African Americans on the Western Frontier*. Boulder: University Press of Colorado, 1998.

Birkner, Michael J., ed. *James Buchanan and the Political Crisis of the 1850s*. Selinsgrove, Pa.: Susquehanna University Press, 1996.

Birnbaum, Jonathan, and Clarence Taylor, eds. *Civil Rights since 1787: A Reader on the Black Struggle*. New York: New York University Press, 2000.

Blackburn, Robin. *The Making of New World Slavery: From the Baroque to the Modern, 1492–1800*. London: Verso, 1997.

————. *The Overthrow of Colonial Slavery, 1776–1848*. London: Verso, 1988.

Blackett, R. J. M. *Building an Anti-Slavery Wall: Black Americans in the Atlantic Abolitionist Movement, 1830–1860*. Baton Rouge: Louisiana State University Press, 1983.

————. "Freedom, or the Martyr's Grave: Black Pittsburgh's Aid to the Fugitive Slave." In *African Americans in Pennsylvania: Shifting Historical Perspectives*, edited by Joe William Trotter, Jr., and Eric Ledell Smith. University Park: Pennsylvania State University Press, 1997.

Blake, Gregory. *To Pierce the Tyrant's Heart: A Military History of the Battle for the Eureka Stockade 3 December 1854*. Loftus, New South Wales: Australian Military History Publications, 2008.

Blanchard, Peter. *Under the Flags of Freedom: Slave Soldiers and the Wars of Independence in Spanish South America*. Pittsburgh: University of Pittsburgh Press, 2008.

Blankaert, Claude. "Of Monstrous Métis? Hybridity, Fear of Miscegenation, and Patriotism from Buffon to Paul Broca." In *The Color of Liberty: Histories of Race in France*, edited by Sue Peabody and Tyler Stovall. Durham, N.C.: Duke University Press, 2003.

Blassingame, John W. *Black New Orleans 1860–1880*. Chicago: University of Chicago Press, 1976.

————, ed. *The Frederick Douglass Papers, Series One: Speeches, Debates, and Interviews*. 5 vols. New Haven, Conn.: Yale University Press, 1979–92.

Blight, David W. *Frederick Douglass' Civil War: Keeping Faith in Jubilee*. Baton Rouge: Louisiana State University Press, 1989.

Bluett, Thomas. *Some Memories of the Life of Job, the Son of the Solomon High Priest of Boonda in Africa; Who Was a Slave about Two Years in Maryland; and Afterwards Being Brought to England, Was Set Free, and Sent to His Native Land in the Year 1734*. London: Richard Ford, 1734. Available online. URL: http://docsouth.unc.edu/neh/bluett/bluett.html/. Accessed January 13, 2011.

Bocanegra José María. *Memorias para la historia de México independiente*. México: Instituto Cultural Helénico-INERM, 1986–87.

Boley, G. E. Saigbe. *Liberia: The Rise and Fall of the First Republic*. New York: MacMillan, 1983.

Bolland, O. Nigel. *Colonialism and Resistance in Belize*. Benque Viejo del Carmen, Belize: Cubola Press, 1988.

———. *The Formation of a Colonial Society: Belize from Conquest to Crown Colony.* Baltimore: Johns Hopkins University Press, 1977.

Bolland, O. Nigel, and Assad Shoman. *Land in Belize, 1765–1781.* Kingston, Jamaica: University of the West Indies Press, 1977.

Bolster, W. Jeffrey. *Black Jacks: African-American Seamen in the Age of Sail.* Cambridge, Mass.: Harvard University Press, 1998.

Bond, Bradley G. *Political Culture in the Nineteenth-Century South.* Baton Rouge: Louisiana State University Press, 1995.

Bonner, Thomas D. *The Life and Adventures of James P. Beckwourth.* New York: Harper and Brothers, 1856.

Bordewich, Fergus M. *Bound for Canaan: The Underground Railroad and the War for the Soul of America.* New York: HarperCollins, 2005.

Borome, Joseph A. "The Autobiography of Hiram Rhodes Revels Together with Some Letters by and about Him." *Midwest Journal* 5 (Winter 1952–1953): 79–92.

Boucher, Morris Raymond. "The Free Negro in Alabama Prior to 1860." Ph.D. diss, University of Iowa, 1950.

Boyer, Richard, and Geoffrey Spurling. *Colonial Lives: Documents on Latin American History, 1550–1850.* New York: Oxford University Press, 1999.

Brace, Jeffrey. *The Blind African Slave, or Memoirs of Boyrereau Brinch, Nick-Named Jeffrey Brace.* Chapel Hill: University of North Carolina at Chapel Hill, 1810. Available online. URL: http://docsouth.unc.edu/neh/brinch/brinch.html. Accessed January 13, 2011.

Brackett, Jeffrey R. *The Negro in Maryland.* Baltimore: Jos. Murphy, 1889.

Bradford, Sarah. *Harriet Tubman: The Moses of Her People,* 1881. Reprint, New York: Corinth Books, 1961.

———. *Scenes in the Life of Harriet Tubman.* 1867. Reprint, Freeport: Books for Libraries Press, 1971.

Breen, T. H., and Stephen Innes. *"Myne Own Ground": Race and Freedom on Virginia's Eastern Shore, 1640–1676.* New York: Oxford University Press, 1980.

Bridikhina, Eugenia. *La mujer negra en Bolivia.* La Paz, Bolivia: Librería Editorial Juventud, 1995.

Brière, Jean-François. "Abbé Grégoire and Haitian Independence." *Research in African Literatures* 35, no. 2 (2004): 34–43.

Brizan, George. *Grenada, Island of Conflict.* London and Basingstoke, England: Macmillan Education, 1998.

Brodie, Fawn M. *Thomas Jefferson: An Intimate History.* New York: W. W. Norton & Company, 1974.

Brooks, Charles H. *The Official History and Manual of the Grand United Order of Odd Fellows in the United States.* Philadelphia: 1902. Available online. URL: http://books.google.com/books?id=Sj-jv2g7utcC&source=gbs_navlinks_s. Accessed January 13, 2011.

Brooks James F., ed. *Confounding the Color Line: The Indian-Black Experience in North America.* Lincoln: University of Nebraska Press, 2002.

Brown, Christopher Leslie. *Moral Capital: Foundations of British Abolitionism.* Chapel Hill: University of North Carolina Press, 2006.

Brown, Eliza Smith, ed. *African American Historic Sites Survey of Allegheny County.* Harrisburg: Pennsylvania Historical and Museum Commission, 1994.

Brown, Henry Box. *Narrative of the Life of Henry Box Brown,* edited by Richard Newman. New York: Oxford University Press, 2002.

Brown, Rose. *American Emperor: Dom Pedro II of Brazil.* New York: Viking, 1945.

Brown, Thomas, and Leah Sims. "'To Swear Him Free': Ethnic Memory as Social Capital in 18th Century Freedom Petitions." In *Colonial Chesapeake: New Perspectives,* edited by Debra Meyers and Melanie Perreault. New York: Lexington Books, 2006.

Brown, William Wells. *The Black Man, His Antecedents, His Genius, and His Achievements.* New York: Thomas Hamilton, 1863.

Bryant, Linda. *I Cannot Tell a Lie: The True Story of George Washington's African American Descendants.* Bloomington, Ind.: iUniverse Star, 2004.

Budiansky, Stephen. *The Bloody Shirt: Terror after Appomattox.* New York: Viking, 2008.

Bullock, H. A. *A History of Negro Education in the South from 1619 to the Present.* New York: Praeger, 1970.

Bullock, Steven. *Revolutionary Brotherhood: Freemasonry and the Transformation of the American Social Order, 1730–1840.* Chapel Hill: University of North Carolina Press, 1998.

Burin, Eric. *Slavery and the Peculiar Solution: A History of the American Colonization Society.* Miami: University Press of Florida, 2005.

Burns, E. Bradford. "The Intellectuals as Agents of Change and the Independence of Brazil." In *From Colony to Nation: Essays on the Independence of Brazil,* edited by A. J. R. Russell-Wood. Baltimore: Johns Hopkins University Press, 1975.

Burton, Art T. *Black Gun, Silver Star: The Life and Legend of Frontier Marshal Bass Reeves.* Lincoln: University of Nebraska Press, 2006.

Busdiecker, Sara. "Where Blackness Resides: Afro-Bolivians and the Spatializing and Racializing of the African Diaspora." *Radical History Review* 103 (Winter 2009): 105–116.

Bush, Barbara. "White 'Ladies,' Coloured 'Favourites' and Black 'Wenches': Some Considerations on Sex, Race, and Class Factors in Social Relations in White Creole Society in the British Caribbean." *Slavery and Abolition* 2 (1981): 245–262.

Bushnell, David. "The Independence of Spanish South America." In *The Independence of Spanish America,* edited by David Bushnell. Cambridge: University of Cambridge Press, 1987.

———. *The Making of Modern Colombia: A Nation in Spite of Itself.* Berkeley: University of California Press, 1993.

———. *Reform and Reaction in the Platine Provinces, 1810–1852.* Gainesville: University of Florida Press, 1983.

Busto Duthurburu, José Antonio del. *Breve historia de los negros del Perú.* Lima: Congreso de la República, 2000.

Butchart, Ronald. *Northern Schools, Southern Blacks, and Reconstruction: Freedmen's Education, 1862–1875.* Westport, Conn.: Greenwood Press, 1980.

Butler, Kim D. *Freedom Given, Freedom Won: Afro-Brazilians in Post-Abolition Sao Paulo and Salvador.* New Brunswick, N.J.: Rutgers University Press, 1998.

Byrd, Alexander X. *Captives and Voyagers: Black Migrants across the Eighteenth-Century British Atlantic World.* Baton Rouge: Loiusiana State University Press, 2008.

Cabeza de Vaca, Alvar Nuñez. *Chronicle of the Narváez Expedition.* Translated by Fanny Bandelier; revised and annotated by Harold Augenbraum; introduction by Ilan Stavans. New York: Penguin, 2002.

Cáceres Gómez, Rina. "The African Origins of San Fernando de Omoa." In *Trans-Atlantic Dimensions of Ethnicity in the African Diaspora*, edited by Paul Lovejoy and David Trotman, 115–138. London: Continuum, 2003.

———. *Negros, mulatos, esclavos y libertos en la Costa Rica del siglo XVII.* México-D.F.: Instituto Panamericano de Geografía e Historia, 2000.

Caldwell, Helen. *Machado de Assis: Reflections on a Brazilian Master Writer.* Berkeley: University of California Press, 1970.

California State University Sacramento Library. "The California Underground Railroad." Available online. URL: http://digital.lib.csus.edu/curr/. Accessed January 13, 2011.

Calloway, Bertha W., and Alonzo N. Smith. *Visions of Freedom on the Great Plains: An Illustrated History of African Americans in Nebraska.* Virginia Beach, Va.: Donning, 1998.

Campbell, James T. *Songs of Zion: The African Methodist Episcopal Church in the United States and South Africa.* New York: Oxford University Press, 1995.

Campbell, Mavis. *The Dynamics of Change in Slave Society: A Socio-Political History of the Free Coloreds Jamaica, 1800–1865.* London: Associated University Presses, 1976.

Campos, Luís Eugenio. "Negros y morenos: La población afromexicana de la Costa Chica de Oaxaca." In *Configuraciones étnicas en Oaxaca.* Perspectivas etnográficas para las autonomías, vol. 2. Mexico City: Editorial CONACULTA-INAH-NI, 2000.

Carboni, Raffello. *The Eureka Stockade.* Carlton, Australia: Miegunyah Press, 2004.

Caretta, Vincent. *Equiano the African: Biography of a Self-Made Man.* Athens: University of Georgia Press, 2005.

Carmagnani, Marcello. "Colonial Latin American Demography: Growth of Chilean Population." *Journal of Social History* 1 (1967): 179–191.

Caroll, Patrick. *Blacks in Colonial Veracruz: Race, Ethnicity, and Regional Development.* Austin: University of Texas Press, 2001.

Carpentier, Alejo. *The Kingdom of this World.* Translated by Harriet Onis. New York: Knopf, 1957.

Carretta, Vincent. *Equiano the African: Biography of a Self-Made Man.* Athens: University of Georgia Press, 2005.

———, ed. *Ignatius Sancho: Letters of the Late Igatius Sancho, an African.* New York: Penguin Books, 1998.

———. "Sancho, (Charles) Ignatius (1729?–1780)." In *Oxford Dictionary of National Biography*, edited by H. C. G. Matthew and Brian Harrison. Oxford: Oxford University Press, 2004. Available online. URL: www.oxforddnb.com.library.unl.edu/view/article/24609. Accessed June 1, 2011.

Carretta, Vincent, and Philip Gould, eds. *Genius in Bondage: Literature of the Early Black Atlantic.* Lexington: University Press of Kentucky, 2001.

Carroll, Patrick. *Blacks in Colonial Veracruz: Race, Ethnicity and Regional Development.* Austin: University of Texas Press, 1991.

Carson, James Taylor. *Searching for the Bright Path: The Mississippi Choctaws from Prehistory to Removal.* Lincoln: University of Nebraska Press, 1999.

Castellanos, Jorge. *Placido, poeta social y politico.* Ediciones Universal, 1984.

Castillero Calvo, Alfredo. *Historia general de Panamá.* Vol. 1, T. 1 and 2. Panamá: Comité Nacional del Centenario, 2004.

Castro, Hebe Maria Mattos de. "'Terras de Quilombo': Land Rights, Memory of Slavery, and Ethnic Identification in Contemporary Brazil." In *Africa, Brazil, and the Construction of Trans-Atlantic Black Identities*, edited by Boubacar Barry, Elisee Akpo Soumonni, and Livio Sansone. Trenton, N.J.: Africa World Press, 2008.

Cavallini, Giuliana. *St. Martin de Porres: Apostle of Charity.* Charlotte, N.C.: T A N Books, 1979.

Chace, Russel. "Protest in Post-Emancipation Dominica: The 'Guerre Nègre' of 1844." Paper presented at the Conference [Association] of Caribbean Historians, UWI Mona, Jamaica, 15–20 April 1983.

Cha-Jua, Sundiata Keita. *America's First Black Town: Brooklyn, Illinois, 1830–1915.* Urbana: University of Illinois Press, 2000.

Chasteen, John Charles. *Americanos: Latin America's Struggle for Independence.* New York: Oxford University Press, 2008.

———. *Heroes on Horseback: A Life and Times of the Last Gaucho Caudillos.* Albuquerque: University of New Mexico Press, 1995.

Cheek, William F., and Aimee Lee Cheek. *John Mercer Langston and the Fight for Black Freedom, 1829–65.* Urbana: University of Illinois Press, 1996.

———. "John Mercer Langston: Principle and Politics." In *Black Leaders of the Nineteenth Century*, edited by Leon Litwack and August Meier, eds., Urbana: University of Illinois Press, 1998.

Chesnutt, Helen M. *Charles Waddell Chesnutt: Pioneer of the Color Line*. Chapel Hill: University of North Carolina Press, 1952.

"Le Chevalier de Saint-Georges (1745–1799), Afro-French Composer, Violinist and Conductor, France's Best Fencer and Colonel of Black Legion." Available online. URL: http://chevalierdesaintgeorges.homestead.com/page1.html#33. Accessed January 13, 2011.

Christian, Charles M. *Black Saga: The African American Experience*. Boston: Houghton Mifflin, 1995.

Christopher, R. Reed. "African American Life in Antebellum Chicago, 1833–1860." *Journal of the Illinois State Historical Society* 94 (Winter 2001–2002): 356–382.

———. *Black Chicago's First Century*. Vol. 1, *1833–1900*. Columbia: University of Missouri Press, 2005.

Clamorgan, Cyprian. *The Colored Aristocracy of St. Louis*. Columbia: Missouri University Press, 1999.

Clark, John, Walter Dendy, James Mursell Phillippo, and David J. East. *The Voice of Jubilee: A Narrative of the Baptist Mission, Jamaica*. London: J. Snow, 1865.

Clark, Kenneth M. "James Madison and Slavery." Madison Museum Website. Available online. URL: http://www.jamesmadisonmus.org/textpages/clark.htm. Accessed January 13, 2011.

Clarkson, John. "Mission to America." Birchtown, Nova Scotia, Canada: Black Loyalist Heritage Society Online Digital Project. Available online. URL: http://www.blackloyalist.com/canadiandigitalcollection/documents/diaries/mission.htm. Accessed February 28, 2010.

Clifford, Mary Louise. *From Slavery to Freetown: Black Loyalists after the American Revolution*. London: McFarland, 1999.

Clinton, Catherine. *Harriet Tubman: The Road to Freedom*. New York: Little, Brown, 2004.

Clinton, Catherine, and Michele Gillespie, eds. *The Devil's Lane: Sex and Race in the Early South*. New York: Oxford University Press, 1997.

Cohen, David, and Jack Greene, eds. *Neither Slave nor Free: The Freedman of African Descent in the Slave Societies of the New World*. Baltimore: Johns Hopkins University Press, 1974.

Cole, Hubert. *Christophe: King of Haiti*. New York: Viking Press, 1967.

Congar, Yves, O. P. *The Catholic Church and the Race Question*. Geneva: UNESCO, 1953.

Conrad, Robert. *The Destruction of Brazilian Slavery*. Berkeley: University of California Press, 1972.

Cooper, Zachary. *Black Settlers in Rural Wisconsin*. Madison: State Historical Society of Wisconsin, 1977.

Cormack, William S. "Victor Hugues and the Reign of Terror on Guadeloupe, 1794–1798." In *Essays in French Colonial History*, edited by A. J. B. Johnson. East Lansing: Michigan State University Press, 1997.

Cornish, Dudley Taylor. *The Sable Arm: Black Troops in the Union Army, 1861–1865*. Reprint, Lawrence: University of Kansas Press, 1987.

Cortner, Richard C. *A Mob Intent on Death: The NAACP and the Arkansas Riot Cases*. Middletown, Conn.: Wesleyan University Press, 1988.

Corzo, Gabino La Rosa. *Runaway Slave Settlements in Cuba: Resistance and Repression*. Translated by Mary Todd. Chapel Hill: University of North Carolina Press, 2003.

Costeloe Michael P. *La primera república federal de México (1824–1835): Un estudio de los partidos políticos en el México independiente*. México: Fondo de Cultura Económica, 1975.

Coughtry, Jay. *The Notorious Triangle: Rhode Island and the African Slave Trade, 1700–1807*. Philadelphia: Temple University Press, 1981.

Coulter, E. Merton. *Georgia: A Short History*. Chapel Hill: University of North Carolina Press, 1960.

Courlander, Harold. *The Drum and the Hoe: Life and Lore of the Haitian People*. Berkeley: University of California Press, 1986.

Cox, Edward, *Free Coloreds in the Slave Societies of St. Kitts and Grenada, 1763–1833*. Knoxville: University of Tennessee Press, 1984.

Crafts, Hannah. *The Bondwoman's Narrative*. Introduction by Henry Louis Gates, Jr. New York: Warner Books, 2002.

Craton, Michael. *Empire, Enslavement, and Freedom in the Caribbean*. Kingston, Jamaica: Ian Randle, 1997.

———. *Testing the Chains: Resistance to Slavery in the British West Indies*. Ithaca, N.Y.: Cornell University Press, 1982.

Crespo, Alberto. *Esclavos negros en Bolivia*. La Paz, Bolivia: Librería Editorial Juventud, 1977.

Crété, Liliane. *Daily Life in Louisiana, 1815–1830*. Baton Rouge: Louisiana State University Press, 1981.

Crouch, Barry A. *The Dance of Freedom: African Americans during Reconstruction*. Austin.: University of Texas Press, 2007.

———. *The Freedmen's Bureau and Black Texans*. Austin: University of Texas Press, 1992.

Crummell, Alexander. "Eulogium on Henry Highland Garnet, D.D." In *Africa and America*. Springfield, Mass.: Willey and Co., 1891. Reprint, New York: Negro Universities Press, 1969.

Cruz, Shamil. "African Americans in the Caribbean and Latin America." Available online. URL: http://www.ipoaa.com/blacks_latin_america_etc.htm. Accessed January 13, 2011.

Cudjoe, Selwin. *Beyond Boundaries: The Intellectual Tradition of Trinidad and Tobago in the Nineteenth Century*. Amherst: University of Massachusetts Press, 2003.

Cugoano, Q. O. *Thoughts and Sentiments on the Evil of Slavery*. Edited by Vincent Caretta. London: Penguin, 1999.

Cuny-Hare, Maud. *Negro Musicians and Their Music*. Washington, D.C.: Associated Publishers, 1936.

Curtin, Philip. *Africa Remembered: Narratives by West Africans from the Era of the Slave Trade.* Long Grove, Ill.: Waveland Press, 1967.

———. *The Atlantic Slave Trade: A Census.* Madison: University of Wisconsin Press, 1969.

———. *Cross-Cultural Trade in World History.* Cambridge: Cambridge University Press, 1984.

———. *Economic Change in Precolonial Africa: Senegambia in the Era of the Slave Trade.* Madison: University of Wisconsin Press, 1975.

Curtis, Edward IV. *Muslims in America: A Short History.* Oxford: Oxford University Press, 2009.

Curto, Jose C., and Renee Soulodre-La France, eds. *Africa and the Americas: Interconnections during the Slave Trade.* Trenton, N.J.: Africa World Press, 2004.

Dabydeen, David, John Gilmore, and Cecily Jones, eds. *The Oxford Companion to Black British History.* Oxford: Oxford University Press, 2000.

da Costa, Emilia Viotti. *Crowns of Glory, Tears of Blood: The Demerara Slave Rebellion of 1823.* New York: Oxford University Press, 1994.

Dain, Bruce. *A Hideous Monster of the Mind: American Race Theory in the Early Republic.* Cambridge, Mass.: Harvard University Press, 2002.

Daly, Vere. *The Making of Guyana.* New York: MacMillan, 1974.

Daniel, G. Reginald. *Race and Multiraciality in Brazil and the United States: Converging Paths?* College Station: Pennsylvania State University Press, 2001.

Dantas, Mariana L. R. "For the Benefit of the Common Good": Regiments of Cacadores do Mato in Minas Gerais, Brazil." *Journal of Colonialism and Colonial History* 5, no. 2 (Fall 2004).

David, Barry Gaspar, and David Patrick Geggus, eds. *A Turbulent Time: The French Revolution and the Greater Caribbean.* Bloomington: Indiana University Press, 1997.

David, Vassar Taylor. *African Americans in Minnesota.* St. Paul: Minnesota Historical Society Press, 2002.

Davis, David Brion. *Inhuman Bondage: The Rise and Fall of Slavery in the New World.* Oxford: Oxford University Press, 2006.

———. *The Problem of Slavery in the Age of Revolution.* Ithaca, N.Y.: Cornell University Press, 1975.

———. *The Problem of Slavery in Western Culture.* Ithaca, N.Y.: Cornell University Press, 1966.

Deagan, Kathleen, and Darcie MacMahon. *Fort Mose: Colonial America's Black Fortress of Freedom.* Gainesville: University Press of Florida, 1995.

Dédé, Edmond. *Edmond Dédé* (audio CD). Hot Springs Music Festival, Richard Rosenberg, Conductor. Naxos 8.559038, 2000.

De Ganda, Enrique. *Historia politica Argentina.* Tomo 8, *Rivadavia y su tiempo.* Buenos Aires: Claridad, 1998.

Degler, Carl. *Neither Black nor White: Slavery and Race Relations in Brazil and the United States.* Madison: University of Wisconsin Press, 1971.

———. "Slavery and the Genesis of American Race Prejudice." *Comparative Studies in Society and History* 2 (1959): 49–66. Reprinted in *Interpreting Colonial America: Selected Readings,* edited by James Kirby Martin, 124–139. New York: Harper & Row, 1978.

Deive, Carlos Esteban. *La esclavitud del negro en Santo Domingo (1492–1844).* Santo Domingo: Museo del Hombre Dominicano, 1980.

———. *Los guerrilleros negros: Esclavos fugitivos y cimarrones en Santo Domingo.* Santo Domingo: Fundación Cultural Dominicana, 1989.

de Jesus, Ursula. *The Souls of Purgatory: The Spiritual Diary of a Seventeenth-Century Afro-Peruvian Mystic, Ursula de Jesus.* Edited and translated by Nancy van Deusen. Albuquerque: University of New Mexico Press, 2004.

de la Fuente, Alejandro. "Slaves and the Creation of Legal Rights in Cuba: *Coartacion* and *Papel.*" *Hispanic American Historical Review* 87, no. 4 (2007): 659–692.

De León, Arnoldo. *Racial Frontiers: Africans, Chinese, and Mexicans in Western America, 1848–1890.* Albuquerque: University of New Mexico Press, 2002.

Deming, Brian. "Slaves and Free Blacks in Colonial Boston." *American History.* American History Suite 101. Available online. URL: http://www.colonial-suite101.com/article. cfm/slaves-and-free-blacks-in-colonial-boston-9174078. Accessed January 13, 2011.

Des Champs, Margaret B. "John Chavis as a Preacher to Whites." *North Carolina Historical Review* 32 (April 1955): 165–172.

Dessalles, Pierre. *Sugar and Slavery, Family and Race: The Letters and Diary of Pierre Dessalles, Planter in Martinique, 1808–1856.* Edited and translated by Elborg Forster and Robert Forster. Baltimore: Johns Hopkins University Press, 1996.

Diamond, Jared. *The Third Chimpanzee: The Biological Roots of Human Behavior.* New York: Harper Perennial, 2006.

Diaz, Maria Elena. *The Virgin, the King, and the Royal Slaves of El Cobre: Negotiating Freedom in Colonial Cuba, 1670–1780.* Palo Alto, Calif.: Stanford University Press, 2000.

Diaz Soler, Luis Manuel. *Historia de la esclavitud negra en Puerto Rico.* 4th ed. Rio Piedras: Editorial Universitaria, 1974.

———. *Puerto Rico: desde sus orígenes hasta el cese de la dominación española.* Río Piedras: Editorial de la Universidad de Puerto Rico, 1996.

Dickinson, Richard B. *Entitled! Free Papers in Appalachia concerning Antebellum Freeborn Negroes and Emancipated Blacks in Montgomery County, Virginia.* Washington D.C.: National Geographic Society, 1981.

Diderot, Denis, and Jean le Rond d'Alembert. *Encyclopédie ou dictionnaire raisonné des sciences, des arts et des métiers.* (Originally published Paris, 1750–1772). Available online URL: encyclopedie.uchicago.edu. Accessed January 13, 2011.

Diedrich, Maria. *Love across Color Lines: Ottilie Assing and Frederick Douglass.* New York: Hill & Wang, 1999.

Diggs, Irene. "The Negro in the Viceroyalty of the Rio de la Plata." *Journal of Negro History* 36, no. 3 (1951): 281–301.

Dillard, Tom W. *The Black Moses of the West: A Biography of Mifflin Wistar Gibbs, 1823–1915.* M.A. thesis, University of Arkansas, Fayetteville, 1975.

———. "Golden Prospects and Fraternal Amenities: Mifflin W. Gibbs's Arkansas Years." *Arkansas Historical Quarterly* 35 (Winter 1976): 307–333.

Diouf, Sylviane. *Servants of Allah: African Muslims Enslaved in the Americas.* New York: New York University Press, 1998.

Ditchfield, G. M. "Granville Sharp." In *Oxford Dictionary of National Biography,* Vol. 50, 15–18. Oxford: Oxford University Press, 2004.

Dixon, Chris. *African America and Haiti: Emigration and Black Nationalism in the Nineteenth Century.* Westport, Conn.: Greenwood Press, 2000.

Dominguez, Virginia R. *White by Definition: Social Classification in Creole Louisiana.* New Brunswick, N.J.: Rutgers University, 1986.

Donald, Cleveland, Jr. "Slave Resistance and Abolitionism in Brazil: The Campista Case, 1879–1888." *Luso-Brazilian Review* 13, no. 2 (Winter 1976): 182–193.

Donaldson, Gary A. "A Window on Slave Culture: Dances at Congo Square in New Orleans, 1800–1862." *Journal of Negro History* 69, no. 2 (Spring 1984): 63–72.

Dorsey, Bruce Allen. "A Gendered History of African Colonization in the Antebellum United States." *Journal of Social History* 34, no. 1 (2000): 77–103.

Dorsey, Jennifer Hull. *Free People of Color in Rural Maryland, 1783–1832.* Ph.D. diss., Georgetown University, 2002.

dos Reis, Maria Firmina. "A escrava." *Revista Maranhense* 3 (1887).

———. *Ursula.* São Luis, Maranhão: Typografia Progresso, 1859. Modern edition, Presença, 1988.

Dougan, Michael B. *Confederate Arkansas: The People and Policies of a Frontier State in Wartime.* Tuscaloosa: University of Alabama Press, 1976.

Douglass, Frederick. *Frederick Douglass, Autobiographies.* Edited by Henry Louis Gates, Jr. New York: Library of America, 1994.

———. *The Heroic Slave.* In *Two Slave Rebellions at Sea: "The Heroic Slave" by Frederick Douglass and "Benito Cereno" by Herman Melville,* edited by George Hendrick and Willene Hendrick. New York: Wiley-Blackwell, 2000.

Downing, David C. *A South Divided: Portraits of Dissent in the Confederacy.* Nashville: Cumberland House, 2007.

Drescher, Seymour. "Brazilian Abolition in Comparative Perspective." *Hispanic American Historical Review* 68, no. 3 (August 1988): 429–460.

———. *From Slavery to Freedom: Comparative Studies in the Rise and Fall of Atlantic Slavery.* New York: NYU Press, 1999.

Dubois, Laurent. *Avengers of the New World: The Story of the Haitian Revolution.* Cambridge, Mass.: Belknap, 2005.

———. "'Citoyens et amis!' Esclavage, citoyenneté et république dans les Antilles françaises à l'époque révolutionnaire." *Annales* 58, no. 2 (March–April 2003): 281–304.

———. *A Colony of Citizens: Revolution and Slave Emancipation in the French Caribbean, 1787–1804.* Chapel Hill: University of North Carolina Press, 2004.

DuBois, W. E. B. *Black Reconstruction in America: 1863–1880.* 1935. Reprint, New York: Free Press, 1998.

———. "The Freedmen's Bureau." *Atlantic Monthly* 87 (1901): 354–365.

———. "Of Alexander Crummell." In *Souls of Black Folk.* New York: Oxford University Press, 2007, 145–152.

———. "Of the Black Belt" and "Of the Quest of the Golden Fleece." In *The Souls Of Black Folk: Essays and Sketches.* Chicago: McLurg & Co, 1903.

———. *The Philadelphia Negro: A Social Study.* Philadelphia: University of Pennsylvania Press, 1899.

———. *The Suppression of the African Slave Trade to the United States, 1638–1870.* New York: Dover, 1970.

———. "The Talented Tenth." In *The Negro Problem: A Series of Articles by Representative American Negroes of Today,* edited by Booker T. Washington. New York: James Pott and Company, 1903. Available online. URL: http://teachingamericanhistory.org/library/index.asp?document=174. Accessed March 8, 2010.

———. "The Upbuilding of Black Durham. The Success of the Negroes and Their Value to a Tolerant and Helpful Southern City." University of North Carolina at Chapel Hill. Available online. URL: http://docsouth.unc.edu/nc/dubois/dubois.html. Accessed January 13, 2011.

Dunbar, Erica Armstrong. *A Fragile Freedom: African American Women and Emancipation in the Antebellum City.* New Haven, Conn.: Yale University Press, 2008.

Dyde, Brian. *A History of Antigua: The Unsuspected Isle.* London: Macmillan Caribbean, 2000.

Dykeman, Wilma. *Tennessee: A Bicentennial History.* New York: W. W. Norton, 1975.

Dykstra, Robert R. *Bright Radical Star: Black Freedom and White Supremacy on the Hawkeye Frontier.* Cambridge, Mass.: Harvard University Press, 1993.

Earle, T. F., and K. J. P. Lowe, eds. *Black Africans in Renaissance Europe.* Cambridge: Cambridge University Press, 2005.

Eckberg, Carl J. *Code Noir: The Colonial Slave Laws of French Mid-America.* Naperville, Ill.: Center for French Colonial Studies, 2005.

Edwards, Paul, and James Walvin. *Black Personalities in the Era of the Slave Trade*. Baton Rouge: Louisiana State University Press, 1983.

Egerton, Douglas R. *Death or Liberty: African-Americans and Revolutionary America*. Oxford: Oxford University Press, 2009.

———. "Gabriel's Conspiracy and the Election of 1800." *The Journal of Southern History* 56, no. 2 (May 1990): 191–214.

———. *Gabriel's Rebellion: The Virginia Slave Conspiracies of 1800 and 1802*. Chapel Hill: University of North Carolina Press, 1993.

———. *He Shall Go Out Free: The Lives of Denmark Vesey*. New York: Rowman & Littlefield, 2004.

Ehrlich, Walter. *They Have No Rights: Dred Scott's Struggle for Freedom*. Westport, Conn.: Greenwood Press, 1979.

El Colegio de México. *Historia general de Mexico*. México: El Colegio de México, 2000.

Eldridge, Carrie. *Cabell County's Empire for Freedom: The Manumission of Sampson Sanders' Slaves*. Huntington, W.Va.: John Deaver Drinko Academy, Marshall University, 1999.

Elmer, Lucius Q. C. *The Constitution and Government of the Province and State of New Jersey, with Biographical Sketches of the Governors from 1776 to 1845*. . 1872. Reprint, Memphis, Tenn.: General Books LLC, 2010.

Eltis, David, and James Welvin et al., eds. *The Abolition of the Atlantic Slave Trade: Origins and Effects in Europe, Africa, and the Americas*. Madison: University of Wisconsin Press, 1981.

Ely, Melvin P. *Israel on the Appomattox: A Southern Experiment in Black Freedom from the 1790s to the Civil War*. New York: Knopf, 2005.

Emmer, Pieter Cornelis. "Jesus Christ Was Good, but Trade Was Better': An Overview of the Transit Trade of the Dutch Antilles, 1634–1795." In *The Lesser Antilles in the Age of European Expansion*, edited by Robert L. Paquette and Stanley L. Engerman, 206–222. Gainesville: University Press of Florida, 1996.

England, Sara. *Afro-Central Americans in New York City: Garifuna Tales of Transnational Movements in Racialized Space*. Gainesville: University Press of Florida, 2006.

Engs, Robert. *Freedom's First Generation: Black Hampton, Virginia, 1861–1890*. New York: Fordham University Press, 2004.

Equiano, Olaudah. *The Interesting Narrative of the Life of Olaudah Equiano*. 1791. Reprint, edited by Robert Allison, Boston: Bedford Books of St. Martin's Press, 1995.

Ernest, John, "Outside the Box: Henry Box Brown and the Politics of Antislavery Agency." *Arizona Quarterly: A Journal of American Literature, Culture, and Theory* 63, no. 4 (Winter 2007): 1–24.

Essah, Patience. *A House Divided: Slavery and Emancipation in Delaware, 1638–1865*. Charlottesville: University Press of Virginia, 1996.

Everett, Donald E. "Free Persons of Color in Colonial Louisiana." *Louisiana History* 7, no. 1 (1966): 21–50.

Exquemelin, Alexandre. *The Buccaneers of America*. Translated by Alexia Brown. Originally published in Dutch. *De Americaensche Zee-Roovers*. Amsterdam: 1678. Reprint, New York: Dover, 2000.

Eze, Emmanuel, ed. *Race and the Enlightenment: A Reader*. New York: Wiley-Blackwell, 1997.

Fagerstrom, René Peri. *La raza negra en Chile: una presencia negada*. Santiago, Chile: Editora Hilda López Aguilar, 1999.

Fandrich, Ina Johanna. *The Mysterious Voodoo Queen, Marie Laveaux: A Study of Powerful Female Leadership in Nineteenth-Century New Orleans*. New York: Routledge, 2005.

Farrow, Anne, Joel Lang, and Jenifer Frank. *How the North Promoted, Prolonged, and Profited from Slavery*. New York: Ballantine Books, 2005.

Fehrenbacher, Don E. *The Dred Scott Case: Its Significance in American Law and Politics*. New York: Oxford University Press, 1978.

Feldman, Eugene Pieter Romany. *Black Power in Old Alabama: The Life and Stirring Times of James T. Rapier, Afro-American Congressman from Alabama, 1839–1883*. Chicago: Museum of African-American History, 1968.

Ferguson, James. *Dominican Republic: Beyond the Lighthouse*. London: Latin America Books, 1992.

Fergusson, Charles Bruce, *A Documentary Study of the Establishment of the Negroes in Nova Scotia between the War of 1812 and the Winning of Responsible Government*. Halifax: Public Archives of Nova Scotia, 1948.

Ferling, John. *John Adams; A Life*. Knoxville: University of Tennessee Press, 1992.

Fernández Méndez, Eugenio. *Historia cultural de Puerto Rico, 1493–1968*. Río Piedras, Puerto Rico: Editorial Universitaria, 1980.

Ferrer, Ada. *Insurgent Cuba: Race, Nation, and Revolution, 1868–1898*. Chapel Hill: University of North Carolina Press, 1999.

Fick, Carolyn. "The French Revolution in Saint-Domingue: A Triumph or a Failure?" In *A Turbulent Time: The French Revolution and the Greater Caribbean*, edited by David Barry Gaspar and David Patrick Geggus, 51–77. Bloomington: Indiana University Press, 1997.

———. *The Making of Haiti: The Saint-Domingue Revolution from Below*. Knoxville: University of Tennessee Press, 1990.

Fields, Barbara J. *Slavery and Freedom on the Middle Ground: Maryland during the Nineteenth Century*. New Haven, Conn.: Yale University Press, 1987.

Figueredo, H. D., and Frank Argote-Freyre. *A Brief History of the Caribbean*. New York: Facts On File, 2008.

Figueroa, Luis A. *Sugar and Slavery in Nineteenth-Century Puerto Rico*. Chapel Hill: University of North Carolina Press, 2005.

Filho, José Nascimento Filho. *Maria Firmina dos Reis: Fragmentos de Uma Vida*. São Luis, Maranhão: Estado do Maranhão, 1975.

Finkelman, Paul. "Evading the Ordinance: The Persistence of Bondage in Indiana and Illinois." *Journal of the Early Republic* 9 (Spring 1989): 21–51.

———. *Slavery and the Founders: Race and Liberty in the Age of Jefferson*. Armonk, N.Y., and London: M. E. Sharpe, 2001.

———. "Slavery, the 'More Perfect Union,' and the Prairie State." *Illinois Historical Journal* 80 (Winter 1987): 248–269.

Finley, Randy. *From Slavery to Uncertain Freedom: The Freedmen's Bureau in Arkansas, 1865–1869*. Fayetteville: University of Arkansas Press, 1996.

Fitzgerald, Michael W. *Splendid Failure: Postwar Reconstruction in the American South*. Chicago: Ivan Dee, 2008.

Fleischner, J. *Mastering Slavery, Memory, Family and Identity in Women's Slave Narratives*. New York: New York University Press, 1996.

Flusche, Della M., and Eugene H. Korth. *Forgotten Females: Women of African and Indian Descent in Colonial Chile, 1535–1800*. Detroit: Blain Ethridge Books, 1983.

Foner, Eric. *Forever Free: The Story of Emancipation and Reconstruction*. New York: Alfred A. Knopf, 2005.

———. *Freedom's Lawmakers*. Baton Rouge: Louisiana State University Press, 1996.

———. *Nothing but Freedom: Emancipation and Its Legacy*. Baton Rouge: Louisiana State University Press, 2007.

———. *Reconstruction: America's Failed Revolution, 1863–1877*. New York: HarperCollins, 1988.

Foner, Philip. *Antonio Maceo: The "Bronze Titan" of Cuba's Struggle for Independence*. New York: Monthly Review Press, 1978.

———. *History of Black Americans: From the Emergence of the Cotton Kingdom to the Eve of the Compromise of 1850*. Santa Barbara, Calif.: Greenwood Press, 1983.

———. *The Spanish-Cuban-American War and the Birth of American Imperialism*. New York: Monthly Review Press, 1972.

Foner, Philip S., and Robert James Branham, eds. *Lift Every Voice: African American Oratory 1787–1900*. Tuscaloosa: University of Alabama Press, 1998.

Foner, Philip S., and Yuval Taylor, eds. *Frederick Douglass. Selected Speeches and Writings*. Chicago: Lawrence Hill Books, 1999.

Forbes, Ella. *African American Women during the Civil War*. New York: Routledge, 1998.

———. *But We Have No Country: The 1851 Christiana, Pennsylvania Resistance*. Cherry Hill, N.J.: Africana Homestead Legacy, 1998.

Foster, Eugene et al. "Jefferson Fathered Slave's Last Child." *Nature* 196 (November 1998): 27–28.

Foster, Francis, Smith. *Written by Herself: Literary Production by African American Women, 1746–1892*. Bloomington: Indiana University Press, 1993

Fouchard, Jean. *The Haitian Maroons: Liberty or Death*. New York: Blyden Press, 1981.

Frank, Zephyr. *Dutra's World: Wealth and Family in Nineteenth-Century Rio de Janeiro*. Albuquerque: University of New Mexico Press, 1982.

Franklin, Jimmie Lewis. *Journey toward Hope: A History of Blacks in Oklahoma*. Norman: University of Oklahoma Press, 1982.

Franklin, John Hope. *The Free Negro in North Carolina, 1790–1860*. Chapel Hill: University of North Carolina Press, 1943.

Franklin, John H., and Alfred A. Moss, Jr. *From Slavery to Freedom: A History of African Americans*. New York: Alfred A. Knopf, 1994.

Fraser, Walter J., Jr. *Charleston! Charleston! The History of a Southern City*. Columbia: University of South Carolina Press, 1989.

Frazier, Donald S., ed. *The United States and Mexico at War: Nineteenth-Century Expansionism and Conflict*. New York: MacMillan Reference USA, 1998.

Frederickson, George. *Racism: A Short History*. Princeton, N.J.: Princeton University Press, 2003.

"Free Blacks." The Handbook of Texas Online. Available online. URL: http://www.tshaonline.org/handbook/online/articles/FF/pkfbs.html.Accessed January 13, 2011.

Frese, Stephen J. "From Emancipation to Equality: Alexander Clark's Stand for Civil Rights in Iowa." *History Teacher* 40 no. 1 (November 2006). Available online. URL: http://www.historycooperative.org/journals/ht/40.1/frese.html. Accessed January 13, 2011.

Frey, Sylvia R. *Water from the Rock: Black Resistance in a Revolutionary Age*. Princeton, N.J.: Princeton University Press, 1991.

Frey, Sylvia R., and Betty Wood. *Come Shouting to Zion: African American Protestantism in the American South and British Caribbean to 1830*. Durham, N.C.: Duke University Press, 1998.

Freyre, Gilberto. *The Masters and the Slaves: A Study in the Development of Brazilian Civilization*. Translated by Samuel Putnam. New York: Alfred A. Knopf, 1946.

Fryer, Peter. *Staying Power: Black People in Britain since 1504*. Atlantic Highlands, N.J.: Humanities Press, 1984.

Fuller, J. *Men of Color, to Arms! Vermont African Americans in the Civil War*. San Jose, Calif.: University Press, 2001.

Fumet, Stanislas. *Life of St. Martín de Porres: Saint of Interracial Justice*. New York: Doubleday, 1964.

Furtado, Júnia Ferreira. *Chica da Silva: A Brazilian Slave of the Eighteenth Century*. Cambridge: Cambridge University Press, 2009.

Gage, Thomas. "Maroons and Free Blacks in Spanish America in the 1600s: Three Documents." Available online. URL: http://nationalhumanitiescenter.org/pds/amerbegin/power/text9/GageSpanishMaroons.pdf. Accessed January 30, 2011.

Gallup-Díaz, Ignacio. "'Haven't We Come to Kill the Spaniards?' The Tule Upheaval in Eastern Panama, 1727–1728." *Colonial Latin American Review* 10, no. 2 (2001): 251–271.

Garcia-Rivera, Alex. *St. Martín de Porres: The "Little Stories" and the Semiotics of Culture*. New York: Orbis, 1995.

Garnet, Henry Highland. *An Address to the Slaves of the United States of America*. Troy, New York: J. H. Tobbitt, 1843 and 1848. Widely reprinted. For example, Richard Newman et al., eds. *Pamphlets of Protest: An Anthology of Early African-American Protest Literature, 1790–1860*. New York: Routledge, 2001.

———. *A Memorial Discourse Delivered in the Hall of the House of Representatives, Washington, D.C. on Sabbath, February 12, 1865*. Philadelphia: Joseph M. Wilson, 1865.

———. *The Past and Present Condition, and the Destiny, of the Colored Race: A Discourse Delivered at the Fifteenth Anniversary of the Female Benevolent Society of Troy, N.Y., Feb. 14, 1848*. Troy: Steam Press of J. C. Kneeland and Co., 1848. Reprinted in *Negro Social and Political Thought, 1850–1920*, edited by Howard Brotz. New York: Basic Books, 1966.

Garrido, Margarita. "'Free Men of All Colors' in New Granada: Identity and Obedience before Independence." In *Political Cultures in the Andes, 1750–1950*, edited by Nils Jacobsen and Cristóbal Aljovín de Losada, 165–182. Durham, N.C.: Duke University Press, 2005.

Garrigus, John. *Before Haiti: Race and Citizenship in French Saint-Domingue*. New York: Palgrave McMillan, 2006.

———. "Opportunist or Patriot: Julien Raimond (1744–1801) and the Haitian Revolution." *Slavery and Abolition* 28, no. 1 (April 2007): 1–21.

Garrison, William Lloyd. *Thoughts on African Colonization*. Boston, 1832. Reprint, New York: Arno Press, 1968.

Gaspar, David Barry, and David Patrick Geggus, eds. *A Turbulent Time: The French Revolution and the Greater Caribbean*. Bloomington: Indiana University Press, 1997.

Gaspar, David Barry, and Darlene Hine, eds. *More than Chattel: Black Women and Slavery in the Americas*. Bloomington: Indiana University Press, 1996.

Gates, Henry Louis, Jr., and Hollis Robbins, eds. *In Search of Hannah Crafts: Critical Essays on* The Bondwoman's Narrative. New York: Basic Civitas Books, 2004.

Gates, H. L. *The Signifying Monkey*. Oxford and New York: Oxford University Press, 1988.

Gates, H. L., and C. T. Davis. *The Slave's Narrative*. Oxford and New York: Oxford University Press, 1985.

Geggus, David P. *The Impact of the Haitian Revolution in the Atlantic World*. Columbia: University of South Carolina Press, 2002.

———. "The Major Port Towns of Saint-Domingue in the Later Eighteenth Century." In *Atlantic Port Cities: Economy, Culture, and Society in the Atlantic World, 1650-1850*, edited by Franklin Knight and Peggy Liss. Knoxville: University of Tennessee Press, 1991.

———. "Slave and Free Colored Women in Saint-Domingue." In *More than Chattel: Black Women and Slavery in the Americas*, edited by David B. Gaspar and Darlene C. Hine, 259–278. Bloomington: Indiana University Press, 1996.

Gehman, Mary. *The Free People of Color: An Introduction*. New Orleans: Margaret Media, Inc., 1994.

George, Carol. *Segregated Sabbaths: Richard Allen and the Emergence of Independent Black Churches, 1760–1840*. New York: Oxford University Press, 1973.

Gerber, David A. *Black Ohio and the Color Line: African Americans and the Color Line in Ohio 1860–1912*. Champaign: University of Illinois Press, 1976.

Gerhard, Peter. "A Black Conquistador in Mexico." *Hispanic American Historical Review* 58, no. 3 (August 1978): 451–459.

Gernes, Todd. "Poetic Justice: Sarah Forten, Eliza Earle, and the Paradox of Intellectual Property." *New England Quarterly* 71 (June 1998): 229–265.

Gerzina, Gretchen. *Black London: Life before Emancipation*. London: John Murray, 1995.

———. *Mr. and Mrs. Prince*. New York: HarperCollins, 2008.

Gibbes, F. E, N. C. Römer-Kenepa, and M. A. Scriwanek. *De bewoners van Curaçao, vijf eeuwen lief en leed, 1499–1999*. Willemstad, Curaçao: Netherlands Antilles: Nationaal Archief, 2002.

Gibbs, Mifflin W. *Shadow and Light. An Autobiography with Reminiscences of the Last and Present Century*. Washington, 1902. Reprint, Lincoln: University of Nebraska Press, 1995.

Giffin, William W. *African Americans and the Color Line in Ohio 1915–1930*. Columbus: Ohio State University Press, 2005.

Gilder Lehrman Center for the Study of Slavery, Resistance, and Abolition, *Citizens ALL: African-Americans in Connecticut, 1700–1850*. Yale University. Available online. URL: http://cmi2.yale.edu/citizens_all/index.html. Accessed June 1, 2011.

Gillen, Mollie, and Chris Cunneen. "Caesar, John Black (c. 1763–1796) Biographical Entry." *Australian Dictionary of Biography, Online Edition*, Australian National University. Available online. URL: http://www.adb.online.anu.edu.au/biogs/AS10070b.htm. Accessed October 30, 2008.

Glasco, Laurence, ed. *The WPA History of the Negro in Pittsburgh*. Pittsburgh: University of Pittsburgh Press, 2004.

Glasrud, Bruce A., and James M. Smallwood, eds. *The African American Experience in Texas: An Anthology*. Lubbock: Texas Tech University Press, 1999.

Gliozzo, Charles A. "John Jones and the Black Convention Movement, 1848–1856." *Journal of Black Studies* 3 no. 2 (December 1972): 227–236.

———. "John Jones: A Study of a Black Chicagoan." *Illinois Historical Journal* 80 (Autumn 1987): 177–188.

Gomes, Flavio dos Santos, and H. Sabrina Gledhill. "A 'Safe Haven': Runway Slaves, Mocambos, and Borders in Colonial Amazonia, Brazil." *Hispanic American Historical Review* 82, no. 3 (2002): 469–498.

Gondim, Eunice Ribeiro. *Vida e obra de Paula Brito*. Rio de Janeiro: Livraria Brasiliana Editora, 1965.

Gonzalez, Nancie L. "The Garifuna of Central America." In *The Indigenous People of the Caribbean*, edited by Samuel M. Wilson, 197–205. Virgin Islands Humanities Council. Gainesville: University Press of Florida, 1997.

———. *Sojourners of the Caribbean: Ethnogenesis and Ethnohistory of the Garifuna*. Urbana: University of Illinois Press, 1988.

Goodman, Paul. *Of One Blood: Abolitionism and the Origins of Racial Equality*. Los Angeles: University of California Press, 1998.

Goodstein, Anita S. "Black History on the Nashville Frontier, 1780–1810." In *Trial and Triumph: Essays in Tennessee's African American History*, edited by Carroll Van West. Knoxville: University of Tennessee Press, 2002.

Goodwin, Robert. *Crossing the Continent, 1527–1540: The Story of the First African-American Explorer of the American South*. New York: HarperCollins, 2008.

Gordon-Reed, Annette. *The Hemingses of Monticello: An American Family*. New York: W. W. Norton, 2008.

Gottheimer, Josh. *Ripples of Hope: Great American Civil Rights Speeches*. Jackson, Tenn.: Basic Civitas Books, 2004.

Gould, Virginia Meacham. "The Free Creoles of Color of the Antebellum Gulf Ports of Mobile and Pensacola: A Struggle for the Middle Ground." In *Creoles of Color of the Gulf South*, edited by James H. Dormon. Knoxville: University of Tennessee Press, 1996.

———. "In Defense of their Creole Culture: The Free Creoles of Color of New Orleans, Mobile, and Pensacola." *Gulf Coast Historical Review* 9 (Fall 1993): 27–46.

———. "The Parish Identities of Free Creoles of Color in Pensacola and Mobile, 1698–1860." *U.S. Catholic Historian* 14 (Fall 1996): 1–10.

Government of Dominica, eds. *Aspects of Dominican History*. Dominica: Government Printing Division, 1972.

Government Printing Office. "James Thomas Rapier." In *Black Americans in Congress, 1870–2007*. Prepared under the direction of the Committee on House Administration by the Office of History & Preservation, U.S. House of Representatives, 2008.

Graden, Dale. *From Slavery to Freedom in Brazil: Bahía, 1835–1900*. Albuquerque: University of New Mexico Press, 2006.

———. "The Origins, Evolution, and Demise of the 'Myth of Racial Democracy' in Brazil, 1848–1998." In *La reconstrucción del mundo en América Latina*, edited by Enrique Pérez Arias. Lund, Sweden: Heterogenesis, 1998.

Graham, Richard. "Free African Brazilians and the State in Slavery Times." In *Racial Politics in Contemporary Brazil*, edited by Michael Hanchard. Austin: University of Texas Press, 1999.

———, ed. *Machado de Assis: Reflections on a Brazilian Master Writer*. Austin: University of Texas Press, 1999.

Grahn, Lance. "Cartagena and Its Hinterland in the Late Eighteenth Century." In *Atlantic Port Cities: Economy, Culture, and Society in the Atlantic World, 1650–1850*, edited by Franklin Knight and Peggy Liss. Knoxville: University of Tennessee Press, 1991.

Grant, Madison. *The Passing of the Great Race*. New York: C. Scribner's Sons, 1916.

Grant, Ulysses S. *Personal Memoirs*. New York: C. L. Webster, 1885–86. Available online. URL: http://www.bartleby.com/1011/. Accessed January 13, 2011.

Green, William D. *A Peculiar Imbalance: The Fall and Rise of Racial Equality in Early Minnesota*. St. Paul: Minnesota Historical Society Press, 2007.

Greene, Lorenzo J. *The Negro in Colonial New England, 1620–1776*. New York: Columbia University Press, 1942.

Grégoire, Henri. *De la littérature des nègres, ou recherches sur leurs facultés intellectuelles, leurs qualités morales et leur littérature*. Paris: 1808. [*An Enquiry Concerning the Intellectual and Moral Faculties, and Literature of Negroes*. Translated by D. B. Warden. Brooklyn: Thomas Kirk, 1810]. Available online. English translation digitized by the University of South Carolina Library's Digital Collections. URL: http://www.sc.edu/library/digital/collections/gregoire.html. Original French document digitized by Project Gutenberg: http://www.gutenberg.org/etext/15907. Accessed January 13, 2011.

———. *Mémoire en faveur des gens de couleur ou sang-mêlés de St.-Domingue & des autres isles françoises de l'Amérique, adressé à l'Assemblée Nationale*. Paris: Chez Belin, 1789. [Report to the National Assembly in favor of people of color or mixed blood from St.-Domingue and the other French islands in America]

Grey, David. *Inside Prince Hall*. New York: Anchor Communications, 2004.

Griffith, R. Marie, and Barbara Dianne Savage, eds. *Women and Religion in the African Diaspora: Knowledge, Power, and Performance*. Baltimore: Johns Hopkins University Press, 2006.

Grinberg, Keila. *O fiador dos brasileiros: Cidadania, escravidão e direito civil no tempo de Antonio Pereira Rebouças*. Rio de Janeiro: Civilização Brasileira, 2002.

Grivno, Max L. "'Black Frenchmen' and 'White Settlers': Race, Slavery, and the Creation of African-American Identities along the Northwest Frontier, 1790–1840." *Slavery and Abolition* 21, no. 3 (December 2000): 75–93.

Guédé, Alain. *Monsieur de Saint-George: Virtuoso, Swordsman, Revolutionary*. New York: Picador, 2003.

Guedea, Virginia. "The Process of Mexican Independence." *American Historical Review* 105, no. 1 (February 2000): 116–130.

Guevara Sangines, Maria. *Guanajuato diverso: sabores y sinsabores de su ser mestizo, siglos XVI a XVII*. Guanajuato, Mexico: La Rana, 2001.

Guitar, Lynne. "Boiling It Down: Slavery and Rebellion on the First Commercial Sugarcane Ingenios in the Americas (Hispaniola, 1530–1545)." In *Slaves, Subjects, and Subversives: Blacks in Colonial Latin America*, edited by Jane G. Landers and Barry M. Robinson, 39–82. Albuquerque: University of New Mexico Press, 2006.

Gutiérrez Brockington, Lolita. *Blacks, Indians, and Spaniards in the Eastern Andes: Reclaiming the Forgotten in Colonial Mizque, 1550–1782*. Lincoln: University of Nebraska Press, 2006.

Gutman, Herbert G. *The Black Family in Slavery and Freedom: 1750–1925*. New York: Pantheon, 1976.

Guyette, Elise A. *Revealing a Hidden Black Community: Hinesburgh, Vermont 1790s–1860s*. Dartmouth, N.H.: University Press of New England, 2009.

———. "The Working Lives of African Vermonters in Census and Literature, 1790–1870." *Vermont History* 61, no. 2 (1993): 69–84.

Habib, Imtiaz. *Black Lives in the English Archives, 1500–1677: Imprints of the Invisible*. Burlington, Vt.: Ashgate, 2008.

Hagedorn, Ann. *Beyond the River: The Untold Story of the Heroes of the Underground Railroad*. New York: Simon & Schuster, 2002.

Hahn, Steven. *A Nation under Our Feet: Black Political Struggles in the Rural South from Slavery to the Great Migration*. Cambridge, Mass.: Belknap Press of Harvard University Press, 2003.

Hakluyt, Richard. *Voyages and Discoveries: The Principal Navigations, Voyages, Traffiques and Discoveries of the English Nation*. Edited by Jack Beeching. Harmondsworth, England: Baltimore: Penguin Books, 1972.

Hales, Douglas. *A Southern Family in White and Black: The Cuneys of Texas*. College Station: Texas A&M University Press, 2003.

Hall, Neville, and B. W. Higman. *Slave Society in the Danish West Indies*. Mona, Jamaica; University of the West Indies Press, 1992.

Hallewell, L. *Books in Brazil: A History of the Publishing Trade*. Metuchen, N.J.: Scarecrow Press, 1982, 60–68.

Handler, Jerome C. *The Unappropriated People: Freedmen in the Slave Society of Barbados*. Baltimore: Johns Hopkins University Press, 1974.

Handlin, Oscar, and Mary F. Handlin. "Origins of the Southern Labor System." *William & Mary Quarterly, Third Series*, 7 (1950): 199–222.

Handy, Jim. *Gift of the Devil: A History of Guatemala*. Cambridge, Mass. South End Press, 1998.

Hanger, Kimberly. *Bounded Lives, Bounded Places: Free Black Society in Colonial New Orleans 1769–1803*. Durham, N.C.: Duke University Press, 1997.

Hardin, John A. *Fifty Years of Segregation: Black Higher Education in Kentucky, 1904–1954*. Lexington: University Press of Kentucky, 1997.

Harold, Schoen. "The Free Negro in the Republic of Texas." *Southwestern Historical Quarterly* 39, no. 4 (April 1936): 292–308; 41, no. 1 (July 1937): 83–108; 40, no. 1 (July 1936) 26–34.

Harper, Douglas. "Slavery in the North." Available online. URL: http://www.slavenorth.com/. Accessed January 13, 2011.

Harris, Jonathan. "Bernardino Rivadavia and Benthamite 'discipleship.'" *Latin American Research Review* 33, no. 1 (1998): 129–150.

Harris, Joseph E. *Africans and Their History*. New York: Meridian Press, 1998.

———, ed. *Global Dimensions of the African Diaspora*. Washington, D.C.: Howard University Press, 1982.

———. *In the Shadow of Slavery: African Americans in New York City, 1626–1863*. Chicago: University of Chicago Press, 2003.

Harris, J. William. *The Hanging of Thomas Jeremiah: A Free Black Man's Encounter with Liberty*. New Haven, Conn.: Yale University Press, 2009.

Harris, Sheldon. *Paul Cuffe: Black America and the African Return*. New York: Simon & Schuster, 1972.

Harrison, Maureen, and Steve Gilbert. *Landmark Decisions of the United States Supreme Court*. Vol. 5. La Jolla, Calif.: Excellent Books, 1995.

Harrold, Stanley. *American Abolitionists*. Harlow, Essex, England: Pearson Education Limited, 2001.

Hart, Richard E. "Springfield's African Americans as a Part of the Lincoln Community." *Journal of the Abraham Lincoln Association* 20, no. 1 (1999): 35–54.

Harvey, Robert. *Liberators: Latin America's Struggle for Independence*. Woodstock, N.Y.: Overlook Press, 2000.

Hashaw, Tim. *The Birth of Black America: The First African Americans and the Pursuit of Freedom at Jamestown*. Kindle Books, 2007.

Haskins, James. *African American Religious Leaders*. Hoboken, N.J.: John Wiley & Sons, 1941.

Healy, Claire. "Afro-Argentines and Argentine History." *Atlantic Studies* 3, no. 1 (2006): 111–120.

Heinegg, Paul. *Free African Americans of Maryland and Delaware: From the Colonial Period to 1810*. Baltimore: Clearfield, 2000.

Helg, Aline. *Liberty and Equality in Caribbean Colombia, 1770–1835*. Chapel Hill: University of North Carolina Press, 2004.

———. *Our Rightful Share: The Afro-Cuban Struggle for Equality, 1886–1912*. Chapel Hill: University of North Carolina Press, 1995.

———. "Simon Bolivar and the Spectre of Pardocracia: Jose Padilla in Post-Independence Cartagena." *Journal of Latin American Studies* 35 (2003): 447–471.

Hemenway, Abby, ed. *Vermont Historical Gazetteer, a Local History of All the Towns in the State, Civil, Educational, Biographical, Religious and Military*. Vol. 2. Burlington: Author, 1871.

Hemsath, Sr. Caroline. *From Slave to Priest: A Biography of the Reverend Augustine Tolton (1854–1897): First Black American Priest of the United States.* Chicago: Ignatius Press, 2006.

Henderson, George, Capt. *An Account of the British Settlement of Honduras: Being a Brief View of Its Commercial and Agricultural Resources, Soil, Climate, Natural History, &c.* London: C. & R. Baldwin, 1809.

Henderson, Timothy J. *A Glorious Defeat: Mexico and Its War with the United States.* New York: Hill & Wang, 2008.

Hernández Chávez, Alicia. *Mexico: A Brief History.* Translated by Andy Klatt. Berkeley: University of California Press, 2006.

Heuman, Gad. *Between Black and White: Race, Politics, and the Free Coloreds of Jamaica, 1792–1865.* Westport, Conn.: Greenwood Press, 1981.

Higginbotham, Leon. *In the Matter of Color: Race and the American Legal Process: The Colonial Period.* New York: Oxford University Press, 1978.

Higgins, Billy D. "The Origins and Fate of the Marion County Free Black Community." *Arkansas Historical Quarterly* 54 (Winter 1995): 427–443.

Higginson, Thomas. *Black Soldiers/Blue Uniforms: The Story of the First South Carolina Volunteers.* Tuscon, Ariz. Fireship Press, 2009. Originally published 1870 as *Army Life in a Black Regiment.*

Higman, Barry, *Slave Populations of the British Caribbean, 1807–1834.* Kingston: University of the West Indies Press, 1997.

Hinks, Peter P., ed. *David Walker's Appeal to the Coloured Citizens of the World.* University Park: Pennsylvania State University Press, 2000.

———. "Digging Deeper." In *Citizens ALL: African-Americans in Connecticut, 1700–1850.* A Website produced by Gilder Lehrman Center for the Study of Slavery, Resistance & Abolition. New Haven, Conn.: Yale University Press, 2007. Available online. URL: http://www.yale.edu/glc/citizens/index.html. Accessed January 13, 2011.

Hirsch, Arnold R., and Joseph Logsdon. *Creole New Orleans: Race and Americanization.* Baton Rouge: Louisiana State University Press, 1992.

Hodges, Carl G., and Helene H. Levene. *Illinois Negro Historymakers.* Springfield: Illinois Emancipation Centennial Commission, 1964.

Hodges, Graham Russell. *Root and Branch: African Americans in New York and East Jersey, 1613–1863.* Chapel Hill: University of North Carolina Press, 1999.

Hogan, James E. "Antônio Francisco Lisboa, O Aleijadinho: An Annotated Bibliography." *Latin American Research Review* 9, no. 2 (Summer 1974), 83–94.

Hogan, William, and Edwin Davis, eds. *William Johnson's Natchez: The Diary of a Free Negro in Ante-Bellum Natchez.* Baton Rouge: Louisiana State University Press, 1951.

Hollandsworth, James G. *The Louisiana Native Guards: The Black Military Experience during the Civil War.* Baton Rouge: Louisiana State University Press, 1998.

Holmes, Jack D. L. "The Role of Blacks in Spanish Alabama: The Mobile District, 1780–1813." *Alabama Historical Quarterly* 37 (Spring 1975): 5–18.

Holt, Michael. *By One Vote: The Disputed Election of 1876.* Lawrence: University Press of Kansas, 2008.

Holt, Thomas C. *The Problem of Freedom: Race, Labor, and Politics in Jamaica and Britain, 1832–1938.* Baltimore: Johns Hopkins University Press, 1992.

Holton, Woody. *Forced Founders: Indians, Debtors, Slaves, and the Making of the American Revolution in Virginia.* Chapel Hill: University of North Carolina Press, 1999.

Holzer, Harold, Edna Greene Medford, and Frank J. Williams. *The Emancipation Proclamation: Three Views (Conflicting Worlds: New Dimensions of the American Civil War).* Baton Rouge: Louisiana State University Press, 2006.

Honychurch, Lenox. *The Dominica Story: A History of the Island.* 1975. Reprint, London: Macmillan Education, 1995.

Horton, James Oliver, and Lois E. Horton. *Black Bostonians: Family Life and Community Struggle in the Antebellum North.* Holmes & Meier, 1979.

———. *In Hope of Liberty: Culture, Community and Protest among Northern Free Blacks, 1700–1860.* New York: Oxford University Press, 1997.

Horton, James Oliver and Lois E. Horton, eds. *Slavery and Public History: The Tough Stuff of American Memory.* New York: New Press, 2006.

Howard, Philip A. *Changing History: Afro-Cuban Cabildos and Societies of Color in the Nineteenth Century.* Baton Rouge: Louisiana State University Press, 1998.

Hoyles, Asher, and Martin Hoyles. *Remember Me: Achievements of Mixed Race People Past and Present.* London: Hansib Publications & Ethos Publishing, 1999.

Hudson, Gossie H. "John Chavis, 1763–1838: A Social-Psychological Study." *Journal of Negro History* 64 (Spring 1979): 142–154.

———. "William Florville: Lincoln's Barber and Friend." *Negro History Bulletin* 37, no. 5 (1974): 279–281.

Huggins, Nathan Irvin. *Slave and Citizen: The Life of Frederick Douglass.* Boston: Little, Brown, 1980.

Hyde, Samuel C., ed. *Plain Folk of the South Revisited.* Baton Rouge: Louisiana State University Press, 1997.

Irvine, Russell W. "Martin H. Freeman of Rutland, America's First Black College Professor and Pioneering Black Social Activist." *Rutland Historical Society Quarterly* 26, no. 3 (1996): 71–98.

Jackson, Marilyn. "Alexander Clark: A Rediscovered Black Leader." *Iowan* 23 (Spring 1975): 45.

Jackson, Wanda Faye. "John Mercer Langston: A Troubled African-American Leader." *Griot* 23 (Spring 2004): 61–72.

Jacobs, Harriet. *Incidents in the Life of a Slave Girl.* New York: Oxford University Press, 1988.

Jaén Suárez, Omar. *La población del Istmo de Panamá del siglo XVI al siglo XX.* Panama: Instituto Nacional de Cultura, 1979.

James, Sydney V. *Colonial Rhode Island—a History*. New York: Charles Scribner's Sons, 1975.

Jefferson, Thomas. *Notes on the State of Virginia*. London: 1797. Available online. URL: http://etext.lib.virginia.edu/toc/modeng/public/JefVirg.html. Accessed January 13, 2011.

Jenkins, H. J. K. "'The Colonial Robespierre': Victor Hugues on Guadeloupe, 1794–98." *History Today* 27, no. 11 (1977): 734–740.

Jennings, Judith, ed. *The Business of Abolishing the British Slave Trade, 1783–1807*. London: F. Cass, 1997.

Jennings, Lawrence C. *French Anti-Slavery: The Movement for the Abolition of Slavery in France, 1802–1848*. New York: Cambridge University Press, 2000.

Jennings, Paul. *A Colored Man's Reminiscences of James Madison*. New York: George C. Beadle, 1865. Available online. URL: http://docsouth.unc.edu/neh/jennings/jennings.html. Accessed January 13, 2011.

John D. Rockefeller Library. *The Network, a Colonial Williamsburg Publication*. Williamsburg, Va.: Colonial Williamsburg Foundation, 1999.

Johnson, Charles (pseudonym for Daniel Defoe). *A General History of the Robberies and Murders of the Most Notorious Pirates*. London: 1724. Reprint, New York: Caroll & Graf, 1999.

Johnson, Kevin R., ed. *Mixed Race America and the Law: A Reader*. New York: New York University Press, 2003.

Johnson, Michael P. "Denmark Vesey and His Co-Conspirators." *William and Mary Quarterly* 58, no. 4 (October 2001): 915–976.

Johnson, Michael P., and James L. Roak. *Black Masters. A Free Family of Color in the Old South*. New York: W. W. Norton, 1984.

Johnson, Michael P. et al. Responses in "Forum." *William and Mary Quarterly* 59, no. 1 (January 2002): 123–202.

Johnson, Paul Christopher. *Secrets, Gossip, and Gods: The Transformation of Brazilian Candomblé*. Oxford: Oxford University Press, 2002.

Johnson, Reinhard O. *The Liberty Party, 1840–1848: Antislavery Third-Party Politics in the United States*. Baton Rouge: Louisiana State University Press, 2009.

Jones, George Fenwick. "The Black Hessians: Negroes Recruited by the Hessians in South Carolina and Other Colonies." *South Carolina History Magazine* 83 (October 1982): 287–302.

Jones, Howard. *Mutiny on the Amistad: The Saga of a Slave Revolt and Its Impact on American Abolition, Law, and Diplomacy*. New York: Oxford University Press, 1987.

Jordan, Winthrop. *White over Black: American Attitudes toward the Negro, 1550–1812*. Chapel Hill: University of North Carolina Press, 1968.

Joseph, Gilbert M. "John Coxon and the Role of Buccaneering in the Settlement of the Yucatán Colonial Frontier." *Belizean Studies* 17, no. 3 (1989): 2–21.

———. "The Logwood Trade and Its Settlements." In *Readings in Belizean History*, 2nd ed., edited by Lita Hunter Krohn, 32–47. Belize City: St. John's College, 1987.

Josephs, Aleric. "Mary Seacole: Jamaican Nurse and 'Doctress.'" *Jamaica Historical Review* 17 (1991): 48–65.

Junior, R. Magalhães. *A vida turbulenta de José do Patrocínio*. São Pualo: Lisa-Livros Irradiantes, SP, 1969.

Juster, Susan, and Lisa McFarlane, eds. *A Mighty Baptism: Race, Gender, and the Creation of American Protestantism*. Ithaca, N.Y.: Cornell University Press, 1996.

Kaplan, Sidney, and Emma Nogrady Kaplan. *The Black Presence in the Era of the American Revolution*. Amherst, Mass.: University of Massachusetts Press, 1989.

Katz, Loren. *The Black West: A Documentary and Pictorial History of the African American Role in the Westward Expansion of the United States*. Beaverton, Oreg.: Touchstone, 1996.

Katzew, Ilona. *Casta Paintings: Images of Race in Colonial Mexico*. New Haven, Conn.: Yale University Press, 2004.

Keckley, Elizabeth. *Behind the Scenes: Thirty Years a Slave and Four in the White House*. New York: Penguin, 2005.

Kein, Sybil, ed. *Creole: The History and Legacy of Louisiana's Free People of Color*. Baton Rouge: Louisiana State University Press, 2000.

Keith, Robert G. *Conquest and Agrarian Change: The Emergence of the Hacienda System on the Peruvian Coast*. Cambridge, Mass.: Harvard University Press, 1976.

Kendrick, Stephen, and Paul Kendrick. *Sarah's Long Walk: The Free Blacks of Boston and How Their Struggle for Equality Changed America*. Boston: Beacon Press, 2004.

Kennedy, Thomas. *A History of Southland College: The Society of Friends and Black Education in Arkansas*. Fort Smith: University of Arkansas Press, 2009.

Kerr, Paulette A. "Victims or Strategists? Female Lodging-house Keepers Jamaica." In *Engendering History—Caribbean Women in Historical Perspective*, edited by Verene Shepherd et al., 197–212. Kingston: Ian Randle Publishers, 1995.

Keyssar, Alexander. *The Right to Vote: The Contested History of Democracy in the United States*. New York: Basic Books, 2000.

Kidd, Colin. *The Forging of Races: Race and Scripture in the Protestant Atlantic World, 1600–2000*. Cambridge: Cambridge University Press, 2006.

Kiddy, Elizabeth W. *Blacks of the Rosary: Memory and History in Minas Gerais, Brazil*. University Park: Pennsylvania State University Press, 2005.

Kielstra, Paul Michael. *The Politics of Slave Trade Suppression in Britain and France, 1814–48: Diplomacy, Morality and Economics*. New York: St. Martin's Press, 2000.

Kilian, Crawford. *Go Do Some Great Thing: The Black Pioneers of British Columbia*. Vancouver: Douglas & McIntyre, 1978.

King, Johannes. "Guerrilla Warfare: A Bush Negro's View." In *Maroon Societies: Rebel Slave Communities in the Americas,* edited by Richard Price, 298–304. Baltimore: Johns Hopkins University Press, 1996.

King, Stewart. *Blue Coat or Powdered Wig: Free Coloreds In Pre-Revolutionary Saint-Domingue*. Athens: University of Georgia Press, 2000.

———. "The Maréchaussée of Saint-Domingue: Balancing the Ancien Regime and Modernity." *Journal of Colonialism and Colonial History* 5, no. 2 (Fall 2004).

Kinsbruner, Jay. *Not of Pure Blood: The Free People of Color and Racial Prejudice in Nineteenth-Century Puerto Rico*. Durham, N.C.: Duke University Press, 1996.

Kleijwegt, Marc. *The Faces of Freedom: The Manumission and Emancipation of Slaves in Old World and New World Slavery*. Leiden: Brill Academic, 2006.

Klein, Herbert S. *African Slavery in Latin America and the Caribbean*. New York: Oxford University Press, 1986.

———. *Bolivia: The Evolution of a Multi-Ethnic Society*. 2nd ed. New York: Oxford University Press, 1992.

———. "Nineteenth-Century Brazil." In *Neither Slave nor Free: The Freedmen of African Descent in the Slave Societies of the New World*, edited by David W. Cohen and Jack Greene. Baltimore: Johns Hopkins University Press, 1972.

Klinghoffer Judith Apter, and Lois Elkis. "'The Petticoat Electors': Women's Suffrage in New Jersey, 1776–1807." *Journal of the Early Republic* 159 (Summer 1992): 12.

Knepper, George W. *A History of Ohio and Its People*. Kent, Ohio: Kent State University Press, 2003.

Knight, Edgar W. "Notes on John Chavis." *North Carolina Historical Review* 7 (July 1930): 326–345.

Knight, Franklin. *Slave Society in Cuba in the Nineteenth Century*. Madison: University of Wisconsin Press, 1970.

Koger, Larry. *Free Black Slave Masters in South Carolina, 1790–1860*. Jefferson, N.C: McFarland, 1985.

Koster, Rick. *Louisiana Music: A Journey from R&B to Zydeco, Jazz to Country, Blues to Gospel, Cajun Music to Swamp Pop to Carnival Music and Beyond*. Cambridge: Da Capo Press, 2002.

Kraay, Hendrik. *Afro-Brazilian Culture and Politics: Bahía, 1790s–1990s (Latin American Realities)*. Armonk, N.Y.: M. E. Sharpe, 1998.

———. "'As Terrifying as Unexpected': The Bahían Sabinada, 1837–1838." *Hispanic American Historical Review* 72, no. 4 (November 1992): 501–527.

———. "Patriotic Mobilization in Brazil: The Zuavos and Other Black Companies." In *I Die with My Country: Perspectives on the Paraguayan War, 1864–1870*, edited by Hendrik Kraay and Thomas L. Whigham, 61–80. Lincoln: University of Nebraska Press, 2004.

———. "The Politics of Race in Independence-Era Bahía: The Black Militia Officers of Salvador, 1790–1840." In *Afro-Brazilian Culture and Politics: Bahía, 1790s–1840s*, 31–56. Armonk, N.Y.: M. E. Sharpe, 1998.

———. *Race, State, and Armed Forces in Independence-Era Brazil: Bahía, 1790s–1840s*. Palo Alto, Calif.: Stanford University Press, 2001.

Kremer, Gary R., and Antonio F. Holland. *Missouri's Black Heritage*. Columbia: University of Missouri Press, 2005.

Kusmer, Kenneth L. *A Ghetto Takes Shape: Black Cleveland 1870–1930*. Urbana: University of Illinois Press, 1976.

Kutler, Stanley I. *The Dred Scott Decision: Law or Politics?* Boston: Houston Mifflin, 1967.

Labat, Jean-Baptiste. *The Memoirs of Père Labat, 1693–1705*. Edited and translated by John Eaden. London: Routledge, 1970.

LaFarge, John. *The Race Question and the Negro: A Study of the Catholic Doctrine on Interracial Justice*. Toronto: Longman's, 1943.

Lafragua, José María. *Vicente Guerrero el mártir de Cuilapan*. Mexico: Secretaria de Educación Pública, 1946.

Lamon, Lester C. *Blacks in Tennessee, 1791–1970*. Knoxville: University of Tennessee Press, 1981.

Lampe, A. "Yo te nombro libertad. Iglesia y estado en la sociedad esclavista de Curazao (1816–1863)." Ph.D. diss., Free University of Amsterdam, 1988.

Lampe, Gregory P. *Frederick Douglass: Freedom's Voice*. East Lansing: Michigan State University Press, 1998.

Landers, Jane. *Black Society in Spanish Florida*. Urbana: University of Illinois Press, 2001.

Lane, Roger. *Roots of Violence in Black Philadelphia*. Cambridge, Mass.: Harvard University Press, 1986.

Lane-Poole, Stanley. *The Story of the Moors in Spain*. 1886. Reprint, Baltimore, Md.: Black Classic Press, 1996.

Langley, Loudon's Letters to Editors. Vermont Civil War Database. Available online. URL: http://vermontcivilwar.org/units/afam. Accessed January 13, 2011.

Langston, John Mercer. *From the Virginia Plantation to the National Capital; or, the First and Only Negro Representative in Congress from the Old Dominion*. Hartford, Conn.: American Publishing, Co., 1894.

Lanning, Michael Lee. *African Americans in the Revolutionary War*. New York: Citadel, 2000.

Lapp, Rudolph M. *Blacks in Gold Rush California*. New Haven, Conn.: Yale University Press, 1977.

Lapsansky-Werner, Emma J. *The Black Presence in Pennsylvania: "Making It Home."* 2nd ed. University Park: Pennsylvania Historical Association, 2001.

Larson, Kate Clifford. *Bound for the Promised Land: Harriet Tubman, Portrait of an American Hero*. New York: Ballantine Books, 2004.

Lascelles, E. C. P. *Granville Sharp and the Freedom of Slaves in England*. New York: Negro University Press, 1969.

Lasso, Marixa. *Myths of Harmony: Race and Republicanism during the Age of Revolution, Colombia 1795–1831*. Pittsburgh: University of Pittsburgh Press, 2007.

Law, Robin. *The Slave Coast of West Africa 1550–1750: The Impact of the Atlantic Slave Trade on an African Society.* Oxford: Clarendon Press, 1991.

Lawson, Bill E., and Frank M. Kirkland eds. *Frederick Douglass: A Critical Reader.* Oxford: Blackwell, 1999.

Lawson, Elizabeth. *The Gentleman from Mississippi: Our First Negro Senator.* New York: University of Chicago Library, 1960.

Learning, Hugo Prosper. *Hidden Americans: Maroons of Virginia and the Carolinas.* New York: Garland, 1995.

Lee, Byron A. *Naval Warrior: The Life of Commodore Isaac Mayo.* Linthicum, Md.: Anne Arundel County Historical Society, 2002.

Lemelson Center. "Fixing a Gin: Math and History at Your Desk." Available online. URL: http://invention.smithsonian.org/centerpieces/whole_cloth/u2ei/u2ma. Accessed December 11, 2008.

Lepore, Jill. *New York Burning: Liberty, Slavery, and Conspiracy in Eighteenth-Century Manhattan.* New York: Alfred A. Knopf, 2005.

Levin, Carole. "Backgrounds and Echoes of Othello: From Leo Africanus to Ignatius Sancho." *Lamar Journal of the Humanities* 22, no. 2 (Fall 1996): 45–68.

———. "Shakespeare and the Marginalized 'Others.'" In *A Concise Companion to English Renaissance Literature*, edited by Donna B. Hamilton. Oxford: Blackwell, 2006.

Levine, Robert. *Martin Delany, Frederick Douglass and the Politics of Representative Identity.* Chapel Hill: University of North Carolina Press, 1997.

———, ed. *Martin R. Delany: A Documentary Reader.* Chapel Hill: University of North Carolina Press, 2003.

Levi-Strauss, Claude. *Race and History.* New York: UNESCO, 1952.

Lewis, Jan Ellen, and Peter S. Onuf, eds. *Sally Hemings and Thomas Jefferson: History, Memory, and Civic Culture.* Charlottesville: University Press of Virginia, 1999.

Lewis, John W. *The Life, Labors and Travels of Elder Charles Bowles of the Free Will Baptist Denomination.* Watertown, N.Y.: Ingalls and Stowell's Steam Press, 1852.

Lewis, Marvin A. *Afro-Argentine Discourse: Another Dimension of the Black Diaspora.* Columbia: University of Missouri Press, 1996.

Linebaugh, Peter, and Marcus Rediker. *The Many-Headed Hydra: Sailors, Slaves, Commoners and the Hidden History of the Revolutionary Atlantic.* Boston: Beacon Press, 2000.

Lipski, John M. "Afro-Bolivian Language Today: The Oldest Surviving Afro-Hispanic Speech Community." *Afro-Hispanic Review* 25, no. 1 (Spring 2006): 179–200.

———. "The Negros Congos of Panama: Afro-Hispanic Creole Language and Culture." *Journal of Black Studies* 16, no. 14 (June 1986): 409–428.

Litwack, Leon. *Been in the Storm So Long.* New York: Vintage Books, 1980.

———. *North of Slavery: The Negro in the Free States, 1790–1860.* Chicago: University of Chicago Press, 1961.

Lockart, James. *El mundo hispano-peruano.* Mexico: Fondo de Cultura Económica, 1982.

Lockett, James D. "Abraham Lincoln and Colonization: An Episode That Ends in Tragedy at L'Ile à Vache, Haiti, 1863–1864." *Journal of Black Studies* 21, no. 4 (June 1991): 428–444.

Logan, Rayford W., and Michael R. Winston, eds. *Dictionary of American Negro Biography.* New York: W. W. Norton, 1982.

Lokken, Paul. "Génesis de una comunidad afro-indígena en Guatemala: la villa de San Diego de la Gomera en el siglo XVII." *Mesoamérica, Mesoamérica/Antigua* 29, no. 50, (2008): 37–65.

———. "Useful Enemies: Seventeenth-Century Piracy and the Rise of Pardo Militias in Spanish Central America." *Journal of Colonialism and Colonial History* 5, no. 2 (Fall 2004).

Long, Carolyn Morrow. *A New Orleans Voudou Priestess: The Legend and Reality of Marie Laveau.* Gainesville: University Press of Florida, 2006.

Longacre, Edward. *A Regiment of Slaves: The 4th United States Colored Infantry, 1863–1866.* Mechanicsburg, Pa.: Stackpole Books, 2003.

Longo, James McMurtry. *Isabel Orleans-Braganza: The Brazilian Princess Who Freed the Slaves.* Jefferson, N.C.: McFarland, 2007.

Lopez Cantos, Ángel. *Miguel Enríquez.* Sevilla: Consejo Superior de Investigaciones Científicas, Escuela de Estudios Hispano-Americanos, 1998.

López Martínez, Héctor. *El protomédico limeño José Manuel Valdés.* Lima: Dirección de Intereses Marítimos, 1993.

Love, Nat. *The Life and Adventures of Nat Love, Better Known in the Cattle Country as "Deadwood Dick," by Himself.* 1907. Reprint, Lincoln: University of Nebraska Press, 1995.

Lovejoy, Paul. "Autobiography and Memory: Gustavus Vassa, alias Olaudah Equiano, the African." *Slavery and Abolition* 27, no. 3 (December 2006): 317–347.

Lucas, Marion B. *A History of Blacks in Kentucky: From Slavery to Segregation, 1760–1891.* Frankfort: Kentucky Historical Society, 2003.

Lunn, Arnold. *A Saint in the Slave Trade: Peter Claver, 1581–1654.* Sheed & Ward, 1937. Reprint, Whitefish, Mont.: Kessinger Publishing, 2007.

Lynch, John. *Simon Bolivar: A Life.* New Haven, Conn.: Yale University Press, 2006.

———. *The Spanish American Revolution, 1808–1826.* New York: W. W. Norton, 1986.

Mabee, Carleton. "Sojourner Truth and President Lincoln." *New England Quarterly* 61, no. 4 (December 1988): 519–529.

MacAdoo, Harriet Pipes, ed. *Black Families.* London: Sage, 2007.

Macaulay, Neill. *Dom Pedro: The Struggle for Liberty in Brazil and Portugal, 1798–1834.* Durham, N.C.: Duke University Press, 1986.

Machado, Maria Helena Pereira Toledo. "From Slave Rebels to Strikebreakers: The Quilombo of Jabaquara and the Problem of Citizenship in Late-Nineteenth-Century Brazil." *Hispanic American Historical Review* 86, no. 2 (2006): 247–274.

MacLean, Nancy. *Behind the Mask of Chivalry: The Making of the Second Ku Klux Klan.* New York: Oxford University Press, 1994.

Madiou, Thomas. *Histoire d'Haiti.* 7 vols. Port-au-Prince: 1847. Reprint, Port-au-Prince: Éditions Henri Deschamps, 1987.

Malavet Vega. *De las bandas al Trío Borinquen, 1900–1927.* Ponce, Puerto Rico: Ediciones Lorena, 2002.

Malcom, Joyce Lee. *Peter's War: A New England Slave Boy and the American Revolution.* New Haven, Conn.: Yale University Press, 2009.

Mancisidor José. *Hidalgo, Morelos, Guerrero.* Mexico: Grijalbo, 1970.

Maquivar, Consuelo, coordinadora. *Memoria del coloquio: El arte en tiempos de Juan Correa.* Mexico: Museo Nacional del Virreinato, Instituto Nacional de Antropologia e Historia, 1994.

Marable, Manning. *How Capitalism Underdeveloped Black America: Problems in Race, Political Economy, and Society.* New York: South End Press, 2000.

Marfo, Florence. "Marks of the Slave Lash: Black Women's Writing of the 19th Century Anti-Slavery Novel." *Diáspora: Journal of the Annual Afro-Hispanic Literature and Culture Conference* 11 (2001): 80–86.

Markovitz, Jonathan. *Legacies of Lynching: Racial Violence and Memory.* Minneapolis: University of Minnesota Press, 2004.

Marks, Carole, ed. *A History of African Americans of Delaware and Maryland's Eastern Shore.* 2nd ed. Wilmington: Delaware Heritage Commission, 1998.

Martin, Harold H. *Georgia: A Bicentennial History.* New York: W. W. Norton, 1977.

Martin, S. I. *Britain's Slave Trade.* New York: Macmillan, 1999.

Martinez, Maria Elena. "The Black Blood of New Spain: *Limpieza de Sangre,* Racial Violence, and Gendered Power in Early Colonial Mexico." *William and Mary Quarterly* 61, no. 3 (July 2004): 479–520.

Massachusetts Historical Society. "Adams Family Papers: An Electronic Archive." Available online. URL: http://www.masshist.org/digitaladams/aea. Accessed January 13, 2011.

Mathurin, Lucille. *A Historical Study of Women in Jamaica, 1655–1844.* Ph.D. diss., University of the West Indies, 1974.

Matthews, Pat. *Joseph Jenkins Roberts, the Father of Liberia.* Richmond: Virginia State Library, 1973.

Mattos, Hebe. "'Black Troops' and the Hierarchies of Color in the Portuguese Atlantic World: The Case of Henrique Dias and His Black Regiment." *Luso-Brazilian Review* 45, no. 1 (2008): 6–29.

Maurois, Andre. *The Titans: A Three-Generation Biography of the Dumas.* Translated by Gerard Hopkins. New York: Harper, 1957.

May, Philip S. "Zephaniah Kingsley, Nonconformist." *Florida Historical Society* 23 (January 1945): 145–159.

Mayer, Henry. *All on Fire: William Lloyd Garrison and the Abolition of Slavery.* New York: St. Martin's Press, 1998.

Mayo Santana, Raíl, Mariano Negrón Portillo, and Manuel Mayo López. *Cadenas de esclavitud . . . y de solidaridad: Esclavos y libertos en San Juan, siglo XIX.* Río Piedras, Puerto Rico: Centro de Investigaciones Sociales, Universidad de Puerto Rico Recinto de Río Piedras, 1997.

McCalman, I. D. *Radical Underworld: Prophets, Revolutionaries and Pornographers in London, 1795–1840.* New York: Oxford University Press, 1993.

McClintock, Thomas C. "James Saules, Peter Burnett, and the Oregon Black Exclusion Law of June 1844." *Pacific Northwest Quarterly* 86 (1995): 121–130.

McCormick, Richard P. *The History of Voting in New Jersey: A Study of the Development of Election Machinery, 1664–1911.* New Brunswick, N.J.: Rutgers University Press, 1953.

McCullough, David. *John Adams.* New York: Simon & Schuster, 2001.

McDermott, John Francis, ed. *The Spanish in the Mississippi Valley, 1762–1804.* Urbana: University of Illinois Press, 1974.

McDonald, Archie. "William Goyens." TexasEscapes.com Online Magazine. Available online. URL: http://www.texasescapes.com/DEPARTMENTS/Guest_Columnists/East_Texas_all_things_historical/WilliamGoyensamd102.htm. Accessed January 13, 2011.

McDonnell, Michael. *The Politics of War: Race, Class, and Conflict in Revolutionary Virginia.* Chapel Hill: University of North Carolina Press, 2007.

McFarlane, Anthony. *Columbia before Independence: Economy, Society and Politics under Bourbon Rule.* New York: Cambridge University Press, 1993.

McFeely, William S. *Frederick Douglass.* New York: Norton, 1991.

McGlynn, Frank, and Seymour Drescher, eds. *The Meaning of Freedom: Economics, Politics, and Culture after Slavery.* Pittsburgh: University of Pittsburgh Press, 1992.

McGraw, Marie Tyler. "Richmond Free Blacks and African Colonization, 1816–1832." *Journal of American Studies* 21, no. 2 (August 1987): 207–224.

McKinley, P. Michael. *Pre-Revolutionary Caracas: Politics, Economy and Society, 1777–1811.* New York: Cambridge University Press, 1997.

MacLachlan, Colin, and William H. Beezley. *El Gran Pueblo: A History of Greater Mexico.* Upper Saddle River, N.J.: Prentice Hall, 2004.

McLagen, Elizabeth. "A Peculiar Paradise: A History of Blacks in Oregon." The Oregon Black History Project. Available online. URL: www.upa.pdx.edu/IMS/currentprojects/

TAHv3/Content/PDFs/Oregon-Statehood.pdf. Accessed January 13, 2011.

McLeod, Cynthia. *The Free Negress Elisabeth: Prisoner of Color.* London: Waterfront Press, 2004.

McLeroy, Sherrie. *Strangers in Their Midst: The Free Black Population of Amherst County, Virginia.* Bowie, Md.: Heritage Books, 1993.

McManus, Edgar J. *Black Bondage in the North.* Syracuse, N.Y.: Syracuse University Press, 1973.

———. *Law and Liberty in Early New England: Criminal Justice and Due Process, 1620–1692.* Reprint, Amherst: University of Massachusetts Press, 2009.

McMickle, Marvin Andrew. *An Encyclopedia of African American Christian Heritage.* Valley Forge, Pa.: Judson Press, 2002.

McPherson, James. *The Negro's Civil War: How American Blacks Felt and Acted during the War for the Union.* New York: Vintage, 2003.

Meade, Teresa A. *A Brief History of Brazil.* New York: Facts On File, 2003.

Mehlinger, Louis R. "The Attitude of the Free Negro Toward African Colonization." *Journal of Negro History* 1, no. 3 (June 1916): 276–301.

Meléndez, Carlos, and Quince Duncan. *El negro en Costa Rica.* San José: Editorial Costa Rica, 1989.

Melish, Joanne. *Disowning Slavery: Gradual Emancipation and Race in New England, 1780–1860.* Ithaca, N.Y.: Cornell University Press, 2000.

Mellafe R., Rolando. *La introducción de la esclavitud negra en Chile. Tráfico y rutas.* 2nd ed. Santiago, Chile: Editorial Universitaria, 1984.

Mello, José Antônio Gonçalves de. *Henrique Dias: Governador dos crioulos, negros e mulatos do Brasil.* Recife: Massangana, 1988.

Melton, J. Gordon. *A Will to Choose: The Origins of African American Methodism.* Lanham, Md.: Roman & Littlefield, 2007.

Mennucci, Sud. *O precursor do abolicionismo no Brasil—Luiz Gama.* Coleção Brasiliana, série 5, v. 119. São Paulo: Companhia Editora Nacional, 1938.

Merrill, Marlene. *Sarah Margru Kinson: The Two Worlds of an Amistad Captive.* Oberlin, Ohio: Oberlin Historical and Improvement Organization, 2003.

Metraux, Alfred. *Voodoo in Haiti.* New York: Pantheon, 1989.

Meyer, Michael C., and William H. Beezley. *The Oxford History of Mexico.* Oxford and New York: Oxford University Press, 2000.

Middleton, Stephen. *The Black Laws in the Old Northwest: A Documentary History.* Westport, Conn.: Greenwood Press, 1993.

———. *The Black Laws: Race and the Legal Process in Early Ohio.* Athens: Ohio University Press, 2005.

Miller, Edward A. *The Black Civil War Soldiers of Illinois: The Story of the Twenty-Ninth U.S. Colored Infantry.* Columbia: University of South Carolina Press, 1998.

———. *Gullah Statesman: Robert Smalls from Slavery to Congress, 1839–1915.* Columbia: University of South Carolina Press, 1995.

Miller, Floyd L. *The Search for a Black Nationality: Black Colonization and Emigration, 1787–1863.* Urbana: University of Illinois Press, 1975.

Miller, Joseph C. *Way of Death: Merchant Capitalism and the Angolan Slave Trade, 1730–1830.* Madison: University of Wisconsin Press, 1988.

Mills, Gary B. "Free African Americans in Pre-Civil War 'Anglo' Alabama: Slave Manumissions Gleaned from County Court Records." *National Genealogical Society Quarterly* 83 (June 1995): 127–142 and (September 1995): 197–214.

———. "Miscegenation and the Free Negro in Antebellum 'Anglo' Alabama: A Reexamination of Southern Race Relations." *The Journal of American History* 68 (June 1981): 16–34.

———. "Shades of Ambiguity: Comparing Antebellum Free People of Color in 'Anglo' Alabama and 'Latin' Louisiana." In *Plain Folk of the South Revisited,* edited by Samuel C. Hyde, Jr. Baton Rouge: Louisiana State University Press, 1997.

Mintz, Sidney W. *Caribbean Transformations.* Chicago: Aldine, 1974.

———. *Sweetness and Power: The Place of Sugar in Modern History.* New York: Viking, 1985.

Mitre, Bartolomé. "Falucho." *Phylon* 5, no. 2 (1944): 136–137.

Moedano Gabriel, "Notas etnohistóricas sobre la población negra de la Costa Chica." In *Arqueología e Etnohistoria del Estado de Guerrero.* Mexico: SEP-INAH—Gobierno del Estado de Guerrero, 1986.

Mohr, Clarence L. *On the Threshold of Freedom: Masters and Slaves in Civil War Georgia.* Athens: University of Georgia Press, 1986.

Moitt, Bernard. *Women and Slavery in the French Antilles, 1635–1848.* Bloomington: Indiana University Press, 2001.

Montaño, Oscar D. *Umkhonto: la lanza negra. Historia del aporte negro-africano en la formación del Uruguay.* Montevideo: Rosebud Ediciones, 1997.

Montoya, Salvador. "Milicias negras y mulatas en el Reino de Guatemala, siglo XVIII." *Caravelle: Cahiers du monde hispanique et luso-brésilien* 49 (1987): 93–104.

Moore, John Preston. *Revolt in Louisiana: The Spanish Occupation, 1766–1770.* Baton Rouge: Louisiana State University Press, 1976.

Moore, Leonard M. *Carl B. Stokes and the Rise of Black Political Power.* Champaign: University of Illinois Press, 2003.

Moreau de St.-Méry, M. L. E. *Description topographique, physique civile, politique et historique de la partie française de l'isle de Saint-Domingue*. 3 vols. Paris: printed privately, 1788 [Philadelphia 1796–1797]. Reprint of second edition, Blanche Maurel and Etienne Taillemite, eds., Paris: Société de l'Histoire des Colonies Françaises, 1958. Portion of volume 1 in English translation available as *Civilization That Perished*. Translated by I. D. Spencer. New York: University Press of America, 1986.

Morgan, Edmund. *American Slavery American Freedom: The Ordeal of Colonial Virginia*. New York: W. W. Norton, 1995.

Morgan, Phillip D. "The Black Experience in the British Empire, 1680–1810." In *Black Experience and Empire*, edited by Phillip D. Morgan and Sean Hawkins. Oxford: Oxford University Press, 2004.

Mörner, Magnus. *Race Mixture in the History of Latin America*. Boston: Little, Brown, 1967.

Morris, Robert C. *Reading, 'Riting, and Reconstruction: The Education of Freedmen in the South, 1861–1870*. Chicago: University of Chicago Press.

Morris, Roy. *Fraud of the Century: Rutherford B. Hayes, Samuel Tilden, and the Stolen Election of 1876*. New York: Simon & Schuster, 2003.

Morris, Thomas D. *Free Men All: The Personal Liberty Laws of the North, 1780–1861*. Baltimore: Johns Hopkins University Press, 1974.

Moses, Wilson Jeremiah. *Alexander Crummell: A Study of Civilization and Discontent*. New York: Oxford University Press, 1989.

Moya Pons, Frank. *The Dominican Republic, a National History*. New Rochelle, N.Y.: Hispaniola Books, 1995.

Múnera, Alfonso. "En busca del mestizaje." In *Fronteras imaginadas. La construcción de las razas y de la geografía en el siglo XIX colombiano*, 129–152. Bogota: Planeta, 2005.

Murphy, Thomas J., S. J. *Jesuit Slaveholding in Maryland, 1717–1838*. New York: Routledge, 2001.

Murray, David R. *Odious Commerce: Britain, Spain, and the Abolition of the Cuban Slave Trade*. Cambridge: Cambridge University Press, 1980.

Murray, Pauli, ed. *States Laws on Race and Color*. Athens: University of Georgia Press, 1997.

Muzart, Zahidé Lupinacci. "Maria Firmina dos Reis." In *Escritoras Brasileiras do SéculoXIX*. Florianópolis, Santa Catarina: Editora Mulheres, 1999.

Myers, Norma. *Reconstructing the Black Past: Blacks in Britain, 1780–1830*. London: Frank Cass, 1996.

Nabokov, Vladimir. *Notes on Prosody: And Abram Gannibal*. Princeton, N.J.: Princeton University Press, 1964.

Nabuco, Joaquim. *Abolitionism: The Brazilian Antislavery Struggle*. Translated and edited by Robert Conrad. Urbana: University of Illinois Press, 1977.

Nafafe, José Lingna. *Colonial Encounters: Issues of Culture, Hybridity and Creolisation: Portuguese Mercantile Settlers in West Africa*. Bern: Peter Lang, 2007.

Naro, Nancy Priscilla. *Cultures of the Lusophone Black Atlantic (Studies of the Americas)*. New York: Palgrave Macmillan, 2007.

——, ed. *Blacks, Coloureds and National Identity in Nineteenth-Century Latin America*. London: ILAS, University of London, 2003.

Nash, Gary B. *Forging Freedom: The Formation of Philadelphia's Black Community, 1720–1840*. Cambridge, Mass.: Harvard University Press, 1988.

——. *Race and Revolution*. Madison, Wis.: Madison House, 1990.

Nash, Gary B., and Graham Russell Gao Hodges. *Friends of Liberty: Thomas Jefferson, Tadeuz Kosciuszko, and Agrippa Hull; A Tale of Three Patriots, Two Revolutions, and a Tragic Betrayal of Freedom in the New Nation*. New York: Basic Books, 2008.

Nash, Gary B., and Jean R. Soderlund. *Freedom by Degrees: Emancipation in Pennsylvania and Its Aftermath*. New York: Oxford University Press, 1991.

Nash, Roderick W. "William Parker and the Christiana Riot." *Journal of Negro History* 46, no. 1 (January 1961): 24–31.

Necheles, Ruth F. *The Abbé Grégoire, 1787–1831: The Odyssey of an Egalitarian*. Westport, Conn.: Greenwood, 1971.

Neiman, Fraser D. "Coincidence or Causal Connection? The Relationship between Thomas Jefferson's Visits to Monticello and Sally Hemings's Conceptions." *William and Mary Quarterly* 57, no. 1 (January 2000): 198–210.

Nelson, Larry E. "Black Leaders and the Presidential Election of 1864." *Journal of Negro History* 63: 1 (January 1978): 42–58.

Newcombe, Covelle. *Black Fire: A Story of Henri Christophe*. New York: Longman's, 1940.

Newman, Richard S. *Freedom's Prophet: Bishop Richard Allen, the AME Church, and the Black Founding Fathers*. New York: New York University Press, 2008.

——. *The Transformation of American Abolitionism: Fighting Slavery in the Early Republic*. Chapel Hill: University of North Carolina Press, 2002.

Newton, Melanie. *The Children of Africa in the Colonies: Free People of Color in Barbados in the Age of Emancipation*. Baton Rouge: Louisiana State University Press, 2008.

Newton, Velma. *The Silver Men: West Indian Labour Migration to Panama, 1850–1914*. Kingston, Jamaica: Ian Randle, 2004.

New York Public Library. "Preliminary Emancipation Proclamation: A Virtual Visit." Available online. URL: http://www.nysl.nysed.gov/library/features/ep/. Accessed January 13, 2011.

Nicholls, David. *From Dessalines to Duvalier: Race, Color, and National Independence in Haiti*. New Brunswick, N.J.: Rutgers University Press, 1995.

Nieman, Donald G. *To Set the Law in Motion: The Freemen's Bureau and the Legal Rights of Blacks, 1865–1868*. Millwood, N.Y.: KTO Press, 1979.

Nishida, Mieko. *Slavery and Identity. Ethnicity, Gender and Race in Salvador, Brazil, 1808–1888*. Bloomington: Indiana University Press, 2003.

Nordmann, Christopher Andrew. "Free Negroes in Mobile County, Alabama." Ph.D. diss., University of Alabama, 1990.

Oakes, James. *The Radical and the Republican: Frederick Douglass, Abraham Lincoln, and the Triumph of Antislavery Politics*. New York: Norton, 2007.

Ochs, Stephen J. *A Black Patriot and a White Priest: Andre Cailloux and Claude Paschal Maistre in Civil War New Orleans*. Baton Rouge: Louisiana State University Press, 2000.

Ofari, Earl. *"Let Your Motto Be Resistance": The Life and Thought of Henry Highland Garnet*. Boston: Beacon Press, 1972.

Ogg, Frederic Austin. "Slave Property as an Issue in Anglo-American Diplomacy, 1782–1828." Unpublished Ph.D. thesis, Harvard University, 1908.

Oldham, James. *The Mansfield Manuscripts and the Growth of English Law in the Eighteenth Century*. Chapel Hill: University of North Carolina Press 1992.

———. "New Light on Mansfield and Slavery." *Journal of British Studies* 27 (1988): 45–68.

Oostindie, Gerrit Jan. *Het paradijs overzee. De 'Nederlandse' Caraïben en Nederland*. Amsterdam, Netherlands: Bert Bakker, 1997.

Opie, Frederick. *Black Labor Migration in Caribbean Guatemala, 1882–1923*. Gainesville: University Press of Florida, 2009.

Othow, Helen C. *John Chavis: African American Patriot, Preacher, Teacher, and Mentor (1783–1838)*. New York: McFarland, 2001.

O'Toole, James. *Passing for White: Race, Religion, and the Healy Family, 1820–1920*. Amherst: University of Massachusetts Press, 2003.

———. "Passing Free." *Boston College Magazine* (Summer 2003). Available online. URL: http://bcm.bc.edu/issues/summer_2003/ft_passing.html. Accessed January 13, 2011.

Oubre, Claude F. *Forty Acres and a Mule: The Freedmen's Bureau and Black Land Ownership*. Baton Rouge: Louisiana State University Press, 1978.

Oviedo y Valdés, Gonzalo Fernández de. *General and Natural History of the Indies*. Book 35. Translated by Basil Hendrick. Published as *The Journey of the Vaca Party: The Account of The Narváez Expedition, 1528–1536*. Carbondale: Southern Illinois University Press, 1974.

Painter, Nell Irvin. *Sojourner Truth: A Life, a Symbol*. New York: W. W. Norton, 1996.

Pame, Stella. *Cyrille Bissette, Un martyre de la liberté*. Paris: Editions Désormeaux, 1999.

Paquette, Robert L. "From Rebellion to Revisionism: The Continuing Debate about the Denmark Vesey Affair." *Journal of the Historical Society* 4 (Fall 2004): 291–334.

———. *Sugar Is Made with Blood: The Conspiracy of La Escalera and the Conflict between Empires over Slavery in Cuba*. Middletown, Conn.: Wesleyan University Press, 1990.

Park, Eunjin. *"White" Americans in "Black" Africa: Black and White American Methodist Missionaries in Liberia, 1820–1875*. New York: Routledge, 2001.

Pascoe, Peggy. *What Comes Naturally: Miscegenation Law and the Making of Race in America*. Oxford: Oxford University Press, 2009.

Pasternak, Martin B. *Rise Now and Fly to Arms: The Life of Henry Highland Garnet*. New York: Garland, 1995.

Paula, A. F. "Van slaaf tot quasi-slaaf: een sociaal-historische studie over de dubbelzinnige slavenemancipatie op Nederlands Sint Maarten, 1816–1863." Ph.D. thesis, University of Utrecht, 1992.

Payne, Daniel. *History of the African Methodist Episcopal Church*. 1891. New York: Arno Press, 1969.

———. "Slavery Brutalizes Man." *Lutheran Herald and Journal of the Fort Plain, New York, Franckean Synod* 1, no. 15 (August 1, 1839): 113–114.

Peabody, Sue. "A Dangerous Zeal: Catholic Missions to Slaves in the French Antilles, 1635–1800." *French Historical Studies* 25, no. 1 (2002): 53–90.

———. *"There Are No Slaves in France": The Political Culture of Race and Slavery in the Ancien Regime*. Oxford: Oxford University Press, 2002.

Peabody, Sue, and Keila Grinberg. *Slavery, Freedom, and the Law in the Atlantic World: A Brief History with Documents*. Boston: Bedford/St. Martin's, 2007.

Pearson, Edward, ed. *Designs against Charleston: The Trial Record of the Denmark Vesey Conspiracy of 1822*. Chapel Hill: University of North Carolina Press, 1999.

Pendelton, Anthony, Capt. USAF. "From Slave to Spy: Mary Elizabeth Bowser." *Air Intelligence Spokesman Magazine*, November, 2004.

Pereda Valdés, Ildefonso. *El negro en el Uruguay: pasado y presente*. Montevideo, Uruguay: Revista del Instituto Histórico y Geográfico del Uruguay, 1965.

Pérez, Louis A., Jr. *Cuba: Between Reform and Revolution*. 3rd ed. New York: Oxford University Press, 2006.

Philippe, Jean-Baptiste. *A Free Mulatto*. Port of Spain: Paria, 1987.

Phillips, Christopher. *Freedom's Port: The African American Community of Baltimore, 1790–1860*. Urbana: University of Illinois Press, 1997.

Piersen, William D. *Black Yankees: The Development of an Afro-American Subculture in 18th Century New England*. Amherst: University of Massachusetts Press, 1988.

Pike, Ruth. "Black Rebels: The Cimarrons of Sixteenth-Century Panama." *Americas* 64, no. 2 (October 2007): 243–266.

Pinckard, George. *Notes on the West Indies: Written during the Expedition under the Command of the Late General Sir Ralph Abercromby: Including Observations on the Island of Barbadoes, and the Settlements Captured by the British Troops, Upon the Coast of Guiana. . .* London: Longman, Hurst, Rees, and Orme, 1806.

Pineda, Baron L. *Shipwrecked Identities: Navigating Race on Nicaragua's Mosquito Coast.* New Brunswick, N.J.: Rutgers University Press, 2006.

Piñero de Rivera, Flor. *Arturo Schomburg un puertorriqueño descubre el legado histórico del negro.* San Juan: Centro de Estudios Avanzados de Puerto Rico y el Caribe, 2004.

Pittsburgh History and Landmarks Commission. *A Legacy in Bricks and Mortar: African American Landmarks in Allegheny County.* Pittsburgh: Pittsburgh History and Landmarks Commission, 1995.

Polk, Donna Mays. *Black Men and Women of Nebraska.* Lincoln: Nebraska Black History Preservation Society, 1981.

Popkin, Jeremy. *Facing Racial Revolution: Eyewitness Accounts of the Haitian Revolution.* Chicago: University of Chicago Press, 2007.

Popkin, Jeremy D., and Richard H. Popkin, eds. *The Abbé Grégoire and His World.* Dordrecht: Kluwer Academic, 2001.

Potter, David M., and Don E. Fehrenbacher. *The Impending Crisis, 1848–1861.* New York: Harper & Row, 1976.

Potts, E. Daniel, and Annette Potts. *Young America and Australian Gold—Americans and the Gold Rush of the 1850s.* St. Lucia: University of Queensland Press, 1974.

Powers, Bernard E., Jr. *Black Charlestonians: A Social History, 1882–1885.* Fayetteville: University of Arkansas Press, 1994.

Prados-Torreira, Teresa. *Mambisas: Rebel Women in Nineteenth-Century Cuba.* Gainesville: University of Florida Press, 2005.

Price, H. H. "Blacks in 19th-Century Maine." *Maine Archives and Museums (MAM) Newsletter* 4, no. 4 (November 2001).

Price, H. H., and Gerald E. Talbot. *Maine's Visible Black History: The First Chronicle of Its People.* Gardiner, Maine: Tillbury House, 2006.

Price, Richard. *Maroon Societies: Rebel Slave Communities in the Americas.* 3rd ed. Baltimore: Johns Hopkins University Press, 1996.

Prince, Hoare. *Memoirs of Granville Sharp, Esq. Composed from His Own Manuscripts, and Other Authentic Documents.* London: Henry Colburn, 1820.

Public Broadcasting Service. "Africans in America/Part 2/Lemuel Haynes." Available online. URL: http://www.pbs.org/wgbh/aia/part2/2p29.html. Accessed January 13, 2011.

Public Broadcasting Service. "Africans in America/Part 2/Venture Smith." Available online. URL: http://www.pbs.org/wgbh/aia/part2/2p80.html. Accessed January 13, 2011

Public Broadcasting System, "The Rise and Fall of Jim Crow: The Ku Klux Klan (1866)." Available online. URL: http://www.pbs.org/wnet/jimcrow/stories_events_kkk.html. Accessed January 13, 2011.

Pulis, John W., ed. *Moving On: Black Loyalists in the Afro-Atlantic World.* New York: Garland, 1999.

Pushkin, Alexander. "The Moor of Peter the Great." In *The Complete Prose Tales of Alexander Pushkin,* translated by Gillon R. Aitken. London: Barrie Books, 1966.

Pybus, Cassandra. *Black Founders: The Unknown Story of Australia's First Black Settlers.* Sydney: University of New South Wales Press, 2006.

———. *Epic Journeys of Freedom: Runaway Slaves of the American Revolution and Their Global Quest for Liberty.* Boston: Beacon Press, 2006.

———. "A Touch of Tar: African Settlers in Colonial Australia and the Implications for Issues of Aboriginality." *London Papers in Australian Studies,* no. 3. London: Menzies Centre for Australian Studies—Kings College London, 2001.

Quarles, Benjamin. *Black Abolitionists.* New York: Oxford University Press, 1969.

———. *Frederick Douglass.* Washington, D.C.: Associated Publishers, 1948.

———. *Lincoln and the Negro.* New York: Oxford University Press, 1962.

———. *The Negro in the Civil War.* Boston: Little, Brown, 1953.

Quiroz, Francisco. *Artesanos y manufactureros en Lima colonial.* Lima: Instituto de Estudios Peruanos, 2008.

Rabinowitz, Howard N., ed. *Southern Black Leaders of the Reconstruction Era.* Champaign: University of Illinois Press, 1982.

Raboteau, Albert J. *Slave Religion: The Invisible Institution in the Antebellum South.* Oxford: Oxford University Press, 1978.

Rahier, Jean Muteba. "Blackness, the Racial/Spatial Order, Migrations, and Miss Ecuador, 1995–1996." *American Anthropologist* 100, no. 2 (June 1998): 421–430.

Raimond, Julien. *Observations sur l'origine et les progrès du préjugé des colons blancs contre les hommes de couleur.* Paris: Belin, Desenne, Bailly, 1791.

Rama, Carlos M. *Los afrouruguayos.* 3rd ed. Montevideo, Uruguay: Editorial "El Siglo Ilustrado," 1969.

Ramos Rosado, Marie. *La mujer negra en la lietratura puertorriqueña.* Río Piedras: Editorial de la Universidad de Puerto Rico, Instituto de Cultura Puertorriqueña and Editorial Cultural, 2003.

Randall, Laura. "Making a Living: African-Americans in Nineteenth-Century New England." *Humanities* 16, no. 1 (January–February 1995).

Randel, John M., ed. "Bland, James A(llen)." In *Harvard Biographical Dictionary of Music.* Cambridge, Mass.: Harvard University Press, 1996.

Ravage, John W. *Black Pioneers: Images of the Black Experience on the North American Frontier.* Salt Lake City: University of Utah Press, 1997.

Raynal, Guillaume, and Peter Jimack. *A History of the Two Indies: A Translated Selection of Writings from Raynal's* Histoire philosophique et politique des établissements & du commerce des européens dans les deux Indes. Ashgate Publishing, 2006.

Rediker, Marcus. *The Slave Ship: A Human History.* New York: Viking, 2007.

———. *Villains of All Nations: Atlantic Pirates in the Golden Age.* Boston: Beacon Press, 2004.

Redkey, Adam. *A Grand Army of Black Men: Letters from African-American Soldiers in the Union Army, 1861–1865.* Cambridge Studies in American Literature and Culture. Cambridge: Cambridge University Press, 1992.

Rehnquist, William H. *Centennial Crisis: The Disputed Election of 1876.* New York: Knopf, 2004.

Reid, Michele. "Protesting Service: Free Black Response to Cuba's Reestablished Militia of Color." *Journal of Colonialism and Colonial History* 5, no. 2 (Fall 2004).

Reidy, Joseph P. "Black Men in Navy Blue during the Civil War." *Prologue Magazine* 33, no. 3 (Fall 2001): Washington DC: National Archives and Records Administration. Available online. URL: http://www.archives.gov/publications/prologue/2001/fall/black-sailors-1.html. Accessed January 13, 2011.

Reinders, Robert C. "The Decline of the New Orleans Free Negro in the Decade before the Civil War." *Journal of Mississippi History* 24 (January-October 1962): 88–99.

Reis, João José. *Death Is a Festival: Funeral Rites and Rebellion in Nineteenth-Century Brazil.* Chapel Hill: University of North Carolina Press, 2003.

———. *Slave Rebellion in Brazil: The Muslim Uprising of 1835 in Bahía.* Johns Hopkins Studies in Atlantic History and Culture. Baltimore: Johns Hopkins University Press, 1993.

Reiss, Oscar. *Blacks in Colonial America.* Jefferson, N.C.: McFarland, 2006.

Renfro, Herbert G. *Life and Works of Phillis Wheatley.* Salem, Mass.: Ayer, 1993.

Renkema, W. E. "Het Curaçaose plantagebedrijf in de negentiende eeuw." Zutphen, Netherlands: De Walburg Pers. Ph.D. thesis, Free University of Amsterdam, 1981.

Report of Mr. Kennedy, of Maryland, from the Committee on Commerce of the House of Representatives of the United States on the African Slave Trade. Washington, D.C.: Gales and Seaton, 1843. Reprint, Salem, Mass.: Ayer, ass. 1971.

Restall, Matthew. *Beyond Black and Red: African-Native Relations in Colonial Latin America.* Albuquerque: University of New Mexico Press, 2005.

———. "Black Conquistadors: Armed Africans in Early Spanish America." *Americas* 57, no. 2 (2000): 171–205.

———. "Conquistadores negros africanos armados en la temprana Hispanoamérica." In *Pautas de convivencia étnica en América latina colonial (indios, negros, mulatos, pardos y esclavos),* edited by Juan M. de la Serna, 19–72. Mexico City: UNAM-Gob Edo Guanajuato, 2005.

Richard, K. Keith. "Unwelcome Settlers: Black and Mulatto Oregon Pioneers." *Oregon Historical Quarterly* 84 (1983): Part 1, 29–55; Part 2, 172–205.

Richardson, M. *Maria Stewart: America's First Black Woman Political Writer: Essays and Speeches.* Bloomington: Indiana University Press, 1987.

Ripley, C. Peter, ed. *The Black Abolitionist Papers.* 5 vols. Chapel Hill: University of North Carolina Press, 1986–1992.

Roberson, Jere W. "Edward P. McCabe and the Langston Experiment." *Chronicles of Oklahoma* 51, no. 3 (Fall 1973): 343–355.

Robinson, David. *Denmark Vesey: The Buried History of America's Largest Slave Rebellion and the Man Who Led It.* New York: Alfred A. Knopf, 1999.

Robinson, Lloyd. *The Stolen Election: Hayes versus Tilden, 1876.* New York: Tom Doherty Associates, 2001.

Rodríguez O, Jaime E., ed. *The Independence of Mexico and the Creation of the New Nation.* UCLA Latin American Studies. Los Angeles: UCLA Latin American Center Publications, 1989.

Rogers, Dominique. "Réussir dans un monde d'hommes: les stratégies des femmes de couleur libres du Cap-Français." *Journal of Haitian Studies* 9, no. 1 (Spring 2003): 40-51.

Rogers, Dominique, and Stewart King. "Housekeepers, Merchants, *Rentières*: Free Women of Color in the Port Cities of Colonial Saint-Domingue, 1750–1790." In *Women in Port: Gendering Communities, Economies, and Social Networks in Atlantic Port Cities, 1500–1800,* edited by Doug Catterall and Jodi Campbell. Leiden: Brill, forthcoming.

Römer, René Antonio. "Un pueblo na kaminda. Een sociologisch historische studie van de Curaçaose samenleving." Zutphen, Netherlands: De Walburg Pers. Ph.D. thesis, University of Leiden, 1979.

Rose, Willie Lee. *Rehearsal for Reconstruction: The Port Royal Experiment.* New York: Vintage Books, 1964.

Roseboom, Eugene H., and Francis P. Weisenburger. *A History of Ohio.* Columbus: Ohio Historical Society, 1991.

Roundtree, Alton G., and Paul M. Bessel. *Out of the Shadows: Prince Hall Freemasonry in America, 200 Years of Endurance.* Forestville, Md.: KLR, 2006.

Roussève, Charles Barthelemy. *The Negro in Louisiana: Aspects of His History and His Literature.* New Orleans: Xavier University Press, 1937.

Rupert, Linda M. "Inter Imperial Trade and Local Identity: Curaçao in the Colonial Atlantic World." Ph.D. thesis, Duke University, 2006.

Russell-Wood, A. J. R. *The Black Man in Slavery and Freedom in Colonial Brazil.* New York: Palgrave Macmillan, 1982.

Rycenga, J. "A Greater Awakening: Women's Intellect as a Factor in Early Abolitionist Movements, 1824–1834." *Journal of Feminist Studies in Religion* 21, no. 2 (Fall 2005): 31–59.

Safford, Frank, and Marco Palacios. *Colombia: Fragmented Land, Divided Society.* New York: Oxford University Press, 2002.

Saillant, John. *Black Puritan, Black Republican: The Life and Thought of Lemuel Haynes, 1753–1833.* New York: Oxford University Press, 2003.

Sammons, Mark J., and Valerie Cunningham. *Black Ports-mouth: Three Centuries of African-American Heritage.* Durham, N.H.: University of New Hampshire Press, 2004.

Sandburg, Carl. *Abraham Lincoln: The War Years.* Vol. 2. New York: Harcourt, Brace, 1939.

Sanders, James E. *Contentious Republicans: Popular Politics, Race, and Class in Nineteenth-Century Colombia.* Durham, N.C.: Duke University Press, 2004.

Santos, Rodulfo Cortes. *El regimen de "las gracias al sacar" en Venezuela durante el período hispánico.* Caracas: Academia Nacional de la Historia, 1978.

Sater, William F. "The Black Experience in Chile." In *Slavery and Race Relations in Latin America,* edited by Robert Brent Toplin, 13–50. Westport, Conn.: Greenwood Press, 1974.

Saunders, A. C. de C. M. *A Social History of Black Slaves and Freedmen in Portugal, 1441–1555.* Cambridge: Cambridge University Press, 2010.

Savage, W. Sherman. "The Influence of John Chavis and Lunsford Lane on the History of North Carolina." *Journal of Negro History* 25 (January 1940): 14–24.

Scarano, Francisco A. *Puerto Rico: Cinco siglos de historia.* San Juan: McGraw-Hill, 1993.

Schafer, Daniel L. *Anna Kingsley.* 1994. Reprint, Saint Augustine, Fla.: Saint Augustine Historical Society, 1997.

Schafer, Judith K. *Becoming Free, Remaining Free: Manumission and Enslavement in New Orleans, 1846–1862.* Baton Rouge: Louisiana State University Press, 2003.

Schama, Simon. *Rough Crossings: Britain, the Slaves and the American Revolution.* New York: HarperCollins, 2006.

Schecter, Barnet. *The Devil's Own Work: The Civil War Draft Riots and the Fight to Reconstruct America.* New York: Walker, 2005.

Scherr, Arthur. "Governor James Monroe and the Southampton Slave Resistance of 1799." *Historian* 61, no. 3 (1999): 557–578.

Schor, Joel. *Henry Highland Garnet, a Voice of Black Radicalism in the Nineteenth Century.* Westport, Conn.: Greenwood Press, 1977.

Schwalm, Leslie A. *Emancipation's Diaspora: Race and Reconstruction in the Upper Midwest.* Chapel Hill: University of North Carolina Press, 2009.

Schwarcz, Lilia Moritz. *The Emperor's Beard: Dom Pedro II and His Tropical Monarchy in Brazil.* New York: Hill & Wang, 2003.

Schwartz, Rosalie. *Across the Rio to Freedom: U.S. Negroes in Mexico.* El Paso: Western Press, University of Texas at El Paso, 1975.

Schwartz, Stuart. "The Manumission of Slaves in Colonial Brazil: Bahía 1648–1745." *Hispanic American Historical Review* 54, no. 4 (1974): 603–635.

———. *Slaves, Peasants, and Rebels: Reconsidering Brazilian Slavery.* Blacks in the New World. Urbana: University of Illinois Press, 1992.

———. *Sugar Plantations in the Formation of Brazilian Society: Bahía, 1550–1835.* New York: Cambridge University Press, 1985.

———. "Tapanhuns, Negros da Terra, and Curibocas: Common Cause and Confrontation between Blacks and Natives in Colonial Brazil." In, *Beyond Black and Red: African-Native Relations in Colonial Latin America,* edited by Matthew Restall. Albuquerque: University of New Mexico Press, 2005.

Schweninger, Loren. "James Rapier and the Negro Labor Movement, 1869–1872." *Alabama Review* 28 (July 1975): 185–201.

———. *James T. Rapier and Reconstruction.* Chicago: University of Chicago Press, 1978.

Sciway.net. The South Carolina Information Highway. "South Carolina African Americans, 1525–1865." Available online. URL: http://www.sciway.net/afam/slavery/indexs.html. Accessed January 13, 2011.

Scobie, Edward. *Black Britannia: A History of Blacks in Britain.* Chicago: Johnson, 1972.

Scott, Rebecca J. *Slave Emancipation in Cuba: The Transition to Free Labor, 1860–1899.* Princeton, N.J.: Princeton University Press, 1985.

Seacole, Mary. *The Wonderful Adventures of Mrs. Seacole in Many Lands.* 1857. Reprint, London: Penguin, 2005.

Selig, Robert A. "The Revolution's Black Soldiers." Available online. URL: http://www.americanrevolution.org/blk.html. Accessed December 9, 2009.

Senior Angulo, Diana. "La incorporación social en Costa Rica de la población Afrocostarricense durante el siglo XX, 1927–1963." Tesis de Maestría en Historia, Universidad de Costa Rica, 2007.

Sensbach, Jon. *Rebecca's Revival: Creating Black Christianity in the Atlantic World.* Cambridge, Mass.: Harvard University Press, 2005.

Sepinwall, Alyssa Goldstein. *The Abbé Grégoire and the French Revolution: The Making of Modern Universalism.* Berkeley: University of California Press, 2005.

Seraile, William. "The Brief Diplomatic Career of Henry Highland Garnet." *Phylon* 46, no. 1 (1st Quarter 1985): 71–81.

Shannon, Ronald. *Profiles in Ohio: A Legacy of African American Achievement.* Bloomington, Ind.: Universe Inc., 2008.

Sherlock, Philip, and Hazel Bennett. *The Story of the Jamaican People.* New York: Marcus Weiner, 1998.

Sherwood, Marika. *After Abolition: Britain and the Slave Trade since 1807.* New York: Palgrave MacMillan, 2007.

Shick, Tom. *Behold the Promised Land: A History of Afro-American Settler Society in Nineteenth-Century Liberia.* Baltimore: Johns Hopkins University Press, 1980.

Shumway, Nicholas. *The Invention of Argentina.* Berkeley and Los Angeles: University of California Press, 1991.

Shyllon, F. O. *Black Slaves in Britain.* New York: Oxford University Press, 1974.

Shyllon, Folarin. *Black People in Britain, 1555–1833*. New York: Oxford University Press, 1977.

Sibley, Inez Knibb. *Baptists of Jamaica*. Kingston: Jamaica Baptist Union, 1965.

Sidbury, James. *Becoming African in America: Race and Nation in the Early Black Atlantic*. New York: Oxford University Press, 2007, esp. chap. 6, "African Churches in the Atlantic World."

Silva, Eduardo. "Black Abolitionists in the Quilombo of Leblon, Rio de Janeiro: Symbols, Organizers and Revolutionaries." In *Beyond Slavery: The Multilayered Legacy of Africans in Latin America and the Caribbean*, edited by Darin J. Davis Lanham, Md.: Rowman & Littlefield, 2006.

———. *Prince of the People: The Life and Times of a Brazilian Free Man of Colour*. Translated by Moyra Ashford. London: Verso, 1993.

Silverblatt, Irene. *Modern Inquisitions: Peru and the Colonial Origins of the Civilized World*. Durham, N.C.: Duke University Press, 2004.

Silverman, Jason H. *Unwelcome Guests: Canada West's Response to American Fugitive Slaves, 1800–1865*. Port Washington, N.Y.: Associated Faculty University Press, 1985.

Simpson, Brooks D. "Quandaries of Command: Ulysses S. Grant and Black Soldiers." In *Union and Emancipation: Essays on Politics and Race in the Civil War Era*, edited by David Blight and Brooks Simpson, 123–152. Kent, Ohio: Kent State University Press, 1997.

Simpson, Donald George. *Under the North Star: Black Communities in Upper Canada before Confederation*. Trenton, N.J.: Africa World Press, 2005.

Simpson, George E. *Black Religions in the New World*. New York: Columbia University Press, 1978.

Singleton, Theresa A., ed. *"I, Too, Am America": Archaeological Studies of African American Life*. Charlottesville: University Press of Virginia, 1999.

Sinkler, George. *The Racial Attitudes of American Presidents from Lincoln to Theodore Roosevelt*. New York: Doubleday, 1971.

Skates, John Ray. *Mississippi: A Bicentennial History*. New York: W. W. Norton, 1979.

Skidmore, Thomas E. *Black into White: Race and Nationality in Brazilian Thought*. New York: Oxford University Press, 1974.

Skocpol, Theda, Ariane Liazos, and Marshall Ganz. *What a Mighty Power We Can Be: African American Fraternal Groups and the Struggle for Racial Equality*. Princeton, N.J.: Princeton University Press, 2006.

Slatta, Richard. *Cowboys of the Americas*. New Haven, Conn.: Yale University Press, 1990.

Slaughter, Thomas P. *Bloody Dawn: The Christiana Riot and Racial Violence in the Antebellum North*. New York: Oxford University Press, 1991.

Smith, Elbert B. *The Presidencies of Zachary Taylor and Millard Fillmore*. Lawrence: University Press of Kansas, 1988.

Smith, Eric Ledell. "The Pittsburgh Memorial." *Pittsburgh History* 80, no. 3 (Fall 1997).

Smith, J. Douglas. "The Campaign for Racial Purity and the Erosion of Paternalism in Virginia, 1922–1930: 'Nominally White, Biologically Mixed, and Legally Negro.'" *Journal of Southern History* 68, no. 1 (2002): 65–106.

Smith, Julia Floyd. *Slavery and Plantation Growth in Antebellum Florida, 1821–1860*. Gainesville: University Press of Florida, 1973.

———. *Slavery and Rice Culture in Low Country Georgia: 1750–1860*. Knoxville: University of Tennessee Press, 1985.

Smith, Venture. *A Narrative of the Life and Adventures of Venture, a Native of Africa, but Resident above Sixty Years in the United States of America, Related by Himself*. Middletown, Conn.: J.S. Stewart, 1897. Available online. URL: http://docsouth.unc.edu/neh/venture2/menu.html. Accessed January 13, 2011.

Socolow, Susan. "Economic Roles of the Free Women of Color of Cap Francais." In *More Than Chattel: Black Women and Slavery in the Americas*, edited by David Gaspar and Darlene Hine, 279–297. Bloomington: Indiana University Press, 1996.

Sollors, Werner, ed. *Interracialism: Black-White Intermarriage in American History, Literature, and Law*. Oxford: Oxford University Press, 2000.

Southern, Eileen. *Biographical Dictionary of Afro-American and African Musicians*. Westport, Conn.: Greenwood Press, 1982.

———. *The Music of Black Americans: A History*. 3rd ed. New York: W. W. Norton, 1997.

Souza, Paulo Cesar. *A Sabinada: A revolta separatista da Bahia*. 1837. São Paulo: Brasiliense, 1987.

Spitzer, Leo. *Lives in Between: Assimilation and Marginality in Austria, Brazil, West Africa, 1780–1945*. Cambridge: Cambridge University Press, 1989, 101–126.

Stakeman, Randolph. "The Black Population of Maine, 1764–1900." *New England Journal of Black Studies* 8 (1989): 19–33.

Stalcup, Brenda, ed. *Reconstruction: Opposing Viewpoints*. Farmington Hills, Mich.: Greenhaven Press, 1995.

Stanley, Harrold. *American Abolitionists*. Essex: Pearson Education, 2001.

Stansell, Christine. *City of Women: Sex and Class in New York 1789–1860*. New York: Knopf, 1986.

Starobin, Robert, ed. *Denmark Vesey: The Slave Conspiracy of 1822*. Englewood Cliffs, N.J.: Prentice Hall, 1970.

State Trials, Queen v. Joseph, 1855, Library of the Supreme Court of Victoria.

Stauffer, John. *Giants: The Parallel Lives of Frederick Douglass and Abraham Lincoln*. New York: Twelve, 2008.

Stearns, Peter N. "The Free People of Color in Louisiana and St. Domingue: A Comparative Portrait of Two Three-Caste

Slave Societies." *Journal of Social History* 3, no. 4 (1970): 406–430.

Stedman, John Gabriel. *Stedman's Surinam: Life in an Eighteenth-Century Slave Society. An Abridged, Modernized Edition of Narrative of a Five Years Expedition against the Revolted Negroes of Surinam,* edited by Richard Price. Baltimore: Johns Hopkins University Press, 1992.

Steele, Beverley. *Grenada: A History of Its People.* London: Oxford: Macmillan Education, 2003.

Stein, Robert Louis. *The French Sugar Business in the Eighteenth Century.* Baton Rouge: Louisiana State University Press, 1988.

Stein, Stanley L. *Vassouras: A Brazilian Coffee County, 1850–1900: The Roles of Planter and Slave in a Plantation Society.* Princeton, N.J.: Princeton University Press, 1986.

Stewart, Maria, "An Address Delivered at the African Masonic Hall" and "A Lecture Given at Franklin Hall." In *Early Negro Writing, 1760–1837,* edited by Dorothy Porter, 129–140. Baltimore, Md.: Black Classic Press, 1995.

Stone, Frank Andrews. *African American Connecticut: The Black Scene in a New England State; Eighteenth to Twenty-First Century.* Bloomington, Ind.: Trafford, 2008.

Stovall, Tyler. "Race and the Making of the Nation: Blacks in Modern France." In *Diasporic Africa: A Reader.* New York: New York University Press, 2006.

Stowell, Daniel, ed. *Balancing Evils Judiciously: The Proslavery Writings of Zephaniah Kingsley.* Gainesville: University Press of Florida, 2000.

Sued Badillo, Jalil, and Angel Lopez Cantos. *Puerto Rico Negro.* Rio Piedras: Editorial Culture, 1986.

Swanson, Gail. *Slave Ship Guerrero.* West Conshohocken, Pa.: Infinity, 2005.

Sweet, Frank W. *Legal History of the Color Line: The Rise and Triumph of the One-Drop Rule.* Palm Coast, Fla.: Backintyme, 2005.

Sweet, James. "The Iberian Roots of American Racist Thought." *William and Mary Quarterly* 54 (1997): 143–166. Reprinted in *The Worlds of Unfree Labour from Indentured Servitude to Slavery,* edited by Colin A. Palmer. Aldershot, England: Ashgate, 1998, 1–24.

Swift, David E. *Black Prophets of Justice: Activist Clergy before the Civil War.* Baton Rouge: Louisiana State University Press, 1987.

Switala, William J. *Underground Railroad in Pennsylvania.* Mechanicsburg, Pa.: Stackpole Books, 2001.

Sylvester, Melvin. "African-American Freedom Fighters: Soldiers for Liberty." C. W. Post Campus of Long Island University, February 1995. Available online. URL: http://www2.liu.edu/cwis/cwp/library/aaffsfl.htm. Accessed January 13, 2011.

Tabbert, Mark A. "The Odd Fellows." Available online. URL: http://www.freemasons-freemasonry.com/tabbert5.html. Accessed January 13, 2011.

Taffin, Dominique, ed. *Moreau de Saint-Méry, ou les ambiguïtés d'un créole des Lumières.* Martinique: Société des amis des archives, 2006.

Tannenbaum, Frank. *Slave and Citizen: The Negro in the Americas.* New York: Vintage Books, 1946.

Tardieu, Jean-Pierre. *El negro en el Cuzco: los caminos de la alienación en la segunda mitad del siglo XVII.* Lima: Pontificia Universidad Católica del Perú, Banco Central de Reserva del Perú, 1998.

Taylor, Joe Gray. *Louisiana: A Bicentennial History.* New York: W. W. Norton, 1976.

Taylor, Michael J. C. "Governing the Devil in Hell: 'Bleeding Kansas' and the Destruction of the Franklin Pierce Presidency (1854–1856)." *White House Studies* 1 (2001): 185–205.

Taylor, Quintard. *In Search of the Racial Frontier: African Americans in the American West, 1528–1990.* New York: Norton, 1998.

Taylor, Quintard, and Shirley Ann Wilson Moore, eds. *African American Women Confront the West, 1600–2000.* Norman: University of Oklahoma Press, 2003.

Taylor, Rosser Howard. *The Free Negro in North Carolina.* James Sprunt Historical Publications, vol. 17, no. 1. Chapel Hill: University of North Carolina, 1920.

Taylor, Susie King. *Reminiscences of My Life in Camp.* Boston: privately published, 1902. Reprinted in *Collected Black Women's Narratives,* edited by Anthony Barthelemy. Oxford: Oxford University Press, 1988.

Tazewell, C. W. *Virginia's Ninth President, Joseph Jenkins Roberts.* Virginia Beach, Va.: W. S. Dawson, 1992.

Telles, Edward E. *Race in Another America: The Significance of Skin Color in Brazil.* Princeton, N.J.: Princeton University Press, 2006.

Tennessee Historical Society. "Callie House: 1861–1928." 1998. Available online. URL: http://tennesseeencyclopedia.net/imagegallery.php?entryID=C005a. Accessed December 9, 2008.

Thames Valley University. "Mary Seacole." Thames Valley University. Available online. URL: http://www.maryseacole.com/maryseacole/pages/. Accessed January 13, 2011.

Thomas, Hugh. *The Slave Trade: The Story of the Atlantic Slave Trade, 1440–1870.* New York: Simon & Schuster, 1999.

Thomas, Lamont. *Paul Cuffe: Black Entrepreneur and Pan-Africanist.* Champaign-Urbana: University of Illinois Press, 1988.

Thome, James, and J. Horace Kimball. *Emancipation in the West Indies, a Six Month's Tour in Antigua, Barbados, and Jamaica in the Year 1837.* New York: American Anti-Slavery Society, 1839. Available online. URL: http://books.google.com/books?id=BlwSAAAAIAAJ&dq=edward+jordon+jamaica&source=gbs_navlinks_s. Accessed March 30, 2010.

Thompson, Julius Eric. "Hiram Rhodes Revels, 1827–1901: A Reappraisal." *Journal of Negro History* 79 (Summer 1994): 297–303.

———. *Hiram R. Revels, 1827–1901: A Biography*. New York: Arno Press, 1982.

Thornell, Paul N.D. "The Absent Ones and the Providers: A Biography of the Vashons." *Journal of Negro History* 83, no. 4 (Autumn 1998): 284–301.

Thornton, John. *Africa and Africans in the Making of the Atlantic World (Studies in Comparative World History)*. Cambridge: Cambridge University Press, 1998.

Timmons, Wilbert. *Morelos of Mexico: Priest, Soldier, Statesman*. El Paso: Texas Western Press, 1970.

Toplin, Robert. *The Abolition of Slavery in Brazil*. New York: Atheneum, 1972.

Treece, David. *Exiles, Allies, Rebels: Brazil's Indianist Movement, Indigenist Politics, and the Imperial Nation-State*. Westport, Conn.: Greenwood, 2000.

Trefousse, Hans L. *Rutherford B. Hayes*. New York: Times Books, 2002.

Trexler, Harrison A. *Slavery in Missouri, 1804–1865*. Baltimore: Johns Hopkins University Press, 1914. Available online. URL: http://www.dinsdoc.com/trexler-1-0b.htm. Accessed January 13, 2011.

Trial of the Prisoners of the Amistad on the Writ of Habeas Corpus, before the Circuit Court of the United States. New York: 1839.

Tripp, Bernell. *Origins of the Black Press: New York, 1827–1847*. Northport, Ala.: Vision Press, 1992.

Trotter, James M. *Music and Some Highly Musical People*. Boston: Lee and Shepard, Publishers, 1881.

Trotter, Joe William, Jr., and Eric Ledell Smith, eds. *African Americans in Pennsylvania: Shifting Historical Perspectives*. University Park: Pennsylvania State University Press, 1997.

Trouillot, Michel-Rolph. *Haiti: State against Nation: The Origins and Legacy of Duvalierism*. New York: Monthly Review, 1989.

———. "The Inconvenience of Freedom: Free People of Color and the Political Aftermath of Slavery in Dominica and Saint-Domingue/Haiti." In *The Meaning of Freedom: Economics, Politics, and Culture after Slavery*, edited by Frank McGlynn and Seymour Drescher, 147–182. Pittsburgh: University of Pittsburgh Press, 1992.

———. "Motion in the System: Coffee, Color, and Slavery in Eighteenth-Century Saint-Domingue." *Review* 3 (Winter 1982): 331–388.

Truth, Sojourner. *Narrative of Sojourner Truth*. New York: Penguin Classics, 1998.

Turley, David. *The Culture of English Antislavery, 1780–1860*. New York: Routledge, 1991.

Turner, Edward Raymond. *The Negro in Pennsylvania: Slavery, Servitude, Freedom, 1639–1861*. Washington, D.C.: American Historical Association, 1911.

Turner, Mary. *Slaves and Missionaries: The Disintegration of Jamaican Slave Society, 1787–1834*. Barbados: University Press of the West Indies, 1998.

Twinam, Ann. *Public Lives, Private Secrets: Gender, Honor, Sexuality and Illegitimacy in Colonial Latin America*. Palo Alto, Calif.: Stanford University Press, 1999.

Tyler, Ronnie C. "Fugitive Slaves in Mexico." *Journal of Negro History* 57, no. 1 (January 1972): 1–12.

Ullman, Victor. *Martin R. Delany: The Beginnings of Black Nationalism*. Boston: Beacon Press, 1971.

University of Kentucky Library. "Notable Kentucky African Americans Database." University of Kentucky Library. Available online. URL: http://www.uky.edu/Libraries/NKAA/index.php. Accessed January 13, 2011.

Uya, Okon Edet. *From Slavery to Public Service: Robert Smalls (1839–1915)*. New York: Oxford University Press, 1971.

Valdés, José Manuel. *Salterio peruano o paráfrasis de los ciento cincuenta salmos de David y algunos cánticos sagrados*. Lima: 1833.

———. *Vida admirable del bienaventurado fray Martín de Porres, natural de Lima y donado profeso en el convento del Rosario del orden de predicadores de esta ciudad*. Lima: 1840.

Vandercook, John. *Black Majesty: The Life of Christophe, King of Haiti*. New York: Harper and Brothers, 1928.

van Deusen, Nancy. "Ursula de Jesus: A Seventeenth-Century Afro-Peruvian Mystic." In *The Human Tradition in Colonial Latin America*, edited by Kenneth J. Andrien, 88–103. Lanham, Md.: SR Books, 2002.

Van West, Carroll, ed. *Trial and Triumph: Essays in Tennessee's African American History*. Knoxville: University of Tennessee Press, 2002.

Van Young, Eric. *The Other Rebellion: Popular Violence, Ideology, and the Mexican Struggle for Independence, 1810–1821*. Palo Alto, Calif.: Stanford University Press, 2001.

Vargas Lugo, Elisa, and Gustavo Curiel. *Juan Correa, su vida y su obra. Cuerpo de documentos*. Mexico: Universidad Nacional Autonoma de Mexico, 1991.

Varon, Elizabeth. *"Southern Lady, Yankee Spy": The True Story of Elizabeth Van Lew, a Union Agent in the Heart of the Confederacy*. New York: Oxford University Press, 2003.

Vasconcellos, Sylvio de. *Vida e obra de Antônio Francisco Lisboa, o Aleijadinho*. São Paulo: Companhia Editora Nacional, 1979. Available online. URL: http://www.aleijadinho.net/. Accessed January 13, 2011.

Velazquez, Maria Elisa. *Juan Correa, mulato libre, maestro de pintor*. Mexico: Consejo Nacional para la Cultura y las Artes, 1998.

Vermont Folklife Center Media. "Journey's End: The Memories and Traditions of Daisy Turner and her Family." Available online. URL: http://www.prx.org/series/16101. Accessed January 13, 2011.

Vianna, Hélio. "Francisco Gê Acaiaba de Montezuma, Visconde de Jequitinhohna." *Revista do Instituto Histórico e Geográfico Brasileiro* 244 (July–September 1959): 104–135.

Vinson Ben III. "Articulating Space: The Free-Colored Military Establishment in Colonial Mexico from the Conquest to Independence." *Callaloo* 27, no. 1 (Winter 2004): 150–171.

———. "The Racial Profile of a Rural Mexican Province in the Costa Chica: Igualapa In 1791." *Americas* 57, no. 2 (October 2000): 269–282.

Vinson, Ben III, and Matthew Restall, eds. *Black Mexico: Race and Society from Colonial to Modern Times.* Albuquerque: University of New Mexico Press, 2009.

Virtual Vermont. "Vermont History: Lemuel Haynes." Available online. URL: http://www.virtualvermont.com/history/haynes.html. Accessed January 13, 2011.

Voelz, Peter. *Slave and Soldier: The Military Impact of Blacks in the Colonial Americas.* New York: Routledge, 1993.

von Germeten, Nicole. *Black Blood Brothers: Confraternities and Social Mobility for Afro-Mexicans.* Tallahassee: University Press of Florida, 2006.

Vorenberg, Michael. "Slave Reparations: The Untold Story." *Concord Monitor* (September 29, 2005).

Wade, Peter. *Blackness and Race Mixture: The Dynamics of Racial Identity in Colombia.* Baltimore: Johns Hopkins University Press, 1993.

Wade, Wyn Craig. *The Fiery Cross: The Ku-Klux Klan in America.* New York: Oxford University Press, 1987.

Wald, Elijah. *Escaping the Delta: Robert Johnson and the Invention of the Blues.* New York: HarperCollins, 2004.

Waldrep, Christopher. "Substituting Law for the Lash: Emancipation and Legal Formalism in a Mississippi County Court." *Journal of American History* 82, no. 4 (1996): 1,425–1,451.

Walker, David. *David Walker's Appeal.* Baltimore, Md.: Black Classic Press, 1997.

Walker, James W. St. G. *The Black Loyalists: The Search for a Promised Land in Nova Scotia and Sierra Leone, 1783–1870.* 1976. Reprint, Toronto: University of Toronto Press, 1992.

Walker, Juliet E. K. *Free Frank: A Black Pioneer on the Antebellum Frontier.* Lexington: University Press of Kentucky, 1983.

Walker, Sheila S., ed. *African Roots/American Cultures: Africa in the Creation of the Americas.* Lanham, Md.: Rowman & Littlefield, 2001.

Ward, Martha. *Voodoo Queen: The Spirited Lives of Marie Laveau.* Jackson: University Press of Mississippi, 2004.

Watson, Elinor. *Jim Beckwourth: Black Mountain Man and War Chief of the Crows.* Norman: University of Oklahoma Press, 1972.

Weiner, Mark S. *Black Trials: Citizenship from the Beginnings of Slavery to the End of Caste.* Westminster, Md.: Knopf, 2004.

———. "Notes and Documents: New Biographical Evidence on Somersett's Case." *Slavery and Abolition* 23 (2002): 121–136.

Welch, Pedro. *Slave Society in the City: Bridgetown, Barbados, 1680–1834.* Oxford: Ian Randle Publishers and James Currey Publishers, 2003.

Welch, Pedro, and Richard Goodridge. *"Red" and Black over White: Free Colored Women in Pre-Emancipation Barbados.* Bridgetown: Carib Research, 2000.

Wells, Ida B. *Southern Horrors: Lynch Law in All Its Phases.* Project Gutenberg. New York: 1892. Available online. URL: http://www.gutenberg.org/etext/14975. Accessed January 13, 2011.

Wesley, Charles H. "Negro Suffrage in the Period of Constitution Making, 1787–1865." *Journal of Negro History* 143 (April 1947): 32.

West, Cornel. *Race Matters.* New York: Vintage, 1993.

West, Jean M. "Slavery in America: History." *King Cotton: The Fiber of Slavery.* Available online. URL: http://www.slaveryinamerica.org/history/hs_es_cotton.htm. Accessed May 12, 2008.

Wheeler, Gerald E. "Hiram R. Revels: Negro Educator and Statesman." M.A. thesis, University of California at Berkeley, 1949.

White, A. O. "Prince Sauders: An Instance of Social Mobility among Antebellum New England Blacks." *Journal of Negro History* 60, no. 4 (1975): 526–535.

White, E. Frances. *Sierra Leone's Settler Women Traders: Women on the Afro-European Frontier.* Ann Arbor: University of Michigan Press, 1987.

White, Ellen Gibson. *John Clarkson and the African Adventure.* London: Macmillan Press, 1980.

White, Shane. *Somewhat More Independent: The End of Slavery in New York City, 1770–1810.* Athens: University of Georgia Press, 1991.

Whitfield, Harvey Amani. "African Americans in Burlington, 1880–1900." *Vermont History* 75, no. 2 (2007): 101–123.

———. *Black Refugees in British North America, 1815–1860.* Burlington: University of Vermont Press (University Press of New England), 2006.

Whitman, T. Stephen. *The Price of Freedom: Slavery and Manumission in Baltimore and Early National Maryland.* Frankfort: University of Kentucky Press, 1997.

Whitten, Norman E., Jr. *Class, Kinship, and Power in an Ecuadorian Town: The Negroes of San Lorenzo.* Palo Alto, Calif.: Stanford University Press, 1965.

———, ed. *Cultural Transformations and Ethnicity in Modern Ecuador.* Urbana: University of Illinois Press, 1981.

———, ed. *Millennial Ecuador: Critical Essays on Cultural Transformations and Social Dynamics.* Iowa City: University of Iowa Press, 2003.

Whitten, Norman E., Jr., and Diego Quiroga. "Ecuador." In *No Longer Invisible: Afro-Latin Americans Today.* London: Minority Rights Publications, 1995, 287–317.

Wiebe, Robert H. *The Opening of American Society.* New York: Alfred A. Knopf, 1984.

Wiencek, Henry. *An Imperfect God: George Washington, His Slaves, and the Creation of America.* New York: Farrar, Strauss & Giroux, 2004.

Wild, Anthony. *Coffee: A Dark History.* New York: Norton, 2007.

Wilkins, Ron. "Mexico's Legacy: A Refuge for Fugitive Slaves and Black Job-Seekers. New Perspectives on the Immigration Debate." *Black Commentator* 182 (May 4, 2006). Available online. URL: http://www.blackcommentator.com/182/182_mexico_black_history.html. Accessed January 13, 2011.

Wilkramangrake, Marina. *A World in Shadow: The Free Black in Antebellum South Carolina.* Columbia: University of South Carolina Press, 1989.

Williams, Adebayo. "Of Human Bondage and Literary Triumphs: Hannah Crafts and the Morphology of the Slave Narrative." *Research in African Literatures* 34, no. 1 (Spring 2003): 137–150.

Williams, David. *Bricks without Straw: A Comprehensive History of African Americans in Texas.* Austin, Tex.: Eakin Press, 1997.

Williams, Eric. *History of the People of Trinidad and Tobago.* London: Andre Deutsch, 1964.

Williams, John H. "Observations on Blacks and Bondage in Uruguay." *Americas* 43 (1987): 410–428.

Williams, Lou Falkner. *The Great South Carolina Ku Klux Klan Trials, 1871–1872.* Athens: University of Georgia Press, 1996.

Williams, William Henry. *Slavery and Freedom in Delaware, 1639–1865.* Wilmington, Del.: SR Books, 1996.

Williamson, Jane. "'I Don't Get Fair Play Here': A Black Vermonter Writes Home." *Vermont History* 75, no. 1 (2007): 35–38.

Wills, Garry. *Lincoln at Gettysburg: The Words That Remade a Nation.* New York: Simon & Schuster, 1992.

———. *The Negro President: Jefferson and the Slave Power.* Boston: Houghton Mifflin, 2003.

Wilson, Charles Reagan. *Baptized in Blood: The Religion of the Lost Cause, 1865–1920.* Athens: University of Georgia Press, 1980.

Wilson, Ellen Gibson. *The Loyal Blacks.* New York: G. P. Putnam's Sons, 1976.

Wilson, Joseph T. *The Black Phalanx: African American Soldiers in the War of Independence, the War of 1812 and the Civil War.* Hartford, Connecticut: 1887.

Wilson, Keith. *Campfires of Freedom: The Camp Life of Black Soldiers during the Civil War.* Kent, Ohio: Kent State University Press, 2002.

Winch, Julie. *A Gentleman of Color: The Life of James Forten.* Oxford: Oxford University Press, 2002.

———. *Philadelphia's Black Elite: Activism, Accommodation, and the Struggle for Autonomy, 1787–1848.* Philadelphia: Temple University Press, 1988.

Winders, Bruce. *Mr. Polk's Army: The American Military Experience in the Mexican-American War.* College Station: Texas A&M University Press, 1997.

Winegarten, Ruth. *Black Texas Women: 150 Years of Trial and Triumph.* Austin: University of Texas Press, 1995.

Wise, Steven M. *Though the Heavens May Fall: The Landmark Trial That Led to the End of Human Slavery.* Jackson, Tenn.: Da Capo Press, 2005.

Wolf, Eva. *Race and Liberty in the New Nation: Emancipation in Virginia from the Revolution to Nat Turner's Rebellion.* Baton Rouge: Louisiana State University Press, 2006.

Wood, Betty. *Slavery in Colonial Georgia.* Athens: University of Georgia Press, 1984.

Wood, Peter H. *Black Majority: Negroes in Colonial South Carolina from 1670 through the Stono Rebellion.* New York: W. W. Norton, 1974.

Woods, James M. *Rebellion and Realignment: Arkansas's Road to Secession.* Fayetteville: University of Arkansas Press, 1987.

Woodson, Carter G. *The Education of the Negro Prior to 1861.* New York: Putnam, 1915. Available online. URL: http://www.gutenberg.org/ebooks/11089. Accessed January 13, 2011.

———. "The Gibbs Family." *Negro History Bulletin* (October 1947): 3–12, 22.

Wright, James M. *The Free Negro in Maryland, 1634–1860.* Studies in History, Economics and Public Law. Edited by the Faculty of Political Science of Columbia University, Volume XC VII, 1921.

Wright, Richard R. *The Negro in Pennsylvania: A Study in Economic History.* New York: Arno Press, 1969.

Wright, Winthrop R. *Café con Leche: Race, Class and National Image in Venezuela.* Austin: University of Texas Press, 1990.

"Writing, Reading and Reflections Famous Women You've Never Heard Of—#2." Available online. URL: http://writingreadingandreflections.wordpress.com/2008/06. Accessed December 14, 2008.

Yellin, J. F. *Harriet Jacobs: A Life.* New York: Basic Books, 2004.

Young, Sandra Sandiford. "John Brown Russwurm's Dilemma: Citizenship or Emigration?" In *Prophets of Protest: Reconsidering the History of American Abolitionism,* edited by Timothy Patrick McCarthy and John Stauffer. New York: New Press, 2006.

Zagano, Phyllis. *The Dominican Tradition (Spirituality in History).* Collegeville, Minn.: Liturgical Press, 2006.

Zenón Cruz, Isabelo. *Narciso descubre su trasero: El negro en la cultura puertorriqueña.* 2 vols. Humacao, Puerto Rico: Editorial Furidi, 1974, 1975.

Zilversmit, Arthur. "Quok Walker, Mumbet, and the Abolition of Slavery in Massachusetts." *William and Mary Quarterly* Third Series, 25, no. 4 (October 1968): 614–624.

Index

Bréda, Toussaint. *See*
   Louverture, *Toussaint*
Brewton, Daniel 296
Bridenbaugh, Carl 53
Bridges, Robert 178, 296
Bridgetower, George
   Augustus Polgreen 452
Bridgetown, Barbados 57
Bridgetown Methodist
   Chapel incident 335
Brigands' War 284
Brindis de Salas, Claudio 424
Brindis de Salas, Virginia
   792
Brissot de Warville, Jacques
   Pierre 525, 663, 668
Britain xxv*c*–xxviii*c*, xxx*c*,
   xxxi*c*, **106–109**. *See also*
   London, England
   abolitionism and resistance
      to slavery 5
   Australia 44
   Barbados 56, 57
   Belize 62–64
   Bideau, Jean-Baptiste 68,
      69
   Black Carib 72–73
   black Seminole 80, 81
   Brazil, laws on race and
      slavery 102
   Brown, Henry "Box"
      120–121
   Captain Cudjoe 135
   Charleston, South Carolina
      146
   Clarkson, John 163
   cotton cultivation 199
   Crowther, Samuel Ajayi
      202
   Crummell, Alexander 203
   Cuba 206
   Danish Virgin Islands 215
   Delaware 219, 220
   Delgrès, Louis 223
   Dominica 226, 227
   Douglas, Sir James 236
   Douglass, Frederick 237
   emigration and
      colonization 265
   Enríquez, Miguel 269
   Equiano, Olaudah 271–272
   family relationships with
      whites 283
   Fédon's Rebellion 284–285
   Florida 291, 292
   France 300
   freemasonry 309, 310
   French Caribbean 313, 315
   French Revolution 318

Georgia 330, 331
Grand United Order of
   Odd Fellows 337
Guatemala 342
Guyana 348–349
Haitian Revolution 352,
   353
Honduras 366
Illinois 374
interracial marriage 388
Jamaica 396–399
Lecesne and Escoffery case
   430–432
legal discrimination on the
   basis of race 436, 442
Louisiana 454
Louverture, Toussaint
   460
manumission 474, 479
marriage between free and
   slave 485
Michigan 514
Mississippi 526–527
Montezuma, Francisco Gê
   Acaiaba de 538
navy 542
New Jersey 551
New Orleans, Louisiana
   554
Nicaragua 565
Pedro I 596
Pélage, Magloire 597, 598
personal liberty laws
   603–604
piracy 621
police 629, 630
Polk, James 631
Port-au-Prince 634, 635
Protestant mainline
   churches 645
Sancho, Ignatius 715–716
Seacole, Mary 720–721
Seven Years' War 724–725
Sharp, Granville 725–726
Sierra Leone 727, 728
Somerset v. Stewart 736–
   737
South Carolina 742–743
Spain 750, 751
Strong, Jonathan 753
Surinam 756, 757
Tannenbaum hypothesis
   758–760
Tennessee 765
Trinidad and Tobago
   776–778
Tye, Colonel 783
Uruguay 790
Vermont 808

Virginia and West Virginia
   813–814
War of American
   Independence 822–825
Washington Territory 836
Wedderburn, Robert 837
"whitening" and racial
   promotion 840
Britain, abolitionist
   movements in **109–112**,
   110, 118
British and Spanish Mixed
   Commission for the
   Suppression of the Slave
   Trade 205
British anti-slavery acts
   112–114
British Caribbean xxiv*c*
   artisans 42
   Baptists and Pietists 51
   Britain, abolitionist
      movements in 112
   commerce and trade
      179–180
   creole 201
   higher education 364
   Jamaica 396–397
   manumission 474
   militia 520
   planters and planter agents
      627
   Protestant mainline
      churches 644, 646
   War of American
      Independence 827
British Columbia xxxv*c*, 123,
   126, 130, 235–236, 334
British Empire 74, 202, 751,
   777
British Honduras 61
British Israelitism 660
British Lesser Antilles 42,
   72–73, **114–119**, 115*m*, 265,
   313, 482
British North America 201
British North American
   Mission Annual Conference
   129
British Slavery Abolition Act
   (1833) xxxi*c*
Brittle v. The People 545
Brown, Henry "Box" xxxiii*c*,
   109, **119–121**, *120*, 786
Brown, John (abolitionist) 4,
   238, 415, 619, 782
Brown, John (slave merchant)
   684
Brown, Morris 18
Brown, Moses 686

Brown, Robert 563
Brown, William Wells 27
Brown Fellowship Society
   148, 150
Brown Privilege Bill
   (Barbados) 58
Brown v. Board of Education
   xxxvi*c*, 277, 493
Bruce, Blanche 161
Brudenell, George 716
Brunes, John 290
Brunias, Agostino 116–117,
   227
Bryant, Sherrod 767
buccaneers xxiii*c*, 300, 705
Buchanan, James xxxv*c*, **121–
   122**, 386, 415, 619, 794, 797
Buena Vista, Battle of 764
Buenos Aires, Argentina
   xxix*c*, 32–37, 522, 590, 740
Buffalo, New York, National
   Negro Convention (1843)
   xxxiii*c*, 547
Buffalo Soldiers 82, 381, 386,
   579
Buley, Noah 158
Bunker Hill, Battle of xxv*c*,
   492, 710, 711, 823
Bureau of Colored Troops 24
Bureau of Refugees,
   Freedmen, and Abandoned
   Lands. *See* Freedmen's
   Bureau
Burgoyne, John 711
Burlingame, O. H. 287
Burlington, Vermont 810–811
Burnett, James 584
Burnett, Peter 584
Burns, Anthony xxxiv*c*, 89,
   288, 494, 676, 788
Burton, Walter 774
Bush, George Washington
   xxxiii*c*, **122–123**, 385, 583,
   836
"bush freedom" 709
"bush negroes" 480, 756
Bush Prairie 122–123
Bustamante, Anastasio 346
Butler, Benjamin F. xxxv*c*
   American Civil War 23
   Fleetwood, Christian
      Abraham 290
   Freedmen's Bureau 303
   New Orleans, Louisiana
      557
   Reconstruction in the
      United States 673
   Virginia and West Virginia
      818

G